Auditing and Assurance Services
An Integrated Approach, 11th Edition

Arens · Elder · Beasley

Highlights of Sarbanes-Oxley and Section 404 Coverage

Extensive coverage of the Sarbanes-Oxley Act of 2002 and Section 404 audits is integrated throughout the book.

Overview information about key components of the Act and factors leading to its issuance are provided in the opening chapter.

Detailed coverage of the creation of the Public Company Accounting Oversight Board (PCAOB) and its responsibilities for auditing, independence, quality control, and ethics standards for audits of public companies are included in Chapter 2 on the CPA Profession.

Coverage of changes to the profession resulting from the issuance of the Act, including implications for the Auditing Standards Board of the AICPA, is provided.

Entire section of Chapter 3 on Audit Reports highlights the combined audit report for an integrated audit of financial statements and internal control for a public company.

Chapter on Professional Ethics (Chapter 4) highlights independence requirements of the PCAOB for audits of public companies, with emphasis on the prohibition of specific non-audit services.

Completely re-written Chapter 10 on internal control emphasizes Section 404 audits of internal control over financial reporting, with extensive coverage of the PCAOB Auditing Standard 2 requirements.

Detailed descriptions of management's and the auditor's responsibilities for documenting, testing, and reporting on internal control over financial reporting for audits of public companies is provided in the internal control chapter.

Coverage is integrated throughout all transaction cycle chapters illustrating how auditor tests of controls are combined to provide assurance in both the audit of financial statements and audit of internal control over financial reporting.

New reporting and communication requirements for consideration of significant deficiencies and material weaknesses in internal control are described throughout the book and Section 404 implications for the management representation letter are provided in the Completing the Audit chapter (Chapter 24).

Eleventh Edition

AUDITING AND ASSURANCE SERVICES
An Integrated Approach

Includes coverage of the Sarbanes–Oxley Act and Section 404 Audits

Alvin A. Arens
PricewaterhouseCoopers
Auditing Professor
Michigan State University

Randal J. Elder
Syracuse University

Mark S. Beasley
North Carolina State University

with Web Content provided by
J. Gregory Jenkins
Virginia Tech

PEARSON
Prentice Hall

Pearson Education International

Library of Congress Cataloging-in-Publication Data

Arens, Alvin A.
        Auditing and assurance services: an integrated approach/Alvin A. Arens, Randal J.
        Elder, Mark S. Beasley.--11th ed.
                p.   cm.
        Includes index.
        ISBN 0-13-186712-1
        1. Auditing. I. Elder, Randal J. II. Beasley, Mark S. III. Title.

        HF5667 .A69 2005
        657′ .45--dc22
                                                                        2005006768

Senior Acquisitions Editor: Bill Larkin
Editorial Director: Jeff Shelstad
Editorial Assistant: Joanna Doxey
Media Project Manager: Caroline Kasterine
Director of Marketing: Eric Frank
Marketing Assistant: Tina Panagiotou
Senior Managing Editor (Production): Cynthia Regan
Production Editor: Michael Reynolds
Permissions Supervisor: Charles Morris
Manufacturing Buyer: Diane Peirano
Creative Director: Maria Lange
Designer: Kevin Kall
Interior Design: Steve Frim
Cover Design: Karen Quigley
Cover Illustration/Photo: Aurora
Manager, Print Production: Christy Mahon
Print Production Liaison: Suzanne Duda
Composition/Full-Service Project Management: Progressive Information Technologies
Printer/Binder: Quebecor/Dubuque
Typeface: 10/12 ITC Franklin Gothic Book

Credits and acknowledgments borrowed from other sources and reproduced, with permission, in this textbook appear on appropriate page within text.

Pearson Education LTD.   Pearson Education Australia PTY, Limited
Pearson Education Singapore, Pte. Ltd   Pearson Education North Asia Ltd
Pearson Education, Canada, Ltd   Pearson Educación de Mexico, S.A. de C.V.
Pearson Education–Japan   Pearson Education Malaysia, Pte. Ltd

10 9 8 7 6 5
ISBN 0-13-186712-1

CONTENTS

9   Materiality and Risk   231

10   Section 404 Audits of Internal Control and Control Risk   269

11   Fraud Auditing   313

PART 4   Application of the Audit Process to Other Cycles

18   Audit of the Payroll and Personnel Cycle 559

19   Audit of the Acquisition and Payment Cycle: Tests of Controls, Substantive Tests of Transactions, and Accounts Payable 581

20   Completing the Tests in the Acquisition and Payment Cycle: Verification of Selected Accounts 611

PART 6   Other Assurance and Nonassurance Services

25   Other Assurance Services 741

26   Internal and Governmental Financial Auditing and Operational Auditing 769

PREFACE

OBJECTIVE

Auditing and Assurance Services: An Integrated Approach is an introduction to auditing and other assurance services for students who have not had significant experience in providing such services. It is intended for either a one-quarter or one-semester course at the undergraduate or graduate level. This book is also appropriate for introductory professional development courses for CPA firms, internal auditors, and government auditors.

The primary emphasis in this text is on the auditor's decision-making process in both an audit of financial statements and an audit of internal control over financial reporting. We believe that the most fundamental concepts in auditing relate to determining the nature and amount of evidence the auditor should accumulate after considering the unique circumstances of each engagement. If a student of auditing understands the objectives to be accomplished in a given audit area, the circumstances of the engagement, and the decisions to be made, he or she should be able to determine the appropriate evidence to gather and how to evaluate the evidence obtained.

Thus, as the title of this book reflects, our purpose is to integrate the most important concepts of auditing, including key provisions of the Sarbanes–Oxley Act and the related Section 404 audits, in a logical manner to assist students in understanding audit decision making and evidence accumulation in today's complex auditing environment. For example, internal control is integrated into each of the chapters dealing with a particular functional area and is related to tests of controls and substantive tests of transactions that are performed in both an audit of financial statements and an audit of internal control over financial reporting; tests of controls and substantive tests of transactions are, in turn, related to the tests of details of financial statement balances for the area; and audit sampling is applied to the accumulation of audit evidence rather than treated as a separate topic. Technology, e-commerce, fraud, and auditing on internal control issues are integrated throughout the chapters.

KEY FEATURES IN THE ELEVENTH EDITION

Coverage of the Sarbanes–Oxley Act and Section 404 Reporting

The requirements of the Sarbanes–Oxley Act, including Section 404 and PCAOB Auditing Standard 2, are integrated throughout the text. The requirements for an integrated audit of financial statements and an audit of internal control over financial reporting have had the most significant effect on the auditing profession as anything in several decades. This edition provides extensive, integrated coverage of audits of internal control for public companies required by Section 404 of the Act and related auditor responsibilities as outlined in PCAOB Auditing Standard 2. Chapter 10 has been entirely re-written to illustrate the auditor's consideration of internal control in an integrated audit. It outlines management's and the auditor's separate responsibilities related to documentation and assessment of the operating effectiveness of internal control, including identification of significant deficiencies and material weaknesses. All chapters in this edition include integrated discussions of implications related to Section 404 audits of internal control. We believe our integrated approach will help professors emphasize coverage of these important professional issues as they cover the entire audit process. We hope our approach will ultimately improve student understanding of these major professional issues.

In addition, Chapter 1 has been entirely restructured to emphasize the impact that the Act is having on the auditing profession, particularly the requirements of the integrated audit of financial statements and internal control. Chapter 2 emphasizes the lead role that the PCAOB is taking in the regulation of the profession, including an entire section featuring the Sarbanes–Oxley Act. A specific section of Chapter 3 illustrates requirements related to issuing a combined report on the audit of the financial statements and audit of internal control for public companies.

Chapter 11 on fraud auditing provides expanded coverage of the auditor's responsibility for assessing the risk of fraud and detecting material misstatements due to fraud based on the fraud triangle in SAS 99. The chapter includes coverage of corporate governance and other factors that reduce fraud risk. Specific fraud risk areas and procedures to detect fraud are also discussed. Most other text chapters include new vignettes highlighting specific examples of fraud.

Chapter 11 on Fraud Auditing and Expanded Fraud Coverage

The annual report for the Hillsburg Hardware Company is included as a four-color insert to the text. Financial statements and other information included in the annual report are used in examples throughout the text to illustrate chapter concepts. The annual report also includes management's report on internal control that is required by Section 404.

Hillsburg Hardware Annual Report

The Pinnacle Manufacturing integrated case has been modified to represent a larger, multi-division company, and expanded from four to six parts. Each part of the case is included at the end of the chapter to which that part relates. The parts of the case are connected so that students will gain a better understanding of how the parts of the audit are interrelated and integrated by the audit process.

Pinnacle Manufacturing Integrated Case Example

All chapters include an Internet-based case/homework assignment that requires students to use the Internet to research relevant auditing issues. New and updated Internet-based margin links appear in every chapter, providing information on current events, companies, and professional standards.

Internet Problems and Margin Links

ORGANIZATION

The text is divided into six parts.

Part 1, The Auditing Profession (Chapters 1–5) The book begins with an opening vignette, featuring the WorldCom fraud, to help students begin to see the connection between recent frauds and the new responsibilities for auditing internal control and other requirements of the Sarbanes–Oxley Act. Chapter 1 introduces key provisions of the Act, including the creation of the PCAOB and Section 404 internal control reporting requirements. Chapter 2 covers the CPA profession, with particular emphasis on the standards setting responsibilities of the PCAOB and how those responsibilities differ from those of the Auditing Standards Board (ASB) of the AICPA. Chapter 3 provides a detailed discussion of audit reports, including a separate section on the combined report for the integrated audit of financial statements and internal control for a public company. The chapter also emphasizes conditions affecting the type of report the auditor must issue and the type of audit report applicable to each condition under varying levels of materiality. Chapter 4 explains ethical dilemmas, professional ethics, independence, and the AICPA *Code of Professional Conduct*. Chapter 5 ends this part with an investigation of auditors' legal liability.

Part 2, The Audit Process (Chapters 6–13) The first two of these chapters deal with auditors' and managements' responsibilities, audit objectives, general concepts of evidence accumulation, and audit documentation. Chapter 8 deals with planning the engagement and using analytical procedures as an audit tool. Chapter 9 introduces materiality and risk and shows their effect on the audit. Chapter 10 shows how effective internal controls can reduce planned audit evidence in the audit of financial statements. Most of the chapter describes how public company auditors integrate evidence to provide a basis for their report on the effectiveness of internal control over financial reporting with the assessment of control risk in the financial statement audit. Fraud auditing is the focus of Chapter 11. That chapter describes the auditor's responsibility for assessing fraud risk and detecting fraud. The chapter also includes specific examples of fraud and discusses warning signs and procedures to detect fraud. Chapter 12 addresses the most important effects of information technology on internal controls in businesses, risks the auditor must consider, and audit evidence changes. Chapter 13 summarizes Chapters 6 through 12 and integrates them with the remainder of the text.

Part 3, Application of the Audit Process to the Sales and Collection Cycle (Chapters 14–17) These chapters apply the concepts from Part 2 to the audit of sales, cash receipts, and the related income statement and balance sheet accounts. The appropriate audit procedures for accounts in the sales and collection cycle are related to internal control and audit objectives for tests of controls, substantive tests of transactions, and tests of details of balances in the context of both the audit of financial statements and audit of internal control over financial reporting. Students learn to apply audit sampling to the audit of sales, cash receipts, and accounts receivable.

In response to an increased emphasis on nonstatistical sampling by practitioners, Chapters 15 and 17 emphasize nonstatistical sampling rather than statistical methods. Chapter 15 begins with a general discussion of audit sampling for tests of controls and substantive tests of transactions. Similarly, Chapter 17 begins with general sampling concepts for tests of details of balances. The next topic in each chapter is extensive coverage of nonstatistical sampling. The last part of each chapter covers statistical sampling techniques.

Part 4, Application of the Audit Process to Other Cycles (Chapters 18–23) Each of these chapters deals with a specific transaction cycle or part of a transaction cycle in much the same manner as Chapters 14 through 17 cover the sales and collection cycle. Each chapter in Part IV is meant to demonstrate the relationship of internal controls, tests of controls, and substantive tests of transactions for each broad category of transactions to the related balance sheet and income statement accounts. We have integrated discussion of implications related to the audit of internal control throughout all these transaction cycle chapters. Cash in the bank is studied late in the text to demonstrate how the audit of cash balances is related to most other audit areas.

Part 5, Completing the Audit (Chapter 24) This part includes only one chapter, which deals with summarizing all audit tests, reviewing audit documentation, obtaining management representations in an integrated audit of financial statements and internal control, and all other aspects of completing an audit.

Part 6, Other Assurance and Nonassurance Services (Chapters 25 and 26) The last two chapters deal with various types of engagements and reports, other than the audit of financial statements using generally accepted accounting principles. Topics covered include *WebTrust*, *SysTrust*, other assurance services, review and compilation services, agreed-upon procedures engagements, attestation engagements, other audit engagements, internal financial auditing, governmental financial auditing, and operational auditing.

SUPPLEMENTS

Supplements for the Instructor

Instructor's Resource CD-ROM The **Instructor CD** contains print and technology (e.g., spreadsheets, videos) supplements on a single CD-ROM. Enjoy the freedom to transport the entire package from office, to home, to classroom. The CD-ROM enables you to customize any of the ancillaries, print only the chapters or materials you wish to use, or access any item from the package within the classroom!

Electronic Art Log The **Electronic Art Log** contains every table, graph, and piece of art from the book. Enjoy the freedom to create your own PowerPoint presentations or overhead transparencies. Available online at **www.prenhall.com** and on the Instructor's Resource CD-ROM.

Instructor's Manual Suggestions for each chapter include: Homework problems, how learning objectives correlate with chapter problem material, and transparency masters. Chapters have been designed so that their arrangement and selection provides maximum flexibility in course design. Sample syllabi and suggested term projects are provided. The Instructor's Manual is also available to adopters on the Instructor's Resource CD-ROM and online at **www.prenhall.com.**

Solutions Manual Included are detailed solutions to all the end-of-chapter exercises, problems, and cases. Guidelines for replies to review questions and discussion questions are offered. The Solutions Manual is also available to adopters on the Instructor's Resource CD-ROM and online at **www.prenhall.com.**

Test Item File & TestGen The printed **Test Item File** includes multiple choice exercises, true/false, essay questions, and questions related to the chapter vignettes. To assist the instructor in selecting questions for use in examinations and quizzes, each question has been assigned one of three difficulty ratings—easy, medium, or challenging. In addition, questions that uniquely relate to the integrated audits of public companies or to the provisions of the Sarbanes–Oxley Act and Section 404 have been separately labeled for easy identification by the professor. Formatted for easy copying, **TestGen** testing software is an easy-to-use computerized testing program. It can create exams, evaluate, and track student results.

PowerPoint Slides PowerPoint presentations are available for each chapter of the text. Instructors have the flexibility to add slides and/or modify the existing slides to meet the courses' needs. The PowerPoint Slides are also available to adopters on the Instructor's Resource CD-ROM and online at **www.prenhall.com.**

Videos featuring Al Arens Al Arens briefly introduces 1) auditing concepts and 2) video clips of real companies facing auditing challenges via videos on the text web site at **www.prenhall.com/arens.** Free upon adoption.

Enhanced Companion Web Site Prentice Hall's Learning on the Internet Partnership offers the most expansive Internet-based support available. Our Web site provides a wealth of resources for students and faculty. Resources include:

- Twice a year, faculty will be able to access newsletter **summaries of the most recent changes to professional standards** and summaries of major issues affecting the auditing profession. This will help instructors to stay informed of emerging issues.
- **"Internet Margin Links,"** included in each chapter, encourage students to use the Internet to learn more about issues, services, or organizations covered in the text.
- **"Internet Problems,"** end-of-chapter assignments available for most chapters, require students to utilize the Internet to conduct research in order to develop a solution.
- **"Faculty Web Links"** provided for most chapters take interested instructors to related Internet sites.

Free Online "Study Guide" Students receive immediate feedback on tests, including total score, an explanation provided for each incorrect answer, and the ability to e-mail the results to a faculty member. All questions are created specifically for the Study Guide and there is no duplication of questions taken from the text or test bank.

CAST: Comprehensive Assurance and Systems Tool by Buckless/Ingraham/Jenkins This *integrated* practice set enables students to complete accounting transactions based on the day-to-day operations of a *real* winery. Three modules are available—assurance, manual AIS, and computerized AIS. **Appropriate for use in auditing, AIS, or intermediate courses.**

The Lakeside Company: Case Studies in Auditing, 10th ed., by Hoyle/Trussel This practice set guides the student through the life cycle of an audit from beginning to end. The cases are designed to create a realistic view of how an auditor organizes and carries out an audit.

Auditing Cases, 2nd ed., **Beasley/Buckless/Glover/Prawitt** This collection of 36 auditing cases addresses most major activities performed during the conduct of an audit, from client acceptance to issuance of an audit report. Several cases ask students to work with realistic audit evidence to prepare and evaluate audit schedules. The cases are available as a collection or as part of the Pearson Custom Publishing Resources Program. For details, go to: **www.prenhall.com.**

ACKNOWLEDGMENTS

We acknowledge the American Institute of Certified Public Accountants for permission to quote extensively from statements on auditing standards, the *Code of Professional Conduct,* Financial Accounting Standards Board, Uniform CPA Examinations, and other publications. The willingness of this major accounting organization to permit the use of its materials is a significant contribution to the book.

The continuing generous support of the PricewaterhouseCoopers Foundation is acknowledged, particularly in regard to the word processing, editing, and moral support of this text.

We gratefully acknowledge the contributions of the following reviewers for their suggestions and support:

Sherri Anderson, Sonoma State University
Stephen K. Asare, University of Florida
David Baglia, Grove City College
Brian Ballou, Miami University
William E. Bealing, Jr., Bloomsburg University
Stanley F. Biggs, University of Connecticut
Joe Brazel, North Carolina State University
Frank Buckless, North Carolina State University
Joseph V. Calmie, Thomas Nelson Community College
Eric Carlsen, Kean College of New Jersey
Freddie Choo, San Francisco State University
Frank Daroca, Loyola Marymount University
William L. Felix, University of Arizona
David S. Gelb, Seton Hall University
John Giles, North Carolina State University
Charles L. Holley, Virginia Commonwealth University
Gary L. Holstrum, University of South Florida
C. Randy Howard, Montana State University at Billings
Rita P. Hull, Virginia Commonwealth University
Steve Hunt, Western Illinois University
Greg Jenkins, North Carolina State University
James Jiambalvo, University of Washington

David S. Kerr, Texas A & M University
Dennis Lee Kimmell, University of Akron
William R. Kinney, Jr., University of Texas at Austin
W. Robert Knechel, University of Florida
Heidi H. Meier, Cleveland State University
Alfred R. Michenzi, Loyola College in Maryland
Charles R. (Tad) Miller, California Polytechnic State University
Lawrence C. Mohrweis, Northern Arizona University
Patricia M. Myers, East Carolina University
Frederick L. Neumann, University of Illinois
Kristine N. Palmer, Longwood College
Vicki S. Peden, Cal Poly—Pomona
Pankaj Saksena, Indiana University
Cindy Seipel, New Mexico State University
Philip H. Siegel, Fairleigh Dickinson University
Robert R. Tucker, Fordham University
Barb Waddington, Eastern Michigan University
D. Dewey Ward, Michigan State University
Robert J. Warth, Rochester Institute of Technology
Jeanne H. Yamamura, University of Nevada, Reno
Doug Ziegenfuss, Old Dominion University

A special recognition goes to Carol Borsum for her editorial, production, and moral support throughout the last six editions. Her concern for quality is beyond the ordinary.

We especially thank the Prentice Hall book team for their hard work and dedication, including Bill Larkin, Acquisitions Editor; Sam Goffinet, Assistant Editor; Jane Avery, Editorial Assistant; Cindy Regan, Managing Editor; Nancy Welcher, Senior Media Project Manager; Eric Frank, Director of Marketing; Anne Graydon, Senior Production Editor; Mike Reynolds, Production Editor; Maria Lange, Design Director; Kevin Kall, Art Director; Michelle Klein, Manufacturing Buyer, and Lisa McClanahan, Project Manager at Progressive Publishing Alternatives.

A. A. A.
R. J. E.
M. S. B.

ABOUT THE AUTHORS

Al Arens is PricewaterhouseCoopers Auditing Professor of Accounting at Michigan State University. His primary teaching and research area is auditing and he teaches undergraduate auditing at least one term annually. Al is a past president of the American Accounting Association and a former member of the AICPA Auditing Standards Board. He practiced public accounting with both a local CPA firm and the predecessor firm to Ernst & Young. He has received many awards including the AAA Auditing Section Outstanding Educator award, the AICPA Outstanding Educator award, the national Beta Alpha Psi Professor of the Year award and many teaching and other awards at Michigan State.

Randy Elder is an Associate Professor of Accounting at Syracuse University. He teaches undergraduate and graduate auditing courses, and has received several teaching awards. His research focuses on audit quality and current audit firm practices. He has extensive public accounting experience with a large regional CPA firm, and is a Certified Fraud Examiner and member of the AICPA and Michigan Association of CPAs.

Mark S. Beasley is a Professor of Accounting at North Carolina State University. He teaches undergraduate and graduate auditing courses, and has received several teaching awards including membership in NC State's Academy of Outstanding Teachers. He has extensive professional audit experience with the predecessor firm to Ernst & Young and has extensive standards-setting experience working with the Auditing Standards Board as a Technical Manager in the Audit and Assurance Division of the AICPA. He served on the ASB's Fraud Standard Task Force responsible for developing SAS 99, the ASB's Antifraud Programs and Controls Task Force, the Advisory Council overseeing COSO's Enterprise Risk Management Framework project. He is now a member of the COSO Board, representing the AAA.

PART 1

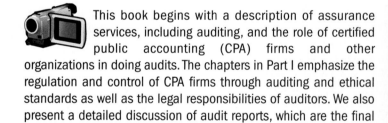 CHAPTERS 1–5

THE AUDITING PROFESSION

These first five chapters provide background for performing financial audits, which is our primary focus. This background will help you understand why auditors perform audits the way they do.

This book begins with a description of assurance services, including auditing, and the role of certified public accounting (CPA) firms and other organizations in doing audits. The chapters in Part I emphasize the regulation and control of CPA firms through auditing and ethical standards as well as the legal responsibilities of auditors. We also present a detailed discussion of audit reports, which are the final products of audits.

CHAPTER 1

THE DEMAND FOR AUDIT AND OTHER ASSURANCE SERVICES

AUDITORS HAVE A GREAT RESPONSIBILITY

"Oh my!" Gene Morse was stunned. He stared at the computer screen in his cubicle, unable to believe that he had found an unsupported entry for $500 million in computer acquisitions. He immediately took his discovery to his supervisor, Cynthia Cooper, vice president for internal audit at WorldCom. "Keep going," directed Cooper. Her team of internal auditors kept digging. They worked late into the night to avoid detection, concerned that they would be fired if superiors found what they were up to. They burned data onto CDs because they feared the data might be destroyed.

Major frauds often begin at the top, and such was the case at WorldCom. Bernie Ebbers, WorldCom's founder and CEO, had told Cooper not to use the term "internal controls" claiming that he did not understand it. However, Cooper fought for respect and more resources for the internal audit department. She told Ebbers that her division could save millions of dollars of wasteful operations with internal controls. In the years that followed, "we paid for ourselves many times over" said Cooper.

As she pursued the trail of fraud, Cooper was obstructed at every turn. In late May 2002, Cooper's team found a gaping hole in the books. The company had recorded billions of dollars of regular fees paid to local telephone companies as capital assets. This accounting trick allowed the company to turn a $662 million loss into a $2.4 billion profit in 2001. The company's CFO, Scott Sullivan, called her in and asked her what they were up to. He then asked her to delay her investigation to the following quarter, but she refused. In June 2002, the company announced that it had inflated assets by $3.8 billion, the largest accounting fraud in history. When the investigation was complete, the total amount of the fraud had grown to an astonishing $11 billion.

Sources: Adapted from 1. Amanda Ripley, "The Night Detective," *Time* (December 30, 2002); 2. Susan Pulliam and Deborah Solomon, "Uncooking the Books: How Three Unlikely Sleuths Discovered Fraud at WorldCom," *The Wall Street Journal* (October 30, 2002) p. A1.

Each chapter's opening vignette illustrates important auditing principles based on realistic situations. Some vignettes are based on public information about the audits of real companies, whereas others are fictitious. Any resemblance in the latter vignettes to real firms, companies, or individuals is unintended and purely coincidental.

LEARNING OBJECTIVES

After studying this chapter, you should be able to

1-1 Describe auditing.

1-2 Distinguish between auditing and accounting.

1-3 Explain the importance of auditing in reducing information risk.

1-4 List the causes of information risk, and explain how this risk may be reduced.

1-5 Describe assurance services and distinguish audit services from other assurance and nonassurance services provided by CPAs.

1-6 Differentiate the three main types of audits.

1-7 Identify the primary types of auditors.

1-8 Describe the requirements for becoming a CPA.

The opening vignette involving Cynthia Cooper and WorldCom illustrates the importance of company controls and the role of internal and external auditors in detecting fraud. In the aftermath of WorldCom and other major financial reporting frauds, in July 2002, Congress passed the **Sarbanes–Oxley Act,** called by many the most significant securities legislation since the 1933 and 1934 Securities Acts. The provisions of the Act apply to publicly held companies and their audit firms.

A key provision of the Sarbanes–Oxley Act is the creation of the Public Company Accounting Oversight Board (PCAOB) to provide oversight for auditors of public companies. The Act also includes provisions to improve corporate governance, and it requires the CEO and CFO of public companies to certify the company's financial statements.

Perhaps the most significant provision of the Act is the requirement in Section 404 that management assess and report on the effectiveness of internal control over financial reporting. The company's auditor must also report on the effectiveness of the company's internal controls over financial reporting, in addition to reporting on the results of their audit of the company's financial statements. These new requirements and their implications are dealt with throughout the text. This chapter introduces auditing and other assurance services and their role in society. There is also discussion of certified public accountants (CPAs) and the services they provide.

NATURE OF AUDITING

OBJECTIVE 1-1

Describe auditing.

We have introduced how auditors' responsibilities have been increased to include reporting on the effectiveness of internal control over financial reporting. We now examine auditing more specifically using the following definition:

> **Auditing** is the accumulation and evaluation of evidence about information to determine and report on the degree of correspondence between the information and established criteria. Auditing should be done by a competent, independent person.

The definition includes several key words and phrases. For ease of understanding, we'll discuss the terms in a different order than they occur in the description.

Information and Established Criteria

To do an audit, there must be information in a *verifiable form* and some standards (*criteria*) by which the auditor can evaluate the information. Information can and does take many forms. Auditors routinely perform audits of quantifiable information, including companies' financial statements and individuals' federal income tax returns. Auditors also perform audits of more subjective information, such as the effectiveness of computer systems and the efficiency of manufacturing operations.

The criteria for evaluating information also vary depending on the information being audited. In the audit of historical financial statements by CPA firms, the criteria are usually generally accepted accounting principles (GAAP). This means that in an audit of Boeing's financial statements, the CPA firm will determine whether Boeing's financial statements have been prepared in accordance with GAAP. For an audit of internal control over financial reporting, the criteria will be a recognized framework for establishing internal control, such as *Internal Control—Integrated Framework* issued by the Committee of Sponsoring Organizations of the Treadway Commission.

For the audit of tax returns by the IRS, the criteria are found in the Internal Revenue Code. In an IRS audit of Boeing's corporate tax return, the internal revenue agent uses the Internal Revenue Code as the criteria for correctness, rather than GAAP.

For more subjective information, it is more difficult to establish criteria. Typically, auditors and the entities being audited agree on the criteria well before the audit starts. For example, in an audit of the effectiveness of specific aspects of computer operations, the criteria might include the allowable level of input or output errors.

Evidence is any information used by the auditor to determine whether the information being audited is stated in accordance with the established criteria. Evidence takes many different forms, including:

Accumulating and Evaluating Evidence

- Oral testimony of the auditee (client)
- Written communication with outsiders
- Observations by the auditor
- Electronic data about transactions

To satisfy the purpose of the audit, auditors must obtain a sufficient quality and volume of evidence. Auditors must determine the types and amount of evidence necessary and evaluate whether the information corresponds to the established criteria. This is a critical part of every audit and the primary subject of this book.

The auditor must be qualified to understand the criteria used and must be *competent* to know the types and amount of evidence to accumulate to reach the proper conclusion after the evidence has been examined. The auditor must also have an *independent mental attitude*. The competence of the individual performing the audit is of little value if he or she is biased in the accumulation and evaluation of evidence.

Competent, Independent Person

Although absolute independence is impossible, auditors strive to maintain a high level of independence to keep the confidence of users relying on their reports. Auditors reporting on company financial statements are often called **independent auditors.** Even though such auditors are paid fees by the company, they are normally sufficiently independent to conduct audits that can be relied on by users. Even internal auditors—those employed by the companies they audit—usually report directly to top management, keeping the auditors independent of the operating units they audit.

The final stage in the auditing process is preparing the **audit report,** which is the communication of the auditor's findings to users. Reports differ in nature, but all must inform readers of the degree of correspondence between information and established criteria. Reports also differ in form and can vary from the highly technical type usually associated with financial statement audits to a simple oral report in the case of an operational audit of a small department's effectiveness.

Reporting

The important ideas in the description of auditing are illustrated in Figure 1-1 using an IRS agent's audit of an individual's tax return as an example. To determine whether the tax return was prepared in a manner consistent with the requirements of the federal

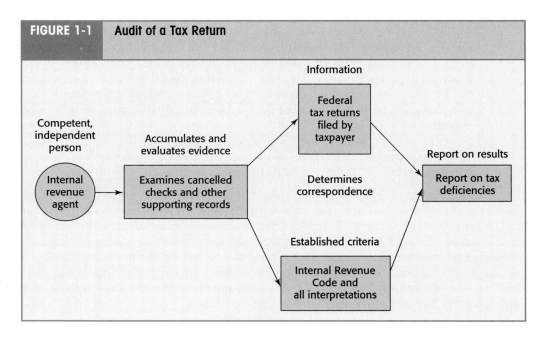

FIGURE 1-1   Audit of a Tax Return

Internal Revenue Code, the agent examines supporting records provided by the taxpayer and from other sources, such as the taxpayer's employer. After completing the audit, the internal revenue agent issues a report to the taxpayer assessing additional taxes, advising that a refund is due, or stating that there is no change in the status of the tax return.

DISTINCTION BETWEEN AUDITING AND ACCOUNTING

OBJECTIVE 1-2

Distinguish between auditing and accounting.

Many financial statement users and members of the general public confuse auditing with accounting. The confusion results because most auditing is usually concerned with accounting information, and many auditors have considerable expertise in accounting matters. The confusion is increased by giving the title "certified public accountant" to many individuals who perform audits.

Accounting is the recording, classifying, and summarizing of economic events in a logical manner for the purpose of providing financial information for decision making. To provide relevant information, accountants must have a thorough understanding of the principles and rules that provide the basis for preparing the accounting information. In addition, accountants must develop a system to make sure that the entity's economic events are properly recorded on a timely basis and at a reasonable cost.

When auditing accounting data, auditors focus on determining whether recorded information properly reflects the economic events that occurred during the accounting period. Because GAAP provide the criteria for evaluating whether the accounting information is properly recorded, auditors must also thoroughly understand GAAP.

In addition to understanding accounting, the auditor must possess expertise in the accumulation and interpretation of audit evidence. It is this expertise that distinguishes auditors from accountants. Determining the proper audit procedures, deciding the number and types of items to test, and evaluating the results are problems unique to the auditor.

ECONOMIC DEMAND FOR AUDITING

OBJECTIVE 1-3

Explain the importance of auditing in reducing information risk.

To illustrate the need for auditing, consider the decision of a bank officer in making a loan to a business. This decision will be based on such factors as previous financial relationships with the business and the financial condition of the business as reflected by its financial statements. If the bank makes the loan, it will charge a rate of interest determined primarily by three factors:

1. *Risk-free interest rate.* This is approximately the rate the bank could earn by investing in U.S. treasury notes for the same length of time as the business loan.
2. *Business risk for the customer.* This risk reflects the possibility that the business will not be able to repay its loan because of economic or business conditions, such as a recession, poor management decisions, or unexpected competition in the industry.
3. *Information risk.* **Information risk** reflects the possibility that the information upon which the business risk decision was made was inaccurate. A likely cause of the information risk is the possibility of inaccurate financial statements.

Auditing has no effect on either the risk-free interest rate or business risk, but it can have a significant effect on information risk. If the bank officer is satisfied that there is minimal information risk because a borrower's financial statements are audited, the bank's risk is substantially reduced and the overall interest rate to the borrower can be reduced. The reduction of information risk can have a significant effect on the borrower's ability to obtain capital at a reasonable cost. For example, assume a large company has total interest-bearing debt of approximately $10 billion. If the interest rate on that debt is reduced by only 1 percent, the annual savings in interest is $100 million.

As society becomes more complex, decision makers are more likely to receive unreliable information. There are several reasons for this: remoteness of information, biases and motives of the provider, voluminous data, and the existence of complex exchange transactions.

Remoteness of Information In a global economy, it is virtually impossible for a decision maker to have much firsthand knowledge about the organization with which they do business. Information provided by others must be relied upon. When information is obtained from others, the likelihood of it being intentionally or unintentionally misstated increases.

Biases and Motives of the Provider If information is provided by someone whose goals are inconsistent with those of the decision maker, the information may be biased in favor of the provider. The reason could be an honest optimism about future events or an intentional emphasis designed to influence users in a certain manner. In either case, the result is a misstatement of information. For example, when a borrower provides financial statements to a lender, there is considerable likelihood that the borrower will bias the statements to increase the chance of obtaining a loan. The misstatement could be in the form of outright incorrect dollar amounts or inadequate or incomplete disclosures of information.

Voluminous Data As organizations become larger, so does the volume of their exchange transactions. This increases the likelihood that improperly recorded information will be included in the records—perhaps buried in a large amount of other information. For example, if a large government agency overpays a vendor's invoice by $2,000, there is a fairly good chance that it will not be uncovered unless the agency has instituted reasonably complex procedures to find this type of misstatement. If many minor misstatements remain undiscovered, the combined total could be significant.

Complex Exchange Transactions In the past few decades, exchange transactions between organizations have become increasingly complex and therefore more difficult to record properly. For example, the correct accounting treatment of the acquisition of one entity by another poses relatively difficult and important accounting problems. Other examples include properly combining and disclosing the results of operations of subsidiaries in different industries and properly disclosing derivative financial instruments under Financial Accounting Standards Board Statements No. 133 and No. 138 (SFAS 133 and SFAS 138).

Causes of Information Risk

OBJECTIVE 1-4
List the causes of information risk, and explain how this risk may be reduced.

Reducing Information Risk

After comparing costs and benefits, business managers and financial statement users may conclude that the best way to deal with information risk is simply to have it remain reasonably high. A small company may find it less expensive to pay higher interest costs than to increase the costs of reducing information risk.

For larger businesses, it is usually practical to incur costs to reduce information risk. There are three main ways to do so.

User Verifies Information The user may go to the business premises to examine records and obtain information about the reliability of the statements. Normally, this is impractical because of costs. In addition, it would be economically inefficient for all users to verify the information individually. Nevertheless, some users perform their own verification. For example, the Internal Revenue Service (IRS) does considerable verification of businesses and individuals to determine whether tax returns filed reflect the actual tax due the federal government. Similarly, if a business intends to purchase another business, it is common for the purchaser to use a special audit team to independently verify and evaluate key information of the prospective business.

User Shares Information Risk with Management There is considerable legal precedent indicating that management is responsible for providing reliable information to users. If users rely on inaccurate financial statements and as a result incur a financial loss, they may have a basis for a lawsuit against management. A difficulty with sharing information risk with management is

According to an article in *Accounting Today,* corporate America is paying too much for new capital, and independent auditors are part of the solution. Robert Elliott, a senior partner with KPMG, believes the cost of capital could shrink significantly as a result of advances in technology, streamlined regulations, and broader audit coverage.

Elliott uses a hypothetical example to illustrate his prediction. Assuming a cost of capital of 13%, he estimates this rate is composed of the following:

- 5.5% risk-free interest rate
- 3.5% economic risk premium *(business risk)*
- 4% information cost *(information risk)*

According to Elliott's example, information risk comprises approximately 30% of the cost of capital. Elliott believes the following factors will drastically reduce information risk:

- Technological advances will drastically decrease the cost of providing relevant and timely information to investors.

- As more companies go "online," the risk of investors obtaining outdated information decreases.
- New accounting and auditing standards already require better disclosures about segment operations, risks, and uncertainties. New rules may require data on nonfinancial performance and forward-looking information.
- Auditors will find more efficient ways to audit, such as continuous auditing of computerized control systems, which may provide new levels of assurance.

Elliott predicts that if and when all of the preceding factors materialize, the cost of capital in his hypothetical example could be reduced from 13% to 11.5%. The entire reduction would result from reduced information risk.

Source: Adapted from *Accounting Today* (December 11, 1995), p. 16.

that users may not be able to collect on losses. If a company is unable to repay a loan because of bankruptcy, it is unlikely that management will have sufficient funds to repay users.

Audited Financial Statements Are Provided The most common way for users to obtain reliable information is to have an independent audit performed. Decision makers can then use the audited information on the assumption that it is reasonably complete, accurate, and unbiased.

Typically, management of a private company or the audit committee for a public company engages the auditor to provide assurances to users that the financial statements are reliable. If the financial statements are ultimately determined to be incorrect, the auditor can be sued by both the users and management. Auditors obviously have considerable legal responsibility for their work.

ASSURANCE SERVICES

OBJECTIVE 1-5

Describe assurance services and distinguish audit services from other assurance and nonassurance services provided by CPAs.

Assurance services are independent professional services that improve the quality of information for decision makers. Such services are valued because the assurance provider is independent and perceived as being unbiased with respect to the information examined. Individuals who are responsible for making business decisions seek assurance services to help improve the reliability and relevance of the information used as the basis for their decisions.

Assurance services can be performed by CPAs or by a variety of other professionals. For example, Consumers Union, a nonprofit organization, tests a wide variety of products used by consumers and reports their evaluations of the quality of the products tested in *Consumer Reports.* The organization provides the information to help consumers make intelligent decisions about the products they buy. Many consumers consider the information in *Consumer Reports* more reliable than information provided by the product manufacturers because Consumers Union is independent of the manufacturers. Similarly, the Better Business Bureau (BBB) online reliability program, BBB*OnLine* Reliability, allows

BBB*OnLine*[1]

[1]To illustrate or emphasize text material, the authors have identified interesting company or organization Web sites on the Internet. Internet links are noted by icons in the margins, and a brief description and hot link for each site can be found at Prentice Hall's Companion Web Site (CW site), www.prenhall.com/arens.

Web shoppers to check BBB information about a company and be assured the company will stand behind its service. Other assurance services provided by firms other than CPAs include the Nielsen television ratings and Arbitron radio ratings.

The need for assurance is not new. CPAs have provided many assurance services for years, particularly assurances about historical financial statement information. CPA firms have also performed assurance services related to lotteries and contests to provide assurance that winners were determined in an unbiased fashion in accordance with contest rules. More recently, CPAs have been expanding the types of assurance services they perform to include forward-looking and other types of information, such as company financial forecasts and Web site controls. For example, businesses and consumers using communication networks such as the Internet to conduct business and make decisions need independent assurances about the reliability and security of that electronic information. The demand for assurance services is expected to grow as the demand for information increases and as more real-time information becomes available through the Internet.

One category of assurance services provided by CPAs is attestation services. An **attestation service** is a type of assurance service in which the CPA firm issues a report about the reliability of an assertion that is made by another party. Attestation services fall into four categories:

Attestation Services

1. Audit of historical financial statements
2. Effectiveness of internal control over financial reporting
3. Review of historical financial statements
4. Other attestation services that may be applied to a broad range of subject matter

Audit of Historical Financial Statements An **audit of historical financial statements** is a form of attestation service in which the auditor issues a written report expressing an opinion about whether the financial statements are fairly stated in accordance with GAAP. Audits represent the predominant form of assurance performed by CPA firms.

Publicly traded companies in the United States are required to have audits under the federal securities acts. Auditor reports can be found in any public company's annual financial report, and most companies' audited financial statements can be accessed over the Internet from the Securities and Exchange Commission (SEC) EDGAR database or directly from the company's Web site. Many privately held companies also have annual financial statement audits to obtain financing from banks and other financial institutions. Government and not-for-profit entities often have audits to meet the requirements of lenders or funding sources.

Report Gallery

When presenting information in the form of financial statements, the company makes various assertions about its financial condition and results of operations. External users such as stockholders and lenders who rely on those financial statements to make business decisions look to the auditor's report as an indication of the statements' reliability. They value the auditor's assurance because of the auditor's independence from the client and knowledge of financial statement reporting matters. Figure 1-2 illustrates the relationships among the auditor, client, and financial statement users.

Attestation on Internal Control over Financial Reporting CPAs also attest to the effectiveness of **internal control over financial reporting**. Section 404 of the Sarbanes–Oxley Act requires public companies to report management's assessment of the effectiveness of internal control over financial reporting. The Act further requires auditors to attest to the effectiveness of internal control over financial reporting. This evaluation, which is integrated with the audit of the financial statements, provides forward-looking information, because effective internal controls reduce the likelihood of future misstatements in the financial statements.

Review of Historical Financial Statements Whereas an audit provides a high level of assurance, a **review of historical financial statements** provides a moderate amount of assurance on the financial statements, and less evidence is necessary to support this level of assurance. A review is often adequate to meet financial statement users' needs, and it can be provided by the CPA firm at a much lower fee than an audit. Many nonpublic companies

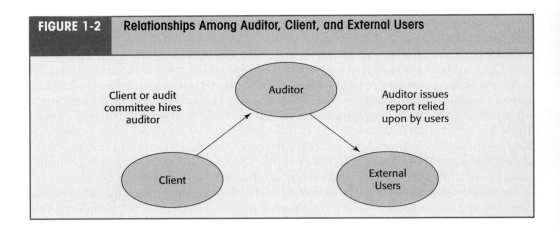

FIGURE 1-2 Relationships Among Auditor, Client, and External Users

Client or audit committee hires auditor

Auditor

Auditor issues report relied upon by users

Client

External Users

take advantage of this attestation option to provide moderate assurance on their financial statements without incurring the cost of an audit.

Other Attestation Services CPAs provide numerous other attestation services, many of which are natural extensions of the audit of historical financial statements, as users seek independent assurances about other types of information. When a bank loans money to a company, for example, the loan agreement may require the company to hire CPAs who will provide assurance about the company's compliance with the financial provisions of the loan. CPAs can also attest to the information in a client's forecasted financial statements, which are often used to obtain financing. We discuss attestation services further in Chapter 25.

Other Assurance Services

Most of the other assurance services that CPAs provide do not meet the formal definition of attestation services, although the CPA must be independent and must provide assurance about information used by decision makers. They differ in that the CPA is not required to issue a written report, and the assurance does not have to be about the reliability of another party's assertion about compliance with specified criteria. Rather, in these other assurance services engagements, the assurance is about the reliability and relevance of information, which may or may not have been asserted by another party. For example, a CPA might provide assurances on a company's data backup procedures.

The common feature of all assurance services, including audits and attestation services, is the focus on improving the quality of information used by decision makers. With new types of risks faced by businesses and increases in the amount of available information sources, the demand for assurance on other types of information is expected to grow substantially in the near future.

CPA firms face a larger field of competitors in the market for other assurance services. Audits and many types of attestation services are limited by regulation to licensed CPAs, but the market for other forms of assurance is open to non-CPA competitors. For example, CPAs must compete with market research firms to assist clients in the preparation of customer surveys and in the evaluation of the reliability and relevance of survey information. However, CPA firms have the competitive advantage of their reputation for competence and independence.

"AND THE OSCAR GOES TO ..."
"THERE SHE IS, MISS AMERICA ..."
"WELCOME TO THE NEW YORK STATE LOTTERY ..."

You probably recognize these statements from the Academy Awards, the Miss America Pageant, and the New York State Lottery drawing. What you may not recognize is what these well-known events have to do with assurance services. Each event is observed by CPAs from a major accounting firm to assure viewers that the contests were fairly conducted. So when you become a member of a CPA firm, you might not win an Oscar—but you could be on the Oscars!

Because of the increased demand for other forms of assurance, the American Institute of Certified Public Accountants (AICPA) formed the Special Committee on Assurance Services (SCAS) to research and develop new assurance service opportunities for CPAs. The SCAS has developed business plans for six services with potential revenues of over $1 billion each. The *WebTrust* and *SysTrust* services are briefly described in the next section. Additional information on the performance of assurance services is included in Chapter 25.

AICPA Assurance Services

Assurance Services on Information Technology The growth of the Internet and new ways of conducting business electronically, often referred to as **e-commerce,** is driving the demand for other assurance services. Because of the volume of real-time information available on the Internet, marketplace needs are shifting from assurance about historical information, such as financial statements, to assurance about the reliability of processes generating information in a real-time format. Many business functions, such as ordering and making payments, are conducted over the Internet or directly between computers using electronic data interchange (EDI). As transactions and information are shared online and in real time, business-people demand even greater assurances about information, transactions, and the security protecting them. CPAs can help provide assurance about these functions, such as assurance services over Web site controls and assurances about information system reliability.

- *WebTrust services.* To respond to the growing need for assurance related to business transacted over the Internet, the AICPA and the Canadian Institute of Chartered Accountants (CICA) jointly created the *WebTrust* assurance service. CPA firms that are licensed by the AICPA to perform this service provide assurance to users of Web sites through the CPA's electronic *WebTrust* seal displayed on the Web site. This seal assures the user that the Web site owner has met established criteria related to business practices, transaction integrity, and information processes. *WebTrust* is an attestation service, and the *WebTrust* seal is a symbolic representation of the CPA's report on management's assertions about its disclosure of electronic commerce practices.

Trust Services

- *SysTrust services.* The AICPA and CICA jointly created the *SysTrust* service to provide assurance on information system reliability. *SysTrust* is an attest-type engagement to evaluate and test system reliability in areas such as security and data integrity. Whereas the *WebTrust* assurance service is primarily designed to provide assurance to third-party users of a Web site, *SysTrust* services might be performed by CPAs to provide assurance to management, the board of directors, or third parties about the reliability of information systems used to generate real-time information.

The AICPA and CICA have developed five principles related to online privacy, security, processing integrity, availability, and confidentiality to be used in performing services such as *WebTrust* and *SysTrust*. Table 1-1 includes a description of the assurance provided for each principle. The table also includes a description of assurance for certification authorities, which applies only to the *WebTrust* service.

TABLE 1-1	Principles for *WebTrust* and *SysTrust* Services
***Trust* Principles**	**Description of Assurance**
Online privacy	Provides assurance that the system protects the privacy of personal information provided by individuals, such as social security numbers
Security	Provides assurance that access to the system and data is restricted to authorized individuals
Processing integrity	Provides assurance that transactions are processed completely and accurately
Availability	Provides assurance that systems and data will be available to users when they need it
Confidentiality	Provides assurance that information designated as confidential is protected
Certification authorities (*WebTrust* only)	Provides assurance on the adequacy and effectiveness of controls used by certification authorities with responsibility for verifying electronic transactions

Assurance Services on Other Types of Information The types of assurance services that CPAs can provide are almost limitless. A survey of large CPA firms performed by the SCAS identified more than 200 assurance services that are currently being provided. Table 1-2 lists some of the other assurance service opportunities for CPAs.

Nonassurance Services Provided by CPAs

CPA firms perform numerous other services that generally fall outside the scope of assurance services. Three specific examples are:

1. Accounting and bookkeeping services
2. Tax services
3. Management consulting services

Most accounting and bookkeeping services, tax services, and management consulting services fall outside the scope of assurance services, although there is some common area of overlap between consulting and assurance services. While the primary purpose of an

TABLE 1-2	Other Assurance Services Examples

Other Assurance Services	Service Activities
Controls over and risks related to investments, including policies related to derivatives	Assess the processes in a company's investment practices to identify risks and to determine the effectiveness of those processes
Mystery shopping	Perform anonymous shopping to assess sales personnel dealings with customers and procedures they follow
Assess risks of accumulation, distribution, and storage of digital information	Assess security risks and related controls over electronic data, including the adequacy of backup and off-site storage
Fraud and illegal acts risk assessment	Develop fraud risk profiles, and assess the adequacy of company systems and policies in preventing and detecting fraud and illegal acts
Compliance with trading policies and procedures	Examine transactions between trading partners to ensure that transactions comply with agreements; identify risks in the agreements
Compliance with entertainment royalty agreements	Assess whether royalties paid to artists, authors, and others comply with royalty agreements
ISO 9000 certifications	Certify a company's compliance with ISO 9000 quality control standards, which help ensure company products are of high quality
Environmental audit	Assess whether company policies and practices ensure the company's compliance with environmental standards and laws

Source: AICPA Special Committee on Assurance Services.

assurance service is to improve the quality of information, the primary purpose of a management consulting engagement is to generate a recommendation to management.

Although the quality of information is often an important criterion in management consulting, this goal is normally not the primary purpose. For example, a CPA may be engaged to design and install a new information technology system for a client as a consulting engagement. The purpose of that engagement is to install the new system, with the goal of improved information being a by-product of that engagement. Occasionally, consulting engagements and assurance services overlap when improving the quality of information for decision makers is a primary goal.

CPA firm revenues from management consulting services have increased significantly in recent years. Many large CPA firms have departments involved exclusively in performing management consulting services, which are often called management advisory services (MAS). As these consulting services have expanded, some CPA firms have sold their consulting businesses to other firms, spun off their consulting practices as separate entities, or offered shares in the consulting businesses in public offerings of stock. In addition, the Sarbanes–Oxley Act and SEC rules do not allow auditors to provide most consulting services to public company audit clients. As a result, consulting services are no longer significant sources of revenue for several of the largest CPA firms.

Figure 1-3 reflects the relationship between assurance and nonassurance services. Audits, reviews, reports on the effectiveness of internal control over financial reporting, and other attestation services are all examples of attestation services, which fall under the scope of assurance services. Some of the new assurance services identified by the AICPA, such as *WebTrust* and *SysTrust*, are also attestation services.

FIGURE 1-3 Relationships Among Assurance Services, Attestation Services, and Nonassurance Services

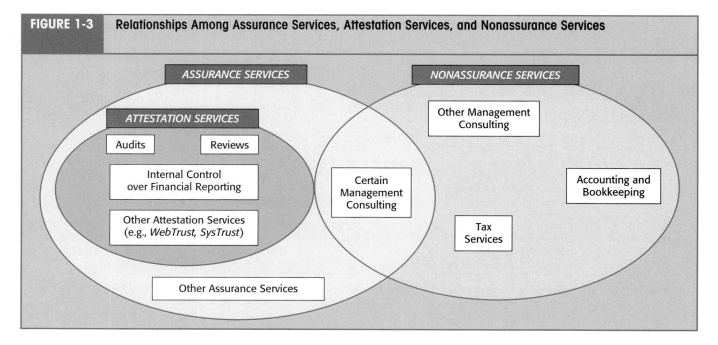

TYPES OF AUDITS

CPAs perform three primary types of audits, as illustrated with examples in Table 1-3:

1. Operational audit
2. Compliance audit
3. Financial statement audit

Operational Audits

An **operational audit** evaluates the *efficiency* and *effectiveness* of any part of an organization's operating procedures and methods. At the completion of an operational audit, management normally expects recommendations for improving operations. For example, auditors might evaluate the efficiency and accuracy of processing payroll transactions in a newly installed computer system. Another example, where most accountants would feel less qualified, is evaluating the efficiency, accuracy, and customer satisfaction in processing the distribution of letters and packages by a company such as Federal Express.

In operational auditing, the reviews are not limited to accounting. They can include the evaluation of organizational structure, computer operations, production methods, marketing, and any other area in which the auditor is qualified. Because of the many different areas in which operational effectiveness can be evaluated, it is impossible to characterize the conduct of a typical operational audit. In one organization, the auditor might evaluate the relevancy and sufficiency of the information used by management in making decisions to acquire new fixed assets. In a different organization, the auditor might evaluate the efficiency of the information flow in processing sales.

Efficiency and effectiveness of operations are far more difficult to evaluate objectively than compliance or the presentation of financial statements in accordance with GAAP. In addition, establishing criteria for evaluating the information in an operational audit is an extremely subjective matter. In this sense, operational auditing is more like management consulting than what is generally regarded as auditing. Operational auditing is discussed in greater depth in Chapter 26.

Compliance Audits

A **compliance audit** is conducted to determine whether the auditee is following specific procedures, rules, or regulations set by some higher authority. A compliance audit for a private business could include:

- determining whether accounting personnel are following the procedures prescribed by the company controller,
- reviewing wage rates for compliance with minimum wage laws, or
- examining contractual agreements with bankers and other lenders to be sure the company is complying with legal requirements.

TABLE 1-3	Examples of the Three Types of Audits			
Type of Audit	**Example**	**Information**	**Established Criteria**	**Available Evidence**
Operational audit	Evaluate whether the computerized payroll processing for subsidiary H is operating efficiently and effectively	Number of payroll records processed in a month, costs of the department, and number of errors made	Company standards for efficiency and effectiveness in payroll department	Error reports, payroll records, and payroll processing costs
Compliance audit	Determine whether bank requirements for loan continuation have been met	Company records	Loan agreement provisions	Financial statements and calculations by the auditor
Financial statement audit	Annual audit of Boeing's financial statements	Boeing's financial statements	Generally accepted accounting principles	Documents, records, and outside sources of evidence

Governmental units, such as school districts, are subject to considerable compliance auditing because of extensive regulation by higher government authorities. In virtually every private and not-for-profit organization, prescribed policies, contractual agreements, and legal requirements may require compliance auditing. Compliance audits for federally funded grant programs are widely performed by CPAs and are discussed in detail in Chapter 26.

Results of compliance audits are typically reported to someone within the organizational unit being audited rather than to a broad spectrum of users. Management, as opposed to outside users, is the primary group concerned with the extent of compliance with certain prescribed procedures and regulations. Therefore, a significant portion of work of this type is done by auditors employed by the organizational units themselves. There are exceptions, however. When an organization wants to determine whether individuals or organizations are complying with its requirements, the auditor is employed by the organization issuing the requirements, such as when an auditor is employed by the government to audit tax returns.

A **financial statement audit** is conducted to determine whether the overall financial statements (the information being verified) are stated in accordance with specified criteria. Normally, the criteria are GAAP, although it is also common to conduct audits of financial statements prepared using the cash basis or some other basis of accounting appropriate for the organization. In determining whether financial statements are fairly stated in accordance with GAAP, the auditor performs appropriate tests to determine whether the statements contain material errors or other misstatements.

As businesses increase in complexity, it is no longer sufficient for auditors to focus narrowly on accounting transactions. An integrated approach to auditing considers both the risk of errors and operating controls intended to prevent errors. Increasingly, this integrated approach incorporates a strategic perspective of the business entity.

In a **strategic systems audit** approach, the auditor must have a thorough understanding of the entity and its environment. This holistic, top-level understanding includes knowledge of the client's industry and its regulatory and operating environment, including external relationships, such as suppliers, customers, and creditors. In addition, the auditor considers the client's business strategies and processes and measurement indicators for critical success factors related to those strategies. This analysis helps the auditor identify risks associated with the client's strategies that may affect whether the financial statements are fairly stated. Many of the skills necessary for the strategic systems audit approach are similar to those needed to provide other types of assurance services that can provide added value to the audit function.

TYPES OF AUDITORS

Several types of auditors are in practice today. The most common are certified public accounting firms, government accountability office auditors, internal revenue agents, and internal auditors.

OBJECTIVE 1-7

Identify the primary types of auditors.

Certified Public Accounting Firms

Certified public accounting firms are responsible for auditing the published historical financial statements of all publicly traded companies, most other reasonably large companies, and many smaller companies and noncommercial organizations. Because of the widespread use of audited financial statements in the U.S. economy, as well as businesspersons' and other users' familiarity with these statements, it is common to use the terms *auditor* and *CPA firm* synonymously, even though several different types of auditors exist. The title *certified public accounting firm* reflects the fact that auditors who express audit opinions on financial statements must be licensed as CPAs. CPA firms are often called *external auditors* or *independent auditors* to distinguish them from internal auditors.

Government Accountability Office Auditors

A **government accountability office auditor** is an auditor working for the U.S. Government Accountability Office (GAO), a nonpartisan agency in the legislative branch of the federal government. Headed by the Comptroller General, the GAO reports to and is responsible solely to Congress.

Auditing Careers

The GAO's primary responsibility is to perform the audit function for Congress, and it has many of the same audit responsibilities as a CPA firm. The GAO audits much of the financial information prepared by various government agencies before it is submitted to Congress. Because the authority for expenditures and receipts of governmental agencies is defined by law, there is considerable emphasis on compliance in these audits.

An increasing portion of the GAO's audit efforts has been devoted to evaluating the operational efficiency and effectiveness of various federal programs. Also, because of the immense size of many federal agencies and the similarity of their operations, the GAO has made significant advances in developing better methods of auditing through the widespread use of highly sophisticated statistical sampling and computer risk assessment techniques.

In many states, experience as a GAO auditor fulfills the experience requirement for becoming a CPA. In those states, if an individual passes the CPA examination and fulfills the experience stipulations by becoming a GAO auditor, he or she may then obtain a CPA certificate.

As a result of their great responsibility for auditing the expenditures of the federal government, their use of advanced auditing concepts, their eligibility to be CPAs, and their opportunities for performing operational audits, GAO auditors are highly regarded in the auditing profession.

Internal Revenue Agents

The IRS, under the direction of the Commissioner of Internal Revenue, is responsible for enforcing the *federal tax laws* as they have been defined by Congress and interpreted by the courts. A major responsibility of the IRS is to audit the taxpayers' returns to determine whether they have complied with the tax laws. These audits are solely compliance audits. The auditors who perform these examinations are called **internal revenue agents.**

It might seem that the audit of returns for compliance with the federal tax laws would be a simple and straightforward problem, but nothing could be farther from the truth. The tax laws are highly complicated, and there are hundreds of volumes of interpretations. The tax returns being audited vary from the simple returns of individuals who work for only one employer and take the standard tax deduction to the highly complex returns of multinational corporations. Taxation problems may involve individual taxpayers, gift taxes, estate taxes, corporate taxes, trusts, and so on. An auditor involved in any of these areas must have considerable tax knowledge and auditing skills to conduct an effective audit.

Internal Auditors

Internal auditors are employed by individual companies to audit for management, much as the GAO does for Congress. Internal auditors' responsibilities vary considerably, depending on the employer. Some internal audit staffs consist of only one or two employees doing routine compliance auditing. Other internal audit staffs may have more than 100 employees who have diverse responsibilities, including many outside the accounting area. Many internal auditors are involved in operational auditing or have expertise in evaluating computer systems.

To maintain independence from other business functions, the internal audit group typically reports directly to the president, another high executive officer, or the audit committee of the board of directors. However, internal auditors cannot be entirely independent of the entity as long as an employer–employee relationship exists. Users from outside the entity are unlikely to want to rely on information verified solely by internal auditors because of their lack of independence. This lack of independence is the major difference between internal auditors and CPA firms.

In many states, internal audit experience can be used to fulfill the experience requirement for becoming a CPA. Many internal auditors pursue certification as a certified internal auditor (CIA), and some internal auditors pursue both the CPA and CIA designations.

CERTIFIED PUBLIC ACCOUNTANT

Use of the title **certified public accountant** (CPA) is regulated by state law through the licensing departments of each state. Within any state, the regulations usually differ for becoming a CPA and retaining a license to practice after the designation has been initially achieved. To become a CPA, three requirements must be met. These are summarized in Figure 1-4.

For a person planning to become a CPA, it is essential to know the requirements in the state where he or she plans to obtain and maintain the CPA designation. The best source of that information is the State Board of Accountancy for the state in which the person plans to be certified. It is possible to transfer the CPA designation from one state to another, but additional requirements often must be met for formal education, practice experience, or continuing education.

Most young professionals who want to become CPAs start their careers working for a CPA firm. After they become CPAs, many leave the firm to work in industry, government, or education. These people may continue to be CPAs but often give up their right to practice as independent auditors. To maintain the right to practice as independent auditors in most states, CPAs must meet defined continuing education and licensing requirements. Therefore, it is common for accountants to be CPAs who do not practice as independent auditors.

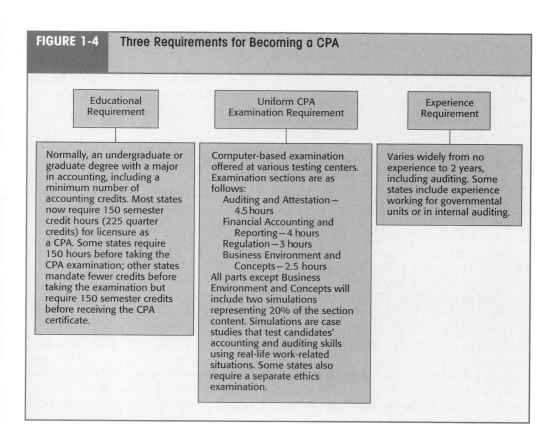

FIGURE 1-4   Three Requirements for Becoming a CPA

Educational Requirement	Uniform CPA Examination Requirement	Experience Requirement
Normally, an undergraduate or graduate degree with a major in accounting, including a minimum number of accounting credits. Most states now require 150 semester credit hours (225 quarter credits) for licensure as a CPA. Some states require 150 hours before taking the CPA examination; other states mandate fewer credits before taking the examination but require 150 semester credits before receiving the CPA certificate.	Computer-based examination offered at various testing centers. Examination sections are as follows: Auditing and Attestation—4.5 hours; Financial Accounting and Reporting—4 hours; Regulation—3 hours; Business Environment and Concepts—2.5 hours. All parts except Business Environment and Concepts will include two simulations representing 20% of the section content. Simulations are case studies that test candidates' accounting and auditing skills using real-life work-related situations. Some states also require a separate ethics examination.	Varies widely from no experience to 2 years, including auditing. Some states include experience working for governmental units or in internal auditing.

**CPA Information
and Requirements**

Information about the CPA examination can be found in *Information for Uniform CPA Examination Candidates* and the *Revised CPA Examination Content Specification Outline,* both of which can be downloaded from the CPA Exam Web site (www.cpa-exam.org). The AICPA also publishes selected examination questions with unofficial answers indexed to the content specification outlines of the examination.

Some of the questions and problems at the end of the chapters in this book have been taken from past CPA examinations. They are designated "AICPA" or "AICPA adapted."

SUMMARY

This chapter defined auditing and distinguished auditing from accounting. Audits are valuable because they reduce information risk, which lowers the cost of obtaining capital. The chapter also described attestation and assurance services, including reports on the effectiveness of internal control over financial reporting, and described the relationships among audits, attestation services, and assurance services. The market for assurance services is expected to grow with increases in technology and information. The chapter also described different types of audits and auditors and requirements for becoming a CPA.

ESSENTIAL TERMS

Accounting—the recording, classifying, and summarizing of economic events in a logical manner for the purpose of providing financial information for decision making

Assurance services—independent professional services that improve the quality of information for decision makers

Attestation service—a type of assurance service in which the CPA firm issues a report about the reliability of an assertion that is the responsibility of another party

Audit of historical financial statements—a form of attestation service in which the auditor issues a written report stating whether the financial statements are in material conformity with generally accepted accounting principles

Audit report—the communication of audit findings to users

Auditing—the accumulation and evaluation of evidence about information to determine and report on the degree of correspondence between the information and established criteria

Certified public accountant—a person who has met state regulatory requirements, including passing the Uniform CPA Examination, and has thus been certified; a CPA may have as his or her primary responsibility the performance of the audit function on published historical financial statements of commercial and noncommercial financial entities

Compliance audit—(1) a review of an organization's financial records performed to determine whether the organization is following specific procedures, rules, or regulations set by some higher authority; (2) an audit performed to determine whether an entity that receives financial assistance from the federal government has complied with specific laws and regulations

E-commerce—the use of information technology and electronic communication networks to exchange information and conduct transactions in electronic form

Evidence—any information used by the auditor to determine whether the information being audited is stated in accordance with established criteria

Financial statement audit—an audit conducted to determine whether the overall financial statements of an entity are stated in accordance with specified criteria (usually generally accepted accounting principles)

Government accountability office auditor—an auditor working for the U.S. Government Accountability Office (GAO); the GAO reports to and is responsible solely to Congress

Independent auditors—certified public accountants or accounting firms that perform audits of commercial and noncommercial financial entities

Information risk—the risk that information upon which a business decision is made is inaccurate

Internal auditors—auditors employed by a company to audit for the company's board of directors and management

Internal control over financial reporting—an attestation engagement in which the auditor reports on the effectiveness of internal control over financial reporting; such reports are required for public companies under Section 404 of the Sarbanes–Oxley Act

Internal revenue agents—auditors who work for the Internal Revenue Service (IRS) and conduct examinations of taxpayers' returns

Operational audit—a review of any part of an organization's operating procedures and methods for the purpose of evaluating efficiency and effectiveness

Review of historical financial statements—a form of attestation in which a CPA firm issues a written report that provides less assurance than an audit as to whether the financial statements are in material conformity with generally accepted accounting principles

Sarbanes–Oxley Act—a federal securities law passed in 2002 that provides for additional regulation of public companies and their auditors; the Act established the Public Company Accounting Oversight Board and also requires auditors to attest to management reports on the effectiveness of internal control over financial reporting

Strategic systems audit—audit approach based on understanding the client's business strategies and processes and external relations and factors that impact those strategies

REVIEW QUESTIONS

1-1 (Objective 1-5) Explain the relationships among audit services, attestation services, and assurance services, and give examples of each.

1-2 (Objective 1-3) Discuss the major factors in today's society that have made the need for independent audits much greater than it was 50 years ago.

1-3 (Objective 1-3) Distinguish among the following three risks: risk-free interest rate, business risk, and information risk. Which one or ones does the auditor reduce by performing an audit?

1-4 (Objective 1-4) Identify the major causes of information risk and identify the three main ways information risk can be reduced. What are the advantages and disadvantages of each?

1-5 (Objective 1-1) Explain what is meant by determining the degree of correspondence between information and established criteria. What are the information and established criteria for the audit of Jones Company's tax return by an internal revenue agent? What are they for the audit of Jones Company's financial statements by a CPA firm?

1-6 (Objectives 1-1, 1-7) Describe the nature of the evidence the internal revenue agent will use in the audit of Jones Company's tax return.

1-7 (Objective 1-2) In the conduct of audits of financial statements, it would be a serious breach of responsibility if the auditor did not thoroughly understand accounting. However, many competent accountants do not have an understanding of the auditing process. What causes this difference?

1-8 (Objective 1-6) What are the differences and similarities in audits of financial statements, compliance audits, and operational audits?

1-9 (Objectives 1-6, 1-7) List five examples of specific operational audits that could be conducted by an internal auditor in a manufacturing company.

1-10 (Objectives 1-5, 1-6) What knowledge does the auditor need about the client to follow a strategic systems audit approach in an audit of historical financial statements? Explain how this knowledge may be useful in performing other assurance or consulting services for the client.

1-11 (Objective 1-7) What are the major differences in the scope of the audit responsibilities for CPAs, GAO auditors, IRS agents, and internal auditors?

1-12 (Objective 1-8) Identify the four parts of the Uniform CPA Examination.

1-13 (Objective 1-5) Explain why CPAs need to be knowledgeable about e-commerce technologies.

MULTIPLE CHOICE QUESTIONS FROM CPA EXAMINATIONS

1-14 (Objectives 1-1, 1-3, 1-5) The following questions deal with audits by CPA firms. Choose the best response.

a. Which of the following best describes why an independent auditor is asked to express an opinion on the fair presentation of financial statements?
   (1) It is difficult to prepare financial statements that fairly present a company's financial position, operations, and cash flows without the expertise of an independent auditor.
   (2) It is management's responsibility to seek available independent aid in the appraisal of the financial information shown in its financial statements.

(3) The opinion of an independent party is needed because a company may not be objective with respect to its own financial statements.

(4) It is a customary courtesy that all stockholders of a company receive an independent report on management's stewardship of the affairs of the business.

b. Independent auditing can best be described as
(1) a branch of accounting.
(2) a discipline that attests to the results of accounting and other functional operations and data.
(3) a professional activity that measures and communicates financial and business data.
(4) a regulatory function that prevents the issuance of improper financial information.

c. Which of the following professional services would be considered an attestation engagement?
(1) A consulting service engagement to provide computer-processing advice to a client.
(2) An engagement to report on statutory requirements.
(3) An income tax engagement to prepare federal and state tax returns.
(4) The compilation of financial statements from a client's financial records.

d. In performing an attestation engagement, a CPA typically
(1) supplies litigation support services.
(2) assesses control risk at a low level.
(3) expresses a conclusion about an assertion.
(4) provides management consulting advice.

1-15 (Objectives 1-6, 1-7) The following questions deal with types of audits and auditors. Choose the best response.

a. Operational audits generally have been conducted by internal auditors and governmental audit agencies but may be performed by certified public accountants. A primary purpose of an operational audit is to provide
(1) a means of assurance that internal accounting controls are functioning as planned.
(2) a measure of management performance in meeting organizational goals.
(3) the results of internal examinations of financial and accounting matters to a company's top-level management.
(4) aid to the independent auditor, who is conducting the audit of the financial statements.

b. In comparison to the external auditor, an internal auditor is more likely to be concerned with
(1) internal administrative control.
(2) cost accounting procedures.
(3) operational auditing.
(4) internal control.

c. Which of the following best describes the operational audit?
(1) It requires the constant review by internal auditors of the administrative controls as they relate to the operations of the company.
(2) It concentrates on implementing financial and accounting control in a newly organized company.
(3) It attempts and is designed to verify the fair presentation of a company's results of operations.
(4) It concentrates on seeking aspects of operations in which waste could be reduced by the introduction of controls.

d. Compliance auditing often extends beyond audits leading to the expression of opinions on the fairness of financial presentation and includes audits of efficiency, economy, effectiveness, as well as
(1) accuracy.
(2) evaluation.
(3) adherence to specific rules or procedures.
(4) internal control.

DISCUSSION QUESTIONS AND PROBLEMS

1-16 (Objective 1-5) The list below indicates various audit, attestation, and assurance engagements involving auditors.

1. An auditor's report on whether the financial statements are fairly presented in accordance with GAAP.
2. An electronic seal indicating that an electronic seller observes certain practices.
3. A report indicating whether a governmental entity has complied with certain government regulations.

4. A report on the examination of a financial forecast.
5. A report on the effectiveness of internal control over financial reporting as required by Section 404 of the Sarbanes–Oxley Act.
6. A review report that provides moderate assurance about whether financial statements are fairly stated in accordance with GAAP.
7. A report on compliance with a royalty agreement.
8. A report about management's assertion on the effectiveness of controls over the availability, reliability, integrity, and maintainability of its accounting information system.
9. An evaluation of the effectiveness of key measures used to assess an entity's success in achieving specific targets linked to an entity's strategic plan and vision.

a. Explain or use a diagram to indicate the relationships among audit services, attestation services, and assurance services.

Required

b. For each of the services listed above, indicate the type of service from the list that follows.
   (1) An audit of historical financial statements.
   (2) An attestation service other than an audit service.
   (3) An assurance service that is not an attestation service.

1-17 (Objective 1-3) Vial-tek has an existing loan in the amount of $1.5 million with an annual interest rate of 9.5%. The company provides an internal company-prepared financial statement to the bank under the loan agreement. Two competing banks have offered to replace Vial-tek's existing loan agreement with a new one. First National Bank has offered to loan Vial-tek $1.5 million at a rate of 8.5% but would require Vial-tek to provide financial statements that have been reviewed by a CPA firm. City First Bank has offered to loan Vial-tek $1.5 million at a rate of 7.5% but would require Vial-tek to provide financial statements that have been audited by a CPA firm. The controller of Vial-tek approached a CPA firm and was given an estimated cost of $12,000 to perform a review and $20,000 to perform an audit.

a. Explain why the interest rate for the loan that requires a review report is lower than that for the loan that did not require a review. Explain why the interest rate for the loan that requires an audit report is lower than the interest rate for the other two loans.

Required

b. Calculate Vial-tek's annual costs under each loan agreement, including interest and costs for the CPA firm's services. Indicate whether Vial-tek should keep its existing loan, accept the offer from First National Bank, or accept the offer from City First Bank.

c. Discuss why Vial-tek may desire to have an audit performed, ignoring the potential reduction in interest costs.

d. Explain how knowledge of e-commerce technologies and use of a strategic systems audit approach may increase the value of the audit service.

1-18 (Objectives 1-3, 1-4, 1-5) Consumers Union is a nonprofit organization that provides information and counsel on consumer goods and services. A major part of its function is the testing of different brands of consumer products that are purchased on the open market and then the reporting of the results of the tests in *Consumer Reports,* a monthly publication. Examples of the types of products it tests are middle-sized automobiles, residential dehumidifiers, canned tuna, and boys' jeans.

a. In what ways are the services provided by Consumers Union similar to assurance services provided by CPA firms?

Required

b. Compare the concept of information risk introduced in this chapter with the information risk problem faced by a buyer of an automobile.

c. Compare the four causes of information risk faced by users of financial statements as discussed in this chapter with those faced by a buyer of an automobile.

d. Compare the three ways users of financial statements can reduce information risk with those available to a buyer of an automobile.

1-19 (Objective 1-1) Fred Oatly is the loan officer of the National Bank of Dallas. National has a loan of $260,000 outstanding to Regional Delivery Service, a company specializing in delivering products of all types on behalf of smaller companies. National's collateral on the loan consists of 35 small delivery trucks with an average original cost of $17,000.

Oatly is concerned about the collectibility of the outstanding loan and whether the trucks still exist. He therefore engages Susan Virms, CPA, to count the trucks, using registration information held by Oatly. She was engaged because she spends most of her time auditing used automobile and truck dealerships and has extensive specialized knowledge about used trucks. Oatly requests that Virms issue a report stating the following:

1. Which of the 35 trucks is parked in Regional's parking lot on the night of June 30, 2005.
2. Whether all of the trucks are owned by Regional Delivery Service.
3. The condition of each truck, using the guidelines of poor, good, and excellent.
4. The fair market value of each truck, using the current "blue book" for trucks, which states the approximate wholesale prices of all used truck models, and also using the poor, good, and excellent condition guidelines.

Required

a. For each of the following parts of the definition of auditing, state which part of the preceding narrative fits the definition:
   (1) Information
   (2) Established criteria
   (3) Accumulating and evaluating evidence
   (4) Competent, independent person
   (5) Reporting results

b. Identify the greatest difficulties Virms is likely to have doing this audit.

1-20 (Objective 1-7) Five college seniors with majors in accounting are discussing alternative career plans. The first senior plans to become an internal revenue agent because his primary interest is income taxes. He believes the background in tax auditing will provide him with better exposure to income taxes than will any other available career choice. The second senior has decided to go to work for a CPA firm for at least 5 years, possibly as a permanent career. She believes the variety of experience in auditing and related fields offers a better alternative than any other available choice. The third senior has decided on a career in internal auditing with a large industrial company because of the many different aspects of the organization with which internal auditors become involved. The fourth senior plans to become an auditor for the GAO because she believes that this career will provide excellent experience in computer risk assessment techniques. The fifth senior plans to pursue some aspect of auditing as a career but has not decided on the type of organization to enter. He is especially interested in an opportunity to continue to grow professionally, but meaningful and interesting employment is also an important consideration.

Required

a. What are the major advantages and disadvantages of each of the four types of auditing careers?

b. What other types of auditing careers are available to those who are qualified?

1-21 (Objectives 1-6, 1-7) In the normal course of performing their responsibilities, auditors often conduct audits or reviews of the following:

1. Federal income tax returns of an officer of the corporation to determine whether he or she has included all taxable income in his or her return.
2. Disbursements of a branch of the federal government for a special research project to determine whether it would have been possible to accomplish the same research results at a lower cost to the taxpayers.
3. Computer operations of a corporation to evaluate whether the computer center is being operated as efficiently as possible.
4. Annual statements for the use of management.
5. Operations of the IRS to determine whether the internal revenue agents are using their time efficiently in conducting audits.
6. Statements for bankers and other creditors when the client is too small to have an audit staff.
7. Financial statements of a branch of the federal government to make sure that the statements present fairly the actual disbursements made during a period of time.
8. Federal income tax returns of a corporation to determine whether the tax laws have been followed.
9. Financial statements for use by stockholders when there is an internal audit staff.
10. A bond indenture agreement to make sure a company is following all requirements of the contract.
11. The computer operations of a large corporation to evaluate whether the internal controls are likely to prevent misstatements in accounting and operating data.
12. Disbursements of a branch of the federal government for a special research project to determine whether the expenditures were consistent with the legislative bill that authorized the project.

Required

a. For these 12 examples, state the most likely type of auditor (CPA, GAO, IRS, or internal) to perform each.

b. In each example, state the type of audit (financial statement audit, operational audit, or compliance audit).

1-22 (Objectives 1-6, 1-7) A large conglomerate is considering acquiring a medium-sized manufacturing company in a closely related industry. A major consideration by the management of the conglomerate in deciding whether to pursue the merger is the operational efficiency of the company. Management has decided to obtain a detailed report based on an intensive investigation of the operational efficiency of the sales department, production department, and research and development department.

a. Whom should the conglomerate engage to conduct the operational audit?

Required

b. What major problems are the auditors likely to encounter in conducting the investigation and writing the report?

1-23 (Objective 1-5) A small, but expanding, specialty home-products retailer recently implemented an Internet portal that allows customers to order merchandise online. In the first few months of operation, their Internet site attracted a large number of visitors; however, very few placed orders online. The retailer conducted several focus-group sessions with potential shoppers to identify reasons why shoppers were visiting the Web site without placing orders. Shoppers in the focus groups made these comments:

1. "I am nervous about doing business with this retailer because it is relatively unknown in the marketplace. How do I know the product descriptions on the Web site are accurate, and that the stated return policies are followed?"
2. "I am reluctant to provide my credit card information online. How do I know the transmission of my personal credit card information to the retailer's Web site is protected?"
3. "Retailers are notorious for selling information about customers to others. The last thing I want to do is enter personal information online, such as my name, address, telephone number, and e-mail address. I am afraid this retailer will sell that information to third parties and then I'll be bombarded with a bunch of junk e-mail messages!"
4. "Web sites go down all the time due to system failures. How do I know the retailer's Web site will be operating when I need it?"

a. Discuss whether this situation provides an opportunity for CPAs to address these customer concerns.

Required

b. For each customer comment, identify the appropriate *WebTrust* principle that a *WebTrust* licensed CPA could apply to the retailer to address the concerns noted. Choose from the following:
   (1) *WebTrust* Online Privacy
   (2) *WebTrust* Security
   (3) *WebTrust* Processing Integrity
   (4) *WebTrust* Availability
   (5) *WebTrust* Confidentiality
   (6) *WebTrust* Certification Authorities

INTERNET PROBLEM 1-1: ASSURANCE SERVICES

Reference Prentice Hall's Companion Web Site (CW site).[2] Businesses must have access to more decision-relevant information than ever before. Furthermore, businesses and individuals need independent assurance that the information on which their decisions are based is reliable. By virtue of their training, experience, and reputation for integrity, CPAs are the logical choice to provide this assurance. To assist the profession's move forward, the AICPA formed the Special Committee on Assurance Services. This problem requires students to use the Internet to (1) research assurance services recommended by the committee, (2) examine components of assurance service business plans, and (3) identify and describe competencies needed by assurance providers in the upcoming decade.

---

[2] Internet problems can be found at Prentice Hall's Companion Web Site (CW site), www. prenhall.com/arens.

THE CPA PROFESSION

GOOD AUDITING INCLUDES GOOD CLIENT SERVICE

"It had been a good week," thought Jeanine Wilson, as she drove out of the parking lot of Solberg Paints on Friday afternoon. Just a few months earlier, she graduated from State University and sat for the CPA examination. Still, Jeanine did not think her transition to professional life had been all that smooth, and she was surprised at how much there still was to learn. But she had made great progress on the Solberg job.

John Hernandez was the audit senior on the Solberg Paints audit, and he had a reputation as a patient teacher and supervisor. Jeanine was not disappointed. At the start of the engagement, John told her, "Don't be afraid to ask questions. If you see anything that seems unusual, let's discuss it. And most importantly, if you have any ideas that will help the client, bring them up. The client expects us to deliver more than an audit report."

"I'd say I delivered," thought Jeanine. She found an error in the way the company had calculated LIFO inventory that was going to save the client a significant amount of taxes. But her biggest contribution almost did not happen. Jeanine read as much as she could about paint manufacturers and learned about some new production control methods that seemed like they could apply to Solberg. She was afraid to bring it up, thinking that she couldn't possibly know anything that the client didn't already know, but John encouraged her to discuss it with the client. The result was that the client wanted to meet further with Jeanine's firm to better understand how they could improve their production processes.

Friday was the last day of field work on the audit, and the partner, Bill Marlow, was at the client's office to complete his review of the audit files. Jeanine was surprised to hear him say to her, "What are you doing on the 15th? We're going to meet with the client to discuss our audit findings. You've made a real contribution on this audit, and I'd like you to be there." Jeanine tried not to show her excitement too much, but she couldn't hide the smile on her face. "Yes, it *had* been a good week."

LEARNING OBJECTIVES

After studying this chapter, you should be able to

2-1 Describe the nature of CPA firms, what they do, and their structure.

2-2 Understand the role of the Public Company Accounting Oversight Board and the effects of the Sarbanes–Oxley Act on the CPA profession.

2-3 Summarize the role of the Securities and Exchange Commission in accounting and auditing.

2-4 Describe the key functions performed by the AICPA.

2-5 Use generally accepted auditing standards as a basis for further study.

2-6 Discuss the role of international auditing standards.

2-7 Identify quality control standards and practices within the accounting profession.

We learned in the first chapter that auditing plays an important role in society by reducing information risk and facilitating access to capital and that audit firms provide additional, value-added service to their clients. As the opening vignette to this chapter demonstrates, audit professionals at all experience levels serve as valued advisors to their clients. This chapter describes the organization of CPA firms and the types of services they provide. We also discuss the effects on auditing of the Sarbanes–Oxley Act and the Public Company Accounting Oversight Board (PCAOB), as well as other standards and regulatory agencies that influence auditor performance.

CERTIFIED PUBLIC ACCOUNTING FIRMS

Except for certain governmental organizations, the audits of all general use financial statements in the United States are done by CPA firms. The legal right to perform audits is granted to CPA firms by regulation of each state. CPA firms also provide many other services to their clients, such as tax and consulting services.

More than 40,000 CPA firms exist in the United States, ranging in size from 1 person to 20,000 partners and staff. *Accounting Today* publishes an annual list of the 100 largest accounting firms. As Table 2-1 illustrates, most of these are CPA firms, although the list includes a few companies such as H&R Block Tax Services. Four size categories are used to describe CPA firms: Big Four international firms, national firms, regional and large local firms, and small local firms.

- *Big Four international firms.* The four largest CPA firms in the United States are called the "Big Four" international CPA firms. They are the first four firms listed in Table 2-1. These four firms have offices throughout the United States and

TABLE 2-1	**Revenue and Other Data for the Largest CPA Firms in the United States**					
2003 Size by Revenue	Firm (1)	Net Revenue— U.S. Only (in $ millions)	Partners	Professionals	U.S. Offices	Percentage of Total Revenue from Accounting and Auditing/Taxes/ Management Consulting and Other
		Big Four				
1	Deloitte & Touche	$6,511.0	2,613	20,487	91	39/25/36
2	Ernst & Young	$5,260.0	2,000	14,400	86	62/35/03
3	PricewaterhouseCoopers	$4,850.0	2,000	21,000	125	62/33/05
4	KPMG	$3,793.0	1,622	11,529	94	67/33/00
		National				
5	RSM McGladrey/McGladrey & Pullen	$ 595.9	498	2,701	91	39/42/19
6	Grant Thornton	$ 484.8	328	2,217	48	52/33/15
7	BDO Seidman	$ 350.0	281	1,243	36	46/37/17
		Regional				
8	Crowe Group	$ 247.3	153	925	16	24/19/57
9	BKD	$ 215.7	194	952	27	42/36/22
10	Moss Adams	$ 181.0	185	825	23	36/38/26
11	Plante & Moran	$ 174.0	156	760	15	46/31/23
		Large Local				
50	Rubin, Brown, Gornstein & Co.	$ 30.0	21	209	1	45/30/25
75	Katz, Sapper & Miller	$ 22.9	22	101	1	25/30/45

(1) List includes only CPA firms and does not include national accounting firms that do not provide audit or attest services. Regional firms exclude alternative practice structures and similar arrangements.
Source: Accounting Today, March 15–April 4, 2004/www.webcpa.com.

throughout the world. The Big Four firms audit nearly all of the largest companies both in the United States and worldwide and many smaller companies as well.

- *National firms.* Three CPA firms in the United States are called national firms because they have offices in most major cities. These are firms 5 through 7 in Table 2-1. These firms are large but considerably smaller than the Big Four. The national firms perform the same services as the Big Four firms and compete directly with them for clients. Each national firm is affiliated with firms in other countries and therefore has an international capability.

Big Four, National, and Regional Firms

- *Regional and large local firms.* There are less than 200 CPA firms with professional staffs of more than 50 people. Some have only one office and serve clients primarily within commuting distances. Others have several offices in a state or region and serve a larger radius of clients. For example, Table 2-1 shows that the largest regional firms are not dramatically smaller than the three national firms. Regional and large local firms compete for clients with other CPA firms, including national and Big Four firms. Many of the regional and large local firms are affiliated with associations of CPA firms to share resources for such things as technical information and continuing education. Many of these firms also have international affiliations.

- *Small local firms.* More than 95 percent of all CPA firms have fewer than 25 professionals in a single-office firm. They perform audits and related services primarily for smaller businesses and not-for-profit entities, although some have one or two clients with public ownership. Many small local firms do not perform audits and primarily provide accounting and tax services to their clients.

ACTIVITIES OF CPA FIRMS

As discussed in Chapter 1, CPA firms provide audit services and have expanded their scope of services to provide additional attestation and assurance services. Additional services commonly provided by CPA firms include accounting and bookkeeping services, tax services, and management consulting services. CPA firms continue to develop new products and services, including financial planning, business valuation, forensic accounting, internal audit outsourcing, and information technology advisory services.

- *Accounting and bookkeeping services.* Many small clients with limited accounting staff rely on CPA firms to prepare their financial statements. Some small clients lack the personnel or expertise to use accounting software for preparing their own journals and ledgers. Thus, CPA firms perform a variety of accounting and bookkeeping services to meet the needs of these clients. In many cases in which the financial statements are to be given to a third party, a review or even an audit is also performed. When neither of these is done, the financial statements are accompanied by a type of report by the CPA firm called a compilation report, which provides no assurance to third parties. As Table 2-1 shows, attestation services and accounting and bookkeeping services account for approximately one-third to more than one-half of the revenue for most large CPA firms.

• *Tax services.* CPA firms prepare corporate and individual tax returns for both audit and nonaudit clients. Almost every CPA firm performs tax services, which may include estate tax, gift tax, tax planning, and other aspects of tax services. For many small firms, such services are far more important to their practice than auditing, as most of their revenue may be generated from tax services.

• *Management consulting services.* Most CPA firms provide certain services that enable their clients to operate their businesses more effectively. These services are called management consulting or management advisory services. These services range from simple suggestions for improving the client's accounting system to advice in risk management, information technology and e-commerce system design, mergers and acquisitions due diligence, and actuarial benefit consulting. Many large CPA firms have departments involved exclusively in management consulting services with little interaction with the audit or tax staff.

Revenues from management consulting increased significantly in the late 1990s, and consulting at one time was the largest source of revenue for all the Big Four firms. Three of the Big Four accounting firms, as well as the former Andersen firm, have sold or otherwise disposed of their consulting practices. These dispositions were partially due to independence concerns and restrictions placed on consulting practices. These changes originated well before passage of the Sarbanes–Oxley Act, and before the SEC issued revisions to its auditor independence rules in November 2000. Table 2-1 shows that management consulting and other services continue to be a significant source of revenue for Deloitte & Touche, the only Big Four firm that has not disposed of all or most of its consulting practice. Consulting continues to be an important source of revenue for other accounting firms.

STRUCTURE OF CPA FIRMS

CPA firms vary in the nature and range of services offered, which will affect the organization and structure of the firms. Three main factors influence the organizational structure of all firms:

1. *The need for independence from clients.* Independence permits auditors to remain unbiased in drawing conclusions about the financial statements.
2. *The importance of a structure to encourage competence.* Competence permits auditors to conduct audits and perform other services efficiently and effectively.
3. *The increased litigation risk faced by auditors.* In the last decade, firms have experienced increases in litigation-related costs. Some organizational structures afford a degree of protection to individual firm members.

Organizational Structures

Six organizational structures are available to CPA firms. Except for the proprietorship, each structure results in an entity separate from the CPA personally, which helps promote auditor independence. The last four organizational structures provide some protection from litigation loss.

Proprietorship Only firms with one owner can operate in this form. Traditionally, all one-owner firms were organized as proprietorships, but in recent years, most of them have changed to organizational forms with more limited liability because of litigation risks.

General Partnership This form of organization is the same as a proprietorship, except that it applies to multiple owners. This organizational structure has also become less popular as other forms of ownership that offer some legal liability protection became authorized under state laws.

General Corporation The advantage of a corporation is that shareholders are liable only to the extent of their investment in the corporation. Most CPA firms do not organize as general corporations because they are prohibited by law from doing so in most states.

Professional Corporation A professional corporation (PC) provides professional services and is owned by one or more shareholders. PC laws in some states offer personal liability protection similar to that of general corporations, whereas the protection in other states is minimal. This variation makes it difficult for a CPA firm with clients in different states to operate as a PC.

Limited Liability Company A limited liability company (LLC) combines the most favorable attributes of a general corporation and a general partnership. An LLC is typically structured and taxed like a general partnership, but its owners have limited personal liability similar to that of a general corporation. Currently, nearly all of the states have LLC laws, and most also allow accounting firms to operate as LLCs.

Limited Liability Partnership A limited liability partnership (LLP) is owned by one or more partners. It is structured and taxed like a general partnership, but the personal liability protection of an LLP is less than that of a general corporation or an LLC. Partners of an LLP are personally liable for the partnership's debts and obligations, their own acts, and acts of others under their supervision. Partners are not personally liable for liabilities arising from negligent acts of other partners and employees not under their supervision. It is not surprising that all of the Big Four firms and many smaller firms now operate as LLPs.

Hierarchy of a Typical CPA Firm

The organizational hierarchy in a typical CPA firm includes partners or shareholders, managers, supervisors, seniors or in-charge auditors, and assistants. A new employee usually starts as an assistant and spends 2 or 3 years in each classification before achieving partner status. The titles of the positions vary from firm to firm, but the structure is similar in all. When we refer in this text to the *auditor*, we mean the person performing some aspect of an audit. It is common to have one or more auditors from each level on larger engagements.

Table 2-2 summarizes the experience and responsibilities of each classification level within CPA firms. Advancement in CPA firms is fairly rapid, with evolving duties and responsibilities. In addition, audit staff members usually gain diversity of experience across client engagements. Because of advances in computer and audit technology, beginning assistants on the audit are rapidly given greater responsibility and challenges.

The hierarchical nature of CPA firms helps promote competence. Individuals at each level of the audit supervise and review the work of others at the level just below them in the organizational structure. A new staff assistant is supervised directly by the senior or in-charge auditor. The staff assistant's work is then reviewed by the in-charge as well as by the manager and partner.

TABLE 2-2	Staff Levels and Responsibilities	
Staff Level	**Average Experience**	**Typical Responsibilities**
Staff Assistant	0–2 years	Performs most of the detailed audit work.
Senior or in-charge auditor	2–5 years	Coordinates and is responsible for the audit field work, including supervising and reviewing staff work.
Manager	5–10 years	Helps the in-charge plan and manage the audit, reviews the in-charge's work, and manages relations with the client. A manager may be responsible for more than one engagement at the same time.
Partner	10+ years	Reviews the overall audit work and is involved in significant audit decisions. A partner is an owner of the firm and therefore has the ultimate responsibility for conducting the audit and serving the client.

To promote competence and to better serve their clients, many CPA firms have also organized along industry specialization lines. Auditors at each staff level may specialize in the performance of audits of certain industries, such as financial institutions. By specializing along industry lines, auditors gain a greater understanding of the client's business. To facilitate a total service approach, industry specialization groups may cross functional lines. For example, a health care specialization group may include auditors, tax professionals, and consultants specializing in health care.

E-Commerce and CPA Firm Operations

Like all industries, CPA firms are using the Internet to market their services. Firms of all sizes use the Internet to highlight such things as office locations or affiliations, service lines, and industry specializations and provide reference tools and materials to existing and potential clients. Firm Web sites feature news and insights about business issues, such as updates on changes in tax laws and interactive forms to determine which type of retirement account to choose. Firm Web sites also feature online software tools and databases to subscribers who pay a fee. For example, Ernst and Young sells its *Accounting and Auditing Tool Kit* to subscribers through its Ernst and Young *Online* Web site. PricewaterhouseCoopers LLP, through an alliance with Watchfire[sm], offers a privacy management software tool, *WatchfireWebCPO*, that provides protection to online information.

CPA firms also use the Internet to connect their global professional staff. Firm personnel from around the world can contribute services to a client on a timely basis without having to be physically present at the client's location. Communicating electronically among firm personnel is especially advantageous for firms that serve multinational clients with operations around the globe. For example, personnel in New York, Tokyo, and London who have expertise in local regulations and business cultures can serve local clients and branches of international clients with operations in those cities and can also communicate with engagement team personnel serving those clients in other locations.

CPA firms take advantage of online resources and databases to help their staffs stay current on emerging business and standards-setting issues. By subscribing to online databases, such as *Standard and Poor's Net Advantage Database* and *Goldman Sachs Research Database*, CPAs can keep informed about specific companies and industry developments and obtain up-to-date industry data that are useful for auditing and consulting purposes.

SARBANES–OXLEY ACT AND PUBLIC COMPANY ACCOUNTING OVERSIGHT BOARD

OBJECTIVE 2-2

Understand the role of the Public Company Accounting Oversight Board and the effects of the Sarbanes–Oxley Act on the CPA profession.

Triggered by the bankruptcies and alleged audit failures involving such companies as Enron and WorldCom, the Sarbanes–Oxley Act was signed into legislation on July 30, 2002. Considered by many to be the most important legislation affecting the auditing profession since the 1933 and 1934 Securities Acts, the provisions of the Act dramatically changed the relationship between publicly held companies and their audit firms.

The Sarbanes–Oxley Act established the **Public Company Accounting Oversight Board (PCAOB),** appointed and overseen by the Securities and Exchange Commission (SEC). The PCAOB provides oversight for auditors of public companies, establishes auditing and quality control standards for public company audits, and performs inspections of the quality controls at audit firms performing those audits. These activities were formerly the responsibility of the AICPA.

Prior to passage of the Sarbanes–Oxley Act, the Auditing Standards Board (ASB) of the AICPA established auditing standards for private and public companies. The PCAOB now has responsibility for auditing standards for public companies, while the ASB continues to provide auditing standards for private companies.

The PCAOB adopted auditing standards established by the ASB as interim audit standards. As a result, auditing standards for public and private companies are similar and are based on standards established by the ASB. When reference is made to a Statement on Auditing Standards (SAS) issued by the ASB, it is assumed that the standard applies to both public and private companies unless noted otherwise. The PCAOB has begun to issue its own auditing standards, including establishing standards for audits of the effectiveness of internal control over financial reporting. These standards are referred to as PCAOB Auditing Standards when referenced in the text.

The PCAOB conducts inspections of registered accounting firms to assess their compliance with the rules of the PCAOB and SEC, professional standards, and each firm's own quality control policies. The PCAOB requires annual inspections of accounting firms that audit more than 100 issuers and inspections of other registered firms at least once every three years. Any violations could result in disciplinary action by the PCAOB and be reported to the SEC and state accountancy boards.

SECURITIES AND EXCHANGE COMMISSION

The **Securities and Exchange Commission (SEC),** an agency of the federal government, assists in providing investors with reliable information upon which to make investment decisions. The Securities Act of 1933 requires most companies planning to issue *new securities* to the public to submit a registration statement to the SEC for approval. The Securities Exchange Act of 1934 provides additional protection by requiring public companies and others to file detailed annual reports with the commission. The commission examines these statements for completeness and adequacy before permitting the company to sell its securities through the securities exchanges.

Although the SEC requires considerable information that is not of direct interest to CPAs, the securities acts of 1933 and 1934 require financial statements, accompanied by the opinion of an independent public accountant, as part of a registration statement and subsequent reports.

SEC

Of special interest to auditors are several specific reports that are subject to the reporting provisions of the securities acts. The most important of these are as follows:

- *Forms S-1 to S-16.* These forms must be completed and registered with the SEC when a company plans to issue new securities to the public. The S-1 form is the general form used when there is no specifically prescribed form. The others are specialized forms. For example, S-11 is for registration of securities of certain real estate companies. All "S" forms apply to the Securities Act of 1933.
- *Form 8-K.* This report is filed to report significant events that are of interest to public investors. Such events include the acquisition or sale of a subsidiary, a change in officers or directors, an addition of a new product line, or a change in auditors.
- *Form 10-K.* This report must be filed annually within 60 days after the close of each fiscal year for companies with more than $75 million in public equity, and within 90 days for all other companies. Extensive detailed financial information, including audited financial statements, is contained in this report.
- *Form 10-Q.* This report must be filed quarterly for all publicly held companies. It contains certain financial information and requires timely auditor reviews of the financial statements before filing with the commission.

Because large CPA firms usually have clients that must file one or more of these reports each year, and the rules and regulations affecting filings with the SEC are extremely complex, most CPA firms have specialists who spend a large portion of their time ensuring that their clients satisfy all SEC requirements.

The SEC has considerable influence in setting generally accepted accounting principles (GAAP) and disclosure requirements for financial statements as a result of its authority for specifying reporting requirements considered necessary for fair disclosure to investors. The SEC has power to establish rules for any CPA associated with audited financial statements submitted to the commission. The SEC's attitude is generally considered in any major change proposed by the Financial Accounting Standards Board (FASB), the independent organization that establishes GAAP.

OBJECTIVE 2-3

Summarize the role of the Securities and Exchange Commission in accounting and auditing.

The SEC requirements of greatest interest to CPAs are set forth in the commission's Regulation S-X, Accounting Series Releases, and Accounting and Auditing Enforcement Releases. These publications constitute important regulations, as well as decisions and opinions on accounting and auditing issues affecting any CPA dealing with publicly held companies. Some of the major influences the SEC has had on auditors in the past few decades are discussed in the text under the topics of independence, legal liability, and audit reports.

AMERICAN INSTITUTE OF CERTIFIED PUBLIC ACCOUNTANTS (AICPA)

OBJECTIVE 2-4

Describe the key functions performed by the AICPA.

CPAs are licensed by the state in which they practice, but the most important influence on CPAs is exerted by their national professional organization, the American Institute of Certified Public Accountants (**AICPA**). Membership in the AICPA is restricted to CPAs, but not all members are practicing as independent auditors. Many members formerly worked for CPA firms but are currently working in government, industry, and education. AICPA membership is voluntary, so not all CPAs join. However, the AICPA estimates that three out of every four CPAs in the United States are members.

The AICPA sets professional requirements for CPAs, conducts research, and publishes materials on many different subjects related to accounting, auditing, attestation and assurance services, management consulting services, and taxes. The AICPA also promotes the accounting profession through organizing national advertising campaigns, promoting new assurance services, and developing specialist certifications to help market and ensure the quality of services in specialized practice areas. For example, the association currently offers specialty designations in business valuation, financial planning, and information technology.

Establishing Standards and Rules

The AICPA sets standards and rules that all members and other practicing CPAs must follow. The five major areas in which the AICPA has authority to set standards and make rules are as follows:

1. *Auditing standards.* The Auditing Standards Board (ASB) is responsible for issuing pronouncements on auditing matters for all entities other than publicly traded companies. ASB pronouncements are called **Statements on Auditing Standards** (**SASs**). They are further discussed later in this chapter and throughout the text.

2. *Compilation and review standards.* The Accounting and Review Services Committee is responsible for issuing pronouncements of the CPA's responsibilities when a CPA is associated with financial statements of privately owned companies that are not audited. They are called Statements on Standards for Accounting and Review Services (SSARS), and they provide guidance for performing compilation and review services. In a compilation service, the accountant helps the client prepare financial statements without providing any assurance. In a review service, the accountant performs inquiry and analytical procedures that provide a reasonable basis for expressing limited assurance on the financial statements.

3. *Other attestation standards.* The first Statement on Standards for Attestation Engagements was issued in 1986 to provide a framework for the development of standards for attestation engagements performed by practitioners. As the demand for attestation engagements increased, the ASB developed detailed standards for specific types of attestation services, such as reports on prospective financial information in forecasts and projections. In 2001, the board issued SSAE 10, updating the standards to improve their usefulness and to provide greater flexibility to practitioners who provide assurance services. Attestation standards are studied in Chapter 25.

4. *Consulting standards.* The Management Consulting Services Executive Committee issues pronouncements on consulting services performed by CPAs. These services differ fundamentally from attestation services, in which a CPA reports on an assertion that is the responsibility of another party. In a consulting service, the CPA takes responsibility for developing findings, conclusions, and recommendations that are presented to the client, rather than reporting on an assertion.

5. *Code of Professional Conduct.* The AICPA Committee on Professional Ethics sets rules of conduct that CPAs are required to meet. These rules apply to all services performed by CPAs and provide a framework for the technical standards. The rules and their relationships to ethical conduct are the subject of Chapter 4.

Other AICPA Functions

In addition to writing and grading the CPA examination, the AICPA performs many educational and other functions for CPAs. The association supports research by its own research staff and provides grants to others. It also publishes a variety of materials, including journals such as the *Journal of Accountancy,* industry audit guides for several industries, periodic updates of the *Codification of Statements on Auditing Standards,* and the *Code of Professional Conduct.*

CPAs must meet continuing education requirements to maintain their licenses to practice and to stay current on the extensive and ever-changing body of knowledge in accounting, auditing, attestation and assurance services, management consulting services, and taxes. The AICPA provides a considerable number of seminars and educational aids in a variety of subjects, such as online continuing education opportunities and reference materials in its *InfoBytes Learning Library.*

GENERALLY ACCEPTED AUDITING STANDARDS

OBJECTIVE 2-5

Use generally accepted auditing standards as a basis for further study.

Auditing standards are general guidelines to aid auditors in fulfilling their professional responsibilities in the audit of historical financial statements. They include consideration of professional qualities such as competence and independence, reporting requirements, and evidence.

The broadest guidelines available are the 10 **generally accepted auditing standards (GAAS),** which have seen minimal changes since they were developed by the AICPA in 1947. These standards, detailed in Table 2-3 (p. 34), are not sufficiently specific to provide any meaningful guide to practitioners, but they do represent a framework upon which the AICPA can provide interpretations.

As illustrated in Figure 2-1 (p. 35), the 10 generally accepted auditing standards fall into three categories:

- General standards
- Standards of field work
- Reporting standards

General Standards

The general standards stress the important personal qualities that the auditor should possess.

Adequate Technical Training and Proficiency The first general standard is normally interpreted as requiring the auditor to have formal education in auditing and accounting, adequate practical experience for the work being performed, and continuing professional education. Recent court cases clearly demonstrate that auditors must be technically qualified and experienced in those industries in which their audit clients are engaged.

TABLE 2-3	Generally Accepted Auditing Standards

General Standards

1. The audit is to be performed by a person or persons having adequate technical training and proficiency as an auditor.
2. In all matters relating to the assignment, an independence in mental attitude is to be maintained by the auditor or auditors.
3. Due professional care is to be exercised in the planning and performance of the audit and the preparation of the report.

Standards of Field Work

1. The work is to be adequately planned and assistants, if any, are to be properly supervised.
2. A sufficient understanding of internal control is to be obtained to plan the audit and to determine the nature, timing, and extent of tests to be performed.
3. Sufficient competent evidential matter is to be obtained through inspection, observation, inquiries, and confirmations to afford a reasonable basis for an opinion regarding the financial statements under audit.

Standards of Reporting

1. The report shall state whether the financial statements are presented in accordance with generally accepted accounting principles.
2. The report shall identify those circumstances in which such principles have not been consistently observed in the current period in relation to the preceding period.
3. Informative disclosures in the financial statements are to be regarded as reasonably adequate unless otherwise stated in the report.
4. The report shall either contain an expression of opinion regarding the financial statements, taken as a whole, or an assertion to the effect that an opinion cannot be expressed. When an overall opinion cannot be expressed, the reasons therefor should be stated. In all cases where an auditor's name is associated with financial statements, the report should contain a clear-cut indication of the character of the auditor's work, if any, and the degree of responsibility the auditor is taking.

In any case in which the CPA or the CPA's assistants are not qualified to perform the work, a professional obligation exists to acquire the requisite knowledge and skills, suggest someone else who is qualified to perform the work, or decline the engagement.

Independence in Mental Attitude The importance of independence was emphasized in Chapter 1 under the definition of auditing. The *Code of Professional Conduct* and SASs stress the need for independence. CPA firms are required to follow several practices to increase the likelihood of independence of all personnel. For example, there are established procedures on larger audits when there is a dispute between management and the auditors. Specific methods to ensure that auditors maintain their independence are studied in Chapter 4.

Due Professional Care The third general standard involves due care in the performance of all aspects of auditing. Simply stated, this means that auditors are professionals responsible for fulfilling their duties diligently and carefully. Due care includes consideration of the completeness of the audit documentation, the sufficiency of the audit evidence, and the appropriateness of the audit report. As professionals, auditors must not act negligently or in bad faith, but they are not expected to be infallible.

Standards of Field Work

The standards of field work concern evidence accumulation and other activities during the actual conduct of the audit.

Adequate Planning and Supervision The first standard requires that the audit be sufficiently planned to ensure an adequate audit and proper supervision of assistants. Supervision is essential in auditing because a considerable portion of the field work is done by less experienced staff members.

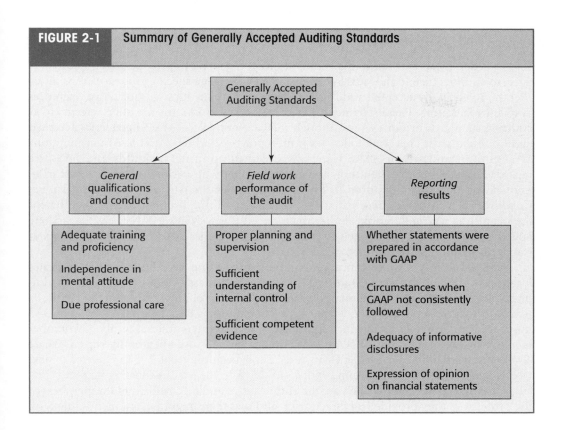

FIGURE 2-1 Summary of Generally Accepted Auditing Standards

Generally Accepted Auditing Standards

General qualifications and conduct

Field work performance of the audit

Reporting results

General qualifications and conduct
- Adequate training and proficiency
- Independence in mental attitude
- Due professional care

Field work performance of the audit
- Proper planning and supervision
- Sufficient understanding of internal control
- Sufficient competent evidence

Reporting results
- Whether statements were prepared in accordance with GAAP
- Circumstances when GAAP not consistently followed
- Adequacy of informative disclosures
- Expression of opinion on financial statements

Understand the Client's Internal Control One of the most widely accepted concepts in the theory and practice of auditing is the importance of the client's system of internal control for safeguarding assets and records and generating reliable financial information. If the auditor is convinced that the client has an excellent system of internal control, one that includes adequate internal controls for providing reliable data, the amount of audit evidence to be accumulated can be significantly less than when controls are not adequate. In some instances, internal control may be so inadequate as to preclude conducting an effective audit.

Sufficient Competent Evidence Decisions about how much and what types of evidence to accumulate for a given set of circumstances require professional judgment. A major portion of this book is concerned with the study of evidence accumulation and the circumstances affecting the amount and types needed.

Standards of Reporting

The four reporting standards require the auditor to prepare a report on the financial statements taken as a whole, including informative disclosures. The reporting standards also require that the report state whether the statements are presented in accordance with GAAP and also identify any circumstances in which GAAP have not been consistently applied in the current year compared with the previous one.

Relationship Between GAAS and PCAOB Auditing Standards

Because the PCAOB establishes auditing standards for public company audits, the term generally accepted auditing standards is no longer used for public company audits. The term generally accepted auditing standards continues to be used for audits of private companies, while public company audits refer to PCAOB auditing standards. When we refer to "auditing standards," the term includes GAAS for private companies and PCAOB auditing standards for public companies. Note that because the PCAOB adopted GAAS as interim auditing standards, these standards continue to apply to public company audits unless changed by PCAOB auditing standards.

STATEMENTS ON AUDITING STANDARDS

The 10 generally accepted auditing standards are too general to provide meaningful guidance, so auditors turn to the SASs issued by the ASB for more specific guidance. SASs interpret the 10 generally accepted auditing standards and are the most authoritative references available to auditors. These statements have the status of GAAS and are often referred to as auditing standards or GAAS, even though they are not part of the 10 generally accepted auditing standards. This book follows common practice and refers to these interpretations as auditing standards or SASs. Generally accepted auditing standards and SASs are regarded as *authoritative* literature, and every member who performs audits of historical financial statements is required to follow them under the AICPA *Code of Professional Conduct*. The ASB issues new statements when an auditing problem arises of sufficient importance to warrant an official interpretation. At this writing, SAS 101 was the last one issued and incorporated into the text materials, but readers should be alert to subsequent standards that influence auditing requirements.

All SASs are given two classification numbers: an SAS and an AU number that indicates location in the *Codification of Auditing Standards.* Both classification systems are used in practice. For example, the Statement on Auditing Standards, *The Relationship of Generally Accepted Auditing Standards to Quality Control Standards*, is SAS 25 and AU 161. The SAS number identifies the order in which it was issued in relation to other SASs; the AU number identifies its location in the AICPA codification of all SASs. AUs beginning with a "2" are always interpretations of the general standards. Those beginning with a "3" are related to field work standards, and those beginning with a "4," "5," or "6" deal with reporting standards.

Although GAAS and the SASs are the authoritative auditing guidelines for members of the profession, they provide less direction to auditors than might be assumed. Almost no specific audit procedures are required by the standards, and there are no specific requirements for auditors' decisions, such as determining sample size, selecting sample items from the population for testing, or evaluating results. Many practitioners believe that the standards should provide more clearly defined guidelines for determining the extent of evidence to be accumulated. Such specificity would eliminate some difficult audit decisions and provide a line of defense for a CPA firm charged with conducting an inadequate audit. However, highly specific requirements could turn auditing into mechanistic evidence gathering, devoid of professional judgment. From the point of view of both the profession and the users of auditing services, there is probably greater harm in defining authoritative guidelines too specifically than too broadly.

GAAS and the SASs should be looked on by practitioners as *minimum standards* of performance rather than as maximum standards or ideals. Any professional auditor who seeks means of reducing the scope of the audit by relying only on the standards, rather than evaluating the substance of the situation, fails to satisfy the spirit of the standards. At the same time, the existence of auditing standards does not mean the auditor must always follow them blindly. If an auditor believes that the requirement of a standard is impractical or impossible to perform, the auditor is justified in following an alternative course of action. Similarly, if the issue in question is immaterial in amount, it is also unnecessary to follow the standard. However, the burden of justifying departures from the standards falls on the auditor.

When auditors desire more specific guidelines, they must turn to less authoritative sources, including textbooks, journals, and technical publications. Materials published by the AICPA, such as the *Journal of Accountancy* and industry audit guides, furnish assistance on specific questions. We provide further study of the standards and make frequent reference to the SASs throughout the text.

INTERNATIONAL STANDARDS ON AUDITING

OBJECTIVE 2-6

Discuss the role of international auditing standards.

The globalization of business and capital markets has created a strong interest and trend toward developing uniform accounting and auditing standards throughout the world. Currently, representatives from different countries are working together on standards-setting projects to coordinate new international auditing standards.

International Standards on Auditing (ISAs) are issued by the International Auditing Practices Committee (IAPC) of the International Federation of Accountants (IFAC). IFAC is the worldwide organization for the accountancy profession, with 157 member organizations in 118 countries, representing more than 2.5 million accountants throughout the world. The IAPC works to improve the uniformity of auditing practices and related services throughout the world by issuing pronouncements on a variety of audit and attest functions and by promoting their acceptance worldwide.

IFAC

ISAs are generally similar to the U.S. GAAS, although there are some differences. If an auditor in the United States is auditing historical financial statements in accordance with ISAs, the auditor must meet any ISA requirements that extend beyond GAAS.

ISAs do not override a country's regulations governing the audit of financial or other information, as each country's own regulations generally govern audit practices. These regulations may be either government statutes or statements issued by regulatory or professional bodies, such as the Australian Auditing & Assurance Standards Board or Spain's Instituto de Contabilidad y Auditoría de Cuentas.

QUALITY CONTROL

For a CPA firm, **quality control** comprises the methods used to ensure that the firm meets its professional responsibilities to clients and others. These methods include the organizational structure of the CPA firm and the procedures the firm establishes. For example, a CPA firm might have an organizational structure that ensures the technical review of every engagement by a partner who has expertise in the client's industry.

> **OBJECTIVE 2-7**
> Identify quality control standards and practices within the accounting profession.

Quality control is closely related to but distinct from GAAS. To ensure that generally accepted auditing standards are followed on every audit, a CPA firm follows specific quality control procedures that help it meet those standards consistently on every engagement. Quality controls are therefore established for the entire CPA firm, whereas GAAS are applicable to individual engagements.

In 1978, the AICPA established the Quality Control Standards Committee and gave it responsibility to help CPA firms develop and implement quality control standards. SAS 25 (AU 161) requires a CPA firm to establish quality control policies and procedures. The standard recognizes that a quality control system can provide only reasonable assurance, not a guarantee, that GAAS are followed.

Elements of Quality Control

The AICPA has not set specific quality control procedures for CPA firms. Procedures should depend on such things as the size of the firm, the number of practice offices, and the nature of the practice. The quality control procedures of a 150-office international firm with many complex multinational clients should differ considerably from those of a five-person firm specializing in small audits in one or two industries.

The Quality Control Standards Committee has identified five elements of quality control that firms should consider in setting up their own policies and procedures. These are listed in Table 2-4 (p. 38) with brief descriptions and procedural examples that firms might use to satisfy the requirement.

Division of CPA Firms

The AICPA has established a **division of CPA firms** and created two sections: the SEC Practice Section (SECPS) and the Private Companies Practice Section (The AICPA Alliance for CPA Firms). The intent is to improve the quality of practice by CPA firms consistent with AICPA quality control standards. Each practice section has membership requirements and the authority to impose sanctions for noncompliance by members. A firm can choose to belong to one section, both sections, or neither.

Many of the self-regulatory activities of the SECPS have been taken over by the PCAOB. As a result, the SECPS has reorganized as the Center for Public Company Audit Firms to share information and promote member firms' positions before the SEC and PCAOB.

Peer Review

Peer review is the review, by CPAs, of a CPA firm's compliance with its quality control system. The purpose of a peer review is to determine and report whether the CPA firm

TABLE 2-4	Five Elements of Quality Control	
Element	**Summary of Requirements**	**Example of a Procedure**
Independence, integrity, and objectivity	All personnel on engagements should maintain independence in fact and in appearance, perform all professional responsibilities with integrity, and maintain objectivity in performing their professional responsibilities.	Each partner and employee must answer an "independence questionnaire" annually, dealing with such things as stock ownership and membership on boards of directors.
Personnel management	Policies and procedures should be established to provide the firm with reasonable assurance that · All new personnel should be qualified to perform their work competently. · Work is assigned to personnel who have adequate technical training and proficiency. · All personnel should participate in continuing professional education and professional development activities that enable them to fulfill their assigned responsibilities. · Personnel selected for advancement have the qualifications necessary for the fulfillment of their assigned responsibilities.	Each professional must be evaluated on every engagement using the firm's individual engagement evaluation report.
Acceptance and continuation of clients and engagements	Policies and procedures should be established for deciding whether to accept or continue a client relationship. These policies and procedures should minimize the risk of associating with a client whose management lacks integrity. The firm should also only undertake engagements that can be completed with professional competence.	A client evaluation form, dealing with such matters as predecessor auditor comments and evaluation of management, must be prepared for every new client before acceptance.
Engagement performance	Policies and procedures should exist to ensure that the work performed by engagement personnel meets applicable professional standards, regulatory requirements, and the firm's standards of quality.	The firm's director of accounting and auditing is available for consultation and must approve all engagements before their completion.
Monitoring	Policies and procedures should exist to ensure that the other four quality control elements are being effectively applied.	The quality control partner must test the quality control procedures at least annually to ensure the firm is in compliance.

being reviewed has developed adequate policies and procedures for the five elements of quality control and follows them in practice. Unless a firm has a peer review, all members of the CPA firm lose their eligibility for AICPA membership.

The peer review program for SECPS member firms has been replaced by the quality inspections conducted by the PCAOB for registered firms responsible for auditing public companies. CPA firms that are members of the Private Companies Practice Section (PCPS) must be reviewed at least once every 3 years. Peer reviews of PCPS member firms are administered through the state CPA societies under the overall direction of the AICPA peer review board. Typically, a review is conducted by a CPA firm selected by the firm being reviewed, although a firm may also request the AICPA or state society to send a review team. After a review is completed, the reviewers issue a report stating their conclusions and recommendations. Only firms that satisfactorily pass peer review can be members of the practice section.

AICPA member firms that are not members of the SECPS or PCPS are also required to have peer reviews every 3 years. This type of peer review has the same objective as a peer review of an SECPS or PCPS member, but it is typically less extensive in the review of the implementation of the firm's quality control system. These peer reviews are also administered through the state CPA societies under the overall direction of the AICPA peer review board.

Peer review benefits individual firms by helping them meet quality control standards, which, in turn, benefits the profession through improved practitioner performance and

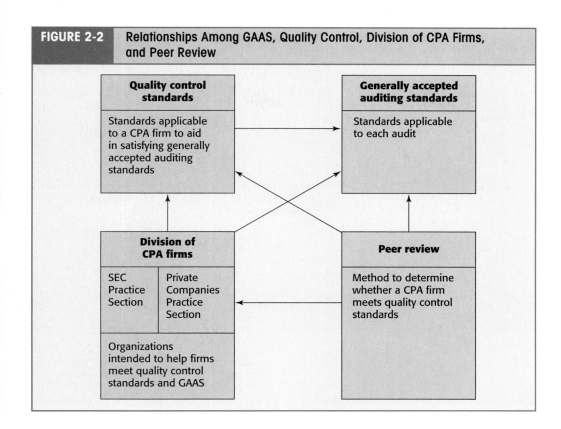

FIGURE 2-2 Relationships Among GAAS, Quality Control, Division of CPA Firms, and Peer Review

higher-quality audits. A firm having a peer review can further benefit if the review improves the firm's practice, thereby enhances its reputation and effectiveness, and reduces the likelihood of lawsuits. Of course, peer reviews are expensive to conduct, so the benefits come at a cost. Figure 2-2 summarizes the relationships among GAAS, quality control, division of CPA firms, and peer review in ensuring audit quality.

SUMMARY

This chapter discussed the nature of the CPA profession and the activities of CPA firms. Because CPA firms play an important social role, several organizations, including the PCAOB, SEC, and AICPA provide oversight to increase the likelihood of appropriate audit quality and professional conduct. These are summarized in Figure 2-3 (p. 40). Shaded circles in the figure indicate items discussed in this or the last chapter. The AICPA *Code of Professional Conduct* provides a standard of conduct for practitioners and is discussed in Chapter 4. The potential for legal liability is also a significant influence on auditor conduct and is discussed in Chapter 5.

ESSENTIAL TERMS

AICPA—American Institute of Certified Public Accountants, a voluntary organization of CPAs that sets professional requirements, conducts research, and publishes materials relevant to accounting, auditing, management consulting services, and taxes

Division of CPA firms—a division of the AICPA established for CPA firms and consisting of two sections: the SEC Practice Section and the Private Companies Practice Section;

the division was established to improve the quality of practice by CPA firms consistent with AICPA quality control standards

Generally accepted auditing standards (GAAS)—10 auditing standards, developed by the AICPA, consisting of general standards, standards of field work, and standards of reporting, along with interpretations; often called *auditing standards*

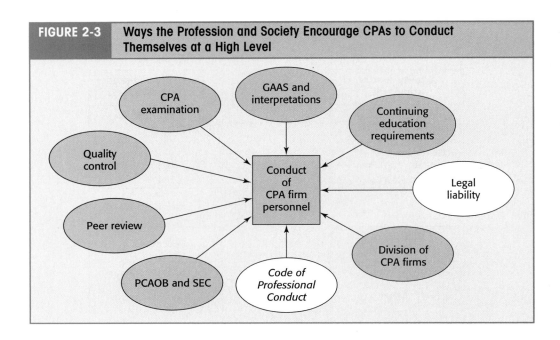

FIGURE 2-3 Ways the Profession and Society Encourage CPAs to Conduct Themselves at a High Level

International Standards on Auditing (ISAs)—statements issued by the International Auditing Practices Committee of the International Federation of Accountants to promote international acceptance of auditing standards

Peer review—the review by CPAs of a CPA firm's compliance with its quality control system

Public Company Accounting Oversight Board (PCAOB)—Board created by the Sarbanes–Oxley Act to oversee auditors of public companies, including establishing auditing and quality control standards and performing inspections of registered accounting firms

Quality control—methods used by a CPA firm to ensure that the firm meets its professional responsibilities to clients and others

Securities and Exchange Commission (SEC)—a federal agency that oversees the orderly conduct of the securities markets; the SEC assists in providing investors in public corporations with reliable information upon which to make investment decisions

Statements on Auditing Standards (SASs)—pronouncements issued by the AICPA to interpret generally accepted auditing standards

REVIEW QUESTIONS

2-1 (Objective 2-1) State the four major types of services CPAs perform, and explain each.

2-2 (Objectives 2-1, 2-7) What major characteristics of the organization and conduct of CPA firms permit them to fulfill their social function competently and independently?

2-3 (Objective 2-2) What is the role of the Public Company Accounting Oversight Board?

2-4 (Objective 2-3) Describe the role of the SEC in society and discuss its relationship with and influence on the practice of auditing.

2-5 (Objective 2-4) What roles are played by the American Institute of Certified Public Accountants for its members?

2-6 (Objective 2-4) What are the purposes of the AICPA *Statement on Standards for Attestation Engagements*?

2-7 (Objectives 2-2, 2-4, 2-5) Who is responsible for establishing auditing standards for audits of public companies? Who is responsible for establishing auditing standards for private companies? Explain.

2-8 (Objective 2-5) Distinguish between generally accepted auditing standards and generally accepted accounting principles, and give two examples of each.

2-9 (Objective 2-5) The first standard of field work requires the performance of the audit by a person or persons having adequate technical training and proficiency as an auditor. What are the various ways in which auditors can fulfill the requirement of the standard?

2-10 (Objective 2-5) Generally accepted auditing standards have been criticized by different sources for failing to provide useful guidelines for conducting an audit. The critics believe the standards should be more specific to enable practitioners to improve the quality of their performance. As the standards are now stated, some critics believe that they provide little more than an excuse to conduct inadequate audits. Evaluate this criticism of the 10 generally accepted auditing standards.

2-11 (Objective 2-6) Describe the role of International Standards on Auditing. Discuss whether a CPA who conducts an audit in accordance with generally accepted auditing standards simultaneously complies with international standards on auditing.

2-12 (Objective 2-7) What is meant by the term *quality control* as it relates to a CPA firm?

2-13 (Objective 2-7) The following is an example of a CPA firm's quality control procedure requirement: "Any person being considered for employment by the firm must have completed a basic auditing course and have been interviewed and approved by an audit partner of the firm before he or she can be hired for the audit staff." Which element of quality control does this procedure affect and what is the purpose of the requirement?

2-14 (Objective 2-7) State what is meant by the term *peer review*. What are the implications of peer review for the profession?

2-15 (Objective 2-7) What are the two sections of practice to which CPA firms may belong? What are the primary purposes of the sections?

MULTIPLE CHOICE QUESTIONS FROM CPA EXAMINATIONS

2-16 (Objective 2-5) The following questions deal with generally accepted auditing standards. Choose the best response.

a. The first general standard, which states in part that the audit is to be performed by a person or persons having adequate technical training, requires that an auditor have
   (1) education and experience in the field of auditing.
   (2) ability in the planning and supervision of the audit work.
   (3) proficiency in business and financial matters.
   (4) knowledge in the areas of financial accounting.

b. Which of the following best describes what is meant by generally accepted auditing standards?
   (1) Acts to be performed by the auditor.
   (2) Measures of the quality of the auditor's performance.
   (3) Procedures to be used to gather evidence to support financial statements.
   (4) Audit objectives generally determined on audit engagements.

c. The general group of the generally accepted auditing standards includes a requirement that
   (1) field work be adequately planned and supervised.
   (2) the auditor's report state whether or not the financial statements conform to generally accepted accounting principles.
   (3) due professional care be exercised by the auditor.
   (4) informative disclosures in the financial statements be reasonably adequate.

d. What is the general character of the three generally accepted auditing standards classified as standards of field work?
   (1) The competence, independence, and professional care of persons performing the audit.
   (2) Criteria for the content of the auditor's report on financial statements and related footnote disclosures.
   (3) The criteria of audit planning and evidence gathering.
   (4) The need to maintain an independence in mental attitude in all matters pertaining to the audit.

2-17 (Objective 2-7) The following questions concern quality control standards. Choose the best response.

   a. A CPA firm is reasonably assured of meeting its responsibility to provide services that conform with professional standards by
   (1) adhering to generally accepted auditing standards.
   (2) having an appropriate system of quality control.
   (3) joining professional societies that enforce ethical conduct.
   (4) maintaining an attitude of independence in its engagements.

   b. Which of the following are elements of a CPA firm's quality control that should be considered in establishing its quality control policies and procedures?

	Personnel Management	Monitoring	Engagement Performance
(1)	Yes	Yes	No
(2)	Yes	Yes	Yes
(3)	No	Yes	Yes
(4)	Yes	No	Yes

   c. Which of the following is an element of a CPA firm's quality control system that should be considered in establishing its quality control policies and procedures?
   (1) Complying with laws and regulations.
   (2) Using statistical sampling techniques.
   (3) Managing personnel.
   (4) Considering audit risk and materiality.

DISCUSSION QUESTIONS AND PROBLEMS

2-18 (Objectives 2-2, 2-7) The following comments summarize the beliefs of some practitioners about the Sarbanes–Oxley Act and the PCAOB.

> The Sarbanes–Oxley Act is unnecessary regulation of the profession. The costs of requirements such as reporting on the effectiveness of internal control over financial reporting greatly exceed the benefits. These increased costs will discourage companies from issuing publicly traded stock in the United States. The regulation also gives a competitive advantage to national CPA firms because they are best prepared to meet the increased requirements of the Act. Three things already provide sufficient assurance that quality audits are performed without PCAOB oversight. They are competitive pressures to do quality work, legal liability for inadequate performance, and a code of professional conduct requiring that CPA firms follow generally accepted auditing standards.

Required
   a. State the pros and cons of those comments.

   b. Evaluate whether the Sarbanes–Oxley Act and PCAOB regulation are worth their cost.

2-19 (Objective 2-7) For each of the following procedures taken from the quality control manual of a CPA firm, identify the applicable element of quality control from Table 2-4 on page 38.

Required
   a. Appropriate accounting and auditing research requires adequate technical reference materials. Each firm professional has online password access through the firm's Internet Web site to electronic reference materials on accounting, auditing, tax, SEC, and other technical information, including industry data.

   b. Each audit engagement of the firm is directed by a partner and, in most instances, a manager of the firm. On every engagement, an attempt is made to maintain continuity of at least a portion of the personnel.

   c. Audit engagement team members enter their electronic signatures in the firm's engagement management software to indicate the completion of specific audit program steps. At the end of the audit engagement, the engagement management software will not allow archiving of the engagement file until all audit program steps have been electronically signed.

   d. At all stages of any engagement, an effort is made to involve professional staff at appropriate levels in the accounting and auditing decisions. Various approvals of the manager or senior accountant are obtained throughout the audit.

e. No employee will have any direct or indirect financial interest, association, or relationship (for example, a close relative serving a client in a decision-making capacity) not otherwise disclosed that might be adverse to the firm's best interest.

f. Each office of the firm shall be visited at least annually by review persons selected by the director of accounting and auditing. Procedures to be undertaken by the reviewers are illustrated by the office review program.

g. Existing clients of the firm are reviewed on a continuing basis by the engagement partner. Termination may result if circumstances indicate that there is reason to question the integrity of management or our independence, or if accounting and auditing differences of opinion cannot be reconciled. Doubts concerning whether the client–auditor relationship should be continued must be promptly discussed with the director of accounting and auditing.

h. Individual partners submit the nominations of those persons whom they wish to be considered for partner. To become a partner, an individual must have exhibited a high degree of technical competence; must possess integrity, motivation, and judgment; and must have a desire to help the firm progress through the efficient dispatch of the job responsibilities to which he or she is assigned.

i. Through our continuing employee evaluation and counseling program and through the quality control review procedures as established by the firm, educational needs are reviewed and formal staff training programs modified to accommodate changing needs. At the conclusion of practice office reviews, apparent accounting and auditing deficiencies are summarized and reported to the firm's director of personnel.

2-20 (Objectives 2-2, 2-3, 2-5) The Mobile Home Manufacturing Company is audited by Rossi and Montgomery, CPAs. Mobile Home has decided to issue stock to the public and wants Rossi and Montgomery to perform all the audit work necessary to satisfy the requirements for filing with the SEC. The CPA firm has never had a client go public before.

a. What are the ethical implications of Rossi and Montgomery's accepting the engagement? **Required**

b. List the additional problems confronting the auditors when they file with the SEC as compared to dealing with a regular audit client.

2-21 (Objective 2-5) Ray, the owner of a small company, asked Holmes, a CPA, to conduct an audit of the company's records. Ray told Holmes that an audit was to be completed in time to submit audited financial statements to a bank as part of a loan application. Holmes immediately accepted the engagement and agreed to provide an auditor's report within 3 weeks. Ray agreed to pay Holmes a fixed fee plus a bonus if the loan was granted.

Holmes hired two accounting students to conduct the audit and spent several hours telling them exactly what to do. Holmes told the students not to spend time reviewing the controls but instead to concentrate on proving the mathematical accuracy of the ledger accounts and summarizing the data in the accounting records that support Ray's financial statements. The students followed Holmes's instructions and after 2 weeks gave Holmes the financial statements, which did not include footnotes. Holmes reviewed the statements and prepared an unqualified auditor's report. The report did not refer to generally accepted accounting principles or to the consistent application of such principles.

Briefly describe each of the 10 generally accepted auditing standards and indicate how the action(s) **Required** of Holmes resulted in a failure to comply with each standard.

Organize your answer as follows:*

Brief Description of GAAS	Holmes' Actions Resulting in Failure to Comply with GAAS

2-22 (Objective 2-1) A local CPA, who has been in practice for several years, recently met with representatives of an Internet service provider that is interested in developing a Web site for the CPA's practice. The CPA has been reluctant to develop an Internet site but is willing to learn more about the types of information and resources that CPAs often provide through their Internet sites before making a final decision.

a. Describe the types of resources and Web links that CPAs often provide on their Internet Web **Required** sites.

b. State reasons why CPA firms invest resources in creating sophisticated Internet sites.

c. Discuss how the Internet can be a useful tool for a CPA firm's accounting and auditing practice.

*AICPA adapted.

INTERNET PROBLEM 2-1: CPA VISION PROJECT

Reference the CW site. The CPA Vision Project is all about helping the "CPA profession stay on top of the change curve." With input from CPAs across the nation, the CPA Vision Project has created a comprehensive and integrated vision of the profession's future. This problem requires students to use the Internet (1) to research the CPA Vision Statement, (2) to research the eight forces impacting the profession, and (3) to answer the question, "What is meant by moving up the economic value chain and how are CPAs going to accomplish this?"

AUDIT REPORTS

THE AUDIT REPORT WAS TIMELY, BUT AT WHAT COST?

Halvorson & Co., CPAs was hired as the auditor for Machinetron, Inc., a company that manufactured high-precision, computer-operated lathes. The owner, Al Trent, thought that Machinetron was ready to become a public company, and he hired Halvorson to conduct the upcoming audit and assist in the preparation of the registration statement for a securities offering.

Because Machinetron's machines were large and complex, they were expensive. Each sale was negotiated individually by Trent, and the sales often transpired over several months. As a result, improper recording of one or two machines could represent a material misstatement of the financial statements.

The engagement partner in charge of the Machinetron audit was Bob Lehman, who had significant experience auditing manufacturing companies. He recognized the risk for improper recording of sales, and he insisted that his staff confirm all receivables at year-end directly with customers. Lehman conducted his review of the Machinetron audit files the same day that Trent wanted to make the company's registration statement for the initial public stock offering effective. Lehman saw that a receivable for a major sale at year-end was supported by a fax, rather than the usual written confirmation reply. Apparently, relations with this customer were "touchy," and Trent had discouraged the audit staff from communicating with the customer.

At the end of the day, there was a meeting in Machinetron's office. It was attended by Lehman, Trent, the underwriter of the stock offering, and the company's attorney. Lehman indicated that a better form of confirmation would be required to support the receivable. After hearing this, Trent blew his stack. Machinetron's attorney stepped in and calmed Trent down. He offered to write a letter to Halvorson & Co. stating that in his opinion, a fax had legal substance as a valid confirmation reply. Lehman, feeling tremendous pressure, accepted this proposal and signed off on an unqualified audit opinion.

Six months after the stock offering, Machinetron issued a statement indicating that its revenues for the prior year had been overstated as a result of improperly recorded sales, including the sale supported by the fax confirmation. The subsequent SEC investigation uncovered that the fax had been sent by Trent, not the customer. Halvorson & Co. recalled their unqualified audit report, but this was too late to prevent the harm done to investors. Halvorson & Co. was forced to pay substantial damages, and Bob Lehman was forbidden to practice before the SEC. He subsequently left public accounting.

LEARNING OBJECTIVES

After studying this chapter, you should be able to

3-1	Describe the parts of the standard unqualified audit report.
3-2	Specify the conditions required to issue the standard unqualified audit report.
3-3	Understand combined reporting on financial statements and internal control over financial reporting under Section 404 of the Sarbanes–Oxley Act.
3-4	Describe the five circumstances when an unqualified report with an explanatory paragraph or modified wording is appropriate.
3-5	Identify the types of audit reports that can be issued when an unqualified opinion is not justified.
3-6	Explain how materiality affects audit reporting decisions.
3-7	Draft appropriately modified audit reports under a variety of circumstances.
3-8	Determine the appropriate audit report for a given audit situation.
3-9	Discuss the impact of e-commerce on audit reporting.

Reports are essential to audit and assurance engagements because they communicate the auditor's findings. Users of financial statements rely on the auditor's report to provide assurance on the company's financial statements. As the vignette at the beginning of this chapter illustrates, the auditor is likely to be held responsible if an incorrect audit report is issued.

The audit report is the final step in the entire audit process. The reason for studying it now is to permit reference to different audit reports as evidence accumulation is studied throughout this text. These evidence concepts are more meaningful after you understand the form and content of the final product of the audit. We begin by describing the content of the standard auditor's report.

STANDARD UNQUALIFIED AUDIT REPORT

To enable users to understand the language of audit reports, AICPA professional standards provide uniform wording for the auditor's report, as illustrated in the auditor's standard unqualified audit report in Figure 3-1. Different auditors may alter the wording or presentation slightly, but the meaning will be the same.

Parts of Standard Unqualified Audit Report

The auditor's **standard unqualified audit report** contains seven distinct parts, and these are labeled in bold letters in the margin beside Figure 3-1.

1. *Report title.* Auditing standards require that the report be titled and that the title include the word *independent*. For example, appropriate titles would be "independent auditor's report," "report of independent auditor," or "independent accountant's opinion." The requirement that the title include the word *independent* is intended to convey to users that the audit was unbiased in all aspects.

2. *Audit report address.* The report is usually addressed to the company, its stockholders, or the board of directors. In recent years, it has become customary to address the report to the board of directors and stockholders to indicate that the auditor is independent of the company.

3. *Introductory paragraph.* The first paragraph of the report does three things: First, it makes the simple statement that the CPA firm has done an *audit*. This is intended to distinguish the report from a compilation or review report. The scope paragraph (see part 4) clarifies what is meant by an audit.

Second, it lists the financial statements that were audited, including the balance sheet dates and the accounting periods for the income statement and statement of cash flows. The wording of the financial statements in the report should be identical to those used by management on the financial statements. Notice that the report in Figure 3-1 is on comparative financial statements. Therefore, a report on both years' statements is needed.

Third, the introductory paragraph states that the statements are the responsibility of management and that the auditor's responsibility is to express an opinion on the statements based on an audit. The purpose of these statements is to communicate that management is responsible for selecting the appropriate generally accepted accounting principles and making the measurement decisions and disclosures in applying those principles and to clarify the respective roles of management and the auditor.

4. *Scope paragraph.* The scope paragraph is a factual statement about what the auditor did in the audit. This paragraph first states that the auditor followed U.S. generally accepted auditing standards. For an audit of a public company, the paragraph will indicate that the auditor followed standards of the Public Company Accounting Oversight Board.

Financial statements prepared in accordance with U.S. accounting principles and audited in accordance with U.S. auditing standards are increasingly available throughout the world on the Internet. Accordingly, SAS 93 requires that the country of origin of the accounting principles used in preparing the financial statements and auditing standards followed by the auditor be identified in the audit report.

FIGURE 3-1	Standard Unqualified Report on Comparative Statements

ANDERSON and ZINDER, P.C.
Certified Public Accountants
Suite 100
Park Plaza East
Denver, Colorado 80110
303/359-0800

Independent Auditor's Report   **Report Title**

To the Stockholders   **Audit Report Address**
General Ring Corporation

We have audited the accompanying balance sheets of General Ring Corporation as of December 31,   **Introductory Paragraph**
2005 and 2004, and the related statements of income, retained earnings, and cash flows for the   **(Factual Statement)**
years then ended. These financial statements are the responsibility of the Company's management.
Our responsibility is to express an opinion on these financial statements based on our audits.

We conducted our audits in accordance with auditing standards generally accepted in the United   **Scope Paragraph**
States of America. Those standards require that we plan and perform the audit to obtain reasonable **(Factual Statement)**
assurance about whether the financial statements are free of material misstatement. An audit
includes examining, on a test basis, evidence supporting the amounts and disclosures in the
financial statements. An audit also includes assessing the accounting principles used and significant
estimates made by management, as well as evaluating the overall financial statement presentation.
We believe that our audits provide a reasonable basis for our opinion.

In our opinion, the financial statements referred to above present fairly, in all material respects, the   **Opinion Paragraph**
financial position of General Ring Corporation as of December 31, 2005 and 2004, and the results of   **(Conclusions)**
its operations and its cash flows for the years then ended in conformity with accounting principles
generally accepted in the United States of America.

ANDERSON AND ZINDER, P.C., CPAs   **Name of CPA Firm**

February 15, 2006   **Audit Report Date (Date Audit
Field Work Is Completed)**

The scope paragraph states that the audit is designed to obtain *reasonable assurance* about whether the statements are free of **material misstatement.** The inclusion of the word *material* conveys that auditors are responsible only to search for significant misstatements, not minor misstatements that do not affect users' decisions. The use of the term *reasonable assurance* is intended to indicate that an audit cannot be expected to completely eliminate the possibility that a material misstatement will exist in the financial statements. In other words, an audit provides a high level of assurance, but it is not a guarantee.

Audit Report Search

The remainder of the scope paragraph discusses the audit evidence accumulated and states that the auditor believes that the evidence accumulated was appropriate for the circumstances to express the opinion presented. The words *test basis* indicate that sampling was used rather than an audit of every transaction and amount on the statements. Whereas the introductory paragraph of the report states that management is responsible for the preparation and content of the financial statements, the scope paragraph states that the auditor evaluates the appropriateness of those accounting principles, estimates, and financial statement disclosures and presentations given.

5. *Opinion paragraph.* The final paragraph in the standard report states the auditor's conclusions based on the results of the audit. This part of the report is so important that often the entire audit report is referred to simply as the *auditor's opinion.* The opinion paragraph is stated as an opinion rather than as a statement of absolute fact or a guarantee. The intent is to indicate that the conclusions are based on professional judgment. The phrase *in our opinion* indicates that there may be some information risk associated with the financial statements, even though the statements have been audited.

The opinion paragraph is directly related to the first and fourth generally accepted auditing reporting standards listed on page 34. The auditor is required to state an opinion about the financial statements taken as a whole, including a conclusion about whether the company followed U.S. generally accepted accounting principles.

One of the controversial parts of the auditor's report is the meaning of the term *present fairly*. Does this mean that if generally accepted accounting principles are followed, the financial statements are presented fairly, or something more? Occasionally, the courts have concluded that auditors are responsible for looking beyond generally accepted accounting principles to determine whether users might be misled, even if those principles are followed. Most auditors believe that financial statements are "presented fairly" when the statements are in accordance with generally accepted accounting principles, but that it is also necessary to examine the substance of transactions and balances for possible misinformation.

6. *Name of CPA firm.* The name identifies the CPA firm or practitioner who performed the audit. Typically, the firm's name is used because the entire CPA firm has the legal and professional responsibility to ensure that the quality of the audit meets professional standards.

7. *Audit report date.* The appropriate date for the report is the one on which the auditor has completed the most important auditing procedures in the field. This date is important to users because it indicates the last day of the auditor's responsibility for the review of significant events that occurred after the date of the financial statements. In the audit report in Figure 3-1, the balance sheet is dated December 31, 2005, and the audit report is dated February 15, 2006. This indicates that the auditor has searched for material unrecorded transactions and events that occurred up to February 15, 2006.

INTERNATIONAL AUDIT OPINIONS

Audit Report Comparison

The standard unqualified audit report described in the preceding section is based on auditing standards generally accepted in the United States. Reporting in other countries is based on auditing standards in those countries. For example, the opinion paragraph from an audit report issued in the United Kingdom is as follows:

In our opinion the financial statements give a true and fair view of the state of affairs of the company at 31st December 2005 and of the profit and cash flow of the company for the year then ended and have been properly prepared in accordance with the United Kingdom Companies Act of 1985.

Conditions for Standard Unqualified Audit Report

OBJECTIVE 3-2

Specify the conditions required to issue the standard unqualified audit report.

The standard unqualified audit report is issued when the following conditions have been met:

1. All statements—balance sheet, income statement, statement of retained earnings, and statement of cash flows—are included in the financial statements.
2. The three general standards have been followed in all respects on the engagement.
3. Sufficient evidence has been accumulated, and the auditor has conducted the engagement in a manner that enables him or her to conclude that the three standards of field work have been met.
4. The financial statements are presented in accordance with U.S. generally accepted accounting principles. This also means that adequate disclosures have been included in the footnotes and other parts of the financial statements.
5. There are no circumstances requiring the addition of an explanatory paragraph or modification of the wording of the report.

When these conditions are met, the standard unqualified audit report, as shown in Figure 3-1, is issued. The standard unqualified audit report is sometimes called a clean opinion because there are no circumstances requiring a qualification or modification of the auditor's opinion. The standard unqualified report is the most common audit opinion. Sometimes circumstances beyond the client's or auditor's control prevent the issuance of a clean opinion. However, in most cases, companies make the appropriate changes to their accounting records to avoid a qualification or modification by the auditor.

If any of the five requirements for the standard unqualified audit report are not met, the standard unqualified report cannot be issued. Figure 3-2 indicates the categories of

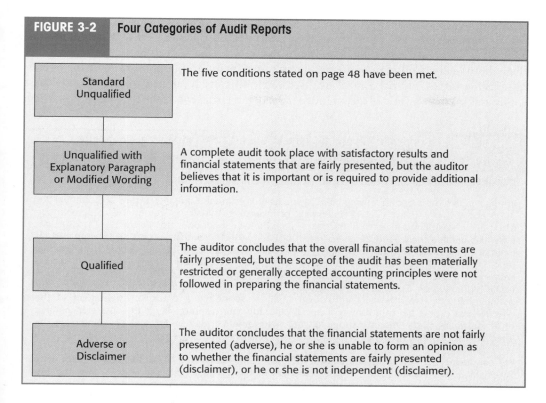

FIGURE 3-2 **Four Categories of Audit Reports**

Standard Unqualified	The five conditions stated on page 48 have been met.
Unqualified with Explanatory Paragraph or Modified Wording	A complete audit took place with satisfactory results and financial statements that are fairly presented, but the auditor believes that it is important or is required to provide additional information.
Qualified	The auditor concludes that the overall financial statements are fairly presented, but the scope of the audit has been materially restricted or generally accepted accounting principles were not followed in preparing the financial statements.
Adverse or Disclaimer	The auditor concludes that the financial statements are not fairly presented (adverse), he or she is unable to form an opinion as to whether the financial statements are fairly presented (disclaimer), or he or she is not independent (disclaimer).

audit reports that can be issued by the auditor. The departures from a standard unqualified report are considered increasingly severe as one moves down the figure. Financial statement users would normally be much more concerned about a disclaimer or adverse opinion than an unqualified report with an explanatory paragraph. These other categories of audit reports are discussed in following sections.

COMBINED REPORTS ON FINANCIAL STATEMENTS AND INTERNAL CONTROL OVER FINANCIAL REPORTING UNDER SECTION 404 OF THE SARBANES–OXLEY ACT

As discussed in Chapter 1, Section 404 of the Sarbanes–Oxley Act requires the auditor of a public company to attest to management's report on the effectiveness of internal control over financial reporting. PCAOB Auditing Standard 2 requires the audit of internal control to be integrated with the audit of the financial statements. However, the auditor may choose to issue separate reports or a combined report, such as the one shown in Figure 3-3 (p. 50). The **combined report on financial statements and internal control over financial reporting** addresses both the financial statements and management's report on internal control over financial reporting:

OBJECTIVE 3-3

Understand combined reporting on financial statements and internal control over financial reporting under Section 404 of the Sarbanes–Oxley Act.

- The introductory, scope, and opinion paragraphs are modified to include reference to management's report on internal control over financial reporting and the scope of the auditor's work and opinion on internal control over financial reporting.
- The introductory and opinion paragraphs also refer to the framework used to evaluate internal control.
- The report includes a paragraph after the scope paragraph defining internal control over financial reporting.
- The report also includes an additional paragraph before the opinion that addresses the inherent limitations of internal control.
- Although the audit opinion on the financial statements addresses multiple reporting periods, management's assertion about the effectiveness of internal control is as of the end of the most recent fiscal year.

The combined report in Figure 3-3 is an unqualified opinion on the financial statements and management's assessment of the effectiveness of internal control over financial reporting. The auditor may issue a qualified opinion, adverse opinion, or disclaimer of opinion on management's assessment of internal control or the operating effectiveness of internal control over financial reporting. Conditions that require the auditor to issue a report other than an unqualified opinion on management's assessment of internal control or the operating effectiveness of internal control are discussed in Chapter 10, along with the effects of these conditions on the wording of the auditor's report on internal control over financial reporting.

FIGURE 3-3	Combined Report on Financial Statements and Internal Control over Financial Reporting

REPORT OF INDEPENDENT REGISTERED PUBLIC ACCOUNTING FIRM

Introductory Paragraph

We have audited the accompanying balance sheets of Westbrook Company, Inc. as of December 31, 2005 and 2004, and the related statements of income, stockholders' equity and comprehensive income, and cash flows for each of the years in the three-year period ended December 31, 2005. We have also audited management's assessment included in the accompanying management report on internal control that Westbrook Company, Inc. maintained effective internal control over financial reporting as of December 31, 2005, based on criteria established in *Internal Control-Integrated Framework* issued by the Committee of Sponsoring Organizations of the Treadway Commission (COSO). Westbrook Company's management is responsible for these financial statements, for maintaining effective internal control over financial reporting, and for its assessment of the effectiveness of internal control over financial reporting. Our responsibility is to express an opinion on these financial statements, an opinion on management's assessment, and an opinion on the effectiveness of the company's internal control over financial reporting based on our audits.

Scope Paragraph

We conducted our audits in accordance with the standards of the Public Company Accounting Oversight Board (United States). Those standards require that we plan and perform the audits to obtain reasonable assurance about whether the financial statements are free of material misstatement and whether effective internal control over financial reporting was maintained in all material respects. Our audit of financial statements included examining, on a test basis, evidence supporting the amounts and disclosures in the financial statements, assessing the accounting principles used and significant estimates made by management, and evaluating the overall financial statement presentation. Our audit of internal control over financial reporting included obtaining an understanding of internal control over financial reporting, evaluating management's assessment, testing and evaluating the design and operating effectiveness of internal control, and performing such other procedures as we considered necessary in the circumstances. We believe that our audits provide a reasonable basis for our opinions.

Definition Paragraph

A company's internal control over financial reporting is a process designed to provide reasonable assurance regarding the reliability of financial reporting and the preparation of financial statements for external purposes in accordance with generally accepted accounting principles. A company's internal control over financial reporting includes those policies and procedures that (1) pertain to the maintenance of records that, in reasonable detail, accurately and fairly reflect the transactions and dispositions of the assets of the company; (2) provide reasonable assurance that transactions are recorded as necessary to permit preparation of financial statements in accordance with generally accepted accounting principles, and that receipts and expenditures of the company are being made only in accordance with authorizations of management and directors of the company; and (3) provide reasonable assurance regarding the prevention or timely detection of unauthorized acquisition, use, or disposition of the company's assets that could have a material effect on the financial statements.

Inherent Limitations Paragraph

Because of its inherent limitations, internal control over financial reporting may not prevent or detect misstatements. Also, projections of any evaluation of effectiveness to future periods are subject to the risk that internal control may become inadequate because of changes in conditions, or that the degree of compliance with the policies or procedures may deteriorate.

Opinion Paragraph

In our opinion, the financial statements referred to above present fairly, in all material respects, the financial position of Westbrook Company, Inc. as of December 31, 2005 and 2004, and the results of its operations and its cash flows for each of the years in the three-year period ended December 31, 2005, in conformity with accounting principles generally accepted in the United States of America. Also in our opinion, management's assessment that Westbrook Company maintained effective internal control over financial reporting as of December 31, 2005, is fairly stated, in all material respects, based on criteria established in *Internal Control-Integrated Framework* issued by the Committee of Sponsoring Organizations of the Treadway Commission (COSO). Furthermore, in our opinion, Westbrook Company maintained, in all material respects, effective internal control over financial reporting as of December 31, 2005, based on criteria established in *Internal Control-Integrated Framework* issued by the Committee of Sponsoring Organizations of the Treadway Commission (COSO).

UNQUALIFIED AUDIT REPORT WITH EXPLANATORY PARAGRAPH OR MODIFIED WORDING

The remainder of this chapter deals with reports, other than standard unqualified reports, on the audit of financial statements. In certain situations, an unqualified audit report on the financial statements is issued, but the wording deviates from the standard unqualified report. The **unqualified audit report with explanatory paragraph or modified wording** meets the criteria of a complete audit with satisfactory results and financial statements that are fairly presented, but the auditor believes it is important or is required to provide additional information. In a qualified, adverse, or disclaimer report, the auditor either has not performed a satisfactory audit, is not satisfied that the financial statements are fairly presented, or is not independent.

OBJECTIVE 3-4
Describe the five circumstances when an unqualified report with an explanatory paragraph or modified wording is appropriate.

The following are the most important causes of the addition of an explanatory paragraph or a modification in the wording of the standard unqualified report:

• Lack of consistent application of generally accepted accounting principles
• Substantial doubt about going concern
• Auditor agrees with a departure from promulgated accounting principles
• Emphasis of a matter
• Reports involving other auditors

The first four reports all require an explanatory paragraph. In each case, the three standard report paragraphs are included without modification, and a separate explanatory paragraph follows the opinion paragraph.

Only reports involving the use of other auditors use a modified wording report. This report contains three paragraphs, and all three paragraphs are modified.

Lack of Consistent Application of GAAP

The second reporting standard requires the auditor to call attention to circumstances in which accounting principles have not been consistently observed in the current period in relation to the preceding period. Generally accepted accounting principles require that changes in accounting principles or their method of application be to a preferable principle and that the nature and impact of the change be adequately disclosed. When a material change occurs, the auditor should modify the report by adding an explanatory paragraph after the opinion paragraph that discusses the nature of the change and points the reader to the footnote that discusses the change. The materiality of a change is evaluated based on the current year effect of the change. An explanatory paragraph is required for both voluntary changes and required changes due to a new accounting pronouncement. Figure 3-4 presents such an explanatory paragraph.

FIGURE 3-4	Explanatory Paragraph Because of Change in Accounting Principle

INDEPENDENT AUDITOR'S REPORT

(Same introductory, scope, and opinion paragraphs as the standard report)

As discussed in Note 8 to the financial statements, the Company changed its method of computing depreciation in 2005.

Fourth Paragraph— Explanatory Paragraph

It is implicit in the explanatory paragraph in Figure 3-4 that the auditor concurs with the appropriateness of the change in accounting principles. If the auditor does not so concur, the change is considered a violation of generally accepted accounting principles, and his or her opinion must be qualified.

Consistency Versus Comparability The auditor must be able to distinguish between changes that affect consistency and those that may affect comparability but do not affect consistency. The following are examples of changes that affect consistency and therefore require an explanatory paragraph if they are material:

1. Changes in accounting principles, such as a change from FIFO to LIFO inventory valuation
2. Changes in reporting entities, such as the inclusion of an additional company in combined financial statements
3. Corrections of errors involving principles, by changing from an accounting principle that is not generally acceptable to one that is generally acceptable, including correction of the resulting error

Changes that affect comparability but not consistency and therefore need not be included in the audit report include the following:

1. Changes in an estimate, such as a decrease in the life of an asset for depreciation purposes
2. Error corrections not involving principles, such as a previous year's mathematical error
3. Variations in format and presentation of financial information
4. Changes because of substantially different transactions or events, such as new endeavors in research and development or the sale of a subsidiary

Items that materially affect the comparability of financial statements generally require disclosure in the footnotes. A qualified audit report for inadequate disclosure may be required if the client refuses to properly disclose the items.

Substantial Doubt About Going Concern

Even though the purpose of an audit is not to evaluate the financial health of the business, the auditor has a responsibility to evaluate whether the company is likely to continue as a going concern. SAS 59 (AU 341) addresses this problem under the heading *The Auditor's Consideration of an Entity's Ability to Continue as a Going Concern*. For example, the existence of one or more of the following factors causes uncertainty about the ability of a company to continue as a going concern:

1. Significant recurring operating losses or working capital deficiencies
2. Inability of the company to pay its obligations as they come due
3. Loss of major customers, the occurrence of uninsured catastrophes such as an earthquake or flood, or unusual labor difficulties
4. Legal proceedings, legislation, or similar matters that have occurred that might jeopardize the entity's ability to operate

The auditor's concern in such situations is the possibility that the client may not be able to continue its operations or meet its obligations for a reasonable period. For this purpose, a reasonable period is considered not to exceed 1 year from the date of the financial statements being audited.

END OF THE CONSISTENCY EXPLANATORY PARAGRAPH?

The Auditing Standards Board has issued a proposal to the PCAOB to eliminate the consistency explanatory paragraph. The ASB believes that the explanatory paragraph duplicates management's required disclosures about accounting changes under GAAP and detracts from other explanatory information that may be included in the auditor's report. The ASB supports eliminating the consistency explanatory paragraph for all accounting changes, but the ASB also provides an alternative to eliminate the consistency explanatory paragraph only for mandatory accounting changes.

If the consistency paragraph is eliminated, it would not be the first explanatory paragraph to be eliminated because it duplicated management's disclosure. The previously required explanatory paragraph for material uncertainties, such as litigation, was eliminated by SAS 79, partially because information about uncertainties was already disclosed by management.

FIGURE 3-5 | **Explanatory Paragraph Because of Substantial Doubt About Going Concern**

INDEPENDENT AUDITOR'S REPORT

(Same introductory, scope, and opinion paragraphs as the standard report)

The accompanying financial statements have been prepared assuming that Fairfax Company will continue as a going concern. As discussed in Note 11 to the financial statements, Fairfax Company has suffered recurring losses from operations and has a net capital deficiency that raise substantial doubt about the company's ability to continue as a going concern. Management's plans in regard to these matters are also described in Note 11. The financial statements do not include any adjustments that might result from the outcome of this uncertainty.

Fourth Paragraph— Explanatory Paragraph

When the auditor concludes that there is substantial doubt about the entity's ability to continue as a going concern, an unqualified opinion with an explanatory paragraph is required, regardless of the disclosures in the financial statements. Figure 3-5 provides an example in which there is substantial doubt about going concern.

SAS 59 permits but does not require a disclaimer of opinion when there is substantial doubt about going concern. The criteria for issuing a disclaimer of opinion instead of adding an explanatory paragraph are not stated in the standards, and this type of opinion is rarely issued in practice. An example for which a disclaimer might be issued is when a regulatory agency, such as the Environmental Protection Agency, is considering a severe sanction against a company and, if the proceedings result in an unfavorable outcome, the company will be forced to liquidate.

Auditor Agrees with a Departure from a Promulgated Principle

Rule 203 of the AICPA *Code of Professional Conduct* states that in unusual situations, a departure from an accounting principle promulgated by a body designated by the AICPA to establish accounting principles may not require a qualified or adverse opinion. However, to justify an unqualified opinion, the auditor must be satisfied and must state and explain, in a separate paragraph or paragraphs in the audit report, that adhering to the principle would have produced a misleading result in that situation.

Emphasis of a Matter

Under certain circumstances, the CPA may want to emphasize specific matters regarding the financial statements, even though he or she intends to express an unqualified opinion. Normally, such explanatory information should be included in a separate paragraph in the report. Examples of explanatory information the auditor may believe should be reported as an emphasis of a matter include the following:

- The existence of significant related party transactions
- Important events occurring subsequent to the balance sheet date
- The description of accounting matters affecting the comparability of the financial statements with those of the preceding year
- Material uncertainties disclosed in the footnotes

Reports Involving Other Auditors

When the CPA relies on a different CPA firm to perform part of the audit, which is common when the client has several widespread branches or subdivisions, the principal CPA firm has three alternatives. Only the second is an unqualified report with modified wording.

1. Make No Reference in the Audit Report When no reference is made to the other auditor, a standard unqualified opinion is given unless other circumstances require a departure. This approach is typically followed when the other auditor audited an immaterial portion of the statements, the other auditor is well known or closely supervised by the principal auditor, or the principal auditor has thoroughly reviewed the other auditor's work. The other auditor is still responsible for his or her own report and work in the event of a lawsuit or SEC action.

2. Make Reference in the Report (Modified Wording Report) This type of report is called a shared opinion or report. A shared unqualified report is appropriate when it is impractical

FIGURE 3-6 | Unqualified Shared Report

INDEPENDENT AUDITOR'S REPORT

Stockholders and Board of Directors
Washington Felp
Midland, Texas

Introductory Paragraph— Modified Wording

We have audited the accompanying consolidated balance sheets of Washington Felp as of July 31, 2005 and 2004, and the related consolidated statements of income, retained earnings, and cash flows for the years then ended. These financial statements are the responsibility of the Company's management. Our responsibility is to express an opinion on these financial statements based on our audits. We did not audit the financial statements of Stewart Pane and Lighting, a consolidated subsidiary in which the Company had an equity interest of 84% as of July 31, 2005, which statements reflect total assets of $2,420,000 and $2,237,000 as of July 31, 2005 and 2004, respectively, and total revenues of $3,458,000 and $3,121,000 for the years then ended. Those statements were audited by other auditors whose report has been furnished to us, and our opinion, insofar as it relates to the amounts included for Stewart Pane and Lighting, is based solely on the report of the other auditors.

Scope Paragraph— Modified Wording

We conducted our audits in accordance with auditing standards generally accepted in the United States of America. Those standards require that we plan and perform the audit to obtain reasonable assurance about whether the financial statements are free of material misstatement. An audit includes examining, on a test basis, evidence supporting the amounts and disclosures in the financial statements. An audit also includes assessing the accounting principles used and significant estimates made by management, as well as evaluating the overall financial statement presentation. We believe that our audits and the report of other auditors provide a reasonable basis for our opinion.

Opinion Paragraph— Modified Wording

In our opinion, based on our audits and the report of other auditors, the consolidated financial statements referred to above present fairly, in all material respects, the financial position of Washington Felp as of July 31, 2005 and 2004, and the results of its operations and its cash flows for the years then ended in conformity with accounting principles generally accepted in the United States of America.

September 16, 2005
Farn, Ross, & Co.
Certified Public Accountants
Dallas, Texas

to review the work of the other auditor or when the portion of the financial statements audited by the other CPA is material in relation to the whole. An example of a shared report that should not be interpreted as a qualification is shown in Figure 3-6. Notice that the report does *not* include a separate paragraph that discusses the shared responsibility, but does so in the introductory paragraph and refers to the other auditor in the scope and opinion paragraphs. The portions of the financial statements audited by the other auditor can be stated as percentages or absolute amounts.

3. Qualify the Opinion A qualified opinion or disclaimer, depending on materiality, is required if the principal auditor is not willing to assume any responsibility for the work of the other auditor. The principal auditor may also decide that a qualification is required in the overall report if the other auditor qualified his or her portion of the audit. Qualified opinions and disclaimers are discussed in a later section.

DEPARTURES FROM AN UNQUALIFIED AUDIT REPORT

OBJECTIVE 3-5

Identify the types of audit reports that can be issued when an unqualified opinion is not justified.

It is essential that auditors and readers of audit reports understand the circumstances when an unqualified report is inappropriate and the type of audit report issued in each circumstance. In the study of audit reports that depart from an unqualified report, there are three closely related topics: the conditions requiring a departure from an unqualified opinion, the types of opinions other than unqualified, and materiality.

First, the three conditions requiring a departure are briefly summarized. Each is discussed in greater depth later in the chapter.

1. The Scope of the Audit Has Been Restricted (Scope Limitation) When the auditor has not accumulated sufficient evidence to conclude whether financial statements are stated in accordance with GAAP, a scope restriction exists. There are two major causes of scope restrictions: restrictions imposed by the client and those caused by circumstances beyond either the client's or auditor's control. An example of a client restriction is management's refusal to permit the auditor to confirm material receivables or to physically examine inventory. An example of a restriction caused by circumstances is when the engagement is not agreed on until after the client's year-end. It may not be possible to physically observe inventories, confirm receivables, or perform other important procedures after the balance sheet date.

2. The Financial Statements Have Not Been Prepared in Accordance with Generally Accepted Accounting Principles (GAAP Departure) For example, if the client insists on using replacement costs for fixed assets or values inventory at selling price rather than historical cost, a departure from the unqualified report is required. When generally accepted accounting principles are referred to in this context, consideration of the adequacy of all informative disclosures, including footnotes, is especially important.

3. The Auditor Is Not Independent Independence ordinarily is determined by Rule 101 of the rules of the *Code of Professional Conduct.*

When any of the three conditions requiring a departure from an unqualified report exists and is material, a report other than an unqualified report must be issued. Three main types of audit reports are issued under these conditions: qualified opinion, adverse opinion, and disclaimer of opinion.

A **qualified opinion** report can result from a limitation on the scope of the audit or failure to follow generally accepted accounting principles. A qualified opinion report can be used *only when the auditor concludes that the overall financial statements are fairly stated.* A disclaimer or an adverse report must be used if the auditor believes that the condition being reported on is highly material. Therefore, the qualified opinion is considered the least severe type of departure from an unqualified report.

Qualified Opinion

A qualified report can take the form of a *qualification of both the scope and the opinion* or of the *opinion alone.* A scope and opinion qualification can be issued only when the auditor has been unable to accumulate all of the evidence required by generally accepted auditing standards. Therefore, this type of qualification is used when the auditor's scope has been restricted by the client or when circumstances exist that prevent the auditor from conducting a complete audit. The use of a qualification of the opinion alone is restricted to situations in which the financial statements are not stated in accordance with GAAP.

When an auditor issues a qualified report, he or she must use the term *except for* in the opinion paragraph. The implication is that the auditor is satisfied that the overall financial statements are correctly stated "except for" a specific aspect of them. Examples of this qualification are given later in this chapter. It is unacceptable to use the phrase *except for* with any other type of audit opinion.

An **adverse opinion** is used only when the auditor believes that the overall financial statements are so *materially misstated or misleading* that they do not present fairly the financial position or results of operations and cash flows in conformity with GAAP. The adverse opinion report can arise only when the auditor has knowledge, after an adequate investigation, of the absence of conformity. This is uncommon and thus the adverse opinion is rarely used.

Adverse Opinion

A **disclaimer of opinion** is issued when the auditor has been *unable to satisfy himself or herself* that the overall financial statements are fairly presented. The necessity for disclaiming an opinion may arise because of a *severe limitation on the scope* of the audit or a *nonindependent relationship* under the *Code of Professional Conduct* between the auditor and the client. Either of these situations prevents the auditor from expressing an opinion

Disclaimer of Opinion

on the financial statements as a whole. The auditor also has the option to issue a disclaimer of opinion for a going concern problem.

The disclaimer is distinguished from an adverse opinion in that it can arise only from a *lack of knowledge* by the auditor, whereas to express an adverse opinion, the auditor must have knowledge that the financial statements are not fairly stated. Both disclaimers and adverse opinions are used only when the condition is highly material.

MATERIALITY

OBJECTIVE 3-6

Explain how materiality affects audit reporting decisions.

Materiality is an essential consideration in determining the appropriate type of report for a given set of circumstances. For example, if a misstatement is immaterial relative to the financial statements of the entity for the current period, it is appropriate to issue an unqualified report. A common instance is the immediate expensing of office supplies rather than carrying the unused portion in inventory because the amount is insignificant.

The situation is totally different when the amounts are of such significance that the financial statements are materially affected as a whole. In these circumstances, it is necessary to issue a disclaimer of opinion or an adverse opinion, depending on the nature of the misstatement. In situations of lesser materiality, a qualified opinion is appropriate.

Levels of Materiality

The common definition of materiality as it applies to accounting and therefore to audit reporting is as follows:

> A misstatement in the financial statements can be considered material if knowledge of the misstatement would affect a decision of a reasonable user of the statements.

In applying this definition, three levels of materiality are used for determining the type of opinion to issue.

Amounts Are Immaterial When a misstatement in the financial statements exists but is unlikely to affect the decisions of a reasonable user, it is considered to be immaterial. An unqualified opinion is therefore appropriate. For example, assume that management recorded prepaid insurance as an asset in the previous year and decides to expense it in the current year to reduce record-keeping costs. Management has failed to follow GAAP, but if the amounts are small, the misstatement would be immaterial and a standard unqualified audit report would be appropriate.

Amounts Are Material but Do Not Overshadow the Financial Statements as a Whole The second level of materiality exists when a misstatement in the financial statements would affect a user's decision, but the overall statements are still fairly stated and therefore useful. For example, knowledge of a large misstatement in fixed assets might affect a user's willingness to loan money to a company if the assets were the collateral. A misstatement of inventory does not mean that cash, accounts receivable, and other elements of the financial statements, or the financial statements as a whole, are materially incorrect.

To make materiality decisions when a condition requiring a departure from an unqualified report exists, the auditor must evaluate all effects on the financial statements. Assume that the auditor is unable to satisfy himself or herself whether inventory is fairly stated in deciding on the appropriate type of opinion. Because of the effect of a misstatement in inventory on other accounts and on totals in the statements, the auditor needs to consider the materiality of the combined effect on inventory, total current assets, total working capital, total assets, income taxes, income taxes payable, total current liabilities, cost of goods sold, net income before taxes, and net income after taxes.

When the auditor concludes that a misstatement is material but does not overshadow the financial statements as a whole, a qualified opinion (using "except for") is appropriate.

Amounts Are So Material or So Pervasive That Overall Fairness of the Statements Is in Question The highest level of materiality exists when users are likely to make incorrect decisions if they rely on the overall financial statements. To return to the previous example, if inventory is the largest balance on the financial statements, a large misstatement would probably be so material that the auditor's report should indicate the financial statements taken as a whole cannot be considered fairly stated. When the highest level of materiality exists, the auditor must issue either a disclaimer of opinion or an adverse opinion, depending on which conditions exist.

When determining whether an exception is highly material, the extent to which the exception affects different parts of the financial statements must be considered. This is called pervasiveness. A misclassification between cash and accounts receivable affects only those two accounts and is therefore not pervasive. On the other hand, failure to record a material sale is highly pervasive because it affects sales, accounts receivable, income tax expense, accrued income taxes, and retained earnings, which in turn affect current assets, total assets, current liabilities, total liabilities, owners' equity, gross margin, and operating income.

As misstatements become more pervasive, the likelihood of issuing an adverse opinion rather than a qualified opinion increases. For example, suppose the auditor decides a misclassification between cash and accounts receivable should result in a qualified opinion because it is material; the failure to record a sale of the same dollar amount may result in an adverse opinion because of pervasiveness.

Regardless of the amount involved, a disclaimer of opinion must be issued if the auditor is determined to lack independence under the rules of the *Code of Professional Conduct*. This harsh requirement reflects the importance of independence to auditors. Any deviation from the independence rule is therefore considered highly material. Table 3-1 summarizes the relationship between materiality and the type of opinion to be issued.

In concept, the effect of materiality on the type of opinion to issue is straightforward. In application, deciding on actual materiality in a given situation is a difficult judgment. There are no simple, well-defined guidelines that enable auditors to decide when something is immaterial, material, or highly material. The evaluation of materiality also depends on whether the situation involves a failure to follow GAAP or a scope limitation.

Materiality Decisions

Materiality Decisions—Non-GAAP Condition When a client has failed to follow GAAP, the audit report will be unqualified, qualified opinion only, or adverse, depending on the materiality of the departure. Several aspects of materiality must be considered.

Dollar Amounts Compared with a Base The primary concern in measuring materiality when a client has failed to follow GAAP is usually the total dollar misstatement in the accounts involved, compared with some base. A $10,000 misstatement might be material for a small company but not for a larger one. Therefore, misstatements must be compared with some measurement base before a decision can be made about the materiality of the failure to follow GAAP. Common bases include net income, total assets, current assets, and working capital.

For example, assume that the auditor believes there is a $100,000 overstatement of inventory because of the client's failure to follow GAAP. Also assume recorded inventory of $1 million, current assets of $3 million, and net income before taxes of $2 million. In this case, the auditor must evaluate the materiality of a misstatement of inventory of 10 percent, current assets of 3.3 percent, and net income before taxes of 5 percent.

TABLE 3-1	Relationship of Materiality to Type of Opinion	
Materiality Level	**Significance in Terms of Reasonable Users' Decisions**	**Type of Opinion**
Immaterial	Users' decisions are unlikely to be affected.	Unqualified
Material	Users' decisions are likely to be affected only if the information in question is important to the specific decisions being made. The overall financial statements are presented fairly.	Qualified
Highly material	Most or all users' decisions based on the financial statements are likely to be significantly affected.	Disclaimer or Adverse

Note: Lack of independence requires a disclaimer regardless of materiality.

To evaluate overall materiality, the auditor must also combine all unadjusted misstatements and judge whether there may be individually immaterial misstatements that, when combined, significantly affect the statements. In the inventory example just given, assume the auditor believes there is also an overstatement of $150,000 in accounts receivable. The total effect on current assets is now 8.3 percent ($250,000 divided by $3,000,000) and 12.5 percent on net income before taxes ($250,000 divided by $2,000,000).

When comparing potential misstatements with a base, the auditor must carefully consider all accounts affected by a misstatement (pervasiveness). For example, it is important not to overlook the effect of an understatement of inventory on cost of goods sold, income before taxes, income tax expense, and accrued income taxes payable.

Measurability The dollar amount of some misstatements cannot be accurately measured. For example, a client's unwillingness to disclose an existing lawsuit or the acquisition of a new company subsequent to the balance sheet date is difficult if not impossible to measure in terms of dollar amounts. The materiality question the auditor must evaluate in such situations is the effect on statement users of the failure to make the disclosure.

Nature of the Item The decision of a user may also be affected by the kind of misstatement in the statement. The following may affect the user's decision and therefore the auditor's opinion in a different way than most misstatements:

1. Transactions are illegal or fraudulent.
2. An item may materially affect some future period, even though it is immaterial when only the current period is considered.
3. An item has a "psychic" effect (for example, the item changes a small loss to a small profit, maintains a trend of increasing earnings, or allows earnings to exceed analysts' expectations).
4. An item may be important in terms of possible consequences arising from contractual obligations (for example, the effect of failure to comply with a debt restriction may result in a material loan being called).

Materiality Decisions—Scope Limitations Condition When there is a scope limitation in an audit, the audit report will be unqualified, qualified scope and opinion, or disclaimer, depending on the materiality of the scope limitation. The auditor will consider the same three factors included in the previous discussion about materiality decisions for failure to follow GAAP, but they will be considered differently. The size of *potential* misstatements, rather than known misstatements, is important in determining whether an unqualified report, a qualified report, or a disclaimer of opinion is appropriate for a scope limitation. For example, if recorded accounts payable of $400,000 was not audited, the auditor must evaluate the potential misstatement in accounts payable and decide how materially the financial statements could be affected. The pervasiveness of these potential misstatements must also be considered.

It is typically more difficult to evaluate the materiality of potential misstatements resulting from a scope limitation than for failure to follow GAAP. Misstatements resulting from failure to follow GAAP are known. Those resulting from scope limitations must usually be subjectively measured in terms of potential or likely misstatements. For example, a recorded accounts payable of $400,000 might be understated by more than $1 million, which may affect several totals, including gross margin, net earnings, and total assets.

DISCUSSION OF CONDITIONS REQUIRING A DEPARTURE

OBJECTIVE 3-7

Draft appropriately modified audit reports under a variety of circumstances.

Auditor's Scope Has Been Restricted

You should now understand the relationships among the conditions requiring a departure from an unqualified report, the major types of reports other than unqualified, and the three levels of materiality. This part of the chapter examines the conditions requiring a departure from an unqualified report in greater detail and shows examples of reports.

Two major categories of scope restrictions exist: those caused by a client and those caused by conditions beyond the control of either the client or the auditor. The effect on the auditor's report is the same for either, but the interpretation of materiality is likely to be different. When there is a scope restriction, the appropriate response is to issue an unqualified report, a qualification of scope and opinion, or a disclaimer of opinion, depending on materiality.

For client-imposed restrictions, the auditor should be concerned about the possibility that management is trying to prevent discovery of misstated information. In such cases, the AICPA has encouraged a disclaimer of opinion when materiality is in question. When restrictions result from conditions beyond the client's control, a qualification of scope and opinion is more likely.

Two restrictions occasionally imposed by clients on the auditor's scope relate to the observation of physical inventory and the confirmation of accounts receivable, but other restrictions may also occur. Reasons for client-imposed scope restrictions may be a desire to save audit fees and, in the case of confirming receivables, to prevent possible conflicts between the client and customer when amounts differ.

The most common case in which conditions beyond the client's and auditor's control cause a scope restriction is an engagement agreed on after the client's balance sheet date. The confirmation of accounts receivable, physical examination of inventory, and other important procedures may be impossible under those circumstances. When the auditor cannot perform procedures he or she considers desirable but can be satisfied with alternative procedures that the information being verified is fairly stated, an unqualified report is appropriate. If alternative procedures cannot be performed, a qualified scope and opinion or disclaimer of opinion is necessary, depending on materiality.

A restriction on the scope of the auditor's examination requires a qualifying paragraph preceding the opinion to describe the restriction. In the case of a disclaimer, the entire scope paragraph is excluded from the report.

For example, the report in Figure 3-7 would be appropriate for an audit in which the amounts were material but not pervasive and the auditor could not obtain audited financial statements supporting an investment in a foreign affiliate and could not satisfy himself or herself by alternate procedures. The entire introductory paragraph and most of the second paragraph are omitted because they use standard wording.

When the amounts are so material that a disclaimer of opinion rather than a qualified opinion is required, the auditor uses only three paragraphs. The first (introductory) paragraph is modified slightly to say "We were engaged to audit . . . ." The second paragraph is the same as the third paragraph in Figure 3-7. The scope paragraph is deleted, and the final (opinion) paragraph is changed to a disclaimer. The reason for deleting the scope paragraph is to avoid stating anything that might lead readers to believe that other parts of the

FIGURE 3-7	Qualified Scope and Opinion Report Due to Scope Restriction

INDEPENDENT AUDITOR'S REPORT

(Same introductory paragraph as standard report)

Except as discussed in the following paragraph, we conducted our audit . . . (remainder is the same as the scope paragraph in the standard report) — **Scope Paragraph— Qualified**

We were unable to obtain audited financial statements supporting the Company's investment in a foreign affiliate stated at $475,000 or its equity in earnings of that affiliate of $365,000, which is included in net income, as described in Note X to the financial statements. Because of the nature of the Company's records, we were unable to satisfy ourselves as to the carrying value of the investment or the equity in its earnings by means of other auditing procedures. — **Third Paragraph— Added**

In our opinion, except for the effects of such adjustments, if any, as might have been determined to be necessary had we been able to examine evidence regarding the foreign affiliate investment and earnings, the financial statements referred to above present fairly, in all material respects, the financial position of Laughlin Corporation as of December 31, 2005, and the results of its operations and its cash flows for the year then ended in conformity with accounting principles generally accepted in the United States of America. — **Opinion Paragraph— Qualified**

FIGURE 3-8   Disclaimer of Opinion Due to Scope Restriction

INDEPENDENT AUDITOR'S REPORT

Introductory Paragraph–Modification of Standard Report

We were engaged to audit . . . (remainder is the same as the introductory paragraph in the standard report)

Second Paragraph–Added

(Same wording as that used for the third paragraph in Figure 3-7)

Opinion Paragraph–Disclaimer

Because we were unable to obtain audited financial statements supporting the Company's investment in a foreign affiliate and we were unable to satisfy ourselves as to the carrying value of the investment or the equity in its earnings by means of other auditing procedures, the scope of our work was not sufficient to enable us to express, and we do not express, an opinion on these financial statements.

Note: In a disclaimer due to a scope restriction, the scope paragraph is omitted entirely.

financial statements were audited and therefore might be fairly stated. Figure 3-8 shows the audit report assuming the auditor had concluded that the facts in Figure 3-7 required a disclaimer rather than a qualified opinion.

Statements Are Not in Conformity with GAAP

When the auditor knows that the financial statements may be misleading because they were not prepared in conformity with GAAP, and the client is unable or unwilling to correct the misstatement, he or she must issue a qualified or an adverse opinion, depending on the materiality of the item in question. The opinion must clearly state the nature of the deviation from accepted principles and the amount of the misstatement, if it is known. Figure 3-9 shows an example of a qualified opinion when a client did not capitalize leases as required by GAAP. The first and second paragraphs are omitted because they include standard wording.

When the amounts are so material or pervasive that an adverse opinion is required, the scope would still be unqualified and the qualifying paragraph could remain the same, but the opinion paragraph might be as shown in Figure 3-10.

When the client fails to include information that is necessary for the fair presentation of financial statements in the body of the statements or in the related footnotes, it is the auditor's responsibility to present the information in the audit report and to issue a qualified or an adverse opinion. It is common to put this type of qualification in an added paragraph preceding the opinion (the scope paragraph will remain unqualified) and to refer to the added paragraph in the opinion paragraph. Figure 3-11 shows an example of an audit report in which the auditor considered the financial statement disclosure inadequate.

Rule 203 Reports Determining whether statements are in accordance with GAAP can be difficult. Rule 203 in the *Code of Professional Conduct* permits a departure from generally

FIGURE 3-9   Qualified Opinion Report Due to Non-GAAP

INDEPENDENT AUDITOR'S REPORT

(Same introductory and scope paragraphs as the standard report)

Third Paragraph–Added

The Company has excluded from property and debt in the accompanying balance sheet certain lease obligations that, in our opinion, should be capitalized to conform with U.S. generally accepted accounting principles. If these lease obligations were capitalized, property would be increased by $4,600,000, long-term debt by $4,200,000, and retained earnings by $400,000 as of December 31, 2005, and net income and earnings per share would be increased by $400,000 and $1.75, respectively, for the year then ended.

Opinion Paragraph–Qualified

In our opinion, except for the effects of not capitalizing lease obligations, as discussed in the preceding paragraph, the financial statements referred to above present fairly, in all material respects, the financial position of Ajax Company as of December 31, 2005, and the results of its operations and its cash flows for the year then ended in conformity with accounting principles generally accepted in the United States of America.

FIGURE 3-10	Adverse Opinion Due to Non-GAAP	

INDEPENDENT AUDITOR'S REPORT

(Same introductory and scope paragraphs as the standard report)

(Same third paragraph as that used for the third paragraph in Figure 3-9)   **Third Paragraph—Added**

In our opinion, because of the effects of the matters discussed in the preceding paragraph, the   **Opinion Paragraph—Adverse**
financial statements referred to above do not present fairly, in conformity with accounting principles
generally accepted in the United States of America, the financial position of Ajax Company as of
December 31, 2005, or the results of its operations and its cash flows for the year then ended.

FIGURE 3-11	Qualified Opinion Due to Inadequate Disclosure	

INDEPENDENT AUDITOR'S REPORT

(Same introductory and scope paragraphs as the standard report)

On January 15, 2005, the company issued debentures in the amount of $3,600,000 for the purpose of   **Third Paragraph—Added**
financing plant expansion. The debenture agreement restricts the payment of future cash dividends to
earnings after December 31, 2005. In our opinion, disclosure of this information is required to
conform with accounting principles generally accepted in the United States of America.

In our opinion, except for the omission of the information discussed in the preceding paragraph, the   **Opinion Paragraph—Qualified**
financial statements referred to above present fairly . . . (remainder is the same as the opinion in the
standard report)

accepted accounting principles when the auditor believes that adherence to these would result in misleading statements.

When the auditor decides that adherence to GAAP would result in misleading statements, there should be a complete explanation in a third paragraph. The paragraph should fully explain the departure and why GAAP would have resulted in misleading statements. The opinion paragraph should then be unqualified except for the reference to the third paragraph. As discussed earlier in the chapter, this is called an unqualified audit report with an explanatory paragraph.

Lack of Statement of Cash Flows The client's unwillingness to include a statement of cash flows is specifically addressed in SAS 58 (AU 508). When the statement is omitted, there must be a third paragraph stating the omission and an "except for" opinion qualification.

If the auditor has not fulfilled the independence requirements specified by the *Code of Professional Conduct,* a disclaimer of opinion is required even though all the audit procedures considered necessary in the circumstances were performed. The wording in Figure 3-12 is recommended when the auditor is not independent.   **Auditor Is Not Independent**

The lack of independence overrides any other scope limitations. Therefore, no other reason for disclaiming an opinion should be cited. There should be no mention in the report of the performance of any audit procedures. It is an example of a one-paragraph audit report.

FIGURE 3-12	Disclaimer Due to Lack of Independence	

We are not independent with respect to Home Decors.com, Inc., and the accompanying balance sheet as of December 31, 2005, and the related statements of income, retained earnings, and cash flows for the year then ended were not audited by us. Accordingly, we do not express an opinion on them.

Note: When the auditor lacks independence, no report title is included.

AUDITOR'S DECISION PROCESS FOR AUDIT REPORTS

OBJECTIVE 3-8

Determine the appropriate audit report for a given audit situation.

Auditors use a well-defined process for deciding the appropriate audit report in a given set of circumstances. The auditor must first assess whether any conditions exist requiring a departure from a standard unqualified report. If any conditions exist, the auditor must then assess the materiality of the condition and determine the appropriate type of report.

Determine Whether Any Condition Exists Requiring a Departure from a Standard Unqualified Report The most important of these conditions are identified in Table 3-2. Auditors identify these conditions as they perform the audit and include information about any condition in the audit files as discussion items for audit reporting. If none of these conditions exist, which is the case in most audits, the auditor issues a standard unqualified audit report.

Decide the Materiality for Each Condition When a condition requiring a departure from a standard unqualified opinion exists, the auditor evaluates the potential effect on the financial statements. For departures from GAAP or scope restrictions, the auditor must decide among immaterial, material, and highly material. All other conditions, except for lack of auditor independence, require only a distinction between immaterial and material. The materiality decision is a difficult one, requiring considerable judgment. For example, assume that there is a scope limitation in auditing inventory. It is difficult to assess the potential misstatement of an account that the auditor does not audit.

Decide the Appropriate Type of Report for the Condition, Given the Materiality Level After making the first two decisions, it is easy to decide the appropriate type of opinion by using a decision aid. An example of such an aid is Table 3-2. For example, assume that the auditor concludes that there is a departure from GAAP and it is material, but not highly material. Table 3-2 shows that the appropriate audit report is a qualified opinion with an additional

TABLE 3-2	Audit Report for Each Condition Requiring a Departure from a Standard Unqualified Report at Different Levels of Materiality		
		Level of Materiality	
Condition Requiring an Unqualified Report with Modified Wording or Explanatory Paragraph		**Immaterial**	**Material**
Accounting principles not consistently applied*		Unqualified	Unqualified report, explanatory paragraph
Substantial doubt about going concern†		Unqualified	Unqualified report, explanatory paragraph
Justified departure from GAAP or other accounting principle		Unqualified	Unqualified report, explanatory paragraph
Emphasis of a matter		Unqualified	Unqualified report, explanatory paragraph
Use of another auditor		Unqualified	Unqualified report, modified wording

		Level of Materiality	
Condition Requiring a Departure from Unqualified Report	**Immaterial**	**Material, But Does Not Overshadow Financial Statements as a Whole**	**So Material That Overall Fairness Is in Question**
Scope restricted by client or other conditions	Unqualified	Qualified scope, additional paragraph, and qualified opinion (except for)	Disclaimer
Financial statements not prepared in accordance with GAAP‡	Unqualified	Additional paragraph and qualified opinion (except for)	Adverse
The auditor is not independent		Disclaimer, regardless of materiality	

*If the auditor does not concur with the appropriateness of the change, the condition is considered a violation of GAAP.
†The auditor has the option of issuing a disclaimer of opinion.
‡If the auditor can demonstrate that GAAP would be misleading, an unqualified report with an explanatory paragraph would be appropriate.

paragraph discussing the departure. The introductory and scope paragraphs will be included using standard wording.

Write the Audit Report Most CPA firms have computer templates that include precise wording for different circumstances to help the auditor write the audit report. Also, one or more partners in most CPA firms have special expertise in writing audit reports. These partners typically write or review all audit reports before they are issued.

Auditors often encounter situations involving more than one of the conditions requiring a departure from an unqualified report or modification of the standard unqualified report. In these circumstances, the auditor should modify his or her opinion for each condition unless one has the effect of neutralizing the others. For example, if there is a scope limitation and a situation in which the auditor is not independent, the scope limitation should not be revealed. The following situations are examples when more than one modification should be included in the report:

More Than One Condition Requiring a Departure or Modification

- The auditor is not independent and the auditor knows that the company has not followed generally accepted accounting principles.
- There is a scope limitation and there is substantial doubt about the company's ability to continue as a going concern.
- There is a substantial doubt about the company's ability to continue as a going concern and information about the causes of the uncertainties is not adequately disclosed in a footnote.
- There is a deviation in the statements' preparation in accordance with GAAP and another accounting principle was applied on a basis that was not consistent with that of the preceding year.

Many readers interpret the number of paragraphs in the report as an important "signal" as to whether the financial statements are correct. A three-paragraph report ordinarily indicates that there are no exceptions in the audit. However, three-paragraph reports are also issued when a disclaimer of opinion is issued due to a scope limitation or for an unqualified shared report involving other auditors. More than three paragraphs indicates some type of qualification or required explanation.

Number of Paragraphs in the Report

An additional paragraph is added before the opinion for a qualified opinion, an adverse opinion, and a disclaimer of opinion for a scope limitation. This results in a four-paragraph report, except for the disclaimer of opinion for a scope limitation. A disclaimer due to a scope limitation results in a three-paragraph report because the scope paragraph is omitted. A disclaimer due to a lack of independence is a one-paragraph report.

TABLE 3-3	Number of Paragraphs, Standard Wording Paragraphs Modified, and Location of Additional Paragraph for Audit Reports		
Type of Report	**Number of Paragraphs**	**Standard Wording Paragraphs Modified**	**Location of Additional Paragraph**
Standard unqualified	3	None	None
Unqualified with explanatory paragraph	4	None	After opinion
Unqualified shared report with other auditors	3	All three paragraphs	None
Qualified—opinion only	4	Opinion only	Before opinion
Qualified—scope and opinion	4	Scope and opinion	Before opinion
Disclaimer—scope limitation	3	Introductory and opinion paragraphs modified; scope paragraph eliminated	Before opinion
Adverse	4	Opinion only	Before opinion

When an unqualified opinion with explanatory paragraph is issued, an explanatory paragraph usually follows the opinion. No explanatory paragraph is required for an unqualified shared report involving other auditors, but the wording in all three paragraphs is modified.

Table 3-3 (p. 63) summarizes the types of reports issued for the audit of financial statements, the number of paragraphs for each type, the standard wording paragraphs modified, and the location of the additional paragraph. The table excludes a disclaimer for a lack of independence, which is a special, one-paragraph report.

IMPACT OF E-COMMERCE ON AUDIT REPORTING

OBJECTIVE 3-9

Discuss the impact of e-commerce on audit reporting.

Most public companies provide access to financial information through their home Web page. Visitors to a company's Web site can view the company's most recent audited financial statements, including the auditor's report. In addition, it is common for the company to include such information as unaudited quarterly financial statements, other selected financial information, and press releases often labeled as "About the Company" or "Investor Relations" on its Web site.

Even before the widespread use of the Internet, companies often published documents that contained information in addition to audited financial statements and the independent auditor's report. The most common example was and still is the company's annual report. Under auditing standards, the auditor has no obligation to perform any procedures to corroborate the other information. The auditor is, however, responsible for reading the other information to determine whether it is materially inconsistent with information in the audited financial statements.

However, under current auditing standards, auditors are not required to read information contained in electronic sites, such as the company's Web site, that also contain the company's audited financial statements and the auditor's report. Auditing standards note that electronic sites are a means of distributing information and are not considered "documents," as that term is used in auditing standards.

SUMMARY

This chapter described the auditor's standard unqualified audit report, as well as combined reports on the financial statements and internal control over financial reporting under Section 404 of the Sarbanes–Oxley Act. The four categories of audit reports and the auditor's decision process in choosing the appropriate audit report to issue were then discussed. In some circumstances, an explanatory paragraph or modification of the unqualified report is required. When there is a material departure from GAAP or a material limitation on the scope of the audit, an unqualified report cannot be issued. The appropriate report to issue in these circumstances depends on whether the situation involves a GAAP departure or a scope limitation, as well as the level of materiality.

ESSENTIAL TERMS

Adverse opinion—a report issued when the auditor believes the financial statements are so materially misstated or misleading as a whole that they do not present fairly the entity's financial position or the results of its operations and cash flows in conformity with GAAP

Combined report on financial statements and internal control over financial reporting—audit report on the financial statements and the effectiveness of internal control over financial reporting required under Section 404 of the Sarbanes–Oxley Act

Disclaimer of opinion—a report issued when the auditor has not been able to become satisfied that the overall financial statements are fairly presented or the auditor is not independent

Material misstatement—a misstatement in the financial statements, knowledge of which would affect a decision of a reasonable user of the statements

Qualified opinion—a report issued when the auditor believes that the overall financial statements are fairly stated but that either the scope of the audit was limited or the financial data indicated a failure to follow GAAP

Standard unqualified audit report—the report a CPA issues when all auditing conditions have been met, no significant misstatements have been discovered and left uncorrected, and it is the auditor's opinion that the financial statements are fairly stated in accordance with GAAP

Unqualified audit report with explanatory paragraph or modified wording—an unqualified report in which the financial statements are fairly presented, but the auditor believes it is important, or is required, to provide additional information

REVIEW QUESTIONS

3-1 (Objective 3-1) Explain why auditors' reports are important to users of financial statements and why it is desirable to have standard wording.

3-2 (Objective 3-1) List the seven parts of a standard unqualified audit report and explain the meaning of each part. How do the parts compare with those found in a qualified report?

3-3 (Objective 3-1) What are the purposes of the scope paragraph in the auditor's report? Identify the most important information included in the scope paragraph.

3-4 (Objective 3-1) What are the purposes of the opinion paragraph in the auditor's report? Identify the most important information included in the opinion paragraph.

3-5 (Objective 3-1) On February 17, 2006, a CPA completed the field work on the financial statements for the Buckheizer Technology Corporation for the year ended December 31, 2005. The audit is satisfactory in all respects except for the existence of a change in accounting principles from FIFO to LIFO inventory valuation, which results in an explanatory paragraph to consistency. On February 26, the auditor completed the tax return and the draft of the financial statements. The final audit report was completed, attached to the financial statements, and delivered to the client on March 7. What is the appropriate date on the auditor's report?

3-6 (Objective 3-2) What five circumstances are required for a standard unqualified report to be issued?

3-7 (Objective 3-3) Describe the additional information included in the introductory, scope, and opinion paragraphs in a combined audit report on financial statements and the effectiveness of internal control over financial reporting. What is the nature of the additional paragraphs in the audit report?

3-8 (Objectives 3-4, 3-7) What type of opinion should an auditor issue when the financial statements are not in accordance with GAAP because such adherence would result in misleading statements?

3-9 (Objectives 3-4, 3-5) Distinguish between an unqualified report with an explanatory paragraph or modified wording and a qualified report. Give examples when an explanatory paragraph or modified wording should be used in an unqualified opinion.

3-10 (Objective 3-4) Describe what is meant by reports involving the use of other auditors. What are the three options available to the principal auditor and when should each be used?

3-11 (Objective 3-4) The client has restated the prior-year statements because of a change from LIFO to FIFO. How should this be reflected in the auditor's report?

3-12 (Objective 3-4) Distinguish between changes that affect consistency and those that may affect comparability but not consistency. Give an example of each.

3-13 (Objective 3-5) List the three conditions that require a departure from an unqualified opinion and give one specific example of each of those conditions.

3-14 (Objective 3-5) Distinguish between a qualified opinion, an adverse opinion, and a disclaimer of opinion, and explain the circumstances under which each is appropriate.

3-15 (Objective 3-6) Define *materiality* as it is used in audit reporting. What conditions will affect the auditor's determination of materiality?

3-16 (Objective 3-6) Explain how materiality differs for failure to follow GAAP and for lack of independence.

3-17 (Objective 3-7) How does the auditor's opinion differ between scope limitations caused by client restrictions and limitations resulting from conditions beyond the client's control? Under which of these two would the auditor be most likely to issue a disclaimer of opinion? Explain.

3-18 (Objective 3-5) Distinguish between a report qualified as to opinion only and one with both a scope and opinion qualification.

3-19 (Objectives 3-6, 3-7) Identify the three alternative opinions that may be appropriate when the client's financial statements are not in accordance with GAAP. Under what circumstance is each appropriate?

3-20 (Objectives 3-5, 3-7) Discuss why the AICPA has such strict requirements on audit opinions when the auditor is not independent.

3-21 (Objective 3-8) When an auditor discovers more than one condition that requires departure from or modification of the standard unqualified report, what should the auditor's report include?

3-22 (Objective 3-9) What responsibility does the auditor have for information on the company's Web site that may be linked to electronic versions of the company's annual financial statements and auditor's report? How does this differ from the auditor's responsibility for other information in the company's annual report that includes the financial statements and auditor's report?

MULTIPLE CHOICE QUESTIONS FROM CPA EXAMINATIONS

3-23 (Objectives 3-1, 3-2, 3-3, 3-4) The following questions concern unqualified audit reports. Choose the best response.

a. Which of the following statements about a combined report on the financial statements and internal control over financial reporting is correct?
   (1) The auditor's report on internal control is for the same period as the financial statements.
   (2) The report includes additional paragraphs for the definition and limitations of internal control.
   (3) The introductory, scope, and opinion paragraphs are unchanged from a report for an audit of the financial statements only.
   (4) GAAP is the framework used to evaluate internal control.

b. The date of the CPA's opinion on the financial statements of the client should be the date of the
   (1) closing of the client's books.
   (2) receipt of the client's letter of representation.
   (3) completion of all important audit procedures.
   (4) submission of the report to the client.

c. If a principal auditor decides to refer in his or her report to the audit of another auditor, he or she is required to disclose the
   (1) name of the other auditor.
   (2) nature of the inquiry into the other auditor's professional standing and extent of the review of the other auditor's work.
   (3) portion of the financial statements audited by the other auditor.
   (4) reasons for being unwilling to assume responsibility for the other auditor's work.

d. An entity changed from the straight-line method to the declining-balance method of depreciation for all newly acquired assets. This change has no material effect on the current year's financial statements but is reasonably certain to have a substantial effect in later years. If the change is disclosed in the notes to the financial statements, the auditor should issue a report with a(n)
   (1) qualified opinion.
   (2) unqualified opinion with explanatory paragraph.
   (3) unqualified opinion.
   (4) qualified opinion with explanatory paragraph regarding consistency.

3-24 (Objectives 3-5, 3-6, 3-7) The following questions concern audit reports other than unqualified audit reports with standard wording. Choose the best response.

a. A CPA will issue an adverse auditor's opinion if
   (1) the scope of the audit is limited by the client.
   (2) the exception to the fairness of presentation is so material that an "except for" opinion is not justified.
   (3) the auditor did not perform sufficient auditing procedures to form an opinion on the financial statements taken as a whole.
   (4) major uncertainties exist concerning the company's future.

b. An auditor would most likely disclaim an opinion because of
   (1) the client's failure to present supplementary information required by the Financial Accounting Standards Board (FASB).
   (2) inadequate disclosure of material information.

(3) a client-imposed scope limitation.

(4) the qualification of an opinion by the other auditor of a subsidiary when responsibility has been divided.

c. Under which of the following sets of circumstances should an auditor issue a qualified opinion?

(1) The financial statements contain a departure from generally accepted accounting principles, the effect of which is material.

(2) The principal auditor decides to make reference to the report of another auditor who audited a subsidiary.

(3) There has been a material change between periods in the method of the application of accounting principles.

(4) There are significant uncertainties affecting the financial statements.

DISCUSSION QUESTIONS AND PROBLEMS

3-25 (Objective 3-1) A careful reading of an unqualified report indicates several important phrases. Explain why each of the following phrases or clauses is used rather than the alternative provided:

a. "In our opinion, the financial statements present fairly" rather than "The financial statements present fairly."

b. "We conducted our audit in accordance with auditing standards generally accepted in the United States of America" rather than "Our audit was performed to detect material misstatements in the financial statements."

c. "The financial statements referred to above present fairly in all material respects the financial position" rather than "The financial statements mentioned above are correctly stated."

d. "In conformity with accounting principles generally accepted in the United States of America" rather than "are properly stated to represent the true economic conditions."

e. "Brown & Phillips, CPAs (firm name)," rather than "James E. Brown, CPA (individual partner's name)."

3-26 (Objectives 3-1, 3-2, 3-4, 3-6, 3-7) Roscoe, CPA, has completed the audit of the financial statements of Excelsior Corporation as of and for the year ended December 31, 2005. Roscoe also audited and reported on the Excelsior financial statements for the prior year. Roscoe drafted the following report for 2005.

> We have audited the balance sheet and statements of income and retained earnings of Excelsior Corporation as of December 31, 2005. We conducted our audit in accordance with generally accepted accounting standards. Those standards require that we plan and perform the audit to obtain reasonable assurance about whether the financial statements are free of misstatement.
>
> We believe that our audits provide a reasonable basis for our opinion.
>
> In our opinion, the financial statements referred to above present fairly the financial position of Excelsior Corporation as of December 31, 2005, and the results of its operations for the year then ended in conformity with generally accepted auditing standards, applied on a basis consistent with those of the preceding year.
>
> Roscoe, CPA
> (Signed)

Other Information

- Excelsior is presenting comparative financial statements.
- Excelsior does not wish to present a statement of cash flows for either year.
- During 2005, Excelsior changed its method of accounting for long-term construction contracts and properly reflected the effect of the change in the current year's financial statements and restated the prior year's statements. Roscoe is satisfied with Excelsior's justification for making the change. The change is discussed in footnote 12.
- Roscoe was unable to perform normal accounts receivable confirmation procedures, but alternative procedures were used to satisfy Roscoe as to the existence of the receivables.
- Excelsior Corporation is the defendant in a litigation, the outcome of which is highly uncertain. If the case is settled in favor of the plaintiff, Excelsior will be required to pay a substantial amount of cash, which might require the sale of certain fixed assets. The litigation and the possible effects have been properly disclosed in footnote 11.
- Excelsior issued debentures on January 31, 2004, in the amount of $10 million. The funds obtained from the issuance were used to finance the expansion of plant facilities. The debenture agreement restricts the payment of future cash dividends to earnings after December 31, 2009. Excelsior declined to disclose this essential data in the footnotes to the financial statements.

a. Identify and explain any items included in "Other Information" that need not be part of the auditor's report.

b. Explain the deficiencies in Roscoe's report as drafted.*

3-27 (Objectives 3-4, 3-5, 3-6, 3-7, 3-8) For the following independent situations, assume that you are the audit partner on the engagement:

1. During your audit of Debold.com, Inc., you conclude that there is a possibility that inventory is materially overstated. The client refuses to allow you to expand the scope of your audit sufficiently to verify whether the balance is actually misstated.

2. You are auditing Woodcolt Linen Services for the first time. Woodcolt has been in business for several years but has never had an audit before. After the audit is completed, you conclude that the current year balance sheet is stated correctly in accordance with GAAP. The client did not authorize you to do test work for any of the previous years.

3. You were engaged to audit the Cutter Steel Company's financial statements after the close of the corporation's fiscal year. Because you were not engaged until after the balance sheet date, you were not able to physically observe inventory, which is highly material. On the completion of your audit, you are satisfied that Cutter's financial statements are presented fairly, including inventory about which you were able to satisfy yourself by the use of alternative audit procedures.

4. Four weeks after the year-end date, a major customer of Prince Construction Co. declared bankruptcy. Because the customer had confirmed the balance due to Prince at the balance sheet date, management refuses to charge off the account or otherwise disclose the information. The receivable represents approximately 10% of accounts receivable and 20% of net earnings before taxes.

5. You complete the audit of Johnson Department Store, and in your opinion, the financial statements are fairly presented. On the last day of the field work, you discover that one of your supervisors assigned to the audit had a material investment in Johnson.

6. Auto Delivery Company has a fleet of several delivery trucks. In the past, Auto Delivery had followed the policy of purchasing all equipment. In the current year, they decided to lease the trucks. The method of accounting for the trucks is therefore changed to lease capitalization. This change in policy is fully disclosed in footnotes.

Required For each situation, do the following:

a. Identify which of the conditions requiring a modification of or a deviation from an unqualified standard report is applicable.

b. State the level of materiality as immaterial, material, or highly material. If you cannot decide the level of materiality, state the additional information needed to make a decision.

c. Given your answers in parts a and b, state the type of audit report that should be issued. If you have not decided on one level of materiality in part b, state the appropriate report for each alternative materiality level.

3-28 (Objectives 3-4, 3-5, 3-6, 3-7, 3-8) For the following independent situations, assume that you are the audit partner on the engagement:

1. Kieko Technology Corporation has prepared financial statements but has decided to exclude the statement of cash flows. Management explains to you that the users of their financial statements find this statement confusing and prefer not to have it included.

2. HardwareFromHome.com is an Internet-based start-up company created to sell home hardware supplies online. Although the company had a promising start, a downturn in e-commerce retailing has negatively affected the company. The company's sales and cash position have deteriorated significantly, and you have reservations about the ability of the company to continue in operation for the next year.

3. Approximately 20% of the audit of Fur Farms, Inc. was performed by a different CPA firm, selected by you. You have reviewed their working papers and believe they did an excellent job on their portion of the audit. Nevertheless, you are unwilling to take complete responsibility for their work.

4. The controller of Fair City Hotels Co. will not allow you to confirm the receivable balance from two of its major customers. The amounts of the receivables are material in relation to Fair City's financial statements. You are unable to satisfy yourself as to the receivable balances by alternative procedures.

*AICPA adapted.

5. In the last 3 months of the current year, Oil Refining Company decided to change direction and go significantly into the oil drilling business. Management recognizes that this business is exceptionally risky and could jeopardize the success of its existing refining business, but there are significant potential rewards. During the short period of operation in drilling, the company has had three dry wells and no successes. The facts are adequately disclosed in footnotes.

6. Your client, Auto Rental Company, has changed from straight-line to sum-of-the-years' digits depreciation. The effect on this year's income is immaterial, but the effect in future years is likely to be material. The facts are adequately disclosed in footnotes.

For each situation, do the following: **Required**

a. Identify which of the conditions requiring a modification of or a deviation from an unqualified standard report is applicable.

b. State the level of materiality as immaterial, material, or highly material. If you cannot decide the level of materiality, state the additional information needed to make a decision.

c. Given your answers in parts a and b, state the appropriate audit report from the following alternatives (if you have not decided on one level of materiality in part b, state the appropriate report for each alternative materiality level):
   (1) Unqualified—standard wording
   (2) Unqualified—explanatory paragraph
   (3) Unqualified—modified wording
   (4) Qualified opinion only—except for
   (5) Qualified scope and opinion
   (6) Disclaimer
   (7) Adverse

d. Based on your answer to part c, indicate which paragraphs, if any, should be modified in the standard audit report. Also indicate whether an additional paragraph is necessary and its location in the report.

3-29 (Objectives 3-4, 3-5, 3-6, 3-7, 3-8) The following are independent situations for which you will recommend an appropriate audit report:

1. Subsequent to the date of the financial statements as part of his post-balance sheet date audit procedures, a CPA learned that a recent fire caused heavy damage to one of a client's two plants; the loss will not be reimbursed by insurance. The newspapers described the event in detail. The financial statements and appended notes as prepared by the client did not disclose the loss caused by the fire.

2. A CPA is engaged in the audit of the financial statements of a large manufacturing company with branch offices in many widely separated cities. The CPA was not able to count the substantial undeposited cash receipts at the close of business on the last day of the fiscal year at all branch offices.

   As an alternative to this auditing procedure used to verify the accurate cutoff of cash receipts, the CPA observed that deposits in transit as shown on the year-end bank reconciliation appeared as credits on the bank statement on the first business day of the new year. He was satisfied as to the cutoff of cash receipts by the use of the alternative procedure.

3. On January 2, 2006, the Retail Auto Parts Company received a notice from its primary supplier that effective immediately, all wholesale prices would be increased 10%. On the basis of the notice, Retail Auto Parts revalued its December 31, 2005, inventory to reflect the higher costs. The inventory constituted a material proportion of total assets; however, the effect of the revaluation was material to current assets but not to total assets or net income. The increase in valuation is adequately disclosed in the footnotes.

4. E-Lotions.com, Inc. is an online retailer of body lotions and other bath and body supplies. The company records revenues at the time customer orders are placed on the Web site, rather than when the goods are shipped, which is usually 2 days after the order is placed. The auditor determined that the amount of orders placed but not shipped as of the balance sheet date is not material.

5. For the past 5 years a CPA has audited the financial statements of a manufacturing company. During this period, the audit scope was limited by the client as to the observation of the annual physical inventory. Because the CPA considered the inventories to be material and he was not able to satisfy himself by other auditing procedures, he was unable to express an unqualified opinion on the financial statements in each of the 5 years.

   The CPA was allowed to observe physical inventories for the current year ended December 31, 2005, because the client's banker would no longer accept the audit reports. In the interest of economy, the client requested the CPA to not extend his audit procedures to the inventory as of January 1, 2005.

6. During the course of his audit of the financial statements of a corporation for the purpose of expressing an opinion on the statements, a CPA is refused permission to inspect the minute books containing the significant decisions from the board of directors meetings. The corporation secretary instead offers to give the CPA a certified copy of all resolutions and actions involving accounting matters.

7. A CPA has completed her audit of the financial statements of a bus company for the year ended December 31, 2005. Prior to 2005, the company had been depreciating its buses over a 10-year period. During 2005, the company determined that a more realistic estimated life for its buses was 12 years and computed the 2005 depreciation on the basis of the revised estimate. The CPA has satisfied herself that the 12-year life is reasonable.

    The company has adequately disclosed the change in estimated useful lives of its buses and the effect of the change on 2005 income in a note to the financial statements.

Required   For each situation, do the following:

a. Identify which of the conditions requiring a deviation from or modification of an unqualified standard report is applicable.

b. State the level of materiality as immaterial, material, or highly material. If you cannot decide the level of materiality, state the additional information needed to make a decision.

c. Given your answers in parts a and b, state the appropriate audit report from the following alternatives (if you have not decided on one level of materiality in part b, state the appropriate report for each alternative materiality level):
    (1) Unqualified—standard wording
    (2) Unqualified—explanatory paragraph
    (3) Unqualified—modified wording
    (4) Qualified opinion only—except for
    (5) Qualified scope and opinion
    (6) Disclaimer
    (7) Adverse*

3-30 (Objective 3-4) Various types of "accounting changes" can affect the second reporting standard of the generally accepted auditing standards. This standard reads, "The report shall identify those circumstances in which such principles have not been consistently observed in the current period in relation to the preceding period."

Assume that the following list describes changes that have a material effect on a client's financial statements for the current year:

1. A change from the completed-contract method to the percentage-of-completion method of accounting for long-term construction contracts.
2. A change in the estimated useful life of previously recorded fixed assets based on newly acquired information.
3. Correction of a mathematical error in inventory pricing made in a prior period.
4. A change from prime costing to full absorption costing for inventory valuation.
5. A change from presentation of statements of individual companies to presentation of consolidated statements.
6. A change from deferring and amortizing preproduction costs to recording such costs as an expense when incurred because future benefits of the costs have become doubtful. The new accounting method was adopted in recognition of the change in estimated future benefits.
7. A change to including the employer share of Social Security (FICA) taxes as "retirement benefits" on the income statement from including it with "other taxes."
8. A change from the FIFO method of inventory pricing to the LIFO method of inventory pricing.

Required   Identify the type of change described in each item above, and state whether any modification is required in the auditor's report *as it relates to the second standard of reporting*. Organize your answer sheet as shown. For example, a change from the LIFO method of inventory pricing to the FIFO method of inventory pricing would appear as shown.

Assume that each item is material.*

Item No.	Type of Change	Should Auditor's Report Be Modified?
Example	An accounting change from one generally accepted accounting principle to another generally accepted accounting principle	Yes

*AICPA adapted.

3-31 (Objective 3-7) The following is an audit report, except for the opinion paragraph, of Tri-Nation Coin Investments.

INDEPENDENT AUDITOR'S REPORT

To the Board of Directors and Stockholders, Tri-Nation Coin Investments, Philadelphia, Pennsylvania

We have audited the accompanying consolidated balance sheet of Tri-Nation Coin Investments and subsidiaries as of July 31, 2005, and the related statements of income, stockholders' equity, and cash flows for the year then ended and the related schedules listed in the accompanying index. These financial statements are the responsibility of the Company's management. Our responsibility is to express an opinion on these financial statements based on our audits.

The company had significant deficiencies in internal control, including the lack of detailed records and certain supporting data, which were not available for our audit. Therefore, we were not able to obtain sufficient evidence in order to form an opinion on the accompanying financial statements including whether the inventory at July 31, 2005 ($670,490), was stated at lower of cost or market, or whether the deferred subscription revenue ($90,260) is an adequate estimate for the applicable liability, as discussed in Notes 5 and 12, respectively.

Required Write the auditor's opinion to accompany this portion of the audit report. Where is the opinion located in this audit report?

3-32 (Objectives 3-5, 3-6, 3-7) The following two paragraphs were taken from the California First Bank audit report, modified for changes in current reporting standards.

INDEPENDENT ACCOUNTANT'S REPORT

To the Shareholders and Board of Directors of California First Bank

We have audited the accompanying consolidated balance sheets of California First Bank (a California chartered state bank and a 76.5% owned subsidiary of The Bank of Tokyo, Ltd.) and subsidiaries as of December 31, 2005 and 2004, and the related consolidated statements of income, changes in shareholders' equity, and cash flows for each of the three years in the period ended December 31, 2005. These financial statements are the responsibility of the Company's management. Our responsibility is to express an opinion on these financial statements based on our audits.

As explained in Note 2 to the financial statements, the Bank has charged goodwill and certain other intangible assets acquired in two separate acquisitions directly to shareholders' equity. Under U.S. generally accepted accounting principles, these intangibles should have been recorded as assets.

Required
a. Which condition requiring a departure from an unqualified opinion exists for the portion of the foregoing report?
b. Should the opinion be unqualified, qualified, disclaimer, or adverse?
c. Assuming a standard-wording scope paragraph, write the opinion paragraph for this audit situation.

3-33 (Objectives 3-1, 3-2, 3-4) The following tentative auditor's report was drafted by a staff accountant and submitted to a partner in the accounting firm of Better & Best, CPAs:

AUDIT REPORT

To the Audit Committee of American Broadband, Inc.

We have examined the consolidated balance sheets of American Broadband, Inc. and subsidiaries as of December 31, 2005 and 2004, and the related consolidated statements of income, retained earnings, and cash flows for the years then ended. These financial statements are the responsibility of the Company's management. Our responsibility is to express an opinion on these financial statements based on our audits.

Our audits were made in accordance with auditing standards generally accepted in the United States of America as we considered necessary in the circumstances. Other auditors audited the financial statements of certain subsidiaries and have furnished us with reports thereon containing no exceptions. Our opinion expressed herein, insofar as it relates to the amounts included for those subsidiaries, is based solely upon the reports of the other auditors.

As fully discussed in Note 7 to the financial statements, in 2005, the company extended the use of the last-in, first-out (LIFO) method of accounting to include all inventories. In examining inventories, we engaged Dr. Irwin Same (Nobel Prize winner 2003) to test check the technical requirements and specifications of certain items of equipment manufactured by the company.

In our opinion, the financial statements referred to above present fairly the financial position of American Broadband, Inc. as of December 31, 2005, and the results of operations for the years then ended, in conformity with accounting principles generally accepted in the United States of America.

To be signed by
Better & Best, CPAs

March 1, 2006

Required Identify deficiencies in the staff accountant's tentative report that constitute departures from the generally accepted standards of reporting.*

3-34 (Objectives 3-1, 3-9) After the completion of the audit of the December 31, 2002, financial statements, IBM Corporation posted on its Web site (www.ibm.com) the following audit report as part of its online 2002 Annual Report:

TO THE STOCKHOLDERS AND BOARD OF DIRECTORS OF
INTERNATIONAL BUSINESS MACHINES CORPORATION

In our opinion, the accompanying consolidated financial statements† present fairly, in all material respects, the financial position of International Business Machines Corporation and subsidiary companies at December 31, 2002 and 2001, and the results of their operations and their cash flows for each of the three years in the period ended December 31, 2002, in conformity with accounting principles generally accepted in the United States of America. These financial statements are the responsibility of the company's management; our responsibility is to express an opinion on these financial statements based on our audits. We conducted our audits of these statements in accordance with auditing standards generally accepted in the United States of America, which require that we plan and perform the audit to obtain reasonable assurance about whether the financial statements are free of material misstatement. An audit includes examining, on a test basis, evidence supporting the amounts and disclosures in the financial statements, assessing the accounting principles used and significant estimates made by management, and evaluating the overall financial statement presentation. We believe that our audits provide a reasonable basis for our opinion.

PricewaterhouseCoopers LLP
New York, New York
January 17, 2003

†For purposes of online presentation, audited financial information is identified as "Audited."

Required a. List the seven parts of the standard unqualified report.

b. Identify the location of each of the seven parts of a standard unqualified report in the preceding audit report.

c. Read the note at the bottom of the report labeled with the "†" and describe why it is important for PricewaterhouseCoopers to include that note in its audit report available on IBM's Web site.

INTERNET PROBLEM 3-1: RESEARCH ANNUAL REPORTS

Reference the CW site. The U.S. Securities and Exchange Commission (SEC) is an independent, nonpartisan, quasi-judicial regulatory agency with responsibility for administering the federal securities laws. Publicly traded companies must electronically file a variety of forms or reports with the SEC (for example, annual financial statements). The SEC makes most of these electronic documents available on the Internet via EDGAR. EDGAR stands for Electronic Data Gathering, Analysis, and Retrieval system. The primary purpose for EDGAR is to increase the efficiency and fairness of the securities market for the benefit of investors, corporations, and the economy by accelerating the receipt, acceptance, dissemination, and analysis of time-sensitive corporate information filed with the agency. This problem requires students to use the EDGAR site (1) to research the definitions of SEC filings (for example, 10-K, 8-K) and (2) to use several companies' 10-K reports to classify types of audit opinions issued.

*AICPA adapted.

CHAPTER 4

PROFESSIONAL ETHICS

THE VALUE OF THE AUDIT DEPENDS ON AUDITOR INDEPENDENCE

Bruce Smith has watched the stock of his audit client, Ultimate Networks, soar for the past 6 months. Ultimate Networks is gaining market share, and he knows that their sales will continue to soar with the new technology they have in the pipeline. Finally, he can't resist any longer. He calls his stockbroker, John Rizzo, and places an order for 200 shares of Ultimate Networks' stock. "Are you sure this is okay?" asked Rizzo. "I thought Ultimate Networks was your client." Rizzo knows about professional responsibilities because he worked with Bruce at the CPA firm before becoming a stockbroker, and they remained friends. "Why don't you check it out and get back to me?" Rizzo added.

The next morning, Bruce is glad that he has John Rizzo for a stockbroker. The SEC just announced that they had uncovered numerous independence violations at another CPA firm. The firm had to recall several audit reports, and a few partners and audit staff were terminated for making stock investments similar to the investment that Bruce contemplated the day before. As he thinks about the requirement that he not own stock in an audit client, he concludes, "There must be other good investments out there."

LEARNING OBJECTIVES

After studying this chapter, you should be able to

4-1 Distinguish ethical from unethical behavior in personal and professional contexts.

4-2 Resolve ethical dilemmas using an ethical framework.

4-3 Explain the importance of ethical conduct for the accounting profession.

4-4 Describe the purpose and content of the AICPA *Code of Professional Conduct*.

4-5 Understand Sarbanes–Oxley Act and other SEC independence requirements and other factors that influence auditor independence.

4-6 Apply the AICPA *Code* rules and interpretations on independence and explain their importance.

4-7 Understand the requirements of other rules under the AICPA *Code*.

4-8 Describe the enforcement mechanisms for the rules of conduct.

In preceding chapters, audit reports and the demand for audit and other assurance services were discussed. The value of the audit report and the demand for audit services depend on public confidence in the independence and integrity of CPAs. This chapter discusses ethics and the independence and other ethical requirements for CPAs under the AICPA *Code of Professional Conduct*. We begin the chapter with a discussion of general ethical principles and their application to the CPA profession.

WHAT ARE ETHICS?

OBJECTIVE 4-1

Distinguish ethical from unethical behavior in personal and professional contexts.

Ethics can be defined broadly as a set of moral principles or values. Each of us has such a set of values, although we may or may not have considered them explicitly. Philosophers, religious organizations, and other groups have defined in various ways ideal sets of moral principles or values. Examples of prescribed sets of moral principles or values at the implementation level include laws and regulations, church doctrine, codes of business ethics for professional groups such as CPAs, and codes of conduct within individual organizations.

An example of a prescribed set of principles is included in Figure 4-1. These principles were developed by the Josephson Institute of Ethics, a nonprofit membership organization for the improvement of the ethical quality of society.

It is common for people to differ in their moral principles and values and the relative importance they attach to these principles. These differences reflect life experiences, successes and failures, as well as the influences of parents, teachers, and friends.

Need for Ethics

Ethical behavior is necessary for a society to function in an orderly manner. It can be argued that ethics is the glue that holds a society together. Imagine, for example, what would happen if we couldn't depend on the people we deal with to be honest. If parents, teachers, employers, siblings, coworkers, and friends all consistently lied, it would be almost impossible for effective communication to occur.

The need for ethics in society is sufficiently important that many commonly held ethical values are incorporated into laws. However, many of the ethical values found in Figure 4-1 cannot be incorporated into laws because of the judgmental nature of certain values. That does not imply, however, that the principles are less important for an orderly society.

Why People Act Unethically

Most people define *unethical behavior* as conduct that differs from what they believe is appropriate given the circumstances. Each of us decides for ourselves what we consider unethical behavior, both for ourselves and others. It is important to understand what causes people to act in a manner that we decide is unethical.

Josephson Institute

FIGURE 4-1	Illustrative Prescribed Ethical Principles

The following are the six core ethical values that the Josephson Institute associates with ethical behavior:

Trustworthiness includes honesty, integrity, reliability, and loyalty. Honesty requires a good faith intent to convey the truth. Integrity means that the person acts according to conscience, regardless of the situation. Reliability means making all reasonable efforts to fulfill commitments. Loyalty is a responsibility to promote and protect the interests of certain people and organizations.

Respect includes notions such as civility, courtesy, dignity, tolerance, and acceptance. A respectful person treats others with consideration and accepts individual differences and beliefs without prejudice.

Responsibility means being accountable for one's actions and exercising restraint. Respon-

sibility also means pursuing excellence and leading by example, including perseverance and engaging in continuous improvement.

Fairness and justice include issues of equality, impartiality, proportionality, openness, and due process. Fair treatment means that similar situations are handled consistently.

Caring means being genuinely concerned for the welfare of others and includes acting altruistically and showing benevolence.

Citizenship includes obeying laws and performing one's fair share to make society work, including such activities as voting, serving on juries, and conserving resources.

There are two primary reasons why people act unethically: The person's ethical standards are different from those of society as a whole, or the person chooses to act selfishly. In many instances, both reasons exist.

Person's Ethical Standards Differ from General Society Extreme examples of people whose behavior violates almost everyone's ethical standards are drug dealers, bank robbers, and larcenists. Most people who commit such acts feel no remorse when they are apprehended because their ethical standards differ from those of society as a whole.

There are also many far less extreme examples when others violate our ethical values. When people cheat on their tax returns, treat other people with hostility, lie on employment applications, or perform below their competence level as employees, most of us regard that as unethical behavior. If the other person has decided that this behavior is ethical and acceptable, there is a conflict of ethical values that is unlikely to be resolved.

The Person Chooses to Act Selfishly The following example illustrates the difference between ethical standards that differ from general society's and acting selfishly. Person A finds a briefcase in an airport containing important papers and $1,000. He tosses the briefcase and keeps the money. He brags to his family and friends about his good fortune. Person A's values probably differ from most of society's. Person B faces the same situation but responds differently. He keeps the money but leaves the briefcase in a conspicuous place. He tells nobody and spends the money on a new wardrobe. It is likely that Person B has violated his own ethical standards, but he decided that the money was too important to pass up. He has chosen to act selfishly.

A considerable portion of unethical behavior results from selfish behavior. Political scandals result from the desire for political power; cheating on tax returns and expense reports is motivated by financial greed; performing below one's competence and cheating on tests typically arise from laziness. In each case, the person knows that the behavior is inappropriate but chooses to do it anyway because of the personal sacrifice needed to act ethically.

ETHICAL DILEMMAS

An **ethical dilemma** is a situation a person faces in which a decision must be made about the appropriate behavior. A simple example of an ethical dilemma is finding a diamond ring, which necessitates deciding whether to attempt to find the owner or to keep it. A far more difficult ethical dilemma to resolve is the following one, taken from *Easier Said Than Done*, a publication dealing with ethical issues. It is the type of case that might be used in an ethics course.

> **OBJECTIVE 4-2**
> Resolve ethical dilemmas using an ethical framework.

- In Europe, a woman was near death from a special kind of cancer. There was one drug that the doctors thought might save her. It was a form of radium that a druggist in the same town had recently discovered. The drug was expensive to make, but the druggist was charging ten times what the drug cost him to make. He paid $200 for the radium and charged $2,000 for a small dose of the drug. The sick woman's husband, Heinz, went to everyone he knew to borrow the money, but he could only get together about $1,000, which is half of what it cost. He told the druggist that his wife was dying and asked him to sell it cheaper or let him pay later. But the druggist said: "No, I discovered the drug and I'm going to make money from it." So Heinz got desperate and broke into the man's store to steal the drug for his wife. Should the husband have done that?[1]

Auditors, accountants, and other businesspeople face many ethical dilemmas in their business careers. Dealing with a client who threatens to seek a new auditor unless an unqualified opinion is issued presents a serious ethical dilemma if an unqualified opinion is inappropriate. Deciding whether to confront a supervisor who has materially overstated

[1] Norman Sprinthall and Richard C. Sprinthall, "Value and Moral Development," *Easier Said Than Done* (Vol. 1, No. 1, Winter 1988); p. 17.

departmental revenues as a means of receiving a larger bonus is a difficult ethical dilemma. Continuing to be a part of the management of a company that harasses and mistreats employees or treats customers dishonestly is a moral dilemma, especially if the person has a family to support and the job market is tight.

Rationalizing Unethical Behavior

There are alternative ways to resolve ethical dilemmas, but care must be taken to avoid methods that are rationalizations of unethical behavior. The following are rationalization methods commonly employed that can easily result in unethical conduct:

Everybody Does It The argument that it is acceptable behavior to falsify tax returns, cheat on exams, or sell defective products is commonly based on the rationalization that everyone else is doing it and therefore it is acceptable.

If It's Legal, It's Ethical Using the argument that all legal behavior is ethical relies heavily on the perfection of laws. Under this philosophy, one would have no obligation to return a lost object unless the other person could prove that it was his or hers.

Likelihood of Discovery and Consequences This philosophy relies on evaluating the likelihood that someone else will discover the behavior. Typically, the person also assesses the severity of the penalty (consequences) if there is a discovery. An example is deciding whether to correct an unintentional overbilling to a customer when the customer has already paid the full billing. If the seller believes that the customer will detect the error and respond by not buying in the future, the seller will inform the customer now; otherwise, the seller will wait to see if the customer complains.

Resolving Ethical Dilemmas

In recent years, formal frameworks have been developed to help people resolve ethical dilemmas. The purpose of such a framework is in identifying the ethical issues and deciding on an appropriate course of action using the person's own values. The six-step approach that follows is intended to be a relatively simple approach to resolving ethical dilemmas:

1. Obtain the relevant facts.
2. Identify the ethical issues from the facts.
3. Determine who is affected by the outcome of the dilemma and how each person or group is affected.
4. Identify the alternatives available to the person who must resolve the dilemma.
5. Identify the likely consequence of each alternative.
6. Decide the appropriate action.

An illustration is used to demonstrate how a person might use this six-step approach to resolve an ethical dilemma.

Ethical Dilemma

Bryan Longview has been working 6 months as a staff assistant for Barton & Barton CPAs. Currently he is assigned to the audit of Reyon Manufacturing Company under the supervision of Charles Dickerson, an experienced audit senior. There are three auditors assigned to the audit, including Bryan, Charles, and a more experienced assistant, Martha Mills. During lunch on the first day, Charles says, "It will be necessary for us to work a few extra hours on our own time to make sure we come in on budget. This audit isn't very profitable anyway, and we don't want to hurt our firm by going over budget. We can accomplish this easily by coming in a half hour early, taking a short lunch break, and working an hour or so after normal quitting time. We just won't enter that time on our time report." Bryan recalls reading in the firm's policy manual that working hours and not charging for them on the time report is a violation of Barton & Barton's employment policy. He also knows that seniors are paid bonuses, instead of overtime, whereas staff are paid for overtime but get no bonuses. Later, when discussing the issue with Martha, she says, "Charles does this on all of his jobs. He is likely to be our firm's next audit manager. The partners think he's great because his jobs always come in under budget. He rewards us by giving us good engagement evaluations, especially under the cooperative attitude category. Several of the other audit seniors follow the same practice."

Relevant Facts There are three key facts in this situation that deal with the ethical issue and how the issue will likely be resolved:

1. The staff person has been informed that he will work hours without recording them as hours worked.
2. Firm policy prohibits this practice.
3. Another staff person has stated that this is common practice in the firm.

Ethical Issue The ethical issue in this situation is not difficult to identify.

- Is it ethical for Bryan to work hours and not record them as hours worked in this situation?

Who Is Affected and How Is Each Affected? There are typically more people affected in situations in which ethical dilemmas occur than might be expected. The following are the key persons involved in this situation:

Who	*How Affected*
Bryan	Being asked to violate firm policy.
	Hours of work will be affected.
	Pay will be affected.
	Performance evaluations may be affected.
	Attitude about firm may be affected.
Martha	Same as Bryan.
Charles	Success on engagement and in firm may be affected.
	Hours of work will be affected.
Barton & Barton	Stated firm policy is being violated.
	May result in underbilling clients in the current and future engagements.
	May affect firm's ability to realistically budget engagements and bill clients.
	May affect the firm's ability to motivate and retain employees.
Staff assigned to Reyon Manufacturing in the future	May result in unrealistic time budgets.
	May result in unfavorable time performance evaluations.
	May result in pressures to continue practice of not charging for hours worked.
Other staff in firm	Following the practice on this engagement may motivate others to follow the same practice on other engagements.

Bryan's Available Alternatives

- Refuse to work the additional hours.
- Perform in the manner requested.
- Inform Charles that he will not work the additional hours or will charge the additional hours to the engagement.
- Talk to a manager or partner about Charles's request.
- Refuse to work on the engagement.
- Quit working for the firm.

Each of these options includes a potential consequence, the worst likely one being termination by the firm.

Consequences of Each Alternative In deciding the consequences of each alternative, it is essential to evaluate both the short- and long-term effects. There is a natural tendency to emphasize the short term because those consequences will occur quickly, even when the long-term consequences may be more important. For example, consider the potential consequences if Bryan decides to work the additional hours and not report them. In the short term, he will likely get good evaluations for cooperation and perhaps a salary increase. In the longer term, what will be the effect of not reporting the hours this time when other ethical conflicts arise? Consider the following similar ethical dilemmas Bryan might face in his career as he advances:

- A supervisor asks Bryan to work 3 unreported hours daily and 15 unreported hours each weekend.
- A supervisor asks Bryan to initial certain audit procedures as having been performed when they were not.
- Bryan concludes that he cannot be promoted to manager unless he persuades assistants to work hours that they do not record.
- Management informs Bryan, who is now a partner, that either the company gets an unqualified opinion for a $40,000 audit fee or the company will change auditors.
- Management informs Bryan that the audit fee will be increased $25,000 if Bryan can find a plausible way to increase earnings by $1 million.

Appropriate Action Only Bryan can decide the appropriate option to select in the circumstances after considering his ethical values and the likely consequences of each option. At one extreme, Bryan can decide that the only relevant consequence is the potential impact on his career. Most of us believe that Bryan is an unethical person if he follows that course. At the other extreme, Bryan can decide to refuse to work for a firm that permits even one supervisor to violate firm policies. Many people consider such an extreme reaction naive.

SPECIAL NEED FOR ETHICAL CONDUCT IN PROFESSIONS

OBJECTIVE 4-3

Explain the importance of ethical conduct for the accounting profession.

Our society has attached a special meaning to the term *professional*. Professionals are expected to conduct themselves at a higher level than most other members of society. For example, when the press reports that a physician, clergyperson, U.S. senator, or CPA has been indicted for a crime, most people feel more disappointment than when the same thing happens to people who are not labeled as professionals.

The term *professional* means a responsibility for conduct that extends beyond satisfying individual responsibilities and beyond the requirements of our society's laws and regulations. A CPA, as a professional, recognizes a responsibility to the public, to the client, and to fellow practitioners, including honorable behavior, even if that means personal sacrifice.

The underlying reason for a high level of professional conduct by any profession is the need for *public confidence* in the quality of service by the profession, regardless of the individual providing it. For the CPA, it is essential that the client and external financial statement users have confidence in the quality of audits and other services. If users of services do not have confidence in physicians, judges, or CPAs, the ability of those professionals to serve clients and the public effectively is diminished.

It is not practical for most customers to evaluate the quality of the performance of professional services because of their *complexity*. A patient cannot be expected to evaluate whether an operation was properly performed. A financial statement user cannot be expected to evaluate audit performance. Most users have neither the competence nor the time for such an evaluation. Public confidence in the quality of professional services is enhanced when the profession encourages high standards of performance and conduct on the part of all practitioners.

In recent years, increased competition has made it more difficult for CPAs and many other professionals to conduct themselves in a professional manner. Increased competition sometimes has the effect of making CPA firms more concerned about keeping clients and maintaining a reasonable profit than with providing high-quality audits for users. Because of the increased competition, many CPA firms have implemented philosophies and practices that are often called improved business practices. These include such things as improved recruiting and personnel practices, better office management, and more effective advertising and other promotional methods. CPA firms are also attempting to provide more efficient audits through the use of engagement management software and more effective audit planning. These changes are desirable, as long as they do not interfere with the conduct of CPAs as professionals.

Difference Between CPA Firms and Other Professionals

CPA firms have a different relationship with users of financial statements than most other professionals have with their customers. Attorneys, for example, are typically engaged and paid by a client and have primary responsibility to be an advocate for that client. CPA firms are engaged by management for private companies and the audit committee for public companies, and are paid by the company issuing the financial statements, but the primary beneficiaries of the audit are statement users. Often, the auditor does not know or have contact with the statement users but has frequent meetings and ongoing relationships with client personnel.

It is essential that users regard CPA firms as competent and unbiased. If users believe that CPA firms do not perform a valuable service (reduce information risk), the value of CPA firms' audit and other attestation reports is reduced and the demand for audits will thereby also be reduced. Therefore, there is considerable incentive for CPA firms to conduct themselves at a high professional level.

Ways CPAs Are Encouraged to Conduct Themselves Professionally

Figure 4-2 summarizes the most important ways in which CPAs can conduct themselves appropriately and perform high-quality audits and related services. We discussed in Chapter 2 GAAS and their interpretations, the CPA examination, quality control, peer review requirements, PCAOB and SEC, division of CPA firms, and continuing education. The legal liability of CPA firms also exerts considerable influence on the way in which practitioners conduct themselves and audits, and this topic is examined in Chapter 5.

Two of the most influential factors—shown shaded in Figure 4-2—are the AICPA *Code of Professional Conduct* and the PCAOB and SEC. The *Code of Professional Conduct* is meant

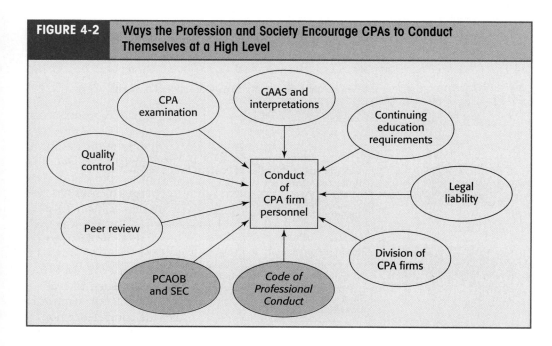

FIGURE 4-2 **Ways the Profession and Society Encourage CPAs to Conduct Themselves at a High Level**

to provide a standard of conduct for all members of the AICPA. The PCAOB is authorized to establish ethical standards for auditors of public companies, and the SEC has also played a significant role in establishing independence standards for auditors of public companies. The remainder of this chapter addresses the AICPA *Code* and related SEC requirements.

CODE OF PROFESSIONAL CONDUCT

AICPA *Code of Professional Conduct*

The AICPA *Code of Professional Conduct* provides both general standards of ideal conduct and specific enforceable rules of conduct. There are four parts to the code: principles, rules of conduct, interpretations of the rules of conduct, and ethical rulings. The parts are listed in order of increasing specificity; the principles provide ideal standards of conduct, whereas ethical rulings are highly specific. The four parts are summarized in Figure 4-3 and discussed on pages 81–82.

A few definitions, taken from the AICPA *Code of Professional Conduct*, must be understood to help interpret the rules.

- *Client.* Any person or entity, other than the member's employer, that engages a member or a member's firm to perform professional services.
- *Firm.* A form of organization permitted by law or regulation whose characteristics conform to resolutions of the Council of the American Institute of Certified Public Accountants that is engaged in the practice of public accounting. Except for the purposes of applying Rule 101, Independence, the firm includes the individual partners thereof.
- *Institute.* The American Institute of Certified Public Accountants.
- *Member.* A member, associate member, or international associate of the American Institute of Certified Public Accountants.
- *Practice of public accounting.* The practice of public accounting consists of the performance for a client, by a member or a member's firm, while holding out as CPA(s), of the professional services of accounting, tax, personal financial planning, litigation support services, and those professional services for which standards are promulgated by bodies designated by Council.

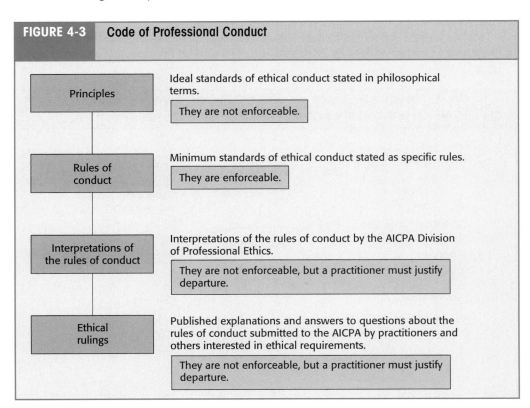

FIGURE 4-3   Code of Professional Conduct

Principles — Ideal standards of ethical conduct stated in philosophical terms.
They are not enforceable.

Rules of conduct — Minimum standards of ethical conduct stated as specific rules.
They are enforceable.

Interpretations of the rules of conduct — Interpretations of the rules of conduct by the AICPA Division of Professional Ethics.
They are not enforceable, but a practitioner must justify departure.

Ethical rulings — Published explanations and answers to questions about the rules of conduct submitted to the AICPA by practitioners and others interested in ethical requirements.
They are not enforceable, but a practitioner must justify departure.

The section of the AICPA *Code* dealing with principles of professional conduct contains a general discussion of certain characteristics required of a CPA. The principles section consists of two main parts: six ethical principles and a discussion of those principles. The ethical principles are listed as follows. Discussions throughout this chapter include ideas taken from the principles section.

Principles of
Professional Conduct

Ethical Principles

1. **Responsibilities** In carrying out their responsibilities as professionals, members should exercise sensitive professional and moral judgments in all their activities.
2. **The Public Interest** Members should accept the obligation to act in a way that will serve the public interest, honor the public trust, and demonstrate commitment to professionalism.
3. **Integrity** To maintain and broaden public confidence, members should perform all professional responsibilities with the highest sense of integrity.
4. **Objectivity and Independence** A member should maintain objectivity and be free of conflicts of interest in discharging professional responsibilities. A member in public practice should be independent in fact and appearance when providing auditing and other attestation services.
5. **Due Care** A member should observe the profession's technical and ethical standards, strive continually to improve competence and quality of services, and discharge professional responsibility to the best of the member's ability.
6. **Scope and Nature of Services** A member in public practice should observe the principles of the *Code of Professional Conduct* in determining the scope and nature of services to be provided.

The first five of these principles are equally applicable to all members of the AICPA, regardless of whether they practice in a CPA firm, work as accountants in business or government, are involved in some other aspect of business, or are in education. One exception is the last sentence of objectivity and independence. It applies only to members in public practice, and then only when they are providing attestation services such as audits. The sixth principle, scope and nature of services, applies only to members in public practice. That principle addresses whether a practitioner should provide a certain service, such as providing personnel consulting when an audit client is hiring a chief information officer (CIO) for the client's IT function. Providing such a service can create a loss of independence if the CPA firm recommends a CIO who is hired and performs incompetently.

This part of the *Code* includes the explicit rules that must be followed by every CPA in the practice of public accounting.[2] Those individuals holding the CPA certificate but not actually practicing public accounting must follow most, but not all, of the requirements. Because the section on rules of conduct is the only enforceable part of the code, it is stated in more precise language than the section on principles. Because of their enforceability, many practitioners refer to the rules as the AICPA *Code of Professional Conduct*.

Rules of Conduct

The difference between the standards of conduct set by the *principles* and those set by the *rules of conduct* is shown in Figure 4-4 (p. 82). When practitioners conduct themselves at the minimum level in Figure 4-4, that does not imply unsatisfactory conduct. The profession has presumably set the standards sufficiently high to make the minimum conduct satisfactory.

At what level do practitioners conduct themselves in practice? As in any profession, the level varies among practitioners. Most practitioners conduct themselves at a high level. Unfortunately, a few conduct themselves below the minimum level set by the profession. The activities designed to encourage CPAs to conduct themselves at a high level described in Figure 4-2 (p. 79) help minimize the extent of any substandard practice.

[2]The AICPA *Code of Professional Conduct* is applicable to every CPA who is a member of the AICPA. Each state also has rules of conduct that are required for licensing by the state. Many states follow the AICPA rules, but some have somewhat different requirements.

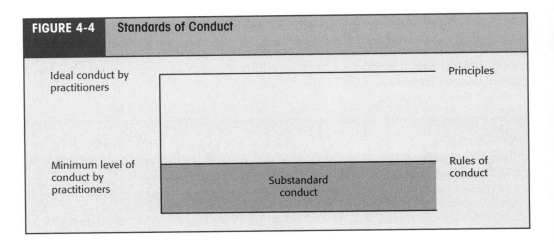

FIGURE 4-4   Standards of Conduct

Ideal conduct by
practitioners

Principles

Minimum level of
conduct by
practitioners

Substandard
conduct

Rules of
conduct

Interpretation of Rules of Conduct

The need for published interpretations of the rules of conduct arises when there are frequent questions from practitioners about a specific rule. The Division of Professional Ethics of the AICPA prepares each interpretation based on a consensus of a committee made up principally of public accounting practitioners. Before interpretations are finalized, they are sent to a large number of key people in the profession for comment. Interpretations are not officially enforceable, but a departure from the interpretations is difficult if not impossible for a practitioner to justify in a disciplinary hearing. The most important interpretations are discussed as a part of each section of the rules.

Ethical Rulings

Rulings are explanations by the executive committee of the professional ethics division of *specific factual circumstances*. A large number of ethical rulings are published in the expanded version of the AICPA *Code of Professional Conduct*. The following is an example (Rule 101—Independence; Ruling No. 16):

- *Question*—A member serves on the board of directors of a nonprofit social club. Is the independence of the member considered to be impaired with respect to the club?
- *Answer*—Independence of the member is considered to be impaired because the board of directors has the ultimate responsibility for the affairs of the club.

Applicability of the Rules of Conduct

The rules of conduct contained in the AICPA *Code of Professional Conduct* apply to all AICPA members for all services provided, whether or not the member is in the practice of public accounting, unless it is specifically stated otherwise in the code. Table 4-1 (p. 98) indicates whether the rule applies to all members or only to members in public practice.

Each of the rules applies to attestation services, and *unless stated otherwise*, each rule also applies to all services provided by CPA firms such as taxes and management services. There are only two rules that exempt certain nonattestation services:

1. Rule 101—Independence. This rule requires independence only when the AICPA has established independence requirements through its rule-setting bodies, such as the Auditing Standards Board. The AICPA requires independence only for attestation engagements. For example, a CPA firm can perform management services for a company in which the partners own stock. Of course, if the CPA firm also does an audit, that violates the independence requirements for attestation services.
2. Rule 203—Accounting Principles. This rule applies only to issuing an audit opinion or review service report on financial statements.

It is a violation of the rules if someone does something on behalf of a member that is a violation if the member does it. An example is a banker who puts in a newsletter that Johnson and Able CPA firm has the best tax department in the state and consistently gets large refunds for its tax clients. That is likely to create false or unjustified expectations and is a violation of Rule 502 on advertising. A member is also responsible for compliance with the rules by employees, partners, and shareholders.

Independence, because of its importance, is the first rule of conduct. Before we discuss the specific independence requirements, we first discuss external factors that may influence auditor independence.

OBJECTIVE 4-5

Understand Sarbanes–Oxley Act and other SEC independence requirements and other factors that influence auditor independence.

The value of auditing depends heavily on the public's perception of the independence of auditors. The reason that many diverse users are willing to rely on the CPA's reports as to the fairness of financial statements is their expectation of an unbiased viewpoint. Not only must auditors be independent in fact, but they must also be independent in appearance. **Independence in fact** exists when the auditor is actually able to maintain an unbiased attitude throughout the audit, whereas **independence in appearance** is the result of others' interpretations of this independence. If auditors are independent in fact but users believe them to be advocates for the client, most of the value of the audit function is lost.

The following sections discuss SEC independence rules, including those required by the Sarbanes–Oxley Act. Organizations and standards other than the AICPA *Code of Professional Conduct* that influence auditor independence are also described.

Sarbanes–Oxley Act and SEC Provisions Addressing Auditor Independence

The SEC adopted rules strengthening auditor independence in January 2003 consistent with the requirements of the Sarbanes–Oxley Act. The SEC rules further restrict the provision of nonaudit services to audit clients, and they also include restrictions on employment of former audit firm employees by the client and provide for audit partner rotation to enhance independence.

Nonaudit Services The Sarbanes–Oxley Act and the revised SEC rules further restrict, but do not completely eliminate, the types of nonaudit services that can be provided to publicly held audit clients. Many of these services were prohibited under the existing SEC rules on independence adopted in November 2000. The new rules clarify many of the existing prohibitions and expand the circumstances in which the services are prohibited. The following nine services are prohibited:

1. Bookkeeping and other accounting services
2. Financial information systems design and implementation
3. Appraisal or valuation services
4. Actuarial services
5. Internal audit outsourcing
6. Management or human resource functions
7. Broker or dealer or investment adviser or investment banker services
8. Legal and expert services unrelated to the audit
9. Any other service that the PCAOB determines by regulation is impermissible

It is important to note that audit firms are not prohibited from performing these services for private companies and for public companies that are not audit clients. In addition, audit firms may still provide other services that are not prohibited for public company audit clients, such as tax services. Nonaudit services that are not prohibited by the Sarbanes–Oxley Act and the SEC rules must be preapproved by the company's audit committee. In addition, an audit firm is not independent if an audit partner receives compensation for selling services to the client other than audit, review, and attest services.

Companies are required to disclose in their proxy statement or annual filings with the SEC the total amount of audit and nonaudit fees paid to the audit firm for the two most recent years. Four categories of fees must be reported: (1) audit fees, (2) audit-related fees, (3) tax fees, and (4) all other fees. Audit-related fees are for services such as comfort letters and reviews of SEC filings that can only be provided by independent accountants. Companies are also required to provide further breakdown of the "other fees" category and to provide qualitative information on the nature of the services provided.

Audit Committees An **audit committee** is a selected number of members of a company's board of directors whose responsibilities include helping auditors remain independent of management. Most audit committees are made up of three to five or sometimes as many as seven directors who are not a part of company management.

The Sarbanes–Oxley Act requires that all members of the audit committee be independent, and companies must disclose whether or not the audit committee includes at least one member who is a financial expert. SEC rules direct the national securities exchanges and national securities associations to prohibit the listing of companies that are not in compliance with the audit committee requirements of the Sarbanes–Oxley Act.

The Sarbanes–Oxley Act further requires the audit committee of a public company to be responsible for the appointment, compensation, and oversight of the work of the auditor. The audit committee must preapprove all audit and nonaudit services, and is responsible for oversight of the work of the auditor, including resolution of disagreements involving financial reporting between management and the auditor. Auditors are responsible for communicating all significant matters identified during the audit to the audit committee.

These provisions increase the independence and role of the audit committee. The requirements enhance auditor independence by effectively making the audit committee the client for public companies, rather than management.

Conflicts Arising from Employment Relationships The employment of former audit team members with an audit client raises independence concerns. Consistent with the requirements of the Sarbanes–Oxley Act, the SEC has added a one-year "cooling off" period before a member of the audit engagement team can work for the client in certain key management positions. This has important implications for an auditor working for a CPA firm who receives an employment offer from a publicly held client, for a position as a chief executive officer, controller, chief financial officer, chief accounting officer, or equivalent position. The CPA firm cannot continue to audit that client if the auditor accepts the position and has participated in any capacity in the audit for one year preceding the start of the audit. This does not affect the CPA firm's ability to continue the audit if the former auditor accepts a position such as assistant controller or accountant without primary accounting responsibilities.

Under SEC rules existing before the Sarbanes–Oxley Act and continuing, a CPA firm is not independent with respect to an audit client if a former partner, principal, shareholder, or professional employee of the firm accepts employment with a client if he or she has a continuing financial interest in the CPA firm or is in a position to influence the CPA firm's operations or financial policies.

Partner Rotation As required by the Sarbanes–Oxley Act, the SEC independence rules require that the lead and concurring audit partner rotate off the audit engagement after a period of five years. Although not addressed in the Sarbanes–Oxley Act, the SEC requires a five-year "time-out" for the lead and concurring partners after rotation before they can return to that audit client. Additional audit partners with significant involvement on the audit must rotate after seven years and are subject to a two-year time-out period.

Ownership Interests Previous rules on ownership interests viewed independence from a firmwide perspective. SEC rules adopted in 2000 on financial relationships take an engagement perspective and narrow the restrictions on ownership in clients to those persons who can influence the audit. For example, under the previous rules, all firm partners and their immediate family were prohibited from having any ownership in the client, regardless of whether the partner was involved with the engagement. The new rules restrict ownership to covered persons and their immediate family, including (a) members of the audit engagement team, (b) those in a position to influence the audit engagement in the firm chain of command, (c) partners and managers who provide more than 10 hours of nonaudit services to the client, and (d) partners in the office of the partner primarily responsible for the audit engagement. These changes were designed to make the independence rules more workable and still safeguard independence.

Independence Standards Board

The **Independence Standards Board (ISB),** a private-sector body, was formed in 1997 to provide a conceptual framework for independence issues related to audits of public companies. In addition to promulgating standards, the ISB provided consultation to auditors and their SEC clients on questions about independence standards.

The Independence Standards Board was dissolved in July 2001. With the adoption of new SEC auditor independence rules, the ISB had largely fulfilled its mission. Existing ISB pronouncements and interpretations remain enforceable unless they conflict with independence rulings issued by the SEC.

Independence Standards Board Standard No. 1, *Independence Discussions with Audit Committees,* requires auditors of companies reporting to the SEC to disclose in writing to the audit committee or board of directors all relationships between the auditing firm and the company that in the auditor's professional judgment may reasonably be thought to bear on independence. The auditing firm must also confirm in writing that in its professional judgment, the firm is independent of the company. The auditor is also required to discuss the auditing firm's independence with the audit committee.

Audit firm professional staff often accept employment with former audit clients. Although this practice is permissible, except as indicated earlier for employment in key management positions, it raises independence concerns. Prior to accepting employment, professionals might compromise their independence to gain employment with the client. After accepting employment with the client, professionals may be able to use their knowledge of the audit plan and staff to circumvent the effectiveness of the audit. ISB Standard No. 3, *Employment with Audit Clients,* recommends safeguards that CPA firms should implement when their professionals consider or accept employment with audit clients. Professionals engaged in employment negotiations with clients should be removed from the audit engagement team and their work reviewed to assess whether they exercised appropriate skepticism. After the professional accepts employment, the engagement team should consider whether changes are necessary in the audit plan to reduce the risk of circumvention.

Both management and representatives of management, such as investment bankers, often consult with other accountants on the application of accounting principles. Although consultation with other accountants is an appropriate practice, it can lead to a loss of independence in certain circumstances. For example, suppose one CPA firm replaces the existing auditors on the strength of accounting advice offered but later finds facts and circumstances that require the CPA firm to change its stance. It may be difficult for the new CPA firm to remain independent in such a situation. SAS 50 (AU 625) sets forth requirements that must be followed when a CPA firm is requested to provide a written or oral opinion on the application of accounting principles or the type of audit opinion that would be issued for a specific or hypothetical transaction of an audit client of another CPA firm. The purpose of the requirement is to minimize the likelihood of management following the practice commonly called opinion shopping and the potential threat to independence of the kind described previously. Primary among the requirements is that the consulted CPA firm should communicate with the entity's existing auditors to ascertain all the available facts relevant to forming a professional judgment on the matters the firm has been requested to report on.

Shopping for Accounting Principles

Engagement and Payment of Audit Fees by Management

Can an auditor be truly independent in fact and appearance if the payment of fees is dependent upon the management of the audited entity? There is probably no satisfactory answer to this question, but it does demonstrate the difficulty of obtaining an atmosphere of complete independence of auditors. The alternative to engagement of the CPA by the audit committee and payment of audit fees by management is probably the use of either government or quasi-government auditors. All things considered, it is questionable whether the audit function would be performed better or more cheaply by the public sector.

INDEPENDENCE RULE OF CONDUCT AND INTERPRETATIONS

OBJECTIVE 4-6

Apply the AICPA *Code* rules and interpretations on independence and explain their importance.

The previous section discussed the importance of auditor independence. It is not surprising that independence is the first subject addressed in the rules of conduct.

> **Rule 101—Independence** A member in public practice shall be independent in the performance of professional services as required by standards promulgated by bodies designated by Council.

CPA firms are required to be independent for certain services that they provide, but not for others. The last phrase in Rule 101, "as required by standards promulgated by bodies designated by Council" is a convenient way for the AICPA to include or exclude independence requirements for different types of services. For example, the Auditing Standards Board requires that auditors of historical financial statements be independent. Rule 101 therefore applies to audits. Independence is also required for other types of attestations, such as review services and audits of prospective financial statements. However, a CPA firm can do tax returns and provide management services without being independent. Rule 101 does not apply to those types of services.

There are more interpretations for independence than for any of the other rules of conduct. Many of the interpretations have been revised to have an "engagement-team" focus and to be consistent with the SEC rules on independence. Some of the more significant issues and interpretations involving independence are discussed in the following sections.

Financial Interests

Interpretations of Rule 101 prohibit covered members from owning *any stock or other direct investment* in audit clients because it is potentially damaging to actual audit independence, and it certainly is likely to affect the users' perceptions of the auditors' independence. *Indirect investments,* such as ownership of stock in a client's company by an auditor's grandparent, are also prohibited, but *only if the amount is material* to the auditor. The ownership of stock rule is more complex than it appears at first glance. A more detailed examination of that requirement is included to aid in understanding and to show the complexity of one of the rules. There are three important distinctions in the rules as they relate to independence and stock ownership.

Covered Members Rule 101 applies to covered members in a position to influence an attest engagement. Covered members include the following:

1. Individuals on the attest engagement team
2. An individual in a position to influence the attest engagement, such as individuals who supervise or evaluate the engagement partner
3. A partner or manager who provides nonattest services to the client
4. A partner in the office of the partner responsible for the attest engagement
5. The firm and its employee benefit plans
6. An entity that can be controlled by any of the covered members listed above or by two or more of the covered individuals or entities operating together

For example, a staff member in a national CPA firm could own stock in a client corporation and not violate Rule 101 if the staff member is not involved in the engagement. However, if the staff member is assigned to the engagement or becomes a partner in the office of the partner responsible for the attest engagement, he or she would have to dispose of the stock or the CPA firm would no longer be independent with respect to that client.

These independence rules also generally apply to the covered member's immediate family. The interpretations of Rule 101 define immediate family as a spouse, spousal equivalent, or dependent.

Some CPA firms do not permit any ownership by staff of a client's stock regardless of which office serves the client. These firms have decided to have higher requirements than the minimums set by the rules of conduct.

Direct Versus Indirect Financial Interest The ownership of stock or other equity shares by members or their immediate family is called a **direct financial interest.** For example, if either a partner in the office in which an audit is conducted or the partner's spouse has a financial interest in a company, the CPA firm is prohibited by Rule 101 from expressing an opinion on the financial statements of that company.

An **indirect financial interest** exists when there is a close, but not a direct, ownership relationship between the auditor and the client. An example of an indirect ownership interest is the covered member's ownership of a mutual fund that has an investment in a client.

Material or Immaterial *Materiality* affects whether ownership is a violation of Rule 101 only for *indirect* ownership. Materiality must be considered in relation to the member person's wealth and income. For example, if a covered member has a significant amount of his or her personal wealth invested in a mutual fund and that fund has a large ownership position in a client company, a violation of the *Code* is likely to exist.

Several interpretations of Rule 101 deal with specific aspects of financial relationships between CPA firm personnel and clients. These are summarized in this section.

Related Financial Interest Issues

Former Practitioners In most situations, the interpretations permit former partners or shareholders who left the firm due to such things as retirement or the sale of their ownership interest to have relationships with clients of the firm of the type that are normally a violation of Rule 101, without affecting a firm's independence. A violation by the firm would occur if the former partner was held out as an associate of the firm or took part in activities that are likely to cause other parties to believe the person was still active in the firm.

Normal Lending Procedures Generally, loans between a CPA firm or its members and an audit client are prohibited because it is a financial relationship. There are several exceptions to the rule, however, including automobile loans, loans fully collateralized by cash deposits at the same financial institution, and unpaid credit card balances not exceeding $5,000 in total. It is also acceptable to accept a financial institution as a client, even if members of the CPA firm have existing home mortgages, other fully collateralized secured loans, and immaterial loans with the institution. No new loans are permitted, however. Both the restrictions and exceptions are reasonable ones, considering the trade-off between independence and the need to permit CPAs to function as businesspeople and individuals.

Financial Interests and Employment of Immediate and Close Family Members The financial interests of immediate family members, defined as a spouse, spousal equivalent, or dependent, are ordinarily treated as if they were the financial interest of the covered member. For example, if the spouse of a professional on the audit engagement team owns any stock in the client, Rule 101 is violated. Independence is also impaired if an immediate family member holds a key position such as financial officer or chief executive officer with the client that allows them to influence accounting functions, preparation of financial statements, or the contents of the financial statements.

Ownership interests of close family members, defined as a parent, sibling, or nondependent child, do not normally impair independence unless the ownership interest is material to the close relative. Imagine the potential difficulty in maintaining independence and objectivity if the firm is asked to audit a client where the parent of the audit partner is chief executive officer and has a significant ownership interest in the client. For individuals on the engagement team, independence is impaired if a close relative has a key position with the client or has a financial interest that is material to the close relative or enables the relative to exercise significant influence over the client. Similar rules apply for other individuals in a position to influence the attest engagement or partners in the attest-engagement office, except the ownership interest must be material to the close relative and allow the close relative to exercise significant influence over the audit client. Independence is not considered impaired if the covered individual is not aware of the close relative's ownership interest.

Joint Investor or Investee Relationship with Client Assume, for example, that a CPA owns stock in a nonaudit client, Jackson Company. Frank Company, which is an audit client, also owns stock in Jackson Company. This may be a violation of Rule 101. Interpretation 101-8 addresses situations where the client is either an investor or investee for a nonclient in which the CPA has an ownership interest.

1. *Client investor.* If the client's investment in the nonclient is material, any direct or material indirect investment by the CPA in the nonclient investee impairs independence. If the client's investment is not material, independence is impaired only if the CPA's investment is material.
2. *Client investee.* If investment in a client is material to a nonclient investor, any direct or material indirect investment by the CPA in the nonclient impairs independence. If the nonclient's investment in the client is not material, independence is not impaired unless the CPA's investment in the nonclient allows the CPA to exercise significant influence over the nonclient.

Director, Officer, Management, or Employee of a Company If a CPA is a member of the board of directors or an officer of a client company, his or her ability to make independent evaluations of the fair presentation of financial statements is affected. Even if holding one of these positions did not actually affect the auditor's independence, the frequent involvement with management and the decisions it makes is likely to affect how statement users perceive the CPA's independence. To eliminate this possibility, interpretations prohibit covered members, partners, and professional staff in the office of the partner responsible for the attest engagement from being a director or officer of an audit client company. Similarly, the auditor cannot be an underwriter, voting trustee, promoter, or trustee of a client's pension fund, or act in any other capacity of management, or be an employee of the company.

Interpretations permit CPAs to do audits and be *honorary* directors or trustees for not-for-profit organizations, such as charitable and religious organizations, as long as the position is purely honorary. To illustrate, it is common for a partner of the CPA firm doing the audit of a city's United Fund drive to also be an honorary director, along with many other civic leaders. The CPA cannot vote or participate in any management functions.

Litigation Between CPA Firm and Client

When there is a lawsuit or intent to start a lawsuit between a CPA firm and its client, the ability of the CPA firm and client to remain objective is questionable. The interpretations regard such litigation as a violation of Rule 101 for the current audit. For example, if management sues a CPA firm claiming a deficiency in the previous audit, the CPA firm is not considered independent for the current year's audit. Similarly, if the CPA firm sues management for fraudulent financial reporting or deceit, independence is lost. The CPA firm and client company or management may be defendants in a suit brought by a third party, such as in a securities class action. This litigation in itself does not affect independence. However, independence may be affected if cross-claims between the auditor and client are filed that have a significant risk of a material loss to the CPA firm or client.

Litigation by the client related to tax or other nonaudit services, or litigation against both the client and the CPA firm by another party, does not usually impair independence. The key consideration in all such suits is the likely effect on the ability of client, management, and CPA firm personnel to remain objective and comment freely.

If a CPA records transactions in the journals for the client, posts monthly totals to the general ledger, makes adjusting entries, and subsequently does an audit, there is some question as to whether the CPA can be independent in the audit role. The interpretations *permit a CPA firm to do both bookkeeping and auditing for the same client.* The AICPA's conclusion is presumably based on a comparison of the effect on independence of having both bookkeeping and auditing services performed by the same CPA firm with the additional cost of having a different CPA firm do the audit. There are three important requirements that the auditor must satisfy before it is acceptable to do bookkeeping and auditing for the client:

Bookkeeping and Other Services

1. The client must accept full responsibility for the financial statements. The client must be sufficiently knowledgeable about the enterprise's activities and financial condition and the applicable accounting principles so that the client can reasonably accept such responsibility, including the fairness of valuation and presentation and the adequacy of disclosure. When necessary, the CPA must discuss accounting matters with the client to be sure that the client has the required degree of understanding.

2. The CPA must not assume the role of employee or of management conducting the operations of an enterprise. For example, the CPA cannot consummate transactions, have custody of assets, or exercise authority on behalf of the client. The client must prepare the source documents on all transactions in sufficient detail to identify clearly the nature and amount of such transactions and maintain accounting control over data processed by the CPA, such as control totals and document counts.

3. The CPA, in making an audit of financial statements prepared from books and records that the CPA has maintained completely or in part, must conform to GAAS. The fact that the CPA has processed or maintained certain records does not eliminate the need to make sufficient audit tests.

The first two requirements are often difficult to satisfy for a smaller company with an owner who may have little knowledge of or interest in accounting or processing transactions. It is important to emphasize that although providing bookkeeping services is allowable under the AICPA *Code*, the SEC does not allow audit firms to provide bookkeeping services to public company audit clients. Recent revisions of the AICPA independence rules require members to adhere to more restrictive independence rules of other regulatory bodies, such as the SEC. As a result, an audit firm that provides bookkeeping services to a public company audit client would violate SEC rules and the AICPA rules on independence. SEC rules do not apply to private companies, and audit firms are not restricted from providing bookkeeping services to private company audit clients.

Consulting and Other Nonaudit Services CPA firms offer many other services to attest clients that may potentially impair independence. Such activities are permissible as long as the member does not perform management functions or make management decisions. For example, a CPA firm may assist in the installation of a client's information system as long as the client makes necessary management decisions about the system. Many CPA firms have also begun providing internal auditing and other extended auditing services to their clients.

The CPA firm must assess the client's willingness and ability to perform all management functions related to the engagement and must document the understanding with the client. The understanding should include a description of the services, the engagement objectives, any limitations on the engagement, the member's responsibilities, and the client's agreement to accept its responsibilities.

As indicated in the discussion of bookkeeping services, the more restrictive SEC independence rules concerning provision of nonaudit services apply to AICPA members when providing services to public company audit clients. As a result, providing nonaudit services that are prohibited by the SEC to a public company audit client would be a violation of both AICPA and SEC rules.

Under Rule 101 and its rulings and interpretations, independence is considered impaired if billed or unbilled fees remain unpaid for professional services provided more than 1 year before the date of the report. Such unpaid fees are deemed to be a loan from the auditor to the client and are therefore a violation of Rule 101. Unpaid fees from a client in bankruptcy do not violate Rule 101.

ETHICS IN PLAIN ENGLISH

Many factors have contributed to increased complexity in the rules of conduct and interpretations, including the engagement-team approach to independence, new practice structures for CPA firms, and new services. In addition, SEC and ISB independence rules may differ from the AICPA rules. In response, the AICPA has published the AICPA *Plain English Guide to Independence*, available online on the AICPA Web site. The guide provides up-to-date answers to ethics questions in straightforward language and also highlights areas where SEC or ISB rules differ from those issued by the AICPA.

Source: www.aicpa.org/members/div/ethics/plaineng.htm

OTHER RULES OF CONDUCT

Although independence is critical to public confidence in CPAs, it is also important that auditors adhere to the other rules of conduct listed in Table 4-1 (p. 98). We begin by discussing the rules for integrity and objectivity.

Integrity and Objectivity

Integrity means impartiality in performing all services. Rule 102 on integrity and objectivity is presented below:

OBJECTIVE 4-7

Understand the requirements of other rules under the AICPA *Code*.

Rule 102—Integrity and Objectivity In the performance of any professional service, a member shall maintain objectivity and integrity, shall be free of conflicts of interest, and shall not knowingly misrepresent facts or subordinate his or her judgment to others.

To illustrate the meaning of integrity and objectivity, assume that an auditor believes that accounts receivable may not be collectible but accepts management's opinion without an independent evaluation of collectibility. The auditor has subordinated his or her judgment and thereby lacks objectivity. Now assume that a CPA is preparing the tax return for a client and, as a client advocate, encourages the client to take a deduction on the returns that the CPA believes is valid, but for which there is some but not complete support. This is not a violation of either objectivity or integrity, because it is acceptable for the CPA to be a client advocate in tax and management services. If the CPA encourages the client to take a deduction for which there is no support but has little chance of discovery by the IRS, a violation has occurred. That is a misrepresentation of the facts; therefore, the integrity of the CPA has been impaired.

Audit staff members should not subordinate their judgment to supervisors on the audit engagement. Staff auditors are responsible for their own judgments documented in the audit files and should not change those conclusions at the request of supervisors on the engagement unless the staff auditor agrees with the supervisor's conclusion. In rare instances where staff members do not agree with a conclusion involving a significant matter, they should document the reasons for the disagreement as a way of disassociating themselves from the resolution of the matter.

Freedom from conflicts of interest means the absence of relationships that might interfere with objectivity or integrity. For example, it would be inappropriate for an auditor who is also an attorney to represent a client in legal matters. The attorney is an advocate for the client, whereas the auditor must be impartial.

An interpretation of Rule 102 states that apparent conflicts of interest may not be a violation of the rules of conduct if the information is disclosed to the member's client or employer. For example, if a partner of a CPA firm recommends that a client have the security of its Internet Web site evaluated by a technology consulting firm that is owned by the partner's spouse, a conflict of interest may appear to exist. No violation of Rule 102 occurs if the partner informs the client's management of the relationship and management proceeded with the evaluation with that knowledge. The interpretation makes it clear that the independence requirements under Rule 101 cannot be eliminated by these disclosures.

The next three standards of the *Code* relate to the auditor's adherence with the requirements of technical standards. The following are the requirements of the technical standards:

Technical Standards

Rule 201—General Standards A member shall comply with the following standards and with any interpretations thereof by bodies designated by Council.

A. *Professional competence.* Undertake only those professional services that the member or the member's firm can reasonably expect to be completed with professional competence.
B. *Due professional care.* Exercise due professional care in the performance of professional services.
C. *Planning and supervision.* Adequately plan and supervise the performance of professional services.
D. *Sufficient relevant data.* Obtain sufficient, relevant data to afford a reasonable basis for conclusions or recommendations in relation to any professional services performed.

Rule 202—Compliance with Standards A member who performs auditing, review, compilation, management consulting, tax, or other professional services shall comply with standards promulgated by bodies designated by Council.

Rule 203—Accounting Principles A member shall not (1) express an opinion or state affirmatively that the financial statements or other financial data of any entity are presented in conformity with generally accepted accounting principles or (2) state that he or she is not aware of any material modifications that should be made to such statements or data in order for them to be in conformity with generally accepted accounting principles, if such statements or data contain any departure from an accounting principle promulgated by bodies designated by Council to establish such principles that has a material effect on the statements or data taken as a whole. If, however, the statements or data contain such a departure and the member can demonstrate that due to unusual circumstances the financial statements or data would otherwise have been misleading, the member can comply with the rule by describing the departure, its approximate effects, if practicable, and the reasons why compliance with the principle would result in a misleading statement.

The primary purpose of the requirements of Rules 201 to 203 is to provide support for the ASB, PCAOB, FASB, and other technical standard-setting bodies. For example, notice that requirements A and B of Rule 201 are the same in substance as general auditing standards 1 and 3, and C and D of Rule 201 have the same intent as field work standards 1 and 3. The only difference is that Rule 201 is stated in terms that apply to all types of services, whereas auditing standards apply only to audits. Rule 202 makes it clear that when a practitioner violates an auditing standard, the rules of conduct are also automatically violated.

It is essential that practitioners not disclose confidential information obtained in any type of engagement without the consent of the client. The specific requirements of Rule 301 related to **confidential client information** are shown in the box at the top of the following page.

Confidentiality

Need for Confidentiality During an audit or other type of engagement, practitioners obtain a considerable amount of information of a confidential nature, including officers' salaries, product pricing and advertising plans, and product cost data. If auditors divulge this information to outsiders or to client employees who have been denied access to the information, their relationship with management can be seriously strained, and in extreme cases, the client can be harmed. The confidentiality requirement applies to all services provided by CPA firms, including tax and management services.

Rule 301—Confidential Client Information A member in public practice shall not disclose any confidential client information without the specific consent of the client.

This rule shall not be construed (1) to relieve a member of his or her professional obligations under Rules 202 and 203, (2) to affect in any way the member's obligation to comply with a validly issued and enforceable subpoena or summons, or to prohibit a member's compliance with applicable laws and government regulations, (3) to prohibit review of a member's professional practice under AICPA or state CPA society or Board of Accountancy authorization, or (4) to preclude a member from initiating a complaint with, or responding to any inquiry made by, the professional ethics division or trial board of the Institute or a duly constituted investigative or disciplinary body of a state CPA society or Board of Accountancy.

Members of any of the bodies identified in (4) above and members involved with professional practice reviews identified in (3) above shall not use to their own advantage or disclose any member's confidential client information that comes to their attention in carrying out those activities. This prohibition shall not restrict members' exchange of information in connection with the investigative or disciplinary proceedings described in (4) above or the professional practice reviews described in (3) above.

Ordinarily, the CPA's audit files can be made available to someone else only with the express permission of the client. This is the case even if a CPA sells the practice to another CPA firm or is willing to permit a successor auditor to examine the audit documentation prepared for a former client. Permission is not required from the client, however, if the audit documentation is subpoenaed by a court or used as part of an authorized peer review program with other CPA firms. If the audit documentation is subpoenaed, the client should be informed immediately. The client and its legal counsel may wish to challenge the subpoena.

Exceptions to Confidentiality As stated in the second paragraph of Rule 301, there are four exceptions to the confidentiality requirements. All four exceptions concern responsibilities that are more important than maintaining confidential relations with the client.

1. *Obligations related to technical standards.* Suppose that 3 months after an unqualified audit report was issued, the auditor discovers that the financial statements were materially misstated. When the chief executive officer is confronted, he responds that even though he agrees that the financial statements are misstated, confidentiality prevents the CPA from informing anyone. This example is similar to an actual legal case, *Yale Express*. Disagreements during the *Yale Express* case resulted in AU 561, which deals with auditors' responsibilities when subsequent facts show that an inappropriate audit report has been issued. (AU 561 is discussed in Chapter 24.) Exception (1) in Rule 301 makes it clear that the auditor's responsibility to discharge professional standards is greater than that for confidentiality. In such a case, a revised, correct audit report must be issued. Note, however, that the conflict seldom occurs.

2. *Subpoena or summons.* Legally, information is called **privileged information** if legal proceedings cannot require a person to provide the information, even if there is a subpoena. Information communicated by a client to an attorney or by a patient to a physician is privileged. *Information obtained by a CPA from a client generally is not privileged.* Exception (2) of Rule 301 is therefore needed to put CPA firms in compliance with the law.

   There have been considerable discussions and disagreements among CPAs, attorneys, and legislators about the need for privileged communication between CPAs and clients. Most CPAs and businesspeople dealing with CPAs support legislation protecting privileged communications. In fact, a number of states have statutes that provide some level of privilege to accountant–client communication. Of course, these statutes would apply only to litigation in state courts and would have no bearing on federal court suits.

3. *Peer review.* When a CPA or CPA firm conducts a peer review of the quality controls of another CPA firm, it is normal practice to examine several sets of audit

files. If the peer review is authorized by the AICPA, state CPA society, or state Board of Accountancy, client permission to examine the audit documentation is not needed. Requiring permission from each client may restrict access of the peer reviewers and would be a time burden on all concerned. Naturally, the peer reviewers must keep the information obtained confidential and cannot use the information for other purposes.

4. *Response to ethics division.* If a practitioner is charged with inadequate technical performance by the AICPA Ethics Division trial board under any of Rules 201 to 203, the board members are likely to want to examine audit documentation. Exception (4) in Rule 301 prevents a CPA firm from denying the inquirers access to audit documentation by saying that it is confidential information. Similarly, a CPA firm that observes substandard audit documentation of another CPA firm cannot use confidentiality as the reason for not initiating a complaint of substandard performance against the firm.

To help CPAs maintain objectivity in conducting audits or other attestation services, basing fees on the outcome of the engagement is prohibited. The requirements of Rule 302 related to contingent fees are shown below:

Rule 302—Contingent Fees A member in public practice shall not

(1) Perform for a contingent fee any professional services for, or receive such a fee from, a client for whom the member or member's firm performs:
   (a) an audit or review of a financial statement; or
   (b) a compilation of a financial statement when the member expects, or reasonably might expect, that a third party will use the financial statement and the member's compilation report does not disclose a lack of independence; or
   (c) an examination of prospective financial information;

or

(2) Prepare an original or amended tax return or claim for a tax refund for a contingent fee for any client.

   The prohibition in (1) above applies during the period in which the member or the member's firm is engaged to perform any of the services listed above and the period covered by any historical financial statements involved in any such listed services.

   Except as stated in the next sentence, a contingent fee is a fee established for the performance of any service pursuant to an arrangement in which no fee will be charged unless a specified finding or result is attained, or in which the amount of the fee is otherwise dependent upon the finding or result of such service. Solely for purposes of this rule, fees are not regarded as being contingent if fixed by courts or other public authorities, or, in tax matters, if determined based on the results of judicial proceedings or the findings of governmental agencies.

   A member's fees may vary depending, for example, on the complexity of services rendered.

To illustrate the need for a rule on contingent fees, suppose a CPA firm was permitted to charge a fee of $50,000 if an unqualified opinion was provided but only $25,000 if the opinion was qualified. Such an agreement may tempt a practitioner to issue the wrong opinion and is a violation of Rule 302. It is also a violation of Rule 302 for members to prepare an original or amended tax return or a claim for tax refunds for a contingent fee.

An agreement between the AICPA and the Federal Trade Commission eliminated the restrictions on contingent fees *for nonattestation services, unless the CPA firm is also performing attestation services* for the same client. The agreement also permits the AICPA to prohibit tax return preparation on a contingent fee basis. Under the agreement, for example, it is *not* a violation for a CPA to charge fees as an expert witness determined by the amount awarded to the plaintiff or to base consulting fees on a percentage of a bond issue *if the CPA firm does not also do an audit or other attestation for the same client.*

The reason for the agreement was a contention by the Federal Trade Commission that contingent fee restrictions reduce competition and therefore are not in the public

CHAPTER 4 / PROFESSIONAL ETHICS   **93**

interest. After considerable negotiation, the AICPA agreed to restrict the contingent fee prohibition only to attestation services clients and for tax return preparation. The Federal Trade Commission agreed to allow the AICPA to prohibit contingent fees for attestation services and tax return preparation because of the importance of independence and objectivity.

Discreditable Acts

Because of the special need for CPAs to conduct themselves in a professional manner, the *Code* has a specific rule prohibiting acts discreditable to the profession.

> **Rule 501—Acts Discreditable** A member shall not commit an act discreditable to the profession.

A discreditable act is not well defined in the rules or interpretations. The following are some of the requirements contained in the interpretations:

1. *Retention of client records.* It is an act discreditable to retain a client's records after a demand is made for them. Assume, for example, that a client did not pay an audit fee and the partners of the CPA firm therefore refused to return client-owned records. The partners have violated Rule 501.
2. *Discrimination and harassment in employment practices.* A member is presumed to have committed an act discreditable whenever the member is found to have violated any federal, state, or local antidiscrimination laws.
3. *Standards on government audits and requirements of government bodies and agencies.* Audits of government units and federal grant recipients must be done in compliance with government auditing standards, in addition to GAAS. Both the government auditing standards and GAAS must be followed unless the audit report discloses the reasons for not following such requirements. When a member accepts an engagement that involves reporting to a regulatory agency such as the SEC, the member must follow the additional requirements of the regulatory agency, in addition to GAAS. If the additional requirements are not followed, the reasons should be noted in the report.
4. *Negligence in the preparation of financial statements or records.* A member is considered to have committed an act discreditable if by his or her negligence others are made or permitted or directed to make materially false and misleading entries in the financial statements and records of an entity, the member fails to correct financial statements that are materially false and misleading, or the member signs or permits or directs another to sign a document containing materially false and misleading information.
5. *Failure to follow requirements of governmental bodies, commissions, or other regulatory agencies.* If a member prepares financial statements or related information for reporting to governmental bodies, commissions, or regulatory agencies, the member should follow the requirements of such organizations in addition to GAAP. A material departure from such requirements is an act discreditable to the profession, unless the member discloses in the financial statements or the report, as applicable, that such requirements were not followed and the reasons therefor.
6. *Solicitation or disclosure of CPA examination questions and answers.* The Uniform CPA Examination became nondisclosed effective with the May 1996 examination. It is an act discreditable to solicit or disclose questions from the May 1996 or later examinations without the permission of the AICPA.
7. *Failure to file tax return or pay tax liability.* A member who fails to comply with federal, state, or local laws regarding the timely filing of personal tax returns or tax returns of the member's firm or the timely remittance of all payroll and other taxes collected on behalf of others may be considered to have committed an act discreditable.

Do excessive drinking, rowdy behavior, or other acts that many people consider unprofessional constitute a discreditable act? Probably not. Determining what constitutes professional behavior continues to be the responsibility of each professional.

For guidance as to what constitutes a discreditable act, the AICPA bylaws provide clearer guidelines than the AICPA *Code of Professional Conduct.* The bylaws state that membership in the AICPA can be terminated without a hearing for judgment of conviction for any of the following four crimes: (1) a crime punishable by imprisonment for more than 1 year; (2) the willful failure to file any income tax return that the CPA, as an individual taxpayer, is required by law to file; (3) the filing of a false or fraudulent income tax return on the CPA's or client's behalf; or (4) the willful aiding in the preparation and presentation of a false and fraudulent income tax return of a client. Observe that three of these deal with income tax matters of the member or a client.

To encourage CPAs to conduct themselves professionally, the rules also prohibit advertising or solicitation that is false, misleading, or deceptive.

Advertising and Solicitation

> **Rule 502—Advertising and Other Forms of Solicitation** A member in public practice shall not seek to obtain clients by advertising or other forms of solicitation in a manner that is false, misleading, or deceptive. Solicitation by the use of coercion, overreaching, or harassing conduct is prohibited.

Solicitation consists of the various means that CPA firms use to engage new clients other than accepting new clients who approach the firm. Examples include taking prospective clients to lunch to explain the CPA's services, offering seminars on current tax law changes to potential clients, and advertising in the Yellow Pages of a phone book. The last example is advertising, which is only one form of solicitation. Advertising is the use of various media, such as magazines and radio, to communicate favorable information about the CPA firm's services.

Until 1978, advertising in any form was prohibited. As a result of the agreement with the Federal Trade Commission discussed earlier, solicitation or advertising that is not *false or deceptive* is acceptable. This change in the rules of conduct is similar to that for other professions. Advertising is now acceptable within most professions.

The effect of these changes has been an increased emphasis on marketing and more competitive pricing of services. Many CPA firms have developed sophisticated advertising for national journals read by businesspeople and for local newspapers. It is common for CPA firms to identify potential clients being serviced by other CPA firms and make formal and informal presentations to convince management to change CPA firms. Price bidding for audits and other services is now common and often highly competitive. As a result of these changes, some companies now change auditors more often than previously to reduce audit cost. Most practitioners believe audits are less profitable than previously.

Has the quality of audits become endangered by these changes? Although there have been several recent high-profile cases involving apparent audit failures, the existing legal exposure of CPAs, peer review requirements, and the potential for interference by the SEC and government has kept audit quality high. In the opinion of the authors, the changes in the rules have caused greater competition in the profession, but not so much that high-quality, efficiently run CPA firms have been significantly harmed. However, for this to continue to be so, CPA firms need to be on guard so that increasing competitive pressures do not cause auditors to reduce quality below an acceptable level.

Commissions and Referral Fees

Commissions are compensation paid for recommending or referring a third party's product or service to a client or recommending or referring a client's product or service to a third party. Restrictions on commissions are similar to the rules on contingent fees. CPAs are generally prohibited from receiving commissions for a client who is receiving attestation services from the CPA firm. Commissions are permissible for other clients, but they must be disclosed. Referral fees related to recommending or referring the services of a

CPA are not considered commissions and are not restricted. However, any referral fees for CPA services must also be disclosed.

Rule 503—Commissions and Referral Fees

A. *Prohibited commissions.* A member in public practice shall not for a commission recommend or refer to a client any product or service, or for a commission recommend or refer any product or service to be supplied by a client, or receive a commission, when the member or the member's firm also performs for that client:
  (a) an audit or review of a financial statement; or
  (b) a compilation of a financial statement when the member expects, or reasonably might expect, that a third party will use the financial statement and the member's compilation report does not disclose a lack of independence; or
  (c) an examination of prospective financial information.
This prohibition applies during the period in which the member is engaged to perform any of the services listed above and the period covered by any historical financial statements involved in such listed services.

B. *Disclosure of permitted commissions.* A member in public practice who is not prohibited by this rule from performing services for or receiving a commission and who is paid or expects to be paid a commission shall disclose that fact to any person or entity to whom the member recommends or refers a product or service to which the commission relates.

C. *Referral fees.* Any member who accepts a referral fee for recommending or referring any service of a CPA to any person or entity or who pays a referral fee to obtain a client shall disclose such acceptance or payment to the client.

The rule for commissions and referral fees means that a CPA firm does not violate AICPA rules of conduct if it sells such things as real estate, securities, and entire firms on a commission basis *if the transaction does not involve a client who is receiving attestation services from the same CPA firm.* This rule enables CPA firms to profit by providing many services to nonattestation services clients that were previously prohibited.

The reason for the AICPA continuing to prohibit commissions for any attestation service client is the need to ensure that the CPA firm is independent. This requirement and the reasons for it are the same as those discussed under contingent fees.

The rationale for the AICPA's less restrictive enforcement of Rule 503 than before is the same as that discussed for contingent fees. The Federal Trade Commission contends that restrictions reduce competition and therefore are not in the public interest.

It is essential to understand that the Board of Accountancy in the state in which the firm is licensed may have more restrictive rules than the AICPA's. The CPA firm must follow the more restrictive requirements if different rules exist.

Form of Organization and Name

The organizational structure of CPA firms was first discussed in Chapter 2. The rules of conduct restrict the permissible forms of organization and prohibit a member from practicing under a firm name that is misleading.

Rule 505 permits practitioners to organize in any of six forms, as long as they are permitted by state law: proprietorship, general partnership, general corporation, professional corporation (PC), limited liability company (LLC), or limited liability partnership (LLP). Each of these forms of organization was discussed in Chapter 2 (pp. 28–29).

Rule 505—Form of Organization and Name A member may practice public accounting only in a form of organization permitted by state law or regulation whose characteristics conform to resolutions of Council.

A member shall not practice public accounting under a firm name that is misleading. Names of one or more past owners may be included in the firm name of a successor organization.

A firm may not designate itself as "Members of the American Institute of Certified Public Accountants" unless all of its CPA owners are members of the Institute.

Prior to April 1994, all owners of a CPA firm had to be CPAs who were qualified to practice. Ownership of CPA firms by non-CPAs is now allowed under the following conditions:

- CPAs must own a majority of the firm's financial interests and voting rights.
- A CPA must have ultimate responsibility for all financial statement attest, compilation, and other services provided by the firm that are governed by Statements on Auditing Standards or Statements on Standards for Accounting and Review Services.
- Owners must at all times own their equity in their own right.
- The following rules apply to all non-CPA owners:

   1. They must actively provide services to the firm's clients as their principal occupation.
   2. They cannot hold themselves out as CPAs but may use any title permitted by state law such as principal, owner, officer, member, or shareholder.
   3. They cannot assume ultimate responsibility for any financial statement attest or compilation engagement.
   4. They are not eligible for AICPA membership but must abide by the AICPA *Code of Professional Conduct*.
   5. New non-CPA owners must have a bachelor's degree. Beginning in 2010, they must also meet the AICPA 150-hour education requirement.
   6. They must meet the same continuing professional education requirements as AICPA members.

A recent development has been the acquisition of CPA firms by corporate entities such as American Express. In such instances, the CPA firm may form a subsidiary to provide attest services to clients. These alternative practice structures are permissible, but an AICPA Council resolution makes it clear that to protect the public interest, CPAs have the same responsibility for the conduct of their attest work as they have in traditional practice structures.

A CPA firm may use any name as long as it is not misleading. Most firms use the name of one or more of the owners. It is not unusual for a firm name to include the names of five or more owners. A CPA firm can use a trade name, although this is unusual in practice. Names such as Marshall Audit Co. or Chicago Tax Specialists are permissible if they are not misleading.

A summary of the rules of conduct is included in Table 4-1 (p. 98).

ENFORCEMENT

OBJECTIVE 4-8
Describe the enforcement mechanisms for the rules of conduct.

Failure to follow the rules of conduct can result in *expulsion* from the AICPA. This by itself does not prevent a CPA from practicing public accounting, but it certainly is a weighty social sanction. All expulsions from the AICPA for a violation of the rules are published in the *CPA Newsletter*, a publication that is sent to all AICPA members, and in *The Wall Street Journal*.

In addition to the rules of conduct, the AICPA bylaws provide for automatic suspension or expulsion from the AICPA for conviction of a crime punishable by imprisonment for more than 1 year and for various tax-related crimes.

Action by AICPA Professional Ethics Division

The AICPA Professional Ethics Division is responsible for investigating other violations of the *Code* and deciding disciplinary action. The division's investigations result from information obtained primarily from complaints of practitioners or other individuals, state societies of CPAs, or governmental agencies. A member can be automatically sanctioned without an investigation if the member has been disciplined by governmental agencies or other organizations that have been granted the authority to regulate accountants, such as the SEC and PCAOB.

There are two primary levels of disciplinary action. For less serious, and probably unintentional violations, the division limits the discipline to a requirement of remedial or corrective action. An example is the unintentional failure to make sure that a small audit

| TABLE 4-1 | Summary of Rules of Conduct |

Rules of Conduct		Applicability		Summary of Rules
Number	**Topic**	**All Members**	**Members in Public Practice**	
101	Independence		x	A member in public practice shall be independent in the performance of professional services as required by standards promulgated by bodies designated by Council.
102	Integrity and objectivity	x		In performing any professional service, a member shall maintain objectivity and integrity, shall be free of conflicts of interest, and shall not knowingly misrepresent facts or subordinate his or her judgment to others.
201	General standards	x		For all services, a member shall comply with the following professional standards and interpretations thereof by bodies designated by Council: (1) undertake only those professional services that the member can reasonably expect to complete with professional competence, (2) exercise due professional care, (3) adequately plan and supervise all engagements, and (4) obtain sufficient relevant data to afford a reasonable basis for all conclusions or recommendations.
202	Compliance with standards	x		A member who performs auditing, review, compilation, management consulting, tax, or other professional services shall comply with standards promulgated by bodies designated by Council.
203	Accounting principles	x		A member shall follow the professional audit reporting standards promulgated by bodies designated by Council in issuing reports about entities' compliance with generally accepted accounting principles.
301	Confidential client information		x	A member in public practice shall not disclose any confidential client information without the specific consent of the client, except for the four specific situations included in Rule 301.
302	Contingent fees		x	A member in public practice shall not perform for a contingent fee any professional service if the member also performs for the client an audit, review, or certain compilations of financial statements, or an examination of prospective financial statements. A member in public practice should also not prepare an original or amended tax return or claim for a tax refund for a contingent fee for any client.
501	Acts discreditable	x		A member shall not commit an act discreditable to the profession.
502	Advertising and other forms of solicitation		x	A member in public practice shall not seek to obtain clients by advertising or other forms of solicitation in a manner that is false, misleading, or deceptive. Solicitation by the use of coercion, overreaching, or harassing conduct is prohibited.
503	Commissions and referral fees		x	A member in public practice shall not receive or pay a commission or referral fee for any client if the member also performs for the client an audit, review, or certain compilations of financial statements, or an examination of prospective financial statements. For nonprohibited commissions or referral fees, a member must disclose the existence of such fees to the client.
505	Form of organization and name		x	A member may practice public accounting only in a form of organization permitted by state law or regulation whose characteristics conform to resolutions of Council and shall not practice public accounting under a firm name that is misleading.

client included all disclosures in its financial statements, which violates Rule 203 of the rules of conduct. The division is likely to require the member to attend a specified number of hours of continuing education courses to improve technical competence. The second level of disciplinary action is action before the Joint Trial Board. This board has authority to *suspend or expel members from the AICPA* for various violations of professional ethics. Typically, action by the board also results in publication in the *CPA Newsletter* of the name and address of the person suspended or expelled and reasons for the action.

Even more important than expulsion from the AICPA is the existence of rules of conduct, similar to the AICPA's, that have been enacted by the Board of Accountancy of each of the 50 states. Because each state grants the individual practitioner a license to practice as a CPA, a significant breach of a state Board of Accountancy's code of conduct can result in the *loss of the CPA certificate and the license to practice.* Although it rarely happens, the loss removes the practitioner from public accounting. Most states adopt the AICPA rules of conduct, but several have more restrictive codes. For example, some states have retained restrictions on advertising and other forms of solicitation. In recent years, an increasing number of states have adopted codes of conduct more restrictive than the AICPA's.

Action by a State Board of Accountancy

State Boards of Accountancy

SUMMARY

The demand for audit and other assurance services provided by CPA firms depends on public confidence in the profession. This chapter discussed the role of ethics in society and the unique ethical responsibilities of CPAs.

The professional activities of CPAs are governed by the AICPA *Code of Professional Conduct,* and auditors of public companies are also subject to oversight by the PCAOB and SEC. Foremost of all ethical responsibilities of CPAs is the need for independence. The rules of conduct and interpretations provide guidance on permissible financial and other interests to help CPAs maintain independence. Other rules of conduct are also designed to maintain public confidence in the profession. The ethical responsibilities of CPAs are enforced by the AICPA for members and by state boards of accountancy for licensed CPAs.

ESSENTIAL TERMS

Audit committee—selected members of a client's board of directors whose responsibilities include helping auditors to remain independent of management

Confidential client information—client information that may not be disclosed without the specific consent of the client except under authoritative professional or legal investigation

Direct financial interest—the ownership of stock or other equity shares by members or their immediate family

Ethical dilemma—a situation in which a decision must be made about the appropriate behavior

Ethics—a set of moral principles or values

Independence in appearance—the auditor's ability to maintain an unbiased viewpoint *in the eyes of others*

Independence in fact—the auditor's ability to take an unbiased viewpoint in the performance of professional services

Independence Standards Board (ISB)—an autonomous private-sector body established under an agreement between the SEC and the AICPA to provide a conceptual framework for independence issues related to audits of public companies

Indirect financial interest—a close, but not direct, ownership relationship between the auditor and the client; an example is the ownership of stock by a member's grandparent

Privileged information—client information that the professional cannot be legally required to provide; information that an accountant obtains from a client is confidential but not privileged

REVIEW QUESTIONS

4-1 (Objective 4-1) What are the six core ethical values described by the Josephson Institute? What are some other sources of ethical values?

4-2 (Objective 4-2) Describe an ethical dilemma. How does a person resolve an ethical dilemma?

4-3 (Objective 4-3) Why is there a special need for ethical behavior by professionals? Why do the ethical requirements of the CPA profession differ from those of other professions?

4-4 (Objective 4-4) List the four parts of the *Code of Professional Conduct*, and state the purpose of each.

4-5 (Objective 4-5) Distinguish between independence in fact and independence in appearance. State three activities that may not affect independence in fact but are likely to affect independence in appearance.

4-6 (Objective 4-5) Why is an auditor's independence so essential?

4-7 (Objective 4-5) What consulting or nonaudit services are prohibited for auditors of public companies? What other restrictions and requirements apply to auditors when providing nonaudit services to public companies?

4-8 (Objective 4-6) Explain how the rules concerning stock ownership apply to partners and professional staff. Give an example of when stock ownership would be prohibited for each.

4-9 (Objective 4-5) Many people believe that a CPA cannot be truly independent when payment of fees is dependent on the management of the client. Explain two approaches that could reduce this appearance of lack of independence.

4-10 (Objective 4-7) After accepting an engagement, a CPA discovers that the client's industry is more technical than he realized and that he is not competent in certain areas of the operation. What are the CPA's options?

4-11 (Objective 4-7) Assume that an auditor makes an agreement with a client that the audit fee will be contingent upon the number of days required to complete the engagement. Is this a violation of the *Code of Professional Conduct*? What is the essence of the rule of professional ethics dealing with contingent fees, and what are the reasons for the rule?

4-12 (Objective 4-7) The auditor's audit files usually can be provided to someone else only with the permission of the client. Give three exceptions to this general rule.

4-13 (Objective 4-7) Identify and explain factors that should keep the quality of audits high even though advertising and competitive bidding are allowed.

4-14 (Objective 4-7) Summarize the restrictions on advertising by CPA firms in the rules of conduct and interpretations.

4-15 (Objective 4-7) What is the purpose of the AICPA's *Code of Professional Conduct* restriction on commissions as stated in Rule 503?

4-16 (Objective 4-7) State the allowable forms of organization a CPA firm may assume.

4-17 (Objective 4-8) Distinguish between the effect on a CPA firm's practice of enforcing the rules of conduct by the AICPA versus a state Board of Accountancy.

MULTIPLE CHOICE QUESTIONS FROM CPA EXAMINATIONS

4-18 (Objective 4-6) The following questions concern independence and the *Code of Professional Conduct* or GAAS. Choose the best response.

a. What is the meaning of the generally accepted auditing standard that requires the auditor be independent?
   (1) The auditor must be without bias with respect to the client under audit.
   (2) The auditor must adopt a critical attitude during the audit.
   (3) The auditor's sole obligation is to third parties.
   (4) The auditor may have a direct ownership interest in the client's business if it is not material.

b. The independent audit is important to readers of financial statements because it
   (1) determines the future stewardship of the management of the company whose financial statements are audited.
   (2) measures and communicates financial and business data included in financial statements.
   (3) involves the objective examination of and reporting on management-prepared statements.
   (4) reports on the accuracy of all information in the financial statements.

c. An auditor strives to achieve independence in appearance to
   (1) maintain public confidence in the profession.
   (2) become independent in fact.
   (3) comply with the generally accepted auditing standards of field work.
   (4) maintain an unbiased mental attitude.

4-19 (Objective 4-7) The following questions concern possible violations of the AICPA *Code of Professional Conduct*. Choose the best response.

a. In which one of the following situations would a CPA be in violation of the AICPA *Code of Professional Conduct* in determining the audit fee?
   (1) A fee based on whether the CPA's report on the client's financial statements results in the approval of a bank loan.
   (2) A fee based on the outcome of a bankruptcy proceeding.
   (3) A fee based on the nature of the service rendered and the CPA's expertise instead of the actual time spent on the engagement.
   (4) A fee based on the fee charged by the prior auditor.

b. The AICPA *Code of Professional Conduct* states that a CPA shall not disclose any confidential information obtained in the course of a professional engagement except with the consent of the client. In which one of the following situations would disclosure by a CPA be in violation of the code?
   (1) Disclosing confidential information in order to properly discharge the CPA's responsibilities in accordance with the profession's standards.
   (2) Disclosing confidential information in compliance with a subpoena issued by a court.
   (3) Disclosing confidential information to another accountant interested in purchasing the CPA's practice.
   (4) Disclosing confidential information during an AICPA authorized peer review.

c. A CPA's retention of client records as a means of enforcing payment of an overdue audit fee is an action that is
   (1) not addressed by the AICPA *Code of Professional Conduct*.
   (2) acceptable if sanctioned by the state laws.
   (3) prohibited under the AICPA rules of conduct.
   (4) a violation of generally accepted auditing standards.

DISCUSSION QUESTIONS AND PROBLEMS

4-20 (Objectives 4-5, 4-6) The following situations involve the provision of nonaudit services. Indicate whether providing the service is a violation of AICPA rules or SEC rules including Sarbanes–Oxley requirements on independence. Explain your answer as necessary.

a. Providing bookkeeping services to a public company. The services were preapproved by the audit committee of the company.

b. Providing internal audit services to a public company that is not an audit client.

c. Designing and implementing a financial information system for a private company.

d. Recommending a tax shelter to a client that is publicly held. The services were preapproved by the audit committee.

e. Providing internal audit services to a public company client with the preapproval of the audit committee.

f. Providing bookkeeping services to an audit client that is a private company.

4-21 (Objectives 4-6, 4-7) Each of the following situations involves a possible violation of the AICPA's *Code of Professional Conduct*. For each situation, state the applicable section of the rules of conduct and whether it is a violation.

a. John Brown is a CPA, but not a partner, with 3 years of professional experience with Lyle and Lyle, CPAs. He owns 25 shares of stock in an audit client of the firm, but he does not take part in the audit of the client, and the amount of stock is not material in relation to his total wealth.

b. In preparing the personal tax returns for a client, Phyllis Allen, CPA, observed that the deductions for contributions and interest were unusually large. When she asked the client for backup information to support the deductions, she was told, "Ask me no questions, and I will tell you no lies." Allen completed the return on the basis of the information acquired from the client.

c. A nonaudit client requests assistance of J. Bacon, CPA, in the installation of a local area network. Bacon had no experience in this type of work and no knowledge of the client's computer system, so he obtained assistance from a computer consultant. The consultant is not in the practice of public accounting, but Bacon is confident of his professional skills. Because of the highly technical nature of the work, Bacon is not able to review the consultant's work.

d. Five small Chicago CPA firms have become involved in an information project by taking part in an interfirm working paper review program. Under the program, each firm designates two partners to review the audit files, including the tax returns and the financial statements of another CPA firm taking part in the program. At the end of each review, the auditors who prepared the working papers and the reviewers have a conference to discuss the strengths and weaknesses of the audit. They do not obtain authorization from the audit client before the review takes place.

e. James Thurgood, CPA, stayed longer than he should have at the annual Christmas party of Thurgood and Thurgood, CPAs. On his way home he drove through a red light and was stopped by a policeman, who observed that he was intoxicated. In a jury trial, Thurgood was found guilty of driving under the influence of alcohol. Because this was not his first offense, he was sentenced to 30 days in jail and his driver's license was revoked for 1 year.

f. Bill Wendal, CPA, set up a casualty and fire insurance agency to complement his auditing and tax services. He does not use his own name on anything pertaining to the insurance agency and has a highly competent manager, Frank Jones, who runs it. Wendal often requests Jones to review the adequacy of a client's insurance with management if it seems underinsured. He believes that he provides a valuable service to clients by informing them when they are underinsured.

g. Rankin, CPA, provides tax services, management advisory services, and bookkeeping services and conducts audits for the same nonpublic client. Because the firm is small, the same person often provides all the services.

4-22 (Objectives 4-6, 4-7) Each of the following situations involves possible violations of the AICPA's *Code of Professional Conduct*. For each situation, state whether it is a violation of the *Code*. In those cases in which it is a violation, explain the nature of the violation and the rationale for the existing rule.

a. Ralph Williams is the partner on the audit of a nonprofit charitable organization. He is also a member of the board of directors, but this position is honorary and does not involve performing a management function.

b. Pickens and Perkins, CPAs, are incorporated to practice public accounting. The only shareholders in the corporation are existing employees of the organization, including partners, staff members who are CPAs, staff members who are not CPAs, and administrative personnel.

c. Fenn and Company, CPAs, has a sophisticated network-based computer server that supports the firm's technology systems and databases. Because of excess capacity available on the server, Fenn and Company agreed to maintain on its server accounting records for one of Fenn's nonpublic audit clients, Delta Equipment Company.

d. Godette, CPA, has a law practice. Godette has recommended one of his clients to Doyle, CPA. Doyle has agreed to pay Godette 10% of the fee for services rendered by Doyle to Godette's client.

e. Theresa Barnes, CPA, has an audit client, Smith, Inc., which uses another CPA for management services work. Barnes sends her firm's literature covering its management services capabilities to Smith on a monthly basis, unsolicited.

f. A bank issued a notice to its depositors that it was being audited and requested them to comply with the CPA's effort to obtain a confirmation on the deposit balances. The bank printed the name and address of the CPA in the notice. The CPA has knowledge of the notice.

g. Myron Jones, CPA, is a member of a national CPA firm. His business card includes his name, the firm's name, address, and telephone number, and the title *IT consultant*.

h. Gutowski, a practicing CPA, has written an e-commerce-related article that is being published in a professional publication. The publication wishes to inform its readers about Gutowski's background. The information, which Gutowski has approved, includes his academic degrees, other articles he has had published in professional journals, and a statement that he is an e-commerce expert.

i. Poust, CPA, has sold his public accounting practice, which includes bookkeeping, tax services, and auditing, to Lyons, CPA. Poust obtained permission from all audit clients for audit-related working papers before making them available to Lyons. He did not get permission before releasing tax- and management services-related working papers.

j. Murphy and Company, CPAs, is the principal auditor of the consolidated financial statements of Lowe, Inc. and subsidiaries. Lowe accounts for approximately 98% of consolidated assets and consolidated net income. The two subsidiaries are audited by Trotman and Company, CPAs, a firm with an excellent professional reputation. Murphy insists on auditing the two subsidiaries because he deems this necessary to warrant the expression of an opinion.*

4-23 (Objective 4-5) The SEC now requires all public companies to have an independent audit committee.

Required

a. Describe an audit committee.

b. What are the typical functions performed by an audit committee?

c. Explain how an audit committee can help an auditor be more independent.

d. Some critics of audit committees believe that they bias companies in favor of larger and perhaps more expensive CPA firms. These critics contend that a primary concern of audit committee members is to reduce their exposure to legal liability. The committees will therefore recommend larger, more prestigious CPA firms, even if the cost is somewhat higher, to minimize the potential criticism of selecting an unqualified firm. Evaluate these comments.

4-24 (Objectives 4-5, 4-6) The following relate to auditors' independence:

a. Why is independence so essential for auditors?

Required

b. Compare the importance of independence of CPAs with that of other professionals, such as attorneys.

c. Explain the difference between independence in appearance and in fact.

d. Assume that a partner of a CPA firm owns two shares of stock of a large audit client on which he serves as the engagement partner. The ownership is an insignificant part of his total wealth.
(1) Has he violated the *Code of Professional Conduct*?
(2) Explain whether the ownership is likely to affect the partner's independence in fact.
(3) Explain the reason for the strict requirements about stock ownership in the rules of conduct.

e. Discuss how each of the following could affect independence in fact and independence in appearance, and evaluate the social consequence of prohibiting auditors from doing each one:
(1) Owning stock in a client company
(2) Having bookkeeping services for an audit client performed by the same person who does the audit
(3) Recommending adjusting entries to the client's financial statements and preparing financial statements, including footnotes, for the client
(4) Having management services for an audit client performed by individuals in a department that is separate from the audit department
(5) Having the annual audit performed by the same audit team, except for assistants, for 5 years in a row
(6) Having the annual audit performed by the same CPA firm for 10 years in a row
(7) Having management select the CPA firm

f. Which of (1) through (7) are prohibited by the AICPA *Code of Professional Conduct*? Which are prohibited by the Sarbanes–Oxley Act or the SEC?

4-25 (Objective 4-6) Marie Janes encounters the following situations in doing the audit of a large auto dealership. Janes is not a partner.

1. The sales manager tells her that there is a sale (at a substantial discount) on new cars that is limited to long-established customers of the dealership. Because her firm has been doing the audit for several years, the sales manager has decided that Janes should also be eligible for the discount.

2. The auto dealership has an executive lunchroom that is available free to employees above a certain level. The controller informs Janes that she can also eat there any time.

3. Janes is invited to and attends the company's annual Christmas party. When presents are handed out, she is surprised to find her name included. The present has a value of approximately $200.

a. Assuming Janes accepts the offer or gift in each situation, has she violated the rules of conduct?

Required

b. Discuss what Janes should do in each situation.

*AICPA adapted.

4-26 (Objective 4-6) Ann Archer serves on the audit committee of JKB Communications, Inc., a telecommunications start-up company. The company is currently a private company. One of the audit committee's responsibilities is to evaluate the external auditor's independence in performing the audit of the company's financial statements. In conducting this year's evaluation, Ann learned that JKB Communications' external auditor also performed the following IT and e-commerce services for the company:

1. Installed JKB Communications' information system hardware and software selected by JKB management
2. Supervised JKB Communications' personnel in the daily operation of the newly installed information system
3. Customized a prepackaged payroll software application, based on options and specifications selected by management
4. Trained JKB Communications' employees on the use of the newly installed information system
5. Determined which JKB Communications' products would be offered for sale on the company's Internet Web site
6. Operated JKB Communications' local area network for several months while the company searched for a replacement after the previous network manager left the company

Required   Consider each of the preceding services separately. Evaluate whether the performance of each service violates the AICPA's *Code of Professional Conduct*.

CASES

4-27 (Objectives 4-6, 4-7) The following are situations that may violate the *Code of Professional Conduct*. Assume, in each case, that the CPA is a partner.

1. Able, CPA, owns a substantial limited partnership interest in an apartment building. Frederick Marshall is a 100% owner in Marshall Marine Co. Marshall also owns a substantial interest in the same limited partnership as Able. Able does the audit of Marshall Marine Co.
2. Baker, CPA, approaches a new audit client and tells the president that he has an idea that could result in a substantial tax refund in the prior year's tax return by application of a technical provision in the tax law that the client had overlooked. Baker adds that the fee will be 50% of the tax refund after it has been resolved by the Internal Revenue Service. The client agrees to the proposal.
3. Contel, CPA, advertises in the local paper that his firm does the audit of 14 of the 36 largest savings and loans in the city. The advertisement also states that the average audit fee, as a percentage of total assets for the savings and loans he audits, is lower than any other CPA firm's in the city.
4. Davis, CPA, sets up a small loan company specializing in loans to business executives and small companies. Davis does not spend much time in the business because he spends full time with his CPA practice. No employees of Davis's CPA firm are involved in the small loan company.
5. Elbert, CPA, owns a material amount of stock in a mutual fund investment company, which in turn owns stock in Elbert's largest audit client. Reading the investment company's most recent financial report, Elbert is surprised to learn that the company's ownership in his client has increased dramatically.
6. Finigan, CPA, does the audit, tax return, bookkeeping, and management services work for Gilligan Construction Company. Mildred Gilligan follows the practice of calling Finigan before she makes any major business decision to determine the effect on her company's taxes and the financial statements. Finigan attends continuing education courses in the construction industry to make sure that she is technically competent and knowledgeable about the industry. Finigan normally attends board of directors meetings and accompanies Gilligan when she is seeking loans. Mildred Gilligan often jokingly introduces Finigan with this statement, "I have my three business partners—my banker, the government, and my CPA, but Finny's the only one that is on my side."

Required   Discuss whether the facts in any of the situations indicate violations of the *Code of Professional Conduct*. If so, identify the nature of the violation(s).

4-28 (Objectives 4-2, 4-7) Barbara Whitley had great expectations about her future as she sat in her graduation ceremony in May 2004. She was about to receive her Master of Accountancy degree, and next week she would begin her career on the audit staff of Green, Thresher & Co., CPAs.

Things looked a little different to Barbara in February 2005. She was working on the audit of Delancey Fabrics, a textile manufacturer with a calendar year-end. The pressure was enormous.

Everyone on the audit team was putting in 70-hour weeks, and it still looked as if the audit wouldn't be done on time. Barbara was doing work in the property area, vouching additions for the year. The audit program indicated that a sample of all items over $20,000 should be selected, plus a judgmental sample of smaller items. When Barbara went to take the sample, Jack Bean, the senior, had left the client's office and couldn't answer her questions about the appropriate size of the judgmental sample. Barbara forged ahead with her own judgment and selected 50 smaller items. Her basis for doing this was that there were about 250 such items, so 50 was a reasonably good proportion of such additions.

Barbara audited the additions with the following results: The items over $20,000 contained no misstatements; however, the 50 small items contained a large number of misstatements. In fact, when Barbara projected them to all such additions, the amount seemed quite significant.

A couple of days later, Jack Bean returned to the client's office. Barbara brought her work to Jack in order to apprise him of the problems she found and got the following response:

> My God, Barbara, why did you do this? You were only supposed to look at the items over $20,000 plus 5 or 10 little ones. You've wasted a whole day on that work, and we can't afford to spend any more time on it. I want you to throw away the schedules where you tested the last 40 small items and forget you ever did them.

When Barbara asked about the possible audit adjustment regarding the small items, none of which arose from the first 10 items, Jack responded, "Don't worry, it's not material anyway. You just forget it; it's my concern, not yours."

a. In what way is this an ethical dilemma for Barbara? **Required**

b. Use the six-step approach discussed in the book to resolve the ethical dilemma.

4-29 (Objectives 4-1, 4-2, 4-3) In 2000, Arnold Diaz was a bright, upcoming audit manager in the South Florida office of a national public accounting firm. He was an excellent technician and a good "people person." Arnold also was able to bring new business into the firm as the result of his contacts in the rapidly growing Hispanic business community.

Arnold was assigned a new client in 2001, XYZ Securities, Inc., a privately held broker–dealer in the secondary market for U.S. government securities. Neither Arnold nor anyone else in the South Florida office had broker–dealer audit experience. However, the AICPA and Arnold's firm had audit aids for the industry, which Arnold used to get started.

Arnold was promoted to partner in 2001. Although this was a great step forward for him (he was a new staff assistant in 1992), Arnold was also under a great deal of pressure. Upon making partner, he was required to contribute capital to the firm. He also thought he must maintain a special image with his firm, with his clients, and within the Hispanic community. To accomplish this, Arnold maintained an impressive wardrobe, bought a BMW and a small speedboat, and traded up to a nicer house. He also entertained freely. Arnold financed much of this higher living with credit cards. He had six American Express and banking cards and ran up a balance of about $40,000.

After the audit was completed and before the 2002 audit was to begin, Arnold contacted Jack Oakes, the CFO of XYZ Securities, with a question. Arnold had noticed an anomaly in the financial statements that he couldn't understand and asked Oakes for an explanation. Oakes's reply was as follows:

> Arnold, the 2001 financial statements were materially misstated and you guys just blew it. I thought you might realize this and call me, so here's my advice to you. Keep your mouth shut. We'll make up the loss we covered up last year, this year, and nobody will ever know the difference. If you blow the whistle on us, your firm will know you screwed up, and your career as the star in the office will be down the tubes.

Arnold said he'd think about this and get back to Oakes the next day. When Arnold called Oakes, he had decided to go along with him. After all, it would only be a "shift" of a loss between two adjacent years. XYZ is a private company and no one would be hurt or know the difference. In reality, only he was the person exposed to any harm in this situation, and he had to protect himself, didn't he?

When Arnold went to XYZ to plan for the 2002 audit, he asked Oakes how things were going, and Oakes assured him they were fine. He then said to Oakes,

> Jack, you guys are in the money business, maybe you can give me some advice. I've run up some debts and I need to refinance them. How should I go about it?

After some discussions, Oakes volunteered a "plan." Oakes would give Arnold a check for $15,000. XYZ would request its bank to put $60,000 in an account in Arnold's name and guarantee the loan security on it. Arnold would pay back the $15,000 and have $45,000 of refinancing. Arnold thought the plan was great and obtained Oakes's check for $15,000.

During 2002 through 2004, three things happened. First, Arnold incurred more debts and went back to the well at XYZ. By the end of 2004, he had "borrowed" a total of $125,000. Second, the company continued to lose money in various "off-the-books" investment schemes. These losses were covered up by falsifying the results of normal operations. Third, the audit team, under Arnold's leadership, "failed to find" the fraud and issued unqualified opinions.

In 2003, Oakes had a tax audit of his personal 2002 return. He asked Arnold's firm to handle it, and the job was assigned to Bob Smith, a tax manager. In reviewing Oakes's records, Smith found a $15,000 check payable from Oakes to Diaz. Smith asked to see Diaz and inquired about the check. Arnold somewhat broke down and confided in Smith about his problems. Smith responded by saying,

Don't worry Arnold, I understand. And believe me, I'll never tell a soul.

In 2004, XYZ's continuing losses caused it to be unable to deliver nonexistent securities when requested by a customer. This led to an investigation and bankruptcy by XYZ. Losses totaled in the millions. Arnold's firm was held liable, and Arnold was found guilty of conspiracy to defraud. He is still in prison today.

Required
a. Try to put yourself in Arnold's shoes. What would you have done (be honest with yourself now) when told of the material misstatement in mid-2002?
b. What do you think of Bob Smith's actions to help Arnold?
c. Where does one draw the line between ethical and unethical behavior?

4-30 (Objective 4-2) Frank Dorrance, a senior audit manager for Bright and Lorren, CPAs, has recently been informed that the firm plans to promote him to partner within the next year or two if he continues to perform at the same high-quality level as in the past. Frank excels at dealing effectively with all people, including client personnel, professional staff, partners, and potential clients. He has recently built a bigger home for entertaining and has joined the city's most prestigious golf and tennis club. He is excited about his future with the firm.

Frank has recently been assigned to the audit of Machine International, a large wholesale company that ships goods throughout the world. It is one of Bright and Lorren's most prestigious clients. During the audit, Frank determines that Machine International uses a method of revenue recognition called "bill and hold" that has recently been questioned by the SEC. After considerable research, Frank concludes that the method of revenue recognition is not appropriate for Machine International. He discusses the matter with the engagement partner, who concludes that the accounting method has been used for more than 10 years by the client and is appropriate, especially considering that the client does not file with the SEC. The partner is certain the firm would lose the client if the revenue recognition method is found inappropriate. Frank argues that the revenue recognition method was appropriate in prior years, but the SEC ruling makes it inappropriate in the current year. Frank recognizes the partner's responsibility to make the final decision, but he feels strongly enough to state that he plans to follow the requirements of SAS 22 (AU 311) and include a statement in the audit files that he disagrees with the partner's decision. The partner informs Frank that she is unwilling to permit such a statement because of the potential legal implications. However, she is willing to write a letter to Frank stating that she takes full responsibility for making the final decision if a legal dispute ever arises. She concludes by saying, "Frank, partners must act like partners, not like loose cannons trying to make life difficult for their partners. You have some growing up to do before I would feel comfortable with you as a partner."

Required
Use the six-step approach discussed in the book to resolve the ethical dilemma.

INTERNET PROBLEM 4-1: PUBLIC COMPANY DISCLOSURE OF AUDIT AND NONAUDIT FEES

Reference the CW site. Companies are required to disclose in their proxy statements or annual filings with the Securities and Exchange Commission the total amount of audit and nonaudit fees paid to the audit firm for the two most recent years. Current rules require that fees be reported under the following four categories: audit fees, audit-related fees, tax fees, and all other fees. This problem requires you to locate fee information for two companies and answer questions regarding the effect of nonaudit fees on auditor independence.

LEGAL LIABILITY

IT TAKES THE NET PROFIT FROM MANY AUDITS TO OFFSET THE COST OF ONE LAWSUIT

Orange & Rankle, a CPA firm in San Jose, audited a small high-tech client that developed software. A significant portion of the client's capital was provided by a syndicate of 40 limited partners. The owners of these interests were knowledgeable business and professional people, including several lawyers.

Orange & Rankle audited the company for 4 consecutive years, from its inception, for an average annual fee of approximately $33,000. The audits were well done by competent auditors. It was clear to the firm and to others who subsequently reviewed the audits that they complied with generally accepted auditing standards in every way.

In the middle of the fifth year of the company's existence, it became apparent that the marketing plan it had developed was overly optimistic and the company was going to require additional capital or a significant strategy change. The limited partners were polled and refused to provide the capital. The company folded its tent and filed bankruptcy. The limited partners lost their investment in the company. They subsequently filed a lawsuit against all parties involved in the enterprise, including the auditors.

Over the next several years, the auditors proceeded through the process of preparing to defend themselves in the lawsuit. They went through complete discovery, hired an expert witness on auditing-related issues, filed motions, and so forth. They attempted a settlement at various times, but the plaintiffs would not agree to a reasonable amount. Finally, during the second day of trial, the plaintiffs settled for a nominal amount.

It was clear that the plaintiffs knew the auditors bore no fault but kept them in the suit anyway. The total *out-of-pocket* cost to the audit firm was $2.5 million, not to mention personnel time, possible damage to their reputation, and general stress and strain. Thus, the cost of this suit, in which the auditors were completely innocent, was more than 75 times the average annual audit fee earned from this client.

LEARNING OBJECTIVES

After studying this chapter, you should be able to

5-1 Understand the litigious environment in which CPAs practice.

5-2 Explain why the failure of financial statement users to differentiate among business failure, audit failure, and audit risk has resulted in lawsuits.

5-3 Use the primary legal concepts and terms concerning accountants' liability as a basis for studying legal liability of auditors.

5-4 Describe accountants' liability to clients and related defenses.

5-5 Describe accountants' liability to third parties under common law and related defenses.

5-6 Describe accountants' civil liability under the federal securities laws and related defenses.

5-7 Specify what constitutes criminal liability for accountants.

5-8 Describe what the profession and the individual CPA can do and what is being done to reduce the threat of litigation.

This chapter on legal liability and the preceding chapter on professional ethics highlight the environment in which CPAs operate. We focus on these chapters now to provide an overview of the importance of protecting the profession's reputation as being one that is viewed as highly ethical and to highlight consequences accountants face when others believe they have failed to live up to that ethical standard. Legal liability and its consequences for the profession are serious. This chapter highlights ways CPAs can be held liable for the professional services they provide.

As the auditors at Orange & Rankle in the opening vignette learned the hard way, legal liability and its consequences are significant for CPAs. It has been estimated that the profession's aggregate legal liability exposure exceeds $40 billion. Although firms have insurance to help alleviate the impact of assessed damages, the premiums are high and the policies available to the firms have large deductible amounts. The deductibles are such that the large firms are essentially self-insured for losses of many millions of dollars.

This chapter focuses on legal liability for CPAs both on a conceptual level and in terms of specific legal suits that have been filed against CPAs. It also highlights actions available to the profession and individual practitioners to minimize liability while still meeting society's needs.

CHANGED LEGAL ENVIRONMENT

OBJECTIVE 5-1

Understand the litigious environment in which CPAs practice.

Professionals have always had a duty to provide a reasonable level of care while performing work for those they serve. Audit professionals have a responsibility under common law to fulfill implied or expressed contracts with clients. They are liable to their clients for negligence and/or breach of contract should they fail to provide the services or not exercise due care in their performance. Auditors may also be held liable under common law in certain circumstances to parties other than their clients. Although the criteria for legal actions against auditors by third parties vary by state, the most common view is that the auditor owes a duty of care to third parties who are part of a limited group of persons whose reliance is "foreseen" by the auditor. In addition to common law, auditors may be held liable to third parties under statutory law. Both the Securities Act of 1933 and the Securities Exchange Act of 1934 contain sections that serve as a basis for actions against auditors. Finally, in rare cases, auditors have also been held liable for criminal acts. A criminal conviction against an auditor can result when it is demonstrated that the auditor intended to deceive or harm others.

Despite efforts to address legal liability of CPAs, both the number of lawsuits and sizes of awards to plaintiffs remain high, including suits involving third parties under both common law and the federal securities acts. There are no simple reasons for this trend, but the following are major factors:

Stanford's Securities
Class Action
Clearinghouse

- There is growing awareness of the responsibilities of public accountants by users of financial statements.
- There is an increased consciousness on the part of the Securities and Exchange Commission (SEC) regarding its responsibility for protecting investors' interests.
- Auditing and accounting are more complex because of factors such as the increasing size of business, the globalization of business, and the intricacies of business operations.
- Society accepts lawsuits by injured parties against anyone who might be able to provide compensation, regardless of who was at fault, coupled with the joint and several liability doctrine. This is often called the deep-pocket concept of liability.
- Large civil court judgments against CPA firms have been awarded in a few cases, which has encouraged attorneys to provide legal services on a contingent-fee basis. This arrangement offers the injured party a potential gain when the suit is successful, but minimal loss when it is unsuccessful.
- Many CPA firms are willing to settle their legal problems out of court in an attempt to avoid costly legal fees and adverse publicity rather than resolve them through the judicial process.

- Courts have difficulty in understanding and interpreting technical accounting and auditing matters.

Litigation costs for accountants are a concern because all members of society bear these costs. Legislative efforts that attempt to control litigation costs focus on discouraging nonmeritorious lawsuits and bringing damages more in line with relative fault. For example, the Private Securities Litigation Reform Act of 1995 was passed to provide relief to accountants in the area of federal securities litigation. Nevertheless, accountants' liability is still onerous and a major consideration in the conduct of a CPA firm's professional practice.

DISTINCTION AMONG BUSINESS FAILURE, AUDIT FAILURE, AND AUDIT RISK

Many accounting and legal professionals believe that a major cause of lawsuits against CPA firms is the lack of understanding by financial statement users of the difference between a business failure and an audit failure and between an audit failure and audit risk. We will now examine these terms and the ways in which not understanding them can lead to lawsuits against auditors.

A **business failure** occurs when a business is unable to repay its lenders or meet the expectations of its investors because of economic or business conditions, such as a recession, poor management decisions, or unexpected competition in the industry. The extreme case of business failure is filing for bankruptcy. **Audit failure** occurs when the auditor issues an erroneous audit opinion as the result of an underlying failure to comply with the requirements of generally accepted auditing standards (GAAS). An example is assigning unqualified assistants to perform audit tasks who then fail to find material misstatements that qualified auditors would discover. **Audit risk** represents the risk that the auditor will conclude that the financial statements are fairly stated and an unqualified opinion can be issued when, in fact, they are materially misstated. Because auditors are able to gather evidence only on a test basis and detecting well-concealed frauds can be extremely difficult, there is always some risk that the auditor will not uncover a material misstatement due to fraud, even though the auditor complied with auditing standards.

OBJECTIVE 5-2

Explain why the failure of financial statement users to differentiate among business failure, audit failure, and audit risk has resulted in lawsuits.

Most accounting professionals agree that in most cases when an audit has failed to uncover material misstatements and the wrong type of audit opinion is issued, a legitimate question may be raised whether the auditor exercised due care. If the auditor failed to use due care in the conduct of the audit, there is an audit failure. In such cases, the law often allows parties who suffered losses as a result of the auditor's breach of a duty of care owed to them to recover some or all of the losses proximately caused by the audit failure. It is difficult in practice to determine when the auditor has failed to use due care because of the complexity of auditing. It is also difficult to determine who has a right to expect the benefits of an audit because of legal traditions. Nevertheless, an auditor's failure to follow due care often may be expected to result in liability and, when appropriate, damages against the CPA firm.

As highlighted by the lawsuit against Orange & Rankle in the opening vignette, the difficulty arises when there has been a business failure, but not an audit failure. For example, when a company goes bankrupt or cannot pay its debts, it is common for statement users to claim that there was an audit failure, especially when the most recently issued auditor's opinion indicates that the financial statements were fairly stated. Even worse, if there is a business failure and the financial statements are later determined to have been misstated, users may claim that the auditor was negligent even if the audit was conducted in accordance with auditing standards. This conflict between statement users and auditors often arises because of what is called the expectation gap between users and auditors. Most auditors believe that the conduct of the audit in accordance with auditing standards is all that can be expected of auditors. Many users believe that auditors guarantee the accuracy of financial statements, and some users even believe that the auditor guarantees the financial viability of the business. Fortunately for the profession, courts continue to support the auditor's view. Unfortunately, the expectation gap often results in unwarranted lawsuits.

Perhaps the profession has a responsibility to educate statement users about the role of auditors and the difference among business failure, audit failure, and audit risk. Realistically, however, auditors must recognize that, in part, the claims of audit failure may also result from the hope of those who suffer a business loss to recover from any source, regardless of who is at fault.

LEGAL CONCEPTS AFFECTING LIABILITY

OBJECTIVE 5-3

Use the primary legal concepts and terms concerning accountants' liability as a basis for studying legal liability of auditors.

The CPA is responsible for every aspect of his or her public accounting work, including auditing, taxes, management advisory services, and accounting and bookkeeping services. For example, if a CPA negligently failed to properly prepare and file a client's tax return, the CPA can be held liable for any penalties and interest that the client was required to pay plus the tax preparation fee charged. In some states, the court can also assess punitive damages.

Most of the major lawsuits against CPA firms have dealt with audited or unaudited financial statements. The discussion in this chapter is restricted primarily to those two aspects of public accounting. Several legal concepts apply to lawsuits against CPAs. These are the prudent person concept, liability for the acts of others, and the lack of privileged communication.

Prudent Person Concept

There is agreement within the profession and the courts that the auditor is not a guarantor or insurer of financial statements. The auditor is expected only to conduct the audit with due care. Even then, the auditor cannot be expected to be perfect.

The standard of due care to which the auditor is expected to be held is often called the **prudent person concept.** It is expressed in *Cooley on Torts* as follows:

- Every man who offers his service to another and is employed assumes the duty to exercise in the employment such skill as he possesses with reasonable care and diligence. In all these employments where peculiar skill is prerequisite, if one offers his service, he is understood as holding himself out to the public as possessing the degree of skill commonly possessed by others in the same employment, and, if his pretentions are unfounded, he commits a species of fraud upon every man who employs him in reliance on his public profession. But no man, whether skilled or unskilled, undertakes that the task he assumes shall be performed successfully, and without fault or error. *He undertakes for good faith and integrity, but not for infallibility,* and he is liable to his employer for negligence, bad faith, or dishonesty, but not for losses consequent upon pure errors of judgment.

Liability for the Acts of Others

Generally, the partners, or shareholders in the case of a professional corporation, are jointly liable for the civil actions against any owner. However, if the firm operates as a limited liability partnership (LLP), a limited liability company (LLC), a general corporation, or a professional corporation with limited liability, the liability for one owner's actions does not extend to another owner's *personal assets,* unless the other owner was directly involved in the actions of the owner causing the liability. Of course, the firm's assets are all subject to the damages that arise.

The partners may also be liable for the work of others on whom they rely under the laws of agency. The three groups an auditor is most likely to rely on are *employees, other CPA firms* engaged to do part of the work, and *specialists* called upon to provide technical information. For example, if an employee performs improperly in doing an audit, the partners can be held liable for the employee's performance.

Lack of Privileged Communication

CPAs do not have the right under common law to withhold information from the courts on the grounds that the information is privileged. As stated in Chapter 4, information in an auditor's documentation can be subpoenaed by a court. Confidential discussions between the client and auditor cannot be withheld from the courts.

A number of states have statutes that permit privileged communication between the client and auditor. Even then, the intent at the time of the communication must have been for the communication to remain confidential. A CPA can refuse to testify in a state with privileged communications statutes. The privilege does not extend to federal courts.

TABLE 5-1	Legal Terms Affecting CPAs' Liability
Legal Term	**Description**
Terms Related to Negligence and Fraud	
Ordinary negligence	Absence of reasonable care that can be expected of a person in a set of circumstances. For auditors, it is in terms of what other competent auditors would have done in the same situation.
Gross negligence	Lack of even slight care, tantamount to reckless behavior, that can be expected of a person. Some states do not distinguish between ordinary and gross negligence.
Constructive fraud	Existence of extreme or unusual negligence even though there was no intent to deceive or do harm. Constructive fraud is also termed *recklessness*. Recklessness in the case of an audit would be present if the auditor knew an adequate audit was not done but still issued an opinion, even though there was no intention of deceiving statement users.
Fraud	Occurs when a misstatement is made and there is both the knowledge of its falsity and the intent to deceive.
Terms Related to Contract Law	
Breach of contract	Failure of one or both parties in a contract to fulfill the requirements of the contract. An example is the failure of a CPA firm to deliver a tax return on the agreed-upon date. Parties who have a relationship that is established by a contract are said to have *privity of contract*.
Third-party beneficiary	A third party who does not have privity of contract but is known to the contracting parties and is intended to have certain rights and benefits under the contract. A common example is a bank that has a large loan outstanding at the balance sheet date and requires an audit as a part of its loan agreement.
Other Terms	
Common law	Laws that have been developed through court decisions rather than through government statutes.
Statutory law	Laws that have been passed by the U.S. Congress and other governmental units. The Securities Acts of 1933 and 1934 are important statutory laws affecting auditors.
Joint and several liability	The assessment against a defendant of the full loss suffered by a plaintiff, regardless of the extent to which other parties shared in the wrongdoing. For example, if management intentionally misstates financial statements, an auditor can be assessed the entire loss to shareholders if the company is bankrupt and management is unable to pay.
Separate and proportionate liability	The assessment against a defendant of that portion of the damage caused by the defendant's negligence. For example, if the courts determine that an auditor's negligence in conducting an audit was the cause of 30% of a loss to a defendant, only 30% of the aggregate damage would be assessed to the CPA firm.

The material in the rest of the chapter can be covered more effectively if the most common legal terms affecting CPAs' liability are understood. Table 5-1 defines many of the terms that will be used throughout the remainder of this chapter.

The distinction between joint and several liability and separate and proportionate liability, which are both defined in Table 5-1, is an extremely significant one, as the amounts will vary greatly between these two bases for assessing damages. Generally, these damage approaches apply in cases of liability to third parties under common law and under the federal securities laws. When lawsuits are filed in state court, the state laws will determine which approach to damages applies. When lawsuits are brought under the federal securities laws, the separate and proportionate approach will apply, except where it can be shown that the CPA defendant has actual knowledge of fraud or has participated in fraud, in which case joint and several liability would apply. It should be noted that under the federal statutes, the amount of damages under separate and proportionate liability can be increased to 150 percent of the amount determined to be proportionate to the CPA's degree of fault, where the main defendant is insolvent.

Legal Terms Affecting
CPAs' Liability

FIGURE 5-1	Four Major Sources of Auditors' Legal Liability

Source of Liability	Example of Potential Claim
Client—liability to client under common law	Client sues auditor for not discovering a material fraud during the audit.
Third party—liability to third parties under common law	Bank sues auditor for not discovering that a borrower's financial statements are materially misstated.
Liability under federal securities laws	Combined group of stockholders sues auditor for not discovering materially misstated financial statements.
Criminal liability	Federal government prosecutes auditor for knowingly issuing an incorrect audit report.

Sources of Legal Liability

The main focus of this chapter is on the four sources of auditor's **legal liability.** These four areas of liability are classified as (1) liability to clients, (2) liability to third parties under common law, (3) liability to third parties under the federal securities laws, and (4) criminal liability. Figure 5-1 provides examples of each of these classifications of liability. Next, each of these liability classifications is examined in more detail.

LIABILITY TO CLIENTS

OBJECTIVE 5-4

Describe accountants' liability to clients and related defenses.

The most common source of lawsuits against CPAs is from clients. The suits vary widely, including such claims as failure to complete a nonaudit engagement on the agreed-upon date, inappropriate withdrawal from an audit, failure to discover a defalcation (theft of assets), and breach of the confidentiality requirements of CPAs. Typically, the amount of these lawsuits is relatively small, and they do not receive the publicity often given to other types of suits. The *Fund of Funds* case, in which the court awarded the company $80 million in a suit against a CPA firm for breach of confidentiality requirements, is a notable exception.

A typical lawsuit involves a claim that the auditor did not discover an employee defalcation as a result of negligence in the conduct of the audit. The lawsuit can be for breach of contract, a tort action for negligence, or both. Tort actions can be based on ordinary negligence, gross negligence, or fraud. Tort actions are common because the amounts recoverable under them are normally larger than under breach of contract.

The principal issue in cases involving alleged negligence is usually the level of care required. Although it is generally agreed that nobody is perfect, not even a professional, in most instances, any significant error or mistake in judgment will create at least a presumption of negligence that the professional will have to rebut. In the auditing environment, failure to meet auditing standards is often conclusive evidence of negligence. A typical example of an audit case raising the question of negligent performance by a CPA firm is the case of *Cenco Incorporated* v. *Seidman & Seidman*. The case, which is described in more detail in Figure 5-2, involved alleged negligence by the auditor in failing to find a fraud. In the legal suit by Cenco's new management, the auditor was able to successfully argue that it was not negligent and that the deceitful actions on the part of the old management team prevented the auditor from uncovering the fraud. The reader should remember from the study of auditing standards in Chapter 2 that determining whether there is a violation is highly subjective.

The question of level of care becomes more difficult in the environment of an unaudited review or compilation of financial statements in which there are fewer accepted standards to evaluate performance. A widely known example of a lawsuit dealing with the failure to uncover fraud in unaudited financial statements is described in Figure 5-3. Although the CPA was never engaged to conduct an audit for the 1136 Tenants Corporation, the CPA was found liable for failing to detect an embezzlement scheme conducted by one of the client's managers. One of the reasons for this outcome was the

FIGURE 5-2 | *Cenco Incorporated* v. *Seidman & Seidman* (1982)—Liability to Clients

Between 1970 and 1975 Cenco's managerial employees, ultimately including top management, were involved in a massive fraud to inflate the value of the company's inventory. This in turn enabled the company to borrow money at a lower interest rate and to obtain higher fire insurance settlements than were proper. After the fraud was discovered by an employee of Cenco and reported to the SEC, a class action suit was filed by stockholders against Cenco, its management, and its auditors. The CPA firm settled out of court on the class action suit by paying $3.5 million.

By now, new management was operating Cenco. They brought a second suit against the CPA firm on behalf of Cenco for breach of contract, professional negligence, and fraud. The primary defense used by the CPA firm was that a diligent attempt was made on the part of the auditors to follow up any indications of fraud, but the combined efforts of a large number of Cenco's management prevented them from uncovering the fraud. The CPA firm argued that the wrongdoings of management were a valid defense against the charges.

The Seventh Circuit Court of Appeals concluded that the CPA firm was not responsible in this case. The wrongdoings of Cenco's management were considered an appropriate defense against the charges of breach of contract, negligence, and fraud, even though the management no longer worked for the company. Considering management's involvement, the CPA firm was not considered negligent.

lack of a clear understanding between the client and the CPA as to the exact nature of the services to be performed by the CPA. As noted in Figure 5-3, *engagement letters* between the client and the CPA firm developed as a result of this case. Now, CPA firms and clients typically sign engagement letters to formalize their agreements about the services to be provided, fees, and timing. There can be *privity of contract* (recall that was defined in

FIGURE 5-3 | *1136 Tenants* v. *Max Rothenberg and Company* (1967)—Liability to Clients

The *1136 Tenants* case was a civil case concerning a CPA's failure to uncover fraud as a part of unaudited financial statements. The tenants recovered approximately $235,000.

A CPA firm was engaged by a real estate management agent for $600 per year to prepare financial statements, a tax return, and a schedule showing the apportionment of real estate taxes for the 1136 Tenants Corporation, a cooperative apartment house. The statements were sent periodically to the tenants. The statements included the words *unaudited*, and there was a cover letter stating that "the statement was prepared from the books and records of the cooperative and no independent verifications were taken thereon."

During the period of the engagement, from 1963 to 1965, the manager of the management firm embezzled significant funds from the tenants of the cooperative. The tenants sued the CPA firm for negligence and breach of contract for failure to find the fraud.

There were two central issues in the case. Was the CPA firm engaged to do an audit instead of only accounting, and was there negligence on the part of the CPA firm? The court answered yes on both counts. The reasoning for the court's conclusion that an audit had taken place was the performance of "some audit procedures" by the CPA firm, including the preparation of a worksheet entitled "missing invoices." Had the CPA followed up on these, the fraud would likely have been uncovered. Most important, the court concluded that even if the engagement had not been considered an audit, the CPA had a duty to follow up on any potential significant exceptions uncovered during an engagement.

Two developments resulted from the *1136 Tenants* case and similar lawsuits concerning unaudited financial statements:

- Engagement letters between the client and CPA firm have been strongly recommended by the AICPA for all engagements, but especially for unaudited engagements. The letter should clearly define the intent of the engagement, the CPA's responsibilities, and any restrictions imposed on the CPA.
- The Accounting and Review Services Committee was formed as a major committee of the AICPA to set forth guidelines for unaudited financial statements of nonpublic companies. They issued their first pronouncement in 1979. The Auditing Standards Board has eliminated all references to unaudited statements for nonpublic companies in SASs to avoid confusion between audited and unaudited engagements.

Table 5-1) without a written agreement, but an engagement letter defines the contract more clearly.

Auditor's Defenses Against Client Suits

The CPA firm normally uses one or a combination of four defenses when there are legal claims by clients: lack of duty to perform the service, nonnegligent performance, contributory negligence, and absence of causal connection.

Lack of Duty The **lack of duty to perform** the service means that the CPA firm claims that there was no implied or expressed contract. For example, the CPA firm might claim that misstatements were not uncovered because the firm did a review service, not an audit. A common way for a CPA firm to demonstrate a lack of duty to perform is by use of an engagement letter. Many litigation experts believe that a well-written engagement letter is one of the most important ways in which CPA firms can reduce the likelihood of adverse legal actions.

Nonnegligent Performance For **nonnegligent performance** in an audit, the CPA firm claims that the audit was performed in accordance with auditing standards. Even if there were undiscovered misstatements, the auditor is not responsible if the audit was conducted properly. The prudent person concept discussed earlier establishes in law that the CPA firm is not expected to be infallible. Similarly, SAS 47 (AU 312) and SAS 99 (AU 316) make it clear that an audit in accordance with GAAS is subject to limitations and cannot be relied on for complete assurance that all misstatements will be found. Requiring auditors to discover all material misstatements would, in essence, make them insurers or guarantors of the accuracy of the financial statements. The courts do not require that.

Contributory Negligence A defense of **contributory negligence** exists when the client's own actions either resulted in the loss that is the basis for damages or interfered with the conduct of the audit in such a way that prevented the auditor from discovering the cause of the loss. As an example of the first circumstance, suppose a client claims that a CPA firm was negligent in not uncovering an employee's theft of cash. If the CPA firm had notified the client (preferably in writing) of a weakness in internal control that would have prevented the theft but management did not correct it, the CPA firm would have a defense of contributory negligence. As an example of the second circumstance, suppose a CPA firm failed to determine that certain accounts receivable were uncollectible and, in reviewing collectibility, were lied to and given false documents by the credit manager. In this circumstance, assuming the audit of accounts receivable was done in accordance with GAAS, a defense of contributory negligence would exist.

Absence of Causal Connection To succeed in an action against the auditor, the client must be able to show that there is a close causal connection between the auditor's breach of the standard of due care and the damages suffered by the client. For example, assume that an auditor failed to complete an audit on the agreed-upon date. The client alleges that this caused a bank not to renew an outstanding loan, which caused damages. A potential auditor defense is that the bank refused to renew the loan for other reasons, such as the weakening financial condition of the client. This defense is called an **absence of causal connection.**

LIABILITY TO THIRD PARTIES UNDER COMMON LAW

OBJECTIVE 5-5

Describe accountants' liability to third parties under common law and related defenses.

In addition to being sued by clients under common law, CPAs may be liable to third parties under common law. Third parties include actual and potential stockholders, vendors, bankers and other creditors, employees, and customers. A CPA firm may be liable to third parties if a loss was incurred by the claimant due to reliance on misleading financial statements. A typical suit might occur when a bank is unable to collect a major loan from an insolvent customer. The bank can claim that misleading audited financial statements were relied on in making the loan and that the CPA firm should be held responsible because it failed to perform the audit with due care.

The leading precedent-setting auditing case in third-party liability is a 1931 case, *Ultramares Corporation* v. *Touche*. It established the traditional common-law approach known as the **Ultramares doctrine.** Take a look at the case, which is summarized in Figure 5-4.

Ultramares Doctrine

| FIGURE 5-4 | *Ultramares Corporation* v. *Touche* (1931)—Liability to Third Parties |

The creditors of an insolvent corporation (Ultramares) relied on the audited financials and subsequently sued the accountants, alleging that they were guilty of negligence and fraudulent misrepresentation. The accounts receivable had been falsified by adding to approximately $650,000 in accounts receivable another item of over $700,000. The creditors alleged that careful investigation would have shown the $700,000 to be fraudulent. The accounts payable contained similar discrepancies.

The court held that the accountants had been negligent but ruled that accountants would not be liable to third parties for honest blunders beyond the bounds of the original contract unless they were primary beneficiaries. The court held that only one who enters into a contract with an accountant for services can sue if those services are rendered negligently.

In this case, the court held that although the accountants were negligent, they were not liable to the creditors because the creditors were not deemed to be *primary beneficiaries*. In this context, a primary beneficiary is one about whom the auditor was informed before conducting the audit (a *known third party*). The key aspect of the *Ultramares* case was that the creditors lacked *privity of contract* with the auditor. This case established a precedent, commonly called the *Ultramares* doctrine, that ordinary negligence is insufficient for liability to third parties because of the lack of *privity of contract* between the third party and the auditor, unless the third party is a *primary beneficiary*. However, in a subsequent trial of the *Ultramares* case, the court pointed out that had there been fraud or gross negligence on the part of the auditor, the auditor could be held liable to more general third parties.

In recent years, many courts have broadened the *Ultramares* doctrine to allow recovery by third parties in more circumstances than previously by introducing the concept of foreseen users. Generally, a **foreseen user** is a member of a limited class of users whom the auditor is aware will rely on the financial statements. For example, a bank that has loans outstanding to a client at the balance sheet date may be a foreseen user. Under this concept, a foreseen user would be treated the same as a known third party.

Although the concept of foreseen users may seem straightforward, its application is not and has developed differently in different jurisdictions. At present, three approaches have emerged: the *Credit Alliance* approach, the *Restatement of Torts* approach, and the *Foreseeable User* approach.

Foreseen Users

Credit Alliance *Credit Alliance* v. *Arthur Andersen & Co.* (1986) was a case in New York in which a lender brought suit against the auditor of one of its borrowers, alleging that it relied on the financial statements of the borrower, who was in default, in granting the loan. The New York State Court of Appeals reversed a lower court's decision that prevented the defendant auditor from using absence of privity as a defense. In so doing, the appellate court upheld the basic concept of privity established by *Ultramares* and stated that to be liable (1) an auditor must know and intend that the work product would be used by the plaintiff third party for a specific purpose, and (2) the knowledge and intent must be evidenced by the auditor's conduct. Approximately 15 states follow some variation of this approach.

Restatement of Torts The approach followed by most states is to apply the rule cited in the *Restatement of Torts*, an authoritative compendium of legal principles. The *Restatement Rule* is that foreseen users must be members of a *reasonably limited and identifiable group of*

CHAPTER 5 / LEGAL LIABILITY   **115**

users that have relied on the CPA's work, such as creditors, even though those persons were not specifically known to the CPA at the time the work was done. A leading case supporting the application of this rule is *Rusch Factors* v. *Levin*, presented in Figure 5-5.

FIGURE 5-5	*Rusch Factors* v. *Levin* (1968)—Liability to Third Parties

The plaintiff, a lender, asked the defendant auditor to audit the financial statements of a company seeking a loan. The auditor issued an unqualified opinion on the financial statements, indicating that the company was solvent when, in fact, it was insolvent. The plaintiff loaned the company money, suffered a subsequent loss, and sued the auditor for recovery.

The auditor's defense in the case was based on the absence of privity on the part of Rusch Factors. The court found in favor of this plaintiff. Although the court could have found in favor of Rusch Factors under *Ultramares* in that it was a primary beneficiary, it chose to rely on the *Restatement of Torts*, stating that the auditor should be liable for ordinary negligence in audits where the financial statements are relied on by *actually foreseen and limited classes of persons*.

Foreseeable User The broadest interpretation of the rights of third-party beneficiaries is to use the concept of **foreseeable users**. Under this concept, any users that the auditor should have reasonably been able to foresee as being likely users of financial statements have the same rights as those with privity of contract. These users are often called an unlimited class. Although a significant number of states have followed this approach in the past, there are now only two that use it, Mississippi and Wisconsin.

There has been confusion caused by differing views of liability to third parties under common law, but the movement is clearly away from the foreseeable user approach, and thus from three approaches to two. And there may be some movement from the *Restatement of Torts* approach toward *Credit Alliance*. For example, in New Jersey, where the foreseeable user approach had been followed by the courts, the legislature recently adopted a strict privity standard. And in *Bily* v. *Arthur Young* (1992), the California Supreme Court reversed a lower court decision against Arthur Young, clearly upholding the *Restatement* doctrine. In its decision, the court stated that "an auditor owes no general duty of care regarding the conduct of an audit to persons other than the client" and reasoned that the potential liability to auditors under the foreseeable user doctrine would be distinctly out of proportion to fault.

Auditor Defenses Against Third-Party Suits

Three of the four defenses available to auditors in suits by clients are also available in third-party lawsuits. Contributory negligence is ordinarily not available because a third party is not in a position to contribute to misstated financial statements.

The preferred defense in third-party suits is nonnegligent performance. If the auditor conducted the audit in accordance with GAAS, the other defenses are unnecessary. On the other hand, nonnegligent performance is difficult to demonstrate to a court, especially if it is a jury trial and the jury is made up of laypeople.

A lack of duty defense in third-party suits contends lack of privity of contract. The extent to which privity of contract is an appropriate defense and the nature of their defense depends heavily on the judicial jurisdiction. As has been shown, there would, for example, be significant differences among New York, Florida, and Wisconsin in the nature of this defense.

Absence of causal connection in third-party suits often means nonreliance on the financial statements by the user. For example, assume that the auditor can demonstrate that a lender relied on an ongoing banking relationship with a customer, rather than the financial statements, in making a loan. The fact that the auditor was negligent in the conduct of the audit would not be relevant in that situation. Of course, it is difficult to prove nonreliance on the financial statements. And, losses can be caused by other factors, such as market behavior.

CIVIL LIABILITY UNDER THE FEDERAL SECURITIES LAWS

Although there has been some growth in actions brought against accountants by their clients and third parties under common law, the greatest growth in CPA liability litigation has been under the federal securities laws.

OBJECTIVE 5-6

Describe accountants' civil liability under the federal securities laws and related defenses.

The emphasis on federal remedies has resulted primarily from the availability of class-action litigation and the relative ease of obtaining massive recovery from defendants. In addition, several sections of the securities laws impose rather strict liability standards on CPAs. Federal courts are often likely to favor plaintiffs in lawsuits in which there are strict standards. However, this may change in light of recent tort reform legislation.

The **Securities Act of 1933** deals with the information in registration statements and prospectuses. It concerns only the reporting requirements for companies issuing new securities. The only parties who can recover from auditors under the 1933 act are original purchasers of securities. The amount of the potential recovery is the original purchase price less the value of the securities at the time of the suit. If the securities have been sold, users can recover the amount of the loss incurred.

Securities Act of 1933

1933 and 1934 Acts

The Securities Act of 1933 imposes an unusual burden on the auditor. Section 11 of the 1933 act defines the rights of third parties and auditors. These are summarized as follows:

- Any third party who purchased securities described in the registration statement may sue the auditor for material misrepresentations or omissions in audited financial statements included in the registration statement.
- Third-party users do not have the burden of proof that they relied on the financial statements or that the auditor was negligent or fraudulent in doing the audit. Users must only prove that the audited financial statements contained a material misrepresentation or omission.
- The auditor has the burden of demonstrating as a defense that (1) an adequate audit (that is, a "reasonable investigation") was conducted in the circumstances or (2) all or a portion of the plaintiff's loss was caused by factors other than the misleading financial statements. The 1933 act is the only common or statutory law where the burden of proof is on the defendant.

Furthermore, the auditor has responsibility for making sure that the financial statements were fairly stated beyond the date of issuance, up to the date the registration statement became effective, which could be several months later. For example, assume that the audit report date for December 31, 2005, financial statements is February 10, 2006, but the registration statement is dated November 1, 2006. In a typical audit, the auditor must review transactions through the audit report date, February 10, 2006. In statements filed under the 1933 act, the auditor is responsible for reviewing transactions through the registration statement date, November 1, 2006.

Although the burden may appear harsh to auditors, there have been relatively few cases tried under the 1933 act. The most significant one is *Escott et al.* v. *BarChris Construction Corporation* (1968). As noted in Figure 5-6 (p. 118), the CPA firm was held liable for a lack of due diligence required under the 1933 act when performing its review of events occurring subsequent to the balance sheet date. Two significant results occurred directly because of this case:

1. Statements on Auditing Standards were changed to require greater emphasis on procedures that the auditor must perform regarding subsequent events, SAS 1 (AU 560).
2. A greater emphasis began to be placed on the importance of the audit staff understanding the client's business and industry.

BarChris filed an S-1 registration statement with the SEC in 1961 for the issuance of convertible sub-ordinated debentures, thereby subjecting the company to the Securities Act of 1933. Approximately 17 months later, BarChris filed for bankruptcy. The purchasers of the debentures filed suit against the CPA firm under the 1933 act.

The most significant issue of the case, especially to audit staff personnel, was the matter of the review for events subsequent to the balance sheet, called an S-1 review for registration statements. The courts concluded that the CPA firm's written audit program was in conformity with GAAS in existence at that time. However, they were highly critical of the auditor conducting the review, who was inexperienced in audits of construction companies, for the failure to appropriately follow up on answers by management. The following is an important part of the court's opinion in the case:

- Accountants should not be held to a higher standard than that recognized in their profession. I do not do so here. Richard's review did not come up to that written standard. He did not take the steps which the CPA firm's written program prescribed. He did not spend an adequate amount of time on a task of this magnitude. *Most important of all, he was too easily satisfied with glib answers to his inquiries.* This is not to say that he should have made a complete audit. But there were enough danger signals in the materials which he did examine to require some further investigation on his part. . . . It is not always sufficient merely to ask questions. (Italics were added and the name used in the case was changed.)

The CPA firm was found liable in the case on the grounds that they had not established due diligence required under the 1933 securities act.

Securities Exchange Act of 1934

The liability of auditors under the **Securities Exchange Act of 1934** often centers on the audited financial statements issued to the public in annual reports or submitted to the SEC as a part of annual Form 10-K reports.

Every company with securities traded on national and over-the-counter exchanges is required to submit audited statements annually. Obviously, a much larger number of statements fall under the 1934 act than under the 1933 act.

In addition to annual audited financial statements, there is potential legal exposure to auditors for quarterly information (Form 10-Q) or other reporting information filed with the SEC, such as an unusual event filed in a Form 8-K. The auditor is required to perform a review of the Form 10-Q before filing with the SEC, and the auditor is frequently involved in reviewing the information in other reports; therefore, there may be legal responsibility. However, few cases have involved auditors for reports other than annual reports.

Rule 10b-5 of the Securities Exchange Act of 1934

The principal focus on CPA liability litigation under the 1934 act has been Rule 10b-5, a section of the federal Securities Exchange Act of 1934, which appears in the rules and regulations of the Securities and Exchange Commission. Rule 10b-5 states the following:

- It shall be unlawful for any person directly or indirectly, by the use of any means or instrumentality of interstate commerce, or of the mails or of any facility of any national securities exchange, (a) to employ any device, scheme, or artifice to defraud, (b) to make any untrue statement of a material fact or omit to state a material fact necessary in order to make the statements made, in the light of the circumstances under which they were made, not misleading, or (c) to engage in any act, practice, or course of business which operates or would operate as a fraud or deceit upon any person in connection with the purchase or sale of any security.

Section 10 and Rule 10b-5 are often called the antifraud provisions of the 1934 act, because they were designed primarily to thwart the commission of fraud by persons selling securities. Numerous federal court decisions have clarified that Rule 10b-5 applies not only to direct sellers but also to accountants, underwriters, and others. Generally, accountants can be held liable under Section 10 and Rule 10b-5 if they intentionally or recklessly misrepresent information intended for third-party use.

FIGURE 5-7 *Hochfelder* v. *Ernst & Ernst* (1976) — Securities Exchange Act of 1934

The case involved the auditor's responsibility for detecting fraud perpetrated by the president of the client firm. Lestor Nay, the president of First Securities Co. of Chicago, fraudulently convinced certain customers to invest funds in escrow accounts that he represented would yield a high return. There were no escrow accounts. Nay converted the customers' funds to his own use.

The transactions were not in the usual form of dealings between First Securities and its customers. First, all correspondence with customers was made solely with Nay. Second, checks of the customers were drawn payable to Nay and because of a *mail rule* that Nay imposed, such mail was opened only by him. Third, the escrow accounts were not reflected on the books of First Securities, or in filings with the SEC, or in connection with customers' other investment accounts. The fraud was uncovered at the time of Nay's suicide.

Respondent customers originally sued in district court for damages against the auditors, Ernst & Ernst, as aiders and abettors under Section 10b-5. They alleged that Ernst & Ernst failed to conduct a proper audit that should have led them to discover the "mail rule" and the fraud. No allegations were made as to Ernst & Ernst's fraudulent and intentional conduct. The action was based solely on a claim that Ernst & Ernst failed to conduct a proper audit. The district court dismissed the action but did not resolve the issue of whether a cause of action could be based merely on allegations of negligence.

The court of appeals reversed the district court. The appeals court held that one who breaches a duty of inquiry and disclosure owed another is liable in damages for aiding and abetting a third party's violation of Rule 10b-5 if the fraud would have been discovered or prevented had the breach not occurred. The court reasoned that Ernst & Ernst had a common-law and statutory duty of inquiry into the adequacy of First Securities' internal control because it had contracted to audit First Securities and to prepare for filing with the commission the annual report of its financial condition.

The U.S. Supreme Court reversed the court of appeals, concluding that the interpretation of Rule 10b-5 required the "intent to deceive, manipulate or defraud." Justice Powell wrote in the Court's opinion that

- When a statute speaks so specifically in terms of manipulation and deception, and of implementing devices and contrivances—the commonly understood terminology of intentional wrongdoing—and when its history reflects no more expansive intent, we are quite unwilling to extend the scope of the statute to negligent conduct.

The Court pointed out that in certain areas of the law, recklessness is considered to be a form of intentional conduct for purposes of imposing liability. This left open the possibility that reckless behavior may be sufficient for liability under Rule 10b-5.

In 1976, in *Hochfelder* v. *Ernst & Ernst,* a leading securities law case as well as CPA liabilities case, the U.S. Supreme Court ruled that knowledge and intent to deceive are required before CPAs could be held liable for violation of Rule 10b-5. A summary of *Hochfelder* is included in Figure 5-7.

Many auditors believed the *Hochfelder* case would significantly reduce auditors' exposure to liability. However, suits have subsequently been brought under Rule 10b-5. In earlier suits, the knowledge and deceit standard was more easily met by plaintiffs in cases in which the auditor knew all the relevant facts but made poor judgments. In such a situation, the courts emphasized that the CPAs had requisite knowledge. The *Solitron Devices* case, described in Figure 5-8 (p. 120), is an example of that reasoning. In that case, the court of appeals ruled that reckless behavior on the part of the auditor was sufficient to hold the auditor liable for violation of Rule 10b-5. However, in two more recent suits, *Worlds of Wonder* and *Software Toolworks,* two key Ninth Circuit decisions stated that poor judgment isn't proof of fraud. This view appears now to be winning in the courts. In a third case, *McLean* v. *Alexander,* the appellate court ruled that the auditors—who were at most guilty of negligence, but not of bad-faith recklessness—were not liable under Rule 10b-5.

It is clear from the previous discussion that Rule 10b-5 continues to be a basis for lawsuits against auditors, even though *Hochfelder* has limited the liability somewhat.

The same three defenses available to auditors in common-law suits by third parties are also available for suits under the 1934 act. These are nonnegligent performance, lack of duty, and absence of causal connection.

Auditor Defenses— 1934 Act

Solitron was a manufacturer of electronic devices, with its stock issued on the American Stock Exchange. It was involved in government contracts that subjected it to assessments on excess profits as determined by the Renegotiations Board. When the board determined that profits were excessive, management admitted that profits had been intentionally overstated to aid in acquiring new companies. It was subsequently shown in court, through an audit by another CPA firm, that earnings had been materially overstated by more than 30 percent in two different years, by overstating inventory.

A jury trial found the auditor responsible for reckless behavior in the conduct of the audit. The trial judge overturned the jury verdict on the grounds that the CPA firm could not be held liable for damages under Rule 10b-5 unless there was proof that the CPA firm *had actual knowledge* of the misstatement. Reckless behavior was not sufficient for damages.

On appeal, the Second Circuit Court of Appeals concluded that there had been sufficient evidence for the jury to conclude that the CPA firm had knowledge of the fraud. It therefore overturned the trial judge's findings and affirmed the original jury's guilty verdict.

The court of appeals also stated that proof of recklessness may meet the requirement of intent in Rule 10b-5, but that it need not address whether there was sufficient recklessness in this case because the CPA firm had knowledge of the misstatement.

As discussed in this section, the use of the lack of duty defense in response to actions under Rule 10b-5 has had varying degrees of success, depending on the jurisdiction. In the *Hochfelder* case, that defense was successful. In other cases, negligent or reckless behavior resulted in liability. Continued court interpretations are likely to clarify this unresolved issue.

SEC Sanctions

Closely related to auditors' liability is the SEC's authority to sanction. The SEC has the power in certain circumstances to sanction or suspend practitioners from doing audits for SEC companies. Rule 2(e) of the SEC's *Rules of Practice* says:

- The commission may deny, temporarily or permanently, the privilege of appearing or practicing before it in any way to any person who is found by the commission . . . (1) not to possess the requisite qualifications to represent others, or (2) to be lacking in character or integrity or to have engaged in unethical or improper professional conduct.

The SEC has temporarily suspended a number of individual CPAs from doing any audits of SEC clients in recent years. It has similarly prohibited a number of CPA firms from accepting any new SEC clients for a period, such as 6 months. At times, the SEC has required an extensive review of a major CPA firm's practices by another CPA firm. In some cases, individual CPAs and their firms have been required to participate in continuing education programs and to make changes in their practices. Sanctions such as these are published by the SEC and are often reported in the business press, making them a significant embarrassment to those involved.

Racketeer Influenced and Corrupt Organization Act

In 1970, Congress passed legislation aimed at preventing organized crime from invading legitimate business enterprises. One of the elements of that legislation is the **Racketeer Influenced and Corrupt Organization Act (RICO).** That act allows an injured party to seek treble (triple) damages and recovery of legal fees in cases where it can be demonstrated that the defendant was engaged in a "pattern of racketeering activity." The statute states that a pattern of racketeering activity means at least two acts of racketeering activity within a 10-year period. In interpreting these requirements, the courts have generally focused on the continuity and relatedness of the acts to determine whether a pattern exists. Prior to 1993, the case law applying RICO to accountants was mixed. Some courts made it clear that a complaint must allege extensive participation by the auditor in the enterprise's affairs beyond conducting an annual audit, while others held that the issuance of a materially false audit report would constitute an act of racketeering activity. Legislation has been considered by the U.S. Congress to clarify the applicability of the act. However, from the auditor's point of view, the issue was essentially resolved by the U.S. Supreme Court. In a 1993 decision, the Court ruled that outside professionals such as accountants who do not help run corrupt businesses cannot be sued under the provisions of RICO.

Another significant congressional action affecting both CPA firms and their clients was the passage of the **Foreign Corrupt Practices Act of 1977.** The act makes it illegal to offer a bribe to an official of a foreign country for the purpose of exerting influence and obtaining or retaining business. The prohibition against payments to foreign officials is applicable to all U.S. domestic firms, regardless of whether they are publicly or privately held, and to foreign companies filing with the SEC.

Foreign Corrupt Practices Act of 1977

Apart from the bribery provisions that affect all companies, the law also requires SEC registrants under the Securities Exchange Act of 1934 to meet additional requirements. These include the maintenance of reasonably complete and accurate records and an adequate system of internal control. The law significantly affects all SEC companies, and may affect auditors through their responsibility to review and evaluate systems of internal control as a part of doing the audit.

To date, there have been no legal cases affecting auditors' legal responsibilities under the Foreign Corrupt Practices Act. But there is considerable disagreement about auditors' responsibilities under the law. There is likely to be ongoing discussion, and perhaps litigation, to resolve the issue.

CRIMINAL LIABILITY

A fourth way CPAs can be held liable is under **criminal liability for accountants.** CPAs can be found guilty for criminal action under both federal and state laws. The most likely statutes to be used under state law are the Uniform Securities Acts, which are similar to parts of the SEC rules. The 1933 and 1934 securities acts, as well as the Federal Mail Fraud Statute and the Federal False Statements Statute, are the most relevant federal laws affecting auditors. All make it a criminal offense to defraud another person through *knowingly being involved* with false financial statements.

OBJECTIVE 5-7

Specify what constitutes criminal liability for accountants.

The Sarbanes–Oxley Act of 2002 makes it a felony to destroy or create documents to impede or obstruct a federal investigation. The Sarbanes–Oxley Act provides for fines and imprisonment of up to 20 years for altering or destroying documents to impede an official investigation. These provisions were adopted following the *United States* v. *Andersen* (2002) case described in Figure 5-9 (p. 122), in which the government charged Andersen with obstruction of justice for the destruction and alteration of documents related to its audit of Enron.

Sarbanes–Oxley Act

Unfortunately, there have been several other criminal cases of notoriety involving CPAs. Although these are not great in absolute number, they have the effect of damaging the integrity of the profession and reducing the profession's ability to attract and retain outstanding people. On the positive side, criminal actions encourage practitioners to use extreme care and exercise good faith in their activities.

A leading case of criminal action against CPAs is *United States* v. *Simon,* which occurred in 1969. In this case, three auditors were prosecuted for filing false financial statements of a client with the government and held to be criminally liable. The consequences for these three men were significant. They lost their CPA certificates under Rule 501 of the *Code of Professional Conduct* (acts discreditable) and were forced to leave the profession. Simon has been followed by three additional major criminal cases. In *United States* v. *Natelli* (1975), two auditors were convicted of criminal liability under the 1934 act for certifying financial statements of National Student Marketing Corporation that contained inadequate disclosures pertaining to accounts receivable.

In *United States* v. *Weiner* (1975), three auditors were convicted of securities fraud in connection with their audit of Equity Funding Corporation of America. Equity Funding was a financial conglomerate with financial statements that had been overstated through a massive fraud by management. The fraud was so extensive and the audit work so poor that the court concluded that the auditors must have been aware of the fraud and were therefore guilty of knowing complicity.

In this case, the government charged Andersen with destruction of documents related to the firm's audit of Enron. During the period between October 19, 2001, when Enron alerted Andersen that the SEC had begun an inquiry into Enron's accounting for certain special purpose entities, and November 8, 2001, when the SEC served Andersen with a subpoena in connection with its work for Enron, Andersen personnel shredded extensive amounts of physical documentation and deleted computer files related to Enron.

The firm was ultimately convicted of one count of obstruction of justice. The conviction was not based on the document shredding, but it was based on the alteration of a memo related to Enron's characterization of charges as nonrecurring in its third quarter 2001 earnings release, in which the company announced a loss of $618 million.

As a result of the conviction, Andersen was no longer able to audit publicly traded U.S. companies, which essentially sealed the fate of the Andersen firm.

In *ESM Government Securities* v. *Alexander Grant & Co.* (1986), it was revealed by management to the partner in charge of the audit of ESM that the previous year's audited financial statements contained a material misstatement. Rather than complying with professional and firm standards in such circumstances, the partner agreed to say nothing in the hope that management would work its way out of the problem during the current year. Instead, the situation worsened, eventually to the point where losses exceeded $300 million. The partner was convicted of criminal charges for his role in sustaining the fraud and was sentenced to a 12-year prison term.

Several critical lessons can be learned from these cases:

• An investigation of the integrity of management is an important part of deciding on the acceptability of clients and the extent of work to perform. SAS 84 (AU 315) gives guidance to auditors in investigating new clients, which will be discussed in a subsequent chapter.
• The auditor can be found criminally guilty in the conduct of an audit even if the person's background indicates integrity in personal and professional life. The criminal liability can extend to partners and staff.
• Independence in appearance and fact by all individuals on the engagement is essential, especially in a defense involving criminal actions. SAS 1 (AU 200) requires a firm to implement policies to help ensure independence in fact and in appearance.
• Transactions with related parties require special scrutiny because of the potential for misstatement. SAS 45 (AU 334) gives guidance in auditing related-party transactions.
• Generally accepted accounting principles cannot be relied on exclusively in deciding whether financial statements are fairly presented. The substance of the statements, considering all facts, is required. The SEC preferability requirement provides guidelines in selecting accounting principles.
• Good documentation may be just as important in the auditor's defense of criminal charges as in a civil suit.
• The potential consequences of the auditor knowingly committing a wrongful act are so severe that it is unlikely that the potential benefits could ever justify the actions.

THE PROFESSION'S RESPONSE TO LEGAL LIABILITY

OBJECTIVE 5-8

Describe what the profession and the individual CPA can do and what is being done to reduce the threat of litigation.

The AICPA and the profession as a whole can do a number of things to reduce practitioners' exposure to lawsuits: by seeking protection from nonmeritorious litigation, improving auditing to better meet users' needs, and educating users about the limits of auditing. Some specific activities are discussed briefly:

• *Research in auditing.* Continued research is important in finding better ways to do such things as uncover unintentional material misstatements or fraud, communicate audit results to statement users, and make sure that auditors are independent.

Significant research already takes place through the AICPA, CPA firms, and universities.

- *Standard and rule setting.* The AICPA and PCAOB must constantly set standards and revise them to meet the changing needs of auditing. For example, changes in auditing standards on the auditor's responsibility to detect fraud and revisions to the auditor independence requirements in the interpretations of the rules of conduct have been issued in recent years to address users' needs and expectations as to auditor performance.

- *Set requirements to protect auditors.* The AICPA can help protect its members by setting certain requirements that better practitioners already follow. Naturally, these requirements should not be in conflict with meeting users' needs. An example of an auditor-set standard is the SAS 85 (AU 333) requirement of a written letter of representation from management in all audits.

- *Establish peer review requirements.* The periodic examination of a firm's practices and procedures is a way to educate practitioners and identify firms not meeting the standards of the profession.

- *Oppose lawsuits.* CPA firms must continue to oppose unwarranted lawsuits even if, in the short run, the costs of winning are greater than the costs of settling. The AICPA has aided practitioners in fighting an unwarranted expansion of legal liability for accountants by filing briefs as "a friend of the court" known as *amicus curiae* briefs.

- *Education of users.* Investors and others who read financial statements must be educated as to the meaning of the auditor's opinion and the extent and nature of the auditor's work. Users must be educated to understand that auditors do not test 100 percent of all records and do not guarantee the accuracy of the financial records or the future prosperity of the company. It is also important to educate users to understand that accounting and auditing are arts, not sciences, and that perfection and precision are not achievable.

- *Sanction members for improper conduct and performance.* One characteristic of a profession is its responsibility for policing its own membership. The AICPA has made progress toward dealing with the problems of inadequate CPA performance, but more rigorous review of alleged failures is still needed.

- *Lobby for changes in laws.* In recent years, several changes in state and federal laws have favorably impacted the legal environment for the profession. Most states have revised their laws to allow accounting firms to practice in different organizational forms, including limited liability organizations that provide some protection from litigation. The passage of the **Private Securities Litigation Reform Act of 1995** (the Reform Act) significantly reduced potential damages in securities-related litigation by providing for proportionate liability in most instances. However, the Reform Act applied only to federal courts, and lawyers began taking their cases to state courts, which the Reform Act did not cover. This loophole was closed by the Securities Litigation Uniform Standards Act of 1998, which requires that class actions involving covered securities be addressed in federal district court. The profession continues to pursue litigation reform at the state level, including application of a strict privity standard for liability to nonclients and proportionate liability in all cases not involving fraud.

1998 Litigation Reform Act

LESSONS LEARNED FROM AUDITOR LITIGATION

In considering the advisability of the laws being considered in reform of accountants' liability, it is useful to consider actual experiences with past accountants' litigation. Accordingly, a review was conducted of 23 cases of alleged audit failure with which I have been involved as a litigation consultant and expert witness. Of these 23 cases, six were clearly without merit and should not have been brought on equitable grounds. Of the 17 that were with merit, 13 did, in fact, represent a real audit failure. In considering the nature of the failure in each case, it was observed that the evidence that would lead the auditor to identify

the misstatement that existed was usually there. In other words, the problem was not any inadequacy in the audit process as presented by professional standards; it was a *lack of professional skepticism* on the part of the auditor. The auditor had evidence in his or her possession that indicated the problem, but did not see it as such.

Source: Presentation by James K. Loebbecke at the Forum on Responsibilities and Liabilities of Accountants and Auditors, United Nations Conference on Trade and Development, March 16, 1995.

PROTECTING INDIVIDUAL CPAs FROM LEGAL LIABILITY

Practicing auditors may also take specific action to minimize their liability. Some of the more common actions are as follows:

- *Deal only with clients possessing integrity.* There is an increased likelihood of having legal problems when a client lacks integrity in dealing with customers, employees, units of government, and others. A CPA firm needs procedures to evaluate the integrity of clients and should dissociate itself from clients found lacking.
- *Hire qualified personnel and train and supervise them properly.* A considerable portion of most audits is done by young professionals with relatively little experience. Given the high degree of risk CPA firms have in doing audits, it is important that these young professionals be qualified and well trained. Supervision of their work by experienced and qualified professionals is also essential.
- *Follow the standards of the profession.* A firm must implement procedures to ensure that all firm members understand and follow the auditing standards, FASB opinions, rules of conduct, and other professional guidelines.
- *Maintain independence.* Independence is more than merely financial. Independence in fact requires an attitude of responsibility separate from the client's interest. Much litigation has arisen from a too-willing acceptance by an auditor of a client's representation or of a client's pressures. The auditor must maintain an attitude of *healthy skepticism.*
- *Understand the client's business.* The lack of knowledge of industry practices and client operations has been a major factor in auditors failing to uncover misstatements in several cases. It is important that the audit team be educated in these areas.
- *Perform quality audits.* Quality audits require that auditors obtain appropriate evidence and make appropriate judgments about the evidence. It is essential, for example, that the auditor understand a client's internal controls and modify the evidence to reflect the findings. Improved auditing reduces the likelihood of misstatements and the likelihood of lawsuits.
- *Document the work properly.* The preparation of good audit documentation helps the auditor organize and perform quality audits. Quality audit documentation is essential if an auditor has to defend an audit in court.
- *Obtain an engagement letter and a representation letter.* These two letters are essential in defining the respective obligations of the client and the auditor. They are helpful especially in lawsuits between the client and auditor, and also in third-party lawsuits.
- *Maintain confidential relations.* Auditors are under an ethical and sometimes legal obligation not to disclose client matters to outsiders.
- *Carry adequate insurance.* It is essential for a CPA firm to have adequate insurance protection in the event of a lawsuit. Although insurance rates have risen considerably as a result of increasing litigation, professional liability insurance is still available for all CPAs.
- *Seek legal counsel.* When serious problems occur during an audit, a CPA would be wise to consult experienced counsel. In the event of a potential or actual lawsuit, the auditor should immediately seek an experienced attorney.
- *Choose a form of organization with limited liability.* As discussed in Chapter 2, many CPA firms now operate as professional corporations, limited liability companies, or limited liability partnerships in order to provide some personal liability protection to owners.
- *Exercise professional skepticism.* Auditors are often liable when they are presented with information indicating a problem that they fail to recognize. Auditors need to strive to maintain a healthy level of skepticism, one that keeps them alert to potential misstatements, so that they can recognize misstatements when they exist.

SUMMARY

This chapter provides insight into the environment in which CPAs operate by highlighting the significance of the legal liability facing the CPA profession. No reasonable CPA would want to eliminate the profession's legal responsibility for fraudulent or incompetent performance. It is certainly in the profession's best interest to maintain public trust in the competent performance of the auditing profession, while avoiding liability for cases involving strictly business failure and not audit failure. To more effectively avoid legal liability, CPAs need to have an adequate understanding of how they can be held liable to their clients or third parties. Knowledge about how CPAs are liable to clients under common law, to third parties under common law, to third parties under federal securities laws, and for criminal liability provides auditors an awareness of issues that may subject them to greater liability. CPAs can protect themselves from legal liability in numerous ways, and the profession has worked diligently to identify ways to help CPAs reduce the profession's potential exposure. Fortunately, recent litigation reform efforts have been successful that are designed to limit abusive securities class-action suits against CPAs. It is necessary for the profession and society to determine a reasonable trade-off between the degree of responsibility the auditor should take for fair presentation and the audit cost to society. CPAs, Congress, the SEC, and the courts will all continue to have a major influence in shaping the final solution.

ESSENTIAL TERMS

Absence of causal connection—an auditor's legal defense under which the auditor contends that the damages claimed by the client were not brought about by any act of the auditor

Audit failure—a situation in which the auditor issues an erroneous audit opinion as the result of an underlying failure to comply with the requirements of auditing standards

Audit risk—the risk that the auditor will conclude that the financial statements are fairly stated and an unqualified opinion can therefore be issued when, in fact, they are materially misstated

Business failure—the situation when a business is unable to repay its lenders or meet the expectations of its investors because of economic or business conditions

Contributory negligence—an auditor's legal defense under which the auditor claims that the client failed to perform certain obligations and that it is the client's failure to perform those obligations that brought about the claimed damages

Criminal liability for accountants—defrauding a person through knowing involvement with false financial statements

Foreign Corrupt Practices Act of 1977—a federal statute that makes it illegal to offer a bribe to an official of a foreign country for the purpose of exerting influence and obtaining or retaining business and that requires U.S. companies to maintain reasonably complete and accurate records and an adequate system of internal control

Foreseeable users—an unlimited class of users that the auditor should have reasonably been able to foresee as being likely users of financial statements

Foreseen user—a member of a limited class of users whom the auditor is aware will rely on the financial statements

Lack of duty to perform—an auditor's legal defense under which the auditor claims that no contract existed with the client; therefore, no duty existed to perform the disputed service

Legal liability—the professional's obligation under the law to provide a reasonable level of care while performing work for those served

Nonnegligent performance—an auditor's legal defense under which the auditor claims that the audit was performed in accordance with auditing standards

Private Securities Litigation Reform Act of 1995—a federal law passed in 1995 that significantly reduced potential damages in securities-related litigation

Prudent person concept—the legal concept that a person has a duty to exercise reasonable care and diligence in the performance of obligations to another

Racketeer Influenced and Corrupt Organization Act (RICO)—a 1970 federal statute designed to discourage fraud, extortion, and other racketeering activities, under which an injured party may recover treble damages and legal fees; in 1993 the Supreme Court ruled that CPA firms are ordinarily exempt from this statute

Securities Act of 1933—a federal statute dealing with companies that register and sell securities to the public; under the statute, third parties who are original purchasers of securities may recover damages from the auditor if the financial statements are misstated, unless the auditor proves that the audit was adequate or that the third party's loss was caused by factors other than misleading financial statements

Securities Exchange Act of 1934—a federal statute dealing with companies that trade securities on national and over-the-counter exchanges; auditors are involved because the annual reporting requirements include audited financial statements

***Ultramares* doctrine**—a common-law approach to third-party liability, established in 1931 in the case of *Ultramares Corporation* v. *Touche,* in which ordinary negligence is insufficient for liability to third parties because of the lack of *privity of contract* between the third party and the auditor, unless the third party is a *primary beneficiary*

REVIEW QUESTIONS

5-1 (Objective 5-1) State several factors that have affected the incidence of lawsuits against CPAs in recent years.

5-2 (Objective 5-1) Lawsuits against CPA firms have increased dramatically in the past decade. State your opinion of the positive and negative effects of the increased litigation on CPAs and on society as a whole.

5-3 (Objective 5-2) Distinguish between business failure and audit risk. Why is business failure a concern to auditors?

5-4 (Objective 5-3) How does the prudent person concept affect the liability of the auditor?

5-5 (Objective 5-3) Distinguish between "fraud" and "constructive fraud."

5-6 (Objectives 5-1, 5-8) Discuss why many CPA firms have willingly settled lawsuits out of court. What are the implications to the profession?

5-7 (Objective 5-4) A common type of lawsuit against CPAs is for the failure to detect a fraud. State the auditor's responsibility for such discovery. Give authoritative support for your answer.

5-8 (Objectives 5-3, 5-4) What is meant by contributory negligence? Under what conditions will this likely be a successful defense?

5-9 (Objective 5-4) Explain how an engagement letter might affect an auditor's liability to clients under common law.

5-10 (Objectives 5-4, 5-5) Compare and contrast traditional auditors' legal responsibilities to clients and third-party users under common law. How has that law changed in recent years?

5-11 (Objective 5-5) Is the auditor's liability affected if the third party was unknown rather than known? Explain.

5-12 (Objective 5-6) Contrast the auditor's liability under the Securities Act of 1933 with that under the Securities Exchange Act of 1934.

5-13 (Objectives 5-4, 5-5, 5-6, 5-7) Distinguish between the auditor's potential liability to the client, liability to third parties under common law, civil liability under the securities laws, and criminal liability. Describe one situation for each type of liability in which the auditor could be held legally responsible.

5-14 (Objective 5-6) What sanctions does the SEC have against a CPA firm?

5-15 (Objective 5-8) In what ways can the profession positively respond and reduce liability in auditing?

MULTIPLE CHOICE QUESTIONS FROM CPA EXAMINATIONS

5-16 (Objectives 5-4, 5-5) The following questions concern CPA firms' liability under common law. Choose the best response.

a. Sharp, CPA, was engaged by Peters & Sons, a partnership, to give an opinion on the financial statements that were to be submitted to several prospective partners as part of a planned expansion of the firm. Sharp's fee was fixed on a per diem basis. After a period of intensive work, Sharp completed about half of the necessary field work. Then, because of unanticipated demands on his time by other clients, Sharp was forced to abandon the work. The planned expansion of the firm failed to materialize because the prospective partners lost interest when the audit report was not promptly available. Sharp offered to complete the task at a later date. This offer was refused. Peters & Sons suffered damages of $400,000 as a result. Under the circumstances, what is the probable outcome of a lawsuit between Sharp and Peters & Sons?
   (1) Sharp will be compensated for the reasonable value of the services actually performed.
   (2) Peters & Sons will recover damages for breach of contract.
   (3) Peters & Sons will recover both punitive damages and damages for breach of contract.
   (4) Neither Sharp nor Peters & Sons will recover against the other.

b. Martin Corporation orally engaged Humm & Dawson to audit its year-end financial statements. The engagement was to be completed within 2 months after the close of Martin's fiscal year for a fixed fee of $75,000. Under these circumstances, what obligation is assumed by Humm & Dawson?
   (1) None. The contract is unenforceable because it is not in writing.
   (2) An implied promise to exercise reasonable standards of competence and care.
   (3) An implied obligation to take extraordinary steps to discover all defalcations.
   (4) The obligation of an insurer of its work, which is liable without fault.

c. If a CPA firm is being sued for common-law fraud by a third party based on materially false financial statements, which of the following is the best defense the accountants could assert?
   (1) Lack of privity.
   (2) Nonnegligent performance.
   (3) A disclaimer contained in the engagement letter.
   (4) Contributory negligence on the part of the client.

d. The *1136 Tenants* case was important chiefly because of its emphasis on the legal liability of the CPA when associated with
   (1) an SEC engagement.
   (2) unaudited financial statements.
   (3) an audit resulting in a disclaimer of opinion.
   (4) letters for underwriters.

5-17 (Objective 5-6) The following questions deal with liability under the 1933 and 1934 securities acts. Choose the best response.

a. Major, Major, & Sharpe, CPAs, are the auditors of MacLain Technologies. In connection with the public offering of $10 million of MacLain securities, Major expressed an unqualified opinion as to the financial statements. Subsequent to the offering, certain misstatements were revealed. Major has been sued by the purchasers of the stock offered pursuant to the registration statement that included the financial statements audited by Major. In the ensuing lawsuit by the MacLain investors, Major will be able to avoid liability if
   (1) the misstatements were caused primarily by MacLain.
   (2) it can be shown that at least some of the investors did *not* actually read the audited financial statements.

(3) it can prove due diligence in the audit of the financial statements of MacLain.

(4) MacLain had expressly assumed any liability in connection with the public offering.

b. Donalds & Company, CPAs, audited the financial statements included in the annual report submitted by Markum Securities, Inc. to the SEC. The audit was improper in several respects. Markum is now insolvent and unable to satisfy the claims of its customers. The customers have instituted legal action against Donalds based on Section 10b and Rule 10b-5 of the Securities Exchange Act of 1934. Which of the following is likely to be Donalds's best defense?

(1) They did *not* intentionally certify false financial statements.

(2) Section 10b does *not* apply to them.

(3) They were *not* in privity of contract with the creditors.

(4) Their engagement letter specifically disclaimed any liability to any party that resulted from Markum's fraudulent conduct.

c. Josephs & Paul is a growing, medium-sized partnership of CPAs. One of the firm's major clients is considering offering its stock to the public. This will be the firm's first client to go public. Which of the following is true with respect to this engagement?

(1) If the client is a service corporation, the Securities Act of 1933 will not apply.

(2) If the client is not going to be listed on an organized exchange, the Securities Exchange Act of 1934 will not apply.

(3) The Securities Act of 1933 imposes important additional potential liability on Josephs & Paul.

(4) As long as Josephs & Paul engages exclusively in intrastate business, the federal securities laws will not apply.

DISCUSSION QUESTIONS AND PROBLEMS

5-18 (Objectives 5-4, 5-5) Verna Cosden & Co., a medium-sized CPA firm, was engaged to audit Joslin Supply Company. Several staff were involved in the audit, all of whom had attended the firm's in-house training program on effective auditing methods. Throughout the audit, Cosden spent most of her time in the field planning the audit, supervising the staff, and reviewing their work.

A significant part of the audit entailed verifying the physical count, cost, and summarization of inventory. Inventory was highly significant to the financial statements, and Cosden knew the inventory was pledged as collateral for a large loan to East City National Bank. In reviewing Joslin's inventory count procedures, Cosden told the president she believed the method of counting inventory at different locations on different days was highly undesirable. The president stated that it was impractical to count all inventory on the same day because of personnel shortages and customer preference. After considerable discussion, Cosden agreed to permit the practice if the president would sign a statement that no other method was practical. The CPA firm had at least one person at each site to audit the inventory count procedures and actual count. There were more than 40 locations.

Eighteen months later, Cosden found out that the worst had happened. Management below the president's level had conspired to materially overstate inventory as a means of covering up obsolete inventory and inventory losses resulting from mismanagement. The misstatement occurred by physically transporting inventory at night to other locations after it had been counted in a given location. The accounting records were inadequate to uncover these illegal transfers.

Both Joslin Supply Company and East City National Bank sued Verna Cosden & Co.

Required

Answer the following questions, setting forth reasons for any conclusions stated:

a. What defense should Verna Cosden & Co. use in the suit by Joslin?

b. What defense should Verna Cosden & Co. use in the suit by East City National Bank?

c. Is Cosden likely to be successful in her defenses?

d. Would the issues or outcome be significantly different if the suit was brought under the Securities Exchange Act of 1934?

5-19 (Objective 5-5) The CPA firm of Bigelow, Barton, and Brown was expanding rapidly. Consequently, it hired several junior accountants, including a man named Small. The partners of the firm eventually became dissatisfied with Small's production and warned him they would be forced to discharge him unless his output increased significantly.

At that time, Small was engaged in audits of several clients. He decided that to avoid being fired, he would reduce or omit some of the standard auditing procedures listed in audit programs prepared by the partners. One of the CPA firm's clients, Newell Corporation, was in serious financial difficulty and had adjusted several of the accounts being audited by Small to appear financially sound. Small prepared fictitious audit documentation in his home at night to support purported completion of auditing procedures assigned to him, although he in fact did not examine the adjusting entries. The CPA firm rendered an unqualified opinion on Newell's financial statements, which were grossly misstated. Several creditors, relying on the audited financial statements, subsequently extended large sums of money to Newell Corporation.

Would the CPA firm be liable to the creditors who extended the money because of their reliance on the erroneous financial statements if Newell Corporation should fail to pay them? Explain.* **Required**

5-20 (Objectives 5-3, 5-5) Watts and Williams, a firm of CPAs, audited the accounts of Sampson Skins, Inc., a corporation that imports and deals in fine furs. Upon completion of the audit, the auditors supplied Sampson Skins with 20 copies of the audited financial statements. The firm knew in a general way that Sampson Skins wanted that number of copies of the auditor's report to furnish to banks and other potential lenders.

The balance sheet in question was misstated by approximately $800,000. Instead of having a $600,000 net worth, the corporation was insolvent. The management of Sampson Skins had doctored the books to avoid bankruptcy. The assets had been overstated by $500,000 of fictitious and nonexisting accounts receivable and $300,000 of nonexisting skins listed as inventory when in fact Sampson Skins had only empty boxes. The audit failed to detect these fraudulent entries. Martinson, relying on the audited financial statements, loaned Sampson Skins $200,000. He seeks to recover his loss from Watts and Williams.

State whether each of the following is true or false and give your reasons: **Required**

a. If Martinson alleges and proves negligence on the part of Watts and Williams, he will be able to recover his loss.

b. If Martinson alleges and proves constructive fraud (that is, gross negligence on the part of Watts and Williams), he will be able to recover his loss.

c. Martinson does not have a contract with Watts and Williams.

d. Unless actual fraud on the part of Watts and Williams could be shown, Martinson could not recover.

e. Martinson is a third-party beneficiary of the contract Watts and Williams made with Sampson Skins.*

5-21 (Objectives 5-4, 5-5, 5-7) Donald Sharpe recently joined the CPA firm of Spark, Watts, and Wilcox. He quickly established a reputation for thoroughness and a steadfast dedication to following prescribed auditing procedures to the letter. On his third audit for the firm, Sharpe examined the underlying documentation of 200 disbursements as a test of acquisitions, receiving, vouchers payable, and cash disbursement procedures. In the process, he found 12 disbursements for the acquisition of materials with no receiving reports in the documentation. He noted the exceptions in his working papers and called them to the attention of the in-charge accountant. Relying on prior experience with the client, the in-charge accountant disregarded Sharpe's comments, and nothing further was done about the exceptions.

Subsequently, it was learned that one of the client's purchasing agents and a member of its accounting department were engaged in a fraudulent scheme whereby they diverted the receipt of materials to a public warehouse while sending the invoices to the client. When the client discovered the fraud, the conspirators had obtained approximately $70,000, $50,000 of which was recovered after the completion of the audit.

Discuss the legal implications and liabilities to Spark, Watts, and Wilcox as a result of the facts just described.* **Required**

5-22 (Objectives 5-3, 5-4, 5-5) In confirming accounts receivable on December 31, 2005, the auditor found 15 discrepancies between the customers' records and the recorded amounts in the accounts receivable master file. A copy of all confirmations that had exceptions was turned over to the company controller to investigate the reason for the difference. He, in turn, had the bookkeeper perform the analysis. The bookkeeper analyzed each exception, determined its cause, and prepared an elaborate spreadsheet explaining each difference. Most of the differences in the bookkeeper's report indicated that the exceptions were caused by timing differences in the client's and customer's records. The auditor reviewed the spreadsheet and concluded that there were no material exceptions in accounts receivable.

Two years subsequent to the audit, it was determined that the bookkeeper had stolen thousands of dollars in the past 3 years by taking cash and overstating accounts receivable. In a lawsuit by the client against the CPA, an examination of the auditor's December 31, 2005, accounts receivable working papers, which were subpoenaed by the court, indicated that one of the explanations in the bookkeeper's analysis of the exceptions was fictitious. The analysis stated the exception was caused by a sales allowance granted to the customer for defective merchandise the day before the end of the year. The difference was actually caused by the bookkeeper's theft.

*AICPA adapted.

Required a. What are the legal issues involved in this situation? What should the auditor use as a defense in the event that he is sued?

b. What was the CPA's deficiency in conducting the audit of accounts receivable?

5-23 (Objectives 5-4, 5-5, 5-7) Smith, CPA, is the auditor for Juniper Manufacturing Corporation, a privately owned company that has a June 30 fiscal year. Juniper arranged for a substantial bank loan that was dependent on the bank's receiving, by September 30, audited financial statements that showed a current ratio of at least 2 to 1. On September 25, just before the audit report was to be issued, Smith received an anonymous letter on Juniper's stationery indicating that a 5-year lease by Juniper, as lessee, of a factory building accounted for in the financial statements as an operating lease was, in fact, a capital lease. The letter stated that there was a secret written agreement with the lessor modifying the lease and creating a capital lease.

Smith confronted the president of Juniper, who admitted that a secret agreement existed but said it was necessary to treat the lease as an operating lease to meet the current ratio requirement of the pending loan and that nobody would ever discover the secret agreement with the lessor. The president said that if Smith did not issue his report by September 30, Juniper would sue Smith for substantial damages that would result from not getting the loan. Under this pressure and because the audit files contained a copy of the 5-year lease agreement that supported the operating lease treatment, Smith issued his report with an unqualified opinion on September 29.

Despite the fact that the loan was received, Juniper went bankrupt within 2 years. The bank is suing Smith to recover its losses on the loan, and the lessor is suing Smith to recover uncollected rents.

Required Answer the following questions, setting forth reasons for any conclusions stated:

a. Is Smith liable to the bank?

b. Is Smith liable to the lessor?

c. Is there potential for criminal action against Smith?*

5-24 (Objective 5-4) Ward & East, CPAs, were the auditors of Southern Development, Inc., a real estate company that owned several shopping centers. It was Southern's practice to let each shopping center manager negotiate that center's leases; they thought that such an arrangement resulted in much better leases because a local person did the negotiating.

Two of the center managers were killed in a plane accident returning home from a company meeting at the head office in Phoenix. In both cases, the new managers appointed to take their places discovered kickback schemes in operation; the managers had negotiated lower rents than normal in return for kickbacks from the tenants.

Southern brought in a new CPA firm, Jasper & Co., to investigate the extent of the fraud at those two locations and the possibility of similar frauds at other centers. Jasper & Co. completed their investigation and found that four locations were involved quite independently of each other and that the total loss over 5 years was more than $1 million. Southern sued Ward & East for negligence for $1 million plus interest.

Required What defense would Ward & East use? What would they have to prove?

5-25 (Objective 5-6) Gordon & Groton, CPAs, were the auditors of Bank & Company, a brokerage firm and member of a national stock exchange. Gordon & Groton audited and reported on the financial statements of Bank, which were filed with the Securities and Exchange Commission.

Several of Bank's customers were swindled by a fraudulent scheme perpetrated by Bank's president, who owned 90% of the voting stock of the company. The facts establish that Gordon & Groton were negligent but not reckless or grossly negligent in the conduct of the audit, and neither participated in the fraudulent scheme or knew of its existence.

The customers are suing Gordon & Groton under the antifraud provisions of Section 10b and Rule 10b-5 of the Securities Exchange Act of 1934 for aiding and abetting the fraudulent scheme of the president. The customers' suit for fraud is predicated exclusively on the nonfeasance of the auditors in failing to conduct a proper audit, thereby failing to discover the fraudulent scheme.

Required Answer the following questions, setting forth reasons for any conclusions stated:

a. What is the probable outcome of the lawsuit?

b. What other theory of liability might the customers have asserted?*

5-26 (Objective 5-5) Sarah Robertson, CPA, had been the auditor of Majestic Co. for several years. As she and her staff prepared for the audit for the year ended December 31, 2004, Herb Majestic told her that he needed a large bank loan to "tide him over" until sales picked up as expected in late 2005.

In the course of the audit, Robertson discovered that the financial situation at Majestic was worse than Majestic had revealed and that the company was technically bankrupt. She discussed the

*AICPA adapted.

situation with Majestic, who pointed out that the bank loan would "be his solution"—he was sure he would get it as long as the financial statements didn't look too bad.

Robertson stated that she believed the statements would have to include a going concern note. Majestic said that such a note really wasn't needed because the bank loan was so certain and that inclusion of such a note would certainly cause the management of the bank to change its mind about the loan.

Robertson finally acquiesced and the audited statements were issued without the note. The company received the loan, but things did not improve as Majestic thought they would and the company filed for bankruptcy in August 2005.

The bank sued Sarah Robertson for fraud.

Indicate whether or not you think the bank would succeed. Support your answer.   **Required**

CASE

5-27 (**Objectives 5-5, 5-6**) *Part 1.* Whitlow & Company is a brokerage firm registered under the Securities Exchange Act of 1934. The act requires such a brokerage firm to file audited financial statements with the SEC annually. Mitchell & Moss, Whitlow's CPAs, performed the annual audit for the year ended December 31, 2005, and rendered an unqualified opinion, which was filed with the SEC along with Whitlow's financial statements. During 2005, Charles, the president of Whitlow & Company, engaged in a huge embezzlement scheme that eventually bankrupted the firm. As a result, substantial losses were suffered by customers and shareholders of Whitlow & Company, including Thaxton, who had recently purchased several shares of stock of Whitlow & Company after reviewing the company's 2005 audit report. Mitchell & Moss's audit was deficient; if they had complied with GAAS, the embezzlement would have been discovered. However, Mitchell & Moss had no knowledge of the embezzlement, nor could their conduct be categorized as reckless.

Answer the following questions, setting forth reasons for any conclusions stated: **Required**

a. What liability to Thaxton, if any, does Mitchell & Moss have under the Securities Exchange Act of 1934?

b. What theory or theories of liability, if any, are available to Whitlow & Company's customers and shareholders under common law?

Part 2. Jackson is a sophisticated investor. As such, she was initially a member of a small group that was going to participate in a private placement of $1 million of common stock of Clarion Corporation. Numerous meetings were held between management and the investor group. Detailed financial and other information was supplied to the participants. Upon the eve of completion of the placement, it was aborted when one major investor withdrew. Clarion then decided to offer $2.5 million of Clarion common stock to the public pursuant to the registration requirements of the Securities Act of 1933. Jackson subscribed to $300,000 of the Clarion public stock offering. Nine months later, Clarion's earnings dropped significantly, and as a result, the stock dropped 20% beneath the offering price. In addition, the Dow Jones Industrial Average was down 10% from the time of the offering.

Jackson has sold her shares at a loss of $60,000 and seeks to hold all parties liable who participated in the public offering, including Clarion's CPA firm of Allen, Dunn, and Rose. Although the audit was performed in conformity with GAAS, there were some relatively minor misstatements. The financial statements of Clarion Corporation, which were part of the registration statement, contained minor misleading facts. It is believed by Clarion and Allen, Dunn, and Rose that Jackson's asserted claim is without merit.

Answer the following questions, setting forth reasons for any conclusions stated: **Required**

a. If Jackson sues under the Securities Act of 1933, what will be the basis of her claim?

b. What are the probable defenses that might be asserted by Allen, Dunn, and Rose in light of these facts?*

INTERNET PROBLEM 5-1: SEC ENFORCEMENT

Reference the CW site. The SEC's Enforcement Division posts Litigation Releases, which are descriptions of SEC civil and selected criminal suits in the federal courts proceedings. This problem requires students to use the Internet to look up and answer questions associated with litigation releases.

*AICPA adapted.

PART 2 CHAPTERS 6 – 13

THE AUDIT PROCESS

Part 2 presents the audit process in a manner that will enable you to apply the concepts developed in these chapters to any audit area. It is essential to understand the material in these chapters because the information will be used extensively in almost all chapters throughout the rest of the book. We also highlight the importance of audit planning.

 Chapters 6 and 7 deal with auditors' and managements' responsibilities, audit objectives, and general concepts of evidence accumulation. The next five chapters study various aspects of audit planning in depth, including auditors' responsibility for detecting fraud. Chapter 13 summarizes and integrates audit planning and audit evidence. You will use these planning concepts throughout the rest of the book.

Many of the concepts throughout the remainder of the book are illustrated with examples based on the Hillsburg Hardware Company. The financial statements and other information from the company's annual report are included in the glossy insert material to the textbook.

CHAPTER 6

AUDIT RESPONSIBILITIES AND OBJECTIVES

WHERE WERE THE AUDITORS?

Barry Minkow was a true "whiz kid." He started ZZZZ Best Company, a high-flying carpet cleaning company specializing in insurance restoration contracts, at the age of 16. In 1982, when Minkow started the business, it was run out of his garage, but a mere 5 years later he had taken the company public and it had sales of $50 million and earnings of more than $5 million. The market value of Minkow's stock in ZZZZ Best exceeded $100 million.

As it turned out, Minkow's genius lay not in business but in deception. Instead of being a solid operation company, ZZZZ Best was an illusion. There were no large restoration jobs and no real revenues and profits. They were only on paper and supported by an effective network of methods to deceive shareholders, the SEC, and the reputable professionals who served the company, including its auditors. Many, including members of Congress, asked, "How could this happen? Where were the auditors?"

When ZZZZ Best first started to grow, Minkow ran into the common problem of needing credit. He devised a scheme with an insurance adjuster to validate nonexistent jobs to potential creditors. Minkow could then get large sums of cash or credit despite not doing any real work. The scam was broadened when ZZZZ Best started needing audits. To fool the auditors, the coconspirator insurance adjuster was kept busy running a company that generated false contracts for ZZZZ Best. When the auditors tried to check on those contracts, the adjuster confirmed them. Minkow even went so far as taking auditors to real work sites, sites that weren't actually his. He even leased a partially completed building and hired subcontractors to perform work on the site, all for the sake of a visit by the auditors.

As incredible as the ZZZZ Best story may seem, when asked about it, most knowledgeable observers would answer: "It's not the first time, and it won't be the last." It is also not the last time people will ask, "Where were the auditors?"

LEARNING OBJECTIVES

After studying this chapter, you should be able to

6-1 Explain the objective of conducting an audit of financial statements and an audit of internal controls.

6-2 Distinguish management's responsibility for the financial statements and internal control from the auditor's responsibility for verifying the financial statements and effectiveness of internal control.

6-3 Explain the auditor's responsibility for discovering material misstatements.

6-4 Classify transactions and account balances into financial statement cycles and identify benefits of a cycle approach to segmenting the audit.

6-5 Describe why the auditor obtains a combination of assurance by auditing classes of transactions and ending balances in accounts.

6-6 Distinguish among the five categories of management assertions about financial information.

6-7 Link the six general transaction-related audit objectives to the five management assertions.

6-8 Link the nine general balance-related audit objectives to the five management assertions.

6-9 Explain the relationship between audit objectives and the accumulation of audit evidence.

Before beginning the study of how to conduct an audit, it is necessary to understand the overall objectives of the audit, the auditor's responsibilities in conducting the audit, and the specific objectives the auditor tries to accomplish. Without an understanding of these topics, planning and accumulating audit evidence during the audit has no relevance. Figure 6-1 summarizes the five topics that provide keys to understanding evidence accumulation. These are the steps used to develop specific audit objectives.

OBJECTIVE OF CONDUCTING AN AUDIT OF FINANCIAL STATEMENTS

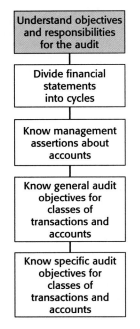

OBJECTIVE 6-1

Explain the objective of conducting an audit of financial statements and an audit of internal controls.

SAS 1 (AU 110) states

> The objective of the ordinary audit of financial statements by the independent auditor is the expression of an opinion on the fairness with which they present fairly, in all material respects, financial position, results of operations, and its cash flows in conformity with generally accepted accounting principles.

That section of the SAS emphasizes issuing an opinion on *financial statements,* which is our primary focus. For public companies, the auditor also issues a report on internal control as required by Section 404 of the Sarbanes–Oxley Act. Auditors accumulate evidence to allow them to reach conclusions about whether the financial statements are fairly stated and the effectiveness of internal control, and they issue the appropriate audit report.

When, on the basis of adequate evidence, the auditor concludes that the financial statements are unlikely to mislead a prudent user, the auditor gives an audit opinion on their fair presentation and associates his or her name with the statements. If facts subsequent to their issuance indicate that the statements were actually not fairly presented, the auditor is likely to have to demonstrate to the courts or regulatory agencies that he or she conducted the audit in a proper manner and drew reasonable conclusions. Although not an insurer or a guarantor of the fairness of the presentations in the statements, the auditor has considerable responsibility for notifying users whether the

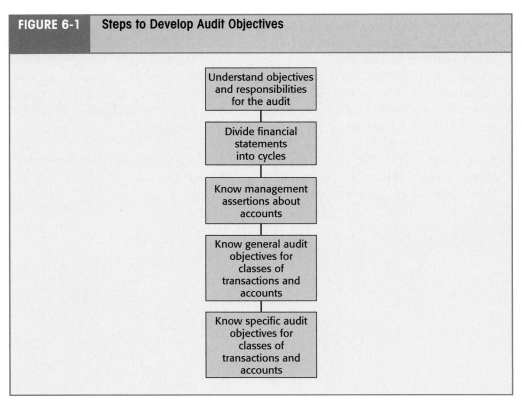

FIGURE 6-1   Steps to Develop Audit Objectives

statements are properly stated. If the auditor believes that the statements are not fairly presented or is unable to reach a conclusion because of insufficient evidence or prevailing conditions, the auditor has the responsibility of notifying the users through the auditor's report.

MANAGEMENT'S RESPONSIBILITIES

The responsibility for adopting sound accounting policies, maintaining adequate internal control, and making fair representations in the financial statements *rests with management* rather than with the auditor. Because they operate the business daily, a company's management knows more about the company's transactions and related assets, liabilities, and equity than the auditor does. In contrast, the auditor's knowledge of these matters and internal control is limited to that acquired during the audit.

In recent years, the annual reports of many public companies have included a statement about management's responsibilities and relationship with the CPA firm. Figure 6-2

FIGURE 6-2	The Boeing Company's Report of Management

2003 ANNUAL REPORT

REPORT OF MANAGEMENT

To the Shareholders of The Boeing Company:

The accompanying consolidated financial statements of The Boeing Company and subsidiaries have been prepared by management who are responsible for their integrity and objectivity. The statements have been prepared in conformity with accounting principles generally accepted in the United States of America and include amounts based on management's best estimates and judgments. Financial information elsewhere in this Annual Report is consistent with that in the financial statements.

Management has established and maintains a system of internal control designed to provide reasonable assurance that errors or fraud that could be material to the financial statements are prevented or would be detected within a timely period. In addition, management has also established and maintains a system of disclosure controls designed to provide reasonable assurance that information required to be disclosed is accumulated and reported in an accurate and timely manner. The systems of internal control and disclosure control include widely communicated statements of policies and business practices that are designed to require all employees to maintain high ethical standards in the conduct of Company affairs. The internal controls and disclosure controls are augmented by organizational arrangements that provide for appropriate delegation of authority and division of responsibility and by a program of internal audit with management follow-up.

The financial statements have been audited by Deloitte & Touche LLP, independent certified public accountants. Their audit was conducted in accordance with auditing standards generally accepted in the United States of America and included a review of internal controls and selective tests of transactions. The Independent Auditors' Report appears in this report.

The Audit Committee of the Board of Directors, composed entirely of outside directors, meets periodically with the independent certified public accountants, management and internal auditors to review accounting, auditing, internal accounting controls, litigation and financial reporting matters. The independent certified public accountants and the internal auditors have free access to this committee without management present.

Harry C. Stonecipher
President and
Chief Executive Officer

James A. Bell
Executive Vice President
and Chief Financial Officer

Harry S. McGee
Vice President of Finance
and Corporate Controller

presents a report of management for the Boeing Company as a part of its annual report. Read the report carefully to determine what management states about its responsibilities.

Management's responsibility for the fairness of the representations (assertions) in the financial statements carries with it the privilege of determining which disclosures it considers necessary. Although management has the responsibility for the preparation of the financial statements and the accompanying footnotes, it is acceptable for an auditor to draft the financial statements for the client or to offer suggestions for clarification. In the event that management insists on financial statement disclosure that the auditor finds unacceptable, the auditor can either issue an adverse or qualified opinion or withdraw from the engagement.

The Sarbanes–Oxley Act increases management's responsibility for the financial statements by requiring the chief executive officer (CEO) and the chief financial officer (CFO) of public companies to certify the quarterly and annual financial statements submitted to the SEC. In signing those statements, management certifies that the financial statements fully comply with the requirements of the Securities Exchange Act of 1934 and that the information contained in the report fairly presents, in all material respects, the financial condition and results of operations. The Sarbanes–Oxley Act provides for criminal penalties, including significant monetary fines or imprisonment up to 20 years, for anyone who knowingly falsely certifies those statements.

AUDITOR'S RESPONSIBILITIES

OBJECTIVE 6-3

Explain the auditor's responsibility for discovering material misstatements.

SAS 1 (AU 110) states

> The auditor has a responsibility to plan and perform the audit to obtain reasonable assurance about whether the financial statements are free of material misstatement, whether caused by error or fraud. Because of the nature of audit evidence and the characteristics of fraud, the auditor is able to obtain reasonable, but not absolute, assurance that material misstatements are detected. The auditor has no responsibility to plan and perform the audit to obtain reasonable assurance that misstatements, whether caused by errors or fraud, that are not material to the financial statements are detected.

This paragraph discusses the auditor's responsibility for detecting material misstatements in the financial statements. When the auditor also reports on the effectiveness of internal control over financial reporting, the auditor is also responsible for identifying material weaknesses in internal control. The auditor's responsibilities for audits of internal control are discussed in Chapter 10.

This paragraph and the related discussion in the standards about the auditor's responsibility to detect material misstatements include several important terms and phrases.

Material Versus Immaterial Misstatements Misstatements are usually considered material if the combined uncorrected errors and fraud in the financial statements would likely have changed or influenced the decisions of a reasonable person using the statements. Although it is extremely difficult to quantify a measure of materiality, auditors are responsible for obtaining reasonable assurance that this materiality threshold has been satisfied. It would be extremely costly (and probably impossible) for auditors to have responsibility for finding all immaterial errors and fraud.

Objectives of Financial
Statement Audits

Reasonable Assurance Assurance is a measure of the level of certainty that the auditor has obtained at the completion of the audit. Reasonable assurance is not defined in the literature, but it is presumably less than certainty or absolute assurance and more than a low level of assurance. The concept of reasonable, but not absolute, assurance indicates that the auditor is not an insurer or guarantor of the correctness of the financial statements.

There are several reasons why the auditor is responsible for reasonable but not absolute assurance. First, most audit evidence results from testing a sample of a population such as accounts receivable or inventory. Sampling inevitably includes some risk of not uncovering a material misstatement. Also, the areas to be tested; the type, extent, and timing of those tests; and the evaluation of test results require significant auditor judgment. Even with good faith and integrity, auditors can make mistakes and errors in judgment. Second, accounting presentations contain complex estimates, which inherently involve uncertainty and can be affected by future events. As a result, the auditor has to rely on evidence that is persuasive, but not convincing. Third, fraudulently prepared financial statements are often extremely difficult, if not impossible, for the auditor to detect, especially when there is collusion among management.

If the auditor was responsible for making certain that all the assertions in the statements were correct, evidence requirements and the resulting cost of the audit function would increase to such an extent that audits would not be economically practical. Even then, auditors would be unlikely to uncover all material misstatements in every audit. The auditor's best defense when material misstatements are not uncovered in the audit is that the audit was conducted in accordance with auditing standards.

Errors Versus Fraud SAS 99 (AU 316) distinguishes between two types of misstatements: errors and fraud. Either type of misstatement can be material or immaterial. An **error** is an *unintentional* misstatement of the financial statements, whereas **fraud** is *intentional*. Two examples of errors are a mistake in extending prices times quantity on a sales invoice and overlooking older raw materials in determining the lower of cost or market for inventory.

For fraud, there is a distinction between **misappropriation of assets,** often called defalcation or employee fraud, and **fraudulent financial reporting,** often called management fraud. An example of misappropriation of assets is a clerk taking cash at the time a sale is made and not entering the sale in the cash register. An example of fraudulent financial reporting is the intentional overstatement of sales near the balance sheet date to increase reported earnings.

Professional Skepticism SAS 1 (AU 230) requires that an audit be designed to provide reasonable assurance of detecting *both* material errors and fraud in the financial statements. To accomplish this, the audit must be planned and performed with an *attitude of professional skepticism* in all aspects of the engagement. Professional skepticism is an attitude that includes a questioning mind and a critical assessment of audit evidence. The auditor should not assume that management is dishonest, but the possibility of dishonesty must be considered. The auditor also should not assume that management is unquestionably honest.

Auditors spend a great portion of their time planning and performing audits to detect the unintentional mistakes made by management and employees. Auditors find a variety of errors resulting from such things as mistakes in calculations, omissions, misunderstanding and misapplication of accounting standards, and incorrect summarizations and descriptions. Most of the remainder of this book deals with how the auditor plans and performs audits for detecting both errors and fraud.

Auditor's Responsibilities for Detecting Material Errors

Auditor's Responsibilities for Detecting Material Fraud

Auditing standards make no distinction between the auditor's responsibilities for searching for errors and fraud, whether from fraudulent financial reporting or misappropriation of assets. For both errors and fraud, the auditor must obtain reasonable assurance about whether the statements are free of material misstatements.

The standards also recognize that it is often more difficult to detect fraud than errors because management or the employees perpetrating the fraud *attempt to conceal the fraud.* The difficulty of detection does not change the auditor's responsibility to properly plan and perform the audit.

AICPA Antifraud & Corporate Responsibility Resource Center

Fraud Resulting from Fraudulent Financial Reporting Versus Misappropriation of Assets There is an important difference between fraudulent financial reporting and misappropriation of assets. Fraudulent financial reporting harms users by providing incorrect financial statement information for their decision making. When assets are misappropriated, stockholders, creditors, and others are harmed because assets are no longer available to their rightful owners. Both types of fraud are potentially harmful to users.

Typically, fraudulent financial reporting is committed by management, sometimes without the knowledge of employees. Management is in a position to make accounting and reporting decisions without employees' knowledge. An example is the decision to omit an important footnote about pending litigation.

Usually, but not always, theft of assets is perpetrated by employees and not by management, and the amounts are often immaterial. However, there are well-known examples of extremely material misappropriation of assets by employees and management.

An important concept for misappropriation of assets is the distinction between the theft of assets and misstatements arising from the theft of assets. To illustrate, following are three situations involving the theft of assets:

1. Assets were taken and the theft was covered by overstating assets. For example, cash collected from a customer was stolen, and the account receivable for the customer's account was not credited. The misstatement has not been discovered.
2. Assets were taken and the theft was covered by understating revenues or overstating expenses. For example, cash from a cash sale was stolen, and the transaction was not recorded. The misstatement has not been discovered.
3. Assets were taken, but the misappropriation was discovered. The income statement and related footnotes clearly describe the misappropriation.

In all three situations, there has been a misappropriation of assets, but the financial statements are misstated only in situations 1 and 2. In situation 1, the balance sheet is misstated, whereas in situation 2, revenues or expenses are misstated.

Auditor's Responsibilities for Discovering Illegal Acts

Illegal acts are defined in SAS 54 (AU 317) as violations of laws or government regulations *other than fraud.* Two examples of illegal acts are a violation of federal tax laws and a violation of the federal environmental protection laws.

Direct-Effect Illegal Acts Certain violations of laws and regulations have a direct financial effect on specific account balances in the financial statements. For example, a violation of federal tax laws directly affects income tax expense and income taxes payable. The auditor's responsibilities under SAS 54 for these direct-effect illegal acts is the same as for errors and fraud. On each audit, therefore, the auditor will normally evaluate whether or not there is evidence available to indicate material violations of federal or state tax laws. This might be done by discussions with client personnel and examination of reports issued by the Internal Revenue Service after they have completed an examination of the client's tax return.

Indirect-Effect Illegal Acts Most illegal acts affect the financial statements only indirectly. For example, if the company violates environmental protection laws, there is an effect on the financial statements only if there is a fine or sanction. Potential material fines and sanctions indirectly affect financial statements by creating the need to disclose a contingent liability for the potential amount that might ultimately be paid. This is called an indirect-effect illegal act. Other examples of illegal acts that are likely to have only an indirect effect are violations of insider securities trading regulations, civil rights laws, and federal employee safety requirements.

Auditing standards clearly state that the auditor provides *no assurance* that indirect-effect illegal acts will be detected. Auditors lack legal expertise, and the frequent indirect relationship between illegal acts and the financial statements makes it impractical for auditors to assume responsibility for discovering those illegal acts.

There are three levels of responsibility that the auditor has for finding and reporting illegal acts.

Evidence Accumulation When There Is No Reason to Believe Indirect-Effect Illegal Acts Exist Many audit procedures normally performed on audits to search for errors and fraud may also uncover illegal acts. Examples include reading the minutes of the board of directors and inquiring of the client's attorneys about litigation. The auditor should also inquire of management about policies they have established to prevent illegal acts and whether management knows of any laws or regulations that the company has violated. Other than these procedures, the auditor should not search for indirect-effect illegal acts unless there is reason to believe they may exist.

Evidence Accumulation and Other Actions When There Is Reason to Believe Direct- or Indirect-Effect Illegal Acts May Exist The auditor may find indications of possible illegal acts in a variety of ways. For example, the minutes may indicate that an investigation by a government agency is in process or the auditor may have identified unusually large payments to consultants or government officials.

When the auditor believes that an illegal act may have occurred, it is necessary to take several actions: First, the auditor should inquire of management at a level above those likely to be involved in the potential illegal act. Second, the auditor should consult with the client's legal counsel or other specialist who is knowledgeable about the potential illegal act. Third, the auditor should consider accumulating additional evidence to determine whether there actually is an illegal act. All three of these actions are intended to provide the auditor with information about whether the suspected illegal act actually exists.

Actions When the Auditor Knows of an Illegal Act The first course of action when an illegal act has been identified is to consider the effects on the financial statements, including the adequacy of disclosures. These effects may be complex and difficult to resolve. For example, a violation of civil rights laws could involve significant fines, but it could also result in the loss of customers or key employees, which could materially affect future revenues and expenses. If the auditor concludes that the disclosures relative to an illegal act are inadequate, the auditor should modify the audit report accordingly.

The auditor should also consider the effect of such illegal acts on its relationship with management. If management knew of the illegal act and failed to inform the auditor, it is questionable whether management can be believed in other discussions.

The auditor should communicate with the audit committee or others of equivalent authority to make sure that they know of the illegal act. The communication can be oral or written. If it is oral, the nature of the communication and discussion should be documented in the audit files. If the client either refuses to accept the auditor's modified report or fails to take appropriate remedial action concerning the illegal act, the auditor may find it necessary to withdraw from the engagement. If the client is publicly held, the auditor must also report the matter directly to the SEC. Such decisions are complex and normally involve consultation by the auditor with the auditor's legal counsel.

FINANCIAL STATEMENT CYCLES

Audits are performed by dividing the financial statements into smaller segments or components. The division makes the audit more manageable and aids in the assignment of tasks to different members of the audit team. For example, most auditors treat fixed assets and notes payable as different segments. Each segment is audited separately but not on a completely independent basis. (For example, the audit of fixed assets may reveal an unrecorded note payable.) After the audit of each segment is completed, including

OBJECTIVE 6-4

Classify transactions and account balances into financial statement cycles and identify benefits of a cycle approach to segmenting the audit.

interrelationships with other segments, the results are combined. A conclusion can then be reached about the financial statements taken as a whole.

There are different ways of segmenting an audit. One approach would be to treat every account balance on the statements as a separate segment. Segmenting that way is usually inefficient. It would result in the independent audit of such closely related accounts as inventory and cost of goods sold.

Cycle Approach to Segmenting an Audit

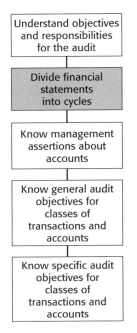

A more common way to divide an audit is to keep closely related types (or classes) of transactions and account balances in the same segment. This is called the **cycle approach.** For example, sales, sales returns, cash receipts, and charge-offs of uncollectible accounts are the four classes of transactions that cause accounts receivable to increase and decrease. Therefore, they are all part of the sales and collection cycle. Similarly, payroll transactions and accrued payroll are a part of the payroll and personnel cycle.

The logic of using the cycle approach can be seen by thinking about the way transactions are recorded in journals and summarized in the general ledger and financial statements. Figure 6-3 shows that flow. To the extent that it is practical, the cycle approach combines transactions recorded in different journals with the general ledger balances that result from those transactions.

The cycles used in this text follow and are then explained in detail. Observe that each of these cycles is so important that it is part of the title of one or more chapters in the remainder of this book:

• Sales and collection cycle
• Acquisition and payment cycle
• Payroll and personnel cycle
• Inventory and warehousing cycle
• Capital acquisition and repayment cycle

To illustrate the application of cycles to audits, Figure 6-4 presents the December 31, 2004, trial balance for Hillsburg Hardware Company. The financial statements prepared from this trial balance are included in the glossy insert to the textbook. Prior-year figures

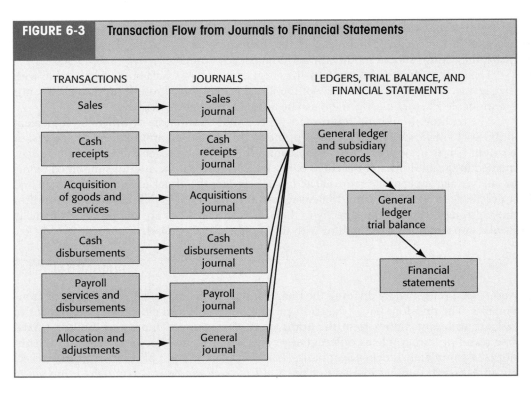

FIGURE 6-3 Transaction Flow from Journals to Financial Statements

FIGURE 6-4   Hillsburg Hardware Co. Adjusted Trial Balance

HILLSBURG HARDWARE CO.
TRIAL BALANCE
December 31, 2004

		Debit	Credit
S,A,P,C	Cash in bank	$ 827,568	
S	Trade accounts receivable	20,196,800	
S	Allowance for uncollectible accounts		$ 1,240,000
S	Other accounts receivable	945,020	
A,I	Inventories	29,864,621	
A	Prepaid expenses	431,558	
A	Land	3,456,420	
A	Buildings	32,500,000	
A	Computer and other equipment	3,758,347	
A	Furniture and fixtures	2,546,421	
A	Accumulated depreciation		31,920,126
A	Trade accounts payable		4,719,989
C	Notes payable		4,179,620
P	Accrued payroll		1,349,800
P	Accrued payroll taxes		119,663
C	Accrued interest		149,560
C	Dividends payable		1,900,000
A	Accrued income tax		795,442
C	Long-term notes payable		24,120,000
A	Deferred tax		738,240
A	Other accrued payables		829,989
C	Capital stock		5,000,000
C	Capital in excess of par value		3,500,000
C	Retained earnings		11,929,075
S	Sales		144,327,789
S	Sales returns and allowances	1,241,663	
I	Cost of goods sold	103,240,768	
P	Salaries and commissions	7,738,900	
P	Sales payroll taxes	1,422,100	
A	Travel and entertainment—selling	1,110,347	
A	Advertising	2,611,263	
A	Sales and promotional literature	321,620	
A	Sales meetings and training	924,480	
A	Miscellaneous sales expense	681,041	
P	Executive and office salaries	5,523,960	
P	Administrative payroll taxes	682,315	
A	Travel and entertainment—administrative	561,680	
A	Computer maintenance and supplies	860,260	
A	Stationery and supplies	762,568	
A	Postage	244,420	
A	Telephone and fax	722,315	
A	Rent	312,140	
A	Legal fees and retainers	383,060	
A	Auditing and related services	302,840	
A	Depreciation	1,452,080	
S	Bad debt expense	3,323,084	
A	Insurance	722,684	
A	Office repairs and maintenance	843,926	
A	Miscellaneous office expense	643,680	
A	Miscellaneous general expense	323,842	
A	Gain on sale of assets		719,740
A	Income taxes	1,746,600	
C	Interest expense	2,408,642	
C	Dividends	1,900,000	
		$237,539,033	$237,539,033

Note: Letters in the left-hand column refer to the following transaction cycles:

S = Sales and collection   *I* = Inventory and warehousing
A = Acquisition and payment   *C* = Capital acquisition and repayment
P = Payroll and personnel

usually included for comparative purposes are excluded from Figure 6-4 in order to focus on transaction cycles. A trial balance is used to prepare financial statements and is a primary focus of every audit. The letter representing a cycle is shown for each account in the left column beside the account name. Observe that each account has at least one cycle associated with it, and only cash and inventory are a part of two or more cycles.

The cycles used in this text are shown again in Table 6-1. The accounts for Hillsburg Hardware Co. are summarized in Table 6-1 by cycle, and include the related journals and financial statements in which the accounts appear. The observations on the following page expand the information contained in Table 6-1.

TABLE 6-1	Cycles Applied to Hillsburg Hardware Co.		
Cycle	**Journals Included in the Cycle (See Figure 6-3)**	**General Ledger Accounts Included in the Cycle (See Figure 6-4)**	
		Balance Sheet	**Income Statement**
Sales and collection	Sales journal Cash receipts journal General journal	Cash in bank Trade accounts receivable Other accounts receivable Allowance for uncollectible accounts	Sales Sales returns and allowances Bad debt expense
Acquisition and payment	Acquisitions journal Cash disbursements journal General journal	Cash in bank Inventories Prepaid expenses Land Buildings Computer and other equipment Furniture and fixtures Accumulated depreciation Trade accounts payable Other accrued payables Accrued income tax Deferred tax	Advertising^S Travel and entertainment^S Sales meetings and training^S Sales and promotional literature^S Miscellaneous sales expense^S Travel and entertainment^A Stationery and supplies^A Postage^A Telephone and fax^A Computer maintenance and supplies^A Depreciation^A Rent^A Legal fees and retainers^A Auditing and related services^A Insurance^A Office repairs and maintenance expense^A Miscellaneous office expense^A Miscellaneous general expense^A Gain on sale of assets Income taxes
Payroll and personnel	Payroll journal General journal	Cash in bank Accrued payroll Accrued payroll taxes	Salaries and commissions^S Sales payroll taxes^S Executive and office salaries^A Administrative payroll taxes^A
Inventory and warehousing	Acquisitions journal Sales journal General journal	Inventories	Cost of goods sold
Capital acquisition and repayment	Acquisitions journal Cash disbursements journal General journal	Cash in bank Notes payable Long-term notes payable Accrued interest Capital stock Capital in excess of par value Retained earnings Dividends Dividends payable	Interest expense

S = Selling expense; A = general and administrative expense.

- All general ledger accounts and journals for Hillsburg Hardware Co. are included at least once. For a different company, the number and titles of journals and general ledger accounts would differ, but all would be included.
- Some journals and general ledger accounts are included in more than one cycle. When that occurs, it means that the journal is used to record transactions from more than one cycle and indicates a tie-in between the cycles. The most important general ledger account included in and affecting several cycles is general cash (cash in bank). General cash connects most cycles.
- The capital acquisition and repayment cycle is closely related to the acquisition and payment cycle. The acquisition of goods and services includes the purchase of inventory, supplies, and general services in performing the main business operations. Transactions in the capital acquisition and repayment cycle are related to financing the business, such as issuing stock or debt, paying dividends, and repayment of debt. The same three journals are used to record transactions for both cycles, and the transactions are similar. There are two reasons for treating capital acquisition and repayment separately from the acquisition of goods and services. First, the transactions are related to financing a company rather than to its operations. Second, most capital acquisition and repayment cycle accounts involve few transactions, but each is often highly material and therefore should be audited extensively. Considering both reasons, it is more convenient to separate the two cycles.
- The inventory and warehousing cycle is closely related to all other cycles, especially for a manufacturing company. The cost of inventory includes raw materials (acquisition and payment cycle), direct labor (payroll and personnel cycle), and manufacturing overhead (acquisition and payment and payroll and personnel cycles). The sale of finished goods involves the sales and collection cycle. Because inventory is material for most manufacturing companies, it is common to borrow money using inventory as security. In those cases, the capital acquisition and repayment cycle is also related to inventory and warehousing.

Figure 6-5 illustrates the relationships of the cycles. In addition to the five cycles, general cash is also shown. Each cycle is studied in detail in later chapters. Figure 6-5 shows that cycles have no beginning or end except at the origin and final disposition of a company. A company begins by obtaining capital, usually in the form of cash. In a manufacturing company, cash is used to acquire raw materials, fixed assets, and related goods and services to produce inventory (acquisition and payment cycle). Cash is also used to acquire labor for the same reason (payroll and personnel cycle). Acquisition and payment and payroll and personnel are similar in nature, but the functions are sufficiently different to justify separate cycles. The combined result of these two cycles is inventory (inventory and

Relationships Among Cycles

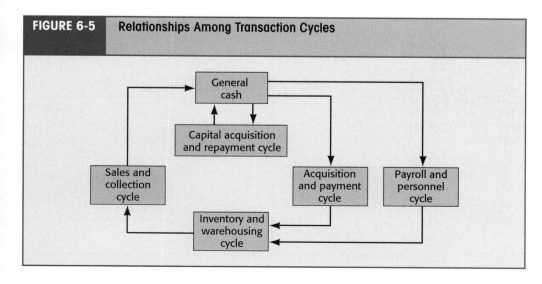

FIGURE 6-5	Relationships Among Transaction Cycles

warehousing cycle). At a subsequent point, the inventory is sold and billings and collections result (sales and collection cycle). The cash generated is used to pay dividends and interest or finance capital expansion and to start the cycles again. The cycles interrelate in much the same way in a service company, where there will be no inventory, but there may be unbilled receivables.

Transaction cycles are of major importance in the conduct of the audit. For the most part, auditors treat each cycle separately during the audit. Although care should be taken to interrelate different cycles at different times, the auditor must treat the cycles somewhat independently to manage complex audits effectively.

SETTING AUDIT OBJECTIVES

OBJECTIVE 6-5

Describe why the auditor obtains a combination of assurance by auditing classes of transactions and ending balances in accounts.

Auditors conduct financial statement audits using the cycle approach by performing audit tests of the transactions making up ending balances and also by performing audit tests of the account balances themselves. Figure 6-6 illustrates this important concept by showing the four classes of transactions that determine the ending balance in accounts receivable for Hillsburg Hardware Co. Assume that the beginning balance of $17,521 (thousand) was audited in the prior year and is therefore considered reliable. If the auditor could be completely sure that each of the four classes of transactions was correctly stated, the auditor could also be sure that the ending balance of $20,197 (thousand) was correctly stated. But it may be impractical for the auditor to obtain complete assurance about the correctness of each class of transactions, resulting in less than complete assurance about the ending balance in accounts receivable. In such a case, overall assurance can be increased by auditing the ending balance of accounts receivable. Auditors have found that, generally, the most efficient way to conduct audits is to *obtain some combination of assurance for each class of transactions and for the ending balance in the related account.*

For any given class of transactions, there are several audit objectives that must be met before the auditor can conclude that the transactions are properly recorded. They are called **transaction-related audit objectives** in the remainder of this book. For example, there are specific sales transaction-related audit objectives and specific sales returns and allowances transaction-related audit objectives.

Similarly, there are several audit objectives that must be met for each account balance. They are called **balance-related audit objectives.** For example, there are specific accounts receivable balance-related audit objectives and specific accounts payable balance-related

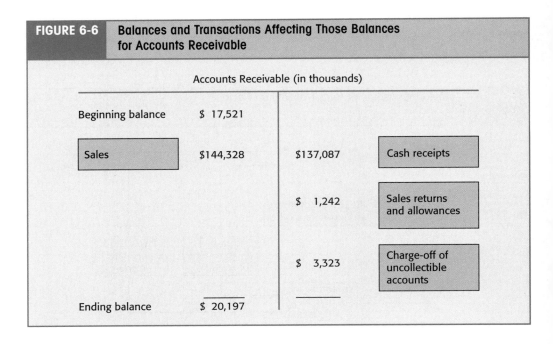

FIGURE 6-6	Balances and Transactions Affecting Those Balances for Accounts Receivable

Accounts Receivable (in thousands)

Beginning balance	$ 17,521		
Sales	$144,328	$137,087	Cash receipts
		$ 1,242	Sales returns and allowances
		$ 3,323	Charge-off of uncollectible accounts
Ending balance	$ 20,197		

audit objectives. It will be shown later that the transaction-related and balance-related audit objectives are somewhat different but closely related. Throughout the remainder of this text, the term *audit objectives* refers to both transaction-related and balance-related audit objectives.

Before examining audit objectives in more detail, it is necessary to understand management assertions. These are studied next.

Management assertions are implied or expressed representations by management about classes of transactions and the related accounts in the financial statements. As an illustration, the management of Hillsburg Hardware Co. asserts that cash of $827,568 (see Figure 6-4 on page 141) was present in the company's bank accounts as of the balance sheet date. Unless otherwise disclosed in the financial statements, management also asserts that the cash was unrestricted and available for normal use. Similar assertions exist for each asset, liability, owners' equity, revenue, and expense item in the financial statements. These assertions apply to both classes of transactions and account balances.

Management assertions are directly related to generally accepted accounting principles (GAAP). These assertions are part of the *criteria that management uses to record and disclose accounting information in financial statements*. Return to the definition of auditing in Chapter 1. It states, in part, that auditing is a comparison of information (financial statements) to established criteria (assertions established according to GAAP). Auditors must therefore understand the assertions to do adequate audits.

SAS 31 (AU 326) classifies assertions into five broad categories:

1. Existence or occurrence
2. Completeness
3. Valuation or allocation
4. Rights and obligations
5. Presentation and disclosure

Assertions About Existence or Occurrence Assertions about existence deal with whether assets, obligations, and equities included in the balance sheet actually existed on the balance sheet date. Assertions about occurrence concern whether recorded transactions included in the financial statements actually occurred during the accounting period. For example, management asserts that merchandise inventory included in the balance sheet exists and is available for sale at the balance sheet date. Similarly, management asserts that recorded sales transactions represent exchanges of goods or services that actually took place.

Assertions About Completeness These management assertions state that all transactions and accounts that should be presented in the financial statements are included. For example, management asserts that all sales of goods and services are recorded and included in the financial statements. Similarly, management asserts that notes payable in the balance sheet include all such obligations of the entity.

The completeness assertion deals with matters opposite from those of the existence or occurrence assertion. The completeness assertion is concerned with the possibility of omitting items from the financial statements that should have been included, whereas the existence or occurrence assertion is concerned with inclusion of amounts that should not have been included. Thus, violations of the existence assertion relate to account overstatements, whereas violations of the completeness assertion relate to account understatements.

The recording of a sale that did not take place would be a violation of the occurrence assertion, whereas the failure to record a sale that did occur would be a violation of the completeness assertion.

Assertions About Valuation or Allocation These assertions deal with whether asset, liability, equity, revenue, and expense accounts have been included in the financial statements at appropriate amounts. For example, management asserts that property is recorded at historical cost and that such cost is systematically allocated to appropriate accounting periods

---

Management Assertions

OBJECTIVE 6-6

Distinguish among the five categories of management assertions about financial information.

Understand objectives and responsibilities for the audit

Divide financial statements into cycles

Know management assertions about accounts

Know general audit objectives for classes of transactions and accounts

Know specific audit objectives for classes of transactions and accounts

through depreciation. Similarly, management asserts that trade accounts receivable included in the balance sheet are stated at net realizable value.

Assertions About Rights and Obligations These management assertions deal with whether assets are the rights of the entity and liabilities are the obligations of the entity at a given date. For example, management asserts that assets are owned by the company or that amounts capitalized for leases in the balance sheet represent the cost of the entity's rights to leased property and that the corresponding lease liability represents an obligation of the entity.

Assertions About Presentation and Disclosure These assertions deal with whether components of the financial statements are properly combined or separated, described, and disclosed. For example, management asserts that obligations classified as long-term liabilities in the balance sheet will not mature within 1 year. Similarly, management asserts that amounts presented as extraordinary items in the income statement are properly classified and described.

TRANSACTION-RELATED AUDIT OBJECTIVES

OBJECTIVE 6-7

Link the six general transaction-related audit objectives to the five management assertions.

The auditor's transaction-related audit objectives follow and are closely related to management assertions. That is not surprising because the auditor's primary responsibility is to determine whether management assertions about financial statements are justified.

These transaction-related audit objectives are intended to provide a *framework* to help the auditor accumulate sufficient competent evidence required by the third standard of field work and decide the proper evidence to accumulate for classes of transactions given the circumstances of the engagement. The objectives remain the same from audit to audit, but the evidence varies, depending on the circumstances.

A distinction must be made between general transaction-related audit objectives and specific transaction-related audit objectives for each class of transactions. The general transaction-related audit objectives discussed here are applicable to every class of transactions but are stated in broad terms. Specific transaction-related audit objectives are also applied to each class of transactions but are stated in terms tailored to a class of transactions such as sales transactions. Once you know the general transaction-related audit objectives, they can be used to develop specific transaction-related audit objectives for each class of transactions being audited. The six general transaction-related audit objectives are discussed next.

General Transaction-Related Audit Objectives

Existence—Recorded Transactions Exist This objective deals with whether recorded transactions have actually occurred. Inclusion of a sale in the sales journal when no sale occurred violates the existence objective. This objective is the auditor's counterpart to the management assertion of existence or occurrence.

Completeness—Existing Transactions Are Recorded This objective deals with whether all transactions that should be included in the journals have actually been included. Failure to include a sale in the sales journal and general ledger when a sale occurred violates the completeness objective. The objective is the counterpart to the management assertion of completeness.

The existence and completeness objectives emphasize opposite audit concerns; existence deals with potential overstatement and completeness with unrecorded transactions (understatement).

Accuracy—Recorded Transactions Are Stated at the Correct Amounts This objective deals with the accuracy of information for accounting transactions. For sales transactions, there would be a violation of the accuracy objective if the quantity of goods shipped was different from the quantity billed, the wrong selling price was used for billing, extension or adding errors occurred in billing, or the wrong amount was included in the sales journal. Accuracy is one part of the valuation or allocation assertion.

It is important to distinguish between accuracy and existence or completeness. For example, if a recorded sales transaction should not have been recorded because the shipment was on consignment, the existence objective has been violated, even if the amount of the invoice was accurately calculated. If the recorded sale was for a valid shipment but the amount was calculated incorrectly, there is a violation of the accuracy objective but not of existence. The same relationship exists between completeness and accuracy.

Classification—Transactions Included in the Client's Journals Are Properly Classified Examples of misclassifications for sales are including cash sales as credit sales, recording a sale of operating fixed assets as revenue, and misclassifying commercial sales as residential sales. Classification is also a part of the valuation or allocation assertion.

Timing—Transactions Are Recorded on the Correct Dates A timing error occurs if transactions are not recorded on the dates the transactions took place. A sales transaction, for example, should be recorded on the date of shipment. Timing is also a part of the valuation or allocation assertion.

Posting and Summarization—Recorded Transactions Are Properly Included in the Master Files and Are Correctly Summarized This objective deals with the accuracy of the transfer of information from recorded transactions in journals to subsidiary records and the general ledger. For example, if a sales transaction is recorded in the wrong customer's record or at the wrong amount in the master file, it is a violation of this objective. Posting and summarization is also a part of the valuation or allocation assertion.

Because the posting of transactions from journals to subsidiary records, the general ledger, and other related master files is typically accomplished automatically by computerized accounting systems, the risk of random human error in posting is minimal. Once the auditor can establish that the computer is functioning properly, there is a reduced concern about posting process errors.

The general transaction-related audit objectives must be applied to each material type (class) of transaction in the audit. Such transactions typically include sales, cash receipts, acquisitions of goods and services, payroll, and so on. Table 6-2 summarizes the six transaction-related audit objectives. It includes the general form of the objectives, the application of the objectives to sales transactions, and the assertions. Notice that only three assertions are associated with transaction-related audit objectives. This shows that two of the assertions are not satisfied by performing transaction-related audit tests.

| Understand objectives and responsibilities for the audit |
| Divide financial statements into cycles |
| Know management assertions about accounts |
| Know general audit objectives for classes of transactions and accounts |
| Know specific audit objectives for classes of transactions and accounts |

Specific Transaction-Related Audit Objectives

TABLE 6-2	Transaction-Related Audit Objectives and Management Assertions for Sales Transactions	
Management Assertions	**General Transaction-Related Audit Objectives**	**Specific Sales Transaction-Related Audit Objectives**
Existence or occurrence	Existence	Recorded sales are for shipments made to nonfictitious customers.
Completeness	Completeness	Existing sales transactions are recorded.
Valuation or allocation	Accuracy	Recorded sales are for the amount of goods shipped and are correctly billed and recorded.
	Classification	Sales transactions are properly classified.
	Timing	Sales are recorded on the correct dates.
	Posting and summarization	Sales transactions are properly included in the master file and are correctly summarized.
Rights and obligations	N/A	N/A
Presentation and disclosure	N/A	N/A

BALANCE-RELATED AUDIT OBJECTIVES

OBJECTIVE 6-8

Link the nine general balance-related audit objectives to the five management assertions.

Balance-related audit objectives are similar to the transaction-related audit objectives just discussed. They also follow from management assertions and they provide a framework to help the auditor accumulate sufficient competent evidence. There are also both general and specific balance-related audit objectives.

There are two differences between balance-related and transaction-related audit objectives. First, as the terms imply, balance-related audit objectives are applied to account balances, whereas transaction-related audit objectives are applied to classes of transactions such as sales transactions and cash disbursements transactions. Second, there are more audit objectives for account balances than for classes of transactions. There are nine balance-related audit objectives compared to six transaction-related audit objectives.

Because of the way audits are done, balance-related audit objectives are almost *always* applied to the ending balance in balance sheet accounts, such as accounts receivable, inventory, and notes payable. However, some balance-related objectives are applied to certain income statement accounts. These usually involve nonroutine transactions and unpredictable expenses, such as legal expense or repairs and maintenance. Other income statement accounts are closely related to balance sheet accounts and are tested simultaneously, such as depreciation expense with accumulated depreciation and interest expense with notes payable.

When using the balance-related audit objectives as a framework for auditing account balances, the auditor accumulates evidence to verify detail that supports the account balance, rather than verifying the account balance itself. For example, in auditing accounts receivable, the auditor obtains a listing of the accounts receivable master file from the client that agrees to the general ledger balance (see page 491 for an illustration). The accounts receivable balance-related audit objectives are applied to the customer accounts in that listing.

Following is a brief discussion of the nine general balance-related audit objectives. Throughout the discussion, there is reference to a supporting schedule, which refers to a client-provided schedule or electronic file such as the accounts receivable listing just described.

General Balance-Related Audit Objectives

Existence—Amounts Included Exist This objective deals with whether the amounts included in the financial statements should actually be included. For example, inclusion of an account receivable from a customer in the accounts receivable trial balance when there is no receivable from that customer violates the existence objective. This objective is the auditor's counterpart to the management assertion of existence or occurrence.

Completeness—Existing Amounts Are Included This objective deals with whether all amounts that should be included have actually been included. Failure to include an account receivable from a customer in the accounts receivable trial balance when a receivable exists violates the completeness objective. This objective is the counterpart to the management assertion of completeness.

The existence and completeness objectives emphasize opposite audit concerns; existence deals with potential overstatement and completeness with unrecorded transactions and amounts (understatement).

Accuracy—Amounts Included Are Stated at the Correct Amounts The accuracy objective refers to amounts being included at the correct arithmetic amount. An inventory item on a client's inventory listing could be wrong because the number of units of inventory on hand was misstated, the unit price was wrong, or the total was incorrectly extended. Each of these violates the accuracy objective. Accuracy is one part of the valuation or allocation assertion.

Classification—Amounts Included in the Client's Listing Are Properly Classified Classification involves determining whether items on a client's listing are included in the correct accounts. For example, on the accounts receivable listing, receivables must be separated into short-term and long-term, and amounts due from affiliates, officers, and directors must be classified separately from amounts due from customers. Classification is also a part of the valuation or allocation assertion.

Cutoff—Transactions Near the Balance Sheet Date Are Recorded in the Proper Period In testing for cutoff, the objective is to determine whether transactions are recorded in the proper period. The transactions that are most likely to be misstated are those recorded near the end of the accounting period. It is proper to think of cutoff tests as a part of verifying either the balance sheet accounts or the related transactions, but for convenience, auditors usually perform them as a part of auditing balance sheet accounts. Cutoff is also a part of the valuation or allocation assertion.

Detail Tie-In—Details in the Account Balance Agree with Related Master File Amounts, Foot to the Total in the Account Balance, and Agree with the Total in the General Ledger Account balances on financial statements are supported by details in master files and schedules prepared by clients. The detail tie-in objective is concerned that the details on lists are accurately prepared, correctly added, and agree with the general ledger. For example, individual accounts receivable on a listing of accounts receivable should be the same in the accounts receivable master file, and the total should equal the general ledger control account. Detail tie-in is also a part of the valuation or allocation assertion.

Realizable Value—Assets Are Included at the Amounts Estimated to Be Realized This objective concerns whether an account balance has been reduced for declines from historical cost to net realizable value. Examples when the objective applies are considering the adequacy of the allowance for uncollectible accounts receivable and write-downs of inventory for obsolescence. The objective applies only to asset accounts and is also a part of the valuation or allocation assertion.

Rights and Obligations In addition to existing, most assets must be owned before it is acceptable to include them in the financial statements. Similarly, liabilities must belong to the entity. Rights are always associated with assets and obligations with liabilities. This objective is the auditor's counterpart to the management assertion of rights and obligations.

Presentation and Disclosure—Account Balances and Related Disclosure Requirements Are Properly Presented in the Financial Statements In fulfilling the presentation and disclosure objective, the auditor tests to make certain that all balance sheet and income statement accounts and related information are correctly set forth in the financial statements and properly described in the body and footnotes of the statements. This objective has its counterpart in the management assertion of presentation and disclosure.

Presentation and disclosure is closely related to, but distinct from, classification. Accounting information for balance-related audit objectives is correctly classified if all information on a detailed schedule supporting an account balance is summarized in the appropriate accounts. The information is correctly disclosed if those account balances and related footnote information are properly combined, described, and presented in the financial statements. For example, if a long-term note receivable is included on an accounts receivable listing, there is a violation of the classification objective. If the long-term note receivable is correctly classified but combined with accounts receivable on the financial statements, there is a violation of the presentation and disclosure objective.

After the general balance-related audit objectives are understood, specific balance-related audit objectives for each account balance on the financial statements can be developed. There should be at least one specific balance-related audit objective for each general balance-related audit objective unless the auditor believes that the general balance-related audit objective is not relevant or is unimportant in the circumstances. There may be more than one specific balance-related audit objective for a general balance-related audit objective. For example, specific balance-related audit objectives for rights and obligations of the inventory of Hillsburg Hardware Co. could include (1) the company has title to all inventory items listed and (2) inventory is not pledged as collateral unless it is disclosed.

Specific Balance-Related Audit Objectives

TABLE 6-3	Hillsburg Hardware Co.: Management Assertions and Balance-Related Audit Objectives Applied to Inventory	
Management Assertions	**General Balance-Related Audit Objectives**	**Specific Balance-Related Audit Objectives Applied to Inventory**
Existence or occurrence	Existence	All recorded inventory exists at the balance sheet date.
Completeness	Completeness	All existing inventory has been counted and included in the inventory summary.
Valuation or allocation	Accuracy	Inventory quantities on the client's perpetual records agree with items physically on hand. Prices used to value inventories are materially correct. Extensions of price times quantity are correct and details are correctly added.
	Classification	Inventory items are properly classified as to raw materials, work in process, and finished goods.
	Cutoff	Purchase cutoff at year-end is proper. Sales cutoff at year-end is proper.
	Detail tie-in	Total of inventory items agrees with general ledger.
	Realizable value	Inventories have been written down where net realizable value is impaired.
Rights and obligations	Rights and obligations	The company has title to all inventory items listed. Inventories are not pledged as collateral.
Presentation and disclosure	Presentation and disclosure	Major categories of inventories and their bases of valuation are disclosed. The pledge or assignment of any inventories is disclosed.

Relationships Among Management Assertions and Balance-Related Audit Objectives

The reason there are more general balance-related audit objectives than management assertions is to provide additional guidance to auditors in deciding what evidence to accumulate. Table 6-3 illustrates this by showing the relationships among management assertions, the general balance-related audit objectives, and specific balance-related audit objectives as applied to inventory for Hillsburg Hardware Co. Notice that there is a one-to-one relationship between assertions and objectives, except for the valuation or allocation assertion. The valuation or allocation assertion has multiple objectives because of the complexity of valuation issues and the need to provide auditors with additional guidance.

HOW AUDIT OBJECTIVES ARE MET

OBJECTIVE 6-9

Explain the relationship between audit objectives and the accumulation of audit evidence.

The auditor must obtain sufficient competent audit evidence to support all management assertions in the financial statements. As stated earlier, this is done by accumulating evidence in support of some appropriate combination of transaction-related audit objectives and balance-related audit objectives. A comparison of Tables 6-2 and 6-3 shows a significant overlap between the two types of audit objectives. The only assertions that must be addressed through balance-related audit objectives, rather than some combination of balance- and transaction-related audit objectives, are rights and obligations and presentation and disclosure.

The auditor plans the appropriate combination of audit objectives and the evidence that must be accumulated to meet them by following an audit process. An audit process is

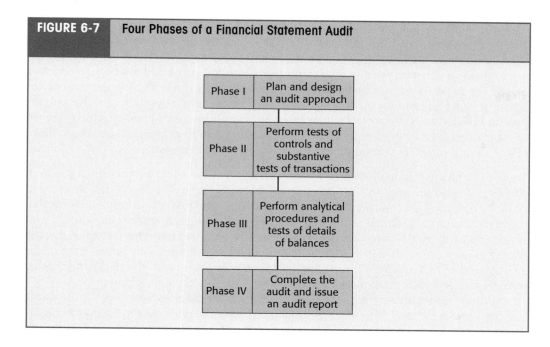

FIGURE 6-7 Four Phases of a Financial Statement Audit

```
Phase I      Plan and design
             an audit approach

Phase II     Perform tests of
             controls and
             substantive
             tests of transactions

Phase III    Perform analytical
             procedures and
             tests of details
             of balances

Phase IV     Complete the
             audit and issue
             an audit report
```

a well-defined methodology for organizing an audit to ensure that the evidence gathered is both sufficient and competent and that all appropriate audit objectives are both specified and met. If the client is a public company, the auditor must also plan to meet the objectives associated with reporting on the effectiveness of internal control over financial reporting. PCAOB Auditing Standard 2 requires that the audit of the effectiveness of internal control be integrated with the audit of the financial statements. The audit process described in this text has four specific phases. These are shown in Figure 6-7. The remainder of this chapter provides a brief introduction to each of the four **phases of the audit process.**

For any given audit, there are many ways in which an auditor can accumulate evidence to meet the overall audit objectives. Two overriding considerations affect the approach the auditor selects: *sufficient competent evidence must be accumulated to meet the auditor's professional responsibility*, and *the cost of accumulating the evidence should be minimized.* The first consideration is the most important, but cost minimization is necessary if CPA firms are to be competitive and profitable. If there were no concern for controlling costs, evidence decision making would be easy. Auditors would keep adding evidence, without concern for efficiency, until they were sufficiently certain that there were no material misstatements.

Concern for sufficient competent evidence and cost control necessitates planning the engagement. The plan should result in an effective audit approach at a reasonable cost. Planning and designing an audit approach can be broken down into several parts. Two key aspects of audit planning are briefly introduced here and are discussed in subsequent chapters.

Obtain Knowledge of the Client's Business Strategies and Processes and Assess Risks To adequately assess the risk of misstatements in the financial statements and interpret information obtained throughout the audit, an understanding of the client's business strategies and processes is essential. For example, the auditor should study the client's business model and perform analytical procedures and other comparisons to competitors. In addition, the auditor must understand any unique accounting requirements of the client's industry. For example, when auditing an insurance company, an auditor must understand how loss reserves are calculated.

Once the auditor has an understanding of the client's industry and business strategies, he or she assesses the risk of misstatements in the financial statements. For example, the client may be expanding sales by taking on new customers with poor credit ratings. The auditor would assess a higher risk of misstatement for net realizable value of accounts receivable and plan to expand testing in this area.

Plan and Design an Audit Approach (Phase I)

Understand Internal Control and Assess Control Risk The risk of misstatement in the financial statements is reduced if the client has effective controls over computer operations and transaction processing. It was pointed out in Chapter 2 that the ability of the client's internal controls to generate reliable financial information and safeguard assets and records is one of the most important and widely accepted concepts in the theory and practice of auditing. When the auditor identifies internal controls and evaluates their effectiveness, the process is called *assessing control risk*. If internal controls are considered effective, planned assessed control risk can be reduced and the amount of audit evidence to be accumulated can be significantly less than when internal controls are not adequate.

Perform Tests of Controls and Substantive Tests of Transactions (Phase II)

To justify reducing planned assessed control risk when internal controls are considered effective, the auditor must test the effectiveness of the controls. The procedures involved in this type of testing are commonly referred to as **tests of controls**. For example, assume that the client's internal controls require the verification by an independent clerk of all unit selling prices on sales before sales invoices are mailed to customers. This control is directly related to the accuracy transaction-related audit objective for sales. One possible test of the effectiveness of this control is for the auditor to examine a sample of the clerk's initials that were required on each duplicate sales invoice after verifying the unit selling price.

Auditors also evaluate the client's recording of transactions by verifying the monetary amounts of transactions. This is called **substantive tests of transactions**. An example is for the auditor to compare the unit selling price on a duplicate sales invoice with the approved price list as a test of the accuracy objective for sales transactions. Like the test of control in the previous paragraph, this test satisfies the accuracy transaction-related audit objective for sales. Often, auditors perform tests of controls and substantive tests of transactions at the same time.

Perform Analytical Procedures and Tests of Details of Balances (Phase III)

There are two general categories of phase III procedures: analytical procedures and tests of details of balances. **Analytical procedures** use comparisons and relationships to assess whether account balances or other data appear reasonable. An example of an analytical procedure that would provide some assurance for the accuracy objective for both sales transactions (transaction-related audit objective) and accounts receivable (balance-related audit objective) is to examine sales transactions in the sales journal for unusually large amounts and to compare total monthly sales with prior years. If a company is consistently using incorrect sales prices, significant differences are likely.

Tests of details of balances are specific procedures intended to test for monetary misstatements in the balances in the financial statements. An example related to the accuracy objective for accounts receivable (balance-related audit objective) is direct written communication with the client's customers. Tests of details of ending balances are essential to the conduct of the audit because most of the evidence is obtained from a source independent of the client and therefore is considered to be of high quality.

Complete the Audit and Issue an Audit Report (Phase IV)

After the auditor has completed all procedures for each audit objective and for each financial statement account, it is necessary to combine the information obtained to reach an *overall conclusion* as to whether the financial statements are fairly presented. This is a highly subjective process that relies heavily on the auditor's professional judgment. When the audit is completed, the CPA must issue an audit report to accompany the client's published financial statements. These reports have already been studied in Chapter 3.

SUMMARY

This chapter discussed the objectives of the audit and the way the auditor subdivides an audit to result in specific audit objectives. The auditor then accumulates evidence to obtain assurance that each audit objective has been satisfied. The illustration on meeting the accuracy objectives for sales transactions and accounts receivable shows that the auditor can obtain assurance by accumulating evidence using tests of controls, substantive tests of transactions, analytical procedures, and tests of details of balances. In some audits, there is more emphasis on certain tests such as analytical procedures and tests of controls, whereas in others, there is emphasis on substantive tests of transactions and tests of details of balances.

ESSENTIAL TERMS

Analytical procedures—use of comparisons and relationships to assess whether account balances or other data appear reasonable

Balance-related audit objectives—nine audit objectives that must be met before the auditor can conclude that any given account balance is fairly stated; the general balance-related audit objectives are existence, completeness, accuracy, classification, cutoff, detail tie-in, realizable value, rights and obligations, and presentation and disclosure

Cycle approach—a method of dividing an audit by keeping closely related types of transactions and account balances in the same segment

Error—an unintentional misstatement of the financial statements

Fraud—an intentional misstatement of the financial statements

Fraudulent financial reporting—intentional misstatements or omissions of amounts or disclosures in financial statements to deceive users

Illegal acts—violations of laws or government regulations other than fraud

Management assertions—implied or expressed representations by management about classes of transactions and related accounts in the financial statements

Misappropriation of assets—a fraud involving the theft of an entity's assets

Phases of the audit process—the four aspects of a complete audit: (1) plan and design an audit approach, (2) perform tests of controls and substantive tests of transactions, (3) perform analytical procedures and tests of details of balances, and (4) complete the audit and issue an audit report

Substantive tests of transactions—audit procedures testing for monetary misstatements to determine whether the six transaction-related audit objectives have been satisfied for each class of transactions

Tests of controls—audit procedures to test the effectiveness of controls in support of a reduced assessed control risk

Tests of details of balances—audit procedures testing for monetary misstatements to determine whether the nine balance-related audit objectives have been satisfied for each significant account balance

Transaction-related audit objectives—six audit objectives that must be met before the auditor can conclude that the total for any given class of transactions is fairly stated; the general transaction-related audit objectives are existence, completeness, accuracy, classification, timing, and posting and summarization

REVIEW QUESTIONS

6-1 (Objective 6-1) State the objective of the audit of financial statements. In general terms, how do auditors meet that objective?

6-2 (Objectives 6-2, 6-3) Distinguish between management's and the auditor's responsibility for the financial statements being audited.

6-3 (Objective 6-3) Distinguish between the terms *errors* and *fraud*. What is the auditor's responsibility for finding each?

6-4 (Objective 6-3) Distinguish between fraudulent financial reporting and misappropriation of assets. Discuss the likely difference between these two types of fraud on the fair presentation of financial statements.

6-5 (Objective 6-3) "It is well accepted in auditing that throughout the conduct of the ordinary audit, it is essential to obtain large amounts of information from management and to rely heavily on management's judgments. After all, the financial statements are management's representations, and the primary responsibility for their fair presentation rests with management, not the auditor. For example, it is extremely difficult, if not impossible, for the auditor to evaluate the obsolescence of inventory as well as management can in a highly complex business. Similarly, the collectibility of accounts receivable and the continued usefulness of machinery and equipment are heavily dependent on management's willingness to provide truthful responses to questions." Reconcile the auditor's responsibility for discovering material misrepresentations by management with these comments.

6-6 (Objective 6-3) List two major characteristics that are useful in predicting the likelihood of fraudulent financial reporting in an audit. For each of the characteristics, state two things that the auditor can do to evaluate its significance in the engagement.

6-7 (Objective 6-4) Describe what is meant by the cycle approach to auditing. What are the advantages of dividing the audit into different cycles?

6-8 (Objective 6-4) Identify the cycle to which each of the following general ledger accounts would ordinarily be assigned: sales, accounts payable, retained earnings, accounts receivable, inventory, and repairs and maintenance.

6-9 (Objectives 6-4, 6-5) Why are sales, sales returns and allowances, bad debts, cash discounts, accounts receivable, and allowance for uncollectible accounts all included in the same cycle?

6-10 (Objective 6-6) Define what is meant by a management assertion about financial statements. Identify the five broad categories of management assertions.

6-11 (Objectives 6-6, 6-7) Distinguish between the general audit objectives and management assertions. Why are the general audit objectives more useful to auditors?

6-12 (Objective 6-7) An acquisition of a fixed-asset repair by a construction company is recorded on the wrong date. Which transaction-related audit objective has been violated? Which transaction-related audit objective has been violated if the acquisition had been capitalized as a fixed asset rather than expensed?

6-13 (Objective 6-8) Distinguish between the existence and completeness balance-related audit objectives. State the effect on the financial statements (overstatement or understatement) of a violation of each in the audit of accounts receivable.

6-14 (Objectives 6-7, 6-8) What are specific audit objectives? Explain their relationship to the general audit objectives.

6-15 (Objectives 6-6, 6-8) Identify the management assertion and general balance-related audit objective for the specific balance-related audit objective: All recorded fixed assets exist at the balance sheet date.

6-16 (Objectives 6-6, 6-8) Explain how management assertions, general balance-related audit objectives, and specific balance-related audit objectives are developed for an account balance such as accounts receivable.

6-17 (Objective 6-9) Identify the four phases of the audit. What is the relationship of the four phases to the objective of the audit of financial statements?

MULTIPLE CHOICE QUESTIONS FROM CPA EXAMINATIONS

6-18 (Objective 6-1) The following questions concern the reasons auditors do audits. Choose the best response.

    a. Which of the following *best* describes the reason why an independent auditor reports on financial statements?
- (1) A misappropriation of assets may exist, and it is more likely to be detected by independent auditors.
- (2) Different interests may exist between the company preparing the statements and the persons using the statements.
- (3) A misstatement of account balances may exist and is generally corrected as the result of the independent auditor's work.
- (4) Poorly designed internal controls may be in existence.

    b. An independent audit aids in the communication of economic data because the audit
- (1) confirms the accuracy of management's financial representations.
- (2) lends credibility to the financial statements.
- (3) guarantees that financial data are fairly presented.
- (4) assures the readers of financial statements that any fraudulent activity has been corrected.

    c. The major reason an independent auditor gathers audit evidence is to
- (1) form an opinion on the financial statements.
- (2) detect fraud.
- (3) evaluate management.
- (4) assess control risk.

6-19 (Objective 6-3) The following questions deal with errors and fraud. Choose the best response.

    a. An independent auditor has the responsibility to design the audit to provide reasonable assurance of detecting errors and fraud that might have a material effect on the financial statements. Which of the following, if material, would be a fraud as defined in auditing standards?
- (1) Misappropriation of an asset or groups of assets.
- (2) Clerical mistakes in the accounting data underlying the financial statements.

(3) Mistakes in the application of accounting principles.

(4) Misinterpretation of facts that existed when the financial statements were prepared.

b. What assurance does the auditor provide that errors, fraud, and direct-effect illegal acts that are material to the financial statements will be detected?

Errors	Fraud	Direct-Effect Illegal Acts
(1) Limited	Negative	Limited
(2) Reasonable	Reasonable	Reasonable
(3) Limited	Limited	Reasonable
(4) Reasonable	Limited	Limited

6-20 (Objectives 6-2, 6-3, 6-6) The following are miscellaneous questions from this chapter. Choose the best response.

a. An auditor most likely would analyze inventory turnover rates to obtain evidence concerning management's assertions about

(1) existence or occurrence.

(2) rights and obligations.

(3) valuation or allocation.

(4) presentation and disclosure.

b. The audit client's board of directors and audit committee refused to take any action with respect to an immaterial illegal act that was brought to their attention by the auditor. Because of their failure to act, the auditor withdrew from the engagement. The auditor's decision to withdraw was primarily because of doubts concerning

(1) inadequate financial statement disclosures.

(2) compliance with the Foreign Corrupt Practices Act of 1977.

(3) scope limitations resulting from their inaction.

(4) reliance on management's representations.

c. The primary responsibility for the adequacy of disclosure in the financial statements and footnotes rests with the

(1) partner assigned to the engagement.

(2) auditor in charge of field work.

(3) staff member who drafts the statements and footnotes.

(4) client.

DISCUSSION QUESTIONS AND PROBLEMS

6-21 (Objectives 6-2, 6-3) The following two reports are taken from the same page of a published annual report.

REPORT OF MANAGEMENT

The management of American Express Company (the company) is responsible for the preparation and fair presentation of its Consolidated Financial Statements, which have been prepared in conformity with accounting principles generally accepted in the United States, and include amounts based on the best judgment of management. The company's management is also responsible for the accuracy and consistency of other financial information included in this annual report.

In recognition of its responsibility for the integrity and objectivity of data in the financial statements, the company maintains a system of internal control over financial reporting which is designed to provide reasonable, but not absolute, assurance with respect to the reliability of the company's financial statements. The concept of reasonable assurance is based on the notion that the cost of the internal control system should not exceed the benefits derived.

The internal control system is founded on an ethical climate and includes: (i) an organizational structure with clearly defined lines of responsibility, policies and procedures; (ii) a Code of Conduct; and (iii) the careful selection and training of employees. Internal auditors monitor and assess the effectiveness of the internal control system and report their findings to management and the Board of Directors throughout the year. The company's independent auditors are engaged to express an opinion on the year-end financial statements and, with the coordinated support of the internal auditors, review the financial records and related data and test the internal control system over financial reporting to the extent they believed necessary to support their report.

The Audit Committee of the Board of Directors, which has only outside directors, meets regularly with the internal auditors, management and independent auditors to review their work and discuss the company's financial controls and audit and reporting practices. The independent auditors and the internal auditors independently have full and free access to the Audit Committee, without the presence of management, to discuss any matters which they feel require attention.

REPORT OF ERNST & YOUNG LLP INDEPENDENT AUDITORS
The Shareholders and Board of Directors of American Express Company

(First two paragraphs of standard unqualified report have been omitted.)

In our opinion, the financial statements referred to above present fairly, in all material respects, the consolidated financial position of American Express Company at December 31, 2003 and 2002, and the consolidated results of its operations and its cash flows for each of the three years in the period ended December 31, 2003, in conformity with accounting principles generally accepted in the United States.

As discussed in Note 1 to the consolidated financial statements, in 2003 the Company adopted the provisions of Financial Accounting Standards Board Interpretation No. 46 (revised December 2003), "Consolidation of Variable Interest Entities," and the fair value recognition provisions of Statement of Financial Accounting Standards (SFAS) No. 123, "Accounting for Stock-Based Compensation," prospectively for all stock options granted after December 31, 2002. Additionally, as discussed in Note 5 to the consolidated financial statements, in 2002 the Company adopted SFAS No. 142, "Goodwill and Other Intangible Assets."

Ernst & Young LLP
New York, New York
January 26, 2004

Required

a. What are the purposes of the two reports and who was responsible for writing each?

b. What information does the report of management provide to users of financial statements?

c. Explain the purpose of the audit committee as described in the fourth paragraph of management's report. What is the relevance of the phrase "which has only outside directors"?

d. Is the audit report a standard wording unqualified, qualified—except for, or something else? Explain your answer.

e. How long after the balance sheet date did the CPA firm complete the audit field work?

6-22 (Objectives 6-1, 6-3) Often, questions have been raised "regarding the responsibility of the independent auditor for the discovery of fraud (including misappropriation of assets and fraudulent financial reporting), and concerning the proper course of conduct of the independent auditor when his or her audit discloses specific circumstances that arouse suspicion as to the existence of fraud."

Required

a. What are (1) the function and (2) the responsibilities of the independent auditor in the audit of financial statements? Discuss fully, but in this part do not include fraud in the discussion.

b. What are the responsibilities of the independent auditor for the detection of fraud? Discuss fully.

c. What is the independent auditor's proper course of conduct when the audit discloses specific circumstances that arouse suspicion as to the existence of fraud?*

6-23 (Objectives 6-2, 6-3) A competent auditor has done a conscientious job of conducting an audit, but because of a clever fraud by management, a material fraud is included in the financial statements. The fraud, which is an overstatement of inventory, took place over several years, and it covered up the fact that the company's financial position was rapidly declining. The fraud was accidentally discovered in the latest audit by an unusually capable audit senior, and the SEC was immediately informed. Subsequent investigation indicated that the company was actually near bankruptcy, and the value of the stock dropped from $26 per share to $1 in less than 1 month. Among the losing stockholders were pension funds, university endowment funds, retired couples, and widows. The individuals responsible for perpetrating the fraud were also bankrupt.

After making an extensive investigation of the audit performance in previous years, the SEC was satisfied that the auditor had done a high-quality audit and had followed generally accepted auditing standards in every respect. The commission concluded that it would be unreasonable to expect auditors to uncover this type of fraud.

Required

State your opinion as to who should bear the loss of the fraudulent financial reporting. Include in your discussion a list of potential bearers of the loss, and state why you believe they should or should not bear the loss.

6-24 (Objective 6-4) The following are the classes of transactions and the titles of the journals used for Phillips Equipment Rental Co.

*AICPA adapted.

Classes of Transactions	Titles of Journals
Purchase returns	Cash receipts journal
Rental revenue	Cash disbursements journal
Charge-off of uncollectible accounts	Acquisitions journal
Acquisition of goods and services (except payroll)	Revenue journal
Rental allowances	Payroll journal
Adjusting entries (for payroll)	Adjustments journal
Payroll service and payments	
Cash disbursements (except payroll)	
Cash receipts	

Required

a. Identify one financial statement balance that is likely to be affected by each of the nine classes of transactions.

b. For each class of transactions, identify the journal that is likely to be used to record the transactions.

c. Identify the transaction cycle that is likely to be affected by each of the nine classes of transactions.

d. Explain how total rental revenue, as cited on the financial statements of Phillips Equipment Rental Co., is accumulated in journals and is summarized on the financial statements. Assume that there are several adjusting entries for rental revenue at the balance sheet date.

6-25 (Objective 6-4) The following general ledger accounts are included in the trial balance for an audit client, Jones Wholesale Stationery Store.

Income tax expense	Allowance for doubtful accounts
Income tax payable	Inventory
Accounts receivable	Property tax expense
Advertising expense	Interest expense
Travel expense	Depreciation expense—furniture and
Accounts payable	equipment
Bonds payable	Retained earnings
Common stock	Sales
Unexpired insurance	Salaries, office and general
Furniture and equipment	Telephone and fax expense
Cash	Bad debt expense
Notes receivable—trade	Insurance expense
Purchases	Interest receivable
Sales salaries expense	Interest income
Accumulated depreciation	Accrued sales salaries
of furniture and equipment	Rent expense
Notes payable	Prepaid interest expense
	Property tax payable

Required

a. Identify the accounts in the trial balance that are likely to be included in each transaction cycle. Some accounts will be included in more than one cycle. Use the format that follows.

Cycle	Balance Sheet Accounts	Income Statement Accounts
Sales and collection		
Acquisition and payment		
Payroll and personnel		
Inventory and warehousing		
Capital acquisition and repayment		

b. How would the general ledger accounts in the trial balance most likely differ if the company were a retail store rather than a wholesale company? How would they differ for a hospital or a government unit?

6-26 (Objectives 6-6, 6-8) The following are specific balance-related audit objectives applied to the audit of accounts receivable (a through h) and management assertions (1 through 5). The list referred to in the specific balance-related audit objectives is the list of the accounts receivable from each customer at the balance sheet date.

Specific Balance-Related Audit Objective

a. There are no unrecorded receivables.

b. Receivables have not been sold or discounted.

c. Uncollectible accounts have been provided for.

d. Receivables that have become uncollectible have been written off.

e. All accounts on the list are expected to be collected within 1 year.

f. Any agreement or condition that restricts the nature of trade receivables is known and disclosed.

g. All accounts on the list arose from the normal course of business and are not due from related parties.

h. Sales cutoff at year-end is proper.

Management Assertion

1. Existence or occurrence
2. Completeness
3. Valuation or allocation
4. Rights and obligations
5. Presentation and disclosure

Required   For each specific balance-related audit objective, identify the appropriate management assertion. (*Hint:* See Table 6-3.)

6-27 (Objectives 6-6, 6-7) The following are specific transaction-related audit objectives applied to the audit of cash disbursement transactions (a through f), management assertions (1 through 5), and general transaction-related audit objectives (6 through 11).

Specific Transaction-Related Audit Objective

a. Recorded cash disbursement transactions are for the amount of goods or services received and are correctly recorded.

b. Cash disbursement transactions are properly included in the accounts payable master file and are correctly summarized.

c. Recorded cash disbursements are for goods and services actually received.

d. Cash disbursement transactions are properly classified.

e. Existing cash disbursement transactions are recorded.

f. Cash disbursement transactions are recorded on the correct dates.

Management Assertion

1. Existence or occurrence
2. Completeness
3. Valuation or allocation
4. Rights and obligations
5. Presentation and disclosure

General Transaction-Related Audit Objective

6. Existence
7. Completeness
8. Accuracy
9. Classification
10. Timing
11. Posting and summarization

Required   a. Explain the differences among management assertions, general transaction-related audit objectives, and specific transaction-related audit objectives and their relationships to each other.

b. For each specific transaction-related audit objective, identify the appropriate management assertion.

c. For each specific transaction-related audit objective, identify the appropriate general transaction-related audit objective.

6-28 (**Objective 6-8**) The following are two specific balance-related audit objectives in the audit of accounts payable. The list referred to is the list of accounts payable taken from the accounts payable master file. The total of the list equals the accounts payable balance on the general ledger.

1. All accounts payable included on the list represent amounts due to valid vendors.
2. There are no unrecorded accounts payable.

a. Explain the difference between these two specific balance-related audit objectives.

Required

b. Which of these two specific balance-related audit objectives applies to the general balance-related audit objective of existence, and which one applies to completeness?

c. For the audit of accounts payable, which of these two specific balance-related audit objectives would usually be more important? Explain.

6-29 (**Objective 6-8**) The following are 9 general balance-related audit objectives for the audit of any balance sheet account (1 through 9) and 11 specific balance-related audit objectives for the audit of property, plant, and equipment (a through k).

General Balance-Related Audit Objective

1. Existence
2. Completeness
3. Accuracy
4. Classification
5. Cutoff
6. Detail tie-in
7. Realizable value
8. Rights and obligations
9. Presentation and disclosure

Specific Balance-Related Audit Objective

a. There are no unrecorded fixed assets in use.

b. The company has valid title to the assets owned.

c. Details of property, plant, and equipment agree with the general ledger.

d. Fixed assets physically exist and are being used for the purpose intended.

e. Property, plant, and equipment are recorded at the correct amounts.

f. The company has a contractual right for use of assets leased.

g. Liens or other encumbrances on property, plant, and equipment items are known and disclosed.

h. Cash disbursements and/or accrual cutoff for property, plant, and equipment items are proper.

i. Expense accounts do not contain amounts that should have been capitalized.

j. Depreciation is determined in accordance with an acceptable method and is materially correct as computed.

k. Fixed asset accounts have been properly adjusted for declines in historical cost.

a. What are the purposes of the general balance-related audit objectives and the specific balance-related audit objectives? Explain the relationship between these two sets of objectives.

Required

b. For each general balance-related audit objective, identify one or more specific balance-related audit objectives. No letter can be used for more than one general balance-related audit objective.

CASE

6-30 (**Objectives 6-1, 6-3**) Rene Ritter opened a small grocery and related-products convenience store in 1982 with money she had saved working as an A&P store manager. She named it Ritter Dairy and Fruits. Because of the excellent location and her fine management skills, Ritter Dairy and Fruits grew to three locations by 1987. By that time, she needed additional capital. She obtained financing through a local bank at 2 percent above prime, under the condition that she submit quarterly financial statements reviewed by a CPA firm approved by the bank. After interviewing several firms, she decided to use the firm of Gonzalez & Fineberg CPAs, after obtaining approval from the bank.

In 1991, the company had grown to six stores, and Rene developed a business plan to add another 10 stores in the next several years. Ritter's capital needs had also grown, so Rene decided to add two business partners who both had considerable capital and some expertise in convenience stores. After further discussions with the bank and continued conversations with the future business partners, she decided to have an annual audit and quarterly reviews done by Gonzalez & Fineberg, even though the additional cost was almost $15,000 annually. The bank agreed to reduce the interest rate on the $4,000,000 of loans to 1 percent above prime.

By 1996, things were going smoothly, with the two business partners heavily involved in day-to-day operations and the company adding two new stores each year. The company was growing steadily and was more profitable than they had expected. By the end of 1997, one of the business partners, Fred Worm, had taken over responsibility for accounting and finance operations, as well as some marketing. Annually Gonzalez & Fineberg did an in-depth review of the accounting system, including internal controls, and reported their conclusions and recommendations to the board of directors. Specialists in the firm provided tax and other advice. The other partner, Ben Gold, managed most of the stores and was primarily responsible for building new stores. Rene was president and managed four stores.

In 2001, the three partners decided to go public to enable them to add more stores and modernize existing ones. The public offering was a major success, resulting in $25 million in new capital and nearly 1,000 shareholders. Ritter Dairy and Fruits added stores rapidly under the three managers, and the company remained highly profitable under the leadership of Ritter, Worm, and Gold.

Rene retired in 2004 after a highly successful career. During the retirement celebration, she thanked her business partners, employees, and customers. She also added a special thanks to the bank management for their outstanding service and to Gonzalez & Fineburg for being partners in the best and most professional sense of the word. She mentioned their integrity, commitment, high-quality service in performing their audits and reviews, and considerable tax and business advice for more than two decades.

Required

a. Explain why the bank imposed a requirement of a quarterly review of the financial statements as a condition of obtaining the loan at 2 percent above prime. Also explain why the bank didn't require an audit and why the bank demanded the right to approve which CPA firm was engaged.

b. Explain why Ritter Dairy and Fruits agreed to have an audit performed rather than a review, considering the additional annual cost of $15,000.

c. What did Rene mean when she referred to Gonzalez & Fineberg as partners? Does the CPA firm have an independence problem?

d. What benefit does Gonzalez & Fineberg provide to stockholders, creditors, and management in performing the audit and related services?

e. What are the responsibilities of the CPA firm to stockholders, creditors, management, and other users?

INTERNET PROBLEM 6-1: ASSERTIONS AND EVIDENCE ASSOCIATED WITH NEW ASSURANCE SERVICES

Reference the CW site. The AICPA has developed a business plan for CPA ElderCare, a new assurance service. This problem requires students to use the Internet to (1) identify possible performance criteria associated with a client living in a long-term care facility, (2) determine in what form and to whom CPAs would report findings, and (3) identify what assertions would be tested and how.

2004 Annual Report

HILLSBURG HARDWARE COMPANY 2004 ANNUAL REPORT

CONTENTS

Rick Chulick, President and Chief Operating Officer

DEAR SHAREHOLDERS: March 29, 2005

We are proud to announce another year of noticeable improvement.

In last year's letter we stated, "We are committed to increasing the efficiency and effectiveness of operations through cost savings and productivity improvements. In addition, we intend to maintain and further develop our customer base through recently implemented post-sale service programs." The operating results in this report demonstrate that our objectives have been achieved, resulting in a net income increase of $740,000 from 2003 to 2004. This amounts to 15 cents per share, a 23.2% increase from last year. Our goal in the current year is to further improve the results of operations and create value for shareholders. In doing so, we will focus primarily on the following three strategic components of our business plan:

1. Post-sale service arrangements designed to further develop and maintain our customer base.

2. Aggressive advertising campaigns that allow us to penetrate markets dominated by national wholesale hardware store chains.

3. Implementation of new warehouse technology designed to increase productivity and reduce stocking and distribution costs.

We will report our progress throughout the year.

Christopher J. Kurran
Chief Executive Officer

Rick Chulick
President and Chief Operating Officer

3

HISTORY

Hillsburg Stores Inc. began operations in 1980 in Gary, Indiana, as a retail hardware store chain. On September 25, 1986, Hillsburg merged with Handy Hardware and Lumber Company, which established the concept of selling high-quality hardware through wholesale distribution outlets in 1981, to form Handy-Hillsburg, Inc., a Washington corporation. On June 5, 1990, after spinning off all of its lumber-related assets to Handy Corporation, the company changed its name to Hillsburg Hardware, Inc. On October 22, 1992, the company reincorporated from Washington to Delaware and changed its name to Hillsburg Hardware Company (heareafter referred to as "the Company"), which trades on the NASDAQ under the symbol "HLSB."

OVERVIEW

Hillsburg Hardware Company is a wholesale distributor of hardware equipment to a variety of independent, high-quality hardware stores in the midwestern part of the United States. The primary products are power and hand tools, landscaping equipment, electrical equipment, residential and commercial construction equipment, and a wide selection of paint products.

More than 90% of the Company's products are purchased from manufacturers and shipped either directly to customers or to the main warehouse in Gary, Indiana, where shipments are combined to minimize the costs of freight and handling.

Hardware retailers, now more than ever, find it advantageous to purchase from us rather than directly from manufacturers. We make it possible for smaller, independent retailers to purchase on an as-needed basis, rather than in bulk. Moreover, we offer our customers a range of high-quality products that cannot be found at most national chains.

We also offer far more post-sale services to customers than are offered by manufacturers and other national distributors. We simplify the purchasing process by assigning each customer a permanent salesperson. Each salesperson becomes involved in the sales process, and also acts as a liaison between the customer and post-sale service areas. For example, when customers experience technical problems with recently purchased hardware, their salesperson has the responsibility to coordinate both exchanges and warranty repairs with the manufacturer. This process adds value for customers and makes post-sales service more efficient and less problematic. Low turnover and extensive training of our salespeople enhance this service.

To further encourage customer loyalty, each customer is given access to our internal database system—ONHAND (Online Niche-Hardware Availability Notification Database). The ONHAND system lets customers check the availability of hard-to-find products instantly over the Internet. Moreover, the system includes data such as expected restock dates for items that are currently sold out and expected availability dates for items that will soon be introduced to the market.

Because of the two aforementioned processes, we have managed to maintain a repeat-customer base. Nearly 75% of all first-time customers make at least one additional purchase within one year of their first purchase.

Recently, there have been major consolidations in the wholesale hardware industry. We believe this consolidation trend is advantageous to our operations as a distributor of hard-to-find, high-quality hardware equipment. The recent consolidation of Builder's Plus Hardware, Inc., one of the top ten largest national hardware store chains, is a case in point. One month after the consolidation, Builder's Plus decided not to carry high-end construction and landscaping equipment in order to focus on what it called the "typical hardware customer."

PRODUCTS

To more effectively manage inventory, we carefully monitor the composition of net sales by category of items sold. The following chart indicates the percentage of net sales by class of merchandise sold during the years 2004, 2003, and 2002:

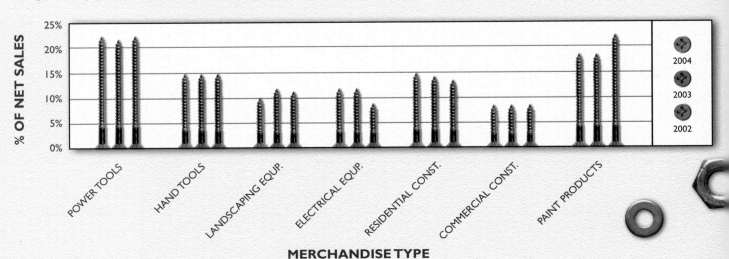

MARKETING PROGRAM

This year, the Company made a significant investment in a new advertising campaign. Various radio, newspaper, magazine, and television advertisements were purchased at the local and regional levels using the Company's new catchphrase, "Hardware for Hard Workers." The new jingle has been partially responsible for the fiscal 2004 increase in sales of 9%.

CUSTOMERS

The majority of our customers are located in Illinois, Michigan, Wisconsin, Ohio, and Missouri. Our current customer base consists of more than 400 independently owned hardware stores. Approximately 25% of our customers make up more than 80% of total sales revenue. To promote long-standing relationships with customers, we offer an array of incentive and customer appreciation programs. Since these programs were implemented in 1997, customer satisfaction ratings have improved steadily in each subsequent year.

SUPPLIERS

We purchase hardware and other products from more than 300 manufacturers in the United States. No single vendor accounted for more than 5% of our purchases during fiscal 2004, but our 25 largest vendors accounted for nearly 35%. We currently have long-term supply agreements with two vendors: Mechanical Tools and Painter's Paradise. These agreements are in effect until the end of fiscal year 2005. The combined dollar amount of each contract is not expected to exceed 5% of total purchases for the year.

COMPETITORS

There are other regional wholesale hardware distributors that compete with the Company, but national wholesale hardware store chains dominate the industry. Most of our competitors are not only larger, but have greater financial resources than our company. Ten national chains exist in the geographic area in which Hillsburg Hardware Co. operates. Of the ten national chains, Hardware Bros., Tools & Paint, and Construction City account for a significant portion of the wholesale hardware market share and also carry the hard-to-find and high-quality items we provide. The success of our business depends on our ability to keep distribution costs to a minimum and our customers satisfied through superior customer service.

The chart that follows is a breakdown of market share in the wholesale hardware market by competitor category, including the 2% market share held by the Company. The chart illustrates that we have considerable opportunity for sales growth.

EMPLOYEES

Hillsburg Hardware currently employs 319 individuals. The majority of our employees are involved in day-to-day sales. Because of our marketing and customer relations strategy, we make significant investments in ongoing training and professional development activities. Each year employees are required to attend 75 hours of professional training. Each employee receives a performance evaluation at least four times per year, usually once each quarter. Our turnover is among the lowest in the industry because of our compensation, training, and evaluation programs. We regard our employees as our most valuable asset.

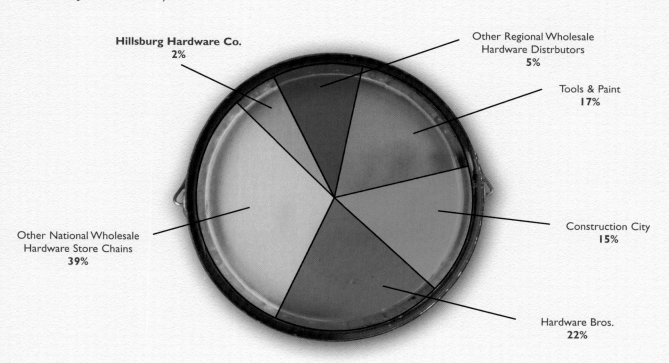

Hillsburg Hardware Co. 2%

Other Regional Wholesale Hardware Distrbutors 5%

Tools & Paint 17%

Construction City 15%

Hardware Bros. 22%

Other National Wholesale Hardware Store Chains 39%

PROPERTIES

The Company owns and operates its main warehouse and an administrative office. The main warehouse and administrative office are in the same 475,000 square-foot building. We also rent a second warehouse for which rental fees are $312,000 annually. The building, located in Detroit, Michigan, serves as an off-site storage facility.

LEGAL PROCEEDINGS

On September 3, 2003, a suit was filed in the Circuit Court in Gary, Indiana, against the Company. The product liability suit, "*Don Richards* v. *Hillsburg Hardware Co.*" is related to injuries that resulted from an alleged defective design of a tractor manufactured by Silo-Tractor, a U.S. corporation. The suit is currently in pretrial proceedings. In the opinion of our legal counsel the suit is without merit. We intend to vigorously defend our position.

The Company does not believe any other legal issues materially affect its finances.

EXECUTIVE OFFICERS

The following list provides names, ages, and present positions of the Company's officers:

NAME	AGE	POSITION
John P. Higgins	55	Chairman of the Board
Rick Chulick	54	President and Chief Operating Officer (a)
Christopher J. Kurran	67	Chief Executive Officer (b)
Avis A. Zomer	44	Chief Financial Officer
Brandon S. Mack	64	Vice President Sales and Marketing
Mary R. Moses	46	Vice President Merchandising
Vanessa M. Namie	53	Vice President Operations (c)
Joseph A. Akuroi	64	Vice President Quality Assurance (d)

(a) Mr. Chulick has been President and Chief Operating Officer of the Company for ten years, since November 1993. Mr. Chulick was Chairman of the Board from 1996 to 1998.

(b) Mr. Kurran has been Chief Executive Officer of the Company since September 1999. Prior to his role as CEO, Mr. Kurran was employed from 1990-1998 by Trini Enterprises, an industrial distributor.

(c) Ms. Namie has been employed by the company since its inception in 1992. She has held her current position since 1998 and served as an operations manager from 1992-1998.

(d) Mr. Akuroi was Chief Operating Officer and President of Hardware Bros., one of the ten largest wholesale hardware chains in the nation, from 1996-2001.

BUSINESS

CONTROLS AND PROCEDURES

Pursuant to Section 404 of the Sarbanes–Oxley Act of 2002 and related Exchange Act Rules, we have carefully evaluated the design and operating effectiveness of our internal control over financial reporting. After careful review of all key controls over financial reporting, our Chief Executive Officer and Chief Financial Officer implemented new controls over the internal verification and timely recording of sales transactions. In compliance with Section 404 and related Exchange requirements, management has issued its report that internal controls over financial reporting are operating effectively as of December 31, 2004 based on criteria established in the COSO *Internal Control-Integrated Framework.*

INFORMATION REGARDING COMMON EQUITY

Hillsburg Hardware Company's common stock currently trades on the NASDAQ under the symbol "HLSB." The following chart shows the high and low prices of the Company's common stock by quarter for the years 2004 and 2003:

	2004		2003	
	High	Low	High	Low
Quarter 1	12.50	9.05	13.30	10.00
Quarter 2	12.55	10.10	12.75	10.25
Quarter 3	12.30	10.99	14.10	9.75
Quarter 4	12.40	8.95	11.50	8.20

On March 23, 2005, there were 1,250 shareholders of our common stock.

DIVIDEND POLICY

Dividend payments on common stock are authorized annually by the Board of Directors. For 2004, dividend payments totaled $1.9 million, which is $.38 per share.

HLSB +12.40

Board of Directors and Stockholders
Hillsburg Hardware Company

We have audited the accompanying balance sheets of Hillsburg Hardware Company as of December 31, 2004 and 2003, and the related statements of income, stockholders' equity and comprehensive income, and cash flows for each of the years in the three-year period ended December 31, 2004. We have also audited management's assessment included in the accompanying management report on internal control that Hillsburg Hardware Company, Inc. maintained effective internal control over financial reporting as of December 31, 2004, based on criteria established in *Internal Control-Integrated Framework* issued by the Committee of Sponsoring Organizations of the Treadway Commission (COSO). Hillsburg Hardware Company's management is responsible for these financial statements, for maintaining effective internal control over financial reporting, and for its assessment of the effectiveness of internal control over financial reporting. Our responsibility is to express an opinion on these financial statements, an opinion on management's assessment, and an opinion on the effectiveness of the company's internal control over financial reporting based on our audits.

We conducted our audits in accordance with the standards of the Public Company Accounting Oversight Board (United States). Those standards require that we plan and perform the audits to obtain reasonable assurance about whether the financial statements are free of material misstatement and whether effective internal control over financial reporting was maintained in all material respects. Our audit of financial statements included examining, on a test basis, evidence supporting the amounts and disclosures in the financial statements, assessing the accounting principles used and significant estimates made by management, and evaluating the overall financial statement presentation. Our audit of internal control over financial reporting included obtaining an understanding of internal control over financial reporting, evaluating management's assessment, testing and evaluating the design and operating effectiveness of internal control, and performing such other procedures as we considered necessary in the circumstances. We believe that our audits provide a reasonable basis for our opinions.

A company's internal control over financial reporting is a process designed to provide reasonable assurance regarding the reliability of financial reporting and the preparation of financial statements for external purposes in accordance with generally accepted accounting principles. A company's internal control over financial reporting includes those policies and procedures that (1) pertain to the maintenance of records that, in reasonable detail, accurately and fairly reflect the transactions and dispositions of the assets of the company; (2) provide reasonable assurance that transactions are recorded as necessary to permit preparation of financial statements in accordance with generally accepted accounting principles, and that receipts and expenditures of the company are being made only in accordance with authorizations of management and directors of the company; and (3) provide reasonable assurance regarding the prevention or timely detection of unauthorized acquisition, use, or disposition of the company's assets that could have a material effect on the financial statements.

Because of its inherent limitations, internal control over financial reporting may not prevent or detect misstatements. Also, projections of any evaluation of effectiveness to future periods are subject to the risk that internal control may become inadequate because of changes in conditions, or that the degree of compliance with the policies or procedures may deteriorate.

In our opinion, the financial statements referred to above present fairly, in all material respects, the financial position of Hillsburg Hardware Company, Inc. as of December 31, 2004 and 2003, and the results of its operations and its cash flows for each of the years in the three-year period ended December 31, 2004 in conformity with accounting principles generally accepted in the United States of America. Also in our opinion, management's assessment that Hillsburg Hardware Company maintained effective internal control over financial reporting as of December 31, 2004, is fairly stated, in all material respects, based on criteria established in *Internal Control-Integrated Framework* issued by the Committee of Sponsoring Organizations of the Treadway Commission (COSO). Furthermore, in our opinion, Hilllsburg Hardware Company maintained, in all material respects, effective internal control over financial reporting as of December 31, 2004, based on criteria established in *Internal Control-Integrated Framework* issued by the Committee of Sponsoring Organizations of the Treadway Commission (COSO).

Berger & Associates, LLP

Berger and Associates, LLP
March 21, 2005

FINANCIAL STATEMENTS

Management's Responsibility for the Financial Statements

To Our Shareholders:

The accompanying financial statements of Hillsburg Hardware Company have been prepared by management, who is responsible for their integrity and objectivity. The statements have been prepared in conformity with accounting principles generally accepted in the United States of America and include amounts based on management's best estimates and judgments. Management has also prepared information elsewhere in this Annual Report that is consistent with data in the financial statements. The Company's financial statements have been audited by Berger and Anthony, independent Certified Public Accountants. Our auditors were given unrestricted access to all financial records and related data, including minutes of the meetings of the Board of Directors. We believe all representations made to Berger and Anthony were legitimate and appropriate.

The management of Hillsburg Hardware Company is responsible for establishing and maintaining adequate internal control over financial reporting. Hillsburg Hardware Company's internal control system was designed to provide reasonable assurance to the company's management and board of directors regarding the preparation and fair presentation of published financial statements.

Hillsburg Hardware Company management assessed the effectiveness of the company's internal control over financial reporting as of December 31, 2004. In making this assessment, it used the criteria set forth by the Committee of Sponsoring Organizations of the Treadway Commission (COSO) in *Internal Control-Integrated Framework*. Based on our assessment we believe that, as of December 31, 2004, the company's internal control over financial reporting is effective based on those criteria.

Hillsburg Hardware Company's independent auditors have issued an audit report on our assessment of the company's internal control over financial reporting. This report appears on the preceding page.

John P. Higgins
Chairman of the Board

Christopher J. Kurran
Chief Executive Officer

Avis A. Zomer
Chief Financial Officer

HILLSBURG HARDWARE COMPANY
BALANCE SHEETS (in thousands)

December 31

ASSETS		2004		2003
Current assets				
Cash and cash equivalents	$	828	$	743
Trade receivables (net of allowances of $1,240 and $1,311)		18,957		16,210
Other receivables		945		915
Merchandise inventory		29,865		31,600
Prepaid expenses		432		427
Total current assets		51,027		49,895
Property and equipment				
Land		3,456		3,456
Buildings		32,500		32,000
Equipment, furniture, and fixtures		6,304		8,660
Less: accumulated depreciation		(31,920)		(33,220)
Total property and equipment (net)		10,340		10,896
Total assets	$	**61,367**	$	**60,791**
LIABILITIES AND STOCKHOLDERS' EQUITY				
Current liabilities				
Trade accounts payable	$	4,720	$	4,432
Notes payable		4,180		4,589
Accrued payroll		1,350		715
Accrued payroll tax		120		116
Accrued interest and dividends payable		2,050		1,975
Accrued income tax		796		523
Total current liabilities		13,216		12,350
Long-term notes payable		24,120		26,520
Deferred income taxes		738		722
Other long-term payables		830		770
STOCKHOLDERS' EQUITY				
Capital stock ($1 par value; 5,000,000 shares issued)		5,000		5,000
Capital in excess of par value		3,500		3,500
Retained earnings		13,963		11,929
Total stockholders' equity:		**22,463**		**20,429**
Total liabilities and stockholders' equity	$	**61,367**	$	**60,791**

See Notes to Financial Statements.

"We offer our customers a range of high-quality products that cannot be found at most national chains."

STATEMENT OF OPERATIONS

HILLSBURG HARDWARE COMPANY
STATEMENT OF OPERATIONS (in thousands)
Year Ended December 31

	2004	2003	2002
Net sales	$143,086	$131,226	$122,685
Cost of sales	103,241	94,876	88,724
Gross profit	39,845	36,350	33,961
Selling, general and administrative expenses	32,475	29,656	28,437
Operating income	7,370	6,694	5,524
Other income and expense			
Interest expense	2,409	2,035	2,173
Gain on sale of assets	(720)	—	—
Total other income/expense (net)	1,689	2,035	2,173
Earnings before income taxes	5,681	4,659	3,351
Provision for income taxes	1,747	1,465	1,072
Net income	$3,934	$3,194	$2,279
Earnings per share	$0.79	$0.64	$0.46

See Notes to Financial Statements.

STOCKHOLDERS' EQUITY

HILLSBURG HARDWARE COMPANY
STATEMENTS OF STOCKHOLDERS' EQUITY (in thousands)

| | Common Stock | | Paid-in | Retained | Total |
	Shares	Par value	Capital	Earnings	Stockholders' Equity
Balance as of December 31, 2001	5,000	$5,000	$3,500	$10,256	$18,756
Net income				2,279	2,279
Dividends paid				(1,900)	(1,900)
Balance as of December 31, 2002	5,000	5,000	3,500	10,635	19,135
Net income				3,194	3,194
Dividends paid				(1,900)	(1,900)
Balance as of December 31, 2003	5,000	5,000	3,500	11,929	20,429
Net income				3,934	3,934
Dividends paid				(1,900)	(1,900)
Balance as of December 31, 2004	5,000	$5,000	$3,500	$13,963	$22,463

See Notes to Financial Statements.

HILLSBURG HARDWARE COMPANY
STATEMENTS OF CASH FLOWS (in thousands)
Year Ended December 31

Operating activities	2004	2003	2002
Net income	$ 3,934	$ 3,194	$ 2,279
Adjustments to reconcile net income to net cash provided by (used in) operating activities:			
Depreciation and amortization	1,452	1,443	1,505
(Gain) or Loss on sale of assets	(720)	—	—
Deferred income taxes increase (decrease)	16	(8)	43
Changes in assets and liabilities:			
Trade and other receivables	(2,777)	(393)	(918)
Merchandise inventory	1,735	(295)	(430)
Prepaid expenses	(5)	(27)	(55)
Accounts payable	288	132	76
Accrued liabilities	714	77	142
Income taxes payable	273	23	13
Net cash provided by operating activities	4,910	4,146	2,655
Investing activities			
Capital expenditures	(10,500)	(1,800)	(2,292)
Sale of equipment	10,324	—	—
Net cash used in investing activities	(176)	(1,800)	(2,292)
Financing activities			
Dividend payment	(1,900)	(1,900)	(1,900)
Proceeds (repayments) from borrowings (net)	(2,749)	(423)	1,602
Net cash used in financing activities	(4,649)	(2,323)	(298)
Net increase in cash and cash equivalents	85	23	65
Cash and cash equivalents at beginning of year	743	720	655
Cash and cash equivalents at end of year	$ 828	$ 743	$ 720

See Notes to Financial Statements.

NOTES TO FINANCIAL STATEMENTS

1. DESCRIPTION OF SIGNIFICANT ACCOUNTING POLICIES AND BUSINESS

We are a wholesale distributor of high-quality power tools, hand tools, electrical equipment, landscaping equipment, residential and commercial construction equipment, and paint products. The majority of our customers are smaller, independent hardware stores located in Illinois, Michigan, Wisconsin, Ohio, and Missouri.

Allowance for Doubtful Accounts: Our allowance for doubtful accounts is maintained to account for expected credit losses. Estimates of bad debts are based on individual customer risks and historical collection trends. Allowances are evaluated and updated when conditions occur that give rise to collection issues.

Merchandise Inventory: Merchandise inventory is presented at the lower of average cost or market. To present accurately the estimated net realizable value of the accounts, we adjust inventory balances when current and expected future market conditions, as well as recent and historical turnover trends, indicate adjustments are necessary.

Property, Plant and Equipment: Land, buildings, computers and other equipment, and furniture and fixtures are stated at historical cost. Depreciation is calculated on a straight-line basis over estimated useful lives of the assets. Estimated useful lives are 20 to 35 years for buildings and 2 to 10 years for equipment and furniture and fixtures.

Revenue Recognition: Revenues are recognized when goods are shipped, title has passed, the sales price is fixed, and collectibility is reasonably assured. A sales returns and allowance account is maintained to reflect estimated future returns and allowances. Adjustments to the sales returns and allowance account are made in the same period as the related sales are recorded and are based on historical trends, as well as analyses of other relevant factors. Sales are recorded net of returns and allowances in the statements referred to in this report.

Income Taxes: The deferred income tax account includes temporary differences between book (financial accounting) income and taxable income (for IRS reporting purposes). The account consists largely of temporary differences related to (1) the valuation of inventory, (2) depreciation, and (3) other accruals.

2. OTHER RECEIVABLES

The other receivables balance consists largely of vendor allowances and vendor rebates. When vendor allowances and vendor rebates are recognized (all activities required by the supplier are completed, the amount is determinable, and collectibility is reasonably certain), they are recorded as reductions of costs of goods sold.

3. NOTES PAYABLE

Notes payable for the year ended December 31, 2004, consists of three notes payable to the bank. Each note carries a fixed interest rate of 8.5%. One note for $4,180,000 matures in June 2005 and the other two

mature on December 31, 2007. During 2004, there was an additional note outstanding in the amount of $4,400,000, which was paid off during October 2004.

4. COMMITMENTS

The Company is currently committed to an operating lease that expires in 2008. Rental payments for the remainder of the contract are set at $312,000 per annum.

5. SEGMENT REPORTING

The Company operates in one segment. The breakdown of revenues (in thousands) from different products is listed in the chart below:

SEGMENT REPORTING			
	2004	**2003**	**2002**
Power Tools	$ 31,479	$ 27,557	$ 26,991
Hand Tools	21,463	19,684	18,403
Landscaping Equipment	14,309	15,645	13,494
Electrical Goods	17,170	15,849	11,042
Residential Construction Equipment	21,463	18,372	15,949
Commercial Construction Equipment	11,447	10,498	9,815
Paint Products	25,755	23,621	26,991
	$143,086	**$131,226**	**$122,685**

6. EARNINGS PER SHARE

Earnings per share calculations for 2004, 2003, and 2002 were computed as follows:

Numerators
(net income in thousands): $3,934, $3,194, and $2,279

Denominators
(shares of common stock): 5,000,000
(unchanged for all years)

Diluted earnings per share was the same as basic earnings per share for all years.

**Management's Discussion and Analysis
of Financial Condition and Results of Operations**

The following discussion and analysis of the results of our operations and our financial condition are based on the financial statements and related notes included in this report. When preparing the financial statements, we are frequently required to use our best estimates and judgments. These estimates and judgments affect certain asset, liability, revenue, and expense account balances. Therefore, estimates are evaluated constantly based on our analyses of historical trends and our understanding of the general business environment in which we operate. There are times, however, when different circumstances and assumptions cause actual results to differ from those expected when judgments were originally made. The accounting policies referred to in Note 1 to the financial statements, in our opinion, influence the judgments and estimates we use to prepare our financial statements.

RESULTS OF OPERATIONS

For the year ended December 31, 2004, gross profit increased by 9.6% or $3,495,000 from 2003. This increase in gross profit more than offsets the increase in operating expenses from 2003 to 2004 of $2,819,000 or 9.5%. The increase in gross margin largely explains the operating income increase of $676,000.

For the year ended December 31, 2003, gross profit increased by $2,389,000 or 7% from 2002. Total operating expenses increased by $1,219,000 or approximately 4.3% from 2002. The increase in gross profit offset the total operating expense increase, and the net result was a $1,170,000 increase in operating income.

Net Sales: From 2003 to 2004 net sales increased by $11,860,000 or 9%. The increase in net sales can be explained largely by an aggressive advertising campaign that the Company organized during the second half of 2004. Net sales for 2003 increased by $8,541,000 or 7.0% from 2002, which is consistent with industrywide average revenue growth of 7% from 2002 to 2003.

Gross Profit: Gross profit as a percentage of net sales stayed relatively stable at 27.68% and 27.70% in 2002 and 2003, respectively, but increased to 27.85% in 2004. The 2004 increase is mostly due to improved vendor incentive programs, our focus on cost containment, and increases in the resale values of certain commodities such as PVC piping material and certain types of metal wiring. While gross profit percentages in the industry have declined somewhat, our position as a niche provider in the overall hardware market allows us to charge premium prices without losing customers.

Selling, General and Administrative Expenses: Selling expenses increased by $1,911,000 or 14.8% from 2003 to 2004 and by $805,000 or 6.7% from 2002 to 2003. As a percentage of net sales, selling expens-es increased by 0.52% since 2003 and decreased by 0.03% from 2002 to 2003. The increase in selling expenses as a percentage of net sales from 2003 to 2004 is due to our new advertising campaign and increased expenditures on sales meetings and training.

General and administrative expenses increased by $908,000 or 5.4% from 2003 to 2004 and by $414,000 or 2.5% from 2002 to 2003. As a percentage of net sales, general and administrative expenses decreased by 0.42% since 2003 and decreased by 0.55% from 2002 to 2003. The overall increase from 2003 to 2004 was caused mostly by unexpected repairs needed to reattach and replace damaged shelving units in our main warehouse building.

Interest Expense: In 2004, interest expense increased by $374,000, or approximately 18.4%, compared to 2003. The increase was due to an overall interest rate increase and the restructuring of debt covenants that are less restrictive but demand higher interest rates. In 2003 interest expense decreased by $138,000 or 6.4% compared to 2002. The 2003 decrease was mainly due to the Company's decision to decrease the level of long-term debt. The average interest rates on short- and long-term debt during 2004 were approximately 10.5% and 8.5% respectively.

LIQUIDITY

During 2004, our working capital requirements were primarily financed through our line of credit, under which we are permitted to borrow up to the lesser of $7,000,000 or 75% of accounts receivable outstanding less than 30 days. The average interest rate on these short-term borrowings in 2004 was approximately 10.5%

Cash provided by operating activities for 2004 and 2003 was $4,910,000 and $4,146,000 respectively. The change from 2003 to 2004 is primarily due to the increase in net income. Increases in receivables were largely offset by decreases in inventories and increases in payables and other current liabilities. The increase in cash provided from operating activities of $1,491,000 from 2002 to 2003 is largely the result of the increase in net income and smaller increases in receivables and merchandise inventory in 2003 compared to 2002. We believe that cash flow from operations and the available short-term line of credit will continue to allow us to finance operations throughout the current year.

STATEMENT OF CONDITION

Merchandise inventory and trade accounts receivable together accounted for over 95% of current assets in both 2004 and 2003. Merchandise inventory turned over approximately 3.4 times in 2004 and 3.0 times in 2003. Average days to sell inventory were 108.6 and 120.9 in 2004 and 2003 respectively. Net trade receivables turned over approximately 7.6 times in 2004 and in 2003. Days to collect accounts receivable computations were 48.1 and 48.0 in 2004 and 2003 respectively. Both inventory and accounts receivable turnover are lower than industry averages. We plan for this difference to satisfy the market in which we operate. Our market consists of smaller, independent hardware stores that need more favorable receivable collection terms and immediate delivery of inventory. Because we hold large amounts of inventory, we are able to fill orders quicker than most of our competitors even during the busiest times of the year.

OUTLOOK

During 2004 we experienced another year of noticeable improvement. The Company's financial performance can largely be attributed to (1) a continued focus on cost containment, (2) productivity improvements, (3) aggressive advertising, and (4) the implementation of programs designed to enhance customer satisfaction.

During 2005, we will continue to apply the same strategic efforts that improved 2004 performance. We are also implementing a new warehouse information system designed to increase productivity and reduce stocking and distribution costs. Management believes that earnings growth will be primarily driven by (1) continued focus on customer satisfaction, (2) penetration into markets currently dominated by national wholesale hardware store chains, and (3) the use of technology to attract additional customers and promote more efficient operations.

INFORMATION CONCERNING FORWARD-LOOKING STATEMENTS

This report contains certain forward-looking statements (referenced by such terms as "expects" or "believes") that are subject to the effects of various factors including (1) changes in wholesale hardware prices, (2) changes in the general business environment, (3) the intensity of the competitive arena, (4) new national wholesale hardware chain openings, and (5) certain other matters influencing the Company's ability to react to changing market conditions. Therefore, management wishes to make readers aware that the aforementioned factors could cause the actual results of our operations to differ considerably from those indicated by any forward-looking statements included in this report.

HILLSBURG HARDWARE COMPANY
FIVE-YEAR FINANCIAL SUMMARY (in thousands, except for per share amounts)

BALANCE SHEET DATA:	2004	2003	2002	2001	2000
Current assets	$ 51,027	$ 49,895	$ 49,157	$ 47,689	$ 46,504
Total assets	61,367	60,791	59,696	57,441	51,580
Current liabilities	13,216	12,350	12,173	12,166	9,628
Long-term notes payable	24,120	26,520	26,938	25,432	25,223
Total stockholders' equity	22,463	20,429	19,135	18,756	15,764
INCOME STATEMENT DATA:					
Net sales	$ 143,086	$ 131,226	$ 122,685	$ 120,221	$ 117,115
Cost of sales	103,241	94,876	88,724	88,112	85,663
Gross profit	39,845	36,350	33,961	32,109	31,452
Earnings before income taxes	5,681	4,659	3,351	3,124	1,450
Net income	3,934	3,194	2,279	2,142	994
Cash provided by operating activities	4,910	4,146	2,655	1,811	1,232
Per common share data:					
Net income	$ 0.79	$ 0.64	$ 0.46	$ 0.43	$ 0.22
Cash dividends per share	$ 0.38	$ 0.38	$ 0.38	$ —	$ —
Common shares outstanding	5,000	5,000	5,000	5,000	4,500
KEY OPERATING RESULTS AND FINANCIAL POSITION RATIOS:					
Gross profit (%)	27.85%	27.70%	27.68%	26.71%	26.86%
Return on assets (%)	9.30%	7.73%	5.72%	5.73%	2.86%
Return on common equity (%)	26.49%	23.55%	17.69%	18.10%	9.50%

AUDIT EVIDENCE

SOMETIMES THE MOST IMPORTANT EVIDENCE IS NOT FOUND IN THE ACCOUNTING RECORDS

Crenshaw Properties was a real estate developer that specialized in self-storage facilities that it sold to limited partner investors. Crenshaw's role was to identify projects, serve as general partner with a small investment, and raise capital from pension funds. Crenshaw had an extensive network of people who marketed these investments on a commission basis. As general partner, Crenshaw earned significant fees for related activities, including promotional fees, investment management fees, and real estate commissions.

As long as the investments were successful, Crenshaw prospered. Because the investments were reasonably long-term, the underlying investors did not pay careful attention to them. However, in the mid-1980s, the market for self-storage units in many parts of the country became oversaturated. Occupancy rates, rental rates, and market values declined.

Ralph Smalley, of Hambusch, Robinson & Co., did the annual audit of Crenshaw. As part of the audit, Smalley obtained financial statements for all of the partnerships in which Crenshaw was the general partner. He traced amounts back to the original partnership documents and determined that amounts agreed with partnership records. Smalley also determined that they were mathematically accurate. The purpose of doing these tests was to determine that the partnership assets, at original cost, exceeded liabilities, including the mortgage on the property and loans from investors. Under the law, Crenshaw, as general partner, was liable for any deficiency.

Every year, Smalley concluded that there were no significant deficiencies in partnership net assets for which Crenshaw would be liable. What Smalley failed to recognize in the late 1980s, however, was that current market prices had declined significantly because cash flows were lower than those projected in the original partnership offering documents. In fact, Crenshaw went bankrupt in 1989, and Hambusch, Robinson & Co. was named in a suit to recover damages filed by the bankruptcy trustee.

LEARNING OBJECTIVES

After studying this chapter, you should be able to

7-1 Contrast audit evidence with evidence used by other professions.

7-2 Identify the four audit evidence decisions that are needed to create an audit program.

7-3 Specify the characteristics that determine the persuasiveness of evidence.

7-4 Identify and apply the seven types of evidence used in auditing.

7-5 Understand the purposes of audit documentation.

7-6 Prepare organized audit documentation.

7-7 Describe how e-commerce affects audit evidence and audit documentation.

The foundation of any audit is the evidence gathered and evaluated by the auditor. The auditor must have the knowledge and skill to accumulate sufficient competent evidence on every audit to meet the standards of the profession. As described in the opening vignette, Ralph Smalley learned the effect of not accumulating the appropriate evidence after being sued over his audit of Crenshaw Properties. This chapter deals with the types of evidence decisions auditors make, the evidence available to auditors, and the use of that evidence in performing audits.

NATURE OF EVIDENCE

OBJECTIVE 7-1

Contrast audit evidence with evidence used by other professions.

Evidence was defined in Chapter 1 as any *information used by the auditor* to determine whether the information being audited is stated in accordance with the established criteria. The information varies greatly in the extent to which it persuades the auditor whether financial statements are stated in accordance with generally accepted accounting principles. Evidence includes information that is highly persuasive, such as the auditor's count of marketable securities, and less persuasive information, such as responses to questions of client employees.

Audit Evidence Contrasted with Legal and Scientific Evidence

The use of evidence is not unique to auditors. Evidence is also used extensively by scientists, lawyers, and historians.

Through television, most people are familiar with the use of evidence in legal cases dealing with the guilt or innocence of a party charged with a crime such as robbery. In legal cases, there are well-defined rules of evidence enforced by a judge for the protection of the innocent. It is common, for example, for legal evidence to be judged inadmissible on the grounds that it is irrelevant, prejudicial, or based on hearsay.

Similarly, in scientific experiments, the scientist obtains evidence to draw conclusions about a theory. Assume, for example, that a medical scientist is evaluating a new medicine that may provide relief for asthma sufferers. The scientist will gather evidence from a large number of controlled experiments over an extended period to determine the effectiveness of the medicine.

The auditor also gathers evidence to draw conclusions. Different evidence is used by auditors than by scientists and in cases of law, and it is used in different ways, but in all

TABLE 7-1	Characteristics of Evidence for a Scientific Experiment, Legal Case, and Audit of Financial Statements		
Basis of Comparison	Scientific Experiment Involving Testing a Medicine	Legal Case Involving an Accused Thief	Audit of Financial Statements
Use of the evidence	Determine effects of using the medicine	Decide guilt or innocence of accused	Determine whether statements are fairly presented
Nature of evidence used	Results of repeated experiments	Direct evidence and testimony by witnesses and parties involved	Various types of audit evidence generated by the auditor, third parties, and the client
Party or parties evaluating evidence	Scientist	Jury and judge	Auditor
Certainty of conclusions from evidence	Vary from uncertain to near certainty	Requires guilt beyond a reasonable doubt	High level of assurance
Nature of conclusions	Recommend or not recommend use of medicine	Innocence or guilt of party	Issue one of several alternative types of audit reports
Typical consequences of incorrect conclusions from evidence	Society uses ineffective or harmful medicine	Guilty party is not penalized or innocent party is found guilty	Statement users make incorrect decisions and auditor may be sued

three cases, evidence is used to reach conclusions. Table 7-1 (p. 162) illustrates key characteristics of evidence from the perspective of a scientist doing an experiment, an attorney prosecuting an accused thief, and an auditor of financial statements. There are six bases of comparison. Note the similarities and differences among the three professions.

AUDIT EVIDENCE DECISIONS

OBJECTIVE 7-2

Identify the four audit evidence decisions that are needed to create an audit program.

A major decision facing every auditor is determining the *appropriate types and amounts* of evidence to accumulate to be satisfied that the components of the client's financial statements and the overall statements are fairly stated, or that the client maintained effective internal control over financial reporting. This judgment is important because of the prohibitive cost of examining and evaluating all available evidence. For example, in an audit of financial statements of most organizations, it is impossible for the CPA to examine the contents of all computer files or available evidence such as cancelled checks, vendors' invoices, customer orders, payroll time cards, and the many other types of documents and records.

The auditor's *decisions* on evidence accumulation can be broken down into the following four subdecisions:

1. Which audit procedures to use
2. What sample size to select for a given procedure
3. Which items to select from the population
4. When to perform the procedures

Audit Procedures

An **audit procedure** is the detailed instruction for the collection of a type of audit evidence that is to be obtained at some time during the audit. In designing audit procedures, it is common to spell them out in sufficiently specific terms to permit their use as instructions during the audit. For example, the following is an audit procedure for the verification of cash disbursements:

• Obtain the cash disbursements journal and compare the payee name, amount, and date on the cancelled check with the cash disbursements journal.

Sample Size

Once an audit procedure is selected, it is possible to vary the sample size from one to all the items in the population being tested. In the preceding audit procedure, suppose 6,600 checks are recorded in the cash disbursements journal. The auditor might select a sample size of 50 checks for comparison with the cash disbursements journal. The decision of how many items to test must be made by the auditor for each audit procedure. The sample size for any given procedure is likely to vary from audit to audit.

Items to Select

After the sample size has been determined for an audit procedure, it is still necessary to decide which items in the population to test. If the auditor decides, for example, to select 50 cancelled checks from a population of 6,600 for comparison with the cash disbursements journal, several different methods can be used to select the specific checks to be examined. The auditor could (1) select a week and examine the first 50 checks, (2) select the 50 checks with the largest amounts, (3) select the checks randomly, or (4) select those checks that the auditor thinks are most likely to be in error. Or a combination of these methods could be used.

Timing

An audit of financial statements usually covers a period such as a year, and an audit is usually not completed until several weeks or months after the end of the period. The timing of audit procedures can therefore vary from early in the accounting period to long after it has ended. In part, the timing decision is affected by when the client needs the audit to be completed. In the audit of financial statements, the client normally wants the audit completed 1 to 3 months after year-end. The SEC currently requires that all public companies file audited financial statements with the SEC within 3 months of the companies' fiscal year-end. However, timing is also influenced by when the auditor believes the audit evidence will be most effective and when audit staff is available. For example, auditors often prefer to do counts of inventory as close to the balance sheet date as possible.

Audit procedures often incorporate sample size, items to select, and timing into the procedure. The following is a modification of the audit procedure previously used to include all four audit evidence decisions. (Italics identify the timing, items to select, and sample size decisions.)

• Obtain the *October* cash disbursements journal and compare the payee name, amount, and date on the cancelled check with the cash disbursements journal for a *randomly selected sample of 40* check numbers.

Audit Program

Audit Programs Resource

The list of audit procedures for an audit area or an entire audit is called an **audit program.** The audit program always includes a list of the audit procedures. It usually also includes sample sizes, items to select, and the timing of the tests. Normally, there is an audit program, including several audit procedures, for each component of the audit. Therefore, there will be an audit program for accounts receivable, for sales, and so on. An example of an audit program that includes audit procedures, sample size, items to select, and timing is given on page 392 in Table 13-4. The right side of the audit program also includes the balance-related audit objectives for each procedure, as studied in Chapter 6.

Most auditors use computers to facilitate the preparation of audit programs. The simplest computer application involves typing the audit program on a word processor and saving it from one year to the next to facilitate changes and updating. A more sophisticated application involves the use of a specialized program designed to help the auditor think through the planning considerations of the audit and select appropriate procedures using audit program generator software or other audit planning database templates.

PERSUASIVENESS OF EVIDENCE

OBJECTIVE 7-3

Specify the characteristics that determine the persuasiveness of evidence.

The third standard of field work that was introduced in Chapter 2 requires the auditor to accumulate *sufficient competent evidence to support the opinion issued.* Because of the nature of audit evidence and the cost considerations of doing an audit, it is unlikely that the auditor will be completely convinced that the opinion is correct. However, the auditor must be persuaded that the opinion is correct with a high level of assurance. By combining all evidence from the entire audit, the auditor is able to decide when he or she is persuaded to issue an audit report.

The two determinants of the **persuasiveness of evidence** are *competence* and *sufficiency,* which are taken directly from the third standard of field work.

Competence

Competence of evidence refers to the degree to which evidence can be considered believable or worthy of trust. If evidence is considered highly competent, it is a great help in persuading the auditor that financial statements are fairly stated. For example, if an auditor counted the inventory, that evidence would be more competent than if management gave the auditor its own figures. Most auditors, as well as the authors of this text, use the term **reliability of evidence** as being synonymous with competence.

Competence of evidence deals only with the audit procedures selected. Competence cannot be improved by selecting a larger sample size or different population items. It can be improved only by selecting audit procedures that contain a higher quality of one or more of the following seven characteristics of competent evidence.

Relevance Evidence must *pertain to or be relevant to the audit objective* that the auditor is testing before it can be reliable. For example, assume that the auditor is concerned that a client is failing to bill customers for shipments (completeness objective). If the auditor selected a sample of duplicate sales invoices and traced each to related shipping documents, the evidence would *not be relevant* for the completeness objective and therefore would not be considered reliable evidence for that objective. A relevant procedure would be to trace a sample of shipping documents to related duplicate sales invoices to determine whether each had been billed. The second audit procedure is relevant and the first is not because the shipment of goods is the normal criterion used for determining whether a sale has occurred and should have been billed. By tracing from shipping documents to duplicate sales invoices, the auditor can determine whether shipments have been billed to customers. When the auditor traces from duplicate sales invoices to shipping documents, it is impossible to find unbilled shipments.

Relevance can be considered only in terms of specific audit objectives. Evidence may be relevant to one audit objective but not to a different one. In the previous example, when the auditor traced from the duplicate sales invoices to related shipping documents, the evidence was relevant to the existence objective. Most evidence is relevant to more than one, but not all, audit objectives.

Independence of Provider Evidence obtained from a source outside the entity is more reliable than that obtained from within. For example, external evidence such as communications from banks, attorneys, or customers is generally considered more reliable than answers obtained from inquiries of the client. Similarly, documents that originate from outside the client's organization are considered more reliable than are those that originate within the company and have never left the client's organization. An example of the former is an insurance policy and of the latter a purchase requisition.

Effectiveness of Client's Internal Controls When a client's internal controls are effective, evidence obtained is more reliable than when they are weak. For example, if internal controls over sales and billing are effective, the auditor could obtain more competent evidence from sales invoices and shipping documents than if the controls were inadequate.

Auditor's Direct Knowledge Evidence obtained directly by the auditor through physical examination, observation, computation, and inspection is more competent than information obtained indirectly. For example, if the auditor calculates the gross margin as a percentage of sales and compares it with previous periods, the evidence would be more reliable than if the auditor relied on the calculations of the controller.

Qualifications of Individuals Providing the Information Although the source of information is independent, the evidence will not be reliable unless the individual providing it is qualified to do so. Therefore, communications from attorneys and bank confirmations are typically more highly regarded than accounts receivable confirmations from persons not familiar with the business world. Also, evidence obtained directly by the auditor may not be reliable if the auditor lacks the qualifications to evaluate the evidence. For example, examination of an inventory of diamonds by an auditor not trained to distinguish between diamonds and glass would not provide reliable evidence of the existence of diamonds.

Degree of Objectivity Objective evidence is more reliable than evidence that requires considerable judgment to determine whether it is correct. Examples of objective evidence include confirmation of accounts receivable and bank balances, the physical count of securities and cash, and adding (footing) a list of accounts payable to determine whether it agrees with the balance in the general ledger. Examples of subjective evidence include a letter written by a client's attorney discussing the likely outcome of outstanding lawsuits against the client, observation of obsolescence of inventory during physical examination, and inquiries of the credit manager about the collectibility of noncurrent accounts receivable. When the reliability of subjective evidence is being evaluated, the qualifications of the person providing the evidence are important.

Timeliness The timeliness of audit evidence can refer either to when it is accumulated or to the period covered by the audit. Evidence is usually more reliable for balance sheet accounts when it is obtained as close to the balance sheet date as possible. For example, the auditor's count of marketable securities on the balance sheet date would be more reliable than a count 2 months earlier. For income statement accounts, evidence is more reliable if there is a sample from the entire period under audit rather than from only a part of the period. For example, a random sample of sales transactions for the entire year would be more reliable than a sample from only the first 6 months.

Sufficiency

The *quantity* of evidence obtained determines its sufficiency. **Sufficiency of evidence** is measured primarily by the sample size the auditor selects. For a given audit procedure, the evidence obtained from a sample of 100 would ordinarily be more sufficient than from a sample of 50.

Several factors determine the appropriate sample size in audits. The two most important ones are the auditor's expectation of misstatements and the effectiveness of the client's internal controls. To illustrate, assume in the audit of Jones Computer Parts Co. that the auditor concludes that there is a high likelihood of obsolete inventory because of the nature of the

Star Technology reported its advance of funds to Glen Culler as a note receivable on its balance sheet. Star Technology's auditors obtained a draft of the loan agreement and used that as the primary audit evidence to support the accounting treatment. The auditors, however, failed to obtain the final executed loan agreement. Unfortunately, there were big differences between the draft and final versions of the agreement that materially impacted the substance of the transaction. Instead of supporting the inclusion of the advanced funds as a receivable on Star

The audit firm learned about its oversight when its national office received an anonymous memo alleging the audit failure. The audit firm's follow-up on the matter ultimately led to an SEC investigation. The SEC eventually charged the audit firm partner for failure to obtain sufficient competent evidential matter and for failing to exercise due professional care. As a result of the partner's negligence, the SEC barred him from working in any capacity with a public company for a period of five years, among other penalties imposed by the SEC and the audit firm.

Source: *Accounting and Auditing Enforcement Release No. 455*, Commerce Clearing House, Inc., Chicago.

client's industry. The auditor would sample more inventory items for obsolescence in an audit such as this than one where the likelihood of obsolescence was low. Similarly, if the auditor concludes that a client has effective rather than ineffective internal controls over recording fixed assets, a smaller sample size in the audit of acquisitions of fixed assets is warranted.

In addition to sample size, the individual items tested affect the sufficiency of evidence. Samples containing population items with large dollar values, items with a high likelihood of misstatement, and items that are representative of the population are usually considered sufficient. In contrast, most auditors would usually consider samples insufficient that contain only the largest dollar items from the population unless these items make up a large portion of the total population amount.

Combined Effect

The persuasiveness of evidence can be evaluated only after considering the combination of competence and sufficiency, including the effects of the factors influencing competence and sufficiency. A large sample of evidence provided by an independent party is not persuasive unless it is relevant to the audit objective being tested. A large sample of evidence that is relevant but not objective is also not persuasive. Similarly, a small sample of only one or two pieces of highly competent evidence also typically lacks persuasiveness. The auditor must evaluate the degree to which both competence and sufficiency, including all factors influencing them, have been met when determining the persuasiveness of evidence.

There are direct relationships among the four evidence decisions and the two qualities that determine the persuasiveness of evidence. Table 7-2 shows those relationships.

To illustrate the relationships shown in Table 7-2, assume an auditor is verifying inventory that is a major item in the financial statements. Auditing standards require that the auditor be reasonably persuaded that inventory is not materially misstated. The auditor must therefore obtain a sufficient amount of competent evidence about inventory. This means deciding which procedures to use for auditing inventory to satisfy the competency requirements, as well as determining the appropriate sample size and items to select from the population to satisfy the sufficiency requirement. The combination of these four evidence decisions must result in sufficiently persuasive evidence to satisfy the auditor that inventory is materially correct. The audit program section for inventory will reflect these decisions. In practice, the auditor applies the four evidence decisions to specific audit objectives in deciding sufficient competent evidence.

Persuasiveness and Cost

In making decisions about evidence for a given audit, both persuasiveness and cost must be considered. It is rare when only one type of evidence is available for verifying information. The persuasiveness and cost of all alternatives should be considered before selecting the best type or types. The auditor's goal is to obtain a sufficient amount of competent

TABLE 7-2 — Relationships Among Evidence Decisions and Persuasiveness

Audit Evidence Decisions	Qualities Affecting Persuasiveness of Evidence

Audit procedures and timing	Competence
	  Relevance
	  Independence of provider
	  Effectiveness of internal controls
	  Auditor's direct knowledge
	  Qualifications of provider
	  Objectivity of evidence
	  Timeliness
	    When procedures are performed
	    Portion of period being audited

Sample size and items to select	Sufficiency
	  Adequate sample size
	  Selection of appropriate population items

evidence at the lowest possible total cost. However, cost is never an adequate justification for omitting a necessary procedure or not gathering an adequate sample size.

TYPES OF AUDIT EVIDENCE

OBJECTIVE 7-4

Identify and apply the seven types of evidence used in auditing.

In deciding which audit procedures to use, the auditor can choose from seven broad categories of evidence. These categories, called types of evidence, are listed below and are defined and discussed in this section:

1. Physical examination
2. Confirmation
3. Documentation
4. Analytical procedures
5. Inquiries of the client
6. Reperformance
7. Observation

Before beginning the study of types of evidence, it is useful to show the relationships among auditing standards, which were studied in Chapter 2, types of evidence, and the four evidence decisions discussed earlier in this chapter. These relationships are shown in Figure 7-1 (p. 168).

Notice that the standards are general, whereas audit procedures are specific. Types of evidence are broader than procedures and narrower than the standards. Every audit procedure obtains one or more types of evidence.

Physical examination is the inspection or count by the auditor of a *tangible asset*. This type of evidence is most often associated with inventory and cash, but it is also applicable to the verification of securities, notes receivable, and tangible fixed assets. The distinction between the physical examination of assets, such as marketable securities and cash, and the examination of documents, such as cancelled checks and sales documents, is important for auditing purposes. If the object being examined, such as a sales invoice, has no inherent value, the evidence is called documentation. For example, before a check is signed, it is a document; after it is signed, it becomes an asset; and when it is cancelled, it becomes a document again. Technically, physical examination of the check can occur only while the check is an asset.

Physical examination, which is a direct means of verifying that an asset actually exists (existence objective), is regarded as one of the most reliable and useful types of audit evidence. Generally, physical examination is an objective means of ascertaining both the quantity and the description of the asset. In some cases, it is also a useful method for evaluating an asset's condition or quality. However, physical examination is not sufficient evidence to

Physical Examination

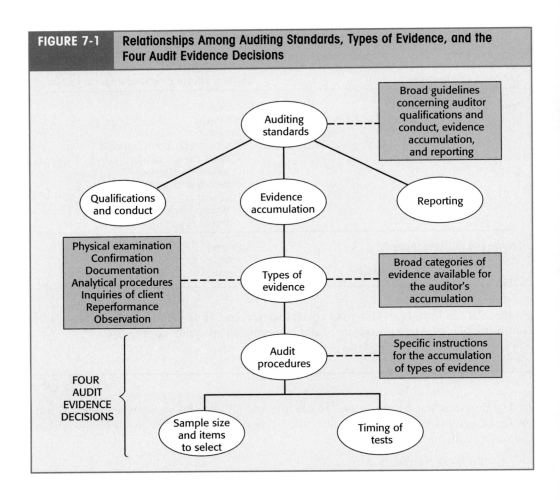

FIGURE 7-1 Relationships Among Auditing Standards, Types of Evidence, and the Four Audit Evidence Decisions

Auditing standards

Broad guidelines concerning auditor qualifications and conduct, evidence accumulation, and reporting

Qualifications and conduct

Evidence accumulation

Reporting

Physical examination
Confirmation
Documentation
Analytical procedures
Inquiries of client
Reperformance
Observation

Types of evidence

Broad categories of evidence available for the auditor's accumulation

FOUR AUDIT EVIDENCE DECISIONS

Audit procedures

Specific instructions for the accumulation of types of evidence

Sample size and items to select

Timing of tests

verify that existing assets are owned by the client (rights and obligations objective), and in many cases the auditor is not qualified to judge qualitative factors such as obsolescence or authenticity (net realizable value objective). Also, proper valuation for financial statement purposes usually cannot be determined by physical examination (accuracy objective).

Confirmation

Confirmation describes the *receipt* of a *written or oral response* from an *independent third party* verifying the accuracy of information that was *requested by the auditor*. The request is made to the client, and the client asks the independent third party to respond directly to the auditor. Because confirmations come from sources independent of the client, they are a highly regarded and often-used type of evidence. However, confirmations are relatively costly to obtain and may cause some inconvenience to those asked to supply them. Therefore, they are not used in every instance in which they are applicable. Because of the high reliability of confirmations, auditors typically obtain written responses rather than oral ones when it is practical. Written confirmations are easier for supervisors to review, and they provide better support if it is necessary to demonstrate that a confirmation was received.

Whether or not confirmations should be used depends on the reliability needs of the situation as well as the alternative evidence available. Traditionally, confirmations are seldom used in the audit of fixed asset additions because these can be verified adequately by documentation and physical examination. Similarly, confirmations are ordinarily not used to verify individual transactions between organizations, such as sales transactions, because the auditor can use documents for that purpose. Naturally, there are exceptions. Assume the auditor determines that there are two extraordinarily large sales transactions recorded 3 days before year-end. Confirmation of these two transactions may be appropriate.

SAS 67 (AU 330) identifies two common types of confirmation requests: positive confirmations and negative confirmations. A positive confirmation asks the recipient to respond in all circumstances. In contrast, with a negative confirmation the recipient is asked to respond only when the information is incorrect. Because confirmations are considered significant evidence only when returned, negative confirmations are less competent than positive confirmations.

A positive confirmation may request the recipient to provide the information (called a blank form), or the confirmation may include the information and request the respondent to indicate whether he or she agrees with the information. The latter type of positive confirmation is often used because the response rate is higher than for the blank form. However, because recipients may sign the request without verifying the information, this type of confirmation is considered less reliable.

When the auditor does not receive a response to a positive confirmation, it is common to send a second or third request and in some cases even request the client to contact the independent third party and ask for a response to the auditor. If other efforts fail or are considered too costly, the auditor may be able to use different evidence to satisfy the audit objective. This evidence is called alternative procedures.

When practical and reasonable, the confirmation of a sample of accounts receivable is *required* of CPAs. This requirement, imposed by SAS 67, exists because accounts receivable usually represent a significant balance on the financial statements, and confirmations are a highly reliable type of evidence.

Although confirmation is not required for any account other than accounts receivable, this type of evidence is useful in verifying many types of information. The major types of information that are often confirmed, along with the source of the confirmation, are indicated in Table 7-3.

To be considered reliable evidence, confirmations must be controlled by the auditor from the time they are prepared until they are returned. If the client controls the preparation of the confirmation, does the mailing, or receives the responses, the auditor has lost control and with it independence; thus, the reliability of the evidence is reduced.

TABLE 7-3	Information Often Confirmed
INFORMATION	**SOURCE**
Assets	
Cash in bank	Bank
Accounts receivable	Customer
Notes receivable	Maker
Owned inventory out on consignment	Consignee
Inventory held in public warehouses	Public warehouse
Cash surrender value of life insurance	Insurance company
Liabilities	
Accounts payable	Creditor
Notes payable	Lender
Advances from customers	Customer
Mortgages payable	Mortgagor
Bonds payable	Bondholder
Owners' Equity	
Shares outstanding	Registrar and transfer agent
Other Information	
Insurance coverage	Insurance company
Contingent liabilities	Bank, lender, and client's legal counsel
Bond indenture agreements	Bondholder
Collateral held by creditors	Creditor

Documentation

Documentation is the auditor's examination of the *client's documents and records* to substantiate the information that is or should be included in the financial statements. The documents examined by the auditor are the records used by the client to provide information for conducting its business in an organized manner. Because each transaction in the client's organization is normally supported by at least one document, there is a large volume of this type of evidence available. For example, the client often retains a customer order, a shipping document, and a duplicate sales invoice for each sales transaction. These same documents are useful evidence for verification by the auditor of the accuracy of the client's records for sales transactions. Documentation is a form of evidence widely used in every audit because it is usually readily available to the auditor at a relatively low cost. Sometimes it is the only reasonable type of evidence available.

Documents can be conveniently classified as internal and external. An **internal document** is one that has been prepared and used within the client's organization and is retained without ever going to an outside party such as a customer or a vendor. Examples of internal documents include duplicate sales invoices, employees' time reports, and inventory receiving reports. An **external document** is one that has been in the hands of someone outside the client's organization who is a party to the transaction being documented, but which is either currently in the hands of the client or readily accessible. In some cases, external documents originate outside the client's organization and end up in the hands of the client. Examples of this type of external document are vendors' invoices, cancelled notes payable, and insurance policies. Other documents, such as cancelled checks, originate with the client, go to an outsider, and are finally returned to the client.

The primary determinant of the auditor's willingness to accept a document as reliable evidence is whether it is internal or external and, when internal, whether it was created and processed under conditions of good internal control. Internal documents created and processed under conditions of weak internal control may not constitute reliable evidence.

Because external documents have been in the hands of both the client and another party to the transaction, there is some indication that both members are in agreement about the information and the conditions stated on the document. Therefore, external documents are considered more reliable evidence than internal ones. Some external documents have exceptional reliability because they are prepared with considerable care and often have been reviewed by attorneys or other qualified experts. Examples include title papers to property such as land, insurance policies, indenture agreements, and contracts.

When auditors use documentation to support recorded transactions or amounts, it is often called **vouching.** To vouch recorded acquisition transactions, the auditor might, for example, trace from the acquisitions journal to supporting vendors' invoices and receiving reports and thereby satisfy the existence objective. If the auditor traces from receiving reports to the acquisitions journal to satisfy the completeness objective, it would not be appropriate to call it vouching.

It is common in many companies for a considerable portion of clients' documentation to be available only in electronic form. For example, some companies use Electronic Data Interchange (EDI) to transact business electronically and complete purchase, shipping, billing, cash receipt, and cash disbursement transactions entirely by the exchange of electronic messages. Companies also use image processing systems to convert traditional documents into electronic images to facilitate storage and reference. Typically, the traditional documents are not retained.

Electronic Evidence

Both written and electronic information, such as records of electronic transfers, are valid and useful. SAS 80 recognizes these changes in the nature of documentary audit evidence.

Analytical Procedures

Analytical procedures use comparisons and relationships to assess whether account balances or other data appear reasonable. An example is comparing the gross margin percent in the current year with the preceding year's. Analytical procedures are used extensively in practice, and their use has increased with the availability of computers to perform the calculations. The Auditing Standards Board has concluded that analytical procedures are so important that they are *required during the planning and completion phases on all audits.* Analytical procedures are used for different purposes on an audit. The purposes are discussed next.

Understand the Client's Industry and Business Auditors must obtain knowledge about a client's industry and business as a part of planning an audit. By conducting analytical procedures in which the current year's unaudited information is compared with prior years' audited information or industry data, changes are highlighted. These changes can represent important trends or specific events, all of which will influence audit planning. For example, a decline in gross margin percentages over time may indicate increasing competition in the company's market area and the need to consider inventory pricing more carefully during the audit. Similarly, an increase in the balance in fixed assets may indicate a significant acquisition that must be reviewed.

Industry Information

Assess the Entity's Ability to Continue as a Going Concern Analytical procedures are often useful as an indication that the client company has financial problems. Certain analytical procedures can be helpful to the auditor in assessing the likelihood of failure. For example, if a higher-than-normal ratio of long-term debt to net worth is combined with a lower-than-average ratio of profits to total assets, a relatively high risk of financial failure may be indicated. Not only would such conditions affect the audit plan, they may indicate that substantial doubt exists about the entity's ability to continue as a going concern, which, as discussed in Chapter 3, would require a report modification.

Indicate the Presence of Possible Misstatements in the Financial Statements Significant unexpected differences between the current year's unaudited financial data and other data used in comparisons are commonly called **unusual fluctuations.** Unusual fluctuations occur when significant differences are not expected but do exist or when significant differences are expected but do not exist. In either case, one of the possible reasons for an unusual fluctuation is the presence of an accounting misstatement. Thus, if the unusual fluctuation is large, the auditor must determine the reason and be satisfied that the cause is a valid economic event and not a misstatement. For example, in comparing the ratio of the allowance for uncollectible accounts receivable to gross accounts receivable with that of the previous year, suppose that the ratio had decreased while, at the same time, accounts receivable turnover also decreased. The combination of these two pieces of information would indicate a possible understatement of the allowance. This aspect of analytical procedures is often called attention directing because it results in more detailed procedures in the specific audit areas where misstatements might be found.

Reduce Detailed Audit Tests When an analytical procedure reveals no unusual fluctuations, the implication is that the possibility of a material misstatement is minimized. In that case, the analytical procedure constitutes substantive evidence in support of the fair statement of the related account balances, and it is possible to perform fewer detailed tests in connection with those accounts. For example, if analytical procedures results of a small account balance such as prepaid insurance are favorable, no detailed tests may be necessary. In other cases, certain audit procedures can be eliminated, sample sizes can be reduced, or the timing of the procedures can be moved farther away from the balance sheet date.

Inquiry is the obtaining of *written* or *oral* information from the client in response to questions from the auditor. Although considerable evidence is obtained from the client through inquiry, it usually cannot be regarded as conclusive because it is not from an independent source and may be biased in the client's favor. Therefore, when the auditor obtains evidence through inquiry, it is normally necessary to obtain further corroborating evidence through other procedures. As an illustration, when the auditor wants to obtain information about the client's method of recording and controlling accounting transactions, the auditor usually begins by asking the client how the internal controls operate. Later, the auditor performs audit tests using documentation and observation to determine whether the transactions are recorded (completeness objective) and authorized (existence objective) in the manner stated.

Inquiries of the Client

As the word implies, **reperformance** involves rechecking a sample of the computations and transfers of information made by the client during the period under audit. Rechecking of computations consists of testing the client's arithmetical accuracy. It includes such procedures as extending sales invoices and inventory, adding journals and subsidiary records, and checking the calculation of depreciation expense and prepaid expenses. Rechecking of

Reperformance

transfers of information consists of tracing amounts to be confident that when the same information is included in more than one place, it is recorded at the same amount each time. For example, the auditor normally makes limited tests to ascertain that the information in the sales journal has been included for the proper customer and at the correct amount in the subsidiary accounts receivable records and is accurately summarized in the general ledger. A considerable portion of auditors' reperformance is done by computer-assisted audit software.

Observation

Observation is the use of the senses to assess certain activities. Throughout the audit, there are many opportunities to exercise sight, hearing, touch, and smell to evaluate a wide range of items. For example, the auditor may tour the plant to obtain a general impression of the client's facilities, observe whether equipment is rusty to evaluate whether it is obsolete, and watch individuals perform accounting tasks to determine whether the person assigned a responsibility is performing it. Observation is rarely sufficient by itself because there is a risk that the client personnel involved in those activities are aware of the auditor's presence. Therefore, they may perform their responsibilities in accordance with company policy but resume normal activities once the auditor is not in sight. It is necessary to follow up initial impressions with other kinds of corroborative evidence. Nevertheless, observation is useful in most parts of the audit.

Competence of Types of Evidence

The characteristics discussed earlier in the chapter for determining the competence of evidence are related to the seven types of evidence in Table 7-4. Note that two of the characteristics that determine the competency of evidence—relevance and timeliness—are not included in Table 7-4. Each of the seven types of evidence included in the table has the potential to be both relevant and timely, depending on its source and when the evidence is obtained. Several other observations are apparent from a study of Table 7-4.

First, the effectiveness of the client's internal controls has a significant impact on the competence of most types of evidence. For example, internal documentation from a company with effective internal control is more reliable because the documents are more likely to be accurate. Similarly, analytical procedures will not be competent evidence if the controls that produced the data provide inaccurate information.

TABLE 7-4	Competence of Types of Evidence				
	Criteria to Determine Competence				
Type of Evidence	**Independence of Provider**	**Effectiveness of Client's Internal Controls**	**Auditor's Direct Knowledge**	**Qualifications of Provider**	**Objectivity of Evidence**
Physical examination	High (auditor does)	Varies	High	Normally high (auditor does)	High
Confirmation	High	Not applicable	Low	Varies—usually high	High
Documentation	Varies—external more independent than internal	Varies	Low	Varies	High
Analytical procedures	High/low (auditor does/ client responds)	Varies	Low	Normally high (auditor does/ client responds)	Varies—usually low
Inquiries of client	Low (client provides)	Not applicable	Low	Varies	Varies—low to high
Reperformance	High (auditor does)	Varies	High	High (auditor does)	High
Observation	High (auditor does)	Varies	High	Normally high (auditor does)	Medium

Second, both physical examination and reperformance are likely to be highly reliable if the internal controls are effective, but their use differs considerably. These two types of evidence effectively illustrate that equally reliable evidence may be completely different.

Third, a specific type of evidence is rarely sufficient by itself to provide competent evidence to satisfy any audit objective. It is apparent from examining Table 7-4 that observation, inquiries of the client, and analytical procedures are examples of this.

Cost of Types of Evidence

The two most expensive types of evidence are physical examination and confirmation. Physical examination is costly because it normally requires the auditor's presence when the client is counting the asset, often on the balance sheet date. For example, physical examination of inventory can result in several auditors traveling to widely separated geographical locations. Confirmation is costly because the auditor must follow careful procedures in the confirmation preparation, mailing, and receipt, and in the follow-up of nonresponses and exceptions.

Documentation and analytical procedures are moderately costly. If client personnel locate documents for the auditor and organize them for convenient use, documentation usually has a fairly low cost. When auditors must find those documents themselves, documentation can be extremely costly. Even under ideal circumstances, information and data on documents are sometimes complex and require interpretation and analysis. For example, it is usually time-consuming to read and evaluate a client's contracts, lease agreements, and minutes of the board of directors meetings. Analytical procedures are considerably less expensive than confirmations and physical examination. Therefore, most auditors prefer to replace tests of details with analytical procedures when possible. To illustrate, it may be far less expensive to calculate and review sales and accounts receivable ratios than to confirm accounts receivable. If it is possible to reduce or replace confirmation by performing analytical procedures, considerable cost savings can occur. But analytical procedures require the auditor to decide which analytical procedures to use, make the calculations, and evaluate the results. Doing so often takes considerable time.

The three least-expensive types of evidence are observation, inquiries of the client, and reperformance. Observation is normally done concurrently with other audit procedures. An auditor can easily observe whether client personnel are following appropriate inventory counting procedures at the same time he or she counts a sample of inventory (physical examination). Inquiries of clients are done extensively on every audit and normally have a low cost. Certain inquiries may be costly, such as obtaining written statements from the client documenting discussions throughout the audit. Reperformance is usually low cost because it involves simple calculations and tracing that can be done at the auditor's convenience. Often, the auditor's computer software is used to perform many of these tests.

Application of Types of Evidence to the Four Evidence Decisions

An application of three types of evidence to the four evidence decisions for one balance-related audit objective—inventory quantities on the client's perpetual records agree with items physically on hand—is shown in Table 7-5 (p. 174). First, examine column 3 in Table 6-3 on page 150. These are the balance-related audit objectives for the audit of inventory for Hillsburg Hardware Co. The overall objective is to obtain persuasive evidence at minimum cost to verify that inventory is materially correct. The auditor must therefore decide which audit procedures to use to satisfy each balance-related audit objective, what the sample size should be for each procedure, which items from the population to include in the sample, and when to perform each procedure.

For the objective "inventory quantities on the client's perpetual records agree with items physically on hand," the auditor selected the three types of evidence included in Table 7-5. The auditor decided that the other four types of evidence studied in this chapter were not relevant or necessary for this objective. Only one audit procedure is included for each type of evidence, and illustrative decisions for sample size, items to select, and timing are shown for each procedure.

Terms Used in Audit Procedures

As stated earlier, audit procedures are the detailed steps, usually written in the form of instructions, for the accumulation of the seven types of audit evidence. They should be sufficiently clear to enable members of the audit team to understand what is to be done.

TABLE 7-5	Types of Evidence and Four Evidence Decisions for a Balance-Related Audit Objective for Inventory*			
		Evidence Decisions		
Type of Evidence	Audit Procedure	Sample Size	Items to Select	Timing
Observation	Observe client's personnel counting inventory to determine whether they are properly following instructions	All count teams	Not applicable	Balance sheet date
Physical examination	Count a sample of inventory and compare quantity and description to client's counts	120 items	40 items with large dollar value, plus 80 randomly selected	Balance sheet date
Documentation	Compare quantity on client's perpetual records to quantity on client's counts	70 items	30 items with large dollar value, plus 40 randomly selected	Balance sheet date

*Balance-related audit objective: Inventory quantities on the client's perpetual records agree with items physically on hand.

Several different terms are commonly used to describe audit procedures. These are presented and defined in Table 7-6. To help you understand each term, an illustrative audit procedure and the type of evidence that it is associated with are shown.

AUDIT DOCUMENTATION

According to auditing standards, **audit documentation** is the *principal record of auditing procedures applied, evidence obtained, and conclusions reached by the auditor in the engagement.* Audit documentation should include all the information the auditor considers necessary to conduct the audit adequately and to provide support for the audit report. Audit documentation may also be referred to as working papers. Increasingly, audit documentation is maintained in computerized files.

Purposes of Audit Documentation

The overall objective of audit documentation is to aid the auditor in providing reasonable assurance that an adequate audit was conducted in accordance with auditing standards. More specifically, audit documentation, as it pertains to the current year's audit, provides a basis for planning the audit, a record of the evidence accumulated and the results of the tests, data for determining the proper type of audit report, and a basis for review by supervisors and partners.

If the auditor is to plan the current year's audit adequately, the necessary reference information must be available in the audit files. The files include such diverse planning information as descriptive information about internal control, a time budget for individual audit areas, the audit program, and the results of the preceding year's audit.

Audit documentation is the primary means of documenting that an adequate audit was conducted in accordance with GAAS. If the need arises, the auditor must be able to demonstrate to regulatory agencies and courts that the audit was well planned and adequately supervised; the evidence accumulated was competent, sufficient, and timely; and the audit report was proper, considering the results of the audit.

Audit documentation provides an important source of information to assist the auditor in deciding the appropriate audit report to issue in a given set of circumstances. The data in the files are useful for evaluating the adequacy of audit scope and the fairness of the financial statements. In addition, the audit files contain information needed to assist the client in the preparation of the financial statements.

The audit files are the primary frame of reference used by supervisory personnel to evaluate whether sufficient competent evidence was accumulated to justify the audit report. When audit procedures involve inspection of documents or confirmation of balances, the audit documentation should include an identification of the items tested. The audit files should also include documentation about significant audit findings or

TABLE 7-6   **Terms, Audit Procedures, and Types of Evidence**

Term and Definition	Illustrative Audit Procedure	Type of Evidence
Examine—A reasonably detailed study of a document or record to determine specific facts about it.	*Examine* a sample of vendors' invoices to determine whether the goods or services received are reasonable and of the type normally used by the client's business.	Documentation
Scan—A less-detailed examination of a document or record to determine whether there is something unusual warranting further investigation.	*Scan* the sales journal, looking for large and unusual transactions.	Analytical procedures
Read—An examination of written information to determine facts pertinent to the audit.	*Read* the minutes of a board of directors meeting and summarize all information that is pertinent to the financial statements in an audit file.	Documentation
Compute—A calculation done by the auditor independent of the client.	*Compute* the inventory turnover ratios and compare with those of previous years as a test of inventory obsolescence.	Analytical procedures
Recompute—A calculation done to determine whether a client's calculation is correct.	*Recompute* the unit sales price times the number of units for a sample of duplicate sales invoices and compare the totals with the calculations.	Reperformance
Foot—Addition of a column of numbers to determine whether the total is the same as the client's.	*Foot* the sales journal for a 1-month period and compare all totals with the general ledger.	Reperformance
Trace—An instruction normally associated with documentation or reperformance. The instruction should state what the auditor is tracing and where it is being traced from and to. Often, an audit procedure that includes the term *trace* will also include a second instruction, such as *compare* or *recalculate*.	*Trace* a sample of sales transactions from the sales journal to sales invoices, and *compare* customer name, date, and the total dollar value of the sale.	Documentation
	Trace postings from the sales journal to the general ledger accounts.	Reperformance
Compare—A comparison of information in two different locations. The instruction should state which information is being compared in as much detail as practical.	Select a sample of sales invoices and *compare* the unit selling price as stated on the invoice to the list of unit selling prices authorized by management.	Documentation
Count—A determination of assets on hand at a given time. This term should be associated only with the type of evidence defined as physical examination.	*Count* a sample of 100 inventory items and compare quantity and description to client's counts.	Physical examination
Observe—The act of observation should be associated with the type of evidence defined as observation.	*Observe* whether the two inventory count teams independently count and record inventory costs.	Observation
Inquire—The act of inquiry should be associated with the type of evidence defined as inquiry.	*Inquire* of management whether there is any obsolete inventory on hand at the balance sheet date.	Inquiries of client
Vouch—The use of documents to verify recorded transactions or amounts.	*Vouch* a sample of recorded acquisition transactions to vendors' invoices and receiving reports.	Documentation

issues, actions taken to address them, and the basis for the conclusions reached. For example, the auditor may test several transactions at year-end to determine whether transactions were recorded in the proper period. The auditor should document the specific transactions tested. If misstatements are uncovered during these cutoff tests, the auditor should document additional procedures performed to determine the extent of cutoff misstatements, the conclusion as to whether the account balances affected are fairly stated, and whether any audit adjustments should be proposed.

In addition to the purposes directly related to the audit report, the audit files have other uses. They often serve as the basis for preparing tax returns, filings with the SEC, and other reports. They are a source of information for issuing communications to the audit committee and management concerning various matters such as internal control weaknesses or operational recommendations. Audit files are also a useful frame of reference for training personnel and as an aid in planning and coordinating subsequent audits.

Ownership of Audit Files

Audit documentation prepared during the engagement, including schedules prepared by the client for the auditor, is the *property of the auditor.* The only time anyone else, including the client, has a legal right to examine the files is when they are subpoenaed by a court as legal evidence. At the completion of the engagement, audit files are retained on the CPA's premises for future reference.

Confidentiality of Audit Files

The need to maintain a confidential relationship with the client is expressed in Rule 301 of the *Code of Professional Conduct,* which states

- A member shall not disclose any confidential information obtained in the course of a professional engagement except with the consent of the client.

During the course of the audit, auditors obtain a considerable amount of information of a confidential nature, including officers' salaries, product pricing and advertising plans, and product cost data. If auditors divulged this information to outsiders or to client employees who have been denied access, their relationship with management would be seriously strained. Furthermore, having access to the audit files would give employees an opportunity to alter information on them. For these reasons, care must be taken to protect the audit files at all times.

Ordinarily, audit documentation can be provided to someone else only with the express permission of the client. This is the case even if a CPA sells the practice to another CPA firm. Permission is not required from the client, however, if the audit documentation is subpoenaed by a court or is used as part of an AICPA or state society approved peer review program with other CPA firms.

Sarbanes–Oxley Requirements for Retention of Audit Documentation

The Sarbanes–Oxley Act requires auditors of public companies to prepare and maintain audit working papers and other information related to any audit report in sufficient detail to support the auditor's conclusions, for a period of not less than seven years. The Sarbanes–Oxley Act makes the knowing and willful destruction of audit documentation within the seven-year period a criminal offense subject to financial fines and imprisonment up to ten years.

As required by the Sarbanes–Oxley Act, the SEC has issued final rules on the retention of records for audits and reviews that require public company auditors to maintain the following documentation:

- Working papers or other documents that form the basis for the audit of the company's annual financial statements or review of the company's quarterly financial statements.
- Memos, correspondence, communications, other documents, and records, including electronic records, that meet the following two criteria.
  (1) The materials are created, sent, or received in connection with the audit or review.
  (2) The materials contain conclusions, opinions, analyses, or financial data related to the audit or review.

These rules significantly increase the audit documentation that must be retained for audits of public companies. For example, auditors of public companies will now be required to retain e-mail correspondence that contains information meeting the preceding criteria. The rules acknowledge that administrative records and other documents not containing relevant financial data or the auditor's conclusions, opinions, or analyses do not meet the retention criteria.

Existing auditing standards for audits of nonpublic entities do not include a mandated audit documentation retention period. Instead, those standards require auditors of nonpublic entities to retain audit documentation for a period sufficient to meet the needs of the audit firm's practice and to satisfy any pertinent legal requirements of records retention.

Each CPA firm establishes its own approach to preparing and organizing audit files, and the beginning auditor must adopt the firm's approach. The emphasis in this text is on the general concepts common to all audit documentation.

Figure 7-2 illustrates the contents and organization of a typical set of audit files. They contain virtually everything involved in the audit. There is a definite logic to the type of audit documentation prepared for an audit and the way it is arranged in the files, even though different firms may follow somewhat different approaches. In the figure, the audit files start with more general information, such as corporate data in the permanent files, and end with the financial statements and audit report. In between are the audit files supporting the auditor's tests.

Permanent files are intended to contain data of a *historical or continuing nature* pertinent to the current audit. These files provide a convenient source of information about the audit

Contents and Organization

OBJECTIVE 7-6

Prepare organized audit documentation.

Permanent Files

FIGURE 7-2	Audit File Contents and Organization

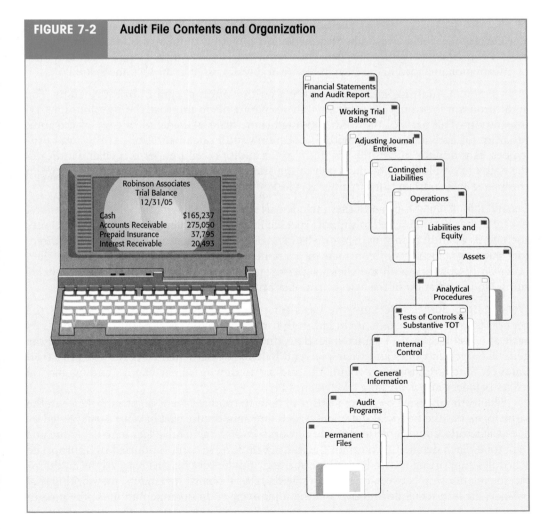

that is of continuing interest from year to year. The permanent files typically include the following:

- *Extracts or copies of such company documents of continuing importance as the articles of incorporation, bylaws, bond indentures, and contracts.* The contracts are pension plans, leases, stock options, and so on. Each of these documents is of significance to the auditor for as many years as it is in effect.
- *Analyses from previous years of accounts that have continuing importance to the auditor.* These include accounts such as long-term debt, stockholders' equity accounts, goodwill, and fixed assets. Having this information in the permanent files enables the auditor to concentrate on analyzing only the changes in the current year's balance while retaining the results of previous years' audits in a form accessible for review.
- *Information related to the understanding of internal control and assessment of control risk.* This includes organization charts, flowcharts, questionnaires, and other internal control information, including enumeration of controls and weaknesses in the system.
- *The results of analytical procedures from previous years' audits.* Among these data are ratios and percentages computed by the auditor and the total balance or the balance by month for selected accounts. This information is useful in helping the auditor decide whether there are unusual changes in the current year's account balances that should be investigated more extensively.

Analytical procedures and the understanding of internal control and assessment of control risk are included in the current period audit files rather than in the permanent file by many CPA firms.

Current Files

The **current files** include all audit documentation applicable to the year under audit. There is one set of permanent files for the client and a set of current files for each year's audit. The types of information included in the current file are briefly discussed in the sections that follow.

Audit Program Auditing standards require a written audit program for every audit. The audit program is ordinarily maintained in a separate file to improve the coordination and integration of all parts of the audit, although some firms also include a copy of the audit program for each audit section with that section's audit documentation. As the audit progresses, each auditor initials the program for the audit procedures performed and indicates the date of completion. The inclusion in the audit files of a well-designed audit program completed in a conscientious manner is evidence of a high-quality audit.

General Information Some audit files include current period information that is of a general nature rather than designed to support specific financial statement amounts. This includes such items as audit planning memos, abstracts or copies of minutes of the board of directors meetings, abstracts of contracts or agreements not included in the permanent files, notes on discussions with the client, supervisors' review comments, and general conclusions. Documentation of the assessment of control risk may also be included.

Working Trial Balance Because the basis for preparing the financial statements is the general ledger, the amounts included in that record are the focal point of the audit. As early as possible after the balance sheet date, the auditor obtains or prepares a listing of the general ledger accounts and their year-end balances. This schedule is the **working trial balance**. Software programs enable the auditor to download the client's ending general ledger balances into a working trial balance file.

The technique used by many firms is to have the auditor's working trial balance in the same format as the financial statements. Each line item on the trial balance is supported by a **lead schedule**, containing the detailed accounts from the general ledger making up the line item total. Each detailed account on the lead schedule is, in turn, supported by appropriate schedules supporting the audit work performed and the conclusions reached. As an example, the relationship between cash as it is stated on the financial statements, the working trial balance, the lead schedule for cash, and the supporting audit documentation is presented in Figure 7-3. As the figure indicates, cash on the financial statements is the same as on the

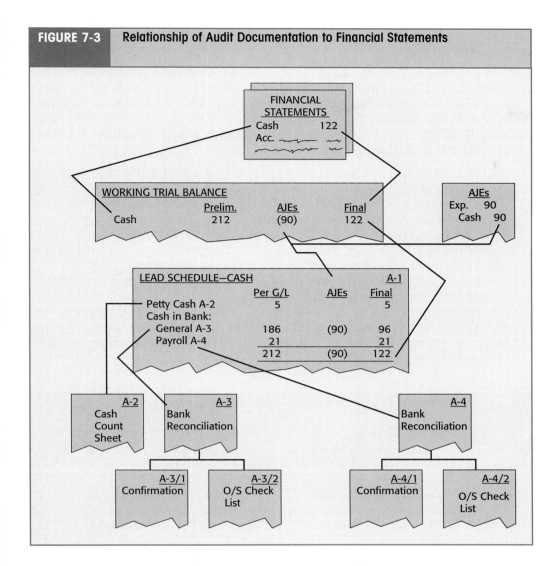

FIGURE 7-3   Relationship of Audit Documentation to Financial Statements

working trial balance and the total of the detail on the cash lead schedule. Initially, figures for the lead schedule were taken from the general ledger. The audit work performed resulted in an adjustment to cash that would be evidenced in the detail schedules and reflected on the lead schedule, the working trial balance, and the financial statements.

Adjusting and Reclassification Entries When the auditor discovers material misstatements in the accounting records, the financial statements must be corrected. For example, if the client failed to properly reduce inventory for obsolete raw materials, an adjusting entry can be made by the auditor to reflect the realizable value of the inventory. Even though adjusting entries discovered in the audit are typically prepared by the auditor, they must be approved by the client because management has primary responsibility for the fair presentation of the statements. Figure 7-3 illustrates an adjustment of the general cash account for $90.

Reclassification entries are frequently made in the statements to present accounting information properly, even when the general ledger balances are correct. A common example is the reclassification for financial statement purposes of material credit balances in accounts receivable to accounts payable. Because the balance in accounts receivable on the general ledger reflects the accounts receivable properly from the point of view of operating the company on a day-to-day basis, the reclassification entry is not included in the client's general ledger.

Only those adjusting and reclassification entries that significantly affect the fair presentation of financial statements must be made. The determination of when a misstatement should be adjusted is based on materiality. The auditor should keep in mind that several immaterial misstatements that are not adjusted could result in a material overall misstatement when they are combined. It is common for auditors to summarize all entries that have not been recorded in a separate audit file as a means of determining their cumulative effect.

Supporting Schedules The largest portion of audit documentation includes the detailed **supporting schedules** prepared by the client or the auditors in support of specific amounts on the financial statements. Many different types of schedules are used. Use of the appropriate type for a given aspect of the audit is necessary to document the adequacy of the audit and to fulfill the other objectives of audit documentation. Following are the major types of supporting schedules:

- *Analysis.* An analysis is designed to show the *activity in a general ledger account* during the entire period under audit, tying together the beginning and ending balances. This type of schedule is normally used for accounts such as marketable securities; notes receivable; allowance for doubtful accounts; property, plant, and equipment; long-term debt; and all equity accounts. The common characteristic of these accounts is the significance of the activity in the account during the year. In most cases, the analysis has cross-references to other audit files.
- *Trial balance or list.* This type of schedule consists of the *details that make up a year-end balance* of a general ledger account. It differs from an analysis in that it includes only those items constituting the end-of-the-period balance. Common examples include trial balances or lists in support of trade accounts receivable, trade accounts payable, repair and maintenance expense, legal expense, and miscellaneous income. An example is included in Figure 7-4.

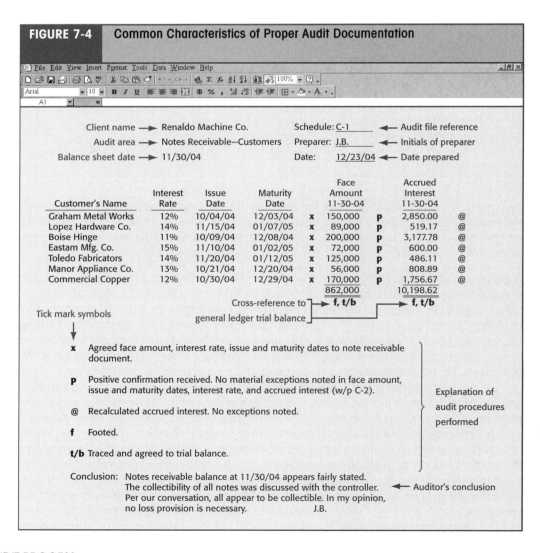

FIGURE 7-4   Common Characteristics of Proper Audit Documentation

Rhonda McMillan had been the in-charge auditor on the audit of Blaine Construction Company in 1999. Now she is sitting here, in 2005, in a room full of attorneys who are asking her questions about the 1999 audit. Blaine was sold to another company in 2000 at a purchase price that was based primarily on the 1999 audited financial statements. Several of the large construction contracts showed a profit in 1999 using the percentage of completion method, but they ultimately resulted in large losses for the buyer. Because Rhonda's firm audited the 1999 financial statements, the buyer is trying to make the case that Rhonda's firm failed in their audit of contract costs and revenues.

The buyer's attorney is taking Rhonda's deposition and is asking her about the audit work she did on contracts. Referring to the audit files, his examination goes something like this:

ATTORNEY Do you recognize this exhibit, and if you do, would you please identify it for us?

RHONDA Yes, this is the summary of contracts in progress at the end of 1999.

ATTORNEY Did you prepare this document?

RHONDA I believe the client prepared it, but I audited it. My initials are right here in the upper right-hand corner.

ATTORNEY When did you do this audit work?

RHONDA I'm not sure, I forgot to date this one. But it must have been about the second week in March, because that's when we did the field work.

ATTORNEY Now I'd like to turn your attention to this tick mark next to the Baldwin contract. You see where it shows Baldwin, and then the red sort of cross-like mark?

RHONDA Yes.

ATTORNEY In the explanation for that tick mark it says: "Discussed status of job with Elton Burgess. Job is going according to schedule and he believes that the expected profit will be earned." Now my question is, Ms. McMillan, what exactly was the nature and content of your discussion with Mr. Burgess?

RHONDA Other than what is in the explanation to this tick mark, I have no idea. I mean, this all took place over 5 years ago. I only worked on the engagement that 1 year, and I can hardly even remember that.

• *Reconciliation of amounts.* A reconciliation *supports a specific amount* and is normally expected to tie the amount recorded in the client's records to another source of information. Examples include the reconciliation of bank balances with bank statements, the reconciliation of subsidiary accounts receivable balances with confirmations from customers, and the reconciliation of accounts payable balances with vendors' statements. An example is included on page 693.

• *Tests of reasonableness.* A test of reasonableness schedule, as the name implies, contains information that enables the auditor to evaluate whether the client's balance appears to include a misstatement considering the circumstances in the engagement. Frequently, auditors test depreciation expense, the provision for federal income taxes, and the allowance for doubtful accounts by tests of reasonableness. These tests are primarily analytical procedures.

• *Summary of procedures.* Another type of schedule *summarizes the results* of a specific audit procedure performed. Examples are the summary of the results of accounts receivable confirmation and the summary of inventory observations.

• *Examination of supporting documents.* A number of special-purpose schedules are designed to *show detailed tests performed,* such as examination of documents during tests of controls and substantive tests of transactions or cutoffs. These schedules show no totals, and they do not tie in to the general ledger because they document only the tests performed and the results found. However, the schedules must state a definite positive or negative conclusion about the objective of the test.

• *Informational.* This type of schedule contains information as opposed to audit evidence. These schedules include information for tax returns and SEC Form 10-K data and data such as time budgets and the client's working hours, which are helpful in administration of the engagement.

• *Outside documentation.* Much of the content of the audit files consists of the outside documentation gathered by auditors, such as confirmation replies and copies of client agreements. Although not "schedules" in the real sense, these are indexed and interfiled, and procedures are indicated on them in the same manner as on the other schedules.

Preparation of
Audit Documentation

The proper preparation of schedules to document the audit evidence accumulated, the results found, and the conclusions reached is an important part of the audit. Read the insert on page 181 about Rhonda and imagine yourself in her position several years after completing an audit.

Although the design depends on the objectives involved, audit documentation should possess certain characteristics:

- Each audit file should be properly identified with such information as the client's name, the period covered, a description of the contents, the initials of the preparer, the date of preparation, and an index code.
- Audit documentation should be indexed and cross-referenced to aid in organizing and filing. One type of indexing is illustrated in Figure 7-3 (p. 179). The lead schedule for cash has been indexed as A-1, and the individual general ledger accounts making up the total cash on the financial statements are indexed as A-2 through A-4. The final indexing is for the schedules supporting A-3 and A-4.
- Completed audit documentation must clearly indicate the audit work performed. This is accomplished in three ways: by a written statement in the form of a memorandum, by initialing the audit procedures in the audit program, and by notations directly on the schedules. Notations on schedules are accomplished by the use of **tick marks**, which are symbols adjacent to the detail on the body of the schedule. These notations must be clearly explained at the bottom of the schedule.
- Audit documentation should include sufficient information to fulfill the objectives for which it was designed. If the auditor is to prepare audit documentation properly, the auditor must be aware of his or her goals. For example, if a schedule is designed to list the detail and show the verification of support of a balance sheet account, such as prepaid insurance, it is essential that the detail on the schedule reconcile with the trial balance.
- The conclusions that were reached about the segment of the audit under consideration should be plainly stated.

The common characteristics of proper audit documentation preparation are indicated in Figure 7-4 (p. 180).

Effect of E-Commerce on Audit Evidence and Audit Documentation

OBJECTIVE 7-7

Describe how e-commerce affects audit evidence and audit documentation.

ACL and IDEA

Audit evidence is increasingly in electronic form, and auditors must evaluate how electronic information affects their ability to gather sufficient, competent evidence. In certain instances, electronic evidence may exist only at a point in time. That evidence may not be retrievable later if files are changed and if the client lacks backup files. Therefore, auditors must consider the availability of the electronic evidence and plan their evidence gathering appropriately.

When evidence can be examined only in machine-readable form, auditors use computers to read and examine evidence. There are commercial audit software programs designed specifically for use by auditors. These software programs are typically Windows-based and can easily be operated on the auditor's desktop or laptop computer. Examples are ACL Software and Interactive Data Extraction and Analysis (IDEA) software. The auditor obtains copies of client databases or master files in machine-readable form and uses the software to perform a variety of tests of the client's electronic data. These audit software packages are relatively easy to use, even by auditors with little audit-related IT training, and can be applied to a wide variety of clients with minimal customization. Auditors also use spreadsheet software packages to perform audit tests.

Auditors also use technology to convert traditional paper-based documentation into electronic files and to organize audit documentation. Some firms develop their own software, while others buy commercial audit documentation software. An example of such software is ACE (Automated Client Engagement). Using ACE, an auditor can prepare a trial balance, lead schedules, supporting audit documentation, and financial statements, as well as perform ratio analysis. Tick marks and other explanations, such as reviewer notes, can be entered directly into computerized files. In addition, data can be imported and exported to other applications. Examples include downloading a client's general ledger into ACE and exporting tax information to a commercial tax preparation package. Auditors also use local area networks and groupshare software programs to access audit documentation simultaneously from remote locations.

SUMMARY OF AUDIT DOCUMENTATION

Audit documentation is an essential part of every audit for effectively planning the audit, providing a record of the evidence accumulated and the results of the tests, deciding the proper type of audit report, and reviewing the work of assistants. CPA firms establish their own policies and approaches to audit documentation to make sure that these objectives are met. High-quality CPA firms make sure that audit documentation is properly prepared and is appropriate for the circumstances in the audit.

ESSENTIAL TERMS

Analytical procedures—use of comparisons and relationships to assess whether account balances or other data appear reasonable

Audit documentation—the principal record of auditing procedures applied, evidence obtained, and conclusions reached by the auditor in the engagement

Audit procedure—detailed instruction for the collection of a type of audit evidence

Audit program—list of audit procedures for an audit area or an entire audit; the audit program always includes audit procedures and may also include sample sizes, items to select, and timing of the tests

Competence of evidence—the degree to which evidence can be considered believable or worthy of trust; evidence is competent when it is obtained (1) from a relevant source, (2) from an independent provider, (3) from a client with effective internal controls, (4) from the auditor's direct knowledge, (5) from qualified providers such as law firms and banks, (6) from objective sources, and (7) in a timely manner

Confirmation—the auditor's receipt of a written or oral response from an independent third party verifying the accuracy of information requested

Current files—all audit files applicable to the year under audit

Documentation—the auditor's examination of the client's documents and records to substantiate the information that is or should be included in the financial statements

External document—a document, such as a vendor's invoice, that has been used by an outside party to the transaction being documented and that the client now has or can easily obtain

Inquiry—the obtaining of written or oral information from the client in response to specific questions during the audit

Internal document—a document, such as an employee time report, that is prepared and used within the client's organization

Lead schedule—an audit schedule that contains the detailed accounts from the general ledger making up a line item total in the working trial balance

Observation—the use of the senses to assess certain activities

Permanent files—auditors' files that contain data of a *historical or continuing nature* pertinent to the current audit such as copies of articles of incorporation, bylaws, bond indentures, and contracts

Persuasiveness of evidence—the degree to which the auditor is convinced that the evidence supports the audit opinion; the two determinants of persuasiveness are the competence and sufficiency of the evidence

Physical examination—the auditor's inspection or count of a tangible asset

Reliability of evidence—see *competence of evidence*

Reperformance—the rechecking of a sample of the computations and transfers of information made by the client during the period under audit

Sufficiency of evidence—the quantity of evidence; appropriate sample size

Supporting schedules—detailed schedules prepared by the client or the auditor in support of specific amounts on the financial statements

Tick marks—symbols used on an audit schedule that provide additional information or details of audit procedures performed

Unusual fluctuations—significant unexpected differences indicated by analytical procedures between the current year's unaudited financial data and other data used in comparisons

Vouching—the use of documentation to support recorded transactions or amounts

Working trial balance—a listing of the general ledger accounts and their year-end balances

REVIEW QUESTIONS

7-1 (Objective 7-1) Discuss the similarities and differences between evidence in a legal case and evidence in an audit of financial statements.

7-2 (Objective 7-2) List the four major evidence decisions that must be made on every audit.

7-3 (Objective 7-2) Describe what is meant by an audit procedure. Why is it important for audit procedures to be carefully worded?

7-4 (Objective 7-2) Describe what is meant by an audit program for accounts receivable. What four things should be included in an audit program?

7-5 (Objective 7-3) State the third standard of field work. Explain the meaning of each of the major phrases of the standard.

7-6 (Objective 7-3) Explain why the auditor can be persuaded only with a reasonable level of assurance, rather than convinced, that the financial statements are correct.

7-7 (Objective 7-3) Identify the two factors that determine the persuasiveness of evidence. How are these two factors related to audit procedures, sample size, items to select, and timing?

7-8 (Objective 7-3) Identify the seven characteristics that determine the competence of evidence. For each characteristic, provide one example of a type of evidence that is likely to be competent.

7-9 (Objective 7-4) List the seven types of audit evidence included in this chapter and give two examples of each.

7-10 (Objective 7-4) What are the four characteristics of the definition of a confirmation? Distinguish between a confirmation and external documentation.

7-11 (Objective 7-4) Distinguish between internal documentation and external documentation as audit evidence and give three examples of each.

7-12 (Objective 7-4) Explain the importance of analytical procedures as evidence in determining the fair presentation of the financial statements.

7-13 (Objective 7-4) Identify the most important reasons for performing analytical procedures.

7-14 (Objective 7-4) Your client, Harper Company, has a contractual commitment as a part of a bond indenture to maintain a current ratio of 2.0. If the ratio falls below that level on the balance sheet date, the entire bond becomes payable immediately. In the current year, the client's financial statements show that the ratio has dropped from 2.6 to 2.05 over the past year. How should this situation affect your audit plan?

7-15 (Objective 7-4) Distinguish between attention-directing analytical procedures and those intended to eliminate or reduce detailed substantive procedures.

7-16 (Objective 7-4) Explain why the statement "Analytical procedures are essential in every part of an audit, but these tests are rarely sufficient by themselves for any audit area" is correct or incorrect.

7-17 (Objective 7-5) List the purposes of audit documentation and explain why each purpose is important.

7-18 (Objectives 7-5, 7-6) What are the two criteria that auditors of public companies consider when determining whether memos, correspondence, and other documents must be maintained in the audit files?

7-19 (Objectives 7-5, 7-6) For how long does the Sarbanes–Oxley Act require auditors of public companies to retain audit documentation?

7-20 (Objective 7-6) Explain why it is important for audit documentation to include each of the following: identification of the name of the client, period covered, description of the contents, initials of the preparer, date of the preparation, and an index code.

7-21 (Objective 7-6) Define what is meant by a permanent file, and list several types of information typically included. Why does the auditor not include the contents of the permanent file with the current year's audit file?

7-22 (Objective 7-6) Distinguish between the following types of current period supporting schedules and state the purpose of each: analysis, trial balance, and tests of reasonableness.

7-23 (Objective 7-6) Why is it essential that the auditor not leave questions or exceptions in the audit documentation without an adequate explanation?

7-24 (Objective 7-6) Define what is meant by a tick mark. What is its purpose?

7-25 (Objective 7-5) Who owns the audit files? Under what circumstances can they be used by other people?

7-26 (Objective 7-5) A CPA sells his auditing practice to another CPA firm and includes all audit files as a part of the purchase price. Under what circumstances is this a violation of the *Code of Professional Conduct*?

7-27 (Objective 7-7) How does the auditor read and evaluate information that is available only in machine-readable form?

7-28 (Objective 7-7) Explain the purposes and benefits of audit documentation software.

MULTIPLE CHOICE QUESTIONS FROM CPA EXAMINATIONS

7-29 (Objectives 7-3, 7-4) The following questions concern persuasiveness of evidence. Choose the best response.

a. Which of the following types of documentary evidence should the auditor consider to be the most reliable?
   (1) A sales invoice issued by the client and supported by a delivery receipt from an outside trucker.
   (2) Confirmation of an account payable balance mailed by and returned directly to the auditor.
   (3) A check, issued by the company and bearing the payee's endorsement, that is included with the bank statements mailed directly to the auditor.
   (4) An audit schedule prepared by the client's controller and reviewed by the client's treasurer.

b. The most reliable type of audit evidence that an auditor can obtain is
   (1) physical examination by the auditor.
   (2) calculations by the auditor from company records.
   (3) confirmations received directly from third parties.
   (4) external documents.

c. Audit evidence can come in different forms with different degrees of persuasiveness. Which of the following is the *least* persuasive type of evidence?
   (1) Vendor's invoice.
   (2) Bank statement obtained from the client.
   (3) Computations made by the auditor.
   (4) Prenumbered sales invoices.

d. Which of the following is the *least* persuasive documentation in support of an auditor's opinion?
   (1) Schedules of details of physical inventory counts conducted by the client.
   (2) Notation of inferences drawn from ratios and trends.
   (3) Notation of appraisers' conclusions documented in the auditor's files.
   (4) Lists of negative confirmation requests for which *no* response was received by the auditor.

7-30 (Objectives 7-5, 7-6) The following questions concern audit documentation. Choose the best response.

a. Which of the following is *not* a primary purpose of audit documentation?
   (1) To coordinate the audit.
   (2) To assist in preparation of the audit report.
   (3) To support the financial statements.
   (4) To provide evidence of the audit work performed.

b. During an audit engagement, pertinent data are compiled and included in the audit files. The audit files primarily are considered to be
   (1) a client-owned record of conclusions reached by the auditors who performed the engagement.
   (2) evidence supporting financial statements.
   (3) support for the auditor's representations as to compliance with auditing standards.
   (4) a record to be used as a basis for the following year's engagement.

c. Although the quantity, type, and content of audit documentation will vary with the circumstances, audit documentation generally would include the
   (1) copies of those client records examined by the auditor during the course of the engagement.

(2) evaluation of the efficiency and competence of the audit staff assistants by the partner responsible for the audit.

(3) auditor's comments concerning the efficiency and competence of client management personnel.

(4) auditing procedures followed and the testing performed in obtaining evidential matter.

DISCUSSION QUESTIONS AND PROBLEMS

7-31 (Objective 7-4) The following are examples of documentation typically obtained by auditors:

1. Vendors' invoices
2. General ledgers
3. Bank statements
4. Cancelled payroll checks
5. Payroll time cards
6. Purchase requisitions
7. Receiving reports (documents prepared when merchandise is received)
8. Minutes of the board of directors
9. Remittance advices
10. Signed W-4s (Employees' Withholding Exemption Certificates)
11. Signed lease agreements
12. Duplicate copies of bills of lading
13. Subsidiary accounts receivable records
14. Cancelled notes payable
15. Duplicate sales invoices
16. Articles of incorporation
17. Title insurance policies for real estate
18. Notes receivable

Required
a. Classify each of the preceding items according to type of documentation: (1) internal or (2) external.

b. Explain why external evidence is more reliable than internal evidence.

7-32 (Objective 7-4) The following are examples of audit procedures:

1. Review the accounts receivable with the credit manager to evaluate their collectibility.
2. Stand by the payroll time clock to determine whether any employee "punches in" more than one time.
3. Count inventory items and record the amount in the audit files.
4. Obtain a letter from the client's attorney addressed to the CPA firm stating that the attorney is not aware of any existing lawsuits.
5. Extend the cost of inventory times the quantity on an inventory listing to test whether it is accurate.
6. Obtain a letter from an insurance company to the CPA firm stating the amount of the fire insurance coverage on buildings and equipment.
7. Examine an insurance policy stating the amount of the fire insurance coverage on buildings and equipment.
8. Calculate the ratio of cost of goods sold to sales as a test of overall reasonableness of gross margin relative to the preceding year.
9. Obtain information about internal control by requesting the client to fill out a questionnaire.
10. Trace the total on the cash disbursements journal to the general ledger.
11. Watch employees count inventory to determine whether company procedures are being followed.
12. Examine a piece of equipment to make sure that a major acquisition was actually received and is in operation.
13. Calculate the ratio of sales commissions expense to sales as a test of sales commissions.
14. Examine corporate minutes to determine the authorization of the issue of bonds.
15. Obtain a letter from management stating that there are no unrecorded liabilities.
16. Review the total of repairs and maintenance for each month to determine whether any month's total was unusually large.
17. Compare a duplicate sales invoice with the sales journal for customer name and amount.
18. Add the sales journal entries to determine whether they were correctly totaled.
19. Make a petty cash count to make sure that the amount of the petty cash fund is intact.
20. Obtain a written statement from a bank stating that the client has $15,671 on deposit and liabilities of $500,000 on a demand note.

Classify each of the preceding items according to the seven types of audit evidence: (1) physical examination, (2) confirmation, (3) documentation, (4) analytical procedures, (5) inquiries of the client, (6) reperformance, and (7) observation. **Required**

7-33 (Objective 7-4) List two examples of audit evidence the auditor can use in support of each of the following:

a. Recorded amount of entries in the acquisitions journal

b. Physical existence of inventory

c. Accuracy of accounts receivable

d. Ownership of fixed assets

e. Liability for accounts payable

f. Obsolescence of inventory

g. Existence of petty cash

7-34 (Objective 7-4) Seven different types of evidence were discussed. The following questions concern the reliability (competence) of that evidence:

a. Explain why confirmations are normally more reliable evidence than inquiries of the client.

b. Describe a situation in which confirmation would be considered highly reliable and another in which it would not be reliable.

c. Under what circumstances is the physical observation of inventory considered relatively unreliable evidence?

d. Explain why reperformance tests are highly reliable but of relatively limited use.

e. Give three examples of relatively reliable documentation and three examples of less reliable documentation. What characteristics distinguish the two?

f. Give several examples in which the qualifications of the respondent or the qualifications of the auditor affect the reliability of the evidence.

g. Explain why analytical procedures are important evidence even though they are relatively unreliable by themselves.

7-35 (Objective 7-4) As auditor of the Star Manufacturing Company, you have obtained

a. A trial balance taken from the books of Star one month before year-end:

	Dr. (Cr.)
Cash in bank	$ 87,000
Trade accounts receivable	345,000
Notes receivable	125,000
Inventories	317,000
Land	66,000
Buildings, net	350,000
Furniture, fixtures, and equipment, net	325,000
Trade accounts payable	(235,000)
Mortgages payable	(400,000)
Capital stock	(300,000)
Retained earnings	(510,000)
Sales	(3,130,000)
Cost of sales	2,300,000
General and administrative expenses	622,000
Legal and professional fees	3,000
Interest expense	35,000

b. There are no inventories consigned either in or out.

c. All notes receivable are due from outsiders and held by Star.

Which accounts should be confirmed with outside sources? Briefly describe from whom they should be confirmed and the information that should be confirmed. Organize your answer in the following format:* **Required**

Account Name	From Whom Confirmed	Information to Be Confirmed

*AICPA adapted.

7-36 (Objective 7-4) The following audit procedures were performed in the audit of inventory to satisfy specific balance-related audit objectives as discussed in Chapter 6. The audit procedures assume that the auditor has obtained the inventory count sheets that list the client's inventory. The general balance-related audit objectives from Chapter 6 are also included.

Audit Procedures

1. Test extend unit prices times quantity on the inventory list, test foot the list, and compare the total to the general ledger.
2. Trace selected quantities from the inventory list to the physical inventory to make sure that it exists and the quantities are the same.
3. Question operating personnel about the possibility of obsolete or slow-moving inventory.
4. Select a sample of quantities of inventory in the factory warehouse and trace each item to the inventory count sheets to determine if it has been included and if the quantity and description are correct.
5. Compare the quantities on hand and unit prices on this year's inventory count sheets with those in the preceding year as a test for large differences.
6. Examine sales invoices and contracts with customers to determine whether any goods are out on consignment with customers. Similarly, examine vendors' invoices and contracts with vendors to determine whether any goods on the inventory listing are owned by vendors.
7. Send letters directly to third parties who hold the client's inventory and request that they respond directly to the auditors.

General Balance-Related Audit Objectives

Existence
Completeness
Accuracy
Classification
Cutoff
Detail tie-in
Realizable value
Rights and obligations
Presentation and disclosure

Required
a. Identify the type of audit evidence used for each audit procedure.
b. Identify the general balance-related audit objective or objectives satisfied by each audit procedure.

7-37 (Objectives 7-3, 7-4) The following are nine situations, each containing two means of accumulating evidence:

1. Confirm receivables with consumers versus confirming accounts receivable with business organizations.
2. Physically examine 3-inch steel plates versus examining electronic parts.
3. Examine duplicate sales invoices when several competent people are checking each other's work versus examining documents prepared by a competent person on a one-person staff.
4. Physically examine inventory of parts for the number of units on hand versus examining them for the likelihood of inventory being obsolete.
5. Discuss the likelihood and amount of loss in a lawsuit against the client with client's in-house legal counsel versus discussion with the CPA firm's own legal counsel.
6. Confirm the oil and gas reserves with a geologist specializing in oil and gas versus confirming a bank balance.
7. Confirm a bank balance versus examining the client's bank statements.
8. Physically count the client's inventory held by an independent party versus confirming the count with an independent party.
9. Obtain a physical inventory count from the company president versus physically counting the client's inventory.

Required
a. Identify the seven factors that determine the competence of evidence.
b. For each of the nine situations, state whether the first or second type of evidence is more reliable.
c. For each situation, state which of the seven factors affected the competence of the evidence.

7-38 (Objective 7-4) Following are 10 audit procedures with words missing and a list of several terms commonly used in audit procedures.

Audit Procedures

1. _____ whether the accounts receivable bookkeeper is prohibited from handling cash.
2. _____ the ratio of cost of goods sold to sales and compare the ratio to previous years.
3. _____ the sales journal and _____ the total to the general ledger.
4. _____ the sales journal, looking for large and unusual transactions requiring investigation.
5. _____ of management whether all accounting employees are required to take annual vacations.
6. _____ the balance in the bank account directly with the East State Bank.
7. _____ all marketable securities as of the balance sheet date to determine whether they equal the total on the client's list.
8. _____ a sample of duplicate sales invoices to determine if the controller's approval is included and _____ each duplicate sales invoice to the sales journal for agreement of name and amount.
9. _____ the unit selling price times quantity on the duplicate sales invoice and compare the total to the amount on the duplicate sales invoice.
10. _____ the agreement between Johnson Wholesale Company and the client to determine whether the shipment is a sale or a consignment.

Terms

a. Examine	g. Trace
b. Scan	h. Compare
c. Read	i. Count
d. Compute	j. Observe
e. Recompute	k. Inquire
f. Foot	l. Confirm

Required

a. For each of the 12 blanks in procedures 1 through 10, identify the most appropriate term. No term can be used more than once.

b. For each of the procedures 1 through 10, identify the type of evidence that is being used.

7-39 (Objectives 7-5, 7-6) The preparation of audit documentation is an integral part of a CPA's audit of financial statements. On a recurring engagement, a CPA reviews audit programs and audit documentation from the prior audit while planning the current audit to determine their usefulness for the current engagement.

Required

a. What are the purposes or functions of audit documentation?

b. What records may be included in audit files?

c. What factors affect the CPA's judgment of the type and content of the audit files for an engagement?*

7-40 (Objectives 7-5, 7-6) Do the following with regard to the audit schedule for the Vandervoort Company shown on page 190:

a. List the deficiencies in the audit schedule.

b. For each deficiency, state how the audit schedule could be improved.

c. Prepare an improved audit schedule, using an electronic spreadsheet software program. Include an indication of the audit work done as well as the analysis of the client data (instructor's option).

CASES

7-41 (Objective 7-4) Grande Stores is a large discount catalog department store chain. The company has recently expanded from 6 to 43 stores by borrowing from several large financial institutions and from a public offering of common stock. A recent investigation has disclosed that Grande materially overstated net income. This was accomplished by understating accounts payable and recording fictitious supplier credits that further reduced accounts payable. An SEC investigation was critical of the evidence gathered by Grande's audit firm, Montgomery & Ross, in testing accounts payable and the supplier credits.

The following is a description of some of the fictitious supplier credits and unrecorded amounts in accounts payable, as well as the audit procedures.

1. McClure Advertising Credits—Grande had arrangements with some vendors to share the cost of advertising the vendor's product. The arrangements were usually agreed to in advance by

*AICPA adapted.

	APEX CO.		AJAX, INC.		J.J. CO.		P. SMITH		MARTIN-PETERSON		TENT CO.			
Date made	6/15/03		11/21/03		11/1/03		7/26/04		5/12/03		9/3/04			
Date due	6/15/05		Demand		$ 200/mo.		$1,000/mo.		Demand		$400/mo.			
Paid to date	None		Paid		12/31/04		9/30/04		Paid		11/30/04			
Face amount	$5,000	x	$ 3,591	x	$ 13,180	x	$ 25,000	x	$ 2,100	x	$ 12,000	x		
Interest rate	5%		5%		5%		5%		5%		6%			
Value of security	None		None		$ 24,000		$ 50,000		None		$ 10,000			

Note Receivable:

	APEX CO.		AJAX, INC.		J.J. CO.		P. SMITH		MARTIN-PETERSON		TENT CO.			
12/31/03 bal.	$4,000	py	$ 3,591	py	$ 12,780	py	$ 0		$ 2,100	py	$ 0			
Additions							25,000				12,000			
Payments	(1,000)	x	$(3,591)	x	(2,400)	x	(5,000)	x	(2,100)	x	(1,600)	x		
12/31/04 bal.	$3,000		$ 0		$ 10,380		$ 20,000		$ 0		$ 10,400		TOTALS	
Current	$3,000		–		$ 2,400		$ 12,000		–		$ 4,800		$22,200	tb
Long-term	–		–		7,980		8,000		–		5,600		21,580	tb
Total end. bal.	$3,000	@	$ 0		$ 10,380	@	$ 20,000	@	$ 0		$ 10,400	@	$43,780	tb

Interest Receivable:

	APEX CO.		AJAX, INC.		J.J. CO.		P. SMITH		MARTIN-PETERSON		TENT CO.			
12/31/03 bal.	$ 104	py	$ 0	py	$ 24	py	$ 0		$ 0	py	$ 0		$ 128	
Interest earned	175	x	102	x	577	x	468	x	105	x	162	x	1,589	#
Interest received	0		(102)	x	(601)	x	(200)	x	(105)	x	(108)	x	(1,116)	
12/31/04 bal.	$ 279		$ 0		$ 0		$ 268		$ 0		$ 54		$ 601	a/r

x = Tested
py = Agrees with prior year's audit schedules.
tb = Agrees with working trial balance.
\# = Agrees with miscellaneous income analysis in operations w/p.
a/r = Agrees with A/R lead schedule.

Vandervoort Company
A/C # 110—Notes Receivable
12-31-04

Schedule	N-1	Date
Prepared by JD		1-21-05
Approved by PP		2-15-05

the vendor and supported by evidence of the placing of the ad. Grande created a 114-page list of approximately 1,100 vendors, supporting advertising credits of $300,000. Grande's auditors selected a sample of 4 of the 1,100 items for direct confirmation. One item was confirmed by telephone, one traced to cash receipts, one to a vendor credit memo for part of the amount and cash receipts for the rest, and one to a vendor credit memo. Two of the amounts confirmed differed from the amount on the list, but the auditors did not seek an explanation for the differences because the amounts were not material.

The rest of the credits were tested by selecting 20 items (one or two from each page of the list). Twelve of the items were supported by examining the ads placed, and eight were supported by Grande debit memos charging the vendors for the promotional allowances.

2. Springbrook Credits—Grande created 28 fictitious credit memos totaling $257,000 from Springbrook Distributors, the main supplier of health and beauty aids to Grande. Grande's controller initially told the auditor that the credits were for returned goods, then said they were a volume discount, and finally stated they were a payment so that Grande would continue to use Springbrook as a supplier. One of the Montgomery & Ross staff auditors concluded that a $257,000 payment to retain Grande's business was too large to make economic sense.

The credit memos indicated that the credits were for damaged merchandise, volume rebates, and advertising allowances. The audit firm requested a confirmation of the credits. In response, Jon Steiner, the president of Grande Stores, placed a call to Mort Seagal, the president of Springbrook, and handed the phone to the staff auditor. In fact, the call had been placed to an officer of Grande. The Grande officer, posing as Seagal, orally confirmed the credits. Grande refused to allow Montgomery & Ross to obtain written confirmations supporting the credits. Although the staff auditor doubted the validity of the credits, the audit partner, Mark Franklin, accepted the credits based on the credit memoranda, telephone confirmation of the credits, and oral representations of Grande officers.

Index		K-1	
		Initials	Date
Prepared by		AA	3/22/05
Approved by			

American Widgets, Inc.
Long-Term Debt
December 31, 2004

Lender	Interest Rate	Payment Terms	Collateral	Balance 12/31/03	2004 Borrowings	2004 Reductions	Balance 12/31/04	Interest paid to	Accrued Interest Payable 12/31/04	Comments
Φ First Commercial Bank	12%	Interest only on 25th of month, principal due in full 1/1/08; no prepayment penalty	Inventories	$ 50,000 √	$300,000 A 1/31/04	$100,000 ● 6/30/04	$ 250,000 CX	12/25/04	$2,500 NR	Dividend of $80,000 paid 9/2/04 (W/P N-3) violates a provision of the debt agreement, which thereby permits lender to demand immediate payment; lender has refused to waive this violation
Φ Lender's Capital Corp.	Prime plus 1%	Interest only on last day of month, principal due in full 3/5/06	2nd Mortgage on Park St. Building	100,000 √	50,000 A 2/29/04	–	200,000 C	12/31/04	–	Prime rate was 8% to 9% during the year
Φ Gigantic Building & Loan Assoc.	12%	$5,000 principal plus interest due on 5th of month, due in full 12/31/15	1st Mortgage on Park St. Building	720,000 √	–	60,000 ⊖	660,000 C	12/5/04	5,642 R	Reclassification entry for current portion proposed (See RJE-3)
Φ J. Lott, majority stockholder	0%	Due in full 12/31/07	Unsecured	300,000 √	–	100,000 N 12/31/04	200,000 C	–	–	Borrowed additional $100,000 from J. Lott on 1/7/05
				$1,170,000 √ F	$350,000 F	$260,000 F	$1,310,000 T/B F		$8,142 T/B F	

Interest Costs from Long-Term Debt

Interest expense for year	$ 281,333	T/B
Average loan balance outstanding	$1,406,667	R

Five-Year Maturities (for disclosure purposes)

Year-end	12/31/05	$ 60,000
	12/31/06	260,000
	12/31/07	260,000
	12/31/08	310,000
	12/31/09	60,000
	Thereafter	360,000
		$1,310,000 F

Tick Mark Legend

F	Readded, foots correctly
C	Confirmed without exception, W/P K-2
CX	Confirmed with exception, W/P K-3
NR	Does not recompute correctly
A	Agreed to loan agreement, validated bank deposit ticket, and board of directors authorization, W/P W-7
⊖	Agreed to cancelled checks and lender's monthly statements
	Agreed to cash disbursements journal and cancelled check dated 12/31/04, clearing 1/8/05
N	Agreed to cash disbursements journal and cancelled check dated 12/31/04, clearing 1/8/05
T/B	Traced to working trial balance
√	Agreed to 12/31/03 audit files
Φ	Agreed interest rate, term, and collateral to copy of note and loan agreement
●	Agreed to cancelled check and board of directors authorization, W/P W-7

Overall Conclusions

Long-term debt, accrued interest payable, and interest expense are correct and complete at 12/31/04

3. Ridolfi Credits—$130,000 in credits based on 35 credit memoranda from Ridolfi, Inc., were purportedly for the return of overstocked goods from several Grande stores. A Montgomery & Ross staff auditor noted the size of the credit and that the credit memos were dated subsequent to year-end. He further noticed that a sentence on the credit memos from Ridolfi had been obliterated by a felt-tip marker. When held to the light, the accountant could read that the marked-out sentence read, "Do not post until merchandise received." The staff auditor thereafter called Harold Ridolfi, treasurer of Ridolfi, Inc., and was informed that the $130,000 in goods had not been returned and the money was not owed to Grande by Ridolfi. Steiner advised Franklin, the audit partner, that he had talked to Harold Ridolfi, who claimed he had been misunderstood by the staff auditor. Steiner told Franklin not to have anyone call Ridolfi to verify the amount because of pending litigation between Grande and Ridolfi, Inc.

4. Accounts Payable Accrual—Montgomery & Ross assigned a senior with experience in the retail area to audit accounts payable. Although Grande had poor internal control, Montgomery & Ross selected a sample of 50 for confirmation of the several thousand vendors who did business with Grande. Twenty-seven responses were received, and 21 were reconciled to Grande's records. These tests indicated an unrecorded liability of approximately $290,000 when projected to the population of accounts payable. However, the investigation disclosed that Grande's president made telephone calls to some suppliers who had received confirmation requests from Montgomery & Ross and told them how to respond to the request.

   Montgomery & Ross also performed a purchases cutoff test by vouching accounts payable invoices received for nine weeks after year-end. The purpose of this test was to identify invoices received after year-end that should have been recorded in accounts payable. Thirty percent of the sample ($160,000) was found to relate to the prior year, indicating a potential unrecorded liability of approximately $500,000. The audit firm and Grande eventually agreed on an adjustment to increase accounts payable by $260,000.

Required   Identify deficiencies in the sufficiency and competency of the evidence gathered in the audit of accounts payable of Grande Stores.

7-42 (Objectives 7-5, 7-6) The long-term debt schedule on page 191 (indexed K-1) was prepared by client personnel and audited by AA, an audit assistant, during the calendar year 2004 audit of American Widgets, Inc., a continuing audit client. The engagement supervisor is reviewing the audit documentation thoroughly.*

Required   Identify the deficiencies in the audit schedule that the engagement supervisor should discover.

INTERNET PROBLEM 7-1: ELECTRONIC EVIDENCE

Reference the CW site. This problem requires students to use the Internet to research and consider how electronic evidence affects the audit process.

    *AICPA adapted.

AUDIT PLANNING AND ANALYTICAL PROCEDURES

THE FALL OF ENRON: DID ANYONE UNDERSTAND THEIR BUSINESS?

The bankruptcy of Enron Corporation, the nation's largest energy wholesaling company, represents the biggest corporate collapse in American history. Despite being listed as No. 7 on the Fortune 500 list with a market capitalization of $75 billion before its collapse, the meltdown of Enron was rapid. The fall began in October 2001 when Enron officials reported a shocking $618 million quarterly loss related to allegedly mysterious and hidden related party partnerships with company insiders. Then, in early November 2001, company officials were forced to admit that they had falsely claimed almost $600 million in earnings dating back to 1997, requiring the restatement of four years of audited financial statements. By the end of 2001, the company was in bankruptcy.

Enron, which was created in 1985 out of a merger of two gas pipelines, was a pioneer in trading natural gas and electricity in the newly deregulated utilities markets. In its earlier years, Enron made its money from hard assets like pipelines. However, by the end of the 1990s, 80% of Enron's earnings were coming from a more vague business known as "wholesale energy operations and services." Enron had built new markets, such as trading of weather securities, and believed that it could handle trades for almost anything, including electrons and advertising space.

In early 2001, speculation about Enron's business dealings began to surface. One highly regarded investment banker publicly stated that no one could explain how Enron actually made money. Additionally, he pointed to an odd and opaque mention in Enron documents about transactions that Enron and other "Entities" had done with a "Related Party" that was run by a "senior officer of Enron." However, the disclosure was difficult to understand.

Now, in the wake of the collapse, many are wondering how such a collapse could go undetected for so long. Many point to the incredibly complicated business structure at Enron and Enron's related vague and confusing financial statements. "What we are looking at here is an example of superbly complex financial reports. They didn't have to lie. All they had to do was to obfuscate it with sheer complexity," noted John Dingell, U.S. Congressman from Michigan. Others even allege that the men running the company never even understood their business concept because it was too complicated.

Apparently, the complexity and uncertainty surrounding Enron's business and financial statements fooled their auditors, too. Enron's auditor faced a flurry of attacks, class action lawsuits, and a criminal conviction that ultimately led to the firm's demise. In December 2001 congressional testimony, the audit firm's CEO admitted that the firm's professional judgment "turned out to be wrong" and that they mistakenly let Enron keep the related entities separate when they should have been consolidated.

Several lessons will likely come out of the Enron disaster. One to be underscored for auditors is the paramount importance of understanding the company's business and industry. Without that understanding, it's almost impossible to identify significant business risks impacting financial statements.

Source: Adapted from Bethany McLean, "Why Enron Went Bust," *Fortune* (December 24, 2001), pp. 58–68.

LEARNING OBJECTIVES

After studying this chapter, you should be able to

8-1 Discuss why adequate audit planning is essential.

8-2 Make client acceptance decisions and perform initial audit planning.

8-3 Gain an understanding of the client's business and industry.

8-4 Assess client business risk.

8-5 Perform preliminary analytical procedures.

8-6 State the purposes of analytical procedures and the timing of each purpose.

8-7 Select the most appropriate analytical procedure from among the five major types.

8-8 Compute common financial ratios.

As the chapter vignette illustrates, Enron's complex and confusing business structure helped disguise material misstatements in Enron financial statements for several years. Gaining an understanding of the client's business and industry is one of the most important steps in audit planning. This chapter explains audit planning in detail, including gaining an understanding of the client's business and industry, assessing client business risk, and performing preliminary analytical procedures.

PLANNING

OBJECTIVE 8-1

Discuss why adequate audit planning is essential.

The first generally accepted auditing standard of field work requires adequate planning.

> The work is to be adequately planned, and assistants, if any, are to be properly supervised.

There are three main reasons why the auditor should properly plan engagements: to enable the auditor to obtain sufficient competent evidence for the circumstances, to help keep audit costs reasonable, and to avoid misunderstandings with the client. Obtaining sufficient competent evidence is essential if the CPA firm is to minimize legal liability and maintain a good reputation in the business community. Keeping costs reasonable helps the firm remain competitive and thereby retain or expand its client base, assuming the firm has a reputation for doing high-quality work. Avoiding misunderstandings with the client is important for good client relations and for facilitating high-quality work at reasonable cost. For example, suppose that the auditor informs the client that the audit will be completed before June 30 but is unable to finish it until August because of inadequate scheduling of staff. The client is likely to be upset with the CPA firm and may even sue for breach of contract.

Figure 8-1 presents the eight major parts of audit planning. Each of the first seven parts is intended to help the auditor develop the last part, an effective and efficient overall audit plan and audit program. The first four parts of the planning phase of an audit are studied in this chapter. The last four are studied separately in later chapters.

Before beginning the discussion of the first four parts of the planning phase, it is useful to briefly introduce two risk terms: *acceptable audit risk* and *inherent risk*. These two risks have a significant effect on the conduct and cost of audits. Much of the early planning on audits deals with obtaining information to help auditors assess these risks.

Acceptable audit risk is a measure of how willing the auditor is to accept that the financial statements may be materially misstated after the audit is completed and an unqualified opinion has been issued. When the auditor decides on a lower acceptable audit risk, it means that the auditor wants to be more certain that the financial statements are *not* materially misstated. Zero risk would be certainty, and a 100 percent risk would be complete uncertainty.

Inherent risk is a measure of the auditor's assessment of the likelihood that there are material misstatements in an account balance before considering the effectiveness of internal control. If, for example, the auditor concludes that there is a high likelihood of material misstatement in an account such as accounts receivable, the auditor would conclude that inherent risk for accounts receivable is high.

Assessments of acceptable audit risk and inherent risk are an important part of audit planning, because they affect the amount of evidence to be accumulated and staff to be assigned to the engagement. For example, if inherent risk for inventory is high because of complex valuation issues, more evidence will be accumulated in the audit of inventory and more experienced staff will be assigned to perform testing in this area.

ACCEPT CLIENT AND PERFORM INITIAL AUDIT PLANNING

OBJECTIVE 8-2

Make client acceptance decisions and perform initial audit planning.

Initial audit planning involves four things, all of which should be done early in the audit. First, the auditor decides whether to accept a new client or continue serving an existing one. This is typically done by an experienced auditor who is in a position to make important decisions. The auditor wants to make that decision early, before incurring any significant

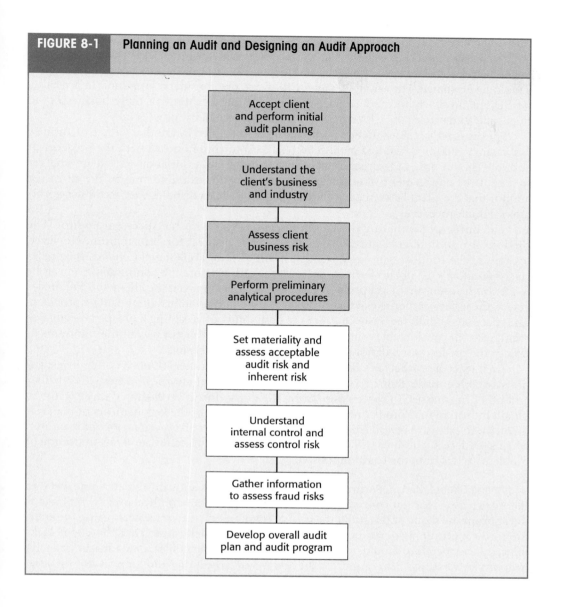

| FIGURE 8-1 | Planning an Audit and Designing an Audit Approach |

Accept client
and perform initial
audit planning

Understand the
client's business
and industry

Assess client
business risk

Perform preliminary
analytical procedures

Set materiality and
assess acceptable
audit risk and
inherent risk

Understand
internal control and
assess control risk

Gather information
to assess fraud risks

Develop overall audit
plan and audit program

costs that cannot be recovered. Second, the auditor identifies why the client wants or needs an audit. This information is likely to affect the remaining parts of the planning process. Third, the auditor obtains an understanding with the client about the terms of the engagement to avoid misunderstandings. Finally, the staff for the engagement is selected, including any required audit specialists.

Even though obtaining and retaining clients is not easy in a competitive profession such as public accounting, a CPA firm must use care in deciding which clients are acceptable. The firm's legal and professional responsibilities are such that clients who lack integrity or argue constantly about the proper conduct of the audit and fees can cause more problems than they are worth. Some CPA firms now refuse any clients in certain high-risk industries, such as savings and loans, health, and casualty insurance companies, and may even discontinue auditing existing clients in those industries. Some smaller CPA firms will not do audits of publicly held clients because of the risk of litigation or because of costs associated with registering the audit firm with the Public Company Accounting Oversight Board (PCAOB). Stated in terms of audit risk, an auditor is unlikely to accept a new client or continue serving an existing client if acceptable audit risk is lower than the CPA firm's threshold.

Client Acceptance and Continuance

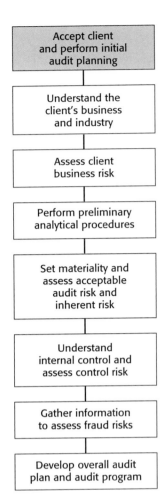

Accept client
and perform initial
audit planning

Understand the
client's business
and industry

Assess client
business risk

Perform preliminary
analytical procedures

Set materiality and
assess acceptable
audit risk and
inherent risk

Understand
internal control and
assess control risk

Gather information
to assess fraud risks

Develop overall audit
plan and audit program

New Client Investigation Before accepting a new client, most CPA firms investigate the company to determine its acceptability. To the extent possible, the prospective client's standing in the business community, financial stability, and relations with its previous CPA firm should be evaluated. For example, many CPA firms use considerable caution in accepting new clients in newly formed, rapidly growing businesses. Many of these businesses fail financially and expose the CPA firm to significant potential liability.

For prospective clients that have previously been audited by another CPA firm, the new (successor) auditor is *required* by SAS 84 (AU 315) to communicate with the predecessor auditor. The purpose of the requirement is to help the successor auditor evaluate whether to accept the engagement. The communication may, for example, inform the successor auditor that the client lacks integrity or that there have been disputes over accounting principles, audit procedures, or fees.

The burden of initiating the communication rests with the successor auditor. The predecessor auditor is required to respond to the request for information. However, because of the confidentiality requirement in the *Code of Professional Conduct,* the predecessor auditor must obtain permission from the client before the communication can be made. In the event that legal problems or disputes arise between the client and the predecessor, the latter's response can be limited to stating that no information will be provided. The successor should seriously consider the desirability of accepting a prospective engagement, without considerable other investigation, if a client will not permit the communication or the predecessor will not provide a comprehensive response.

Even when a prospective client has been audited by another CPA firm, other investigations are often made. Sources of information include local attorneys, other CPAs, banks, and other businesses. In some cases, the auditor may hire a professional investigator to obtain information about the reputation and background of the key members of management. More extensive investigation is appropriate when there has been no previous auditor, when a predecessor auditor will not provide the desired information, or if any indication of problems arises from the communication.

Continuing Clients Many CPA firms evaluate existing clients annually to determine whether there are reasons for not continuing to do the audit. Previous conflicts over such things as the appropriate scope of the audit, the type of opinion to issue, or fees may cause the auditor to discontinue association. The auditor may also determine that the client lacks integrity and therefore should no longer be a client. If the client files a lawsuit against a CPA firm or vice versa, the firm cannot do the audit. Similarly, if there are unpaid fees for services performed more than 1 year previously, the CPA firm cannot do the current year audit. To do an audit in either of these circumstances violates the AICPA *Code of Professional Conduct* rules on independence.

Even if none of the previously discussed conditions exist, the CPA firm may decide not to continue doing audits for a client because of excessive risk when acceptable audit risk is below the CPA firm's threshold. For example, a CPA firm might decide that there is considerable risk of a regulatory conflict between a governmental agency and a client, which could result in financial failure of the client and ultimately lawsuits against the CPA firm. Even if the engagement is profitable, the risk may exceed the short-term benefits of doing the audit.

Investigation of new clients and reevaluation of existing ones is an essential part of deciding acceptable audit risk. Assume a potential client in a reasonably risky industry, where management has a reputation of integrity but is also known to take aggressive financial risks. If the CPA firm decides that acceptable audit risk is extremely low, it may choose not to accept the engagement. If the CPA firm concludes that acceptable audit risk is low but the client is still acceptable, that is likely to affect the fee proposed to the client. Audits with a low acceptable audit risk will normally result in higher audit costs, which should be reflected in higher audit fees.

**Identify Client's Reasons
for Audit**

Two major factors affecting acceptable audit risk are the likely statement users and their intended uses of the statements. The auditor is likely to accumulate more evidence when the statements are to be used extensively. This is often the case for publicly held companies, those with extensive indebtedness, and companies that are to be sold in the near future.

The most likely uses of the statements can be determined from previous experience with the client and discussion with management. Throughout the engagement, the auditor may get additional information about why the client is having an audit and the likely uses of the financial statements. This information may affect the auditor's assessment of acceptable audit risk.

A clear understanding of the terms of the engagement should exist between the client and the CPA firm. SAS 83 (AU 310) requires that auditors must document their understanding of an engagement in the audit files, including the engagement's objectives, the responsibilities of the auditor and management, and the engagement's limitations. This is typically done with an **engagement letter**, even though one is not required.

The engagement letter is an agreement between the CPA firm and the client for the conduct of the audit and related services. It should specify whether the auditor will perform an audit, a review, or a compilation, plus any other services such as tax returns or management consulting. It should also state any restrictions to be imposed on the auditor's work, deadlines for completing the audit, assistance to be provided by the client's personnel in obtaining records and documents, and schedules to be prepared for the auditor. It often includes an agreement on fees. The engagement letter is also a means of informing the client that the auditor cannot guarantee that all acts of fraud will be discovered.

The engagement letter does not affect the CPA firm's responsibility to external users of audited financial statements, but it can affect legal responsibilities to the client. For example, if the client sued the CPA firm for failing to find a material misstatement, one defense a CPA firm could use would be a signed engagement letter stating that a review service, rather than an audit, was agreed upon.

Because the Sarbanes–Oxley Act explicitly shifts responsibility for hiring and firing of the auditor from management to the audit committee for public companies, the audit committee is viewed as "the client" in those engagements. Auditors of public companies should now obtain an understanding of the terms of the engagement with the audit committee and document that understanding in the audit files. In some cases, auditors may obtain signed engagement letters directly from the audit committee. The engagement letter will also include the agreement for the audit of the effectiveness of internal control over financial reporting, and may also include any nonaudit services that must be preapproved by the audit committee. For audits of nonpublic companies, the understanding is generally established through an engagement letter signed by management.

Engagement letter information is important in planning the audit principally because it affects the timing of the tests and the total amount of time the audit and other services will take. If the deadline for submitting the audit report is soon after the balance sheet date, a significant portion of the audit must be done before the end of the year. When the auditor is preparing tax returns and a management letter, or if client assistance is not available, arrangements must be made to extend the amount of time for the engagement. Client-imposed restrictions on the audit could affect the procedures performed and possibly even the type of audit opinion issued. An example of an engagement letter is given in Figure 8-2 (p. 198).

Obtain an Understanding with the Client

Assigning the appropriate staff to the engagement is important to meet generally accepted auditing standards and to promote audit efficiency. The first general standard states the following:

Select Staff for the Engagement

> The audit is to be performed by a person or persons having adequate technical training and proficiency as an auditor.

Staff must therefore be assigned with that standard in mind, and those assigned to the engagement must be knowledgeable about the client's industry. On larger engagements, there are likely to be one or more partners and staff at several experience levels doing the

FIGURE 8-2   **Engagement Letter**

HILYER AND RIDDLE, CPAs
Macon, Georgia 31212

June 14, 2005

Mr. Chuck Milsaps, President
Babb Clothing Co.
4604 Oakley St.
Macon, Georgia 31212

Dear Mr. Milsaps:

This will confirm our understanding of the arrangements for our audit of the financial statements of Babb Clothing Co. for the year ending December 31, 2005.

We will audit the company's financial statements for the year ending December 31, 2005, for the purpose of expressing an opinion on the fairness with which they present, in all material respects, the financial position, results of operations, and cash flows in conformity with generally accepted accounting principles.

We will conduct our audit in accordance with generally accepted auditing standards. Those standards require that we obtain reasonable, rather than absolute, assurance that the financial statements are free of material misstatement, whether caused by error or fraud. Accordingly, a material misstatement may remain undetected. Also, an audit is not designed to detect error or fraud that is immaterial to the financial statements; therefore, the audit will not necessarily detect misstatements less than this materiality level that might exist because of error, fraudulent financial reporting, or misappropriation of assets. If, for any reason, we are unable to complete the audit or are unable to form or have not formed an opinion, we may decline to express an opinion or decline to issue a report as a result of the engagement.

Although an audit includes obtaining an understanding of internal control sufficient to plan the audit and to determine the nature, timing, and extent of audit procedures to be performed, it is not designed to provide assurance on internal control or to identify significant deficiencies. However, we are responsible for ensuring that the audit committee is aware of any significant deficiencies that come to our attention.

The financial statements are the responsibility of the company's management. Management is also responsible for (1) establishing and maintaining effective internal control over financial reports, (2) identifying and ensuring the company complies with the laws and regulations applicable to its activities, (3) making all financial records and related information available to us, and (4) providing to us at the conclusion of the engagement a representation letter that, among other things, will confirm management's responsibility for the preparation of the financial statements in conformity with generally accepted accounting principles, the availability of financial records and related data, the completeness and availability of all minutes of the board and committee meetings, and to the best of its knowledge and belief, the absence of fraud involving management or those employees who have a significant role in the entity's internal control.

The timing of our audit and the assistance to be supplied by your personnel, including the preparation of schedules and analyses of accounts, are described on a separate attachment. Timely completion of this work will facilitate the completion of our audit.

As part of our engagement for the year ending December 31, 2005, we will also prepare the federal and state income tax returns for Babb Clothing Co.

Our fees will be billed as work progresses and are based on the amount of time required at various levels of responsibility, plus actual out-of-pocket expenses. Invoices are payable upon presentation. We will notify you immediately of any circumstances we encounter that could significantly affect our initial estimate of total fees of $135,000.

If this letter correctly expresses your understanding, please sign the enclosed copy and return it to us. We appreciate the opportunity to serve you.

Yours very truly:

Alan Hilyer

Alan Hilyer
Partner

Accepted:

By: *Chuck Milsaps*
Date: 6-21-05

audit. Specialists in such technical areas as statistical sampling and computer risk assessment may also be assigned. On smaller audits, there may be only one or two staff members.

A major consideration affecting staffing is the need for continuity from year to year. An inexperienced staff assistant is likely to become the most experienced nonpartner on the engagement within a few years. Continuity helps the CPA firm maintain familiarity with the technical requirements and closer interpersonal relations with client personnel.

To illustrate the importance of assigning appropriate staff to engagements, consider a computer manufacturing client with extensive inventory of computers and computer parts. Inherent risk for inventory has been assessed as high. It is essential for the staff person doing the inventory portion of the audit to be experienced in auditing inventory. In addition, the auditor should have a good understanding of the computer manufacturing industry.

If the audit of a client requires specialized knowledge, it may be necessary to consult a specialist. SAS 73 (AU 336) establishes the requirements for selecting specialists and reviewing their work. Examples include using a diamond expert in evaluating the replacement cost of diamonds and an actuary for determining the appropriateness of the recorded value of insurance loss reserves. Another common use of specialists is consulting with attorneys on the legal interpretation of contracts and titles. In the previously discussed example of a large inventory of computers and computer parts, the CPA firm may decide to engage a specialist if no one within the firm is qualified to evaluate whether the inventory is obsolete.

The auditor should have a sufficient understanding of the client's business to recognize the need for a specialist. The auditor should evaluate the specialist's professional qualifications and understand the objectives and scope of the specialist's work. The auditor should also consider the specialist's relationship to the client, including circumstances that might impair the specialist's objectivity.

**Evaluate Need
for Outside Specialists**

UNDERSTAND THE CLIENT'S BUSINESS AND INDUSTRY

A thorough understanding of the client's business and industry and knowledge about the company's operations are essential for doing an adequate audit. The nature of the client's business and industry affects client business risk and the risk of material misstatements in the financial statements. The auditor uses knowledge of these risks to determine the appropriate extent of audit evidence.

Several factors have increased the importance of understanding the client's business and industry:

- Information technology connects client companies with major customers and suppliers. As a result, auditors need greater knowledge about major customers and suppliers and risks related to those relationships.

OBJECTIVE 8-3

Gain an understanding of the client's business and industry.

Industry Information

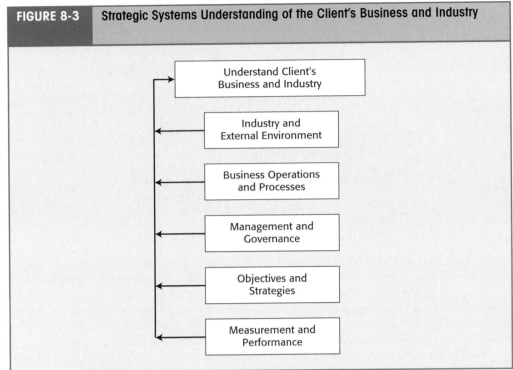

FIGURE 8-3 | Strategic Systems Understanding of the Client's Business and Industry

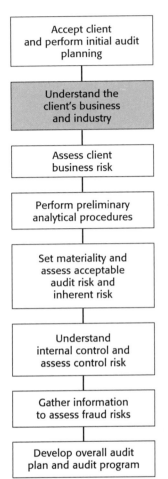

- Accept client and perform initial audit planning
- Understand the client's business and industry
- Assess client business risk
- Perform preliminary analytical procedures
- Set materiality and assess acceptable audit risk and inherent risk
- Understand internal control and assess control risk
- Gather information to assess fraud risks
- Develop overall audit plan and audit program

- Clients have expanded operations globally, often through joint ventures or strategic alliances.
- Information technology affects internal client processes, improving the quality and timeliness of accounting information.
- The increased importance of human capital and other intangible assets has increased accounting complexity and the importance of management judgments and estimates.
- Auditors need a better understanding of the client's business and industry to provide additional value-added services to clients. For example, audit firms often provide assurance and consulting services related to information technology and risk management services for nonpublic audit clients that require an extensive knowledge of the client's industry.

Auditors consider these factors using the strategic systems approach to understanding the client's business that was introduced in Chapter 1. Figure 8-3 provides an overview of the strategic systems approach to understanding the client's business and industry. Important aspects of this understanding are discussed in the following sections.

Industry and External Environment

There are three primary reasons for obtaining a good understanding of the client's industry and external environment. First, there are risks associated with specific industries. These risks may affect the auditor's assessment of client business risk and acceptable audit risk, or

MANY CPA FIRMS ORGANIZE TO FOCUS ON INDUSTRIES

A high level of knowledge of a client's industry and business is so critical to conducting quality audits and providing value-added tax and consulting services that many CPA firms are organized to focus on industry lines. For example, PricewaterhouseCoopers, LLP has organized its practice using multidisciplinary teams across 21 industry sectors. The firm groups these industry sectors into one of three clusters: Consumer and Industrial Products & Services; Financial Services; and Technology Info-Com and Entertainment. Organizing along industry lines helps CPA firms such as PricewaterhouseCoopers better understand their clients' businesses and provide value-added services.

even whether auditing companies in the industry is advisable. As stated earlier, certain industries are more risky than others, such as the savings and loan and health insurance industries.

Second, there are inherent risks that are typically common to all clients in certain industries. Understanding those risks aids the auditor in assessing the client's inherent risks. Examples include potential inventory obsolescence in the fashion clothing industry, accounts receivable collection inherent risk in the consumer loan industry, and reserve for loss inherent risk in the casualty insurance industry.

Third, many industries have unique accounting requirements that the auditor must understand to evaluate whether the client's financial statements are in accordance with generally accepted accounting principles. For example, if the auditor is doing an audit of a city, the auditor must understand governmental accounting and auditing requirements. There are also unique accounting requirements for construction companies, railroads, not-for-profit organizations, financial institutions, and many other organizations.

Several auditor litigation cases described in Chapter 5 resulted from the auditor's failure to understand the nature of the client's industry. For example, several major accounting firms paid large settlements to the federal government related to audits of failed savings and loans. In some of these audits, the auditors failed to understand the nature of significant real estate transactions.

The auditor must also understand the client's external environment, including such things as economic conditions, extent of competition, and regulatory requirements. For example, auditors of utility companies need an understanding of the unique regulatory accounting requirements in this industry. In addition, in recent years deregulation in this industry has introduced competition that threatens the survival of less-efficient companies, and utilities are increasingly susceptible to fluctuations in energy prices. Auditors of these companies must assess these risks in developing effective audit plans.

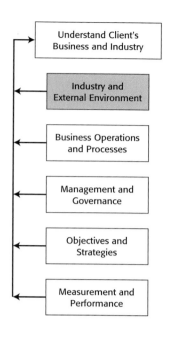

The auditor should understand factors such as major sources of revenue, key customers and suppliers, sources of financing, and information about related parties that may indicate areas of increased client business risk. For example, many technology firms are dependent on one or a few products that may become obsolete due to new technologies or stronger competitors. Dependence on a few major customers may result in highly material losses from bad debts or obsolete inventory. For example, many suppliers of Internet and telecommunications equipment provided significant sales financing to customers and suffered losses when the customers were unable to pay for equipment.

The ability to obtain financing is an important factor in determining whether the company is likely to continue as a going concern. This is especially true for Internet and other new companies that are expected to lose money for several years before becoming profitable.

Business Operations and Processes

Tour the Plant and Offices A tour of the client's facilities is helpful in obtaining a better understanding of the client's business operations because it provides an opportunity to observe operations firsthand and to meet key personnel. The actual viewing of the physical facilities aids in understanding physical safeguards over assets and in interpreting accounting data by providing a frame of reference in which to visualize such assets as inventory in process and factory equipment. Knowledge of the physical layout also facilitates getting answers to questions later in the audit. The tour may also help the auditor identify inherent risks. As an example, if the auditor observes unused equipment and potentially unsalable inventory, it will affect the assessment of inherent risks for equipment and inventory. Discussions with nonaccounting employees during the tour and throughout the audit are useful in maintaining a broad perspective.

Identify Related Parties Transactions with related parties are important to auditors because generally accepted accounting principles require that they be *disclosed in the financial statements* if they are material. Transactions with a related party are not arm's-length transactions. Therefore, there is a risk that they were not valued at the same amount as they would

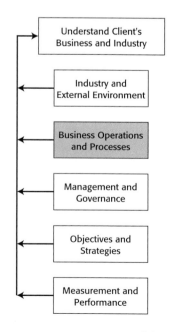

have been if the transactions had been with an independent third party. The disclosure requirements include the nature of the related party relationship; a description of transactions, including dollar amounts; and amounts due from and to related parties. Most auditors assess inherent risk as high for related parties and related party transactions, both because of the accounting disclosure requirements and the lack of independence between the parties involved in the transactions.

A **related party** is defined in SAS 45 (AU 334) as an affiliated company, a principal owner of the client company, or any other party with which the client deals, where one of the parties can influence the management or operating policies of the other. A **related party transaction** is any transaction between the client and a related party. Common examples include sales or purchase transactions between a parent company and its subsidiary, exchanges of equipment between two companies owned by the same person, and loans to officers. A less common example is the exercise of significant management influence on an audit client by its most important customer.

Because material related party transactions must be disclosed, it is important that all related parties be *identified and included in the permanent files* early in the engagement. Finding undisclosed related party transactions is thereby enhanced. Common ways of identifying related parties include inquiry of management, review of SEC filings, and examination of stockholders' listings to identify principal stockholders.

Because of the lack of independence between the parties involved, the Sarbanes–Oxley Act prohibits related party transactions that involve personal loans to executives. It is now unlawful for any public company to provide personal credit or loans to any director or executive officer of the company. Banks or other financial institutions are permitted to make normal loans to their directors and officers using market rates, such as for residential mortgages. In light of these prohibitions, auditors should be alert for any such loans to executives or other employees to ensure those transactions do not exist and, if they do, to deal with them as illegal acts.

Management and Governance

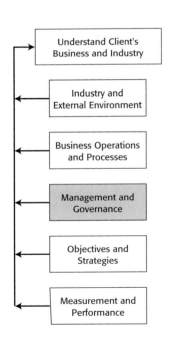

Management establishes the strategies and business processes followed by the client's business. Management's philosophy and operating style, and ability to identify and respond to risk, significantly impact the risk of material misstatements in the financial statements. For example, one of the major financial accounting scandals in the late 1990s involved the aggressive CEO of a consumer products company. The significant annual increase in sales and earnings reported by the company was ultimately determined to be based on various improper accounting techniques encouraged by the CEO.

Governance includes the client's organizational structure, as well as the activities of the board of directors and the audit committee. An effective board of directors helps ensure that the company takes appropriate risks. The audit committee, through oversight of financial reporting, can reduce the likelihood of overly aggressive accounting. As part of understanding the client's governance system, the auditor should gain knowledge of the corporate charter and bylaws, consider its code of ethics, and read the corporate minutes.

Corporate Charter and Bylaws The **corporate charter** is granted by the state in which the company is incorporated and is the legal document necessary for recognizing a corporation as a separate entity. It includes the exact name of the corporation, the date of incorporation, the kinds and amounts of capital stock the corporation is authorized to issue, and the types of business activities the corporation is authorized to conduct. In specifying the kinds of capital stock, there is also included such information as the voting rights of each class of stock, par or stated value of the stock, preferences and conditions necessary for dividends, and prior rights in liquidation.

The **bylaws** include the rules and procedures adopted by the stockholders of the corporation. They specify such things as the fiscal year of the corporation, the frequency of stockholder meetings, the method of voting for directors, and the duties and powers of the corporate officers.

Code of Ethics Companies frequently communicate the entity's values and ethical standards through policy statements and codes of conduct. In response to requirements in the

Sarbanes–Oxley Act, the SEC requires each public company to disclose whether it has adopted a code of ethics that applies to senior management, including the CEO, CFO, and principal accounting officer or controller. A company that has not adopted such a code must disclose this fact and explain why it has not done so. The SEC also requires companies to promptly disclose amendments and waivers to the code of ethics for any of those officers.

As a part of the understanding of the client's governance system, auditors should gain knowledge of the company's code of ethics. In particular, auditors should examine any changes and waivers of the code of conduct that have implications about the governance system and related integrity and ethical values of senior management.

Minutes of Meetings The **corporate minutes** are the official record of the meetings of the board of directors and stockholders. They include summaries of the most important topics discussed at these meetings and the decisions made by the directors and stockholders. The auditor should read the minutes to obtain information that is relevant to performing the audit.

Common authorizations in the minutes include compensation of officers, new contracts and agreements, acquisitions of property, loans, and dividend payments. While reading the minutes, the auditor should identify relevant authorizations and include the information in the audit files by making an abstract of the minutes or by obtaining a copy and underlining significant portions. Some time before the audit is completed, there must be a follow-up of this information to be sure that management has complied with actions taken by the stockholders and the board of directors. As an illustration, the authorized compensation of officers should be traced to each individual officer's payroll record as a test of whether the correct total compensation was paid. Similarly, the auditor should compare the authorizations of loans with notes payable to make certain that these liabilities are recorded.

Client Objectives and Strategies

Strategies are approaches followed by the entity to achieve organizational objectives. Auditors should understand client objectives related to (1) reliability of financial reporting, (2) effectiveness and efficiency of operations, and (3) compliance with laws and regulations.

Management is primarily concerned with the effectiveness and efficiency of operations. Auditors need knowledge about operations to assess client business risk and inherent risk in the financial statements. For example, product quality can have a significant impact on the financial statements through lost sales and warranty and product liability claims. One auto manufacturer recently recalled more than $3 billion of tires, which affected the financial statements of the auto company and its tire supplier.

As part of understanding the client's objectives related to compliance with laws and regulations, the auditor should become familiar with the terms of contracts and other legal obligations. These can include such diverse items as long-term notes and bonds payable, stock options, pension plans, contracts with vendors for future delivery of supplies, government contracts for completion and delivery of manufactured products, royalty agreements, union contracts, and leases.

Most contracts are of primary interest in individual parts of the audit and, in practice, receive special attention during the different phases of the detailed tests. For example, the provisions of a pension plan would receive substantial emphasis as a part of the audit of the unfunded liability for pensions. The auditor should review and abstract the documents early in the engagement to gain a better perspective of the organization and to become familiar with potential problem areas. Later, these documents can be examined more carefully as a part of the tests of individual audit areas.

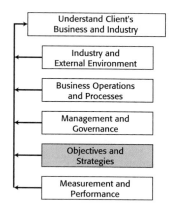

Measurement and Performance

The client's performance measurement system includes the key performance indicators that management uses to measure progress toward objectives. These indicators go beyond financial statement figures such as sales and net income and include measures that are tailored to the client and its objectives. Examples of such key performance indicators include market share and sales per employee, unit sales growth, unique visitors to a Web site, or same-store sales and sales per square foot for a retailer.

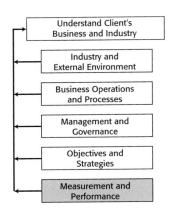

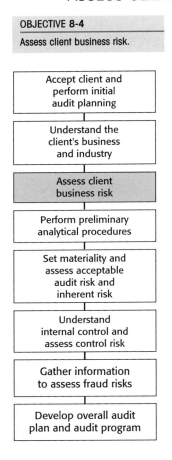

The risk of financial misstatements may be increased if the client has set unreasonable objectives or if the performance measurement system encourages aggressive accounting. For example, a company may have as an objective obtaining the leading market share of industry sales. If management and salespeople are compensated based on achieving this sales objective, there is increased incentive to record sales before they have been earned or record sales for nonexistent transactions. In this situation, the auditor is likely to increase assessed inherent risk and the extent of testing for the existence of sales.

Performance measurement includes ratio analysis and benchmarking against key competitors. As part of understanding the client's business, the auditor should perform ratio analysis or review the client's calculations of key performance ratios. Performing preliminary analytical procedures is the fourth step in the planning process and is discussed later in this chapter.

ASSESS CLIENT BUSINESS RISK

OBJECTIVE 8-4

Assess client business risk.

The auditor uses knowledge gained from the strategic systems understanding of the client's business and industry to assess client business risk. **Client business risk** is the risk that the client will fail to achieve its objectives. Client business risk can arise from any of the factors affecting the client and its environment. For example, a new technology may erode a client's competitive advantage, or the client may fail to execute its strategies as well as its competitors.

The auditor's primary concern is the risk of material misstatements in the financial statements due to client business risk. In a recent example, a company that provides Internet networking equipment recorded a $3 billion write-down of inventory when actual sales were less than forecast sales due to an economic downturn. For technology companies and clients in other industries with short product cycles, the auditor should be concerned with whether production plans and inventory levels are appropriate for current economic conditions. Similarly, companies often make strategic acquisitions that depend on successfully combining the operations of two or more companies. If the planned synergies do not develop, the fixed assets and goodwill recorded in the acquisition may be impaired, affecting the fair presentation of the financial statements.

Figure 8-4 summarizes the relationship among the client's business and industry, client business risk, and the auditor's assessment of the risk of material financial statement misstatements. The client's industry and other external factors and the client's business strategies, processes, and other internal factors are considered in the auditor's assessment of

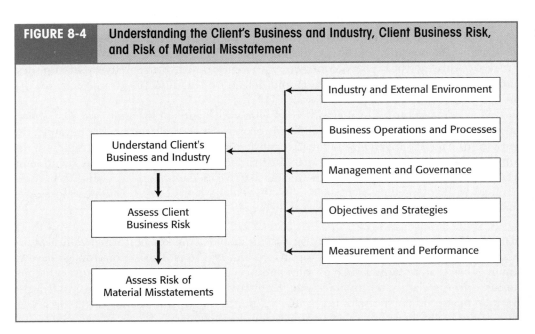

FIGURE 8-4   Understanding the Client's Business and Industry, Client Business Risk, and Risk of Material Misstatement

client business risk. The auditor also considers management controls that may mitigate business risk, such as effective risk assessment practices and corporate governance. Client business risk, after considering the effectiveness of top management controls, is sometimes called residual risk. Client business risk is then evaluated to assess the risk of material misstatement in the financial statements. The risk of material misstatements is used to classify risks using the audit risk model to determine the appropriate extent of audit evidence. Use of the audit risk model is discussed in the next chapter.

Management is a primary source for identifying client business risks. To be in a position to certify quarterly and annual financial statements and to evaluate the effectiveness of disclosure controls and procedures now required by the Sarbanes–Oxley Act, management of public companies should conduct thorough evaluations of relevant client business risks affecting financial reporting.

The Sarbanes–Oxley Act requires that management certify it has designed disclosure controls and procedures to ensure that material information about business risks is made known to them. The SEC believes these procedures are intended to cover a broader range of information than is covered by an issuer's internal controls for financial reporting. In the SEC's view, the procedures should capture information that is relevant to assess the need to disclose developments and *risks* that pertain to the company's business. Inquiries of management about client business risks identified by them in advance of certifying quarterly and annual financial statements may provide a significant source of information for auditors about client business risks affecting financial reporting.

The Sarbanes–Oxley Act also requires that management certify it has informed the auditor and audit committee of any significant deficiencies in internal control, including material weaknesses. Such information is useful to auditors as they evaluate the impact of internal control on the likelihood of material misstatements in financial statements.

PERFORM PRELIMINARY ANALYTICAL PROCEDURES

An important part of understanding the client's business and assessing client business risk is performing preliminary analytical procedures. Comparison of client ratios to industry or competitor benchmarks provides an indication of the company's performance. Unusual changes in ratios compared to prior years or to industry averages help identify areas having increased risk of misstatements that require further attention during the audit.

Analytical procedures are also an important part of testing throughout the audit. The use of preliminary analytical procedures as part of audit planning is first illustrated for the

> **OBJECTIVE 8-5**
> Perform preliminary analytical procedures.

```
┌─────────────────────────┐
│   Accept client and     │
│   perform initial       │
│   audit planning        │
└─────────────────────────┘
           │
┌─────────────────────────┐
│   Understand the        │
│   client's business     │
│   and industry          │
└─────────────────────────┘
           │
┌─────────────────────────┐
│   Assess client         │
│   business risk         │
└─────────────────────────┘
           │
┌─────────────────────────┐
│   Perform preliminary   │
│   analytical procedures │
└─────────────────────────┘
           │
┌─────────────────────────┐
│   Set materiality and   │
│   assess acceptable     │
│   audit risk and        │
│   inherent risk         │
└─────────────────────────┘
           │
┌─────────────────────────┐
│   Understand            │
│   internal control and  │
│   assess control risk   │
└─────────────────────────┘
           │
┌─────────────────────────┐
│   Gather information    │
│   to assess fraud risks │
└─────────────────────────┘
           │
┌─────────────────────────┐
│   Develop overall audit │
│   plan and audit program│
└─────────────────────────┘
```

Hillsburg Hardware Co. After a summary of the audit planning process, the remainder of the chapter studies the use of analytical procedures throughout the audit.

Table 8-1 presents key financial ratios for Hillsburg Hardware Co. that auditors might consider during audit planning, along with comparative industry information. These ratios are based on the Hillsburg Hardware Co. financial statements, which are included in the glossy insert to the textbook. As described more fully in the Annual Report to Shareholders (also included in the glossy insert material), Hillsburg is a wholesale distributor of hardware equipment to independent, high-quality hardware stores in the midwestern part of the United States. The company is a niche provider in the overall hardware market, which is recently becoming dominated by huge hardware and building supply national chains. Hillsburg's auditors identified potential increased competition from national chains as a specific client business risk. Hillsburg's market consists of smaller, independent hardware stores. Increased competition could affect the sales and profitability of these customers, which would likely impact Hillsburg's sales and the value of assets such as accounts receivable and inventory. The following discussion indicates how the auditor might use ratio information to further understand Hillsburg's operations and identify areas with increased risk of material misstatements.

The profitability measures indicate that Hillsburg is performing fairly well, despite the increased competition from larger national chains. Although lower than the industry averages, the liquidity measures indicate that the company is in good financial condition, and the leverage ratios indicate additional borrowing capacity. Because Hillsburg's market consists of smaller, independent hardware stores, the company holds more inventory and takes longer to collect receivables than the industry average.

In identifying areas of specific risk, the auditor would likely focus on the liquidity activity ratios. Inventory turnover has improved but is still lower than the industry average. Accounts receivable turnover has declined slightly and is lower than the industry average. The collectibility of accounts receivable and inventory obsolescence will likely warrant attention in the current year's audit. These areas also likely received additional attention during the prior year's audit.

TABLE 8-1	Examples of Planning Analytical Procedures			
SELECTED RATIOS	**HILLSBURG 12/31/04**	**INDUSTRY 12/31/04**	**HILLSBURG 12/31/03**	**INDUSTRY 12/31/03**
Short-Term Debt-Paying Ability				
Cash ratio	0.06	0.22	0.06	0.20
Quick ratio	1.57	3.10	1.45	3.00
Current ratio	3.86	5.20	4.04	5.10
Liquidity Activity Ratios				
Accounts receivable turnover	7.59	12.15	7.61	12.25
Days to collect accounts receivable	48.09	30.04	47.96	29.80
Inventory turnover	3.36	5.20	3.02	4.90
Days to sell inventory	108.63	70.19	120.86	74.49
Ability to Meet Long-Term Obligations				
Debt to equity	1.73	2.51	1.98	2.53
Times interest earned	3.06	5.50	3.29	5.60
Profitability Ratios				
Gross profit percent	27.85	31.00	27.70	32.00
Profit margin	0.05	0.07	0.05	0.08
Return on assets	0.09	0.09	0.08	0.09
Return on common equity	0.26	0.37	0.24	0.35

SUMMARY OF THE PURPOSES OF AUDIT PLANNING

There are several purposes of the planning procedures discussed in this section. A major purpose is to gain an understanding of the client's business and industry. This is used to assess client business risk and the risk of material misstatements in the financial statements.

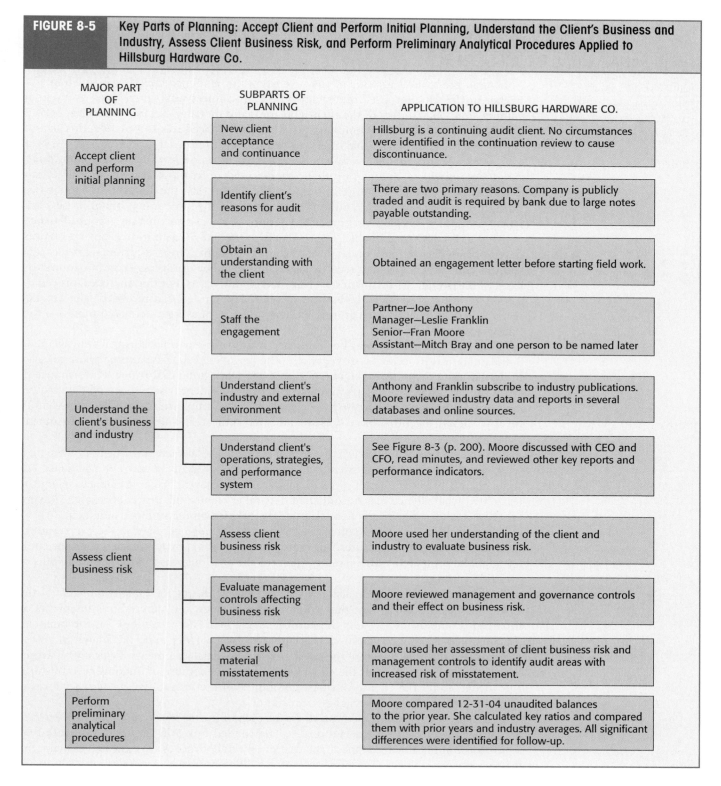

FIGURE 8-5 Key Parts of Planning: Accept Client and Perform Initial Planning, Understand the Client's Business and Industry, Assess Client Business Risk, and Perform Preliminary Analytical Procedures Applied to Hillsburg Hardware Co.

MAJOR PART OF PLANNING	SUBPARTS OF PLANNING	APPLICATION TO HILLSBURG HARDWARE CO.
Accept client and perform initial planning	New client acceptance and continuance	Hillsburg is a continuing audit client. No circumstances were identified in the continuation review to cause discontinuance.
	Identify client's reasons for audit	There are two primary reasons. Company is publicly traded and audit is required by bank due to large notes payable outstanding.
	Obtain an understanding with the client	Obtained an engagement letter before starting field work.
	Staff the engagement	Partner—Joe Anthony Manager—Leslie Franklin Senior—Fran Moore Assistant—Mitch Bray and one person to be named later
Understand the client's business and industry	Understand client's industry and external environment	Anthony and Franklin subscribe to industry publications. Moore reviewed industry data and reports in several databases and online sources.
	Understand client's operations, strategies, and performance system	See Figure 8-3 (p. 200). Moore discussed with CEO and CFO, read minutes, and reviewed other key reports and performance indicators.
Assess client business risk	Assess client business risk	Moore used her understanding of the client and industry to evaluate business risk.
	Evaluate management controls affecting business risk	Moore reviewed management and governance controls and their effect on business risk.
	Assess risk of material misstatements	Moore used her assessment of client business risk and management controls to identify audit areas with increased risk of misstatement.
Perform preliminary analytical procedures		Moore compared 12-31-04 unaudited balances to the prior year. She calculated key ratios and compared them with prior years and industry averages. All significant differences were identified for follow-up.

Keep in mind that there are four additional parts of audit planning, each of which is discussed in subsequent chapters: set materiality and assess acceptable audit risk and inherent risk (Chapter 9), understand internal control and assess control risk (Chapter 10), gather information to assess fraud risks (Chapter 11), and develop an overall audit plan and audit program (Chapter 13). Figure 8-5 (p. 207) summarizes the four major parts of audit planning discussed in this section and the key components of each part, with a brief illustration of how a CPA firm applied each component to a continuing client, Hillsburg Hardware Co.

ANALYTICAL PROCEDURES

OBJECTIVE 8-6

State the purposes of analytical procedures and the timing of each purpose.

Analytical procedures are one of the seven types of evidence introduced in Chapter 7. Earlier in this chapter, preliminary analytical procedures were introduced as a part of gaining an understanding of the client's business and industry. Because of the importance of this topic and increased emphasis on analytical procedures in practice, this section expands on the subject. Analytical procedures are defined by SAS 56 (AU 329) as *evaluations of financial information made by a study of plausible relationships among financial and nonfinancial data . . . involving comparisons of recorded amounts to expectations developed by the auditor.* This definition is more formal than the description of analytical procedures used in Chapter 7, but both say essentially the same thing. In both cases, analytical procedures use comparisons and relationships to assess whether account balances or other data appear reasonable. The emphasis in the SAS 56 definition is on expectations developed by the auditor. For example, the auditor might compare current-year recorded commissions expense to total recorded sales multiplied by the average commission rate as a test of the overall reasonableness of recorded commissions. For this analytical procedure to be relevant and reliable, the auditor has likely concluded that recorded sales are correctly stated, all sales earn a commission, and there is an average actual commission rate that is readily determinable.

Analytical procedures may be performed at any of three times during an engagement. Some analytical procedures are *required* to be performed in the *planning phase* to assist in determining the nature, extent, and timing of work to be performed. Performance of analytical procedures during planning helps the auditor identify significant matters requiring special consideration later in the engagement. For example, the calculation of inventory turnover before inventory price tests are done may indicate the need for special care during those tests.

Analytical procedures done in the planning phase typically use data aggregated at a high level, and the sophistication, extent, and timing of the procedures vary among clients. For some clients, the comparison of prior-year and current-year account balances using the unaudited trial balance may be sufficient. For other clients, the procedures might involve extensive analysis of quarterly financial statements based on the auditor's judgment.

Analytical procedures are often done *during the testing phase* of the audit in conjunction with other audit procedures. For example, the prepaid portion of each insurance policy might be compared with the same policy for the previous year as a part of doing tests of prepaid insurance.

Analytical procedures are also *required* to be done *during the completion phase* of the audit. Such tests are useful at that point as a final review for material misstatements or financial problems and to help the auditor take a final "objective look" at the financial statements that have been audited. It is common for a partner to do the analytical procedures during the final review of the audit files and financial statements. Typically, a partner has a good understanding of the client and its business because of ongoing relationships. Knowledge about the client's business combined with effective analytical procedures is a way to identify possible oversights in an audit.

The purposes of analytical procedures for each of the three different phases when they are performed are shown in Figure 8-6. The shaded boxes in the figure indicate that a purpose is applicable for a phase. In addition, several purposes are indicated as being the primary purpose. Notice that purposes vary for different phases. Analytical procedures are

FIGURE 8-6   Timing and Purposes of Analytical Procedures

Purpose	Phase		
	(Required) Planning Phase	Testing Phase	**(Required)** Completion Phase
Understand client's industry and business	Primary purpose		
Assess going concern	Secondary purpose		Secondary purpose
Indicate possible misstatements (attention directing)	Primary purpose	Secondary purpose	Primary purpose
Reduce detailed tests	Secondary purpose	Primary purpose	

performed during the planning phase for all four purposes, whereas the other two phases are used primarily to determine appropriate audit evidence and to reach conclusions about the fair presentation of financial statements.

FIVE TYPES OF ANALYTICAL PROCEDURES

The usefulness of analytical procedures as audit evidence depends significantly on the auditor developing an *expectation* of what a recorded account balance or ratio based on account balances *should be*, regardless of the type of analytical procedures used. Auditors develop an expectation of an account balance or ratio by considering information from prior periods, industry trends, client-prepared budgeted expectations, and nonfinancial information. The auditor typically compares the client's balances and ratios with expected balances and ratios using one or more of the following types of analytical procedures:

OBJECTIVE 8-7

Select the most appropriate analytical procedure from among the five major types.

- Compare client and industry data
- Compare client data with similar prior-period data
- Compare client data with client-determined expected results
- Compare client data with auditor-determined expected results
- Compare client data with expected results, using nonfinancial data

Suppose that you are doing an audit and obtain the following information about the client and the average company in the client's industry:

Compare Client and Industry Data

	Client		Industry	
	2005	2004	2005	2004
Inventory turnover	3.4	3.5	3.9	3.4
Gross margin percent	26.3%	26.4%	27.3%	26.2%

Analytical Procedures—
Apple and Dell

If we look only at client information for the two ratios shown, the company appears to be stable with no apparent indication of difficulties. However, if the auditor uses industry data to develop expectations about the two ratios for 2005, the auditor would expect both ratios for the client to increase. Although these two ratios by themselves may not indicate significant problems, the example illustrates how developing expectations using industry data may provide useful information about the client's performance. For example, the company may have lost market share, its pricing may not be competitive, it may have incurred abnormal costs, or it may have obsolete items in inventory.

Dun & Bradstreet, Robert Morris Associates, and other analysts accumulate financial information for thousands of companies and compile the data for different lines of business. Many CPA firms purchase this information for use as a basis for industry comparisons in their audits.

The most important benefits of industry comparisons are as an aid to understanding the client's business and as an indication of the likelihood of financial failure. The ratios in Robert Morris Associates, for example, are primarily of a type that bankers and other credit executives use in evaluating whether a company will be able to repay a loan. That same information is useful to auditors in assessing the relative strength of the client's capital structure, its borrowing capacity, and the likelihood of financial failure.

A major weakness in using industry ratios for auditing is the difference between the nature of the client's financial information and that of the firms making up the industry totals. Because the industry data are broad averages, the comparisons may not be meaningful. Often, the client's line of business is not the same as the industry standards. In addition, different companies follow different accounting methods, and this affects the comparability of data. If most companies in the industry use FIFO inventory valuation and straight-line depreciation and the audit client uses LIFO and double-declining-balance depreciation, comparisons may not be meaningful. This does not mean that industry comparisons should not be made. Rather, it is an indication of the need for care in interpreting the results. One approach to overcome the limitations of industry averages is to compare the client to one or more benchmark firms in the industry.

Compare Client Data with Similar Prior-Period Data

Suppose that the gross margin percent for a company has been between 26 and 27 percent for each of the past 4 years but is 23 percent in the current year. This decline in gross margin should be a concern to the auditor if there is no expectation of a decline. The cause of the decline could be a change in economic conditions. However, it could also be caused by misstatements in the financial statements, such as sales or purchase cutoff errors, unrecorded sales, overstated accounts payable, or inventory costing errors. The auditor should determine the cause of the decline in gross margin and consider the effect, if any, on evidence accumulation.

There are a wide variety of analytical procedures in which client data are compared with similar data from one or more prior periods. The following are common examples.

Compare the Current Year's Balance with That for the Preceding Year One of the easiest ways to make this test is to include the preceding year's adjusted trial balance results in a separate column of the current year's trial balance spreadsheet. The auditor can easily compare the current year's balance and previous year's balance to decide early in the audit whether an account should receive more than the normal amount of attention because of a significant change in the balance. For example, if the auditor observes a substantial increase in supplies expense, the auditor should determine whether the cause was an increased use of supplies, an error in the account due to a misclassification, or a misstatement of supplies inventory.

Compare the Detail of a Total Balance with Similar Detail for the Preceding Year If there have been no significant changes in the client's operations in the current year, much of the detail making up the totals in the financial statements should also remain unchanged. By briefly comparing the detail of the current period with similar detail of the preceding period, it is often possible to isolate information that needs further examination. Comparison of details may take the form of details over time or details at a point in time. A common example of the former is comparing the monthly totals for the current year and preceding year for sales, repairs, and other accounts. An example of the latter is comparing the details of loans payable at the end of the current year with those at the end of the preceding year. In each of these examples, the auditor should first develop an expectation of a change or lack thereof before making the comparison.

Compute Ratios and Percentage Relationships for Comparison with Previous Years The comparison of totals or details with previous years as described in the two preceding paragraphs has two shortcomings. First, it fails to consider growth or decline in business activity. Second, relationships of data to other data, such as sales to cost of goods sold, are ignored. Ratio and percentage relationships overcome both shortcomings. The example discussed earlier about the decline in gross margin is a common percentage relationship used by auditors.

A few types of ratios and internal comparisons are included in Table 8-2 to show the widespread use of ratio analysis. In all cases, the comparisons should be with calculations made in previous years for the same client. There are many potential ratios and comparisons available for use by an auditor. Subsequent chapters dealing with specific audit areas describe other examples.

Many of the ratios and percentages used for comparison with previous years are the same ones used for comparison with industry data. For example, it is useful to compare

TABLE 8-2	Internal Comparisons and Relationships
Ratio or Comparison	**Possible Misstatement**
Raw material turnover for a manufacturing company	Misstatement of inventory or cost of goods sold or obsolescence of raw material inventory
Sales commissions divided by net sales	Misstatement of sales commissions
Sales returns and allowances divided by gross sales	Misclassified sales returns and allowances or unrecorded returns or allowances subsequent to year-end
Cash surrender value of life insurance (current year) divided by cash surrender value of life insurance (preceding year)	Failure to record the change in cash surrender value or an error in recording the change
Each of the individual manufacturing expenses as a percentage of total manufacturing expense	Significant misstatement of individual expenses within a total

HILLSBURG HARDWARE CO.
COMMON-SIZE INCOME STATEMENT
Three Years Ending December 31, 2004

	2004		2003		2002	
	(000) Preliminary	% of Net Sales	(000) Audited	% of Net Sales	(000) Audited	% of Net Sales
Sales	$144,328	100.87	$132,421	100.91	$123,737	100.86
Less: Returns and allowances	1,242	0.87	1,195	0.91	1,052	0.86
Net sales	143,086	100.00	131,226	100.00	122,685	100.00
Cost of goods sold	103,241	72.15	94,876	72.30	88,724	72.32
Gross profit	39,845	27.85	36,350	27.70	33,961	27.68
Selling expense						
Salaries and commissions	7,739	5.41	7,044	5.37	6,598	5.38
Sales payroll taxes	1,422	0.99	1,298	0.99	1,198	0.98
Travel and entertainment	1,110	0.78	925	0.70	797	0.65
Advertising	2,611	1.82	1,920	1.46	1,790	1.46
Sales and promotional literature	322	0.22	425	0.32	488	0.40
Sales meetings and training	925	0.65	781	0.60	767	0.62
Miscellaneous sales expense	681	0.48	506	0.39	456	0.37
Total selling expense	14,810	10.35	12,899	9.83	12,094	9.86
Administration expense						
Executive and office salaries	5,524	3.86	5,221	3.98	5,103	4.16
Administrative payroll taxes	682	0.48	655	0.50	633	0.52
Travel and entertainment	562	0.39	595	0.45	542	0.44
Computer maintenance and supplies	860	0.60	832	0.63	799	0.65
Stationery and supplies	763	0.53	658	0.50	695	0.57
Postage	244	0.17	251	0.19	236	0.19
Telephone and fax	722	0.51	626	0.48	637	0.52
Rent	312	0.22	312	0.24	312	0.25
Legal fees and retainers	383	0.27	321	0.25	283	0.23
Auditing and related services	303	0.21	288	0.22	265	0.22
Depreciation	1,452	1.01	1,443	1.10	1,505	1.23
Bad debt expense	3,323	2.32	3,394	2.59	3,162	2.58
Insurance	723	0.51	760	0.58	785	0.64
Office repairs and maintenance	844	0.59	538	0.41	458	0.37
Miscellaneous office expense	644	0.45	621	0.47	653	0.53
Miscellaneous general expense	324	0.23	242	0.18	275	0.22
Total administrative expenses	17,665	12.35	16,757	12.77	16,343	13.32
Total selling and administrative expenses	32,475	22.70	29,656	22.60	28,437	23.18
Earnings from operations	7,370	5.15	6,694	5.10	5,524	4.50
Other income and expense						
Interest expense	2,409	1.68	2,035	1.55	2,173	1.77
Gain on sale of assets	(720)	(0.50)	0	0.00	0	0.00
Earnings before income taxes	5,681	3.97	4,659	3.55	3,351	2.73
Income taxes	1,747	1.22	1,465	1.12	1,072	0.87
Net income	$ 3,934	2.75	$ 3,194	2.43	$ 2,279	1.86

current year gross margin with industry averages and previous years. The same can be said for most of the ratios described in the following section.

There are also numerous potential comparisons of current- and prior-period data beyond those normally available from industry data. For example, the percentage of each expense category to total sales can be compared with that of previous years. Similarly, in a multiunit operation (for example, a retail chain), internal comparisons for each unit can be made with previous periods.

Auditors often prepare common-size financial statements for one or more years to compare changes in account balances and their relation to a common base, such as sales. Common-size income statement data for the last three years for Hillsburg Hardware are included in Figure 8-7 (p. 212). Calculating income statement account balances as a percentage of sales is especially important when the level of sales has changed from the prior year, which is likely in many businesses. Hillsburg's sales have increased significantly compared to the prior year. Note that accounts such as cost of goods sold and sales salaries and commissions have also increased significantly but are fairly consistent as a percentage of sales, which would be expected for these accounts.

The auditor would likely require further explanation and corroborating evidence for the changes in advertising, bad debt expense, and office repairs and maintenance. Advertising expense has increased as a percentage of sales. One possible explanation is the development of a new advertising campaign. The dollar amount of bad debt expense has not changed significantly but has decreased as a percentage of sales. The auditor would need to gather additional evidence to determine whether bad debt expense and the allowance for doubtful accounts are understated. Repairs and maintenance expense has also increased. Fluctuations in this account are not unusual if the client has incurred unexpected repairs. The auditor would likely investigate major expenditures in this account to determine whether they include any amounts that should be capitalized as a fixed asset.

Compare Client Data with Client-Determined Expected Results

Most companies prepare **budgets** for various aspects of their operations and financial results. Because budgets represent the client's expectations for the period, an investigation of the most significant areas in which differences exist between budgeted and actual results may indicate potential misstatements. The absence of differences may also indicate that misstatements are unlikely. It is common, for example, in the audit of local, state, and federal governmental units to use this type of analytical procedure.

When client data are compared with budgets, there are two special concerns. First, the auditor must evaluate whether the budgets were realistic plans. In some organizations, budgets are prepared with little thought or care and therefore are not realistic expectations. Such information has little value as audit evidence. The second concern is the possibility that current financial information was changed by client personnel to conform to the budget. If that has occurred, the auditor will find no differences in comparing actual data with budgeted data, even if there are misstatements in the financial statements. A discussion of budget procedures with client personnel is used to satisfy the first concern. Assessment of control risk and detailed audit tests of actual data are usually done to minimize the likelihood of the latter concern.

Compare Client Data with Auditor-Determined Expected Results

A second common type of comparison of client data with expected results occurs when the *auditor calculates the expected balance for comparison with the actual balance.* In this type of analytical procedure, the auditor makes an estimate of what an account balance should be by relating it to some other balance sheet or income statement account or accounts or by making a projection based on some historical trend. An example of calculating an expected value based on relationships of accounts is the independent calculation of interest expense on long-term notes payable by multiplying the ending monthly balance in notes payable by the average monthly interest rate (see Figure 8-8) (p. 214). An example of using a historical trend would be when the moving average of the allowance for uncollectible accounts receivable as a percentage of gross accounts receivable is applied to the balance of gross accounts receivable at the end of the audit year to determine an expected value for the current allowance.

File Edit View Insert Format Tools Data Window Help

Arial   10   B I U $ %   100%

A1

Hillsburg Hardware Co.
Overall Test of Interest Expense
12/31/04

Schedule N-3   Date
Prepared by TM   3/06/05
Approved by JW   3/12/05

Interest expense per general ledger   2,408,642 ①

Computation of estimate:

Short-term loans:

Balance outstanding at month-end: ②

Jan.	2,950,000
Feb.	3,184,000
Mar.	3,412,000
Apr.	3,768,000
May	2,604,000
June	1,874,000
July	1,400,000
Aug.	1,245,000
Sept.	1,046,000
Oct.	854,000
Nov.	2,526,000
Dec.	4,180,000
Total	29,043,000

Average (÷12) 2,420,250 @ 10.5% ③ 254,126

Long-term loans:

Beginning balance 26,520,000 ②
Ending balance   24,120,000 ②
                  50,640,000

Average (÷2) 25,320,000 @ 8.5% ④ 2,152,200

Estimated total interest expense   2,406,326

Difference   2,316 ⑤

Legend and Comments

① Agrees with general ledger and working trial balance.
② Obtained from general ledger.
③ Estimated based on examination of several notes throughout the
  year with rates ranging from 10% to 11%.
④ Agrees with permanent file schedule of long-term debt.
⑤ Difference not significant. Indicates that interest expense per books is reasonable.

Compare Client Data with Expected Results Using Nonfinancial Data

Suppose that in auditing a hotel, you can determine the number of rooms, room rate for each room, and occupancy rate. Using those data, it is relatively easy to estimate total revenue from rooms to compare with recorded revenue. The same approach can sometimes be used to estimate such accounts as tuition revenue at universities (average tuition times enrollment), factory payroll (total hours worked times wage rate), and cost of materials sold (units sold times materials cost per unit).

The major concern in using nonfinancial data is the accuracy of the data. In the previous illustration, it is not appropriate to use an estimated calculation of hotel revenue as audit evidence unless the auditor is satisfied with the reasonableness of the count of the number of rooms, room rate, and occupancy rate. It would be more difficult for the auditor to evaluate the accuracy of the occupancy rate than the other two items.

COMMON FINANCIAL RATIOS

OBJECTIVE 8-8

Compute common financial ratios.

Auditors' analytical procedures often include the use of general financial ratios during planning and final review of the audited financial statements. These are useful for understanding recent events and the financial status of the business and for viewing the statements from the perspective of a user. The general financial analysis may be effective for identifying possible problem areas for additional analysis and audit testing as well as business problem areas for which the auditor can provide other assistance. In using these ratios, it is important to make appropriate comparisons. The most important comparisons are to those of previous years for the company and to industry averages or similar companies for the same year.

Ratios and other analytical procedures are normally calculated using spreadsheets and other types of audit software. These ratios are linked to the trial balance so that the calculations are automatically updated when adjusting entries are made to the client's statements. For example, a change in inventory and cost of goods sold affects a large number of ratios. Several years of client and industry data can be maintained in the computer files for comparative purposes.

The following sections present a number of widely used financial ratios. Computation of the various ratios is illustrated using the 2004 financial statements of Hillsburg Hardware Co. The financial statements appear in the glossy insert to the textbook and were prepared from the trial balance in Figure 6-4 on page 141.

Short-term Debt-Paying Ability

$$\text{Cash ratio} = \frac{\text{cash + marketable securities}}{\text{current liabilities}} \qquad \frac{828}{13,216} = 0.06$$

$$\text{Quick ratio} = \frac{\text{cash + marketable securities + net accounts receivable}}{\text{current liabilities}} \qquad \frac{828 + 18,957 + 945}{13,216} = 1.57$$

$$\text{Current ratio} = \frac{\text{current assets}}{\text{current liabilities}} \qquad \frac{51,027}{13,216} = 3.86$$

Companies need a reasonable level of liquidity to pay their debts as they come due. These three ratios are measures of liquidity. It is apparent by examining the three ratios that the cash ratio may be useful to evaluate the ability to pay debts immediately, whereas the current ratio requires the conversion of assets such as inventory and accounts receivable to cash before debts can be paid. The most important difference between the quick and current ratios is the inclusion of inventory in current assets for the current ratio.

Liquidity Activity Ratios

$$\frac{\text{Accounts receivable}}{\text{turnover}} = \frac{\text{net sales}}{\text{average gross receivables}} \qquad \frac{143,086}{((18,957 + 1,240) + (16,210 + 1,311))/2} = 7.59$$

$$\frac{\text{Days to collect}}{\text{receivables}} = \frac{365 \text{ days}}{\text{accounts receivable turnover}} \qquad \frac{365 \text{ days}}{7.59} = 48.09 \text{ days}$$

$$\frac{\text{Inventory}}{\text{turnover}} = \frac{\text{cost of goods sold}}{\text{average inventory}} \qquad \frac{103,241}{(29,865 + 31,600)/2} = 3.36$$

$$\frac{\text{Days to sell}}{\text{inventory}} = \frac{365 \text{ days}}{\text{inventory turnover}} \qquad \frac{365 \text{ days}}{3.36} = 108.63 \text{ days}$$

If a company does not have sufficient cash and cash-like items to meet its obligations, the key to its debt-paying ability is the time it takes the company to convert less liquid current assets into cash. This is measured by the liquidity activity ratios.

The activity ratios for accounts receivable and inventory are especially useful to auditors. Trends in the accounts receivable turnover ratio are often used in assessing the reasonableness of the allowance for uncollectible accounts. Trends in the inventory turnover ratio are used in identifying potential inventory obsolescence. Average days to collect is a different way of looking at the average accounts receivable turnover data. The same is true of average days to sell compared to average inventory turnover.

Ability to Meet Long-term Debt Obligations

$$\text{Debt to equity} = \frac{\text{total liabilities}}{\text{total equity}} \qquad \frac{13,216 + 25,688}{22,463} = 1.73$$

$$\text{Times interest earned} = \frac{\text{operating income}}{\text{interest expense}} \qquad \frac{7,370}{2,409} = 3.06$$

A company's long-run solvency depends on the success of its operations and on its ability to raise capital for expansion, as well as its ability to make principal and interest payments. These two ratios are key measures used by creditors and investors to assess a company's ability to pay its debts.

The debt-to-equity ratio shows the extent of the use of debt in financing a company. If the debt-to-equity ratio is too high, it may indicate that the company has used up its borrowing capacity and has no cushion for additional debt. If it is too low, it may mean that available leverage is not being used to the owners' benefit.

The ability to make interest payments is dependent on the company's ability to generate positive cash flows from operations. Thus, times interest earned shows how comfortably the company should be able to make interest payments, assuming that earnings trends are stable.

Profitability Ratios

A company's ability to generate cash for payment of obligations, expansion, and dividends is heavily dependent on profitability. The most widely used profitability ratio is earnings per share. Additional ratios can be calculated that provide further insights into operations.

Gross profit percent shows the portion of sales available to cover all expenses and profit after deducting the cost of the product. It is especially useful to auditors in assessing misstatements in sales, cost of goods sold, accounts receivable, and inventory.

Profit margin is similar to gross profit margin but subtracts both cost of goods sold and operating expenses in making the calculations. This ratio is especially useful to auditors in assessing potential misstatements in operating expenses and related balance sheet accounts.

$$\text{Earnings per share} = \frac{\text{net income}}{\text{average common shares outstanding}} \qquad \frac{3,934}{5,000} = 0.79$$

$$\text{Gross profit percent} = \frac{\text{net sales} - \text{cost of goods sold}}{\text{net sales}} \qquad \frac{143,086 - 103,241}{143,086} = 27.85\%$$

$$\text{Profit margin} = \frac{\text{operating income}}{\text{net sales}} \qquad \frac{7,370}{143,086} = 0.05$$

$$\text{Return on assets} = \frac{\text{income before taxes}}{\text{average total assets}} \qquad \frac{5,681}{(61,367 + 60,791)/2} = 0.09$$

$$\text{Return on common equity} = \frac{\text{income before taxes} - \text{preferred dividends}}{\text{average stockholders' equity}} \qquad \frac{5,681 - 0}{(22,463 + 20,429)/2} = 0.26$$

Two measures of overall profitability of a company are return on assets and return on equity. These ratios show a company's ability to generate profit for each dollar of assets and equity.

SUMMARY OF ANALYTICAL PROCEDURES

Analytical procedures involve the computation of ratios and other comparisons of recorded amounts to auditor expectations. Analytical procedures are used in planning to understand the client's business and industry and throughout the audit to identify possible misstatements, reduce detailed tests, and to assess going-concern issues. The use of analytical procedures has increased because of their effectiveness at identifying possible misstatements at a low cost, and they are required in the planning and completion phases of the audit.

ESSENTIAL TERMS

Acceptable audit risk—a measure of how willing the auditor is to accept that the financial statements may be materially misstated after the audit is completed and an unqualified opinion has been issued

Budgets—written records of the client's expectations for the period; a comparison of budgets with actual results may indicate whether or not misstatements are likely

Bylaws—the rules and procedures adopted by a corporation's stockholders, including the corporation's fiscal year and the duties and powers of its officers

Client business risk—the risk that the client will fail to achieve its objectives related to (1) reliability of financial reporting, (2) effectiveness and efficiency of operations, and (3) compliance with laws and regulations

Corporate charter—a legal document granted by the state in which a company is incorporated that recognizes a corporation as a separate entity; it includes the name of the corporation, the date of incorporation, capital stock the corporation is authorized to issue, and the types of business activities the corporation is authorized to conduct

Corporate minutes—the official record of the meetings of a corporation's board of directors and stockholders, in which corporate issues, such as the declaration of dividends and the approval of contracts, are documented

Engagement letter—an agreement between the CPA firm and the client as to the terms of the engagement for the conduct of the audit and related services

Inherent risk—a measure of the auditor's assessment of the likelihood that there are material misstatements in a segment before considering the effectiveness of internal control

Initial audit planning—involves deciding whether to accept or continue doing the audit for the client, identifying the client's reasons for the audit, obtaining an engagement letter, and selecting staff for the engagement

Related party—affiliated company, principal owner of the client company, or any other party with which the client deals, where one of the parties can influence the management or operating policies of the other

Related party transaction—any transaction between the client and a related party

REVIEW QUESTIONS

8-1 (Objective 8-1) What benefits does the auditor derive from planning audits?

8-2 (Objective 8-1) Identify the eight major steps in planning audits.

8-3 (Objective 8-2) What are the responsibilities of the successor and predecessor auditors when a company is changing auditors?

8-4 (Objective 8-2) What factors should an auditor consider prior to accepting an engagement? Explain.

8-5 (Objective 8-2) What is the purpose of an engagement letter? What subjects should be covered in such a letter?

8-6 (Objective 8-2) Who is considered "the client" when auditing public companies?

8-7 (Objective 8-2) Which services must be preapproved by the audit committee of a public company?

8-8 (Objective 8-3) Explain why auditors need an understanding of the client's industry. What sources are commonly used by auditors to learn about the client's industry?

8-9 (Objective 8-3) When a CPA has accepted an engagement from a new client who is a manufacturer, it is customary for the CPA to tour the client's plant facilities. Discuss the ways in which the CPA's observations made during the course of the plant tour will be of help in planning and conducting the audit.

8-10 (Objective 8-3) An auditor often tries to acquire background knowledge of the client's industry as an aid to audit work. How does the acquisition of this knowledge aid the auditor in distinguishing between obsolete and current inventory?

8-11 (Objective 8-3) Define what is meant by a related party. What are the auditor's responsibilities for related parties and related party transactions?

8-12 (Objective 8-3) Which types of loans to executives are permitted by the Sarbanes–Oxley Act?

8-13 (Objective 8-3) Your firm has performed the audit of the Rogers Company for several years and you have been assigned the audit responsibility for the current audit. How would your review of the corporate charter and bylaws for this audit differ from that of the audit of a client who was audited by a different CPA firm in the preceding year?

8-14 (Objective 8-3) For the audit of Radline Manufacturing Company, the audit partner asks you to carefully read the new mortgage contract with the First National Bank and abstract all pertinent information. List the information in a mortgage that is likely to be relevant to the auditor.

8-15 (Objective 8-3) Identify two types of information in the client's minutes of the board of directors meetings that are likely to be relevant to the auditor. Explain why it is important to read the minutes early in the engagement.

8-16 (Objective 8-3) Identify the three categories of client objectives. Indicate how each objective may affect the auditor's assessment of inherent risk and evidence accumulation.

8-17 (Objective 8-3) What is the purpose of the client's performance measurement system? Give examples of key performance indicators for the following businesses: (1) a chain of retail clothing stores; (2) an Internet portal; (3) a hotel chain.

8-18 (Objective 8-4) Define client business risk and describe several sources of client business risk. What is the auditor's primary concern when evaluating client business risk?

8-19 (Objective 8-4) Describe top management controls and their relation to client business risk. Give examples of effective management and governance controls.

8-20 (Objectives 8-5, 8-6) What are the purposes of preliminary analytical procedures? What types of comparisons are useful when performing preliminary analytical procedures?

8-21 (Objective 8-6) When are analytical procedures required to be performed during the audit? What is the primary purpose of analytical procedures performed during the completion phase of the audit?

8-22 (Objective 8-7) Gale Gordon, CPA, has found ratio and trend analysis relatively useless as a tool in conducting audits. For several engagements, he computed the industry ratios included in publications by Robert Morris Associates and compared them with industry standards. For most engagements, the client's business was significantly different from the industry data in the publication and the client would automatically explain away any discrepancies by attributing them to the unique nature of its operations. In cases in which the client had more than one branch in different industries, Gordon found the ratio analysis no help at all. How could Gordon improve the quality of his analytical procedures?

8-23 (Objective 8-7) At the completion of every audit, Roger Morris, CPA, calculates a large number of ratios and trends for comparison with industry averages and prior-year calculations. He believes the calculations are worth the relatively small cost of doing them because they provide him with an excellent overview of the client's operations. If the ratios are out of line, Morris discusses the reasons with the client and often makes suggestions on how to bring the ratio back in line in the future. In some cases, these discussions with management have been the basis for management consulting engagements. Discuss the major strengths and shortcomings in Morris's use of ratio and trend analysis.

8-24 (Objective 8-8) Name the four categories of financial ratios and give an example of a ratio in each category. What is the primary information provided by each financial ratio category?

MULTIPLE CHOICE QUESTIONS FROM CPA EXAMINATIONS

8-25 (Objectives 8-1, 8-3) The following questions concern the planning of the engagement. Select the best response.

a. Which of the following is an effective audit planning procedure that helps prevent misunderstandings and inefficient use of audit personnel?
   (1) Arrange to make copies, for inclusion in the audit files, of those client supporting documents examined by the auditor.
   (2) Arrange to provide the client with copies of the audit programs to be used during the audit.
   (3) Arrange a preliminary conference with the client to discuss audit objectives, fees, timing, and other information.

(4) Arrange to have the auditor prepare and post any necessary adjusting or reclassification entries prior to final closing.

b. An auditor is planning an audit engagement for a new client in a business with which he is unfamiliar. Which of the following would be the most useful source of information during the preliminary planning stage, when the auditor is trying to obtain a general understanding of audit problems that might be encountered?
(1) Client manuals of accounts and charts of accounts.
(2) AICPA Industry Audit Guides.
(3) Prior-year audit files of the predecessor auditor.
(4) Latest annual and interim financial statements issued by the client.

c. An auditor obtains knowledge about a new client's business and industry to
(1) make constructive suggestions concerning improvements in the client's internal control.
(2) develop an attitude of professional skepticism concerning management's financial statement assertions.
(3) evaluate whether the sum of known misstatements causes the financial statements as a whole to be materially misstated.
(4) understand the events and transactions that may have an effect on the client's financial statements.

8-26 (Objective 8-2) The following questions pertain to client acceptance. Choose the best response.

a. In assessing whether to accept a client for an audit engagement, a CPA should consider

	Client Business Risk	Acceptable Audit Risk
(1)	Yes	Yes
(2)	Yes	No
(3)	No	Yes
(4)	No	No

b. When approached to perform an audit for the first time, the CPA should make inquiries of the predecessor auditor. This is a necessary procedure because the predecessor may be able to provide the successor with information that will assist the successor in determining whether
(1) the predecessor's work should be used.
(2) the company follows the policy of rotating its auditors.
(3) in the predecessor's opinion internal control of the company has been satisfactory.
(4) the engagement should be accepted.

c. What is the responsibility of a successor auditor with respect to communicating with the predecessor auditor in connection with a prospective new audit client?
(1) The successor auditor has *no* responsibility to contact the predecessor auditor.
(2) The successor auditor should obtain permission from the prospective client to contact the predecessor auditor.
(3) The successor auditor should contact the predecessor regardless of whether the prospective client authorizes contact.
(4) The successor auditor need *not* contact the predecessor if the successor is aware of all available relevant facts.

8-27 (Objectives 8-5, 8-6, 8-7, 8-8) The following questions concern the use of analytical procedures during the planning phase of an audit. Select the best response.

a. Analytical procedures used in planning an audit should focus on identifying
(1) material weaknesses of internal control.
(2) the predictability of financial data from individual transactions.
(3) the various assertions that are embodied in the financial statements.
(4) areas that may represent specific risks relevant to the audit.

b. For all audits of financial statements made in accordance with generally accepted auditing standards, the use of analytical procedures is required to some extent

	In the Planning Stage	As a Substantive Test	In the Completion Stage
(1)	Yes	No	Yes
(2)	No	Yes	No
(3)	No	Yes	Yes
(4)	Yes	No	No

c. Which of the following would be *least* likely to be comparable between similar corporations in the same industry line of business?
   (1) Accounts receivable turnover.
   (2) Earnings per share.
   (3) Gross profit percent.
   (4) Return on assets before interest and taxes.

d. Which of the following situations has the best chance of being detected when a CPA compares 2005 revenues and expenses with the prior year and investigates all changes exceeding a fixed percentage?
   (1) An increase in property tax rates has not been recognized in the company's 2005 accrual.
   (2) The cashier began lapping accounts receivable in 2005.
   (3) Because of worsening economic conditions, the 2005 provision for uncollectible accounts was inadequate.
   (4) The company changed its capitalization policy for small tools in 2005.

DISCUSSION QUESTIONS AND PROBLEMS

8-28 (Objectives 8-2, 8-3, 8-4, 8-5) In late spring, you are advised of a new assignment as in-charge accountant of your CPA firm's recurring annual audit of a major client, the Lancer Company. You are given the engagement letter for the audit covering the current calendar year and a list of personnel assigned to this engagement. It is your responsibility to plan and supervise the field work for the engagement.

Required Discuss the necessary preparation and planning for the Lancer Company annual audit before beginning field work at the client's office. In your discussion, include the sources you should consult, the type of information you should seek, the preliminary plans and preparation you should make for the field work, and any actions you should take relative to the staff assigned to the engagement.*

8-29 (Objective 8-3) Generally accepted accounting principles set certain requirements for disclosure of related parties and related party transactions. Similarly, the SASs set requirements for the audit of related parties and related party transactions. For this problem, you are expected to research appropriate SFASs and SASs.

Required a. Define *related party* as used for generally accepted accounting principles and explain the disclosure requirements for related parties and related party transactions.

b. Explain why disclosure of related party transactions is relevant information for decision makers.

c. List the most important related parties who are likely to be involved in related party transactions.

d. List several different types of related party transactions that could take place in a company.

e. Discuss ways the auditor can determine the existence of related parties and related party transactions.

f. For each type of related party transaction, discuss different ways the auditor can evaluate whether it is recorded on an arm's-length basis, assuming that the auditor knows the transactions exist.

g. Assume that you know the material related party transactions occurred and were transacted at significantly less favorable terms than ordinarily occur when business is done with independent parties. The client refuses to disclose these facts in the financial statements. What are your responsibilities?

8-30 (Objective 8-3) The minutes of the board of directors of the Marygold Catalog Company for the year ended December 31, 2005, were provided to you.

MEETING OF FEBRUARY 15, 2005

Ruth Jackson, chairman of the board, called the meeting to order at 4:00 PM. The following directors were in attendance:

John Aronson	Licorine Phillips
Fred Brick	Lucille Renolds
Oron Carlson	J. T. Smith
Homer Jackson	Raymond Werd
Ruth Jackson	Ronald Wilder

*AICPA adapted.

The minutes of the meeting of October 11, 2004, were read and approved.

Homer Jackson, president, discussed the new marketing plan for wider distribution of catalogs in the southwestern U.S. market. He made a motion for approval of increased expenditures of approximately $500,000 for distribution costs that was seconded by Wilder and unanimously passed.

The unresolved dispute with the Internal Revenue Service over the tax treatment of leased office buildings was discussed with Cecil Makay, attorney. In Mr. Makay's opinion, the matter would not be resolved for several months and may result in an unfavorable settlement.

J. T. Smith moved that the computer equipment that was no longer being used in the Kingston office, because of new equipment acquired in 2004, be donated to the Kingston vocational school for use in their repair and training program. John Aronson seconded the motion and it unanimously passed.

Annual cash dividends were unanimously approved as being payable April 30, 2005, for stockholders of record April 15, 2005, as follows:

Class A common—$10 per share
Class B common—$5 per share

Officers' bonuses for the year ended December 31, 2004, were approved for payment March 1, 2005, as follows:

Homer Jackson—President	$130,000
Lucille Renolds—Vice president	60,000
Ronald Wilder—Controller	60,000
Fred Brick—Secretary-treasurer	45,000

Meeting adjourned 6:30 PM.

Fred Brick, Secretary

MEETING OF SEPTEMBER 16, 2005

Ruth Jackson, chairman of the board, called the meeting to order at 4:00 PM. The following directors were in attendance:

John Aronson	Licorine Phillips
Fred Brick	Lucille Renolds
Oron Carlson	J. T. Smith
Homer Jackson	Raymond Werd
Ruth Jackson	Ronald Wilder

The minutes of the meeting of February 15, 2005, were read and approved.

Homer Jackson, president, discussed the improved sales and financial condition for 2005. He was pleased with the results of the catalog distribution and cost control for the company. No action was taken.

The nominations for officers were made as follows:

President—Homer Jackson
Vice president—Lucille Renolds
Controller—Ronald Wilder
Secretary-treasurer—Fred Brick

The nominees were elected by unanimous voice vote.

Salary increases of 5%, exclusive of bonuses, were recommended for all officers for the year 2006. Homer Jackson moved that such salary increases be approved, seconded by J. T. Smith, and unanimously approved.

	Salary	
	2005	**2006**
Homer Jackson, President	$240,000	$252,000
Lucille Renolds, Vice president	160,000	168,000
Ronald Wilder, Controller	160,000	168,000
Fred Brick, Secretary-treasurer	120,000	126,000

Ronald Wilder moved that the company consider adopting a pension/profit-sharing plan for all employees as a way to provide greater incentive for employees to stay with the company. Considerable discussion ensued. It was agreed without adoption that Wilder should discuss the legal and tax implications with attorney Cecil Makay and a CPA firm reputed to be knowledgeable about pension and profit-sharing plans, Able and Better, CPAs.

Ronald Wilder discussed expenditure of $58,000 for acquisition of a new computer system for the Kingston office to replace equipment that was purchased in 2004 and has proven ineffective. A settlement has been tentatively reached to return the equipment for a refund of $21,000. Wilder moved that both transactions be approved, seconded by Jackson, and unanimously adopted.

Fred Brick moved that a loan of $360,000, from the Kingston Federal Bank and Trust, be approved. The interest is floating at 2% above prime. The loan is collateralized by accounts receivable, with the loan balance not to exceed 75% of current accounts receivable. Seconded by Phillips and unanimously approved.

Lucille Renolds, chair of the audit committee, moved that the CPA firm of Moss and Lawson be selected again for the company's annual audit and related tax work for the year ended December 31, 2005. Seconded by Aronson and unanimously approved.

Meeting adjourned 6:40 PM.

Fred Brick, Secretary

Required

a. How do you, as the auditor, know that all minutes have been made available to you?

b. Read the minutes of the meetings of February 15 and September 16. Use the following format to list and explain information that is relevant for the 2005 audit:

Information Relevant to 2005 Audit	Audit Action Required
1.	
2.	

c. Read the minutes of the meeting of February 15, 2005. Did any of that information pertain to the December 31, 2004, audit? Explain what the auditor should have done during the December 31, 2004, audit with respect to 2005 minutes.

8-31 (Objectives 8-3, 8-4, 8-5) You are engaged in the annual audit of the financial statements of Maulack Company, a medium-sized wholesale company that manufactures light fixtures. The company has 25 stockholders. During your review of the minutes, you observe that the president's salary has been increased substantially over the preceding year by action of the board of directors. His present salary is much greater than salaries paid to presidents of companies of comparable size and is clearly excessive. You determine that the method of computing the president's salary was changed for the year under audit. In previous years, the president's salary was consistently based on sales. In the latest year, however, his salary was based on net income before income taxes. The Maulack Company is in a cyclical industry and would have had an extremely profitable year except that the increase in the president's salary siphoned off much of the income that would have accrued to the stockholders. The president is a substantial stockholder.

Required

a. What is the implication of this condition on the fair presentation of the financial statements?

b. Discuss your responsibility for disclosing this situation.

c. Discuss the effect, if any, that the situation has on your auditor's opinion as to
(1) the fairness of the presentation of the financial statements.
(2) the consistency of the application of accounting principles.*

8-32 (Objectives 8-5, 8-6, 8-7, 8-8) In auditing the financial statements of a manufacturing company that were prepared using information technology, the CPA has found that the traditional audit trail has been obscured. As a result, the CPA may place increased emphasis on analytical procedures of the data under audit. These tests, which are also applied in auditing visibly posted accounting records, include the computation of ratios that are compared with prior-year ratios or with industrywide norms. Examples of analytical procedures are the computation of the rate of inventory turnover and the computation of the number of days in receivables.

Required

a. Discuss the advantages to the CPA of the use of analytical procedures in an audit.

b. In addition to the computations described, list ratios that an auditor may compute during an audit on balance sheet accounts and related income accounts. For each ratio listed, name the two (or more) accounts used in its computation.

*AICPA adapted.

c. When there has been a significant change in a ratio when compared with the preceding year's, the auditor considers the possible reasons for the change. Give the possible reasons for the following significant changes in ratios:

    (1) The rate of inventory turnover (ratio of cost of sales and average inventory) has decreased from the preceding year's rate.

    (2) The number of days' sales in receivables (ratio of average daily accounts receivable and sales) has increased over the prior year.*

8-33 (Objectives 8-3, 8-7, 8-8) Your comparison of the gross margin percentage for Jones Drugs for the years 2002 through 2005 indicates a significant decline. This is shown by the following information:

	2005	2004	2003	2002
Sales (thousands)	$14,211	$12,916	$11,462	$10,351
CGS (thousands)	9,223	8,266	7,313	6,573
Gross margin	$4,988	$4,650	$4,149	$3,778
Percent	35.1	36.0	36.2	36.5

A discussion with Marilyn Adams, the controller, brings to light two possible explanations. She informs you that the industry gross profit percentage in the retail drug industry declined fairly steadily for 3 years, which accounts for part of the decline. A second factor was the declining percentage of the total volume resulting from the pharmacy part of the business. The pharmacy sales represent the most profitable portion of the business, yet the competition from discount drugstores prevents it from expanding as fast as the nondrug items such as magazines, candy, and many other items sold. Adams feels strongly that these two factors are the cause of the decline.

The following additional information is obtained from independent sources and the client's records as a means of investigating the controller's explanations:

	Jones Drugs ($ in thousands)				Industry Gross Profit Percent for Retailers of Drugs and Related Products
	Drug Sales	Nondrug Sales	Drug Cost of Goods Sold	Nondrug Cost of Goods Sold	
2005	$5,126	$9,085	$3,045	$6,178	32.7
2004	5,051	7,865	2,919	5,347	32.9
2003	4,821	6,641	2,791	4,522	33.0
2002	4,619	5,732	2,665	3,908	33.2

Required

a. Evaluate the explanation provided by Adams. Show calculations to support your conclusions.

b. Which specific aspects of the client's financial statements require intensive investigation in this audit?

8-34 (Objectives 8-7, 8-8) In the audit of the Worldwide Wholesale Company, you performed extensive ratio and trend analysis. No material exceptions were discovered except for the following:

1. Commission expense as a percentage of sales has stayed constant for several years but has increased significantly in the current year. Commission rates have not changed.
2. The rate of inventory turnover has steadily decreased for 4 years.
3. Inventory as a percentage of current assets has steadily increased for 4 years.
4. The number of days' sales in accounts receivable has steadily increased for 3 years.
5. Allowance for uncollectible accounts as a percentage of accounts receivable has steadily decreased for 3 years.
6. The absolute amounts of depreciation expense and depreciation expense as a percentage of gross fixed assets are significantly smaller than in the preceding year.

Required

a. Evaluate the potential significance of each of the exceptions just listed for the fair presentation of financial statements.

b. State the follow-up procedures you would use to determine the possibility of material misstatements.

8-35 (Objectives 8-3, 8-5) As part of the analytical procedures of Mahogany Products, Inc., you perform calculations of the following ratios:

*AICPA adapted.

Ratio	Industry Averages 2005	Industry Averages 2004	Mahogany Products 2005	Mahogany Products 2004
1. Current ratio	3.30	3.80	2.20	2.60
2. Days to collect receivables	87.00	93.00	67.00	60.00
3. Days to sell inventory	126.00	121.00	93.00	89.00
4. Purchases divided by accounts payable	11.70	11.60	8.50	8.60
5. Inventory divided by current assets	.56	.51	.49	.48
6. Operating income divided by tangible assets	.08	.06	.14	.12
7. Operating income divided by net sales	.06	.06	.04	.04
8. Gross profit percentage	.21	.27	.21	.19
9. Earnings per share	$14.27	$13.91	$2.09	$1.93

Required   For each of the preceding ratios:

    a. State whether there is a need to investigate the results further and, if so, the reason for further investigation.

    b. State the approach you would use in the investigation.

    c. Explain how the operations of Mahogany Products appear to differ from those of the industry.

8-36 (Objectives 8-3, 8-5, 8-7) Following are the auditor's calculations of several key ratios for Cragston Star Products. The primary purpose of this information is to understand the client's business and assess the risk of financial failure, but any other relevant conclusions are also desirable.

Ratio	2005	2004	2003	2002	2001
Current ratio	2.08	2.26	2.51	2.43	2.50
Quick ratio	.97	1.34	1.82	1.76	1.64
Times interest earned	3.50	3.20	4.10	5.30	7.10
Accounts receivable turnover	4.20	5.50	4.10	5.40	5.60
Days to collect receivables	86.90	66.36	89.02	67.59	65.18
Inventory turnover	2.03	1.84	2.68	3.34	3.36
Days to sell inventory	179.80	198.37	136.19	109.28	108.63
Net sales divided by tangible assets	.68	.64	.73	.69	.67
Profit margin	.13	.14	.16	.15	.14
Return on assets	.09	.09	.12	.10	.09
Return on equity	.05	.06	.10	.10	.11
Earnings per share	$4.30	$4.26	$4.49	$4.26	$4.14

Required   a. What major conclusions can be drawn from this information about the company's future?

    b. What additional information would be helpful in your assessment of this company's financial condition?

    c. Based on the preceding ratios, which aspects of the company do you believe should receive special emphasis in the audit?

e-biz

8-37 (Objectives 8-3, 8-4) The Internet has dramatically increased global e-commerce activities. Both traditional "brick and mortar" businessess and new dot-com businesses use the Internet to meet business objectives. For example, traditional retailer Toys "R" Us, Inc., also sells toys and other products through its Web site, which is operated in partnership with Amazon.com.

Required   a. Identify three specific business strategies that are likely reasons why Toys "R" Us is offering products for sale online.

    b. Describe three business risks related to Toys "R" Us offering online sales.

    c. Discuss possible reasons why Toys "R" Us decided to partner with Amazon.com to handle online sales.

    d. Identify possible risks that could lead to material misstatements in the Toys "R" Us financial statements if its business risks related to online sales are not effectively managed.

CASES

8-38 (Objectives 8-2, 8-3, 8-4) Winston Black was an audit partner in the firm of Henson, Davis & Company. He was in the process of reviewing the audit files for the audit of a new client, McMullan

Resources. McMullan was in the business of heavy construction. Black was conducting his first review after the field work was substantially complete. Normally, he would have done an initial review during the planning phase as required by his firm's policies; however, he had been overwhelmed by an emergency with his largest and most important client. He rationalized not reviewing audit planning information because (1) the audit was being overseen by Sarah Beale, a manager in whom he had confidence, and (2) he could "recover" from any problems during his end-of-audit review.

Now, Black found that he was confronted with a couple of problems. First, he found that the firm may have accepted McMullan without complying with its new-client acceptance procedures. McMullan came to Henson, Davis on a recommendation from a friend of Black's. Black got "credit" for the new business, which was important to him because it would affect his compensation from the firm. Because Black was busy, he told Beale to conduct a new-client acceptance review and let him know if there were any problems. He never heard from Beale and assumed everything was okay. In reviewing Beale's preaudit planning documentation, he saw a check mark in the box "Contact prior auditors" but found no details indicating what was done. When he asked Beale about this, she responded with the following:

> I called Gardner Smith [the responsible partner with McMullan's prior audit firm] and left a phone mail message for him. He never returned my call. I talked to Ted McMullan about the change, and he told me that he informed Gardner about the change and that Gardner said, "Fine, I'll help in any way I can." Ted said Gardner sent over copies of analyses of fixed assets and equity accounts, which Ted gave to me. I asked Ted why they replaced Gardner's firm, and he told me it was over the tax contingency issue and the size of their fee. Other than that, Ted said the relationship was fine.

The tax contingency issue that Beale referred to was a situation in which McMullan had entered into litigation with a bank from which it had received a loan. The result of the litigation was that the bank forgave several hundred thousand dollars in debt. This was a windfall to McMullan, and they recorded it as a gain, taking the position that it was nontaxable. The prior auditors disputed this position and insisted that a contingent tax liability existed that required disclosure. This upset McMullan, but the company agreed in order to receive an unqualified opinion. Before hiring Henson, Davis as their new auditors, McMullan requested that Henson, Davis review the situation. Henson, Davis believed the contingency was remote and agreed to the elimination of the disclosure.

The second problem involved a long-term contract with a customer in Montreal. Under GAAP, McMullan was required to recognize income on this contract using the percentage-of-completion method. The contract was partially completed as of year-end and had a material effect on the financial statements. When Black went to review the copy of the contract in the audit files, he found three things. First, there was a contract summary that set out its major features. Second, there was a copy of the contract written in French. Third, there was a signed confirmation confirming the terms and status of the contract. The space requesting information about any contract disputes was left blank, indicating no such problems.

Black's concern about the contract was that to recognize income in accordance with GAAP, the contract had to be enforceable. Often, contracts contain a cancellation clause that might mitigate enforceability. Because he was not able to read French, Black couldn't tell whether the contract contained such a clause. When he asked Beale about this, she responded that she had asked the company's vice president for the Canadian division about the contract and he told her that it was their standard contract. The company's standard contract did have a cancellation clause in it, but it required mutual agreement and could not be cancelled unilaterally by the buyer.

Required

a. Evaluate and discuss whether Henson, Davis & Company complied with generally accepted auditing standards in their acceptance of McMullan Resources as a new client. What can they do at this point in the engagement to resolve deficiencies if they exist?

b. Evaluate and discuss whether sufficient audit work has been done with regard to McMullan's Montreal contract. If not, what more should be done?

c. Evaluate and discuss whether Black and Beale conducted themselves in accordance with generally accepted auditing standards.

8-39 (Objectives 8-3, 8-4, 8-7) Solomon is a highly successful, closely held Boston, Massachusetts, company that manufactures and assembles automobile specialty parts that are sold in auto parts stores in the East. Sales and profits have expanded rapidly in the past few years, and the prospects for future years are every bit as encouraging. In fact, the Solomon brothers are currently considering either selling out to a large company or going public to obtain additional capital.

The company originated in 1970 when Frank Solomon decided to manufacture tooled parts. In 1985, the company changed over to the auto parts business. Fortunately, it has never been necessary to expand the facilities, but space problems have recently become severe and expanded facilities will be necessary. Land and building costs in Boston are currently extremely inflated.

Management has always relied on you for help in its problems because the treasurer is sales-oriented and has little background in the controllership function. Salaries of all officers have been fairly modest in order to reinvest earnings in future growth. In fact, the company is oriented toward long-run wealth of the brothers more than toward short-run profit. The brothers have all of their personal wealth invested in the firm.

A major reason for the success of Solomon has been the small but excellent sales force. The sales policy is to sell to small auto shops at high prices. This policy is responsible for fairly high credit losses, but the profit margin is high and the results have been highly successful. The firm has every intention of continuing this policy in the future.

Your firm has been auditing Solomon since 1980, and you have been on the job for the past 3 years. The client has excellent internal controls and has always been cooperative. In recent years, the client has attempted to keep net income at a high level because of borrowing needs and future sellout possibilities. Overall, the client has always been pleasant to deal with and willing to help in any way possible. There have never been any major audit adjustments, and an unqualified opinion has always been issued.

In the current year, you have completed the tests of the sales and collection area. The tests of controls and substantive tests of transactions for sales and sales returns and allowances were excellent, and an extensive confirmation yielded no material misstatements. You have carefully reviewed the cutoff for sales and for sales returns and allowances and find these to be excellent. All recorded bad debts appear reasonable, and a review of the aged trial balance indicates that conditions seem about the same as in past years.

Required

a. Evaluate the information in the case (see below) to provide assistance to management for improved operation of its business. Prepare the supporting analysis using an electronic spreadsheet program (instructor option).

b. Do you agree that sales, accounts receivable, and allowance for doubtful accounts are probably correctly stated? Show calculations to support your conclusion.

	12-31-05 (Current Year)	12-31-04	12-31-03	12-31-02
Balance Sheet				
Cash	$ 49,615	$ 39,453	$ 51,811	$ 48,291
Accounts receivable	2,366,938	2,094,052	1,756,321	1,351,470
Allowance for doubtful accounts	(250,000)	(240,000)	(220,000)	(200,000)
Inventory	2,771,833	2,585,820	2,146,389	1,650,959
Current assets	4,938,386	4,479,325	3,734,521	2,850,720
Fixed assets	3,760,531	3,744,590	3,498,930	3,132,133
Total assets	$8,698,917	$8,223,915	$7,233,451	$5,982,853
Current liabilities	$2,253,422	$2,286,433	$1,951,830	$1,625,811
Long-term liabilities	4,711,073	4,525,310	4,191,699	3,550,481
Owners' equity	1,734,422	1,412,172	1,089,922	806,561
Total liabilities and owners' equity	$8,698,917	$8,223,915	$7,233,451	$5,982,853
Income Statement Information				
Sales	$6,740,652	$6,165,411	$5,313,752	$4,251,837
Sales returns and allowances	(207,831)	(186,354)	(158,367)	(121,821)
Sales discounts allowed	(74,147)	(63,655)	(52,183)	(42,451)
Bad debts	(248,839)	(245,625)	(216,151)	(196,521)
Net sales	$6,209,835	$5,669,777	$4,887,051	$3,891,044
Gross margin	$1,415,926	$1,360,911	$1,230,640	$1,062,543
Net income after taxes	$ 335,166	$ 322,250	$ 283,361	$ 257,829
Aged Accounts Receivable				
0–30 days	$ 942,086	$ 881,232	$ 808,569	$ 674,014
31–60 days	792,742	697,308	561,429	407,271
61–120 days	452,258	368,929	280,962	202,634
>120 days	179,852	146,583	105,361	67,551
Total	$2,366,938	$2,094,052	$1,756,321	$1,351,470

INTEGRATED CASE APPLICATION—PINNACLE MANUFACTURING: PART I

8-40 (Objectives 8-3, 8-4, 8-5)

Introduction

This case study is presented in six parts. Each part deals largely with the material in the chapter to which that part relates. However, the parts are connected in such a way that in completing all six, you will gain a better understanding of how the parts of the audit are interrelated and integrated by the audit process. The parts of this case appear in the following textbook chapters:

- Part I— Perform analytical procedures for different phases of the audit, **Chapter 8.**
- Part II—Understand factors influencing risks and the relationship of risks to audit evidence, **Chapter 9.**

FIGURE 8-9	Pinnacle Manufacturing Financial Statements

Pinnacle Manufacturing Company
Income Statement
For the Year ended December 31

	2004	2003	2002
Net sales	$ 149,245,176	$ 137,579,664	$ 125,814,272
Cost of goods sold	104,807,966	96,595,908	88,685,361
Gross profit	44,437,210	40,983,756	37,128,911
Operating expenses	38,265,708	34,985,293	32,383,572
Income from operations	6,171,502	5,998,463	4,745,339
Other revenues and gains	—	—	—
Other expenses and losses	1,897,346	2,128,905	2,085,177
Income before income tax	4,274,156	3,869,558	2,660,162
Income tax	1,013,745	1,399,001	1,166,553
Net income for the year	3,260,411	2,470,557	1,493,609
Earnings per share	3.26	2.47	1.49

Pinnacle Manufacturing Company
Balance Sheet
As of December 31

Assets	2004	2003	2002
Current assets			
Cash and cash equivalents	$ 6,714,156	$ 6,369,431	$ 7,014,387
Net receivables	9,601,883	7,495,528	6,901,225
Inventory	28,031,323	22,206,259	21,975,220
Other current assets	149,807	124,527	114,558
Total current assets	44,497,169	36,195,745	36,005,390
Property, plant and equipment	58,489,606	53,596,113	50,668,463
Total assets	$ 102,986,775	$ 89,791,858	$ 86,673,853
Liabilities			
Current liabilities			
Accounts payable	$ 11,277,988	$ 8,200,059	$ 6,466,412
Short/current long-term debt	12,935,495	7,868,407	8,411,017
Other current liabilities	1,712,675	1,536,835	1,463,088
Total current liabilities	25,926,158	17,605,301	16,340,517
Long-term debt	21,234,861	19,427,831	19,460,800
Total liabilities	47,161,019	37,033,132	35,801,317
Stockholders' equity			
Common stock	1,000,000	1,000,000	1,000,000
Additional paid-in capital	13,667,517	13,667,517	13,667,517
Retained earnings	41,158,239	38,091,209	36,205,019
Total stockholders' equity	55,825,756	52,758,726	50,872,536
Total liabilities & stockholders' equity	$ 102,986,775	$ 89,791,858	$ 86,673,853

- Part III—Understand internal control and assess control risk for the acquisition and payment cycle, **Chapter 10.**
- Part IV—Design tests of controls and substantive tests of transactions, **Chapter 14.**
- Part V—Determine sample sizes using audit sampling and evaluate results, **Chapter 15.**
- Part VI—Design, perform, and evaluate results for tests of details of balances, **Chapter 16.**

Background Information

One of the partners of the CPA firm you work for has engaged a new audit client, Pinnacle Manufacturing, for the year ended December 31, 2004. Pinnacle is a medium-sized corporation, with its headquarters located in Detroit, Michigan. The company is made up of three divisions. The first division, Welburn, has been in existence for 35 years and creates powerful diesel engines for boats, trucks, and commercial farming equipment. The second division, Solar-Electro, was recently acquired from a high-tech manufacturing firm based out of Dallas, Texas. Solar-Electro produces state-of-the-art, solar-powered engines. The solar-powered engine market is relatively new, and Pinnacle's top management believes that the Solar-Electro division will be extremely profitable in the future when highly anticipated EPA regulations make solar-powered engines mandatory for certain public transportation vehicles. Finally, the third division, Machine-Tech, engages in a wide variety of machine service and repair operations. This division, also new to Pinnacle, is currently in its second year of operations. Pinnacle's board of directors has recently considered selling the Machine-Tech division in order to focus more on core operations—engine manufacturing. However, before any sale will be made, the board has agreed to evaluate this year's operating results. Excellent operating results may have the effect of keeping the division a part of Pinnacle for the next few years. The vice president for Machine-Tech is committed to making it profitable.

PART I

The purpose of Part I is to perform preliminary analytical procedures. You have been asked to focus your attention on two purposes of analytical procedures: assess going concern and indicate where there is an increased likelihood of misstatements.

Required

a. Calculate at least five ratios that are useful to assess going concern using Pinnacle's financial statements, which are included in Figure 8-9 (p. 227). Document the ratios in a format similar to the following:

Ratio	2004	2003	2002
Current ratio			

b. Based on your calculations, assess the likelihood (high, medium, or low) that Pinnacle is likely to fail financially in the next 12 months.

c. Go to the Pinnacle link on the textbook Web site (www.prenhall.com/arens) and open the Pinnacle income statement, which is located in the Pinnacle Income Statement worksheet of the Pinnacle_Financials Excel file. Use the income statement information to prepare a common-size income statement for all three years. See Figure 8-7 (p. 212) for an example. Use the information to identify accounts for which you believe there is a concern about material misstatements. Use a format similar to the following:

Account Balance	Estimate of $ Amount of Potential Misstatement

d. Use the three divisional income statements in the Pinnacle_Financials Excel file on the Web site to prepare a common-size income statement for each of the three divisions for all three years. Each division's income statement is in a separate worksheet in the Excel file. Use the information to identify accounts for which you believe there is a concern about material misstatements. Use a format similar to the one in requirement c.

e. Explain whether you believe the information in requirement c or d provides the most useful data for evaluating the potential for misstatements. Explain why.

f. Your aging analysis of accounts receivable and discussions with management indicate that collections of accounts receivable have been somewhat slower than in the previous year. Evaluate whether or not you believe the allowance for uncollectible accounts is fairly valued. If you believe the account is misstated, calculate the potential misstatement.

INTERNET PROBLEM 8-1: INDUSTRY RESEARCH AND CLIENT ACCEPTANCE

Reference the CW site. The vignette at the beginning of Chapter 6 in the text contains a brief description of the ZZZZ Best fraud. One area in which the auditors were criticized in that audit was the auditors' lack of industry knowledge. With hindsight, it appeared that the fraud should have been easily detected because ZZZZ Best's large restoration contracts were in excess of $7 million, whereas the largest restoration jobs on record in the insurance restoration industry were less than $3 million. This problem requires students to use the Internet to research industry data to determine the reasonableness of reported unit sales.

INTERNET PROBLEM 8-2: OBTAIN CLIENT BACKGROUND INFORMATION

Planning is one of the most demanding and important aspects of an audit. A carefully planned audit increases auditor efficiency and provides greater assurance that the audit team addresses the critical issues. Auditors prepare audit planning documents that summarize client and industry background information and discuss important accounting and auditing issues related to the client's financial statements.

Your assignment is to find and document information for inclusion in the audit planning memorandum. Obtain the necessary information by downloading a public company's most recent annual report from its Web site (the company will be selected by you or your instructor). You may also use other sources of information such as recent 10-K filings to find additional information. You should address the following matters in four brief bulleted responses:

- Brief company history.
- Description of the company's business (for example, related companies, competitors).
- Key accounting issues identified from a review of the company's most recent annual report. (Note: Do not concentrate solely on the company's basic financial statements. Careful attention should be given to Management's Discussion and Analysis as well as the Footnotes.)
- Necessary experience levels (that is, years of experience, industry experience) required of the auditors to be involved in the audit.

MATERIALITY AND RISK

EXPLAIN TO ME ONE MORE TIME THAT YOU DID A GOOD JOB, BUT THE COMPANY WENT BROKE

Maxwell Spencer is a senior partner in his firm, and one of his regular duties is to attend the firm's annual training session for newly hired auditors. He loves doing this because it gives him a chance to share his many years of experience with inexperienced people who have bright and receptive minds. He covers several topics formally during the day and then sits around and "shoots the breeze" with participants during the evening hours. Here we listen to what he is saying.

Suppose you are a retired 72-year-old man. You and your wife, Minnie, live on your retirement fund which you elected to manage yourself, rather than receive income from an annuity. You decide that your years in business prepared you with the ability to earn a better return than the annuity would provide.

So when you retired and got your bundle, you called your broker and discussed with him what you should do with it. He tells you the most important thing is to protect your principal and recommends that you buy bonds. You settle on three issues that your broker and his firm believe are good ones, with solid balance sheets: (1) a utility company, (2) a fast-growing alternative energy company, and (3) a major county in Southern California. Now all you have to do is sit back and clip your coupons.

Ah, but the best laid plans of mice and men. . . . First, the utility company goes broke, and you can look forward to recovering only a few cents on the dollar over several years. Then, the alternative energy company fails, and you might get something back—eventually. Finally, the county has a scandal and has to default on all of its outstanding bonds. A recovery plan is initiated, but don't hold your breath. Your best strategy is to apply for a job at McDonald's. They hire older people, don't they?

Now what could the auditors of these three entities ever say to you about how they planned and conducted their audits and decided to issue an unqualified opinion that would justify that opinion in your mind? You don't care about business failure versus audit failure, or risk assessment and reliability of audit evidence, or any of that technical mumbo jumbo. The auditors were supposed to be there for you when you needed them, and they weren't. And materiality? Anything that would have indicated a problem is material to you.

The message is, folks, that it's a lot easier to sweat over doing a tough audit right than it is to justify your judgments and decisions after it's too late. And good luck if you think that a harmed investor will ever see things from your point of view.

LEARNING OBJECTIVES

After studying this chapter, you should be able to

9-1 Apply the concept of materiality to the audit.

9-2 Make a preliminary judgment about what amounts to consider material.

9-3 Allocate preliminary materiality to segments of the audit during planning.

9-4 Use materiality to evaluate audit findings.

9-5 Define risk in auditing.

9-6 Describe the audit risk model and its components.

9-7 Consider the impact of engagement risk on acceptable audit risk.

9-8 Consider the impact of several factors on the assessment of inherent risk.

9-9 Discuss the relationship of risks to audit evidence.

9-10 Discuss how materiality and risk are related and integrated into the audit process.

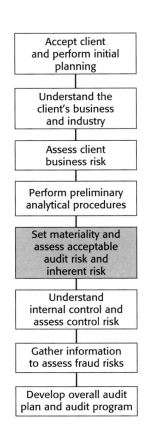

Accept client
and perform initial
planning

Understand the
client's business
and industry

Assess client
business risk

Perform preliminary
analytical procedures

Set materiality and
assess acceptable
audit risk and
inherent risk

Understand
internal control and
assess control risk

Gather information
to assess fraud risks

Develop overall audit
plan and audit program

The scope paragraph in auditors' reports includes two important phrases that are directly related to materiality and risk. These phrases are emphasized in italic print in the following two sentences of a standard scope paragraph.

• We conducted our audits in accordance with auditing standards generally accepted in the United States of America. Those standards require that we plan and perform the audit to *obtain reasonable assurance* about whether the financial statements are *free of material misstatement.*

The phrase *obtain reasonable assurance* is intended to inform users that auditors do not guarantee or ensure the fair presentation of the financial statements. The phrase communicates that there is some *risk* that the financial statements are not fairly stated even when the opinion is unqualified.

The phrase *free of material misstatement* is intended to inform users that the auditor's responsibility is limited to *material* financial information. Materiality is important because it is impractical for auditors to provide assurances on immaterial amounts.

Thus, materiality and risk are fundamental concepts that are important to planning the audit and designing the audit approach. This chapter shows how these concepts fit into the planning phase of the audit.

There is a close relationship between this chapter and Chapters 6 and 8. Chapter 6 discussed the auditor's responsibilities, transaction cycles, and audit objectives. In this chapter, both materiality and risk are applied to the concepts studied in these topics. The first part of Chapter 8 dealt with planning the audit, primarily the first four parts, which are shown in the margin. This chapter deals with the fifth part, which is shaded in the margin. A considerable amount of the information that auditors acquire and document during the first four parts of planning is used when the auditor decides materiality and assesses risks.

MATERIALITY

OBJECTIVE 9-1

Apply the concept of materiality to the audit.

As was shown in Chapter 3, materiality is a major consideration in determining the appropriate audit report to issue. The concepts of materiality discussed in this chapter are directly related to those in Chapter 3.

FASB 2 has defined **materiality** as

• The magnitude of an omission or misstatement of accounting information that, in the light of surrounding circumstances, makes it *probable* that the judgment of a reasonable person relying on the information would have been changed or influenced by the omission or misstatement. [italics added]

The auditor's responsibility is to determine whether financial statements are materially misstated. If the auditor determines that there is a material misstatement, he or she will bring it to the client's attention so that a correction can be made. If the client refuses to correct the statements, a qualified or an adverse opinion must be issued, depending on how material the misstatement is. Therefore, auditors must have a thorough knowledge of the application of materiality.

A careful reading of the FASB definition reveals the difficulty that auditors have in applying materiality in practice. The definition emphasizes reasonable users who rely on the statements to make decisions. Therefore, auditors must have knowledge of the likely users of their clients' statements and the decisions that are being made. For example, if an auditor knows that financial statements will be relied on in a buy–sell agreement for the entire business, the amount that the auditor considers material may be smaller than that for an otherwise similar audit. In practice, auditors may not know who all users are or what decisions will be made.

There are five closely related steps in applying materiality. They are shown in Figure 9-1 and discussed in the next few sections of this chapter. The steps start with setting a preliminary judgment about materiality and allocating this estimate to the segments of the audit. As shown in the first bracket in Figure 9-1, these two steps are done as part of planning and

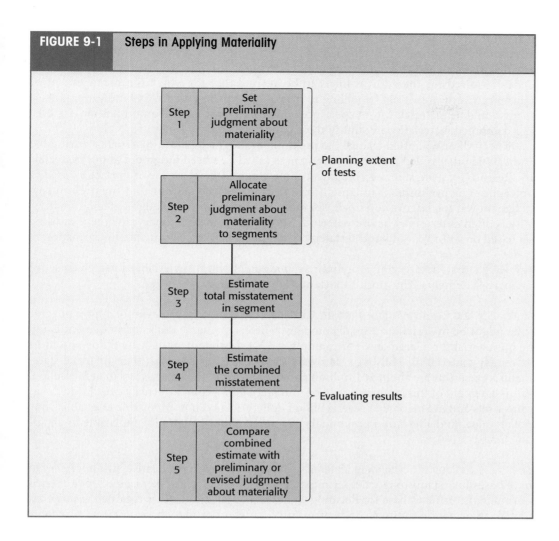

FIGURE 9-1 | Steps in Applying Materiality

Step 1 — Set preliminary judgment about materiality

Step 2 — Allocate preliminary judgment about materiality to segments

Planning extent of tests

Step 3 — Estimate total misstatement in segment

Step 4 — Estimate the combined misstatement

Step 5 — Compare combined estimate with preliminary or revised judgment about materiality

Evaluating results

are the primary topics of the discussion of materiality in this chapter. Estimation of the amount of misstatements in each segment takes place throughout the audit. The final two steps are done near the end of the audit during the engagement completion phase. These three steps are shown in the second bracket in Figure 9-1 and are done as part of evaluating the results of audit tests.

SET PRELIMINARY JUDGMENT ABOUT MATERIALITY

OBJECTIVE **9-2**

Make a preliminary judgment about what amounts to consider material.

Ideally, an auditor decides early in the audit the combined amount of misstatements in the financial statements that would be considered material. SAS 47 (AU 312) defines the amount as the **preliminary judgment about materiality**. This judgment need not be quantified but often is. It is called a preliminary judgment about materiality because it is a professional judgment and may change during the engagement if circumstances change.

The preliminary judgment about materiality (step 1 in Figure 9-1) is thus the maximum amount by which the auditor believes the statements could be misstated and still *not* affect the decisions of reasonable users. (Conceptually, this would be an amount that is $1 less than materiality as defined by the FASB. Preliminary materiality is defined in this manner as a convenience in application.) This judgment is one of the most important decisions the auditor makes. It requires considerable professional judgment.

The reason for setting a preliminary judgment about materiality is to help the auditor plan the appropriate evidence to accumulate. If the auditor sets a low dollar amount, more evidence is required than for a high amount. Examine the financial statements of Hillsburg

Hardware Co., which are included in the glossy insert to the textbook. What do you think is the combined amount of misstatements that would affect decisions of reasonable users? Do you believe that a $100 misstatement would affect users' decisions? If so, the amount of evidence required for the audit is likely to be beyond that for which the management of Hillsburg Hardware would be willing to pay. Do you believe that a $10 million misstatement would be material? Most experienced auditors would say that amount is far too large as a combined materiality amount in these circumstances.

The auditor will often change the preliminary judgment about materiality during the audit. When that is done, the new judgment is called a **revised judgment about materiality**. Reasons for using a revised judgment can include a change in one of the factors used to determine the preliminary judgment or a decision by the auditor that the preliminary judgment was too large or too small. For example, the preliminary judgment about materiality is often determined before year-end. In this case, the preliminary judgment must be set based on prior years' financial statements or interim financial statement information.

Factors Affecting Judgment

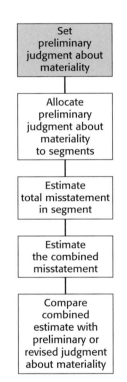

Set preliminary judgment about materiality

Allocate preliminary judgment about materiality to segments

Estimate total misstatement in segment

Estimate the combined misstatement

Compare combined estimate with preliminary or revised judgment about materiality

Several factors affect setting a preliminary judgment about materiality for a given set of financial statements. The most important of these are discussed next.

Materiality Is a Relative Rather Than an Absolute Concept A misstatement of a given magnitude might be material for a small company, whereas the same dollar misstatement could be immaterial for a large one. For example, a total misstatement of $10 million would be extremely material for Hillsburg Hardware Co. because, as shown in their financial statements, total assets are about $61 million and net income before taxes is less than $6 million. A misstatement of this amount would be immaterial for a company such as IBM, which has total assets and net income of several billion dollars. Hence, it is impossible to establish any dollar-value guidelines for a preliminary judgment about materiality applicable to all audit clients.

Bases Are Needed for Evaluating Materiality Because materiality is relative, it is necessary to have bases for establishing whether misstatements are material. *Net income before taxes* is normally the primary base for deciding what is material because it is regarded as a critical item of information for users. Some firms use a different primary base because net income often fluctuates considerably from year to year and therefore does not provide a stable base. Examples of other primary bases used by firms are net sales, gross profit, and total assets. In addition to establishing a primary base, it also is important to decide whether the misstatements could materially affect the reasonableness of other possible bases such as current assets, total assets, current liabilities, and owners' equity.

Assume that for a given company, an auditor decided that a misstatement of income before taxes of $100,000 or more would be material, but a misstatement of $250,000 or more would be material for current assets. It would be inappropriate for the auditor to use a preliminary judgment about materiality of $250,000 for both income before taxes and current assets. The auditor must therefore plan to find all misstatements affecting income before taxes that exceed the preliminary judgment about materiality of $100,000. Because most misstatements affect both the income statement and balance sheet, the auditor will not be greatly concerned about the possibility of misstatement of current assets exceeding $250,000 and will use a materiality level of $100,000 for most tests. However, some misstatements, such as misclassifying a long-term asset as a current one, affect only the balance sheet. The auditor will therefore also need to plan the audit with the $250,000 preliminary judgment about materiality for certain tests of current assets.

Qualitative Factors Also Affect Materiality Certain types of misstatements are likely to be more important to users than others, even if the dollar amounts are the same. For example:

• Amounts involving fraud are usually considered more important than unintentional errors of equal dollar amounts because fraud reflects on the honesty and reliability of the management or other personnel involved. To illustrate, most users would consider an intentional misstatement of inventory as being more important than clerical errors in inventory of the same dollar amount.

- Misstatements that are otherwise minor may be material if there are possible consequences arising from contractual obligations. An example is when net working capital included in the financial statements is only a few hundred dollars more than the required minimum in a loan agreement. If the correct net working capital were less than the required minimum, putting the loan in default, the current and noncurrent liability classifications would be materially affected.
- Misstatements that are otherwise immaterial may be material if they affect a trend in earnings. For example, if reported income has increased 3 percent annually for the past 5 years but income for the current year has declined 1 percent, that change of trend may be material. Similarly, a misstatement that would cause a loss to be reported as a profit would be of concern.

SAB No. 99

Accounting and auditing standards do not provide specific materiality guidelines to practitioners. The concern is that such guidelines might be applied without considering all the complexities that should affect the auditor's final decision. Therefore, this chapter provides illustrative guidelines to show the application of materiality. They are intended only to help you better understand the concept of applying materiality in practice. The guidelines are stated in Figure 9-2 in the form of a policy guideline for a CPA firm. Notice that the guidelines are formulas using one or more bases and a range of percentages. Guidelines such as the ones presented require considerable professional judgment.

Illustrative Guidelines

FIGURE 9-2	Illustrative Materiality Guidelines

BERGER AND ANTHONY, CPAs
Gary, Indiana 46405

POLICY STATEMENT   Charles G. Berger
No. 32IC   Joe Anthony
Title: Materiality Guidelines

Professional judgment is to be used at all times in setting and applying materiality guidelines. As a general guideline, the following policies are to be applied:

1. The combined total of misstatements in the financial statements exceeding 10 percent is normally considered material. A combined total of less than 5 percent is presumed to be immaterial in the absence of qualitative factors. Combined misstatements between 5 percent and 10 percent require the greatest amount of professional judgment to determine their materiality.

2. The 5 percent to 10 percent must be measured in relation to the appropriate base. Many times there is more than one base to which misstatements should be compared. The following guides are recommended in selecting the appropriate base:
   a. *Income statement.* Combined misstatements in the income statement should ordinarily be measured at 5 percent to 10 percent of operating income before taxes. A guideline of 5 percent to 10 percent may be inappropriate in a year in which income is unusually large or small. When operating income in a given year is not considered representative, it is desirable to substitute as a base a more representative income measure. For example, average operating income for a 3-year period may be used as the base.
   b. *Balance sheet.* Combined misstatements in the balance sheet should originally be evaluated for current assets, current liabilities, and total assets. For current assets and current liabilities, the guidelines should be between 5 percent and 10 percent, applied in the same way as for the income statement. For total assets, the guidelines should be between 3 percent and 6 percent, applied in the same way as for the income statement.

3. Qualitative factors should be carefully evaluated on all audits. In many instances, they are more important than the guidelines applied to the income statement and balance sheet. The intended uses of the financial statements and the nature of the information in the statements, including footnotes, must be carefully evaluated.

Using the illustrative guidelines in Figure 9-2, we will now present a preliminary judgment about materiality for Hillsburg Hardware Co. The guidelines are as follows:

Preliminary Judgment About Materiality (Rounded, in Thousands)				
	Minimum		Maximum	
	Percentage	Dollar Amount	Percentage	Dollar Amount
Earnings from operations	5	$ 368	10	$ 737
Current assets	5	2,551	10	5,103
Total assets	3	1,841	6	3,682
Current liabilities	5	661	10	1,322

If the auditor for Hillsburg Hardware decides that the general guidelines are reasonable, the first step is to evaluate whether any qualitative factors significantly affect the materiality judgment. If not, the auditor must decide that if combined misstatements of operating income before taxes were less than $368,000, the statements would be considered fairly stated. If the combined misstatements exceeded $737,000, the statements would not be considered fairly stated. If the misstatements were between $368,000 and $737,000, a more careful consideration of all facts would be required. The auditor then applies the same process to the other three bases.

ALLOCATE PRELIMINARY JUDGMENT ABOUT MATERIALITY TO SEGMENTS (TOLERABLE MISSTATEMENT)

OBJECTIVE 9-3

Allocate preliminary materiality to segments of the audit during planning.

The **allocation of the preliminary judgment about materiality** to segments (step 2 in Figure 9-1) is necessary because evidence is accumulated by segments rather than for the financial statements as a whole. If auditors have a preliminary judgment about materiality for each segment, it helps them decide the appropriate audit evidence to accumulate. For example, an auditor is likely to accumulate more evidence for an accounts receivable balance of $1,000,000 when a misstatement of $50,000 in accounts receivable is considered material than if $300,000 were material.

Most practitioners allocate materiality to balance sheet rather than income statement accounts. Most income statement misstatements have an equal effect on the balance sheet because of the double-entry bookkeeping system. Therefore, the auditor can allocate materiality to either income statement or balance sheet accounts. Because there are fewer balance sheet than income statement accounts in most audits and most audit procedures focus on balance sheet accounts, allocating materiality to balance sheet accounts is the most appropriate alternative.

When auditors allocate the preliminary judgment about materiality to account balances, the materiality allocated to any given account balance is referred to in SAS 39 (AU 350) as **tolerable misstatement.** For example, if an auditor decides to allocate $100,000 of a total preliminary judgment about materiality of $200,000 to accounts receivable, tolerable misstatement for accounts receivable is $100,000. This means that the auditor is willing to consider accounts receivable fairly stated if it is misstated by $100,000 or less.

There are three major difficulties in allocating materiality to balance sheet accounts (segments): Auditors expect certain accounts to have more misstatements than others, both overstatements and understatements must be considered, and relative audit costs affect the allocation. All three of these difficulties are considered in the allocation in Figure 9-3.

Figure 9-3 illustrates the allocation approach followed by the senior, Fran Moore, for the audit of Hillsburg Hardware Co. It summarizes the balance sheet, combining certain accounts, and shows the allocation of total materiality of $737,000 (10 percent of earnings from operations). The allocation approach followed by Moore for Hillsburg Hardware Co. is to use judgment in the allocation, subject to two arbitrary requirements established by Berger and Anthony, CPAs: Tolerable misstatement for any account cannot exceed

FIGURE 9-3 — Tolerable Misstatement Allocated to Hillsburg Hardware Co.

	Balance 12-31-04 (in Thousands)	Tolerable Misstatement (in Thousands)	
Cash	$ 828	$ 10	(a)
Trade accounts receivable (net)	18,957	442	(b)
Inventories	29,865	442	(b)
Other current assets	1,377	100	(c)
Property, plant, and equipment	10,340	80	(d)
Total assets	$61,367		
Trade accounts payable	$ 4,720	180	(e)
Notes payable—total	28,300	0	(a)
Accrued payroll and payroll tax	1,470	100	(c)
Accrued interest and dividends payable	2,050	0	(a)
Other liabilities	2,364	120	(c)
Capital stock and capital in excess of par	8,500	0	(a)
Retained earnings	13,963	NA	(f)
Total liabilities and equity	$61,367	$1,474	(2 × $737)

NA = Not applicable

(a) Zero or small tolerable misstatement because account can be completely audited at low cost and no misstatements are expected.
(b) Large tolerable misstatement because account is large and requires extensive sampling to audit the account.
(c) Large tolerable misstatement as a percent of account because account can be verified at extremely low cost, probably with analytical procedures, if tolerable misstatement is large.
(d) Small tolerable misstatement as a percent of account balance because most of the balance is in land and buildings, which is unchanged from the prior year and need not be audited.
(e) Moderately large tolerable misstatement because a relatively large number of misstatements are expected.
(f) Not applicable—retained earnings is a residual account that is affected by the net amount of the misstatements in the other accounts.

60 percent of the preliminary judgment (60 percent of $737,000 = $442,000, rounded), and the sum of all tolerable misstatements cannot exceed twice the preliminary judgment about materiality (2 × $737,000 = $1,474,000).

The reason for the first requirement is to keep the auditor from allocating all of total materiality to one account. If, for example, all of the preliminary judgment of $737,000 is allocated to trade accounts receivable, a $737,000 misstatement in that account would be acceptable. However, it may not be acceptable to have such a large misstatement in one account, and even if it is acceptable, it would not allow for any misstatements in other accounts.

There are two reasons for permitting the sum of the tolerable misstatement to exceed overall materiality. First, it is unlikely that all accounts will be misstated by the full amount of tolerable misstatement. If, for example, other current assets have a tolerable misstatement of $100,000 but no misstatements are found in auditing those accounts, it means that the auditor, after the fact, could have allocated zero or a small tolerable misstatement to other current assets. It is common for auditors to find fewer misstatements than tolerable misstatement. Second, some accounts are likely to be overstated, whereas others are likely to be understated, resulting in a net amount that is likely to be less than overall materiality.

Notice in the allocation that the auditor is concerned about the combined effect on operating income of the misstatement of each balance sheet account. An overstatement of an asset account will therefore have the same effect on the income statement as an understatement of a liability account. In contrast, a misclassification in the balance sheet, such as a classification of a note payable as an account payable, will have no effect on operating income. The materiality of items not affecting the income statement must be considered separately.

Figure 9-3 also includes the rationale that Fran Moore followed in deciding tolerable misstatement for each account. For example, she concluded that it was unnecessary to assign any tolerable misstatement to notes payable, even though it is as large as inventories. If she

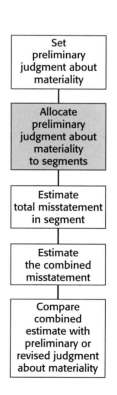

Set preliminary judgment about materiality

Allocate preliminary judgment about materiality to segments

Estimate total misstatement in segment

Estimate the combined misstatement

Compare combined estimate with preliminary or revised judgment about materiality had assigned $221,000 to each of those two accounts, more evidence would have been required in inventories, but the confirmation of the balance in notes payable would still have been required. It was therefore more efficient to allocate $442,000 to inventories and none to notes payable. Similarly, she allocated $100,000 to other current assets and accrued payroll and payroll tax, both of which are large compared with the recorded account balance. Moore did so because she believes that these accounts can be verified within $100,000 by using only analytical procedures, which are low cost. If tolerable misstatement were set lower, she would have to use more costly audit procedures such as documentation and confirmation.

In practice, it is often difficult to predict in advance which accounts are most likely to be misstated and whether misstatements are likely to be overstatements or understatements. Similarly, the relative costs of auditing different account balances often cannot be determined. It is therefore a difficult professional judgment to allocate the preliminary judgment about materiality to accounts. Accordingly, many accounting firms have developed rigorous guidelines and sophisticated statistical methods for doing so.

To summarize, the purpose of allocating the preliminary judgment about materiality to balance sheet accounts is to help the auditor decide the appropriate evidence to accumulate for each account. An aim of the allocation should be to minimize audit costs. Regardless of how the allocation is done, when the audit is completed, the auditor must be confident that the combined misstatements in all accounts are less than or equal to the preliminary (or revised) judgment about materiality.

ESTIMATE MISSTATEMENT AND COMPARE WITH PRELIMINARY JUDGMENT

OBJECTIVE 9-4

Use materiality to evaluate audit findings.

The first two steps in applying materiality involve planning, whereas the last three (steps 3, 4, and 5 in Figure 9-1) result from performing audit tests. The last three steps are discussed in greater detail in later chapters. This section only shows their relationship to the first two.

When the auditor performs audit procedures for each segment of the audit, a worksheet is kept of all misstatements found. For example, assume that the auditor finds six client misstatements in a sample of 200 in testing inventory costs. These misstatements are used to estimate the *total* misstatements in inventory (step 3). The total is called an estimate or often a "projection" because only a sample, rather than the entire population, was audited. Estimation of projected misstatement is required by SAS 39 (AU 350). The projected misstatement amounts for each account are combined on the worksheet (step 4), and then the combined misstatement is compared with materiality (step 5).

Table 9-1 is used to illustrate the last three steps in applying materiality. For simplicity, only three accounts are included. The estimated misstatements are calculated based on actual audit tests. Assume, for example, that in auditing inventory, the auditor found $3,500 of net overstatement amounts in a sample of $50,000 of the total population

TABLE 9-1	Illustration of Comparison of Estimated Total Misstatement to Preliminary Judgment about Materiality			
		Estimated Misstatement Amount		
Account	**Tolerable Misstatement**	**Direct Projection**	**Sampling Error**	**Total**
Cash	$ 4,000	$ 0	$ NA	$ 0
Accounts receivable	20,000	12,000	6,000	18,000
Inventory	36,000	31,500	15,750	47,250
Total estimated misstatement amount		$43,500	$16,800	$60,300
Preliminary judgment about materiality	$50,000			

NA=Not applicable.
Cash audited 100 percent.

of $450,000. One way to calculate the estimate of the misstatements is to make a direct projection from the sample to the population and add an estimate for sampling error. The calculation of the **direct projection estimate of misstatement** is

$$\frac{\text{Net misstatements in the sample (\$3,500)}}{\text{Total sampled (\$50,000)}} \times \begin{array}{c}\text{Total recorded}\\ \text{population value}\\ (\$450,000)\end{array} = \begin{array}{c}\text{Direct projection}\\ \text{estimate of}\\ \text{misstatement}\\ (\$31,500)\end{array}$$

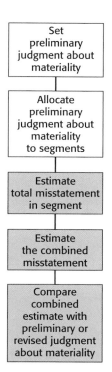

The direct projection for accounts receivable of $12,000 is not illustrated.

The estimate for **sampling error** results because the auditor has sampled only a portion of the population (this is discussed in detail in Chapters 15 and 17). In this simplified example, the estimate for sampling error is assumed to be 50 percent of the direct projection of the misstatement amounts for the accounts where sampling was used (accounts receivable and inventory).

In combining the misstatements in Table 9-1, observe that the direct projection misstatements for the three accounts add to $43,500. However, the total sampling error is less than the sum of the individual sampling errors. This is because sampling error represents the maximum misstatement in account details not audited. It is unlikely that this maximum misstatement amount would exist in all accounts subjected to sampling. Thus, sampling methodology provides for determining a combined sampling error that takes this into consideration. Again, this is discussed in detail in Chapters 15 and 17.

Table 9-1 shows that total estimated misstatement of $60,300 exceeds the preliminary judgment about materiality of $50,000. Furthermore, the major area of difficulty is inventory, where estimated misstatement of $47,250 is significantly greater than tolerable misstatement of $36,000. Because the estimated combined misstatement exceeds the preliminary judgment, the financial statements are not acceptable. The auditor can either determine whether the estimated misstatement actually exceeds $50,000 by performing additional audit procedures or require the client to make an adjustment for estimated misstatements. If additional audit procedures are performed, they would be concentrated in the inventory area.

If the estimated net overstatement amount for inventory had been $28,000 ($18,000 plus $10,000 sampling error), the auditor probably would not need to expand audit tests because it would have met both the tests of tolerable misstatement ($36,000) and the preliminary judgment about materiality ($18,000 + $28,000 = $46,000 < $50,000). In fact, there would be some leeway with that amount because the results of cash and accounts receivable procedures indicate that those accounts are well within their tolerable misstatement limits. If the auditor were to approach the audit of the accounts in a sequential manner, the findings of the audit of the earlier accounts can be used to revise the tolerable misstatement established for other accounts. For example, in the illustration, if the auditor had audited cash and accounts receivable before inventories, tolerable misstatement for inventories could be increased.

RISK

There is a close relationship between materiality and risk. In the example in Table 9-1, the auditor estimated a $6,000 sampling error for accounts receivable, which was used to calculate the total estimated misstatement of $18,000 for comparison to tolerable misstatement of $20,000. The $6,000 sampling error *includes a risk* resulting from sampling. This is only one of several kinds of risks auditors must address.

As we saw in Chapter 8, auditors accept some level of **risk** or uncertainty in performing the audit function. The auditor recognizes, for example, that there is uncertainty about the competence of evidence, uncertainty about the effectiveness of a client's internal controls, and uncertainty about whether the financial statements are fairly stated when the audit is completed. An effective auditor recognizes that risks exist and deals with those risks in an appropriate manner. Most risks auditors encounter are difficult to measure and require careful thought to respond to appropriately. Responding to these risks properly is critical to achieving a high-quality audit.

OBJECTIVE 9-5

Define risk in auditing.

As discussed in Chapter 8, the auditor gains an understanding of the client's business and industry and assesses client business risk to assess the likelihood of material misstatements in the client's financial statements. Auditors use the audit risk model to further identify the potential for misstatements and where they are most likely to occur. Before discussing the audit risk model, an illustration for a hypothetical company is provided in Table 9-2 as a frame of reference for the discussion. The table first shows that there are differences among cycles in the frequency and size of expected misstatements (A). For example, there are almost no misstatements expected in payroll and personnel but many in inventory and warehousing. The reason may be that the payroll transactions are highly routine, whereas there may be considerable complexities in recording inventory. Similarly, internal control is believed to differ in effectiveness among the five cycles (B). For example, internal controls in payroll and personnel are considered highly effective, whereas those in inventory and warehousing are considered ineffective. Finally, the auditor has decided on a low willingness that material misstatements exist after the audit is complete for all five cycles (C). It is common for auditors to want an equally low likelihood of misstatements for each cycle after the audit is finished to permit the issuance of an unqualified opinion.

The previous considerations (A, B, C) affect the auditor's decision about the appropriate extent of evidence to accumulate (D). For example, because the auditor expects few misstatements in payroll and personnel (A) and internal controls are effective (B), the auditor plans for less evidence (D) than for inventory and warehousing. Notice that the auditor has the same

TABLE 9-2	Illustration of Differing Evidence Among Cycles				
		Sales and Collection Cycle	Acquisition and Payment Cycle	Payroll and Personnel Cycle	Inventory and Warehousing Cycle	Capital Acquisition and Repayment Cycle
A	Auditor's assessment of expectation of material misstatement before considering internal control (inherent risk)	Expect some misstatements (medium)	Expect many misstatements (high)	Expect few misstatements (low)	Expect many misstatements (high)	Expect few misstatements (low)
B	Auditor's assessment of effectiveness of internal controls to prevent or detect material misstatements (control risk)	Medium effectiveness (medium)	High effectiveness (low)	High effectiveness (low)	Low effectiveness (high)	Medium effectiveness (medium)
C	Auditor's willingness to permit material misstatements to exist after completing the audit (acceptable audit risk)	Low willingness (low)	Low willingness (low)	Low willingness (low)	Low willingness (low)	Low willingness (low)
D	Extent of evidence the auditor plans to accumulate (planned detection risk)	Medium level (medium)	Medium level (medium)	Low level (high)	High level (low)	Medium level (medium)

level of willingness to accept material misstatements after the audit is finished for all five cycles, but a different extent of evidence is needed for various cycles. The difference is caused by differences in the auditor's expectations of misstatements and assessment of internal control.

The primary way that auditors deal with risk in planning audit evidence is through the application of the **audit risk model.** The source of the audit risk model is the professional literature in SAS 39 (AU 350) on audit sampling and SAS 47 (AU 312) on materiality and risk. A thorough understanding of the model is essential to effective audit planning and to the study of the remaining chapters of this book.

The audit risk model is used primarily for planning purposes in deciding how much evidence to accumulate in each cycle. It is usually stated as follows:

$$PDR = \frac{AAR}{IR \times CR}$$

where:

$$PDR = \text{planned detection risk}$$
$$AAR = \text{acceptable audit risk}$$
$$IR = \text{inherent risk}$$
$$CR = \text{control risk}$$

A numerical example is provided for discussion, even though it is not practical to measure as precisely as these numbers imply. The numbers used are for the inventory and warehousing cycle in Table 9-2.

$$IR = 100\%$$
$$CR = 100\%$$
$$AAR = 5\%$$
$$PDR = \frac{.05}{1.0 \times 1.0} = .05 \text{ or } 5\%$$

TYPES OF RISKS

The four risks in the audit risk model are sufficiently important to merit detailed discussion. All four risks are discussed briefly in this section to provide an overview of the risks. Acceptable audit risk and inherent risk are then discussed in greater detail later in this chapter. Control risk is studied in detail in Chapter 10.

Planned detection risk is a measure of the risk that audit evidence for a segment will fail to detect misstatements exceeding a tolerable amount, should such misstatements exist. There are two key points about planned detection risk. First, it is dependent on the other three factors in the model. Planned detection risk will change only if the auditor changes one of the other factors. Second, it determines the amount of substantive evidence that the auditor plans to accumulate, inversely with the size of planned detection risk. If planned detection risk is reduced, the auditor needs to accumulate more evidence to achieve the reduced planned risk. For example, in Table 9-2 (D), planned detection risk is low for inventory and warehousing, which causes planned evidence to be high. The opposite is true for payroll and personnel.

The planned detection risk of .05 in the previous numerical example means the auditor plans to accumulate evidence until the risk of misstatements exceeding tolerable misstatement is reduced to 5 percent. If control risk had been .50 instead of 1.0, planned detection risk would be .10, and planned evidence could therefore be reduced.

Inherent risk is a measure of the auditor's assessment of the likelihood that there are material misstatements (errors or fraud) in a segment before considering the effectiveness of internal control. Inherent risk is the susceptibility of the financial statements to material misstatement, assuming no internal controls. If the auditor concludes that there is a high likelihood of misstatement, ignoring internal controls, the auditor would conclude that inherent risk is high. Internal controls are ignored in setting inherent risk because they are considered separately in the audit risk model as control risk. In Table 9-2 inherent risk (A) has been assessed high for inventory and warehousing and lower for payroll and personnel and capital acquisition and repayment. The assessment was likely based on discussions with management, knowledge of the company, and results in audits of previous years.

The relationship of inherent risk to planned detection risk and planned evidence is that inherent risk is inversely related to planned detection risk and directly related to evidence. Inherent risk for inventory and warehousing in Table 9-2 is high, and in the numerical example 1.0, which will result in a lower planned detection risk and more planned evidence than would be necessary had inherent risk been lower. Inherent risk is examined in greater detail later in the chapter.

In addition to increasing audit evidence for a higher inherent risk in a given audit area, it is also common to assign more experienced staff to that area and review the completed audit tests more thoroughly. For example, if inherent risk for inventory obsolescence is extremely high, it makes sense for the CPA firm to have an experienced staff person perform more extensive tests for inventory obsolescence and to have the audit results more carefully reviewed.

| Control Risk | **Control risk** is a measure of the auditor's assessment of the likelihood that misstatements exceeding a tolerable amount in a segment will not be prevented or detected by the client's internal controls. Control risk represents (1) an assessment of whether a client's internal controls are effective for preventing or detecting misstatements, and (2) the auditor's intention to make that assessment at a level below the maximum (100 percent) as part of the audit plan. For example, assume that the auditor concludes that internal controls are completely ineffective to prevent or detect misstatements. That is the likely conclusion for inventory and warehousing in Table 9-2 (B). The auditor would therefore assign a high, perhaps 100 percent, risk factor to control risk. The more effective the internal controls, the lower the risk factor that *could* be assigned to control risk. |

The audit risk model shows the close relationship between inherent and control risks. For example, an inherent risk of 40 percent and a control risk of 60 percent affect planned detection risk and planned evidence the same as an inherent risk of 60 percent and a control risk of 40 percent. In both cases, multiplying *IR* by *CR* results in a denominator in the audit risk model of 24 percent. The combination of inherent risk and control risk can be thought of as the *expectation of misstatements after considering the effect of internal control*. Inherent risk is the expectation of misstatements before considering the effect of internal control.

As with inherent risk, the relationship between control risk and planned detection risk is inverse, whereas the relationship between control risk and substantive evidence is direct. For example, if the auditor concludes that internal controls are effective, planned detection risk can be increased and evidence therefore decreased. The auditor can increase planned detection risk when controls are effective because effective internal controls reduce the likelihood of misstatements in the financial statements.

Before auditors can set control risk less than 100 percent, they must obtain an understanding of internal control, evaluate how well it should function based on the understanding, and test the internal controls for effectiveness. The first of these is the *understanding* requirement that relates to all audits. The latter two are the *assessment of control risk* steps that are required when the auditor *chooses* to assess control risk below maximum.

Auditors of public companies will generally choose to rely on controls because of the required testing of the effectiveness of internal control over financial reporting required by the Sarbanes–Oxley Act. Auditors of private companies and other entities may rely on controls if they are effective and if it is cost-effective to rely on the controls based on the audit risk model; that is, the benefit from reduced planned evidence exceeds the cost of testing and relying on the client's controls.

Understanding internal control, assessing control risk, and evaluating their impact on evidence requirements are so important that the entire next chapter is devoted to that topic. However, it should be noted here that if the auditor elects not to assess control risk below maximum, control risk must be set at 100 percent regardless of the actual effectiveness of the underlying controls. Use of the audit risk model in this circumstance then causes the auditor to control acceptable audit risk entirely through a low level of planned detection risk (assuming that inherent risk is high).

Acceptable audit risk is a measure of how willing the auditor is to accept that the financial statements may be materially misstated after the audit is completed and an unqualified opinion has been issued. When the auditor decides on a lower acceptable audit risk, it means the auditor wants to be more certain that the financial statements are *not* materially misstated. Zero risk would be certainty, and a 100 percent risk would be complete uncertainty. Complete assurance (zero risk) of the accuracy of the financial statements is not economically practical. It has already been established in Chapter 6 that the auditor cannot guarantee the complete absence of material misstatements.

Often, auditors refer to the terms **audit assurance**, **overall assurance**, or **level of assurance** instead of acceptable audit risk. Audit assurance or any of the equivalent terms is the complement of acceptable audit risk, that is, one minus acceptable audit risk. For example, acceptable audit risk of 2 percent is the same as audit assurance of 98 percent.

The concept of acceptable audit risk can be more easily understood by thinking in terms of a large number of audits, say, 10,000. What portion of these audits could include material misstatements without having an adverse effect on society? Certainly, the portion would be below 10 percent. It is probably much closer to 1 or one-half of 1 percent or perhaps even one-tenth of 1 percent. If an auditor believes that the appropriate percentage is 1 percent, then acceptable audit risk should be set at 1 percent, or perhaps lower, based on the specific circumstances.

Using the audit risk model, there is a direct relationship between acceptable audit risk and planned detection risk, and an inverse relationship between acceptable audit risk and planned evidence. For example, if the auditor decides to reduce acceptable audit risk, planned detection risk is thereby reduced, and planned evidence must be increased. As stated in Chapter 8, auditors also often assign more experienced staff or review the audit files more extensively for a client with lower acceptable audit risk.

ASSESSING ACCEPTABLE AUDIT RISK

Auditors must decide the appropriate acceptable audit risk for an audit, preferably during audit planning. First, auditors decide engagement risk and use engagement risk to modify acceptable audit risk.

Engagement risk is the risk that the auditor or audit firm will suffer harm because of a client relationship, even though the audit report rendered for the client was correct. Engagement risk is closely related to client business risk. For example, if a client declares bankruptcy after an audit is completed, the likelihood of a lawsuit against the CPA firm is reasonably high, even if the quality of the audit was good.

OBJECTIVE 9-7

Consider the impact of engagement risk on acceptable audit risk.

Auditors disagree about whether engagement risk should be considered in planning the audit. Opponents of modifying evidence for engagement risk contend that auditors do not provide audit opinions for different levels of assurance and therefore should not provide more or less assurance because of engagement risk. Proponents contend that it is appropriate for auditors to accumulate additional evidence, assign more experienced personnel, and review the audit more thoroughly on audits where legal exposure is high, as long as the assurance level is not decreased below a reasonably high level when there is low engagement risk.

When auditors modify evidence for engagement risk, it is done by control of acceptable audit risk. The authors believe that a reasonably low acceptable audit risk is always desirable, but in some circumstances an even lower risk is needed because of engagement risk factors. Research has indicated that several factors affect engagement risk and therefore acceptable audit risk. Only three of those are discussed here: the degree to which external users rely on the statements, the likelihood that a client will have financial difficulties after the audit report is issued, and the integrity of management.

The Degree to Which External Users Rely on the Statements When external users place heavy reliance on the financial statements, it is appropriate that acceptable audit risk be decreased. When the statements are heavily relied on, a great social harm could result if a significant misstatement were to remain undetected in the financial statements. The cost of additional evidence can be more easily justified when the loss to users from material misstatements is substantial. Several factors are good indicators of the degree to which statements are relied on by external users:

- *Client's size.* Generally speaking, the larger a client's operations, the more widely the statements will be used. The client's size, measured by total assets or total revenues, will have an effect on the acceptable audit risk.
- *Distribution of ownership.* The statements of publicly held corporations are normally relied on by many more users than those of closely held corporations. For these companies, the interested parties include the SEC, financial analysts, and the general public.
- *Nature and amount of liabilities.* When statements include a large amount of liabilities, they are more likely to be used extensively by actual and potential creditors than when there are few liabilities.

The Likelihood That a Client Will Have Financial Difficulties After the Audit Report Is Issued If a client is forced to file for bankruptcy or suffers a significant loss after completion of the audit, there is a greater chance of the auditor being required to defend the quality of the audit than if the client were under no financial strain. There is a natural tendency for those who lose money in a bankruptcy or because of a stock price reversal to file suit against the auditor. This can result from the honest belief that the auditor failed to conduct an adequate audit or from the users' desire to recover part of their loss regardless of the adequacy of the audit work.

In situations in which the auditor believes the chance of financial failure or loss is high and there is a corresponding increase in engagement risk, acceptable audit risk should be reduced. If a subsequent challenge does occur, the auditor will then be in a better position to defend the audit results successfully. The total audit evidence and costs will increase, but this is justifiable because of the additional risk of lawsuits that the auditor faces.

It is difficult for an auditor to predict financial failure before it occurs, but certain factors are good indicators of its increased probability:

- *Liquidity position.* If a client is constantly short of cash and working capital, it indicates a future problem in paying bills. The auditor must assess the likelihood and significance of a steadily declining liquidity position.
- *Profits (losses) in previous years.* When a company has rapidly declining profits or increasing losses for several years, the auditor should recognize the future solvency problems that the client is likely to encounter. It is also important to consider the changing profits relative to the balance remaining in retained earnings.
- *Method of financing growth.* The more a client relies on debt as a means of financing, the greater the risk of financial difficulty if the client's operations become less successful. It is also important to evaluate whether fixed assets are being financed with short- or long-term loans. Large amounts of required cash outflows during a short time can force a company into bankruptcy.

ASSESSING ACCEPTABLE AUDIT RISK IN PRACTICE

Henry Rinsk, of Links, Rinsk, and Rodman, CPAs, is the partner responsible for the audit of Hungry Food Restaurants, a chain of nine Midwestern family restaurants. The firm has audited Hungry Food for 10 years and has always found management competent, cooperative, and easy to deal with. Hungry Food is family-owned with a business succession plan in place; it is profitable, is liquid, and has little debt. Management has a reputation in the community for high integrity and good relationships with employees, customers, and suppliers.

After meeting with the other partners as part of the firm's annual client continuation meeting, Henry recommends that acceptable audit risk for Hungry Food be assessed at high. For Links, Rinsk, and Rodman, this means no expansion of evidence, a "standard" review of audit documentation, and a "standard" assignment of personnel to the engagement.

TABLE 9-3	Methods Practitioners Use to Assess Acceptable Audit Risk	
Factors	**Methods Used to Assess Acceptable Audit Risk**	
External users' reliance on financial statements	• Examine the financial statements, including footnotes. • Read minutes of board of directors meetings to determine future plans. • Examine Form 10K for a publicly held company. • Discuss financing plans with management.	
Likelihood of financial difficulties	• Analyze the financial statements for financial difficulties using ratios and other analytical procedures. • Examine historical and projected cash flow statements for the nature of cash inflows and outflows.	
Management integrity	Follow the procedures discussed in Chapter 8 for client acceptance and continuance.	

• *Nature of the client's operations.* Certain types of businesses are inherently riskier than others. For example, other things being equal, a start-up technology company dependent on one product is much more likely to go bankrupt than a diversified food manufacturer.
• *Competence of management.* Competent management is constantly alert for potential financial difficulties and modifies its operating methods to minimize the effects of short-run problems. The ability of management must be assessed as a part of the evaluation of the likelihood of bankruptcy.

The Auditor's Evaluation of Management's Integrity As discussed in Chapter 8 as a part of new client investigation and continuing client evaluation, if a client has questionable integrity, the auditor is likely to assess acceptable audit risk lower. Companies with low integrity often conduct their business affairs in a manner that results in conflicts with their stockholders, regulators, and customers. In turn, these conflicts often reflect on the users' perceived quality of the audit and can result in lawsuits and other disagreements. An obvious example of a situation in which management's integrity is questionable is prior criminal convictions of key management personnel. Other examples of questionable integrity might include frequent disagreements with previous auditors, the Internal Revenue Service, and the SEC. Frequent turnover of key financial and internal audit personnel and ongoing conflicts with labor unions and employees may also indicate integrity problems.

To assess acceptable audit risk, the auditor must first assess each of the factors affecting acceptable audit risk. Table 9-3 illustrates the methods used by auditors to assess each of the three factors already discussed. It is easy to see after examining Table 9-3 that the assessment of each of the factors is highly subjective, which means that the overall assessment is also highly subjective. A typical evaluation of acceptable audit risk is high, medium, or low, where a low acceptable audit risk assessment means a "risky" client requiring more extensive evidence, assignment of more experienced personnel, and/or a more extensive review of audit documentation. As the audit progresses, additional information about the client is obtained, and acceptable audit risk may be modified.

Making the Acceptable Audit Risk Decision

ASSESSING INHERENT RISK

The inclusion of inherent risk in the audit risk model is one of the most important concepts in auditing. It implies that auditors should attempt to predict where misstatements are most and least likely in the financial statement segments. This information affects the total amount of evidence that the auditor is required to accumulate and influences how the auditor's efforts to gather the evidence are allocated among the segments of the audit.

OBJECTIVE 9-8

Consider the impact of several factors on the assessment of inherent risk.

At the start of the audit, there is not much that can be done about changing inherent risk. Instead, the auditor must *assess the factors* that make up the risk and *modify audit evidence* to take them into consideration. The auditor should consider several major factors when assessing inherent risk:

Factors Affecting Inherent Risk

- Nature of the client's business
- Results of previous audits
- Initial versus repeat engagement
- Related parties
- Nonroutine transactions
- Judgment required to correctly record account balances and transactions
- Makeup of the population

Nature of the Client's Business Inherent risk for certain accounts is affected by the nature of the client's business. For example, there is a greater likelihood of obsolete inventory for an electronics manufacturer than for a steel fabricator. Inherent risk is most likely to vary from business to business for accounts such as inventory, accounts and loans receivable, and property, plant, and equipment. The nature of the client's business should have little or no effect on inherent risk for accounts such as cash, notes, and mortgages payable. Information gained while obtaining knowledge about the client's business and industry and assessing client business risk, as discussed in Chapter 8, is useful for assessing this factor.

Results of Previous Audits Misstatements found in the previous year's audit have a high likelihood of occurring again in the current year's audit. This is because many types of misstatements are systemic in nature, and organizations are often slow in making changes to eliminate them. Therefore, an auditor would be negligent if the results of the preceding year's audit were ignored during the development of the current year's audit program. For example, if the auditor found a significant number of misstatements in pricing inventory, inherent risk would likely be high, and extensive testing would have to be done in the current audit as a means of determining whether the deficiency in the client's system had been corrected. If, however, the auditor has found no misstatements for the past several years in conducting tests of an audit area, the auditor is justified in reducing inherent risk, provided that changes in relevant circumstances have not occurred.

Initial Versus Repeat Engagement Auditors gain experience and knowledge about the likelihood of misstatements after auditing a client for several years. The lack of previous years' audit results would cause most auditors to assess a higher inherent risk for initial audits than for repeat engagements in which no material misstatements had been found. Most auditors set a high inherent risk in the first year of an audit and reduce it in subsequent years as they gain experience.

Related Parties Transactions between parent and subsidiary companies and those between management and the corporate entity are examples of related-party transactions as defined by SFAS 57. Because these transactions do not occur between two independent parties dealing at "arm's length," a greater likelihood exists that they might be misstated, causing an increase in inherent risk. Determining the existence of related parties was discussed in Chapter 8.

Nonroutine Transactions Transactions that are unusual for the client are more likely to be incorrectly recorded by the client than routine transactions because the client lacks experience in recording them. Examples include fire losses, major property acquisitions, and lease agreements. Knowledge of the client's business and review of minutes of meetings, as discussed in Chapter 8, are useful to learn about nonroutine transactions.

Judgment Required to Correctly Record Account Balances and Transactions Many account balances require estimates and a great deal of management judgment. Examples are allowance for uncollectible accounts receivable, obsolete inventory, liability for warranty payments, and bank loan loss reserves. Similarly, transactions for major repairs or partial replacement of assets are examples where considerable judgment is needed to correctly record the information.

Makeup of the Population Often, the individual items making up the total population also affect the auditor's expectation of material misstatement. For example, most auditors would use a higher inherent risk for accounts receivable where most accounts are significantly overdue than where most accounts are current. Transactions with affiliated companies, amounts due from officers, cash disbursements made payable to cash, and accounts receivable outstanding for several months are examples of situations requiring a higher inherent risk and therefore greater investigation because there is usually a greater likelihood of misstatement than for more typical transactions.

The auditor must evaluate the information affecting inherent risk and decide on an appropriate inherent risk factor for each cycle, account, and, many times, for each audit objective. Some factors, such as the integrity of management, will affect many or perhaps all cycles, whereas others, such as nonroutine transactions, will affect only specific accounts or audit objectives. Although the profession has not established standards or guidelines for setting inherent risk, the authors believe that auditors are generally conservative in making such assessments. For example, assume that in the audit of inventory the auditor notes that (1) a large number of misstatements were found in the previous year and (2) inventory turnover has slowed in the current year. Many auditors would probably set inherent risk at a relatively high level (some would use 100 percent) for each audit objective for inventory in this situation.

Making the Inherent Risk Decision

Auditors begin their assessments of inherent risk during the planning phase and update the assessments throughout the audit. A considerable portion of Chapter 8 dealt with information that is relevant to inherent risk assessment during the planning phase. For example, the discussion of obtaining knowledge about the client's business and industry, touring the client's plant and offices, and identifying related parties all pertain directly to inherent risk assessment. As the auditor performs the wide variety of tests on an audit, additional information is obtained that often affects the original assessment.

Obtain Information to Assess Inherent Risk

RELATIONSHIP OF RISKS TO EVIDENCE AND FACTORS INFLUENCING RISKS

OBJECTIVE 9-9

Discuss the relationship of risks to audit evidence.

Figure 9-4 summarizes the factors that determine each of the risks, the effect of the three component risks on the determination of planned detection risk, and the relationship of all four risks to planned audit evidence. "D" in the figure indicates a direct relationship between a component risk and planned detection risk or planned evidence. "I" indicates an inverse relationship. For example, an increase in acceptable audit risk results in an increase in planned detection risk (D) and a decrease in planned audit evidence (I). Compare Figure 9-4 to Table 9-2 on page 240 and observe that these two illustrations include the same concepts.

In addition to modifying audit evidence, there are two other ways that auditors can change the audit to respond to risks. For example:

1. *The engagement may require more experienced staff.* CPA firms should staff all engagements with qualified staff, but for low acceptable audit risk clients, special care is appropriate in staffing. Similarly, if an audit area such as inventory has a high inherent risk, it is important to assign that area to someone with experience in auditing inventory.

2. *The engagement will be reviewed more carefully than usual.* CPA firms need to be sure that the audit files that document the auditor's planning, evidence accumulation and conclusions, and other matters in the audit are adequately reviewed. When acceptable audit risk is low, there is often more extensive review, including a review by personnel who were not assigned to the engagement. If inherent risk or control risk is high for certain accounts, the reviewer will likely spend more time making sure the evidence was appropriate and correctly evaluated.

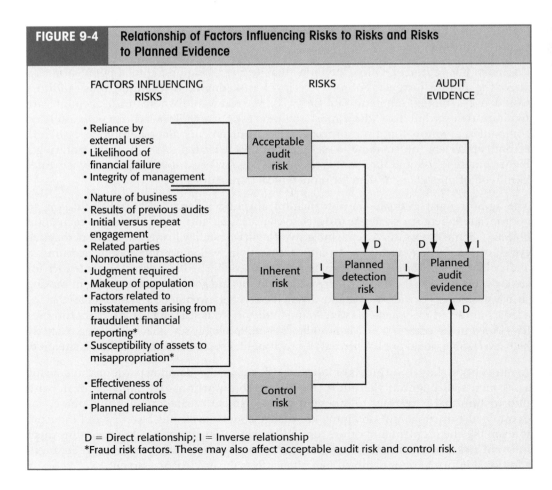

FIGURE 9-4 Relationship of Factors Influencing Risks to Risks and Risks to Planned Evidence

Both control risk and inherent risk are typically set for each cycle, each account, and often even each audit objective, not for the overall audit, and are likely to vary from cycle to cycle, account to account, and objective to objective on the same audit. Internal controls may be more effective for inventory-related accounts than for those related to fixed assets. Control risk would therefore also be different for different accounts depending on the effectiveness of the controls. Factors affecting inherent risk, such as susceptibility to defalcation and routineness of the transactions, are also likely to differ from account to account. For that reason, it is normal to have inherent risk vary for different accounts in the same audit unless there is some strong overriding factor of concern, such as management integrity.

Acceptable audit risk is ordinarily set by the auditor during planning and held constant for each major cycle and account. Auditors normally use the same acceptable audit risk for each segment because the factors affecting acceptable audit risk are related to the entire audit, not individual accounts. For example, the extent to which financial statements are relied on for external users' decisions is usually related to the overall financial statements, not just one or two accounts.

In some cases, however, a *lower* acceptable audit risk may be more appropriate for one account than for others. In the previous example, even though the auditor decided to use a medium acceptable audit risk for the audit as a whole, the auditor might decide to reduce acceptable audit risk to low for inventory if inventory is used as collateral for a short-term loan.

Some auditors use the same acceptable audit risk for each segment as overall acceptable audit risk, whereas others use a higher acceptable audit risk for each segment. The argument for using a higher acceptable audit risk for each segment is the effect of the interactions of the various accounts and transactions making up the financial statements and the synergy of multiple tests. Stated differently, if all individual segments of the audit are completed at an acceptable audit risk of a given level, the auditor can be assured that the audit risk for the financial statements as a whole will be lower. Other auditors use the same acceptable audit risk for segments as overall acceptable audit risk because of the difficulties of measurement. The latter approach is followed in the illustrations in this and subsequent chapters, but either approach is acceptable.

Because control risk and inherent risk vary from cycle to cycle, account to account, or objective to objective, planned detection risk and required audit evidence will also vary. This conclusion should not be surprising. The circumstances of each engagement are different, and the extent of evidence needed will depend on the unique circumstances. For example, inventory might require extensive testing on an engagement because of weak internal controls and concern about obsolescence resulting from technological changes in the industry. On the same engagement, accounts receivable may require little testing because of effective internal controls, fast collection of receivables, excellent relationships between the client and customers, and good audit results in previous years. Similarly, for a given audit of inventory, an auditor may assess that there is a higher inherent risk of a realizable value misstatement because of the higher potential for obsolescence but a low inherent risk of a classification misstatement because there is only purchased inventory.

There was a discussion in Chapter 6 of the auditor's responsibilities to assess the risk of fraud arising from fraudulent financial reporting and misappropriation of assets. It is difficult in concept and practice to separate fraud risk factors into acceptable audit risk, inherent risk, or control risk. For example, management that lacks integrity and is motivated to misstate financial statements is one of the factors in acceptable audit risk, but it may also affect control risk. Similarly, it will be shown in Chapter 10 that several of the other risk factors influencing management characteristics are a part of the control environment. An example is the attitude, actions, and policies that reflect the overall attitudes of top management about integrity, ethical values, and commitment to competence.

To satisfy the requirements of auditing standards, it is more important for the auditor to assess the risks and to respond to them than it is to identify them as acceptable audit risk, inherent risk, or control risk. For this reason, many audit firms assess fraud risk separately from the assessment of the risk model components.

The risk of fraud can be assessed for the entire audit or by cycle, account, and objective. For example, a strong incentive for management to meet unduly aggressive earnings expectations may affect the entire audit, while the susceptibility of inventory to theft may affect the inventory account. For both the risk of fraudulent financial reporting and the risk of misappropriation of assets, the focus is on specific areas of increased fraud risk and designing audit procedures or changing the overall conduct of the audit to respond to those risks. The specific response to an identified risk of fraud could include revising assessments of acceptable audit risk, inherent risk, and control risk. Figure 9-4 (p. 248) shows how risks related to fraud may influence each of the audit risk model components. Assessing fraud risk will be the focus of Chapter 11.

Relating Tolerable Misstatement and Risks to Balance-Related Audit Objectives

Although it is common in practice to assess inherent and control risks for each balance-related audit objective, it is not common to allocate materiality to objectives. Auditors are able to effectively associate most risks with different objectives. It is reasonably easy to determine the relationship between a risk and one or two objectives. For example, obsolescence in inventory would be unlikely to affect any objective other than realizable value. It is more difficult to decide how much of the materiality allocated to a given account should in turn be allocated to one or two objectives. Most auditors do not attempt to do so.

Measurement Limitations

Activity-Based Risk Evaluation Model

One major limitation in the application of the audit risk model is the difficulty of measuring the components of the model. Despite the auditor's best efforts in planning, the assessments of acceptable audit risk, inherent risk, and control risk and therefore planned detection risk are highly subjective and are approximations of reality at best. Imagine, for example, attempting to precisely assess inherent risk by determining the impact of factors such as the misstatements discovered in prior years' audits and technology changes in the client's industry.

To offset this measurement problem, many auditors use broad and subjective measurement terms, such as *low, medium,* and *high*. Table 9-4 shows how auditors can use the information to decide on the appropriate amount of evidence to accumulate. For example, in situation 1, the auditor has decided to accept a high audit risk for an account or objective. The auditor has concluded that there is a low risk of misstatement in the financial statements and that internal controls are effective. Therefore, a high planned detection risk is appropriate. As a result, a low level of evidence is needed. Situation 3 is at the opposite extreme. If both inherent and control risks are high and the auditor wants a low audit risk, considerable evidence is required. The other three situations fall between the two extremes.

It is equally difficult to measure the amount of evidence implied by a given planned detection risk. A typical audit program that is intended to reduce detection risk to the planned level is a combination of several audit procedures, each using a different type of evidence that is applied to different audit objectives. Auditors' measurement methods are too imprecise to permit an accurate quantitative measure of the combined evidence. Instead, auditors subjectively evaluate whether sufficient evidence has been planned to

TABLE 9-4	Relationships of Risk to Evidence				
Situation	Acceptable Audit Risk	Inherent Risk	Control Risk	Planned Detection Risk	Amount of Evidence Required
1	High	Low	Low	High	Low
2	Low	Low	Low	Medium	Medium
3	Low	High	High	Low	High
4	Medium	Medium	Medium	Medium	Medium
5	High	Low	Medium	Medium	Medium

satisfy a planned detection risk of low, medium, or high. Presumably, measurement methods are sufficient to permit an auditor to know that more evidence is needed to satisfy a low planned detection risk than for medium or high. Considerable professional judgment is needed to decide how much more.

In applying the audit risk model, auditors are concerned about both overauditing and underauditing, but most auditors are more concerned about the latter. Underauditing exposes the CPA firm to legal liability and loss of professional reputation.

Because of the concern to avoid underauditing, auditors typically assess risks conservatively. For example, an auditor might not assess either control risk or inherent risk below .5 even when the likelihood of misstatement is low. In these audits, a low risk might be .5, medium .8, and high 1.0, if the risks are quantified.

Practicing auditors develop various types of worksheets to aid in relating the considerations affecting audit evidence to the appropriate evidence to accumulate. One such worksheet is included in Figure 9-5 for the audit of accounts receivable for Hillsburg Hardware Co. The nine balance-related audit objectives introduced in Chapter 6 are included in the

Tests of Details of Balances Evidence-Planning Worksheet

| FIGURE 9-5 | Evidence-Planning Worksheet to Decide Tests of Details of Balances for Hillsburg Hardware Co.—Accounts Receivable |

	Detail tie-in	Existence	Completeness	Accuracy	Classification	Cutoff	Realizable value	Rights	Presentation and disclosure
Acceptable audit risk	High	High	High	High	High	High	High	High	High
Inherent risk	Low	Medium	Low	Low	Low	Medium	Medium	Low	Low
Control risk—Sales									
Control risk—Cash receipts									
Control risk—Additional controls									
Substantive tests of transactions—Sales									
Substantive tests of transactions—Cash receipts									
Analytical procedures									
Planned detection risk for tests of details of balances									
Planned audit evidence for tests of details of balances									

Tolerable misstatement $442,000

columns at the top of the worksheet. Rows one and two are acceptable audit risk and inherent risk, which were studied in this chapter. Tolerable misstatement is included at the bottom of the worksheet. The engagement in-charge, Fran Moore, made the following decisions in the audit of Hillsburg Hardware Co.:

- *Tolerable misstatement.* The preliminary judgment about materiality was set at $737,000 (approximately 10 percent of earnings from operations of $7,370,000). She allocated $442,000 to the audit of accounts receivable (see p. 237).
- *Acceptable audit risk.* Fran assessed acceptable audit risk as high because of the good financial condition of the company, high management integrity, and the relatively few users of the financial statements. Although Hillsburg is a publicly traded company, its stock is not widely held or extensively followed by financial analysts.
- *Inherent risk.* Fran assessed inherent risk as medium for existence and cutoff because of concerns over revenue recognition. Fran also assessed inherent risk as medium for realizable value. In past years, there have been audit adjustments to the allowance for uncollectible accounts because it was found to be understated. Inherent risk was assessed as low for all other objectives.

Planned detection risk would be approximately the same for each balance-related audit objective in the audit of accounts receivable for Hillsburg Hardware Co. if the only three factors the auditor needs to consider are acceptable audit risk, inherent risk, and tolerable misstatement. The evidence-planning worksheet shows that other factors must be considered before making the final evidence decisions. These are studied in subsequent chapters and will be integrated into the evidence-planning worksheet at that time.

Relationship of Risk and Materiality to Audit Evidence

The concepts of materiality and risk in auditing are closely related and inseparable. Risk is a measure of uncertainty, whereas materiality is a measure of magnitude or size. Taken together, they measure the uncertainty of amounts of a given magnitude. For example, the statement that the auditor plans to accumulate evidence such that there is only a 5 percent risk (acceptable audit risk) of failing to uncover misstatements exceeding tolerable misstatements of $442,000 (materiality) is a precise and meaningful statement. If the statement eliminates either the risk or materiality portion, it would be meaningless. A 5 percent risk without a specific materiality measure could imply that a $100 or $1 million misstatement is acceptable. A $442,000 overstatement without a specific risk could imply that a 1 percent or 80 percent risk is acceptable.

The relationships among tolerable misstatement and the four risks to planned audit evidence are shown in Figure 9-6. This figure expands Figure 9-4 to include tolerable misstatement. Observe that tolerable misstatement does not affect any of the four risks, and the risks have no effect on tolerable misstatement, but together they determine the planned evidence.

EVALUATING RESULTS

After the auditor plans the engagement and accumulates audit evidence, results can also be stated in terms of the evaluation version of the audit risk model. The audit risk model for evaluating audit results is stated in SAS 47 as

$$AcAR = IR \times CR \times AcDR$$

where:

AcAR = Achieved audit risk. A measure of the risk the auditor has taken that an account in the financial statements is materially misstated after the auditor has accumulated audit evidence.

IR = Inherent risk. It is the same inherent risk factor discussed in planning unless it has been revised as a result of new information.

CR = Control risk. It is also the same control risk discussed previously unless it has been revised during the audit.

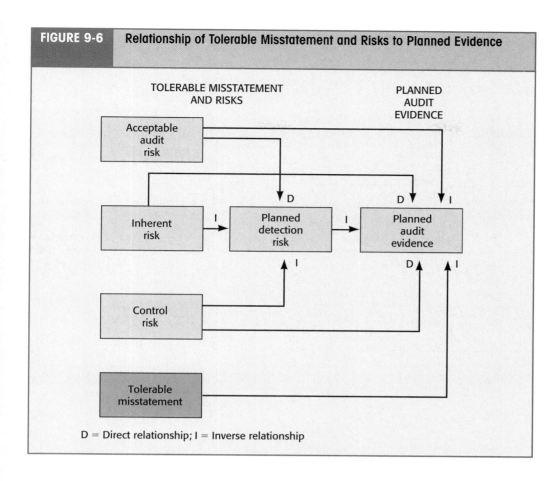

FIGURE 9-6 | Relationship of Tolerable Misstatement and Risks to Planned Evidence

TOLERABLE MISSTATEMENT AND RISKS

PLANNED AUDIT EVIDENCE

Acceptable audit risk

Inherent risk

Planned detection risk

Planned audit evidence

Control risk

Tolerable misstatement

D = Direct relationship; I = Inverse relationship

AcDR = Achieved detection risk. A measure of the risk that audit evidence for a segment did not detect misstatements exceeding a tolerable amount, if such misstatements existed. The auditor can reduce achieved detection risk only by accumulating substantive evidence.

Research subsequent to the issuance of SAS 47 has shown that it is *not appropriate to use this evaluation formula* in the way it is stated in SAS 47. The research indicates that using the formula can result in an understatement of achieved audit risk. Even though it is not appropriate to use the formula to calculate achieved audit risk, the relationships in the formula are valid and should be used in practice. The formula shows that there are three ways to reduce achieved audit risk to an acceptable level:

1. *Reduce inherent risk.* Because inherent risk is assessed by the auditor based on the client's circumstances, this assessment is done during planning and is typically not changed unless new facts are uncovered as the audit progresses.
2. *Reduce control risk.* Assessed control risk is affected by the client's internal controls and the auditor's tests of those controls. Auditors can reduce control risk by more extensive tests of controls if the client has effective controls.
3. *Reduce achieved detection risk by increasing substantive audit tests.* Auditors reduce achieved detection risk by accumulating evidence using analytical procedures, substantive tests of transactions, and tests of details of balances. Additional audit procedures, assuming that they are effective, and larger sample sizes both reduce achieved detection risk.

Subjectively combining these three factors to achieve an acceptably low audit risk requires considerable professional judgment. Some firms develop sophisticated approaches to help their auditors make those judgments, whereas other firms leave those decisions to each audit team.

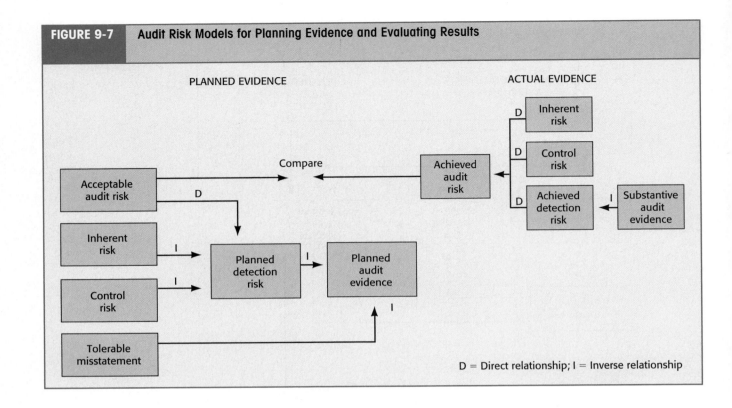

Figure 9-7 graphically shows both the planning and evaluating results versions of the audit risk model. The right side of the figure shows that accumulating more substantive evidence reduces achieved detection risk. A lower achieved detection risk along with lower inherent and control risk reduce achieved audit risk.

Revising Risks and Evidence

As already stated, the audit risk model is primarily a *planning* model and is therefore of limited use in evaluating results. Great care must be used in revising the risk factors when the actual results are not as favorable as planned.

No difficulties occur when the auditor accumulates planned evidence and concludes that the assessment of each of the risks was reasonable or better than originally thought. The auditor will conclude that sufficient competent evidence has been collected for that account or cycle.

Special care must be exercised when the auditor decides, on the basis of accumulated evidence, that the original assessment of control risk or inherent risk was understated or acceptable audit risk was overstated. In such a circumstance, the auditor should follow a two-step approach. First, the auditor must revise the original assessment of the appropriate risk. It would violate due care to leave the original assessment unchanged if the auditor knows it is inappropriate. Second, the auditor should consider the effect of the revision on evidence requirements, *without use of the audit risk model.* Research in auditing has shown that if a revised risk is used in the audit risk model to determine a revised planned detection risk, there is a danger of not increasing the evidence sufficiently. Instead, the auditor should carefully evaluate the implications of the revision of the risk and modify evidence appropriately, outside of the audit risk model. An example is used to illustrate revision of a factor in the audit risk model. Assume that the auditor confirms accounts receivable and, based on the misstatements found, concludes that the original control risk assessment as low was inappropriate. The auditor should revise the estimate of control risk upward and carefully consider the effect of the revision on the additional evidence needed in the sales and collection cycle. That should be done without recalculating planned detection risk.

ESSENTIAL TERMS

Acceptable audit risk—a measure of how willing the auditor is to accept that the financial statements may be materially misstated after the audit is completed and an unqualified audit opinion has been issued; see also *audit assurance*

Allocation of the preliminary judgment about materiality—the process of assigning to each balance sheet account the misstatement amount to be considered material for that account based on the auditor's preliminary judgment

Audit assurance—a complement to acceptable audit risk; an acceptable audit risk of 2 percent is the same as audit assurance of 98 percent; also called *overall assurance* and *level of assurance*

Audit risk model—a formal model reflecting the relationships between acceptable audit risk (AAR), inherent risk (IR), control risk (CR), and planned detection risk (PDR); $PDR = AAR/(IR \times CR)$

Control risk—a measure of the auditor's assessment of the likelihood that misstatements exceeding a tolerable amount in a segment will not be prevented or detected by the client's internal controls

Direct projection estimate of misstatement—estimate of likely misstatement in a population based on a sample, excluding sampling risk, and calculated as net misstatements in the sample, divided by the total sampled, multiplied by the total recorded population value

Engagement risk—the risk that the auditor or audit firm will suffer harm because of a client relationship, even though the audit report rendered for the client was correct

Inherent risk—a measure of the auditor's assessment of the likelihood that there are material misstatements in a segment before considering the effectiveness of internal control

Materiality—the magnitude of an omission or misstatement of accounting information that, in the light of surrounding circumstances, makes it *probable* that the judgment of a reasonable person relying on the information would have been changed or influenced by the omission or misstatement

Planned detection risk—a measure of the risk that audit evidence for a segment will fail to detect misstatements exceeding a tolerable amount, should such misstatements exist; $PDR = AAR/(IR \times CR)$

Preliminary judgment about materiality—the maximum amount by which the auditor believes that the statements could be misstated and still *not* affect the decisions of reasonable users; used in audit planning

Revised judgment about materiality—a change in the auditor's preliminary judgment made when the auditor determines that the preliminary judgment was too large or too small

Risk—the acceptance by auditors that there is some level of uncertainty in performing the audit function

Sampling error—results because the auditor has sampled only a portion of the population

Tolerable misstatement—the materiality allocated to any given account balance; used in audit planning

REVIEW QUESTIONS

9-1 (Objective 9-1) Chapter 8 introduced the eight parts of the planning phase of an audit. Which part is the evaluation of materiality and risk?

9-2 (Objective 9-1) Define the meaning of the term *materiality* as it is used in accounting and auditing. What is the relationship between materiality and the phrase *obtain reasonable assurance* used in the auditor's report?

9-3 (Objectives 9-1, 9-2) Explain why materiality is important but difficult to apply in practice.

9-4 (Objective 9-2) What is meant by setting a preliminary judgment about materiality? Identify the most important factors affecting the preliminary judgment.

9-5 (Objective 9-2) What is meant by using bases for setting a preliminary judgment about materiality? How would those bases differ for the audit of a manufacturing company and a government unit such as a school district?

9-6 (Objective 9-2) Assume that Rosanne Madden, CPA, is using 5% of net income before taxes, current assets, or current liabilities as her major guidelines for evaluating materiality. What qualitative factors should she also consider in deciding whether misstatements may be material?

9-7 (Objectives 9-2, 9-3) Distinguish between the terms *tolerable misstatement* and *preliminary judgment about materiality*. How are they related to each other?

9-8 (Objective 9-3) Assume a company with the following balance sheet accounts:

Account	Amount
Cash	$10,000
Fixed assets	60,000
	$70,000
Long-term loans	$30,000
M. Johnson, proprietor	40,000
	$70,000

You are concerned only about overstatements of owner's equity. Set tolerable misstatement for the three relevant accounts such that the preliminary judgment about materiality does not exceed $5,000. Justify your answer.

9-9 (Objective 9-4) Explain what is meant by making an estimate of the total misstatement in a segment and in the overall financial statements. Why is it important to make these estimates? What is done with them?

9-10 (Objective 9-2) How would the conduct of an audit of a medium-sized company be affected by the company's being a small part of a large conglomerate as compared with it being a separate entity?

9-11 (Objective 9-6) Define the audit risk model and explain each term in the model.

9-12 (Objective 9-6) What is meant by planned detection risk? What is the effect on the amount of evidence the auditor must accumulate when planned detection risk is increased from medium to high?

9-13 (Objective 9-6) Explain the causes of an increased or decreased planned detection risk.

9-14 (Objectives 9-6, 9-8) Define what is meant by inherent risk. Identify four factors that make for *high* inherent risk in audits.

9-15 (Objective 9-8) Explain why inherent risk is set for segments rather than for the overall audit. What is the effect on the amount of evidence the auditor must accumulate when inherent risk is increased from medium to high for a segment? Compare your answer with the one for question 9-12.

9-16 (Objective 9-8) Explain the effect of extensive misstatements found in the prior year's audit on inherent risk, planned detection risk, and planned audit evidence.

9-17 (Objectives 9-6, 9-7) Explain what is meant by the term *acceptable audit risk*. What is its relevance to evidence accumulation?

9-18 (Objective 9-7) Explain the relationship between acceptable audit risk and the legal liability of auditors.

9-19 (Objective 9-7) State the three categories of factors that affect acceptable audit risk and list the factors that the auditor can use to indicate the degree to which each category exists.

9-20 (Objective 9-9) Auditors have not been successful in measuring the components of the audit risk model. How is it possible to use the model in a meaningful way without a precise way of measuring the risk?

9-21 (Objective 9-10) Explain the circumstances when the auditor should revise the components of the audit risk model and the effect of the revisions on planned detection risk and planned evidence.

MULTIPLE CHOICE QUESTIONS FROM CPA EXAMINATIONS

9-22 (Objectives 9-1, 9-2) The following questions deal with materiality. Choose the best response.

    a. Which one of the following statements is correct concerning the concept of materiality?
        (1) Materiality is determined by reference to guidelines established by the AICPA.
        (2) Materiality depends only on the dollar amount of an item relative to other items in the financial statements.
        (3) Materiality depends on the nature of an item rather than the dollar amount.
        (4) Materiality is a matter of professional judgment.

b. The concept of materiality will be least important to the CPA in determining the
   (1) scope of the audit of specific accounts.
   (2) specific transactions that should be reviewed.
   (3) effects of audit exceptions upon the opinion.
   (4) effects of the CPA's direct financial interest in a client upon the CPA's independence.

9-23 (Objectives 9-1, 9-6, 9-8) The following questions concern materiality and risk. Choose the best response.

a. Edison Corporation has a few large accounts receivable that total $1,400,000. Victor Corporation has a great number of small accounts receivable that also total $1,400,000. The importance of a misstatement in any one account is therefore greater for Edison than for Victor. This is an example of the auditor's concept of
   (1) materiality.
   (2) comparative analysis.
   (3) reasonable assurance.
   (4) relative risk.

b. Which of the following elements ultimately determines the specific auditing procedures that are necessary in the circumstances to afford a reasonable basis for an opinion?
   (1) Auditor judgment
   (2) Materiality
   (3) Inherent risk
   (4) Reasonable assurance

c. Which of the following *best* describes the element of inherent risk that underlies the application of generally accepted auditing standards, specifically the standards of field work and reporting?
   (1) Cash audit work may have to be carried out in a more conclusive manner than inventory audit work.
   (2) Intercompany transactions are usually subject to less detailed scrutiny than arm's-length transactions with outside parties.
   (3) Inventories may require more attention by the auditor on an engagement for a merchandising enterprise than on an engagement for a public utility.
   (4) The scope of the audit need *not* be expanded if misstatements that arouse suspicion of fraud are of relatively insignificant amounts.

9-24 (Objectives 9-1, 9-2, 9-5, 9-6, 9-8) The following questions deal with materiality and risk. Choose the best response.

a. Which of the following statements is *not* correct about materiality?
   (1) The concept of materiality recognizes that some matters are important for fair presentation of financial statements in conformity with GAAP, whereas other matters are *not* important.
   (2) An auditor considers materiality for planning purposes in terms of the largest aggregate level of misstatements that could be material to any one of the financial statements.
   (3) Materiality judgments are made in light of surrounding circumstances and necessarily involve both quantitative and qualitative judgments.
   (4) An auditor's consideration of materiality is influenced by the auditor's perception of the needs of a reasonable person who will rely on the financial statements.

b. Inherent risk and control risk differ from planned detection risk in that they
   (1) arise from the misapplication of auditing procedures.
   (2) may be assessed in either quantitative or nonquantitative terms.
   (3) exist independently of the financial statement audit.
   (4) can be changed at the auditor's discretion.

c. In considering materiality for planning purposes, an auditor believes that misstatements aggregating $10,000 would have a material effect on an entity's income statement, but that misstatements would have to aggregate $20,000 to materially affect the balance sheet. Ordinarily, it would be appropriate to design auditing procedures that would be expected to detect misstatements that aggregate
   (1) $10,000
   (2) $15,000
   (3) $20,000
   (4) $30,000

DISCUSSION QUESTIONS AND PROBLEMS

9-25 (Objectives 9-2, 9-3, 9-4) You are evaluating audit results for current assets in the audit of Quicky Plumbing Co. You set the preliminary judgment about materiality for current assets at $12,500 for overstatements and at $20,000 for understatements. The preliminary and actual estimates are shown below.

	Tolerable Misstatement		Estimate of Total Misstatement	
Account	Overstatements	Understatements	Overstatements	Understatements
Cash	$ 2,000	$ 3,000	$ 2,000	$ 0
Accounts receivable	12,000	18,000	4,000	19,000
Inventory	8,000	14,000	3,000	10,000
Prepaid expenses	3,000	5,000	2,000	1,000
Total	$25,000	$40,000	$11,000	$30,000

Required

a. Justify a lower preliminary judgment about materiality for overstatements than understatements in this situation.

b. Explain why the totals of the tolerable misstatements exceed the preliminary judgments about materiality for both understatements and overstatements.

c. Explain how it is possible that three of the estimates of total misstatement have both an overstatement and an understatement.

d. Assume that you are not concerned whether the estimate of misstatement exceeds tolerable misstatement for individual accounts if the total estimate is less than the preliminary judgment.
   (1) Given the audit results, should you be more concerned about the existence of material overstatements or understatements at this point in the audit of Quicky Plumbing Co.?
   (2) Which account or accounts would you be most concerned about in (1)? Explain.

e. Assume that the estimate of total overstatement amount for each account is less than tolerable misstatement, but that the total overstatement estimate exceeds the preliminary judgment of materiality.
   (1) Explain why this would occur.
   (2) Explain what the auditor should do.

9-26 (Objectives 9-2, 9-3, 9-4) On pages 259–260 are statements of earnings and financial position for Wexler Industries.

Required

a. Use professional judgment in deciding on the preliminary judgment about materiality for earnings, current assets, current liabilities, and total assets. Your conclusions should be stated in terms of percents and dollars.

b. Assume that you define materiality for this audit as a combined misstatement of earnings from continuing operations before income taxes of 5%. Also assume that you believe there is an equal likelihood of a misstatement of every account in the financial statements, and each misstatement is likely to result in an overstatement of earnings. Allocate materiality to these financial statements as you consider appropriate.

c. As discussed in part b, net earnings from continuing operations *before* income taxes was used as a base for calculating materiality for the Wexler Industries audit. Discuss why most auditors use *before*-tax net earnings instead of *after*-tax net earnings when calculating materiality based on the income statement.

d. Now, assume that you have decided to allocate 75% of your preliminary judgment to accounts receivable, inventories, and accounts payable because you believe all other accounts have a low inherent and control risk. How does this affect evidence accumulation on the audit?

e. Assume that you complete the audit and conclude that your preliminary judgment about materiality for current assets, current liabilities, and total assets has been met. The actual estimate of misstatements in *earnings* exceeds your preliminary judgment. What should you do?

Consolidated Statements of Earnings
Wexler Industries (in Thousands)

	For the 53 Weeks Ended March 30, 2005	For the 52 Weeks Ended March 31, 2004	April 1, 2003
Revenue			
Net sales	$8,351,149	$6,601,255	$5,959,587
Other income	59,675	43,186	52,418
	8,410,824	6,644,441	6,012,005
Costs and expenses			
Cost of sales	5,197,375	4,005,548	3,675,369
Marketing, general, and administrative expenses	2,590,080	2,119,590	1,828,169
Provision for loss on restructured operations	64,100	—	—
Interest expense	141,662	46,737	38,546
	7,993,217	6,171,875	5,542,084
Earnings from continuing operations before income taxes	417,607	472,566	469,921
Income taxes	(196,700)	(217,200)	(214,100)
Earnings from continuing operations	220,907	255,366	255,821
Provision for loss on discontinued operations, net of income taxes	(20,700)	—	—
Net earnings	$ 200,207	$ 255,366	$ 255,821

Consolidated Statements of Financial Position
Wexler Industries (in Thousands)

Assets	March 30, 2005	March 31, 2004
Current assets		
Cash	$ 39,683	$ 37,566
Temporary investments, including time deposits of $65,361 in 2005 and $181,589 in 2004 (at cost, which approximates market)	123,421	271,639
Receivables, less allowances of $16,808 in 2005 and $17,616 in 2004	899,752	759,001
Inventories		
Finished product	680,974	550,407
Raw materials and supplies	443,175	353,795
	1,124,149	904,202
Deferred income tax benefits	9,633	10,468
Prepaid expenses	57,468	35,911
Current assets	2,254,106	2,018,787
Land, buildings, and equipment, at cost, less accumulated depreciation	1,393,902	1,004,455
Investments in affiliated companies and sundry assets	112,938	83,455
Goodwill and other intangible assets	99,791	23,145
Total	$3,860,737	$3,129,842

Liabilities and Stockholders' Equity	March 30, 2005	March 31, 2004
Current liabilities		
Notes payable	$ 280,238	$ 113,411
Current portion of long-term debt	64,594	12,336
Accounts and drafts payable	359,511	380,395
Accrued salaries, wages, and vacations	112,200	63,557
Accrued income taxes	76,479	89,151
Other accrued liabilities	321,871	269,672
Current liabilities	**1,214,893**	**928,522**
Long-term debt	**730,987**	**390,687**
Other noncurrent liabilities	**146,687**	**80,586**
Deferred income taxes	**142,344**	**119,715**
Stockholders' equity		
Common stock issued, 51,017,755 shares in		
2005 and 50,992,410 in 2004	51,018	50,992
Additional paid-in capital	149,177	148,584
Cumulative foreign currency translation adjustment	(76,572)	—
Retained earnings	1,554,170	1,462,723
Common stock held in treasury, at cost,		
1,566,598 shares	(51,967)	(51,967)
Stockholders' equity	**1,625,826**	**1,610,332**
Total	**$3,860,737**	**$3,129,842**

9-27 (Objectives 9-2, 9-3, 9-4, 9-6, 9-7, 9-8, 9-10) The following are concepts discussed in this chapter:

1. Preliminary judgment about materiality
2. Estimate of the combined misstatement
3. Acceptable audit risk
4. Tolerable misstatement
5. Inherent risk
6. Risk of fraud
7. Estimated total misstatement in a segment
8. Control risk
9. Planned detection risk

Required
a. Identify which items are *audit planning decisions* requiring professional judgment.
b. Identify which items are *audit conclusions* resulting from application of audit procedures and requiring professional judgment.
c. Under what circumstances is it acceptable to change those items in part a after the audit is started? Which items can be changed after the audit is 95% completed?

9-28 (Objectives 9-6, 9-7) Describe what is meant by acceptable audit risk. Explain why each of the following statements is true:

a. A CPA firm should attempt to achieve the same audit risk for all audit clients when circumstances are similar.
b. A CPA firm should decrease acceptable audit risk for audit clients when external users rely heavily on the statements.
c. A CPA firm should decrease acceptable audit risk for audit clients when there is a reasonably high likelihood of a client's filing bankruptcy.
d. Different CPA firms should attempt to achieve reasonably similar audit risks for clients with similar circumstances.

9-29 (Objectives 9-5, 9-6, 9-7, 9-8) State whether each of the following statements is true or false, and give your reasons:

a. The audit evidence accumulated for every client should be approximately the same, regardless of the circumstances.
b. If acceptable audit risk is the same for two different clients, the audit evidence for the two clients should be approximately the same.
c. If acceptable audit risk, inherent risk, and control risk are approximately the same for two different clients, the audit evidence for the two clients should be approximately the same.

9-30 (Objectives 9-6, 9-7, 9-8) The following questions deal with the use of the audit risk model.

a. Assume that the auditor is doing a first-year municipal audit of Redwood City, Missouri, and concludes that the internal controls are not likely to be effective.
   (1) Explain why the auditor is likely to set both inherent and control risks at 100% for most segments.
   (2) Assuming (1), explain the relationship of acceptable audit risk to planned detection risk.
   (3) Assuming (1), explain the effect of planned detection risk on evidence accumulation compared with its effect if planned detection risk were larger.

b. Assume that the auditor is doing the third-year municipal audit of Redwood City, Missouri, and concludes that internal controls are effective and inherent risk is low.
   (1) Explain why the auditor is likely to set inherent and control risks for material segments at a higher level than, say, 40%, even when the two risks are low.
   (2) For the audit of fixed asset accounts, assume inherent and control risks of 50% each, and an acceptable audit risk of 5%. Calculate planned detection risk.
   (3) For (2), explain the effect of planned detection risk on evidence accumulation compared with its effect if planned detection risk were smaller.

c. Assume that the auditor is doing the fifth-year municipal audit of Redwood City, Missouri, and concludes that acceptable audit risk can be set high and inherent and control risks should be set low.
   (1) What circumstances would result in these conclusions?
   (2) For the audit of repairs and maintenance, inherent and control risk are set at 20% each. Acceptable audit risk is 5%. Calculate planned detection risk.
   (3) How much evidence should be accumulated in this situation?

9-31 (Objective 9-6) Following are six situations that involve the audit risk model as it is used for planning audit evidence requirements. Numbers are used only to help you understand the relationships among factors in the risk model.

			Situation			
Risk	1	2	3	4	5	6
Acceptable audit risk	5%	5%	5%	5%	1%	1%
Inherent risk	100%	40%	60%	20%	100%	40%
Control risk	100%	60%	40%	30%	100%	60%
Planned detection risk	—	—	—	—	—	—

a. Explain what each of the four risks means.

b. Calculate planned detection risk for each situation.

c. Using your knowledge of the relationships among the foregoing factors, state the effect on planned detection risk (increase or decrease) of changing each of the following factors while the other two remain constant:
   (1) A decrease in acceptable audit risk
   (2) A decrease in control risk
   (3) A decrease in inherent risk
   (4) An increase in control risk and a decrease in inherent risk of the same amount

d. Which situation requires the greatest amount of evidence and which requires the least?

9-32 (Objectives 9-6, 9-9) Following are six situations that involve the audit risk model as it is used for planning audit evidence requirements in the audit of inventory.

			Situation			
Risk	1	2	3	4	5	6
Acceptable audit risk	High	High	Low	Low	High	Medium
Inherent risk	Low	High	High	Low	Medium	Medium
Control risk	Low	Low	High	High	Medium	Medium
Planned detection risk	—	—	—	—	—	—
Planned evidence	—	—	—	—	—	—

a. Explain what low, medium, and high mean for each of the four risks and planned evidence.

b. Fill in the blanks for planned detection risk and planned evidence using the terms *low, medium,* or *high*.

c. Using your knowledge of the relationships among the foregoing factors, state the effect on planned evidence (increase or decrease) of changing each of the following five factors, while the other three remain constant:
   (1) An increase in acceptable audit risk
   (2) An increase in control risk
   (3) An increase in planned detection risk
   (4) An increase in inherent risk
   (5) An increase in inherent risk and a decrease in control risk of the same amount

9-33 (Objectives 9-6, 9-10) Using the audit risk model, state the effect on control risk, inherent risk, acceptable audit risk, and planned evidence for each of the following independent events. In each of the events a to j, circle one letter for each of the three independent variables and planned evidence: I = increase, D = decrease, N = no effect, and C = cannot determine from the information provided.

a. The client's management materially increased long-term contractual debt:
   Control risk   I D N C   Acceptable audit risk   I D N C
   Inherent risk   I D N C   Planned evidence   I D N C

b. The company changed from a privately held company to a publicly held company:
   Control risk   I D N C   Acceptable audit risk   I D N C
   Inherent risk   I D N C   Planned evidence   I D N C

c. The auditor decided to set assessed control risk below maximum (it was previously assessed at maximum):
   Control risk   I D N C   Acceptable audit risk   I D N C
   Inherent risk   I D N C   Planned evidence   I D N C

d. The account balance increased materially from the preceding year without apparent reason:
   Control risk   I D N C   Acceptable audit risk   I D N C
   Inherent risk   I D N C   Planned evidence   I D N C

e. You determined through the planning phase that working capital, debt-to-equity ratio, and other indicators of financial condition had improved during the past year:
   Control risk   I D N C   Acceptable audit risk   I D N C
   Inherent risk   I D N C   Planned evidence   I D N C

f. This is the second year of the engagement, and there were few misstatements found in the previous year's audit. The auditor also decided to increase reliance on internal control:
   Control risk   I D N C   Acceptable audit risk   I D N C
   Inherent risk   I D N C   Planned evidence   I D N C

g. The client began selling products online to customers through its Web page during the year under audit. The online customer ordering process is not integrated with the company's accounting system. Client sales staff print out customer order information and enter that data into the sales accounting system:
   Control risk   I D N C   Acceptable audit risk   I D N C
   Inherent risk   I D N C   Planned evidence   I D N C

h. In discussions with management, you conclude that management is planning to sell the business in the next few months. Because of the planned changes, several key accounting personnel quit several months ago for alternative employment. You also observe that the gross margin percent has significantly increased compared with that of the preceding year:
   Control risk   I D N C   Acceptable audit risk   I D N C
   Inherent risk   I D N C   Planned evidence   I D N C

i. There has been a change in several key management personnel. You believe that management is somewhat lacking in personal integrity compared with the previous management. You believe it is still appropriate to do the audit:
   Control risk   I D N C   Acceptable audit risk   I D N C
   Inherent risk   I D N C   Planned evidence   I D N C

j. In auditing inventory, you obtain an understanding of internal control and perform tests of controls. You find it significantly improved compared with that of the preceding year. You also observe that because of technology changes in the industry, the client's inventory may be somewhat obsolete:
   Control risk   I D N C   Acceptable audit risk   I D N C
   Inherent risk   I D N C   Planned evidence   I D N C

CASES

9-34 (Objectives 9-6, 9-7, 9-8) In the audit of Whirland Chemical Company, a large publicly traded company, you have been assigned the responsibility for obtaining background information for the audit. Your firm is auditing the client for the first time in the current year as a result of a dispute between Whirland and the previous auditor over the proper valuation of work-in-process inventory and the inclusion in sales of inventory that has not been delivered but has for practical purposes been completed and sold.

Whirland Chemical has been highly successful in its field in the past two decades, primarily because of many successful mergers negotiated by Bert Randolph, the president and chairman of the board. Even though the industry as a whole has suffered dramatic setbacks in recent years, Whirland continues to prosper, as evidenced by its constantly increasing earnings and growth. Only in the last 2 years have the company's profits turned downward. Randolph has a reputation for having been able to hire an aggressive group of young executives by the use of relatively low salaries combined with an unusually generous profit-sharing plan.

A major difficulty you face in the new audit is the lack of highly sophisticated accounting records for a company the size of Whirland. Randolph believes that profits come primarily from intelligent and aggressive action based on forecasts, not by relying on historical data that come after the fact. Most of the forecast data are generated by the sales and production department rather than by the accounting department. The personnel in the accounting department do seem competent but somewhat overworked and underpaid relative to other employees. One of the recent changes that will potentially improve the record keeping is the installation of sophisticated computer equipment. All the accounting records are not computerized yet, but such major areas as inventory and sales are included in the new system. Most of the computer time is being reserved for production and marketing because these areas are more essential to operations than the record-keeping function.

The first 6 months' financial statements for the current year include a profit of approximately only 10% less than the first 6 months of the preceding year, which is somewhat surprising, considering the reduced volume and the disposal of a segment of the business, Mercury Supply Co. The disposal of this segment was considered necessary because it had become increasingly unprofitable over the past 4 years. At the time of its acquisition from Roger Randolph, who is a brother of Bert Randolph, the company was highly profitable and it was considered a highly desirable purchase. The major customer of Mercury Supply Co. was the Mercury Corporation, which is owned by Roger Randolph. Gradually, the market for its products declined as the Mercury Corporation began diversifying and phasing out its primary products in favor of more profitable business. Even though Mercury Corporation is no longer buying from Mercury Supply Co., it compensates for it by buying a large volume of other products from Whirland Chemical.

The only major difficulty Whirland faces right now, according to financial analysts, is underfinancing. There is an excessive amount of current debt and long-term debt because of the depressed capital markets. Management is reluctant to obtain equity capital at this point because the increased number of shares would decrease the earnings per share even more than 10%. At the present time, Randolph is negotiating with several cash-rich companies in the hope of being able to merge with them as a means of overcoming the capital problems.

Required

a. List the major concerns you should have in the audit of Whirland Company and explain why they are potential problems.

b. State the appropriate approach to investigating the significance of each item you listed in a.

9-35 (Objectives 9-2, 9-3, 9-6, 9-7, 9-8) Pamela Albright is the manager of the audit of Stanton Enterprises, a public company that manufactures formed steel subassemblies for other manufacturers. Albright is planning the 2005 audit and is considering an appropriate amount for planning materiality, what tolerable misstatement should be allocated to the financial statement accounts, and the appropriate inherent risks. Summary financial statement information is shown in Figure 9-8 (p. 264). Additional relevant planning information is summarized next.

1. Stanton has been a client for 4 years, and Albright's firm has always had a good relationship with the company. Management and the accounting people have always been cooperative, honest, and positive about the audit and financial reporting. No material misstatements were found in the prior year's audit. Albright's firm has monitored the relationship carefully, because when the audit was obtained, Leonard Stanton, the CEO, had the reputation of being a "high-flyer" and had been through bankruptcy at an earlier time in his career.

2. Stanton runs the company in an autocratic way, primarily because of a somewhat controlling personality. He believes that it is his job to make all the tough decisions. He delegates responsibility to others but is not always willing to delegate a commensurate amount of authority.

FIGURE 9-8 Stanton Enterprises Summary Financial Statements

Balance Sheet

	Preliminary 12-31-05	Audited 12-31-04
Cash	$ 243,689	$ 133,981
Trade accounts receivable	3,544,009	2,224,921
Allowance for uncollectible accounts	(120,000)	(215,000)
Inventories	4,520,902	3,888,400
Prepaid expenses	29,500	24,700
Total current assets	8,218,100	6,057,002
Property, plant, and equipment:		
At cost	12,945,255	9,922,534
Less accumulated depreciation	(4,382,990)	(3,775,911)
Total prop., plant, and equipment	8,562,265	6,146,623
Goodwill	1,200,000	345,000
Total assets	$17,980,365	$12,548,625
Accounts payable	$ 2,141,552	$ 2,526,789
Bank loan payable	150,000	—
Accrued liabilities	723,600	598,020
Federal income taxes payable	1,200,000	1,759,000
Current portion of long-term debt	240,000	240,000
Total current liabilities	4,455,152	5,123,809
Long-term debt	960,000	1,200,000
Stockholders' equity:		
Common stock	1,250,000	1,000,000
Additional paid-in capital	2,469,921	1,333,801
Retained earnings	8,845,292	3,891,015
Total stockholders' equity	12,565,213	6,224,816
Total liabilities and stockholders' equity	$17,980,365	$12,548,625

Combined Statement of Income and Retained Earnings

	Preliminary 12-31-05	Audited 12-31-04
Sales	$43,994,931	$32,258,015
Cost of goods sold	24,197,212	19,032,229
Gross profit	19,797,719	13,225,786
Selling, general, and administrative expenses	10,592,221	8,900,432
Pension cost	1,117,845	865,030
Interest expense	83,376	104,220
Total operating expenses	11,793,442	9,869,682
Income before taxes	8,004,277	3,356,104
Income tax expense	1,800,000	1,141,000
Net income	6,204,277	2,215,104
Beginning retained earnings	3,891,015	2,675,911
	10,095,292	4,891,015
Dividends declared	(1,250,000)	1,000,000
Ending retained earnings	$ 8,845,292	$ 3,891,015

3. The industry in which Stanton participates has been in a favorable cycle the past few years and that trend is continuing in the current year. Industry profits are reasonably favorable, and there are no competitive or other apparent threats on the horizon.

4. Internal controls for Stanton are evaluated as reasonably effective for all cycles but not unusually strong. Although Stanton supports the idea of control, Albright has been disappointed that management has continually rejected Albright's recommendation to establish an internal audit function.

5. Stanton has a contract with its employees that if earnings before taxes, interest expense, and pension cost exceed $7.8 million for the year, an additional contribution must be made to the pension fund equal to 5% of the excess.

FIGURE 9-9 **Stanton Enterprises Evidence-Planning Worksheet to Decide Tests of Details of Balances for Accounts Receivable**

	Detail tie-in	Existence	Completeness	Accuracy	Classification	Cutoff	Realizable value	Rights	Presentation and disclosure
Acceptable audit risk									
Inherent risk									
Control risk—Sales									
Control risk—Cash receipts									
Control risk—Additional controls									
Substantive tests of transactions—Sales									
Substantive tests of transactions—Cash receipts									
Analytical procedures									
Planned detection risk for tests of details of balances									
Planned audit evidence for tests of details of balances									

Tolerable misstatement _____

Required

a. You are to play the role of Pamela Albright in the 12-31-05 audit of Stanton Enterprises. Make a preliminary judgment of materiality and allocate tolerable misstatement to financial statement accounts. Prepare an audit schedule showing your calculations. (Instructor option: prepare the schedule using an electronic spreadsheet.)

b. Make an acceptable audit risk decision for the current year as high, medium, or low, and support your answer.

c. Perform analytical procedures for Stanton Enterprises that will help you identify accounts that may require additional evidence in the current year's audit. Document the analytical procedures you perform and your conclusions. (Instructor option: use an electronic spreadsheet to calculate analytical procedures.)

d. The evidence planning worksheet to decide tests of details of balances for Stanton's accounts receivable is shown in Figure 9-9. Use the information in the case and your conclusions in parts a–c to complete the following rows of the evidence-planning worksheet: Acceptable audit risk, Inherent risk, and Analytical procedures. Also fill in tolerable misstatement for accounts receivable at the bottom of the worksheet. Make any assumptions you believe are reasonable and appropriate and document them.

INTEGRATED CASE APPLICATION—PINNACLE MANUFACTURING: PART II

9-36 (Objectives 9-7, 9-8)

In Part I of the case, you performed preliminary analytical procedures for Pinnacle (pp. 227–228). The purpose of Part II is to identify factors influencing risks and the relationship of risks to audit evidence.

During the planning phase of the audit, you met with Pinnacle's management team and performed other planning activities. You encounter the following situations that you believe may be relevant to the audit:

1. Your firm has an employee who reads and saves articles about issues that may affect key clients. You read an article in the file titled, "EPA Regulations Encouraging Solar-Powered Engines Postponed?" After reading the article, you realize that the regulations management is relying upon to increase sales of this division might not go into effect for at least ten years. A second article is titled, "Stick to Diesel Pinnacle!" The article claims that although Pinnacle has proven itself within the diesel engine industry, they lack the knowledge and people necessary to perform well in the solar-powered engine industry.

2. You ask management for a tour of the Solar-Electro facilities. While touring the warehouse, you notice a section of solar-powered engines that do not look like the ones advertised on Pinnacle's Web site. You ask the warehouse manager when those items were first manufactured. He responds by telling you, "I'm not sure. I've been here a year and they were here when I first arrived."

3. You also observe that new computerized manufacturing equipment has been installed at Solar-Electro. The machines have been stamped with the words, "Product of Welburn Manufacturing, Detroit, Michigan."

4. During a meeting with the facilities director, you learn that the board of directors has decided to raise a significant amount of debt to finance the construction of a new manufacturing plant for the Solar-Electro division. The company also plans to make a considerable investment in modifications to the property on which the plant will be built.

5. While standing in line at a vending machine, you see a Pinnacle vice president wearing a golf shirt with the words "Todd-Machinery." You are familiar with the company and noticed some of its repairmen working in the plant earlier. You tell the man you like the shirt and he responds by saying, "Thank you. My wife and I own the company, but we hire people to manage it."

6. After inquiry of the internal audit team, you realize there is significant turnover in the internal audit department. You conclude the turnover is only present at the higher-level positions.

7. While reviewing Pinnacle's long-term debt agreements, you identify several restrictive covenants. Two requirements are to keep the current ratio above 2.0 and debt-to-equity below 1.0 at all times.

8. While reading the footnotes of the previous year's financial statements, you note that one customer, Auto-Electro, accounts for nearly 15% of the company's accounts receivable balance. You investigate this receivable and learn it has been outstanding for several months.

9. The engagement partner from your CPA firm called today notifying you that Brian Sioux, an industry specialist and senior tax manager from the firm's Ontario office, will be coming on-site to Pinnacle's facilities to investigate an ongoing dispute between the Internal Revenue Service and Pinnacle.

10. A member of your CPA firm, who is currently on-site in Detroit at the Welburn division, calls you to see how everything is going while you are visiting Solar-Electro in Texas. During your conversation, he asks if you know anything about the recent intercompany loan from Welburn to Solar-Electro.

11. During discussions with the Pinnacle controller, you learn that Pinnacle employees did a significant amount of the construction work for a building addition. The controller stated that the work was carefully coordinated with the construction company responsible for the addition.

Required

a. Identify specific considerations from Parts I and II of the case that affect your assessments of engagement risk and acceptable audit risk. Use each of the three factors in the text to categorize your conclusions:

External users' reliance on financial statements

Likelihood of financial difficulties

Management integrity

b.   Assess acceptable audit risk as high, medium, or low considering the items you identified in requirement a. (A risky client will be assessed as a low acceptable audit risk.)

c.   Identify inherent risks for the audit of Pinnacle using the information from Parts I and II. For each inherent risk, identify the account or accounts that may be affected.

Inherent Risk	Account or Accounts Affected

INTERNET PROBLEM 9-1:
MATERIALITY AND TOLERABLE MISSTATEMENT

Reference the CW site. This problem requires students to apply specific materiality and tolerable misstatement guidelines to actual financial statements obtained from the Internet.

SECTION 404 AUDITS OF INTERNAL CONTROL AND CONTROL RISK

GOOD INTERNAL CONTROL PREVENTS MORE DEFALCATIONS THAN GOOD AUDITORS FIND

Shortly after its tenth consecutive audit of the Foundation for Youth Bible Studies (FYBS), Able & Co. was informed that FYBS's head accountant was found to have embezzled $2 million during the past four years. FYBS wanted to know how this could have occurred without Able discovering it. Able responded that he would have to know how the fraud was carried out to answer the question.

The FYBS's camp facility was in a different state than its home office. Funds were collected from campers and sent in the form of a cashier's check to the head accountant, who was supposed to forward the check to the home office cash receipts clerk. The head accountant recorded the revenue using the information on the cashier's check. No record of the source or amount of the cash receipts was maintained at the FYBS camp, which allowed her to occasionally pocket some of the checks. Obviously, she did not record the revenue for these defalcations.

When the auditors gained an understanding of internal control at FYBS, they regularly interviewed employees about how the system functioned. During the course of those discussions, they were never told about the procedure for transmitting funds from the camp. It was not clear that anyone in the home office, other than the embezzler, was aware of it. Fortunately, Able & Co.'s audit report contained a qualification that they could verify only those revenues that were actually recorded. Given the qualification in the audit report and the conduct of their audit, Able & Co. was not held responsible for the loss. They helped FYBS implement new controls to prevent a similar occurrence, but nevertheless, FYBS changed auditors.

LEARNING OBJECTIVES

After studying this chapter, you should be able to

10-1 Describe the three primary objectives of effective internal control.

10-2 Contrast management's responsibilities for maintaining and reporting on internal controls with the auditor's responsibilities for understanding, testing, and reporting on internal controls.

10-3 Explain the five components of the COSO internal control framework.

10-4 Obtain and document an understanding of internal control.

10-5 Assess control risk by linking key controls, significant deficiencies, and material weaknesses to transaction-related audit objectives.

10-6 Describe the process of designing and performing tests of controls.

10-7 Understand Section 404 requirements for auditor reporting on internal control.

10-8 Describe the differences in evaluating, reporting, and testing internal control for nonpublic companies.

The opening vignette involving FYBS demonstrates how deficiencies in internal control can result in material misstatements in financial statements. Financial reporting problems at companies such as Enron and WorldCom also exposed serious deficiencies in internal control. To address these concerns, Section 404 of the Sarbanes–Oxley Act (Section 404) requires auditors of public companies to assess and report on the effectiveness of internal control over financial reporting, in addition to their report on the audit of the financial statements.

This is the third chapter dealing with planning the audit. It shows how effective internal controls can reduce planned audit evidence in the audit of financial statements. To support the assessment of the control risk component of the audit risk model, auditors must obtain an understanding of internal control and gather related evidence to support that assessment. The chart in the margin shows where these tasks fit into planning the audit. Most of the chapter describes how public company auditors integrate evidence to provide a basis for their report on the effectiveness of internal control over financial reporting with the assessment of control risk in the financial statement audit. The end of the chapter identifies and discusses the differences in assessing control risk and testing controls for nonpublic companies compared to public companies. By the end of the chapter, you will see that there are more similarities than differences in the approach.

INTERNAL CONTROL OBJECTIVES

OBJECTIVE 10-1

Describe the three primary objectives of effective internal control.

Accept client and perform initial planning

Understand the client's business and industry

Assess client business risk

Perform preliminary analytical procedures

Set materiality and assess acceptable audit risk and inherent risk

Understand internal control and assess control risk

Gather information to assess fraud risks

Develop overall audit plan and audit program

A system of internal control consists of policies and procedures designed to provide management with reasonable assurance that the company achieves its objectives and goals. These policies and procedures are often called controls, and collectively, they comprise the entity's **internal control**. Management typically has three broad objectives in designing an effective internal control system:

1. *Reliability of financial reporting.* As we discussed in Chapter 6, management is responsible for preparing financial statements for investors, creditors, and other users. Management has both a legal and professional responsibility to be sure that the information is fairly presented in accordance with reporting requirements such as GAAP. The objective of effective internal control over financial reporting is to fulfill these financial reporting responsibilities.

2. *Efficiency and effectiveness of operations.* Controls within an organization are meant to encourage efficient and effective use of its resources to optimize the company's goals. An important objective of these controls is accurate financial and nonfinancial information about the entity's operations for decision making.

3. *Compliance with laws and regulations.* Section 404 requires all public companies to issue a report about the operating effectiveness of internal control over financial reporting. In addition to the legal provisions of Section 404, public, nonpublic, and not-for-profit organizations are required to follow many laws and regulations. Some relate to accounting only indirectly, such as environmental protection and civil rights laws. Others are closely related to accounting, such as income tax regulations and fraud.

Management designs systems of internal control to accomplish all three objectives. The auditor's focus in both the audit of financial statements and the audit of internal controls is on those controls related to the reliability of financial reporting plus those controls related to operations and to compliance with laws and regulations objectives that could materially affect financial reporting.

MANAGEMENT AND AUDITOR RESPONSIBILITIES RELATED TO INTERNAL CONTROL

Responsibilities related to internal controls differ between management and the auditor. Management has responsibility for establishing and maintaining the entity's internal controls. Management is also required by Section 404 to publicly report on the operating effectiveness of those controls. In contrast, the auditor's responsibilities include understanding and testing internal control over financial reporting. The auditor is also required by Section 404 to issue an audit report on management's assessment of its internal controls, including the auditor's opinion on the operating effectiveness of those controls.

Management, not the auditor, must establish and maintain the entity's internal controls. This concept is consistent with the requirement that management, not the auditor, is responsible for the preparation of financial statements in accordance with GAAP. Two key concepts underlie management's design and implementation of internal control—reasonable assurance and inherent limitations.

Management's Responsibilities for Establishing Internal Control

Reasonable Assurance A company should develop internal controls that provide *reasonable, but not absolute, assurance* that the financial statements are fairly stated. Internal controls are developed by management after considering both the costs and benefits of the controls. As defined by the PCAOB, reasonable assurance allows for only a remote likelihood that material misstatements will not be prevented or detected on a timely basis by internal control.

Inherent Limitations Internal controls can never be regarded as completely effective, regardless of the care followed in their design and implementation. Even if systems personnel can design an ideal system, its effectiveness will depend on the competency and dependability of the people using it. Assume, for example, that a carefully developed procedure for counting inventory requires two employees to count independently. If neither of the employees understands the instructions or if both are careless in doing the counts, the inventory count is likely to be wrong. Even if the count is correct, management might override the procedure and instruct an employee to increase the count of quantities to improve reported earnings. Similarly, the employees might decide to overstate the counts to intentionally cover up a theft of inventory by one or both of them. An act of two or more employees to steal assets or misstate records is called **collusion**.

Prior to the issuance of the Sarbanes–Oxley Act, some public companies voluntarily issued reports on internal control, and such reports were required by regulators in certain industries, such as banking. Section 404 requires management of all public companies to issue an internal control report that includes the following:

Management's Section 404 Reporting Responsibilities

- A statement that management is responsible for establishing and maintaining an adequate internal control structure and procedures for financial reporting
- An assessment of the effectiveness of the internal control structure and procedures for financial reporting as of the end of the company's fiscal year

KPMG's 404 Institute

In addition to a statement that management is responsible for establishing and maintaining internal control, management's internal control report must identify the framework used to evaluate the effectiveness of internal control. The internal control framework for most U.S. companies is the Committee of Sponsoring Organizations of the Treadway Commission (COSO) *Internal Control—Integrated Framework*, issued in 1992.

Management's assessment of internal control over financial reporting consists of two key components. First, management must evaluate the *design* of internal control over financial reporting. Second, management must test the *operating effectiveness* of those controls.

Design of Internal Control When evaluating the design of internal control over financial reporting, management evaluates whether the control is designed to prevent or detect material misstatements in the financial statements. Management's focus is on controls over all relevant assertions related to all significant accounts and disclosures in the financial statements. As part of the assessment, management evaluates information about how significant transactions are initiated, authorized, recorded, processed, and reported to identify points in the flow of transactions where material misstatements due to error or fraud could occur. Management must determine whether existing controls will be effective if they operate as designed and whether all the necessary controls are in place.

Operating Effectiveness of Controls In addition to evaluating the design of internal control over financial reporting, management must test the operating effectiveness of controls. The testing objective is to determine whether the control is operating as designed and whether the person performing the control possesses the necessary authority and qualifications to perform the control effectively. Management's test results, which must also be documented, form the basis for management's assertion at the end of the fiscal year about the controls' operating effectiveness. Management must disclose any material weakness in internal control. Even if only one material weakness is present, management is unable to conclude that the company's internal control over financial reporting is effective.

Management's tests of operating effectiveness include a mix of inquiries of personnel, inspection of relevant documentation, observation of the company's operations, and reperformance of the application of the controls. Management conducts tests of controls over a period of time to be able to adequately determine whether the controls are operating effectively. For example, the timing of tests of controls performed daily differs from the timing of tests of controls performed monthly or quarterly. Testing in earlier periods also allows management time to implement corrective actions, if necessary, before auditors test the controls.

The SEC requires management to include its report on internal control in its annual Form 10-K report filed with the SEC. Figure 10-1 includes an example of management's report on internal control that complies with Section 404 requirements and related SEC rules.

Auditor Responsibilities for Understanding Internal Control

Because it is sufficiently important to the audit process, knowledge about a client's internal control merits a separate generally accepted auditing standard. Recall that the second GAAS field work standard states "A sufficient understanding of internal control is to be obtained to plan the audit and to determine the nature, timing, and extent of tests to be performed." The auditor obtains the understanding of internal control to assess control risk in every audit. Auditors are primarily concerned about controls related to the reliability of financial reporting and controls over classes of transactions.

FIGURE 10-1	Example Section 404 Management Report on Internal Control Over Financial Reporting

The management of Marble Corporation is responsible for establishing and maintaining adequate internal control over financial reporting. Marble's internal control system was designed to provide reasonable assurance to the company's management and board of directors regarding the preparation and fair presentation of published financial statements.

Marble management assessed the effectiveness of the company's internal control over financial reporting as of December 31, 2005. In making this assessment, it used the criteria set forth by the Committee of Sponsoring Organizations of the Treadway Commission (COSO) in *Internal Control—Integrated Framework*. Based on our assessment, we believe that, as of December 31, 2005, the company's internal control over financial reporting is effective based on those criteria.

Marble's independent auditors have issued an audit report on our assessment of the company's internal control over financial reporting. This report appears on the following page.

February 15, 2006

Fred Narsky, President   Karen Wilson, Chief Financial Officer

Controls Related to the Reliability of Financial Reporting To comply with the second standard of field work, the auditor may focus primarily on controls that relate to the first of management's internal control concerns: reliability of financial reporting. This area directly affects the financial statements and their related assertions and, therefore, affects the auditor's ability to determine that the financial statements are fairly stated. The financial statements are not likely to correctly reflect GAAP if these controls are inadequate. Unlike the client, the auditor is less concerned with controls that affect the efficiency and effectiveness of company operations, because such controls may not influence the fair presentation of financial statements.

As stated in Chapter 6, auditors have significant responsibility for the discovery of material fraudulent financial reporting and misappropriation of assets (fraud) and direct-effect illegal acts. Auditors are therefore also concerned with a client's internal control over the safeguarding of assets and compliance with laws and regulations if they affect the fairness of the financial statements. Internal controls, if properly designed and implemented, can be effective in preventing and detecting fraud.

Although auditors should concentrate on controls that ensure the reliability of data for external reporting purposes, they should not ignore controls affecting internal management information, such as budgets and internal performance reports. These types of information are often important sources of evidence in helping the auditor decide whether the financial statements are fairly presented. If the controls over these internal reports are considered inadequate, the value of the reports as evidence diminishes.

Controls over Classes of Transactions An auditor's primary emphasis is the internal control over classes of transactions rather than account balances, because the accuracy of accounting system outputs (account balances) depends heavily on the accuracy of inputs and processing (transactions). For example, if products sold, units shipped, or unit selling prices are wrong in billing customers for sales, both sales and accounts receivable will be misstated. On the other hand, if controls are adequate to ensure correct billings, cash receipts, sales returns and allowances, and charge-offs, the ending balance in accounts receivable is likely to be correct.

When gaining an understanding of internal control and assessing control risk, auditors are primarily concerned with the transaction-related audit objectives discussed in Chapter 6. These objectives were discussed in detail on pages 146–147. Table 10-1 illustrates the development of transaction-related audit objectives for sales transactions.

While gaining an understanding of internal control and assessing control risk, the auditor does not, however, ignore internal control over account balances. For example, transaction-related audit objectives typically have no effect on three balance-related audit objectives: realizable value, rights and obligations, and presentation and disclosure. The

TABLE 10-1	Sales Transaction-Related Audit Objectives
Transaction-Related Audit Objective—General Form	**Sales Transaction-Related Audit Objectives**
Recorded transactions exist (existence).	Recorded sales are for shipments made to existing customers.
Existing transactions are recorded (completeness).	Existing sales transactions are recorded.
Recorded transactions are stated at the correct amounts (accuracy).	Recorded sales are for the amount of goods shipped and are correctly billed and recorded.
Transactions are properly classified (classification).	Sales transactions are properly classified.
Transactions are recorded on the correct dates (timing).	Sales are recorded on the correct dates.
Recorded transactions are properly included in the master files and are correctly summarized (posting and summarization).	Sales transactions are properly included in the master files and are correctly summarized.

Public companies and their auditing firms are working diligently to comply with the Section 404 management and auditor reporting requirements. The magnitude of work necessary to comply with these new requirements is tremendous. By November 2004, it was estimated that the Big Four CPA firms had collectively spent approximately 12 million hours on activities related to Section 404 compliance. And, public companies had spent about 10 hours for each hour by external auditors. As a result, about 132 million hours have been incurred in preparation for the Section 404 requirements. Conservative estimates suggest this represents costs ranging between $10 billion and $13 billion.

A July 2004 survey by the Financial Executives International (FEI) found that companies expected to pay additional audit fees for the auditor report required by Section 404 averaging $823,200 or about 53% of the total annual financial statement audit fee. Companies with annual revenues over $5 billion expect to pay audit fees of over $2,000,000 for the auditor's report on internal control.

Sources: Adapted from 1. Ira Solomon and Mark Peecher, "SOX 404—A Billion Here, A Billion There. . ." *The Wall Street Journal,* November 9, 2004, page B2, and 2. Financial Executives International, *FEI Special Survey on Sarbanes–Oxley Section 404 Implementation Executive Summary,* July 2004, www.fei.org.

auditor is likely to evaluate separately whether management has implemented internal controls for each of these three balance-related audit objectives.

Because of the inherent limitations of internal controls and because auditors cannot obtain more than reasonable assurance of their effectiveness, the level of control risk is almost always greater than zero. Therefore, even with the most effectively designed internal controls, the auditor must obtain audit evidence beyond testing the controls for every material financial statement account.

Auditor Responsibilities for Testing Internal Control

Section 404 requires that the auditor attest to and issue a report on management's assessment of internal control over financial reporting. To express an opinion on internal controls, the auditor obtains an understanding of and performs tests of controls related to *all* significant account balances, classes of transactions, and disclosures and related assertions in the financial statements. We will discuss tests of controls later in the chapter and in considerable detail in several other chapters throughout the text.

Auditor Responsibilities for Reporting on Internal Control

The required audit report on internal control over financial reporting under the Sarbanes–Oxley Act must include the auditor's opinion as to whether management's assessment of the design and operating effectiveness of internal control over financial reporting is fairly stated in all material respects. This involves both evaluating management's assessment process and arriving at the auditor's independent assessment of the design and operating effectiveness of internal control. Auditor reporting on internal control is discussed later in the chapter.

COSO COMPONENTS OF INTERNAL CONTROL

OBJECTIVE 10-3

Explain the five components of the COSO internal control framework.

COSO's *Internal Control—Integrated Framework,* the most widely accepted internal control framework in the United States, describes internal control as consisting of five components that management designs and implements to provide reasonable assurance that its control objectives will be met. Each component contains many controls, but auditors concentrate on those designed to prevent or detect material misstatements in the financial statements. The COSO internal control components include the following:

1. Control environment
2. Risk assessment
3. Control activities
4. Information and communication
5. Monitoring

As illustrated in Figure 10-2, the control environment serves as the umbrella for the other four components. Without an effective control environment, the other four are unlikely to result in effective internal control, regardless of their quality.

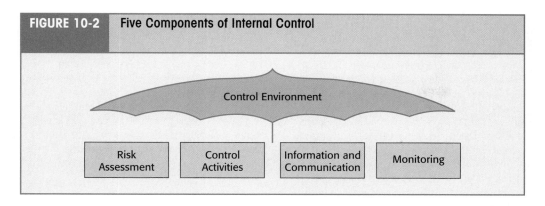

FIGURE 10-2 Five Components of Internal Control

Control Environment

| Risk Assessment | Control Activities | Information and Communication | Monitoring |

The essence of an effectively controlled organization lies in the attitude of its management. If top management believes that control is important, others in the organization will sense that and respond by conscientiously observing the controls established. If members of the organization believe that control is not an important concern to top management, it is almost certain that management's control objectives will not be effectively achieved.

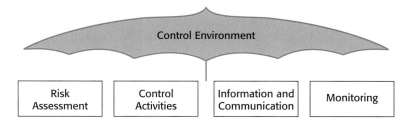

Control Environment

| Risk Assessment | Control Activities | Information and Communication | Monitoring |

The **control environment** consists of the actions, policies, and procedures that reflect the overall attitudes of top management, directors, and owners of an entity about internal control and its importance to the entity. To understand and assess the control environment, auditors should consider the most important control subcomponents.

Integrity and Ethical Values Integrity and ethical values are the product of the entity's ethical and behavioral standards, as well as how they are communicated and reinforced in practice. They include management's actions to remove or reduce incentives and temptations that might prompt personnel to engage in dishonest, illegal, or unethical acts. They also include the communication of entity values and behavioral standards to personnel through policy statements, codes of conduct, and by example.

Commitment to Competence Competence is the knowledge and skills necessary to accomplish tasks that define an individual's job. Commitment to competence includes management's consideration of the competence levels for specific jobs and how those levels translate into requisite skills and knowledge.

Board of Directors or Audit Committee Participation An effective board of directors is independent of management, and its members stay involved in and scrutinize management's activities. Although the board delegates responsibility for internal control to management, it is charged with providing regular independent assessments of management-established internal control. In addition, an active and objective board can often effectively reduce the likelihood that management overrides existing controls. To assist the board in its oversight, the board creates an audit committee that is charged with oversight responsibility for the financial reporting process. The audit committee is also responsible for maintaining ongoing communication with both external and internal auditors, including the approval of audit and nonaudit services performed by auditors for public companies. This allows the auditors and directors to discuss matters that might relate to such things as the integrity or actions of management.

Audit Committee Requirements

The audit committee's independence from management and knowledge of financial reporting issues are important determinants of their ability to effectively evaluate internal controls and financial statements prepared by management. The major exchanges (NYSE, AMEX, and NASDAQ) require that listed companies have an audit committee composed entirely of independent directors who are financially literate. PCAOB Standard 2 requires the auditor to evaluate the effectiveness of the audit committee's oversight of the company's external financial reporting and internal control over financial reporting. Many privately held companies also create effective audit committees, recognizing the importance of effective financial reporting and internal control oversight.

Management's Philosophy and Operating Style Management, through its activities, provides clear signals to employees about the importance of internal control. For example, does management take significant risks, or is it risk averse? Are sales and earnings targets unrealistic, and are employees encouraged to take aggressive actions to meet those targets? Can management be described as "fat and bureaucratic," "lean and mean," dominated by one or a few individuals, or is it "just right"? Understanding these and similar aspects of management's philosophy and operating style gives the auditor a sense of management's attitude about internal control.

Organizational Structure The entity's organizational structure defines the existing lines of responsibility and authority. By understanding the client's organizational structure, the auditor can learn the management and functional elements of the business and perceive how controls are implemented.

Assignment of Authority and Responsibility In addition to the informal aspects of communication made by management and the board as part of day-to-day operations, formal methods of communication about authority and responsibility and similar control-related matters are equally important. These might include such methods as memoranda from top management about the importance of control and control-related matters, formal organizational and operating plans, and employee job descriptions and related policies.

Human Resource Policies and Practices The most important aspect of internal control is personnel. If employees are competent and trustworthy, other controls can be absent, and reliable financial statements will still result. Incompetent or dishonest people can reduce the system to a shambles—even if there are numerous controls in place. Honest, efficient people are able to perform at a high level even when there are few other controls to support them. However, even competent and trustworthy people can have certain innate shortcomings. For example, they can become bored or dissatisfied, personal problems can disrupt their performance, or their goals may change.

Because of the importance of competent, trustworthy personnel in providing effective control, the methods by which persons are hired, evaluated, trained, promoted, and compensated are an important part of internal control.

After obtaining information about each of the subcomponents of the control environment, the auditor uses this understanding as a basis for assessing management's and the directors' attitudes and awareness about the importance of control. For example, the auditor might determine the nature of a client's budgeting system as a part of understanding the design of the control environment. The operation of the budgeting system might then be evaluated in part by inquiry of budgeting personnel to determine budgeting procedures and follow-up of differences between budget and actual. The auditor might also examine client schedules, comparing actual results to budgeted amounts.

Risk assessment for financial reporting is *management's* identification and analysis of risks relevant to the preparation of financial statements in conformity with GAAP. For example, if a company frequently sells products at a price below inventory cost because of rapid technology changes, it is essential for the company to incorporate adequate controls to overcome the risk of overstating inventory.

Risk Assessment

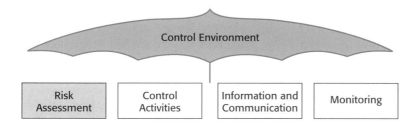

All entities, regardless of size, structure, nature, or industry, face a variety of risks from external and internal sources that must be managed. Because economic, industry, regulatory, and operating conditions constantly change, management is challenged with developing mechanisms to identify and deal with risks associated with change. Internal control under one set of conditions will not necessarily be effective under another.

Risk Advisory Services

Identifying and analyzing risk is an ongoing process and a critical component of effective internal control. Management must focus on risks at all levels of the organization and take necessary actions to manage them. An important first step is for management to identify factors that may increase risk. Failure to meet prior objectives, quality of personnel, geographic dispersion of company operations, significance and complexity of core business processes, introduction of new information technologies, and entrance of new competitors all represent examples of factors that may lead to increased risk. Once management identifies a risk, it estimates the significance of that risk, assesses the likelihood of the risk occurring, and develops specific actions that need to be taken to reduce the risk to

HELPING CLIENTS MANAGE RISK

Many CPAs assist clients in developing processes to identify and manage enterprisewide risks. The AICPA and the Canadian Institute of Chartered Accountants issued a report, *Managing Risk in the New Economy*, for CPAs who provide risk management services to their clients or employers. The report highlights how successful organizations take calculated risks to achieve objectives. They weigh opportunities against threats and act decisively. The traditional, negative definitions of risk—harm, loss, danger, and hazard—are only part of the story. The other and equally important part is opportunity.

Although each organization has its own unique approach to risk management, the report highlights a number of consistent steps that represent current best practices. Risk management steps include:

◆ Establishing the context
◆ Identifying risks
◆ Analyzing and assessing risks
◆ Designing strategies for managing risk
◆ Implementing and integrating risk management
◆ Measuring, monitoring, and reporting

These steps can be applied to an entire enterprise, to a part of the organization, or to a specific project. Although an enterprisewide program is the most effective, it is often desirable to initially focus on a few critical areas.

Source: Adapted from *Managing Risk in the New Economy*, American Institute of Certified Public Accountants and The Canadian Institute of Chartered Accountants, 2000.

an acceptable level. Of course, there is no cost-beneficial way to eliminate risk entirely. However, management must assess how much risk is prudently acceptable and strive to maintain risk within this level.

Management's risk assessment differs from but is closely related to the auditor's risk assessment discussed in Chapter 9. While management assesses risks as a part of designing and operating internal controls to minimize errors and fraud, auditors assess risks to decide the evidence needed in the audit. If management effectively assesses and responds to risks, the auditor will typically accumulate less evidence than when management fails to identify or respond to significant risks.

The auditor obtains knowledge about management's risk assessment process by determining how management identifies risks relevant to financial reporting, and how they evaluate their significance and likelihood of occurrence, and decide the actions needed to address the risks. Questionnaires and discussions with management are the most common ways for the auditor to obtain this understanding.

Control Activities

Control activities are the policies and procedures, in addition to those included in the other four components, that help ensure that necessary actions are taken to address risks in the achievement of the entity's objectives. There are potentially many such control activities in any entity, including both manual and automated controls. SAS 94 and COSO note that control activities generally relate to policies and procedures that pertain to (1) segregation of duties, (2) information processing, (3) physical controls, and (4) performance reviews. The development of control activities related to these types of policies and procedures generally falls into the following five types of specific control activities, which are discussed next:

1. Adequate separation of duties
2. Proper authorization of transactions and activities
3. Adequate documents and records
4. Physical control over assets and records
5. Independent checks on performance

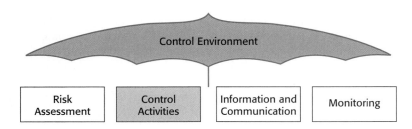

Adequate Separation of Duties Four general guidelines for adequate **separation of duties** to prevent both fraud and errors are of special significance to auditors.

Separation of the Custody of Assets from Accounting To protect a company against defalcation, a person who has temporary or permanent custody of an asset should not account for that asset. Allowing one person to perform both functions increases the risk of that person disposing of the asset for personal gain and adjusting the records to cover up the theft. If the cashier, for example, receives cash and is responsible for data entry for cash receipts and sales, that person could pocket the cash received and adjust the customer's account by failing to record a sale or by recording a fictitious credit to the account.

Separation of the Authorization of Transactions from the Custody of Related Assets If possible, it is desirable to prevent persons who authorize transactions from having control over the related asset, as this raises the possibility of defalcation. For example, the same person should not authorize the payment of a vendor's invoice and also sign the check in payment of the bill.

Separation of Operational Responsibility from Record-Keeping Responsibility To ensure unbiased information, record keeping is typically included in a separate department under the controller. For example, if a department or division prepares its own records and reports, it might bias the results to improve its reported performance.

Separation of IT Duties from User Departments As the level of complexity of IT systems increases, the segregation of authorization, record keeping, and custody often becomes blurred. For example, sales agents may enter customer orders online. The computer authorizes those sales based on its comparison of customer credit limits to the master file and posts all approved sales in the sales cycle journals. Therefore, the computer plays a significant role in the authorization and record keeping of sales transactions. To compensate for these potential overlaps of duties, it is important for companies to separate major IT-related functions from key user department functions. In this example, responsibility for designing and controlling accounting software programs that contain the sales authorization and posting controls should be under the authority of IT, whereas the ability to update information in the master file of customer credit limits should reside in the company's credit department outside the IT function.

Naturally, the extent of separation of duties depends heavily on the size of the organization. In many small companies, it is not practical to segregate the duties to the extent suggested. In these cases, audit evidence may require modification.

Proper Authorization of Transactions and Activities Every transaction must be properly authorized if controls are to be satisfactory. If any person in an organization could acquire or expend assets at will, complete chaos would result. Authorization can be either *general* or *specific*. Under **general authorization**, management establishes policies for the organization to follow, and subordinates are instructed to implement these general authorizations by approving all transactions within the limits set by the policy. General authorization decisions might include the issuance of fixed price lists for the sale of products, credit limits for customers, and fixed reorder points for making acquisitions.

Specific authorization applies to individual transactions. For certain transactions, management is often unwilling to establish a general policy of authorization. Instead, management prefers to make authorizations on a case-by-case basis. An example is the authorization of a sales transaction by the sales manager for a used-car company.

The distinction between authorization and approval also is important. Authorization is a policy decision for either a general class of transactions or specific transactions. Approval is the implementation of management's general authorization decisions. For example, assume that management sets a policy authorizing the ordering of inventory when less than a 3-week supply is on hand. That is a general authorization. When a department orders inventory, the clerk responsible for maintaining the perpetual record approves the order to indicate that the authorization policy has been met. In other cases, the computer performs the general approval of transactions. The comparison of quantities of inventory on hand to a master file of reorder points may be performed by the computer, and the computer

---

PHANTOM BOOKS

Senior executives at Livent Inc., the Toronto theater owner and producer of Broadway-style shows including *Show Boat, Ragtime,* and *Phantom of the Opera,* took their theatrics to a new level when they allegedly engaged in a pervasive fraud to materially distort their financial statements over an eight-year period. According to charges filed by the Securities and Exchange Commission, the former chairman and CEO and former president together coaxed several of their longtime company associates, including the CFO and IT manager, to participate in a multifaceted scheme to manipulate profits.

In addition to orchestrating vendor kickback schemes to siphon off millions of dollars and numerous customer side-agreements to falsify revenues, senior management manipulated the accounting records to shift costs of shows to fixed assets from expenses. Their techniques included alteration of computer programs to lower expenses without a trace in order to hide the fraud from Livent auditors. In addition, they created "phantom" accounting records showing the adjustments so senior management could track the fraudulent entries and know the company's true financial condition. Ultimately, their distortions were revealed, and the executives faced charges both in the United States and Canada. Livent filed for bankruptcy and was subsequently sold to a team headed by a former Walt Disney Company executive.

Sources: 1. Securities and Exchange Commission, *Litigation Release No. 16022,* Washington, DC, January 1999. 2. Canadian Broadcasting Company, "Livent Founders Charged with Fraud," *Arts Now,* Toronto, October 10, 2002.

CHAPTER 10 / SECTION 404 AUDITS OF INTERNAL CONTROL AND CONTROL RISK   **279**

may use that comparison to decide whether to submit purchase orders to authorized suppliers in the vendor master file. In that case, the computer is performing the general approval function using preauthorized information contained in the master files. The authorization in this case is performed by purchasing department personnel when they authorize changes to reorder points and vendors in the inventory and vendor master files, respectively.

Adequate Documents and Records Documents and records are the physical objects upon which transactions are entered and summarized. They include such diverse items as sales invoices, purchase orders, subsidiary records, sales journals, and employee time cards. Many of these documents and records are maintained in the form of computer files until they are printed out for specific purposes. Both documents of original entry and records upon which transactions are entered are important, but the inadequacy of documents typically causes greater control problems.

Documents perform the function of transmitting information throughout the client's organization and between different organizations. The documents must be adequate to provide reasonable assurance that all assets are properly controlled and all transactions are correctly recorded. For example, if the receiving department fills out a receiving report when material is obtained, the accounts payable department can verify the quantity and description on the vendor's invoice by comparing it with the information on the receiving report.

Certain relevant principles dictate the proper design and use of documents and records. Documents and records should be

- Prenumbered consecutively to facilitate control over missing documents and as an aid in locating documents when they are needed at a later date (significantly affects the transaction-related audit objective of completeness).
- Prepared at the time a transaction takes place, or as soon as possible thereafter. When there is a longer time interval, records are less credible and the chance for misstatement increases (affects the transaction-related audit objective of timing).
- Sufficiently simple to ensure that they are clearly understood.
- Designed for multiple use, when possible, to minimize the number of different forms. For example, a properly designed and used shipping document can be the basis for releasing goods from storage to the shipping department, informing billing of the quantity of goods to bill to the customer and the appropriate billing date, and updating the perpetual inventory records.
- Constructed in a manner that encourages correct preparation. This can be done by providing internal checks within the form or record. For example, a document might include instructions for proper routing, blank spaces for authorizations and approvals, and designated column spaces for numerical data.

When data related to transactions are entered online into the computer, the design of the input screen is important to minimize errors and to improve efficiencies in the input process. For example, automatic prompts that provide instructional messages assist input personnel in identifying information needed for input. Automatic cursor movement to the next desired cell of information requested helps guide the input process in a systematic and organized way, which increases input accuracy and completeness. Input screen controls often validate information entered. For example, a general ledger account code entered may be automatically rejected when the account number does not match the chart of accounts master file. Other input screen controls automatically assign sequential document numbers and prevent the input clerk from changing that sequence number.

A control closely related to documents and records is the **chart of accounts**, which classifies transactions into individual balance sheet and income statement accounts. The chart of accounts is an important control because it provides the framework for determining the information presented to management and other financial statement users. The chart of accounts is helpful in preventing classification errors if it accurately and precisely describes which type of transactions should be in each account.

The procedures for proper record keeping should be spelled out in systems manuals to encourage consistent application. The manuals should provide sufficient information to facilitate adequate record keeping and maintain proper control over assets. Many software applications contain Help screens, which assist in the proper use of accounting software.

Physical Control Over Assets and Records To maintain adequate internal control, it is essential to protect assets and records. If assets are left unprotected, they can be stolen. If records are not adequately protected, they can be stolen, damaged, or lost. In the event of such an occurrence, the accounting process and normal operations could be seriously disrupted. When a company is highly computerized, it is especially important to protect its computer equipment, programs, and data files. The equipment and programs are expensive and essential to operations. The data files are the records of the company and, if damaged, could be costly or even impossible to reconstruct.

The most important type of protective measure for safeguarding assets and records is the use of physical precautions. An example is the use of storerooms for inventory to guard against theft. When the storeroom is under the control of a competent employee, there is further assurance that obsolescence is minimized. Fireproof safes and safety deposit vaults for the protection of assets such as currency and securities are other important physical safeguards.

Independent Checks on Performance The last category of control activities is the careful and continuous review of the other four, often called **independent checks** or internal verification. The need for independent checks arises because internal control tends to change over time unless there is a mechanism for frequent review. Personnel are likely to forget or intentionally fail to follow procedures, or they may become careless unless someone observes and evaluates their performance. Regardless of the quality of the controls, personnel can make both fraudulent actions and unintentional mistakes.

An essential characteristic of the persons performing internal verification procedures is independence from the individuals originally responsible for preparing the data. The least expensive means of internal verification is the separation of duties in the manner previously discussed. For example, when the bank reconciliation is performed by a person independent of the accounting records and handling of cash, there is an opportunity for verification without incurring significant additional costs.

Computerized accounting systems can be designed so that many internal verification procedures can be automated as part of the system. For example, the computer will prevent the processing of payment on a vendor invoice if there is no matching purchase order number or receiving report number for that invoice recorded in the system.

Auditors obtain an understanding of the control environment and risk assessment in a similar manner for most audits, but obtaining an understanding of control activities varies considerably. For smaller clients, it is common to identify few or even no control activities because controls are often ineffective because of limited personnel. In that case, the auditor sets a high assessed control risk. For clients with extensive controls that the auditor believes to be excellent, it is often appropriate to identify many controls during the understanding phase. In other audits, the auditor may identify a limited number of controls during this phase and then identify additional controls later in the process. The extent to which controls are identified is a matter of audit judgment. A methodology for identifying controls is studied later in the chapter.

The purpose of an entity's accounting **information and communication** system is to initiate, record, process, and report the entity's transactions and to maintain accountability for the related assets. An accounting information and communication system has several subcomponents, typically made up of classes of transactions such as sales, sales returns, cash receipts, acquisitions, and so on. For each class of transactions, the accounting system must

Information and Communication

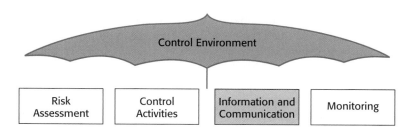

satisfy all of the six transaction-related audit objectives identified earlier in Table 10-1 (p. 273). For example, the sales accounting system should be designed to ensure that all shipments of goods by a company are correctly recorded as sales (completeness and accuracy objectives) and are reflected in the financial statements in the proper period (timing objective). The system must also avoid duplicate recording of sales and recording a sale if a shipment did not occur (existence objective).

To understand the design of the accounting information system, the auditor determines (1) the major classes of transactions of the entity; (2) how those transactions are initiated and recorded; (3) what accounting records exist and their nature; (4) how the system captures other events that are significant to the financial statements, such as declines in asset values; and (5) the nature and details of the financial reporting process followed, including procedures to enter transactions and adjustments in the general ledger.

Monitoring

Monitoring activities deal with ongoing or periodic assessment of the quality of internal control performance by management to determine that controls are operating as intended and that they are modified as appropriate for changes in conditions. The information being assessed comes from a variety of sources, including studies of existing internal controls, internal auditor reports, exception reporting on control activities, reports by regulators such as bank regulatory agencies, feedback from operating personnel, and complaints from customers about billing charges.

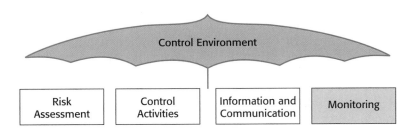

The most important things the auditor needs to know about monitoring are the major types of monitoring activities a company uses and how these activities are used to modify internal controls when necessary. Discussion with management is the most common way to obtain this understanding.

For many companies, especially larger ones, an internal audit department is essential for effective monitoring. To be effective, the internal audit function must be performed by staff independent of both the operating and accounting departments and that report directly to a high level of authority within the organization, either top management or the audit committee of the board of directors.

In addition to its role in monitoring an entity's internal control, an adequate internal audit staff can reduce external audit costs by providing direct assistance to the external auditor. SAS 65 (AU 322) defines the way internal auditors affect the external auditor's evidence accumulation. PCAOB Standard 2 defines the extent that auditors can use the work performed by internal auditors when reporting on internal control under Section 404. If the external auditor obtains evidence that supports the competence, integrity, and objectivity of internal auditors, the external auditor can rely on the internal auditor's work in a number of ways.

How the Size of the Business Affects Internal Control Responsibilities

As companies work toward complying with Section 404, many believe there is an increased burden on smaller-sized public companies. As a general matter, the SEC believes that small businesses should be expected to adhere to the same internal control standards that apply to larger public companies that engage in similar transactions. However, the SEC has publicly stated that the burden to smaller companies can be disproportionate and that it will continue to closely monitor the Section 404 impact on small businesses.

COSO's five components of internal control discussed in the preceding sections are summarized in Table 10-2.

TABLE 10-2   COSO Components of Internal Control

INTERNAL CONTROL

Components	Description of Component	Further Subdivision (if applicable)
Control environment	Actions, policies, and procedures that reflect the overall attitude of top management, directors, and owners of an entity about internal control and its importance	Subcomponents of the control environment: • Integrity and ethical values • Commitment to competence • Board of directors or audit committee participation • Management's philosophy and operating style • Organizational structure • Assignment of authority and responsibility • Human resource policies and practices
Risk assessment	Management's identification and analysis of risks relevant to the preparation of financial statements in accordance with GAAP	Risk assessment processes: • Identify factors affecting risks • Assess significance of risks and likelihood of occurrence • Determine actions necessary to manage risks Management assertions that must be satisfied: • Existence or occurrence • Completeness • Valuation or allocation • Rights and obligations • Presentation and disclosure
Control activities	Policies and procedures that management has established to meet its objectives for financial reporting	Types of specific control activities: • Adequate separation of duties • Proper authorization of transactions and activities • Adequate documents and records • Physical control over assets and records • Independent checks on performance
Information and communication	Methods used to initiate, record, process, and report an entity's transactions and to maintain accountability for related assets	Transaction-related audit objectives that must be satisfied: • Existence • Completeness • Accuracy • Classification • Timing • Posting and summarization
Monitoring	Management's ongoing and periodic assessment of the quality of internal control performance to determine whether controls are operating as intended and are modified when needed	Not applicable

OBTAIN AND DOCUMENT UNDERSTANDING OF INTERNAL CONTROL

Figure 10-3 (p. 284) provides an overview of the process of understanding internal control and assessing control risk for an integrated audit of the financial statements and the effectiveness of internal control over financial reporting. The figure shows that there are four phases in the process of understanding internal control and assessing control risk. In the first phase, auditors obtain an understanding of internal controls. Next, auditors must make a preliminary assessment of internal control and perform tests of controls in every audit as part of their integrated audits. The auditor uses the results of tests of controls for both the audit report on internal control over financial reporting and to assess control risk and to ultimately decide planned detection risk and substantive tests for the audit of financial statements, which is phase 4.

> **OBJECTIVE 10-4**
>
> Obtain and document an understanding of internal control.

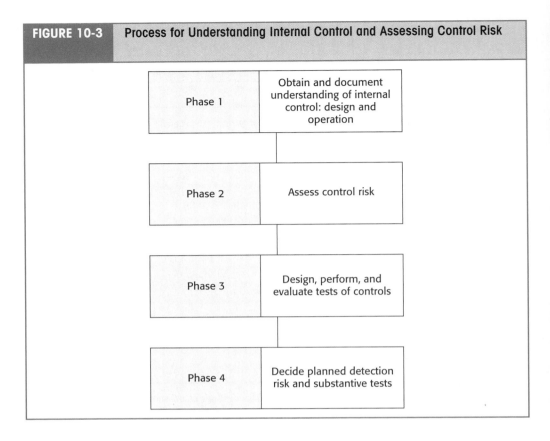

| FIGURE 10-3 | Process for Understanding Internal Control and Assessing Control Risk |

Phase 1 — Obtain and document understanding of internal control: design and operation

Phase 2 — Assess control risk

Phase 3 — Design, perform, and evaluate tests of controls

Phase 4 — Decide planned detection risk and substantive tests

The level of understanding internal control and extent of testing required for the audit of internal controls exceeds that which would be required for only an audit of the financial statements. The effect is to permit the auditor to focus on the internal control understanding and testing needed for the audit of internal controls. When the audit of internal control is completed, the auditor can use the results to decide planned detection risk and substantive tests for the audit of financial statements—the last box in Figure 10-3.

As discussed earlier, Section 404 requires management to document its processes for assessing the effectiveness of the company's internal control over financial reporting. Management must document the design of controls, including all five control components, and also the results of its testing and evaluation. The types of information gathered by management to assess and document internal control effectiveness can take many forms, including policy manuals, flowcharts, narratives, documents, questionnaires, and other forms that are in either paper or electronic formats. PCAOB Standard 2 requires the auditor to evaluate the client's documentation when auditing internal control over financial reporting.

Obtain and Document Understanding of Internal Control

SAS 55 and PCAOB Standard 2 both require the auditor to obtain an understanding of internal control for every audit. This understanding is necessary for both the audit of internal controls over financial reporting and the audit of financial statements. Management's documentation is a major source of information in gaining the understanding. The auditor must also document his or her understanding.

To obtain an understanding of internal control, the auditor uses **procedures to obtain an understanding**, which include gathering evidence about the *design* of internal controls and whether they have been *placed in operation,* and then uses that information as a basis for the integrated audit.

Three methods commonly used by auditors to obtain and document their understanding of the design of internal control are narratives, flowcharts, and internal control questionnaires. Because Section 404 requires management to assess the design effectiveness of internal control over financial reporting, in most instances these forms of documentation have already been prepared by management as part of their internal control assessment. Narratives, flowcharts, and internal control questionnaires, used by the auditor separately or in combination to document internal control, are discussed next.

Narrative A **narrative** is a written description of a client's internal controls. A proper narrative of an accounting system and related controls includes four characteristics:

1. *The origin of every document and record in the system.* For example, the description should state where customer orders come from and how sales invoices are generated.
2. *All processing that takes place.* For example, if sales amounts are determined by a computer program that multiplies quantities shipped by standard prices contained in price master files, that process should be described.
3. *The disposition of every document and record in the system.* The filing of documents, sending them to customers, or destroying them should be shown.
4. *An indication of the controls relevant to the assessment of control risk.* These typically include separation of duties (such as separating recording cash from handling cash), authorizations and approvals (such as credit approvals), and internal verification (such as comparison of unit selling price to sales contracts).

Flowchart An internal control **flowchart** is a diagram of the client's documents and their sequential flow in the organization. An adequate flowchart includes the same four characteristics identified for narratives.

Flowcharting is advantageous primarily because it can provide a concise overview of the client's system, which is useful to the auditor as an analytical tool in evaluation. A well-prepared flowchart aids management and the auditor in identifying inadequacies by facilitating a clear understanding of how the system operates. Flowcharts have two advantages over narratives: typically they are easier to read and easier to update.

It would be unusual to use both a narrative and a flowchart to describe the same system because both present the same information. Sometimes presentations combine narratives and flowcharts. The decision to use either or a combination of the two is dependent on two factors: (1) the relative ease of understanding by current- and subsequent-year auditors and (2) the relative cost of preparation. Flowcharting software is readily available.

Internal Control Questionnaire An **internal control questionnaire** asks a series of questions about the controls in each audit area as a means of uncovering aspects of internal control that may be inadequate. In most instances, questionnaires require a "yes" or a "no" response, with "no" responses indicating potential internal control deficiencies.

By using a questionnaire, management or auditors cover each audit area reasonably quickly. The primary disadvantage is that individual parts of the client's systems are examined without providing an overall view. In addition, a standard questionnaire is often inapplicable to some audit clients, especially smaller ones.

Figure 10-4 (p. 286) illustrates part of an internal control questionnaire for the sales and collection cycle of Hillsburg Hardware Co. Notice how the questionnaire incorporates the six transaction-related audit objectives A through F as each applies to sales transactions (see shaded portions). The same is true for all other audit areas.

The use of questionnaires and flowcharts is highly desirable for understanding the client's internal control design. Flowcharts provide an overview of the system, while questionnaires offer useful checklists to remind the auditor of many different types of internal controls that should exist. When properly used, a combination of these two approaches should provide the auditor with an excellent description of the system.

Evaluating Internal Control Operation

In addition to understanding the design of the internal controls, the auditor must also evaluate whether the designed controls are actually placed in operation. In practice, the understanding of the design and operation may be done simultaneously. Following are common methods.

[Obtain and document understanding of internal control: design and operation]

[Assess control risk]

[Design, perform, and evaluate tests of controls]

[Decide planned detection risk and substantive tests]

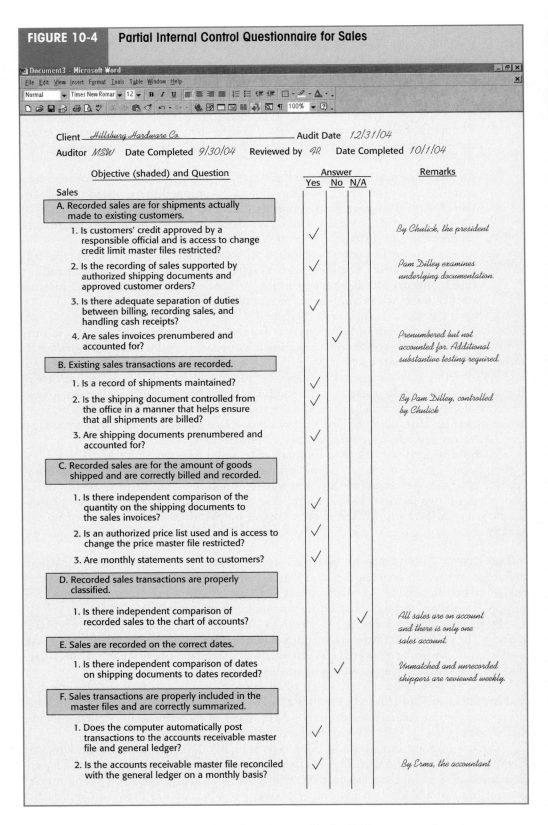

FIGURE 10-4 Partial Internal Control Questionnaire for Sales

Client _Hillsburg Hardware Co._ ———————————— Audit Date _12/31/04_

Auditor _MSW_   Date Completed _9/30/04_   Reviewed by _GR_   Date Completed _10/1/04_

Objective (shaded) and Question	Answer			Remarks
	Yes	No	N/A	
Sales				
A. Recorded sales are for shipments actually made to existing customers.				
1. Is customers' credit approved by a responsible official and is access to change credit limit master files restricted?	✓			*By Chulick, the president*
2. Is the recording of sales supported by authorized shipping documents and approved customer orders?	✓			*Pam Dilley examines underlying documentation.*
3. Is there adequate separation of duties between billing, recording sales, and handling cash receipts?	✓			
4. Are sales invoices prenumbered and accounted for?		✓		*Prenumbered but not accounted for. Additional substantive testing required.*
B. Existing sales transactions are recorded.				
1. Is a record of shipments maintained?	✓			
2. Is the shipping document controlled from the office in a manner that helps ensure that all shipments are billed?	✓			*By Pam Dilley, controlled by Chulick*
3. Are shipping documents prenumbered and accounted for?	✓			
C. Recorded sales are for the amount of goods shipped and are correctly billed and recorded.				
1. Is there independent comparison of the quantity on the shipping documents to the sales invoices?	✓			
2. Is an authorized price list used and is access to change the price master file restricted?	✓			
3. Are monthly statements sent to customers?	✓			
D. Recorded sales transactions are properly classified.				
1. Is there independent comparison of recorded sales to the chart of accounts?			✓	*All sales are on account and there is only one sales account.*
E. Sales are recorded on the correct dates.				
1. Is there independent comparison of dates on shipping documents to dates recorded?		✓		*Unmatched and unrecorded shippers are reviewed weekly.*
F. Sales transactions are properly included in the master files and are correctly summarized.				
1. Does the computer automatically post transactions to the accounts receivable master file and general ledger?	✓			
2. Is the accounts receivable master file reconciled with the general ledger on a monthly basis?	✓			*By Erma, the accountant*

Update and Evaluate Auditor's Previous Experience with the Entity Most audits of a company are done annually by the same CPA firm. Except for initial engagements, the auditor begins the audit with a great deal of information from prior years about the client's internal control. It is especially useful to determine whether controls that were not previously operating effectively have been improved.

Make Inquiries of Client Personnel An essential element of determining if the system operates as designed is to ask management, supervisors, and staff to explain their duties. Careful questioning of the appropriate personnel will help the auditor evaluate whether employees actually do what is described in the client's control documentation.

Examine Documents and Records The five components of internal control all involve the creation of many documents and records. By examining completed documents, records, and computer files, the auditor can evaluate whether information in flowcharts and narratives has been placed in operation.

Observe Entity Activities and Operations In addition to examining completed documents and records, the auditor can observe client personnel carrying out their normal accounting and control activities, including their preparation of documents and records. This further enhances understanding and knowledge that controls have been placed in operation.

Perform Walkthroughs of the Accounting System Observation, documentation, and inquiry can be conveniently and effectively combined in the form of a transaction walkthrough. PCAOB Standard 2 requires the auditor to perform at least one walkthrough for each major class of transactions. In a **walkthrough**, the auditor selects one or a few documents for the initiation of a transaction type and traces them through the entire accounting process. At each stage of processing, the auditor makes inquiries and observes current activities, in addition to examining completed documentation for the transaction or transactions selected.

ASSESS CONTROL RISK

Now that the auditor's procedures for gaining an understanding of internal control design and operation have been discussed, the chapter focuses on how the auditor uses that information to assess control risk. Once the auditor obtains an understanding of internal control sufficient for audit planning, a preliminary assessment of control risk must be made. Two specific assessments must be made to arrive at the preliminary assessment.

The first assessment is whether the entity is auditable. Two primary factors determine auditability: the integrity of management and the adequacy of accounting records. Many audit procedures rely to some extent on the representations of management. For example, it is difficult for the auditor to evaluate whether inventory is obsolete without an honest assessment by management. If management lacks integrity, management may provide false representations, causing the auditor to rely on unreliable evidence.

The accounting records serve as a direct source of audit evidence for most audit objectives. If the accounting records are deficient, necessary audit evidence may not be available. For example, if the client has not kept duplicate sales invoices and vendors' invoices, it would usually be impractical to do an audit. Unless the auditor can identify an alternative source of reliable evidence or appropriate records can be constructed for the auditor's use, the only recourse may be to consider the entity unauditable.

In complex IT environments, much of the transaction information is available only in electronic form without generating a visible audit trail of documents and records. In that case, the company is generally still auditable; however, auditors must assess whether they have the necessary skills to gather evidence that is in electronic form and can assign personnel with adequate IT training and experience.

When the auditor concludes that the entity is not auditable, the circumstances are discussed with the client (usually at the highest level), and the auditor either withdraws from the engagement or issues a disclaimer form of audit report. In practice, this assessment is likely to be made early in the engagement, normally at the time of client acceptance. The control environment factors discussed in this chapter are similar to those included in Chapter 8 under client acceptance and continuance.

OBJECTIVE 10-5

Assess control risk by linking key controls, significant deficiencies, and material weaknesses to transaction-related audit objectives.

Assess Whether the Financial Statements Are Auditable

Obtain and document understanding of internal control: design and operation

Assess control risk

Design, perform, and evaluate tests of controls

Decide planned detection risk and substantive tests

After obtaining an understanding of internal control, the auditor makes a preliminary **assessment of control risk**. This assessment is a measure of the auditor's expectation that internal controls *will neither prevent material misstatements* from occurring *nor detect and correct them* if they have occurred.

The preliminary assessment is made for each transaction-related audit objective for each major type of transaction in each transaction cycle. For example, in the sales and collection cycle, the types of transactions usually involve sales, sales returns and allowances, cash receipts, and the provision for and write-off of uncollectible accounts.

Many auditors use a **control risk matrix** to assist in the control risk assessment process. The purpose is to provide a convenient way to organize the elements that go into assessing control risk for each transaction-related audit objective. Figure 10-5 illustrates the use of a control risk matrix for sales transactions of Hillsburg Hardware Co. We now discuss the preparation of the matrix.

Identify Transaction-Related Audit Objectives The first step in the assessment is to identify the transaction-related audit objectives for each type of transaction to which the assessment applies. This is done by applying the specific transaction-related audit objectives introduced earlier, which were stated in general form, to each major type of transaction for the entity. For example, the auditor makes an assessment of the existence objective for sales and a separate assessment of the completeness objective. This is shown for sales transactions for Hillsburg Hardware at the top of Figure 10-5.

Identify Existing Controls The next step is to identify the specific controls that contribute to accomplishing transaction-related audit objectives. The auditor identifies pertinent controls by proceeding through the descriptive information about the client's system. Those policies, procedures, and activities that in the auditor's judgment provide control over the transactions involved are identified. In doing this, it is often helpful to refer back to the types of controls that might exist, and ask whether they do exist. For example: Is there adequate separation of duties and how is it achieved? Are the documents used well designed? Are prenumbered documents properly accounted for? Are key master files properly restricted from unauthorized access?

In making this analysis, it is not necessary to consider every control. The auditor should identify and include controls that are expected to have the greatest effect on meeting the transaction-related audit objectives. These are often called **key controls**. The reason for including only key controls is that they will be sufficient to achieve the transaction-related audit objectives and should provide audit efficiency. Examples of key controls for Hillsburg Hardware are shown in Figure 10-5.

Associate Controls with Transaction-Related Audit Objectives Each control satisfies one or more transaction-related audit objectives. This can be seen in Figure 10-5. The body of the matrix is used to show how each control contributes to the accomplishment of the transaction-related audit objectives. In this illustration, a C was entered in each cell where a control partially or fully satisfied an objective. For example, the mailing of statements to customers satisfies three objectives in the audit of Hillsburg Hardware, which is indicated by the placement of each C on the row in Figure 10-5 describing that control.

Identify and Evaluate Control Deficiencies, Significant Deficiencies, and Material Weaknesses Auditors must evaluate whether key controls are absent in the design of internal control over financial reporting as a part of evaluating control risk and the likelihood of financial statement misstatements. There are three levels of evaluating the absence of internal controls for each transaction-related audit objective:

1. *Control deficiency.* A **control deficiency** exists if the design or operation of controls does not permit company personnel to prevent or detect misstatements on a timely basis. A *design deficiency* exists if a necessary control is missing or not properly designed. An *operation deficiency* exists if a well-designed control does not

	SALES TRANSACTION-RELATED AUDIT OBJECTIVES					
INTERNAL CONTROL	Recorded sales are for shipments actually made to nonfictitious customers (existence).	Existing sales transactions are recorded (completeness).	Recorded sales are for the amount of goods shipped and are correctly billed and recorded (accuracy).	Sales transactions are properly classified (classification).	Sales are recorded on the correct dates (timing).	Sales transactions are properly included in the accounts receivable master file and are correctly summarized (posting and summarization).
Credit is approved automatically by computer by comparison to authorized credit limits (C1).	C					
Recorded sales are supported by authorized shipping documents and approved customer orders (C2).	C		C			
Separation of duties between billing, recording of sales, and handling of cash receipts (C3).	C	C				C
Shipping documents are forwarded to billing daily and are billed the subsequent day (C4).	C				C	
Shipping documents are prenumbered and accounted for weekly (C5).		C			C	
Batch totals of quantities shipped are compared with quantities billed (C6).	C	C	C			
Unit selling prices are obtained from the price list master file of approved prices (C7).			C			
Sales transactions are internally verified (C8).				C		
Statements are mailed to customers each month (C9).	C		C			C
Computer automatically posts transactions to the accounts receivable subsidiary records and to the general ledger (C10).						C
Accounts receivable master file is reconciled to the general ledger on a monthly basis (C11).						C
There is a lack of internal verification for the possibility of sales invoices being recorded more than once (W1).	W					
There is a lack of control to test for timely recording (W2).					W	
Assessed control risk	Medium	Low	Low	Low*	Medium	Low

*Because there are no cash sales, classification is not a problem.
C = Control; W = Significant Deficiency or Material Weakness.
Note: This matrix was developed using an internal control questionnaire, part of which is included in Figure 10-4 (p. 286), as well as flowcharts and other documentation of the auditor's understanding of internal control.

operate as designed or when the person performing the control is insufficiently qualified or authorized.

2. *Significant deficiency.* A **significant deficiency** exists if one or more control deficiencies exist that, *more than remotely,* adversely affect a company's ability to

initiate, authorize, record, process, or report external financial statements reliably such that there is more than a remote likelihood that a misstatement that is more than inconsequential will not be prevented or detected. The interpretation of what is "more than remotely" is highly subjective in both concept and practice. Auditing standards define it as "a slight chance of occurrence." A misstatement is inconsequential if a reasonable person would conclude that the misstatement would clearly be immaterial to the financial statements.

If the auditor concludes that one or more control deficiencies for a specific objective do not exceed the more than remote level or are inconsequential, they can be ignored.

3. *Material weakness.* A **material weakness** exists if a significant deficiency, by itself, or in combination with other significant deficiencies, results in a more than remote likelihood that internal control will not prevent or detect material financial statement misstatements.

To determine if a significant internal control deficiency or deficiencies are a material weakness, they must be evaluated along two dimensions: likelihood and significance. The horizontal line in Figure 10-6 depicts the likelihood of a misstatement resulting from the significant deficiency, while the vertical line depicts its significance. If there is more than a remote chance (likelihood) that a material misstatement (significance) could result from the significant deficiency or deficiencies, then it is considered a material weakness.

Identify Deficiencies, Significant Deficiencies, and Material Weaknesses

A five-step approach can be used to identify deficiencies, significant deficiencies, and material weaknesses:

1. *Identify existing controls.* Because deficiencies and material weaknesses are the absence of adequate controls, the auditor must first know which controls exist. The methods for identifying controls have already been discussed.
2. *Identify absence of key controls.* Internal control questionnaires, flowcharts, and walkthroughs are useful tools to identify where controls are lacking and in which the likelihood of misstatement is therefore increased.
3. *Consider the possibility of compensating controls.* A compensating control is one elsewhere in the system that offsets the absence of a key control. A common example in a small business is the active involvement of the owner. When a compensating control exists, there is no longer a significant deficiency or material weakness.
4. *Decide whether there is a significant deficiency or material weakness.* The likelihood of misstatements and their materiality are used to evaluate if there are significant deficiencies or material weaknesses.
5. *Determine potential misstatements that could result.* This step is intended to identify specific misstatements that are likely to result because of the significant deficiency or material weakness. The importance of a significant deficiency or material weakness is directly related to the likelihood and materiality of potential misstatements.

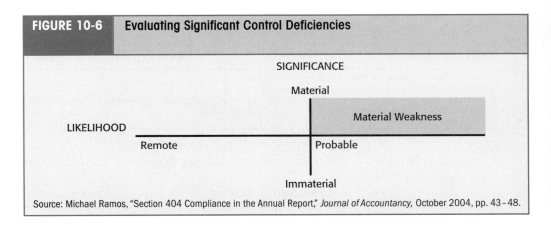

FIGURE 10-6	Evaluating Significant Control Deficiencies

Source: Michael Ramos, "Section 404 Compliance in the Annual Report," *Journal of Accountancy*, October 2004, pp. 43–48.

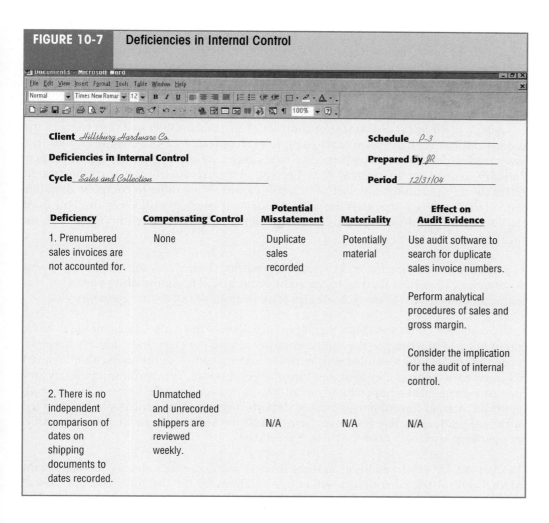

FIGURE 10-7 Deficiencies in Internal Control

Client _Hillsburg Hardware Co._   Schedule _P-3_

Deficiencies in Internal Control   Prepared by _JR_

Cycle _Sales and Collection_   Period _12/31/04_

Deficiency	Compensating Control	Potential Misstatement	Materiality	Effect on Audit Evidence
1. Prenumbered sales invoices are not accounted for.	None	Duplicate sales recorded	Potentially material	Use audit software to search for duplicate sales invoice numbers. Perform analytical procedures of sales and gross margin. Consider the implication for the audit of internal control.
2. There is no independent comparison of dates on shipping documents to dates recorded.	Unmatched and unrecorded shippers are reviewed weekly.	N/A	N/A	N/A

Figure 10-7 for Hillsburg Hardware includes two significant deficiencies but no material weaknesses.

Associate Significant Deficiencies and Material Weaknesses with Transaction-Related Audit Objectives The same as for controls, each significant deficiency or material weakness can apply to one or more transaction-related audit objectives. In the case of Hillsburg Hardware in Figure 10-5, there are two significant deficiencies, and each applies to only one objective. The significant deficiencies are shown in the body of the figure by a W in the appropriate objective column.

Assess Control Risk for Each Transaction-Related Audit Objective Once controls, significant deficiencies, and material weaknesses are identified and related to transaction-related audit objectives, the auditor can assess control risk. This is the critical decision in the evaluation of internal control. The auditor uses all of the information discussed previously to make a subjective control risk assessment for each objective. There are different ways to express this assessment. Some auditors use a subjective expression such as high, moderate, or low. Others use numerical probabilities such as 1.0, 0.6, or 0.2.

Again, the control risk matrix is a useful tool for making the assessment. Referring to Figure 10-5, the auditor assessed control risk for each objective for Hillsburg's sales by reviewing each column for pertinent controls and significant deficiencies and asking, "What is the likelihood that a significant material misstatement would not be prevented or detected, or corrected if it occurred, by these controls, and what is the effect of the deficiencies or weaknesses?" If the likelihood is low, then control risk is low, and so forth. Figure 10-5 for Hillsburg Hardware shows that all objectives are assessed as low except existence and timing, which are medium.

This assessment is not the final one. Before making the final assessment at the end of the integrated audit, the auditor will test controls and perform substantive tests of details. These procedures can either support the preliminary assessment or cause the auditor to make changes. In some cases, management can correct deficiencies and material weaknesses before the auditor does significant testing, which may permit a reduction in control risk.

After a preliminary assessment of control risk is made for sales and cash receipts, the auditor can complete the three control risk rows of the evidence-planning worksheet that was introduced in Chapter 9 on page 251. If tests of controls results do not support the preliminary assessment of control risk, the auditor must modify the worksheet later. Alternatively, the auditor can wait until tests of controls are done to complete the three control risk rows of the worksheet. An evidence-planning worksheet for Hillsburg Hardware with the three rows for control risk completed is illustrated in Figure 15-6 on page 464.

Audit Committee Communications and Management Letters

As part of understanding internal control and assessing control risk, the auditor is required to communicate certain matters to the audit committee. This information and other recommendations related to controls are also often communicated to management.

Audit Committee Communications Significant deficiencies and material weaknesses must be communicated in writing to the audit committee as a part of every audit. Usually the auditor communicates any identified deficiencies in internal control to the audit committee and management as soon as they become aware of their existence. Timely communications may provide management an opportunity to address control deficiencies before management's report on internal control must be issued. In some instances, deficiencies can be corrected sufficiently early such that both management and the auditor can conclude that controls are operating effectively as of the balance sheet date.

Management Letters In addition to these matters, auditors often observe less significant internal control-related issues, as well as opportunities for the client to make operational improvements. These types of matters should also be communicated to the client. The form of communication is often a separate letter for that purpose, called a **management letter**. Although management letters are not required by auditing standards, auditors generally prepare them as a value-added service of the audit.

TESTS OF CONTROLS

OBJECTIVE 10-6

Describe the process of designing and performing tests of controls.

Now that we've examined how auditors link controls, significant deficiencies, and material weaknesses in internal control to transaction-related audit objectives to assess control risk for each objective, we'll address how auditors test those controls that are used to support a control risk assessment. For example, each key control in Figure 10-5 (p. 289) that the auditor intends to rely on to support a control risk of medium or low must be supported by sufficient tests of controls. We will deal with tests of controls for both audits of internal control for financial reporting and audits of financial statements.

Purpose of Tests of Controls

Assessing control risk requires the auditor to consider both the design and operation of controls to evaluate whether they will likely be effective in meeting transaction-related audit objectives. During the understanding phase, the auditor will have already gathered some evidence in support of the design of the controls, as well as evidence that they have been placed in operation. In most cases, sufficient evidence *will not* have been gathered to reduce assessed control risk to a sufficiently low level. The auditor must therefore obtain additional evidence about their operating effectiveness throughout all, or at least most, of the period under audit. The procedures to test effectiveness of controls in support of a reduced assessed control risk are called **tests of controls**.

If the results of tests of controls support the design and operation of controls as expected, the auditor uses the same assessed control risk as the preliminary assessment. If, however, the tests of controls indicate that the controls did not operate effectively, the assessed control risk must be reconsidered. For example, the tests may indicate that the application of a control was curtailed midway through the year or that the person applying it made frequent misstatements. In such situations, the auditor uses a higher assessed control risk, unless compensating controls for the same transaction-related audit objectives are identified and found to be effective. Of course, the auditor must also consider the impact of those controls that are not operating effectively on the auditor's report on internal control.

The auditor is likely to use four types of procedures to support the operating effectiveness of internal controls. Management's testing of internal control will likely include the same four types of procedures. Recall that PCAOB Standard 2 requires auditors to not only evaluate management's documentation of its tests of internal control but also perform their own tests of controls for the integrated audit.

Procedures for Tests of Controls

The four types of procedures are as follows:

1. *Make inquiries of appropriate client personnel.* Although inquiry is not generally a strong source of evidence about the effective operation of controls, it is an appropriate form. For example, to determine that unauthorized personnel are not allowed access to computer files, the auditor may make inquiries of the person who controls the computer library and of the person who controls online access security password assignments.

2. *Examine documents, records, and reports.* Many controls leave a clear trail of documentary evidence. Suppose, for example, that when a customer order is received, it is used to create a customer sales order, which is approved for credit. (See the first and second key controls in Figure 10-5 on page 289.) The customer order is attached to the sales order as authorization for further processing. The auditor examines the documents to make sure that they are complete and properly matched and that required signatures or initials are present.

3. *Observe control-related activities.* Some controls do not leave an evidence trail, which means that it is not possible to examine evidence that the control was executed at a later date. For example, separation of duties relies on specific persons performing specific tasks, and there is typically no documentation of the separate performance. (See the third key control in Figure 10-5.) For controls that leave no documentary evidence, the auditor generally observes them being applied at various points during the year.

4. *Reperform client procedures.* There are also control-related activities for which there are related documents and records, but their content is insufficient for the auditor's purpose of assessing whether controls are operating effectively. For example, assume that prices on sales invoices are to be verified with a standard price list by client personnel as an internal verification procedure, but no indication of performance is entered on the sales invoices. (See the seventh key control in Figure 10-5.) In these cases, it is common for the auditor to reperform the control activity to see whether the proper results were obtained. For this example, the auditor can reperform the procedure by tracing the sales prices to the authorized price list in effect at the date of the transaction. If no misstatements are found, the auditor can conclude that the procedure is operating as intended.

Obtain and document understanding of internal control: design and operation

Assess control risk

Design, perform, and evaluate tests of controls

Decide planned detection risk and substantive tests

Extent of Procedures

The extent to which tests of controls are applied depends on the preliminary assessed control risk. If the auditor wants a lower assessed control risk, more extensive tests of controls are applied, both in terms of the number of controls tested and the extent of the tests for each control. For example, if the auditor wants to use a low assessed control risk, a larger sample size for documentation, observation, and reperformance procedures should be applied.

Reliance on Evidence from the Prior Year's Audit PCAOB Standard 2 requires a public company auditor to test controls each year for all relevant assertions for significant accounts and transactions. However, if evidence was obtained in the prior year's audit that indicates that a key control was operating effectively, and the auditor determines that it is still in place, the extent of the tests of that control may be reduced somewhat in the current year. For example, in such circumstances, the auditor might use a reduced sample size in testing a control that leaves documentary evidence.

Testing Less Than the Entire Audit Period Recall that management's report on internal control deals with the effectiveness of internal controls as of the end of the fiscal year. PCAOB Standard 2 requires the auditor to perform tests of controls that are adequate to determine whether controls are operating effectively at year-end. The timing of the auditor's tests of controls will therefore depend on the nature of the controls and the frequency at which they are performed. For certain controls, it is practical to test the controls at an interim date. The auditor will then determine later if changes in controls occurred in the period not tested and decide the implication of any change. Certain controls dealing with financial statement preparation occur only quarterly or at year-end and must therefore also be tested at quarter and year-end.

Relationship Between Tests of Controls and Procedures to Obtain an Understanding

There is a significant overlap between tests of controls and procedures to obtain an understanding. Both include inquiry, documentation, and observation. There are two primary differences in the application of these common procedures. First, in obtaining an understanding of internal control, the procedures to obtain an understanding are applied to all controls identified during that phase. Tests of controls, on the other hand, are applied only when the assessed control risk has not been satisfied by the procedures to obtain an understanding. Second, procedures to obtain an understanding are performed only on one or a few transactions or, in the case of observations, at a single point in time. Tests of controls are performed on larger samples of transactions (perhaps 20 to 100), and often, observations are made at more than one point in time.

For key controls, tests of controls other than reperformance are essentially an extension of procedures to obtain an understanding. Therefore, assuming the auditors plan to obtain a low assessed control risk from the beginning of the integrated audit, they will likely combine both types of procedures and perform them simultaneously. Table 10-3 illustrates this concept in more detail. One option is to perform the audit procedures separately, as shown in Table 10-3, where minimum procedures to obtain an understanding of design and operation are performed, followed by additional tests of controls. An alternative is to combine both columns and do them simultaneously. The same amount of evidence is accumulated in the second approach, but more efficiently.

The determination of the appropriate sample size for tests of controls is an important audit decision. That topic is covered in Chapter 15.

TABLE 10-3	Relationship of Assessed Control Risk and Extent of Procedures	
	Assessed Control Risk	
Type of Procedure	**High Level: Procedures to Obtain an Understanding**	**Lower Level: Tests of Controls***
Inquiry	Yes—extensive	Yes—some
Documentation	Yes—with transaction walk-through	Yes—using sampling
Observation	Yes—with transaction walk-through	Yes—at multiple times
Reperformance	No	Yes—using sampling

Note: In an integrated audit for a public company, the auditor will likely combine procedures to obtain an understanding with tests of controls and perform them simultaneously.

DECIDE PLANNED DETECTION RISK AND DESIGN SUBSTANTIVE TESTS

We've focused on how auditors assess control risk for each transaction-related audit objective and support control risk assessments with tests of controls. The completion of these activities is sufficient for the audit of internal control over financial reporting, even though the report will not be finalized until the auditor completes the audit of financial statements.

The auditor uses the results of the control risk assessment process and tests of controls to determine the planned detection risk and related substantive tests for the audit of financial statements. The auditor does this by linking the control risk assessments to the balance-related audit objectives for the accounts affected by the major transaction types. The appropriate level of detection risk for each balance-related audit objective is then decided using the audit risk model. The relationship of transaction-related audit objectives to balance-related audit objectives and the selection and design of audit procedures for substantive tests of financial statement balances are discussed and illustrated in Chapter 13.

Obtain and document understanding of internal control: design and operation
Assess control risk
Design, perform, and evaluate tests of controls
Decide planned detection risk and substantive tests

SECTION 404 REPORTING ON INTERNAL CONTROL

Earlier in this chapter, we discussed the auditor's responsibilities for reporting on the operating effectiveness of internal control required by Section 404. As described in Chapter 3, the auditor may issue separate or combined audit reports on the financial statements and on internal control over financial reporting. An example of the combined report is illustrated in Figure 3-3 on page 50.

The auditor's report on internal control must include two auditor opinions:

1. The auditor's opinion on whether management's assessment of the effectiveness of internal control over financial reporting as of the end of the fiscal period is fairly stated, in all material respects.
2. The auditor's opinion on whether the company maintained, in all material respects, effective internal control over financial reporting as of the specified date.

In practice, it is unlikely for the auditor to issue anything other than an unqualified report on whether management's assessment is fairly stated. If the auditor concludes that management has not identified and reported all significant deficiencies and material weaknesses, it will be in management's best interests to revise its assessment to conform to the auditor's conclusions. For example, management's assessment would be revised to reflect that it did not maintain effective internal control and the auditor's opinion would state that such an assessment is fairly stated. In contrast, there is likely to be more variety in the auditor's opinion about the operating effectiveness of the company's internal control, depending on the presence of material weaknesses.

The scope of the auditor's report on internal control as required by PCAOB Standard 2 is limited to obtaining reasonable assurance that material weaknesses in internal control are identified. Thus, the audit is not designed to detect deficiencies in internal control that individually, or in the aggregate, are less severe than a material weakness. The distinction between deficiencies, significant deficiencies, and material weaknesses was discussed earlier.

Unqualified Opinion The auditor may issue an unqualified opinion on internal control over financial reporting when two conditions are present:

- There are no identified material weaknesses.
- There have been no restrictions on the scope of the auditor's work.

OBJECTIVE 10-7

Understand Section 404 requirements for auditor reporting on internal control.

Types of Opinions

Adverse Opinion When material weaknesses exist, the auditor must express an *adverse opinion* on the effectiveness of internal control. The most common cause of an adverse opinion in the auditor's report on internal control is when management identified a material weakness in its report.

Qualified or Disclaimer of Opinion A scope limitation requires the auditor to express a *qualified opinion* or a *disclaimer of opinion* on internal control over financial reporting. This type of opinion is issued when the auditor is unable to determine if there are material weaknesses, due to a restriction on the scope of the audit of internal control over financial reporting or other circumstances where the auditor is unable to obtain sufficient evidence.

Because the audit of the financial statements and the audit of internal control over financial reporting are integrated, the auditor must consider the results of audit procedures performed to issue the audit report on the financial statements when issuing the audit report on internal control. For example, if the auditor identifies a material misstatement in the financial statements that was not initially identified by the company's internal controls, the auditor should consider this as at least a significant deficiency, if not a material weakness for purposes of reporting on internal control. In such circumstances, the auditor's report on the financial statements may be unqualified as long as management corrected the misstatement before issuing the financial statements. In contrast, however, the auditor's report on internal control must include an adverse opinion if the auditor concludes it is a material weakness. In addition, the auditor will likely request management to change its report on internal control to include the significant deficiency or material weakness.

Figure 10-8 illustrates the introductory and opinion paragraphs from an auditor's separate report on internal control when the auditor expresses an unqualified opinion on management's assessment of internal control and an adverse opinion on the effectiveness of internal control over financial reporting because of the existence of a material weakness. Notice that the report refers to management's separate report on internal control that

FIGURE 10-8	Partial Section 404 Auditor Report on Internal Control when Material Weaknesses Exist (bold added)*

Report of Independent Registered Public Accounting Firm

[*Introductory paragraph*]

We have audited **management's assessment,** included in the accompanying Management Report on Internal Control, that Kincannon Company **did not maintain effective internal control** over financial reporting as of December 31, 2005, because of the effect of a material weakness identified in management's assessment, based on criteria established in *Internal Control—Integrated Framework* issued by the Committee of Sponsoring Organizations of the Treadway Commission (COSO).

[*Opinion paragraph*]

In our opinion, management's assessment that Kincannon Company **did not maintain effective internal control** over financial reporting as of December 31, 2005, **is fairly stated,** in all material respects, based on criteria established in *Internal Control—Integrated Framework* issued by the Committee of Sponsoring Organizations of the Treadway Commission (COSO). **Also, in our opinion, because of the effect of the material weakness described above on the achievement of the objectives of the control criteria, Kincannon Company has not maintained effective internal control** over financial reporting as of December 31, 2005, based on criteria established in *Internal Control—Integrated Framework* issued by the Committee of Sponsoring Organizations of the Treadway Commission (COSO).

Kellum & Kellum, LLP
Brentwood, Tennessee

February 2, 2006

*The scope paragraph, definition of internal control, and inherent limitations of internal control paragraphs use standard wording and are not included. The explanatory paragraph describing the nature of the weakness is also not included.

includes an assessment by management that controls are not operating effectively due to the presence of the material weakness. Because management's assessment of internal control recognizes the presence of the material weakness, the auditor's opinion about management's assessment is that the assessment is fairly stated. However, the separate adverse opinion about the operating effectiveness of internal control over financial reporting is issued by the auditor because of the material weakness.

EVALUATING, REPORTING, AND TESTING INTERNAL CONTROL FOR NONPUBLIC COMPANIES

OBJECTIVE 10-8

Describe the differences in evaluating, reporting, and testing internal control for nonpublic companies.

The chapter to this point has discussed internal control and an integrated audit of internal control and financial statements for public companies under Sarbanes–Oxley and PCAOB Standard 2. Most of the concepts in the chapter also apply equally to nonpublic companies. This section deals with the differences in evaluating, reporting, and testing internal control for nonpublic companies.

A common misconception of nonpublic companies is that they are automatically small and less sophisticated than public companies. While it is often true that many nonpublic companies are small, others are large and have sophisticated internal controls. This section assumes there is considerable variation in the size and complexity of the controls in nonpublic companies.

Following is an identification and discussion of the most important differences in evaluating, reporting, and testing internal control for nonpublic companies.

1. Reporting requirements. The most important difference related to internal controls between public and nonpublic company audits is the lack of a requirement for an audit of internal controls over financial reporting for nonpublic companies. The auditor, therefore, focuses on internal control only to the extent that is needed to do a quality audit of financial statements.

The auditor is required by auditing standards to issue a report on significant deficiencies and material weaknesses in internal control to the audit committee or other senior management, the same as for public companies. The report in Figure 10-9 on page 298 would be used in the audit of a nonpublic company.

2. Extent of required internal controls. Management, not the auditor, has responsibility for establishing adequate internal controls in nonpublic companies, just like management for public companies. If the control environment or documentation is inadequate, the auditor may decide to withdraw from the engagement or issue a disclaimer of opinion. Also, well-run nonpublic companies understand the importance of effective controls to reduce the likelihood of errors and fraud, and to improve effectiveness and efficiency.

A company's size has a significant effect on the nature of internal control and the specific controls that are placed in operation. Obviously, it is more difficult to establish adequate separation of duties in a small company. It would also be unreasonable to expect a small firm to have internal auditors. However, if the various subcomponents of internal control are examined, it becomes apparent that most are applicable to both large and small companies. Even though it may not be common to formalize policies in manuals, it is certainly possible for a small company to have (1) competent, trustworthy personnel with clear lines of authority; (2) proper procedures for authorization, execution, and recording of transactions; (3) adequate documents, records, and reports; (4) physical controls over assets and records; and, to a limited degree, (5) independent checks on performance.

A major control available in a small company is the knowledge and concern of the top operating person, who is often an owner–manager. A personal interest in the organization and a close relationship with personnel make careful evaluation of the competence of the employees and the effectiveness of the overall system possible. For example, internal control can be significantly strengthened if the owner conscientiously performs such duties as signing all checks after carefully reviewing supporting documents, reviewing bank reconciliations, examining accounts receivable statements sent to customers, approving credit, examining all correspondence from customers and vendors, and approving bad debts.

JOHNSON AND SEYGROVES
Certified Public Accountants
2016 Village Boulevard
Troy, Michigan 48801

February 12, 2006

Audit Committee
Airtight Machine Company
1729 Athens Street
Troy, MI 48801

In planning and performing our audit of the financial statements of Airtight Machine Company for the year ended December 31, 2005, we considered its internal control in order to determine our auditing procedures for the purpose of expressing our opinion on the financial statements and not to provide assurance on internal control. Our consideration of internal control would not necessarily disclose all deficiencies in internal control that might be significant deficiencies. However, as discussed below, we noted certain deficiencies involving internal control that we consider to be significant deficiencies under standards issued by the American Institute of Certified Public Accountants. A significant deficiency is an internal control deficiency that could adversely affect the entity's ability to initiate, record, process, and report financial data consistent with the assertions of management in the financial statements.

The matter noted is that there is a lack of independent verification of the key entry of the customer's name, product number, quantity shipped, prices used, and the related mathematical extensions on sales invoices and credit memos. As a consequence, errors in these activities could occur and remain uncorrected, adversely affecting both recorded net sales and accounts receivable. This deficiency is significant because of the large size of the average sale of Airtight Machine Company.

This report is intended solely for the information and use of the audit committee, board of directors, management, and others in Airtight Machine Company.

Very truly yours,
Johnson and Seygroves

Johnson and Seygroves, CPAs

Some nonpublic companies are unwilling to implement ideal internal control systems because of costs. For a small nonpublic company, hiring additional personnel might achieve only small improvements in the reliability of accounting data. Instead, it is often less expensive for nonpublic companies to have auditors do more extensive auditing than to incur higher internal control costs.

3. Extent of understanding needed. Auditing standards require that the auditor obtain a sufficient understanding of internal control to assess control risk. In practice, the procedures to gain an understanding of internal control vary considerably from client to client. For smaller nonpublic clients, many auditors obtain a level of understanding sufficient only to assess whether the statements are auditable, evaluate the control environment for management's attitude toward internal control and financial reporting, and determine the adequacy of the client's accounting system. In those engagements, the auditor often assesses control risk at maximum because it is more efficient to perform increased substantive tests than tests of controls. For larger clients, the understanding can be the same as that described for public companies.

It is common for nonpublic companies to lack understandable and reliable narratives or flowcharts. In those instances, the auditor must either prepare them or assist the client in their preparation.

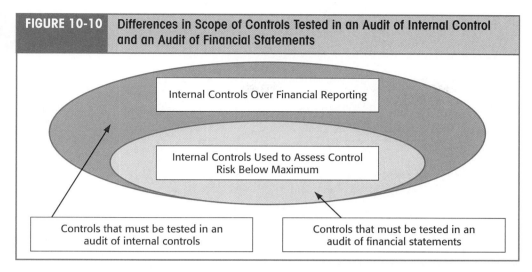

FIGURE 10-10 Differences in Scope of Controls Tested in an Audit of Internal Control and an Audit of Financial Statements

Internal Controls Over Financial Reporting

Internal Controls Used to Assess Control Risk Below Maximum

Controls that must be tested in an audit of internal controls

Controls that must be tested in an audit of financial statements

4. Assessing control risk. The most important difference in a nonpublic company in assessing control risk is the ability to assess control risk at maximum for any or all control-related objectives. The auditor can make that assessment for any objective for either of two reasons: (1) internal controls for the objective are nonexistent or ineffective, or (2) it is more costly to perform tests of controls than the cost reductions that would result from reduced substantive tests. This important concept is discussed in Chapter 13.

As with public company audits, it is useful for auditors to use a control risk matrix for nonpublic company audits. The same format suggested in Figure 10-5 (p. 289) is appropriate.

5. Extent of tests of controls needed. Whenever the auditor assesses control risk below maximum, the auditor must perform tests of controls to support that control risk assessment. The auditor *will not perform tests of controls* when the auditor assesses control risk at maximum, either because of inadequate controls or because it is inefficient to test those controls. When control risk is assessed below the maximum, the auditor designs and performs a combination of tests of controls and substantive procedures. This illustrates that tests of controls vary based on the auditor's assessment of control risk.

In contrast, the number of controls tested by auditors to express an opinion on internal controls for a public company is significantly greater than that tested solely to express an opinion on the financial statements. This is illustrated in Figure 10-10. To express an opinion on internal controls for a public company, the auditor obtains an understanding of and performs tests of controls for *all* significant account balances, classes of transactions, and disclosures and related assertions in the financial statements. Those controls might or might not be tested in a financial statement audit.

SUMMARY

This chapter focused on management's and the auditor's responsibility for understanding, evaluating, and testing internal control for an integrated audit of financial statements and internal control over financial reporting under Section 404 of the Sarbanes–Oxley Act and PCAOB requirements. To rely on a client's internal controls to report on internal control over financial reporting and to reduce planned audit evidence for audits of financial statements, the auditor must first obtain an understanding of each of the five components of internal control. Knowledge about the design of the client's control environment, risk assessment, control activities, information and communication, and monitoring activities and information about whether internal control components have been placed in operation assist the auditor in assessing control risk for each transaction-related audit objective.

The chapter ended with a discussion of the differences in the audit of nonpublic companies because they are not subject to Section 404 and PCAOB requirements to report on internal control over financial reporting. For nonpublic companies, auditors have the option of assessing a higher level of control risk, depending on the quality of the client's internal controls and cost–benefit considerations.

The process followed by auditors in assessing control risk for public and nonpublic companies is summarized in Figure 10-11 (p. 300).

Nonpublic Company		Public Company	
Sufficient to audit financial statements	Obtain an understanding of internal control: design and operation	Sufficient to audit internal control over financial reporting	PHASE 1
	Decide control risk at the objective level for each transaction type	Decide low for all objectives unless there are significant deficiencies or material weaknesses	PHASE 2
	Three alternatives		
	Maximum Intermediate Low		
Varies depending on alternative selected and cost–benefit of testing controls	Plan and perform tests of controls and evaluate results	Extensive tests for all objectives	PHASE 3
Revise for tests of controls results	Revise assessed control risk if appropriate	Revise for tests of controls results	
Likely to be more reliance on substantive tests, depending on assessed control risk option selected	Plan detection risk and perform substantive tests considering control risk and other audit risk model factors	Likely to be less reliance on substantive tests due to tests of controls	PHASE 4
Must communicate, preferably in writing, to the audit committee or equivalent describing significant deficiencies or material weaknesses	Issue internal control report or letter	Must issue report on internal control over financial reporting and issue a written communication to audit committee describing significant deficiencies or material weaknesses	

ESSENTIAL TERMS

Assessment of control risk—a measure of the auditor's expectation that internal controls will neither prevent material misstatements from occurring nor detect and correct them if they have occurred; control risk is assessed for each transaction-related audit objective in a cycle or class of transactions

Chart of accounts—a listing of all the entity's accounts, which classifies transactions into individual balance sheet and income statement accounts

Collusion—a cooperative effort among employees to steal assets or misstate records

Control activities—policies and procedures, in addition to those included in the other four components of internal control, that help ensure that necessary actions are taken to address risks in the achievement of the entity's objectives; they typically include the following five specific control activities: (1) adequate separation of duties, (2) proper authorization of transactions and activities, (3) adequate documents and records, (4) physical control over assets and records, and (5) independent checks on performance

Control deficiency—a deficiency in the design or operation of controls that does not permit company personnel to prevent or detect misstatements on a timely basis

Control environment—the actions, policies, and procedures that reflect the overall attitudes of top management, directors, and owners of an entity about internal control and its importance to the entity

Control risk matrix—a methodology used to help the auditor assess control risk by matching key internal controls and internal control deficiencies with transaction-related audit objectives

Flowchart—a diagrammatic representation of the client's documents and records and the sequence in which they are processed

General authorization—companywide policies for the approval of all transactions within stated limits

Independent checks—internal control activities designed for the continuous internal verification of other controls

Information and communication—the set of manual and/or computerized procedures that initiates, records, processes, and reports an entity's transactions and maintains accountability for the related assets

Internal control—a process designed to provide reasonable assurance regarding the achievement of management's objectives in the following categories: (1) reliability of financial reporting, (2) effectiveness and efficiency of operations, and (3) compliance with applicable laws and regulations

Internal control questionnaire—a series of questions about the controls in each audit area used as a means of indicating to the auditor aspects of internal control that may be inadequate

Key controls—controls that are expected to have the greatest effect on meeting the transaction-related audit objectives

Management letter—an optional letter written by the auditor to a client's management containing the auditor's recommendations for improving any aspect of the client's business

Material weakness—a significant deficiency in internal control that, by itself, or in combination with other significant deficiencies, results in more than a remote likelihood that a mate-

rial misstatement of the financial statements will not be prevented or detected

Monitoring—management's ongoing and periodic assessment of the quality of internal control performance to determine that controls are operating as intended and are modified when needed

Narrative—a written description of a client's internal controls, including the origin, processing, and disposition of documents and records, and the relevant control procedures

Procedures to obtain an understanding—procedures used by the auditor to gather evidence about the design and placement in operation of specific controls

Risk assessment—management's identification and analysis of risks relevant to the preparation of financial statements in accordance with generally accepted accounting principles

Separation of duties—segregation of the following activities in an organization: (1) custody of assets from accounting, (2) authorization from custody of assets, (3) operational responsibility from record keeping, and (4) IT duties from outside users of IT

Significant deficiency—one or more control deficiencies exist that, *more than remotely*, adversely affect a company's ability to initiate, authorize, record, process, or report external financial statements reliably

Specific authorization—case-by-case approval of transactions not covered by companywide policies

Tests of controls—audit procedures to test the operating effectiveness of controls in support of reduced assessed control risk

Walkthrough—the tracing of selected transactions through the accounting system to determine that controls are in place

REVIEW QUESTIONS

10-1 (Objective 10-1) Describe the three broad objectives management has when designing effective internal control.

10-2 (Objective 10-1) Describe which of the three categories of broad objectives for internal controls would be considered by the auditor in an audit of both the financial statements and internal control over financial reporting.

10-3 (Objective 10-2) Section 404 of the Sarbanes–Oxley Act requires management to issue a report on internal control over financial reporting. Identify the specific Section 404 reporting requirements for management.

10-4 (Objective 10-2) What two components of internal control must management assess when reporting on internal control to comply with Section 404 of the Sarbanes–Oxley Act?

10-5 (Objective 10-2) Chapter 8 introduced the eight parts of the planning phase of audits. Which part is understanding internal control and assessing control risk? What parts precede and follow that understanding and assessing?

10-6 (Objectives 10-2, 10-4, 10-8) What is the auditor's responsibility for obtaining an understanding of internal control? How does that responsibility differ for audits of public and nonpublic companies?

10-7 (Objective 10-2) When auditing a public company, what are the auditor's responsibilities related to internal control as required by PCAOB Standard 2?

10-8 (Objectives 10-2, 10-5) State the six transaction-related audit objectives.

10-9 (Objectives 10-2, 10-3) Management must identify the framework used to evaluate the effectiveness of internal control over financial reporting. What framework is used by most U.S. public companies?

10-10 (Objective 10-3) What are the five components of internal control in the COSO internal control framework?

10-11 (Objective 10-3) What is meant by the control environment? What are the factors the auditor must evaluate to understand it?

10-12 (Objective 10-3) What is the relationship among the five components of internal control?

10-13 (Objective 10-3) List the types of specific control activities and provide one specific illustration of a control in the sales area for each control activity.

10-14 (Objective 10-3) The separation of operational responsibility from record keeping is meant to prevent different types of misstatements than the separation of the custody of assets from accounting. Explain the difference in the purposes of these two types of separation of duties.

10-15 (Objective 10-3) For each of the following, give an example of a physical control the client can use to protect the asset or record:
1. Petty cash
2. Cash received by retail clerks
3. Accounts receivable records
4. Raw material inventory
5. Perishable tools
6. Manufacturing equipment
7. Marketable securities

10-16 (Objective 10-3) Explain what is meant by independent checks on performance and give five specific examples.

10-17 (Objective 10-4) Describe the four phases performed by the auditor when obtaining an understanding of internal control and assessing control risk.

10-18 (Objective 10-4) What are management's responsibilities for documenting internal control over financial reporting in a public company? How would the lack of documentation affect an auditor's report on internal control over financial reporting required by PCAOB Standard 2?

10-19 (Objective 10-4) What two aspects of internal control must the auditor assess when performing procedures to obtain an understanding of internal control?

10-20 (Objective 10-4) What is a walkthrough of internal control? What is the PCAOB Standard 2 requirement related to auditor walkthroughs of internal control in an integrated audit?

10-21 (Objective 10-5) Describe what is meant by a key control and a control deficiency.

10-22 (Objectives 10-5, 10-7) Distinguish a significant deficiency in internal control from a material weakness in internal control. How would the presence of one significant deficiency affect an auditor's report on internal control required by PCAOB Standard 2? How would the presence of one material weakness affect an auditor's report on internal control required by PCAOB Standard 2?

10-23 (Objectives 10-3, 10-5) Frank James, a highly competent employee of Brinkwater Sales Corporation, had been responsible for accounting-related matters for two decades. His devotion to the firm and his duties had always been exceptional, and over the years, he had been given increased responsibility. Both the president of Brinkwater and the partner of an independent CPA firm in charge of the audit were shocked and dismayed to discover that James had embezzled more than $500,000 over a 10-year period by not recording billings in the sales journal and subsequently diverting the cash receipts. What major factors permitted the defalcation to take place?

10-24 (Objective 10-5) Jeanne Maier, CPA, believes that it is appropriate to obtain an understanding of internal control about halfway through the audit, after she is familiar with the client's operations and the way the system actually works. She has found through experience that filling out internal control questionnaires and flowcharts early in the engagement is not beneficial because the system rarely functions the way it is supposed to. Later in the engagement, the auditor can prepare flowcharts and questionnaires with relative ease because of the knowledge already obtained on the audit. Evaluate her approach.

10-25 (Objectives 10-6, 10-8) Distinguish the auditor's responsibility for testing controls in an audit of a public company from the responsibility to test controls in an audit of a nonpublic company.

10-26 (Objective 10-6) How does the sufficiency of evidence differ between procedures performed to obtain an understanding of internal control and tests of controls?

10-27 (Objective 10-6) During the prior-year audit of McKimmon Inc., a public company, the auditor performed tests of controls for all relevant financial statement assertions. What are the PCAOB Standard 2 requirements for testing those same controls in the current year?

10-28 (Objective 10-7) What are the two opinions that must be included in the auditor's report on internal control over financial reporting required by PCAOB Standard 2?

10-29 (Objective 10-7) What two conditions must be present for the auditor to issue an unqualified opinion on internal control over financial reporting? What type of condition would cause the auditor to issue a qualified or disclaimer of opinion on internal control over financial reporting?

10-30 (Objective 10-7) Describe the concept of an integrated audit of the financial statements and internal control required by PCAOB Standard 2.

MULTIPLE CHOICE QUESTIONS FROM CPA EXAMINATIONS

10-31 (Objectives 10-1, 10-2, 10-7) The following are general questions about internal control. Choose the best response.

  a. When considering internal control, an auditor must be aware of the concept of reasonable assurance, which recognizes that the
    (1) employment of competent personnel provides assurance that management's control objectives will be achieved.
    (2) establishment and maintenance of internal control is an important responsibility of the management and not of the auditor.
    (3) cost of internal control should not exceed the benefits expected to be derived therefrom.
    (4) separation of incompatible functions is necessary to ascertain that the internal control is effective.

  b. When an auditor issues an unqualified opinion about internal control over financial reporting for a public company, the auditor has obtained reasonable assurance that
    (1) the likelihood of fraud is minimal.
    (2) there are no control deficiencies.
    (3) internal control over financial reporting is operating effectively.
    (4) the financial statements are fairly presented in all material respects.

  c. Which of the following most accurately describe the auditor's responsibilities for reporting on internal control required by PCAOB Standard 2? The auditor tested
    (1) all controls related to the objectives of reliable financial reporting, efficiency and effectiveness of operations, and compliance with laws and regulations.
    (2) controls solely related to the reliability of financial reporting objective.
    (3) controls related to the compliance with laws and regulations objective.
    (4) controls related to the reliability of financial reporting objective in addition to those controls related to operations and compliance with laws and regulations objectives that could materially affect financial reporting.

  d. What is the independent auditor's principal purpose for obtaining an understanding of internal control and assessing control risk in a financial statement audit?
    (1) To comply with generally accepted accounting principles.
    (2) To obtain a measure of assurance of management's efficiency.
    (3) To maintain a state of independence in mental attitude during the audit.
    (4) To determine the nature, timing, and extent of subsequent audit work.

10-32 (Objectives 10-5, 10-7) The following questions deal with deficiencies in internal control. Choose the best response.

a. In general, an internal control deficiency may be defined as a condition under which misstatements would ordinarily not be detected within a timely period by
   (1) an auditor during the typical obtaining of an understanding of internal control and assessment of control risk.
   (2) a controller when reconciling accounts in the general ledger.
   (3) employees in the normal course of performing their assigned functions.
   (4) the chief financial officer when reviewing interim financial statements.

b. A material weakness in internal control represents a control deficiency that
   (1) more than remotely adversely affects a company's ability to initiate, authorize, record, process, or report external financial statements reliably.
   (2) results in more than a remote likelihood that internal control will not prevent or detect material financial statement misstatements.
   (3) exists because a necessary control is missing or not properly designed.
   (4) reduces the efficiency and effectiveness of the entity's operations.

c. An auditor of a public company identifies a material weakness in internal control. The auditor
   (1) will be unable to issue an unqualified opinion on the financial statements.
   (2) must issue a qualified or disclaimer of opinion on internal control over financial reporting.
   (3) may still be able to issue an unqualified opinion on internal control over financial reporting.
   (4) must issue an adverse opinion on internal control over financial reporting.

10-33 (Objectives 10-5, 10-6, 10-8) The following questions deal with assessing control risk in a financial statement audit. Choose the best response.

a. The ultimate purpose of assessing control risk is to contribute to the auditor's evaluation of the
   (1) factors that raise doubts about the auditability of the financial statements.
   (2) operating effectiveness of internal controls.
   (3) risk that material misstatements exist in the financial statements.
   (4) possibility that the nature and extent of substantive tests may be reduced.

b. An auditor uses assessed control risk to
   (1) evaluate the effectiveness of the entity's internal controls.
   (2) identify transactions and account balances where inherent risk is at the maximum.
   (3) indicate whether materiality thresholds for planning and evaluation purposes are sufficiently high.
   (4) determine the acceptable level of detection risk for financial statement assertions.

c. On the basis of audit evidence gathered and evaluated, an auditor decides to increase assessed control risk from that originally planned. To achieve an audit risk level (*AcAR*) that is substantially the same as the planned audit risk level (*AAR*), the auditor would
   (1) increase inherent risk.
   (2) increase materiality levels.
   (3) decrease substantive testing.
   (4) decrease planned detection risk.

d. Which of the following statements about tests of controls is incorrect? Tests of controls
   (1) must be performed in every audit of a public company's financial statements.
   (2) provide persuasive evidence that a material misstatement exists when the auditor determines that the control is not being consistently applied.
   (3) are often based on the same types of audit techniques used to gain an understanding of internal controls, except the extent of testing is generally greater when testing controls.
   (4) allow a reduction in the extent of substantive testing, as long as the results of the tests of controls are equal to or better than what the auditor expects.

DISCUSSION QUESTIONS AND PROBLEMS

10-34 (Objectives 10-3, 10-4, 10-5, 10-6) Each of the following internal controls has been taken from a standard internal control questionnaire used by a CPA firm for assessing control risk in the payroll and personnel cycle.

1. Approval of department head or foreman on time cards is required before preparing payroll.
2. All prenumbered time cards are accounted for before beginning data entry for preparation of checks.
3. The payroll accounting software application will not accept data input for an employee number not contained in the employee master file.
4. Persons preparing the payroll do not perform other payroll duties (timekeeping, distribution of checks) or have access to payroll data master files or cash.
5. The computer calculates gross and net pay based on hours inputted and information in employee master files, and payroll accounting personnel double-check the mathematical accuracy on a test basis.
6. All voided and spoiled payroll checks are properly mutilated and retained.
7. Personnel requires an investigation of an employment application from new employees. Investigation includes checking the employee's background, former employers, and references.
8. Written termination notices, with properly documented reasons for termination, and approval of an appropriate official are required.
9. All checks not distributed to employees are returned to the treasurer for safekeeping.
10. Online ability to add employees or change pay rates to the payroll master file is restricted via passwords to authorized human resource personnel.

a. For each internal control, identify the type(s) of specific control activity (activities) to which it applies (such as adequate documents and records or physical control over assets and records). **Required**

b. For each internal control, identify the transaction-related audit objective(s) to which it applies.

c. For each internal control, identify a specific misstatement that is likely to be prevented if the control exists and is effective.

d. For each control, list a specific misstatement that could result from the absence of the control.

e. For each control, identify one audit test that the auditor could use to uncover misstatements resulting from the absence of the control.

10-35 (Objectives 10-3, 10-4, 10-5) The following are misstatements that have occurred in Fresh Foods Grocery Store, a retail and wholesale grocery company:

1. The incorrect price was used on sales invoices for billing shipments to customers because the wrong price was entered into the computer master file of prices.
2. A vendor's invoice was paid twice for the same shipment. The second payment arose because the vendor sent a duplicate copy of the original 2 weeks after the payment was due.
3. Employees in the receiving department took sides of beef for their personal use. When a shipment of meat was received, the receiving department filled out a receiving report and forwarded it to the accounting department for the amount of goods actually received. At that time, two sides of beef were put in an employee's pickup truck rather than in the storage freezer.
4. During the physical count of inventory of the retail grocery, one counter wrote down the wrong description of several products and miscounted the quantity.
5. A salesperson sold an entire carload of lamb at a price below cost because she did not know the cost of lamb had increased in the past week.
6. On the last day of the year, a truckload of beef was set aside for shipment but was not shipped. Because it was still on hand the inventory was counted. The shipping document was dated the last day of the year, so it was also included as a current-year sale.
7. A vendor invoice was paid even though no merchandise was ever received. The accounts payable software application does not require the input of a valid receiving report number before payment can be made.
8. An accounts payable clerk processed payments to himself by adding a fictitious vendor address to the approved vendor master file.

a. For each misstatement, identify one or more types of controls that were absent. **Required**

b. For each misstatement, identify the transaction-related audit objectives that have not been met.

c. For each misstatement, suggest a control to correct the deficiency.

10-36 (Objective 10-3) The division of the following duties is meant to provide the best possible controls for the Meridian Paint Company, a small wholesale store:

†1. Assemble supporting documents for general and payroll cash disbursements.
†2. Sign general cash disbursement checks.

†3. Input information to prepare checks for signature, record checks in the cash disbursements journal, and update the appropriate master files.

†4. Mail checks to suppliers and deliver checks to employees.

5. Cancel supporting documents to prevent their reuse.

†6. Approve credit for customers included in the customer credit master file.

†7. Input shipping and billing information to bill customers, record invoices in the sales journal, and update the accounts receivable master file.

†8. Open the mail and prepare a prelisting of cash receipts.

†9. Enter cash receipts data to prepare the cash receipts journal and update the accounts receivable master file.

†10. Prepare daily cash deposits.

†11. Deliver daily cash deposits to the bank.

†12. Assemble the payroll time cards and input the data to prepare payroll checks and update the payroll journal and payroll master files.

†13. Sign payroll checks.

14. Update the general ledger at the end of each month and review all accounts for unexpected balances.

15. Reconcile the accounts receivable master file with the control account and review accounts outstanding more than 90 days.

16. Prepare monthly statements for customers by printing the accounts receivable master file; then mail the statements to customers.

17. Reconcile the monthly statements from vendors with the accounts payable master file.

18. Reconcile the bank account.

Required
You are to divide the accounting-related duties 1 through 18 among Robert Smith, James Cooper, and Bill Miller. All of the responsibilities marked with a dagger are assumed to take about the same amount of time and must be divided equally between Smith and Cooper. Both employees are equally competent. Miller, who is president of the company, is not willing to perform any functions designated by a dagger and will perform only a maximum of two of the other functions.*

10-37 (Objectives 10-2, 10-3, 10-5) Recently, while eating lunch with your family at a local cafeteria, you observe a practice that is somewhat unusual. As you reach the end of the cafeteria line, an employee asks how many persons are in your party. He then totals the food purchases on the trays for all of your family and enters the number of persons included in the group. He hands you the receipt and asks you to pay when you finish eating. Near the end of the meal, you decide you want a piece of pie and coffee so you return to the line, select your food, and again go through the line. The employee goes through the same procedures, but this time he staples the second receipt to the original and returns it to you.

When you leave the cafeteria, you hand the stapled receipts to the cash register operator, who totals the two receipts, takes your money, and puts the receipts on a spindle.

Required
a. What internal controls has the cafeteria instituted for its operations?

b. How can the manager of the cafeteria evaluate the effectiveness of the controls?

c. How do these controls differ from those used by most cafeterias?

d. What are the costs and benefits of the cafeteria's system?

10-38 (Objectives 10-2, 10-4, 10-8) Lew Pherson and Vera Collier are friends who are employed by different CPA firms. One day during lunch they are discussing the importance of internal control in determining the amount of audit evidence required for an engagement. Pherson expresses the view that internal control must be evaluated carefully in all companies, regardless of their size or whether they are publicly held, in a similar manner. His CPA firm requires a standard internal control questionnaire on every audit as well as a flowchart of every transaction area. In addition, he says the firm requires a careful evaluation of the system and a modification in the evidence accumulated based on the controls and deficiencies in the system.

Collier responds by saying she believes that internal control cannot be adequate in many of the small companies she audits; therefore, she simply ignores internal control and acts under the assumption of inadequate controls. She goes on to say, "Why should I spend a lot of time obtaining an understanding of internal control and assessing control risk when I know it has all kinds of weaknesses before I start? I would rather spend the time it takes to fill out all those forms in testing whether the statements are correct."

*AICPA adapted.

a. Express in general terms the most important difference between the nature of the potential controls available for large and small companies.

b. Criticize the positions taken by Pherson and Collier, and express your own opinion about the similarities and differences that should exist in understanding internal control and assessing control risk for different-sized companies.

c. Discuss whether Collier's approach is acceptable when auditing a public company's financial statements.

d. Describe what additional procedures Pherson must perform if auditing the financial statements of a public company.

Required

10-39 (Objectives 10-3, 10-5) The following are partial descriptions of internal controls for companies engaged in the manufacturing business:

1. When Mr. Clark orders materials for his machine-rebuilding plant, he sends a duplicate purchase order to the receiving department. During the delivery of materials, Mr. Smith, the receiving clerk, records the receipt of shipment on this purchase order. After recording, Mr. Smith sends the purchase order to the accounting department, where it is used to record materials purchased and accounts payable. The materials are transported to the storage area by forklifts. The additional purchased quantities are recorded on storage records.

2. Every day, hundreds of employees clock in using time cards at Generous Motors Corporation. The timekeepers collect these cards once a week and deliver them to the computer department. There, the data on these time cards are entered into the computer. The information entered into the computer is used in the preparation of the labor cost distribution records, the payroll journal, and the payroll checks. The treasurer, Mrs. Webber, compares the payroll journal with the payroll checks, signs the checks, and returns them to Mr. Strode, the supervisor of the computer department. The payroll checks are distributed to the employees by Mr. Strode.

3. The smallest branch of Connor Cosmetics in South Bend employs Mary Cooper, the branch manager, and her sales assistant, Janet Hendrix. The branch uses a bank account in South Bend to pay expenses. The account is kept in the name of "Connor Cosmetics—Special Account." To pay expenses, checks must be signed by Mary Cooper or by the treasurer of Connor Cosmetics, John Winters. Cooper receives the cancelled checks and bank statements. She reconciles the branch account herself and files cancelled checks and bank statements in her records. She also periodically prepares reports of cash disbursements and sends them to the home office.

a. List the deficiencies in internal control for each of these situations. To identify the deficiencies, use the methodology that was discussed in this chapter.

b. For each deficiency, state the type(s) of misstatement(s) that is (are) likely to result. Be as specific as possible.

c. How would you improve internal controls for each of the three companies?*

Required

10-40 (Objective 10-5) Anthony, CPA, prepared the flowchart on page 308, which portrays the raw materials purchasing function of one of Anthony's clients, Medium-Sized Manufacturing Company, from the preparation of initial documents through the vouching of invoices for payment in accounts payable. Assume that all documents are prenumbered.

Identify the deficiencies in internal control that can be determined from the flowchart. Use the methodology discussed in this chapter. Include internal control deficiencies resulting from activities performed or not performed.*

Required

10-41 (Objective 10-7) The following are independent situations for which you will recommend an appropriate audit report on internal control over financial reporting as required by PCAOB Standard 2:

1. The auditor identified a material misstatement in the financial statements that was not detected by management of the company.

2. The auditor was unable to obtain any evidence about the operating effectiveness of internal control over financial reporting.

3. The auditor determined that a deficiency in internal control exists that will not prevent or detect a material misstatement in the financial statements.

4. During interim testing, the auditor identified and communicated to management a significant control deficiency. Management immediately corrected the deficiency and the auditor was able to sufficiently test the newly instituted internal control before the end of the fiscal period.

*AICPA adapted.

5. As a result of performing tests of controls, the auditor identified a significant deficiency in internal control over financial reporting; however, the auditor does not believe that it represents a material weakness in internal control.

Required
For each situation, state the appropriate audit report from the following alternatives:

- Unqualified opinion on internal control over financial reporting.
- Qualified or disclaimer of opinion on internal control over financial reporting.
- Adverse opinion on internal control over financial reporting.

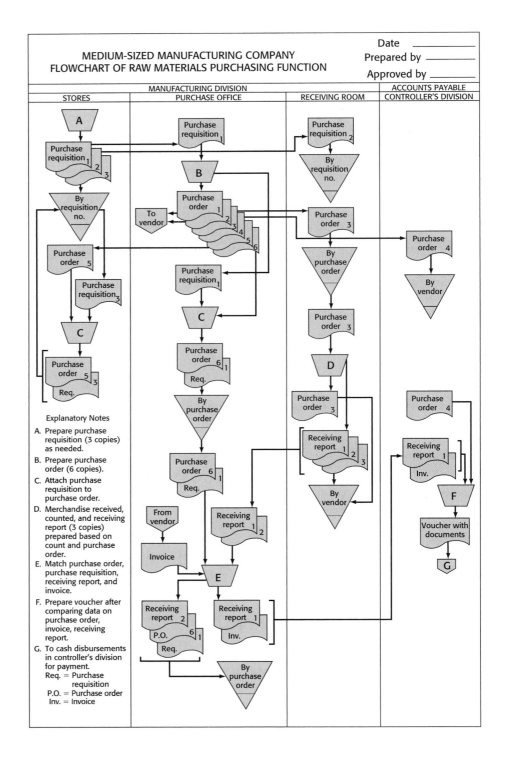

CASE

10-42 (Objective 10-5) The following is the description of sales and cash receipts for the Lady's Fashion Fair, a retail store dealing in expensive women's clothing. Sales are for cash or credit, using the store's own billing rather than credit cards.

Each salesclerk has her own sales book with prenumbered, three-copy, multicolored sales slips attached, but perforated. Only a central cash register is used. It is operated by the store supervisor, who has been employed for 10 years by Alice Olson, the store owner. The cash register is at the store entrance to control theft of clothes.

Salesclerks prepare the sales invoices in triplicate. The original and the second copy are given to the cashier. The third copy is retained by the salesclerk in the sales book. When the sale is for cash, the customer pays the salesclerk, who marks all three copies "paid" and presents the money to the cashier with the invoice copies.

All clothing is put into boxes or packages by the supervisor after comparing the clothing to the description on the invoice and the price on the sales tag. She also rechecks the clerk's calculations. Any corrections are approved by the salesclerk. The clerk changes her sales book at that time.

A credit sale is approved by the supervisor from an approved credit list after the salesclerk prepares the three-part invoice. Next, the supervisor enters the sale in her cash register as a credit or cash sale. The second copy of the invoice, which has been validated by the cash register, is given to the customer.

At the end of the day, the supervisor recaps the sales and cash and compares the totals to the cash register tape. The supervisor deposits the cash at the end of each day in the bank's lockbox. The cashier's copies of the invoices are sent to the accounts receivable clerk along with a summary of the day's receipts. The bank mails the deposit slip directly to the accounts receivable clerk.

Each clerk summarizes her sales each day on a daily summary form, which is used in part to calculate employees' sales commissions. Marge, the accountant, who is prohibited from handling cash, receives the supervisor's summary and the clerk's daily summary form. Daily, she puts all sales invoice information into the firm's computer, which provides a complete printout of all input and summaries. The accounting summary includes sales by salesclerk, cash sales, credit sales, and total sales. Marge compares this output with the supervisor's and salesclerks' summaries and reconciles all differences.

The computer updates accounts receivable, inventory, and general ledger master files. After the update procedure has been run on the computer, Marge's assistant files all sales invoices by customer number. A list of the invoice numbers in numerical sequence is included in the sales printout.

The mail is opened each morning by a secretary in the owner's office. All correspondence and complaints are given to the owner. The secretary prepares a prelist of cash receipts. He totals the list, prepares a deposit slip, and deposits the cash daily. A copy of the prelist, the deposit slip, and all remittances returned with the cash receipts are given to Marge. She uses this list and the remittances to record cash receipts and update accounts receivable, again by computer. She reconciles the total receipts on the prelist to the deposit slip and to her printout. At the same time, she compares the deposit slip received from the bank for cash sales to the cash receipts journal.

A weekly aged trial balance of accounts receivable is automatically generated by the computer. A separate listing of all unpaid bills over 60 days is also automatically prepared. These are given to Mrs. Olson, who acts as her own credit collector. She also approves all charge-offs of uncollectible items and forwards the list to Marge, who writes them off.

Each month Marge mails statements generated by the computer to customers. Complaints and disagreements from customers are directed to Mrs. Olson, who resolves them and informs Marge in writing of any write-downs or misstatements that require correction.

The computer system also automatically totals the journals and posts the totals to the general ledger. A general ledger trial balance is printed out, from which Marge prepares financial statements. Marge also prepares a monthly bank reconciliation and reconciles the general ledger to the aged accounts receivable trial balance.

Because of the importance of inventory control, Marge prints out the inventory perpetual totals monthly, on the last day of each month. Salesclerks count all inventory after store hours on the last day of each month for comparison with the perpetuals. An inventory shortages report is provided to Mrs. Olson. The perpetuals are adjusted by Marge after Mrs. Olson has approved the adjustments.

Required

a. For each sales transaction-related audit objective, identify one or more existing controls.

b. For each cash receipts transaction-related audit objective, identify one or more existing controls.

c. Identify deficiencies of internal control for sales and cash receipts.

INTEGRATED CASE APPLICATION—PINNACLE MANUFACTURING: PART III

10-43 (Objective 10-5) In Parts I and II of this case, you performed preliminary analytical procedures and assessed acceptable audit risk and inherent risk for Pinnacle Manufacturing. Your team has been assigned the responsibility of auditing the acquisition and payment cycle and one related balance sheet account, accounts payable. The general approach to be taken will be to reduce assessed control risk to a low level, if possible, for the two main types of transactions affecting accounts payable: acquisitions and cash disbursements. The following are furnished as background information:

- A summary of key information from the audit of the acquisition and payment cycle and accounts payable in the prior year, which was extracted from the previous audit firm's audit files (Figure 10-12)

- A flowchart description of the accounting system and internal controls for the acquisition and payment cycle (Figure 10-13)—the flowchart shows that although each of the company's three divisions has its own receiving department, the purchasing and accounts payable functions are centralized

The purpose of Part III is to obtain an understanding of internal control and assess control risk for Pinnacle Manufacturing's acquisition and cash disbursement transactions.

Required

a. Familiarize yourself with the internal control system for acquisitions and cash disbursements by studying the information in Figure 10-12 and Figure 10-13.

b. Prepare a control risk matrix for acquisitions and a separate one for cash disbursements using Figure 10-5 on page 289 as a guide. A formatted control risk matrix is provided on the textbook Web site. The objectives should be specific transaction-related audit objectives for acquisitions

FIGURE 10-12	Information for Audit of Accounts Payable—Previous Year

Accounts payable, 12-31-03	
Number of accounts	452
Total accounts payable	$8,200,060
Range of individual balances	$27.83–$614,819.62
Tolerable misstatement for accounts payable	$210,000
Transactions, 2003	
Acquisitions:	
Number of acquisitions	15,103
Total acquisitions	$81,573,000
Cash disbursements:	
Number of disbursements	25,412
Total cash disbursements	$82,916,500
Results of audit procedures—tests of controls and substantive tests of transactions for acquisitions (sample size of 100):	
Purchase order not approved	2
Purchase quantities, prices, and/or extensions not correct	1
Transactions charged to wrong general ledger account	1
Transactions recorded in wrong period	1
No other exceptions	
Results of audit procedures—cash disbursements (sample size of 100):	
Cash disbursement recorded in wrong period	1
No other exceptions	
Results of audit procedures—accounts payable:	
(50% of vendors' balances were verified; combined net understatement amounts were projected to the population as follows):	
Three cutoff misstatements	$48,673
One difference in amounts due to disputes and discounts	$11,103
No adjustment was necessary because the total projected misstatement was not material.	

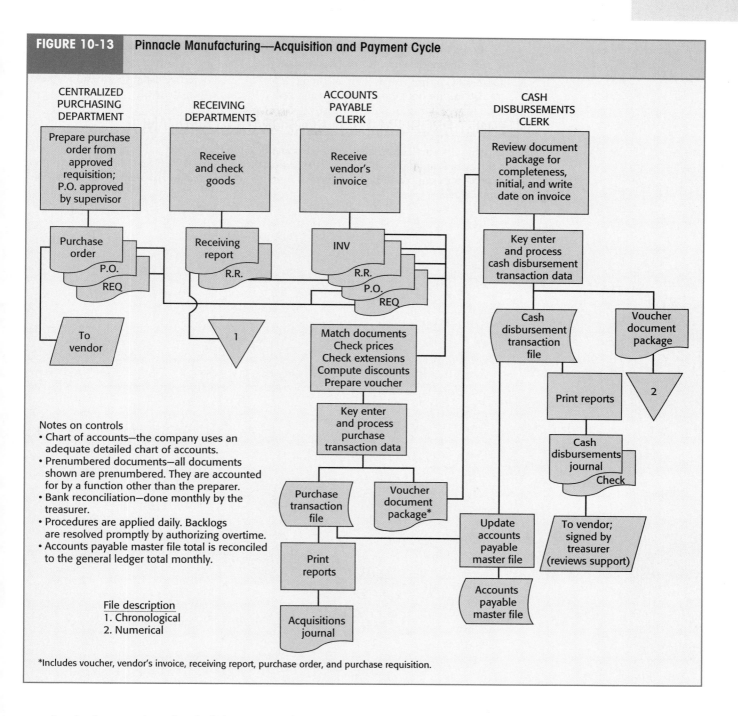

FIGURE 10-13 | Pinnacle Manufacturing—Acquisition and Payment Cycle

CENTRALIZED PURCHASING DEPARTMENT

Prepare purchase order from approved requisition; P.O. approved by supervisor

Purchase order
P.O.
REQ

To vendor

Notes on controls
• Chart of accounts—the company uses an adequate detailed chart of accounts.
• Prenumbered documents—all documents shown are prenumbered. They are accounted for by a function other than the preparer.
• Bank reconciliation—done monthly by the treasurer.
• Procedures are applied daily. Backlogs are resolved promptly by authorizing overtime.
• Accounts payable master file total is reconciled to the general ledger total monthly.

File description
1. Chronological
2. Numerical

RECEIVING DEPARTMENTS

Receive and check goods

Receiving report
R.R.

1

ACCOUNTS PAYABLE CLERK

Receive vendor's invoice

INV
R.R.
P.O.
REQ

Match documents
Check prices
Check extensions
Compute discounts
Prepare voucher

Key enter and process purchase transaction data

Purchase transaction file

Voucher document package*

Print reports

Acquisitions journal

CASH DISBURSEMENTS CLERK

Review document package for completeness, initial, and write date on invoice

Key enter and process cash disbursement transaction data

Cash disbursement transaction file

Voucher document package

Print reports

2

Cash disbursements journal
Check

To vendor; signed by treasurer (reviews support)

Update accounts payable master file

Accounts payable master file

*Includes voucher, vendor's invoice, receiving report, purchase order, and purchase requisition.

for the first matrix and cash disbursements for the second matrix. See pages 589–592 in Chapter 19 for transaction-related audit objectives for acquisitions and cash disbursements. In doing Part III, the following steps are recommended:

(1) *Controls*

a. Identify key controls for acquisitions and for cash disbursements. After you decide on the key controls, include each control in one of the two matrices.

b. Include a "C" in the matrix in each column for the objective(s) to which each control applies. Several of the controls should satisfy multiple objectives.

(2) *Deficiencies*

a. Identify key deficiencies for acquisitions and for cash disbursements. After you decide on the deficiencies, include each significant deficiency or material weakness in the bottom portion of one of the two matrices.

b. Include a "W" in the matrix in each column for the objective(s) to which each significant deficiency or material weakness applies.

(3) Assess control risk as high, medium, or low for each objective using your best judgment. Do this for both the acquisitions and cash disbursements matrices.

INTERNET PROBLEM 10-1: CORPORATE GOVERNANCE

Reference the CW site. The problem requires students to use the Internet to research (1) the purpose of the Business Roundtable (BR) and (2) specific issues within the BR's Statement on Corporate Governance (for example, board of directors' function with respect to risk management, controls, and compliance).

CHAPTER 11

FRAUD AUDITING

ACCOUNTING SCANDAL ROCKS PUBLIC TRUST

The accounting profession was under fire. Throughout the long hot summer, newspapers were filled with new details of a corporate accounting scandal. One of the largest, most respected companies in the United States had been caught inflating earnings and assets through blatant manipulation of the accounting rules. Thousands of investors and employees had suffered. Congressional hearings were called to examine and understand the fraud, and everyone asked, "Where were the auditors?" The accounting profession was under immense political pressure from reform-minded lawmakers, and the negative publicity surrounding the perceived audit failure cast all CPAs in the most unfavorable light.

The year was 1938. The corporate accounting scandal was McKesson-Robbins, and it arguably had a greater impact on the way audits are performed than any subsequent scandal, including Enron and WorldCom. McKesson-Robbins inflated assets and earnings by $19 million through the reporting of nonexistent inventory and fictitious sales.

In 1924, Philip Musica, a high school dropout with fraud convictions and a prison record, reinvented himself as F. Donald Coster and awarded himself a medical degree. "Dr. Coster" took control of McKesson-Robbins and embarked on a massive fraud to inflate its share prices. Coster duped McKesson's auditors, and the investing public, into believing that the company had a huge drug inventory, worth multimillions of dollars, that didn't exist. Coster created phony purchase orders, sales invoices, and other documents, all of which McKesson's auditors dutifully reviewed as evidence of the imaginary inventory. The fraud succeeded because the auditing standards of the day permitted auditors to confine themselves to reviewing documents and talking to management. They were not required to physically observe and verify inventories.

During an emergency board meeting, hastily called after the fraud came to light, word was received that Coster had committed suicide. An investment bank partner who served as a McKesson outside director, concerned about his responsibilities, responded to the news by exclaiming, "Let's fire him anyway!"

LEARNING OBJECTIVES

After studying this chapter, you should be able to

11-1 Define fraud and distinguish between fraudulent financial reporting and misappropriation of assets.

11-2 Describe the fraud triangle and identify conditions for fraud.

11-3 Understand the auditor's responsibility for assessing the risk of fraud and detecting material misstatements due to fraud.

11-4 Identify corporate governance and other control environment factors that reduce fraud risks.

11-5 Develop responses to identified fraud risks.

11-6 Recognize specific fraud risk areas and develop procedures to detect fraud.

11-7 Understand interview techniques and other activities after fraud is suspected.

Sources: Adapted from 1. Michael Ramos, "SAS 99 Gives CPAs New Chance to Reclaim Reputation," December 2002 (www.CPA2biz.com/News/Viewpoint). 2. Presentation by PCAOB Board Member Daniel L. Goelzer at Investment Company Institute's 2003 Tax & Accounting Conference, September 15, 2003 (www.pcaobus.org/transcripts/Goelzer_09-15-03.asp).

The classic fraud at McKesson-Robbins illustrates that financial statement fraud is not something new. In the wake of that scandal, the auditing profession responded by setting the first formal standards for auditing procedures. Those standards required confirmation of receivables and observation of physical inventories, procedures that are standard today. The standards also included guidance on the auditor's responsibilities for detecting fraud.

In response to more recent frauds, Congress passed the Sarbanes–Oxley Act and specific auditing standards have been developed dealing with fraud risk assessment and detection. This chapter discusses the auditor's responsibility to assess the risk of fraud and detect material misstatements due to fraud. The chapter also describes major areas of fraud risk, as well as controls to prevent fraud and audit procedures to detect fraud.

TYPES OF FRAUD

OBJECTIVE 11-1

Define fraud and distinguish between fraudulent financial reporting and misappropriation of assets.

While fraud is a broad legal concept, in the context of auditing financial statements, fraud is defined as an intentional misstatement of financial statements. The two main categories of fraud are fraudulent financial reporting and misappropriation of assets, which were introduced in Chapter 6 in defining the auditor's responsibilities for detecting material misstatements.

Fraudulent Financial Reporting

Fraudulent financial reporting is an intentional misstatement or omission of amounts or disclosures with the intent to deceive users. Most cases of fraudulent financial reporting involve the intentional misstatement of amounts, not disclosures. For example, WorldCom is reported to have capitalized as fixed assets, billions of dollars that should have been expensed. Omissions of amounts are less common, but a company can overstate income by omitting accounts payable and other liabilities.

Although most cases of fraudulent financial reporting involve overstatement of assets and income or omission of liabilities and expenses in an attempt to overstate income, it is important to note that companies often deliberately understate income. For privately held companies, this may be done in an attempt to reduce income taxes. Companies may also intentionally understate income when earnings are high to create a reserve of earnings or "cookie jar reserves" that may be used to increase earnings in future periods. This practice is called income smoothing or earnings management. **Earnings management** involves deliberate actions taken by management to meet earnings objectives. **Income smoothing** is a form of earnings management in which revenues and expenses are shifted between periods to reduce fluctuations in earnings. One technique to smooth income is to reduce the value of inventory and other assets of an acquired company at the time of acquisition, resulting in higher earnings when the assets are later sold. Companies may also deliberately overstate inventory obsolescence reserves and allowances for doubtful accounts in periods of higher earnings.

Although less frequent, several notable cases of fraudulent financial reporting involved inadequate disclosure. For example, a central issue in the Enron case was whether the company had adequately disclosed obligations to affiliates known as special-purpose entities. E. F. Hutton, a now defunct brokerage firm, was charged with intentionally overdrawing accounts at various banks to increase interest earnings. These overdrafts were included as liabilities on the balance sheet, but the balance sheet description of the obligations was unclear.

Misappropriation of Assets

Misappropriation of assets is fraud that involves theft of an entity's assets. In many cases, the amounts involved are not material to the financial statements. However, the loss of company assets is an important management concern, and management's materiality threshold for fraud will likely be much lower than the materiality threshold used by the auditor for financial reporting purposes.

The term misappropriation of assets is normally used to refer to theft involving employees and others internal to the organization. For example, the Association of Certified Fraud Examiners estimates that the average company loses 6 percent of its revenues to fraud. However, much of this fraud involves external parties, such as shoplifting and cheating by suppliers.

Misappropriation of assets is normally perpetrated at lower levels of the organization hierarchy. In some notable cases, however, top management is involved in the theft of company assets. Because of management's greater authority and control over organization assets, defalcations involving top management can involve significant amounts. In one extreme example, the former CEO of Tyco International was charged by the SEC with stealing over $100 million in assets. In a fraud survey conducted by the Association of Certified Fraud Examiners, the median loss in frauds involving top management was more than three times larger than frauds involving other employees.

CONDITIONS FOR FRAUD

Three conditions for fraud arising from fraudulent financial reporting and misappropriations of assets are described in SAS 99 (AU 316). As shown in Figure 11-1 (p. 316), these three conditions are referred to as the **fraud triangle.**

OBJECTIVE 11-2

Describe the fraud triangle and identify conditions for fraud.

1. *Incentives/Pressures.* Management or other employees have incentives or pressures to commit fraud.

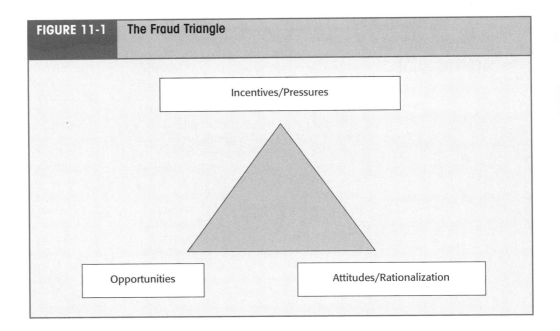

FIGURE 11-1 | **The Fraud Triangle**

Incentives/Pressures

Opportunities

Attitudes/Rationalization

2. *Opportunities.* Circumstances provide opportunities for management or employees to commit fraud.
3. *Attitudes/Rationalization.* An attitude, character, or set of ethical values exists that allows management or employees to commit a dishonest act, or they are in an environment that imposes sufficient pressure that causes them to rationalize committing a dishonest act.

Risk Factors for Fraudulent Financial Reporting

An essential consideration by the auditor in uncovering fraud is identifying factors that increase the risk of fraud. These are referred to as **fraud risk factors.** Table 11-1 provides examples of fraud risk factors for each of the three conditions of fraud for fraudulent financial reporting. Even though the three conditions in the fraud triangle are the same for fraudulent financial reporting and misappropriation of assets, the risk factors are different. First, the risk factors for fraudulent financial reporting are discussed, followed by those for misappropriation of assets. Later in the chapter, there is a discussion of the auditor's use of the risk factors in uncovering fraud.

LAST DEAL FOR TURNAROUND ARTIST

Albert J. "Chainsaw Al" Dunlap was a legendary turnaround artist known for his reputation of slashing jobs and other costs. The news in July 1996 that he was joining Sunbeam caused its stock to rise by nearly 60 percent, at that time, the largest one-day jump in the history of the New York Stock Exchange. However, 2 years later, he was ousted from the company by the board of directors amid charges that he had cooked the books to hide Sunbeam's true financial condition from investors.

To increase income and create the impression of revenue growth, the company borrowed revenues from future periods through a procedure known as "channel stuffing." Sunbeam offered discounts and inducements to customers to buy merchandise immediately that was normally sold in later periods. For example,

customers were encouraged to take delivery of outdoor grills during the winter, even though there was little demand for these items at that time.

Sunbeam ultimately entered bankruptcy in 2001. Al Dunlap was fined $500,000 by the SEC, a proverbial slap on the wrist compared to his compensation from Sunbeam and his accumulated wealth. He also agreed to a lifetime ban from serving as an officer or director of a public company.

Sources: Adapted from 1. John Byrne, "Chainsaw Al Dunlap Cuts His Last Deal," *BusinessWeek* (September 5, 2002). 2. Securities and Exchange Commission Accounting and Auditing Enforcement Release 1623, September 4, 2002 (www.sec.gov/litigation/litreleases/lr17710.htm).

THREE CONDITIONS OF FRAUD		
Incentives/Pressures	**Opportunities**	**Attitudes/Rationalization**
Management or other employees have incentives or pressures to materially misstate financial statements.	Circumstances provide an opportunity for management or employees to misstate financial statements.	An attitude, character, or set of ethical values exists that allows management or employees to intentionally commit a dishonest act, or they are in an environment that imposes sufficient pressure that causes them to rationalize committing a dishonest act.
Examples of Risk Factors	**Examples of Risk Factors**	**Examples of Risk Factors**
Financial stability or profitability is threatened by economic, industry, or entity operating conditions. Examples include significant declines in customer demand and increasing business failures in either the industry or overall economy. Excessive pressure for management to meet debt repayment or other debt covenant requirements. Management or the board of directors' personal net worth is materially threatened by the entity's financial performance.	Significant accounting estimates involve subjective judgments or uncertainties that are difficult to verify. Ineffective board of director or audit committee oversight over financial reporting. High turnover or ineffective accounting, internal audit, or information technology staff.	Inappropriate or ineffective communication and support of the entity's values. Known history of violations of securities laws or other laws and regulations. Management's practice of making overly aggressive or unrealistic forecasts to analysts, creditors, and other third parties.

Incentives/Pressures A common incentive for companies to manipulate financial statements is a decline in the company's financial prospects. A decline in earnings may threaten the company's ability to obtain financing and continue as a going concern. Companies may also manipulate earnings to meet analysts' forecasts or benchmarks such as prior-year earnings, to meet debt covenant restrictions, or to artificially inflate stock prices. In some cases, management may manipulate earnings just to preserve their reputation.

Opportunities Financial statements of all companies are potentially subject to manipulation. However, the risk of fraudulent financial reporting is greater for companies in industries where significant judgments and estimates are involved. For example, valuation of inventories is subject to greater risk of misstatement for companies with diverse inventories in many locations. The risk of misstatement of inventories is further increased if those inventories are potentially obsolete.

Opportunities for misstatement are greater if there is turnover in accounting personnel or other weaknesses in accounting and information processes. In many cases of fraudulent financial reporting, the company had an ineffective audit committee and board of director oversight of financial reporting.

Attitudes/Rationalization The attitude of top management toward financial reporting is a critical risk factor in assessing the likelihood of fraudulent financial statements. If the CEO or other top managers display a significant disregard for the financial reporting process, for example, by consistently issuing overly optimistic forecasts or by being overly concerned about meeting analysts' earnings forecasts, fraudulent financial reporting is more likely. Also, management's character or set of ethical values may make it easier for them to rationalize a fraudulent act.

The same three fraud triangle conditions apply to misappropriation of assets. However, in assessing risk factors, greater emphasis is placed on individual incentives and opportunities for theft. Table 11-2 (p. 318) provides examples of fraud risk factors for each of the three conditions of fraud for misappropriation of assets.

Risk Factors for Misappropriation of Assets

TABLE 11-2	Examples of Risk Factors for Misappropriation of Assets	

THREE CONDITIONS OF FRAUD

Incentives/Pressures	Opportunities	Attitudes/Rationalization
Management or other employees have incentives or pressures to misappropriate material assets.	Circumstances provide an opportunity for management or employees to misappropriate assets.	An attitude, character, or set of ethical values exists that allows management or employees to intentionally commit a dishonest act, or they are in an environment that imposes sufficient pressure that causes them to rationalize committing a dishonest act.
Examples of Risk Factors	**Examples of Risk Factors**	**Examples of Risk Factors**
Personal financial obligations create pressure for those with access to cash or other assets susceptible to theft to misappropriate those assets. Adverse relationships between management and employees with access to assets susceptible to theft motivate employees to misappropriate those assets. Examples include the following: • Known or expected employee layoffs. • Promotions, compensation, or other rewards inconsistent with expectations.	Presence of large amounts of cash on hand or inventory items that are small, of high value, or are in high demand. Inadequate internal control over assets due to lack of the following: • Appropriate segregation of duties or independent checks. • Job applicant screening for employees with access to assets. • Mandatory vacations for employees with access to assets.	Disregard for the need to monitor or reduce risk of misappropriating assets. Disregard for internal controls by overriding existing controls or failing to correct known internal control deficiencies.

Incentives/Pressures Financial pressures are a common incentive for employees who misappropriate assets. Employees with excessive financial obligations or with drug abuse or gambling problems may steal to meet their personal financial or other needs. Managers should be alert for signs of these problems in employees with access to assets or accounting records. A credit investigation may be included in the hiring background check for potential employees who will have access to assets. Dissatisfied employees may steal from a sense of entitlement or as a form of attack against their employers. Companies can reduce fraud risk by dealing fairly with employees and monitoring employee morale.

Opportunities Opportunities for theft exist in all companies. However, opportunities are greater in companies with accessible cash or with inventory or other valuable assets, especially if they are small or readily portable. For example, thefts of laptop computers are fairly common and much more frequent than thefts of desktop systems. Retail establishments and other organizations that receive revenue in the form of cash are also susceptible to theft.

EMPLOYERS BEWARE

One small business owner knew him as David Shelton, but he had at least a dozen aliases. Hired as a bookkeeper by seven small Southern California businesses, authorities believe he has stolen at least $600,000 by pocketing cash receipts and issuing checks to fake suppliers that he controlled.

One company hired Shelton after he responded to an ad for a bookkeeper. His resume indicated that he had been a bookkeeper for over 20 years with two companies. The company owner called the number for his "current employer," and a woman answered with the name of the firm. The call was then transferred to a man who gave a glowing recommendation. Shelton disappeared the day before the company's outside auditor was scheduled to appear, after apparently stealing $44,000 from the company.

Police detective Jeff Nelson continues to try to track down Mr. Shelton, often on his own time. He has tracked Shelton through 15 aliases and concedes he may never learn his true identity. However, he is sure of one thing: "He is doing it to some other business as we speak."

Source: John Emshwiller, "Looking for a New Bookkeeper? Beware of This One," *The Wall Street Journal* (April 19, 1994).

Surveillance methods and inventory coding and tracking systems can reduce the potential for theft. For example, casinos handle extensive amounts of cash with little formal records of cash received. As a result, casinos make extensive use of video and human surveillance.

Weak internal controls create opportunities for theft. Inadequate separation of duties is practically a license for employees to steal. Whenever employees have custody or even temporary access to assets and maintain the accounting records for those assets, the potential for theft exists. As an example, if inventory storeroom employees also maintain inventory records, it is relatively easy for them to take inventory items and cover the theft by adjusting the accounting records.

Fraud is more prevalent in smaller businesses and not-for-profit organizations because it is more difficult for these entities to maintain adequate separation of duties. However, even large organizations may fail to maintain adequate separation in critical areas. As an illustration, Barings Bank incurred losses in excess of $1 billion from the activities of one trader because of inadequate separation of duties.

Attitudes/Rationalization Management's attitude toward controls and ethical conduct may allow employees and managers to rationalize the theft of assets. If management cheats customers through overcharging for goods or engaging in high-pressure sales tactics, employees may feel that it is acceptable for them to behave in the same fashion by cheating on expense or time reports.

ASSESSING THE RISK OF FRAUD

SAS 99 provides guidance to auditors in assessing the risk of fraud. Auditors must maintain a level of professional skepticism as they consider a broad set of information, including fraud risk factors, to identify and respond to fraud risk. As discussed in Chapter 6, the auditor has a responsibility to respond to fraud risk by planning and performing the audit to obtain reasonable assurance that material misstatements, whether due to errors or fraud, are detected.

OBJECTIVE 11-3

Understand the auditor's responsibility for assessing the risk of fraud and detecting material misstatements due to fraud.

SAS 1 states that, in exercising **professional skepticism,** an auditor "*neither assumes that management is dishonest nor assumes unquestioned honesty.*" In practice, maintaining this attitude of professional skepticism can be difficult because, despite some recent high-profile examples of fraudulent financial statements, material frauds are infrequent compared to the number of audits of financial statements conducted annually. Most auditors will never encounter a material fraud during their careers. Also, through client acceptance and continuance evaluation procedures, auditors reject most potential clients perceived as lacking honesty and integrity. SAS 99 emphasizes consideration of a client's susceptibility to fraud, regardless of the auditor's beliefs about the likelihood of fraud and management's honesty and integrity.

Professional Skepticism

Fraud-Related
Web Sites

Questioning Mind During audit planning for every audit, the engagement team must discuss the need to maintain a questioning mind throughout the audit in identifying fraud risks and critically evaluating audit evidence. In maintaining a questioning mind, auditors should set

| PCAOB CONSIDERATION OF AUDITOR RESPONSIBILITY FOR FRAUD DETECTION | While SAS 99 currently provides authoritative guidance about the auditor's responsibility for detecting material misstatements due to fraud, the PCAOB has identified auditor detection of fraud as a top standards-setting priority. The PCAOB staff has developed a briefing paper outlining issues related to its consideration of a new auditing standard related to fraud detection that would apply to audits of public companies. In that briefing paper, the PCAOB questions whether the level of responsibility for fraud detection articulated in SAS 99 is sufficient to meet stock- | holder expectations for auditor detection of fraud and whether auditors should be held to a higher level of fraud detection than that required by SAS 99. The briefing paper contains 50 discussion questions related to specific auditor fraud detection issues that the PCAOB will be considering as it develops a new auditing standard related to fraud detection.

Source: Public Company Accounting Oversight Board, "Financial Fraud" Briefing Paper, September 8–9, 2004 (www.pcaobus.org). |

aside any prior beliefs about management's integrity and honesty and should consider the potential for management override of controls, given that fraud is possible in any audit.

Critical Evaluation of Audit Evidence Auditors should thoroughly probe the issues, acquire additional evidence as necessary, and consult with other team members rather than rationalize or dismiss information or other conditions that indicate a material misstatement due to fraud may have occurred. For example, an auditor may uncover a current-year sale that should properly be reflected as a sale in the following year. Rather than conclude that the error is an isolated incident, the auditor should evaluate the reasons for the error, determine whether it was intentional or unintentional, and consider whether other such errors are likely to have occurred.

Sources of Information About Fraud Risks

Information used to assess fraud risk is summarized in Figure 11-2. This information is considered in the context of the three conditions for fraud: incentives/pressures, opportunities, and attitudes/rationalization. Auditors should consider the following:

- Information obtained from communications among audit team members about their knowledge of the company and its industry, including how and where the company might be susceptible to material misstatements due to fraud.
- Responses to auditor inquiries of management about their views of the risks of fraud and about existing programs and controls to address specific identified fraud risks.
- Specific risk factors for fraudulent financial reporting and misappropriations of assets.
- Analytical procedures results obtained during planning that indicate possible implausible or unexpected analytical relationships.
- Knowledge obtained through other procedures, such as client acceptance and retention decisions, interim review of financial statements, and consideration of inherent or control risks.

Communications Among Audit Team SAS 99 requires the audit team to conduct discussions to share insights from more experienced audit team members and to "brainstorm" ideas that address the following:

1. How and where they believe the entity's financial statements might be susceptible to material misstatement due to fraud—this should include consideration of known external and internal factors affecting the entity that might

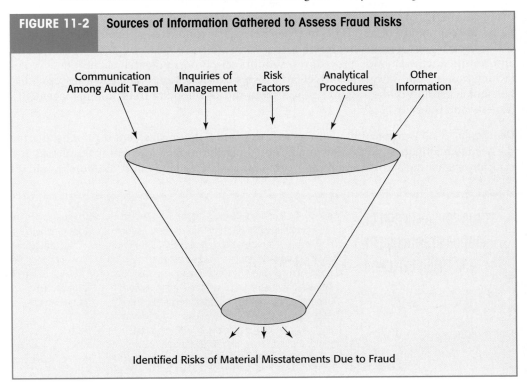

FIGURE 11-2 | **Sources of Information Gathered to Assess Fraud Risks**

Communication Among Audit Team   Inquiries of Management   Risk Factors   Analytical Procedures   Other Information

Identified Risks of Material Misstatements Due to Fraud

- create an incentive or pressure for management to commit fraud.
- provide the opportunity for fraud to be perpetrated.
- indicate a culture or environment that enables management to rationalize fraudulent acts.

2. How management could perpetrate and conceal fraudulent financial reporting.
3. How assets of the entity could be misappropriated.
4. How the auditor might respond to the susceptibility of material misstatements due to fraud.

Inquiries of Management SAS 99 requires the auditor to make specific inquiries about fraud in every audit. Inquiries of management and others within the company are important because the likelihood of fraud is often revealed through information received in response to the auditor's questions. Inquiries provide employees an opportunity to tell the auditor information that otherwise might not be communicated.

The auditor's inquiries of management should include whether management has knowledge of any fraud or suspected fraud within the company. Auditor inquiries about management's process of assessing fraud risks, the nature of fraud risks identified by management, and any internal controls implemented to address those risks provide useful information. The auditor should also inquire about any information reported by management to the audit committee about fraud risks and related controls.

The audit committee often assumes an active role in overseeing management's fraud risk assessment and response processes. SAS 99 requires the auditor to inquire of the audit committee about its views of the risks of fraud and whether the audit committee has knowledge of any fraud or suspected fraud. For entities with an internal audit function, the auditor inquires about internal audit's views of fraud risks and whether they have performed any procedures to identify or detect fraud during the year.

SAS 99 also requires the auditor to make inquiries of others within the entity whose duties lie outside the normal financial reporting lines of responsibility. When coming into contact with company personnel throughout the audit, such as the inventory warehouse manager or purchasing agents, the auditor may inquire about the existence or suspicion of fraud. Inquiries of executives and a wide variety of other employees provide opportunities for the auditor to learn about risks of fraud. When responses are inconsistent, the auditor should obtain additional audit evidence to resolve the inconsistency and to support or refute the original risk assessment.

Risk Factors SAS 99 requires the auditor to evaluate whether fraud risk factors exist that indicate incentives or pressures to perpetrate fraud, opportunities to carry out fraud, or attitudes or rationalizations used to justify a fraudulent action. Examples of fraud risk factors considered by auditors are included in Table 11-1 (p. 317) and 11-2 (p. 318). Fraud risk factors do not mean that fraud exists, only that the likelihood of fraud is higher. Auditors should consider these factors along with other information used to assess the risks of fraud.

Analytical Procedures As discussed in Chapter 7, auditors must perform analytical procedures during the planning and completion phases of the audit. Analytical procedures help the auditor identify unusual transactions or events that might indicate the presence of material misstatements in the financial statements.

Analytical procedures performed during planning may be helpful in identifying fraud risks. When results from analytical procedures differ from the auditor's expectations, the auditor evaluates those results along with other information to assess whether there is a heightened risk of fraud.

Because occurrences of fraudulent financial reporting often involve manipulation of revenue, SAS 99 requires the auditor to perform analytical procedures on revenue accounts. The objective is to identify unusual or unexpected relationships involving revenue accounts that may indicate fraudulent financial reporting. For example, comparing the sales volume based on recorded revenue with actual production capacity could reveal revenues beyond the entity's production capabilities.

Other Information Auditors should consider all information they have obtained in any part of the audit as they assess the risk of fraud. Examples include information about management's integrity and honesty obtained during client acceptance procedures, inquiries and analytical procedures done in connection with the auditor's review of the client's quarterly financial statements, and information considered in assessing inherent and control risks.

As shown in Figure 11-2 (p. 320), the auditor considers, individually and in combination, all information gathered to assess fraud risks. The outcome of the assessment process is the identification of specific risks of material misstatements due to fraud. Before determining audit responses to identified fraud risks, the auditor considers management's programs and controls that may address those risks, as described later in this chapter.

Documenting Fraud Assessment

SAS 99 requires that auditors document the following matters related to the auditor's consideration of material misstatements due to fraud:

- The discussion among engagement team personnel in planning the audit about the susceptibility of the entity's financial statements to material fraud.
- Procedures performed to obtain information necessary to identify and assess the risks of material fraud.
- Specific risks of material fraud that were identified, and a description of the auditor's response to those risks.
- Reasons supporting a conclusion that there is not a significant risk of material improper revenue recognition.
- Results of the procedures performed to address the risk of management override of controls.
- Other conditions and analytical relationships indicating that additional auditing procedures or other responses were required, and the actions taken by the auditor.
- The nature of communications about fraud made to management, the audit committee, or others.

After fraud risks are identified and documented, the auditor should evaluate factors that reduce fraud risk before developing an appropriate response to the risk of fraud. Corporate governance and other control factors that reduce fraud risks are discussed in the next section.

CORPORATE GOVERNANCE OVERSIGHT TO REDUCE FRAUD RISKS

OBJECTIVE 11-4

Identify corporate governance and other control environment factors that reduce fraud risks.

AICPA Antifraud & Corporate Responsibility Resource Center

Management is responsible for implementing corporate governance and control procedures to minimize fraud. The risk of fraud can be reduced through a combination of prevention, deterrence, and detection measures. Because fraud is difficult to detect due to collusion and false documentation, a focus on fraud prevention and deterrence is often more effective and less costly. Programs and controls implemented by management to prevent fraud help reduce opportunities for fraud. Programs and controls implemented to deter fraud help persuade employees that they should not commit fraud because of the likelihood of detection and punishment.

The AICPA, in conjunction with several professional organizations, has issued *Management Antifraud Programs and Controls: Guidance to Help Prevent, Deter, and Detect Fraud*, to assist management and boards of directors in their antifraud efforts. This guidance identifies three actions to prevent, deter, and detect fraud:

1. Create and maintain a culture of honesty and high ethics.
2. Evaluate fraud risks and implement programs and controls to mitigate identified fraud risks.
3. Develop an appropriate fraud oversight process.

We discuss the elements of these corporate governance and other control environment actions next. Understanding these actions is helpful to auditors in assessing the extent to which clients have implemented these fraud-reducing activities.

Creating a Culture of Honesty and High Ethics

Research indicates that the most effective way to prevent and deter fraud is to implement programs and controls that are based on core values embraced by the company. These values create an environment that reinforces acceptable behavior and expectations of each employee that they can use to guide their actions. These values help create a culture of honesty and ethics that provides the foundation for employees in their job responsibilities. Creating a culture of honesty and high ethics includes six elements.

Setting the Tone at the Top Management and the board of directors are responsible for setting the "tone at the top" for ethical behavior in the company. Honesty and integrity by management reinforces honesty and integrity to employees throughout the organization.

EthicsLine

Management cannot act one way and expect others in the company to behave differently. Through its actions and communications, management can show that dishonest and unethical behaviors are not tolerated, even if the results benefit the company. Statements by management about the absolute need to meet operating and financial targets create undue pressures that may lead employees to commit fraud to achieve them. In contrast, statements indicating management's desire to aggressively pursue entity goals and targets, while at the same time requiring honest and ethical actions to achieve those goals, clearly indicate to employees that integrity is a requirement. Such a message demonstrates that management and the board have zero tolerance for unethical behavior.

A tone at the top based on honesty and integrity provides the foundation upon which a more detailed code of conduct can be developed to provide more specific guidance about permitted and prohibited behavior. Table 11-3 contains an example of the key contents of an effective code of conduct.

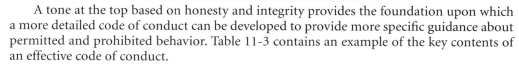

TABLE 11-3	Example Elements for a Code of Conduct

Code of Conduct Element	Description
Organizational Code of Conduct	The organization and its employees must at all times comply with all applicable laws and regulations, with all business conduct well above the minimum standards required by law.
General Employee Conduct	The organization expects its employees to conduct themselves in a businesslike manner and prohibits unprofessional activities, such as drinking, gambling, fighting, and swearing, while on the job.
Conflicts of Interest	The organization expects that employees will perform their duties conscientiously, honestly, and in accordance with the best interests of the organization and will not use their positions or knowledge gained for private or personal advantage.
Outside Activities, Employment, and Directorships	All employees share a responsibility for the organization's good public relations. Employees should avoid activities outside the organization that create an excessive demand on their time or create a conflict of interest.
Relationships with Clients and Suppliers	Employees should avoid investing in or acquiring a financial interest in any business organization that has a contractual relationship with the organization.
Gifts, Entertainment, and Favors	Employees must not accept entertainment, gifts, or personal favors that could influence or appear to influence business decisions in favor of any person with whom the organization has business dealings.
Kickbacks and Secret Commissions	Employees may not receive payment or compensation of any kind, except as authorized under organizational remuneration policies.
Organization Funds and Other Assets	Employees who have access to organization funds must follow prescribed procedures for recording, handling, and protecting money.
Organization Records and Communications	Employees responsible for accounting and record keeping must not make or engage in any false record or communication of any kind, whether external or internal.
Dealing with Outside People and Organizations	Employees must take care to separate their personal roles from their organizational positions when communicating on matters not involving the organization's business.
Prompt Communications	All employees must make every effort to achieve complete, accurate, and timely communications in all matters relevant to customers, suppliers, government authorities, the public, and others within the organization.
Privacy and Confidentiality	When handling financial and personal information about customers and others with whom the organization has dealings, employees should collect, use, and retain only the information necessary for the organization's business; internal access to information should be limited to those with a legitimate business reason for seeking that information.

Source: AICPA, "CPA's Handbook of Fraud and Commercial Crime Prevention."

Creating a Positive Workplace Environment Research shows that wrongdoing occurs less frequently when employees have positive feelings about their employer than when they feel abused, threatened, or ignored. In a positive workplace, there is improved employee morale, which may reduce employees' likelihood of committing fraud against the company.

Management should build a positive culture and work environment by implementing programs and initiatives to increase employee morale. Employees should be encouraged to contribute to that environment and support the entity's values and code of conduct. Employees should also have the ability to obtain advice internally before making decisions that appear to have legal or ethical implications.

Many organizations have a "whistle-blowing" process for employees to report actual or suspected wrongdoing or potential violations of the code of conduct or ethics policy. Some organizations have a telephone "hotline" directed to or monitored by an ethics officer or other trusted individual responsible for investigating and reporting fraud or illegal acts.

Hiring and Promoting Appropriate Employees To be successful in preventing fraud, well-run companies implement effective screening policies to reduce the likelihood of hiring and promoting individuals with low levels of honesty, especially those who hold positions of trust. Effective hiring and promotion policies may include background checks on individuals being considered for employment or for promotion to positions of trust. Background checks verify a candidate's education, employment history, and personal references, including references about character and integrity. After an employee is hired, continuous evaluation of employee compliance with the company's values and code of conduct reduce the likelihood of fraud.

Training All new employees should be trained about the company's expectations of employees' ethical conduct. Employees should be told of their duty to communicate actual or suspected fraud and the appropriate way to do so. Fraud awareness training should be tailored to employees' job responsibilities. For example, training for purchasing agents should be different than training for sales agents.

Confirmation Most companies require employees to periodically confirm their responsibilities for complying with the code of conduct. Employees are asked to state that they understand the company's expectations and have complied with the code, and that they are unaware of any violations. These confirmations help reinforce the code of conduct policies and also help deter employees from committing fraud or other ethics violations. Most employees want to avoid making a false statement in writing and would rather disclose what they know. Follow-up by internal audit or others on disclosures and nonreplies may uncover significant issues.

Discipline Employees must know that they are held accountable for failing to follow the company's code of conduct. Enforcement of violations of the code, regardless of the level of the employee committing the act, sends clear messages to all employees that compliance with the code of conduct and other ethical standards is important and expected. Thorough investigation of all violations and appropriate and consistent responses can be effective deterrents to fraud.

Codes of Conduct

Fraud cannot occur without a perceived opportunity to commit and conceal the act. Management is responsible for identifying and measuring fraud risks, taking steps to mitigate identified risks, and monitoring internal controls that prevent and detect fraud.

Management's Responsibility to Evaluate Risks of Fraud

Identifying and Measuring Fraud Risks Effective fraud oversight begins with management's recognition that fraud is possible and that almost any employee is capable of committing a dishonest act under the right circumstances. This recognition increases the likelihood that effective fraud prevention, deterrence, and detection programs and controls are implemented. Figure 11-3 summarizes factors that management should consider that may contribute to fraud in an organization.

Management has the primary responsibility to assess fraud risks and establish corporate governance programs and controls to prevent, deter, and detect fraud. The assessment process should focus on the company's vulnerability to fraud. For example, the company's industry may create incentives or opportunities for employees to manipulate financial results, such as inventory reserves for a manufacturer, or to misappropriate cash for a bank. Assessing fraud risk may be part of management's overall enterprise risk management or it may be a separate process.

Mitigating Fraud Risks Management is responsible for designing and implementing programs and controls to mitigate fraud risks. Management can change business activities and processes prone to fraud in order to reduce incentives and opportunities for fraud. For example, management can outsource certain operations, such as transferring cash

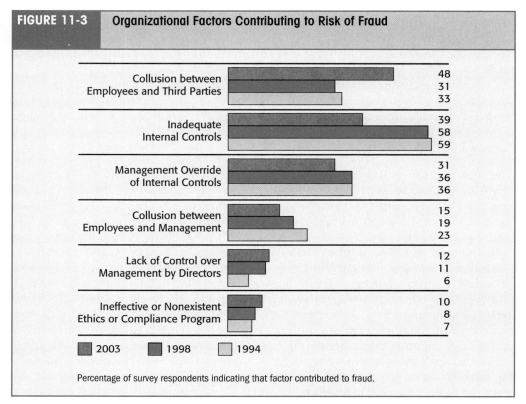

FIGURE 11-3 Organizational Factors Contributing to Risk of Fraud

Collusion between Employees and Third Parties
- 48
- 31
- 33

Inadequate Internal Controls
- 39
- 58
- 59

Management Override of Internal Controls
- 31
- 36
- 36

Collusion between Employees and Management
- 15
- 19
- 23

Lack of Control over Management by Directors
- 12
- 11
- 6

Ineffective or Nonexistent Ethics or Compliance Program
- 10
- 8
- 7

■ 2003   ■ 1998   □ 1994

Percentage of survey respondents indicating that factor contributed to fraud.

Source: *Fraud Survey 2003*, KPMG Forensics. Copyright © 2003 KPMG LLP. Reprinted with permission.

collections from company personnel to a bank lockbox system. Other programs and controls may be implemented at a company-wide level, such as the training of all employees about fraud risks, and strengthening employment and promotion policies.

Monitoring Fraud Prevention Programs and Controls For high fraud risk areas, management should periodically evaluate whether appropriate antifraud programs and controls have been implemented and are operating effectively. For example, management's review and evaluation of operating units' or subsidiaries' financial results increase the likelihood that manipulated results will be detected.

Internal audit plays a key role in monitoring activities to ensure that antifraud programs and controls are operating effectively. Internal audit activities can both deter and detect fraud. Internal auditors assist in deterring fraud by examining and evaluating internal controls that reduce fraud risk. Internal auditors assist in fraud detection by performing audit procedures to search for fraudulent financial reporting and misappropriation of assets.

Because management is often in a position to override internal controls, there is a strong need for corporate governance oversight for senior management actions. One of the strongest internal corporate governance mechanisms over senior management is the audit committee of the board of directors. The audit committee's role in fraud risk oversight is discussed next.

Audit Committee Oversight

The audit committee has primary responsibility to oversee the organization's financial reporting and internal control processes. In fulfilling this responsibility, the audit committee considers the potential for management override of internal controls and oversees management's fraud risk assessment process, as well as antifraud programs and controls. The audit committee also assists in creating an effective "tone at the top" about the importance of honesty and ethical behavior by reinforcing management's zero tolerance for fraud.

Audit committee oversight also serves as a deterrent to fraud by senior management. For example, direct reporting of key findings by internal audit to the audit committee, periodic reports by ethics officers about whistle-blowing, and other reports about lack of ethical behavior or suspected fraud increase the likelihood that any attempt by senior management to involve employees in committing or concealing fraud is promptly disclosed. An open line of communication between the audit committee and members of management one or two levels below senior management can also assist the audit committee in identifying fraud by senior management. Information received from external auditors can also assist the audit committee in assessing the strength of the company's internal controls and the potential for fraudulent financial reporting.

Most audit committee charters authorize the audit committee to investigate any matters within the scope of its financial reporting oversight responsibilities. Audit committees usually have the authority to retain legal, accounting, and other professional advisers to assist in any fraud investigation.

Because the audit committee plays an important role in establishing a proper tone at the top and in overseeing the actions of management, PCAOB Standard 2 requires auditors of public companies to evaluate the effectiveness of the audit committee as part of the auditor's evaluation of the operating effectiveness of internal control over financial reporting. As part of their evaluation, auditors might consider the audit committee's independence from management and the level of understanding about the audit committee's responsibilities between management and the audit committee. Observed interactions between the audit committee and internal audit and the external auditor may also provide useful insights about the level of audit committee commitment to overseeing the financial reporting process. PCAOB Standard 2 notes that ineffective oversight by the audit committee is at least a significant deficiency and may be a strong indicator of a material weakness in internal control over financial reporting.

RESPONDING TO THE RISK OF FRAUD

When risks of material misstatements due to fraud are identified, the auditor should first discuss these findings with management and obtain management's views of the potential fraud and existing controls designed to prevent or detect misstatements. As described in the last section, management may have programs designed to prevent, deter, and detect fraud, as well as controls designed to mitigate specific risks of fraud. Auditors should then consider whether such programs and controls mitigate the identified risks of material misstatements due to fraud or whether control deficiencies increase the risk of fraud. Auditor responses to fraud risk include the following:

OBJECTIVE 11-5

Develop responses to identified fraud risks.

1. Change the overall conduct of the audit to respond to identified fraud risks.
2. Design and perform audit procedures to address identified risks.
3. Design and perform procedures to address the risk of management override of controls.

There are several overall responses to an increased fraud risk. If the risk of misstatement due to fraud is increased, more experienced personnel may be assigned to the audit. In some cases, a fraud specialist may be assigned to the audit team.

Change the Overall Conduct of the Audit

Auditors should also consider management's choice of accounting principles. Careful attention should be placed on accounting principles that involve subjective measurements or complex transactions. Because there is a presumption of fraud risk in revenue recognition, auditors should also evaluate the company's revenue recognition policies.

Fraud perpetrators are often knowledgeable about audit procedures. For this reason, SAS 99 requires auditors to incorporate unpredictability in the audit plan. For example, auditors may visit inventory locations or test accounts that were not tested in prior periods. Auditors should also consider tests that address misappropriation of assets, even when the amounts are not typically material.

Design and Perform Audit Procedures to Address Fraud Risks

The appropriate audit procedures used to address specific fraud risks depend on the account being audited and type of fraud risk identified. For example, if concerns are raised about revenue recognition because of cutoff or channel stuffing, the auditor may review the sales journal for unusual activity near the end of the period and review the terms of sales. Specific procedures are described in the discussion of specific fraud risk areas later in this chapter.

Design and Perform Procedures to Address Management Override of Controls

The risk of management override of controls exists in almost all audits. Because management is in a unique position to perpetrate fraud by overriding controls that are otherwise operating effectively, auditors must perform procedures in every audit to address the risk of management override. Three procedures must be performed in every audit.

Examine Journal Entries and Other Adjustments for Evidence of Possible Misstatements Due to Fraud Fraud often results from adjustments to amounts reported in the financial statements, even when there are effective internal controls in the rest of the recording processes. The auditor should first obtain an understanding of the entity's financial reporting process and controls over journal entries and other adjustments, and inquire of employees involved in the financial reporting process about inappropriate or unusual activity in processing journal entries and other adjustments. SAS 99 requires testing of journal entries and other financial statement adjustments. The extent of testing is affected by the effectiveness of controls and results of the inquiries.

Review Accounting Estimates for Biases Fraudulent financial reporting is often accomplished through intentional misstatement of accounting estimates. SAS 99 requires the auditor to consider the potential for management bias when reviewing current-year estimates. The auditor is required to "look back" at significant prior-year estimates to identify any changes in the company's processes or management's judgments and assumptions that might indicate a potential bias. For example, management's estimates may have been clustered at the high end of the range of acceptable amounts in the prior year and at the low end in the current year.

Evaluate the Business Rationale for Significant Unusual Transactions SAS 99 places greater focus than was previously required on understanding the underlying business rationale for significant unusual transactions that might be outside the normal course of business for the company. The auditor should gain an understanding of the purposes of significant transactions to assess whether transactions have been entered into to engage in fraudulent financial reporting. For example, the company may engage in financing transactions to avoid reporting liabilities on the balance sheet. The auditor should determine whether the accounting treatment for any unusual transaction is appropriate in the circumstances, and whether information about the transaction is adequately disclosed in the financial statements.

Update Risk Assessment Process

The auditor's assessment of the risks of material misstatement due to fraud should be ongoing throughout the audit. Conditions may be identified during field work that change or support a judgment about the initial assessment of fraud risks. For example, the auditor should be alert for the following conditions during field work:

- Discrepancies in the accounting records.
- Conflicting or missing evidential matter.
- Problematic or unusual relationships between the auditor and management.
- Results from substantive or final review stage analytical procedures that indicate a previously unrecognized fraud risk.
- Responses to inquiries made throughout the audit that have been vague or implausible or that have produced evidence that is inconsistent with other evidence.

Depending on the client's industry, certain accounts are especially susceptible to manipulation or theft. Figure 11-4 indicates that rates of fraud are increasing, especially theft of assets. The following sections discuss specific high-risk accounts, including warning signs of fraud. Even with knowledge of these warning signs, fraud is extremely difficult to detect. However, awareness of these warning signs and fraud detection techniques increases the auditor's likelihood of identifying misstatements due to fraud.

OBJECTIVE 11-6

Recognize specific fraud risk areas and develop procedures to detect fraud.

Revenue and Accounts Receivable Fraud Risks

Revenue and related accounts receivable and cash accounts are especially susceptible to manipulation and theft. A study sponsored by the Committee of Sponsoring Organizations (COSO) found that more than half of financial statement frauds involve revenues and accounts receivable. Similarly, because sales are often made for cash or are quickly converted to cash, they are also highly susceptible to theft.

Fraudulent Financial Reporting Risk for Revenue As a result of the frequency of financial reporting frauds involving revenue recognition, the AICPA and SEC issued guidance in the late 1990s dealing with revenue recognition. SAS 99 issued by the Auditing Standards Board specifically requires auditors to identify revenue recognition as a fraud risk in most audits.

Revenue is susceptible to manipulation for several reasons. Overstatement of revenues often increases net income by an equal amount, because related costs of sales are often not recognized on fictitious or prematurely recognized revenues. Also, financial analysts and other market participants place increasing emphasis on revenue growth. There are three main types of revenue manipulations: fictitious revenues, premature revenue recognition, and manipulation of adjustments to revenues.

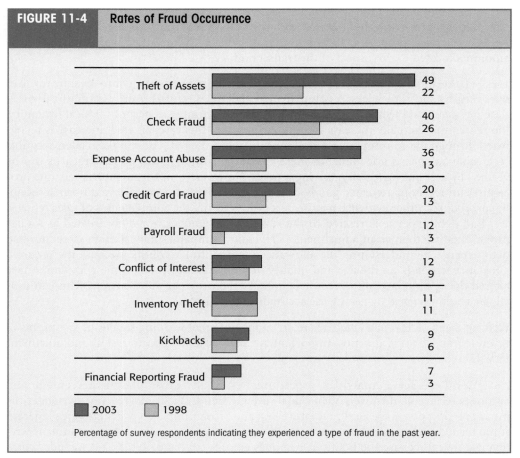

FIGURE 11-4 Rates of Fraud Occurrence

	2003	1998
Theft of Assets	49	22
Check Fraud	40	26
Expense Account Abuse	36	13
Credit Card Fraud	20	13
Payroll Fraud	12	3
Conflict of Interest	12	9
Inventory Theft	11	11
Kickbacks	9	6
Financial Reporting Fraud	7	3

Percentage of survey respondents indicating they experienced a type of fraud in the past year.

Source: *Fraud Survey 2003*, KPMG Forensics. Copyright © 2003 KPMG LLP. Reprinted with permission.

Fictitious Revenues The most egregious forms of revenue fraud involve creating fictitious revenues. Although there have been several recent cases involving fictitious revenues, there are also many earlier examples. For example, the *Ultramares* case described in Chapter 5 (p. 115) involved fictitious revenue entries in the general ledger.

Fraud perpetrators often go to great lengths to support fictitious revenue. The *Equity Funding* case involved issuing fictitious insurance policies. The perpetrators held file-stuffing parties to create the fictitious policies. In the *ZZZZ Best* case, the company even took the auditors to visit a fictitious construction site.

Premature Revenue Recognition Companies often accelerate the timing of revenue recognition to meet earnings or sales forecasts. **Premature revenue recognition** is the recognition of revenue before GAAP requirements for recording revenue have been met. Premature revenue recognition should be distinguished from cutoff errors, in which transactions are inadvertently recorded in the incorrect period. In the simplest form of accelerated revenue recognition, sales that should have been recorded in the subsequent period are recorded as current period sales. One method of fraudulently accelerating revenue is a "bill-and-hold" sale. Sales are normally recognized at the time goods are shipped. In a bill-and-hold sale, the goods are invoiced before they are shipped. Another method involves issuing side agreements that modify the terms of the sales transaction. For example, revenue recognition is likely to be inappropriate if a major customer agrees to take a significant amount of inventory at year-end, but a side agreement provides for more favorable pricing and unrestricted return of the goods if not sold by the customer. In some cases, as a result of the terms of the side agreement, the transaction does not qualify as a sale under generally accepted accounting principles.

Two notable recent examples of premature revenue recognition involve Bausch and Lomb and Xerox Corporation. In the Bausch and Lomb case, items were shipped that were not ordered by customers, with unrestricted right of return and promises that the goods did not have to be paid for until sold. The revenue recognition issues at Xerox were more complex. Capital equipment leases include sales, financing, and service components. Because the sales component is recognized immediately, Xerox attempted to maximize the amount allocated to this aspect of the transaction.

Manipulation of Adjustments to Revenues The most common adjustment to revenue involves sales returns and allowances. A company may hide sales returns from the auditor to overstate net sales and income. If the returned goods are counted as part of physical inventory, the return may actually increase reported income. In this case, an asset increase is recognized through the counting of physical inventory, but the reduction in the related accounts receivable balance is not made. In these cases, the completeness of sales returns can be verified by accounting for all receiving reports. However, if management has separate procedures for receiving returned goods, or if attempts are made to circumvent normal receiving procedures, other evidence may be necessary to verify the completeness of sales returns.

Bad debt expense is related to the revenue cycle but is normally treated as a sales expense, rather than as an adjustment to revenue. Companies may attempt to reduce bad debt expense by understating the allowance for doubtful accounts. Because the required allowance depends on the age and quality of accounts receivable, some companies have altered the aging of accounts receivable to make them appear more current. This can usually be readily verified by testing the accuracy of the aging.

Warning Signs of Revenue Fraud There are many potential warning signals or symptoms of revenue fraud. Two of the most important are analytical procedures results and documentary discrepancies.

Analytical Procedures Analytical procedures, especially gross margin percentage and accounts receivable turnover, often signal revenue frauds. Fictitious revenue overstates the gross margin percentage, and premature revenue recognition also overstates gross margin if the related cost of sales is not recognized. Fictitious revenues also lower accounts receivable turnover, because the fictitious revenues are not collected. Table 11-4 includes comparative sales, cost of sales, and accounts receivable data for Regina Vacuum. Notice how

TABLE 11-4	Example of the Effect of Fictitious Receivables on Accounting Ratios Based on Regina Vacuum Company		
	Year Ended June 30		
	1988	**1987**	**1986**
Sales	$181,123	$126,234	$76,144
Cost of sales	(94,934)	(70,756)	(46,213)
Gross profit	86,189	55,478	29,931
Gross profit percentage	47.6%	43.9%	39.3%
Year-end accounts receivable	51,076	27,801	14,402
Accounts receivable turnover[a]	3.55	4.54	5.29

[a]Accounts receivable turnover calculated as Sales/Ending accounts receivable

both a higher gross profit percentage and lower accounts receivable turnover ratio helped signal fictitious accounts receivable.

In some frauds, management generated fictitious revenues to make analytical procedures results, such as gross margin, similar to the prior year. In frauds like this, analytical procedures are typically not useful to signal the fraud.

Documentary Discrepancies Despite the best efforts of fraud perpetrators, fictitious transactions rarely have the same level of documentary evidence as legitimate transactions. For example, in the well-known fraud at *ZZZZ Best*, insurance restoration contracts worth millions of dollars were supported by one- or two-page agreements and lacked many of the supporting details and evidence, such as permits, that are normally associated with such contracts.

Auditors should be aware of unusual markings and alterations on documents, and they should rely on original rather than duplicate copies of documents. Because fraud perpetrators attempt to conceal fraud, even one unusual transaction in a sample should be considered to be a potential indicator of fraud that should be investigated.

Misappropriation of Receipts Involving Revenue Although misappropriation of cash receipts is rarely as material as fraudulent reporting of revenues, such frauds can be costly to the organization because of the direct loss of assets. The objective of the misappropriation of assets is usually theft of cash. Many thefts of cash receipts are closely tied to the revenue cycle and are considered separately from other thefts of cash. A typical misappropriation of assets involves failure to record a sale or adjustments made to customer accounts to hide thefts of cash receipts.

Failure to Record a Sale One of the most difficult frauds to detect is when a sale is not recorded and the cash from the sale is stolen. Such frauds are somewhat easy to detect when goods are shipped on credit to customers. Tracing shipping documents to sales entries in the sales journal and accounting for all shipping documents can be used to verify that all sales have been recorded.

It is much more difficult to verify that all cash sales have been recorded, because there are no shipping documents to verify the completeness of sales, and there are no customer account receivable records supporting the sale. In such cases, other documentary evidence is necessary to verify that all sales are recorded. For example, a retail establishment may require that all sales be recorded on a cash register. Recorded sales can then be compared to the total amount of sales on the cash register tape.

Theft of Cash Receipts After a Sale is Recorded It is much more difficult to hide the theft of cash receipts after a sale is recorded. If a customer's payment is stolen, regular billing of unpaid accounts will quickly uncover the fraud. As a result, to hide the theft, the fraud perpetrator must reduce the customer's account in one of three ways: (1) record a sales return or allowance, (2) write off the customer's account, or (3) apply the payment from another customer to the customer's account, which is also known as lapping.

Warning Signs of Misappropriation of Revenues and Cash Receipts Relatively small thefts of sales and related cash receipts are normally best prevented and detected by internal controls designed to minimize the opportunity for fraud. Analytical procedures and other comparisons may be useful in detecting larger frauds.

Inventory Fraud Risks

Inventory is often the largest account on many companies' balance sheets and it is often difficult to verify the existence and valuation of inventories. As a result, inventory is susceptible to manipulation to achieve financial reporting objectives. Because inventory is also usually readily saleable, it is also susceptible to misappropriation.

Fraudulent Financial Reporting Risk for Inventory Fictitious inventory has been at the center of several major cases of fraudulent financial reporting. Many large companies have varied and extensive inventory in multiple locations, making it relatively easy for the company to add fictitious inventory to accounting records.

Auditors are required to verify the existence of physical inventories. However, audit testing is done on a sample basis, and not all locations with inventory are typically tested. In some cases involving fictitious inventories, auditors informed the client in advance which inventory locations were to be tested. As a result, it was relatively easy for the client to transfer inventories to the locations being tested.

Warning Signs of Inventory Fraud As for accounts receivable, there are many potential warning signals or symptoms of inventory fraud. Analytical procedures are especially important for detecting inventory fraud.

Analytical Procedures Analytical procedures, especially gross margin percentage and inventory turnover, often signal inventory fraud. Fictitious inventory understates cost of goods sold and overstates the gross margin percentage. Fictitious inventory also lowers inventory turnover. Table 11-5 is an example of the effects of fictitious inventory on inventory turnover based on the Crazy Eddie fraud. Note that the gross profit percentage did not signal the existence of fictitious inventories, but the significant decrease in inventory turnover was a sign of fictitious inventories.

Purchases and Accounts Payable Fraud Risks

Cases of fraudulent financial reporting involving accounts payable are relatively common, although less frequent than frauds involving inventory or accounts receivable. The deliberate understatement of accounts payable generally results in an understatement of purchases and cost of goods sold and an overstatement of net income. Significant misappropriations involving purchases can also occur in the form of payments to fictitious vendors, as well as kickbacks and other illegal arrangements with suppliers.

Fraudulent Financial Reporting Risk for Accounts Payable Companies may engage in deliberate attempts to understate accounts payable and overstate income. This can be accomplished by not recording accounts payable until the subsequent period or by recording fictitious reductions to accounts payable.

TABLE 11-5	Example of the Effect of Fictitious Inventory on Inventory Turnover Based on Crazy Eddie, Inc.		
	Year Ended March 1, 1987	Year Ended March 2, 1986	9 Months Ended March 3, 1985
Sales	$352,523	$262,268	$136,319
Cost of sales	(272,255)	(194,371)	(103,421)
Gross profit	80,268	67,897	32,898
Gross profit percentage	22.8%	25.9%	24.1%
Year-end inventories	109,072	59,864	26,543
Inventory turnover[a]	2.50	3.2	5.20[b]

[a]Inventory turnover calculated as Cost of sales/Ending inventory.
[b]Inventory turnover calculated based on annualized Cost of sales.

Source: Copyright © 2004, *Conducting Internal Auditing Interviews* by the Institute of Internal Auditing Research Foundation, 247 Maitland Avenue, Altamonte Springs, FL 32701-4201. USA. Reprinted with permission.

All purchases received before the end of the year should be recorded as liabilities. This is relatively easy to verify if the company accounts for prenumbered receiving reports. However, if the receiving reports are not prenumbered or the company deliberately omits receiving reports from the accounting records, it may be difficult for the auditor to verify whether all liabilities have been recorded. In such cases, analytical evidence, such as unusual changes in ratios, may signal that accounts payable are understated.

Companies often have complex arrangements with suppliers that result in reductions to accounts payable for advertising credits and other allowances. These arrangements are often not as well documented as acquisition transactions. Some companies have used fictitious reductions to accounts payable to overstate net income. Auditors should read agreements with suppliers when amounts are material and make sure the financial statements reflect the substance of the agreements.

Misappropriations in the Acquisition and Payment Cycle The most common fraud in the acquisitions area is for the perpetrator to issue payments to fictitious vendors and deposit the cash in a fictitious account. These frauds can be prevented by allowing payments to be made only to approved vendors and by carefully scrutinizing documentation supporting the acquisitions by authorized personnel before payments are made. In other misappropriation cases, the accounts payable clerk or other employee steals a check to a legitimate vendor. The purchases information is then resubmitted for payment to the vendor. Such fraud can be prevented by canceling supporting documents to prevent their use as support for multiple payments.

Almost every account is subject to manipulation. The following sections discuss other accounts with specific risks of fraudulent financial reporting or misappropriation.

Other Areas of Fraud Risk

Fixed Assets Fixed assets are a large balance sheet account for many companies and are often based on subjectively determined valuations. As a result, fixed assets may be a target for manipulation, especially for companies without material receivables or inventories. For example, companies may capitalize repairs or other operating expenses as fixed assets. Such frauds are relatively easy to detect if the auditor examines evidence supporting fixed asset additions. Nevertheless, several recent cases of fraudulent financial reporting have involved improper capitalization of assets.

Because of their value and salability, fixed assets are also targets for theft. This is especially true for fixed assets that are readily portable, such as laptop computers. To reduce the potential for theft, fixed assets should be physically protected whenever possible, engraved, or otherwise permanently labeled, and should be periodically inventoried.

Payroll Expenses Payroll is rarely a significant risk area for fraudulent financial reporting. However, companies may overstate inventories and net income by recording excess labor costs in inventory. Company employees are sometimes used to construct fixed assets. Excess labor cost may also be capitalized as fixed assets in these circumstances. Material fringe benefits, such as retirement benefits, are also subject to manipulation.

Payroll fraud involving misappropriation of assets is fairly common, but the amounts involved are often immaterial. The two most common areas of fraud are the creation of fictitious employees and overstatement of individual payroll hours. The existence of fictitious employees can usually be prevented by separation of the human resource and payroll functions. Overstatement of hours is typically prevented by use of time clocks or approval of payroll hours.

RESPONSIBILITIES WHEN FRAUD IS SUSPECTED

Responding to Misstatements that May be the Result of Fraud

As might be expected, more frauds are detected by internal controls or the internal audit function than by external auditors. However, as indicated in Figure 11-5, the percentage of frauds detected by external auditors is increasing.

Throughout an audit, the auditor continually evaluates whether evidence gathered and other observations made indicate material misstatement due to fraud. All misstatements the auditor finds during the audit should be evaluated for any indication of fraud. When fraud is suspected, the auditor gathers additional information to determine whether fraud actually exists. Often, the auditor begins by making additional inquiries of management and others.

Types of Inquiry Techniques As described in Chapter 7, inquiry can be an effective audit evidence gathering technique. Interviewing allows the auditor to clarify unobservable issues and observe the respondent's verbal and nonverbal responses. Interviewing can also help identify issues omitted from documentation or confirmations. The auditor can also modify questions during the interview based on the interviewee's responses.

FIGURE 11-5	Methods for Uncovering Fraud		
		(Percentages)	
	2003	1998	1994
Internal Controls	77	51	52
Internal Audit	65	43	47
Notification by Employee	63	58	51
Accident	54	37	28
Anonymous Tip	41	35	26
Notification by Customer	34	41	34
Notification by Regulatory or Law Enforcement Agency	19	16	8
Notification by Vendor	16	11	15
External Audit	12	4	5

Percentage of survey respondents indicating method used to uncover fraud in the past year.

Source: *Fraud Survey 2003*, KPMG Forensics. Copyright © 2003 KPMG LLP. Reprinted with permission.

Inquiry as an audit evidence technique should be tailored to the purpose for which it is being used. Depending on the purpose, the auditor may ask different types of questions and change the tone of the interview. One or more of three categories of inquiry can be used, depending on the auditor's objectives: informational inquiry, assessment inquiry, and interrogative inquiry.

Informational Inquiry Auditors use **informational inquiry** to obtain information about facts and details that the auditor does not have. Usually the auditor wants information from the interviewee about past or current events or processes. Often the inquiry is cordial, with the auditor posing open-ended questions that allow the respondent to provide details of events, processes, or circumstances. Auditors often use informational inquiry when gathering follow-up evidence about programs and controls or other evidence involving a misstatement or suspected fraud uncovered in the audit.

Assessment Inquiry Auditors also use inquiry to assess whether information already obtained is correct, factual, or truthful. The auditor uses **assessment inquiry** to corroborate or contradict prior information. The auditor often starts assessment inquiry with broad, open-ended questions that allow the interviewee to provide detailed responses that can later be followed up with more specific questions. One common use of assessment inquiry is to corroborate management responses to earlier inquiries by asking questions of other employees.

Interrogative Inquiry This category of inquiry is used when the auditor seeks responses from the interview subject about his or her knowledge of an event or circumstance. **Interrogative inquiry** is often used to determine if the individual is being deceptive or purposefully omitting disclosure of key knowledge of facts, events, or circumstances, especially when the auditor suspects the interviewee is being deceptive or concealing information. Often, interrogative inquiry is confrontational, given that subjects may be defensive, as they cover up their knowledge of specific facts, events, or circumstances. When using interrogative inquiry, the auditor often asks specific directed questions that seek either a "yes" or "no" response. Interrogative interviewing should typically be done by senior members of the audit team who are experienced and knowledgeable about the client's affairs.

Evaluating Responses to Inquiry For inquiry to be effective, auditors need to be skilled at listening and evaluating responses to questions. Typically, the interviewee's initial response will omit important information. Effective follow-up questions often lead to better information to assess whether fraud exists. Good listening techniques and observation of behavioral cues strengthen the auditor's inquiry techniques.

Listening Techniques It is critical for the auditor to use effective listening skills throughout the inquiry process. The auditor should stay attentive by maintaining eye contact, nodding in agreement, or demonstrating other signs of comprehension. Auditors should also attempt to avoid preconceived ideas about the information being provided. Good listeners also take advantage of silence to think about the information provided and to prioritize and review information heard.

Observing Behavioral Cues Auditors who are skilled in using inquiry evaluate verbal and nonverbal cues as they listen to the interviewee. Verbal cues, such as those outlined in Table 11-6 (p. 336), may indicate the responder's nervousness, lack of knowledge, or even deceit. In addition to observing verbal cues, the use of inquiry allows the auditor to observe nonverbal behaviors. Expert investigators note that subjects who are uncomfortable providing a response to an inquiry often exhibit many of the nonverbal behaviors shown in Table 11-7 (p. 336).

Of course, not everyone who exhibits these behaviors is uncomfortable responding to the auditor's inquiry. The key is to identify when the individual's behavior begins to change from his or her normal behavior. Less-experienced auditors should be cautious when they start to observe unusual behaviors, and they should discuss their concerns with senior members of the audit team before doing anything in response to those behaviors.

TABLE 11-6	Observing Verbal Cues During Inquiry

Verbal Cue Examples	Implications
Extensive use of modifiers, such as "generally," "usually," "often," "normally," etc.	Auditors should probe further to determine whether the use of the modifier indicates that there are exceptions to the processes or circumstances being examined.
Frequent rephrasing by the interviewee of the auditor's question.	Skilled auditors recognize that rephrasing often indicates that the interviewee is uncertain about his or her response or is attempting to stall for time.
Filler terms, such as "um," "well," "to tell you the truth," etc.	Auditors should be alert for filler terms, given that they often suggest that the interviewee is hesitant or unable to respond to the inquiry.
Forgetfulness and acknowledgments of nervousness, such as "I'm a bit nervous" or "I just can't remember."	When this continues to occur, auditors should be concerned about the possibility of deception.
Tolerant attitudes, such as "it depends on the circumstances," and overqualified responses, such as "to the best of my memory."	Dishonest people are often tolerant toward someone who may have committed fraud.
Reluctance to end an interview.	Someone who has been honest generally is ready to terminate an interview. Those trying to deceive may try to continue the inquiry process to convince the auditor that they are telling the truth.

Source: Reprinted by permission of The Association of Fraud Examiners.

Other Responsibilities When Fraud Is Suspected When the auditor suspects that fraud may be present, SAS 99 requires the auditor to obtain additional evidence to determine whether material fraud has occurred. Auditors often use inquiry, as previously discussed, as part of that information-gathering process. SAS 99 also requires the auditor to consider the implications for other aspects of the audit. For example, fraud involving the misappropriation of cash from a small petty cash fund normally is of little significance to the auditor, unless the matter involves higher-level management. In the latter situation, the petty cash fraud may indicate a more pervasive problem involving management's integrity. This may indicate to the auditor a need to re-evaluate the fraud risk assessment and the impact on the nature, timing, and extent of audit evidence.

When the auditor determines that fraud may be present, SAS 99 requires the auditor to discuss the matter and audit approach for further investigation with an appropriate level of management, even if the matter might be considered inconsequential. The appropriate level of management should be at least one level above those involved, as well as senior

TABLE 11-7	Observing Nonverbal Cues During Inquiry

Nonverbal Cue Examples	Implications
Physical Barriers—Interviewees may • Block their mouth with their hands, pens, pencils, papers, etc. • Cross their arms or legs. • Use distracting noises, such as finger tapping or drumming. • Lean away from the auditor, usually toward the door or window, in an effort to create spatial distance.	When the interviewee feels uncomfortable with a specific inquiry, he or she may put up nonverbal barriers to try to keep the auditor at a comfortable distance.
Signs of Stress—Interviewees under stress may • Show signs of having a dry mouth. • Lick lips, swallow, or clear their throats frequently. • Fidget, tap their foot, or shake a leg. • Sweat or become flushed in the face. • Avoid eye contact.	In most people, lying will produce stress, which can manifest itself physically.

Source: Institute of Internal Auditors, *Conducting Internal Audit Interviews*, Altamonte Springs, Florida.

management and the audit committee. If the auditor believes that senior management may be involved in the fraud, the auditor should discuss the matter directly with the audit committee.

The discovery that fraud exists also has implications for the public company auditor's report on internal control over financial reporting. PCAOB Standard 2 states that fraud of any magnitude by senior management is at least a significant deficiency and may be a material weakness in internal control over financial reporting. This includes fraud by senior management that results in even immaterial misstatements. If the auditor decides the fraud by senior management is a material weakness, the auditor's report on internal control over financial reporting will contain an adverse opinion.

Sometimes, auditors identify risks of material misstatements due to fraud that have internal control implications. There may also be cases where the auditor's consideration of management's antifraud programs and controls identify deficiencies that fail to mitigate these risks of fraud. The auditor must communicate those items to the audit committee if they are considered significant deficiencies or material weaknesses. When auditing the financial statements of a public company, the auditor should consider those deficiencies when auditing internal controls over financial reporting, as described in Chapter 10.

The disclosure of possible fraud to parties other than the client's senior management and its audit committee ordinarily is not part of the auditor's responsibility. As described in Chapter 4, such disclosure is prevented by the auditor's professional code of conduct and may violate legal obligations of confidentiality.

The results of the auditor's procedures may indicate such a significant risk of material misstatement due to fraud that the auditor should consider withdrawing from the audit. Withdrawal may depend on management's integrity and the diligence and cooperation of management and the board of directors in investigating the potential fraud and taking appropriate action.

SUMMARY

This chapter examined the two types of fraud considered by auditors when auditing financial statements: fraudulent financial reporting and misappropriations of assets. Auditors are responsible for obtaining reasonable assurance that material misstatements, whether due to errors or fraud, are detected. The chapter described the way auditors gather information to assess fraud risk in every audit and develop appropriate responses to identified fraud risks, after considering the effectiveness of management's antifraud programs and controls. Several illustrations of typical fraud techniques highlighted areas often subject to high fraud risk and provided examples of effective audit procedures to address those risk areas. Once fraud is suspected, auditors gather additional evidence, often through inquiry, and are responsible for making certain communications about suspected or detected fraud to senior management and the audit committee. Auditors of public companies must consider the implications of their fraud risk assessments, including any suspected fraud, when arriving at their opinion on the operating effectiveness of internal control over financial reporting.

ESSENTIAL TERMS

Assessment inquiry—inquiry to corroborate or contradict prior information obtained

Earnings management—deliberate actions taken by management to meet earnings objectives

Fraud risk factors—entity factors that increase the risk of fraud

Fraud triangle—represents the three conditions of fraud: incentives/pressures, opportunities, and attitudes/rationalization

Income smoothing—form of earnings management in which revenues and expenses are shifted between periods to reduce fluctuations in earnings

Informational inquiry—inquiry to obtain information about facts and details the auditor does not have

Interrogative inquiry—inquiry used to determine if the interviewee is being deceptive or purposefully omitting disclosure of key knowledge of facts, events, or circumstances

Premature revenue recognition—recognition of revenue before GAAP requirements for recording revenue have been met

Professional skepticism—an attitude of the auditor that neither assumes management is dishonest nor assumes unquestioned honesty

REVIEW QUESTIONS

11-1 (Objective 11-1) Define fraudulent financial reporting and give two examples that illustrate fraudulent financial reporting.

11-2 (Objective 11-1) Define misappropriation of assets and give two examples of misappropriation of assets.

11-3 (Objective 11-1) Distinguish fraudulent financial reporting from misappropriation of assets.

11-4 (Objective 11-2) What are the three conditions of fraud often referred to as "the fraud triangle?"

11-5 (Objective 11-2) Give examples of risk factors for fraudulent financial reporting for each of the three fraud conditions: incentives/pressures, opportunities, and attitudes/rationalization.

11-6 (Objective 11-2) Give examples of risk factors for misappropriation of assets for each of the three fraud conditions: incentives/pressures, opportunities, and attitudes/rationalization.

11-7 (Objective 11-3) What sources are used by the auditor to gather information to assess fraud risks?

11-8 (Objective 11-3) What should the audit team consider in its planning discussion about fraud risks?

11-9 (Objective 11-3) Auditors are required to make inquiries of individuals in the company when gathering information to assess fraud risk. Identify those with whom the auditor must make inquiries.

11-10 (Objective 11-4) Describe the purpose of corporate codes of conduct and identify three examples of items addressed in a typical code of conduct.

11-11 (Objective 11-4) Discuss the importance of the control environment, or "setting the tone at the top," in establishing a culture of honesty and integrity in a company.

11-12 (Objective 11-4) Distinguish management's responsibility from the audit committee's responsibility for designing and implementing antifraud programs and controls within a company.

11-13 (Objective 11-5) What are the three categories of auditor responses to fraud risks?

11-14 (Objective 11-5) What three auditor actions are required to address the potential for management override of controls?

11-15 (Objective 11-6) Describe the three main techniques used to manipulate revenue.

11-16 (Objective 11-6) You go through the drive-through window of a fast food restaurant and notice a sign that reads "your meal is free if we fail to give you a receipt." Why would the restaurant post this sign?

11-17 (Objective 11-7) Name the three categories of inquiry and describe the purpose of each when used by an auditor to obtain additional information about a suspected fraud.

11-18 (Objective 11-7) Identify three verbal and three nonverbal cues that may be observed when making inquiries of an individual who is being deceitful.

11-19 (Objective 11-7) You have identified a suspected fraud involving the company's controller. What must you do in response to this discovery? How might this discovery affect your report on internal control when auditing a public company?

MULTIPLE CHOICE QUESTIONS FROM CPA EXAMINATIONS

11-20 (Objectives 11-2, 11-3) The following questions address fraud risk factors and the assessment of fraud risk.

    a. Because of the risk of material misstatements due to fraud (fraud risk), an audit of financial statements in accordance with generally accepted auditing standards should be performed with an attitude of
        (1) objective judgment.
        (2) independent integrity.
        (3) professional skepticism.
        (4) impartial conservatism.

    b. Which of the following circumstances is most likely to cause an auditor to consider whether material misstatements due to fraud exist in an entity's financial statements?

(1) Management places little emphasis on meeting earnings projections of external parties.

(2) The board of directors oversees the financial reporting process and internal control.

(3) Significant deficiencies in internal control previously communicated to management have been corrected.

(4) Transactions selected for testing are not supported by proper documentation.

c. Which of the following characteristics is most likely to heighten an auditor's concern about the risk of material misstatements due to fraud in an entity's financial statements?

(1) The entity's industry is experiencing declining customer demand.

(2) Employees who handle cash receipts are not bonded.

(3) Internal auditors have direct access to the board of directors and the entity's management.

(4) The board of directors is active in overseeing the entity's financial reporting policies.

d. Which of the following circumstances is most likely to cause an auditor to increase the assessment of the risk of material misstatement of the financial statements due to fraud?

(1) Property and equipment are usually sold at a loss before being fully depreciated.

(2) Unusual discrepancies exist between the entity's records and confirmation replies.

(3) Monthly bank reconciliations usually include several in-transit items.

(4) Clerical errors are listed on a computer-generated exception report.

11-21 (Objective 11-5) The following questions concern the auditor's responses to the possibility of fraud.

a. If an independent audit leading to an opinion on financial statements causes the auditor to believe that a material misstatement due to fraud exists, the auditor should first

(1) consider the implications for other aspects of the audit and discuss the matter with the appropriate levels of management.

(2) make the investigation necessary to determine whether fraud has actually occurred.

(3) request that management investigate to determine whether fraud has actually occurred.

(4) consider whether fraud was the result of a failure by employees to comply with existing controls.

b. As a result of analytical procedures, the auditor determines that the gross profit percentage has increased from 30 percent in the preceding year to 40 percent in the current year. The auditor should

(1) document management's plans for maintaining this trend.

(2) evaluate management's performance in causing the improvement in gross profit.

(3) require footnote disclosure.

(4) consider the possibility of fraud or other misstatements in the financial statements.

11-22 (Objective 11-6) The following questions address fraud risks in specific audit areas and accounts.

a. Cash receipts from sales on account have been misappropriated. Which of the following acts would conceal this defalcation and be least likely to be detected by the auditor?

(1) Understating the sales journal.

(2) Overstating the accounts receivable control account.

(3) Overstating the accounts receivable subsidiary records.

(4) Understating the cash receipts journal.

b. An auditor discovers that a client's accounts receivable turnover is substantially lower for the current year than for the prior year. This trend may indicate that

(1) fictitious credit sales have been recorded during the year.

(2) employees have stolen inventory just before year-end.

(3) the client recently tightened its credit-granting policies.

(4) an employee has been lapping receivables in both years.

c. Which of the following audit procedures will best detect the theft of valuable items from an inventory that consists of hundreds of different items selling for $1 to $10 and a few items selling for hundreds of dollars?

(1) Maintain a perpetual inventory of only the more valuable items, with frequent periodic verification of the validity of the perpetual inventory records.

(2) Have an independent auditing firm examine and report on management's assertion about the design and operating effectiveness of the control activities relevant to inventory.

(3) Have separate warehouse space for the more valuable items, with sequentially numbered tags.

(4) Require an authorized officer's signature on all requisitions for the more valuable items.

DISCUSSION QUESTIONS AND PROBLEMS

11-23 (Objective 11-2) During audit planning, an auditor obtained the following information:
1. Management has a strong interest in employing inappropriate means to minimize reported earnings for tax-motivated reasons.
2. Assets and revenues are based on significant estimates that involve subjective judgments and uncertainties that are hard to corroborate.
3. The company is marginally able to meet exchange listing and debt covenant requirements.
4. Significant operations are located and conducted across international borders in jurisdictions where differing business environments and cultures exist.
5. There are recurring attempts by management to justify marginal or inappropriate accounting on the basis of materiality.
6. The company's financial performance is threatened by a high degree of competition and market saturation.

Required Classify each of the six factors into one of these fraud conditions: incentives/pressures, opportunities, or attitudes/rationalization.

11-24 (Objectives 11-1, 11-2, 11-3) Recently, there have been a significant number of highly publicized cases of management fraud involving the misstatement of financial statements. Although most client managements possess unquestioned integrity, a very small number, given sufficient incentive and opportunity, may be predisposed to fraudulently misstate reported financial condition and operating results.

Required
a. What distinguishes management fraud from a defalcation?
b. What are an auditor's responsibilities under generally accepted auditing standards to detect management fraud?
c. What are the characteristics of management fraud that an auditor should consider to fulfill the auditor's responsibilities for detecting management fraud required by auditing professional standards?
d. Three factors that heighten an auditor's concern about the existence of management fraud include (1) an intended public placement of securities in the near future, (2) management compensation dependent on operating results, and (3) a weak internal control environment evidenced by lack of concern for basic controls and disregard of the auditor's recommendations. What other factors should heighten an auditor's concern about the existence of management fraud?*

11-25 (Objectives 11-2, 11-6) The Art Appreciation Society operates a museum for the benefit and enjoyment of the community.

When the museum is open to the public, two clerks who are positioned at the entrance collect a $5.00 admission fee from each nonmember patron. Members of the Art Appreciation Society are permitted to enter free of charge upon presentation of their membership cards.

At the end of each day, one of the clerks delivers the proceeds to the treasurer. The treasurer counts the cash in the presence of the clerk and places it in a safe. Each Friday afternoon, the treasurer and one of the clerks deliver all cash held in the safe to the bank and receive an authenticated deposit slip that provides the basis for the weekly entry in the accounting records.

The Art Appreciation Society board of directors has identified a need to improve its internal controls over cash admission fees. The board has determined that the cost of installing turnstiles, sales booths, or otherwise altering the physical layout of the museum will greatly exceed any benefits. However, the board has agreed that the sale of admission tickets must be an integral part of its improvement efforts.

Smith has been asked by the board of directors of the Art Appreciation Society to review the internal control over cash admission fees and provide suggestions for improvements.

Required
a. Indicate deficiencies in the existing internal controls over cash admission fees that Smith should identify, and recommend one improvement for each of the deficiencies identified. Organize the answer as indicated in the following illustrative example.*

Deficiencies	Recommendation
1. There is no basis for establishing the number of paying patrons.	1. Prenumbered admission tickets should be issued upon payment of the admission fee.

b. Indicate which of the deficiencies, if any, increase the likelihood of misappropriation of assets.
c. Indicate which of the deficiencies, if any, increase the likelihood of fraudulent financial reporting.

*AICPA adapted.

11-26 (Objectives 11-1, 11-4, 11-6) The following misstatements are included in the accounting records of the Joyce Manufacturing Company:

1. A sales invoice was misadded by $1,000 as a result of a key-entry mistake.
2. A material sale was unintentionally recorded for the second time on the last day of the year. The sale had originally been recorded 2 days earlier.
3. Cash paid on accounts receivable was stolen by the mail clerk when the mail was opened.
4. Cash paid on accounts receivable that had been prelisted by a secretary was stolen by the bookkeeper who records cash receipts and accounts receivable. He failed to record the transactions.
5. A shipment to a customer was not billed because of the loss of the bill of lading.
6. Merchandise was shipped to a customer, but no bill of lading was prepared. Because billings are prepared from bills of lading, the customer was not billed.
7. A sale to a residential customer was unintentionally classified as a commercial sale.
8. Sales generated through the company's Web site are recorded at the point the customers submit the orders online.

a. Identify whether each misstatement is an error or fraud.

b. For each misstatement, list one or more controls that should have prevented it from occurring on a continuing basis.

c. For each misstatement, identify evidence the auditor could use to uncover it.

Required

11-27 (Objectives 11-2, 11-4, 11-6) Appliances Repair and Service Company bills all customers rather than collecting in cash when services are provided. All mail is opened by Tom Gyders, treasurer. Gyders, a CPA, is the most qualified person in the company who is in the office daily. Therefore, he can solve problems and respond to customers' needs quickly. Upon receipt of cash, he immediately prepares a listing of the cash and a duplicate deposit slip. Cash is deposited daily. Gyders uses the listing to enter the financial transactions in the computerized accounting records. He also contacts customers about uncollected accounts receivable. Because he is so knowledgeable about the business and each customer, he grants credit, authorizes all sales allowances, and charges off uncollectible accounts. The owner is extremely pleased with the efficiency of the company. He can run the business without spending much time there because of Gyders' effectiveness.

Imagine the owner's surprise when he discovers that Gyders has committed a major theft of the company's cash receipts. He did so by not recording sales, recording improper credits to recorded accounts receivable, and overstating receivables.

a. Given that cash was prelisted, went only to the treasurer, and was deposited daily, what internal control deficiency permitted the fraud?

b. What are the benefits of a prelisting of cash? Who should prepare the prelisting and what duties should that person not perform?

c. Assume that an appropriate person, as discussed in part b, prepares a prelisting of cash. What is to prevent that person from taking the cash after it is prelisted but before it is deposited?

d. Who should deposit the cash, given your answer to part b?

Required

11-28 (Objectives 11-2, 11-4, 11-6) The Kowal Manufacturing Company employs about 50 production workers and has the following payroll procedures:

The factory foreman interviews applicants and on the basis of the interview either hires or rejects them. When applicants are hired, they prepare a W-4 form (Employee's Withholding Exemption Certificate) and give it to the foreman. The foreman writes the hourly rate of pay for the new employee in the corner of the W-4 form and then gives the form to a payroll clerk as notice that the worker has been employed. The foreman verbally advises the payroll department of rate adjustments.

A supply of blank time cards is kept in a box near the entrance to the factory. Each worker takes a time card on Monday morning, fills in his or her name, and notes in pencil their daily arrival and departure times. At the end of the week, the workers drop the time cards in a box near the door to the factory.

On Monday morning, the completed time cards are taken from the box by a payroll clerk. One of the payroll clerks then records the payroll transactions using a computer system, which records all information for the payroll journal that was calculated by the clerk and automatically updates the employees' earnings records and general ledger. Employees are automatically removed from the payroll when they fail to turn in a time card.

The payroll checks are manually signed by the chief accountant and given to the foreman. The foreman distributes the checks to the workers in the factory and arranges for the delivery of the checks to the workers who are absent. The payroll bank account is reconciled by the chief accountant, who also prepares the various quarterly and annual payroll tax reports.

a. List the most important deficiency in internal control and state the misstatements that are likely to result from the deficiency.

b. For each deficiency that increases the likelihood of fraud, identify whether the likely fraud is misappropriation of assets or fraudulent financial reporting.*

11-29 (Objectives 11-2, 11-3, 11-4, 11-6) Each year near the balance sheet date, when the president of Bargon Construction, Inc. takes a 3-week vacation to Hawaii, she signs several checks to pay major bills during the period she is absent. Jack Morgan, head bookkeeper for the company, uses this practice to his advantage. Morgan makes out a check to himself for the amount of a large vendor's invoice, and because there is no acquisitions journal, he records the amount in the cash disbursements journal as an acquisition from the supplier listed on the invoice. He holds the check until several weeks into the subsequent period to make sure that the auditors do not get an opportunity to examine the cancelled check. Shortly after the first of the year when the president returns, Morgan resubmits the invoice for payment and again records the check in the cash disbursements journal. At that point, he marks the invoice "paid" and files it with all other paid invoices. Morgan has been following this practice successfully for several years and feels confident that he has developed a fool-proof method.

a. What is the auditor's responsibility for discovering this type of embezzlement?

b. What deficiencies exist in the client's internal control?

c. What evidence could the auditor use to uncover the fraud?

11-30 (Objective 11-1) The following are activities that occurred at Franklin Manufacturing, a non-public company.

1. Franklin's accountant did not record checks written in the last few days of the year until the next accounting period to avoid a negative cash balance in the financial statements.
2. Franklin's controller prepared and mailed a check to a vendor for a carload of material that was not received. The vendor's chief accountant, who is a friend of Franklin's controller, mailed a vendor's invoice to Franklin, and the controller prepared a receiving report. The vendor's chief accountant deposited the check in an account he had set up with a name almost identical to the vendor's.
3. The accountant recorded cash received in the first few days of the next accounting period in the current accounting period to avoid a negative cash balance.
4. Discounts on checks to Franklin's largest vendor are never taken, even though they are paid before the discount period expires. The president of the vendor's company provides free use of his ski lodge to the accountant who processes the checks in exchange for the lost discounts.
5. Franklin shipped and billed goods to a customer in New York on December 23, and the sale was recorded on December 24, with the understanding that the goods will be returned on January 31 for a full refund plus a 5 percent handling fee.
6. Franklin's factory superintendent routinely takes scrap metal home in his pickup and sells it to a scrap dealer to make a few extra dollars.
7. Franklin's management decided not to include a footnote about a material uninsured lawsuit against the company on the grounds that the primary users of the statements, a small local bank, would probably not understand the footnote anyway.

a. Identify which of these activities are frauds.

b. For each fraud, state whether it is a misappropriation of assets or fraudulent financial reporting.

CASE

11-31 (Objectives 11-2, 11-3, 11-4) Kent, CPA, is the engagement partner on the financial statement audit of Super Computer Services Co. (SCS) for the year ended April 30, 2005. On May 6, 2005, Smith, the senior auditor assigned to the engagement, had the following conversation with Kent concerning the planning phase of the audit:†

Kent: Do you have all the audit programs updated yet for the SCS engagement?

Smith: Mostly. I still have work to do on the fraud risk assessment.

*AICPA adapted.

†Copyright 1998, 2003 by the American Institute of Certified Public Accountants, Inc. Reprinted with permission.

Kent: Why? Our "errors and irregularities" program from last year is still OK. It has passed peer review several times. Besides, we don't have specific duties regarding fraud. If we find it, we'll deal with it then.

Smith: I don't think so. That new CEO, Mint, has almost no salary, mostly bonuses and stock options. Doesn't that concern you?

Kent: No. Mint's employment contract was approved by the Board of Directors just three months ago. It was passed unanimously.

Smith: I guess so, but Mint told those stock analysts that SCS's earnings would increase 30 percent next year. Can Mint deliver numbers like that?

Kent: Who knows? We're auditing the '05 financial statements, not '06. Mint will probably amend that forecast every month between now and next May.

Smith: Sure, but all this may change our other audit programs.

Kent: No, it won't. The programs are fine as is. If you find fraud in any of your tests, just let me know. Maybe we'll have to extend the tests. Or maybe we'll just report it to the audit committee.

Smith: What would they do? Green is the audit committee's chair, and remember, Green hired Mint. They've been best friends for years. Besides, Mint is calling all the shots now. Brown, the old CEO, is still on the Board, but Brown's never around. Brown's even been skipping the Board meetings. Nobody in management or on the Board would stand up to Mint.

Kent: That's nothing new. Brown was like that years ago. Brown caused frequent disputes with Jones, CPA, the predecessor auditor. Three years ago, Jones told Brown how ineffective the internal audit department was then. Next thing you know, Jones is out and I'm in. Why bother? I'm just as happy that those understaffed internal auditors don't get in our way. Just remember, the bottom line is . . . are the financial statements fairly presented? And they always have been. We don't provide any assurances about fraud. That's management's job.

Smith: But what about the lack of segregation of duties in the cash disbursements department? That clerk could write a check for anything.

Kent: Sure. That's a material weakness every year and probably will be again this year. But we're talking cost-effectiveness here, not fraud. We just have to do lots of testing on cash disbursements and report it again.

Smith: What about the big layoffs coming up next month? It's more than a rumor. Even the employees know it's going to happen, and they're real uptight about it.

Kent: I know, it's the worst kept secret at SCS, but we don't have to consider that now. Even if it happens, it will only improve next year's financial results. Brown should have let these people go years ago. Let's face it, how else can Mint even come close to the 30 percent earnings increase next year?

Required

a. Describe the fraud risk factors that are indicated in the dialogue above.

b. Describe Kent's misconceptions regarding the consideration of fraud in the audit of SCS's financial statements that are contained in the preceding dialogue, and explain why each is a misconception.

c. Describe an auditor's audit documentation requirements regarding the assessment of the risk of material misstatement due to fraud.

INTERNET PROBLEM 11-1: FRAUD BEST PRACTICES

Reference the CW site. This problem requires students to use the Internet to explore best practice resources available to auditors at the AICPA's Antifraud & Corporate Responsibility Resource Center.

THE IMPACT OF INFORMATION TECHNOLOGY ON THE AUDIT PROCESS

JUST BECAUSE THE COMPUTER DID THE WORK DOESN'T MEAN IT'S RIGHT

Foster Wellman's audit client, Manion's Department Stores Inc., installed a software program that processed and aged customer accounts receivable. The aging, which indicated how long the customers' accounts were outstanding, was useful to Foster when evaluating the collectibility of those accounts.

Because Foster did not know whether the aging totals were computed correctly, he decided to test Manion's aging by using his own firm's audit software to recalculate the aging, using an electronic copy of Manion's accounts receivable data file. He reasoned that if the aging produced by his audit software was in reasonable agreement with Manion's aging, he would have evidence that Manion's aging was correct.

Foster was shocked when he found a material difference between his and Manion's calculated aging. Manion's manager of the information technology (IT) function, Rudy Rose, investigated the discrepancy and discovered that programmer errors had resulted in design flaws in Manion's software used to calculate the aging. This outcome caused Foster to substantially increase the amount of his testing of the year-end balance of the allowance for uncollectible accounts.

LEARNING OBJECTIVES

After studying this chapter, you should be able to

12-1 Describe how IT improves internal control.

12-2 Identify risks that arise from using an IT-based accounting system.

12-3 Explain how general controls and application controls reduce IT risks.

12-4 Describe how general controls affect the auditor's testing of application controls.

12-5 Use test data, parallel simulation, and embedded audit module approaches when auditing through the computer.

12-6 Identify issues for e-commerce systems and other specialized IT environments.

In Chapter 10, the components of internal control and how the auditor obtains an understanding of internal control, assesses control risk, and performs tests of controls were discussed. This chapter examines how the client's integration of information technology (IT) into the accounting system affects risks and internal control. The use of IT can enhance internal control by adding new control procedures performed by the computer and by replacing manual controls subject to human error. IT can also introduce new risks, which the client can manage through the implementation of controls specific to IT environments. This chapter highlights risks specific to IT environments, identifies controls that can be implemented to address those risks, and highlights how IT-related controls affect the audit process.

Auditors must be careful to not overrely on information merely because it is generated by the computer. As shown in the chapter vignette, Manion's overreliance on the accuracy of the computer-produced accounts receivable aging highlights a risk associated with the use of computer-generated information. A common assumption is that "the information is correct because the computer produced it." Too often, reliance is placed on the untested accuracy of computer-generated output because auditors fail to remember that computers perform only what they are programmed to do. Auditors must understand and test computer-based controls before concluding that computer-generated information is reliable. We begin by focusing on how IT can enhance internal control.

HOW INFORMATION TECHNOLOGIES ENHANCE INTERNAL CONTROL

OBJECTIVE 12-1

Describe how IT improves internal control.

Most entities, including small, family-owned businesses, rely on IT to record and process business transactions. As a result of explosive advancements in IT, even relatively simple businesses use personal computers with purchased accounting software for their accounting processes to replace inefficient and less effective manual accounting systems. As businesses grow and evolve, they often upgrade their IT systems to handle continually increasing information needs. The use of complex network environments, the Internet, and centralized IT functions is common in businesses today.

Enhancements to internal control resulting from the integration of IT into accounting systems include the following:

- *Computer controls replace manual controls.* The obvious benefits of IT, such as the ability to handle tremendous volumes of complex business transactions cost-effectively, cause organizations to use IT throughout their financial reporting processes. One advantage of IT is the ability to improve internal controls by incorporating computer-performed controls in day-to-day transaction processing activities. Replacing manual procedures with programmed controls that apply checks and balances to each processed transaction can reduce human error that is likely to occur in traditional manual environments. A well-controlled IT system offers greater potential for reducing misstatements because computers process information consistently. Examples of internal controls performed by computers that once were processed by employees are comparing customer and product numbers with master files and comparing sales transaction amounts with preprogrammed credit limits. Online security controls in applications, databases, and operating systems also provide opportunities to enhance segregation of duties.
- *Higher-quality information is available.* Once management is confident about the reliability of information produced by IT, management's use of the information offers further potential for improved management decisions. First, complex IT environments are usually administered effectively because the complexity requires effective organization, procedures, and documentation. Second, IT systems typically provide management with more and higher-quality information faster than most manual systems.

ASSESSING RISKS OF INFORMATION TECHNOLOGY

Although IT can enhance a company's internal control, it can also affect a company's overall control risk. Many risks associated with manual systems are reduced and in some cases eliminated. However, new risks specific to IT environments are created and can lead to substantial losses if ignored. For example, the inability to retrieve important information because of IT systems failure or use of unreliable information because of processing errors produced by that technology could paralyze organizations. These risks increase the likelihood of material misstatements in financial statements that must be considered by management and the auditor. The following highlights key risks specific to IT environments:

OBJECTIVE 12-2

Identify risks that arise from using an IT-based accounting system.

- *Reliance on the functioning capabilities of hardware and software.* Without proper physical protection, hardware or software may not function. Therefore, it is critical to physically protect hardware, software, and related data from physical damage that might result from inappropriate use, sabotage, or environmental damage (such as fire, heat, humidity, or water).

- *Visibility of audit trail.* Because much of the information is entered directly into the computer, the use of IT often reduces or even eliminates source documents and records that allow the organization to trace accounting information. These documents and records are called the audit trail. Because of the loss of the audit trail, other controls must be put into place to replace the traditional ability to compare output information with hard-copy data.

- *Reduced human involvement.* In many IT environments, employees who deal with the initial processing of transactions never see the final results. Therefore, they are less able to identify processing misstatements. Even if they see the final output, it is often difficult to recognize misstatements because the results are often highly summarized. Also, employees tend to regard output generated through the use of technology as "correct" because a computer produced it.

- *Systematic versus random errors.* As organizations replace manual procedures with technology-based procedures, the risk of random errors decreases. However, the risk of systematic error increases because of the uniformity of computer processing. Once procedures are programmed into computer software, the computer processes information consistently for all transactions until the programmed procedures are changed. Unfortunately, flaws in software programming and changes to that software affect the reliability of computer processing, often resulting in many significant misstatements. This risk is heightened if the system is not programmed to recognize unusual transactions or when transaction audit trails are inadequate.

- *Unauthorized access.* IT-based accounting systems often allow online access to data in master files and other records stored in electronic form. Because online access can occur from many remote access points, including by external parties with remote access through the Internet, there is potential for illegitimate access. Without proper online restrictions such as passwords and user IDs, unauthorized activity may be initiated through the computer, resulting in improper changes in software programs and master files. Also, confidential information may be improperly obtained.

- *Loss of data.* Much of the underlying data in an IT environment are stored in centralized electronic files. When data are centralized, there is an increased risk of loss or destruction of entire data files with severe ramifications. There is potential for misstated financial statements, and in certain cases, the organization may incur serious business interruptions.

- *Reduced segregation of duties.* As organizations convert from manual to computer processes, computers perform many duties that were traditionally segregated, such as authorization and record keeping. Therefore, combining activities from different parts of the organization into one IT function centralizes responsibilities that were traditionally divided. IT personnel with access to software and master files may be able to steal assets unless key duties are appropriately segregated within the IT function.

- *Lack of traditional authorization.* It is common in advanced IT systems for certain types of transactions to be initiated automatically by the computer. Examples include calculating interest on savings accounts and ordering inventory when prespecified order levels are reached. Therefore, proper authorization depends on software procedures and the accuracy of master files used in making the authorization decision.

- *Need for IT experience.* Even when companies purchase relatively simple computer systems that include purchased software, personnel with knowledge and experience to install, maintain, and use the system are essential. As the use of IT systems increases in organizations, the need for qualified IT specialists often arises. Many companies create an entire function of IT personnel that includes programmers, operators, network supervisors, librarians, data entry clerks, quality assurance specialists, and database administrators. Other companies outsource the management of IT operations. For example, some companies rely on outside Web site providers to create Internet-based inventory ordering and sales applications. The reliability of an IT system and the information it generates often depends on the ability of the organization to employ personnel or hire consultants with appropriate technology knowledge and experience.

INTERNAL CONTROLS SPECIFIC TO INFORMATION TECHNOLOGY

OBJECTIVE 12-3

Explain how general controls and application controls reduce IT risks.

To address many of the risks associated with greater reliance on IT, organizations often implement controls specific to the IT function. Auditing standards describe two broad control groupings for IT systems: general controls and application controls.

General controls relate to all aspects of the IT function, including administration; software acquisition and maintenance; physical and online security over access to hardware,

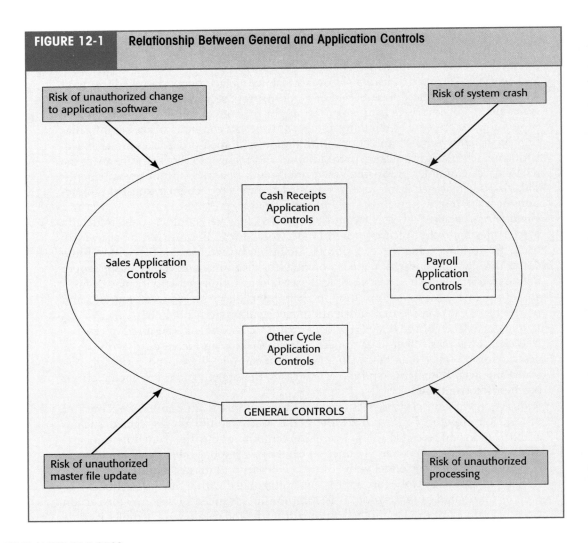

FIGURE 12-1 Relationship Between General and Application Controls

Risk of unauthorized change to application software

Risk of system crash

Cash Receipts Application Controls

Sales Application Controls

Payroll Application Controls

Other Cycle Application Controls

GENERAL CONTROLS

Risk of unauthorized master file update

Risk of unauthorized processing

software, and related data; backup planning in the event of unexpected emergencies; and hardware controls.

Application controls apply to the processing of individual transactions, such as controls over the processing of sales or cash receipts. Therefore, application controls are specific to certain software applications and typically do not affect all IT functions. Processing controls must therefore be evaluated for every audit area (account or class of transactions) affected by an application in which the auditor plans to reduce assessed control risk.

As shown in Figure 12-1, general controls are designed to protect all application controls to ensure that those controls are effective. Strong general controls mitigate the types of risks identified in the boxes outside the general controls oval in Figure 12-1.

Table 12-1 describes six categories of general controls and three categories of application controls, with specific examples of each category. The next two sections discuss each of the categories of general and application controls in more detail.

Similar to the effect that the control environment has on other components of internal control discussed in Chapter 10, the six categories of general controls have an overriding effect on all IT functions. Auditors typically evaluate general controls early in the audit because of the impact of general controls on application controls. The six categories of general controls are now examined in more detail.

General Controls

Administration of the IT Function As reliance on IT in business increases, managing and administrating the IT function becomes more important. Management must allocate sufficient resources to support technology.

The perceived importance of IT within an organization is often dictated by the attitude of the board of directors and senior management. Their oversight, resource allocation, and involvement in key IT decisions provide a strong signal about the importance of the function. In complex environments, management often establishes IT steering committees to help monitor the organization's technology needs. In less complex organizations, the board may rely on regular reporting by a chief information officer (CIO) or other senior IT manager to keep management informed.

In contrast, when technology functions are delegated exclusively to lower-level employees or outside consultants, an implied message is given that IT may not be a high priority. The result is often an understaffed, underfunded, and poorly controlled IT function.

TABLE 12-1	Categories of General and Application Controls	
Control Type	**Category of Control**	**Example of Control**
General controls	Administration of the IT function	Chief information officer or IT manager reports to senior management and board.
	Segregation of IT duties	Responsibilities for programming, operations, and data control are separated.
	Systems development	Teams of users, systems analysts, and programmers develop and thoroughly test software.
	Physical and online security	Access to hardware is restricted, passwords and user IDs limit access to software and data files, and encryption and firewalls protect data and programs from external parties.
	Backup and contingency planning	Written backup plans are prepared and tested regularly throughout the year.
	Hardware controls	Memory failure or hard drive failure causes error messages on the monitor.
Application controls	Input controls	Preformatted screens prompt data input personnel for information to be entered.
	Processing controls	Reasonableness tests review unit-selling prices used to process a sale.
	Output controls	The sales department performs postprocessing review of sales transactions.

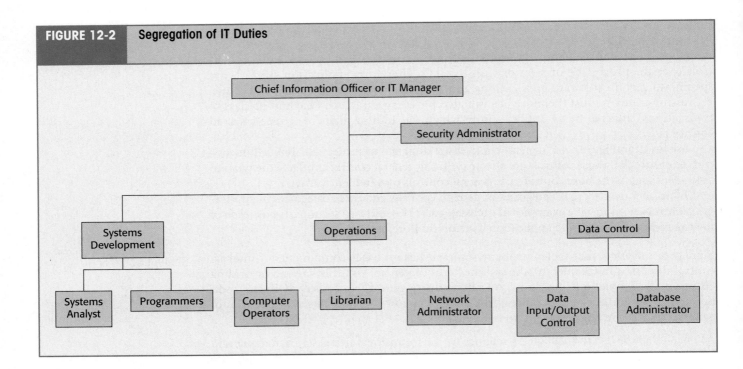

FIGURE 12-2   Segregation of IT Duties

IFAC Guidance on IT Governance

Segregation of IT Duties To respond to the risk of combining traditional custody, authorization, and record-keeping responsibilities under the IT function, well-controlled organizations respond by segregating key duties within IT. One concern is preventing IT personnel from authorizing and recording transactions to cover the theft of assets. Another concern is minimizing errors. To reduce these concerns, software programming, computer operations (including security surrounding physical and online access to hardware, software, and data files), and controls over data entry and output should be segregated as depicted in Figure 12-2.

Ideally, responsibilities for IT management, systems development, operations, and data control should be separated as follows:

- *IT management.* Oversight of the IT function is generally the responsibility of the CIO or IT manager. This individual is responsible for the oversight of all IT functions to ensure that activities are carried out consistently with the IT strategic plan. In addition to the CIO, a security administrator monitors both physical and online access to hardware, software, and data files and performs follow-up investigative procedures for detected security breaches.
- *Systems development.* Development and changes to IT systems are generally coordinated by a systems analyst who is responsible for the overall design of each application system and serves as the liaison between IT personnel responsible for programming the application and personnel outside the IT function who will be the primary system users (such as accounts receivable personnel). Programmers develop special flowcharts for the application, prepare computer instructions, test programs, and document the results based on direction from the systems analyst. Programmers should not have access to input data or computer operation because understanding the program logic can easily be used for personal benefit. Access to copies of actual programs used to produce accounting information and access to data should be restricted so that programmers are not able to implement software programming changes without proper authorization. Instead, programmers should be allowed to work only with test copies of programs and data.
- *Operations.* The day-to-day operations of the computer are the responsibility of computer operators who are responsible for executing jobs in accordance with the job schedule established by the CIO and for monitoring computer consoles for messages about computer efficiency and malfunctions. A librarian is responsible for maintaining

computer programs, transaction files, and other important computer records and documentation. The librarian maintains control over these programs and records by releasing them to operators only as indicated on the job schedule. The librarian releases a test copy to programmers only on approval by senior management. In networked environments, the network administrator is responsible for planning, implementing, and maintaining a network of servers that link users to various applications and data files.

- *Data control.* Data input/output control personnel independently verify the quality of input and the reasonableness of output. For organizations that use databases to store information shared by accounting and other functions, database administrators are responsible for the operation and access security of shared databases.

Naturally, the extent of segregation of duties depends on the organization's size and complexity. In many small companies, it is not practical to segregate the duties to the extent illustrated in Figure 12-2.

Systems Development To increase confidence that tested software continues to process information as intended, management must design and implement internal controls designed to reduce the risk of unauthorized software changes. These internal controls are called systems development methodology procedures.

A key to successful software purchase decisions or to in-house programming of software is to involve a team of both IT and non-IT personnel, including key users of the software and internal auditors. This combination of personnel increases the likelihood that information needs as well as software design and implementation problems are properly addressed. A team approach usually results in more effective systems and better acceptance by key users.

Whether software is purchased or developed internally, extensive testing of the software with realistic data is critical. The purpose is to ensure that the new software is compatible with existing hardware and software components and to determine whether the hardware and software can handle realistic volumes of transactions. Two typical test strategies companies use are pilot testing and parallel testing. **Pilot testing** involves implementing a new system in one part of the organization while other locations continue to rely on the old system. **Parallel testing** involves operating the old and new systems simultaneously in all locations.

Once successfully tested, the software supporting the new system is transferred from the programming staff to the librarian. Controls over this transfer process are critical to be certain that only approved changes are implemented. The librarian should accept the new or modified software only when proper documentation of the systems development is provided. In addition, to avoid implementation problems, conversion should be scheduled during off-peak time periods, when reliance on the system is reduced.

COMPUTER GLITCHES BRING BIG PROBLEMS

The installation of a new computer system brings new risks. Hershey's Foods found this out when it flipped the switch on a new $112 million computer system in July 1999. The new system was supposed to automate everything from candy orders to placing pallets on trucks. Instead, the system gummed up the ordering and distribution system, and some customers found themselves unable to obtain candy bars during the crucial Halloween season.

For small businesses, the impact of computer problems can be even more severe. Texas Textbooks closed its doors after computer problems made it difficult for students to find the books they needed. The loss of sales and unhappy customers created a downward spiral from which the company never recovered.

Sources: Adapted from Emily Nelson and Evan Ramstad, "Trick or Treat: Hershey's Biggest Dud Has Turned Out to Be Its New Technology," *The Wall Street Journal* (October 29, 1999), p. A1. Jerry Mahoney, "Texas Textbooks Closes Doors in Austin, Texas, In Wake of Yearlong Demise," *Knight-Ridder Tribune Business News: Austin American Statesman* (April 6, 2001).

Physical and Online Security Effective physical controls over computers and online restrictions to software and related data files decrease the risk that unauthorized changes are made to software programs and data files. Security plans should be in writing and continually monitored. Following is a brief description of typical physical controls and online access controls:

- *Physical controls.* Physical control over computer equipment begins with restricting access to hardware, software, and backup data files on magnetic tapes or disks, hard drives, CDs, and external disks. Examples of ways to restrict unauthorized use include keypad entrances, badge-entry systems, security cameras, and security personnel. For higher levels of security, physical and online access are granted only after employee fingerprints are read or employee retinas are scanned and matched with an approved database. Other physical controls include monitoring of cooling and humidity to ensure that the equipment functions properly. Readily available fire-extinguishing equipment reduces potential damage from fire.
- *Online access controls.* Appropriately enforced user IDs and passwords to access software and related data files reduce the likelihood that unauthorized changes are made to software applications and data files. The operating systems of many computers provide user ID and password control features. In more advanced IT systems, separate add-on security software packages can be installed to strengthen security.

Disaster Recovery Plan Example

Backup and Contingency Planning Disasters such as power failures, fire, excessive heat or humidity, water damage, or even sabotage have serious consequences to businesses using IT. To address such risks, organizations develop detailed backup and contingency plans. One key to a backup and contingency plan is to make sure that all critical copies of software and data files are backed up and stored off the premises. Also, the plans should identify alternative hardware to process company data.

For smaller IT systems, replacement computers and servers can be purchased and used with backup copies of software and data files. In more advanced systems, organizations install battery backups for temporary power outages and have generators on-site, and they may also contract for backup facilities.

Hardware Controls Controls that are built into computer equipment by the manufacturer to detect and report equipment failures are called **hardware controls**. Independent auditors are more concerned with the client's methods of handling the errors identified by the computer than with the adequacy of the hardware controls in the system. Regardless of the quality of hardware controls, output will remain uncorrected unless the client's organization has made provisions for handling machine errors.

Application Controls

Application controls are designed for each software application and are intended to help a company satisfy the six transaction-related audit objectives discussed in previous chapters. Although some application controls affect one or only a few transaction-related audit objectives, most controls prevent or detect several types of misstatements.

Application controls may be performed by computers or by people. Application controls performed by people interacting with computers are often referred to as user controls. The effectiveness of user controls, such as reviews of computer-produced exception reports, often depends on the accuracy of the information produced. For example, credit department personnel review of exception reports highlighting credit sales exceeding a customer's authorized credit limit is dependent on both the quality of the person's review and the accuracy of the information on the report.

Although the objectives for input, processing, and output controls are the same, the procedures for meeting the objectives vary considerably. We will now discuss these three types of application controls.

Input Controls Controls designed by an organization to ensure that the information being processed by the computer is authorized, accurate, and complete are called **input controls**. Input controls are critical because a large portion of errors in IT systems result from errors in entering data. Errors in input result in output errors, regardless of the quality of the information processing. Typical controls found in manual systems continue to be important. Examples include management's authorization of transactions, adequate

TABLE 12-2 | Batch Input Controls

Control	Definition	Examples
Financial total	Summary total of field amounts for all records in a batch that represent a meaningful total such as dollars or amounts	The total of dollars of all vendor invoices to be paid
Hash total	Summary total of codes from all records in a batch that do not represent a meaningful total	The total of all vendor account numbers for vendor invoices to be paid
Record count	Summary total of physical records in a batch	The total number of vendor invoices to be processed

preparation of input source documents, and competent personnel. Other controls are specific to IT. Examples include adequately designed input screens with preformatted prompts for transaction information, pull-down menu lists of available software options, and computer-performed validation tests of input accuracy, such as the validation of customer numbers against the customer master files. Also, immediate error correction procedures and accumulation of errors in an error file for subsequent follow-up by data input personnel provide for early detection and correction of input errors. Online-based input controls are especially important for e-commerce applications, where external parties, such as customers and suppliers, perform the initial input of transaction information.

For IT environments that group similar transactions together into batches, the use of financial batch totals, hash totals, and record count totals helps increase the accuracy and completeness of input. Batch input controls are described in Table 12-2.

Processing Controls Controls that prevent and detect errors when transaction data are processed are called **processing controls.** Even though general controls, especially controls related to systems development and security, provide some of the best control for minimizing errors, application processing controls are often embedded in software to prevent, detect, and correct processing errors. Table 12-3 includes examples of processing controls.

Output Controls Controls that focus on detecting errors after processing is completed rather than on preventing errors are called **output controls.** The most important output control is review of the data for reasonableness by someone knowledgeable about the output. Users can often identify errors because they know the approximate correct amounts. In addition, reconciliation of computer-produced output to manual control totals and comparisons of the number of units processed to the number of units submitted for processing help identify errors in output. In some cases, sample comparisons of transaction output to input

TABLE 12-3 | Processing Controls

Type of Processing Control	Description	Example
Validation test	Ensures the use of the correct master file, database, and programs in processing	Does the internal label on the payroll master file tape match the file label indicated in the application software?
Sequence test	Determines that data submitted for processing are in the correct order	Has the file of payroll input transactions been sorted in departmental order before processing?
Arithmetic accuracy test	Checks the accuracy of processed data	Does the sum of net pay plus withholdings equal gross pay for the entire payroll?
Data reasonableness test	Determines whether data exceed prespecified amounts	Does employee's gross pay exceed 60 hours or $1,999 for the week?
Completeness test	Determines that every field in a record has been completed	Are employee number, name, number of regular hours, number of overtime hours, department number, etc., included for each employee?

source documents are performed. Similarly, verification of dates and times of processing may help identify out-of-sequence processing. For sensitive output, such as payroll checks automatically generated by computer, control is enhanced by requiring the presentation of proper employee identification before distribution of checks. Also, access to sensitive output viewed on computer screens or transmitted across public networks such as the Internet can be restricted by using passwords, user IDs, and encryption techniques.

IMPACT OF INFORMATION TECHNOLOGY ON THE AUDIT PROCESS

OBJECTIVE 12-4

Describe how general controls affect the auditor's testing of application controls.

The last section provided an overview of general controls and application controls. Auditors must be knowledgeable about these controls because they are responsible for gaining an understanding of internal control, including general and application controls, regardless of whether the client's use of IT is simple or complex. Also, knowledge about general controls increases the auditor's ability to rely on effective application controls to reduce control risk for transaction-related audit objectives. Knowledge of both general and application IT controls is particularly relevant for public company auditors who must issue an opinion on internal control over financial reporting. Because general controls can have a pervasive effect on the operating effectiveness of application controls, auditors must consider general controls to arrive at an opinion on the operating effectiveness of key application controls. This section highlights how general and application controls affect the audit process.

Effect of General Controls on Control Risk

ISACA

Most auditors evaluate the effectiveness of general controls before evaluating application controls. If general controls are ineffective, there is potential for material misstatement in each computer-based accounting application, regardless of the quality of application controls. For example, if duties are inadequately segregated such that computer operators are also programmers and have access to computer programs and files, the auditor should be concerned about the potential for fictitious transactions or unauthorized data and omissions in accounts such as sales, purchases, and salaries. Similarly, if the auditor observes that data files are inadequately safeguarded, the auditor may conclude that there is a significant risk of loss of data because the general controls affect each application. In this situation, audit testing to satisfy the completeness objective may need to be expanded in several areas such as cash receipts, cash disbursements, and sales.

On the other hand, if good general controls are in place, there is an increased likelihood of placing greater reliance on application controls. Auditors can therefore test specific application controls for operating effectiveness and rely on the results to reduce substantive testing. And, the presence of effective general controls may allow the auditor of a public company to test a single operation of an automated application control in an audit of internal control over financial reporting. This use of effective general and application controls can result in significant audit efficiencies.

One challenge, however, in IT environments is the effect of changes in software on the auditor's reliance on controls. When the client changes the software, the auditor must evaluate whether additional testing is needed. If general controls are effective, the auditor will be able to easily identify when software changes are made. In environments where general controls are weak, there is greater likelihood of unidentified changes in application software. As a result, auditors must consider performing tests of application control operating effectiveness on a continual basis throughout the year when general controls are weak.

Auditors typically obtain information about general and application controls through interviews with IT personnel and key users; examination of system documentation such as flowcharts, user manuals, program change requests, and testing results; and review of detailed questionnaires completed by IT staff. In most cases, it is desirable to use several approaches in understanding internal control because each offers different information. Interviews with the chief information officer and systems analysts provide useful information about the operation of the entire IT function, the extent of software development and hardware changes made to key accounting application software, and an overview of planned changes. Reviews of program change requests and system test results are useful in identifying program changes in application software. Questionnaires are useful to identify specific internal controls.

Recall from Chapter 10 that auditors relate strengths and deficiencies in internal control to specific transaction-related audit objectives. Based on those strengths and weaknesses, the auditor assesses control risk for each transaction-related audit objective. That same approach is used in IT environments, but now the auditor may be able to rely on application controls performed by the computer to reduce control risk.

Auditors do not normally link strengths and weaknesses in general controls to specific transaction-related audit objectives. Like the control environment discussed in Chapter 10, general controls affect transaction-related audit objectives in several cycles. If the general controls are ineffective, the auditor's ability to rely on application controls to reduce control risk is reduced. Conversely, if general controls are effective, it increases the auditor's ability to rely on application controls to reduce control risk.

Auditors identify both manual and computer-performed application controls and control deficiencies for each transaction-related audit objective using a control risk matrix in much the same manner as discussed in Chapter 10. For example, the computer's comparison of inputted employee identification numbers with the employee master file might reduce control risk for the existence objective for payroll expense by preventing payments to fictitious employees.

Similar to the discussion in Chapter 10, when the auditor identifies specific application controls that can be used to reduce control risk, the auditor can reduce substantive testing. In addition, effective application controls performed by the computer are likely to be more consistent than manually performed controls because of the absence of random human errors. The systematic nature of controls performed by the computer may reduce sample sizes used to test automated application controls in both an audit of financial statements and an audit of internal control over financial reporting. Also, the auditor may be able to reduce the audit costs of tests of controls by using the audit firm's software to test the controls. These factors, when combined, often lead to extremely effective and efficient audits.

The impact of general controls and application controls on audits is likely to vary depending on the level of complexity in the IT environment. The next two sections highlight issues in auditing clients with relatively simple IT environments and ones with more complex environments.

Many organizations use IT to process business transactions and design those systems so that source documents are retrievable in readable form and can be traced easily through the accounting system to output. In those instances, many of the traditional source documents such as customer purchase orders, shipping and receiving records, and sales and vendor invoices are maintained. The related accounting software also produces printed journals and ledgers that allow the auditor to trace individual transactions through the accounting records. In addition, internal controls often include client comparison of computer-produced records with source documents.

In these situations, the use of IT does not significantly impact the audit trail. Typically, the auditor obtains an understanding of internal control and performs tests of controls, substantive tests of transactions, and account balance verification procedures in the same manner as if the accounting system were entirely manual. The auditor is still responsible for gaining an understanding of general and application computer controls because such knowledge is useful in identifying risks that may affect the financial statements. However, the auditor does not typically perform tests of computer controls. This approach to auditing is often called **auditing around the computer** because the auditor is not using computer controls to reduce assessed control risk. Instead, the auditor uses non-IT controls to support reduced control risk assessment in a manner similar to that presented in Chapter 10.

For audits of internal control over financial reporting required for public companies, the ability to audit around the computer is dependent on the extent of noncomputer-performed controls. To audit around the computer in a public company audit, there must be sufficient noncomputer-performed controls over all relevant financial statement assertions for all significant accounts and disclosures in the financial statements. Otherwise, the auditor must test the operating effectiveness of key automated controls. For audits of financial statements of a nonpublic company, the auditor may decide not to reduce control risk by testing automated controls and may instead increase substantive tests.

OBJECTIVE 12-5

Use test data, parallel simulation,
and embedded audit module
approaches when auditing
through the computer.

As organizations expand their use of IT, internal controls are often embedded in applications that are visible only in electronic form. When traditional source documents such as invoices, purchase orders, billing records, and accounting records such as sales journals, inventory listings, and accounts receivable subsidiary records are only in electronic form rather than hard copy, the auditor must change the approach to auditing. This approach to the audit is often called **auditing through the computer.** Table 12-4 contains examples that highlight differences in auditing around the computer and auditing through the computer.

There are three categories of testing strategies when auditing through the computer: the test data approach, parallel simulation, and the embedded audit module approach.

Test Data Approach The **test data approach** involves processing the auditor's test data using the client's computer system and the client's application program to determine whether the computer-performed controls correctly process the test data. Because the auditor designs the test data, the auditor is able to identify which test items should be accepted or rejected by the client's system. The auditor compares the output generated by the system from the test data to the expected output to assess the effectiveness of the application program's internal controls. Figure 12-3 illustrates the use of the test data approach.

When using the test data approach, there are three main auditor considerations:

1. Test data should include all relevant conditions that the auditor wants tested. The auditor should design test data to test key computer-based controls. The auditor's test data should contain realistic data items that are likely to be a part of the client's normal processing, including both valid and invalid transactions.

For example, assume the client's payroll application contains a limit check that disallows a payroll transaction that exceeds 80 hours per week. To test this control, the auditor can prepare payroll transactions with 79, 80, and 81 hours for each sampled week and process them through the client's system in a manner shown in Figure 12-3. If the limit check control is operating effectively, the client's system should reject the transaction for 81 hours, and the client's error listing should report the 81-hour transaction error.

2. Application programs tested by the auditor's test data must be the same as those the client used throughout the year. One approach is to run the test data on a surprise basis, possibly at random times throughout the year, even though doing so is costly and time consuming. Another method is to rely on the client's general controls in the librarian and

TABLE 12-4	Examples of Auditing Around and Through the Computer	
Internal Control	**Auditing Around the Computer Approach**	**Auditing Through the Computer Approach**
Credit is approved for sales on account.	Select a sample of sales transactions from the sales journal and obtain the related customer sales order to determine that the credit manager's initials are present, indicating approval of sales on account.	Obtain a copy of the client's sales application program and related credit limit master file and process a test data sample of sales transactions to determine whether the application software properly rejects those test sales transactions that exceed the customer's credit limit amount and accepts all other transactions.
Payroll is processed only for individuals currently employed.	Select a sample of payroll disbursements from the payroll journal and verify by reviewing human resource department files that the payee is currently employed.	Create a test data file of valid and invalid employee ID numbers and process that file using a controlled copy of the client's payroll application program to determine that all invalid employee ID numbers are rejected and that all valid employee ID numbers are accepted.
Column totals for the cash disbursements journal are subtotaled automatically by the computer.	Obtain a printout of the cash disbursements journal and manually foot each column to verify the accuracy of the printed column totals.	Obtain an electronic copy of the cash disbursements journal transactions and use generalized audit software to verify the accuracy of the column totals.

FIGURE 12-3   Test Data Approach

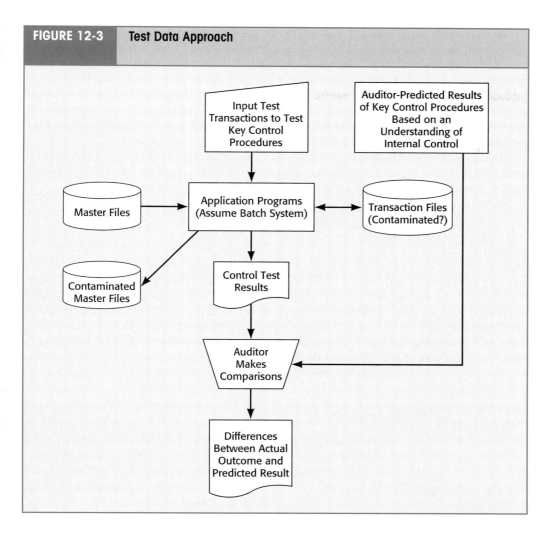

systems development functions for assurance that the program tested is the one used in normal processing.

3. Test data must be eliminated from the client's records. If testing of the client's software involves processing test data while simultaneously processing actual client transactions, the auditor must eliminate test data in client master files once testing is complete. It is not appropriate to permit fictitious transactions to remain permanently in the client's master file. To remove the fictitious transactions, the auditor submits additional input that reverses the effect of those transactions.

Because of the complexities of many clients' application software programs, auditors who plan to use the test data approach often obtain assistance from a computer audit specialist. Many larger accounting firms have staff dedicated to assisting in testing client application controls.

Parallel Simulation A variety of software is available to assist auditors in determining the effectiveness of controls in software and to obtain evidence about account balances that are in an electronic format. The auditor uses auditor-controlled software to perform parallel operations to the client's software by using the same data files. Whether testing controls or ending balances, the auditor compares the output to output from the client's software to test the effectiveness of the client's software. The lack of differences in output indicates effectively functioning client software, whereas differences indicate potential deficiencies. Because the auditor's software is designed to parallel an operation performed by the client's software, this testing strategy is called **parallel simulation testing.**

ACL and IDEA

A tool commonly used by auditors to perform parallel simulation testing is **generalized audit software (GAS)**, which is software designed specifically for use by auditors. Purchased audit software, such as ACL or IDEA discussed in Chapter 7, can be easily operated on an auditor's desktop or laptop computer. The auditor obtains copies of client databases or master files in machine-readable form and uses the generalized audit software to perform a variety of tests of the client's electronic data. Some auditors use spreadsheet software to perform basic parallel simulation tests. Others may develop their own customized audit software. Figure 12-4 depicts a typical parallel simulation.

There are two advantages of generalized audit software. First, it is relatively easy to train audit staff in its use, even if they have had little audit-related IT training. Second, generalized audit software can be applied to a wide variety of clients with minimal customization.

One use of generalized audit software is to test IT controls. For example, the auditor can obtain copies of a client's customer credit limit master file and input file of customer orders and instruct the auditor's computer to list transactions that fall below the customer's authorized credit limit. The auditor can then reconcile the audit software output tests to the client's recorded transactions to verify the accuracy and completeness of the client's files. A second use of generalized audit software is to verify the client's account balances. For example, the auditor can use the software to add the master file of customer accounts receivable to determine whether the total agrees with the general ledger balance. A significant benefit of generalized audit software is the ability to perform audit tests much faster and in more detail than using traditional manual procedures. Table 12-5 highlights other common uses of generalized audit software.

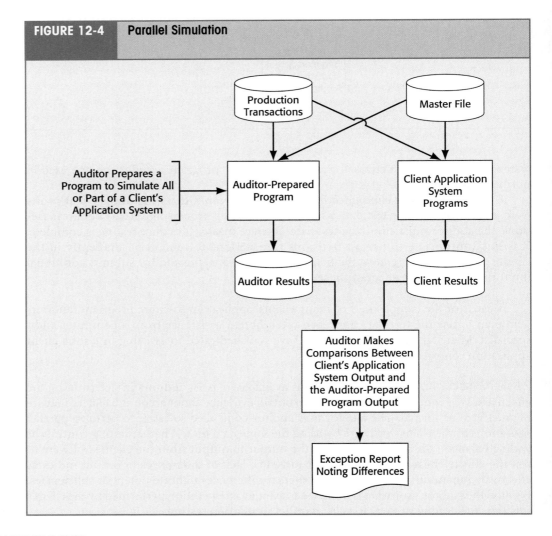

FIGURE 12-4 | Parallel Simulation

TABLE 12-5 Common Uses of Generalized Audit Software

Uses	Description	Examples
Verify extensions and footings.	Verify the accuracy of the client's computations by calculating information independently.	Foot accounts receivable trial balance.
Examine records for quality, completeness, consistency, and correctness.	Scan all records using specified criteria.	Review payroll files for terminated employees.
Compare data on separate files.	Determine that information in two or more data files agrees.	Compare changes in accounts receivable balances between two dates using sales and cash receipts in transaction files.
Summarize or resequence data and perform analyses.	Change or aggregate data.	Resequence inventory items by location to facilitate physical observation.
Select audit samples.	Select samples from machine-readable data.	Randomly select accounts receivable for confirmation.
Print confirmation requests.	Print data for sample items selected for confirmation testing.	Print customer name, address, and account balance information from master files.
Compare data obtained through other audit procedures with company records.	Compare machine-readable data with audit evidence gathered manually, which is converted to machine-readable form.	Compare confirmation responses with accounts receivable master files.

Embedded Audit Module Approach When using the **embedded audit module approach**, an auditor inserts an audit module in the client's application system to capture transactions with characteristics that are of specific interest to the auditor. For example, the auditor might capture all purchases exceeding a set dollar amount in order to examine all large transactions processed through the acquisition and payment cycle. With the embedded audit module approach, the auditor is able to continuously audit transactions by identifying actual transactions processed by the client. An important advantage is the auditor's ability to test continuously, compared with the test data and parallel simulation approaches, which are done at points in time. Another advantage of embedded audit modules is the ability to identify all unusual transactions for auditor evaluation. In some cases, these unusual transactions are copied to a separate data file, which is processed by an auditor-designed software program to duplicate the function performed by the client's system. The computer then compares the client's output with the auditor's output. Discrepancies are printed on an exception report for auditor follow-up. In this case, the embedded audit module permits the auditor to perform a real-time parallel simulation test.

An auditor may use one or a combination of the test data, parallel simulation, and embedded audit module approaches. Auditors typically use test data to perform tests of controls and substantive tests of transactions. Parallel simulation is often used for substantive testing, such as recalculating transaction amounts and footing master file subsidiary records of account balances. Auditors use the embedded audit module approach to identify unusual transactions for substantive testing.

ISSUES FOR DIFFERENT IT ENVIRONMENTS

OBJECTIVE 12-6

Identify issues for e-commerce systems and other specialized IT environments.

Much of the material presented in this chapter thus far addresses the effect of IT on the audit process for organizations that centralize the IT function. Although all organizations need a strong general control environment regardless of the structure of their IT function, some general control issues vary depending on the IT environment. The next five sections highlight IT issues for clients who use microcomputers, networks, database management systems, e-commerce systems, and outsourced computer service centers.

Issues for Microcomputer Environments

Microcomputers are widely used in most businesses, regardless of the organization's size. They usually play an important role for small businesses in processing or analyzing accounting data through the use of purchased or tailored accounting and electronic spreadsheet software.

General controls in smaller companies are usually less effective than in more complex IT environments. Often, there are no dedicated IT personnel, or the client relies on periodic involvement of IT consultants to assist in installing and maintaining hardware and software. Also, the responsibility of the IT function is often assigned to user departments, such as in the accounting department, where the hardware physically resides. However, even in these IT environments, controls over software acquisition, physical and online access security, and backup planning are important.

Often, auditors of clients that use microcomputers in less sophisticated general control environments do most of their auditing around the computer. These systems often produce sufficient audit trails that permit the auditor to reconcile input source documentation to output. And, there may be manual controls over the input and output processes that operate effectively in the prevention and detection of material financial statement misstatements. However, even in less sophisticated IT environments, there are situations in which computer controls can be relied on. For example, software programs in microcomputers can be loaded on the computer's hard drive in a format that does not permit changes by client personnel. The risk of unauthorized changes in the software is therefore low. Before relying on controls built into that software, the auditor must have confidence in the software vendor's reputation for quality.

A concern in a microcomputer environment is access to master files by unauthorized people. For example, the usefulness of comparing customer sales orders and customer accounts receivable balances with the master file of credit limits depends on the accuracy of customer credit limits. Unlike sophisticated IT environments, microcomputers often lack data file password protection. Without such protection, a user may be able to enter changes that make the control useless. An example is raising a customer credit limit high enough to avoid rejection. In such situations, appropriate segregation of duties between personnel with access to master files and responsibilities for processing in such situations is critical. In addition, regular owner–manager review of transaction output increases internal control.

Another risk with microcomputers is the loss of data and programs because of computer viruses, which can infect other programs and the entire system. Certain viruses can damage disk files or shut down an entire network of computers. Regularly updated virus protection software that continually screens for virus infections enhances controls.

A public company's use of microcomputers in the financial reporting process may affect the audit of internal control over financial reporting. If the auditor concludes that general controls are ineffective, the auditor's tests of key automated application controls may need to be increased. The auditor must also consider the implications of the lack of effective general controls on the opinion about the operating effectiveness of internal control over financial reporting.

Issues for Network Environments

The explosive use of networks that link equipment such as microcomputers, midrange computers, mainframes, workstations, servers, and printers is changing the IT function for many businesses. **Local area networks (LANs)** link equipment within a single or small cluster of buildings and are used only for intracompany purposes. A common use of LANs is to transfer data and programs from one computer or workstation to another using network system software to allow all of the devices to function together. **Wide area networks (WANs)** link equipment in larger geographic regions, including global operations.

In network environments, the application software and data files used to process transactions reside on servers, which are devices to manipulate data. Access to the application from microcomputers or workstations is managed by network server software. Companies often have several servers.

For many large client network environments, most of the general controls discussed in this chapter apply because the IT support and user involvement is centralized. For other companies, the network environment often presents control issues that the auditor must consider in planning the audit. Many organizations decentralize their network's servers, which often increases control risk because of a lack of security and overall management supervision of network operations. Also, many network environments lack standardized equipment and procedures. Organizations that need fast communication and easy access to data often create networks outside the control of the IT function. Responsibility for purchasing equipment and software, maintenance, administration, and physical security often resides with key user groups rather than with a centralized IT function, which often leads to lack of adequate controls. Also, network-related software often lacks the security features, including segregation of duties, typically available in traditionally centralized environments because of the ready access to software and data by multiple users.

When clients have accounting applications processed in a network environment, the auditor's understanding of internal control should include knowledge of the network configuration, including the location of servers, workstations, and computers linked to one another, and knowledge of network software used to manage the system. Auditors should also know about controls over access and changes to application programs and data files located on servers. Such knowledge may have important implications for the auditor's control risk assessment when planning the audit of the financial statements and when testing controls in an audit of internal control over financial reporting.

Auditors often encounter accounting applications that use database management systems to process transactions and maintain data files. **Database management systems** allow clients to create databases that contain information that can be shared in multiple applications. In nondatabase environments, each application contains its own data file, whereas in database management systems, many applications share files. Clients implement database management systems to reduce data redundancy, improve control over data, and provide better information for decision making by integrating information throughout functions and departments. For example, customer data, such as the customer's name and address, can be shared in the sales, credit, accounting, marketing, and shipping functions, resulting in significant cost reductions. Companies often integrate database management systems across the entire organization. Such programs are called enterprise software.

Controls often improve when data are centralized in a database management system by eliminating the redundant data files. However, database management systems also can create internal control risks. For example, there are risks associated with multiple users, including individuals outside of accounting, accessing and updating data files. Without proper database administration and access control, risks of unauthorized, inaccurate, and incomplete data files increase. Also, the centralization of data into a single file increases the importance of proper backup of data information on a regular basis.

Issues for Database Management Systems

VIRUSES WREAK HAVOC

Computer viruses, including the "Blaster" and "SoBig.F" worms that spread rapidly in August 2003, can wreak havoc on global computer systems in a matter of hours. Computer security experts claim that the Blaster and SoBig.F viruses affected more than 500,000 computers worldwide and cost North American companies $1.3 billion. The original Blaster worm struck computer systems on August 11, 2003, and was among the most damaging computer viruses to date. It struck days before the SoBig.F virus was sent to millions of e-mail addresses throughout the world. The Blaster worm was aimed at corporations and brought computer traffic to a halt and compromised company data. The SoBig.F worm was aimed at home personal computer users and small companies; however, Starbucks Corp., FedEx Corp., and the New York Times Co. were hurt by SoBig's spread, and it prompted the shutdown of the U.S. passport agency's computers.

According to computer experts, there have been about 150 writers of major harmful computer viruses in the last 5 years. Of those, roughly 20 have been identified, and only about 10 have been prosecuted. Sophisticated hackers are able to cover their tracks by connecting to a variety of anonymous servers scattered throughout the world. U.S. Attorney General John Ashcroft issued a statement saying, "Cyber-hacking is not joyriding. Hacking disrupts lives and innocent victims across the nation." As a result, federal investigators, including the FBI, are actively tracking the origins of these viruses. A Minnesota teenager has already been arrested for writing a variant of the Blaster virus, known as "Blaster B."

Sources: 1. Sarah Kershaw, Laurie Flynn, and Matthew Preusch, "Arrest Made in Attacks on Computers," *The New York Times*, August 30, 2003, Section C, p. 1. 2. Joseph Menn, "Computers Bearing Virus Orders Isolated," *The Los Angeles Times*, August 23, 2003, Business, Part 3, p. 1.

Auditors of clients using database management systems should understand the clients' planning, organization, and policies and procedures to determine how well the systems are managed. This understanding may affect the auditor's assessment of control risk and the auditor's opinion about the operating effectiveness of internal control over financial reporting.

<table>
<tr><td>

**Issues for
E-commerce Systems**

</td><td>

Companies using e-commerce systems to transact business electronically link their internal accounting systems to systems maintained by external parties, such as customers and suppliers. As a result, risks that a company faces when engaging in e-commerce activities are partly dependent on how well its e-commerce partners identify and manage risks in their own IT systems. To manage these interdependency risks, companies must ensure that their business partners effectively manage IT system risks before conducting business with them electronically. Some of the assurance services discussed in Chapter 1, such as *SysTrust,* may provide objective information about the reliability of a business partner's IT system.

</td></tr>
</table>

The use of e-commerce systems also exposes sensitive company data, programs, and hardware to potential interception or sabotage by external parties. To limit these exposures, companies use firewalls, encryption techniques, and digital signatures. A **firewall** protects data, programs, and other IT resources from external users accessing the system through networks, such as the Internet. A firewall is a system of hardware and software that monitors and controls the flow of e-commerce communications by channeling all network connections through a control gateway. Firewalls can be used to verify an external user of the network, grant authorized access, and direct the user to the program or data requested.

Companies use **encryption techniques** to protect the security of electronic communication during the transmission process. Encryption techniques are based on computer programs that transform a standard message into a coded (encrypted) form. The receiver of the electronic message must use a decryption program to decode the encrypted message. Often, a public key encryption technique is used, whereby one key (the public key) is used for encoding the message and the other key (the private key) is used to decode the message. The public key is distributed to all approved users of the e-commerce system and can only be used to encode messages. The private key, which is used to decode the message, becomes the focal point of the control. The protection of the private key is often the responsibility of the IT security administrator and it is only distributed to internal users with the authority to decode the message.

To help authenticate the validity of a trading partner conducting business electronically, companies may rely on external certification authorities who verify the source of the public key through the use of **digital signatures.** A trusted certification authority issues a digital certificate to individuals and companies engaging in e-commerce. The digital signature contains the holder's name and its public key. It also contains the name of the certification authority and the certificate's expiration date and other specified information. To guarantee integrity and authenticity, each signature is digitally signed by the private key maintained by the certification authority.

<table>
<tr><td>

**Issues When Clients
Outsource IT**

</td><td>

Many clients outsource some or all of their IT needs to an independent computer **service center,** including **application service providers** (**ASPs**), rather than maintain an internal IT center. Many smaller companies outsource their payroll function because payroll is reasonably standard from company to company and there are reliable providers of payroll services. Companies also outsource their e-commerce systems to external Web site service providers. Like all outsourcing decisions, companies decide whether to outsource IT on a cost-benefit basis.

</td></tr>
</table>

When outsourcing to a computer service center, the client submits input data, which the service center processes for a fee, and returns the agreed-upon output and the original input. For payroll, the company submits time cards, pay rates, and W-4s to the service center. The service center returns payroll checks, journals, and input data each week and W-2s at the end of each year. The service center is responsible for designing the computer system and providing adequate controls to ensure that the processing is reliable.

The auditor faces a difficulty when obtaining an understanding of the client's internal controls because many of the controls reside at the service center, and the auditor cannot assume that the controls are adequate simply because it is an independent enterprise. Auditing standards require the auditor to consider the need to understand and test the service center's controls if the service center application involves processing significant financial data.

The extent of obtaining an understanding and testing the service center's controls should be based on the same criteria that the auditor follows in evaluating a client's internal controls. The depth of the understanding depends on the complexity of the system and the extent to which the auditor intends to reduce assessed control risk to reduce substantive audit tests. The depth of understanding also depends on the extent to which key controls over financial reporting reside at the service center for audits of internal control for public companies. If the auditor concludes that active involvement at the service center is the only way to conduct the audit, it may be necessary to obtain an understanding of internal controls at the service center and test controls using test data and other tests of controls.

In recent years, it has become increasingly common to have one independent auditor obtain an understanding and test internal controls of the service center for use by all customers and their independent auditors. The purpose of this independent assessment is to provide service center customers with a reasonable level of assurance of the adequacy of the service center's general and application controls and to eliminate the need for redundant audits by customers' auditors. If the service center has many customers and each requires an understanding of the service center's internal control by its own independent auditor, the inconvenience and cost to the service center can be substantial.

SAS 70 (AU 324), as amended by SAS 78 and SAS 80, provides guidance to (1) auditors who issue reports on the internal control of service organizations (*service auditors*) and (2) auditors of user organizations (*user auditors*) about reliance on the service auditor's report. Service auditors may issue two types of reports:

- Report on controls placed in operation
- Report on controls placed in operation and tests of operating effectiveness

A report on controls placed in operation is helpful in obtaining an understanding of internal control to plan the audit. However, evidence concerning the operating effectiveness of controls is necessary to assess control risk below the maximum or when auditing internal control over financial reporting for public companies. This evidence can be based on the service auditor's report on controls placed in operation and tests of operating effectiveness. This evidence can also come from tests of the user organization's controls over the activities of the service organization, or the user auditor may perform appropriate tests at the service organization. If the user auditor decides to rely on the service auditor's report, appropriate inquiries should be made regarding the service auditor's reputation. The user auditor should not make reference to the report of the service auditor in the opinion on the user organization's financial statements.

SUMMARY

This chapter studied the impact of IT on the audit process. Even when a client's use of IT leads to enhanced internal control, the use of IT-based accounting systems introduces new risks typically not associated with traditional manual systems. Well-managed companies recognize these new risks and respond by implementing effective general and application controls in the IT system to reduce the impact of those risks on financial reporting. The auditor must be knowledgeable about these risks and obtain an understanding of the client's general and application controls to effectively plan an audit. Obtaining knowledge about general controls provides a basis for the auditor to rely on application controls and may reduce the extent of tests of key automated controls in audits of financial statements and internal controls. Some of the auditor's tests of controls can be performed by the computer, often as a way to achieve more effective and efficient audits. Reliance on general and application controls to reduce control risk is likely to change when clients use microcomputers, networks, database management systems, e-commerce systems, and outsourced computer service centers instead of centralized IT systems.

ESSENTIAL TERMS

Application controls—controls related to a specific use of IT, such as the inputting, processing, and outputting of sales or cash receipts

Application service providers (ASPs)—a third-party entity that manages and supplies software applications or software-related services to customers through the Internet

Auditing around the computer—auditing without relying on and testing controls embedded in computer application programs, which is acceptable when the auditor has access to source documents in a readable form that can be reconciled to detailed listings of output or when sufficient nonautomated controls exist

Auditing through the computer—auditing by testing computer-performed internal controls and account balances electronically, generally because strong general controls exist

Database management systems—hardware and software systems that allow clients to establish and maintain databases shared by multiple applications

Digital signatures—electronic certificates that are used to authenticate the validity of individuals and companies conducting business electronically

Embedded audit module approach—a method of auditing transactions processed by IT whereby the auditor embeds a module in the client's application system to capture transactions with characteristics that are of interest to the auditor; the auditor is then able to analyze the captured transactions on a real-time, continuous basis as client transactions are processed

Encryption techniques—computer programs that transform a standard message into a coded form that is decoded by the recipient using a decryption program

Firewall—a system of hardware and software that monitors and controls the flow of e-commerce communications by channeling all network connections through a control gateway

General controls—controls that relate to all parts of the IT function

Generalized audit software (GAS)—computer programs used by auditors that provide data retrieval, data manipulation, and reporting capabilities specifically oriented to the needs of auditors

Hardware controls—controls built into the computer equipment by the manufacturer to detect and report equipment failure

Input controls—controls designed by an organization to ensure that the information to be processed by the computer is authorized, accurate, and complete

Local area networks (LANs)—networks that connect computer equipment, data files, software, and peripheral equipment within a local area, such as a single building or a small cluster of buildings, for intracompany use

Output controls—controls designed to ensure that computer-generated data are valid, accurate, complete, and distributed only to authorized people

Parallel simulation testing—an audit testing strategy that involves the auditor's use of audit software, either purchased or programmed by the auditor, to replicate some part of a client's application system

Parallel testing—a company's computer testing strategy that involves operating the old and new systems simultaneously

Pilot testing—a company's computer testing strategy that involves implementing a new system in just one part of the organization, while maintaining the old system at other locations

Processing controls—controls designed to ensure that data input into the system are accurately and completely processed

Service center—an organization that provides IT services for companies on an outsourcing basis

Test data approach—a method of auditing an IT system that uses the auditor's test data to determine whether the client's computer program can correctly process valid and invalid transactions

Wide area networks (WANs)—networks that connect computer equipment, databases, software, and peripheral equipment that reside in many geographic locations, such as client offices located around the world

REVIEW QUESTIONS

12-1 (Objective 12-1) Explain how client internal controls can be enhanced through the proper installation of IT.

12-2 (Objective 12-2) Identify risks for accounting systems that rely heavily on IT functions.

12-3 (Objective 12-2) Define what is meant by an audit trail and explain how it can be affected by the client's integration of IT.

12-4 (Objective 12-2) Distinguish between random error resulting from manual processing and systematic error resulting from IT processing and give an example of each category of error.

12-5 (Objective 12-2) Identify the traditionally segregated duties in noncomplex IT environments and explain how increases in the complexity of the IT function affect that segregation.

12-6 (Objective 12-3) Distinguish between general controls and application controls and give two examples of each.

12-7 (Objective 12-3) Identify the typical duties within an IT function and describe how those duties should be segregated among IT personnel.

12-8 (Objective 12-4) Explain how the strength of general controls affects the auditor's tests of application controls.

12-9 (Objective 12-4) Explain the relationship between application controls and transaction-related audit objectives.

12-10 (Objective 12-4) Explain what is meant by auditing around the computer and describe what must be present for this strategy to be effective when auditing clients who use IT to process accounting information.

12-11 (Objective 12-5) Explain what is meant by the test data approach. What are the major difficulties with using this approach? Define parallel simulation with audit software and provide an example of how it could be used to test a client's payroll system.

12-12 (Objective 12-6) Describe risks that are associated with purchasing software to be installed on microcomputer hard drives. What precautions can clients take to reduce those risks?

12-13 (Objective 12-6) Compare the risks associated with network environments to those associated with centralized IT functions.

12-14 (Objective 12-6) How does the use of a database management system affect risks?

12-15 (Objective 12-6) An audit client is in the process of creating an online Web-based sales ordering system for customers to purchase products using personal credit cards for payment. Identify three risks related to an online sales system that management should consider. For each risk, identify an internal control that could be implemented to reduce that risk.

12-16 (Objective 12-6) Explain why it is unacceptable for an auditor to assume that an independent computer service center is providing reliable accounting information to an audit client. What can the auditor do to test the service center's internal controls?

MULTIPLE CHOICE QUESTIONS FROM CPA EXAMINATIONS

12-17 (Objectives 12-1, 12-4) The following questions concern the characteristics of IT systems. Choose the best response.

a. An IT system is designed to ensure that management possesses the information it needs to carry out its functions through the integrated actions of
   (1) data-gathering, analysis, and reporting functions.
   (2) a computer-based information retrieval and decision-making system.
   (3) statistical and analytical procedures functions.
   (4) production budgeting and sales forecasting activities.

b. Which of the following conditions would *not* normally cause the auditor to question whether material misstatements exist?
   (1) Bookkeeping errors are listed on an IT-generated error listing.
   (2) Differences exist between control accounts and supporting master files.
   (3) Transactions are not supported by proper documentation.
   (4) Differences are disclosed by confirmations.

c. As the strength of general IT controls weakens, the auditor is most likely to
   (1) reduce testing of application controls performed by the computer.
   (2) increase testing of general IT controls to conclude whether they are operating effectively.
   (3) expand testing of application controls used to reduce control risk to cover greater portions of the fiscal year under audit.
   (4) ignore gaining knowledge about the design of general IT controls and whether they have been placed in operation.

d. Which of the following is an example of an application control?
  (1) The client uses access security software to limit access to each of the accounting applications.
  (2) Employees are assigned a user ID and password that must be changed every quarter.
  (3) The sales system automatically computes the total sale amount and posts the total to the sales journal master file.
  (4) Systems programmers are restricted from performing applications programming functions.

12-18 (Objectives 12-2, 12-4) The following questions concern auditing complex IT systems. Choose the best response.

a. Which of the following client IT systems generally can be audited without examining or directly testing the computer programs of the system?
  (1) A system that performs relatively uncomplicated processes and produces detailed output.
  (2) A system that affects a number of essential master files and produces limited output.
  (3) A system that updates a few essential master files and produces no printed output other than final balances.
  (4) A system that performs relatively complicated processing and produces little detailed output.

b. Which of the following is true of generalized audit software programs?
  (1) They can be used only in auditing online computer systems.
  (2) They can be used on any computer without modification.
  (3) They each have their own characteristics that the auditor must carefully consider before using in a given audit situation.
  (4) They enable the auditor to perform all manual tests of control procedures less expensively.

c. Assume that an auditor estimates that 10,000 checks were issued during the accounting period. If an IT application control that performs a limit check for each check request is to be subjected to the auditor's test data approach, the sample should include
  (1) approximately 1,000 test items.
  (2) a number of test items determined by the auditor to be sufficient under the circumstances.
  (3) a number of test items determined by the auditor's reference to the appropriate sampling tables.
  (4) one transaction.

d. An auditor will use the test data approach to gain certain assurances with respect to the
  (1) input data.
  (2) machine capacity.
  (3) procedures contained within the program.
  (4) degree of data entry accuracy.

DISCUSSION QUESTIONS AND PROBLEMS

12-19 (Objectives 12-2, 12-3) The following are misstatements that can occur in the sales and collection cycle:

1. A customer order was filled and shipped to a former customer that had already filed for bankruptcy.
2. The sales manager approved the price of goods ordered by a customer, but he wrote down the wrong price.
3. Several remittance advices were batched together for inputting. The cash receipts clerk stopped for coffee, set them on a box, and failed to deliver them to the data input personnel.
4. A customer number on a sales invoice was transposed and, as a result, charged to the wrong customer. By the time the error was found, the original customer was no longer in business.
5. A former computer operator, who is now a programmer, entered information for a fictitious sales return and ran it through the computer system at night. When the money came in, he took it and deposited it in his own account.
6. A computer operator picked up a computer-based data file for sales of the wrong week and processed them through the system a second time.
7. For a sale, a data entry operator erroneously failed to enter the information for the salesman's department. As a result, the salesman received no commission for that sale.
8. A nonexistent part number was included in the description of goods on a shipping document. Therefore, no charge was made for those goods.

a. Identify the transaction-related audit objective(s) to which the misstatement pertains. **Required**

b. Identify one computer-based control that would have likely prevented each misstatement.

12-20 (Objectives 12-2, 12-3) You are doing the audit of Phelps College, a private school with approximately 2,500 students. With your firm's consultation, they have instituted an IT system that separates the responsibilities of the computer operator, systems analyst, librarian, programmer, and data control group by having a different person do each function. Now, a budget reduction is necessary and one of the five people must be laid off. You are requested to give the college advice as to how the five functions could be performed with reduced personnel and minimal negative effects on internal control. The amount of time the functions take is not relevant because all five people also perform nonaccounting functions.

a. Divide the five functions among four people in such a way as to maintain the best possible control system. **Required**

b. Assume that economic times become worse for Phelps College and it must terminate employment of another person. Divide the five functions among three people in such a way as to maintain the best possible internal control. Again, the amount of time each function takes should not be a consideration in your decision.

c. Assume that economic times become so severe for Phelps College that only two people can be employed to perform IT functions. Divide the five functions between two people in such a way as to maintain the best possible control system.

d. If the five functions were performed by one person, would internal controls be so inadequate that an audit could not be performed? Discuss.

12-21 (Objectives 12-2, 12-3, 12-4, 12-5) The Meyers Pharmaceutical Company has the following system for billing and recording accounts receivable:

1. An incoming customer's purchase order is received in the order department by a clerk who prepares a prenumbered company sales order form on which the pertinent information, such as the customer's name and address, customer's account number, and items and quantities ordered, is inserted. After the sales order form has been prepared, the customer's purchase order is stapled to it.

2. The sales order form is then passed to the credit department for credit approval. Rough approximations of the billing values of the orders are made in the credit department for those accounts on which credit limitations are imposed. After investigation, approval of credit is noted on the form.

3. Next the sales order form is passed to the billing department, where a clerk key-enters the sales order information onto a data file, including unit sales prices obtained from an approved price list. The data file is used to prepare sales invoices.

   The billing application automatically accumulates daily totals of customer account numbers and invoice amounts to provide "hash" totals and control amounts. These totals, which are inserted in a daily record book, serve as predetermined batch totals for verification of computer inputs. The billing is done on prenumbered, continuous, carbon-interleaved forms that have the following designations:

   (a) Customer's copy
   (b) Sales department copy, for information purposes
   (c) File copy
   (d) Shipping department copy, which serves as a shipping order

   Bills of lading are also prepared as carbon copy by-products of the invoicing procedure.

4. The shipping department copy of the invoice and the bills of lading are then sent to the shipping department. After the order has been shipped, copies of the bill of lading are returned to the billing department. The shipping department copy of the invoice is filed in the shipping department.

5. In the billing department, one copy of the bill of lading is attached to the customer's copy of the invoice and both are mailed to the customer. The other copy of the bill of lading, together with the sales order form, is then stapled to the invoice file copy and filed in invoice numerical order.

6. The data file is updated for shipments that are different from those billed earlier. After these changes are made, the file is used to prepare a sales journal in sales invoice order and to update the accounts receivable master file. Daily totals are printed to match the control totals prepared earlier. These totals are compared with the "hash" and control totals by an independent person.

a. Identify the important controls and related sales transaction-related audit objectives.

b. List the procedures that a CPA would use in an audit of sales transactions to test the identified controls and the substantive aspects of the sales transactions.

12-22 (Objective 12-5) The following are audit procedures taken from a CPA firm's audit program for acquisitions and cash disbursements:

1. Foot the list of accounts payable and trace the balance to the general ledger.
2. Select a sample of accounts payable for confirmation, emphasizing vendors with a large balance and those that the client transacts with frequently, but include several with small and zero balances.
3. Compare all transactions recorded for 4 days before and after the balance sheet date with related receiving reports and vendors' invoices to determine the appropriate recording period.
4. Examine a random sample of 100 acquisition transactions to determine whether each was authorized by an appropriate official and paid within the discount period to obtain the maximum cash discount.
5. Compare the total of each account payable outstanding, including zero balances, with those in the preceding year, and examine vendors' statements for any total with a difference in excess of $500.
6. Compare the unit cost on a random sample of 100 vendors' invoices with catalogs or other price lists and investigate any with a difference of more than 3%.

Required

a. For each audit procedure, identify whether it is a test of control, a substantive test of transactions, or a test of details of balances.

b. Explain how generalized audit software could be used, at least in part, to perform some or all of each audit procedure. Assume all information is in both machine- and non-machine-readable form. Also, identify audit procedures or parts of procedures to which the general audit software is not likely to be applicable. Use the following format:

Procedure	Data File or Files Needed	Kind of Test or Tests the Auditor Can Perform Using GAS	Procedure for which GAS is Likely to Be Inappropriate

12-23 (Objectives 12-1, 12-2, 12-3, 12-4, 12-5) You are conducting an audit of sales for the James Department Store, a retail chain store with a computer-based sales system in which computer-based cash registers are integrated directly with accounts receivable, sales, perpetual inventory records, and sales commission expense. At the time of sale, the salesclerks key-enter the following information directly into the cash register:

- Product number
- Quantity sold
- Unit selling price
- Store code number
- Salesclerk number
- Date of sale
- Cash sale or credit sale
- Customer account number for all credit sales

The total amount of the sale, including sales tax, is automatically computed by the system and indicated on the cash register's visual display. The only printed information for cash sales is the cash register receipt, which is given to the customer. For credit sales, a credit slip is prepared and one copy is retained by the clerk and submitted daily to the accounting department.

A summary of sales is printed out daily in the accounting department. The summary includes daily and monthly totals by salesclerks for each store as well as totals for each of 93 categories of merchandise by store. Perpetual inventory and accounts receivable records are updated daily on magnetic tape, but supporting records are limited primarily to machine-readable records.

Required

a. What major problems does the auditor face in verifying sales and accounts receivable?

b. How can the concept of test data be used in the audit? Explain the difficulties the auditor would have to overcome in using test data.

c. How can generalized audit software be used in this audit? List several tests that can be conducted by using this approach.

d. The client would also like to reduce the time it takes to key-enter the information into the cash register. Suggest several ways in which this could be accomplished, considering the information now being key-entered manually.

12-24 (Objective 12-5) A CPA's client, Boos & Baumkirchner, Inc., is a medium-size manufacturer of products for the leisure-time activities market (camping equipment, scuba gear, bows and arrows, and so forth). During the past year, a computer system was installed and inventory records of finished goods and parts were converted to computer processing. The inventory master file is maintained on a disk. Each record of the file contains the following information:

- Item or part number
- Description
- Size
- Unit-of-measure code
- Quantity on hand
- Cost per unit
- Total value of inventory on hand at cost
- Date of last sale or usage
- Quantity used or sold this year
- Economic order quantity
- Code number of major vendor
- Code number of secondary vendor

In preparation for year-end inventory, the client has two identical sets of preprinted inventory count cards. One set is for the client's inventory counts, and the other is for the CPA's use to make audit test counts. The following information is on each card:

- Item or part number
- Description
- Size
- Unit-of-measure code

In taking the year-end inventory, the client's personnel will write the actual counted quantity on the face of each card. When all counts are complete, the counted quantity will be entered into the system. The cards will be processed against the inventory database, and quantity-on-hand figures will be adjusted to reflect the actual count. A computer-generated edit listing will be prepared to show any missing inventory count cards and all quantity adjustments of more than $100 in value. These items will be investigated by client personnel, and all required adjustments will be made. When adjustments have been completed, the final year-end balances will be computed and posted to the general ledger.

The CPA has available generalized audit software that will run on the client's computer and can process both card and disk files.

Required

a. In general and without regard to the facts in this case, discuss the nature of generalized audit software and list the various types and uses.

b. List and describe at least five ways generalized audit software can be used to assist in all aspects of the audit of the inventory of Boos & Baumkirchner, Inc. (For example, the software can be used to read the disk inventory master file and list items and parts with a high unit cost or total value. Such items can be included in the test counts to increase the dollar coverage of the audit verification.)*

12-25 (Objectives 12-2, 12-3) One of the firm's audit partners, Alice Goodwin, just had lunch with a good friend, Sara Hitchcock, who is president of Granger Container Corporation. Granger Container Corp. is a fast-growing company that has been in business for only a few years. During lunch, Sara asked Alice for some advice and direction on how Granger Container should structure its systems development process within the Information Systems Department. Sara noted that because Granger has experienced such tremendous growth, the systems development process has evolved into its current state without much direction. Given Granger Container's current size, Sara questions whether their current processes are reasonable. Sara's concern is magnified by the fact that she has little understanding of information systems processes. Alice told Sara about your information systems evaluation experience and agreed to have you look at Granger Container's current systems development procedures. Sara gave Alice the following summary of the current processes:

*AICPA adapted.

Eric Winecoff is the information systems manager at Granger Container and has been at the company for 3 years. Before becoming an employee, Eric provided software consulting services for Granger Container. Granger Container purchased a basic software package from Eric's former employer. Granger Container has the capability to make extensive modifications to the purchased software to adapt the software to Granger Container's specific business needs.

Program change requests are initiated by either the operations staff (two employees) or the programming staff (two employees), depending on the nature of the change. All change requests are discussed in Eric's office with the initiating staff. Based on that discussion, Eric provides a verbal approval or denial of the requested change. For approved projects, he encourages the programmers to visit with him from time to time to discuss progress on the projects. Eric's long and varied experience with this particular software is helpful in the evaluation of work performed, and he is able to make substantive suggestions for improvement. Eric has complete faith in his programmers. He believes that if he controlled their activities too carefully, he would stifle their creativity.

Upon completion of the technical programming, Eric reviews the programs and related systems flowcharts. Eric only rarely identifies last-minute changes before granting his final approval for implementation. One evening a week is set aside in the computer room for program debugging and testing.

The programmers stay late on those evenings so that they can load the programs themselves. To speed up the coding, debugging, and testing process, the programmers work with the actual production program. As a safeguard, however, testing is performed on copies of the data files. The original data files are locked carefully in the file storage room. Eric is the only person who has access to the room.

When program changes are tested to the satisfaction of the programmers, Eric reviews the test results. If he approves the test results, he personally takes care of all the necessary communications and documentation. This involves preparing a short narrative description of the change, usually no longer than a paragraph. A copy of the narrative is sent to the user. Another copy is filed with the systems documentation. When the narrative is complete, Eric instructs operations to resume normal production with the new program.

Required

a. Describe strengths in Granger Container's systems development and program change processes.

b. Describe deficiencies in Granger Container's systems development and program change processes.

c. Provide recommendations for how Granger Container could improve its processes.

12-26 (Objective 12-4) Following are 10 key internal controls in the payroll cycle for Gilman Stores, Inc.

Key Controls

1. To input hours worked, payroll accounting personnel input the employee's Social Security number. The system does not allow input of hours worked for invalid employee numbers.
2. The system automatically computes pay at time and a half once hours worked exceed 80 in a 2-week pay period.
3. The system accumulates totals each pay period of employee checks processed and debits the payroll expense general ledger account for the total amount.
4. Each pay period, payroll accounting clerks count the number of time cards submitted by department heads for processing and compare that total with the number of checks printed by the system to ensure that each time card has a check.
5. For factory personnel, the payroll system matches employee ID numbers with ID numbers listed on job costing tickets as direct labor per the cost accounting system. The purpose of the reconciliation is to verify that the amount paid to each employee matches the amount charged to production during the time period.
6. The system generates a listing by employee name of checks processed. Department heads review these listings to ensure that each employee actually worked during the pay period.
7. The payroll application is programmed so that only human resource personnel are able to add employee names to the employee master files.
8. On a test basis, payroll accounting personnel obtain a listing of pay rates and withholding information for a sample of employees from human resources to recalculate gross and net pay.
9. Input menus distinguish executive payroll, administrative payroll, and factory payroll.
10. The system automatically rejects processing an employee's pay if inputted hours exceed 160 hours for a 2-week pay period.

For each control,

    a. identify whether the control is an application control performed by the computer (AC) or a manual control performed by Gilman employees (MC).

    b. identify the transaction-related audit objective that is affected by the control.

Required

12-27 (Objectives 12-2, 12-3) Your new audit client, Hardwood Lumber Company, has a computerized accounting system for all financial statement cycles. During planning, you visited with the information systems vice president and learned that personnel in information systems are assigned to one of four departments: systems programming, applications programming, operations, or data control. Job tasks are specific to the individual and no responsibilities overlap with other departments. Hardwood Lumber relies on the operating system software to restrict online access to individuals. The operating system allows an employee with "READ" capabilities to only view the contents of the program or file. "CHANGE" allows the employee to update the contents of the program or file. "RUN" allows the employee to use a program to process data. Programmers, both systems and applications, are restricted to a READ-only access to all live application software program files but have READ and CHANGE capabilities for test copies of those software program files. Operators have READ and RUN capabilities for live application programs. Data control clerks have CHANGE access to data files only and no access to software program files. The person in charge of operations maintains access to the operating software security features and is responsible for assigning access rights to individuals. The computer room is locked and requires a card-key to access the room. Only operations staff have a card-key to access the room. Security cameras monitor access to the room. A TV screen is in the information systems vice president's office to allow periodic monitoring of access. The TV presents the live picture and no tape record is maintained. The librarian, who is in the operations department, is responsible for maintaining the library of program tapes and files. The librarian has READ and CHANGE access rights to program tapes and files. The files, when not being used, are stored in shelves located in a room adjacent to the computer room. They are filed numerically based on the tape label physically attached on the outside of the tape cartridge to allow for easy identification by operators as they access tapes from the shelves for processing.

What recommendations for change can you suggest to improve Hardwood's information systems function?

Required

12-28 (Objective 12-6) Parts for Wheels, Inc. has historically sold auto parts directly to consumers through its retail stores. Due to competitive pressure, Parts for Wheels installed an Internet-based sales system that allows customers to place orders through the company's Web site. The company hired an outside Web site design consultant to create the sales system because the company's IT personnel lack the necessary experience.

    Customers use the link to the inventory parts listing on the Web site to view product descriptions and prices. The inventory parts listing is updated weekly. To get the system online quickly, management decided not to link the order system to the sales and inventory accounting systems. Customers submit orders for products through the online system and provide credit card information for payment. Each day, accounting department clerks print submitted orders from the online system. After credit authorization is verified with the credit card agency, the accounting department enters the sale into the sales journal. After that, the accounting department sends a copy of the order to warehouse personnel who process the shipment. The inventory system is updated based on bills of lading information forwarded to accounting after shipment.

    Customers may return parts for full refund if returned within 30 days of submitting the order online. The company agrees to refund shipping costs incurred by the customer for returned goods.

    a. Describe deficiencies in Parts for Wheels' online sales system that may lead to material misstatements in the financial statements.

Required

    b. Identify changes in manual procedures that could be made to minimize risks, without having to reprogram the current online system.

    c. Describe customer concerns about doing business online with Parts for Wheels. What types of controls could be implemented to address those concerns?

CASE

12-29 (Objectives 12-2, 12-3) The information systems (IS) department at Jacobsons Inc. consists of eight employees, including the IS Manager, Melinda Cullen. Melinda is responsible for the day-to-day oversight of the IS function and reports to Jacobsons' chief operating officer (COO). The COO is a senior vice president responsible for the overall retail operations. The COO reports directly to the president and chief executive officer. The COO attends board of director meetings to provide an update of key operating performance issues. Because Melinda takes an active role in managing the IS department, the COO rarely discusses IS issues with the board or CEO. Melinda and the COO identify hardware and software needs and are authorized to approve those purchases.

In addition to Melinda, the IS department is composed of seven other individuals: three programmers, three operators, and one data control clerk. Melinda has been employed by Jacobsons for 12 years, working her way up through various positions in the department. Fortunately, she has been able to retain a fairly stable staff and has experienced minimal turnover. All IS personnel have been employed in their current positions since mid-2003. When hiring personnel, Melinda performs extensive background checks on prospective employees, including reference, credit, and criminal checks. Melinda has developed a trust with each employee and, as a result, delegates extensively to each individual. This is especially beneficial because Melinda spends most of her time working with user departments in a systems analyst role, identifying changes needed to existing applications. She conducts weekly IS departmental meetings on Tuesday mornings. Each staff member attends, including night operators, to discuss issues affecting the performance of the department.

The three programmers are responsible for maintaining and updating systems and application software. The lead programmer is responsible for assigning duties among the programming staff. All three programmers have extensive experience with the operating, utility, security, and library software as well as all of Jacobsons' application software packages. Programming assignments are made based on who is least busy among the programming staff at the time. This method of management keeps all programmers familiar with most software packages in use at Jacobsons and keeps programmers excited about the job tasks because of the variety of assignments they receive. Melinda encourages each programmer to take continuing education courses to keep current with the latest technical developments. In addition to programming responsibilities, the programming staff maintains the library of programs and data tapes, which is located in a locked room nearby. The programming staff maintains extensive logs of tape use and of changes made to program files.

The three operators consist of a day operator and two night operators. Most of the applications are based on online inputting from various user departments for batch processing overnight. Thus, the heaviest volume of processing occurs during the night shift, although there is some daytime processing of payroll and general ledger applications. All operators are responsible for monitoring the operation of the equipment and correcting system-caused errors. In addition, they perform routine monthly backup procedures. The computer operators have programming experience with the program language used in application programs. Occasionally, when a small change is identified for an application program, Melinda asks the day shift operator to implement that change to avoid overburdening the programming staff. Operators follow the production schedule prepared by Melinda, who consults with user departments to develop the schedule. The day shift operator reviews the job processed log (which chronologically details the jobs processed) generated at the end of the previous night shift for deviations from the schedule, and the lead night shift operator reviews the job processed log generated at the end of the previous day shift for deviations from the schedule. If jobs processed reconcile to the job schedule, the job processed log is discarded. When there are deviations, the operator performing the review leaves a copy for Melinda, highlighting the deviation. Before performing batch processing jobs, the operators generate an input listing report that summarizes the number of online input entries submitted during the day for processing. This number is recorded and then later compared by the operators with the computer output generated after batch processing and file updating occur. This provides a check figure of the number of transactions processed. When the numbers agree, the output is submitted to the data control clerk. When the numbers disagree, the operators identify the error and resubmit the application for processing.

The data control clerk collates all computer output, including output reports and exception listings. The data control clerk reviews exception reports and prepares correction forms for reprocessing. Examples of changes that the data control clerk might make include corrections for inputting errors (that is, amounts accidentally transposed) and preparation of change request forms for changes to existing master files (that is, revising sales price lists and inventory product numbers in the sales master file and adding new employee names, addresses, and Social Security numbers to the payroll master file). After all corrections are made, the data control clerk distributes all computer output to the various user departments. User departments have high regard for the IS staff. Output reports are reconciled to input reports by users on a test basis quarterly.

Required   You are the senior auditor assigned to the audit of Jacobsons. The audit partner has asked you to assist in performing the IS general controls review. The partner has asked you to review this narrative information and respond to the following questions:

1. What strengths and weaknesses exist in the lines of reporting from IS to senior management? If you note any weaknesses, provide recommendations that can be included in the management letter.

2. What is your assessment of how Melinda Cullen fulfills her IS management responsibilities? What tasks performed by her do you believe strengthen the department? Which of her tasks cause you concern? What changes in her day-to-day responsibilities would you make?
3. What is your assessment of the programming function at Jacobsons? What are the strengths? What are the weaknesses? Make recommendations for improvement.
4. What is your assessment of the IS operations function at Jacobsons? What are the strengths? What are the weaknesses? Make recommendations for improvement.
5. What is your assessment of the data control function at Jacobsons? What are the strengths? What are the weaknesses? Make recommendations for improvement.
6. Make recommendations for improving controls over the involvement of users.

INTERNET PROBLEM 12-1: COBIT

Reference the CW site. The mission of COBIT is to research, develop, publicize, and promote an authoritative, up-to-date, international set of generally accepted information technology control objectives for day-to-day use by business managers and auditors.

The third edition of COBIT, released by the IT Governance Institute, is available at the ISACA Web site (www.isaca.org/cobit.htm). The Web site also contains a number of articles related to COBIT. Based on the information available at the ISACA Web site, answer the following questions:

1. What does the COBIT acronym mean?
2. COBIT is divided into six parts. (*Hint*: the first part is the "Executive Summary," which explains for management the need for controlling IT activities and highlights a method that is useful regardless of the IT configuration, size, industry, or location.) Please list and describe the other five parts.

OVERALL AUDIT PLAN AND AUDIT PROGRAM

HOW MUCH AND WHAT KIND OF TESTING WILL GET THE JOB DONE?

Terry Holland and Al Baker have known each other for years. Terry is a partner in the Southern California office of a national accounting firm. Al is an auditing professor at a nearby university. They get together once a month faithfully for lunch, and the conversation always gets around to auditing theory versus practice. Following is their most recent conversation:

PROFESSOR AL: Now that PCAOB Standard 2 requires the audit of a public company's financial statements and internal control over financial reporting to be integrated, I'm afraid that auditors will overrely on tests of controls and perform virtually no testing of details of balances. Given significant time pressures required to complete the testing of controls to comply with the new requirements, firms will take the low-cost approach and reduce substantive testing instead of being concerned enough about audit quality, especially the audit of the financial statements.

PARTNER TERRY: Auditors must understand internal control in every audit, regardless if the client is publicly traded or not. For all public companies and for nonpublic companies where control risk is assessed below maximum, the auditor will be performing tests of controls. But, don't forget that auditing standards also require that substantive tests be performed in *all* audits, even audits of public companies. So, while our extent of testing of controls may be extensive, we will always be performing some mix of substantive tests. We might concentrate on larger items in tests of details of balances. Where risks are high, we pull out all the stops and do a lot of detailed testing.

PROFESSOR AL: That sounds fine, but there are certain things that only detailed testing will find. I'm thinking specifically about misappropriation of assets. I'm sure your clients expect you to find it, but analytical procedures and tests of large items at year-end won't get that job done. What about that?

PARTNER TERRY: Well, Al, our clients also tell us they want our opinion on their financial statements at as low a cost as possible. If we went looking for misappropriation of assets in every audit, our costs would go through the roof. And I'll tell you, the best way for the client to deal with fraud is to have good controls. And, now that we must audit internal control over financial reporting in every public company audit, we will be conducting tests of controls that should address the risk of material misstatements due to misappropriations of assets.

PROFESSOR AL: I'm not convinced. I'm concerned about the reduction in testing to search for errors as well as fraud. It seems to me you guys are taking the auditing standards requirements and figuring out how to audit so efficiently that you're not allowing any slack in the process. I think you're creeping more and more toward being an insurer rather than an assurer of the financial statements.

PARTNER TERRY: What do you mean, Al? I don't understand your theory at all.

PROFESSOR AL: Well, you guys are counting on most of your clients not having misstated financial statements, doing minimal audit work at relatively high fees, and then banking on the fact that you'll be able to absorb the cost of any damages you suffer from bad audit opinions.

PARTNER TERRY: Oh come on, Al, sitting in this ivory tower of yours has turned you into a cynic. I hope you don't talk to your students this way. Auditors do a terrific job, and there is tremendous focus on the auditing profession right now. We want people to come into the profession with a positive attitude. Let's talk about something else. Say, I believe it's your turn to pay.

This chapter deals with the eighth and last step in the planning phase of an audit. It is a critical step because it results in the entire audit program the auditor plans to follow in the audit, including all audit procedures, sample sizes, items to select, and timing. This chapter's opening vignette deals with the importance of making the correct decisions in forming the overall audit plan and developing the detailed audit program, considering both the effectiveness of evidence and the efficiency of the audit process.

The first part of this chapter discusses the overall audit plan, which means selecting a mix of five types of tests that will result in an effective and efficient audit. This topic includes discussion of the trade-offs among the types of tests and consideration of the cost of each type of test. After the auditor decides on the most cost-effective mix of the types of tests, a detailed audit program can be designed. This topic is covered later in the chapter. Because the material in this chapter is the final step in phase I, the planning phase, the relationship of phase I to the other three phases of the audit is discussed at the end of this chapter.

TYPES OF TESTS

OBJECTIVE 13-1

Use the five types of audit tests to determine whether financial statements are fairly stated.

In developing an overall audit plan, auditors have five **types of tests** they can use to determine whether financial statements are fairly stated. These tests are included in Figure 13-1, which shows the relationship of each type of test to the audit risk model. All five of these tests were introduced in earlier chapters and are now discussed in more detail, including the relationships among them. All audit procedures fall into one, and sometimes more than one, of these five categories.

As shown in Figure 13-1, procedures to gain an understanding and tests of controls reduce control risk, whereas analytical procedures and tests of details of balances are used to satisfy planned detection risk. Substantive tests of transactions affect both control risk and planned detection risk because they are used to test the effectiveness of internal controls and the dollar amounts of transactions.

Procedures to Obtain an Understanding of Internal Control

Procedures to obtain an understanding of internal control were studied in Chapter 10. During this part of an audit, the auditor must focus attention on both the *design* and the *operation* of aspects of internal control to the extent necessary to effectively plan the rest of the audit. After appropriately documenting internal controls, it is critical that a system walkthrough be completed to ensure that the described controls have actually been put into place. Five types of audit procedures that relate to the auditor's understanding of internal control were identified in Chapter 10:

- Update and evaluate the auditor's previous experience with the entity.
- Make inquiries of client personnel.
- Examine documents and records.

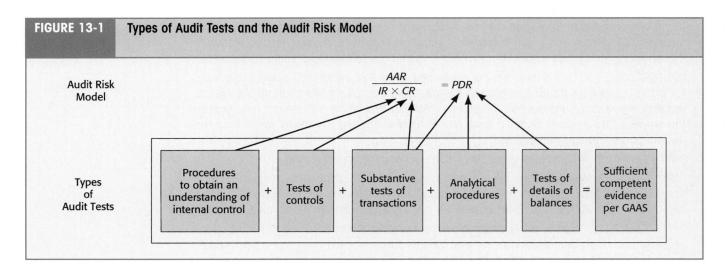

FIGURE 13-1   Types of Audit Tests and the Audit Risk Model

- Observe entity activities and operations.
- Perform walkthroughs of the accounting system.

Tests of Controls

A major use of the auditor's understanding of internal control is to assess control risk for each transaction-related audit objective. Examples are assessing the accuracy objective for sales transactions as low and the existence objective as moderate. When control policies and procedures are believed to be effectively designed and when it is efficient to do so, the auditor will elect to assess control risk at a level that reflects that evaluation. In making this risk assessment, however, assessed control risk must be limited to the level supported by evidence. The procedures used to obtain such evidence are called **tests of controls**.

Tests of controls are performed to determine the appropriateness of the design and operating effectiveness of specific internal controls. The controls may be manual or automated. These tests include the following types of procedures:

- Make inquiries of appropriate client personnel.
- Examine documents, records, and reports.
- Observe control-related activities.
- Reperform client procedures.

The first two procedures are the same as those used to obtain an understanding of internal control. A system walkthrough performed as part of procedures to gain an understanding is used to determine whether controls are in place and is normally applied to one or a few transactions. Tests of controls are used to determine whether those controls are effective and usually involve testing a sample of transactions. For example, the auditor may select one sales transaction for a system walkthrough of the credit approval process. As part of the walkthrough, the auditor would follow the credit approval process from initiation of the sales transaction through the granting of credit. In tests of controls, the auditor might examine a sample of sales transactions from throughout the year to determine whether credit was granted before the shipment of goods as a test of the operating effectiveness of the credit approval process. For some objectives, procedures to gain an understanding may provide sufficient evidential matter to support a reduced level of control risk. The amount of additional evidence required for tests of controls depends on the extent of evidence obtained in gaining the understanding and on the planned reduction in control risk.

The role of tests of controls in the audit of the sales and collection cycle is shown in Figure 13-2 (p. 378) by the circles with no shading and the words "Audited by TOC." Procedures to gain an understanding of internal control and tests of controls are combined in Figure 13-2 because they are essentially the same. For simplicity, two assumptions are made. First, only sales and cash receipts transactions and three general ledger balances make up the sales and collection cycle. Second, the beginning balances in cash and accounts receivable were audited in the previous year and are considered correct. If the auditor verifies that sales and cash receipts transactions are correctly recorded in the accounting records and posted to the general ledger, then the conclusion can be made that the ending balances in accounts receivable and sales are correct. (Cash disbursements transactions will have to be audited before the auditor can reach a conclusion about the ending balance in the cash account.) One way the auditor can verify this is to perform tests of controls. If controls are in place over sales and cash receipts transactions, the auditor can perform tests of controls to determine whether the six transaction-related audit objectives are being met for the cycle. Substantive tests of transactions, which are studied in the next section, also affect audit assurance for sales and cash receipts transactions.

To illustrate typical tests of controls, it is useful to return to the control risk matrix for Hillsburg Hardware Co. in Figure 10-5 (p. 289). For each of the 11 controls included in Figure 10-5, Table 13-1 (p. 379) identifies a test of control that might be performed to test its effectiveness.

Substantive Tests of Transactions

Substantive tests are procedures designed to test for dollar misstatements directly affecting the correctness of financial statement balances. Such misstatements (often termed *monetary misstatements*) are a clear indication of the misstatement of the accounts. There

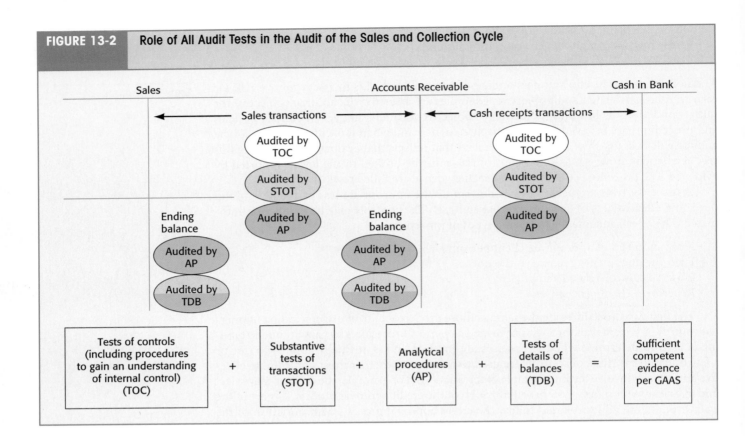

are three types of substantive tests: substantive tests of transactions, analytical procedures, and tests of details of balances.

The purpose of **substantive tests of transactions** is to determine whether all six transaction-related audit objectives have been satisfied for each class of transactions. For example, the auditor performs substantive tests of transactions to test whether recorded transactions exist and existing transactions are recorded. The auditor also performs these tests to determine whether recorded sales transactions are accurately recorded, recorded in the appropriate time period, correctly classified, and accurately summarized and posted to the general ledger and master files. If the auditor is confident that transactions were correctly recorded in the journals and correctly posted, the auditor can be confident that general ledger totals are correct.

The role of substantive tests of transactions in the audit of the sales and collection cycle is illustrated in Figure 13-2 by the circles with partial shading and the words "Audited by STOT." Observe that both tests of controls and substantive tests of transactions are performed for transactions in the cycle, not on the ending account balances. The auditor verifies the recording and summarizing of sales and cash receipts transactions by performing substantive tests of transactions. In this example, there is one set of tests for sales and another for cash receipts.

Tests of controls can be performed separately from all other tests, but for efficiency, they are often done at the same time as substantive tests of transactions. For example, tests of controls involving documentation and reperformance usually are applied to the same transactions tested for monetary misstatements. In fact, reperformance always simultaneously provides evidence about both controls and monetary correctness. This provides a good illustration of how the audit of financial statements and the audit of internal control over financial reporting are integrated in a public company audit. In the remainder of this book, it is assumed that tests of controls and substantive tests of transactions are done at the same time.

TABLE 13-1	Illustration of Tests of Controls
Illustrative Key Controls	**Typical Tests of Controls**
Credit is approved automatically by the computer by comparison to authorized credit limits (C1).	Examine a sample of sales invoices and compare customer order to authorized credit limit (reperformance).
Recorded sales are supported by authorized shipping documents and approved customer orders, which are attached to the duplicate sales invoice (C2).	Examine a sample of duplicate sales invoices to determine that each one is supported by an attached authorized shipping document and approved customer order (documentation).
Separation of duties between billing, recording sales, and handling cash receipts (C3).	Observe whether personnel responsible for handling cash have no accounting responsibilities and inquire as to their duties (observation and inquiry).
Shipping documents are forwarded to billing daily and billed the subsequent day (C4).	Observe whether shipping documents are forwarded daily to billing and observe when they are billed (observation).
Shipping documents are issued in numerical order by the computer and are accounted for weekly (C5).	Account for a sequence of shipping documents and trace each to the sales journal (documentation and reperformance).
Shipping documents are batched daily and compared with quantities billed (C6).	Examine a sample of daily batches, recalculate the shipping quantities, and trace totals to reconciliation with input reports (reperformance).
Unit selling prices are obtained from the price list master file of approved prices (C7).	Examine a sample of sales invoices and agree prices to authorized computer price list. Review changes to price file throughout the year for proper approval (reperformance and documentation).
Sales transactions are internally verified (C8).	Examine document package for internal verification (classification).
Statements are mailed to all customers each month (C9).	Observe whether statements are mailed for 1 month and inquire about who is responsible for mailing the statements (observation and inquiry).
Once the batch of sales transactions is entered, the computer automatically posts transactions to the accounts receivable subsidiary records and to the general ledger (C10).	Use audit software to trace postings from the batch of sales transactions to the subsidiary records and general ledger (reperformance).
Accounts receivable master file is reconciled to the general ledger on a monthly basis (C11).	Examine evidence of reconciliation for test month, and test accuracy of reconciliation (documentation and reperformance).

As first discussed in Chapter 7, **analytical procedures** involve comparisons of recorded amounts to expectations developed by the auditor. They often involve the calculation of ratios by the auditor for comparison with previous years' ratios and other related data.

Analytical Procedures

The two most important purposes of analytical procedures in the audit of account balances are to (1) indicate the presence of possible misstatements in the financial statements and (2) reduce tests of details of balances. There is typically a difference in the analytical procedures done during planning and those done in the testing phase. Even if, for example, the gross margin is calculated during planning, it is probably done using interim data. Later, during the tests of the ending balances, the auditor will recalculate the ratio using full-year data. If the auditor believes that analytical procedures indicate a reasonable possibility of misstatement, additional analytical procedures may be performed or the auditor may decide to modify tests of details of balances.

When the auditor develops expectations using analytical procedures and concludes that the client's ending balances in certain accounts appear reasonable, certain tests of details of balances may be eliminated or sample sizes may be reduced. Auditing standards state that analytical procedures can be used as substantive tests.

The role of analytical procedures in the audit of the sales and collection cycle is illustrated in Figure 13-2 by the circles with dark shading and the words "Audited by AP." Observe that the auditor performs analytical procedures on sales and cash receipts transactions, as well as on the ending balances of the accounts in the cycle.

Tests of Details of Balances

Tests of details of balances focus on the ending general ledger balances for both balance sheet and income statement accounts, but the primary emphasis in most tests of details of balances is on the balance sheet. Examples include confirmation of customer balances for accounts receivable, physical examination of inventory, and examination of vendors' statements for accounts payable. These tests of ending balances are essential because the evidence is usually obtained from a source independent of the client and thus is considered highly reliable.

The role of tests of details of balances is illustrated in Figure 13-2 by the circles with half dark and half light shading and the words "Audited by TDB." Detailed tests of the ending balances are performed for sales and accounts receivable. These include audit procedures such as confirmation of account receivable balances and sales cutoff tests. The extent of these tests depends on the results of tests of controls, substantive tests of transactions, and analytical procedures for these accounts.

Tests of details of balances have the objective of establishing the monetary correctness of the accounts they relate to and therefore are substantive tests. For example, confirmations test for monetary misstatements and are therefore substantive. Similarly, counts of inventory and cash on hand are also substantive tests.

Summary of Types of Tests

Examining Figure 13-2 overall summarizes how the five types of audit tests are used to obtain audit assurance in the audit of the sales and collection cycle. Procedures to gain an understanding of internal control and tests of controls evaluate whether controls over transactions in the cycle are sufficiently effective to reduce control risk and thereby reduce substantive testing. They also form the basis for the auditor's report on internal control over financial reporting. Substantive tests of transactions emphasize the verification of transactions recorded in the journals and then posted in the general ledger. Analytical procedures emphasize the overall reasonableness of transactions and the general ledger balances. Tests of details of balances emphasize the ending balances in the general ledger. By combining the types of audit tests shown in Figure 13-2 (p. 378), the auditor obtains a higher overall assurance for transactions and accounts in the sales and collection cycle than the assurance obtained from any one test. To increase overall assurance for the cycle, the auditor can increase the assurance obtained from any one of the tests.

SELECTING WHICH TYPES OF TESTS TO PERFORM

OBJECTIVE 13-2

Select the appropriate types of audit tests.

Typically, auditors use all five types of tests when performing an audit of the financial statements, but certain types are emphasized, depending on the circumstances. Factors such as the availability of the seven types of evidence, the cost of each type of test, the effectiveness of internal controls, and the existence of inherent risks all affect the mix of the types of tests the auditor selects. Recall, however, that only the first two types of tests are performed in an audit of internal control over financial reporting: procedures to obtain an understanding of internal control and tests of controls.

Types of Evidence

Each of the five types of tests involves only certain types of evidence (confirmation, documentation, and so forth). Table 13-2 summarizes the relationship between types of tests and types of evidence. Several observations about Table 13-2 follow:

- Procedures to obtain an understanding of internal control and tests of controls involve only observation, documentation, inquiry, and reperformance. Substantive tests of transactions involve only the last three of these types of evidence.
- More types of evidence are obtained by using tests of details of balances than by using any other type of test. Only tests of details of balances involve confirmation and physical examination.
- Inquiries of clients are made with every type of test.
- Documentation and reperformance are used for every type of test except analytical procedures.

Relative Costs

In deciding which type of test to select for obtaining sufficient competent evidence, the cost of the evidence is one important consideration. The types of tests are listed in order of increasing cost as follows:

				Type of Evidence				

TABLE 13-2   **Relationship Between Types of Tests and Evidence**

Type of Test	Physical Examination	Confirmation	Documentation	Observation	Inquiries of the Client	Reperformance	Analytical Procedures
Procedures to obtain an understanding of internal control			√	√	√	√	
Tests of controls			√	√	√	√	
Substantive tests of transactions			√		√	√	
Analytical procedures					√		√
Tests of details of balances	√	√	√		√	√	

- Analytical procedures
- Procedures to obtain an understanding of internal control and tests of controls
- Substantive tests of transactions
- Tests of details of balances

The reason analytical procedures are least costly is the relative ease of making calculations and comparisons. Often, considerable information about potential misstatements can be obtained by simply comparing two or three numbers. Auditors often calculate these ratios using computer software at almost no cost.

Tests of controls are also low in cost because the auditor is making inquiries and observations and examining such things as approvals on documents or in computer files and outward indications of other controls. Often, tests of controls can be done on a large number of items in a few minutes. Auditors often take advantage of audit software to test controls included in clients' computerized accounting systems. For example, many computerized accounts receivable systems automatically authorize sales to existing customers by comparing the proposed sales amount and existing accounts receivable balance with the customer's credit limit. The auditor can test this control using audit software.

Substantive tests of transactions are more expensive than tests of controls that do not include reperformance because recalculations and tracings are often required. In a computerized environment, however, the auditor can often perform substantive tests of transactions quickly for a large number of transactions.

Tests of details of balances are almost always considerably more costly than any of the other types of procedures. It is costly to send confirmations and to count assets. Because of the high cost of tests of details of balances, auditors usually try to plan the audit to minimize their use.

Naturally, the cost of each type of evidence varies in different situations. For example, the cost of an auditor's test-counting inventory (a substantive test of the details of the inventory balance) often depends on the nature and dollar value of the inventory, its location, and the number of different items.

To better understand the nature of tests of controls and substantive tests, an examination of how they differ is useful. An exception in a test of control is only an *indication* of the likelihood of misstatements affecting the dollar value of the financial statements, whereas an exception in a substantive test of transactions or a test of details of balances *is* a financial statement misstatement. Exceptions in tests of controls are often called *control test deviations*. Recall from Chapter 10 that there are three levels of control test

Relationship Between Tests of Controls and Substantive Tests

deviations: control deficiencies, significant deficiencies, and material weaknesses. Control test deviations that are considered to be significant deficiencies or material weaknesses are most likely to cause the auditor to believe there may be material dollar misstatements in the financial statements. Substantive tests of transactions or tests of details of balances should then be performed to determine whether dollar misstatements have actually occurred. The auditor must also evaluate the effect of the noted control test deviations on the auditor's report on internal control over financial reporting.

As an illustration, assume that the client's controls require an independent clerk to verify the quantity, price, and extension of each sales invoice, after which the clerk must initial the duplicate invoice to indicate performance. A test of control audit procedure would be to examine a sample of duplicate sales invoices for the initials of the person who verified the quantitative data. If a significant number of documents do not have initials, the auditor should consider implications for the audit of internal control over financial reporting and follow up with substantive tests for the financial statement audit. This can be done by extending the tests of the duplicate sales invoices to include verifying prices, extensions, and footings (substantive tests of transactions) or by increasing the sample size for the confirmation of accounts receivable (substantive test of details of balances). Of course, even though the control is not operating effectively, the invoices may still be correct. This will be the case if the person originally preparing the sales invoices did a conscientious and competent job.

On the other hand, if no or only a few documents have missing initials, the control would be considered effective and the auditor could therefore reduce substantive tests of transactions and tests of details of balances. Some substantive tests are still necessary to provide the auditor assurance that the initials were not written without the clerk performing the control procedures or performing them carelessly. Because of the need to complete some reperformance tests, many auditors prefer to perform them as a part of the original tests of controls. Others prefer to reperform, in the form of a substantive test, only when there is indication of the need to do so.

Relationship Between Analytical Procedures and Substantive Tests

Similar to the relationships discussed in the previous section, analytical procedures also provide only an indication of the likelihood of misstatements affecting the dollar value of the financial statements. Unusual fluctuations in the relationships of an account to other accounts or to nonfinancial information provide an indication of an increased likelihood that material misstatements exist without necessarily providing direct evidence of a material misstatement. When unusual analytical procedure fluctuations are identified, substantive tests of transactions or tests of details of balances should be performed to determine whether dollar misstatements have actually occurred. If the auditor performs analytical procedures and believes that the likelihood of material misstatement is small, other substantive tests can be reduced.

Trade-Off Between Tests of Controls and Substantive Tests

There is a trade-off between tests of controls and substantive tests. The auditor makes a decision during planning whether to assess control risk below the maximum. Tests of controls must be performed to determine whether the assessed control risk is supported. They must also be performed in an audit of internal control over financial reporting. If tests of controls support the control risk assessment, planned detection risk in the audit risk model is increased, and planned substantive tests can therefore be reduced. Figure 13-3 shows the relationship between substantive tests and control risk assessment (including tests of controls) at differing levels of internal control effectiveness.

The shaded area in Figure 13-3 is the maximum assurance obtainable from control risk assessment and tests of controls. For example, at any point to the left of point A, assessed control risk is 1.0 because the auditor evaluates internal controls as ineffective. Any point to the right of point B results in no further reduction of control risk because the CPA firm has established a minimum assessed control risk it will permit. Notice in Figure 13-3 that regardless of the level of audit assurance obtained from control risk assessment and tests of controls, some substantive procedures are always required in an audit of financial statements. Because the audit of financial statements and the audit of internal control over financial reporting are to be integrated, public company audits would most likely be represented by point B.

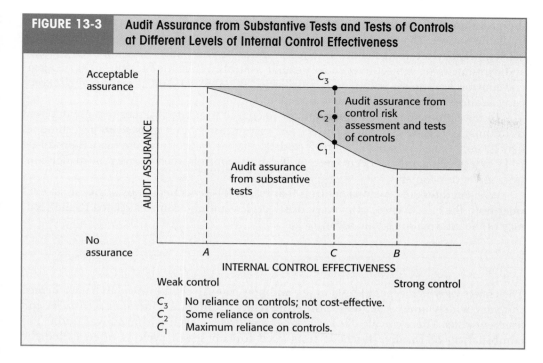

FIGURE 13-3 Audit Assurance from Substantive Tests and Tests of Controls at Different Levels of Internal Control Effectiveness

C_3 No reliance on controls; not cost-effective.
C_2 Some reliance on controls.
C_1 Maximum reliance on controls.

After the auditor decides the effectiveness of the client's internal controls, it is appropriate to select any point within the shaded area of Figure 13-3 consistent with the assessed control risk the auditor decides to support. To illustrate, assume that the auditor contends that internal control effectiveness is at point C. Tests of controls at the C_1 level would provide the minimum control risk, given the internal controls. The auditor could choose to perform no tests of controls (point C_3), which would support a control risk of 1.0. Any point between the two, such as C_2, would also be appropriate. If C_2 is selected, the audit assurance from tests of controls is $C_3 - C_2$ and from substantive tests is $C - C_2$. The auditor will likely select C_1, C_2, or C_3 based on the relative cost of tests of controls and substantive tests.

IMPACT OF INFORMATION TECHNOLOGY ON AUDIT TESTING

OBJECTIVE 13-3

Understand how information technology affects audit testing.

SAS 80 (AU 326) and SAS 94 (AU 319) provide guidance for auditors of entities that transmit, process, maintain, or access significant information electronically. Examples of electronic evidence include records of electronic fund transfers and purchase orders transmitted through electronic data interchange (EDI). The standards recognize that in instances in which a significant amount of audit evidence is in electronic form, it may not be practical or possible to reduce detection risk to an acceptable level by performing only substantive tests. For example, the potential for improper initiation or alteration of information may be greater if information is maintained only in electronic form. In these circumstances, the auditor should perform tests of controls to gather evidence to support an assessed level of control risk below maximum for the affected financial statement assertions. Although some substantive tests are still required, the auditor can significantly reduce substantive tests if the tests of controls results support the effectiveness of computer controls. In the audit of a public company, computer-performed controls must be tested if they are considered to be key controls for reducing the likelihood of material misstatements in the financial statements.

ITAudit.org

Because of the inherent consistency of IT processing, the auditor may be able to reduce the extent of testing of an automated control. For example, a software-based control is almost certain to function consistently unless the program is changed. Once it is determined that an automated control is functioning properly, the auditor can focus subsequent tests on assessing whether any changes have occurred that would limit the effectiveness of the control. Such tests might include determining whether any changes have occurred to the program and whether these changes were properly authorized and tested prior to implementation. This approach leads to significant audit efficiencies when the auditor determines that automated controls tested in the prior year's audit have not been changed and continue to be subject to effective general controls. While the presence of strong general controls leads to significant audit efficiencies, PCAOB Standard 2 requires public company auditors to test controls each year.

To test automated controls, the auditor may need to use techniques that are different from those used to test manual controls. For example, computer-assisted audit techniques may be used to test automated controls or data, and the auditor may use reports produced by IT to test the operating effectiveness of IT general controls, such as program change controls and access controls.

When auditors test manual controls that rely on IT-generated reports, they must consider both the effectiveness of management's review and the controls related to the accuracy of the information in the report.

EVIDENCE MIX

OBJECTIVE 13-4

Understand the concept of evidence mix and how it should be varied in different circumstances.

The choice of which types of tests to use and how extensively they need to be performed can vary widely among audits for differing levels of internal control effectiveness and inherent risks. There can also be variations from cycle to cycle within a given audit. The combination of the five types of tests used for any given cycle is often called the **evidence mix.** Table 13-3 shows the evidence mix for four different audits. In each case, assume that sufficient competent evidence was accumulated. An analysis of each audit follows.

Analysis of Audit 1 This client is a large company with sophisticated internal controls and low inherent risk. Therefore, the auditor performs extensive tests of controls and relies heavily on the client's internal controls to reduce substantive tests. Extensive analytical procedures are also performed to reduce other substantive tests. Substantive tests of transactions and tests of details of balances are therefore minimized. Because of the emphasis on tests of controls and analytical procedures, this audit can be done relatively inexpensively. This audit likely represents the mix of evidence used in the integrated audit of a public company's financial statements and internal control over financial reporting.

Analysis of Audit 2 This company is medium sized, with some controls and a few inherent risks. Therefore, the auditor has decided to do a medium amount of testing for all types of tests except analytical procedures, which will be done extensively. There will be more extensive testing done where there are specific inherent risks.

Analysis of Audit 3 This company is medium sized but has few effective controls and significant inherent risks. Management has decided that it is not cost effective to have better internal controls. Because of the lack of emphasis on internal control, this company

TABLE 13-3	Variations in Evidence Mix				
	Procedures to Obtain an Understanding of Internal Control	Tests of Controls	Substantive Tests of Transactions	Analytical Procedures	Tests of Details of Balances
Audit 1	E	E	S	E	S
Audit 2	M	M	M	E	M
Audit 3	M	N	E	M	E
Audit 4	M	M	E	E	E

E = Extensive amount of testing; M = Medium amount of testing; S = Small amount of testing; N = No testing.

most likely is a nonpublic company. No tests of controls are done because reliance on internal controls is inappropriate when controls are insufficient at a nonpublic company. The emphasis is on tests of details of balances and substantive tests of transactions, but some analytical procedures are also done. Analytical procedures are usually performed to reduce other substantive tests because they provide evidence about the likelihood of material misstatements. The auditor already expects to find material misstatements in the account balances, so additional analytical procedures are not cost effective. The cost of the audit is likely to be relatively high because of the amount of detailed substantive testing.

Analysis of Audit 4 The original plan on this audit was to follow the approach used in Audit 2. However, the auditor found extensive control test deviations and significant misstatements while performing substantive tests of transactions and analytical procedures. Therefore, the auditor concluded that the internal controls were not effective. Extensive tests of details of balances are performed to offset the unacceptable results of the other tests. The cost of this audit is higher because tests of controls and substantive tests of transactions were performed but could not be used to reduce tests of details of balances.

DESIGN OF THE AUDIT PROGRAM

After the auditor determines the appropriate emphasis on each of the five types of tests, the specific audit program for each type must be designed. The audit procedures, when combined, form the audit program. In most audits, the engagement in-charge auditor recommends the evidence mix to the engagement manager. After the evidence mix is approved, the in-charge prepares the audit program or modifies an existing program to satisfy all audit objectives, considering such things as evidence mix, inherent risk, control risk, and any identified fraud risks, as well as the need for an integrated audit for a public company. The in-charge is also likely to get approval from the manager before performing the audit procedures or delegating their performance to an assistant. This part of the chapter focuses on designing audit programs to satisfy transaction-related and balance-related audit objectives.

Audit Programs Resource

The audit program for most audits is designed in three parts: tests of controls and substantive tests of transactions, analytical procedures, and tests of details of balances. There will likely be a separate set of subaudit programs for each transaction cycle. An example in the sales and collection cycle might be tests of controls and substantive tests of transactions audit programs for sales and cash receipts; an analytical procedures audit program for the entire cycle; and tests of details of balances audit programs for cash, accounts receivable, bad debt expense, allowance for uncollectible accounts, and miscellaneous accounts receivable.

Tests of Controls and Substantive Tests of Transactions

The tests of controls and substantive tests of transactions audit program normally includes a descriptive section documenting the understanding obtained about internal control. It is also likely to include a description of the procedures performed to obtain an understanding of internal control and assessed control risk. Both of these affect the tests of controls and substantive tests of transactions audit program. The methodology to design these tests is shown in Figure 13-4 (p. 386). The first three steps in the figure were described in Chapter 10. The audit procedures include both tests of controls and substantive tests of transactions and vary depending on assessed control risk. When controls are effective and assessed control risk is low, there will be heavy emphasis on tests of controls. Some substantive tests of transactions will also be included. If control risk is assessed at 1.0, only substantive tests of transactions will be used, assuming this is an audit of a nonpublic company. The procedures already performed in obtaining an understanding of internal control will affect both tests of controls and substantive tests of transactions.

Audit Procedures The approach to designing tests of controls and substantive tests of transactions emphasizes satisfying the transaction-related audit objectives developed in Chapter 6. A four-step approach is followed when the auditor plans to reduce assessed control risk.

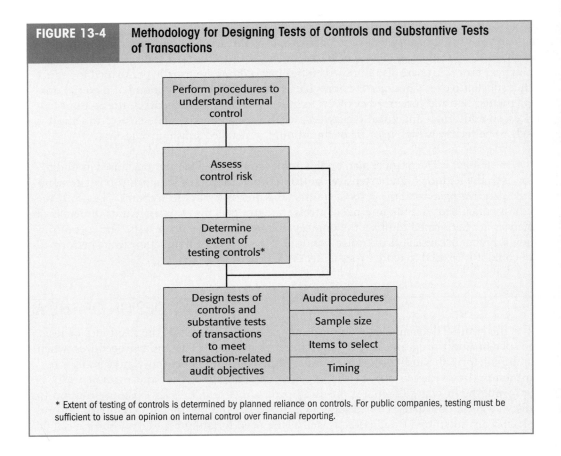

FIGURE 13-4	Methodology for Designing Tests of Controls and Substantive Tests of Transactions

Perform procedures to understand internal control

Assess control risk

Determine extent of testing controls*

Design tests of controls and substantive tests of transactions to meet transaction-related audit objectives

Audit procedures

Sample size

Items to select

Timing

* Extent of testing of controls is determined by planned reliance on controls. For public companies, testing must be sufficient to issue an opinion on internal control over financial reporting.

1. Apply the transaction-related audit objectives to the class of transactions being tested, such as sales.
2. Identify key controls that should reduce control risk for each transaction-related audit objective.
3. For all internal controls used to reduce the initial assessment of control risk below maximum (key controls), develop appropriate tests of controls.
4. For the potential types of misstatements related to each transaction-related audit objective, design appropriate substantive tests of transactions, considering deficiencies in internal control and expected results of the tests of controls in step 3.

This four-step approach to designing tests of controls and substantive tests of transactions is summarized in Figure 13-5. The approach in Figure 13-5 is illustrated in several chapters in the text. For example, see Table 14-2 on pages 420–421 for an application of the four-step procedure for the audit of sales transactions. Each of the steps corresponds to a column in Table 14-2.

Analytical Procedures

Because they are relatively inexpensive, many auditors perform extensive analytical procedures on all audits. As stated in Chapter 8, analytical procedures are performed at three different stages of the audit: (1) in the planning stage to help the auditor understand the client's business and determine the other evidence needed to satisfy acceptable audit risk; (2) during the audit, especially during substantive testing; and (3) near the end of the audit as a final test of reasonableness. Analytical procedures performed during substantive testing, such as for the audit of accounts receivable, are typically more focused and extensive than those done as part of planning. For example, during planning, the auditor might calculate the gross margin percentage for total sales. During substantive testing of accounts receivable, the auditor might calculate gross margin percentage by month or by line of business, or possibly both. Analytical procedures calculated using monthly amounts will typically be more effective in detecting misstatements than those calculated using annual amounts, and

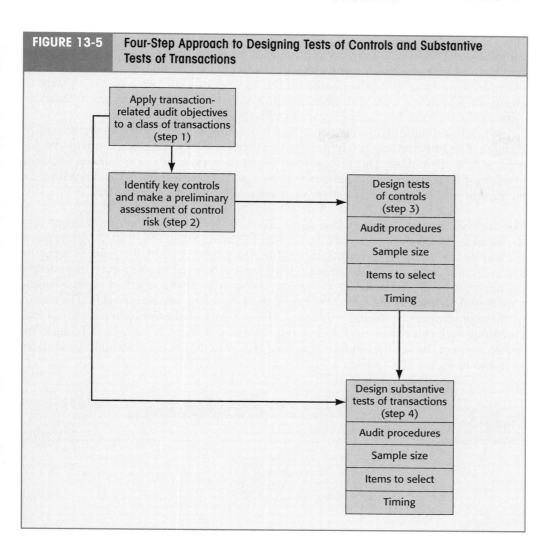

LACK OF AUDIT PROGRAM BRINGS SANCTIONS

William Boettger and P. Robert Wilkinson were partners with the firm Harlan & Boettger, LLP, and were responsible for the audit of Madera International, Inc. Madera was a timber company with international holdings, including timber interests in Nicaragua, Venezuela, and the Brazilian rain forest.

Madera acquired Nicaraguan property by issuing a $5 million convertible note that was converted into 10,200,000 shares of Madera stock. The property was subsequently revalued at $12 million in violation of GAAP provisions that require assets to be recorded at original cost. In fact, the property was worthless because Madera did not hold valid title to the property.

Madera acquired 478,000 acres of timberland and related assets in the Brazilian rain forest for 10 million shares of Madera nontrading convertible preferred stock. The timber properties were valued at $27 million, although Madera never verified that it had title to the property and learned shortly after acquiring the property that it was not economically

feasible to harvest the rain forest timber. Similar issues arose with the acquisition of an additional 988,400 acres valued at $12 million.

The SEC criticized the audits performed by Boettger and Wilkinson. In two of the years, there was no documentation of any audit planning and no written audit programs. In other years, planning documents were incomplete, undated, and unsigned. In addition, the staff person performing the audit received little supervision, and the manager who reviewed the audit lacked knowledge of Madera's operations. Boettger and Wilkinson, as well as the Harlan & Boettger firm, were permanently barred from practicing before the SEC.

Source: Securities and Exchange Commission Accounting and Auditing Enforcement Release No. 1452, September 19, 2001 (www.sec.gov/litigation/admin/34-44817.htm).

comparisons by line of business will usually be more effective than companywide comparisons. If sales and accounts receivable are based on predictable relationships with nonfinancial data, the auditor often uses that information for analytical procedures. For example, if revenue billings are based on the number of hours professionals charge to clients, such as in law firms and other organizations that provide services, the auditor can estimate total revenue by multiplying hours billed by average billing rate.

When the auditor plans to use analytical procedures as a part of the assurance gained through substantive testing, it is important that the data used in the calculations be considered sufficiently reliable. This is important for all data, especially nonfinancial data. For example, if hours billed and the average billing rate are used to estimate total revenue, the auditor must be confident that both of these are reasonably reliable numbers.

Tests of Details of Balances

The methodology for designing tests of details of balances audit procedures is oriented to the balance-related audit objectives developed in Chapter 6 (pp. 148–150). For example, if the auditor is verifying accounts receivable, the planned audit procedures must be sufficient to satisfy each of the balance-related audit objectives. In planning tests of details of balances audit procedures to satisfy these objectives, many auditors follow a methodology such as the one shown in Figure 13-6 for accounts receivable. The design of these procedures is normally the most difficult part of the entire planning process. Designing such procedures is subjective and requires considerable professional judgment. A discussion of the key decisions in designing tests of details of balances audit procedures as shown in Figure 13-6 follows.

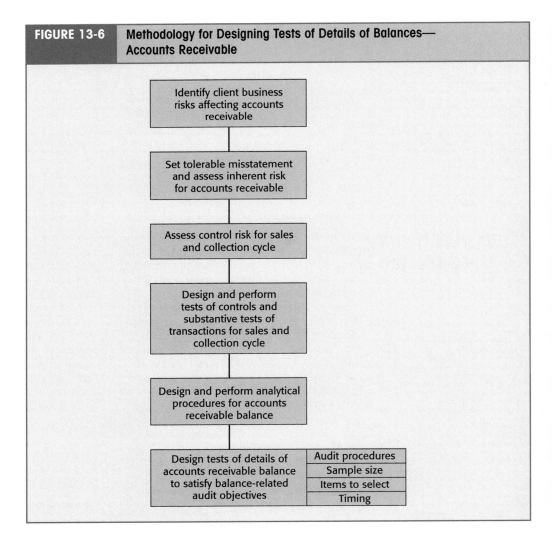

FIGURE 13-6 Methodology for Designing Tests of Details of Balances—Accounts Receivable

Identify client business risks affecting accounts receivable

Set tolerable misstatement and assess inherent risk for accounts receivable

Assess control risk for sales and collection cycle

Design and perform tests of controls and substantive tests of transactions for sales and collection cycle

Design and perform analytical procedures for accounts receivable balance

Design tests of details of accounts receivable balance to satisfy balance-related audit objectives

Audit procedures
Sample size
Items to select
Timing

Identify Client Business Risks Affecting Accounts Receivable As discussed in Chapter 8, as part of gaining an understanding of the client's business and industry, the auditor identifies significant client business risks. These risks are then evaluated to determine whether they result in increased risk of material misstatements in the financial statements. If any of the identified client business risks affect accounts receivable, they should be incorporated in the auditor's evaluation of inherent risk or control risk and the appropriate extent of evidence. For example, the auditor may identify competitive factors or industry conditions that may have a negative impact on sales. If the performance measurement system encourages attainment of overly optimistic sales goals for the current economic environment, the auditor may decide to increase inherent risk and the extent of evidence for the existence and cutoff objectives for sales and accounts receivable.

Set Tolerable Misstatement and Assess Inherent Risk for Accounts Receivable Setting the preliminary judgment about materiality for the audit as a whole and allocating the total to account balances (tolerable misstatement) are auditor decisions that were discussed in Chapter 9. After the preliminary judgment about materiality is made, tolerable misstatement is set for each significant balance. A lower tolerable misstatement would result in more testing of details than a higher amount. Some auditors may allocate tolerable misstatement to individual balance-related audit objectives, but most do not.

Inherent risk is assessed by identifying any aspect of the client's history, environment, or operations that indicates a high likelihood of misstatement in the current year's financial statements. Considerations affecting inherent risk that were discussed in Chapter 9 applied to accounts receivable include makeup of accounts receivable, nature of the client's business, initial engagement, and so on. An account balance for which inherent risk has been assessed as high would result in more evidence accumulation than for an account with low inherent risk.

Inherent risk also can be extended to individual balance-related audit objectives. For example, because of adverse economic conditions in the client's industry, the auditor may conclude that there is a high risk of uncollectible accounts receivable (realizable value objective). Inherent risk could still be low for all other objectives.

Assess Control Risk for the Sales and Collection Cycle Control risk is evaluated in the manner discussed in Chapter 10 and in earlier parts of this chapter. That methodology would be applied to both sales and cash receipts in the audit of accounts receivable. Effective controls reduce control risk and therefore the evidence required for substantive tests of transactions and tests of details of balances; inadequate controls increase the substantive evidence needed.

Design and Perform Tests of Controls and Substantive Tests of Transactions for the Sales and Collection Cycle The methodology for designing tests of controls and substantive tests of transactions was discussed earlier in this section and is illustrated in subsequent chapters. The tests are designed with the expectation that certain results will be obtained. These predicted results affect the design of tests of details of balances.

Design and Perform Analytical Procedures for Accounts Receivable Balance As discussed earlier, the auditor performs analytical procedures for an account such as accounts receivable for two purposes: (1) to identify possible misstatements in the account balance and (2) to reduce detailed audit tests. The results of analytical procedures directly affect the extent of tests of details of balances, as discussed in the following section.

Design Tests of Details of Accounts Receivable Balance to Satisfy Balance-Related Audit Objectives The planned tests of details of balances include audit procedures, sample size, items to select, and timing. Procedures must be selected and designed for each account and each balance-related audit objective within each account. The balance-related audit objectives for accounts receivable are shown on page 484.

A difficulty the auditor faces in designing tests of details of balances is the need to predict the outcome of the tests of controls, substantive tests of transactions, and analytical procedures before they are performed. This is necessary because the auditor should design tests of details of balances during the planning phase, but the appropriate design depends on the outcome of the other tests. In planning tests of details of balances, the auditor usually predicts that there will be few or no exceptions in tests of controls, substantive tests of transactions, and analytical procedures, unless there are reasons to believe otherwise. If the results of the tests of controls, substantive tests of transactions, and analytical procedures are *not* consistent with the predictions, the tests of details of balances will need to be changed as the audit progresses.

The discussion about the approach to designing tests of details of balances applied to accounts receivable is summarized in Figure 13-7. The light shading on the left side of the figure is the design of tests of controls and substantive tests of transactions as presented in Figure 13-5 (p. 387). The figure shows that the tests of controls and substantive tests of transactions affect the design of the tests of details of balances. The darker shading on the right side of the figure shows the design of tests of details of balances and the factors affecting that decision.

One of the most difficult parts of auditing is properly applying the factors that affect tests of details of balances. Each of the factors is subjective, requiring considerable professional judgment. The impact of each factor on tests of details of balances is equally subjective. For example, if inherent risk is reduced from medium to low, there is agreement that tests of details of balances can be reduced. Deciding the specific effect on audit procedures, sample size, timing, and items to select is a difficult decision.

Level of Disaggregation of Planning Activities

The various planning activities discussed in Chapters 6 through 13 are applied at different levels of disaggregation, depending on the nature of the activity. Figure 13-8 shows the primary planning activities and the levels of disaggregation normally applied. These levels

FIGURE 13-7	Approach to Designing Tests of Details of Balances

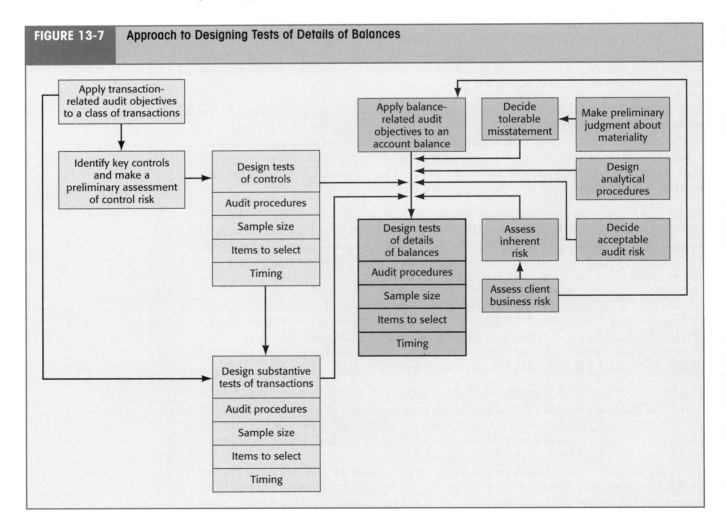

FIGURE 13-8	Disaggregation Level to Which Planning Activities Are Applied

	LEVEL OF DISAGGREGATION				
PLANNING ACTIVITY	Overall Audit	Cycle	Account	Transaction-Related Audit Objective	Balance-Related Audit Objective
Accept client and perform initial planning.	P				
Understand client's business and industry.	P				
Assess client business risk.	P				
Gather information to assess fraud risks.	P				

Understand internal control:
  Control environment
  Risk assessment
  Control activities
  Information and communication
  Monitoring
	P	P
		P
		P
		P			

Identify key internal controls.				P	
Identify internal control weaknesses.				P	
Design tests of controls.				P	
Design substantive tests of transactions.				P	
Assess control risk.				P	
Assess inherent risk.			P		P
Assess acceptable audit risk.	P				
Set preliminary judgment about materiality.	P				
Set tolerable misstatement.			P		
Design analytical procedures.			P		P
Design tests of details of balances.					P

P = Primary level to which planning activity is applied.

of disaggregation range from the overall audit to the balance-related audit objective for each account. For example, when the auditor obtains background information about the client's business and industry, it pertains to the overall audit. As the audit progresses, the information will first be used in assessing acceptable audit risk and assessing inherent risk and later is likely to affect tests of details of balances. Similarly, the auditor first assesses the risk of fraud for the overall audit. In assessing control risk and inherent risk and designing tests of details of balances, the auditor considers whether any fraud risks exist that may affect risk assessments or the nature and extent of tests of details of balances.

SAS 77 (AU 311) requires the auditor to use a written audit program. Table 13-4 shows the tests of details of balances segment of an audit program for accounts receivable. The format used relates the audit procedures to the balance-related audit objectives. Notice that most procedures satisfy more than one objective. Also, more than one audit procedure is used for

Illustrative Audit Program

TABLE 13-4	Tests of Details of Balances Audit Program for Accounts Receivable

Tests of Details of Balances Audit Procedures	Sample Size for Each Audit Procedure	Items to Select from the Population	Timing of the Test	Detail tie-in	Existence	Completeness	Accuracy	Classification	Cutoff	Realizable value	Rights	Presentation and disclosure
1. Obtain an aged list of receivables: trace accounts to the master file, foot schedule, and trace to general ledger.	Trace 20 items; foot 2 pages and all subtotals	Random	I	X								
2. Obtain an analysis of the allowance for doubtful accounts and bad debt expense: test accuracy, examine authorization for write-offs, and trace to general ledger.	All	All	Y	X	X	X	X			X		
3. Obtain direct confirmation of accounts receivable and perform alternative procedures for nonresponses.	50	10 largest 40 random	I		X		X	X	X		X	
4. Review accounts receivable control account for the period. Investigate the nature of and review support for any large or unusual entries or any entries not arising from normal journal sources. Also investigate any significant increases or decreases in sales toward year-end.	NA	NA	Y		X		X	X	X		X	X
5. Review receivables for any that have been assigned or discounted.	All	All	Y								X	X
6. Investigate collectibility of account balances.	NA	NA	Y							X		
7. Review lists of balances for amounts due from related parties or employees, credit balances, and unusual items, as well as notes receivable due after 1 year.	All	All	Y		X			X				X
8. Determine that proper cutoff procedures were applied at the balance sheet date to ensure that sales, cash receipts, and credit memos have been recorded in the correct period.	20 transactions for sales and cash receipts; 10 for credit memos	50% before and 50% after year-end	Y						X			

I = Interim; Y = Year-end; NA = Not applicable.

each objective. Audit procedures can be added or deleted as the auditor considers necessary. Sample size, items to select, and timing can also be changed for most procedures.

The audit program in Table 13-4 was developed after consideration of all the factors affecting tests of details of balances and is based on several assumptions about inherent risk, control risk, and the results of tests of controls, substantive tests of transactions, and analytical procedures. As indicated, if those assumptions are materially incorrect, the planned audit program will require revision. For example, analytical procedures could indicate potential misstatements for several balance-related audit objectives, tests of controls results could indicate weak internal controls, or new facts could cause the auditor to change inherent risk.

Audit programs are often computerized. The simplest form of this application is to type the audit program on a word processor and save it from one year to the next to facilitate changes and updating. A more sophisticated use is to have a special-use program that helps the auditor think through the planning considerations of the audit and select appropriate procedures from an audit procedures database. These are then formulated into an audit program.

City of Tampa Internal
Audit Programs

Relationship of Transaction-Related Audit Objectives to Balance-Related Audit Objectives

It has already been shown that tests of details of balances must be designed to satisfy balance-related audit objectives for each account, and the extent of these tests can be reduced when transaction-related audit objectives have been satisfied by tests of controls or substantive tests of transactions. Therefore, it is important to understand how each transaction-related audit objective relates to each balance-related audit objective. A general presentation of these relationships is shown in Table 13-5. The major implication of Table 13-5 is that even when all transaction-related audit objectives are met, the auditor will still rely primarily on substantive tests of balances to meet the

OBJECTIVE 13-6

Compare and contrast transaction-related audit objectives and balance-related audit objectives.

TABLE 13-5	Relationship of Transaction-Related Audit Objectives to Balance-Related Audit Objectives		
Transaction-Related Audit Objective	Balance-Related Audit Objective	Nature of Relationship	Explanation
Existence	Existence or completeness	Direct	There is a direct relationship of the existence transaction-related audit objective to the existence balance-related audit objective if a class of transactions increases the related account balance (e.g., sales transactions increase accounts receivable). There is a direct relationship of the existence transaction-related audit objective to the completeness balance-related audit objective if a class of transactions decreases the related account balance (e.g., cash receipts transactions decrease accounts receivable).
Completeness	Completeness or existence	Direct	See comments above for existence objective.
Accuracy	Accuracy	Direct	—
Classification	Classification	Direct	—
Timing	Cutoff	Direct	—
Posting and summarization	Detail tie-in	Direct	—
	Realizable value	None	Few internal controls over realizable value are related to classes of transactions, but the credit approval process affects the extent of tests.
	Rights and obligations	None	Few internal controls over rights and obligations are related to classes of transactions.
	Presentation and disclosure	None	Internal controls provide little assurance that proper presentations and disclosures will be made and there are no relevant substantive tests of transactions.

following balance-related audit objectives: realizable value, rights and obligations, and presentation and disclosure. Some substantive tests of balances are also likely for the other balance-related audit objectives, depending on the results of the tests of controls and substantive tests of transactions.

SUMMARY OF KEY EVIDENCE-RELATED TERMS

Several descriptions of evidence-related terms have been used in the past several chapters. It is essential to distinguish among these terms and understand the meaning of each. The following summarizes the terms. Table 13-6 shows the relationship among the terms.

TABLE 13-6	Relationship Among Five Key Evidence-Related Terms			
Phases of the Audit Process	Audit Objectives	Types of Tests	Evidence Decisions	Types of Evidence
Plan and Design an Audit Approach		Analytical procedures	• Audit procedures • Timing	Documentation Inquiries of client Analytical procedures
Perform Tests of Controls and Substantive Tests of Transactions	Transaction-related audit objectives • Existence • Completeness • Accuracy • Classification • Timing • Posting and summarization	Procedures to obtain an understanding and tests of controls Substantive tests of transactions	• Audit procedures • Sample size • Items to select • Timing • Audit procedures • Sample size • Items to select • Timing	Documentation Observation Inquiries of client Reperformance
Perform Analytical Procedures and Tests of Details of Balances	Balance-related audit objectives • Existence • Completeness • Accuracy • Classification • Cutoff • Detail tie-in • Realizable value • Rights and obligations • Presentation and disclosure	Analytical procedures Tests of details of balances	• Audit procedures • Timing • Audit procedures • Sample size • Items to select • Timing	Physical examination Confirmation Documentation Inquiries of client Reperformance Analytical procedures
Complete the Audit and Issue an Audit Report		Analytical procedures Tests of details of balances	• Audit procedures • Timing • Audit procedures • Sample size • Items to select • Timing	Analytical procedures Documentation Inquiries of client

Phases of the Audit Process The four aspects of a complete audit: (1) plan and design an audit approach, (2) perform tests of controls and substantive tests of transactions, (3) perform analytical procedures and tests of details of balances, and (4) complete the audit and issue an audit report.

Audit Objectives The objectives on an audit that must be met before the auditor can conclude that any given class of transactions or account balance is fairly stated. There are six transaction-related and nine balance-related audit objectives.

Types of Tests The five categories of audit tests auditors use to determine whether financial statements are fairly stated: procedures to obtain an understanding of internal control, tests of controls, substantive tests of transactions, analytical procedures, and tests of details of balances.

Evidence Decisions The four subcategories of decisions the auditor makes in accumulating audit evidence: audit procedures, sample size, items to select, and timing of performance.

Types of Evidence The seven broad categories of evidence auditors use: physical examination, confirmation, documentation, analytical procedures, observation, inquiry of the client, and reperformance.

SUMMARY OF THE AUDIT PROCESS

The four **phases of the audit process** were introduced at the end of Chapter 6. Considerable portions of Chapters 7 through 13 have discussed the eight steps in phase I. Figure 13-9 (p. 396) shows the four phases for the entire audit process. Table 13-7 (p. 397) shows the timing of the tests in each phase for an audit with a December 31 balance sheet date.

> **OBJECTIVE 13-7**
>
> Integrate the four phases of the audit process.

Phase I: Plan and Design an Audit Approach

Chapters 7 through 13 have emphasized various aspects of planning the audit. At the end of phase I, the auditor should have a well-defined audit plan and a specific audit program for the entire audit.

Information obtained during client acceptance and initial planning, understanding the client's business and industry, assessing the client's business risks, and performing preliminary analytical procedures (first four boxes in Figure 13-9) is used primarily to assess inherent risk and acceptable audit risk. Assessments of materiality, acceptable audit risk, inherent risk, control risk, and any identified fraud risks are used to develop an overall audit plan and audit program.

Phase II: Perform Tests of Controls and Substantive Tests of Transactions

Performance of the tests of controls and substantive tests of transactions occurs during this phase. The objectives of phase II are to (1) obtain evidence in support of the specific controls that contribute to the auditor's assessed control risk (that is, where it is reduced below the maximum) and to the audit of internal control over financial reporting in a public company and (2) obtain evidence in support of the monetary correctness of transactions. The former objective is met by performing tests of controls, and the latter by performing substantive tests of transactions. Many of both types of tests are conducted simultaneously on the same transactions. When controls are not considered effective or when control deviations are discovered, substantive tests can be expanded in this phase or in phase III, along with considering the implications for the auditor's report on internal control over financial reporting.

Because the results of tests of controls and substantive tests of transactions are a major determinant of the extent of tests of details of balances, the tests are often performed 2 or 3 months before the balance sheet date. This helps the auditor plan for contingencies, revise the audit program for unexpected results, and complete the audit as soon as possible after the balance sheet date. This approach is also used in the audit of public companies to allow management an opportunity to correct control deficiencies in time to allow auditor testing of the newly implemented control before year-end.

For computerized accounting systems, auditors often perform tests of controls and substantive tests of transactions throughout the year to identify significant or unusual transactions and determine whether any changes have been made to the computer programs. This approach is often called continuous auditing. It is likely to be used in the integrated audits of financial statements and internal control for public companies.

FIGURE 13-9 | Summary of the Audit Process

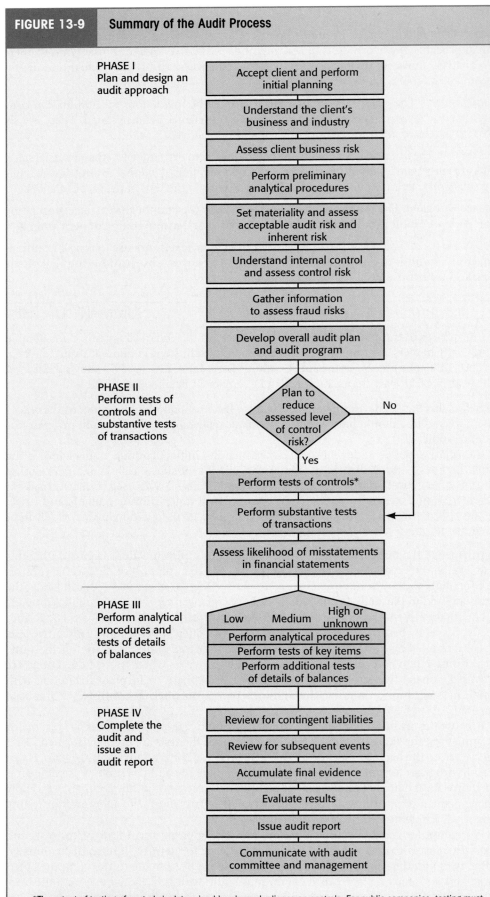

PHASE I
Plan and design an audit approach

- Accept client and perform initial planning
- Understand the client's business and industry
- Assess client business risk
- Perform preliminary analytical procedures
- Set materiality and assess acceptable audit risk and inherent risk
- Understand internal control and assess control risk
- Gather information to assess fraud risks
- Develop overall audit plan and audit program

PHASE II
Perform tests of controls and substantive tests of transactions

- Plan to reduce assessed level of control risk? — No
  - Yes
- Perform tests of controls*
- Perform substantive tests of transactions
- Assess likelihood of misstatements in financial statements

PHASE III
Perform analytical procedures and tests of details of balances

- Low   Medium   High or unknown
- Perform analytical procedures
- Perform tests of key items
- Perform additional tests of details of balances

PHASE IV
Complete the audit and issue an audit report

- Review for contingent liabilities
- Review for subsequent events
- Accumulate final evidence
- Evaluate results
- Issue audit report
- Communicate with audit committee and management

*The extent of testing of controls is determined by planned reliance on controls. For public companies, testing must be sufficient to issue an opinion on internal control over financial reporting.

TABLE 13-7	Timing of Tests		
Phase I	Plan and design audit approach. Update understanding of internal control. Update audit program. Perform preliminary analytical procedures.	8-31-05	
Phase II	Perform tests of controls and substantive tests of transactions for first 9 months of the year.	9-30-05	
Phase III	Confirm accounts receivable. Observe inventory.	10-31-05	
	Count cash. Perform cutoff tests. Request various other confirmations.	12-31-05	Balance sheet date
	Perform analytical procedures, complete tests of controls and substantive tests of transactions, and complete most tests of details of balances.	1-7-06	Books closed
Phase IV	Summarize results, review for contingent liabilities, review for subsequent events, accumulate final evidence (including analytical procedures), and finalize audit.	2-15-06	Last date of field work
	Issue audit report.	2-25-06	

The objective of phase III is to obtain sufficient additional evidence to determine whether the ending balances and footnotes in financial statements are fairly stated. The nature and extent of the work will depend heavily on the findings of the two previous phases.

Phase III: Perform Analytical Procedures and Tests of Details of Balances

There are two general categories of phase III procedures: analytical procedures and tests of details of balances. Analytical procedures are those that assess the overall reasonableness of transactions and balances. Tests of details of balances are specific procedures intended to test for monetary misstatements in the balances in the financial statements. Certain key transactions and amounts are so important that each one must be audited. Other items can be sampled.

Table 13-7 shows analytical procedures being done both before and after the balance sheet date. Because of their low cost, it is common to use analytical procedures when they are relevant. They are often done early with preliminary data before year-end as a means of planning and directing other audit tests to specific areas. But the greatest benefit from calculating ratios and making comparisons occurs after the client has finished preparing its financial statements. Ideally, these analytical procedures are done before tests of details of balances so that they can then be used to determine how extensively to test balances. They are also used as a part of performing tests of balances and during the completion phase of the audit.

Table 13-7 also shows that tests of details of balances are normally done last. On some audits, all are done after the balance sheet date. When clients want to issue statements soon after the balance sheet date, however, the more time-consuming tests of details of balances will be done at interim dates before year-end with additional work being done to "bring up" the audited interim-date balances to year-end. Substantive tests of balances performed before year-end provide less assurance and are not normally done unless internal controls are effective.

After the first three phases are completed, it is necessary to accumulate some additional evidence for the financial statements, summarize the results, issue the audit report, and perform other forms of communication. This phase has several parts.

Phase IV: Complete the Audit and Issue an Audit Report

Review for Contingent Liabilities Contingent liabilities are potential liabilities that must be disclosed in the client's footnotes. Auditors must make sure that the disclosure is adequate. A considerable portion of the search for contingent liabilities is done during the first three phases, but additional testing is done during phase IV. Contingent liabilities are studied in Chapter 24.

Review for Subsequent Events Occasionally, events occurring subsequent to the balance sheet date but before the issuance of the financial statements and auditor's report will have an effect on the information presented in the financial statements. Specific review procedures are designed to bring to the auditor's attention any subsequent events that may require recognition in the financial statements. Review for subsequent events is also studied in Chapter 24.

Accumulate Final Evidence In addition to the evidence obtained for each cycle during phases I and II and for each account during phase III, it is necessary to gather evidence for the financial statements as a whole during the completion phase. This evidence includes performing final analytical procedures, evaluating the going-concern assumption, obtaining a client representation letter, and reading information in the annual report to make sure that it is consistent with the financial statements.

Issue Audit Report The type of audit report issued depends on the evidence accumulated and the audit findings. The appropriate reports for differing circumstances were studied in Chapter 3.

Communicate with Audit Committee and Management The auditor is required to communicate significant deficiencies in internal control to the audit committee or senior management. Auditing standards also require the auditor to communicate certain other matters to the audit committee or a similarly designated body upon completion of the audit or sooner. Although not required, auditors often also make suggestions to management to improve business performance.

ESSENTIAL TERMS

Analytical procedures—use of comparisons and relationships to assess whether account balances or other data appear reasonable

Evidence mix—the combination of the five types of tests to obtain sufficient competent evidence for a cycle; there are likely to be variations in the mix from cycle to cycle depending on the circumstances of the audit

Phases of the audit process—the four aspects of a complete audit: (1) plan and design an audit approach, (2) perform tests of controls and substantive tests of transactions, (3) perform analytical procedures and tests of details of balances, and (4) complete the audit and issue an audit report

Procedures to obtain an understanding of internal control—procedures used by the auditor to gather evidence about the design and placement in operation of specific controls

Substantive tests—audit procedures designed to test for dollar (monetary) misstatements of financial statement balances

Substantive tests of transactions—audit procedures testing for monetary misstatements to determine whether the six transaction-related audit objectives have been satisfied for each class of transactions

Tests of controls—audit procedures to test the effectiveness of controls in support of a reduced assessed control risk

Tests of details of balances—audit procedures testing for monetary misstatements to determine whether the nine balance-related audit objectives have been satisfied for each significant account balance

Types of tests—the five categories of audit tests auditors use to determine whether financial statements are fairly stated: procedures to obtain an understanding of internal control, tests of controls, substantive tests of transactions, analytical procedures, and tests of details of balances

REVIEW QUESTIONS

13-1 (Objective 13-1) What are the five types of tests auditors use to determine whether financial statements are fairly stated? Identify which tests are performed to reduce control risk and which tests are performed to reduce planned detection risk. Also, identify which tests would be used by a public company auditor when auditing internal control over financial reporting.

13-2 (Objective 13-1) What is the purpose of tests of controls? Identify specific accounts on the financial statements that are affected by performing tests of controls for the acquisition and payment cycle.

13-3 (Objective 13-1) Distinguish between a test of control and a substantive test of transactions. Give two examples of each.

13-4 (Objectives 13-1, 13-4) State a test of control audit procedure to test the effectiveness of the following control: Approved wage rates are used in calculating employees' earnings. State a substantive test of transactions audit procedure to determine whether approved wage rates are actually used in calculating employees' earnings.

13-5 (Objective 13-1) A considerable portion of the tests of controls and substantive tests of transactions are performed simultaneously as a matter of audit convenience. But the substantive tests of transactions procedures and sample size, in part, depend on the results of the tests of controls. How can the auditor resolve this apparent inconsistency?

13-6 (Objectives 13-2, 13-4) Evaluate the following statement: "Tests of sales and cash receipts transactions are such an essential part of every audit that I like to perform them as near the end of the audit as possible. By that time I have a fairly good understanding of the client's business and its internal controls because confirmations, cutoff tests, and other procedures have already been completed."

13-7 (Objectives 13-1, 13-2) Explain how the calculation and comparison to previous years of the gross margin percentage and the ratio of accounts receivable to sales are related to the confirmation of accounts receivable and other tests of the accuracy of accounts receivable.

13-8 (Objective 13-1) Distinguish between substantive tests of transactions and tests of details of balances. Give one example of each for the acquisition and payment cycle.

13-9 (Objective 13-3) The auditor of Ferguson's Inc. identified two internal controls in the sales and collection receipts cycle for testing. In the first control, the computer verifies that a planned sale on account will not exceed the customer's credit limit entered in the accounts receivable master file. In the second control, the accounts receivable clerk matches bills of lading, sales invoices, and customer orders before recording in the sales journal. Describe how the presence of general controls over software programs and master file changes affects the extent of audit testing of each of these two internal controls.

13-10 (Objective 13-4) Assume that the client's internal controls over the recording and classifying of fixed asset additions are considered deficient because the individual responsible for recording new acquisitions has inadequate technical training and limited experience in accounting. How would this situation affect the evidence you should accumulate in auditing fixed assets as compared with another audit in which the controls are excellent? Be as specific as possible.

13-11 (Objective 13-2) For each of the seven types of evidence discussed in Chapter 7, identify whether it is applicable for procedures to obtain an understanding of internal control, tests of controls, substantive tests of transactions, analytical procedures, and tests of details of balances.

13-12 (Objective 13-2) Rank the following types of tests from most costly to least costly: analytical procedures, tests of details of balances, procedures to obtain an understanding of internal control and tests of controls, and substantive tests of transactions.

13-13 (Objective 13-2) In Figure 13-3, explain the difference among C_3, C_2, and C_1. Explain the circumstances under which it would be a good decision to obtain audit assurance from substantive tests at point C_1. Do the same for points C_2 and C_3.

13-14 (Objective 13-2) The following are three decision factors related to assessed control risk: effectiveness of internal controls, cost-effectiveness of a reduced assessed control risk, and results of tests of controls. Identify the combination of conditions for these three factors that is required before reduced substantive testing is permitted.

13-15 (Objective 13-4) Table 13-3 illustrates variations in the emphasis on different types of audit tests. What are the benefits to the auditor of identifying the best mix of tests?

13-16 (Objective 13-5) State the four-step approach to designing tests of controls and substantive tests of transactions.

13-17 (Objective 13-5) Explain the relationship between the methodology for designing tests of controls and substantive tests of transactions in Figure 13-4 to the methodology for designing tests of details of balances in Figure 13-6.

13-18 (Objective 13-5) Why is it desirable to design tests of details of balances before performing tests of controls and substantive tests of transactions? State the assumptions that the auditor must make in doing that. What does the auditor do if the assumptions are wrong?

13-19 (Objective 13-5) Explain the relationship of tolerable misstatement, inherent risk, and control risk to planned tests of details of balances.

13-20 (Objective 13-5) List the nine balance-related audit objectives in the verification of the ending balance in inventory and provide one useful audit procedure for each of the objectives.

13-21 (Objective 13-7) Why do auditors often consider it desirable to perform audit tests throughout the year rather than wait until year-end? List several examples of evidence that can be accumulated before year-end.

MULTIPLE CHOICE QUESTIONS FROM CPA EXAMINATIONS

13-22 (Objective 13-1) The following questions concern types of audit tests. Choose the best response.

a. The auditor looks for an indication on duplicate sales invoices to see whether the invoices have been verified. This is an example of

(1) a test of details of balances.
(2) a test of control.
(3) a substantive test of transactions.
(4) both a test of control and a substantive test of transactions.

b. Analytical procedures may be classified as being primarily
(1) tests of controls.
(2) substantive tests.
(3) tests of ratios.
(4) tests of details of balances.

c. To support the auditor's initial assessment of control risk below maximum, the auditor performs procedures to determine that internal controls are operating effectively. Which of the following audit procedures is the auditor performing?
(1) Tests of details of balances
(2) Substantive tests of transactions
(3) Tests of controls
(4) Tests of trends and ratios

d. The auditor faces a risk that the audit will not detect material misstatements that occur in the accounting process. To minimize this risk, the auditor relies primarily on
(1) substantive tests.
(2) tests of controls.
(3) internal control.
(4) statistical analysis.

13-23 (Objective 13-1) The following questions deal with tests of controls. Choose the best response.

a. Which of the following statements about tests of controls is most accurate?
(1) Auditing procedures cannot concurrently provide both evidence of the effectiveness of internal control procedures and evidence required for substantive tests.
(2) Tests of controls include observations of the proper segregation of duties.
(3) Tests of controls provide direct evidence about monetary misstatements in transactions.
(4) Tests of controls ordinarily should be performed as of the balance sheet date or during the period subsequent to that date.

b. Which of the following would be *least* likely to be included in an auditor's tests of controls?
(1) Documentation.
(2) Observation.
(3) Inquiry.
(4) Confirmation.

c. The two phases of the auditor's involvement with internal control are sometimes called "understanding and assessment" and "tests of controls." In the tests of controls phase, the auditor attempts to obtain
(1) a reasonable degree of assurance that the client's internal controls are operating effectively on a consistent basis throughout the year.
(2) sufficient, competent evidential matter to afford a reasonable basis for the auditor's opinion.
(3) assurances that informative disclosures in the financial statements are reasonably adequate.
(4) knowledge and understanding of the client's prescribed procedures and methods.

d. Which of the following is ordinarily considered a test of control audit procedure?
(1) Sending confirmation letters to banks
(2) Counting and listing cash on hand
(3) Examining signatures on checks
(4) Preparing reconciliations of bank accounts as of the balance sheet date

13-24 (Objectives 13-5, 13-7) The following questions concern the sequence and timing of audit tests. Choose the best response.

a. A conceptually logical approach to the auditor's evaluation of internal control consists of the following four steps:
I. Determining the internal controls that should prevent or detect errors and fraud
II. Identifying control deficiencies to determine their effect on the nature, timing, or extent of auditing procedures to be applied and suggestions to be made to the client
III. Determining whether the necessary procedures are prescribed and are being followed satisfactorily
IV. Considering the types of errors and fraud that could occur

What should be the order in which these four steps are performed?
    (1) I, II, III, and IV
    (2) I, III, IV, and II
    (3) III, IV, I, and II
    (4) IV, I, III, and II

b. The sequence of steps in gathering evidence as the basis of the auditor's opinion is
    (1) substantive tests, initial assessment of control risk, and tests of controls.
    (2) initial assessment of control risk, substantive tests, and tests of controls.
    (3) initial assessment of control risk, tests of controls, and substantive tests.
    (4) tests of controls, initial assessment of control risk, and substantive tests.

DISCUSSION QUESTIONS AND PROBLEMS

13-25 (Objectives 13-1, 13-2) The following are 11 audit procedures taken from an audit program:

1. Foot the accounts payable trial balance and compare the total with the general ledger.
2. Examine vendors' invoices to verify the ending balance in accounts payable.
3. Compare the balance in payroll tax expense with previous years. The comparison takes the increase in payroll tax rates into account.
4. Discuss the duties of the cash disbursements clerk with him and observe whether he has responsibility for handling cash or preparing the bank reconciliation.
5. Confirm accounts payable balances directly with vendors.
6. Account for a sequence of checks in the cash disbursements journal to determine whether any have been omitted.
7. Examine the internal auditor's initials on monthly bank reconciliations as an indication of whether they have been reviewed.
8. Examine vendors' invoices and other documentation in support of recorded transactions in the acquisitions journal.
9. Multiply the commission rate by total sales and compare the result with commission expense.
10. Examine vendors' invoices and other supporting documents to determine whether large amounts in the repair and maintenance account should be capitalized.
11. Inquire about the accounts payable supervisor's monthly review of a computer-generated exception report of receiving reports and purchase orders that have not been matched with a vendor invoice.

a. Indicate whether each procedure is a test of control, substantive test of transactions, analytical procedure, or a test of details of balances.
b. Identify the type of evidence for each procedure.

Required

13-26 (Objectives 13-1, 13-2, 13-3, 13-6) The following are audit procedures from different transaction cycles:

1. Use audit software to foot and cross-foot the cash disbursements journal and trace the balance to the general ledger.
2. Select a sample of entries in the acquisitions journal and trace each one to a related vendor's invoice to determine whether one exists.
3. Compute inventory turnover for each major product and compare with previous years.
4. Confirm a sample of notes payable balances, interest rates, and collateral with lenders.
5. Use audit software to foot the accounts payable trial balance and compare the balance with the general ledger.
6. Examine documentation for acquisition transactions before and after the balance sheet date to determine whether they are recorded in the proper period.
7. Inquire of the credit manager whether each account receivable on the aged trial balance is collectible.

a. For each audit procedure, identify the transaction cycle being audited.
b. For each audit procedure, identify the type of evidence.
c. For each audit procedure, identify whether it is a test of control or a substantive test.
d. For each substantive audit procedure, identify whether it is a substantive test of transactions, a test of details of balances, or an analytical procedure.
e. For each test of control or substantive test of transactions procedure, identify the transaction-related audit objective or objectives being satisfied.

Required

f. For each analytical procedure or test of details of balances procedure, identify the balance-related audit objective or objectives being satisfied.

13-27 (Objective 13-1) For each of the following controls, identify whether the control leaves a paper audit trail. Also identify a test of control audit procedure the auditor can use to test the effectiveness of the control.

a. An accounting clerk accounts for all shipping documents on a monthly basis and initials the monthly shipping log.

b. Bank reconciliations are prepared by the controller, who does not have access to cash receipts.

c. As employees check in daily by using time clocks, a supervisor observes to make certain that no individual "punches in" more than one time card.

d. Vendors' invoices are approved by the controller after she examines the purchase order and receiving report attached to each invoice.

e. The cashier, who has no access to accounting records, prepares the deposit slip and delivers the deposit directly to the bank daily.

f. An accounting clerk verifies the price, extensions, and footings of all sales invoices in excess of $300 and initials the duplicate sales invoice when he has completed the procedure.

g. All mail is opened and cash is prelisted daily by the president's secretary, who has no other responsibility for handling assets or recording accounting data.

13-28 (Objectives 13-1, 13-5, 13-6) The following are independent internal controls commonly found in the acquisition and payment cycle. Each control is to be considered independently.

1. At the end of each month, an accounting clerk accounts for all prenumbered receiving reports (documents evidencing the receipt of goods) issued during the month, and he traces each one to the related vendor's invoice and acquisitions journal entry. The clerk's tests do not include testing quantity or description of the merchandise received.

2. The cash disbursements clerk is prohibited from handling cash. The bank account is reconciled by another person even though the clerk has sufficient expertise and time to do it.

3. Before a check is prepared to pay for acquisitions by the accounts payable department, the related purchase order and receiving report are attached to the vendor's invoice being paid. A clerk compares the quantity on the invoice with the receiving report and purchase order, compares the price with the purchase order, recomputes the extensions, re-adds the total, and examines the account number indicated on the invoice to determine whether it is properly classified. He indicates his performance of these procedures by initialing the invoice.

4. Before a check is signed by the controller, she examines the supporting documentation accompanying the check. At that time, she initials each vendor's invoice to indicate her approval.

5. After the controller signs the checks, her secretary writes the check number and the date the check was issued on each of the supporting documents to prevent their reuse.

Required

a. For each of the internal controls, state the transaction-related audit objective(s) the control is meant to fulfill.

b. For each control, list one test of control the auditor could perform to test the effectiveness of the control.

c. For each control, list one substantive test the auditor could perform to determine whether financial misstatements are actually taking place.

13-29 (Objectives 13-1, 13-5, 13-6) The following internal controls for the acquisition and payment cycle were selected from a standard internal control questionnaire.

1. Vendors' invoices are recalculated before payment.
2. Approved price lists are used for acquisitions.
3. Prenumbered receiving reports are prepared as support for acquisitions and numerically accounted for.
4. Dates on receiving reports are compared with vendors' invoices before entry into the acquisitions journal.
5. The accounts payable master file is updated, balanced, and reconciled to the general ledger monthly.
6. Account classifications are reviewed by someone other than the preparer.
7. All checks are signed by the owner or manager.
8. The check signer compares data on supporting documents with checks.
9. All supporting documents are cancelled after the checks are signed.
10. Checks are mailed by the owner or manager or a person under her supervision after signing.

a. For each control, identify which element of the five categories of control activities is applicable (separation of duties, proper authorization, adequate documents or records, physical control over assets and records, or independent checks on performance). **Required**

b. For each control, state which transaction-related audit objective(s) is (are) applicable.

c. For each control, write an audit procedure that could be used to test the control for effectiveness.

d. For each control, identify a likely misstatement, assuming that the control does not exist or is not functioning.

e. For each likely misstatement, identify a substantive audit procedure to determine whether the misstatement exists.

13-30 (Objective 13-3) Beds and Spreads, Inc. specializes in bed and bath furnishings. Its inventory system is linked through the Internet to key suppliers. The auditor identified the following internal controls in the inventory cycle:

1. The computer initiates an order only when perpetual inventory levels fall below prespecified inventory levels in the inventory master file.

2. The sales and purchasing department managers review inventory reorder points on a monthly basis for reasonableness. Approved changes to reorder points are entered into the master file by the purchasing department manager and an updated printout is generated for final review. Both managers verify that all changes were entered correctly and initial the final printout indicating final approval. These printouts are maintained in the purchasing department.

3. The computer will initiate a purchase order only for inventory product numbers maintained in the inventory master file.

4. The purchasing department manager reviews a computer-generated exception report that highlights weekly purchases that exceed $10,000 per vendor.

5. Salesclerks send damaged merchandise on the store shelves to the back storage room. The sales department manager examines the damaged merchandise each month and prepares a listing showing the estimated salvage value by product number. The accounting department uses the listing to prepare a monthly adjustment to recorded inventory values.

a. Consider each of the preceding controls separately. Identify whether the control is a(n) **Required**
   (1) automated control embedded in computer software.
   (2) manual control with effectiveness based significantly on IT-generated information.
   (3) manual control with effectiveness not significantly reliant on IT-generated information.

b. Describe how the extent of testing of each control would be affected in subsequent years if general controls are effective, particularly controls over program and master file changes.

13-31 (Objectives 13-5, 13-7) Jennifer Schaefer, CPA, follows the philosophy of performing interim tests of controls and substantive tests of transactions on every December 31 audit as a means of keeping overtime to a minimum. Typically, the interim tests are performed some time between August and November.

a. Evaluate her decision to perform interim tests of controls and substantive tests of transactions. **Required**

b. Under what circumstances is it acceptable for her to perform no additional tests of controls and substantive tests of transactions work as a part of the year-end audit tests?

c. If she decides to perform no additional testing, what is the effect on other tests she performs during the remainder of the engagement?

d. Evaluate her approach if she is auditing a public company and has to perform an audit of internal control over financial reporting.

13-32 (Objectives 13-4, 13-5) Following are several decisions that the auditor must make in an audit of a nonpublic company. Letters indicate alternative conclusions that could be made.

Decisions	Alternative Conclusions
1. Determine whether it is cost effective to perform tests of controls.	A. It is cost effective B. It is not cost effective
2. Perform substantive tests of details of balances.	C. Perform reduced tests D. Perform expanded tests
3. Complete initial assessment of control risk.	E. Controls are effective F. Controls are ineffective
4. Perform tests of controls.	G. Controls are effective H. Controls are ineffective

a. Identify the sequence in which the auditor should make decisions 1 to 4.

b. For the audit of the sales and collection cycle and accounts receivable, an auditor reached the following conclusions: A, D, E, H. Put the letters in the appropriate sequence and evaluate whether the auditor's logic was reasonable. Explain your answer.

c. For the audit of inventory and related inventory cost records, an auditor reached the following conclusions: B, C, E, G. Put the letters in the appropriate sequence and evaluate whether the auditor used good professional judgment. Explain your answer.

d. For the audit of property, plant, and equipment and related acquisition records, an auditor reached the following conclusions: A, C, F, G. Put the letters in the appropriate sequence and evaluate whether the auditor used good professional judgment. Explain your answer.

e. For the audit of payroll expenses and related liabilities, an auditor recorded the following conclusions: D, F. Put the letters in the appropriate sequence and evaluate whether the auditor used good professional judgment. Explain your answer.

13-33 (Objective 13-4) The following are three situations, all involving nonpublic companies, in which the auditor is required to develop an audit strategy:

1. The client has inventory at approximately 50 locations in a three-state region. The inventory is difficult to count and can be observed only by traveling by automobile. The internal controls over acquisitions, cash disbursements, and perpetual records are considered effective. This is the fifth year that you have done the audit, and audit results in past years have always been excellent. The client is in excellent financial condition and is privately held.

2. This is the first year of an audit of a medium-sized company that is considering selling its business because of severe underfinancing. A review of the acquisition and payment cycle indicates that controls over cash disbursements are excellent but controls over acquisitions cannot be considered effective. The client lacks receiving reports and a policy as to the proper timing to record acquisitions. When you review the general ledger, you observe that there are many large adjusting entries to correct accounts payable.

3. You are doing the audit of a small loan company with extensive receivables from customers. Controls over granting loans, collections, and loans outstanding are considered effective, and there is extensive follow-up of all outstanding loans weekly. You have recommended a new computer system for the past 2 years, but management believes the cost is too great, given their low profitability. Collections are an ongoing problem because many of the customers have severe financial problems. Because of adverse economic conditions, loans receivable have significantly increased and collections are less than normal. In previous years, you have had relatively few adjusting entries.

a. For audit 1, recommend an evidence mix for the five types of tests for the audit of inventory and cost of goods sold. Justify your answer. Include in your recommendations both tests of controls and substantive tests.

b. For audit 2, recommend an evidence mix for the audit of the acquisition and payment cycle, including accounts payable. Justify your answer.

c. For audit 3, recommend an evidence mix for the audit of outstanding loans. Justify your answer.

13-34 (Objectives 13-1, 13-5) Brad Jackson was assigned to the audit of a client that had not been audited by any CPA firm in the preceding year. In conducting the audit, he did no testing of the beginning balance of accounts receivable, inventory, or accounts payable on the grounds that the audit report is being limited to the ending balance sheet, the income statement, and the statement of cash flows. No comparative financial statements are to be issued.

a. Explain the error in Jackson's reasoning.

b. Suggest an approach that Jackson can follow in verifying the beginning balance in accounts receivable.

c. Why does the same problem not exist in the verification of beginning balances on continuing audit engagements?

13-35 (Objective 13-4) Kim Bryan, a new staff auditor, is confused by the inconsistency of the three audit partners she has been assigned to on her first three audit engagements. On the first engagement, she spent a considerable amount of time in the audit of cash disbursements by examining cancelled checks and supporting documentation, but almost no testing was spent in the verification of fixed assets. On the second engagement, a different partner had her do less intensive tests in the cash disbursements area and take smaller sample sizes than in the first audit, even though the company was much larger. On her most recent engagement under a third audit partner, there was a thorough test of cash disbursement transactions, far beyond that of the other two audits, and an extensive verification of fixed assets. In fact, this partner insisted on a complete physical examination of all fixed assets recorded on the books. The total audit time on the most recent audit was longer than that of either of the first two audits despite the smaller size of the company. Bryan's conclusion is that the amount of evidence to accumulate depends on the audit partner in charge of the engagement.

Required

a. State several factors that could explain the difference in the amount of evidence accumulated in each of the three audit engagements as well as the total time spent.

b. What could the audit partners have done to help Bryan understand the difference in the audit emphasis on the three audits?

c. Explain how these three audits are useful in developing Bryan's professional judgment. How could the quality of her judgment have been improved on the audits?

d. Which audit most likely represents an integrated audit of a public company's financial statements and internal control over financial reporting?

13-36 (Objectives 13-5, 13-7) The following are parts of a typical audit for a company with a fiscal year-end of July 31.

1. Confirm accounts payable.
2. Do tests of controls and substantive tests of transactions for the acquisition and payment and payroll and personnel cycles.
3. Do other tests of details of balances for accounts payable.
4. Do tests for review of subsequent events.
5. Accept the client.
6. Issue the audit report.
7. Understand internal control and assess control risk.
8. Do analytical procedures for accounts payable.
9. Set acceptable audit risk and decide preliminary judgment about materiality and tolerable misstatement.

Required

a. Put parts 1 through 9 of the audit in the sequential order in which you would expect them to be performed in a typical audit.

b. Identify those parts that would frequently be done before July 31.

CASES

13-37 (Objectives 13-4, 13-5) Gale Brewer, CPA, has been the partner in charge of the audit of Merkle Manufacturing Company, a nonpublic company, for 13 years. Merkle has had excellent growth and profits in the past decade, primarily as a result of the excellent leadership provided by Bill Merkle and other competent executives. Brewer has always enjoyed a close relationship with the company and prides himself on having made several constructive comments over the years that have aided in the success of the firm. Several times in the past few years, Brewer's CPA firm has considered rotating a different audit team on the engagement, but this has been strongly resisted by both Brewer and Merkle.

For the first few years of the audit, internal controls were inadequate and the accounting personnel had inadequate qualifications for their responsibilities. Extensive audit evidence was required during the audit, and numerous adjusting entries were necessary. However, because of Brewer's constant prodding, internal controls improved gradually and competent personnel were hired. In recent years, there were normally no audit adjustments required, and the extent of the evidence accumulation was gradually reduced. During the past 3 years, Brewer was able to devote less time to the audit because of the relative ease of conducting the audit and the cooperation obtained throughout the engagement.

In the current year's audit, Brewer decided that the total time budget for the engagement should be kept approximately the same as in recent years. The senior in charge of the audit, Phil Warren, was new on the job and highly competent, and he had the reputation of being able to cut time off the budget. The fact that Merkle had recently acquired a new division through merger would probably add to the time, but Warren's efficiency would probably compensate for it.

The interim tests of controls took somewhat longer than expected because of the use of several new assistants, a change in the accounting system to computerize the inventory and other accounting records, a change in accounting personnel, and the existence of a few more errors in the tests of the system. Neither Brewer nor Warren was concerned about the budget deficit, however, because they could easily make up the difference at year-end.

At year-end, Warren assigned the responsibility for inventory to an assistant who also had not been on the audit before but was competent and extremely fast at his work. Even though the total value of inventory increased, he reduced the size of the sample from that of other years because there had been few errors in the preceding year. He found several items in the sample that were overstated as a result of errors in pricing and obsolescence, but the combination of all of the errors in the sample was immaterial. He completed the tests in 25% less time than the preceding year. The entire audit was completed on schedule and in slightly less time than the preceding year. There were only a few adjusting entries for the year, and only two of them were material. Brewer was extremely pleased with the results and wrote a special letter to Warren and the inventory assistant complimenting them on the audit.

Six months later, Brewer received a telephone call from Merkle and was informed that the company was in serious financial trouble. Subsequent investigation revealed that the inventory had been significantly overstated. The major cause of the misstatement was the inclusion of obsolete items in inventory (especially in the new division), errors in pricing as a result of the new computer system, and the inclusion of nonexistent inventory in the final inventory listing. The new controller had intentionally overstated the inventory to compensate for the reduction in sales volume from the preceding year.

Required

a. List the major deficiencies in the audit and state why they took place.

b. What things should have been apparent to Brewer in the conduct of the audit?

c. If Brewer's firm is sued by creditors, what is the likely outcome?

13-38 (Objectives 13-4, 13-5) McClain Plastics has been an audit client of Belcor, Rich, Smith & Barnes, CPAs (BRS&B), for several years. McClain Plastics was started by Evers McClain, who owns 51% of the company's stock. The balance is owned by about 200 stockholders who are investors with no operational responsibilities. McClain Plastics makes products that have plastic as their primary material. Some are made to order, but most products are made for inventory. An example of a McClain-manufactured product is a plastic chair pad that is used in a carpeted office. Another is a plastic bushing that is used with certain fastener systems.

McClain has grown from a small, two-product company, when they first engaged BRS&B, to a successful diverse company. At the time Randall Sessions of BRS&B became manager of the audit, annual sales had grown to $20 million and profits to $1.9 million. Historically, the company presented no unusual audit problems, and BRS&B had issued an unqualified opinion every year.

The audit approach BRS&B always used on the audit of McClain Plastics was a "substantive" audit approach. Under this approach, the in-charge auditor obtained an understanding of internal control, but control risk was assumed to be at the maximum (100%). Extensive analytical procedures were done on the income statement, and unusual fluctuations were investigated. Detailed audit procedures emphasized balance sheet accounts. The theory was that if the balance sheet accounts were correct at year-end and had been audited as of the beginning of the year, then retained earnings and the income statement must be correct.

Part I

In evaluating the audit approach for McClain for the current year's audit, Sessions believed that a substantive approach was really only appropriate for the audits of small nonpublic companies. In his judgment, McClain Plastics, with sales of $20 million and 46 employees, had reached the size where it was not economical, and probably not wise, to concentrate all the tests on the balance sheet. Furthermore, recent requirements in Section 404 of the Sarbanes–Oxley Act and the related PCAOB Standard 2 now require an integrated audit of the financial statements and internal control over financial reporting. Therefore, he designed an audit program that emphasized identifying internal controls in all major transaction cycles and included tests of controls. In addition to satisfying new requirements of the PCAOB, the intended economic benefit of this "reducing control risk" approach was that the time spent testing controls would be more than offset by reduced tests of details of the balance sheet accounts.

In planning tests of inventories, Sessions used the audit risk model included in auditing standards to determine the number of inventory items BRS&B would test at year-end. Because of the number of different products, features, sizes, and colors, McClain's inventory consisted of 2,450 different items. These were maintained on a perpetual inventory management system that used a relational database.

In using the audit risk model for inventories, Sessions believed that an audit risk of 5% was acceptable. He assessed inherent risk as high (100%) because inventory, by its nature, is subject to many types of misstatements. Based on his understanding of the relevant transaction cycles, Sessions believed that internal controls were good. He therefore assessed control risk as low (50%) before performing tests of controls. Sessions also planned to use analytical procedures for tests of inventory. These planned tests included comparing gross profit margins by month and reviewing for slow-moving items. Sessions believed that these tests would provide assurance of 40%. Substantive tests of details would include tests of inventory quantities, costs, and net realizable values at an interim date 2 months before year-end. Cutoff tests would be done at year-end. Inquiries and analytical procedures would be relied on for assurance about events between the interim audit date and fiscal year-end.

a. Decide which of the following would likely be done under both a reducing control risk approach and a substantive approach:

Required

(1) Assess acceptable audit risk.
(2) Assess inherent risk.
(3) Obtain an understanding of internal control.
(4) Assess control risk at less than 100%.
(5) Perform analytical procedures.
(6) Assess planned detection risk.

b. What advantages does the reducing control risk approach Sessions plans to use have over the substantive approach previously used in the audit of McClain Plastics?

c. What advantages did the substantive approach have over the reducing control risk approach?

Part II

The engagement partner agreed with Sessions's recommended approach. In planning the audit evidence for detailed inventory tests, the audit risk model was applied with the following results:

$$TDR = \frac{AAR}{IR \times CR \times APR}$$

where:

$$
\begin{aligned}
TDR &= \text{test of details risk} \\
AAR &= \text{acceptable audit risk} \\
IR &= \text{inherent risk} \\
CR &= \text{control risk} \\
APR &= \text{analytical procedures risk}
\end{aligned}
$$

Therefore, using Sessions's assessments and judgments as described previously,

$$TDR = \frac{.05}{1.0 \times .5 \times .6}$$

$$= .17$$

a. Explain what .17 means in this audit.

Required

b. Calculate *TDR* assuming that Sessions had assessed control risk at 100% and all other risks as they are stated.

c. Explain the effect of your answer in requirement b on the planned audit procedures and sample size in the audit of inventory compared with the .17 calculated by Sessions.

Part III

Although the planning went well, the actual testing yielded some surprises. When conducting tests of controls over acquisitions and additions to the perpetual inventory, the staff person performing the tests found that the exception rates for several important controls were significantly higher than expected. As a result, the staff person considered internal control to not be operating effectively, supporting an 80% control risk rather than the 50% level used. Accordingly, the staff person "reworked" the audit risk model as follows:

$$TDR = \frac{.05}{1.0 \times .8 \times .6}$$

$$TDR = .10$$

A 10% test of details risk still seemed to the staff person to be in the "moderate" range, so he recommended no increase in planned sample size for substantive tests.

Do you agree with the staff person's revised judgments about the effect of tests of controls on planned substantive tests? Explain the nature and basis of any disagreement. Also, describe the implications of these results on the auditor's report on internal control over financial reporting.

Required

INTERNET PROBLEM 13-1: ASSESSING EFFECTS OF EVIDENCE MIX

Reference the CW site. Auditors develop overall audit plans to ensure that they obtain "sufficient competent evidential matter." This problem requires students to visit company Web sites and assess how the date of the completion of field work and company characteristics might affect the timing and mix of evidence procedures.

PART 3 CHAPTERS 14–17

APPLICATION OF THE AUDIT PROCESS TO THE SALES AND COLLECTION CYCLE

To understand how auditing is done in practice, it is important to understand how auditing concepts are applied to specific auditing areas. The sales and collection cycle is the first area we look at for a detailed application of auditing concepts because this cycle is an important part of every audit and because it is reasonably straightforward. These four chapters apply the concepts you learned in Part 2 to the audit of sales, cash receipts, and the related income statement and balance sheet accounts in the cycle.

 The objective of Chapter 14 is to help you learn the methodology for designing tests of controls and substantive tests of transactions audit procedures for sales, cash receipts, and the other classes of transactions in the sales and collection cycle. Chapter 15 deals with both nonstatistical and statistical sampling methods for tests of controls and substantive tests of transactions. Chapter 16 presents the methodology for designing audit procedures for the audit of account balances in the sales and collection cycle. Chapter 17 covers audit sampling, with a focus on sampling for tests of details of balances.

AUDIT OF THE SALES AND COLLECTION CYCLE: TESTS OF CONTROLS AND SUBSTANTIVE TESTS OF TRANSACTIONS

THE CHOICE IS SIMPLE—RELY ON INTERNAL CONTROL OR RESIGN

City Finance is the largest client managed out of the Pittsburgh office of a Big Four firm. It is a financial services conglomerate with almost 1,000 offices in the United States and Canada, as well as correspondent offices overseas. The company's records contain more than a million accounts receivable and it processes millions of sales and other transactions annually.

The company's computer center is in a large, environmentally controlled room that contains several large mainframe computers and a great deal of ancillary equipment. There are two complete online systems, one serving as a backup for the other, as systems failure would preclude operations in all of the company's branches.

The company has an unusual system of checks and balances in which branch office transaction records are reconciled to data processing controls daily, which, in turn, are reconciled to outside bank account records monthly. Whenever this reconciliation process indicates a significant out-of-balance condition, procedures are initiated to resolve the problem as quickly as possible. A large internal audit staff oversees any special investigative efforts that are required.

Because City Finance is a public company, it currently must file its report on Form 10-K with the Securities and Exchange Commission within 60 days after its fiscal year-end. The Form 10-K will contain management's report on internal control over financial reporting along with the auditor's report on those controls. In addition, the company likes to announce annual earnings and issue its annual report as soon after year-end as reasonably feasible. Under these circumstances, there is always a great deal of pressure on the CPA firm to complete the audit quickly.

A standard audit planning question is: "How much shall we rely on internal control?" In the case of the City Finance audit, there is only one possible answer: as much as we can. PCAOB Standard 2 requires the auditor to test controls as part of the audit of internal control over financial reporting. Furthermore, it would be difficult to complete the audit within the reporting deadlines without extensively testing key controls. Accordingly, the CPA firm conducts the audit with significant reliance on IT controls, reconciliation processes, and internal audit procedures. They test these controls extensively and perform many of their substantive procedures up through year-end. In all honesty, if City Finance did not have excellent internal controls, the CPA firm would admit that an audit of the company just could not be done.

LEARNING OBJECTIVES

After studying this chapter, you should be able to

14-1 Identify the accounts and the classes of transactions in the sales and collection cycle.

14-2 Describe the business functions and the related documents and records in the sales and collection cycle.

14-3 Understand how e-commerce activities affect the sales and collection cycle.

14-4 Understand internal control, and design and perform tests of controls and substantive tests of transactions for sales.

14-5 Apply the methodology for controls over sales transactions to controls over sales returns and allowances.

14-6 Understand internal control, and design and perform tests of controls and substantive tests of transactions for cash receipts.

14-7 Apply the methodology for controls over the sales and collection cycle to write-offs of uncollectible accounts receivable.

The circumstances of City Finance in the opening vignette illustrate an audit in which extensive reliance on internal controls in the sales and collection cycle will likely require the auditor to expand tests of controls and substantive tests of transactions. In other situations not involving the audit of a public company, the auditor is likely to rely far less on internal controls but, as was shown in Chapter 10, will still need to understand the internal controls over sales and cash receipts. It is important for auditors to know when they should rely extensively on internal controls and when they should not. This chapter studies assessing control risk and designing tests of controls and substantive tests of transactions for each of the classes of transactions in the sales and collection cycle.

Before studying the process of assessing control risk and designing tests of controls and substantive tests of transactions for each class of transactions in detail, two related topics are covered. First, it is important to know the sales and collection cycle classes of transactions and account balances in a typical company. These were discussed earlier but are reviewed here. Second, because a considerable portion of the audit of transactions in the sales and collection cycle involves documents and records, it is essential to understand the typical documents and records used in the cycle.

ACCOUNTS AND CLASSES OF TRANSACTIONS IN THE SALES AND COLLECTION CYCLE

OBJECTIVE 14-1

Identify the accounts and the classes of transactions in the sales and collection cycle.

The overall objective in the audit of the sales and collection cycle is to evaluate whether the account balances affected by the cycle are fairly presented in accordance with generally accepted accounting principles. Typical accounts included in the sales and collection cycle are shown in Figure 14-1 with the use of T accounts. The nature of the accounts may vary, of course, depending on the industry and client involved. There are differences in account titles for a service industry, a retail company, and an insurance company, but the key concepts are the same. To provide a frame of reference for understanding the material in this chapter, a wholesale merchandising company is assumed.

FIGURE 14-1   Accounts in the Sales and Collection Cycle

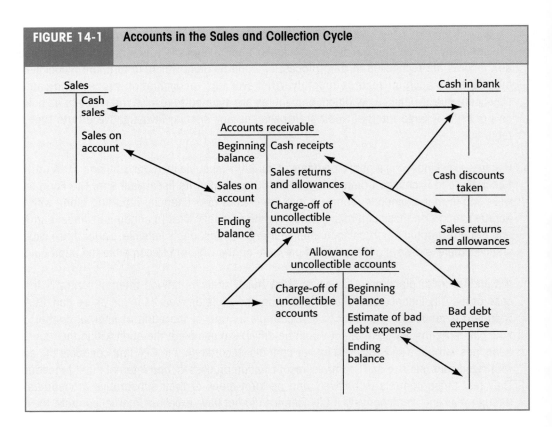

Figure 14-1 shows the way accounting information flows through the various accounts in the sales and collection cycle. This figure shows that there are five **classes of transactions in the sales and collection cycle**:

1. Sales (cash and sales on account)
2. Cash receipts
3. Sales returns and allowances
4. Charge-off of uncollectible accounts
5. Estimate of bad debt expense

Figure 14-1 also shows that with the exception of cash sales, every transaction and amount ultimately is included in one of two balance sheet accounts, accounts receivable or allowance for uncollectible accounts. For simplicity, assume that the same internal controls exist for both cash and credit sales.

BUSINESS FUNCTIONS IN THE CYCLE AND RELATED DOCUMENTS AND RECORDS

The **sales and collection cycle** involves the decisions and processes necessary for the transfer of the ownership of goods and services to customers after they are made available for sale. It begins with a request by a customer and ends with the conversion of material or service into an account receivable, and ultimately into cash.

There are eight **business functions for the sales and collection cycle** shown in the third column of Table 14-1. They occur in every business in the recording of the five classes of transactions in the sales and collection cycle. Observe in Table 14-1 that the first four processes are for recording sales, whereas every other class of transactions includes only one business function. This section explains each of the eight business functions and describes

> **OBJECTIVE 14-2**
>
> Describe the business functions and the related documents and records in the sales and collection cycle.

TABLE 14-1	Classes of Transactions, Accounts, Business Functions, and Related Documents and Records for the Sales and Collection Cycle		
Classes of Transactions	**Accounts**	**Business Functions**	**Documents and Records**
Sales	Sales Accounts receivable	Processing customer orders	Customer order Sales order
		Granting credit	Customer order or sales order
		Shipping goods	Shipping document
		Billing customers and recording sales	Sales invoice Sales transaction file Sales journal or listing Accounts receivable master file Accounts receivable trial balance Monthly statements
Cash receipts	Cash in bank (debits from cash receipts) Accounts receivable	Processing and recording cash receipts	Remittance advice Prelisting of cash receipts Cash receipts transaction file Cash receipts journal or listing
Sales returns and allowances	Sales returns and allowances Accounts receivable	Processing and recording sales returns and allowances	Credit memo Sales returns and allowances journal
Charge-off of uncollectible accounts	Accounts receivable Allowance for uncollectible accounts	Charging off uncollectible accounts receivable	Uncollectible account authorization form General journal
Bad debt expense	Bad debt expense Allowance for uncollectible accounts	Providing for bad debts	General journal

typical documents and records for each function. These documents and records are shown in the fourth column of Table 14-1. It is essential to understand the business functions and documents and records in a business before assessing control risk and designing tests of controls and substantive tests of transactions.

Processing Customer Orders

The request for goods by a customer is the starting point for the entire cycle. Legally, it is an offer to buy goods under specified terms. The receipt of a customer order often results in the immediate creation of a sales order.

Customer Order A request for merchandise by a customer. It may be received by telephone, letter, a printed form that has been sent to prospective and existing customers, through salespeople, or through electronic submission of the customer order through the Internet or other network linkage between the supplier and the customer.

Sales Order A document for communicating the description, quantity, and related information for goods ordered by a customer. This is often used to indicate credit approval and authorization for shipment.

Granting Credit

Credit Reports

Before goods are shipped, a properly authorized person must *approve credit* to the customer for sales on account. Weak practices in credit approval often result in excessive bad debts and accounts receivable that may be uncollectible. An indication of credit approval on the sales order often serves as the approval to ship the goods. In some companies, the computer automatically approves a credit sale based on preapproved credit limits maintained in a customer master file. The computer allows the sale to proceed only when the proposed sales order total plus the existing customer balance is less than the credit limit in the master file.

Shipping Goods

This critical function is the first point in the cycle where company assets are given up. Most companies recognize sales when goods are shipped. A shipping document is prepared at the time of shipment; this can be done automatically by the computer based on sales order information. The shipping document, which is often a multicopy bill of lading, is essential to the proper billing of shipments to customers. Companies that maintain perpetual inventory records also update them based on shipping information.

Shipping Document A document prepared to initiate shipment of the goods, indicating the description of the merchandise, the quantity shipped, and other relevant data. The original is sent to the customer, and one or more copies are retained. It is also used as a signal to bill the customer. One type of shipping document is a bill of lading, which is a written contract between the carrier and the seller of the receipt and shipment of goods. Often, bills of lading include only the number of boxes or pounds shipped, rather than complete details of quantity and description. Throughout the text, we assume that complete details are included on bills of lading. The computer operator informs the computer by a key entry that the goods described on the shipping document have been shipped.

The bill of lading is often transmitted electronically and automatically generates the related sales invoice as well as the entry in the sales journal. Many companies use bar codes and handheld computers to record removal of inventory from the warehouse. This information is used to update the perpetual inventory records in the inventory master file.

Billing Customers and Recording Sales

Because the billing of customers is the means by which the customer is informed of the amount due for the goods, it must be done correctly and on a timely basis. The most important aspects of billing are making sure that all shipments made have been billed, that no shipment has been billed more than once, and that each one is billed for the proper amount. Billing at the proper amount is dependent on charging the customer for the quantity shipped at the authorized price. The authorized price includes consideration for freight charges, insurance, and terms of payments.

In most systems, billing of the customer includes preparation of a multicopy sales invoice and simultaneous updating of the sales transactions file, accounts receivable master file, and general ledger master file for sales and accounts receivable. This information is used to generate the sales journal and, along with cash receipts and miscellaneous credits, allows preparation of the accounts receivable trial balance.

Sales Invoice A document indicating the description and quantity of goods sold, the price, freight charges, insurance, terms, and other relevant data. The sales invoice is the method of indicating to the customer the amount of a sale and due date of a payment. The original is sent to the customer, and one or more copies are retained. Typically, the sales invoice is automatically prepared by the computer after the customer number, quantity, destination of goods shipped, and sales terms are entered. The computer calculates the invoice extensions and total sales amount using the information entered along with prices in the inventory master file.

Sales Transaction File A computer-generated file that includes all sales transactions processed by the accounting system for a period, such as a day, week, or month. It includes all information entered into the system and information for each transaction, such as customer name, date, amount, account classification or classifications, salesperson, and commission rate. The file can also include returns and allowances or there can be a separate file for those transactions.

The information on the sales transaction file is used for a variety of records, listings, or reports, depending on the company's needs. Examples include a sales journal, accounts receivable master file, and transactions for a certain account balance or division.

Sales Journal or Listing A report generated from the sales transaction file that typically includes the customer name, date, amount, and account classification or classifications for each transaction, such as division or product line. It also identifies whether the sale was for cash or accounts receivable. The journal or listing can be for any time period but is often for a month. Typically, the journal or listing includes totals of every account number included for the time period. The same transactions included in the journal or listing are also posted simultaneously to the general ledger and, if they are on account, to the accounts receivable master file. The journal or listing can also include returns and allowances or there can be a separate journal or listing of those transactions.

Accounts Receivable Master File A file used to record individual sales, cash receipts, and sales returns and allowances for each customer and to maintain customer account balances. The master file is updated from the sales, sales returns and allowances, and cash receipts computer transaction files. The total of the individual account balances in the master file equals the total balance of accounts receivable in the general ledger. A printout of the accounts receivable master file shows, by customer, the beginning balance in accounts receivable, each sales transaction, sales returns and allowances, cash receipts, and the ending balance. The term *master file* is used in this book to refer to either the computer file or a printout of that file. It is also sometimes called the accounts receivable subsidiary ledger or subledger.

Accounts Receivable Trial Balance A list of the amount owed by each customer at a point in time. This is prepared directly from the accounts receivable master file. It is most often an *aged* trial balance, showing how old the accounts receivable components of each customer's balance are as of the report date.

Monthly Statement A document sent by mail or electronically to each customer indicating the beginning balance of accounts receivable, the amount and date of each sale, cash payments received, credit memos issued, and the ending balance due. It is, in essence, a copy of the customer's portion of the accounts receivable master file.

Processing and Recording Cash Receipts

Dun & Bradstreet Services

The preceding four functions are necessary for getting the goods into the hands of customers, properly billing them, and reflecting the information in the accounting records. The result of these four functions is sales transactions. The remaining four functions involve the collection and recording of cash, sales returns and allowances, charge-off of uncollectible accounts, and providing for bad debt expense.

Processing and recording cash receipts includes receiving, depositing, and recording cash. Cash includes both currency and checks. The most important concern is the possibility of theft. Theft can occur before receipts are entered in the records or later. The most important consideration in the handling of cash receipts is that all cash must be deposited in the bank at the proper amount on a timely basis and recorded in the cash receipts transaction file, which is used to prepare the cash receipts journal and update the accounts receivable and general ledger master files. Remittance advices are important for this purpose.

Remittance Advice A document that accompanies the sales invoice mailed to the customer and can be returned to the seller with the cash payment. It is used to indicate the customer name, the sales invoice number, and the amount of the invoice when the payment is received. If the customer fails to include the remittance advice with the payment, it is common for the person opening the mail to prepare one at that time. A remittance advice is used to permit the immediate deposit of cash and to improve control over the custody of assets.

Prelisting of Cash Receipts A list prepared when cash is received by someone who has no responsibility for recording sales, accounts receivable, or cash and who has no access to accounting records. It is used to verify whether cash received was recorded and deposited at the correct amounts and on a timely basis.

Cash Receipts Transaction File A computer-generated file that includes all cash receipts transactions processed by the accounting system for a period, such as a day, week, or month. It includes the same type of information discussed for the sales transaction file.

LOCKBOX SYSTEMS AND ELECTRONIC FUNDS TRANSFER

Many companies engage a bank to assist in the processing of cash receipts from customers. Some companies use a lockbox system, whereby customers mail payments to an address maintained by bank personnel. The bank is responsible for opening all receipts, maintaining records of all payments by customers received at the lockbox address, and depositing receipts into the company's bank account on a timely basis. In other cases, receipts are submitted electronically from customers' bank accounts to a company bank account through the use of electronic funds transfer (EFT). For consumer purchases by credit card on Web sites, the issuer of the credit card uses EFT to transfer funds into the company's bank account almost immediately after the sale. For both lockbox systems and EFT, the bank provides information to the company to prepare the cash receipt entries in the company's accounting records. The use of both lockboxes and EFT allows for faster deposit of cash receipts into company bank accounts and often reduces risks associated with company personnel handling cash receipts.

Cash Receipts Journal or Listing A report generated from the cash receipts transaction file that includes all transactions for any time period. The same transactions, including all relevant information, are included in the accounts receivable master file and general ledger.

When a customer is dissatisfied with the goods, the seller often accepts the return of the goods or grants a reduction in the charges. The company normally prepares a receiving report for the returned goods and returns them to storage. Returns and allowances must be correctly and promptly recorded in the sales returns and allowances transaction file and the accounts receivable master file. Credit memos are normally issued for returns and allowances to aid in maintaining control and to facilitate record keeping.

Processing and Recording
Sales Returns
and Allowances

Credit Memo A document indicating a reduction in the amount due from a customer because of returned goods or an allowance granted. It often takes the same general form as a sales invoice, but it supports reductions in accounts receivable rather than increases.

Sales Returns and Allowances Journal A journal used to record sales returns and allowances. It performs the same function as the sales journal. Many companies record these transactions in the sales journal rather than in a separate journal.

Regardless of the diligence of credit departments, it is not unusual if some customers do not pay their bills. When the company concludes that an amount is no longer collectible, it must be charged off. Typically, this occurs after a customer files bankruptcy or the account is turned over to a collection agency. Proper accounting requires an adjustment for these uncollectible accounts.

Charging Off Uncollectible
Accounts Receivable

Uncollectible Account Authorization Form A document used internally to indicate authority to write an account receivable off as uncollectible.

The provision for bad debts must be sufficient to allow for the current period sales that the company will be unable to collect in the future. For most companies, the provision represents a residual, resulting from management's end-of-period adjustment of the allowance for uncollectible accounts.

Providing for Bad Debts

The Internet and other developing technologies allow companies to develop new business models to generate sales through electronic markets. Both existing companies and start-ups use the Internet to engage in business-to-business (B2B) and business-to-consumer (B2C) e-commerce. These Internet-based markets allow companies to expand sales of their products and services by interacting with customers around the world on a 24-hour, seven-day-per-week basis. These e-commerce models often allow companies to charge lower prices by eliminating traditional distributors and other middlemen from the sales distribution process. The Internet also provides additional sources of revenue, such as ads and sponsorships on company Web sites. These ad agreements are often complex, with fees based on the number of hits to the ad links. Other companies engage in barterlike transactions as payment for the exchange of goods and services.

Effect of E-commerce
on the Sales
and Collection Cycle

OBJECTIVE 14-3

Understand how e-commerce activities affect the sales and collection cycle.

Management's assertions for sales and collection activities remain the same, whether sales are generated through traditional or electronic markets. Management also continues to be responsible for adopting sound accounting policies and internal controls when engaging in e-commerce activities. In some companies, the online sales system is effectively integrated with the traditional sales system, while other companies create separate accounting systems and internal controls for online sales.

Auditors should obtain an understanding of the design and operation of key internal controls over e-commerce revenues as part of gaining an understanding of internal controls in the sales and collection cycle. Evidence for e-commerce activities is likely to be in electronic form. The auditor's tests of controls and substantive tests of transactions may therefore need to be modified to ensure that this electronic evidence is available for audit testing.

METHODOLOGY FOR DESIGNING TESTS OF CONTROLS AND SUBSTANTIVE TESTS OF TRANSACTIONS FOR SALES

OBJECTIVE 14-4

Understand internal control, and design and perform tests of controls and substantive tests of transactions for sales.

The account balances, classes of transactions, business functions, and related documents and records for the sales and collection cycle were described in earlier sections of this chapter. With this knowledge, it is now appropriate to study the design of tests of controls and substantive tests of transactions for each of the five classes of transactions in the cycle. This is the topic for the remainder of this chapter.

The methodology for obtaining an understanding of internal control and designing tests of controls and substantive tests of transactions for sales is shown in Figure 14-2. That methodology was studied in general terms in Chapters 10 and 13. It is applied specifically to sales in this section. The bottom box in Figure 14-2 shows the four evidence decisions the auditor must make. This section deals with deciding the appropriate audit procedures. The following sections deal with each of the parts in Figure 14-2, starting with gaining an understanding of internal control for sales.

Understand Internal Control—Sales

Chapter 10 discussed how auditors obtain an understanding of internal control. A typical approach for sales is to study the client's flowcharts, prepare an internal control questionnaire, and perform walkthrough tests of sales. The flowchart of the sales and cash receipts function for Hillsburg Hardware Co. in Figure 14-3 is used to demonstrate the design of tests of controls and substantive tests of transactions audit procedures.

Assess Planned Control Risk—Sales

The auditor uses the information obtained in understanding internal control to assess control risk. There are four essential steps to this assessment, all of which were discussed in Chapter 10.

1. First, the auditor needs a framework for assessing control risk. The framework for all classes of transactions is the six transaction-related audit objectives. For sales, these are shown for Hillsburg Hardware in Figure 10-5 on page 289. These six objectives are the same for every audit of sales.

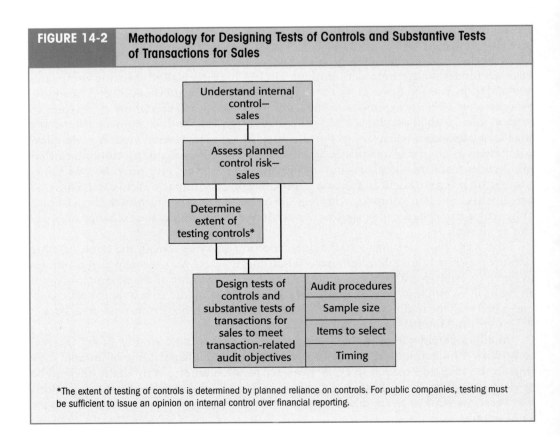

FIGURE 14-2   **Methodology for Designing Tests of Controls and Substantive Tests of Transactions for Sales**

Understand internal control— sales

Assess planned control risk— sales

Determine extent of testing controls*

Design tests of controls and substantive tests of transactions for sales to meet transaction-related audit objectives

Audit procedures

Sample size

Items to select

Timing

*The extent of testing of controls is determined by planned reliance on controls. For public companies, testing must be sufficient to issue an opinion on internal control over financial reporting.

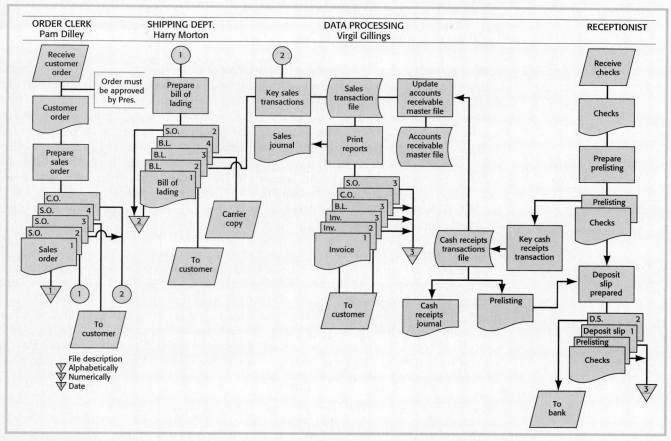

NOTES
1. All correspondence is sent to the president.
2. All sales order numbers are accounted for weekly by the controller.
3. All bills of lading numbers are accounted for weekly by the controller.
4. Sales amount recorded on sales invoice is based on standard price list. It is stored in the inventory master file and can be changed only with authorization of the controller.
5. Duplicate sales invoice is compared with bill of lading daily by Pam Dilley for descriptions and quantities and the sales invoice is reviewed for reasonableness of the extensions and footing. She initials a copy of the invoice before the original is mailed to the customer.
6. Sales are batched daily by Pam Dilley. The batch totals are compared with the sales journal weekly.
7. Statements are sent to customers monthly.
8. Accounts receivable master file total is compared with general ledger by the controller on a monthly basis.
9. Unpaid invoices are filed separately from paid invoices.
10. The receptionist stamps incoming checks with a restrictive endorsement immediately upon receipt.
11. There are no cash sales.
12. Deposits are made daily.
13. Cash receipts are batched daily by the receptionist. The batch totals are compared with the cash receipts journal weekly.
14. The bank account is reconciled by the controller on a monthly basis.
15. All bad debt expense and charge-off of bad debts are approved by the president after being initiated by the controller.
16. Financial statements are printed monthly by the controller and reviewed by the president.
17. All errors are reviewed daily by the controller immediately after the updating run. Corrections are made the same day.

2. Second, the auditor must identify the key internal controls and deficiencies for sales. These are also shown on page 289. The controls and deficiencies will be different for every audit. The controls and deficiencies for Hillsburg Hardware Co. were identified from the flowchart in Figure 14-3 and the internal control checklist in Figure 10-4 (p. 286).

3. After identifying the controls and deficiencies, the auditor associates them with the objectives. This is also shown in Figure 10-5 on page 289 with W's and C's in appropriate columns.

4. Finally, the auditor assesses control risk for each objective by evaluating the controls and deficiencies for each objective. This step is critical because it affects the

auditor's decisions about both tests of controls and substantive tests. It is a highly subjective decision. The bottom of page 289 shows the auditor's conclusions for Hillsburg Hardware.

We will now examine key control activities (see pp. 278–281) for sales. A knowledge of these control activities is important for identifying the key controls and deficiencies for sales, which were first discussed in Chapter 10.

Adequate Separation of Duties Proper separation of duties is useful to prevent various types of misstatements, both intentional and unintentional. To prevent fraud, it is important that anyone responsible for inputting sales and cash receipts transaction information into the computer be denied access to cash. It is also desirable to separate the credit-granting function from the sales function because credit checks are intended to offset the natural tendency of sales personnel to optimize volume even at the expense of high bad debt write-offs. It is equally desirable that personnel responsible for doing internal comparisons are independent of those entering the original data. For example, comparison of batch control totals with summary reports and comparison of accounts receivable master file totals with the general ledger balance should be done by someone independent of those who input sales and cash receipt transactions.

Proper Authorization The auditor is concerned about authorization at *three key points:* credit must be properly authorized before a sale takes place; goods should be shipped only after proper authorization; and prices, including basic terms, freight, and discounts, must be authorized. The first two controls are meant to prevent the loss of company assets by shipping to fictitious customers or those who will fail to pay for the goods. Price authorization is meant to ensure that the sale is billed at the price set by company policy. As discussed in Chapter 10 (pp. 279–280), authorization may be done for each individual transaction or general authorization may be given for specific classes of transactions. General authorizations are often done automatically by computer.

Adequate Documents and Records Because each company has a unique system of originating, processing, and recording transactions, it may be difficult to evaluate whether its procedures are designed for maximum control; nevertheless, adequate record-keeping procedures must exist before most of the transaction-related audit objectives can be met. Some companies, for example, automatically prepare a multicopy prenumbered sales invoice at the time a customer order is received. Copies of this document are used to approve credit, authorize shipment, record the number of units shipped, and bill customers. Under this system, there is almost no chance of the failure to bill a customer if all invoices are accounted for periodically. Under a different system, in which the sales invoice is prepared only after a shipment has been made, the likelihood of failure to bill a customer is high unless some compensating control exists.

Prenumbered Documents An important characteristic of documents for sales is the use of prenumbering, which is meant to prevent both the *failure* to bill or record sales and the occurrence of *duplicate* billings and recordings. Of course, it does not do much good to have prenumbered documents unless they are properly accounted for. An example of the use of this control is the filing, by a billing clerk, of a copy of all shipping documents in sequential order after each shipment is billed, with someone else periodically accounting for all numbers and investigating the reason for any missing documents. Another example is to program the computer to prepare a listing of unused numbers at month's end with follow-up by appropriate personnel.

Monthly Statements Sending monthly statements automatically by computer or by someone who has no responsibility for handling cash or preparing the sales and accounts receivable records is a useful control, because it encourages a response from customers if the balance is improperly stated. For maximum effectiveness, all disagreements about the balance in the account should be directed to a designated official who has no responsibility for handling cash or recording sales or accounts receivable.

Internal Verification Procedures The use of computer programs or independent persons for checking the processing and recording of sales transactions is essential for fulfilling each of the six transaction-related audit objectives. Examples of these procedures include accounting for the numerical sequence of prenumbered documents, checking the accuracy of document preparation, and reviewing reports for unusual or incorrect items.

After the auditor has identified the key internal controls and control deficiencies, control risk is assessed. For audits of public companies, the auditor must perform tests of key controls and evaluate the impact of the noted deficiencies on the auditor's report on internal control over financial reporting. For audits of nonpublic companies, the auditor must decide whether substantive tests will be reduced sufficiently to justify the cost of performing tests of controls. When practical, auditors of nonpublic companies make this decision before completing a matrix such as the one illustrated in Figure 10-5 on page 289. It makes little sense to incur the cost of identifying controls and assessing control risk below the maximum if there will be no reduction of substantive tests in the audit of nonpublic companies.

Determine Extent of Testing Controls

For each key control, one or more tests of controls must be designed to verify its effectiveness. In most audits, it is relatively easy to determine the nature of the test of the control from the nature of the control. For example, if the internal control is to initial customer orders after they have been approved for credit, the test of control is to examine the customer order for a proper initial.

Design Tests of Controls for Sales

The first three columns of Table 14-2 (pp. 420–421) illustrate the design of tests of controls for sales for Hillsburg Hardware Co. Column three in Table 14-2 shows one test of control for each key internal control in column two. Observe that Table 14-2 is organized by transaction-related audit objective. For example, the second key internal control for the existence objective is "sales are supported by authorized shipping documents and approved customer orders." The test of control is to "examine sales invoice for supporting bill of lading and customer order." For this test, the auditor should start with sales invoices and examine documents in support of the sales invoices rather than going in the opposite direction. If the auditor traced from shipping documents to sales invoices, it would be a test of completeness. Direction of tests is discussed further on page 422.

As shown in the third column of Table 14-2 for the completeness objective, a common test of control for sales is to account for a sequence of various types of documents. For example, accounting for a sequence of shipping documents and tracing each one to the duplicate sales invoice and recording in the sales journal provides evidence of completeness.

Accounting for the sequence of sales invoices selected from the sales journal and watching for omitted and duplicate numbers or invoices outside the normal sequence is a test that simultaneously provides evidence of both the existence and completeness objectives. As an illustration, assume that the auditor selects sales invoices #18100 to #18199. The completeness objective will be partially satisfied if all 100 sales invoices are recorded. The existence objective will be satisfied if there is no duplicate recording of any of the invoice numbers. As indicated in Table 14-2, the lack of verification to prevent the possibility of duplicate recording of sales invoices is a deficiency at the Hillsburg Hardware Co.

The appropriate tests of controls for separation of duties are ordinarily restricted to the auditor's observations of activities and discussions with personnel. For example, it is possible to observe whether the billing clerk has access to cash when incoming mail is opened or cash is deposited. It is usually also necessary to ask personnel what their responsibilities are and if there are any circumstances where their responsibilities are different from the normal policy. For example, the employee responsible for billing customers may state that he or she does not have access to cash. Further discussion may bring out that when the cashier is on vacation, that person takes over the cashier's duties.

Transaction-Related Audit Objective	Key Existing Control*	Test of Control†	Deficiencies*	Substantive Tests of Transactions†
Recorded sales are for shipments actually made to customers (existence).	Credit is approved automatically by computer by comparison to authorized credit limits (C1). Sales are supported by authorized shipping documents and approved customer orders (C2). Batch totals of quantities shipped are compared with quantities billed (C6). Statements are sent to customers each month (C9).	Examine customer order for evidence of customer approval (13e). Examine sales invoice for supporting bill of lading and customer order (13b). Examine file of batch totals for initials of data control clerk (8). Observe whether monthly statements are sent (6).	There is a lack of internal verification for the possibility of sales invoices being recorded more than once (W1).	Account for a sequence of sales invoices (12). Review sales journal and master file for unusual transactions and amounts (1). Trace sales journal entries to supporting documents, including duplicate sales invoice, bill of lading, sales order, and customer order (14).
Existing sales transactions are recorded (completeness).	Shipping documents are prenumbered and accounted for weekly (C5). Batch totals of quantities shipped are compared with quantities billed (C6).	Account for a sequence of shipping documents (10). Examine file of batch totals for initials of data control clerk (8).		Trace selected shipping documents to the sales journal to be sure that each one is included (11).
Recorded sales are for the amount of goods shipped and are correctly billed and recorded (accuracy).	Sales are supported by authorized shipping documents and approved customer orders (C2). Batch totals of quantities shipped are compared with quantities billed (C6). Unit selling prices are obtained from the price list master file of approved prices (C7). Statements are sent to customers each month (C9).	Examine sales invoice for supporting documents (13b). Examine file of batch totals for initials of data control clerk (8). Examine the approved price list for accuracy and proper authorization (9). Observe whether monthly statements are sent (6).		Trace entries in sales journal to sales invoices (13). Recompute prices and extensions on sales invoices (13b). Trace details on sales invoices to · shipping documents (13c) · sales order (13d) · customer order (13e)
Sales transactions are properly classified (classification).	Account classifications are internally verified (C8).	Examine document package for internal verification (13b).		Examine duplicate sales invoice for proper account classification (13b).
Sales are recorded on the correct dates (timing).	Shipping documents are prenumbered and accounted for weekly by the accountant (C5).	Account for a sequence of shipping documents (10).	There is a lack of control to test for timely recording (W2).	Compare date of recording of sale in sales journal with duplicate sales invoice and bill of lading (13b and 13c).

(cont. on p. 421)

TABLE 14-2	(Cont.)				

Transaction-Related Audit Objective	Key Existing Control*	Test of Control†	Deficiencies*	Substantive Tests of Transactions†
Sales transactions are properly included in the accounts receivable master file and are correctly summarized (posting and summarization).	Computer automatically posts transactions to the accounts receivable master file and general ledger (C10). Accounts receivable master file is reconciled to the general ledger on a monthly basis (C11). Statements are sent to customers each month (C9).	Examine evidence that accounts receivable master file is reconciled to the general ledger (7). Examine evidence that accounts receivable master file is reconciled to the general ledger (7). Observe whether monthly statements are sent (6).		Trace selected sales invoices from the sales journal to the accounts receivable master file and test for amount, date, and invoice number (13a). Use audit software to foot and cross-foot the sales journal and trace totals to the general ledger (2).

*Controls (C) and Deficiencies (W) are from the control matrix for sales in Figure 10-5 (p. 289). Controls C3 and C4 from the control matrix are not included here.
† The number in parentheses after each test of control and substantive test of transaction refers to an audit procedure in the performance format audit program in Figure 14-6 (p. 430).

Several of the tests of controls in Table 14-2 can be performed using the computer. For example, the auditor can test whether credit is properly authorized by the computer by attempting to initiate transactions that exceed a customer's credit limit. If the control is working effectively, the proposed sales order should be rejected. The existence of sales can be similarly tested by attempting to input nonexistent customer numbers, which should be rejected by the computer. This latter control is a key control for preventing fictitious sales.

Design Substantive Tests of Transactions for Sales

In deciding on substantive tests of transactions, some procedures are commonly used on every audit regardless of the circumstances, whereas others are dependent on the adequacy of the controls and the results of the tests of controls. In Table 14-2, the substantive tests of transactions in column 5 are related to the transaction-related audit objectives in the first column and are designed to determine whether any monetary misstatements for that objective exist in the transaction. The audit procedures used are affected by the internal controls and tests of controls for that objective. Materiality, results of the prior year, and the other factors discussed in Chapter 9 also affect the procedures used. Some of the audit procedures used when internal controls are inadequate are discussed in a later section.

Determining the proper substantive tests of transactions procedures for sales is relatively difficult because they vary considerably depending on the circumstances. In subsequent paragraphs, the procedures often *not* performed are emphasized because they are the ones requiring an audit decision. The substantive tests of transactions procedures are discussed in the order of the sales transaction-related audit objectives in Table 14-2. It should be noted that some procedures fulfill more than one objective.

Recorded Sales Exist For this objective, the auditor is concerned with the possibility of *three types of misstatements:* sales being included in the journals for which no shipment was made, sales recorded more than once, and shipments being made to nonexistent customers and recorded as sales. The first two types of misstatements can be intentional or unintentional. The last type is always intentional. The potential consequences are significant because they lead to an overstatement of assets and income.

There is an important difference between finding intentional and unintentional overstatements of sales. An unintentional overstatement normally also results in a clear overstatement of accounts receivable, which can often be easily found through confirmation procedures. For fraud, the perpetrator will attempt to conceal the overstatement, making it more difficult for auditors to find. Substantive tests of transactions may be necessary to discover overstated sales in these circumstances.

The appropriate substantive tests of transactions for testing the existence objective depend on where the auditor believes the misstatements are likely to take place. Many auditors do substantive tests of transactions for the existence objective only if they believe that a control deficiency exists; therefore, the nature of the tests depends on the nature of the potential misstatement as follows:

Recorded Sale for Which There Was No Shipment The auditor can trace from selected entries in the sales journal to make sure that related copies of the shipping and other supporting documents exist. If the auditor is concerned about the possibility of a fictitious duplicate copy of a shipping document, it may be necessary to trace the amounts to the perpetual inventory records as a test of whether inventory was reduced.

Sale Recorded More Than Once Duplicate sales can be determined by reviewing a numerically sorted list of recorded sales transactions for duplicate numbers. The auditor can also test for the proper cancellation of shipping documents. Proper cancellation decreases the likelihood that a shipping document will be used to record another sale.

Shipment Made to Nonexistent Customers This type of fraud normally occurs only when the person recording sales is also in a position to authorize shipments. When internal controls are weak, it is difficult to detect fictitious shipments.

Another effective approach to detecting the three types of misstatements of sales transactions discussed previously is to trace the *credit* in the accounts receivable master file to its source. If the receivable was actually collected in cash or the goods were returned, there must originally have been a sale. If the credit was for a bad debt charge-off or a credit memo or if the account was still unpaid at the time of the audit, intensive follow-up by examining shipping and customer order documents is required because each of these could indicate an inappropriate sales transaction.

SAS 99 indicates that the auditor should normally identify improper revenue recognition as a fraud risk. However, the preceding substantive tests of transactions should be necessary only if the auditor is concerned about the occurrence of fraud because of inadequate controls.

Existing Sales Transactions Are Recorded In many audits, no substantive tests of transactions are made for the completeness objective on the grounds that overstatements of assets and income are a greater concern in the audit of sales transactions than their understatement. If controls are inadequate, which is likely if the client does no independent internal tracing from shipping documents to the sales journal, substantive tests are necessary.

An effective procedure to test for unbilled shipments is to trace selected shipping documents from a file in the shipping department to related duplicate sales invoices and the sales journal. To conduct a meaningful test using this procedure, the auditor must be confident that all shipping documents are included in the file. This can be done by accounting for a numerical sequence of the documents.

Direction of Tests It is important that auditors understand the difference between tracing from source documents to the journals and tracing from the journals back to source documents. The former is a test for *omitted transactions* (completeness objective), whereas the latter is a test for *nonexistent transactions* (existence objective).

In testing for the existence objective, the starting point is the journal. A sample of invoice numbers is selected *from* the journal and traced *to* duplicate sales invoices, shipping documents, and customer orders. In testing for the completeness objective, the likely starting point is the shipping document. A sample of shipping documents is selected and traced *to* duplicate sales invoices and the sales journal as a test of omissions.

When designing audit procedures for the existence and completeness objectives, the starting point for tracing the document is essential. This is called the direction of tests. For example, if the auditor is concerned about the existence objective but traces in the wrong direction (from shipping documents to the journals), a serious audit deficiency exists. The direction of tests is illustrated in Figure 14-4.

FIGURE 14-4

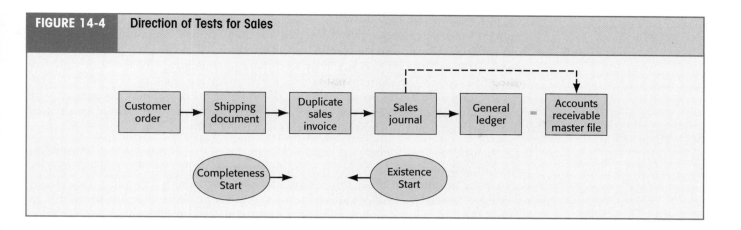

FIGURE 14-4   Direction of Tests for Sales

In testing for the other four transaction-related audit objectives, the direction of tests is usually not relevant. For example, the accuracy of sales transactions can be tested by tracing from a duplicate sales invoice to a shipping document or vice versa.

Sales Are Accurately Recorded The accurate recording of sales transactions concerns shipping the amount of goods ordered, accurately billing for the amount of goods shipped, and accurately recording the amount billed in the accounting records. Substantive tests to ensure that each of these aspects of accuracy is correct are ordinarily conducted in every audit.

Typical substantive tests of transactions include recomputing information in the accounting records to verify whether it is proper. A common approach is to start with entries in the sales journal and compare the total of selected transactions with accounts receivable master file entries and duplicate sales invoices. Prices on the duplicate sales invoices are normally compared with an approved price list, extensions and footings are recomputed, and the details listed on the invoices are compared with shipping records for description, quantity, and customer identification. Often, customer orders and sales orders are also examined for the same information.

The comparison of tests of controls and substantive tests of transactions for the accuracy objective is a good example of how audit time can be saved when effective internal controls exist. It is obvious that the test of control for this objective takes almost no time because it involves examining only an initial or other evidence of internal verification. Because the sample size for substantive tests of transactions can be reduced if this control is effective, a significant savings will result from performing the test of control because of its lower cost.

When sales invoices are automatically calculated and posted by a computer, the auditor may be able to reduce substantive tests of transactions for the accuracy objective. If the auditor determines that the computer is programmed accurately and the price list master file is authorized and correct, detailed invoice computations can be reduced or eliminated. In this case, the auditor focuses on determining that effective computer controls exist to ensure that the computer is properly programmed and has not been altered since it was last tested by the auditor.

Recorded Sales Are Properly Classified Charging the correct general ledger account is less of a problem in sales than in some other transaction cycles, but it is still of some concern. When there are cash and credit sales, it is important not to debit accounts receivable for a cash sale or to credit sales for collection of a receivable. It is also important not to classify sales of operating assets, such as buildings, as sales. For those companies using more than one sales classification, such as companies issuing segmented earnings statements, proper classification is essential.

It is common to test sales for proper classification as part of testing for accuracy. The auditor examines supporting documents to determine the proper classification of a given transaction and compares this with the actual account to which it is charged.

Sales Are Recorded on the Correct Dates Sales should be billed and recorded as soon after shipment takes place as possible to prevent the unintentional omission of transactions from the records and to make sure that sales are recorded in the proper period. Timely recorded transactions are also less likely to contain misstatements. At the same time that substantive tests of transactions procedures for accuracy are being performed, it is common to compare the date on selected bills of lading or other shipping documents with the date on related duplicate sales invoices, the sales journal, and the accounts receivable master file. Significant differences indicate a potential cutoff problem.

Sales Transactions Are Properly Included in the Master File and Correctly Summarized The proper inclusion of all sales transactions in the accounts receivable master file is essential because the accuracy of these records affects the client's ability to collect outstanding receivables. Similarly, the sales journal must be correctly totaled and posted to the general ledger if the financial statements are to be correct. In most audits, it is common to perform some clerical accuracy tests such as footing the journals and tracing the totals and details to the general ledger and the master file to check whether there are intentional or unintentional misstatements in the processing of sales transactions. The extent of such tests is affected by the quality of the internal controls and can often be performed using spreadsheet or generalized audit software. Tracing from the sales journal to the master file is typically done as a part of fulfilling other transaction-related audit objectives, but footing the sales journal and tracing the totals to the general ledger is done as a separate procedure.

The distinction between posting and summarization and other transaction-related audit objectives is that posting and summarization includes footing journals, master file records, and ledgers and tracing from one to the other among these three. When footing and comparisons are restricted to these three records, the process is posting and summarization. In contrast, accuracy involves determining the monetary correctness of transactions and comparing amounts between documents or with journals and master file records. To illustrate, comparing a duplicate sales invoice with either the sales journal or master file entry is an accuracy objective procedure. Tracing an entry from the sales journal to the master file is a posting and summarization procedure.

Summary of Methodology for Sales

Figure 14-2 and Table 14-2 provide summaries of the previous discussion. Figure 14-2 (p. 416) shows the methodology for designing tests of controls and substantive tests of transactions for sales. Table 14-2 (pp. 420–421) combines the four parts of the previous discussion.

Transaction-Related Audit Objectives (Column 1) The transaction-related audit objectives included in the table are derived from the framework developed in Chapters 6 and 10. Although certain internal controls satisfy more than one objective, it is desirable to consider each objective separately to facilitate a better assessment of control risk.

Key Existing Controls (Column 2) The internal controls for sales are designed to achieve the six transaction-related audit objectives discussed in Chapters 6 and 10. If the controls necessary to satisfy any one of the objectives are inadequate, the likelihood of misstatements related to that objective is increased, regardless of the controls for the other objectives. The methodology for determining existing controls was studied in Chapter 10.

The source of the controls in column 2 is the controls from a control risk matrix such as the one illustrated in Figure 10-5 (p. 289). A control will be included in more than one row in Table 14-2 if there is more than one C for that control on the control risk matrix.

Tests of Controls (Column 3) For each internal control in column 2, the auditor designs a test of control to verify its effectiveness. Observe that the tests of controls in Table 14-2 relate directly to the internal controls. For each control, there should be at least one test of control. Test of controls will be performed in all audits of public companies.

Deficiencies (Column 4) Deficiencies identified by the auditor indicate the absence of effective controls. As discussed in Chapter 10, the auditor should evaluate control deficiencies by considering potential misstatements that could occur and any compensating controls. One response in a financial statement audit to a deficiency in internal control is to expand substantive tests of transactions to determine whether the deficiency resulted in a significant number of misstatements.

Substantive Tests of Transactions (Column 5) The purpose of these tests is to determine whether there are monetary misstatements in sales transactions. In Table 14-2, the substantive tests of transactions are related to the objectives in the first column.

It is essential to understand the relationships among the columns in Table 14-2. The first column includes the six transaction-related audit objectives. The general objectives are the same for any class of transactions, but the specific objectives vary for sales, cash receipts, or any other classes of transactions. Column 2 lists one or more illustrative internal controls *for each transaction-related audit objective.* It is essential that any given control be related to one or more specific objective(s). Next, each common test of control in column 3 relates *to a given internal control.* A test of control has no meaning unless it tests a specific control. The table contains at least one test of control in column 3 for each internal control in column 2. Finally, the common substantive tests of transactions in the table's last column are evidence to support *a specific transaction-related audit objective* in column 1. The substantive tests of transactions are not directly related to the key control or test of control columns, but the extent of substantive tests of transactions depends, in part, on which key controls exist and on results of the tests of controls.

The information presented in Table 14-2 is intended to help auditors design audit programs that satisfy the transaction-related audit objectives in a given set of circumstances. If certain objectives are important in a given audit or when the controls are different for different clients, the methodology helps the auditor design an effective and efficient audit program.

After the appropriate audit procedures for a given set of circumstances have been designed, they must be performed. It is likely to be inefficient to do the audit procedures as they are stated in the design format of Table 14-2. In converting from a **design format audit program** to a **performance format audit program,** procedures are combined. This will do the following:

- Eliminate duplicate procedures.
- Make sure that when a given document is examined, all procedures to be performed on that document are done at that time.
- Enable the auditor to do the procedures in the most effective order. For example, by footing the journal and reviewing the journal for unusual items first, the auditor gains a better perspective in doing the detailed tests.

The process of converting from a design to a performance format is illustrated in Figure 14-6 (page 430) for Hillsburg Hardware.

Design and Performance Format Audit Procedures

SALES RETURNS AND ALLOWANCES

The transaction-related audit objectives and the client's methods of controlling misstatements are essentially the same for processing credit memos as those described for sales, with two important differences. The first relates to *materiality.* In many instances, sales returns and allowances are so immaterial that they can be ignored in the audit altogether. The second major difference relates to *emphasis on objectives.* For sales returns and allowances, the primary emphasis is normally on testing the existence of recorded transactions as a means of uncovering any diversion of cash from the collection of accounts receivable that has been covered up by a fictitious sales return or allowance.

Although the emphasis for the audit of sales returns and allowances is often on testing the existence of recorded transactions, the *completeness* objective is especially important at year-end. Unrecorded sales returns and allowances can be material and can be used by

OBJECTIVE 14-5

Apply the methodology for controls over sales transactions to controls over sales returns and allowances.

a company's management to overstate net income. The extent of sales returns and potential liability at year-end varies greatly by industry. Sales returns for mail-order and Web-site sales are typically higher than for in-store sales because the purchaser is not able to physically examine the merchandise prior to purchasing.

Naturally, the other objectives should not be ignored. But because the objectives and methodology for auditing sales returns and allowances are essentially the same as for sales, we will not include a detailed study of the area. The reader should be able to apply the same logic to arrive at suitable controls, tests of controls, and substantive tests of transactions to verify the amounts.

METHODOLOGY FOR DESIGNING TESTS OF CONTROLS AND SUBSTANTIVE TESTS OF TRANSACTIONS FOR CASH RECEIPTS

OBJECTIVE 14-6

Understand internal control, and design and perform tests of controls and substantive tests of transactions for cash receipts.

The same methodology used for designing tests of controls and substantive tests of transactions for sales is used for cash receipts. Similarly, cash receipts tests of controls and substantive tests of transactions audit procedures are developed around the same framework used for sales; that is, given the transaction-related audit objectives, key internal controls for each objective are determined, tests of control are developed for each control, and substantive tests of transactions for the monetary misstatements related to each objective are developed. As in all other audit areas, the tests of controls depend on the controls the auditor has identified, the extent they will be relied on to reduce assessed control risk, and whether the company being audited is publicly traded. Figure 14-5 is the control risk matrix for cash receipts for Hillsburg Hardware. It is based on the information in the sales and cash receipts flowchart in Figure 14-3 (p. 417).

Key internal controls, common tests of controls, and common substantive tests of transactions to satisfy each of the transaction-related audit objectives for cash receipts are listed in Table 14-3 (pp. 428–429) for Hillsburg Hardware Co. Because this summary follows the same format as the previous one for sales, no further explanation of its meaning is necessary. The tests of controls and substantive tests of transactions for cash receipts are combined with those for sales in the performance format audit program in Figure 14-6 (p. 430).

The detailed discussion of the internal controls, tests of controls, and substantive tests of transactions that was included for the audit of sales is not included for cash receipts. Instead, the audit procedures that are most likely to be misunderstood are explained in more detail.

An essential part of the auditor's responsibility in auditing cash receipts is identification of deficiencies in internal control that increase the likelihood of fraud. In expanding on Table 14-3, the emphasis will be on those audit procedures that are designed primarily for the discovery of fraud. Those procedures that are not discussed are omitted only because their purpose and the methodology for applying them should be apparent from their description.

	CASH RECEIPTS TRANSACTION-RELATED AUDIT OBJECTIVES					
INTERNAL CONTROL	Recorded cash receipts are for funds actually received by the company (existence).	Cash received is recorded in the cash receipts journal (completeness).	Cash receipts are deposited at the amount received (accuracy).	Cash receipts transactions are properly classified (classification).	Cash receipts are recorded on the correct dates (timing).	Cash receipts are properly included in the accounts receivable master file and are correctly summarized (posting and summarization).
Accountant independently reconciles bank account (C1).	C		C			
Prelisting of cash receipts is prepared (C2).		C				
Checks are restrictively endorsed (C3).		C				
Batch totals of cash receipts are compared with computer summary reports (C4).	C	C	C			
Statements are sent to customers each month (C5).		C	C			C
Cash receipts transactions are internally verified (C6).				C		
Procedures require recording of cash on a daily basis (C7).					C	
Computer automatically posts transactions to the accounts receivable subsidiary records and to the general ledger (C8).						C
Accounts receivable master file is reconciled to the general ledger on a monthly basis (C9).						C
DEFICIENCY Prelisting of cash is not used to verify recorded cash receipts (W1).		W				
Assessed control risk	Low	Medium	Low	Low	Low	Low

(Left margin labels: CONTROLS, DEFICIENCY)

C = Control; W = Significant deficiency or material weakness

The most difficult type of cash defalcation for the auditor to detect is that which occurs *before the cash is recorded* in the cash receipts journal or other cash listing, especially if the sale and cash receipt are recorded simultaneously. For example, if a grocery store clerk takes cash and intentionally fails to process the receipt of cash on the cash register, it is

Determine Whether Cash Received Was Recorded

extremely difficult to discover the theft. To prevent this type of fraud, internal controls such as those included in the second objective in Table 14-3 are implemented by many companies. The type of control will, of course, depend on the type of business. For example, the controls for a retail store in which the cash is received by the same person who sells the merchandise and rings up the cash receipts should be different from the controls for a company in which all receipts are received through the mail several weeks after the sales have taken place.

It is normal practice to trace from prenumbered remittance advices or prelists of cash receipts to the cash receipts journal and subsidiary accounts receivable records as a substantive test of the recording of actual cash received. This test will be effective only if a cash register tape or some other prelisting was prepared at the time cash was received.

Prepare Proof of Cash Receipts

A useful audit procedure to test whether all recorded cash receipts have been deposited in the bank account is a **proof of cash receipts.** In this test, the total cash receipts recorded in the cash receipts journal for a given period, such as a month, are reconciled with the actual deposits made to the bank during the same period. There may be a difference in the two as a result of deposits in transit and other items, but the amounts can be reconciled and compared. The procedure is not useful in discovering cash receipts that have not been

TABLE 14-3	Transaction-Related Audit Objectives, Key Existing Controls, Tests of Controls, Deficiencies, and Substantive Tests of Transactions for Cash Receipts—Hillsburg Hardware Co.				
Transaction-Related Audit Objective	Key Existing Control*	Test of Control†	Deficiencies*	Substantive Tests of Transactions†	
Recorded cash receipts are for funds actually received by the company (existence).	Accountant independently reconciles bank account (C1). Batch totals of cash receipts are compared with computer summary reports (C4).	Observe whether accountant reconciles bank account (3). Examine file of batch totals for initials of data control clerk (8).		Review cash receipts journal and master file for unusual transactions and amounts (1). Trace cash receipts entries from the cash receipts journal entries to the bank statement (19). Prepare a proof of cash receipts (18).	
Cash received is recorded in the cash receipts journal (completeness).	Prelisting of cash receipts is prepared (C2). Checks are restrictively endorsed (C3). Batch totals of cash receipts are compared with computer summary reports (C4). Statements are sent to customers each month (C5).	Observe prelisting of cash receipts (4). Observe endorsement of incoming checks (5). Examine file of batch totals for initials of data control clerk (8). Observe whether monthly statements are sent (6).	Prelisting of cash is not used to verify recorded cash receipts (W1).	Obtain prelisting of cash receipts and trace amounts to the cash receipts journal, testing for names, amounts, and dates (15). Compare the prelisting with the duplicate deposit slip (16).	
Cash receipts are deposited and recorded at the amounts received (accuracy).	Accountant independently reconciles bank account (C1). Batch totals of cash receipts are compared with computer summary reports (C4). Statements are sent to customers each month (C5).	Observe whether accountant reconciles bank account (3). Examine file of batch totals for initials of data control clerk (8). Observe whether monthly statements are sent (6).		Obtain prelisting of cash receipts and trace amounts to the cash receipts journal, testing for names, amounts, and dates (15). Prepare proof of cash receipts (18).	

(cont. on p. 429)

TABLE 14-3   **(Cont.)**

Transaction-Related Audit Objective	Key Existing Control*	Test of Control†	Deficiencies*	Substantive Tests of Transactions†
Cash receipts transactions are properly classified (classification).	Cash receipts transactions are internally verified (C6).	Examine evidence of internal verification (15).		Examine prelisting for proper account classification (17).
Cash receipts are recorded on the correct dates (timing).	Procedures require recording of cash on a daily basis (C7).	Observe unrecorded cash at a point in time (4).		Compare date of deposit per bank statement to the dates in the cash receipts journal and prelisting of cash receipts (16).
Cash receipts are properly included in the accounts receivable master file and are correctly summarized (posting and summarization).	Statements are sent to customers each month (C5). Computer automatically posts transactions to the accounts receivable master file and general ledger (C8). Accounts receivable master file is reconciled to the general ledger on a monthly basis (C9).	Observe whether monthly statements are sent (6). Examine evidence that accounts receivable master file is reconciled to general ledger (7). Examine evidence that accounts receivable master file is reconciled to general ledger (7).		Trace selected entries from the cash receipts journal to the accounts receivable master file and test for dates and amounts (20). Trace selected credits from the accounts receivable master file to the cash receipts journal and test for dates and amounts (21). Use audit software to foot and cross-foot the sales journal and trace totals to the general ledger (2).

*Controls (C) and Deficiencies (W) are from control matrix for cash receipts in Figure 14-5 (p. 427)
†The number in parentheses after each test of control and substantive test of transaction refers to an audit procedure in the performance format audit program in Figure 14-6 (p. 430).

recorded in the journals or time lags in making deposits, but it can help uncover recorded cash receipts that have not been deposited, unrecorded deposits, unrecorded loans, bank loans deposited directly into the bank account, and similar misstatements. This somewhat time-consuming procedure is ordinarily used only when the controls are deficient. In rare instances in which controls are extremely weak, the period covered by the proof of cash receipts may be the entire year.

Lapping of accounts receivable is the postponement of entries for the collection of receivables to *conceal an existing cash shortage.* The defalcation is perpetrated by a person who handles cash receipts and then enters them into the computer system. He or she defers recording the cash receipts from one customer and covers the shortages with receipts of another. These in turn are covered from the receipts of a third customer a few days later. The employee must continue to cover the shortage through repeated lapping, replace the stolen money, or find another way to conceal the shortage.

Test to Discover Lapping of Accounts Receivable

This defalcation can be easily prevented by separation of duties and a mandatory vacation policy for employees who both handle cash and enter cash receipts into the system. It can be detected by comparing the name, amount, and dates shown on remittance advices with cash receipts journal entries and related duplicate deposit slips. Because the procedure is relatively time-consuming, it is ordinarily performed only when there is specific concern with defalcation because of a deficiency in internal control.

FIGURE 14-6	Audit Program for Tests of Controls and Substantive Tests of Transactions for Sales and Cash Receipts for Hillsburg Hardware Co. (Performance Format)

HILLSBURG HARDWARE CO.
Tests of Controls and Substantive Tests of Transactions Audit Procedures for Sales and Cash Receipts
(Sample size and the items in the sample are not included.)
General

1. Review journals and master file for unusual transactions and amounts.
2. Use audit software to foot and cross-foot the sales and cash receipts journals and trace the totals to the general ledger.
3. Observe whether accountant reconciles the bank account.
4. Observe whether cash is prelisted and the existence of any unrecorded cash.
5. Observe whether restrictive endorsement is used on cash receipts.
6. Observe whether monthly statements are sent.
7. Observe whether accountant compares master file total with general ledger account.
8. Examine file of batch totals for initials of data control clerk.
9. Examine the approved price list in the inventory master file for accuracy and proper authorization.

Shipment of Goods

10. Account for a sequence of shipping documents.
11. Trace selected shipping documents to the sales journal to be sure that each one has been included.

Billing of Customers and Recording the Sales in the Records

12. Account for a sequence of sales invoices in the sales journal.
13. Trace selected sales invoice numbers from the sales journal to
    a. accounts receivable master file and test for amount, date, and invoice number.
    b. duplicate sales invoice and check for the total amount recorded in the journal, date, customer name, and account classification. Check the pricing, extensions, and footings. Examine underlying documents for indication of internal verification.
    c. bill of lading and test for customer name, product description, quantity, and date.
    d. duplicate sales order and test for customer name, product description, quantity, date, and indication of internal verification.
    e. customer order and test for customer name, product description, quantity, date, and credit approval.
14. Trace recorded sales from the sales journal to the file of supporting documents, which includes a duplicate sales invoice, bill of lading, sales order, and customer order.

Processing Cash Receipts and Recording the Amounts in the Records

15. Obtain the prelisting of cash receipts and trace amounts to the cash receipts journal, testing for names, amounts, dates, and internal verification.
16. Compare the prelisting of cash receipts with the duplicate deposit slip, testing for names, amounts, and dates. Trace the total from the cash receipts journal to the bank statement, testing for a delay in deposit.
17. Examine prelisting for proper account classification.
18. Prepare a proof of cash receipts.
19. Trace cash receipt entries from the cash receipts journal to the bank statement, testing for dates and amounts of deposits.
20. Trace selected entries from the cash receipts journal to entries in the accounts receivable master file and test for dates and amounts.
21. Trace selected credits from the accounts receivable master file to the cash receipts journal and test for dates and amounts.

AUDIT TESTS FOR UNCOLLECTIBLE ACCOUNTS

OBJECTIVE 14-7

Apply the methodology for controls over the sales and collection cycle to write-offs of uncollectible accounts receivable.

Existence of recorded write-offs is the most important transaction-related audit objective that the auditor should keep in mind in the verification of the write-off of individual uncollectible accounts. A major concern in testing accounts charged off as uncollectible is the possibility of the client covering up a defalcation by charging off accounts receivable that have already been collected. The major control for preventing this type of misstatement is proper authorization of the write-off of uncollectible accounts by a designated level of management only after a thorough investigation of the reason the customer has not paid.

Normally, verification of the accounts charged off takes relatively little time. A typical procedure is the examination of approvals by the appropriate persons. For a sample of accounts charged off, it is also usually necessary for the auditor to examine correspondence in the client's files establishing their uncollectibility. In some cases, the auditor will also examine credit reports such as those provided by Dun & Bradstreet. After the auditor has concluded that the accounts charged off by general journal entries are proper, selected items should be traced to the accounts receivable master file as a test of the records.

ADDITIONAL INTERNAL CONTROLS OVER ACCOUNT BALANCES

The preceding discussion emphasized internal controls, tests of controls, and substantive tests of transactions for the five classes of transactions that affect account balances in the sales and collection cycle. If the internal controls for these classes of transactions are determined to be effective and the related substantive tests of transactions support the conclusions, the likelihood of misstatements in the financial statements is reduced.

In addition, there may be internal controls directly related to account balances that have not been identified or tested as a part of tests of controls or substantive tests of transactions. For the sales and collection cycle, these are most likely to affect three balance-related audit objectives: realizable value, rights and obligations, and presentation and disclosure.

Realizable value is an essential balance-related audit objective for accounts receivable because collectibility of receivables is often a major financial statement item and has been an issue in a number of accountants' liability cases. Therefore, it is common for inherent risk to be high for the realizable value objective. Several controls are common for the realizable value objective. One that has already been discussed is credit approval by an appropriate person. A second is the preparation of a periodic aged accounts receivable trial balance for review and follow-up by appropriate management personnel. A third control is a policy of charging off uncollectible accounts when they are no longer likely to be collected.

Rights and obligations and presentation and disclosure are rarely a significant problem for accounts receivable. Therefore, competent accounting personnel are typically sufficient controls for these two balance-related audit objectives.

EFFECT OF RESULTS OF TESTS OF CONTROLS AND SUBSTANTIVE TESTS OF TRANSACTIONS

The results of the tests of controls and substantive tests of transactions will have a significant effect on the remainder of the audit, especially on the substantive tests of details of balances. The parts of the audit most affected by the tests of controls and substantive tests of transactions for the sales and collection cycle are the balances in *accounts receivable, cash, bad debt expense,* and *allowance for doubtful accounts.* Furthermore, if the test results are unsatisfactory, it is necessary to do additional substantive testing for the propriety of sales, sales returns and allowances, charge-off of uncollectible accounts, and processing of cash receipts. Auditors of public companies must also consider the impact of the unsatisfactory test results on the audit of internal control over financial reporting.

At the completion of the tests of controls and substantive tests of transactions, it is essential to *analyze each exception* to determine its cause and the implication of the exception on assessed control risk, which may affect the supported detection risk and thereby the remaining substantive tests. The methodology and implications of exceptions analysis are explained more fully in the next chapter.

The most significant effect of the results of the tests of controls and substantive tests of transactions in the sales and collection cycle is on the confirmation of accounts receivable. The type of confirmation, the size of the sample, and the timing of the test are all affected. The effect of the tests on accounts receivable, bad debt expense, and allowance for uncollectible accounts is considered in Chapter 16.

Figure 14-7 (p. 432) illustrates the major accounts in the sales and collection cycle and the types of audit tests used to audit these accounts. This figure was introduced in the last chapter (p. 372) and is presented here for further review.

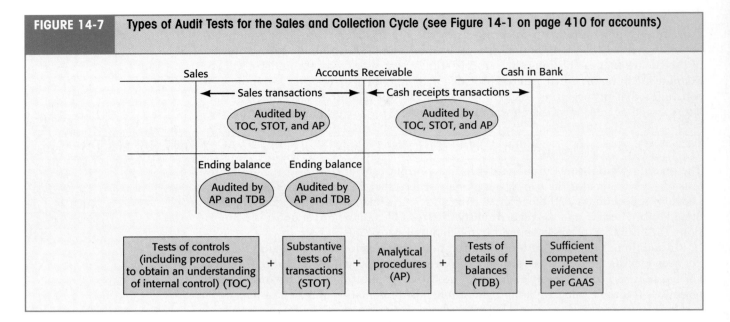

SUMMARY

This chapter deals with designing tests of controls and substantive tests of transactions for each of the five classes of transactions in the sales and collection cycle. The classes of transactions in the cycle are sales, cash receipts, sales returns and allowances, charge-off of uncollectible accounts receivable, and bad debt expense.

The methodology for designing tests of controls and substantive tests of transactions is, in concept, the same for each of the five classes of transactions and includes the following steps:

- Understand internal control
- Assess planned control risk
- Determine the extent of testing controls
- Design tests of controls and substantive tests of transactions to meet transaction-related audit objectives

In designing tests of controls, the emphasis for each class of transactions is on testing internal controls that the auditor intends to rely on to reduce control risk or that the auditor must test to be able to issue an opinion on internal control over financial reporting for a public company. First, the auditor identifies internal controls, if any exist, for each transaction-related audit objective. After assessing control risk for each objective, the auditor then determines the extent of tests of controls that must be performed. For audits of public companies, extensive tests of controls must be performed to provide the basis for the auditor's report on internal control over financial reporting. For audits of nonpublic companies, the decision to perform tests of controls is made on a cost-benefit basis. If it is cost effective, the auditor designs tests of controls to determine the effectiveness of the existing controls.

The auditor also designs substantive tests of transactions for each class of transactions to determine whether the monetary amounts of transactions are correctly recorded. Like tests of controls, substantive tests of transactions are designed for each transaction-related audit objective.

After the design of tests of controls and substantive tests of transactions for each audit objective and each class of transactions is completed, the auditor organizes the audit procedures into a performance format audit program. The purpose of this audit program is to help the auditor complete the audit tests efficiently.

ESSENTIAL TERMS

Business functions for the sales and collection cycle—the key activities that an organization must complete to execute and record business transactions for sales, cash receipts, sales returns and allowances, charge-off of uncollectible accounts, and bad debt expense

Classes of transactions in the sales and collection cycle—the categories of transactions for the sales and collection cycle in a typical company: sales, cash receipts, sales returns and allowances, charge-off of uncollectible accounts, and bad debt expense

Design format audit program—the audit procedures resulting from the auditor's decisions about the appropriate audit procedures for each audit objective; this audit program is used to prepare a performance format audit program

Lapping of accounts receivable—the postponement of entries for the collection of receivables to *conceal an existing cash shortage*

Performance format audit program—the audit procedures for a class of transactions organized in the format in which they will be performed; this audit program is prepared from a design format audit program

Proof of cash receipts—an audit procedure to test whether all recorded cash receipts have been deposited in the bank account by reconciling the total cash receipts recorded in the cash receipts journal for a given period with the actual deposits made to the bank

Sales and collection cycle—involves the decisions and processes necessary for the transfer of the ownership of goods and services to customers after they are made available for sale; it begins with a request by a customer and ends with the conversion of material or service into an account receivable, and ultimately into cash

REVIEW QUESTIONS

14-1 (Objective 14-2) Describe the nature of the following documents and records and explain their use in the sales and collection cycle: bill of lading, sales invoice, credit memo, remittance advice, monthly statement to customers.

14-2 (Objective 14-2) Explain the importance of proper credit approval for sales. What effect do adequate controls in the credit function have on the auditor's evidence accumulation?

14-3 (Objective 14-2) Distinguish between bad debt expense and the charge-off of uncollectible accounts for a company using the allowance method for recording uncollectible accounts receivable. Explain why they are audited in completely different ways.

14-4 (Objective 14-3) BestSellers.com sells fiction and nonfiction books to customers through the company's Web site. Customers place orders for books via the Web site by providing their name, address, credit card number, and expiration date. What internal controls could BestSellers.com implement to ensure that shipments of books occur only for customers who have the ability to pay for those books? At what point would BestSellers.com be able to record the sale as revenue?

14-5 (Objective 14-4) List the transaction-related audit objectives for the verification of sales transactions. For each objective, state one internal control that the client can use to reduce the likelihood of misstatements.

14-6 (Objective 14-4) State one test of control and one substantive test of transactions that the auditor can use to verify the following sales transaction-related audit objective: Recorded sales are stated at the proper amount.

14-7 (Objective 14-4) List the most important duties that should be segregated in the sales and collection cycle. Explain why it is desirable that each duty be segregated.

14-8 (Objective 14-4) Explain how prenumbered shipping documents and sales invoices can be useful controls for preventing misstatements in sales.

14-9 (Objective 14-4) What three types of authorizations are commonly used as internal controls for sales? For each authorization, state a substantive test that the auditor could use to verify whether the control was effective in preventing misstatements.

14-10 (Objective 14-4) Explain the purpose of footing and cross-footing the sales journal and tracing the totals to the general ledger.

14-11 (Objective 14-5) What is the difference between the auditor's approach in verifying sales returns and allowances and that for sales? Explain the reasons for the difference.

14-12 (Objective 14-6) Explain why auditors usually emphasize the detection of fraud in the audit of cash. Is this consistent or inconsistent with the auditor's responsibility in the audit? Explain.

14-13 (Objective 14-6) List the transaction-related audit objectives for the verification of cash receipts. For each objective, state one internal control that the client can use to reduce the likelihood of misstatements.

14-14 (Objective 14-6) List several audit procedures that the auditor can use to determine whether all cash received was recorded.

14-15 (Objective 14-6) Explain what is meant by a proof of cash receipts and state its purpose.

14-16 (Objective 14-6) Explain what is meant by lapping and discuss how the auditor can uncover it. Under what circumstances should the auditor make a special effort to uncover lapping?

14-17 (Objective 14-7) What audit procedures are most likely to be used to verify accounts receivable charged off as uncollectible? State the purpose of each of these procedures.

14-18 (Objectives 14-4, 14-6) State the relationship between the confirmation of accounts receivable and the results of the tests of controls and substantive tests of transactions.

14-19 (Objectives 14-4, 14-6) Under what circumstances is it acceptable to perform tests of controls and substantive tests of transactions for sales and cash receipts at an interim date?

14-20 (Objective 14-4) Diane Smith, CPA, performed tests of controls and substantive tests of transactions for sales for the month of March in an audit of the financial statements for the year ended December 31, 2005. Based on the excellent results of both the tests of controls and the substantive tests of transactions, she decided to significantly reduce her substantive tests of details of balances at year-end. Evaluate this decision.

MULTIPLE CHOICE QUESTIONS FROM CPA EXAMINATIONS

14-21 (Objectives 14-4, 14-5, 14-6, 14-7) The following questions deal with internal controls in the sales and collection cycle. Choose the best response.

    a. When a customer fails to include a remittance advice with a payment, it is common for the person opening the mail to prepare one. Consequently, mail should be opened by which of the following four company employees?
    (1) Credit manager.
    (2) Sales manager.
    (3) Accounts receivable clerk.
    (4) Receptionist.

    b. A key internal control in the sales and collection cycle is the separation of duties between cash handling and record keeping. The objective most directly associated with this control is to verify that
    (1) cash receipts recorded in the cash receipts journal are reasonable.
    (2) cash receipts are properly classified.
    (3) recorded cash receipts result from legitimate transactions.
    (4) existing cash receipts are recorded.

    c. An auditor tests a company's policy of obtaining credit approval before shipping goods to customers in support of management's financial statement assertion of
    (1) valuation or allocation.
    (2) completeness.
    (3) existence or occurrence.
    (4) rights and obligations.

    d. Which of the following internal controls would most likely reduce charge-offs of uncollectible accounts receivable?
    (1) Employees responsible for authorizing sales and charge-offs of uncollectible accounts receivable are denied access to cash.
    (2) Shipping documents and sales invoices are matched by an employee who does not have the authority to charge off uncollectible accounts receivable.
    (3) Employees involved in the credit-granting function are separated from the sales function.
    (4) Accounts receivable master file records are reconciled to the control account by an employee who is not involved in the credit-granting function.

14-22 (Objectives 14-4, 14-5) For each of the following types of misstatements (parts a through d), select the control that should have prevented the misstatement:

    a. A manufacturing company received a substantial sales return in the last month of the year, but the credit memorandum for the return was not prepared until after the auditors had completed their field work. The returned merchandise was included in the physical inventory.

(1) Aged trial balance of accounts receivable is prepared.
(2) Credit memoranda are prenumbered and all numbers are accounted for.
(3) A reconciliation of the trial balance of customers' accounts with the general ledger control is prepared periodically.
(4) Receiving reports are prepared for all materials received and such reports are accounted for on a regular basis.

b. The sales manager credited a salesman, Jack Smith, with sales that were actually "house account" sales. Later, Smith divided his excess sales commissions with the sales manager.
(1) The summary sales entries are checked periodically by persons independent of sales functions.
(2) Sales orders are reviewed and approved by persons independent of the sales department.
(3) The internal auditor compares the sales commission statements with the cash disbursements record.
(4) Sales orders are prenumbered, and all numbers are accounted for.

c. A sales invoice for $5,200 was computed correctly but, by mistake, was key-entered as $2,500 to the sales journal and to the accounts receivable master file. The customer remitted only $2,500, the amount on his monthly statement.
(1) Prelistings and predetermined totals are used to control postings.
(2) Sales invoice numbers, prices, discounts, extensions, and footings are independently checked.
(3) The customers' monthly statements are verified and mailed by a responsible person other than the bookkeeper who prepared them.
(4) Unauthorized remittance deductions made by customers or other matters in dispute are investigated promptly by a person independent of the accounts receivable function.

d. Copies of sales invoices show different unit prices for apparently identical items.
(1) All sales invoices are checked as to all details after their preparation.
(2) Differences reported by customers are satisfactorily investigated.
(3) Statistical sales data are compiled and reconciled with recorded sales.
(4) All sales invoices are compared with the customers' purchase orders.

14-23 (Objectives 14-1, 14-4) The following questions deal with audit evidence for the sales and collection cycle. Choose the best response.

a. Auditors sometimes use comparison of ratios as audit evidence. For example, an unexplained decrease in the ratio of gross profit to sales may suggest which of the following possibilities?
(1) Unrecorded acquisitions.
(2) Unrecorded sales.
(3) Merchandise acquisitions being charged to selling and general expense.
(4) Fictitious sales.

b. An auditor is performing substantive tests of transactions for sales. One step is to trace a sample of debit entries from the accounts receivable master file back to the supporting duplicate sales invoices. What would the auditor intend to establish by this step?
(1) Sales invoices represent existing sales.
(2) All sales have been recorded.
(3) All sales invoices have been properly posted to customer accounts.
(4) Debit entries in the accounts receivable master file are properly supported by sales invoices.

c. To verify that all sales transactions have been recorded, a substantive test of transactions should be completed on a representative sample drawn from
(1) entries in the sales journal.
(2) the billing clerk's file of sales orders.
(3) a file of duplicate copies of sales invoices for which all prenumbered forms in the series have been accounted.
(4) the shipping clerk's file of duplicate copies of bills of lading.

DISCUSSION QUESTIONS AND PROBLEMS

14-24 (Objectives 14-3, 14-4, 14-5, 14-6) Items 1 through 9 are selected questions of the type generally found in internal control questionnaires used by auditors to obtain an understanding of internal control in the sales and collection cycle. In using the questionnaire for a client, a "yes" response to a question indicates a possible internal control, whereas a "no" indicates a potential deficiency.

1. Are sales invoices independently compared with customers' orders for prices, quantities, extensions, and footings?
2. Are sales orders, invoices, and credit memoranda issued and filed in numerical sequence and are the sequences accounted for periodically?
3. Are the selling and cash register functions independent of the cash receipts, shipping, delivery, and billing functions?
4. Are all C.O.D., scrap, equipment, and cash sales accounted for in the same manner as charge sales and is the record keeping independent of the collection procedure?
5. Is the collection function independent of and does it constitute a check on billing and recording sales?
6. Are accounts receivable master files balanced regularly to control accounts by an employee independent of billing functions?
7. Are cash receipts recorded by persons independent of the mail-opening and receipts-listing functions?
8. Are receipts deposited intact daily on a timely basis?
9. Are sales generated through the company's Web site automatically recorded in the sales system?

Required

a. For each of the preceding questions, state the transaction-related audit objectives being fulfilled if the control is in effect.
b. For each control, list a test of control to test its effectiveness.
c. For each of the preceding questions, identify the nature of the potential financial misstatements.
d. For each of the potential misstatements in part c, list a substantive audit procedure to determine whether a material misstatement exists.

14-25 (Objectives 14-4, 14-5, 14-6) The following are commonly performed tests of controls and substantive tests of transactions audit procedures in the sales and collection cycle:

1. Examine sales returns for approval by an authorized official.
2. Account for a sequence of shipping documents and examine each one to make sure that a duplicate sales invoice is attached.
3. Account for a sequence of sales invoices and examine each one to make sure that a duplicate copy of the shipping document is attached.
4. Compare the quantity and description of items on shipping documents with the related duplicate sales invoices.
5. Trace recorded sales in the sales journal to the related accounts receivable master file and compare the customer name, date, and amount for each one.
6. Review the prelisting in the cash receipts book to determine whether cash is prelisted daily.
7. Reconcile the recorded cash receipts on the prelisting with the cash receipts journal and the bank statement for a 1-month period.

Required

a. Identify whether each audit procedure is a test of control or a substantive test of transactions.
b. State which of the six transaction-related audit objectives each of the audit procedures fulfills.
c. Identify the type of evidence used for each audit procedure, such as confirmation and observation.

14-26 (Objective 14-4) The following are selected transaction-related audit objectives and audit procedures for sales transactions:

Transaction-Related Audit Objectives

1. Recorded sales exist.
2. Existing sales are recorded.
3. Sales transactions are properly included in the accounts receivable master file and are correctly summarized.

Procedures

1. Trace a sample of shipping documents to related duplicate sales invoices and the sales journal to make sure that the shipment was billed.
2. Examine a sample of duplicate sales invoices to determine whether each one has a shipping document attached.

3. Examine the sales journal for a sample of sales transactions to determine whether each one has a tick mark in the margin indicating that it has been compared with the accounts receivable master file for customer name, date, and amount.

4. Examine a sample of shipping documents to determine whether each one has a duplicate sales invoice number written on the bottom left corner.

5. Trace a sample of debit entries in the accounts receivable master file to the sales journal to determine whether the date, customer name, and amount are the same.

6. Trace a sample of duplicate sales invoices to related shipping documents filed in the shipping department to make sure that a shipment was made.

a. For each objective, identify at least one specific misstatement that could occur. **Required**

b. Describe the differences between the purposes of the first and second objectives.

c. For each audit procedure, identify it as a test of control or substantive test of transactions. (There are three of each.)

d. For each objective, identify one test of control and one substantive test of transactions.

e. For each test of control, state the internal control that is being tested. Also, identify or describe a misstatement that the client is trying to prevent by use of the control.

14-27 (Objectives 14-2, 14-4) The following sales procedures were encountered during the annual audit of Marvel Wholesale Distributing Company:

Customer orders are received by the sales order department. A clerk computes the approximate dollar amount of the order and sends it to the credit department for approval. Credit approval is stamped on the order and sent to the accounting department. A computer is then used to generate two copies of a sales invoice. The order is filed in the customer order file.

The customer copy of the sales invoice is held in a pending file awaiting notification that the order was shipped. The shipping copy of the sales invoice is routed through the warehouse, and the shipping department has authority for the respective departments to release and ship the merchandise. Shipping department personnel pack the order and manually prepare a three-copy bill of lading: The original copy is mailed to the customer, the second copy is sent with the shipment, and the other is filed in sequence in the bill of lading file. The sales invoice shipping copy is sent to the accounting department with any changes resulting from lack of available merchandise.

A clerk in accounting matches the received sales invoice shipping copy with the sales invoice customer copy from the pending file. Quantities on the two invoices are compared and prices are compared on an approved price list. The customer copy is then mailed to the customer, and the shipping copy is sent to the data processing department.

The data processing clerk in accounting enters the sales invoice data into the computer, which is used to prepare the sales journal and update the accounts receivable master file. She files the shipping copy in the sales invoice file in numerical sequence.

a. To determine whether the internal controls operated effectively to minimize instances of failure to post invoices to customers' accounts receivable master file, the auditor would select a sample of transactions from the population represented by the
   (1) customer order file.
   (2) bill of lading file.
   (3) customers' accounts receivable master file.
   (4) sales invoice file.

b. To determine whether the internal controls operated effectively to minimize instances of failure to invoice a shipment, the auditor would select a sample of transactions from the population represented by the
   (1) customer order file.
   (2) bill of lading file.
   (3) customers' accounts receivable master file.
   (4) sales invoice file.

c. To gather audit evidence that uncollected items in customers' accounts represented existing trade receivables, the auditor would select a sample of items from the population represented by the
   (1) customer order file.
   (2) bill of lading file.
   (3) customers' accounts receivable master file.
   (4) sales invoice file.*

*AICPA adapted.

14-28 (Objectives 14-4, 14-6) The following are common audit procedures for tests of sales and cash receipts:

1. Compare the quantity and description of items on duplicate sales invoices with related shipping documents.
2. Trace recorded cash receipts in the accounts receivable master file to the cash receipts journal and compare the customer name, date, and amount of each one.
3. Examine duplicate sales invoices for an indication that unit selling prices were compared to the approved price list.
4. Examine duplicate sales invoices to determine whether the account classification for sales has been included on the document.
5. Examine the sales journal for related-party transactions, notes receivable, and other unusual items.
6. Select a sample of customer orders and trace the document to related shipping documents, sales invoices, and the accounts receivable master file for comparison of name, date, and amount.
7. Perform a proof of cash receipts.
8. Examine a sample of remittance advices for approval of cash discounts.
9. Account for a numerical sequence of remittance advices and determine whether there is a cross-reference mark for each one, indicating that it has been recorded in the cash receipts journal.

Required
a. Identify whether each audit procedure is a test of control or substantive test of transactions.

b. State which transaction-related audit objective(s) each of the audit procedures fulfills.

c. For each test of control in part a, state a substantive test that could be used to determine whether there was a monetary misstatement.

14-29 (Objective 14-6) You have been asked by the board of trustees of a local church to review its accounting procedures. As part of this review you have prepared the following comments about the collections made at weekly services and record keeping for members' pledges and contributions:

1. The church's board of trustees has delegated responsibility for financial management and audit of the financial records to the finance committee. This group prepares the annual budget and approves major cash disbursements but is not involved in collections or record keeping. No audit has been considered necessary in recent years because the same trusted employee has kept church records and served as financial secretary for 15 years.

2. The collection at the weekly service is taken by a team of ushers. The head usher counts the collection in the church office after each service. He then places the collection and a notation of the amount in the church safe. The next morning, the financial secretary opens the safe and recounts the collection. He withholds about $100 to meet cash expenditures during the coming week and deposits the remainder intact. To facilitate the deposit, members who contribute by check are asked to draw their checks to cash.

3. At their request, a few members are furnished prenumbered predated envelopes in which to insert their weekly contributions. The head usher removes the cash from the envelopes to be counted with the loose cash included in the collection and discards the envelopes. No record is maintained of issuance or return of the envelopes, and the envelope system is not encouraged.

4. Each member is asked to prepare a contribution pledge card annually. The pledge is regarded as a moral commitment by the member to contribute a stated weekly amount. Based on the amounts shown on the pledge cards, the financial secretary furnishes a letter to members, upon request, to support the tax deductibility of their contributions.

Required
Identify the deficiencies and recommend improvements in procedures for collection made at weekly services and record keeping for members' pledges and contributions. Use the methodology for identifying deficiencies that was discussed in Chapter 10. Organize your answer sheets as follows:*

Deficiency	Recommended Improvement

14-30 (Objectives 14-4, 14-6) The customer billing and cash receipts functions of the Robinson Company, a small paint manufacturer, are attended to by a receptionist, an accounts receivable clerk, and a cashier who also serves as a secretary. The company's paint products are sold to wholesalers and retail stores. The following describes all the procedures performed by the employees of the Robinson Company pertaining to customer billings and cash receipts:

*AICPA adapted.

1. The mail is opened by the receptionist, who gives the customers' purchase orders to the accounts receivable clerk. Fifteen to 20 orders are received each day. Under instructions to expedite the shipment of orders, the accounts receivable clerk at once prepares a five-copy sales invoice form that is distributed as follows:

(a) Copy 1 is the customer billing copy and is held by the accounts receivable clerk until notice of shipment is received.

(b) Copy 2 is the accounts receivable department copy and is held for the ultimate updating of the accounting records.

(c) Copies 3 and 4 are sent to the shipping department.

(d) Copy 5 is sent to the storeroom as authority for the release of goods to the shipping department.

2. After the paint order has been moved from the storeroom to the shipping department, the shipping department prepares the bills of lading and labels the cartons. Sales invoice copy 4 is inserted in a carton as a packing slip. After the trucker has picked up the shipment, the customer's copy of the bill of lading and copy 3, on which are noted any undershipments, are returned to the accounts receivable clerk. The company does not "back order" in the event of undershipments; customers are expected to reorder the merchandise. The Robinson Company's copy of the bill of lading is filed by the shipping department.

3. When copy 3 and the customer's copy of the bill of lading are received by the accounts receivable clerk, copies 1 and 2 are completed by numbering them and inserting quantities shipped, unit prices, extensions, discounts, and totals. Copies 2 and 3 are stapled together.

4. The accounts receivable clerk then enters the sales transactions into the computerized accounting records from copy 2. Only the quantities, prices, discounts, and accounts are entered because the computer computes extensions and totals. These extensions and totals are then compared with copy 1. The accounts receivable clerk then mails copy 1 and the copy of the bill of lading to the customer. Copy 2 is then filed, along with staple-attached copy 3, in numerical order.

5. Because the Robinson Company is short of cash, the deposit of cash receipts is also expedited. The receptionist turns over all mail receipts and related correspondence to the accounts receivable clerk, who examines the checks and determines that the accompanying vouchers or correspondence contain enough detail to permit the entering of the transactions into the computer. The accounts receivable clerk then endorses the checks and gives them to the cashier, who prepares the daily deposit. No currency is received in the mail, and no paint is sold over the counter at the factory.

6. The accounts receivable clerk uses the vouchers or correspondence that accompanied the checks to enter the transactions into the computerized accounting records. The accounts receivable clerk is the one who corresponds with customers about unauthorized deductions for discounts, freight or advertising allowances, returns, and so forth, and prepares the appropriate credit memos. Disputed items of large amounts are turned over to the sales manager for settlement. Each month, the accounts receivable clerk prints out a trial balance of accounts receivable and compares the total with the general ledger control accounts for accounts receivable.

a. Identify the internal control deficiencies in the Robinson Company's procedures related to customer billings and cash receipts and the accounting for these transactions. Use the methodology for identifying deficiencies that was discussed in Chapter 10. **Required**

b. For each deficiency, identify the error or fraud that could result.

c. For each deficiency, list one substantive audit procedure for testing the significance of the potential misstatement.*

14-31 (Objectives 14-3, 14-4) YourTeam.com is an online retailer of college and professional sports team memorabilia, such as hats, shirts, pennants and other sports logo products. Consumers select the college or professional team from a pull-down menu on the company's Web site. For each listed team, the Web site provides a product description, picture, and price for all products sold online. Customers click on the product number of the items they wish to purchase. The following are internal controls YourTeam.com has established for its online sales:

1. Only products shown on the Web site can be purchased online. Other company products not shown on the Web site listing are unavailable for online sale.

2. The online sales system is linked to the perpetual inventory system that verifies quantities on hand before processing the sale.

3. Before the sale is authorized, YourTeam.com obtains credit card authorization codes electronically from the credit card agency.

4. Online sales are rejected if the customer's shipping address does not match the credit card's billing address.

*AICPA adapted.

5. Before the sale is finalized, the online screen shows the product name, description, unit price, and total sales price for the online transaction. Customers must click on the Accept or Reject sales buttons to indicate approval or rejection of the online sale.

6. Once customers approve the online sale, the online sales system generates a Pending Sales file, which is an online data file that is used by warehouse personnel to process shipments. Online sales are not recorded in the sales journal until warehouse personnel enter the bill of lading number and date of shipment into the Pending Sales data file.

Required

a. For each control, identify the transaction-related audit objective(s) being fulfilled if each control is in effect.

b. For each control, describe potential financial misstatements that could occur if the control was not present.

CASE

14-32 (Objective 14-4) The Meyers Pharmaceutical Company, a drug manufacturer, has the following internal controls for billing and recording accounts receivable:

1. An incoming customer's purchase order is received in the order department by a clerk who prepares a prenumbered company sales order form in which is inserted the pertinent information, such as the customer's name and address, customer's account number, quantity, and items ordered. After the sales order form has been prepared, the customer's purchase order is stapled to it.

2. The sales order form is then passed to the credit department for credit approval. Rough approximations of the billing values of the orders are made in the credit department for those accounts on which credit limitations are imposed. After investigation, approval of credit is noted on the form.

3. Next, the sales order form is passed to the billing department, where a clerk uses a computer to generate the customer's invoice. It automatically cross-multiplies the number of items with the unit price and adds the extended amounts for the total amount of the invoice. The billing clerk determines the unit prices for the items from a list of billing prices.

   The computer automatically accumulates daily totals of customer account numbers and invoice amounts to provide "hash" totals and control amounts. These totals, which are inserted in a daily record book, serve as predetermined batch totals for verification of inputs into the computerized accounting records.

   The billing is done on prenumbered, continuous, carbon-interleaved forms having the following designations:
   (a) Customer's copy.
   (b) Sales department copy, for information purposes.
   (c) File copy.
   (d) Shipping department copy, which serves as a shipping order. Bills of lading are also prepared as carbon copy by-products of the invoicing procedure.

4. The shipping department copy of the invoice and the bills of lading are then sent to the shipping department. After the order has been shipped, copies of the bill of lading are returned to the billing department. The shipping department copy of the invoice is filed in the shipping department.

5. In the billing department, one copy of the bill of lading is attached to the customer's copy of the invoice and both are mailed to the customer. The other copy of the bill of lading, together with the sales order form, is then stapled to the invoice file copy and filed in invoice numerical order.

6. As the computer is generating invoices, it is also storing the transactions on disk. This disk is then used to update the computerized accounting records. This update procedure is run daily, and a summary report is generated. Hard copy output of all journals and ledgers is prepared.

7. Periodically, an internal auditor traces a sample of sales orders all the way through the system to the journals and ledgers, testing both the procedures and dollar amounts. The procedures include comparing control totals with output, recalculating invoices and refooting journals, and tracing totals to the master file and general ledger.

Required

a. Flowchart the billing function as a means of understanding the system.

b. List the internal controls over sales for each of the six transaction-related audit objectives.

c. For each control, list a useful test of control to verify the effectiveness of the control.

d. For each transaction-related audit objective for sales, list appropriate substantive tests of transactions audit procedures, considering internal controls.

e. Combine the audit procedures from parts c and d into an efficient audit program for sales.

INTEGRATED CASE APPLICATION—PINNACLE MANUFACTURING: PART IV

14-33 (Objectives 14-4, 14-6) In Part III of this case study, you obtained an understanding of internal control and made an initial assessment of control risk for each transaction-related audit objective for acquisition and cash disbursement transactions. The purpose of Part IV is to continue the assessment of control risk by determining the appropriate tests of controls and substantive tests of transactions. In order to do this, you must complete the steps needed to prepare a high-quality performance format audit program for tests of controls and substantive tests of transactions for acquisitions and cash disbursements.

Assume in Part III that you identified the following as the key controls you want to rely on (even though your answers were likely different from these):

1. Segregation of the purchasing, receiving, and cash disbursements functions
2. Independent reconciliation of the monthly bank statements
3. Use of prenumbered voucher packages, properly accounted for
4. Use of prenumbered checks, properly accounted for
5. Use of prenumbered receiving reports, properly accounted for
6. Internal verification of document package before check preparation
7. Review of supporting documents and signing of checks by an independent, authorized person
8. Cancellation of documents prior to signing of the check
9. Monthly reconciliation of the accounts payable master file with the general ledger

Required

a. Prepare an audit file listing the nine controls or download them from the textbook Web site.

b. After each control, identify the transaction-related audit objective(s) that it partially or fully satisfies.

c. Immediately below the control, list one audit procedure to test the control. Use the most reliable test of control evidence that you can think of. Write the audit procedure in good form.

d. Immediately below the test of control, list one substantive test of transactions audit procedure to test whether the control failed to be effective. Use the most reliable substantive tests of transactions evidence that you can think of.

e. Create a separate audit schedule labeled "Acquisitions Substantive Tests of Transactions." Decide and write one substantive test of transactions audit procedure for each transaction-related audit objective for acquisitions. The audit procedures must be different than the ones in requirement d. The schedule should be designed as follows:

Acquisitions Substantive Tests of Transactions

Existence	Write the substantive audit procedure
Completeness	Write the substantive audit procedure
Etc.	

f. Using a separate heading labeled "Cash Disbursements Substantive Tests of Transactions," decide and write one substantive test of transactions audit procedure for each transaction-related audit objective for cash disbursements. The audit procedures must be different than the ones in requirements d and e. The audit schedule should be designed the same as the one in requirement e.

g. Prepare a performance audit program for acquisitions and cash disbursements using all audit procedures in requirements c through f. See Figure 14-6 (p. 430) for a format. To the extent possible, follow the approach in procedure 13 a through e in Figure 14-6 of having "one starting point" procedure followed by other related procedures. Do this for both acquisitions and cash disbursements. Be sure to eliminate any duplicate audit procedures.

INTERNET PROBLEM 14-1: ELECTRONIC SIGNATURES

Reference the CW site. When conducting traditional forms of business, handwritten signatures entered onto contracts and other documents establish a legal basis to enforce the terms of the transaction. However, when companies engage in e-commerce to transact business, the ability to obtain handwritten signatures is absent, requiring companies to rely on electronically generated digital signatures. This problem requires students to learn about legislation, summarized on the Office of Management and Budget's Web site, designed to establish the legal enforceability of certain electronic signatures and documents.

AUDIT SAMPLING FOR TESTS OF CONTROLS AND SUBSTANTIVE TESTS OF TRANSACTIONS

IF YOU ARE NOT GOING TO BELIEVE IT, DON'T USE IT

Brooks & Company, CPAs, uses random samples in performing audit tests whenever possible. They believe that this gives them the best chance of getting representative samples of their clients' accounting information. In the audit of Sensational Products, a random sample of 30 inventory items was taken from a population of 1,800 items in doing a test of unit and total costs. Only 1 of the 30 items was in error, but it was large. In investigating the error, Harold Davis, the audit staff person doing the test, was told by Sensational's controller that the error occurred while the regular inventory clerk was on vacation and was really only an "isolated error."

Harold knew auditing standards require that errors in random samples be projected to the entire population. In this case, such a projection would involve multiplying the error found by a factor of 60 (1,800 divided by 30). This would result in an audit adjustment or additional audit work. Harold knew that the client would not be happy about this because the adjustment would reduce an already "strained" net income figure and additional auditing would increase the audit fee. If the error was, in fact, an isolated one, it would not be significant enough to require an audit adjustment.

Harold decided to look at the situation in terms of the probability of the error being an isolated example. He calculated the chance to be about only 1 in 60 of including an isolated error in a sample of 30 from a population of 1,800. He then looked at accepting the client's representation about the uniqueness of the error as a bet. If he accepted the representation and didn't do the projection and act on it, he was in effect betting his career in a situation where the odds were 60 to 1 against him. It didn't take Harold long to recognize the wisdom of the professional standards and conclude that the projection should be done.

In the last chapter, we learned about designing tests of controls and substantive tests of transactions needed to perform an audit of the sales and collection cycle. Before these tests can be performed, the auditor needs to decide for each audit procedure the sample size and sample items to select from the population. When the auditor decides to select less than 100 percent of the population for testing for the purpose of making inferences about the population, it is called **audit sampling**. As demonstrated by Harold Davis of Brooks & Company in the chapter vignette, evaluating audit samples is an essential, and often challenging, part of the audit process. When is a sample size sufficiently large to evaluate a population? Does a given sample accurately represent the accounting information? This chapter discusses sampling issues for tests of controls and substantive tests of transactions. These sampling concepts are illustrated for the sales and collection cycle, but they are equally applicable to all other cycles.

REPRESENTATIVE SAMPLES

OBJECTIVE 15-1

Explain the concept of representative sampling.

When an auditor selects a sample from a population, the objective is to obtain a representative one. A **representative sample** is one in which the characteristics in the sample of audit interest are approximately the same as those of the population. This means that the sampled items are similar to the items not sampled. For example, assume that a client's internal controls require a clerk to attach a shipping document to every duplicate sales invoice, but the procedure is not followed exactly 3 percent of the time. If the auditor selects a sample of 100 duplicate sales invoices and finds three missing, the sample is highly representative. If two or four such items are found in the sample, the sample is reasonably representative. If no or many missing items are found, the sample is nonrepresentative.

In practice, auditors do not know whether a sample is representative, even after all testing is complete. However, auditors can increase the likelihood of a sample being representative by using care in its design, selection, and evaluation. Two things can cause a sample result to be nonrepresentative: nonsampling error and sampling error. The risk of these occurring is termed nonsampling risk and sampling risk. Both of these can be controlled.

Nonsampling risk is the risk that audit tests do not uncover existing exceptions in the sample. The two causes of nonsampling risk are the auditor's failure to recognize exceptions and inappropriate or ineffective audit procedures. An auditor might fail to recognize an exception because of exhaustion, boredom, or lack of understanding of what to look for. In the previous example in which three shipping documents were not attached to duplicate sales invoices, if the auditor concluded that no exceptions existed, there is a nonsampling error. An ineffective audit procedure for the exceptions in question would be to examine a sample of shipping documents and determine whether each is attached to a set of duplicate sales invoices, rather than to examine a sample of duplicate sales invoices. In this case, the auditor has done the test in the wrong direction by starting with the shipping document instead of the duplicate sales invoice. Careful design of audit procedures, proper instruction, supervision, and review are ways to control nonsampling risk.

Sampling risk is the risk that an auditor reaches an incorrect conclusion because the sample is not representative of the population. Sampling risk is an inherent part of sampling that results from testing less than the entire population. For example, assume that an auditor accepts a population based on a sample of 100 items that contains two exceptions. However, the population actually has an 8 percent exception rate, which the auditor would reject as unacceptable. The auditor has incorrectly accepted the population because the sample was not sufficiently representative of the population.

There are two ways to control sampling risk: by adjusting sample size and by using an appropriate method of selecting sample items from the population. Increasing sample size will reduce sampling risk, and vice versa. At the extreme, a sample of all the items of a population will have a zero sampling risk. Using an appropriate sampling method will reasonably ensure representativeness. This does not eliminate or even reduce sampling risk, but it does allow the auditor to measure the risk associated with a given sample size in a reliable manner. Determining the appropriate sample size to reduce sampling risk to an appropriate level is a major topic of this chapter.

STATISTICAL VERSUS NONSTATISTICAL SAMPLING AND PROBABILISTIC VERSUS NONPROBABILISTIC SAMPLE SELECTION

Before discussing the methods of sample selection to obtain representative samples, it is useful to make two distinctions and discuss the terms involved: statistical versus nonstatistical sampling and probabilistic versus nonprobabilistic sample selection.

Audit sampling methods can be divided into two broad categories: statistical sampling and nonstatistical sampling. These categories have important similarities and differences. They are similar in that they both involve three steps: (1) plan the sample, (2) select the sample and perform the tests, and (3) evaluate the results. The purpose of planning the sample is to make sure that the audit tests are performed in a manner that provides the desired sampling risk and minimizes the likelihood of nonsampling error. Selecting the sample involves deciding how to select sample items from the population. Performing the tests is the examination of documents and doing other audit procedures. Evaluating the results involves drawing conclusions based on the audit tests. To illustrate, assume that an auditor selects a sample of 100 duplicate sales invoices from a population, tests each to determine whether a shipping document is attached, and determines that there are three exceptions. Deciding that a sample size of 100 is needed is a part of planning the sample. Deciding which 100 items to select from the population is a sample selection problem. Doing the audit procedure for each of the 100 items and determining that there were three exceptions constitute performing the tests. Reaching conclusions about the likely exception rate in the total population when there is a sample exception rate of 3 percent is evaluating the results.

Statistical sampling differs from nonstatistical sampling in that, through the application of mathematical rules, it allows the quantification (measurement) of sampling risk in planning the sample (step 1) and evaluating the results (step 3). (You may remember calculating a statistical result at a 95 percent confidence level in a statistics course. The 95 percent confidence level provides a 5 percent sampling risk.)

In **nonstatistical sampling**, the auditor does not quantify sampling risk. Instead, those sample items that the auditor believes will provide the most useful information in the circumstances are selected. Conclusions are reached about populations on a judgmental basis. For that reason, the selection of nonprobabilistic samples is often termed judgmental sampling.

Both probabilistic and nonprobabilistic sample selection are a part of step 2 in using auditing sampling, selecting sample items from the population. **Probabilistic sample selection** is a method of selecting a sample such that each population item has a known probability of being included in the sample and the sample is selected by a random process. To satisfy this definition, the auditor must use great care in selecting samples using one of several methods to be discussed shortly. **Nonprobabilistic sample selection** is a method of selecting a sample in which the auditor uses professional judgment rather than probabilistic methods to select sample items. There are also several nonprobabilistic sample selection methods.

It is equally acceptable under professional standards for auditors to use either statistical or nonstatistical sampling methods. However, it is essential that either method be applied with due care. All steps of the process must be followed carefully. When statistical sampling is used, the sample *must be a probabilistic one* and appropriate statistical evaluation methods must be used with the sample results to make the sampling risk computations.

It is also acceptable to make nonstatistical evaluations by using probabilistic selection. It is *never* acceptable, however, to evaluate a nonprobabilistic sample as if it were a statistical sample.

Three types of sample selection methods are commonly associated with nonstatistical audit sampling. All three methods are nonprobabilistic. Four types of sample selection

Statistical Versus Nonstatistical Sampling

OBJECTIVE 15-2

Distinguish between statistical and nonstatistical sampling and between probabilistic and non-probabilistic sample selection.

Probabilistic Versus Nonprobabilistic Sample Selection

Applying Statistical and Nonstatistical Sampling in Practice and Sample Selection Methods

methods are commonly associated with statistical audit sampling. All four methods are probabilistic.

Nonprobabilistic (judgmental) sample selection methods include the following:

1. Directed sample selection
2. Block sample selection
3. Haphazard sample selection

Probabilistic sample selection methods include the following:

1. Simple random sample selection
2. Systematic sample selection
3. Probability proportional to size sample selection
4. Stratified sample selection

We will now discuss each of these seven sample selection methods, starting with nonprobabilistic methods.

NONPROBABILISTIC SAMPLE SELECTION METHODS

Nonprobabilistic sample selection methods are those that do not meet the technical requirements for probabilistic sample selection. Because these methods are not based on strict mathematical probabilities, the representativeness of the sample may be difficult to determine. The information content of the sample, including its representativeness, will be based on the knowledge and skill of the auditor in applying judgment in the circumstances.

Directed Sample Selection

Directed sample selection is the selection of each item in the sample based on some judgmental criteria established by the auditor. The auditor does not rely on equal chances of selection, but instead deliberately selects items according to the criteria. These criteria may relate to representativeness, or they may not. Commonly used criteria are the following:

Items Most Likely to Contain Misstatements Often, auditors are able to identify which population items are most likely to be misstated. Examples are receivables outstanding for a long time, purchases from and sales to officers and affiliated companies, and unusually large or complex transactions. These kinds of items can be efficiently investigated by the auditor, and the results can be applied to the population on a judgmental basis. The reasoning underlying the evaluation of such samples is often that, if none of the items selected contains misstatements, it is highly unlikely that a material misstatement exists in the population.

Items Containing Selected Population Characteristics The auditor may be able to describe the various types and sources of items that make up the population and design the sample to be representative by selecting one or more items of each type. For example, a sample of cash disbursements might include some from each month, each bank account or location, and each major type of acquisition.

Large Dollar Coverage A sample can often be selected to cover such a large portion of total population dollars that the risk of drawing an improper conclusion by not examining small items is not a concern. This is a practical approach on many audits, especially smaller ones. There are also statistical methods that are intended to accomplish the same effect.

Block Sample Selection

Block sample selection is the selection of several items in sequence. Once the first item in the block is selected, the remainder of the block is chosen automatically. One example of a block sample is the selection of a sequence of 100 sales transactions from the sales journal for the third week of March. A total sample of 100 could also be selected by taking 5 blocks of 20 items each, 10 blocks of 10, or 50 blocks of 2.

It is ordinarily acceptable to use block samples only if a reasonable number of blocks is used. If few blocks are used, the probability of obtaining a nonrepresentative sample is too great, considering the possibility of such things as employee turnover, changes in the accounting system, and the seasonal nature of many businesses. An auditor using block sampling should exercise special care to control sampling risk in designing that sample.

Block sampling can also be used to supplement other samples when there is a high likelihood of misstatement for a known period. For example, selecting all 100 cash receipts from the third week of March may be appropriate if that is when the accounting clerk was on vacation and an inexperienced temporary employee processed the cash receipt transactions.

Haphazard sample selection is the selection of items without any conscious bias on the part of the auditor. In such cases, the auditor selects population items without regard to their size, source, or other distinguishing characteristics.

The most serious shortcoming of haphazard sample selection is the difficulty of remaining completely unbiased in the selection. Because of the auditor's training and "cultural bias," certain population items are more likely than others to be included in the sample.

Although haphazard and block sample selection appear to be less logical than directed sample selection, they are often useful as audit tools and should not be ignored. In some situations, the cost of more complex sample selection methods outweighs the benefits obtained from using them. For example, assume that the auditor wants to trace credits from the accounts receivable master files to the cash receipts journal and other authorized sources as a test for fictitious credits in the master files. A haphazard or block approach is simpler and much less costly than other selection methods in this situation and would be used by many auditors. However, for most nonstatistical sampling applications involving tests of controls and substantive tests of transactions, auditors often prefer to use a probabilistic sample selection method to increase the likelihood of selecting a representative sample. Note that probabilistic selection is required for statistical sampling.

Haphazard Sample Selection (margin)

PROBABILISTIC SAMPLE SELECTION METHODS

As previously indicated, to measure sampling risk, statistical sampling requires a probabilistic sample. For probabilistic samples, the auditor uses no judgment about which sample items are selected, except to select which of the four selection methods to use.

OBJECTIVE 15-3 (margin)
Select representative samples.

A simple **random sample** is one in which every possible combination of elements in the population has an equal chance of constituting the sample. Simple random sampling is used to sample populations that are not segmented for audit purposes. For example, the auditor may wish to sample the client's cash disbursements for the year. A simple random sample of 60 items contained in the cash disbursements journal might be selected for that purpose. Appropriate auditing procedures would be applied to the 60 items selected, and conclusions would be drawn and applied to all cash disbursement transactions recorded for the year.

Simple Random Sample Selection (margin)

Random Number Tables When a simple random sample is obtained, a method must be used that ensures that all items in the population have an equal chance of selection. Suppose that in the preceding example, there were a total of 12,000 cash disbursement transactions for the year. A simple random sample of one transaction would be such that each of the 12,000 transactions would have an equal chance of being selected. This would be done by obtaining a random number between 1 and 12,000. If the number was 3,895, the auditor would select and test the 3,895th cash disbursement transaction recorded in the cash disbursements journal.

Random numbers are a series of digits that have equal probabilities of occurring over long runs and which have no discernible pattern. A **random number table** is a presentation of these random digits in table form with numbered rows and columns. The auditor chooses a random sample by first establishing a correspondence between the client's document numbers to be tested and the digits in the random number table. After selecting a random starting point, the auditor reads down the table and finds the first random number that falls within the sequence of the document numbers being tested. The process continues until the final sample item is selected.

Computer Generation of Random Numbers It is useful to understand the use of random number tables as a means of understanding the concept of selecting simple random samples. However, most random samples obtained by auditors are obtained by using computers. There are three main types: electronic spreadsheet programs, random number generators, and generalized audit software programs.

The advantages of using computer programs in selecting random samples are time savings, reduced likelihood of auditor error in selecting the numbers, and automatic documentation. Because most auditors have access to a computer and to electronic spreadsheets or random number generator programs, auditors often prefer to use computer generation of random numbers over other probabilistic selection methods.

To illustrate computer generation of random numbers, Figure 15-1 shows the random selection of sales invoices for the audit of Hillsburg Hardware Co. using an electronic spreadsheet program. In the application illustrated, the auditor wishes to sample 50 items from a population of sales invoices numbered from 3689 to 9452. The program requires only input parameters by the auditor for a sample to be selected. It possesses great flexibility in the formatting of the numbers. For example, the program can generate random dates or ranges of sets of numbers (such as page and line numbers). It also provides output in both sorted and selection orders.

Random numbers may be obtained with replacement or without replacement. In replacement sampling, an element in the population can be included in the sample more than once, whereas in nonreplacement sampling, an element can be included only once. If the random number corresponding to an element is selected more than once in nonreplacement sampling, it is not included in the sample a second time. Although both selection approaches are consistent with sound statistical theory, auditors rarely use replacement sampling.

FIGURE 15-1   Computer Generation of Random Numbers—Hillsburg Hardware Co.

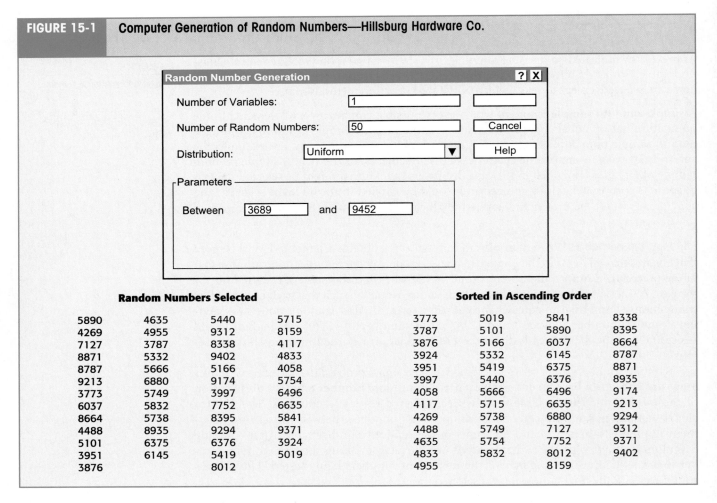

In **systematic sample selection** (also called systematic sampling), the auditor calculates an interval and then methodically selects the items for the sample based on the size of the interval. The interval is determined by dividing the population size by the number of sample items desired. For example, if a population of sales invoices ranges from 652 to 3,151 and the desired sample size is 125, the interval is 20 [(3,151 − 651)/125]. The auditor must now select a random number between 0 and 19 to determine the starting point for the sample. If the randomly selected number is 9, the first item in the sample is invoice number 661 (652 + 9). The remaining 124 items are 681 (661 + 20), 701 (681 + 20), and so on through item 3,141.

The advantage of systematic selection is its ease of use. In most populations, a systematic sample can be drawn quickly, the approach automatically puts the numbers in sequence, and it is easy to develop the appropriate documentation.

A major problem with systematic selection is the possibility of bias. Because of the way systematic selection works, once the first item in the sample is selected, all other items are chosen automatically. This causes no problem if the characteristic of interest, such as a possible control deviation, is distributed randomly throughout the population; however, in some cases, characteristics of interest may not be randomly distributed. For example, if a control deviation occurred at a certain time of the month or with certain types of documents, a systematic sample could have a higher likelihood of failing to be representative than a simple random sample. Therefore, when systematic selection is used, possible patterns in the population data that could cause sample bias must be considered.

There are many situations in auditing when it is advantageous to select samples that emphasize population items that have larger recorded amounts. There are two ways to obtain such samples. The first is to take a sample where the probability of selecting any individual population item is proportional to its recorded amount. This method is called sampling with probability proportional to size (PPS). The second way of emphasizing larger items in the population is to divide the population into subpopulations by size and take larger samples of the larger subpopulations. This is called stratified sampling. The first of these methods is evaluated using monetary unit sampling and the second using variables sampling. These selection methods and their related evaluation methods are discussed in a later chapter.

SAMPLING FOR EXCEPTION RATES

Audit sampling for tests of controls and substantive tests of transactions is used to estimate the proportion of items in a population containing a characteristic or **attribute** of interest. This proportion is called the **occurrence rate** or **exception rate** and is the ratio of the items containing the specific attribute to the total number of population items. The occurrence rate is usually expressed as a percentage. For example, an auditor might conclude that the exception rate for the internal verification of sales invoices is approximately 3 percent, meaning that invoices are not properly verified 3 percent of the time.

Auditors are interested in the occurrence of the following types of exceptions in populations of accounting data: (1) deviations from client's established controls, (2) monetary misstatements in populations of transaction data, and (3) monetary misstatements in populations of account balance details. Knowing the occurrence rate of such exceptions is particularly helpful for the first two types of exceptions, which relate to transactions. Therefore, auditors make extensive use of audit sampling that measures the occurrence or exception rate in performing tests of controls and substantive tests of transactions. With the third type of exception, the auditor usually needs to estimate the total dollar amount of the exceptions because a judgment must be made about whether the exceptions are material. When the auditor wants to know the total amount of a misstatement, then methods that measure dollars, not the exception or occurrence rate, will be used. This topic is studied in a later chapter.

The exception rate in a sample is intended to be an estimate of the exception rate in the entire population. It means that for a given sample, the sample exception rate is the auditor's "best estimate" of the population exception rate. The term *exception* should be understood to refer to both deviations from prescribed controls and situations when amounts are not monetarily correct, whether because of an unintentional accounting error or any other cause. The term *deviation* refers to the specific type of exception of a departure from prescribed controls.

Assume, for example, that the auditor wants to determine the percentage of duplicate sales invoices that do not have shipping documents attached. There is an actual, but unknown, percentage of missing shipping documents. The auditor will obtain a sample of duplicate sales invoices and determine what percentage of the invoices do not have shipping documents attached. The auditor will conclude that the sample exception rate is the best estimate of the population exception rate.

Because it is based on a sample, however, there is a significant likelihood that the sample exception rate and the actual population exception rate differ. This difference is called *sampling error,* a term that was first introduced in Chapter 9. The auditor is concerned with the estimate of the sampling error and the reliability of that estimate, called *sampling risk,* a term that was introduced earlier in this chapter. Assume that the auditor determines that there is a 3 percent sample exception rate and a sampling error of 1 percent with a sampling risk of 10 percent. The auditor can now state an interval estimate of the population exception rate as between 2 percent and 4 percent (3 percent ± 1) at a 10 percent risk of being wrong (and a 90 percent chance of being right).

In using audit sampling in auditing for exception rates, the auditor is primarily interested in knowing the *most* the exception rate might be, rather than the width of the confidence interval. Thus, the auditor focuses on the upper limit of the interval estimate. That limit is called the estimated or **computed upper exception rate (CUER)** in tests of controls and substantive tests of transactions. In the preceding example, the auditor might conclude that the CUER for missing shipping documents is 4 percent at a 5 percent sampling risk. This means that the auditor concludes that the exception rate in the population is no greater than 4 percent with a 5 percent risk of the exception rate exceeding 4 percent. Once the CUER is determined, the auditor can consider it in the context of the specific audit objectives. For example, in testing for missing shipping documents, the auditor must determine whether a 4 percent exception rate indicates an acceptable control risk for the existence objective.

APPLICATION OF NONSTATISTICAL AUDIT SAMPLING

We will now examine the application of nonstatistical audit sampling in testing transactions for control deviations and monetary misstatements. Statistical sampling is examined later in this chapter. Before doing so, the terminology from SAS 39 (AU 350) and other terminology are defined. The same terminology is used for statistical sampling. These are summarized in Table 15-1.

OBJECTIVE 15-5

Use nonstatistical sampling in tests of controls and substantive tests of transactions.

Audit sampling is applied to tests of controls and substantive tests of transactions through a set of 14 well-defined steps. The steps are divided into three sections: plan the sample, select the sample and perform the audit procedures, and evaluate the results. It is important to follow these steps carefully as a means of ensuring that both the auditing and the sampling aspects of the process are properly applied. The steps provide an outline of the discussion that follows and are illustrated for the audit of Hillsburg Hardware Co.

Plan the Sample

1. State the objectives of the audit test.
2. Decide whether audit sampling applies.
3. Define attributes and exception conditions.
4. Define the population.
5. Define the sampling unit.
6. Specify the tolerable exception rate.
7. Specify acceptable risk of assessing control risk too low.
8. Estimate the population exception rate.
9. Determine the initial sample size.

Select the Sample and Perform the Audit Procedures

10. Select the sample.
11. Perform the audit procedures.

Evaluate the Results

12. Generalize from the sample to the population.
13. Analyze exceptions.
14. Decide the acceptability of the population.

TABLE 15-1	Terms Used in Audit Sampling
TERM	**DEfiNITION**
Terms Related to Planning	
Characteristics or attribute	The characteristic being tested in the application
Acceptable risk of assessing control risk too low (ARACR)	The risk that the auditor is willing to take of accepting a control as effective or a rate of monetary misstatements as tolerable, when the true population exception rate is greater than the tolerable exception rate
Tolerable exception rate (TER)	Exception rate that the auditor will permit in the population and still be willing to conclude the control is operating effectively and/or the amount of monetary misstatements in the transactions established during planning is acceptable
Estimated population exception rate (EPER)	Exception rate that the auditor expects to find in the population before testing begins
Initial sample size	Sample size decided after considering the above factors in planning
Terms Related to Evaluating Results	
Exception	Exception from the attribute in a sample item
Sample exception rate (SER)	Number of exceptions in the sample divided by the sample size
Computed upper exception rate (CUER)	The highest estimated exception rate in the population at a given ARACR

State the Objectives of the Audit Test

The overall objectives of the test must be stated in terms of the transaction cycle being tested. Typically, the overall objectives of tests of controls and substantive tests of transactions are to test the operating effectiveness of controls and to determine whether the transactions contain monetary misstatements.

In the tests of the sales and collection cycle, the overall objectives are usually to test the effectiveness of internal controls over sales and cash receipts and to determine whether sales and cash receipts transactions contain monetary misstatements. The objectives of the audit test are normally decided as a part of designing the audit program, which was discussed for the sales and collection cycle in Chapter 14. The audit program for the sales and collection cycle for Hillsburg Hardware is included in Figure 14-6 (p. 430).

Decide Whether Audit Sampling Applies

Audit sampling applies whenever the auditor plans to reach conclusions about a population based on a sample. The auditor should examine the audit program and decide those audit procedures for which audit sampling applies. Assume the following partial audit program:

TABLE 15-2	Audit Procedures—Hillsburg Hardware Co.

PROCEDURE	COMMENT
Shipment of Goods	
10. Account for a sequence of shipping documents.	It is possible to do this by selecting a random sample and accounting for all shipping documents selected. This requires a separate set of random numbers because the sampling unit is different from that used for the other tests.
11. Trace selected shipping documents to the sales journal to be sure that each one has been included.	No exceptions are expected, and a 6 percent TER is considered acceptable at an ARACR of 10 percent. A sample size of 40 is selected. The shipping documents are traced to the sales journal. This is done for all 40 items. There are no exceptions for either test. The results are considered acceptable. There is no further information about this portion of the tests in this illustration.
Billing of Customers and Recording the Sales in the Records	
12. Account for a sequence of sales invoices in the sales journal.	The audit procedures for billing and recording sales (procedures 12 to 14) are the only ones included for illustration throughout this chapter.

13. Trace selected sales invoice numbers from the sales journal to
 	
  a. accounts receivable master file and test for amount, date, and invoice number.
  b. duplicate sales invoice and check for the total amount recorded in the journal, date, customer name, and account classification. Check the pricing, extensions, and footings. Examine underlying documents for indication of internal verification.
  c. bill of lading and test for customer name, product description, quantity, and date.
  d. duplicate sales order and test for customer name, product description, quantity, date, and indication of internal verification by Pam Dilley.
  e. customer order and test for customer name, product description, quantity, date, and credit approval.	

14. Trace recorded sales from the sales journal to the file of supporting documents, which includes a duplicate sales invoice, bill of lading, sales order, and customer order.	

Note: Random selection and statistical sampling are not applicable for the nine general audit procedures in Figure 14-6. Advanced statistical techniques, such as regression analysis, could be applicable for analysis of the results of analytical procedures. Random selection could be used for procedure 2.

1. Review sales transactions for large and unusual amounts (analytical procedure).
2. Observe whether the duties of the accounts receivable clerk are separate from handling cash (test of control).
3. Examine a sample of duplicate sales invoices for

    a. credit approval by the credit manager (test of control).
    b. existence of an attached shipping document (test of control).
    c. inclusion of a chart of accounts number (test of control).

4. Select a sample of shipping documents and trace each to related duplicate sales invoices (test of control).
5. Compare the quantity on each duplicate sales invoice with the quantity on related shipping documents (substantive test of transactions).

Audit sampling is inappropriate for the first two procedures in this audit program. The first is an analytical procedure for which sampling is inappropriate. The second is an observation procedure for which no documentation exists to perform audit sampling. Audit sampling can be used for the remaining three procedures. Table 15-2 (p. 452) indicates the audit procedures for the sales cycle for Hillsburg Hardware Co. for which audit sampling is appropriate.

When audit sampling is used, the auditor must carefully define the characteristics (attributes) being tested and the exception conditions. Unless a precise statement of what constitutes an attribute is made in advance, the staff person who performs the audit procedure will have no guidelines for identifying exceptions.

Attributes of interest and exception conditions come directly from the audit procedures for which the auditor has decided to use audit sampling. Table 15-3 shows nine

Define Attributes and Exception Conditions

TABLE 15-3	Attributes Defined—Tests of Hillsburg Hardware Co.'s Billing Function
Attribute	**Exception Condition**
1. Existence of the sales invoice number in the sales journal (procedure 12).	No record of sales invoice number in the sales journal.
2. Amount and other data in the master file agree with sales journal entry (procedure 13a).	The amount recorded in the master file differs from the amount recorded in the sales journal.
3. Amount and other data on the duplicate sales invoice agree with the sales journal entry (procedure 13b).	Customer name and account number on the invoice differ from the information recorded in the sales journal.
4. Evidence that pricing, extensions, and footings are checked (initials and correct amounts) (procedure 13b).	Lack of initials indicating verification of pricing, extensions, and footings.
5. Quantity and other data on the bill of lading agree with the duplicate sales invoice and sales journal (procedure 13c).	Quantity of goods shipped differs from quantity on the duplicate sales invoice.
6. Quantity and other data on the sales order agree with the duplicate sales invoice (procedure 13d).	Quantity on the sales order differs from the quantity on the duplicate sales invoice.
7. Quantity and other data on the customer order agree with the duplicate sales invoice (procedure 13e).	Product number and description on the customer order differ from information on the duplicate sales invoice.
8. Credit is approved (procedure 13e).	Lack of initials indicating credit approval.
9. For recorded sales in the sales journal, the file of supporting documents includes a duplicate sales invoice, bill of lading, sales order, and customer order (procedure 14).	Bill of lading is not attached to the duplicate sales invoice and the customer order.

attributes of interest and exception conditions taken directly from audit procedures 12 through 14 in the audit of Hillsburg's billing function. Samples of sales invoices will be used to verify these attributes. The absence of the attribute for any sample item will be an exception for that attribute. It is important to note that both missing documents and immaterial misstatements result in exceptions unless the auditor specifically states otherwise in the exception conditions.

Define the Population

The population represents the body of data about which the auditor wishes to generalize. The auditor can define the population to include whatever data are desired but must sample from the entire population as it has been defined. The auditor may generalize *only* about that population that has been sampled. For example, in performing tests of controls and substantive tests of sales transactions, the auditor generally defines the population as all recorded sales for the year. If the auditor samples from only 1 month's transactions, it is invalid to draw conclusions about the invoices for the entire year.

The auditor must carefully define the population in advance, consistent with the objectives of the audit tests. Furthermore, in some cases, it may be necessary to define more than one population for a given set of audit procedures. For example, in the audit of the sales and collection cycle at Hillsburg Hardware Co., the direction of testing in audit procedures 12 through 14 in Table 15-2 is from sales invoices in the sales journal to source documentation. In contrast, the direction of testing for audit procedures 10 and 11 is from the shipping documents to the sales journal. Thus, there are two populations (one population of sales invoices in the sales journal and another of shipping documents). It is also important to test the population for completeness and detail tie-in before a sample is selected to ensure that all population items will be properly subjected to sample selection.

Define the Sampling Unit

The major consideration in defining the sampling unit is to make it consistent with the objectives of the audit tests. Thus, the definition of the population and the planned audit procedures usually dictate the appropriate sampling unit. For example, if the auditor wants to determine how often the client fails to fill a customer's order, the sampling unit must be defined as the customer's order. If, however, the objective is to determine whether the proper quantity of the goods described on the customer's order is correctly shipped and billed, it is possible to define the sampling unit as the customer's order, the shipping document, or the duplicate sales invoice.

Audit procedure 14 in Table 15-2 is a test for the existence of recorded sales. Therefore, the appropriate sampling unit is the duplicate sales invoice. However, it is impossible to test the attribute related to audit procedure 14 if the sampling unit is the shipping document. The appropriate sampling unit for audit procedure 11 is the shipping document because this tests that existing sales are recorded (completeness). The attribute related to audit procedure 11 cannot be tested if the sampling unit is the duplicate sales invoice. Either the duplicate sales invoice or the shipping document is appropriate for audit procedures 13a through 13e because these are all nondirectional tests.

The auditor could define the sampling unit as the duplicate sales invoice to perform audit procedures 12 through 14. Audit procedures 10 and 11 would still have to be tested separately using a sample of shipping documents.

Specify the Tolerable Exception Rate

Establishing the **tolerable exception rate** (TER) requires professional judgment on the part of the auditor. TER represents the exception rate that the auditor will permit in the population and still be willing to conclude the control in operating effectively and/or the amount of monetary misstatements in the transactions established during planning is acceptable. For example, assume that the auditor decides that TER for attribute 8 in Table 15-3 is 9 percent. That means that the auditor has decided that even if 9 percent of the duplicate sales invoices are not approved for credit, the credit approval control is still effective in terms of the assessed control risk included in the audit plan.

TER is the result of an auditor's judgment. The suitable TER is a question of materiality and is therefore affected by both the definition and the importance of the attribute in the audit plan. For example, if only one internal control is used to support a low control risk assessment for an objective, TER will be lower for this attribute than if there are multiple controls used to support a low control risk assessment for the objective. TER will normally be lower for tests of controls in the audit of a public company because the results of the tests of controls provide the basis for the auditor's report on internal control over financial reporting.

TER has a significant impact on sample size. A larger sample size is needed for a low TER than for a high TER. For example, a larger sample is required for a TER of 3 percent for attribute 8 than for a TER of 9 percent in the previous example.

Most auditors use some type of preprinted form to document each sampling application. An example of a commonly used form is given in Figure 15-2. The top part of the form includes a definition of the objective, the population, and the sampling unit.

FIGURE 15-2	Sampling Data Sheet: Tests of Hillsburg Hardware Co.'s Billing Function

Client: Hillsburg Hardware
Audit Area: Tests of Controls and Substantive Tests of Transactions— Billing Function

Year-end: 12/31/04
Pop. size: 5,764

Define the objective(s): Examine duplicate sales invoices and related documents to determine whether the system has functioned as intended and as described in the audit program.

Define the population precisely (including stratification, if any): Sales invoices for the period 1/1/04 to 10/31/04. First invoice number = 3689. Last invoice number = 9452.

Define the sampling unit, organization of population items, and random selection procedures: Sales invoice number, recorded in the sales journal sequentially; computer generation of random numbers.

Description of Attributes	Planned Audit				Actual Results			
	EPER	TER	ARACR	Initial sample size	Sample size	Number of exceptions	Sample exception rate	Calculated Sampling Error (TER − SER)
1. Existence of the sales invoice number in the sales journal (procedure 12).	0	4	Low	75				
2. Amount and other data in the master file agree with sales journal entry (procedure 13a).	1	5	Low	100				
3. Amount and other data on the duplicate sales invoice agree with the sales journal entry (procedure 13b).	1	5	Low	100				
4. Evidence that pricing, extensions, and footings are checked (initials and correct amounts) (procedure 13b).	1	5	Low	100				
5. Quantity and other data on the bill of lading agree with the duplicate sales invoice and sales journal (procedure 13c).	1	5	Low	100				
6. Quantity and other data on the sales order agree with the duplicate sales invoice (procedure 13d).	1	7	Low	65				
7. Quantity and other data on the customer order agree with the duplicate sales invoice (procedure 13e).	1.5	9	Low	50				
8. Credit is approved by Rick Chulick (procedure 13e).	1.5	9	Low	50				
9. For recorded sales in the sales journal, the file of supporting documents includes a duplicate sales invoice, bill of lading, sales order, and customer order (procedure 14).	1	7	Low	65				

Intended use of sampling results:

1. Effect on Audit Plan:

2. Recommendations to Management:

The TER for each attribute being tested in audit procedures 12 through 14 in Table 15-3 (p. 453) is decided on the basis of the auditor's judgment of what exception rate is material. The failure to record a sales invoice would be highly significant, especially considering the system; therefore, as indicated in Figure 15-2 (p. 455), the lowest TER (4 percent) is chosen for attribute 1. The incorrect billing of the customer represents potentially significant misstatements, but no misstatement is likely to be for the full amount of the invoice. As a result, a 5 percent TER is chosen for each of the attributes directly related to the billing of shipments and recording of the amounts in the records. The last four attributes have higher TERs because they are of less importance for the audit and there are other controls for that objective.

Specify Acceptable Risk of Assessing Control Risk Too Low

When a sample is taken, there is a risk that the quantitative conclusions about the population will be incorrect. This is always true unless 100 percent of the population is tested. As has already been stated, this is the case with both nonstatistical and statistical sampling.

For audit sampling in tests of controls and substantive tests of transactions, that risk is called the **acceptable risk of assessing control risk too low (ARACR)**. ARACR is the risk that the auditor is willing to take of accepting a control as effective (or a rate of monetary misstatements as tolerable) when the true population exception rate is greater than TER. ARACR is the auditor's measure of sampling risk. To illustrate, assume that TER is 6 percent, ARACR is 10 percent, and the true population exception rate is 8 percent. The control in this case is not acceptable because the true exception rate of 8 percent exceeds TER. The auditor, of course, does not know the true population exception rate. The ARACR of 10 percent means that the auditor is willing to take a 10 percent risk of concluding that the control is effective after all testing is completed, even when it is ineffective. If the control is found effective in this illustration, the auditor will have overrelied on the system of internal control (used a lower assessed control risk than justified).

In choosing the appropriate ARACR in a situation, auditors must use their best judgment. Because ARACR is a measure of the risk that the auditor is willing to take, the main consideration is the extent to which the auditor plans to reduce assessed control risk as a basis for the extent of tests of details of balances. Referring to Figure 10-11 (p. 300), ARACR will normally be assessed at a lower level when auditing a public company because the auditor will perform extensive tests of controls to support the opinion on internal control over financial reporting. The appropriate ARACR and extent of tests of controls depend on the assessed level of control risk in the audit of a private company.

For nonstatistical sampling, it is common for auditors to use ARACR of high, medium, or low instead of a percentage. A low ARACR implies that the tests of controls are important and would correspond to a low assessed control risk and reduced substantive tests of details of balances. As summarized in Figure 15-2, ARACR for the audit of the billing function at Hillsburg Hardware Co. is assessed as low for all attributes given that Hillsburg Hardware is a public company and the auditor's tests of controls must provide a basis for the opinion on internal control over financial reporting.

The auditor can establish different TER and ARACR levels for different attributes of an audit test. For example, it is common for auditors to use higher TER and ARACR levels for tests of credit approval than for tests of the existence of duplicate sales invoices and bills of lading. This is because the exceptions for the latter are likely to have a more direct impact on the correctness of the financial statements than the former.

Tables 15-4 and 15-5 present illustrative guidelines for establishing TER and ARACR. The guidelines should not be interpreted as representing broad professional standards; however, they are typical of the types of guidelines CPA firms issue to their staff.

Estimate the Population Exception Rate

An advance estimate of the population exception rate should be made to plan the appropriate sample size. If the **estimated population exception rate (EPER)** is low, a relatively small sample size will satisfy the auditor's tolerable exception rate. This is because a less precise estimate is required. In other words, to be more precise, an estimate of the population exception rate must be based on more data, that is, a larger sample. As the EPER approaches the auditor's tolerable exception rate, the need for more precision arises.

It is common to use the results of the preceding year's audit to make this estimate. If prior-year results are not available or if they are considered unreliable, the auditor can take

TABLE 15-4 Guidelines for ARACR and TER for Nonstatistical Sampling: Tests of Controls

Factor	Judgment	Guideline

Assessed control risk. Consider:
   Need to issue a separate report on internal control over financial reporting for public companies
   Nature, extent, and timing of substantive tests (extensive planned substantive tests relate to higher assessed control risk and vice versa)
   Quality of evidence available for tests of controls (a lower quality of evidence available results in a higher assessed control risk and vice versa)
	• Lowest assessed control risk
	• Moderate assessed control risk
	• Higher assessed control risk
	• 100% assessed control risk
		• ARACR of low
		• ARACR of medium
		• ARACR of high
		• ARACR is not applicable

Significance of the transactions and related account balances that the internal controls are intended to affect	• Highly significant balances • Significant balances • Less significant balances	• TER of 4% • TER of 5% • TER of 6%

Note: The guidelines should recognize that there may be variations in ARACRs based on audit considerations. The guidelines above are the most conservative that should be followed.

a small preliminary sample of the current year's population for this purpose. It is not critical that the estimate be precise because the current year's sample exception rate is ultimately used to estimate the population characteristics. Note that if a preliminary sample is used, it can be included in the ultimate sample, as long as appropriate sample selection procedures are followed. For example, assume that an auditor takes a preliminary sample of 30 items to estimate the EPER that considers the entire population. Later, if the auditor decides that a total sample size of 100 is needed, only 70 additional items will need to be properly selected and tested. In the Hillsburg Hardware Co. audit, the estimated population exception rates for the attributes in Figure 15-2 (p. 455) are based on previous years' results, modified slightly to account for the change in personnel.

Four factors determine the **initial sample size** for audit sampling: population size, TER, ARACR, and EPER. Population size is not nearly as significant a factor as the others and typically can be ignored, especially for large populations. An important characteristic of nonstatistical sampling compared with statistical methods is the need to decide the sample size using professional judgment for nonstatistical methods rather than by calculation using a statistical formula. Once the three major factors affecting sample size have been determined, the auditor can decide an initial sample size. The initial sample size is called that because the exceptions in the actual sample must be evaluated before it is possible to know whether the sample is sufficiently large to achieve the objectives of the tests.

Determine the Initial Sample Size

TABLE 15-5 Guidelines for ARACR and TER for Nonstatistical Sampling: Substantive Tests of Transactions

Planned Reduction in Substantive Tests of Details of Balances	Results of Understanding Internal Control and Tests of Controls	ARACR for Substantive Tests of Transactions	TER for Substantive Tests of Transactions
Large	Excellent[1] Good Not good	High Medium Low	Percent or amount based on materiality considerations for related accounts
Moderate	Excellent[1] Good Not good	High Medium Medium-low	Percent or amount based on materiality considerations for related accounts
Small[2]	Excellent[1] Good Not good	High Medium-high Medium	Percent or amount based on materiality considerations for related accounts

Note: The guidelines should also recognize that there may be variations in ARACRs based on audit considerations. The guidelines above are the most conservative that should be followed.
[1]In this situation, both internal control and evidence about it are good. Substantive tests of transactions are least likely to be performed in this situation.
[2]In this situation, little emphasis is being placed on internal controls. Neither tests of controls nor substantive tests of transactions are likely in this situation.

TABLE 15-6	Effect on Sample Size of Changing Factors
Type of Change	**Effect on Initial Sample Size**
Increase acceptable risk of assessing control risk too low	Decrease
Increase tolerable exception rate	Decrease
Increase estimated population exception rate	Increase
Increase population size	Increase (minor effect)

Sensitivity of Sample Size to a Change in the Factors To properly understand the concepts underlying sampling in auditing, it is helpful to understand the effect of changing any of the four factors that determine sample size while the other factors are held constant. Table 15-6 illustrates the effect of increasing each of the four factors; a decrease will have the opposite effect.

A combination of two factors has the greatest effect on sample size: TER minus EPER. The difference is the *precision* of the planned sample estimate. A smaller precision, which is called a more precise estimate, requires a larger sample.

Figure 15-2 (p. 455) summarizes the different sample sizes selected for testing attributes 1 through 9 for the Hillsburg audit. The largest sample (a size of 100) is selected for tests of attributes 2 through 5, given the degree of precision required for those attributes. For those attributes, the difference between TER and EPER is smallest, thus requiring a larger sample size than attributes 6 through 9. Although the difference between TER and EPER for attribute 1 is the same as that between attributes 2 through 5, the estimated population exception rate of zero justifies a smaller sample of 75 items. The degree of precision is smallest for attributes 7 and 8. Thus, a sample size of only 50 items is selected.

Select the Sample

After the initial sample size for the audit sampling application has been computed, the auditor must choose the items in the population to be included in the sample. The sample can be chosen by using any of the probabilistic or nonprobabilistic methods discussed earlier in this chapter. To minimize the possibility of the client altering the sample items, the auditor should not inform the client too far in advance of the sample items selected. The auditor should also control the sample after the client provides the documents. Several additional sample items may be selected as extras to replace any voided items that may be included in the original sample.

The random selection for the Hillsburg audit procedures is straightforward except for different sample sizes for different attributes. This problem can be overcome by selecting a random sample of 50 for use on all nine attributes followed by another sample of 15 for all attributes except attributes 7 and 8, an additional 10 for attributes 1 through 5, and 25 more for attributes 2 through 5. Figure 15-1 on page 448 illustrates the selection of the first 50 sample items for Hillsburg Hardware using computer generation of random numbers.

Perform the Audit Procedures

The auditor performs the audit procedures by examining each item in the sample to determine whether it is consistent with the definition of the attribute and maintains a record of all the exceptions found. When audit procedures have been completed for a sampling application, there will be a sample size and number of exceptions for each attribute.

As means of documenting the tests and providing information for review, it is common to include a schedule of the results. Some auditors prefer to include a schedule containing a listing of all items in the sample; others prefer to limit the documentation to identifying the exceptions. This latter approach is followed in Figure 15-3.

FIGURE 15-3   Inspection of Sample Items for Attributes

CLIENT: Hillsburg Hardware
INSPECTION OF SAMPLE ITEMS
FOR ATTRIBUTES
YEAR-END: DECEMBER 31, 2004

Prepared by   MSW
Date   11/15/04

Attributes   X = Exception

Identity of Item Selected — Invoice no.	1	2	3	4	5	6	7	8	9	10	11
3787					X						
3924				X				X			
3990				X							
4058		X		X							
4117								X			
4222					X						
4488								X			
4635				X	X						
4955						X		X			
4969				X							
5101								X			
5166								X			
5419								X			
5832								X			
5890								X			
6157		X		X							
6229				X							
6376								X			
6635					X						
7127				X							
8338								X			
8871				X							
9174								X			
9371				X							
No. Exceptions	0	2	0	10	4	1	0	12	0		
Sample Size	75	100	100	100	100	65	50	50	65		

The **sample exception rate (SER)** can be easily calculated from the actual sample results. SER equals the actual number of exceptions divided by the actual sample size. Figure 15-3 summarizes the exceptions found for tests of attributes 1 through 9. The auditor uses this information to calculate the SER for each attribute. For example, the auditor found zero exceptions for attribute 1 and two exceptions for attribute 2. Thus, the SER is 0 percent (0 ÷ 75) for attribute 1, while the SER is 2 percent for attribute 2 (2 ÷ 100).

It is improper for the auditor to conclude that the population exception rate is exactly the same as the sample exception rate; the chance that they are exactly the same is too small. For nonstatistical methods, there are two ways to generalize from the sample to the population.

Generalize from the Sample to the Population

1. Add an estimate of sampling error to SER to arrive at a computed upper exception rate (CUER) for a given acceptable risk of assessing control risk too low. It is extremely difficult for auditors to make sampling error estimates using nonstatistical sampling because of the judgment required to do so; therefore, this approach is generally not used.

2. Subtract the sample exception rate from the tolerable exception rate, which is calculated sampling error (TER − SER = calculated sampling error), and evaluate whether calculated sampling error is sufficiently large to indicate that the true population exception rate is acceptable. Under this approach, the auditor does not make an estimate of the computed upper exception rate. Most auditors using nonstatistical sampling follow this approach. For example, if an auditor takes a sample of 100 items for an attribute and finds no exceptions (SER = 0) and TER is 5 percent, calculated sampling error is 5 percent (TER of 5 percent − SER of 0 = 5 percent). On the other hand, if there had been four exceptions, calculated sampling error would have been 1 percent (TER of 5 percent − SER of 4 percent). It is much more likely that the true population exception rate is less than or equal to the tolerable exception rate in the first case than in the second one. Therefore, most auditors would probably find the population acceptable based on the first sample result and not acceptable based on the second. Furthermore, if the SER exceeds the EPER used in designing the sample, it is generally appropriate for the auditor to assume that the sample results do not support the planned assessed level of control risk. In that case, there is likely to be an unacceptably high risk that the true deviation rate in the population exceeds TER.

In addition, the auditor's consideration of whether sampling error is sufficiently large will depend on sample size. For example, if the sample size in the previous example had been only 20 items, the auditor would have been much less confident that finding no exceptions was an indication that the true population exception rate does not exceed TER.

The SER and the calculated sampling error (TER − SER) for Hillsburg Hardware are summarized in Figure 15-4.

Analyze Exceptions

In addition to determining the SER for each attribute and evaluating whether the true but unknown exception rate is likely to exceed the tolerable exception rate, it is necessary to analyze individual exceptions to determine the breakdown in the internal controls that caused them. Exceptions could be caused by carelessness of employees, misunderstood instructions, intentional failure to perform procedures, or many other factors. The nature of an exception and its cause have a significant effect on the qualitative evaluation of the system. For example, if all the exceptions in the tests of internal verification of sales invoices occurred while the person normally responsible for performing the tests was on vacation, this would affect the auditor's evaluation of the internal controls and the subsequent investigation.

Decide the Acceptability of the Population

It was shown under generalizing from the sample to the population that most auditors subtract SER from TER when they use nonstatistical sampling and evaluate whether the difference, which is calculated sampling error, is sufficiently large. If the auditor concludes that the difference is sufficiently large, the control being tested can be used to reduce assessed control risk as planned, provided a careful analysis of the cause of exceptions does not indicate the possibility of other significant problems with internal controls.

As shown in Figure 15-4, SER exceeds TER for attributes 4 and 8. Although SER is less than TER for attributes 2 and 5, the auditor also considered the calculated allowance for sampling error to be too small and the results of the test unacceptable. It is important to analyze the exceptions to determine their causes and to draw conclusions about each attribute tested. The exception analysis is illustrated for Hillsburg in Figure 15-5 on page 462.

When the auditor concludes that TER − SER is too small to conclude that the population is acceptable, or when SER exceeds TER, the auditor must take specific action. Four courses of action can be followed.

Revise TER or ARACR This alternative should be followed only when the auditor has concluded that the original specifications were too conservative. Relaxing either TER or

FIGURE 15-4	Sampling Data Sheet: Tests of Hillsburg Hardware Co.'s Billing Function

Client: Hillsburg Hardware
Audit Area: Tests of Controls and Substantive Tests of Transactions—Billing Function

Year-end: 12/31/04
Pop. size: 5,764

Define the objective(s): Examine duplicate sales invoices and related documents to determine whether the system has functioned as intended and as described in the audit program.

Define the population precisely (including stratification, if any): Sales invoices for the period 1/1/04 to 10/31/04. First invoice number = 3689. Last invoice number = 9452.

Define the sampling unit, organization of population items, and random selection procedures: Sales invoice number, recorded in the sales journal sequentially; computer generation of random numbers.

Description of Attributes	Planned Audit				Actual Results			
	EPER	TER	ARACR	Initial sample size	Sample size	Number of exceptions	Sample exception rate	Calculated Sampling Error (TER − SER)
1. Existence of the sales invoice number in the sales journal (procedure 12).	0	4	Low	75	75	0	0	4.0
2. Amount and other data in the master file agree with sales journal entry (procedure 13a).	1	5	Low	100	100	2	2	3.0
3. Amount and other data on the duplicate sales invoice agree with the sales journal entry (procedure 13b).	1	5	Low	100	100	0	0	5.0
4. Evidence that pricing, extensions, and footings are checked (initials and correct amounts) (procedure 13b).	1	5	Low	100	100	10	10	SER exceeds TER
5. Quantity and other data on the bill of lading agree with the duplicate sales invoice and sales journal (procedure 13c).	1	5	Low	100	100	4	4	1.0
6. Quantity and other data on the sales order agree with the duplicate sales invoice (procedure 13d).	1	7	Low	65	65	1	1.5	5.5
7. Quantity and other data on the customer order agree with the duplicate sales invoice (procedure 13e).	1.5	9	Low	50	50	0	0	9.0
8. Credit is approved by Rick Chulick (procedure 13e).	1.5	9	Low	50	50	12	24	SER exceeds TER
9. For recorded sales in the sales journal, the file of supporting documents includes a duplicate sales invoice, bill of lading, sales order, and customer order (procedure 14).	1	7	Low	65	65	0	0	7.0

Intended use of sampling results:

1. Effect on Audit Plan: Controls tested through attributes 1, 3, 6, 7, and 9 can be viewed as operating effectively given the size of the allowance for sampling error (e.g., TER − SER). Additional emphasis is needed in confirmation, allowance for uncollectible accounts, cutoff tests, and price tests for the financial statement audit due to results of tests for attributes 2, 4, 5, and 8.

2. Effect on Report on Internal Control: The allowance for sampling error is too small or SER exceeds TER for attributes 2, 4, 5, and 8. These findings have been communicated to management to allow an opportunity for correction of the control deficiency to be made before year-end. If timely correction is made by management, the corrected controls will be tested before year-end for purposes of reporting on internal control over financial reporting.

3. Recommendations to Management: Each of the exceptions should be discussed with management. Specific recommendations are needed to correct the internal verification of sales invoices and to improve the approach to credit approvals.

FIGURE 15-5 Analysis of Exceptions

CLIENT: Hillsburg Hardware
ANALYSIS OF EXCEPTIONS
YEAR-END: December 31, 2004

Prepared by: MSW
Date: 11/15/04

Attribute	Number of exceptions	Nature of exceptions	Effect on the financial statement audit and other comments*
2	2	Both errors were posted to the wrong account and were still outstanding after several months. The amounts were for $2,500 and $7,900.	Because the allowance for sampling error is small (e.g., TER – SER), additional substantive work is needed. Perform expanded confirmation procedures and review older uncollected balances thoroughly.
4	10	In six cases there were no initials for internal verification. In two cases the wrong price was used but the errors were under $200 in each case. In one case there was a pricing error of $5,000. In one case freight was not charged. (Three of the last four exceptions had initials for internal verification.)	As a result, have independent client personnel recheck a random sample of 500 duplicate sales invoices under our control. Also, expand the confirmation of accounts receivable.
5	4	In each case the date on the duplicate sales invoice was several days later than the shipping date.	Do extensive tests of the sales cutoff by comparing recorded sales with the shipping documents.
6	1	Just 106 items were shipped and billed though the sales order was for 112 items. The reason for the difference was an error in the perpetual inventory master file. The perpetuals indicated that 112 items were on hand, when there were actually 106. The system does not backorder for undershipments smaller than 25%.	No expansion of tests of controls or substantive tests. The system appears to be working effectively.
8	12	Credit was not approved. Four of these were for new customers. Discussed with Chulick, who stated his busy schedule did not permit approving all sales.	Expand the year-end procedures extensively in evaluating allowance for uncollectible accounts. This includes scheduling of cash receipts subsequent to year-end and for all outstanding accounts receivable to determine collectibility at year-end.

*This column documents conclusions about implications for the financial statement audit. The control deficiencies have been communicated to management to allow an opportunity for correction of the deficiency before year-end. If timely correction is made by management, the corrected controls will be tested before year-end for purposes of reporting on internal control over financial reporting.

ARACR may be difficult to defend if the auditor is ever subject to review by a court or a commission. If these requirements are changed, it should be done on the basis of careful thought.

Expand the Sample Size An increase in the sample size has the effect of decreasing the sampling error if the actual sample exception rate does not increase. Of course, SER may also increase or decrease if additional items are selected.

Sampling Software

Revise Assessed Control Risk If the results of the tests of controls and substantive tests of transactions do not support the planned assessed control risk, the auditor should revise assessed control risk upward. The effect of the revision is likely to increase substantive tests of transactions and tests of details of balances. For example, if tests of controls of internal verification procedures for verifying prices, extensions, and quantities on sales invoices indicate that those procedures are not being followed, the auditor should increase substantive tests of transactions for the accuracy of sales. If the substantive tests of transactions results are unacceptable, the auditor must increase tests of details of balances for accounts receivable.

The decision whether to increase sample size until sampling error is sufficiently small or to revise assessed control risk must be made on the basis of cost versus benefit. If the sample is not expanded, it is necessary to revise assessed control risk upward and therefore perform additional substantive tests. The cost of additional tests of controls must be compared with that of additional substantive tests. If an expanded sample continues to produce unacceptable results, additional substantive tests will still be necessary for the audit of financial statements.

If the original test performed is to test transactions for monetary misstatements and an exception rate higher than that assumed is indicated, the response would generally be the same as for tests of controls.

For public companies, the auditor must evaluate the control deficiencies to determine their effect on the auditor's report on internal control. If any of the deficiencies constitute a material weakness and are not corrected before year-end, then the auditor's report on internal control must be an adverse opinion.

Communicate with the Audit Committee or Management This action is desirable, in combination with one of the other three just described, regardless of the nature of the exceptions. When the auditor determines that the internal controls are not operating effectively, management should be informed in a timely manner. If the tests were performed prior to year-end, this may allow management an opportunity to correct the deficiency before year-end. The auditor is required to communicate in writing significant deficiencies and material weaknesses in internal control to the audit committee.

In some instances, it may be acceptable to limit the action to writing a letter to management when TER − SER is too small. This occurs if the auditor has no intention of reducing the assessed control risk or has already carried out sufficient procedures to his or her own satisfaction as a part of substantive tests of transactions.

For the Hillsburg audit, there were two attributes (4 and 8) where the SER exceeded TER. The sales transactions tested at Hillsburg represented transactions recorded through October 31, 2004. Timely communication of these deficiencies may allow Hillsburg management the opportunity to correct the noted deficiencies in time for the auditor to test those corrected controls before year-end for purposes of auditing internal control over financial reporting. The last column of Figure 15-5 summarizes the follow-up actions that will be conducted in the financial statement audit regardless of whether the control deficiencies are corrected. Because the difference between SER and TER was small for attributes 2 and 5, Figure 15-5 contains follow-up actions in the financial statement audit for those attributes. No follow-up actions are required to address the exception noted for attribute 6, given the large difference between SER and TER. The conclusions reached about each attribute are also documented at the bottom of Figure 15-4 (p. 461).

Adequate Documentation

It is important that the auditor retain adequate records of the procedures performed, the methods used to select the sample and perform the tests, the results found in the tests, and the conclusions drawn. This is necessary as a means of evaluating the combined results of

FIGURE 15-6 — Evidence-Planning Worksheet to Decide Tests of Details of Balances for Hillsburg Hardware Co.—Accounts Receivable

	Detail tie-in	Existence	Completeness	Accuracy	Classification	Cutoff	Realizable value	Rights	Presentation and disclosure
Acceptable audit risk	High	High	High	High	High	High	High	High	High
Inherent risk	Low	Medium	Low	Low	Low	Medium	Medium	Low	Low
Control risk—Sales	Low	Medium	Low	High	Low	Medium	High	Not applicable	Not applicable
Control risk—Cash receipts	Low	Medium	Low	Low	Low	Low	Not applicable	Not applicable	Not applicable
Control risk—Additional controls	None	None	None	None	None	None	None	Low	Low
Substantive tests of transactions—Sales	Good results	Good results	Good results	Fair results	Good results	Unacceptable results	Not applicable	Not applicable	Not applicable
Substantive tests of transactions—Cash receipts	Good results	Good results	Good results	Good results	Good results	Good results	Not applicable	Not applicable	Not applicable
Analytical procedures									
Planned detection risk for tests of details of balances									
Planned audit evidence for tests of details of balances									

Tolerable misstatement $442,000

all tests and as a basis for defending the audit if the need arises. Documentation is equally important for statistical or nonstatistical sampling. Figures 15-2 through 15-6 illustrate the type of documentation commonly found in practice.

After completing tests of controls and substantive tests of transactions, the auditor should complete rows 3 through 7 of the evidence-planning worksheet used in the financial statement audit to decide the tests of balances for accounts receivable. This worksheet is illustrated for Hillsburg Hardware in Figure 15-6.

Recall that rows 1 and 2 were completed in an earlier chapter. Rows 3 through 5 document control risk for sales, cash receipts, and additional controls. The control risk assessments in Figure 15-6 are the same as the planned assessments in the control risk matrices for Hillsburg Hardware on pages 289 and 427, with the following modifications:

- Control risk is high for the accuracy objective for sales because of the unsatisfactory results for attribute 4 (procedure 13b).
- Control risk is high for the realizable value objective for sales based on the results for attribute 8 (procedure 13e).

• Recall that the existence (completeness) objective for cash receipts relates to the completeness (existence) objective for accounts receivable.

Finally, note in Figure 15-6 that all substantive tests of transactions results were satisfactory except for the accuracy and cutoff objectives for sales. The substantive tests of transactions results for the accuracy objective were only fair because of exceptions found for attribute 2 (procedure 13a). Results were unacceptable for the cutoff objective because of unsatisfactory results for attribute 5 (procedure 13c).

The results of these tests of controls and substantive tests of transactions must be evaluated by the auditor to determine their impact on the auditor's report on internal control over financial reporting. If the client corrects the controls, the auditor may be able to test management's corrected controls before year-end. The auditor may also be able to identify additional compensating controls. If the auditor is unable to test corrected controls or identify compensating controls and the deficiencies are deemed to be material weaknesses, the audit report on Hillsburg's internal control over financial reporting would be adverse.

All of the steps involved in nonstatistical sampling are summarized in Figure 15-7. Although this figure deals with nonstatistical sampling, the 14 steps in the figure also apply to statistical sampling, which is studied in the next section.

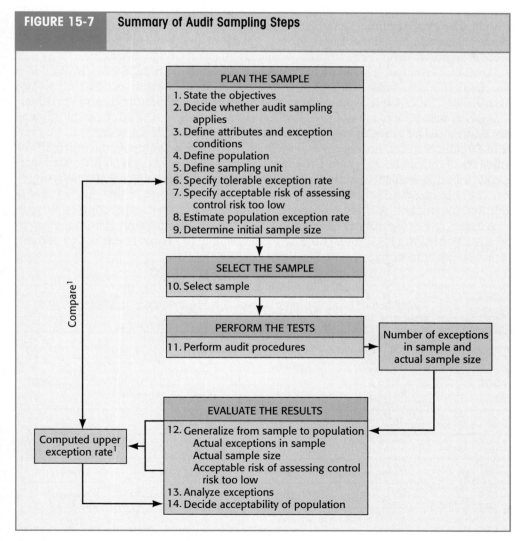

FIGURE 15-7   **Summary of Audit Sampling Steps**

[1]Many auditors using nonstatistical methods calculate tolerable exception rate minus sample exception rate and evaluate whether the difference is sufficiently large.

STATISTICAL AUDIT SAMPLING

OBJECTIVE 15-6

Define and describe attributes sampling and a sampling distribution.

The statistical sampling method most commonly used for tests of controls and substantive tests of transactions is **attributes sampling**. When the term *attributes sampling* is used in this text, it refers to attributes statistical sampling. Both attributes sampling and nonstatistical sampling have attributes, which are the characteristics being tested for in the population, but attributes sampling is a statistical method.

There are far more similarities than differences in applying attributes sampling instead of nonstatistical sampling to tests of controls and substantive tests of transactions. All 14 steps discussed are used for both approaches, and the terminology is essentially the same. The important differences are the calculation of planned sample sizes using tables developed from statistical probability distributions and the calculation of estimated upper exception rates using similar tables. The quantification of these calculations is an extremely important difference to those auditors who prefer statistical to nonstatistical sampling. Before applying attributes sampling using the same 14 steps already discussed, we will discuss sampling distributions.

SAMPLING DISTRIBUTION

Statistical inferences are based on sampling distributions. A **sampling distribution** is a frequency distribution of the results of all possible samples of a specified size that could be obtained from a population containing some specific parameters. The existence of a sampling distribution allows the auditor to make probability statements about the likely degree of representativeness of any sample that is a member of that distribution.

Attributes sampling is based on the binomial distribution. The binomial distribution is a distribution of all possible samples where the items in the population each have one of two possible states, for example, yes/no, black/white, or control deviation/no control deviation.

Assume that a population of sales invoices exists, 5 percent of which have no shipping documents attached as required by the client's internal controls. If the auditor takes a sample of 50 sales invoices, how many will be found that have no shipping documents? The sample could contain no exceptions, or it might contain six or seven. A binomial-based sampling distribution would tell us the probability of each possible number of exceptions occurring. The sampling distribution for the example population is shown in Table 15-7. This distribution shows that, with a sample of 50 items from a very large population with an exception rate of 5 percent, the likelihood of obtaining a sample with at least one exception is 92.31 percent (1 − .0769). (Because the probability of no exceptions is 7.69 percent, the probability of more than 0 is 92.31 percent.)

TABLE 15-7	Probability of Each Exception Rate—5 Percent Population Exception Rate and Sample Size of 50		
Number of Exceptions	Percentage of Exception	Probability	Cumulative Probability
0	0	.0769	.0769
1	2	.2025	.2794
2	4	.2611	.5405
3	6	.2199	.7604
4	8	.1360	.8964
5	10	.0656	.9620
6	12	.0260	.9880
7	14	.0120	1.0000

There is a unique sampling distribution for each population exception rate and sample size. The distribution for a sample size of 100 from a population with a 5 percent exception rate is different from the previous one, as is the distribution for a sample of 50 from a population with a 3 percent exception rate.

In actual audit situations, auditors do not take repeated samples from known populations. They take one sample from an unknown population and get a specific number of exceptions in that sample. But knowledge about sampling distributions enables auditors to make statistical statements about the population. For example, if the auditor selects a sample of 50 sales invoices to test for attached shipping documents and finds one exception, the auditor could examine the probability table in Table 15-7 and know there is a 20.25 percent probability that the sample came from a population with a 5 percent exception rate, and a 79.75 percent (1 − .2025) probability that the sample was taken from a population having some other exception rate. It is also possible to state by examining the cumulative probabilities column in Table 15-7 that there is a 27.94 percent probability that the sample came from a population with *more* than a 5 percent exception rate and a 72.06 percent (1 − .2794) probability that the sample was taken from a population having an exception rate of 5 percent or less. Because it is similarly possible to calculate the probability distributions for other population exception rates, these can be examined in the aggregate to draw more specific statistical conclusions about the unknown population being sampled. These sampling distributions are the basis for the tables used by auditors for attributes sampling.

APPLICATION OF ATTRIBUTES SAMPLING

As already stated, the 14 steps discussed for nonstatistical sampling are equally applicable to attributes sampling. This section focuses on the differences between the two.

Plan the Sample

1. *State the objectives of the audit test.* Same for attributes and nonstatistical sampling.
2. *Decide whether audit sampling applies.* Same for attributes and nonstatistical sampling.
3. *Define attributes and exception conditions.* Same for attributes and nonstatistical sampling.
4. *Define the population.* Same for attributes and nonstatistical sampling.
5. *Define the sampling unit.* Same for attributes and nonstatistical sampling.
6. *Specify the tolerable exception rate.* Same for attributes and nonstatistical sampling.
7. *Specify acceptable risk of assessing control risk too low.*

The concepts of specifying this risk are the same for both statistical and nonstatistical sampling, but the method of quantification is usually different. For nonstatistical sampling, most auditors use low, medium, or high acceptable risk, whereas auditors using attributes sampling assign a specific amount, such as 10 percent or 5 percent risk. The reason for the difference is the need to quantify risk when auditors plan to determine sample size and evaluate results statistically.

8. *Estimate the population exception rate.* Same for attributes and nonstatistical sampling.
9. *Determine the initial sample size.*

Four factors determine the initial sample size for both statistical and nonstatistical sampling: population size, TER, ARACR, and EPER. The difference is that special computer programs or tables developed from statistical formulas are used to determine the sample size for attributes sampling. Tables are used to illustrate determining the sample size. Determining binomial probabilities using computers is not discussed because the software required is complex.

The two tables that make up Table 15-8 (p. 468) are taken from the AICPA *Audit Sampling Guide.* They are the same, except that the first one is for a 5 percent ARACR and the second one a 10 percent ARACR.

Acceptance Sampling

TABLE 15-8 Determining Sample Size for Attributes Sampling

5 PERCENT ARACR

Estimated Population Exception Rate (in Percent)	Tolerable Exception Rate (in Percent)										
	2	3	4	5	6	7	8	9	10	15	20
0.00	149	99	74	59	49	42	36	32	29	19	14
0.25	236	157	117	93	78	66	58	51	46	30	22
0.50	*	157	117	93	78	66	58	51	46	30	22
0.75	*	208	117	93	78	66	58	51	46	30	22
1.00	*	*	156	93	78	66	58	51	46	30	22
1.25	*	*	156	124	78	66	58	51	46	30	22
1.50	*	*	192	124	103	66	58	51	46	30	22
1.75	*	*	227	153	103	88	77	51	46	30	22
2.00	*	*	*	181	127	88	77	68	46	30	22
2.25	*	*	*	208	127	88	77	68	61	30	22
2.50	*	*	*	*	150	109	77	68	61	30	22
2.75	*	*	*	*	173	109	95	68	61	30	22
3.00	*	*	*	*	195	129	95	84	61	30	22
3.25	*	*	*	*	*	148	112	84	61	30	22
3.50	*	*	*	*	*	167	112	84	76	40	22
3.75	*	*	*	*	*	185	129	100	76	40	22
4.00	*	*	*	*	*	*	146	100	89	40	22
5.00	*	*	*	*	*	*	*	158	116	40	30
6.00	*	*	*	*	*	*	*	*	179	50	30
7.00	*	*	*	*	*	*	*	*	*	68	37

10 PERCENT ARACR

	2	3	4	5	6	7	8	9	10	15	20
0.00	114	76	57	45	38	32	28	25	22	15	11
0.25	194	129	96	77	64	55	48	42	38	25	18
0.50	194	129	96	77	64	55	48	42	38	25	18
0.75	265	129	96	77	64	55	48	42	38	25	18
1.00	*	176	96	77	64	55	48	42	38	25	18
1.25	*	221	132	77	64	55	48	42	38	25	18
1.50	*	*	132	105	64	55	48	42	38	25	18
1.75	*	*	166	105	88	55	48	42	38	25	18
2.00	*	*	198	132	88	75	48	42	38	25	18
2.25	*	*	*	132	88	75	65	42	38	25	18
2.50	*	*	*	158	110	75	65	58	38	25	18
2.75	*	*	*	209	132	94	65	58	52	25	18
3.00	*	*	*	*	132	94	65	58	52	25	18
3.25	*	*	*	*	153	113	82	58	52	25	18
3.50	*	*	*	*	194	113	82	73	52	25	18
3.75	*	*	*	*	*	131	98	73	52	25	18
4.00	*	*	*	*	*	149	98	73	65	25	18
4.50	*	*	*	*	*	218	130	87	65	34	18
5.00	*	*	*	*	*	*	160	115	78	34	18
5.50	*	*	*	*	*	*	*	142	103	34	18
6.00	*	*	*	*	*	*	*	182	116	45	25
7.00	*	*	*	*	*	*	*	*	199	52	25
7.50	*	*	*	*	*	*	*	*	*	52	25
8.00	*	*	*	*	*	*	*	*	*	60	25
8.50	*	*	*	*	*	*	*	*	*	68	32

*Sample is too large to be cost effective for most audit applications.

Notes: 1. This table assumes a large population. 2. Sample sizes are the same in certain columns even when estimated population exception rates differ because of the method of constructing the tables. Sample sizes are calculated for attributes sampling by using the expected number of exceptions in the population, but auditors can deal more conveniently with estimated population exception rates. For example, in the 15 percent column for tolerable exception rate, at an ARACR of 5 percent, the initial sample size for most EPERs is 30. One exception, divided by a sample size of 30, is 3.3 percent. Therefore, for all EPERs greater than zero but less than 3.3 percent, the initial sample size is the same.

Use of the Tables Use of the tables to determine initial sample size involves four steps:

1. Select the table corresponding to the ARACR.
2. Locate the TER at the top of the table.
3. Locate the EPER in the far left column.
4. Read down the appropriate TER column until it intersects with the appropriate EPER row. The number at the intersection is the initial sample size.

In the Hillsburg Hardware Co. illustration, assume that an auditor is willing to reduce assessed control risk for the agreement between sales orders and invoices if the number of occurrences where the data differ in the population (attribute 6 in Table 15-3 on page 453) does not exceed 7 percent (TER), at a 5 percent ARACR. On the basis of past experience, EPER is set at 1 percent. Use the 5 percent ARACR table, locate the 7 percent TER column, and read down to where the column intersects with the 1 percent EPER row. The initial sample size is determined to be 66.

Is 66 a large enough sample size for this audit? It is not possible to say until after the tests have been performed. If the actual exception rate in the sample turns out to be greater than 1 percent, the auditor will be unsure of the effectiveness of the internal controls. The reasons for this will become apparent as we proceed.

Effect of Population Size In the preceding discussion, the size of the population was ignored in determining the initial sample size. It may seem strange to some readers, but statistical theory proves that in most types of populations to which attributes sampling applies, the population size is a minor consideration in determining sample size. This is true because representativeness is ensured by the sample selection process more than by sample size. Once a sample is obtained that includes a good cross section of items, additional items are not needed. Because most auditors use attributes sampling for reasonably large populations, the reduction of sample size for smaller populations is ignored here.

Select the Sample and Perform the Audit Procedures

10. *Select the sample.* The only difference in sample selection for statistical and nonstatistical sampling is the requirement that probabilistic methods must be used for statistical sampling. Either simple random or systematic sampling is used for attributes sampling.
11. *Perform the audit procedures.* Same for attributes and nonstatistical sampling.

Evaluate the Results

12. *Generalize from the sample to the population.* For attributes sampling, the auditor calculates an upper precision limit (CUER) at a specified ARACR, again using special computer programs or tables developed from statistical formulas. To illustrate the calculations, tables such as the one for a 5 percent ARACR in Table 15-9 (p. 470) are used. These tables are "one-sided tables," which means that they represent the *upper* exception rate for a given ARACR.

Use of the Tables Use of tables to compute CUER involves four steps:

1. Select the table corresponding to the ARACR. This ARACR should be the same as the ARACR used for determining the initial sample size.
2. Locate the actual number of exceptions found in the audit tests at the top of the table.
3. Locate the actual sample size in the far left column.
4. Read down the appropriate actual number of exceptions column until it intersects with the appropriate sample size row. The number at the intersection is the CUER.

To illustrate the use of the evaluation table for Hillsburg Hardware, assume an actual sample size of 70 and one exception in attribute 6. Using an ARACR of 5 percent, CUER equals 6.6 percent. Stated another way, the result is that the CUER for attribute 6 is 6.6 percent at a 5 percent ARACR. Does this mean that if 100 percent of the population

TABLE 15-9 Evaluating Sample Results Using Attributes Sampling

5 PERCENT ARACR

Sample Size	Actual Number of Exceptions Found										
	0	1	2	3	4	5	6	7	8	9	10
25	11.3	17.6	*	*	*	*	*	*	*	*	*
30	9.5	14.9	19.6	*	*	*	*	*	*	*	*
35	8.3	12.9	17.0	*	*	*	*	*	*	*	*
40	7.3	11.4	15.0	18.3	*	*	*	*	*	*	*
45	6.5	10.2	13.4	16.4	19.2	*	*	*	*	*	*
50	5.9	9.2	12.1	14.8	17.4	19.9	*	*	*	*	*
55	5.4	8.4	11.1	13.5	15.9	18.2	*	*	*	*	*
60	4.9	7.7	10.2	12.5	14.7	16.8	18.8	*	*	*	*
65	4.6	7.1	9.4	11.5	13.6	15.5	17.4	19.3	*	*	*
70	4.2	6.6	8.8	10.8	12.6	14.5	16.3	18.0	19.7	*	*
75	4.0	6.2	8.2	10.1	11.8	13.6	15.2	16.9	18.5	20.0	*
80	3.7	5.8	7.7	9.5	11.1	12.7	14.3	15.9	17.4	18.9	*
90	3.3	5.2	6.9	8.4	9.9	11.4	12.8	14.2	15.5	16.8	18.2
100	3.0	4.7	6.2	7.6	9.0	10.3	11.5	12.8	14.0	15.2	16.4
125	2.4	3.8	5.0	6.1	7.2	8.3	9.3	10.3	11.3	12.3	13.2
150	2.0	3.2	4.2	5.1	6.0	6.9	7.8	8.6	9.5	10.3	11.1
200	1.5	2.4	3.2	3.9	4.6	5.2	5.9	6.5	7.2	7.8	8.4

10 PERCENT ARACR

Sample Size	Actual Number of Exceptions Found										
	0	1	2	3	4	5	6	7	8	9	10
20	10.9	18.1	*	*	*	*	*	*	*	*	*
25	8.8	14.7	19.9	*	*	*	*	*	*	*	*
30	7.4	12.4	16.8	*	*	*	*	*	*	*	*
35	6.4	10.7	14.5	18.1	*	*	*	*	*	*	*
40	5.6	9.4	12.8	16.0	19.0	*	*	*	*	*	*
45	5.0	8.4	11.4	14.3	17.0	19.7	*	*	*	*	*
50	4.6	7.6	10.3	12.9	15.4	17.8	*	*	*	*	*
55	4.1	6.9	9.4	11.8	14.1	16.3	18.4	*	*	*	*
60	3.8	6.4	8.7	10.8	12.9	15.0	16.9	18.9	*	*	*
70	3.3	5.5	7.5	9.3	11.1	12.9	14.6	16.3	17.9	19.6	*
80	2.9	4.8	6.6	8.2	9.8	11.3	12.8	14.3	15.8	17.2	18.6
90	2.6	4.3	5.9	7.3	8.7	10.1	11.5	12.8	14.1	15.4	16.6
100	2.3	3.9	5.3	6.6	7.9	9.1	10.3	11.5	12.7	13.9	15.0
120	2.0	3.3	4.4	5.5	6.6	7.6	8.7	9.7	10.7	11.6	12.6
160	1.5	2.5	3.3	4.2	5.0	5.8	6.5	7.3	8.0	8.8	9.5
200	1.2	2.0	2.7	3.4	4.0	4.6	5.3	5.9	6.5	7.1	7.6

*More than 20 percent.

Note: This table presents computed upper exception rates as percentages. Table assumes a large population.

were tested, the true exception rate would be 6.6 percent? No, the true exception rate is unknown. The result means that if the auditor concludes that the true exception rate does not exceed 6.6 percent, there is a 95 percent chance that the conclusion is right and a 5 percent chance that it is wrong.

It is possible to have a sample size that is not equal to those provided for in the attributes sampling evaluation tables. When this occurs, it is common to interpolate.

These tables assume a very large (infinite) population size, which results in a more conservative CUER than for smaller populations. Because the effect of population size on sample size is typically very small, it is ignored.

13. *Analyze exceptions.* Same for attributes and nonstatistical sampling.
14. *Decide the acceptability of the population.*

Client: Hillsburg Hardware

Audit Area: Tests of Controls and Substantive Tests of Transactions— Billing Function

Year-end: 12/31/04
Pop. size: 5,764

Define the objective(s): Examine duplicate sales invoices and related documents to determine whether the system has functioned as intended and as described in the audit program.

Define the population precisely (including stratification, if any): Sales invoices for the period 1/1/04 to 10/31/04. First invoice number = 3689. Last invoice number = 9452.

Define the sampling unit, organization of population items, and random selection procedures: Sales invoice number, recorded in the sales journal sequentially; computer generation of random numbers.

Description of Attributes	Planned Audit				Actual Results			
	EPER	TER	ARACR	Initial sample size	Sample size	Number of exceptions	Sample exception rate	CUER
1. Existence of the sales invoice number in the sales journal (procedure 12).	0	4	5	74	75	0	0	4.0
2. Amount and other data in the master file agree with sales journal entry (procedure 13a).	1	5	5	93	100	2	2	6.2
3. Amount and other data on the duplicate sales invoice agree with the sales journal entry (procedure 13b).	1	5	5	93	100	0	0	3.0
4. Evidence that pricing, extensions, and footings are checked (initials and correct amounts) (procedure 13b).	1	5	5	93	100	10	10	16.4
5. Quantity and other data on the bill of lading agree with the duplicate sales invoice and sales journal (procedure 13c).	1	5	5	93	100	4	4	9.0
6. Quantity and other data on the sales order agree with the duplicate sales invoice (procedure 13d).	1	7	5	66	70	1	1.5	6.6
7. Quantity and other data on the customer order agree with the duplicate sales invoice (procedure 13e).	1.5	9	5	51	50	0	0	5.9
8. Credit is approved by Rick Chulick (procedure 13e).	1.5	9	5	51	50	12	24	>20
9. For recorded sales in the sales journal, the file of supporting documents includes a duplicate sales invoice, bill of lading, sales order, and customer order (procedure 14).	1	7	5	66	65	0	0	4.6

Intended use of sampling results:

1. Effect on Audit Plan: Controls tested through attributes 1, 3, 6, 7, and 9 can be viewed as operating effectively given that TER equals or exceeds CUER. Additional emphasis is needed in confirmation, allowance for uncollectible accounts, cutoff tests, and price tests for the financial statement audit due to results of tests for attributes 2, 4, 5, and 8.

2. Effect on Report on Internal Control: CUER exceeds TER for attributes 2, 4, 5, and 8. These findings have been communicated to management to allow an opportunity for correction of the control deficiency to be made before year-end. If timely correction is made by management, the corrected controls will be tested before year-end for purposes of reporting on internal control over financial reporting.

3. Recommendations to Management: Each of the exceptions should be discussed with management. Specific recommendations are needed to correct the internal verification of sales invoices and to improve the approach to credit approvals.

The methodology for deciding the acceptability of the population is essentially the same for attributes and nonstatistical sampling. For attributes sampling, the auditor compares CUER with TER for each attribute.

Before the population can be considered acceptable, the CUER determined on the basis of the actual sample results must be *less than or equal to* TER when both are based on ARACR. In the example just given, in which the auditor has specified acceptance of a 7 percent population exception rate at a 5 percent ARACR and the CUER was 6.6 percent, the requirements of the sample have been met. In this case, the control being tested can be used to reduce assessed control risk as planned, provided a careful analysis of the cause of exceptions does not indicate the possibility of a significant problem in an aspect of the control not previously considered.

When the CUER is greater than the TER, it is necessary to take specific action. The four courses of action discussed for nonstatistical sampling are equally applicable to attributes sampling.

Figure 15-8 illustrates the sampling documentation completed for the tests of attributes 1 through 9 in Table 15-3 (p. 453) for Hillsburg Hardware Co. using attributes sampling. Much of the information in Figure 15-8 is consistent with information presented in the nonstatistical sampling example illustrated in Figure 15-4 (p. 461). The key differences between Figures 15-4 and 15-8 relate to the auditor's judgment about ARACR and the initial sample size determined when planning the audit, and the calculation of CUER using the actual test results. Notice that the ARACR judgment is numerical (5 percent) in the attributes sampling application (Figure 15-8). The numerical judgment about ARACR is considered along with the assessments of EPER and TER to determine the initial sample sizes for each attribute using Table 15-8 (p. 468). The CUER in Figure 15-8 is determined using Table 15-9 (p. 470) based on the sample exceptions identified and the actual sample size tested.

Need for Professional Judgment

A criticism occasionally leveled against statistical sampling is that it reduces the use of professional judgment. A comparison of the 14 steps discussed in this chapter for nonstatistical and attributes sampling shows how unwarranted this criticism is. For proper application of attributes sampling, it is necessary to use professional judgment in most of the steps. For example, selection of the initial sample size depends primarily on the TER, ARACR, and EPER. Choosing the first two requires the exercise of high-level professional judgment; the latter requires a careful estimate. Similarly, the final evaluation of the adequacy of the entire application of attributes sampling, including the adequacy of the sample size, must also be based on high-level professional judgment.

ESSENTIAL TERMS

Acceptable risk of assessing control risk too low (ARACR)—the risk that the auditor is willing to take of accepting a control as effective or a rate of monetary misstatements as tolerable when the true population exception rate is greater than the tolerable exception rate

Attribute—the characteristic being tested for in the population

Attributes sampling—a statistical, probabilistic method of sample evaluation that results in an estimate of the proportion of items in a population containing a characteristic or attribute of interest

Audit sampling—testing less than 100 percent of a population for the purpose of making inferences about that population

Block sample selection—a nonprobabilistic method of sample selection in which items are selected in measured sequences

Computed upper exception rate (CUER)—the upper limit of the probable population exception rate; the highest exception rate in the population at a given ARACR

Directed sample selection—a nonprobabilistic method of sample selection in which each item in the sample is selected based on some judgmental criteria established by the auditor

Estimated population exception rate (EPER)—exception rate the auditor expects to find in the population before testing begins

Exception rate—the percent of items in a population that include exceptions in prescribed controls or monetary correctness

Haphazard sample selection—a nonprobabilistic method of sample selection in which items are chosen without regard to their size, source, or other distinguishing characteristics

Initial sample size—sample size determined by professional judgment (nonstatistical sampling) or by statistical tables (attributes sampling)

Nonprobabilistic sample selection—a method of sample selection in which the auditor uses professional judgment to select items from the population

Nonsampling risk—the risk that the auditor fails to identify existing exceptions in the sample; nonsampling risk (nonsampling error) is caused by failure to recognize exceptions and by inappropriate or ineffective audit procedures

Nonstatistical sampling—the auditor's use of professional judgment to select sample items, estimate the population values, and estimate sampling risk

Occurrence rate—the ratio of items in a population that contain a specific attribute to the total number of population items

Probabilistic sample selection—a method of selecting a sample such that each population item has a known probability of being included in the sample and the sample is selected by a random process

Random number table—a listing of independent random digits conveniently arranged in tabular form to facilitate the selection of random numbers with multiple digits

Random sample—a sample in which every possible combination of elements in the population has an equal chance of constituting the sample

Representative sample—a sample with characteristics the same as those of the population

Sample exception rate (SER)—number of exceptions in the sample divided by the sample size

Sampling distribution—a frequency distribution of the results of all possible samples of a specified size that could be obtained from a population containing some specific parameters

Sampling risk—risk of reaching an incorrect conclusion inherent in tests of less than the entire population because the sample is not representative of the population; sampling risk may be reduced by using an increased sample size and an appropriate method of selecting sample items from the population

Statistical sampling—the use of mathematical measurement techniques to calculate formal statistical results and quantify sampling risk

Systematic sample selection—a probabilistic method of sampling in which the auditor calculates an interval (the population size divided by the number of sample items desired) and selects the items for the sample based on the size of the interval and a randomly selected starting point between zero and the length of the interval

Tolerable exception rate (TER)—the exception rate that the auditor will permit in the population and still be willing to conclude the control is operating effectively and/or the amount of monetary misstatements in the transactions established during planning is acceptable

REVIEW QUESTIONS

15-1 (Objective 15-1) State what is meant by a representative sample and explain its importance in sampling audit populations.

15-2 (Objective 15-2) Explain the major difference between statistical and nonstatistical sampling. What are the three main parts of statistical and nonstatistical methods?

15-3 (Objective 15-3) Explain the difference between replacement sampling and nonreplacement sampling. Which method do auditors usually follow? Why?

15-4 (Objective 15-3) What are the two types of simple random sample selection methods? Which of the two methods is used most often by auditors and why?

15-5 (Objective 15-3) Describe systematic sample selection and explain how an auditor would select 35 numbers from a population of 1,750 items using this approach. What are the advantages and disadvantages of systematic sample selection?

15-6 (Objective 15-4) What is the purpose of using nonstatistical sampling for tests of controls and substantive tests of transactions?

15-7 (Objective 15-2) Explain what is meant by block sample selection and describe how an auditor could obtain five blocks of 20 sales invoices from a sales journal.

15-8 (Objective 15-5) Define each of the following terms:
   a. Acceptable risk of assessing control risk too low (ARACR)
   b. Computed upper exception rate (CUER)
   c. Estimated population exception rate (EPER)
   d. Sample exception rate (SER)
   e. Tolerable exception rate (TER)

15-9 (Objective 15-5) Describe what is meant by a sampling unit. Explain why the sampling unit for verifying the existence of recorded sales differs from the sampling unit for testing for the possibility of omitted sales.

15-10 (Objective 15-5) Distinguish between the TER and the CUER. How is each determined?

15-11 (Objective 15-1) Distinguish between a sampling error and a nonsampling error. How can each be reduced?

15-12 (Objective 15-4) What is meant by an attribute in sampling for tests of controls and substantive tests of transactions? What is the source of the attributes that the auditor selects?

15-13 (Objective 15-4) Explain the difference between an attribute and an exception condition. State the exception condition for the audit procedure: The duplicate sales invoice has been initialed indicating the performance of internal verification.

15-14 (Objective 15-5) Identify the factors an auditor uses to decide the appropriate TER. Compare the sample size for a TER of 6% with that of 3%, all other factors being equal.

15-15 (Objective 15-5) Identify the factors an auditor uses to decide the appropriate ARACR. Compare the sample size for an ARACR of 10% with that of 5%, all other factors being equal.

15-16 (Objective 15-5) State the relationship between the following:
   a. ARACR and sample size
   b. Population size and sample size
   c. TER and sample size
   d. EPER and sample size

15-17 (Objective 15-7) Assume that the auditor has selected 100 sales invoices from a population of 100,000 to test for an indication of internal verification of pricing and extensions. Determine the CUER at a 5% ARACR if three exceptions existed in the sample using attributes sampling. Explain the meaning of the statistical results in auditing terms.

15-18 (Objective 15-5) Explain what is meant by analysis of exceptions and discuss its importance.

15-19 (Objective 15-5) When the CUER exceeds the TER, what courses of action are available to the auditor? Under what circumstances should each of these be followed?

15-20 (Objective 15-3) Distinguish between probabilistic selection and statistical measurement. State the circumstances under which one can be used without the other.

15-21 (Objective 15-7) List the major decisions that the auditor must make in using attributes sampling. State the most important considerations involved in making each decision.

MULTIPLE CHOICE QUESTIONS FROM CPA EXAMINATIONS

15-22 (Objectives 15-5, 15-7) The following items apply to determining sample sizes using random sampling from large populations for attributes sampling. Select the most appropriate response for each question.

   a. If all other factors specified in a sampling plan remain constant, changing the ARACR from 10% to 5% would cause the required sample size to
      (1) increase.   (3) decrease.
      (2) remain the same.   (4) become indeterminate.

   b. If all other factors specified in a sampling plan remain constant, changing the TER from 8% to 12% would cause the required sample size to
      (1) increase.   (3) decrease.
      (2) remain the same.   (4) become indeterminate.

   c. If an auditor wishes to select a random sample that must have a 10% ARACR and a TER of 10%, the size of the sample selected will decrease as the estimate of the
      (1) population exception rate increases.
      (2) population exception rate decreases.
      (3) population size increases.
      (4) ARACR increases.

d. In planning a statistical sample for tests of controls, an auditor increases the expected population exception rate from the prior year's rate because of the results of the prior year's tests of controls. As a result, the auditor would most likely increase the planned
   (1) tolerable exception rate.
   (2) allowance for sampling risk.
   (3) acceptable risk of assessing control risk too low.
   (4) sample size.

15-23 (Objectives 15-5, 15-7) The following items concern determining exception rates using random sampling from large populations using attributes sampling. Select the best response.

a. From a random sample of items listed from a client's inventory count, an auditor estimates with a 90% confidence level that the CUER is between 4% and 6%. The auditor's major concern is that there is one chance in twenty that the true exception rate in the population is
   (1) more than 6%.   (3) more than 4%.
   (2) less than 6%.   (4) less than 4%.

b. If, from a random sample, an auditor can state with a 5% ARACR that the exception rate in the population does not exceed 20%, the auditor can state that the exception rate does not exceed 25% with
   (1) 5% risk.
   (2) risk greater than 5%.
   (3) risk less than 5%.
   (4) This cannot be determined from the information provided.

c. As a result of tests of controls, an auditor assessed control risk too low and decreased substantive testing. This assessment occurred because the true deviation rate in the population was
   (1) less than the risk of assessing control risk too low, based on the auditor's sample.
   (2) less than the deviation rate in the auditor's sample.
   (3) more than the risk of assessing control risk too low, based on the auditor's sample.
   (4) more than the deviation rate in the auditor's sample.

15-24 (Objectives 15-1, 15-2) The following questions concern sampling risk. Choose the best response.

a. An advantage of statistical sampling over nonstatistical sampling is that statistical sampling helps an auditor
   (1) minimize the failure to detect errors and fraud.
   (2) eliminate the risk of nonsampling errors.
   (3) design more effective audit procedures.
   (4) measure the sufficiency of evidential matter by quantifying sampling risk.

b. Which of the following is an element of sampling risk?
   (1) Choosing an audit procedure that is inconsistent with the audit objective.
   (2) Choosing a sample size that is too small to achieve the sampling objective.
   (3) The auditor failing to detect an error on a document in the sample.
   (4) Failing to perform audit procedures.

c. Which of the following best illustrates the concept of sampling risk?
   (1) The documents related to the chosen sample may not be available to the auditor for inspection.
   (2) An auditor may fail to recognize errors in the documents from the sample.
   (3) A randomly chosen sample may not be representative of the population as a whole for the characteristic of interest.
   (4) An auditor may select audit procedures that are not appropriate to achieve the specific objective.

DISCUSSION QUESTIONS AND PROBLEMS

15-25 (Objective 15-3)

a. In each of the following independent problems, design an unbiased random sampling plan, using an electronic spreadsheet or a random number generator program. The plan should include defining the sampling unit and establishing a numbering system for the population. After the plan has been designed, select the sample using the computer. Assume that the sample size is 50 for each of (1) through (4).
   (1) Prenumbered sales invoices in a sales journal where the lowest invoice number is 1 and the highest is 6211.

(2) Prenumbered bills of lading where the lowest document number is 21926 and the highest is 28511.

(3) Accounts receivable on 10 pages with 60 lines per page except the last page, which has only 36 full lines. Each line has a customer name and an amount receivable.

(4) Prenumbered invoices in a sales journal where each month starts over with number 1. (Invoices for each month are designated by the month and document number.) There is a maximum of 20 pages per month with a total of 185 pages for the year. All pages have 75 invoices except for the last page for each month.

b. Using systematic sampling, select the first five sample items for populations (1) through (3) from part a, using the random starting points shown. Recall that the sample size is 50 in each case.

(1) Invoice #67

(2) Bill of lading #22011

(3) Page 1, line #8

15-26 (Objectives 15-3, 15-5, 15-7) Lenter Supply Company is a medium-sized distributor of wholesale hardware supplies in the central Ohio area. It has been a client of yours for several years and has instituted excellent internal controls for sales at your recommendation.

In providing control over shipments, the client has prenumbered "warehouse removal slips" that are used for every sale. It is company policy never to remove goods from the warehouse without an authorized warehouse removal slip. After shipment, two copies of the warehouse removal slip are sent to billing for the computerized preparation of a sales invoice. One copy is stapled to the duplicate copy of a prenumbered sales invoice, and the other copy is filed numerically. In some cases, more than one warehouse removal slip is used for billing one sales invoice. The smallest warehouse removal slip number for the year is 14682 and the largest is 37521. The smallest sales invoice number is 47821 and the largest is 68507.

In the audit of sales, one of the major concerns is the effectiveness of the controls in ensuring that all shipments are billed. You have decided to use audit sampling in testing internal controls.

Required

a. State an effective audit procedure for testing whether shipments have been billed. What is the sampling unit for the audit procedure?

b. Assuming that you expect no exceptions in the sample but are willing to accept a TER of 3%, at a 10% ARACR, what is the appropriate sample size for the audit test? You may complete this requirement using attributes sampling.

c. Design a random selection plan for selecting the sample from the population, using either systematic sampling or computer generation of random numbers. Use the sample size determined in part b. If you use systematic sampling, use a random starting point of 14825.

d. Your supervisor suggests the possibility of performing other sales tests with the same sample as a means of efficiently using your audit time. List two other audit procedures that could conveniently be performed using the same sample and state the purpose of each of the procedures.

e. Is it desirable to test the existence of sales with the random sample you have designed in part c? Why?

15-27 (Objective 15-7) The following is a partial audit program for the audit of cash receipts.

1. Review the cash receipts journal for large and unusual transactions.
2. Trace entries from the prelisting of cash receipts to the cash receipts journal to determine whether each is recorded.
3. Compare customer name, date, and amount on the prelisting with the cash receipts journal.
4. Examine the related remittance advice for entries selected from the prelisting to determine whether cash discounts were approved.
5. Trace entries from the prelisting to the deposit slip to determine whether each has been deposited.

Required

a. Identify which audit procedures could be tested by using attributes sampling.

b. What is the appropriate sampling unit for the tests in part a?

c. List the attributes for testing in part a.

d. Assume an ARACR of 5% and a TER of 8% for tests of controls and 6% for substantive tests of transactions. The EPER for tests of controls is 2%, and for substantive tests of transactions it is 1%. What is the initial sample size for each attribute?

15-28 (Objectives 15-5, 15-7) The following questions concern the determination of the proper sample size in audit sampling using the following table:

	1	2	3	4	5	6	7
ARACR (in percent)	10	5	5	5	10	10	5
TER	6	6	5	6	20	20	2
EPER (in percent)	2	2	2	2	8	2	0
Population size	1,000	100,000	6,000	1,000	500	500	1,000,000

Required

a. Assume that the initial sample size for column 1 was determined to be 90 items, using non-statistical sampling. For each of columns 2 through 7, use your judgment to decide the appropriate nonstatistical sample size. In deciding each sample size, consider the effects of changes in each of the four factors (ARACR, TER, EPER, and population size) compared with column 1.

b. For each of the columns numbered 1 through 7, determine the initial sample size needed to satisfy the auditor's requirements using attributes sampling from the appropriate part of Table 15-8.

c. Using your understanding of the relationship between the following factors and sample size, state the effect on the initial sample size (increase or decrease) of changing each of the following factors while the other three are held constant:
   (1) An increase in ARACR   (3) An increase in the EPER
   (2) An increase in the TER   (4) An increase in the population size

d. Explain why there is such a large difference in the sample sizes for columns 3 and 6.

e. Compare your answers in part c with the results you determined in part a (nonstatistical sampling) or part b (attributes sampling). Which of the four factors appears to have the greatest effect on the initial sample size? Which one appears to have the least effect?

f. Why is the sample size called the initial sample size?

15-29 (Objectives 15-5, 15-7) The questions below relate to determining the CUER in audit sampling for tests of controls, using the following table:

	1	2	3	4	5	6	7	8
ARACR (in percent)	10	5	5	5	5	5	5	5
Population size	5,000	5,000	5,000	50,000	500	900	5,000	500
Sample size	200	200	50	200	100	100	100	25
Number of exceptions	4	4	1	4	2	10	0	0

Required

a. Using nonstatistical sampling, calculate TER − SER for each of columns 1 through 8 and evaluate whether or not sampling error is large enough to accept the population. Assume that TER is 5% for each column.

b. For each of the columns 1 through 8, determine CUER using attributes sampling from the appropriate table.

c. Using your understanding of the relationship between the four preceding factors and the CUER, state the effect on the CUER (increase or decrease) of changing each of the following factors while the other three are held constant:
   (1) A decrease in the ARACR
   (2) A decrease in the population size
   (3) A decrease in the sample size
   (4) A decrease in the number of exceptions in the sample

d. Compare your answers in part c with the results you determined in part a (nonstatistical sampling) or part b (attributes sampling). Which of the factors appears to have the greatest effect on the CUER? Which one appears to have the least effect?

e. Why is it necessary to compare the CUER with the TER?

15-30 (Objective 15-7) The following are auditor judgments and attributes sampling results for six populations. Assume large population sizes.

	1	2	3	4	5	6
EPER (in percent)	2	0	3	1	1	8
TER (in percent)	6	3	8	5	20	15
ARACR (in percent)	5	5	10	5	10	10
Actual sample size	100	100	60	100	20	60
Actual number of exceptions in the sample	2	0	1	4	1	8

Required

a. For each population, did the auditor select a smaller sample size than is indicated by using the attributes sampling tables in Table 15-8 for determining sample size? Evaluate selecting either a larger or smaller size than those determined in the tables.

b. Calculate the SER and CUER for each population.

c. For which of the six populations should the sample results be considered unacceptable? What options are available to the auditor?

d. Why is analysis of the exceptions necessary even when the populations are considered acceptable?

e. For the following terms, identify which is an audit decision, a nonstatistical estimate made by the auditor, a sample result, and a statistical conclusion about the population:
   (1) EPER
   (2) TER
   (3) ARACR
   (4) Actual sample size
   (5) Actual number of exceptions in the sample
   (6) SER
   (7) CUER

15-31 (Objective 15-5) For the audit of the financial statements of Mercury Fifo Company, Stella Mason, CPA, has decided to apply nonstatistical audit sampling in the tests of controls and substantive tests of transactions for sales transactions. Based on her knowledge of Mercury's operations in the area of sales, she decides that the EPER is likely to be 3% and that she is willing to accept a 5% risk that the true population exception rate is not greater than 6%. Given this information, Mason selects a random sample of 150 sales invoices from the 5,000 generated during the year and examines them for exceptions. She notes the following exceptions in her audit schedules. There is no other documentation.

Invoice No.	Comment
5028	Sales invoice was originally footed incorrectly but was corrected by client before the bill was sent out.
6791	Voided sales invoice examined by auditor.
6810	Shipping document for a sale of merchandise could not be located.
7364	Sales invoice for $2,875 has not been collected and is 6 months past due.
7625	Client unable to locate the duplicate sales invoice.
8431	Invoice was dated 3 days later than the date entered in the sales journal.
8528	Customer order is not attached to the duplicate sales invoice.
8566	Billing is for $100 less than it should be due to an unintentional pricing error. No indication of internal verification is included on the invoice.
8780	Client unable to locate the duplicate sales invoice.
9169	Credit not authorized, but the sale was for only $7.65.
9974	Lack of indication of internal verification of price extensions and postings of sales invoice.

Required

a. Which of the preceding should be defined as an exception?

b. Explain why it is inappropriate to set a single acceptable TER and EPER for the combined exceptions.

c. Calculate SER for each attribute tested in the population. (You must decide which attributes should be combined, which should be kept separate, and which exceptions are actual exceptions before you can calculate SER.)

d. Calculate TER − SER for each attribute and evaluate whether sampling error is sufficiently large given the 5% ARACR. Assume TER is 6% for each attribute.

e. State the appropriate analysis of exceptions for each of the exceptions in the sample, including additional procedures to be performed.

15-32 (Objectives 15-5, 15-7) In performing tests of controls and substantive tests of transactions of sales for the Oakland Hardware Company, Ben Frentz, CPA, is concerned with the internal verification of pricing, extensions, and footings of sales invoices and the accuracy of the calculations. In testing sales using audit sampling, a separate attribute is used for the test of control (the existence of internal verification) and the substantive test of transactions (the accuracy of calculation).

Because internal controls are considered good, Frentz uses a 10% ARACR, a zero EPER, and a 5% TER for both attributes; therefore, the initial sample size is 45 items, which Ben rounded up to 50.

In conducting the tests, the auditor finds three sample items for which there was no indication of internal verification on the sales invoice, but no sales invoices tested in the sample had a financial misstatement. You may complete the following requirements using either a nonstatistical sampling or an attributes sampling approach.

Required

a. Estimate or determine the CUER for both the attributes, assuming a population of 5,000 sales invoices.

b. Decide whether the control is acceptable and whether the substance of the transaction is acceptable.

c. Discuss the most desirable course of action that the auditor should follow in deciding the effect of the CUER exceeding the TER.

d. Which type of exception analysis is appropriate in this case?

CASE

15-33 (Objectives 15-4, 15-5, 15-7) For the audit of Carbald Supply Company, Carole Wever, CPA, is conducting a test of sales for 9 months of the year ended December 31, 2005. Included among her audit procedures are the following:

1. Foot and cross-foot the sales journal and trace the balance to the general ledger.
2. Review all sales transactions for reasonableness.
3. Select a sample of recorded sales from the sales journal and trace the customer name and amounts to duplicate sales invoices and the related shipping document.
4. Select a sample of shipping document numbers and perform the following tests:

   a. Trace the shipping document to the related duplicate sales invoice.
   b. Examine the duplicate sales invoice to determine whether copies of the shipping document, shipping order, and customer order are attached.
   c. Examine the shipping order for an authorized credit approval.
   d. Examine the duplicate sales invoice for an indication of internal verification of quantity, price, extensions, footings, and tracing the balance to the accounts receivable master file.
   e. Compare the price on the duplicate sales invoice with the approved price list and the quantity with the shipping document.
   f. Trace the balance in the duplicate sales invoice to the sales journal and accounts receivable master file for customer name, amount, and date.

Required

a. For which of these procedures could audit sampling for exceptions be conveniently used?

b. Considering the audit procedures Wever developed, what is the most appropriate sampling unit for conducting most of the audit sampling tests?

c. Set up a sampling data sheet using attributes or nonstatistical sampling. For all tests of controls, assume a TER rate of 5% and an EPER of 1%. For all substantive tests of transactions, use a 4% TER and a 0% EPER. Use a 10% ARACR for all tests.

INTEGRATED CASE APPLICATION—PINNACLE MANUFACTURING: PART V

15-34 (Objectives 15-3, 15-5, 15-7) In Part IV of the Pinnacle Manufacturing case, you prepared a performance format audit program. In Part V, sample sizes will be determined by using nonstatistical or attributes sampling, and the results of the tests will be evaluated. You should use nonstatistical sampling unless your professor tells you to use statistical sampling.

After reviewing the audit program you created in Part IV, the audit manager decided to make some modifications. You agreed with her changes. The modified program is included in Figure 15-9 (p. 480).

The audit manager has decided that the tests should be performed for the first 10 months including the month ended 10/31/04. You determine that document numbers are as follows:

Document	First number	Last number
Voucher	4614	31612
Receiving report	10830	24623
Check	8326	33268
Purchase order	1647	15685

FIGURE 15-9   Audit Program for Acquisitions and Cash Disbursements

General

1. Discuss the following items with client personnel and observe activities:
   a. Segregation of duties
   b. Use of an adequate chart of accounts
   c. Monthly reconciliation of accounts payable master file with the general ledger
2. Foot acquisitions and cash disbursements journals for a test month and trace postings to the general ledger.
3. Examine file of completed bank reconciliations.
4. Account for a sequence of cancelled checks.
5. Reconcile recorded cash disbursements with cash disbursements on the bank statement for a test month.

Acquisitions

6. Trace entries in the acquisitions journal to related vendors' invoices, receiving reports, and purchase orders.
   a. Examine indication of internal verification of dates, unit costs, prices, extensions and footings, account classifications, recording in the journal, and posting and summarization.
   b. Examine supporting documents for propriety.
   c. Compare prices on vendors' invoices with approved price limits established by management.
   d. Recompute information on vendors' invoices.
   e. Examine vendors' invoices for proper account classification.
   f. Compare dates of recorded acquisitions with dates on receiving reports.
   g. Examine voucher document package for indication of internal verification.
7. Account for a sequence of purchase orders and voucher document packages.
8. Trace a sample of receiving reports to the acquisitions journal.

Cash Disbursements

9. Select a sample of cancelled checks.
   a. Trace cancelled check to the related cash disbursements journal entry and date.
   b. Examine check for signature, proper endorsement, and cancellation by the bank.
   c. Compare date on cancelled check with bank cancellation date.
   d. Recompute cash discounts.

Required

a. Using the audit program in Figure 15-9, prepare a nonstatistical sampling data sheet for acquisitions following the format in Figure 15-2 (p. 455). Prepare all parts of the sampling data sheet except those that are blank in Figure 15-2. A formatted sampling data sheet can be downloaded using the Pinnacle link on the textbook Web site. Use the following guidelines.

   (1) Use only one sampling data sheet.
   (2) Select the sampling unit that will permit you to perform the most acquisition audit procedures on the audit program.
   (3) Include all audit procedures on the audit program that are consistent with the sampling unit you selected.
   (4) Decide EPER, TER, and ARACR for each attribute. Consider prior-year results for EPER. [(See Figure 10-12 (p. 310) in Part III.)] Use your judgment for the other two factors.
   (5) Decide the sample size for each attribute.

b. Do the same thing for cash disbursements that you did in requirement a for acquisitions. You will not complete the actual results portion of the cash disbursements sampling data sheet.

c. For acquisitions only, use an Excel spreadsheet to select random numbers for the largest sample size in the acquisitions sampling data sheet. Include the numbers in both random order and sorted numbers, from low to high. Document how you selected the numbers.

d. Assume that you performed all audit procedures included in Figure 15-9 using the sample sizes in requirement a (5). The only exceptions found when you performed the tests include the following: one missing indication of internal verification on a vendor's invoice, one acquisition of inventory transaction recorded for $2,000 more than the amount stated on the vendor's invoice (the vendor was also overpaid by $2,000), and one vendor's invoice recorded as an acquisition 18 days after the receipt of the goods. Complete the sampling data sheet prepared in requirement a. Use Figure 15-4 (p. 461) as a frame of reference for completing the sampling data sheet.

INTERNET PROBLEM 15-1: SAMPLING FOR U.S. CENSUS

Reference the CW site. Sampling concepts are used in a variety of contexts. This problem highlights the use of sampling by the U.S. Census Bureau and emphasizes how key judgments affect the sampling process. Students use the Internet to learn how the U.S. Census Bureau uses sampling techniques to make estimates of the U.S. population.

COMPLETING THE TESTS IN THE SALES AND COLLECTION CYCLE: ACCOUNTS RECEIVABLE

LEARNING OBJECTIVES

After studying this chapter, you should be able to

16-1 Describe the methodology for designing tests of details of balances using the audit risk model.

16-2 Design and perform analytical procedures for accounts in the sales and collection cycle.

16-3 Design and perform tests of details of balances for accounts receivable for each balance-related audit objective.

16-4 Obtain and evaluate accounts receivable confirmations.

16-5 Design audit procedures for the audit of accounts receivable, using an evidence planning worksheet as a guide.

WHEN MORE ISN'T BETTER

On Susan Jackson's first audit assignment, she is asked to handle the confirmation of accounts receivable. She is excited because it was one of the areas in her auditing class that she was confident that she understood. The audit client is a retailer with a large number of customer accounts. In previous years, Susan's firm confirmed these accounts using negative confirmations. Last year, 200 negative confirmations were sent. Confirmations were sent 1 month before year-end. Those that were returned showed only timing differences; none represented a misstatement in the client's books.

The tentative audit plan for the current year is to do about the same as the prior year. Before the current year's planned confirmation date, Susan obtains an understanding of internal controls over sales and cash receipts transactions. She discovers that a new system for sales transactions that includes Internet-based sales has been implemented, but the client is having considerable problems getting the system to work properly. There are a significant number of misstatements in recording sales during the past few months. Susan's tests of controls and substantive tests of sales transactions also identify similar misstatements.

When Susan takes her findings to her supervisor and asks him what to do, he responds, "No problem, Susan. Just send 300 confirmation requests instead of the usual 200. And be sure you get a good random sample so we can get a good projection of the results." Susan is seriously bothered by this instruction. She recalls from her auditing class that negative confirmation requests aren't considered to be good evidence when there are weak controls. Because customers are asked to respond only when there are differences, the auditor cannot be confident of the correct value for each misstatement in the sample. If this is so, then the results of using negative confirmations will be misleading even if a request is sent to *every* account. Susan concludes that expanding the sample size is the wrong solution. When Susan talks with her supervisor about her point of view, this time he responds, "You are absolutely right. I spoke too quickly. We need to sit down and think about a better strategy to find out if accounts receivable is materially misstated."

In the last two chapters, we examined tests of controls and substantive tests of transactions for the sales and collection cycle. Both types of tests are a part of phase II of the audit process. We now move on to phase III and turn our attention to analytical procedures and tests of details of balances for the sales and collection cycle.

As was shown in the vignette introducing this chapter, it is essential for the auditor to select the appropriate evidence, given the conclusions that are reached in evaluating initial controls and performing tests of controls and substantive tests of transactions. Because reliable evidence is available, auditors do extensive analytical procedures and tests of details of balances in almost all audits to reduce detection risk for account balances to a reasonable level. To obtain reasonable assurance that account balances are fairly stated at a reasonable cost, the auditor must carefully design the most appropriate and cost-effective analytical procedures and tests of details of balances. This chapter examines designing analytical procedures and tests of details of balances for accounts receivable.

METHODOLOGY FOR DESIGNING TESTS OF DETAILS OF BALANCES

OBJECTIVE 16-1

Describe the methodology for designing tests of details of balances using the audit risk model.

Figure 16-1 shows the methodology that auditors follow in designing the appropriate tests of details of balances for accounts receivable. Notice that the second to the last step includes designing and performing analytical procedures. The methodology was introduced in Chapter 13 and is now applied to the audit of accounts receivable. The methodology shown in Figure 16-1 relates directly to the evidence planning worksheet first introduced in Chapter 9. The worksheet was partially completed in Chapter 9 for materiality and risk considerations (part of phase I) and was further completed as a part of the study of tests of controls and substantive tests of transactions in the last chapter (phase II). We will continue to complete the worksheet as we proceed through phase III in this chapter.

Deciding the appropriate tests of details of balances evidence is complicated because it must be decided on an objective-by-objective basis, and there are several interactions that affect the evidence decision. For example, the auditor must evaluate the potential for fraud and consider inherent risk, which may vary by objective, as well as the results of substantive tests of sales and cash receipts, which also may vary by objective. The auditor must also consider the results of tests of controls and the related control risk assessment.

In designing tests of details of balances for accounts receivable, it is essential to satisfy each of the nine balance-related audit objectives first discussed in Chapter 6. It was shown in Chapter 6 that these nine general objectives are the same for all accounts. Specifically applied to accounts receivable, they are called **accounts receivable balance-related audit objectives** and are as follows:[1]

1. Accounts receivable in the aged trial balance agree with related master file amounts, and the total is correctly added and agrees with the general ledger. (Detail tie-in)
2. Recorded accounts receivable exist. (Existence)
3. Existing accounts receivable are included. (Completeness)
4. Accounts receivable are accurate. (Accuracy)
5. Accounts receivable are properly classified. (Classification)
6. Cutoff for accounts receivable is correct. (Cutoff)
7. Accounts receivable is stated at realizable value. (Realizable value)
8. The client has rights to accounts receivable. (Rights)
9. Accounts receivable presentation and disclosures are proper. (Presentation and disclosure)

The columns in the evidence planning worksheet in Figure 16-7 (p. 502) include the balance-related audit objectives. The auditor uses the factors in the rows to aid in assessing planned detection risk for accounts receivable, by objective. These factors were studied in earlier chapters.

[1]Detail tie-in is included as the first objective here, compared with being objective 6 in Chapter 6, because tests for detail tie-in are normally done first.

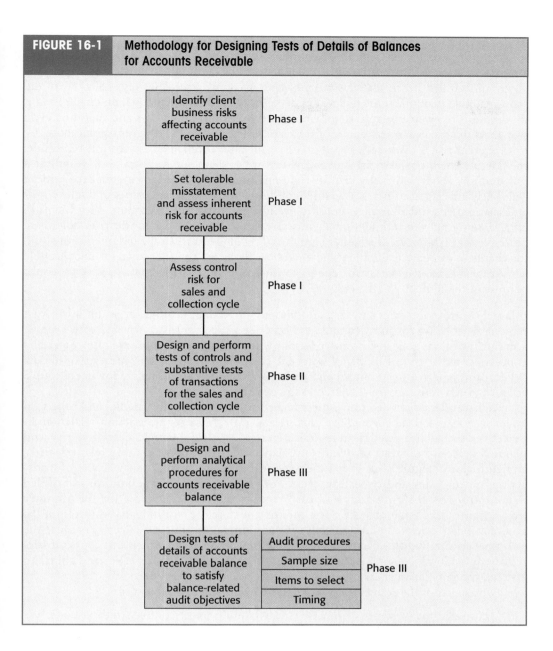

FIGURE 16-1 Methodology for Designing Tests of Details of Balances for Accounts Receivable

Identify client business risks affecting accounts receivable — Phase I

Set tolerable misstatement and assess inherent risk for accounts receivable — Phase I

Assess control risk for sales and collection cycle — Phase I

Design and perform tests of controls and substantive tests of transactions for the sales and collection cycle — Phase II

Design and perform analytical procedures for accounts receivable balance — Phase III

Design tests of details of accounts receivable balance to satisfy balance-related audit objectives

| Audit procedures |
| Sample size |
| Items to select |
| Timing |

Phase III

It is important for students of auditing to understand the entire methodology for designing tests of details of balances for accounts receivable and all other accounts. The following discussion explains the methodology. Portions of the discussion are a review of information studied in earlier chapters, but they are intended to aid in understanding the relationship of each part of Figure 16-1 to designing tests of details of balances.

Identify Client Business Risks Affecting Accounts Receivable (Phase I)

Tests of accounts receivable are based on the auditor's understanding of the client's business and industry, discussed in Chapter 8. As part of this understanding, the auditor studies the client's industry and external environment and evaluates management objectives and business processes to identify significant client business risks that could affect the financial statements, including accounts receivable. As part of gaining this understanding, the auditor also performs preliminary analytical procedures that may indicate increased risk of misstatements in accounts receivable.

Client business risks affecting accounts receivable are considered in the auditor's evaluation of inherent risk and planned evidence for accounts receivable. For example, as a result of adverse changes in the industry's economic environment, the auditor may increase inherent risk for net realizable value of accounts receivable.

Set Tolerable Misstatement and Assess Inherent Risk (Phase I)

As studied in Chapter 9, the auditor first decides the preliminary judgment about materiality for the entire financial statements. Next, the auditor allocates the preliminary judgment amount to each significant balance sheet account, including accounts receivable. This allocation is called *setting tolerable misstatement*. Accounts receivable is typically one of the most material accounts in the financial statements for companies that sell on credit. Even if the accounts receivable balance is not large, the transactions in the sales and collection cycle that affect the balance in accounts receivable are almost certain to be highly significant.

Inherent risk is assessed for each objective for an account such as accounts receivable, considering client business risk and the nature of the client and industry. SAS 99 indicates that auditors should normally identify a specific fraud risk related to revenue recognition. This likely affects the auditor's assessment of inherent risk for the existence and sales cutoff and sales returns and allowances cutoff objectives. In particular, it is common for clients to either intentionally or unintentionally misstate cutoff. Inherent risk for the realizable value objective is also often set at a higher level. It is difficult, because of the judgments involved, for clients to evaluate realizable value and correctly adjust the allowance for uncollectible accounts. It is relatively easy for clients to intentionally misstate the allowance account because of the difficulty of the judgments.

Assess Control Risk for the Sales and Collection Cycle (Phase I)

Internal controls over sales and cash receipts and the related accounts receivable are at least reasonably effective for most companies because management is concerned with keeping accurate records as a means to good relations with customers. Auditors are often especially concerned with three aspects of internal controls: controls that prevent or detect defalcations, controls over cutoff, and controls related to the allowance for uncollectible accounts, such as the approval of credit sales before shipment.

We have already studied transaction-related audit objectives in the sales and collection cycle (see Chapter 14). The auditor must relate control risk for transaction-related audit objectives to balance-related audit objectives in deciding planned detection risk and planned evidence for tests of details of balances. For the most part, the relationship is straightforward. Figure 16-2 shows the relationship for the two primary classes of transactions in the sales and collection cycle. For example, assume the auditor concluded that control risk for both sales and cash receipts transactions is low for the accuracy transaction-related audit objective. The auditor can therefore conclude that controls for the accuracy balance-related audit objective for accounts receivable are effective because the only transactions that affect accounts receivable are sales and cash receipts. Of course, if sales returns and allowances and charge-off of uncollectible accounts receivable are significant, assessed control risk must also be considered for these two classes of transactions.

Two aspects of the relationships in Figure 16-2 deserve special mention:

1. For sales, the existence transaction-related audit objective affects the existence balance-related audit objective, but for cash receipts, the existence transaction-related audit objective affects the completeness balance-related audit objective. A similar relationship exists for the completeness transaction-related audit objective. The reason for this somewhat surprising conclusion is that an increase of sales increases accounts receivable, but an increase of cash receipts decreases accounts receivable. For example, recording a sale that did not occur violates the existence transaction-related audit objective and existence balance-related audit objective (both overstatements). Recording a cash receipt that did not occur violates the existence transaction-related audit objective, but it violates the completeness balance-related audit objective for accounts receivable because a receivable that is still outstanding is no longer included in the records.

2. Three accounts receivable balance-related audit objectives are not affected by assessed control risk for classes of transactions. These are realizable value, rights, and presentation and disclosure. When the auditor wants to reduce assessed control risk below the maximum for these three objectives, separate controls are identified and tested.

Retail Revenue Management

Figure 16-7 on page 502 includes three rows for assessed control risk: one for sales, one for cash receipts, and one for additional controls related to the accounts receivable balance. The source of each control risk for sales and cash receipts is the control risk matrix, assuming that the tests of controls results supported the original assessment. The auditor makes a

FIGURE 16-2 — Relationship Between Transaction-Related Audit Objectives for the Sales and Collection Cycle and Balance-Related Audit Objectives for Accounts Receivable

CLASS OF TRANSACTIONS	TRANSACTION-RELATED AUDIT OBJECTIVES	Detail tie-in	Existence	Completeness	Accuracy	Classification	Cutoff	Realizable value	Rights	Presentation and disclosure
Sales	Existence		X							
	Completeness			X						
	Accuracy				X					
	Classification					X				
	Timing						X			
	Posting and summarization	X								
Cash receipts	Existence			X						
	Completeness		X							
	Accuracy				X					
	Classification					X				
	Timing						X			
	Posting and summarization	X								

separate assessment of control risk for objectives related only to the accounts receivable balance.

Designing audit procedures for tests of controls and substantive tests of transactions, deciding sample size, and evaluating the results of those tests were covered in the last two chapters. The results of the tests of controls determine whether assessed control risk for sales and cash receipts needs to be revised. The results of the substantive tests of transactions are used to determine the extent to which planned detection risk is satisfied for each accounts receivable balance-related audit objective. The evidence planning worksheet in Figure 16-7 shows three rows for control risk and two for substantive tests of transactions, one for sales, and the other for cash receipts.

Design and Perform Tests of Controls and Substantive Tests of Transactions (Phase II)

As discussed in Chapter 8, analytical procedures are often done during three phases of the audit: during planning, when performing detailed tests, and as a part of completing the audit. This chapter covers those done during planning and when performing detailed tests for accounts in the sales and collection cycle.

Design and Perform Analytical Procedures (Phase III)

OBJECTIVE 16-2

Design and perform analytical procedures for accounts in the sales and collection cycle.

Most analytical procedures performed during the detailed testing phase are done after the balance sheet date but before tests of details of balances. It makes little sense to perform extensive analytical procedures before the client has recorded all transactions for the year and finalized the financial statements.

Analytical procedures are done for the entire sales and collection cycle, not only for accounts receivable. This is because of the close relationship between income statement

TABLE 16-1	Analytical Procedures for the Sales and Collection Cycle

Analytical Procedure	Possible Misstatement
Compare gross margin percentage with previous years (by product line).	Overstatement or understatement of sales and accounts receivable.
Compare sales by month (by product line) over time.	Overstatement or understatement of sales and accounts receivable.
Compare sales returns and allowances as a percentage of gross sales with previous years (by product line).	Overstatement or understatement of sales returns and allowances and accounts receivable.
Compare individual customer balances over a stated amount with previous years.	Misstatements in accounts receivable and related income statement accounts.
Compare bad debt expense as a percentage of gross sales with previous years.	Uncollectible accounts receivable that have not been provided for.
Compare number of days that accounts receivable are outstanding with previous years and related turnover of accounts receivable.	Overstatement or understatement of allowance for uncollectible accounts and bad debt expense; also may indicate fictitious accounts receivable.
Compare aging categories as a percentage of accounts receivable with previous years.	Overstatement or understatement of allowance for uncollectible accounts and bad debt expense.
Compare allowance for uncollectible accounts as a percentage of accounts receivable with previous years.	Overstatement or understatement of allowance for uncollectible accounts and bad debt expense.
Compare charge-off of uncollectible accounts as a percentage of total accounts receivable with previous years.	Overstatement or understatement of allowance for uncollectible accounts and bad debt expense.

and balance sheet accounts. If the auditor determines possible misstatement in sales or sales returns and allowances through analytical procedures, accounts receivable will likely be the offsetting misstatement.

Table 16-1 presents examples of the major types of ratios and comparisons for the sales and collection cycle and potential misstatements that may be indicated by the analytical procedures. Although Table 16-1 focuses on the comparison of current year results with previous years, the auditor also considers current year results compared to budgets and industry trends. It is important to observe in the "possible misstatement" column that both balance sheet and income statement accounts are affected. For example, when the auditor performs analytical procedures for sales, evidence is being obtained about both sales and accounts receivable.

In addition to the analytical procedures in Table 16-1, there should also be a review of accounts receivable for large and unusual amounts. Individual receivables that deserve special attention are large balances, accounts that have been outstanding for a long time, receivables from affiliated companies, officers, directors, and other related parties, and credit balances. The auditor should review the listing of accounts (aged trial balance) at the balance sheet date to determine which accounts should be investigated further.

Information about the sales and collection cycle at Hillsburg Hardware Co. is provided as an illustration of the use of analytical procedures during the detailed testing phase. Table 16-2 includes comparative trial balance information for the sales and collection cycle for Hillsburg. Some of that information is used to illustrate several analytical procedures in Table 16-3. None of the analytical procedures indicated potential misstatements except for the ratio of the allowance of uncollectible accounts to accounts receivable. The explanation at the bottom of Table 16-3 describes the potential misstatement.

The auditor's conclusion about analytical procedures for the sales and collection cycle is incorporated into the third row from the bottom on the evidence planning worksheet in

TABLE 16-2 Comparative Information for Hillsburg Hardware Co.—Sales and Collection Cycle

	12-31-04 (in Thousands)	Percent Change 2003–2004	12-31-03 (in Thousands)	Percent Change 2002–2003	12-31-02 (in Thousands)
			Amount		
Sales	$144,328	9.0%	$132,421	7.0%	$123,737
Sales returns and allowances	1,242	3.9	1,195	13.6	1,052
Gross margin	39,845	9.6	36,350	7.0	33,961
Accounts receivable	20,197	15.3	17,521	3.3	16,961
Allowance for uncollectible accounts	1,240	(5.4)	1,311	21.5	1,079
Bad debt expense	3,323	(2.1)	3,394	7.3	3,162
Total current assets	51,027	2.3	49,895	1.5	49,157
Total assets	61,367	.9	60,791	1.8	59,696
Net earnings before taxes	5,681	21.9	4,659	39.0	3,351
Number of accounts receivable	258	16.7	221	5.7	209
Number of accounts receivable with balances over $100,000	37	15.6	32	6.7	30

Figure 16-7. Analytical procedures are substantive tests and therefore reduce the extent to which the auditor needs to test details of balances, if the analytical procedures' results are favorable.

When analytical procedures in the sales and collection cycle uncover unusual fluctuations, the auditor should make additional inquiries of management. Management's responses should be critically evaluated to determine whether they adequately explain the unusual fluctuations and whether they are supported by other corroborative evidence.

TABLE 16-3 Analytical Procedures for Hillsburg Hardware Co.—Sales and Collection Cycle

	12-31-04	12-31-03	12-31-02
Gross margin/net sales	27.85%	27.70%	27.68%
Sales returns and allowances/gross sales	.9%	.9%	.9%
Bad debt expense/net sales	2.3%	2.6%	2.6%
Allowance for uncollectible accounts/ accounts receivable	6.1%	7.5%	6.4%
Number of days receivables outstanding*	48.09	47.96	49.32
Net accounts receivable/total current assets	37.2%	32.5%	32.3%

*Based on year-end accounts receivable only.

Comment: Allowance as a percentage of accounts receivable has declined from 6.4% to 6.1%. Number of days receivables outstanding and economic conditions do not justify this change. Potential misstatement is approximately $60,000 ($20,197,000 × .064 − .061).

The appropriate tests of details of balances depend on the factors incorporated into the evidence planning worksheet in Figure 16-7. The second row from the bottom shows planned detection risk for each accounts receivable balance-related audit objective. Planned detection risk for each objective is an auditor decision, decided by subjectively combining the conclusions reached about each of the factors listed above that row.

Combining the factors that determine planned detection risk is complex because the measurement for each factor is imprecise and the appropriate weight to be given each factor is highly judgmental. Conversely, the relationship between each factor and planned detection risk is well established. For example, the auditor knows that a high inherent risk or control risk decreases planned detection risk and increases planned substantive tests, whereas good results of substantive tests of transactions increase planned detection risk and decrease other planned substantive tests.

The bottom row in Figure 16-7 shows the planned audit evidence for tests of details of balances for accounts receivable, by objective. As discussed in previous chapters, planned audit evidence is the complement of planned detection risk.

The conclusion that planned audit evidence for a given objective is high, medium, or low is implemented by the auditor deciding the appropriate audit procedures, sample size, items to select, and timing. The remainder of this chapter discusses deciding the specific audit procedures and timing decisions for auditing accounts receivable. Chapter 17 deals with sample size and selecting items from the population for testing.

PRACTICE APPLICATION OF ANALYTICAL PROCEDURES FOR GROSS MARGIN

Ron Stopps, CPA, is the auditor for Great Western Lumber Company, a wholesale wood milling company. Ron calculates the gross margin by three product lines and obtains industry information from published data in the table below.

In discussing the results, the controller states that Great Western has always had a higher gross margin on hardwood products than the industry because they focus on the markets where they are able to sell at higher prices instead of emphasizing volume. The opposite is true of plywood, for which they have a reasonably small number of customers, each of whom demands lower prices because of high volume. The controller states that competitive forces have caused reductions in plywood gross margin for both the industry and Great Western in 2004 and 2005. Great Western has traditionally had a somewhat lower gross margin for softwood than the industry until 2005, when gross margin went up significantly due to aggressive selling.

Stopps observed that most of what the controller said was reasonable given the facts. Hardwood gross margin for the industry was stable and approximately 3.5 percent to 4 percent lower than Great Western's every year. Industry gross margin for ply-

wood has declined annually but is about 10 percent higher than Great Western's. Industry gross margin for softwood has been stable for the three years, but Great Western's has increased by a fairly large amount.

The change in Great Western's softwood gross margin from 20.3 percent to 23.9 percent is a concern to Stopps, so he goes through a three-step procedure:

1. Calculate the potential misstatement and evaluate the materiality of that amount. He calculates 23.9% − 20.3% × softwood sales and concludes the amount is potentially material.
2. Identify potential causes of the change.

   ◆ Overstatement of sales
   ◆ Overstatement of inventory (understatement of cost of goods sold)
   ◆ Understatement of purchases (understatement of cost of goods sold)
   ◆ Good results of aggressive selling

3. Indicate in the audit files a concern for the potential overstatement of sales and inventory and understatement of purchases of softwood. This may require an expansion of other substantive audit tests.

	2005 Gross Margin Percent		2004 Gross Margin Percent		2003 Gross Margin Percent	
	Great Western	Industry	Great Western	Industry	Great Western	Industry
Hardwood	36.3	32.4	36.4	32.5	36.0	32.3
Softwood	23.9	22.0	20.3	22.1	20.5	22.3
Plywood	40.3	50.1	44.2	54.3	45.4	55.6

Tests of details of balances for all cycles are directed to balance sheet accounts, but income statement accounts are not ignored because they are verified as a by-product of the balance sheet tests. For example, if the auditor confirms accounts receivable balances and finds overstatements because of mistakes in billing customers, there are overstatements of both accounts receivable and sales.

Confirmation of accounts receivable is the most important test of details of accounts receivable. Confirmation is discussed briefly in studying the appropriate tests for each of the balance-related audit objectives, then separately in more detail later in this chapter.

The discussion of tests of details of balances for accounts receivable that follows assumes that the auditor has completed an evidence planning worksheet similar to the one in Figure 16-7 and has decided planned detection risk for tests of details for each balance-related audit objective. The audit procedures selected and their sample size will depend heavily on whether planned evidence for a given objective is low, medium, or high. The discussion focuses on accounts receivable balance-related audit objectives.

Most tests of accounts receivable and the allowance for uncollectible accounts are based on the aged trial balance. An **aged trial balance** is a listing of the balances in the accounts receivable master file at the balance sheet date. It includes the individual customer balances outstanding and a breakdown of each balance by the time passed between the date of sale and the balance sheet date. An illustration of a typical aged trial balance is given in Figure 16-3 for Hillsburg Hardware. Notice that the total is the same as accounts receivable on the general ledger trial balance on page 141.

Testing the information on the aged trial balance for detail tie-in is a necessary audit procedure. It is ordinarily done before any other tests to assure the auditor that the population being tested agrees with the general ledger and accounts receivable master file. The total column and the columns depicting the aging must be test footed and the total on the trial balance compared with the general ledger. In addition, a sample of individual balances should be traced to supporting documents such as duplicate sales invoices to verify the customer's name, balance, and proper aging. The extent of the testing for detail tie-in depends

OBJECTIVE 16-3

Design and perform tests of details of balances for accounts receivable for each balance-related audit objective.

Accounts Receivable Are Correctly Added and Agree with the Master File and the General Ledger

---

FIGURE 16-3 | Aged Trial Balance for Hillsburg Hardware Co.

PBC	Hillsburg Hardware Co. Accounts Receivable Aged Trial Balance 12/31/04		Schedule Prepared by Client Approved by		Date 1/5/05		

			Aging, Based on Invoice Date				
Account Number	Customer	Balance 12/31/04	0–30 days	31–60 days	61–90 days	91–120 days	over 120
01011	Adams Supply	146,589	90,220	56,369			
01044	Argonaut, Inc.	30,842	30,842				
01100	Atwater Brothers	210,389	210,389				
01191	Beekman Bearings	83,526	73,526		10,000		
01270	Brown and Phillips	60,000				60,000	
01301	Christopher Plumbing	15,789					15,789
09733	Travelers Equipment	59,576	59,576				
09742	Underhill Parts and Maintenance	179,263	179,263				
09810	UJW Co.	102,211	34,911	34,700	32,600		
09907	Zephyr Plastics	286,300	186,000	100,300			
		$20,196,800	$14,217,156	$2,869,366	$1,408,642	$1,038,926	$662,710

---

on the number of accounts involved, the degree to which the master file has been tested as a part of tests of controls and substantive tests of transactions, and the extent to which the schedule has been verified by an internal auditor or other independent person before it is given to the auditor. Audit software can be used to perform footing and cross-footing of the aged trial balance, as well as to recalculate the aging.

Recorded Accounts Receivable Exist

The most important test of details of balances for determining the existence of recorded accounts receivable is the confirmation of customers' balances. Confirmations were defined and discussed in detail in Chapter 7. When customers do not respond to confirmations, auditors also examine supporting documents to verify the shipment of goods and evidence of subsequent cash receipts to determine whether the accounts were collected. Normally, auditors do not examine shipping documents or evidence of subsequent cash receipts for any account in the sample that is confirmed, but these documents are used extensively as alternative evidence for nonresponses.

Existing Accounts Receivable Are Included

It is difficult to test for account balances omitted from the aged trial balance except by relying on the self-balancing nature of the accounts receivable master file. For example, if the client accidentally excluded an account receivable from the trial balance, the only likely way it would be discovered is by footing the accounts receivable trial balance and reconciling the balance with the control account in the general ledger.

If all sales to a customer are omitted from the sales journal, the understatement of accounts receivable is almost impossible to uncover by tests of details of balances. For example, auditors rarely send accounts receivable confirmations to customers with zero balances, in part because research shows that customers are unlikely to respond to requests that indicate their balances are understated. In addition, unrecorded sales to a new customer are difficult to identify for confirmation because that customer is not included in the accounts receivable master file. The understatement of sales and accounts receivable is best uncovered by substantive tests of transactions for shipments made but not recorded (completeness objective for tests of sales transactions) and by analytical procedures.

Accounts Receivable Are Accurate

Confirmation of accounts selected from the trial balance is the most common test of details of balances for the accuracy of accounts receivable. When customers do not respond to confirmation requests, auditors examine supporting documents, in the same way as described for the existence objective. Tests of the debits and credits to individual customers' balances are done by examining supporting documentation for shipments and cash receipts.

Accounts Receivable Are Properly Classified

It is normally relatively easy to evaluate the classification of accounts receivable by reviewing the aged trial balance for material receivables from affiliates, officers, directors, or other related parties. If notes receivable or accounts that should not be classified as a current asset are included with the regular accounts, these should also be segregated. Finally, if credit balances in accounts receivable are significant, it is appropriate to reclassify them as accounts payable.

There is a close relationship between the classification objective as discussed here and the presentation and disclosure objective. Classification concerns determining whether the client has correctly separated different classifications of accounts receivable. Presentation and disclosure concerns making sure that the classifications are properly presented. For example, under the classification objective, the auditor determines whether receivables from related parties have been separated on the aged trial balance. Under the presentation and disclosure objective, the auditor determines whether related party transactions are correctly shown in the financial statements.

Cutoff for Accounts Receivable Is Correct

Cutoff misstatements exist when current period transactions are recorded in the subsequent period or subsequent period transactions are recorded in the current period. The objective of cutoff tests, regardless of the type of transaction, is to verify whether transactions near the end of the accounting period are recorded in the proper period. The cutoff objective is one of the most important in the cycle because misstatements in cutoff can significantly affect current period income. For example, the intentional or unintentional inclusion of several large, subsequent period sales in the current period or the exclusion of several current period sales returns and allowances can materially overstate net earnings.

In determining the reasonableness of cutoff, a threefold approach is needed: (1) decide on the appropriate *criteria for cutoff*, (2) evaluate whether the client has established *adequate procedures* to ensure a reasonable cutoff, and (3) *test* whether a reasonable cutoff was obtained. Cutoff misstatements can occur for *sales, sales returns and allowances,* and *cash receipts.*

Sales Cutoff The criterion used by most merchandising and manufacturing clients for determining when a sale takes place is the *shipment of goods,* but some companies record invoices at the time title passes. The passage of title can take place before shipment (as in the case of custom-manufactured goods), at the time of shipment, or subsequent to shipment. For the correct measurement of current period income, the method must be in accordance with generally accepted accounting principles (GAAP) and consistently applied.

Revenue Recognition

The most important part of evaluating the client's method of obtaining a reliable cutoff is to determine the procedures in use. When a client issues prenumbered shipping documents sequentially, it is usually a simple matter to evaluate and test cutoff. Moreover, the segregation of duties between the shipping and the billing function also enhances the likelihood of recording transactions in the proper period. However, if shipments are made by company truck, if the shipping records are unnumbered, and if shipping and billing department personnel are not independent of each other, it may be difficult, if not impossible, to be assured of an accurate cutoff.

When the client's internal controls are adequate, the cutoff can usually be verified by obtaining the shipping document number for the last shipment made at the end of the period and comparing this number with current and subsequent period recorded sales. As an illustration, assume that the shipping document number for the last shipment in the current period is 1489. All recorded sales before the end of the period should bear a shipping document number preceding number 1490. There should also be no sales recorded in the subsequent period for a shipment with a bill of lading numbered 1489 or lower. This can easily be tested by comparing recorded sales with the related shipping documents for the last few days of the current period and the first few days of the subsequent period.

Sales Returns and Allowances Cutoff GAAP requires that sales returns and allowances be *matched with related sales* if the amounts are material. For example, if current period shipments are returned in the subsequent period, the proper treatment is to include the sales return in the current period. (The returned goods would be treated as current period inventory.) For most companies, however, sales returns and allowances are recorded in the *accounting period in which they occur,* under the assumption of approximately equal, offsetting amounts at the beginning and end of each accounting period. This is acceptable as long as the amounts are not significant.

When the auditor is confident that the client records all sales returns and allowances promptly, the cutoff tests are simple and straightforward. The auditor can examine supporting documentation for a sample of sales returns and allowances recorded during several weeks subsequent to the closing date to determine the date of the original sale. If the amounts recorded in the subsequent period are significantly different from unrecorded returns and allowances at the beginning of the period under audit, an adjustment must be considered. If the internal controls for recording sales returns and allowances are evaluated as ineffective, a larger sample is needed to verify cutoff.

Companies may experience higher returns for Internet sales. Because customers who purchase online are unable to view the actual products before purchase, they may be more likely to return goods after they have received and inspected them. As a result, auditors of companies that have e-commerce sales applications may need to evaluate sales returns from e-commerce-based sales separately from sales returns generated through traditional sales systems.

Cash Receipts Cutoff For most audits, a proper cash receipts cutoff is *less important* than either the sales or the sales returns and allowances cutoff because the improper cutoff of cash affects only the cash and the accounts receivable balances, not earnings. Nevertheless, if the misstatement is material, it could affect the fair presentation of these accounts, especially when cash is a small or negative balance.

It is easy to test for a cash receipts cutoff misstatement (often called *holding the cash receipts book open*) by tracing recorded cash receipts to subsequent period bank deposits on the bank statement. If there is a delay of several days, this could indicate a cutoff misstatement.

The confirmation of accounts receivable may also be relied on to some degree to uncover cutoff misstatements for sales, sales returns and allowances, and cash receipts, especially when there is a long interval between the date the transaction took place and the recording date. However, when the interval is only a few days, mail delivery delays may cause confusion of a cutoff misstatement with a normal **timing difference**. For example, if a customer mails and records a check to a client for payment of an unpaid account on December 30 and the client receives and records the amount on January 2, the records of the two organizations will be different on December 31. This is not a cutoff misstatement, but a timing difference due to the delivery time. It may be difficult for the auditor to evaluate whether a cutoff misstatement or a timing difference occurred when a confirmation reply is the source of information. This type of situation requires additional investigation, such as inspection of underlying documents.

Accounts Receivable Is Stated at Realizable Value	Tests of the **realizable value of accounts receivable** objective are done for the purpose of evaluating the account *allowance for uncollectible accounts*. GAAP requires that accounts receivable be stated at the amount that will ultimately be collected, which is gross accounts receivable less the allowance. The client's estimate of the total amount that is uncollectible is represented by the allowance for uncollectible accounts. Although it is not possible to predict the future precisely, it is necessary for the auditor to evaluate whether the allowance is reasonable, considering all available facts. To assist with this evaluation, the auditor often prepares an audit schedule that analyzes the allowance for uncollectible accounts. An illustration of this schedule for Hillsburg Hardware is shown in Figure 16-4. In the example, the analysis indicates that the allowance is understated. This could be the result of the client failing to adjust the allowance or economic factors. Note that the potential understatement of the reserve was signaled by the analytical procedures in Table 16-3 (p. 489).

The starting point for the evaluation of the allowance for uncollectible accounts is to review the results of the tests of controls that are concerned with the client's credit policy. If the client's credit policy has remained unchanged and the results of the tests of credit policy and credit approval are consistent with those of the preceding year, the change in the balance in the allowance for uncollectible accounts should reflect only changes in economic conditions and sales volume. However, if the client's credit policy or the degree to which it correctly functions has significantly changed, great care must be taken to consider the effects of these changes as well.

FIGURE 16-4

FIGURE 16-4 Analysis of Allowance for Uncollectible Accounts for Hillsburg Hardware Co.

Hillsburg Hardware Co.			**Schedule**	B-4	**Date**
Analysis of Allowance for Uncollectible Accounts			**Prepared by**	TW	1/8/05
12/31/04			**Approved by**	SB	1/10/05

A/R Category	A/R Balance 12/31/04	Estimated Allowance Percentage	Estimated Required Allowance
0–30 days	$14,217,156 ✓	3% ×	$ 426,515
31–60 days	2,869,366 ✓	6% ×	172,162
61–90 days	1,408,642 ✓	15% ×	211,296
91–120 days	1,038,926 ✓	25% ×	259,732
Over 120	662,710 ✓	40% ×	265,084
Total	**$20,196,800**		**$1,334,789**
Recorded Allowance			**$1,240,000** TB
Difference			**$ 94,789**

✓ — Traced to aged accounts receivable trial balance.
× — Allowance percentages are consistent with prior year, and appear reasonable based on historical loss percentages documented in permanent file.
TB — Agreed to trial balance.

Conclusion: Recorded allowance appears understated based on aging analysis. Approximate amount of $95,000 not considered material. Include on Summary of Possible Misstatements schedule on A-3. (See Figure 24-6 on page 725.)

A common way to evaluate the adequacy of the allowance is to carefully examine the noncurrent accounts on the aged trial balance to determine which ones have not been paid subsequent to the balance sheet date. The size and age of unpaid balances can then be compared with similar information from previous years to evaluate whether the amount of noncurrent receivables is increasing or decreasing over time. The examination of credit files, discussions with the credit manager, and review of the client's correspondence file may also provide insights into the collectibility of the accounts. These procedures are especially important if a few large balances are noncurrent and are not being paid on a regular basis.

There are two pitfalls in evaluating the allowance by reviewing individual noncurrent balances on the aged trial balance. First, the current accounts are ignored in establishing the adequacy of the allowance, even though some of these amounts will undoubtedly become uncollectible. Second, it is difficult to compare the results of the current year with those of previous years on such an unstructured basis. If the accounts are becoming progressively uncollectible over several years, this fact could be overlooked. A way to avoid these difficulties is to establish the history of bad debt charge-offs over a period of time as a frame of reference for evaluating the current year's allowance. As an example, if historically a certain percentage of the total of each age category becomes uncollectible, it is relatively easy to compute whether the allowance is properly stated. If 2 percent of current accounts, 10 percent of 30- to 90-day accounts, and 35 percent of all balances over 90 days ultimately become uncollectible, these percentages can easily be applied to the current year's aged trial balance totals, and the result can be compared with the balance in the allowance account. Of course, the auditor has to be careful to modify the calculations for changed conditions.

Bad Debt Expense After the auditor is satisfied with the allowance for uncollectible accounts, it is easy to verify bad debt expense. Assume that (1) the beginning balance in the allowance account was verified as a part of the previous audit, (2) the uncollectible accounts charged off were verified as a part of the substantive tests of transactions, and (3) the ending balance in the allowance account has been verified by various means.

Then bad debt expense is simply a residual balance that can be verified by a reperformance test.

The Client Has Rights to Accounts Receivable

The client's rights to accounts receivable ordinarily cause no audit problems because the receivables usually belong to the client, but in some cases, a portion of the receivables may have been pledged as collateral, assigned to someone else, factored, or sold at discount. Normally, the client's customers are not aware of the existence of such matters; therefore, the confirmation of receivables will not bring them to light. A review of the minutes, discussions with the client, confirmation with banks, the examination of debt contracts for evidence of accounts receivable pledged as collateral, and the examination of correspondence files are usually sufficient to uncover instances in which the client has limited rights to receivables.

Accounts Receivable Presentation and Disclosures Are Proper

In addition to testing for the proper statement of the dollar amount in the general ledger, the auditor must also determine that information about the account balance resulting from the sales and collection cycle is properly presented and disclosed in the financial statements. The auditor must decide whether the client has properly combined amounts and disclosed related party information in the statements. To evaluate the adequacy of the presentation and disclosure, the auditor must have a thorough understanding of generally accepted accounting principles and presentation and disclosure requirements.

An important part of the evaluation involves deciding whether material amounts requiring separate disclosure have actually been separated in the statements. For example, receivables from officers and affiliated companies must be segregated from accounts receivable from customers if the amounts are material. Similarly, under SEC requirements, it is necessary to disclose sales and assets for different business segments separately. The proper aggregation of general ledger balances in the financial statements also requires combining account balances that are not relevant for external users of the statements. If all accounts included in the general ledger were disclosed separately on the statements, most statement users would be more confused than enlightened.

As a part of proper presentation and disclosure, the auditor is also required to evaluate the adequacy of the *footnotes*. One of the major lawsuits in the history of the profession, the Continental Vending case (*United States* v. *Simon*), revolved primarily around the adequacy of the footnote disclosure of a major receivable from an affiliated company. This case was discussed in Chapter 5 in the study of legal liability. The required footnote disclosure for accounts receivable includes information about the pledging, discounting, factoring, assignment of accounts receivable, and amounts due from related parties. Of course, to evaluate the adequacy of these disclosures, it is first necessary to know of their existence and to have complete information about their nature. As discussed in the previous section, this is generally obtained in other parts of the audit.

In the preceding discussion of designing the tests of details of balances, you should have noticed the recurrence of confirmation issues. Confirmation is extremely important because, as discussed in Chapter 7, confirmations are highly reliable evidence. The primary purpose of accounts receivable confirmation is to satisfy the *existence, accuracy,* and *cutoff* objectives.

OBJECTIVE 16-4

Obtain and evaluate accounts receivable confirmations.

Auditing standards require the confirmation of accounts receivable in normal circumstances, but SAS 67 (AU 330) permits an unqualified report even when accounts receivable are not confirmed in any of three circumstances:

AICPA Requirements

1. Accounts receivable are immaterial. This is common for certain companies such as discount stores with primarily cash or credit card sales.

2. The auditor considers confirmations ineffective evidence because response rates will likely be inadequate or unreliable. In certain industries, such as hospitals, response rates to confirmations are very low.

3. The combined level of inherent risk and control risk is low and other substantive evidence can be accumulated to provide sufficient evidence. If a client has effective internal controls and low inherent risk for the sales and collection cycle, the auditor should often be able to satisfy the evidence requirements by tests of controls, substantive tests of transactions, and analytical procedures.

If the auditor decides not to confirm accounts receivable, the justification for doing so must be documented in the audit files.

Although the remaining sections in this chapter refer specifically to the confirmation of accounts receivable from customers, the concepts apply equally to other receivables, such as notes receivable, amounts due from officers, and employee advances. Confirmations are not required by auditing standards for any other accounts.

In performing confirmation procedures, the auditor must decide the type of confirmation to use, timing of the procedures, sample size, and individual items to select.

Confirmation Decisions

Type of Confirmation Two common types of confirmations are used for confirming accounts receivable: positive and negative. A **positive confirmation** is a communication addressed to the debtor requesting the recipient to confirm directly whether the balance as stated on the confirmation request is correct or incorrect. Figure 16-5 (p. 498) illustrates a positive confirmation in the audit of Hillsburg Hardware Co. Notice that this confirmation is for one of the largest accounts on the aged trial balance in Figure 16-3 (p. 491). A second type of positive confirmation, often called a **blank confirmation form,** does not state the amount on the confirmation but requests the recipient to fill in the balance or furnish other information. Because blank forms require the recipient to determine the information requested, they are considered more reliable than confirmations that include balance information. Blank forms are rarely used in practice because they often result in lower response rates.

An **invoice confirmation** is another type of positive confirmation in which an individual invoice is confirmed, rather than the customer's entire accounts receivable balance. Many customers use voucher systems that allow them to confirm individual invoices but not balance information. As a result, invoice confirmations may improve confirmation response rates. Invoice confirmations also result in fewer timing differences and other reconciling items than balance confirmations. However, invoice confirmations have the disadvantage of not directly confirming ending balances.

A **negative confirmation** is also addressed to the debtor but requests a response only when the debtor disagrees with the stated amount. Figure 16-6 (p. 499) illustrates a negative confirmation in the audit of Hillsburg Hardware Co. that has been attached to a customer's monthly statement with a gummed label.

A positive confirmation is *more reliable* evidence because the auditor can perform follow-up procedures if a response is not received from the debtor. With a negative confirmation, failure to reply must be regarded as a correct response, even though the debtor may have ignored the confirmation request.

FIGURE 16-5 | **Positive Confirmation**

HILLSBURG HARDWARE CO.
Gary, Indiana

January 5, 2005

Atwater Brothers
19 South Main Street
Middleton, Ohio 36947

To Whom It May Concern:

In connection with an audit of our financial statements, please confirm directly to our auditors

BERGER & ANTHONY, CPAs
Gary, Indiana

the correctness of the balance of your account with us as of December 31, 2004, as shown below.
This is not a request for payment; please do not send your remittance to our auditors. Your prompt attention to this request will be appreciated. An envelope is enclosed for your reply.

Erma Swanson

Erma Swanson, Controller

BERGER & ANTHONY, CPAs
Gary, Indiana

The balance receivable from us of $210,389 as of December 31, 2004, is correct except as noted below:

_____
_____
_____
_____
_____
_____

Date _____   By _____

Offsetting the reliability disadvantage, negative confirmations are *less expensive* to send than positive confirmations, and thus more can be distributed for the same total cost. Negative confirmations cost less because there are no second requests and no follow-up of nonresponses.

The determination of which type of confirmation to use is an auditor's decision, and it should be based on the facts in the audit. SAS 67 states that it is acceptable to use negative confirmations only when *all* of the following circumstances are present:

• Accounts receivable is made up of a large number of small accounts.
• Combined assessed control risk and inherent risk is low. The combined risk is unlikely to be low if either internal controls are ineffective or there is a high expectation of misstatements. For example, if prior years' audits indicate that there are often disputed or inaccurate accounts receivable, negative confirmations would be inappropriate.
• There is no reason to believe that the recipients of the confirmations are unlikely to give them consideration. For example, if the response rate to positive confirmations in

FIGURE 16-6   Negative Confirmation

AUDITOR'S ACCOUNT CONFIRMATION

Please examine this statement carefully. If it does NOT agree with your records, please report any exceptions directly to our auditors
BERGER & ANTHONY, CPAs
Gary, Indiana
who are conducting an audit of our financial statements as of December 31, 2004. An addressed envelope is enclosed for your convenience in replying.
Do not send your remittance to our auditors.

prior years was extremely high or if there are high response rates on audits of similar clients, it is likely that recipients will give confirmations reasonable consideration.

Typically, when negative confirmations are used, the auditor puts considerable emphasis on the effectiveness of internal controls, substantive tests of transactions, and analytical procedures as evidence of the fairness of accounts receivable and assumes that the large majority of the recipients will provide a conscientious reading and response to the confirmation request. Negative confirmations are often used for audits of hospitals, retail stores, banks, and other industries in which the receivables are due from the general public.

It is also common to use a combination of negative and positive confirmations by sending the latter to accounts with large balances and the former to those with small balances.

The discussion of confirmations to this point shows that there is a continuum for the type of confirmation decision, starting with using no confirmations in some circumstances, to using only negatives, to using both negatives and positives, to using only positives. The primary factors affecting the decision are the materiality of total accounts receivable, the number and size of individual accounts, control risk, inherent risk, the effectiveness of confirmations as audit evidence, and the availability of other audit evidence.

Timing The most reliable evidence from confirmations is obtained when they are sent as close to the balance sheet date as possible, as opposed to confirming the accounts several months before year-end. This permits the auditor to directly test the accounts receivable balance on the financial statements without making any inferences about the transactions taking place between the confirmation date and the balance sheet date. However, as a means of completing the audit on a timely basis, it is often necessary to confirm the accounts at an interim date. This is permissible if internal controls are adequate and can provide reasonable assurance that sales, cash receipts, and other credits are properly recorded between the date of the confirmation and the end of the accounting period. Other factors the auditor is likely to consider in making the decision are the materiality of accounts receivable and the auditor's exposure to lawsuits because of the possibility of client bankruptcy and similar risks.

If the decision is made to confirm accounts receivable before year-end, it may be necessary to test the transactions occurring between the confirmation date and the balance sheet date by examining such internal documents as duplicate sales invoices, shipping documents, and evidence of cash receipts, in addition to performing analytical procedures of the intervening period.

Sample Size The major factors affecting sample size for confirming accounts receivable fall into several categories and include the following:

- Tolerable misstatement
- Inherent risk (relative size of total accounts receivable, number of accounts, prior-year results, and expected misstatements)
- Control risk
- Achieved detection risk from other substantive tests (extent and results of substantive tests of transactions, analytical procedures, and other tests of details)
- Type of confirmation (negatives normally require a larger sample size)

Selection of the Items for Testing Some type of *stratification* is desirable with most confirmations. A typical approach to stratification is to consider both the dollar size of individual accounts and the length of time an account has been outstanding as a basis for selecting the balances for confirmation. In most audits, the emphasis should be on confirming larger and older balances because these are most likely to include a significant misstatement. But it is also important to sample some items from every material segment of the population. In many cases, the auditor selects all accounts above a certain dollar amount and selects a random sample from the remainder.

When selecting a sample of accounts receivable for confirmation, the auditor should be careful to avoid being influenced by the client. If a client tries to discourage the auditor from sending confirmations to certain customers, the auditor should consider the possibility that the client is attempting to conceal fictitious or known misstatements of accounts receivable.

Maintaining Control

After the items for confirmation have been selected, the auditor must maintain control of the confirmations until they are returned from the customer. When the client assists by preparing the confirmations, enclosing them in envelopes, or putting stamps on the envelopes, close supervision by the auditor is required. A return address must be included on all envelopes to make sure that undelivered mail is received by the CPA firm. Similarly, self-addressed return envelopes accompanying the confirmations must be addressed for delivery to the CPA firm's office. It is even important to mail the confirmations *outside* the client's office. All of these steps are necessary to ensure independent communication between the auditor and the customer.

Follow-Up on Nonresponses

It is inappropriate to regard confirmations mailed but not returned by customers as significant audit evidence. For example, nonresponses to positive confirmations do not provide audit evidence. Similarly, for negative confirmations, the auditor should not conclude that the recipient received the confirmation request and verified the information requested. Negative confirmations do, however, provide some evidence of the existence assertion.

When positive confirmations are used, SAS 67 requires follow-up procedures for confirmations not returned by the customer. It is common to send second and sometimes even third requests for confirmations. Even with these efforts, some customers do not return the confirmation, so it is necessary to follow up with **alternative procedures.** The objective of alternative procedures is to determine by a means other than confirmation whether the non-confirmed account existed and was properly stated at the confirmation date. For any positive confirmation not returned, the following documentation can be examined to verify the existence and accuracy of individual sales transactions making up the ending balance in accounts receivable.

Sales Fraud

Subsequent Cash Receipts Evidence of the receipt of cash subsequent to the confirmation date includes examining remittance advices, entries in the cash receipts records, or perhaps even subsequent credits in the accounts receivable master file. On the one hand, the examination of evidence of subsequent cash receipts is a highly useful alternative procedure because it is reasonable to assume that a customer would not make a payment unless it was an existing receivable. On the other hand, the fact of payment does not establish whether there was an obligation on the date of the confirmation. In addition, care should be taken to match each unpaid sales transaction with evidence of its subsequent payment as a test for disputes or disagreements over individual outstanding invoices.

Duplicate Sales Invoices These are useful in verifying the actual issuance of a sales invoice and the actual date of the billing.

Shipping Documents These are important in establishing whether the shipment was actually made and as a test of cutoff.

Correspondence with the Client Usually, the auditor does not need to review correspondence as a part of alternative procedures, but correspondence can be used to disclose disputed and questionable receivables not uncovered by other means.

The extent and nature of the alternative procedures depend primarily on the materiality of the nonresponses, the types of misstatements discovered in the confirmed responses, the subsequent cash receipts from the nonresponses, and the auditor's conclusions about internal control. It is normally desirable to account for all unconfirmed balances with alternative procedures even if the amounts are small, as a means of properly generalizing from the sample to the population. Another acceptable approach is to assume that nonresponses are 100 percent overstatement amounts.

When the confirmation requests are returned by the customer, it is necessary to determine the reason for any reported differences. In many cases, they are caused by timing differences between the client's and the customer's records. It is important to distinguish between these and *exceptions,* which represent misstatements of the accounts receivable balance. The most commonly reported types of differences in confirmations follow.

Analysis of Differences

Payment Has Already Been Made Reported differences typically arise when the customer has made a payment before the confirmation date, but the client has not received the payment in time for recording before the confirmation date. Such instances should be carefully investigated to determine the possibility of a cash receipts cutoff misstatement, lapping, or a theft of cash.

Goods Have Not Been Received These differences typically result because the client records the sale at the date of shipment and the customer records the acquisition when the goods are received. The time that the goods are in transit is often the cause of differences reported on confirmations. These should be investigated to determine the possibility of the customer not receiving the goods at all or the existence of a cutoff misstatement on the client's records.

The Goods Have Been Returned The client's failure to record a credit memo could result from timing differences or the improper recording of sales returns and allowances. Like other differences, these must be investigated.

Clerical Errors and Disputed Amounts The most likely types of reported differences in a client's records are when the customer states that there is an error in the price charged for the goods, the goods are damaged, the proper quantity of goods was not received, and so forth. These differences must be investigated to determine whether the client is in error and what the amount of the error is.

In most instances, the auditor will ask the client to reconcile the difference and, if necessary, will communicate with the customer to resolve any disagreements. Naturally, the auditor must carefully verify the client's conclusions on each significant difference.

When all differences have been resolved, including those discovered in performing alternative procedures, it is important to *reevaluate internal control.* Each client misstatement must be analyzed to determine whether it was consistent or inconsistent with the original assessed level of control risk. If a significant number of misstatements take place that are inconsistent with the assessment of control risk, it is necessary to revise the assessment and consider the effect of the revision on the audit. Auditors of public companies must also consider implications to the audit of internal control over financial reporting.

Drawing Conclusions

It is also necessary to generalize from the sample to the entire population of accounts receivable. Even though the sum of the misstatements in the sample may not significantly affect the financial statements, the auditor must consider whether the population is likely to be materially misstated. This conclusion can be arrived at by using statistical sampling techniques or on a nonstatistical basis. Projection of misstatements was discussed in Chapter 9 and is further explained in Chapter 17.

The auditor should always evaluate the *qualitative* nature of the misstatements found in the sample, regardless of the dollar amount of the projected misstatement. Even if the projected misstatement is less than tolerable misstatement for accounts receivable, the misstatements found in a sample can be symptomatic of a more serious problem.

The final decision about accounts receivable and sales is whether sufficient evidence has been obtained through tests of controls and substantive tests of transactions, analytical procedures, cutoff procedures, confirmation, and other substantive tests to justify drawing conclusions about the correctness of the stated balance.

DEVELOPING TESTS OF DETAILS AUDIT PROGRAM

Design audit procedures for the audit of accounts receivable, using an evidence planning worksheet as a guide.

Hillsburg Hardware Co. is used to illustrate the development of audit program procedures for tests of details in the sales and collection cycle. The determination of these procedures is based on the tests of controls and substantive tests of transactions illustrated in Chapters 14 and 15 and the analytical procedures described in this chapter.

Fran Moore prepared the evidence-planning worksheet in Figure 16-7 as an aid to help her decide the extent of planned tests of details of balances. The source of each of the rows is as follows:

- *Tolerable misstatement.* The preliminary judgment of materiality was set at $737,000 (approximately 10 percent of earnings from operations of $7,370,000). She allocated $442,000 to the audit of accounts receivable (see p. 237).
- *Acceptable audit risk.* Fran assessed acceptable audit risk as high because of the good financial condition of the company, its financial stability, and the relatively few users of the financial statements.

FIGURE 16-7	Evidence-Planning Worksheet to Decide Tests of Details of Balances for Hillsburg Hardware Co.—Accounts Receivable

	Detail tie-in	Existence	Completeness	Accuracy	Classification	Cutoff	Realizable value	Rights	Presentation and disclosure
Acceptable audit risk	High	High	High	High	High	High	High	High	High
Inherent risk	Low	Medium	Low	Low	Low	Medium	Medium	Low	Low
Control risk—Sales	Low	Medium	Low	High	Low	Medium	High	Not applicable	Not applicable
Control risk—Cash receipts	Low	Medium	Low	Low	Low	Low	Not applicable	Not applicable	Not applicable
Control risk—Additional controls	None	None	None	None	None	None	None	Low	Low
Substantive tests of transactions—Sales	Good results	Good results	Good results	Fair results	Good results	Un-acceptable results	Not applicable	Not applicable	Not applicable
Substantive tests of transactions—Cash receipts	Good results	Good results	Good results	Good results	Good results	Good results	Not applicable	Not applicable	Not applicable
Analytical procedures	Good results	Good results	Good results	Good results	Good results	Good results	Un-acceptable results	Not applicable	Not applicable
Planned detection risk for tests of details of balances	High	Medium	High	Medium	High	Low	Low	High	High
Planned audit evidence for tests of details of balances	Low	Medium	Low	Medium	Low	High	High	Low	Low

Tolerable misstatement $442,000

• *Inherent risk.* Fran assessed inherent risk as medium for existence and cutoff because of concerns over revenue recognition identified in SAS 99. Fran also assessed inherent risk as medium for realizable value. In past years, there have been audit adjustments to the allowance for uncollectible accounts because it was found to be understated. Inherent risk was assessed as low for all other objectives.

TABLE 16-4	Balance-Related Audit Objectives and Audit Program for Hillsburg Hardware Co.— Sales and Collection Cycle (Design Format)
Balance-Related Audit Objective	**Audit Procedure**
Accounts receivable in the aged trial balance agree with related master file amounts, and the total is correctly added and agrees with the general ledger (detail tie-in).	Trace 10 accounts from the trial balance to accounts on master file (6). Foot two pages of the trial balance, and total all pages (7). Trace the balance to the general ledger (8).
The accounts receivable on the aged trial balance exist (existence).	Confirm accounts receivable, using positive confirmations. Confirm all amounts over $100,000 and a nonstatistical sample of the remainder (10). Perform alternative procedures for all confirmations not returned on the first or second request (11). Review accounts receivable trial balance for large and unusual receivables (1).
Existing accounts receivable are included in the aged trial balance (completeness).	Trace five accounts from the accounts receivable master file to the aged trial balance (9).
Accounts receivable in the trial balance are accurate (accuracy).	Confirm accounts receivable, using positive confirmations. Confirm all amounts over $100,000 and a nonstatistical sample of the remainder (10). Perform alternative procedures for all confirmations not returned on the first or second request (11). Review accounts receivable trial balance for large and unusual receivables (1).
Accounts receivable on the aged trial balance are properly classified (classification).	Review the receivables listed on the aged trial balance for notes and related party receivables (3). Inquire of management whether there are any related party notes or long-term receivables included in the trial balance (4).
Transactions in the sales and collection cycle are recorded in the proper period (cutoff).	Select the last 20 sales transactions from the current year's sales journal and the first 20 from the subsequent year's and trace each to the related shipping documents, checking for the date of actual shipment and the correct recording (14). Review large sales returns and allowances before and after the balance sheet date to determine whether they are recorded in the correct period (15).
Accounts receivable is stated at realizable value (realizable value).	Trace 10 accounts from the aging schedule to the accounts receivable master file to test for the correct aging on the trial balance (6). Foot the aging columns on the trial balance and total the pages (7). Cross-foot the aging columns (7). Discuss with the credit manager the likelihood of collecting older accounts. Examine subsequent cash receipts and the credit file on all accounts over 90 days and evaluate whether the receivables are collectible (12). Evaluate whether the allowance is adequate after performing other audit procedures for collectibility of receivables (13).
The client has rights to accounts receivable on the trial balance (rights).	Review the minutes of the board of directors meetings for any indication of pledged or factored accounts receivable (5). Inquire of management whether any receivables are pledged or factored (5).
Accounts in the sales and collection cycle and related information are properly presented and disclosed (presentation and disclosure).	Review the minutes of the board of directors meetings for any indication of pledged or factored accounts receivable (5). Inquire of management whether any receivables are pledged or factored (5).

Note: The procedures are summarized into a performance format in Table 16-5 on page 504. The numbers in parentheses after the procedures refer to Table 16-5.

TABLE 16-5	Test of Details of Balances Audit Program for Hillsburg Hardware Co.— Sales and Collection Cycle (Performance Format)

1. Review accounts receivable trial balance for large and unusual receivables.

2. Calculate analytical procedures indicated in carry-forward audit schedules (not included) and follow up on any significant changes from prior years.

3. Review the receivables listed on the aged trial balance for notes and related party receivables.

4. Inquire of management whether there are any related party, notes, or long-term receivables included in the trial balance.

5. Review the minutes of the board of directors meetings and inquire of management to determine whether any receivables are pledged or factored.

6. Trace 10 accounts from the trial balance to the accounts receivable master file for aging and the balance.

7. Foot two pages of the trial balance for aging columns and balance and total all pages and cross-foot the aging.

8. Trace the balance to the general ledger.

9. Trace five accounts from the accounts receivable master file to the aged trial balance.

10. Confirm accounts receivable, using positive confirmations. Confirm all amounts over $100,000 and a nonstatistical sample of the remainder.

11. Perform alternative procedures for all confirmations not returned on the first or second request.

12. Discuss with the credit manager the likelihood of collecting older accounts. Examine subsequent cash receipts and the credit file on all larger accounts over 90 days and evaluate whether the receivables are collectible.

13. Evaluate whether the allowance is adequate after performing other audit procedures for collectibility of receivables.

14. Select the last 20 sales transactions from the current year's sales journal and the first 20 from the subsequent year's and trace each to the related shipping documents, checking for the date of actual shipment and the correct recording.

15. Review large sales returns and allowances before and after the balance sheet date to determine whether they are recorded in the correct period.

- *Control risk.* Control risk assessments for each audit objective are the same as those in Figure 15-6 on page 464. Recall that results of tests of controls and substantive tests of transactions in Chapter 15 were consistent with the auditor's initial control risk assessments, except for the accuracy and realizable value objectives for sales.
- *Substantive tests of transactions results.* These results were also taken from Figure 15-6. Recall from Chapter 15 that all results were acceptable except the accuracy and cutoff objectives for sales.
- *Analytical procedures.* See Tables 16-2 and 16-3 (p. 489).
- *Planned detection risk and planned audit evidence.* These two rows are decided for each objective based on the conclusions in the other rows.

Table 16-4 (p. 503) shows the tests of details audit program for accounts receivable, by objective, and for the allowance for uncollectible accounts. The audit program reflects the conclusions for planned audit evidence on the evidence-planning worksheet in Figure 16-7. Table 16-5 shows the audit program in a performance format. The audit procedures are identical to those in Table 16-4 except for procedure 2, which is an analytical procedure. The numbers in parentheses are a cross reference between the two tables.

ESSENTIAL TERMS

Accounts receivable balance-related audit objectives—the nine specific audit objectives used by the auditor to decide the appropriate audit evidence for accounts receivable

Aged trial balance—a listing of the balances in the accounts receivable master file at the balance sheet date broken down according to the amount of time passed between the date of sale and the balance sheet date

Alternative procedures—the follow-up of a positive confirmation not returned by the debtor with the use of documentation evidence to determine whether the recorded receivable exists and is collectible

Blank confirmation form—a letter, addressed to the debtor, requesting the recipient to fill in the amount of the accounts receivable balance; it is considered a positive confirmation

Cutoff misstatements—misstatements that take place as a result of current period transactions being recorded in a subsequent period, or subsequent period transactions being recorded in the current period

Invoice confirmation—a type of positive confirmation in which an individual invoice is confirmed, rather than the customer's entire accounts receivable balance

Negative confirmation—a letter, addressed to the debtor, requesting a response only if the recipient disagrees with the amount of the stated account balance

Positive confirmation—a letter, addressed to the debtor, requesting that the recipient indicate directly on the letter whether the stated account balance is correct or incorrect and, if incorrect, by what amount

Realizable value of accounts receivable—the amount of the outstanding balances in accounts receivable that will ultimately be collected

Timing difference—a reported difference in a confirmation from a debtor that is determined to be a timing difference between the client's and debtor's records and therefore not a misstatement

REVIEW QUESTIONS

16-1 (Objective 16-1) Distinguish among tests of details of balances, tests of controls, and substantive tests of transactions for the sales and collection cycle. Explain how the tests of controls and substantive tests of transactions affect the tests of details of balances.

16-2 (Objective 16-1) Cynthia Roberts, CPA, expresses the following viewpoint: "I do not believe in performing tests of controls and substantive tests of transactions for the sales and collection cycle. As an alternative, I send a lot of negative confirmations on every audit at an interim date. If I find a lot of misstatements, I analyze them to determine their cause. If internal controls are inadequate, I send positive confirmations at year-end to evaluate the amount of misstatements. If the negative confirmations result in minimal misstatements, which is often the case, I have found that the internal controls are effective without bothering to perform tests of controls and substantive tests of transactions, and the AICPA's confirmation requirement has been satisfied at the same time. In my opinion, the best test of internal controls is to go directly to third parties." Evaluate her point of view.

16-3 (Objective 16-2) List five analytical procedures for the sales and collection cycle. For each test, describe a misstatement that could be identified.

16-4 (Objective 16-3) Identify the nine accounts receivable balance-related audit objectives. For each objective, list one audit procedure.

16-5 (Objective 16-3) Which of the nine accounts receivable balance-related audit objectives can be partially satisfied by confirmations with customers?

16-6 (Objective 16-3) State the purpose of footing the total column in the client's trial balance, tracing individual customer names and amounts to the accounts receivable master file, and tracing the total to the general ledger. Is it necessary to trace each amount to the master file? Why?

16-7 (Objective 16-3) Distinguish between accuracy tests of gross accounts receivable and tests of the realizable value of receivables.

16-8 (Objective 16-3) Explain why you agree or disagree with the following statement: "In most audits, it is more important to test carefully the cutoff for sales than for cash receipts." Describe how you perform each type of test, assuming the existence of prenumbered documents.

16-9 (Objective 16-4) Evaluate the following statement: "In many audits in which accounts receivable is material, the requirement of confirming customer balances is a waste of time and would not be performed by competent auditors if it were not required by the AICPA. When internal controls are excellent and there are a large number of small receivables from customers who do not recognize the function of confirmation, it is a meaningless procedure. Examples include well-run utilities and department stores. In these situations, tests of controls and substantive tests of transactions are far more effective than confirmations."

16-10 (Objective 16-4) Distinguish between a positive and a negative confirmation and state the circumstances in which each should be used. Why do CPA firms often use a combination of positive and negative confirmations on the same audit?

16-11 (Objective 16-4) Under what circumstances is it acceptable to confirm accounts receivable before the balance sheet date?

16-12 (Objective 16-4) State the most important factors affecting the sample size in confirmations of accounts receivable.

16-13 (Objective 16-4) In Chapter 15, one of the points brought out was the need to obtain a representative sample of the population. How can this concept be reconciled with the statement in this chapter that the emphasis should be on confirming larger and older balances because these are most likely to contain misstatements?

16-14 (Objective 16-4) Define what is meant by alternative procedures in the confirmation of accounts receivable and explain their purpose. Which alternative procedures are the most reliable? Why?

16-15 (Objective 16-4) Explain why the analysis of differences is important in the confirmation of accounts receivable, even if the misstatements in the sample are not material.

16-16 (Objective 16-4) State three types of differences that might be observed in the confirmation of accounts receivable that do not constitute misstatements. For each, state an audit procedure that would verify the difference.

16-17 (Objective 16-1) What is the relationship of each of the following to the sales and collection cycle: flowcharts, assessing control risk, tests of controls, and tests of details of balances?

16-18 (Objective 16-3) Describe GAAP requirements for proper recording of sales returns and allowances.

16-19 (Objective 16-3) Customers purchasing products through a company's Internet Web site generally pay for those goods by providing their personal credit card information. Describe how a company's sale of products through its Web site affects the auditor's tests of accounts receivable in the financial statement audit.

MULTIPLE CHOICE QUESTIONS FROM CPA EXAMINATIONS

16-20 (Objective 16-2) The following questions concern analytical procedures in the sales and collection cycle. Choose the best response.

a. As a result of analytical procedures, the independent auditor determines that the gross profit percentage has declined from 30% in the preceding year to 20% in the current year. The auditor should
   (1) express a qualified opinion due to inability of the client company to continue as a going concern.
   (2) evaluate management's performance in causing this decline.
   (3) require footnote disclosure.
   (4) consider the possibility of a misstatement in the financial statements.

b. Once a CPA has determined that accounts receivable have increased as a result of slow collections in a "tight money" environment, the CPA would be likely to
   (1) increase the balance in the allowance for bad debt account.
   (2) review the going concern ramifications.
   (3) review the credit and collection policy.
   (4) expand tests of collectibility.

c. In connection with his review of key ratios, the CPA notes that Pyzi had accounts receivable equal to 30 days' sales at December 31, 2004, and to 45 days' sales at December 31, 2005. Assuming that there had been no changes in economic conditions, clientele, or sales mix, this change most likely would indicate
   (1) a steady increase in sales in 2005.
   (2) an easing of credit policies in 2005.
   (3) a decrease in accounts receivable relative to sales in 2005.
   (4) a steady decrease in sales in 2005.

16-21 (Objective 16-4) The following questions deal with confirmation of accounts receivable. Choose the best response.

a. In connection with his audit of the Beke Supply Company for the year ended August 31, 2005, Derek Lowe, CPA, has mailed accounts receivable confirmations to three groups as follows:

Group Number	Type of Customer	Type of Confirmation
1	Wholesale	Positive
2	Current retail	Negative
3	Past-due retail	Positive

The confirmation responses from each group vary from 10 percent to 90 percent. The most likely response percents are

(1) Group 1—90 percent, group 2—50 percent, group 3—10 percent
(2) Group 1—90 percent, group 2—10 percent, group 3—50 percent
(3) Group 1—50 percent, group 2—90 percent, group 3—10 percent
(4) Group 1—10 percent, group 2—50 percent, group 3—90 percent

b. The negative form of accounts receivable confirmation request is useful *except* when
(1) internal control surrounding accounts receivable is considered to be effective.
(2) a large number of small balances are involved.
(3) the auditor has reason to believe the persons receiving the requests are likely to give them consideration.
(4) individual account balances are relatively large.

c. The return of a positive confirmation of accounts receivable without an exception attests to the
(1) collectibility of the receivable balance.
(2) accuracy of the receivable balance.
(3) accuracy of the aging of accounts receivable.
(4) accuracy of the allowance for uncollectible accounts.

d. In confirming a client's accounts receivable in prior years, an auditor found that there were many differences between the recorded account balances and the confirmation responses. These differences, which were not misstatements, required substantial time to resolve. In defining the sampling unit for the current year's audit, the auditor would most likely choose
(1) individual overdue balances.
(2) individual invoices.
(3) small account balances.
(4) large account balances.

16-22 (Objective 16-3) The following questions concern audit objectives and management assertions for accounts receivable. Choose the best response.

a. When evaluating the adequacy of the allowance for uncollectible accounts, an auditor reviews the entity's aging of receivables to support management's financial assertion of
(1) existence or occurrence.
(2) valuation or allocation.
(3) completeness.
(4) rights and obligations.

b. Which of the following audit procedures would best uncover an understatement of sales and accounts receivable?
(1) Test a sample of sales transactions, selecting the sample from prenumbered shipping documents.
(2) Test a sample of sales transactions, selecting the sample from sales invoices recorded in the sales journal.
(3) Confirm accounts receivable.
(4) Review the aged accounts receivable trial balance.

DISCUSSION QUESTIONS AND PROBLEMS

16-23 (Objective 16-3) The following are common tests of details of balances for the audit of accounts receivable:

1. Obtain a list of aged accounts receivable, foot the list, and trace the total to the general ledger.
2. Trace 35 accounts to the accounts receivable master file for name, amount, and age categories.
3. Examine and document cash receipts on accounts receivable for 20 days after the engagement date.

4. Request 25 positive and 65 negative confirmations of accounts receivable.
5. Perform alternative procedures on accounts not responding to second requests by examining subsequent cash receipts documentation and shipping reports or sales invoices.
6. Test the sales cutoff by tracing entries in the sales journal for 15 days before and after the balance sheet date to shipping documents, if available, and/or sales invoices.
7. Determine and disclose accounts pledged, discounted, sold, assigned, or guaranteed by others.
8. Evaluate the materiality of credit balances in the aged trial balance.

Required For each audit procedure, identify the balance-related audit objective or objectives it partially or fully satisfies.

16-24 (Objective 16-3) The following misstatements are sometimes found in the sales and collection cycle's account balances:

1. Cash received from collections of accounts receivable in the subsequent period is recorded as current period receipts.
2. The allowance for uncollectible accounts is inadequate because of the client's failure to reflect depressed economic conditions in the allowance.
3. Several accounts receivable are in dispute as a result of claims of defective merchandise.
4. The pledging of accounts receivable to the bank for a loan is not disclosed in the financial statements.
5. Goods shipped and included in the current period sales were returned in the subsequent period.
6. Several accounts receivable in the accounts receivable master file are not included in the aged trial balance.
7. One account receivable in the accounts receivable master file is included on the aged trial balance twice.
8. Long-term interest-bearing notes receivable from affiliated companies are included in accounts receivable.
9. The trial balance total does not equal the amount in the general ledger.

Required a. For each misstatement, identify the balance-related audit objective to which it pertains.

b. For each misstatement, list an internal control that should prevent it.

c. For each misstatement, list one test of details of balances audit procedure that the auditor can use to detect it.

16-25 (Objective 16-3) The following are audit procedures in the sales and collection cycle:

1. Examine a sample of shipping documents to determine whether each has a sales invoice number included on it.
2. Discuss with the sales manager whether any sales allowances have been granted after the balance sheet date that may apply to the current period.
3. Add the columns on the aged trial balance and compare the total with the general ledger.
4. Observe whether the controller makes an independent comparison of the total in the general ledger with the trial balance of accounts receivable.
5. Compare the date on a sample of shipping documents throughout the year with related duplicate sales invoices and the accounts receivable master file.
6. Examine a sample of customer orders and see if each has a credit authorization.
7. Compare the date on a sample of shipping documents a few days before and after the balance sheet date with related sales journal transactions.
8. Compute the ratio of allowance for uncollectible accounts divided by accounts receivable and compare with previous years.
9. Examine a sample of noncash credits in the accounts receivable master file to determine if the internal auditor has initialed each, indicating internal verification.

Required a. For each procedure, identify the applicable type of audit evidence.

b. For each procedure, identify which of the following it is:
   (1) Test of control
   (2) Substantive test of transactions
   (3) Analytical procedure
   (4) Test of details of balances

c. For those procedures you identified as a test of control or substantive test of transactions, what transaction-related audit objective or objectives are being satisfied?

d. For those procedures you identified as a test of details of balances, what balance-related audit objective or objectives are being satisfied?

16-26 (Objective 16-3) The following are the nine balance-related audit objectives, seven tests of details of balances for accounts receivable, and seven tests of controls or substantive tests of transactions for the sales and collection cycle:

Balance-Related Audit Objective

Detail tie-in
Existence
Completeness
Accuracy
Classification
Cutoff
Realizable value
Rights
Presentation and disclosure

Test of Details of Balances, Test of Control, or Substantive Test of Transactions Audit Procedure

1. Confirm accounts receivable.
2. Review sales returns after the balance sheet date to determine whether any are applicable to the current year.
3. Compare dates on shipping documents and the sales journal throughout the year.
4. Perform alternative procedures for nonresponses to confirmation.
5. Examine sales transactions for related party or employee sales recorded as regular sales.
6. Examine duplicate sales invoices for consignment sales and other shipments for which title has not passed.
7. Trace a sample of accounts from the accounts receivable master file to the aged trial balance.
8. Trace recorded sales transactions to shipping documents to determine whether a document exists.
9. Examine the financial statements to determine whether all related parties, notes, and pledged receivables are properly presented.
10. Examine duplicate sales invoices for initials that indicate internal verification of extensions and footings.
11. Trace a sample of shipping documents to related sales invoice entries in the sales journal.
12. Compare amounts and dates on the aged trial balance and accounts receivable master file.
13. Trace from the sales journal to the accounts receivable master file to make sure the information is the same.
14. Inquire of management whether there are notes from related parties included with trade receivables.

a. Identify which procedures are tests of details of balances, which are tests of controls, and which are substantive tests of transactions. **Required**

b. Identify one test of details and one test of control or substantive test of transactions that will partially satisfy each balance-related audit objective. (Tests of controls and substantive tests of transactions are not used for presentation and disclosure.) Each procedure must be used at least once.

16-27 (Objective 16-3) Niosoki Auto Parts sells new parts for foreign automobiles to auto dealers. Company policy requires that a prenumbered shipping document be issued for each sale. At the time of pickup or shipment, the shipping clerk writes the date on the shipping document. The last shipment made in the fiscal year ended August 31, 2005, was recorded on document 2167. Shipments are billed in the order that the billing clerk receives the shipping documents.

For late August and early September, shipping documents are billed on sales invoices as follows:

Shipping Document No.	Sales Invoice No.
2163	4332
2164	4326
2165	4327
2166	4330
2167	4331
2168	4328
2169	4329
2170	4333
2171	4335
2172	4334

The August and September sales journals have the following information included:

SALES JOURNAL—AUGUST 2005

Day of Month	Sales Invoice No.	Amount of Sale
30	4326	$ 726.11
30	4329	1,914.30
31	4327	419.83
31	4328	620.22
31	4330	47.74

SALES JOURNAL—SEPTEMBER 2005

Day of Month	Sales Invoice No.	Amount of Sale
1	4332	$4,641.31
1	4331	106.39
1	4333	852.06
2	4335	1,250.50
2	4334	646.58

Required

a. What are the GAAP requirements for a correct sales cutoff?

b. Which sales invoices, if any, are recorded in the wrong accounting period? Prepare an adjusting entry to correct the financial statement for the year ended August 31, 2005. Assume that the company uses a periodic inventory system (inventory and cost of sales do not need to be adjusted).

c. Assume that the shipping clerk accidentally wrote August 31 on shipping documents 2168 through 2172. Explain how that would affect the correctness of the financial statements. How would you, as an auditor, discover that error?

d. Describe, in general terms, the audit procedures you would follow in making sure that cutoff for sales is accurate at the balance sheet date.

e. Identify internal controls that would reduce the likelihood of cutoff misstatements. How would you test each control?

16-28 (Objective 16-4) Dodge, CPA, is auditing the financial statements of a manufacturing company with a significant amount of trade accounts receivable. Dodge is satisfied that the accounts are properly summarized and classified and that allocations, reclassifications, and valuations are made in accordance with GAAP. Dodge is planning to use accounts receivable confirmation requests to satisfy the third standard of field work as to trade accounts receivable.

Required

a. Identify and describe the two forms of accounts receivable confirmation requests and indicate what factors Dodge will consider in determining when to use each.

b. Assume that Dodge has received a satisfactory response to the confirmation requests. Describe how Dodge could evaluate collectibility of the trade accounts receivable.

c. What are the implications to a CPA if during an audit of accounts receivable some of a client's trade customers do not respond to a request for positive confirmation of their accounts?

d. What auditing steps should a CPA perform if there is no response to a second request for a positive confirmation?*

 16-29 (Objective 16-2) Johnson Clock Company sells specialty clocks, watches, and other time-keeping devices. Since its inception, the company has sold items through its home office store and at industry and collector trade shows around the country. To meet the demand from collectors around the world, the company began selling items through its Internet Web site. Recent financial information about Johnson's sales is summarized in the following table.

*AICPA adapted.

	Year Ended 12/31/05	Year Ended 12/31/04	Year Ended 12/31/03
Sales:			
Home office	$1,279,480	$1,218,552	$1,163,851
Trade show	773,265	739,259	704,391
Internet-based	147,772	122,462	52,884
Sales Returns:			
Home office	$ 25,589	$ 23,152	$ 25,605
Trade show	13,946	13,676	12,679
Internet-based	13,254	11,022	4,760
Cost of Goods Sold:			
Home office	$ 831,662	$ 816,429	$ 768,142
Trade show	491,023	480,518	454,332
Internet-based	81,275	66,129	28,822
Receivables Related to Sales from:			
Home office	$ 126,195	$ 123,524	$ 127,545
Trade show	74,149	68,862	67,544
Internet-based	3,239	3,020	1,159

Tolerable misstatement for sales and receivables is $12,000.

Required Using the information given, design and perform analytical procedures for the sales and collection cycle at Johnson Clock Company. Based on the results of your analytical procedures, describe how the results related to the Internet-based sales differ from the home office and trade show sales.

16-30 (Objective 16-4) You have been assigned to the confirmation of aged accounts receivable for the Blank Paper Company audit. You have tested the aged trial balance and selected the accounts for confirming. Before the confirmation requests are mailed, the controller asks to look at the accounts you intend to confirm to determine whether he will permit you to send them.

He reviews the list and informs you that he does not want you to confirm six of the accounts on your list. Two of them are credit balances, one is a zero balance, two of the other three have a fairly small balance, and the remaining balance is highly material. The reason he gives is that he feels the confirmations will upset these customers because "they are kind of hard to get along with." He does not want the credit balances confirmed because it may encourage the customer to ask for a refund.

In addition, the controller asks you to send an additional 20 confirmations to customers he has listed for you. He does this as a means of credit collection for "those stupid idiots who won't know the difference between a CPA and a credit collection agency."

Required
a. Is it acceptable for the controller to review the list of accounts you intend to confirm? Discuss.

b. Discuss the appropriateness of sending the 20 additional confirmations to the customers.

c. Assuming that the auditor complies with all the controller's requests, what is the effect on the auditor's opinion?

16-31 (Objective 16-4) You have been assigned to the first audit of the Chicago Company for the year ending March 31, 2005. Accounts receivable were confirmed on December 31, 2004, and at that date the receivables consisted of approximately 200 accounts with balances totaling $956,750. Seventy-five of these accounts with balances totaling $650,725 were selected for confirmation. All but 20 of the confirmation requests have been returned; 30 were signed without comments, 14 had minor differences that have been cleared satisfactorily, and 11 confirmations had the following comments:

1. We are sorry, but we cannot answer your request for confirmation of our account as the PDQ Company uses an accounts payable voucher system.
2. The balance of $1,050 was paid on December 23, 2004.
3. The balance of $7,750 was paid on January 5, 2005.
4. The balance noted above has been paid.
5. We do not owe you anything at December 31, 2004, as the goods, represented by your invoice dated December 30, 2004, number 25050, in the amount of $11,550, were received on January 5, 2005, on FOB destination terms.

6. An advance payment of $2,500 made by us in November 2004 should cover the two invoices totaling $1,350 shown on the statement attached.
7. We never received these goods.
8. We are contesting the propriety of this $12,525 charge. We think the charge is excessive.
9. Amount okay. As the goods have been shipped to us on consignment, we will remit payment upon selling the goods.
10. The $10,000, representing a deposit under a lease, will be applied against the rent due to us during 2006, the last year of the lease.
11. Your credit memo dated December 5, 2004, in the amount of $440 cancels the balance above.

Required What steps would you take to satisfactorily clear each of the preceding 11 comments.*

16-32 (Objectives 16-2, 16-3, 16-4, 16-5) You have audited the financial statements of the Heft Company for several years. Internal controls for accounts receivable are satisfactory. The Heft Company is on a calendar-year basis. An interim audit, which included confirmation of the accounts receivable, was performed on August 31 and indicated that the accounting for cash, sales, sales returns and allowances, and receivables was reliable.

The company's sales are principally to manufacturing concerns. There are about 1,500 active trade accounts receivable of which about 35% represent 65% of the total dollar amount. The accounts receivable are maintained alphabetically in a master file of accounts receivable.

Shipping document data are keyed into a computerized system that simultaneously produces a sales invoice, sales journal, and an updated accounts receivable master file.

All cash receipts are in the form of customers' checks. Information for cash receipts is obtained from the remittance advice portions of the customers' checks. The computer operator compares the remittance advices with the list of checks that was prepared by another person when the mail was received. As for sales, a cash receipts journal and updated accounts receivable master file are simultaneously prepared after the cash receipts information is entered.

Summary totals are produced monthly by the computer operations department for updating the general ledger master file accounts such as cash, sales, and accounts receivable. An aged trial balance is prepared monthly.

Required Prepare the additional audit procedures necessary for testing the balances in the sales and collection cycle. (Ignore bad debts and allowance for uncollectible accounts.)*

16-33 (Objective 16-4) In the confirmation of accounts receivable for the Reliable Service Company, 85 positive and no negative confirmations were mailed to customers. This represents 35% of the dollar balance of the total accounts receivable. Second requests were sent for all nonresponses, but there were still 10 customers who did not respond. The decision was made to perform alternative procedures on the 10 unanswered confirmation requests. An assistant is requested to conduct the alternative procedures and report to the senior auditor after he has completed his tests on two accounts. He prepared the following information for the audit files:

1. Confirmation request no. 9
   Customer name—Jolene Milling Co.
   Balance—$3,621 at December 31, 2005
   Subsequent cash receipts per the accounts
   receivable master file:

January 15, 2006	$1,837
January 29, 2006	$1,263
February 6, 2006	$1,429

2. Confirmation request no. 26
   Customer name—Rosenthal Repair Service
   Balance—$2,500 at December 31, 2005
   Subsequent cash receipts per the accounts
   receivable master file   February 9, 2006—$500
   Sales invoices per the accounts receivable
   master file (I examined the duplicate invoice)   September 1, 2005—$4,200

Required
a. If you were called on to evaluate the adequacy of the sample size, the type of confirmation used, and the percent of accounts confirmed, what additional information would you need?

b. Discuss the need to send second requests and perform alternative procedures for nonresponses.

c. Evaluate the adequacy of the alternative procedures used for verifying the two nonresponses.

*AICPA adapted.

CASE

16-34 (**Objectives 16-1, 16-3, 16-4, 16-5**) You are auditing the sales and collection cycle for the Smalltown Regional Hospital, a small not-for-profit hospital. The hospital has a reputation for excellent medical services and deficient record keeping. The medical people have a tradition of doing all aspects of their job correctly, but because of a shortage of accounting personnel, there is not time for internal verification or careful performance. In previous years, your CPA firm has found quite a few misstatements in billings, cash receipts, and accounts receivable. As in all hospitals, the two largest assets are accounts receivable and property, plant, and equipment.

The hospital has several large loans payable to local banks, and the two banks have told management that they are reluctant to extend more credit, especially considering the modern hospital that is being built in a nearby city. In the past, county taxes have made up deficits, but in the past year, the county has also been incurring deficits because of high unemployment.

In previous years, your response from patients to confirmation requests has been frustrating at best. The response rate has been extremely low, and those who did respond did not know the purpose of the confirmations or their correct outstanding balance. You have had the same experience in confirming receivables at other hospitals.

You conclude that control over cash is excellent and the likelihood of fraud is extremely small. You are less confident about unintentional errors in billing, recording sales, cash receipts, accounts receivable, and bad debts.

Required

a. Identify the major factors affecting client business risk and acceptable audit risk for this audit.

b. What inherent risks are you concerned about?

c. In this audit of the sales and collection cycle, which types of tests are you likely to emphasize?

d. For each of the following, explain whether you plan to emphasize the tests and give reasons:
   (1) Tests of controls
   (2) Substantive tests of transactions
   (3) Analytical procedures
   (4) Tests of details of balances

INTEGRATED CASE APPLICATION—PINNACLE MANUFACTURING: PART VI

16-35 (**Objectives 16-2, 16-3, 16-4**) Parts III, IV, and V of this case study dealt with obtaining an understanding of internal control and assessing control risk for transactions affecting accounts payable of Pinnacle Manufacturing. In Part VI, you will design analytical procedures and design and perform tests of details of balances for accounts payable.

Assume that your understanding of internal controls over acquisitions and cash disbursements and the related tests of controls and substantive tests of transactions support an assessment of a low control risk. The listing of the 519 accounts making up the accounts payable balance of $11,277,989 at December 31, 2004 is included under the Pinnacle link on the textbook Web site.

Required

a. List those relationships, ratios, and trends that you believe will provide useful information about the overall reasonableness of accounts payable. You should consider income statement accounts that affect accounts payable in selecting the analytical procedures.

b. Study Table 19-5 (p. 596) containing balance-related audit objectives and tests of details of balances for accounts payable to be sure you understand each procedure and its purpose. Prepare an audit program for accounts payable in a performance format, using the audit procedures in Table 19-5. The format of the audit program should be similar to Table 16-5 (page 504). Be sure to include a sample size for each procedure.

c. Assume for requirement b that (1) assessed control risk had been high rather than low for each transaction-related audit objective, (2) inherent risk was high for each balance-related audit objective, and (3) analytical procedures indicated a high potential for misstatement. What would the effect have been on the audit procedures and sample sizes for requirement b?

d. Confirmation requests were sent to a stratified sample of 51 vendors listed in Figure 16-8 (p. 515). Confirmation responses from 45 vendors were returned indicating no difference between the vendor's and the company's records. Figure 16-9 (pp. 516–517) presents the six replies that indicate a difference between the vendor's balance and the company's records. The auditor's follow-up findings are indicated on each reply. Prepare an audit schedule similar to the one illustrated in Figure 16-10 (p. 518) to determine the misstatements, if any, for each difference. The audit schedule format shown in Figure 16-10 can be downloaded using the Pinnacle link on the textbook Web site. The exception for Fiberchem is analyzed as an illustration. Assume that Pinnacle Manufacturing took a complete physical inventory at December 31, 2004, and the auditor concluded that recorded inventory reflects all inventory on hand at the balance sheet date. Include the balances confirmed without exception as one amount on the schedule for each stratum, and total the schedule columns.

e. Estimate the total misstatement in the income statement, not just the misstatements in the sample, based on the income statement misstatements you identified in requirement d. The total misstatement should include a projected misstatement and an estimate for sampling error. Hint: See page 239 for guidance on calculating the point estimate. Note that the misstatements should be projected separately for each stratum. You will need to determine the size of each stratum using the accounts payable listing. Use your judgment to estimate sampling error, considering the size of the population and the amounts tested.

f. Estimate the total misstatement in accounts payable in the same way you did for the income statement in requirement e. Hint: A misstatement caused by the failure to record an FOB origin purchase is an understatement of accounts payable and inventory and has no effect on income.

g. What is your conclusion about the fairness of the recorded balance in accounts payable for Pinnacle Manufacturing as it affects the income statement and balance sheet? How does this affect your assessment of control risk as being low for all transaction-related audit objectives? Assume you decided that tolerable misstatement for accounts payable as it affects the income statement is $230,000.

INTERNET PROBLEM 16-1: REVENUE RECOGNITION

Reference the CW site. In recent years, several high-profile incidents of improper revenue recognition attracted the attention of the business media. The SEC has also expressed concerns about the number of instances of improper revenue recognition identified by SEC staff. In response to the concerns about audit issues associated with revenue recognition, the AICPA put together a "tool kit" summarizing audit guidance in this area. This problem requires students to use the Internet to (1) identify deterrents to improper revenue recognition, (2) define a "bill and hold" sale, and (3) evaluate bill and hold transactions.

FIGURE 16-8

High-Volume Items (>$200,000)

1. American Press	$ 296,319.95	
2. Clean-O-Rama, Co.	276,233.59	
3. Fiberchem	689,608.60	
4. Rufus Austin Antiques	347,866.16	
5. Todd Machinery	461,803.42	
6. Welburn Manufacturing	338,118.32	$2,409,950.04

Large Balance Items ($50,001–$200,000)

1. A & M Sandler Inc.	$ 70,737.86	
2. American Baby/USTC	65,593.68	
3. Beach & Hoover Refining	66,442.43	
4. Bearing Drives Co.	63,493.25	
5. Burton Martin	68,419.60	
6. Cable Sys./Ind. Traf. Cons.	61,990.39	
7. Eddie Ventura, Inc.	52,396.13	
8. Fiberoptics	52,263.29	
9. Finish Metals Inc.	52,843.23	
10. Freeman Furniture–Attn A/P	113,472.62	
11. GP Chambers Co.	55,761.25	
12. Godwin Drug Co.	73,331.35	
13. Holy Family Hospital	102,536.37	
14. Las Flores Designs Inc.	77,082.54	
15. Lean Corp.	59,117.59	
16. MacDonald Svc. Corporation	128,646.91	
17. McCoys Inc.	59,075.06	
18. Metadyne Corp.	74,289.14	
19. Micron Power Systems	118,322.93	
20. Mobil Oil	81,052.59	
21. National Elevator & Mach. Co.	66,888.17	
22. Norris Industries	76,795.34	
23. R & B Products	69,645.62	
24. Remington Supply	107,314.12	
25. Safety Envelope Co.	194,739.43	
26. Scandec USA Inc.	57,341.69	
27. The Dutton Company	55,549.58	
28. The Haberdashery Co.	62,494.92	
29. University of California	70,108.65	
30. ZZZZ Bank Adjustments	56,062.36	$2,313,808.09

Items $50,000 and less

1. Advent Sign Mfg. Co.	$ 45,000.00	
2. B&K Mfg. Co. Inc.	37,103.04	
3. Bellco	37,139.77	
4. Boston Shoecase Co.	45,369.13	
5. Dynamic Metal Products	31,779.17	
6. Everhart Co.	41,320.99	
7. Fuller Travel	28,234.88	
8. Good House Home Video Inc.	40,411.02	
9. Harrah's Metals, Inc.	44,591.17	
10. J C Licht Co.—Glendale Hts.	46,285.63	
11. Liberty Lighting	40,698.07	
12. Long Beach Lawn Service	42,164.31	
13. Premier Whirlpool Bath	5,695.94	
14. Quaker Transanalysis	43,794.51	
15. Tower International	32,434.41	$ 562,022.04
TOTAL TESTED		$5,285,780.17

FIGURE 16-9   Replies to Requests for Information

STATEMENT FROM FIBERCHEM

       Pinnacle Manufacturing
       Detroit, MI

Amounts due as of December 31, 2004:

Invoice No.	Date	Amount	Balance Due
8312	11-22-04	$300,000.00	$300,000.00
8469	12-02-04	178,000.00	478,000.00
8819	12-18-04	211,608.60	689,608.60(1)
9002	12-30-04	27,500.00(2)	717,108.60

Auditor's notes:
(1) Agrees with accounts payable listing.
(2) Goods shipped FOB Fiberchem's plant on December 31, 2004, arrived
*   at Pinnacle Manufacturing on January 4, 2005.*

STATEMENT FROM MOBIL OIL

       Pinnacle Manufacturing
       Detroit, MI

Amounts due as of December 31, 2004:

Invoice No.	Date	Amount	Balance Due
DX14777	12-23-04	$81,052.59	$ 81,052.59(1)
DX16908	12-30-04	26,543.00(2)	107,595.59

Auditor's notes:
(1) Agrees with accounts payable listing.
(2) Goods shipped FOB Mobil Oil on December 30, 2004, arrived on January 4, 2005.

STATEMENT FROM NORRIS INDUSTRIES

       Pinnacle Manufacturing
       Detroit, MI

Amounts due as of December 31, 2004:

Invoice No.	Date	Amount	Balance Due
14896	12-27-04	$ 76,795.34	$ 76,795.34(1)
15111	12-27-04	127,432.00(2)	204,227.34

Auditor's notes:
(1) Agrees with accounts payable listing.
(2) Goods received December 30, 2004; recorded on January 2, 2005.

FIGURE 16-9   Replies to Requests for Information (Cont.)

STATEMENT FROM REMINGTON SUPPLY

Pinnacle Manufacturing
Detroit, MI

Amounts due as of December 31, 2004:

Invoice No.	Date	Amount	Balance Due
141702	11-11-04	$23,067.00(2)	$ 23,067.00
142619	11-19-04	12,000.00(1)	35,067.00
142811	12-04-04	7,100.00(2)	42,167.00
143600	12-21-04	27,715.12(2)	69,882.12
144927	12-29-04(3)	49,432.00(2)	119,314.12

Auditor's notes:
(1) Paid by Pinnacle Manufacturing on December 28, 2004. Payment in transit at year-end.
(2) The total of these items of $107,314.12 agrees with accounts payable listing.
(3) Goods shipped FOB Pinnacle Manufacturing on December 29, 2004, arrived at Pinnacle Manufacturing on January 4, 2005.

STATEMENT FROM ADVENT SIGN MFG. CO.

Pinnacle Manufacturing
Detroit, MI

Amounts due as of December 31, 2004:

First progress billing per contract	$45,000.00(1)
Second progress billing per contract	5,500.00(2)
Total due	$50,500.00

Auditor's notes:
(1) Agrees with accounts payable listing.
(2) Progress payment due as of December 31, 2004, per contract for construction of new custom electric sign. Sign installation completed on January 15, 2005.

STATEMENT FROM FULLER TRAVEL

Pinnacle Manufacturing
Detroit, MI

Amounts due as of December 31, 2004:

Invoice No.	Date	Amount	Balance Due
84360110	12-04-04	$9,411.63(2)	$ 9,411.63
84360181	12-12-04	9,411.63(2)	18,823.26
84360222	12-21-04	7,100.00(1)	25,923.26
84360291	12-26-04	9,411.62(2)	35,334.88

Auditor's notes:
(1) Trip for several executives was cancelled. Credit given on January 2005 statement.
(2) The total of these items of $28,234.88 agrees with accounts payable listing.

Vendor	Balance per Books	Amount Confirmed by Vendor	Books Over (Under) Amount Confirmed	Timing Difference: No Misstatement	Misstatement in Accounts Payable o/s (u/s)*	Other Balance Sheet Misstatement o/s (u/s)*	Income Statement Misstatement o/s (u/s)*	Brief Explanation
Key Accounts (>$200,000)								
Fiberchem	$689,608.60	$717,108.60	$(27,500.00)		$(27,500.00)	$(27,500.00)		F.O.B. Origin error Dr. Inv. Cr. A/P
Accounts in stratum $50,001–$200,000								
Accounts in stratum less than or equal to $50,000								

* o/s = overstatement   u/s = understatement

AUDIT SAMPLING FOR TESTS OF DETAILS OF BALANCES

BOTH STATISTICAL AND NONSTATISTICAL SAMPLING ARE ACCEPTABLE UNDER GAAS, BUT WHICHEVER IS USED, IT MUST BE DONE RIGHT

Bob Lake was the manager on the audit of Images, Inc., a specialty retailer that had shops throughout the Midwest. Images appealed to upscale working women and offered its own credit card. Images' accounting was done centrally. Transactions were captured online and sales and accounts receivable files were maintained on a database.

Bob Lake's firm encouraged the use of statistical sampling in its practice and provided a training program for the development of a statistical coordinator for each office. The coordinator in Bob's office was Barbara Ennis. Bob believed that sales transactions and accounts receivable confirmation tests should be done using statistical sampling and asked Barbara to help design and oversee the statistical aspects of this testing.

Barbara developed a program for the design of confirmation audit procedures as part of doing tests of details of balances for accounts receivable. Her work included determining sample sizes. She left the program with Bob to carry out and said that she would be available to help evaluate the results after the tests were performed.

When all the confirmation replies were received or alternative procedures were completed several weeks later, Bob called Barbara to do the statistical evaluation. Much to his dismay, he found out that Barbara had left the firm, and worse, there was no statistically trained person to take her place. Bob was under a lot of pressure to get the job completed and decided to make the statistical calculations himself. Based on his calculations, he concluded that the potential misstatement was large, but not material, so Bob concluded the objectives of the confirmation tests had been met.

The next year Images, Inc.'s earnings declined sharply, partially because of large write-offs of accounts receivable. The stock price dropped sharply and a class action suit was filed, naming Bob's firm among the defendants. An outside expert was brought in to review the audit documentation. The expert redid all of Bob's work and found errors in the statistical calculations. The expert calculated that the misstatement in accounts receivable, based on the auditor's sample, was significantly more than a material amount. Bob's firm settled the suit for $3.5 million.

In the last chapter, we moved into phase III of the audit process by examining analytical procedures and tests of details of balances for accounts receivable. We will now continue with phase III by determining sample size and items to select from the population for the audit of accounts receivable. Although the concepts discussed in this chapter deal with accounts receivable, they are applicable to the audit of many other account balances.

Both statistical and nonstatistical audit sampling are used extensively for tests of details of balances. Deciding which one to use depends primarily on the auditor's preference, experience, and knowledge about statistical sampling. Both topics are covered in this chapter.

As was demonstrated in the opening vignette, it is extremely important to correctly use the sampling method selected to avoid making wrong conclusions about a population. The study of this chapter is intended to help you make correct inferences about populations using either statistical or nonstatistical methods.

Before starting the study of this chapter, we suggest you refer to Figure 13-9 on page 396 to be sure you understand where we are in the audit process. Before determining sample size and items to select from the population in an audit, all items in phases I and II will have already been completed. The auditor will have also already completed the analytical procedures and designed the audit procedures for tests of details of balances, as studied in Chapter 16 (part of phase III). The auditor cannot perform the audit procedures for tests of details of balances until sample size and items to select from the population are decided.

COMPARISONS OF AUDIT SAMPLING FOR TESTS OF DETAILS OF BALANCES AND FOR TESTS OF CONTROLS AND SUBSTANTIVE TESTS OF TRANSACTIONS

OBJECTIVE 17-1

Differentiate audit sampling for tests of details of balances and for tests of controls and substantive tests of transactions.

Most of the sampling concepts discussed in Chapter 15 for tests of controls and substantive tests of transactions apply equally to sampling for tests of details of balances. In both cases, the auditor wants to make inferences about the entire population based on a sample. Both sampling and nonsampling risks are therefore important for tests of controls, substantive tests of transactions, and tests of details of balances. In dealing with sampling risk, it is acceptable to use either nonstatistical or statistical methods for all three types of tests.

The most important differences among tests of controls, substantive tests of transactions, and tests of details of balances are in what the auditor wants to measure. In tests of controls, the concern is testing the effectiveness of internal controls using tests of controls. When an auditor performs tests of controls, the purpose is to determine whether the exception rate in the population is sufficiently low to conclude that the control is operating effectively for purposes of auditing internal control over financial reporting or for reducing assessed control risk to reduce substantive tests. In substantive tests of transactions, the auditor is concerned about both the effectiveness of controls and the monetary correctness of transactions in the accounting system. In tests of details of balances, the concern is determining whether the dollar amount of an account balance is materially misstated. Tests for the rate of occurrence, therefore, are seldom useful for tests of details of balances. Instead, auditors use sampling methods that provide results in *dollar* terms. There are three primary types of sampling methods used for calculating dollar misstatements in auditing: nonstatistical sampling, monetary unit sampling, and variables sampling. We will now examine each of these, starting with nonstatistical sampling.

ISACA Audit Sampling

NONSTATISTICAL SAMPLING

OBJECTIVE 17-2

Apply nonstatistical sampling to tests of details of balances.

There are 14 steps required in audit sampling for tests of details of balances. These steps parallel the 14 steps used for sampling for tests of controls and substantive tests of transactions, although there are a few differences because of the different objectives of the tests. Understanding the similarities and differences in the application of audit sampling for tests of details of balances compared to those for tests of controls and substantive tests of transactions is essential. The following are the 14 steps, with the steps for tests of controls and substantive tests of transactions included in the right column for comparison:

Steps—Audit Sampling for Tests of Details of Balances	Steps—Audit Sampling for Tests of Controls and Substantive Tests of Transactions (see p. 451)
Plan the Sample	*Plan the Sample*
1. State the objectives of the audit test.	1. State the objectives of the audit test.
2. Decide whether audit sampling applies.	2. Decide whether audit sampling applies.
3. Define misstatement conditions.	3. Define attributes and exception conditions.
4. Define the population.	4. Define the population.
5. Define the sampling unit.	5. Define the sampling unit.
6. Specify tolerable misstatement.	6. Specify the tolerable exception rate.
7. Specify acceptable risk of incorrect acceptance.	7. Specify acceptable risk of assessing control risk too low.
8. Estimate misstatements in the population.	8. Estimate the population exception rate.
9. Determine the initial sample size.	9. Determine the initial sample size.
Select the Sample and Perform the Audit Procedures	*Select the Sample and Perform the Audit Procedures*
10. Select the sample.	10. Select the sample.
11. Perform the audit procedures.	11. Perform the audit procedures.
Evaluate the Results	*Evaluate the Results*
12. Generalize from the sample to the population.	12. Generalize from the sample to the population.
13. Analyze the misstatements.	13. Analyze the exceptions.
14. Decide the acceptability of the population.	14. Decide the acceptability of the population.

When auditors sample for tests of details of balances, the objective is to determine whether the account balance being audited is fairly stated. The population of 40 accounts receivable in Table 17-1 (p. 522), totaling $207,295, is used as an illustration in applying nonstatistical sampling. The objective of the audit test will be to determine whether the total of $207,295 is materially misstated. Typically, materially misstated is defined in terms of tolerable misstatement.

State the Objectives of the Audit Test

As stated in Chapter 15, "Audit sampling applies whenever the auditor plans to reach conclusions about a population based on a sample." Although it is common to sample in many accounts, there are situations when sampling does not apply. For the population in Table 17-1, the auditor may decide to audit only items over $5,000 and ignore all others because the total of the smaller ones is immaterial. In this case, the auditor has not sampled. Similarly, if the auditor is verifying fixed asset additions and there are many small additions and one extremely large purchase of a building, the auditor may decide to ignore the small items entirely. Again, the auditor has not sampled.

Decide Whether Audit Sampling Applies

Audit sampling for tests of details of balances measures monetary misstatements in the population. Thus, the misstatement conditions are any conditions that represent a monetary misstatement in a sample item. In auditing accounts receivable, any client misstatement in a sample item is a misstatement.

Define Misstatement Conditions

The population is defined as the *recorded dollar population*. The auditor then evaluates whether the recorded population is overstated or understated. The recorded population is appropriate for testing for the existence objective. If the completeness objective is a concern, the sample should be selected from a different source, such as customers with zero balances. The population of accounts receivable in Table 17-1 consists of 40 accounts totaling $207,295. Most accounting populations subject to audit would, of course, contain far more items totaling a much larger dollar amount.

Define the Population

TABLE 17-1 Illustrative Accounts Receivable Population

Population Item	Recorded Amount	Population Item (cont.)	Recorded Amount (cont.)
1	$ 1,410	21	$ 4,865
2	9,130	22	770
3	660	23	2,305
4	3,355	24	2,665
5	5,725	25	1,000
6	8,210	26	6,225
7	580	27	3,675
8	44,110	28	6,250
9	825	29	1,890
10	1,155	30	27,705
11	2,270	31	935
12	50	32	5,595
13	5,785	33	930
14	940	34	4,045
15	1,820	35	9,480
16	3,380	36	360
17	530	37	1,145
18	955	38	6,400
19	4,490	39	100
20	17,140	40	8,435
			$207,295

Stratified Sampling For many populations, auditors subdivide the population into two or more subpopulations before applying audit sampling. Subdividing populations is called **stratified sampling**, where each subpopulation is a stratum. The purpose of stratification is to permit the auditor to emphasize certain population items and deemphasize others. In most audit sampling situations, including confirming accounts receivable, auditors want to emphasize the larger recorded dollar values; therefore, stratification is typically done on the basis of the size of recorded dollar values.

When examining the population in Table 17-1, we see that there are different ways to stratify the population. Assume that the auditor decided to stratify as follows:

Stratum	Stratum Criteria	No. in Population	Dollars in Population
1	>$10,000	3	$ 88,955
2	$5,000–$10,000	10	71,235
3	<$5,000	27	47,105
		40	$207,295

Define the Sampling Unit

The sampling unit for nonstatistical audit sampling in tests of details of balances is almost always the item making up the account balance. For accounts receivable, it is usually the customer account balance, which is represented by the customer account name or number on the accounts receivable list. The sampling unit can also be an individual invoice that is part of an account balance.

Specify Tolerable Misstatement

Tolerable misstatement as it was discussed in Chapter 9 is used for determining sample size and evaluating results in nonstatistical sampling. The auditor starts with a preliminary judgment about materiality and uses that total in deciding tolerable misstatement for each account. The required sample size increases as the auditor's tolerable misstatement for the account balance or class of transactions decreases.

Specify Acceptable Risk of Incorrect Acceptance

For all statistical and nonstatistical sampling applications, there is a risk that the quantitative conclusions about the population will be incorrect. This is always true unless 100 percent of the population is tested.

Acceptable risk of incorrect acceptance (ARIA) is the risk that the auditor is willing to take of accepting a balance as correct when the true misstatement in the balance is greater than tolerable misstatement. It is a measure of the auditor's desired assurance for an account balance. If the auditor wants more assurance in auditing a balance, ARIA is set lower. ARIA is the equivalent term to ARACR (acceptable risk of assessing control risk too low) for tests of controls and substantive tests of transactions.

There is an inverse relationship between ARIA and required sample size. If, for example, the auditor decides to reduce ARIA from 10 percent to 5 percent, the required sample size would increase.

The primary factor affecting the auditor's decision about ARIA is assessed control risk in the audit risk model. When internal controls are effective, control risk can be reduced, permitting the auditor to increase ARIA. This, in turn, reduces the sample size required for the test of details of the related account balance.

Understanding how ARACR and ARIA affect evidence accumulation can be difficult. Earlier it was shown that tests of details of balances for monetary misstatements can be reduced if internal controls are found to be effective through assessing control risk and performing tests of controls. The effects of ARACR and ARIA are consistent with that conclusion. If the auditor concludes that internal controls may be effective, control risk can be reduced. A lower control risk requires a lower ARACR in testing the controls, which requires a larger sample size. If controls are found to be effective, control risk can remain low, which permits the auditor to increase ARIA (through use of the audit risk model), thereby requiring a smaller sample size in the related substantive tests of details of balances. This may lead to efficiencies in an integrated audit of the financial statements and internal control for a public company. The effect of ARACR and ARIA on substantive testing in the two different circumstances is shown in Figure 17-1.

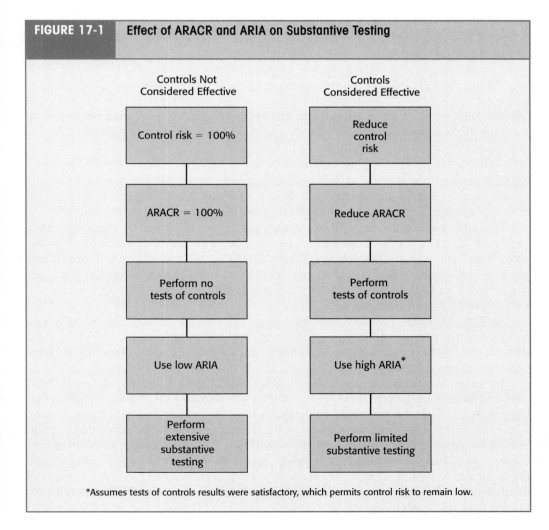

FIGURE 17-1   **Effect of ARACR and ARIA on Substantive Testing**

Controls Not Considered Effective

Control risk = 100%

ARACR = 100%

Perform no tests of controls

Use low ARIA

Perform extensive substantive testing

Controls Considered Effective

Reduce control risk

Reduce ARACR

Perform tests of controls

Use high ARIA*

Perform limited substantive testing

*Assumes tests of controls results were satisfactory, which permits control risk to remain low.

TABLE 17-2 — Relationship Among Factors Affecting ARIA, Effect on ARIA, and Required Sample Size for Audit Sampling

Factor Affecting ARIA	Example	Effect on ARIA	Effect on Sample Size
Effectiveness of internal controls (control risk)	Internal controls are effective (reduced control risk).	Increase	Decrease
Substantive tests of transactions	No exceptions were found in substantive tests of transactions.	Increase	Decrease
Acceptable audit risk	Likelihood of bankruptcy is low (increased acceptable audit risk).	Increase	Decrease
Analytical procedures	Analytical procedures are performed with no indications of likely misstatements.	Increase	Decrease

Besides control risk, ARIA is also directly affected by acceptable audit risk and inversely by other substantive tests already performed or planned for the account balance. For example, if acceptable audit risk is reduced, ARIA should also be reduced. If analytical procedures were performed and indicate that the account balance is fairly stated, ARIA should be increased. Stated differently, the analytical procedures are evidence in support of the account balance; therefore, less evidence from the detailed test using sampling is required to achieve acceptable audit risk. The same conclusion is appropriate for the relationship among substantive tests of transactions, ARIA, and sample size for tests of details of balances. The various relationships affecting ARIA are summarized in Table 17-2.

Estimate Misstatements in the Population

The auditor typically makes this estimate based on prior experience with the client and by assessing inherent risk, considering the results of tests of controls, substantive tests of transactions, and analytical procedures already performed. The planned sample size increases as the amount of misstatements expected in the population approaches tolerable misstatement.

Determine the Initial Sample Size

Auditors using nonstatistical sampling determine the initial sample size judgmentally considering the factors discussed so far. Table 17-3 summarizes the primary factors that influence sample size for nonstatistical sampling and how sample size is affected.

When the auditor uses stratified sampling, the sample size must be allocated among the strata. Typically, auditors allocate a higher portion of the sample items to larger population items. For example, in the example from Table 17-1 on page 522, allocating a sample size of 15, the auditor might decide to select all three accounts from stratum 1, and six each from strata 2 and 3. Observe that audit sampling does not apply to stratum 1 because all population items are being audited.

As Table 17-3 illustrates, determining a nonstatistical sample size is based on several factors and requires considerable judgment. A table for combining these factors and a formula for computing sample size based on the *AICPA Audit Sampling Auditing Guide* are presented in Figure 17-2.

For example, assume that the auditor applied this formula to the population in Table 17-1 and that tolerable misstatement is $20,000. The auditor first eliminates population items 8 and 30 from the recorded population because they exceed tolerable misstatement. These two individually material accounts will be tested separately. The remaining population to be sampled is $135,480 ($207,295 − $44,110 − $27,705). Further, assume that the combined assessed inherent and control risk is moderate and that there is a moderate risk that substantive tests of transactions and analytical procedures will not detect a material misstatement. The required assurance factor is 1.6 based on the table. The computed sample size is 11 [($135,480/$20,000) × 1.6 = 10.8].

TABLE 17-3	Factors Influencing Sample Sizes for Tests of Details of Balances	
Factor	Conditions Leading to Smaller Sample Size	Conditions Leading to Larger Sample Size
Control risk (ARACR)—Affects acceptable risk of incorrect acceptance	Low control risk	High control risk
Results of other substantive tests related to the same assertion (including analytical procedures and other relevant substantive tests)—Affect acceptable risk of incorrect acceptance	Satisfactory results in other related substantive tests	Unsatisfactory results in other related substantive tests
Acceptable audit risk—Affects acceptable risk of incorrect acceptance	High acceptable audit risk	Low acceptable audit risk
Tolerable misstatement for a specific account	Larger tolerable misstatement	Smaller tolerable misstatement
Inherent risk—Affects estimated misstatements in the population	Low inherent risk	High inherent risk
Expected size and frequency of misstatements— Affect estimated misstatements in the population	Smaller misstatements or lower frequency	Larger misstatements or higher frequency
Dollar amount of population	Smaller account balance	Larger account balance
Number of items in the population	Almost no effect on sample size unless population is very small	Almost no effect on sample size unless population is very small

Select the Sample

For nonstatistical sampling, auditing standards permit the auditor to use any of the selection methods discussed in Chapter 15. It is important for the auditor to use a method that will permit meaningful conclusions about the sample results.

For stratified sampling, the auditor selects samples independently from each stratum. For example, in stratum 3 in the previous example, the auditor will select six sample items from the 27 population items in that stratum.

Perform the Audit Procedures

To perform the audit procedures, the auditor applies the appropriate audit procedures to each item in the sample to determine whether it is correct or contains a misstatement. For example, in the confirmation of accounts receivable, the auditor will mail the sample

FIGURE 17-2	Formula for Computing Nonstatistical Tests of Details of Balances Sample Size Based on AICPA Audit Sampling Formula

$$\frac{\text{Population's recorded amount*}}{\text{Tolerable misstatement}} \times \text{Assurance factor} = \text{Sample size}$$

Select the appropriate assurance factor as follows:

Assessed Inherent and Control Risk	Risk That Other Substantive Procedures Will Fail to Detect a Material Misstatement		
	Maximum	Moderate	Low
Maximum	3.0	2.3	2.0
Slightly below maximum	2.7	2.0	1.6
Moderate	2.3	1.6	1.2
Low	2.0	1.2	1.0

*Individual items exceeding tolerable misstatement are tested individually and subtracted from the population for this calculation.

of positive confirmations in the manner described in Chapter 16 and determine the amount of misstatement in each account confirmed. For nonresponses, alternative procedures will be used to determine the misstatements. The auditor cannot expect meaningful results from using audit sampling unless the audit procedures are applied carefully.

Assume that the auditor sends first and second requests for confirmations and performs alternative procedures in the previous example. Assume also that the following conclusions are reached about the sample after reconciling all timing differences:

		Dollars Audited		
Stratum	Sample Size	Recorded Value	Audited Value	Client Misstatement
1	3	$ 88,955	$ 91,695	$(2,740)
2	6	43,995	43,024	971
3	6	13,105	10,947	2,158
	15	$146,055	$145,666	$ 389

Generalize from the Sample to the Population and Decide the Acceptability of the Population

The auditor must generalize from the sample to the population by (1) projecting misstatements from the sample results to the population and (2) considering sampling error and sampling risk (ARIA). For example, in the previous example does the auditor conclude that accounts receivable is overstated by $389? No, the auditor is interested in the *population* results, not those for the sample. It is therefore necessary to project from the sample to the population to estimate the population misstatement. The first step is to make a **point estimate,** which was first shown on page 239 in Chapter 9. There are different ways to calculate the point estimate, but a common way is to assume that misstatements in the unaudited population are proportional to the misstatements in the sample. That calculation must be done for each stratum and then totaled, rather than from the total misstatements in the sample. Thus, the point estimate of the misstatement from the preceding example is determined by using a weighted-average method, as shown next.

Stratum	Client Misstatement ÷ Recorded Value of the Sample	×	Recorded Book Value for the Stratum	=	Point Estimate of Misstatement
1	$(2,740)/$88,955		$88,955		$ (2,740)
2	$ 971 /$43,995		71,235		1,572
3	$ 2,158 /$13,105		47,105		7,757
Total					$ 6,589

The point estimate of the misstatement in the population is $6,589, indicating an overstatement. The point estimate, by itself, is not an adequate measure of the population misstatement, however, because of sampling error. In other words, because the estimate is based on a sample, it will be close to the true population misstatement, but it is unlikely that it is exactly the same. The auditor must consider the possibility that the true population misstatement is greater than the amount of misstatement that is tolerable in the circumstances whenever the point estimate is less than the tolerable misstatement amount. This must be done for both statistical and nonstatistical samples.

An auditor using nonstatistical sampling cannot formally measure sampling error and therefore must subjectively consider the possibility that the true population misstatement exceeds a tolerable amount. This is done by considering (1) the difference between the point estimate and tolerable misstatement, (2) the extent to which items in the population have been audited 100 percent, (3) whether misstatements tend to be offsetting or in only one direction, (4) the amounts of individual misstatements, and (5) the sample size. To continue the example, suppose that tolerable misstatement is $40,000. In that case, the auditor may conclude that there is little chance, given the point estimate of $6,589, that the true population misstatement exceeds the tolerable amount.

Suppose that tolerable misstatement is $12,000, only $5,411 greater than the point estimate. In that case, other factors would be considered. For example, if the larger items in the population were audited 100 percent (as was done here), any unidentified misstatements would be restricted to smaller items. If the misstatements tend to be offsetting and are relatively small in size, the auditor may conclude that the true population misstatement is likely to be less than the tolerable amount. Also, the larger the sample size, the more confident the auditor can be that the point estimate is close to the true population value. Therefore, the auditor would be more willing to accept that the true population misstatement is less than tolerable misstatement in this example where the sample size is considered large, than where it is considered moderate or small. However, if one or more of these other conditions is different, the chance of a misstatement in excess of the tolerable amount may be judged to be high and the recorded population unacceptable.

Even if the amount of likely misstatement is not considered material, the auditor must wait to make a final evaluation until the entire audit is completed. For example, the estimated total misstatement and estimated sampling error in accounts receivable must be combined with estimates of misstatements in all other parts of the audit to evaluate the effect of all misstatements on the financial statements as a whole.

Analyze the Misstatements

As for sampling for tests of controls and substantive tests of transactions, an evaluation of the nature and cause of each misstatement found is essential. For example, in confirming accounts receivable, suppose that all misstatements resulted from the client's failure to record returned goods. The auditor would determine why that type of misstatement occurred so often, the implications of the misstatements on other audit areas, the potential impact on the financial statements, and its effect on company operations.

An important part of misstatement analysis is deciding whether any modification of the audit risk model is needed. If the auditor concluded that the failure to record the returns discussed in the previous paragraph resulted from a breakdown of internal controls, it might be necessary to reassess control risk. That in turn would probably cause the auditor to reduce ARIA, which would increase planned sample size. As discussed in Chapter 9, revisions of the audit risk model must be done with extreme care because the model is intended primarily for planning, not evaluating results.

When the auditor concludes that the misstatement in a population may be larger than tolerable misstatement after considering sampling error, the population is not considered acceptable. There are several possible courses of action.

Take No Action Until Tests of Other Audit Areas Are Completed Ultimately, the auditor must evaluate whether the financial statements taken as a whole are materially misstated. If offsetting misstatements are found in other parts of the audit, such as in inventory, the auditor may conclude that the estimated misstatements in accounts receivable are acceptable. Of course, before the audit is finalized, the auditor must evaluate whether a misstatement in one account may make the financial statements misleading even if there are offsetting misstatements.

Perform Expanded Audit Tests in Specific Areas If an analysis of the misstatements indicates that most of the misstatements are of a specific type, it may be desirable to restrict the additional audit effort to the problem area. For example, if an analysis of the misstatements in confirmations indicates that most of the misstatements result from failure to record sales returns, an extended search could be made of returned goods to make sure that they have been recorded. However, great care must be taken to evaluate the cause of all misstatements in the sample before a conclusion is reached about the proper emphasis in the expanded tests. There may be more than one problem area.

When a problem area is analyzed and corrected by adjusting the client's records, the sample items that led to isolating the problem area can then be shown as "correct." The point estimate can now be recalculated without the misstatements that have been "corrected." Sampling error and the acceptability of the population will also have to be reconsidered with the new facts.

Increase the Sample Size When the auditor increases the sample size, sampling error is reduced if the rate of misstatements in the expanded sample, their dollar amounts, and their direction are similar to those in the original sample. Therefore, increasing the sample size may satisfy the auditor's tolerable misstatement requirements.

Increasing the sample size enough to satisfy the auditor's tolerable misstatement standards is often costly, especially when the difference between tolerable misstatement and projected misstatement is small. Even if the sample size is increased, there is no assurance of a satisfactory result. If the number, amount, and direction of the misstatements in the extended sample are proportionately greater or more variable than in the original sample, the results are still likely to be unacceptable.

For tests such as accounts receivable confirmation and inventory observation, it is often difficult to increase the sample size because of the practical problem of "reopening" those procedures once the initial work is done. By the time the auditor discovers that the sample was not large enough, several weeks have usually passed.

Despite these difficulties, sometimes the auditor must increase the sample size after the original testing is completed. It is much more common to increase sample size in audit areas other than confirmations and inventory observation, but it is occasionally necessary to do so even for these two areas. When stratified sampling is used, increased samples usually focus on the strata containing larger amounts, unless misstatements appear to be concentrated in some other strata.

Adjust the Account Balance When the auditor concludes that an account balance is materially misstated, the client may be willing to adjust the book value based on the sample results. In the previous example, assume the client is willing to reduce book value by the amount of the point estimate ($6,589) to adjust for the estimate of the misstatement. The auditor's estimate of the misstatement is now zero, but it is still necessary to consider sampling error. Again, assuming a tolerable misstatement of $12,000, the auditor must now assess whether sampling error exceeds $12,000, not the $5,411 originally considered. If the auditor believes sampling error is $12,000 or less, accounts receivable is acceptable after the adjustment. If the auditor believes it is more than $12,000, adjusting the account balance is not a practical option.

Request the Client to Correct the Population In some cases, the client's records are so inadequate that a correction of the entire population is required before the audit can be completed. For example, in accounts receivable, the client may be asked to prepare the aging schedule again if the auditor concludes that it has significant misstatements. When the client changes the valuation of some items in the population, the results must be audited again.

Refuse to Give an Unqualified Opinion If the auditor believes that the recorded amount in an account is not fairly stated, it is necessary to follow at least one of the preceding alternatives or to qualify the audit report in an appropriate manner. If the auditor believes that there is a reasonable chance that the financial statements are materially misstated, it would be a serious breach of auditing standards to issue an unqualified opinion. It is also important to keep in mind that when material misstatements are identified by the auditor for a public company, the presence of that misstatement must be considered a material weakness when reporting on internal control over financial reporting.

MONETARY UNIT SAMPLING

Now that we have discussed nonstatistical sampling, we will move on to statistical sampling, starting with monetary unit sampling. **Monetary unit sampling (MUS)** is an innovation in statistical sampling methodology that was developed specifically for use by auditors. It is now the most commonly used statistical method of sampling for tests of details of balances because it has the statistical simplicity of attributes sampling yet provides a statistical result expressed in dollars (or another appropriate currency). MUS is also called dollar unit sampling, cumulative monetary amount sampling, and sampling with probability proportional to size.[1]

There are far more similarities than differences in using MUS and nonstatistical sampling. All 14 of the steps must also be performed for MUS even though some are done differently. Understanding those differences, though, is the key to understanding MUS. The following discussion explains these differences in detail.

Differences Between MUS and Nonstatistical Sampling

Sampling Software

The Definition of the Sampling Unit Is an Individual Dollar A critical feature of MUS is the definition of the sampling unit as an individual dollar in an account balance. The name of the statistical method, monetary unit sampling, results from this distinctive feature. For example, in the population in Table 17-1 on page 522, the sampling unit is 1 dollar and the population size is 207,295 dollars, not the 40 physical units discussed earlier.

The result of the individual dollar being the sampling unit for MUS is its automatic emphasis on physical units with larger recorded balances. Because the sample is selected on the basis of individual dollars, an account with a large balance has a greater chance of being included than an account with a small balance. For example, in accounts receivable confirmation, an account with a $5,000 balance has a 10 times greater probability of selection than one with a $500 balance, as it contains 10 times as many dollar units. As a result, there is no need to use stratified sampling with MUS. Stratification occurs automatically.

The Population Size Is the Recorded Dollar Population For example, the population of accounts receivable in Table 17-1 consists of 207,295 dollars, which is the population size, not the 40 physical units. This definition of population size is consistent with the use of dollar units.

Because of the method of sample selection in MUS, which is discussed later, it is not possible to evaluate the likelihood of unrecorded items in the population. Assume, for example, that MUS is used to evaluate whether inventory is fairly stated. MUS cannot be used to evaluate whether certain inventory items exist but have not been counted. If the completeness objective is important in the audit test, and it usually is, that objective must be satisfied separately from the MUS tests.

Preliminary Judgment of Materiality Is Used for Each Account Instead of Tolerable Misstatement Another unique aspect of MUS is the use of the preliminary judgment about materiality, as discussed in Chapter 9, to directly determine the tolerable misstatement

[1]The currency in many countries will be called something other than "dollars." Thus, in Mexico, for instance, one might use "Peso Unit Sampling." This is why the more universal term, *monetary* unit sampling, has been adopted. We recognize the appropriateness of this term in this text but also refer to dollars as the sampling unit in most cases.

amount for the audit of each account. Other sampling techniques require the auditor to determine tolerable misstatement for each account by allocating the preliminary judgment about materiality. This is not required when MUS is used. For example, assume that the auditor decides that the preliminary judgment about materiality should be $60,000 for the financial statements as a whole. That materiality amount of $60,000, or a derivative of it, would be used as tolerable misstatement in all applications of MUS—inventory, accounts receivable, accounts payable, and so forth.

Sample Size Is Determined Using a Statistical Formula The information used and the calculation of the planned sample size are shown later.

A Formal Decision Rule Is Used for Deciding the Acceptability of the Population The decision rule used for MUS is similar to that used for nonstatistical sampling, but it is sufficiently different to merit discussion. The decision rule is illustrated after the calculation of the misstatement bounds is shown.

Sample Selection Is Done Using PPS Monetary unit samples are samples selected with **probability proportional to size sample selection (PPS).** Such samples are samples of individual dollars in the population. Auditors cannot, however, audit individual dollars. Therefore, the auditor must determine the physical unit to perform the audit tests. For example, in Table 17-4 the auditor will take a random sample of population items between 1 and 7,376 (individual dollars). However, to perform the audit procedures, the auditor must identify the population items between 1 and 12 (physical units). If the auditor selected the random number 3014, the physical unit associated with that number is 6.

PPS samples can be obtained by using computer software, random number tables, or systematic sampling techniques. An illustration of an accounts receivable population, including cumulative totals, is provided in Table 17-4 to demonstrate selecting a sample using computer software.

Assume that the auditor wants to select a PPS sample of four accounts from the population in Table 17-4. Because the sampling unit is defined as an individual dollar, the population size is 7,376, and four random numbers are needed from a computer program. Assume that the computer program generates the following random numbers: 6,586, 1,756, 850, and

TABLE 17-4	Accounts Receivable Population	
Population Item (Physical Unit)	**Recorded Amount**	**Cumulative Total (Dollar Unit)**
1	$ 357	$ 357
2	1,281	1,638
3	60	1,698
4	573	2,271
5	691	2,962
6	143	3,105
7	1,425	4,530
8	278	4,808
9	942	5,750
10	826	6,576
11	404	6,980
12	396	7,376

6,499. The population physical unit items that contain these random dollars are determined by reference to the cumulative total column. They are items 11 (containing dollars 6,577 through 6,980), 4 (dollars 1,699 through 2,271), 2 (dollars 358 through 1,638), and 10 (dollars 5,751 through 6,576). These will be audited, and the result for each physical unit will be applied to the random dollar it contains.

The statistical methods used to evaluate monetary unit samples permit the inclusion of a physical unit in the sample more than once. That is, in the previous example, if the random numbers had been 6,586, 1,756, 850, and 6,599, the sample items would be 11, 4, 2, and 11. Item 11 would be audited once but would be treated as two sample items statistically, and the sample total would be four items because four monetary units were involved.

One problem using PPS selection is that population items with a zero recorded balance have no chance of being selected with PPS sample selection, even though they could contain misstatements. Similarly, small balances that are significantly understated have little chance of being included in the sample. This problem can be overcome by doing specific audit tests for zero- and small-balance items, assuming that they are of concern.

Another problem is the inability to include negative balances, such as credit balances in accounts receivable, in the PPS (monetary unit) sample. It is possible to ignore negative balances for PPS selection and test those amounts by some other means. An alternative is to treat them as positive balances and add them to the total number of monetary units being tested; however, this complicates the evaluation process.

The Auditor Generalizes from the Sample to the Population Using MUS Techniques Regardless of the sampling method selected, the auditor must generalize from the sample to the population by (1) projecting misstatements from the sample results to the population and (2) determining the related sampling error. There are four important aspects in doing this using MUS:

1. Attributes sampling tables are used to calculate the results. Tables such as the one on page 470 can be used, replacing ARACR with ARIA.
2. The attributes results must be converted to dollars. MUS estimates the dollar misstatement in the population, not the percent of items in the population that are misstated. MUS accomplishes this by defining each population item as an individual dollar. Therefore, estimating the rate of population dollars that contain a misstatement is a way of estimating the total dollar misstatement.
3. The auditor must make an assumption about the percentage of misstatement for each population item that is misstated. This assumption enables the auditor to use the attributes sampling tables to estimate dollar misstatements.
4. The statistical results when MUS is used are called **misstatement bounds.** These misstatement bounds are estimates of the likely maximum overstatement (upper misstatement bound) and likely maximum understatement (lower misstatement bound) at a given ARIA. Both an upper misstatement bound and a lower misstatement bound are calculated.

This final step, generalizing from the sample to the population, is an extremely important part of MUS. Generalization is different when the auditor finds no misstatements in the sample compared to when there are misstatements. Generalizing under these two situations is covered next.

Generalizing from the Sample to the Population When No Misstatements Are Found Using MUS

Suppose that the auditor is confirming a population of accounts receivable for monetary correctness. The population totals $1,200,000, and a sample of 100 confirmations is obtained. Upon audit, no misstatements are uncovered in the sample. The auditor wants to determine the maximum amount of overstatement and understatement amounts that could exist in the population even when the sample contains no misstatements. These are the upper misstatement bound and the lower misstatement bound, respectively. Assuming an ARIA of 5 percent, and using the attributes sampling table on page 470, both the upper and lower bounds are determined by locating the intersection of the sample size (100) and the actual number of misstatements (0) in the same manner as for attributes sampling. The CUER of 3 percent on the table represents both the upper and lower bound, *expressed as a percent.* Because the sample misstatement rate was 0 percent, the 3 percent represents an estimate of sampling error.

Thus, based on the sample results and the misstatement bounds from the table, the auditor can conclude with a 5 percent sampling risk that no more than 3 percent of the dollar units in the population are misstated. To convert this percent into *dollars,* the auditor must make an assumption about the average percent of misstatement for population dollars that contain a misstatement. This assumption significantly affects the misstatement bounds. To illustrate this, three sets of example assumptions are examined: (1) a 100 percent misstatement assumption for both overstatements and understatements, (2) a 10 percent misstatement assumption for both overstatements and understatements, and (3) a 20 percent misstatement assumption for overstatements and a 200 percent assumption for understatements.

Assumption 1 Overstatement amounts equal 100 percent; understatement amounts equal 100 percent; misstatement bounds at a 5 percent ARIA are

$$\text{Upper misstatement bound} = \$1,200,000 \times 3\% \times 100\% = \$36,000$$
$$\text{Lower misstatement bound} = \$1,200,000 \times 3\% \times 100\% = \$36,000$$

The assumption is that, on average, those population items that are misstated are misstated by the full dollar amount of the recorded value. Because the misstatement bound is 3 percent, the dollar value of the misstatement is not likely to exceed $36,000 (3 percent of the total recorded dollar units in the population). If all the amounts are overstated, there is an overstatement of $36,000. If they are all understated, there is an understatement of $36,000.

The assumption of 100 percent misstatements is extremely conservative, especially for overstatements. Assume that the actual population exception rate is 3 percent. The following two conditions both have to exist before the $36,000 properly reflects the true overstatement amount:

1. All amounts have to be overstatements. Offsetting amounts would have reduced the amount of the overstatement.
2. All population items misstated have to be 100 percent misstated. There could not, for example, be a misstatement such as a receivable balance of $226 recorded as $262. This would be only a 13.7 percent misstatement ($262 - 226 = 36$ overstatement; $36/262 = 13.7\%$).

In the calculation of the misstatement bounds of $36,000 overstatement and understatement, the auditor did not calculate a point estimate and sampling error (called precision amount in MUS) in the manner discussed earlier in the chapter. This is because the tables used include both a point estimate and a precision amount to derive the upper exception rate. Even though the point estimate and precision amount are not calculated for MUS, they are implicit in the determination of misstatement bounds and can be determined from the tables. For example, in this illustration, the point estimate is zero and the statistical precision is $36,000.

Assumption 2 Overstatement amounts equal 10 percent; understatement amounts equal 10 percent; misstatement bounds at a 5 percent ARIA are

$$\text{Upper misstatement bound} = \$1,200,000 \times 3\% \times 10\% = \$3,600$$
$$\text{Lower misstatement bound} = \$1,200,000 \times 3\% \times 10\% = \$3,600$$

The assumption is that, on average, those items that are misstated are misstated by no more than 10 percent. If all items were misstated in one direction, the misstatement bounds would be +$3,600 and -$3,600. The change in assumption from 100 percent to 10 percent misstatements significantly affects the misstatement bounds. The effect is in direct proportion to the magnitude of the change.

Assumption 3 Overstatement amounts equal 20 percent; understatement amounts equal 200 percent; misstatement bounds at a 5 percent ARIA are

$$\text{Upper misstatement bound} = \$1,200,000 \times 3\% \times 20\% = \$7,200$$
$$\text{Lower misstatement bound} = \$1,200,000 \times 3\% \times 200\% = \$72,000$$

The justification for a larger percent for understatements is the potential for a larger misstatement in percentage terms. For example, an accounts receivable recorded at $20 that should have been recorded at $200 is understated by 900 percent [(200 − 20)/20], whereas one that is recorded at $200 that should have been recorded at $20 is overstated by 90 percent [(200 − 20)/200].

Items containing large understatement amounts may have a small recorded value as a result of those misstatements. As a consequence, because of the mechanics of MUS, few of them will have a chance of being selected in the sample. Because of this, some auditors select an additional sample of small items to supplement the monetary unit sample when understatement amounts are an important audit concern.

Appropriate Percent of Misstatement Assumption The appropriate assumption for the overall percent of misstatement in those population items containing a misstatement is an auditor's decision. The auditor must set these percentages based on professional judgment in the circumstances. In the absence of convincing information to the contrary, most auditors believe that it is desirable to assume a 100 percent amount for both overstatements and understatements unless there are misstatements in the sample results. This approach is considered highly conservative, but it is easier to justify than any other assumption. In fact, the reason upper and lower limits are called misstatement bounds when MUS is used, rather than maximum likely misstatement or the commonly used statistical term *confidence limit,* is because of widespread use of that conservative assumption. Unless stated otherwise, the 100 percent misstatement assumption is used in this chapter and problem materials.

In the preceding section, we assumed there were no misstatements in the sample. What happens, though, if misstatements are found? We will use the example from the preceding section but assume there are five misstatements instead of none. The misstatements are shown in Table 17-5.

Generalizing When Misstatements Are Found

The four aspects of generalizing from the sample to the population discussed earlier still apply, but their use is modified as follows:

1. Overstatement and understatement amounts are dealt with separately and then combined. First, initial upper and lower misstatement bounds are calculated separately for overstatement and understatement amounts. Next, a point estimate of overstatements and understatements is calculated. The point estimate of understatements is used to reduce the initial upper misstatement bound, and the point estimate of overstatements is used to reduce the initial lower misstatement bound. The method and rationale for these calculations will be illustrated by using the four overstatement and one understatement amounts in Table 17-5.

2. A different misstatement assumption is made for each misstatement, including the zero misstatements. When there were no misstatements in the sample, an assumption was required as to

TABLE 17-5	Misstatements Found			
Customer No.	Recorded Accounts Receivable Amount	Audited Accounts Receivable Amount	Misstatement	Misstatement ÷ Recorded Amount
2073	$ 6,200	$ 6,100	$ 100	.016
5111	12,910	12,000	910	.07
5206	4,322	4,450	(128)	(.03)
7642	23,000	22,995	5	.0002
9816	8,947	2,947	6,000	.671

the average percent of misstatement for the population items misstated. The misstatement bounds were calculated showing several different assumptions. Now that misstatements have been found, sample information is available to use in determining the misstatement bounds. The misstatement assumption is still required, but it can be modified based on this actual misstatement data.

Where misstatements are found, a 100 percent assumption for all misstatements is not only exceptionally conservative, it is inconsistent with the sample results. A common assumption in practice, and the one followed in this book, is that the actual sample misstatements are representative of the population misstatements. This assumption requires the auditor to calculate the percent that each sample item is misstated (misstatement ÷ recorded amount) and apply that percent to the population. The calculation of the percent for each misstatement is shown in the last column in Table 17-5. As is explained shortly, a misstatement assumption is still needed for the zero misstatement portion of the computed results. For this example, a 100 percent misstatement assumption is used for the zero misstatement portion for both overstatement and understatement misstatement bounds.

3. The auditor must deal with layers of the computed upper exception rate (CUER) from the attributes sampling table. The reason for doing so is that there is a different misstatement assumption for each misstatement. Layers are calculated by first determining the CUER from the table for each misstatement and then calculating each layer. Table 17-6 shows the layers in the attributes sampling table for the example at hand. The layers were determined by reading across the table for a sample size of 100, from the 0 through 4 exception columns.

4. Misstatement assumptions must be associated with each layer. The most common method of associating misstatement assumptions with layers is to be conservative by associating the largest dollar misstatement percents with the largest layers. Table 17-7 shows the association. For example, the largest average misstatement was .671 for customer 9816. That misstatement is associated with the layer factor of .017, the largest layer where misstatements were found. The portion of the upper precision limit related to the zero misstatement layer has a misstatement assumption of 100 percent, which is still conservative. Table 17-7 shows the calculation of misstatement bounds before consideration of offsetting amounts. The upper misstatement bound was calculated as if there were no understatement amounts, and the lower misstatement bound was calculated as if there were no overstatement amounts.

Most MUS users believe that the approach just discussed is overly conservative when there are offsetting amounts. If an understatement amount is found, it is logical and reasonable that the bound for overstatement amounts should be lower than it would be had no understatement amounts been found, and vice versa. The adjustment of bounds for offsetting amounts is made as follows: (1) A point estimate of misstatements is made for both overstatement and understatement amounts, and (2) each bound is reduced by the opposite point estimate.

TABLE 17-6	Percent Misstatement Bounds	
Number of Misstatements	Upper Precision Limit from Table	Increase in Precision Limit Resulting from Each Misstatement (Layers)
0	.03	.03
1	.047	.017
2	.062	.015
3	.076	.014
4	.089	.013

TABLE 17-7 Illustration of Calculating Initial Upper and Lower Misstatement Bounds

Number of Misstatements	Upper Precision Limit Portion*	Recorded Value	Unit Misstatement Assumption	Misstatement Bound Portion (Columns 2 × 3 × 4)
Overstatements				
0	.030	$1,200,000	1.0	$36,000
1	.017	1,200,000	.671	13,688
2	.015	1,200,000	.07	1,260
3	.014	1,200,000	.016	269
4	.013	1,200,000	.0002	3
Upper precision limit	.089			
Initial misstatement bound				$51,220
Understatements				
0	.030	$1,200,000	1.0	$36,000
1	.017	1,200,000	.03	612
Lower precision limit	.047			
Initial misstatement bound				$36,612

*ARIA of 5%. Sample size of 100.

The point estimate for overstatements is calculated by multiplying the average over-statement amount in the dollar units audited times the recorded value. The same approach is used for calculating the point estimate for understatements. In the example, there is one understatement amount of 3 cents per dollar unit in a sample of 100. The understatement point estimate is therefore $360 (.03/100 × $1,200,000). Similarly, the overstatement point estimate is $9,086 [(.671 + .07 + .016 + .0002)/100 × $1,200,000].

Table 17-8 shows the adjustment of the bounds that follow from this procedure. The initial upper bound of $51,220 is reduced by the estimated most likely understatement amount of $360 to an adjusted bound of $50,860. The initial lower bound of $36,612 is reduced by the estimated most likely overstatement amount of $9,086 to an adjusted bound of $27,526. Thus, given the methodology and assumptions followed, the auditor concludes that there is a 5 percent risk that accounts receivable is overstated by more than $50,860, or understated by more than $27,526. It should be noted that if the mis-statement assumptions are changed, the misstatement bounds will also change. The reader is advised that the method used to adjust the bounds for offsetting amounts is

TABLE 17-8 Illustration of Calculating Adjusted Misstatement Bounds

Number of Misstatements	Unit Misstatement Assumption	Sample Size	Recorded Population	Point Estimate	Bounds
Initial overstatement bound					$51,220
Understatement amount					
1	.03	100	$1,200,000	$ 360	(360)
Adjusted overstatement bound					$50,860
Initial understatement bound					$36,612
Overstatement amounts					
1	.671				
2	.07				
3	.016				
4	.0002				
Sum	.7572	100	$1,200,000	$9,086	(9,086)
Adjusted understatement bound					$27,526

TABLE 17-9   Summary of Steps to Calculate Adjusted Misstatement Bounds

Steps to Calculate Adjusted Misstatement Bounds	Calculation for Overstatements in Tables 17-5, 17-7, and 17-8
1. Determine misstatement for each sample item, keeping overstatements and understatements separate.	Table 17-5; four overstatements
2. Calculate misstatement per dollar unit in each sample item (misstatement/recorded amount).	Table 17-5; .016, .07, .0002, .671
3. Layer misstatements per dollar unit from highest to lowest, including the percent misstatement assumption for sample items not misstated.	Table 17-7; 1.0, .671, .07, .016, .0002
4. Determine upper precision limit from attributes sampling table and calculate the percent misstatement bound for each misstatement (layer).	Table 17-7; Total of 8.9% for four misstatements; calculate five layers
5. Calculate initial upper and lower misstatement bounds for each layer and total.	Table 17-7; Total of $51,220
6. Calculate point estimate for overstatements and understatements.	Table 17-8; $360 for understatements
7. Calculate adjusted upper and lower misstatement bounds.	Table 17-8; $50,860 adjusted overstatement

only one of several in current use. The method illustrated here is taken from Leslie, Teitlebaum, and Anderson.[2]

The seven steps followed in the calculation of the adjusted misstatement bounds for monetary unit sampling when there are offsetting amounts are shown in Table 17-9. The calculation of the adjusted upper misstatement bound for the four overstatement amounts in Table 17-5 (p. 533) is used to illustrate.

Decide the Acceptability of the Population Using MUS

After the misstatement bounds are calculated, the auditor must decide whether the population is acceptable. To do that, a *decision rule* is needed. The decision rule for MUS is as follows: If *both* the lower misstatement bound (LMB) and upper misstatement bound (UMB) fall between the understatement and overstatement tolerable misstatement amounts, *accept* the conclusion that the book value is not misstated by a material amount. Otherwise, conclude that the book value is misstated by a material amount.

This decision rule is illustrated in Figure 17-3. The auditor should conclude that both the LMB and UMB for situations 1 and 2 fall completely within both the understatement and overstatement tolerable misstatement limits. Therefore, the conclusion that the population is not misstated by a material amount is accepted. For situations 3, 4, and 5, either LMB or UMB, or both, are outside tolerable misstatements. Therefore, the population book value is rejected.

Assume in the example being used that the auditor had set a tolerable misstatement amount for accounts receivable of $40,000 (overstatement or understatement). That means the auditor will accept the recorded value if the auditor concludes that accounts receivable is not overstated or understated by more than $40,000. As was previously shown, the auditor selected a sample of 100 items, found five misstatements, and calculated the lower bound to be $27,526 and the upper bound to be $50,860. Application of the decision rule leads the auditor to the conclusion that the population should not be accepted because the upper misstatement bound is more than tolerable misstatement of $40,000 (see p. 537 for illustration).

[2]D. A. Leslie, A. D. Teitlebaum, and R. J. Anderson, *Dollar Unit Sampling: A Practical Guide for Auditors*, Toronto, Copp, Clark and Pitman, 1979.

Tolerable misstatement ($40,000)   Tolerable misstatement $40,000

($27,526) $50,860
LMB   UMB

When one or both of the misstatement bounds lie outside the tolerable misstatement limits and the population is not considered acceptable, the auditor has several options. These are the same as for nonstatistical sampling and have already been discussed.

Action When a Population
Is Rejected

Determining sample size was discussed earlier as one of the steps in MUS, but the method of the calculation was deferred until you had an understanding of average misstatement assumptions. Because you now understand that concept, determining the sample size is covered in more depth. The method used to determine sample size for MUS is similar to that used for physical unit attributes sampling, using the attributes sampling tables. The five things that must be known or specified have already been discussed in this chapter. An example is used to illustrate determining sample size.

Determining Sample Size
Using MUS

Materiality The preliminary judgment about materiality is normally the basis for the tolerable misstatement amount used. If misstatements in non-MUS tests are expected, tolerable misstatement would be materiality less those amounts. Tolerable misstatement may be different for overstatements or understatements. For this example, tolerable misstatement for both overstatements and understatements is $100,000.

Assumption of the Average Percent of Misstatement for Population Items That Contain a Misstatement Again, there may be a separate assumption for the upper and lower bounds. This is also an auditor judgment. It should be based on the auditor's knowledge of the client and past experience, and if less than 100 percent is used, the assumption must be clearly defensible. For this example, 50 percent is used for overstatements and 100 percent for understatements.

Acceptable Risk of Incorrect Acceptance ARIA is an auditor judgment and is often reached with the aid of the audit risk model. It is 5 percent for this example.

Recorded Population Value The dollar value of the population is taken from the client's records. For this example, it is $5 million.

FIGURE 17-3	Illustration of the Auditor's Decision Rule for MUS

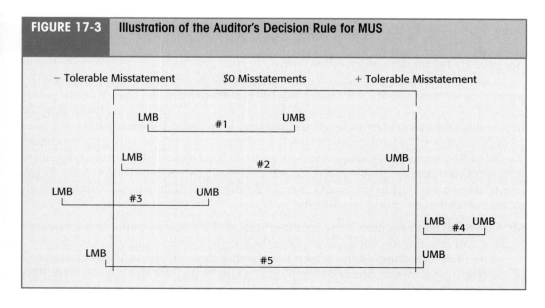

Estimate of the Population Exception Rate Normally, the estimate of the population exception rate for MUS is zero, as it is most appropriate to use MUS when no or only a few misstatements are expected. When misstatements are expected, the total dollar amount of expected population misstatements is estimated and then expressed as a percent of the population recorded value. In this example, a $20,000 overstatement amount is expected. This is equivalent to a .4 percent exception rate. To be conservative, a .5 percent expected exception rate is used.

These assumptions are summarized as follows:

Tolerable misstatement (same for upper and lower)	$100,000
Average percent of misstatement assumption, overstatements	50%
Average percent of misstatement assumption, understatements	100%
ARIA	5%
Accounts receivable—recorded value	$5 million
Estimated misstatement in accounts receivable	$ 20,000

The sample size is calculated as follows:

	Upper Bound	Lower Bound
Tolerable misstatement	100,000	100,000
Average percent of misstatement assumption	÷ .50	÷ 1.00
	200,000	100,000
Recorded population value	÷5,000,000	÷5,000,000
Tolerable exception rate	4%	2%
Estimated population exception rate (EPER)	.5%	0
Sample size from the attributes table (p. 468) 5% ARACR, 4% and 2% TER, and .5% and 0% EPER	117	149

Because only one sample is taken for both overstatements and understatements, the *larger* of the two computed sample sizes is used, in this case 149 items. In auditing the sample, finding any understatement amounts will cause the lower bound to exceed the tolerable limit because the sample size is based on no expected misstatements. Conversely, several overstatement amounts might be found before the tolerable limit for the upper bound is exceeded. When there is concern about unexpectedly finding a misstatement that would cause the population to be rejected, the auditor can guard against it by arbitrarily increasing sample size above the amount determined by the tables. For example, in this illustration, the auditor might use a sample size of 200 instead of 149.

Relationship of the Audit Risk Model to Sample Size for MUS The audit risk model for planning was shown in Chapter 9 and subsequent chapters as

$$PDR = \frac{AAR}{IR \times CR}$$

(see pp. 241–243 for description of the terms).

It was shown in Chapter 16 that the auditor reduces detection risk to the planned level by performing substantive tests of transactions, analytical procedures, and tests of details of balances. MUS is used in performing tests of details of balances. Therefore, understanding the relationship of the three independent factors in the audit risk model plus analytical procedures and substantive tests of transactions to sample size for tests of details of balances is important.

Table 17-2 on page 524 shows that four of these five factors (control risk, substantive tests of transactions, acceptable audit risk, and analytical procedures) all affect ARIA. ARIA in turn determines the planned sample size. The other factor, inherent risk, affects the estimated population exception rate directly.

Audit Uses of Monetary Unit Sampling

MUS is appealing to auditors for at least four reasons. First, it automatically increases the likelihood of selecting high dollar items from the population being audited. Auditors make a practice of concentrating on these items because they generally represent the greatest risk of material misstatements. Stratified sampling can also be used for this purpose, but MUS is often easier to apply.

Second, MUS often reduces the cost of doing the audit testing because several sample items are tested at once. For example, if one large item makes up 10 percent of the total recorded dollar value of the population and the sample size is 100, the PPS sample selection method is likely to result in approximately 10 percent of the sample items from that one large population item. Naturally, that item needs to be audited only once, but it counts as a sample of 10. If the item is misstated, it is also counted as 10 misstatements. Larger population items may be eliminated from the sampled population by auditing them 100 percent and evaluating them separately if the auditor so desires.

Third, MUS is appealing because of its ease of application. Monetary unit samples can be evaluated by the application of simple tables. It is easy to teach and to supervise the use of MUS techniques. Firms that use MUS extensively use computer programs or special tables that streamline sample size determination and evaluation even further than shown here.

Finally, MUS provides a statistical conclusion rather than a nonstatistical one. Many auditors believe that statistical sampling aids them in making better and more defensible conclusions.

The primary disadvantage of MUS is twofold. First, the total misstatement bounds resulting when misstatements are found may be too high to be useful to the auditor. This is because these evaluation methods are inherently conservative when misstatements are found and often produce bounds far in excess of materiality. To overcome this problem, large samples may be required. Second, it may be cumbersome to select PPS samples from large populations without computer assistance.

For all these reasons, MUS is most commonly used when zero or few misstatements are expected, a dollar result is desired, and the population data are maintained on computer files.

VARIABLES SAMPLING

Variables sampling, like monetary unit sampling, is a statistical method used by auditors. Variables sampling and nonstatistical sampling for tests of details of balances have the same objective, which is to measure the true amount of misstatement in an account balance. As with nonstatistical sampling, when it is determined that the misstatement amount exceeds the tolerable amount, the population is rejected and additional actions are taken by the auditor.

OBJECTIVE 17-4

Describe variables sampling.

There are several sampling techniques that constitute the general class of methods called variables sampling. Those studied in this section are difference estimation, ratio estimation, and mean-per-unit estimation. These are discussed more later.

There are far more similarities than differences in using variables methods and nonstatistical sampling. All 14 of the steps discussed for nonstatistical sampling must be performed for variables methods and almost all of them are identical. This section focuses on the differences between variables and nonstatistical sampling on the assumption that you understand the material in the earlier part of this chapter on nonstatistical sampling.

Differences Between Variables and Nonstatistical Sampling

To understand why and how auditors use variables sampling methods in auditing, it is important to understand sampling distributions and how they affect auditors' statistical conclusions. These are studied next.

Sampling Distributions

Although auditors can assess the general nature of populations for the purpose of selecting the most appropriate sampling method, they do not know the mean value (average) or the distribution of the misstatement amounts or the audited values of the populations they are testing in audit engagements. The population characteristics must be *estimated* from samples. That, of course, is the purpose of the audit test. In this section, there is a discussion of sampling distributions, which are essential to drawing conclusions about populations on the basis of samples using variables sampling methods.

Assume that an auditor, as an experiment, took thousands of repeated samples of equal size from a population of accounting data having a mean value of $\overline{X}$. For each sample, the auditor calculates the mean value of the items in the sample as follows:

$$\overline{x} = \frac{\Sigma x_j}{n}$$

FIGURE 17-4   Frequency Distribution of Sample Means

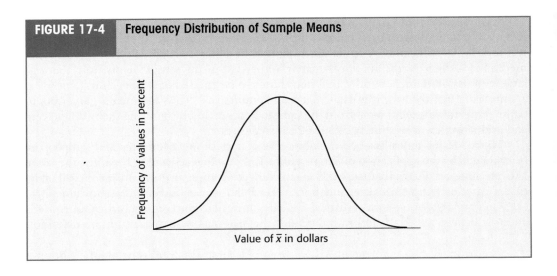

Value of x̄ in dollars

where:

$$\bar{x} = \text{mean value of the sample items}$$

$$x_j = \text{value of each individual sample item}$$

$$n = \text{sample size}$$

After calculating $\bar{x}$ for each sample, the auditor plots them into a frequency distribution. As long as the sample size is sufficient, the frequency distribution of the sample means will appear much like that shown in Figure 17-4.

A distribution of the sample means such as this is normal and has all the characteristics of the normal curve: (1) The curve is symmetrical, and (2) the sample means fall within known portions of the sampling distribution around the average or mean of those means, measured by the distance along the horizontal axis in terms of standard deviations. Furthermore, the mean of the sample means (the midpoint of the sampling distribution) is equal to the population mean, and the standard deviation of the sampling distribution is equal to $SD/\sqrt{n}$, where SD is the population standard deviation and n is the sample size.

To illustrate, assume a population with a mean of $40 and a standard deviation of $15 ($\overline{X} = \$40$ and $SD = \$15$), from which we elected to take many random samples of 100 items each. The standard deviation of our sampling distribution would be $1.50 ($SD/\sqrt{n} = 15/\sqrt{100} = 1.50$). The reference to "standard deviation" of the population and to "standard deviation" of the sampling distribution is often confusing. To avoid confusion, the standard deviation of the distribution of the sample means is often called the standard error of the mean (SE). With this information, the tabulation of the sampling distribution can be made, as shown in Table 17-10.

To summarize, three things are important about the results of the experiment of taking a large number of samples from a known population:

TABLE 17-10	Calculated Sampling Distribution from a Population with a Known Mean and Standard Deviation		
(1) Number of Standard Errors of the Mean (Confidence Coefficient)	(2) Value [(1) × $1.50]	(3) Range Around $\overline{X}$ [$40 ± (2)]	(4) Percent of Sample Means Included in Range
1	$1.50	$38.50 – $41.50	68.2
2	$3.00	$37.00 – $43.00	95.4
3	$4.50	$35.50 – $44.50	99.7
		(taken from table for normal curve)	

1. The mean value of all the sample means is equal to the population mean $(\overline{X})$. A corollary is that the sample mean value $(\overline{x})$ with the highest frequency of occurrence is also equal to the population mean.
2. The shape of the frequency distribution of the sample means is that of a normal distribution (curve), as long as the sample size is sufficiently large, *regardless of the distribution of the population.* A graphic representation of this conclusion is shown in Figure 17-5.
3. The percentage of sample means between any two values of the sampling distribution is measurable. The percentage can be calculated by (1) determining the number of standard errors between any two values and (2) determining the percentage of sample means represented from a table for normal curves.

Naturally, when samples are taken from a population in an actual audit situation, the auditor does not know the population's characteristics and there is ordinarily only one sample taken from the population. But the *knowledge of sampling distributions* enables auditors to draw statistical conclusions, or **statistical inferences**, about the population. For example, assume that the auditor takes a sample from a population and calculates $\overline{x}$ as $46 and SE at $9 (the way to calculate SE is shown later). We can now calculate a confidence interval of the population mean using the logic gained from the study of sampling distributions. It is as follows:

$$\text{CI}_{\overline{x}} = \hat{\overline{X}} \pm Z \cdot \text{SE}$$

where:

$\text{CI}_{\overline{x}} = $ confidence interval for the population mean

$\hat{\overline{X}} = $ point estimate of the population mean

$Z = $ confidence coefficient $\begin{cases} 1 = 68.2\% \ \text{confidence level} \\ 2 = 95.4\% \ \text{confidence level} \\ 3 = 99.7\% \ \text{confidence level} \end{cases}$

$\text{SE} = $ standard error of the mean

$Z \cdot \text{SE} = $ precision interval

For the example:

$\text{CI}_{\overline{x}} = \$46 \pm 1(\$9) = \$46 \pm \$9$ at a 68.2% confidence level

$\text{CI}_{\overline{x}} = \$46 \pm 2(\$9) = \$46 \pm \$18$ at a 95.4% confidence level

$\text{CI}_{\overline{x}} = \$46 \pm 3(\$9) = \$46 \pm \$27$ at a 99.7% confidence level

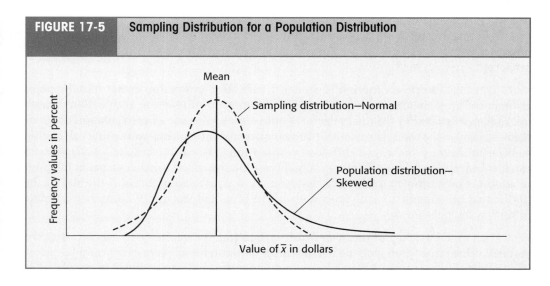

FIGURE 17-5   Sampling Distribution for a Population Distribution

The results can also be stated in terms of confidence limits ($CI_{\bar{x}}$). The upper confidence limit ($UCL_{\bar{x}}$) is $\hat{X} + Z \cdot SE$ ($\$46 + \$18 = \$64$ at a 95 percent confidence level) and a lower confidence limit ($LCL_{\bar{x}}$) is $\hat{X} - Z \cdot SE$ ($\$46 + \$18 = \$28$ at a 95 percent confidence level). Graphically, the results are as follows:

The conclusion that the auditor will draw from a confidence interval using statistical inference can be stated in different ways, but care must be taken to avoid incorrect conclusions. The auditor must remember that the true population value is always unknown. There is always a possibility that the sample is not sufficiently representative of the population to provide a sample mean and/or standard deviation reasonably close to those of the population. The auditor can say, however, that the procedure used to obtain the sample and compute the confidence interval will provide an interval that will contain the true population mean value a given percent of the time. In other words, the auditor knows the reliability of the statistical inference process that is used to draw conclusions.

Variables Methods

The statistical inference process just discussed is used for all the variables sampling methods. The main difference among the various methods is in the characteristic item and thus in the population being measured. The three variables methods are now discussed individually.

Difference Estimation **Difference estimation** is used to measure the estimated total misstatement amount in a population when there is both a recorded value and an audited value for each item in the sample. An example is to confirm a sample of accounts receivable and determine the difference (misstatement) between the client's recorded amount and the amount the auditor considers correct for each selected account. The auditor makes an estimate of the population misstatement based on the number of misstatements, average misstatement size, and individual misstatement size in the sample. The result is stated as a point estimate of the population misstatement plus or minus a computed precision interval at a stated confidence level. For example, in the earlier discussion of sampling distributions, assume the auditor was confirming a random sample of 100 from a population of 1,000 accounts receivable and concluded that the confidence limits of the mean of the misstatement for the population were between $28 and $64 at a 95 percent confidence level. The estimate of the total population misstatement can also be easily calculated as being between $28,000 and $64,000 at a 95 percent confidence level ($1,000 \times 28$ and $1,000 \times 64$). If the auditor's tolerable misstatement is $100,000, the population is clearly acceptable. If it is $40,000, the population is not acceptable. An extended illustration using difference estimation is shown later in the chapter.

Difference estimation frequently results in smaller sample sizes than any other method, and it is relatively easy to use. For that reason, difference estimation is often the preferred variables method.

Ratio Estimation **Ratio estimation** is similar to difference estimation except that the point estimate of the population misstatement is determined by multiplying the portion of sample dollars misstated by the total recorded population book value. The calculation of confidence limits of the total misstatement can be made for ratio estimation with a calculation similar to the one shown for difference estimation. The ratio estimate results in even smaller sample sizes than difference estimation if the size of the misstatements in the population is proportionate to the recorded value of the population items. If the size of the individual misstatements is independent of the recorded value, the difference estimate results in smaller sample sizes.

Mean-per-Unit Estimation In **mean-per-unit estimation,** the auditor is concerned with the audited value rather than with the misstatement amount of each item in the sample. Except for the definition of what is being measured, the mean-per-unit estimate is calculated in exactly the same manner as the difference estimate. The point estimate of the audited value is the average audited value of items in the sample times the population size. The computed precision interval is calculated on the basis of the audited value of the sample items rather than the misstatements. When the auditor has computed the upper and lower confidence limits, a decision is made about the acceptability of the population by comparing these amounts with the recorded book value.

Stratified Statistical Methods

As discussed earlier, stratified sampling is a method of sampling in which all the elements in the total population are divided into two or more subpopulations. Each subpopulation is then independently tested. When auditors use stratified statistical sampling, the results are measured statistically. The calculations are made for each stratum. They are combined into one overall population estimate in terms of a confidence interval. Stratification is applicable to difference, ratio, and mean-per-unit estimation, but it is most commonly used with mean-per-unit estimation.

It was shown earlier that stratifying a population is not unique to statistical sampling, of course. Auditors have traditionally emphasized certain types of items when they are testing a population. For example, in confirming accounts receivable, it has been customary to place more emphasis on large accounts than on small ones. The major difference is that in statistical stratified sampling, the approach is more objective and better defined than it is under nonstatistical stratification methods.

Sampling Risks

Acceptable risk of incorrect acceptance was discussed earlier for nonstatistical sampling. For variables sampling, acceptable risk of incorrect rejection (ARIR) is also used. The distinctions between and uses of the two risks must be understood.

ARIA After an audit test is performed and statistical results are calculated, the auditor must conclude either that the population is not materially misstated or that it is materially misstated. ARIA is the statistical risk that the auditor has accepted a population that is actually materially misstated. ARIA is a serious concern to auditors because there are potential legal implications in concluding that an account balance is fairly stated when it is misstated by a material amount.

An account balance can be either overstated or understated, but not both; therefore, ARIA is a one-tailed statistical test. The confidence coefficients for ARIA are therefore different from the confidence level. (Confidence level = $1 - 2 \times$ ARIA; for example, if ARIA is 10 percent, the confidence level is 80 percent.) The confidence coefficients for various ARIAs are shown in Table 17-11 together with confidence coefficients for the confidence level and ARIR.

ARIR **Acceptable risk of incorrect rejection (ARIR)** is the statistical risk that the auditor has concluded that a population is materially misstated when it is not. The only time that

TABLE 17-11	Confidence Coefficient for Confidence Levels, ARIAs, and ARIRs		
Confidence Level (%)	ARIA (%)	ARIR (%)	Confidence Coefficient
99	.5	1	2.58
95	2.5	5	1.96
90	5	10	1.64
80	10	20	1.28
75	12.5	25	1.15
70	15	30	1.04
60	20	40	.84
50	25	50	.67
40	30	60	.52
30	35	70	.39
20	40	80	.25
10	45	90	.13
0	50	100	.0

TABLE 17-12	ARIA and ARIR	

	Actual State of the Population	
Actual Audit Decision	**Materially Misstated**	**Not Materially Misstated**
Conclude that the population is materially misstated	Correct conclusion— no risk	Incorrect conclusion— risk is ARIR
Conclude that the population is not materially misstated	Incorrect conclusion— risk is ARIA	Correct conclusion— no risk

ARIR affects the auditor's actions is when an auditor concludes that a population is not fairly stated. The most likely action when the auditor finds a balance not fairly stated is to increase the sample size or perform other tests. An increased sample size will usually lead the auditor to conclude that the balance was fairly stated if the account is not materially misstated. ARIR is important only when there is a high cost to increasing the sample size or performing other tests. ARIA is always important. Confidence coefficients for ARIR are also shown in Table 17-11.

ARIA and ARIR are summarized in Table 17-12. It may seem from Table 17-12 that the auditor should attempt to minimize ARIA and ARIR. The way to accomplish that is by increasing the sample size, thus minimizing the risks. Because that is costly, having reasonable ARIA and ARIR is a more desirable goal.

ILLUSTRATION USING DIFFERENCE ESTIMATION

OBJECTIVE 17-5

Use difference estimation in tests of details of balances.

As previously discussed, several different types of variables sampling techniques may be applicable to auditing in different circumstances. One of these, difference estimation using hypothesis testing, has been selected as a means of illustrating the concepts and methodology of variables sampling. The reason for using difference estimation is its relative simplicity. When the method is considered reliable in a given set of circumstances, it is preferred to other variables sampling methods by most auditors.

In explaining difference estimation, the 14 steps in determining whether the account balance in the audit of accounts receivable is correctly stated are illustrated. These steps correspond to the ones used for nonstatistical sampling. Positive confirmations in the audit of Hart Lumber Company are used as a frame of reference to illustrate the use of difference estimation. There are 4,000 accounts receivable listed on the aged trial balance with a recorded value of $600,000. Internal controls are considered somewhat weak, and a large number of small misstatements in recorded amounts are expected in the audit. Total assets are $2,500,000, and net earnings before taxes are $400,000. Acceptable audit risk is reasonably high because of the limited users of the statements and the good financial health of Hart Lumber. Analytical procedures results indicated no significant problems. The assumptions throughout are either that all confirmations were returned or that effective alternative procedures were carried out. Hence, the sample size is the number of positive confirmations mailed.

Plan the Sample and Calculate the Sample Size Using Difference Estimation

State the Objectives of the Audit Test The objective of the audit test in the Hart Lumber Company example is to determine whether accounts receivable before consideration of the allowance for uncollectible accounts is materially misstated.

Decide Whether Audit Sampling Applies Audit sampling applies in the confirmation of the accounts receivable because of the large number of accounts receivable.

Define Misstatement Conditions The misstatement condition is a client error determined in the confirmation of each account or alternative procedure.

Define the Population The population size is determined by count, as it was for attributes sampling. An accurate count is much more important in variables sampling because sample size and the computed precision limits are directly affected by population size. The population size for Hart Lumber's accounts receivable is 4,000.

Define the Sampling Unit The sampling unit is an account on the list of accounts receivable.

Specify Tolerable Misstatement The amount of misstatement the auditor is willing to accept is a materiality question. The auditor decides to accept a tolerable misstatement of $21,000 in the audit of Hart Lumber's accounts receivable.

Specify Acceptable Risk The auditor specifies two risks:

1. *Acceptable risk of incorrect acceptance (ARIA).* It is the risk of accepting accounts receivable as correct if it is actually misstated by more than $21,000. ARIA is affected by acceptable audit risk, results of tests of controls and substantive tests of transactions, analytical procedures, and the relative significance of accounts receivable in the financial statements. In Hart Lumber, an ARIA of 10 percent is used.
2. *Acceptable risk of incorrect rejection (ARIR).* It is the risk of rejecting accounts receivable as incorrect if it is not actually misstated by a material amount. ARIR is affected by the additional cost of resampling. Because it is fairly costly to confirm receivables a second time, an ARIR of 25 percent is used. For audit tests for which it is not costly to increase the sample size, a much higher ARIR is common.

After the auditor specifies the tolerable misstatement and ARIA, the hypothesis can be stated. The auditor's hypothesis for the audit of accounts receivable for Hart Lumber is: Accounts receivable is not misstated by more than $21,000 at an ARIA of 10 percent.

Estimate Misstatements in the Population There are two parts of this estimate:

1. *Estimate an expected point estimate.* An advance estimate of the population point estimate is needed for difference estimation, much as the estimated population exception rate is needed for attributes sampling. The advance estimate is $1,500 (overstatement) for Hart Lumber, based on the previous year's audit tests.
2. *Make an advance population standard deviation estimate—variability of the population.* An advance estimate of the variation in the misstatements in the population as measured by the population standard deviation is needed to determine the initial sample size. The calculation of the standard deviation is shown later. For Hart Lumber, it is estimated to be $20 based on the previous year's audit tests.

Calculate the Initial Sample Size The initial sample size for Hart Lumber can be now calculated from the following formula:

$$n = \left[\frac{SD^*\left(Z_A + Z_R\right)N}{TM - E^*} \right]^2$$

where:

$$n = \text{initial sample size}$$

$$SD^* = \text{advance estimate of the standard deviation}$$

$$Z_A = \text{confidence coefficient for ARIA (see Table 17-11)}$$

$$Z_R = \text{confidence coefficient for ARIR (see Table 17-11)}$$

$$N = \text{population size}$$

$$TM = \text{tolerable misstatement for the population (materiality)}$$

$$E^* = \text{estimated point estimate of the population misstatement}$$

Applied to Hart Lumber, this equation yields

$$n = \left[\frac{20(1.28 + 1.15)4,000}{21,000 - 1,500} \right]^2 = (9.97)^2 = 100$$

TABLE 17-13	Calculation of Confidence Limits	

Step	Statistical Formula	Illustration for Hart Lumber
1. Take a random sample of size n.	n = sample size	100 accounts receivable are selected randomly from the aged trial balance containing 4,000 accounts.
2. Determine the value of each misstatement in the sample.		75 accounts are confirmed by customers, and 25 accounts are verified by alternative procedures. After reconciling timing differences and customer errors, the following 12 items were determined to be client errors (understatements) stated in dollars: 1. $12.75 7. (.87) 2. (69.46) 8. 24.32 3. 85.28 9. 36.59 4. 100.00 10. (102.16) 5. (27.30) 11. 54.71 6. 41.06 12. 71.56 Sum = $226.48
3. Compute the point estimate of the total misstatement.	$$\bar{e} = \frac{\sum e_j}{n}$$ $$\hat{E} = N\bar{e} \text{ or } N\frac{\sum e_j}{n}$$ where: $\bar{e}$ = average misstatement in the sample $\sum$ = summation e_j = an individual misstatement in the sample n = sample size $\hat{E}$ = point estimate of the total misstatement N = population size	$$\bar{e} = \frac{\$226.48}{100} = \$2.26$$ $$\hat{E} = 4{,}000\ (\$2.26) = \$9{,}040$$ or $$\hat{E} = 4{,}000 \left(\frac{\$226.48}{100} \right) = \$9{,}040$$
4. Compute the population standard deviation of the misstatements from the sample.	$$SD = \sqrt{\frac{\sum(e_j)^2 - n(\bar{e})^2}{n-1}}$$ where: SD = standard deviation e_j = an individual misstatement in the sample n = sample size $\bar{e}$ = average misstatement in sample	(rounded to nearest dollar) |	e_j	$(e_j)^2$
1.	$ 13	$ 169
2.	(69)	4,761
3.	85	7,225
4.	100	10,000
5.	(27)	729
6.	41	1,681
7.	(1)	1
8.	24	576
9.	37	1,369
10.	(102)	10,404
11.	55	3,025
12.	72	5,184
	$228	$45,124 | $$SD = \sqrt{\frac{\$45{,}124 - 100\ (\$2.26)^2}{99}}$$ $$SD = \$21.2$$

(cont. on p. 547)

TABLE 17-13	(Cont.)	

Step	Statistical Formula	Illustration for Hart Lumber
5. Compute the precision interval for the estimate of the total population misstatement at the desired confidence level.	$$CPI = NZ_A \frac{SD}{\sqrt{n}} \sqrt{\frac{N-n}{N}}$$ where: CPI = computed precision interval N = population size Z_A = confidence coefficient for ARIA $\left(\text{see Table 17-11}\right)$ SD = population standard deviation n = sample size $$\sqrt{\frac{N-n}{N}} = \text{finite correction factor}$$	$$CPI = 4{,}000 \cdot 1.28 \cdot \frac{\$21.2}{\sqrt{100}} \sqrt{\frac{4{,}000-100}{4{,}000}}$$ $$= 4{,}000 \cdot 1.28 \cdot \frac{\$21.2}{10} \cdot .99$$ $$= 4{,}000 \cdot 1.28 \cdot \$2.12 \cdot .99$$ $$= \$10{,}800 \,(\text{rounded})$$
6. Compute the confidence limits at the CL desired.	$UCL = \hat{E} + CPI$ $LCL = \hat{E} - CPI$ where: UCL = computed upper confidence limit LCL = computed lower confidence limit $\hat{E}$ = point estimate of the total misstatement CPI = computed precision interval at desired CL	$UCL = \$9{,}040 + \$10{,}800 = \$19{,}840$ $LCL = \$9{,}040 - \$10{,}800 = \$(1{,}760)$

Select the Sample Because a random sample (other than PPS) is required, the auditor must use one of the probabilistic sample selection methods discussed in Chapter 15 to select the 100 sample items for confirmation.

Perform the Audit Procedures The auditor must use care in confirming the accounts receivable and performing alternative procedures using the methods discussed in Chapter 16. For confirmations, a misstatement is the *difference* between the confirmation response and the client's balance after the reconciliation of all timing differences and customer errors. For example, if a customer returns a confirmation and states the correct balance is $887.12, and the balance in the client's records is $997.12, the difference of $110 is an overstatement amount if the auditor concludes that the client's records are incorrect. For nonresponses, the misstatements discovered by alternative procedures are treated identically to those discovered through confirmation. At the end of this step, there is a misstatement value for each item in the sample, many of which are likely to be zero. The misstatements for Hart Lumber are shown in Table 17-13.

Generalize from the Sample to the Population In concept, nonstatistical and difference estimation do the same thing in generalizing from the sample to the population. Both methods are measuring the likely population misstatement based on the results of the sample. Difference estimation uses statistical measurement to compute confidence limits. The following four steps describe the calculation of the confidence limits for Hart Lumber Company. Steps 3 through 6 in Table 17-13 illustrate the calculations.

1. Compute the point estimate of the total misstatement. The point estimate is a direct extrapolation from the misstatements in the sample to the misstatements in the population [termed projected misstatement in SAS 39 (AU 350)]. The calculation of the point estimate for Hart Lumber is shown in Table 17-13, step 3.

Select the Sample and Perform the Procedures

Evaluate the Results

It is unlikely, of course, for the actual, but unknown, misstatement to be *exactly* the same as the point estimate. It is more realistic to estimate the misstatement in terms of a confidence interval determined by the point estimate plus and minus a computed precision interval. It should be apparent at this point that the calculation of the confidence interval is an essential part of variables sampling and that the process used to develop it depends on obtaining a representative sample.

2. Compute an estimate of the population standard deviation. The population standard deviation is a statistical measure of the variability in the values of the individual items in the population. If there is a large amount of variation in the values of population items, the standard deviation is larger than when the variation is small. For example, in the confirmation of accounts receivable, misstatements of $4, $14, and $26 have far less variation than the set $2, $275, and $812. Hence, the standard deviation is smaller in the first set.

The standard deviation has a significant effect on the computed precision interval. As might be expected, the ability to predict the value of a population is better when there is a small rather than a large amount of variation in the individual values of the population.

A reasonable estimate of the value of the population standard deviation is computed by the auditor using the standard statistical formula shown in Table 17-13, step 4. The size of the standard deviation estimate is determined solely by the characteristics of the auditor's sample results and is not affected by professional judgment.

3. Compute the precision interval. The precision interval is calculated by a statistical formula. The results are a dollar measure of the inability to predict the true population misstatement because the test was based on a sample rather than on the entire population. For the computed precision interval to have any meaning, it must be associated with ARIA. The formula to calculate the precision interval is shown in Table 17-13, step 5.

An examination of the formula in step 5 of Table 17-13 indicates that the effect of changing each factor while the other factors remain constant is as follows:

Type of Change	Effect on the Computed Precision Interval
Increase ARIA	Decrease
Increase the point estimate of the misstatements	Increase
Increase the standard deviation	Increase
Increase the sample size	Decrease

4. Compute the confidence limits. The confidence limits, which define the confidence interval, are calculated by combining the point estimate of the total misstatements and the computed precision interval at the desired confidence level (point estimate ± computed precision interval). The formula to calculate the confidence limits is shown in Table 17-13, step 6.

The lower and upper confidence limits for Hart Lumber are ($1,760) and $19,840, respectively. There is a 10 percent statistical risk that the population is understated by more than $1,760, and the same risk that it is overstated by more than $19,840. This is because an ARIA of 10 percent is equivalent to a confidence level of 80 percent.

Analyze the Misstatements There are no differences in analyzing misstatements for nonstatistical and statistical methods. The auditor must evaluate misstatements to determine the cause of each misstatement and decide whether modification of the audit risk model is needed.

Decide the Acceptability of the Population When a statistical method is used, a decision rule is needed to decide whether the population is acceptable. The decision rule is as follows: If the two-sided confidence interval for the misstatements is completely within the plus and minus tolerable misstatements, accept the hypothesis that the book value is not misstated by a material amount. Otherwise, accept the hypothesis that the book value is misstated by a material amount.

This decision rule is illustrated in Figure 17-6. The auditor should conclude that both the LCL and UCL for situations 1 and 2 fall completely within both the understatement and overstatement tolerable misstatement limits. Therefore, the conclusion that the population is not misstated by a material amount is accepted. For situations 3, 4, and 5, either LCL or UCL, or both, are outside tolerable misstatements. Therefore, the population book value is rejected.

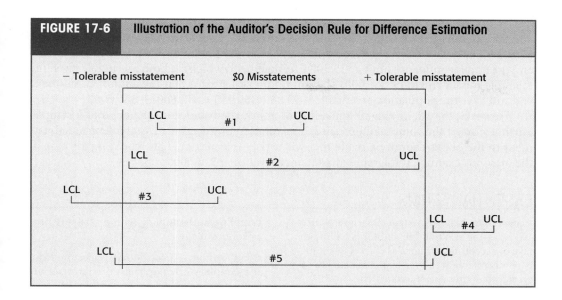

FIGURE 17-6 Illustration of the Auditor's Decision Rule for Difference Estimation

Application of the decision rule to Hart Lumber leads the auditor to the conclusion that the population should be accepted, because both confidence limits are within the tolerable misstatement range:

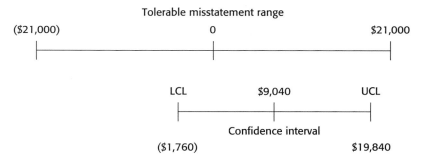

In accepting the population in this way, the auditor is taking a 10 percent chance of being wrong—that is, that the population is in fact misstated by a material amount. However, based on the auditor's planning judgments, this level of risk is appropriate.

Analysis Given that the actual standard deviation (21.2) was larger than the advanced estimate (20), and the actual point estimate ($9,040) was larger than the advanced estimate ($1,500), it may seem surprising that the population was accepted. The reason is that the use of a reasonably small ARIR caused the sample size to be larger than if ARIR had been 100 percent. If ARIR had been 100 percent, which is common when the additional audit cost to increase the sample size is small, the required sample size would have been only 28:

$$\left[\frac{20\,(1.28 + 0)\,4,000}{21,000 - 1,500} \right]^2 = 28$$

Assuming a sample size of 28 and the same actual point estimate and standard deviation, the upper confidence limit would have been $29,559, and therefore, the population book value would have been rejected. One reason that auditors use ARIR is to reduce the likelihood of needing to increase the sample size if the standard deviation or point estimate is larger than was expected.

Action When a Hypothesis Is Rejected

When one or both of the confidence limits lie outside the tolerable misstatement range, the population is not considered acceptable. The courses of action are the same as those discussed for nonstatistical sampling, except that a better estimate of the population misstatement is practical.

For example, in the Hart Lumber case, if the confidence level had been $9,040 ± $15,800 and the client had been willing to reduce the book value by $9,040, the results would be 0 ± $15,800. The new computed lower confidence limit would be an understatement of $15,800, and the upper confidence limit a $15,800 overstatement, which are both acceptable given the tolerable misstatement of $21,000. The minimum adjustment that the auditor could make and still have the population acceptable is $3,840 [($9,040 + $15,800) − $21,000].

However, the client may be unwilling to adjust the balance on the basis of a sample. Furthermore, if the computed precision interval exceeds tolerable misstatement, an adjustment to the books cannot be made that will satisfy the auditor. This would be the case in the previous example if tolerable misstatement was only $15,000.

ESSENTIAL TERMS

Acceptable risk of incorrect acceptance (ARIA)—the risk that the auditor is willing to take of accepting a balance as correct when the true misstatement in the balance is equal to or greater than tolerable misstatement

Acceptable risk of incorrect rejection (ARIR)—the risk that the auditor is willing to take of rejecting a balance as incorrect when it is not misstated by a material amount

Difference estimation—a method of variables sampling in which the auditor estimates the population misstatement by multiplying the average misstatement in the sample by the total number of population items and also calculates sampling risk

Mean-per-unit estimation—a method of variables sampling in which the auditor estimates the audited value of a population by multiplying the average audited value of the sample by the population size and also calculates sampling risk

Misstatement bounds—an estimate of the largest likely overstatements and understatements in a population at a given ARIA, using monetary unit sampling

Monetary unit sampling (MUS)—a statistical sampling method that provides upper and lower misstatement bounds expressed in monetary amounts; also referred to as dollar unit sampling, cumulative monetary amount

sampling, and sampling with probability proportional to size

Point estimate—a method of projecting from the sample to the population to estimate the population misstatement, commonly by assuming that misstatements in the unaudited population are proportional to the misstatements found in the sample

Probability proportional to size sample selection (PPS)—sample selection of individual dollars in a population by the use of random or systematic sample selection

Ratio estimation—a method of variables sampling in which the auditor estimates the population misstatement by multiplying the portion of sample dollars misstated by the total recorded population book value and also calculates sampling risk

Statistical inferences—statistical conclusions that the auditor draws from sample results based on knowledge of sampling distributions

Stratified sampling—a method of sampling in which all the elements in the total population are divided into two or more subpopulations that are independently tested and statistically measured

Variables sampling—sampling techniques for tests of details of balances that use the statistical inference process

REVIEW QUESTIONS

17-1 (Objective 17-1) What major difference between (a) tests of controls and substantive tests of transactions and (b) tests of details of balances makes attributes sampling inappropriate for tests of details of balances?

17-2 (Objective 17-2) Define stratified sampling and explain its importance in auditing. How could an auditor obtain a stratified sample of 30 items from each of three strata in the confirmation of accounts receivable?

17-3 (Objective 17-2) Distinguish between the point estimate of the total misstatements and the true value of the misstatements in the population. How can each be determined?

17-4 (Objective 17-2) Evaluate the following statement made by an auditor: "On every aspect of the audit where it is possible, I calculate the point estimate of the misstatements and evaluate whether the amount is material. If it is, I investigate the cause and continue to test the population until I determine whether there is a serious problem. The use of statistical sampling in this manner is a valuable audit tool."

17-5 (Objective 17-3) Define monetary unit sampling and explain its importance in auditing. How does it combine the features of attributes and variables sampling?

17-6 (Objectives 17-1, 17-2, 17-3, 17-4) Define what is meant by sampling risk. Does sampling risk apply to nonstatistical sampling, MUS, attributes sampling, and variables sampling? Explain.

17-7 (Objectives 17-1, 17-2) What are the major differences in the 14 steps used to do nonstatistical sampling for tests of details of balances versus for tests of controls and substantive tests of transactions?

17-8 (Objective 17-3) The 2,620 inventory items described in Question 17-14 are listed on 44 inventory pages with 60 lines per page. There is a total for each page. The client's data are not in machine-readable form. Describe how a monetary unit sample can be selected in this situation.

17-9 (Objective 17-3) Explain how the auditor determines tolerable misstatement for MUS.

17-10 (Objective 17-2) Explain what is meant by acceptable risk of incorrect acceptance. What are the major audit factors affecting ARIA?

17-11 (Objective 17-4) Evaluate the following statement made by an auditor: "I took a random sample and derived a 90 percent confidence interval of $800,000 to $900,000. That means that the true population value will be between $800,000 and $900,000, 90 percent of the time."

17-12 (Objective 17-2) What is the relationship between ARIA and ARACR?

17-13 (Objective 17-3) What is meant by the "percent of misstatement assumption" for MUS in those population items that are misstated? Why is it common to use a 100% misstatement assumption when it is almost certain to be highly conservative?

17-14 (Objective 17-3) An auditor is determining the appropriate sample size for testing inventory valuation using MUS. The population has 2,620 inventory items valued at $12,625,000. The tolerable misstatement for both understatements and overstatements is $500,000 at a 10% ARIA. No misstatements are expected in the population. Calculate the preliminary sample size using a 100% average misstatement assumption.

17-15 (Objective 17-5) Assume that a sample of 100 units was obtained in sampling the inventory in Question 17-14. Assume further that the following three misstatements were found:

Misstatement	Recorded Value	Audited Value
1	$ 897.16	$ 609.16
2	47.02	0
3	1,621.68	1,522.68

Calculate adjusted misstatement bounds for the population. Draw audit conclusions based on the results.

17-16 (Objective 17-3) Why is it difficult to determine the appropriate sample size for MUS? How should the auditor determine the proper sample size?

17-17 (Objective 17-5) What is meant by a decision rule using difference estimation? State the decision rule.

17-18 (Objective 17-2) What alternative courses of action are appropriate when a population is rejected using nonstatistical sampling for tests of details of balances? When should each option be followed?

17-19 (Objective 17-4) Define what is meant by the population standard deviation and explain its importance in variables sampling. What is the relationship between the population standard deviation and the required sample size?

17-20 (Objective 17-5) In using difference estimation, an auditor took a random sample of 100 inventory items from a large population to test for proper pricing. Several of the inventory items were misstated, but the combined net amount of the sample misstatement was not material. In addition, a review of the individual misstatements indicated that no misstatement was by itself material. As a result, the auditor did not investigate the misstatements or make a statistical evaluation. Explain why this practice is improper.

17-21 (Objectives 17-3, 17-4) Distinguish among difference estimation, ratio estimation, mean-per-unit estimation, and stratified mean-per-unit estimation. Give one example in which each could be used. When would MUS be preferable to any of these?

17-22 (Objective 17-4) An essential step in difference estimation is the comparison of each computed confidence limit with tolerable misstatement. Why is this step so important, and what should the auditor do if one of the confidence limits is larger than the tolerable misstatement?

17-23 (Objective 17-4) Explain why difference estimation is commonly used by auditors.

17-24 (Objectives 17-3, 17-4) Give an example of the use of attributes sampling, MUS, and variables sampling in the form of an audit conclusion.

MULTIPLE CHOICE QUESTIONS FROM CPA EXAMINATIONS

17-25 (Objective 17-2) The following questions refer to the use of stratified sampling in auditing. For each one, select the best response.

a. Mr. Murray decides to use stratified sampling. The reason for using stratified sampling rather than unrestricted random sampling is to
   (1) reduce as much as possible the degree of variability in the overall population.
   (2) give every element in the population an equal chance of being included in the sample.
   (3) allow the person selecting the sample to use personal judgment in deciding which elements should be included in the sample.
   (4) allow the auditor to emphasize larger items from the population.

b. In an audit of financial statements, a CPA will generally find stratified sampling techniques to be most applicable to
   (1) recomputing net wage and salary payments to employees.
   (2) tracing hours worked from the payroll summary back to the individual time cards.
   (3) confirming accounts receivable for residential customers at a large electric utility.
   (4) reviewing supporting documentation for additions to plant and equipment.

c. From prior experience, a CPA is aware that the accounts receivable trial balance contains a few unusually large balances. In using statistical sampling, the CPA's best course of action is to
   (1) eliminate any unusually large balances that appear in the sample.
   (2) continue to draw new samples until no unusually large balances appear in the sample.
   (3) stratify the accounts receivable population so that the unusually large balances are reviewed separately.
   (4) increase the sample size to lessen the effect of the unusually large balances.

17-26 (Objectives 17-1, 17-2) The following apply to audit sampling. For each one, select the best response.

a. The auditor's failure to recognize a misstatement in an amount or a control deviation is described as a
   (1) statistical error.
   (2) sampling error.
   (3) standard error of the mean.
   (4) nonsampling error.

b. An auditor uses audit sampling to perform tests of controls in the acquisition and payment cycle. Those tests indicate that the related controls are operating effectively. The auditor plans to use audit sampling to perform tests of details of balances for accounts payable. The auditor's acceptable risk of incorrect acceptance (ARIA) for the tests of details of balances for accounts payable would most likely be
   (1) the same as the ARACR for tests of controls.
   (2) greater than the ARACR for tests of controls.
   (3) less than the ARACR for tests of controls.
   (4) totally independent from the ARACR used for tests of controls.

c. Which of the following sample planning factors would influence the sample size for a test of details of balances for a specific account?

	Expected Amount of Misstatements	Measure of Tolerable Misstatement
(1)	No	No
(2)	Yes	Yes
(3)	No	Yes
(4)	Yes	No

DISCUSSION QUESTIONS AND PROBLEMS

17-27 (Objective 17-2) You are planning to use nonstatistical sampling to evaluate the results of accounts receivable confirmation for the Meridian Company. You have already performed tests of controls for sales, sales returns and allowances, and cash receipts, and they are considered excellent. Because of the quality of the controls, you decide to use an acceptable risk of incorrect acceptance of 10%. There are 3,000 accounts receivable with a gross value of $6,900,000. The accounts are similar in size and will be treated as a single stratum. An overstatement or understatement of more than $150,000 would be considered material.

Required

a. Calculate the required sample size. Assume your firm uses the following nonstatistical formula to determine sample size:

Sample size = (Book value of population / Tolerable misstatement) × Assurance factor

Assurance factor:
> 5% ARIA = 3
> 10% ARIA = 2
> 20% ARIA = 1

b. Assume that instead of good results, poor results were obtained for tests of controls and substantive tests of transactions for sales, sales returns and allowances, and cash receipts. How would this affect your required sample size? How would you use this information in your sample size determination?

c. Regardless of your answer to part a, assume you decide to select a sample of 100 accounts for testing. Indicate how you would select the accounts for testing using systematic selection.

d. Assume a total book value of $230,000 for the 100 accounts selected for testing. You uncover three overstatements totaling $1,500 in the sample. Evaluate whether the population is fairly stated.

17-28 (Objective 17-3) The accounts receivable population for Jake's Bookbinding Company follows. This table is the same as Table 17-1 on page 522, except that cumulative amounts are included to assist you in completing the problem. The population is smaller than would ordinarily be the case for statistical sampling, but an entire population is useful to show how to select PPS samples.

Required

a. Select a random PPS sample of 10 items, using computer software.

b. Select a sample of 10 items using systematic PPS sampling using the same concepts discussed in Chapter 15 for systematic sampling. Use a starting point of 1857. Identify the physical units associated with the sample dollars. (*Hint:* The interval is 207,295 ÷ 10.)

c. Which sample items will always be included in the systematic PPS sample regardless of the starting point? Will that also be true of random PPS sampling?

d. Which method is preferable in terms of ease of selection in this case?

e. Why would an auditor use MUS?

Population Item	Recorded Amount	Cumulative Amount	Population Item (cont.)	Recorded Amount (cont.)	Cumulative Amount (cont.)
1	$ 1,410	$ 1,410	21	$ 4,865	$117,385
2	9,130	10,540	22	770	118,155
3	660	11,200	23	2,305	120,460
4	3,355	14,555	24	2,665	123,125
5	5,725	20,280	25	1,000	124,125
6	8,210	28,490	26	6,225	130,350
7	580	29,070	27	3,675	134,025
8	44,110	73,180	28	6,250	140,275
9	825	74,005	29	1,890	142,165
10	1,155	75,160	30	27,705	169,870
11	2,270	77,430	31	935	170,805
12	50	77,480	32	5,595	176,400
13	5,785	83,265	33	930	177,330
14	940	84,205	34	4,045	181,375
15	1,820	86,025	35	9,480	190,855
16	3,380	89,405	36	360	191,215
17	530	89,935	37	1,145	192,360
18	955	90,890	38	6,400	198,760
19	4,490	95,380	39	100	198,860
20	17,140	112,520	40	8,435	207,295

17-29 (Objective 17-3) In the audit of Price Seed Company for the year ended September 30, the auditor set a tolerable misstatement of $50,000 at an ARIA of 10%. A PPS sample of 100 was selected from an accounts receivable population that had a recorded balance of $1,975,000. The following table shows the differences uncovered in the confirmation process:

Accounts Receivable per Records	Accounts Receivable per Confirmation	Follow-up Comments by Auditor
1. $2,728.00	$2,498.00	Pricing error on two invoices.
2. $5,125.00	-0-	Customer mailed check 9/26; company received check 10/3.
3. $3,890.00	$1,190.00	Merchandise returned 9/30 and counted in inventory; credit was issued 10/6.
4. $ 791.00	$ 815.00	Footing error on an invoice.
5. $ 548.00	$1,037.00	Goods were shipped 9/28; sale was recorded on 10/6.
6. $3,115.00	$3,190.00	Pricing error on a credit memorandum.
7. $1,540.00	-0-	Goods were shipped on 9/29; customer received goods 10/3; sale was recorded on 9/30.

Required

a. Calculate the upper and lower misstatement bounds on the basis of the client misstatements in the sample.

b. Is the population acceptable as stated? If not, what options are available to the auditor at this point? Which option should the auditor select? Explain.

17-30 (Objective 17-3) You intend to use MUS as a part of the audit of several accounts for Roynpower Manufacturing Company. You have done the audit for the past several years, and there has rarely been an adjusting entry of any kind. Your audit tests of all tests of controls and substantive tests of transactions cycles were completed at an interim date, and control risk has been assessed as low. You therefore decide to use an ARIA of 10% and an EPER of 0% for all tests of details of balances. You also decide to use a 100% misstatement assumption for both overstatements and understatements.

You intend to use MUS in the audit of the three most material asset balance sheet account balances: accounts receivable, inventory, and marketable securities. You feel justified in using the same ARIA for each audit area because of the low assessed control risk.

The recorded balances and related information for the three accounts are as follows:

	Recorded Value
Accounts receivable	$ 3,600,000
Inventory	4,800,000
Marketable securities	1,600,000
	$10,000,000

Net earnings before taxes for Roynpower are $2,000,000. You decide that a combined misstatement of $100,000 is allowable for the client.

The audit approach to be followed will be to determine the total sample size needed for all three accounts. A sample will be selected from all $10 million, and the appropriate testing for a sample item will depend on whether the item is a receivable, inventory, or marketable security. The audit conclusions will pertain to the entire $10 million, and no conclusion will be made about the three individual accounts unless significant misstatements are found in the sample.

Required

a. Evaluate the audit approach of testing all three account balances in one sample.

b. Calculate the required sample size for all three accounts.

c. Calculate the required sample size for each of the three accounts, assuming you decide that the tolerable misstatement in each account is $100,000. (Recall that tolerable misstatement equals preliminary judgment about materiality for MUS.)

d. Assume that you select the random sample using computer software. How would you identify which sample item in the population to audit for the number 4,627,871? What audit procedures would be performed?

e. Assume that you select a sample of 200 sample items for testing and you find one misstatement in inventory. The recorded value is $987.12 and the audit value is $887.12. Calculate the misstatement bounds for the three combined accounts and reach appropriate audit conclusions.

17-31 (Objectives 17-2, 17-3, 17-4, 17-5) An audit partner is developing an office training program to familiarize her professional staff with audit sampling decision models applicable to the audit of dollar-value balances. She wishes to demonstrate the relationship of sample sizes to population size and estimated population exception rate and the auditor's specifications as to tolerable misstatement and ARIA. The partner prepared the following table to show comparative population characteristics and audit specifications of the two populations:

	Characteristics of Population 1 Relative to Population 2		Audit Specifications as to a Sample from Population 1 Relative to a Sample from Population 2	
	Size	Estimated Population Exception Rate	Tolerable Misstatement	ARIA
Case 1	Equal	Equal	Equal	Lower
Case 2	Smaller	Smaller	Equal	Higher
Case 3	Larger	Equal	Equal	Lower
Case 4	Equal	Larger	Larger	Equal
Case 5	Larger	Equal	Smaller	Higher

Required

In items (1) through (5) you are to indicate for the specific case from the table the required sample size to be selected from population 1 relative to the sample from population 2.
  (1) In case 1, the required sample size from population 1 is _____.
  (2) In case 2, the required sample size from population 1 is _____.
  (3) In case 3, the required sample size from population 1 is _____.
  (4) In case 4, the required sample size from population 1 is _____.
  (5) In case 5, the required sample size from population 1 is _____.

Your answer choice should be selected from the following responses:

  a. Larger than the required sample size from population 2.

  b. Equal to the required sample size from population 2.

  c. Smaller than the required sample size from population 2.

  d. Indeterminate relative to the required sample size from population 2.*

17-32 (Objective 17-5) In auditing the valuation of inventory, the auditor, Claire Butler, decided to use difference estimation. She decided to select an unrestricted random sample of 80 inventory items from a population of 1,840 that had a book value of $175,820. Butler decided in advance that she was willing to accept a maximum misstatement in the population of $6,000 at an ARIA of 5 percent. There were eight misstatements in the sample, which were as follows:

Audit Value	Book Value	Sample Misstatements
$ 812.50	$ 740.50	$(72.00)
12.50	78.20	65.70
10.00	51.10	41.10
25.40	61.50	36.10
600.10	651.90	51.80
.12	0	(.12)
51.06	81.06	30.00
83.11	104.22	21.11
Total $1,594.79	$1,768.48	$173.69

Required

a. Calculate the point estimate, the computed precision interval, the confidence interval, and the confidence limits for the population. Label each calculation. Use a computer for this purpose (instructor's option).

*AICPA adapted.

b. Should Butler accept the book value of the population? Explain.

c. What options are available to her at this point?

17-33 (Objective 17-5) Marjorie Jorgenson, CPA, is verifying the accuracy of outstanding accounts payable for Marygold Hardware, a large, single-location retail hardware store. There are 650 vendors listed on the outstanding accounts payable list. She has eliminated from the population 40 vendors that have large ending balances and will audit them separately. There are now 610 vendors.

She plans to do one of three tests for each item in the sample: examine a vendor's statement in the client's hands, obtain a confirmation when no statement is on hand, or extensively search for invoices when neither of the first two is obtained. There is no accounts payable master file available, and a large number of misstatements are expected. Marjorie has obtained facts or made audit judgments as follows:

ARIR	20%	ARIA	10%
Tolerable misstatement	$ 45,000	Expected misstatement	$20,000
Recorded book value	$600,000	Estimated standard deviation	$ 280

Required

a. Under what circumstances is it desirable to use difference estimation in the situation described? Under what circumstances would it be undesirable?

b. Calculate the required sample size for the audit tests of accounts payable using difference estimation, assuming that ARIR is ignored.

c. Assume that the auditor selects exactly the sample size calculated in part b. The point estimate calculated from the sample results is $21,000 and the estimated population standard deviation is 267. Is the population fairly stated as defined by the decision rule? Explain what causes the result to be acceptable or unacceptable.

d. Calculate the required sample size for the audit tests of accounts payable, assuming that the ARIR is considered.

e. Explain the reason for the large increase of the sample size resulting from including ARIR in determining sample size.

f. Marjorie Jorgenson calculates the required sample size using the formula without consideration of ARIR. After the sample size is determined, she increases the sample size by 25%. Marjorie believes that this does the same thing as using ARIR without having to bother to make the calculation. Is this approach appropriate? Evaluate the desirability of the approach.

CASES

17-34 (Objective 17-3) You are doing the audit of Peckinpah Tire and Parts, a wholesale auto parts company. You have decided to use monetary unit sampling (MUS) for the audit of accounts receivable and inventory. The following are the recorded balances:

Accounts receivable	$12,000,000
Inventory	$23,000,000

You have already made the following judgments:

Materiality for planning purposes	$800,000
Acceptable audit risk	5%
Inherent risk:	
Accounts receivable	80%
Inventory	100%
Assessed control risk:	
Accounts receivable	50%
Inventory	80%

Analytical procedures have been planned for inventory, but not for accounts receivable. The analytical procedures for inventory are expected to have a 60% chance of detecting a material misstatement should one exist.

You have concluded that it would be difficult to alter sample size for accounts receivable confirmation once confirmations are sent and replies are received. However, inventory tests could be reopened without great difficulty.

After discussions with the client, you believe that the accounts are in about the same condition this year as they were last year. Last year no misstatements were found in the confirmation of accounts receivable. Inventory tests revealed an overstatement amount of about 1%.

For requirements a–c, make any assumptions necessary in deciding the factors affecting sample size. If no table is available for the ARIA chosen, estimate sample size judgmentally.

Required

a. Plan the sample size for the confirmation of accounts receivable using MUS.

b. Plan the sample size for the test of pricing of inventories using MUS.

c. Plan the combined sample size for both the confirmation of accounts receivable and the price tests of inventory using MUS.

d. (Instructor's option) Using an electronic spreadsheet, generate a list of random dollars in generation order and in ascending order for the sample of accounts receivable items determined in part a.

17-35 (Objectives 17-2, 17-3) You have just completed the accounts receivable confirmation process in the audit of Danforth Paper Company, a paper supplier to retail shops and commercial users. Following are the data related to this process:

Accounts receivable recorded balance	$2,760,000
Number of accounts	7,320
A nonstatistical sample was taken as follows:	
All accounts over $10,000 (23 accounts)	$ 465,000
77 accounts under $10,000	$ 81,500
Tolerable misstatement for the confirmation test	$ 100,000
Inherent and control risk are both high	
No relevant analytical procedures were performed	

The following are the results of the confirmation procedures:

	Recorded Value	Audited Value
Items over $10,000	$465,000	$432,000
Items under $10,000	81,500	77,150
Individual misstatements for items under		
$10,000:		
Item 12	5,120	4,820
Item 19	485	385
Item 33	1,250	250
Item 35	3,975	3,875
Item 51	1,850	1,825
Item 59	4,200	3,780
Item 74	2,405	0

Required

a. Evaluate the results of the nonstatistical sample. Consider both the direct implications of the misstatements found and the effect of using a sample.

b. Assume that the sample was a PPS sample. Evaluate the results using monetary unit sampling.

c. (Instructor's option) Do the above analyses using an electronic spreadsheet.

INTERNET PROBLEM 17-1: AUDIT SAMPLING STRATEGIES

Reference the CW site. The University of Illinois Internet Web site includes a link to the university's audit manual. In this problem, students read the audit sampling guidance contained in the manual to determine when statistical and nonstatistical samples may be used and to determine the most appropriate sampling plan for three different audit situations.

PART 4

APPLICATION OF THE AUDIT PROCESS TO OTHER CYCLES

The chapters in Part 4 apply auditing concepts first presented in Chapters 6 through 13 and then expanded in Chapters 14 through 17 to the other cycles in an audit. Although there are considerable similarities in auditing each cycle, there are also important differences that auditors need to understand.

Each of these chapters deals with a specific transaction cycle or part of a transaction cycle in much the same manner as Chapters 14 through 17 cover the sales and collection cycle. Each chapter in Part 4 demonstrates the relationship of internal controls, tests of controls, substantive tests of transactions, and analytical procedures to the related balance sheet and income statement accounts in the cycle and to tests of details of balances.

AUDIT OF THE PAYROLL AND PERSONNEL CYCLE

THE STAFF AUDITOR MUST NEVER "SIMPLY FOLLOW ORDERS"

Leslie Scott graduated with a Masters of Accountancy degree from a major university before joining the audit staff of a CPA firm. During her first "busy season," she was working on the audit of Sysco, Inc., a software development company. Her immediate supervisor on the Sysco audit was Bob Stith. Bob had been with the firm 3 years longer than Leslie and worked on the Sysco audit the previous year. He was supervising Leslie's work on capitalized software development costs. In preparing herself, Leslie had read FASB Statement 86 and had a good understanding of the accounting rules concerning the capitalization of such costs. She understood, for example, that costs could not be capitalized until after technological feasibility was established, either through detail program design or product design and the completion of a working model, confirmed by testing.

Bob Stith drafted an audit program for capitalized software development costs. He told Leslie to verify the payroll costs that were a significant part of the development cost and to talk to Jack Smart, Sysco's controller, about whether the projects with capitalized costs had reached the technological feasibility stage. Leslie tested the payroll costs and found no misstatements. She also made inquiries of Smart and was told that the appropriate stage was reached. Leslie documented Smart's representation in the audit files and went on to the next area assigned to her.

Later, Leslie began to have second thoughts. She understood that management's representations were a weak form of audit evidence and she was concerned about whether Jack Smart was the most knowledgeable person about the technical status of software projects. To resolve her concerns, she decided to talk to the responsible software engineers about one of the projects to confirm Smart's representations. She intended to clear this with Stith, but he was at another client's office that morning, so she proceeded on her own initiative. The engineer she talked to on the first project told her that he was almost finished with a working model but had not tested it yet. She decided to inquire about another project and discovered the same thing. Leslie documented these findings on an audit schedule and planned to discuss the situation with Stith as soon as he returned to the job. When Leslie told Stith of her findings and showed him the schedule, he told her the following:

> Listen, Leslie, I told you just to talk to Jack. You shouldn't do procedures that you're not instructed to do. I want you to destroy this schedule and don't record the wasted time. We're under a lot of time pressure and we can't bill Sysco for procedures that aren't necessary. There's nothing wrong with the capitalized software development costs. The fact that they have working products that they're selling indicates technological feasibility was reached.

Leslie was extremely distressed with this reaction from Stith but followed his instructions. The following fall, the SEC conducted an investigation of Sysco and found, among other things, that they had overstated capitalized software development costs. The SEC brought an action against both the management of Sysco and its auditors.

LEARNING OBJECTIVES

After studying this chapter, you should be able to

18-1 Identify the accounts and transactions in the payroll and personnel cycle.

18-2 Describe the business functions and the related documents and records in the payroll and personnel cycle.

18-3 Understand internal control and design and perform tests of controls and substantive tests of transactions for the payroll and personnel cycle.

18-4 Design and perform analytical procedures for the payroll and personnel cycle.

18-5 Design and perform tests of details of balances for accounts in the payroll and personnel cycle.

The **payroll and personnel cycle** involves the employment and payment of all employees. Labor is an important consideration in the valuation of inventory in manufacturing, construction, and other industries. As the vignette involving Leslie Scott and the audit of Sysco, Inc., demonstrates, improper valuation and allocation of labor can result in a material misstatement of net income. Payroll is also an area in which large amounts of company resources can be wasted because of inefficiency or stolen through fraud.

As with the sales and collection cycle, the audit of the payroll and personnel cycle includes obtaining an understanding of internal control, assessment of control risk, tests of controls and substantive tests of transactions, analytical procedures, and tests of details of balances. There are several important differences between the payroll and personnel cycle and other cycles in a typical audit.

- *There is only one class of transactions for payroll.* Most cycles include at least two classes of transactions. For example, the sales and collection cycle includes both sales and cash receipts transactions and often sales returns and charge-off of uncollectibles. Payroll has only one class because the receipt of services from employees and the payment for those services through payroll occur within a short time period.
- *Transactions are far more significant than related balance sheet accounts.* Payroll-related accounts such as accrued payroll and withheld taxes are usually small compared to the total amount of transactions for the year.
- *Internal controls over payroll are effective for almost all companies, even small ones.* The reasons for effective controls are harsh federal and state penalties for errors in withholding and paying payroll taxes and employee morale problems if employees are not paid or are underpaid.

Because of these three characteristics, auditors typically emphasize tests of controls, substantive tests of transactions, and analytical procedures in the audit of payroll. Tests of details of balances often take only a few minutes. Before discussing the tests in the cycle, we review the transactions and account balances, as well as the documents and records used in the payroll and personnel cycle for a typical company.

ACCOUNTS AND TRANSACTIONS IN THE PAYROLL AND PERSONNEL CYCLE

OBJECTIVE 18-1

Identify the accounts and transactions in the payroll and personnel cycle.

The overall objective in the audit of the payroll and personnel cycle is to evaluate whether the account balances affected by the cycle are fairly stated in accordance with generally accepted accounting principles. Typical accounts in the payroll and personnel cycle are shown in Figure 18-1 with the use of T accounts.

The way in which accounting information flows through the various accounts in the payroll and personnel cycle is illustrated by the T accounts. In most systems, the accrued wages and salaries account is used only at the end of an accounting period. Throughout the period, expenses are charged when the employees are actually paid rather than when the labor costs are incurred. The accruals for labor are recorded by adjusting entries at the end of the period for any earned but unpaid labor costs.

BUSINESS FUNCTIONS IN THE CYCLE AND RELATED DOCUMENTS AND RECORDS

OBJECTIVE 18-2

Describe the business functions and the related documents and records in the payroll and personnel cycle.

The payroll and personnel cycle begins with the hiring of personnel and ends with payment to the employees for the services performed and to the government and other institutions for the withheld and accrued payroll taxes and benefits. In between, the cycle involves obtaining services from the employees consistent with the objectives of the company and accounting for the services in a proper manner.

560 PART FOUR / APPLICATION OF THE AUDIT PROCESS TO OTHER CYCLES

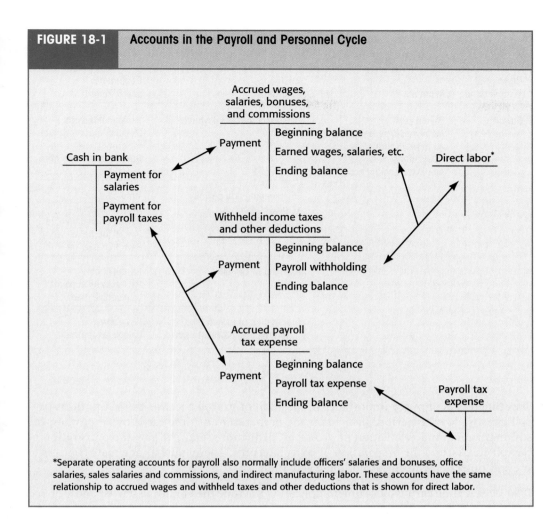

FIGURE 18-1   Accounts in the Payroll and Personnel Cycle

Accrued wages,
salaries, bonuses,
and commissions

	Beginning balance
Payment	Earned wages, salaries, etc.
	Ending balance

Cash in bank

Payment for
salaries

Payment for
payroll taxes

Direct labor*

Withheld income taxes
and other deductions

	Beginning balance
Payment	Payroll withholding
	Ending balance

Accrued payroll
tax expense

	Beginning balance
Payment	Payroll tax expense
	Ending balance

Payroll tax
expense

*Separate operating accounts for payroll also normally include officers' salaries and bonuses, office salaries, sales salaries and commissions, and indirect manufacturing labor. These accounts have the same relationship to accrued wages and withheld taxes and other deductions that is shown for direct labor.

Payroll Services

Column 3 of Table 18-1 on page 562 identifies the four business functions in a typical payroll and personnel cycle. The table also shows the relationships among the business functions, classes of transactions, accounts, and documents and records. Understanding the business functions and documents and records is necessary before assessing control risk and designing tests of controls and substantive tests of transactions.

The human resources department provides an independent source for interviewing and hiring qualified personnel. The department is also an independent source of records for the internal verification of wage information, including additions and deletions from the payroll and changes in wages and deductions.

Personnel and Employment

Personnel Records Records that include such data as the date of employment, personnel investigations, rates of pay, authorized deductions, performance evaluations, and terminations of employment are called **personnel records.**

Deduction Authorization Form A form authorizing payroll deductions, including the number of exemptions for withholding income taxes, 401(K) and other retirement savings plans, U.S. savings bonds, and union dues.

Rate Authorization Form A form authorizing the rate of pay. The source of the information is a labor contract, authorization by management, or in the case of officers, authorization from the board of directors.

TABLE 18-1	Classes of Transactions, Accounts, Business Functions, and Related Documents and Records for the Payroll and Personnel Cycle		
Class of Transactions	Accounts	Business Functions	Documents and Records
Payroll	Payroll cash All payroll expense accounts All payroll withholding accounts All payroll accrual accounts	Personnel and employment	Personnel records Deduction authorization form Rate authorization form
		Timekeeping and payroll preparation	Time card Job time ticket Payroll transaction file Payroll journal or listing Payroll master file
		Payment of payroll	Payroll check Payroll bank account reconciliation
		Preparation of payroll tax returns and payment of taxes	W-2 form Payroll tax returns

Timekeeping and Payroll Preparation

This function is of major importance in the audit of payroll because it directly affects payroll expense for the period. It includes the preparation of time cards by employees; the summarization and calculation of gross pay, deductions, and net pay; the preparation of payroll checks; and the preparation of payroll records. There must be adequate controls to prevent misstatements in each of these activities.

Time Card A **time card** is a document indicating the time the employee started and stopped working each day and the number of hours the employee worked. For many employees, the time card is prepared automatically by time clocks or identification card readers. Time cards are usually submitted weekly. References to time cards in this chapter include both paper and electronic forms.

Salaried employees do not complete time cards. Salaried workers may be required to complete reports of their time when they are compensated for overtime or take vacation or sick days.

Job Time Ticket A document indicating jobs on which an employee worked during a given time period. This form is used only when an employee works on different jobs or in different departments. Job time tickets may be completed electronically by a time and expense reporting system.

Payroll Transaction File A computer-generated file that includes all payroll transactions processed by the accounting system for a period, such as a day, week, or month. It contains all information entered into the system and includes information for each transaction, such as employee name, date, gross and net payments, various withholding amounts, and account classification or classifications.

The information on the payroll transaction file is used for a variety of records, listings, or reports, depending on the company's needs. Examples include the payroll journal, payroll master file, and payroll bank reconciliation.

Payroll Journal or Listing A report generated from the payroll transaction file that typically includes the employee name, date, gross and net payroll amounts, withholding amounts, and account classification or classifications for each transaction. The same transactions included in the journal or listing are also posted simultaneously to the general ledger and to the payroll master file.

Payroll Master File A **payroll master file** is used for recording each payroll transaction for each employee and maintaining total employee wages paid for the year to date. The record for each employee includes gross pay for each payroll period, deductions from gross pay, net pay, check number, and date. The master file is updated from payroll computer transaction files. The total of the individual employee earnings in the master file equals the total balance of gross payroll in various general ledger accounts.

Payment of Payroll

The actual signing and distribution of the checks must be properly handled to prevent their theft. Separate imprest payroll bank accounts are often used to prevent the payment of unauthorized payroll transactions.

Direct Deposit

Payroll Check A check written to the employee for services performed. The check is prepared as part of the payroll preparation function, but the authorized signature makes the check an asset. The amount of the check is the gross pay less taxes and other deductions withheld. After the check is cashed and returned to the company from the bank, it is referred to as a cancelled check. It is now common for payroll to be directly deposited into employees' bank accounts.

Payroll Bank Account Reconciliation An important control is the independent reconciliation of the imprest payroll bank account. An **imprest payroll account** is a separate payroll account in which a small balance is maintained. The exact amount of each net payroll is transferred by check or electronic funds transfer from the general account to the imprest account immediately before distribution of the payroll. The advantages of an imprest account are that it limits the client's exposure to payroll fraud, allows the delegation of payroll check-signing duties, separates routine payroll expenditures from other expenditures, and facilitates cash management. It also simplifies the reconciliation of the payroll bank account if it is done at the low point in the payment cycle.

Preparation of Payroll Tax Returns and Payment of Taxes

The timely preparation and mailing of payroll tax returns is required by federal and state payroll laws. Most computerized payroll systems include the preparation of payroll tax returns using the information on the payroll transaction and master files. Independent verification of the output by a competent individual is an important control to prevent misstatements and potential liability for taxes and penalties.

W-2 Form A form issued for each employee summarizing the earnings record for the calendar year. The information includes gross pay, income taxes withheld, and FICA withheld. The same information is also submitted to the Internal Revenue Service and state and local tax commissions when applicable. This information is prepared from the payroll master file and is normally prepared by the computer.

Payroll Tax Returns Tax forms submitted to local, state, and federal units of government for the payment of withheld taxes and the employer's tax. The nature and due dates of the forms vary depending on the type of taxes. For example, federal withholding and Social Security payments are due weekly or monthly, depending on the amount of withholding, and most state unemployment taxes are due quarterly. These forms are prepared from information on the payroll master file and are often prepared by the computer.

METHODOLOGY FOR DESIGNING TESTS OF CONTROLS AND SUBSTANTIVE TESTS OF TRANSACTIONS

OBJECTIVE 18-3

Understand internal control and design and perform tests of controls and substantive tests of transactions for the payroll and personnel cycle.

Payroll Outsourcing Software

Now that you are familiar with the business functions and related documents and records in the payroll and personnel cycle, we can discuss the assessment of control risk and the design of tests of controls and substantive tests of transactions for the cycle. Figure 18-2 shows the methodology for designing tests of controls and substantive tests of transactions for the payroll and personnel cycle. It is the same methodology as that used in Chapter 14 for the sales and collection cycle.

Internal control for payroll is normally highly structured and well controlled in order to control cash disbursed and to minimize employee complaints and dissatisfaction. Payroll checks and all related journals and payroll records are usually processed by computer. Because the processing of payroll is similar for most organizations, and programs need to be modified annually for changes in withholding schedules, it is common to use an outside payroll service for the processing of payroll. The auditor can often rely on the internal controls of the service organization. This is appropriate if the service organization's auditor issues a report on the internal controls of the service organization.

It is usually not difficult to establish good control in the payroll and personnel cycle. For factory and office employees, there are usually a large number of relatively homogeneous, small-amount transactions. There are fewer executive payroll transactions, but they

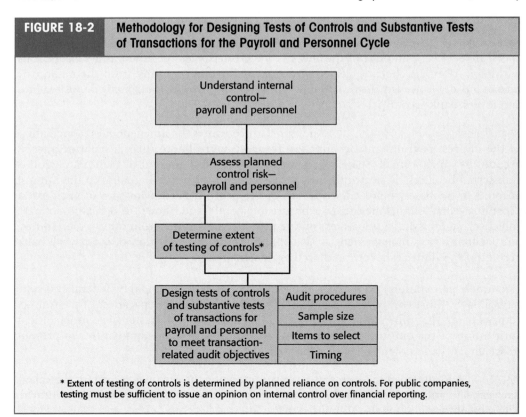

FIGURE 18-2 **Methodology for Designing Tests of Controls and Substantive Tests of Transactions for the Payroll and Personnel Cycle**

Understand internal control—payroll and personnel

Assess planned control risk—payroll and personnel

Determine extent of testing of controls*

Design tests of controls and substantive tests of transactions for payroll and personnel to meet transaction-related audit objectives

- Audit procedures
- Sample size
- Items to select
- Timing

* Extent of testing of controls is determined by planned reliance on controls. For public companies, testing must be sufficient to issue an opinion on internal control over financial reporting.

are ordinarily consistent in timing, content, and amount. Because of relatively consistent payroll concerns from company to company, high-quality computer systems are available. Consequently, auditors seldom expect to find exceptions in testing payroll transactions. Occasionally, control test deviations occur, but most monetary misstatements are corrected by internal verification controls or in response to employee complaints.

Tests of controls and substantive tests of transactions procedures are the *most important* means of verifying account balances in the payroll and personnel cycle. These tests are emphasized because of the lack of independent third-party evidence, such as confirmation, for verifying accrued wages, withheld income taxes, accrued payroll taxes, and other balance sheet accounts. Furthermore, in most audits, the amounts in the balance sheet accounts are small and can be verified with relative ease if the auditor is confident that payroll transactions are correctly entered into the computer and payroll tax returns are properly prepared.

Even though the tests of controls and substantive tests of transactions are the most important parts of testing payroll, the tests in this area are usually not extensive. In many audits, there is a minimal risk of material misstatements, even though payroll is often a significant part of total expenses. There are three reasons for this: Employees are likely to complain to management if they are underpaid, all payroll transactions are typically uniform and uncomplicated, and payroll transactions are subject to audit by federal and state governments for income tax withholding, Social Security, and unemployment taxes.

Following the same approach used in Chapter 14 for tests of sales and cash receipts transactions, the internal controls, tests of controls, and substantive tests of transactions for each transaction-related audit objective are summarized in Table 18-2 (p. 566). Again, the reader should recognize the following:

Understand Internal Control—Payroll and Personnel Cycle

- Internal controls vary from company to company; therefore, the auditor must identify the controls, significant deficiencies, and material weaknesses for each organization.
- Controls the auditor intends to use for reducing assessed control risk must be tested with tests of controls.
- If the client is a public company, the level of understanding controls and extent of tests of controls must be sufficient to issue an opinion on the effectiveness of internal control over financial reporting.
- Substantive tests of transactions vary depending on the assessed control risk and the other considerations of the audit, such as the effect of payroll on inventory.
- Tests are not actually performed in the order given in Table 18-2. The tests of controls and substantive tests of transactions are combined when appropriate and are performed in as convenient a manner as possible, using a performance format audit program.

The purposes of many internal controls and the nature of the tests of controls and substantive tests of transactions are apparent for most tests from their descriptions in Table 18-2. The section that follows discusses some of the key controls for the payroll and personnel cycle for the assessment of control risk.

Adequate Separation of Duties Separation of duties is important in the payroll and personnel cycle, especially to prevent overpayments and payments to nonexistent employees. The human resources department should be independent of the payroll function and is responsible for authorizing the addition and termination of employees, as well as changes in pay rates and deductions. Payroll processing should be separate from the custody of signed payroll checks.

Proper Authorization As noted earlier, the human resources department should be responsible for the authorization of additions and deletions of employees from the payroll. Pay rates and deductions should also be properly authorized. The hours worked by each employee, especially overtime, should be authorized by the employee's supervisor. Approval may be noted on all time cards or done on an exception basis for overtime hours only.

Adequate Documents and Records The appropriate documents and records will depend on the nature of the payroll system. For example, time cards or records are necessary for hourly employees but not for salaried employees. Some employees may be compensated

Transaction-Related Audit Objective	Key Internal Control	Common Test of Control	Common Substantive Tests of Transactions
Recorded payroll payments are for work actually performed by existing employees (existence).	Time cards are approved by supervisor. Time clock is used to record time. Adequate personnel files are maintained. Employment is authorized. There is separation of duties among personnel, timekeeping, and payroll disbursements. Only employees existing in the computer data files are accepted when they are entered. Check is authorized before issuance.	Examine the cards for indication of approvals. Examine time cards. Review personnel policies. Examine personnel files. Review organization chart, discuss with employees, and observe duties being performed. Examine printouts of transactions rejected by the computer as having nonexistent employee numbers. Examine payroll records for indication of approval.	Review the payroll journal, general ledger, and payroll earnings records for large or unusual amounts.* Compare cancelled checks with payroll journal for name, amount, and date. Examine cancelled checks for proper endorsement. Compare cancelled checks with personnel records.†
Existing payroll transactions are recorded (completeness).	Payroll checks are prenumbered and accounted for. Bank accounts are independently reconciled.	Account for a sequence of payroll checks. Discuss with employees and observe reconciliation.	Reconcile the disbursements in the payroll journal with the disbursements on the payroll bank statement. Prove the bank reconciliation.
Recorded payroll transactions are for the amount of time actually worked and are at the proper pay rates; withholdings are properly calculated (accuracy).	Calculations and amounts are internally verified. Batch totals are compared with computer summary reports. Wage rate, salary, or commission rate is properly authorized. Withholdings, including amounts for insurance and payroll savings, are properly authorized.	Examine indication of internal verification. Examine file of batch totals for initials of data control clerk; compare totals to summary reports. Examine payroll records for indication of internal verification. Examine authorizations in personnel file.	Recompute hours worked from time cards. Compare pay rates with union contract, approval by board of directors, or other source. Recompute gross pay. Check withholdings by referring to tax tables and authorization forms in personnel file. Recompute net pay. Compare cancelled check with payroll journal for amount.†
Payroll transactions are properly classified (classification).	An adequate chart of accounts is used. Account classifications are internally verified.	Review chart of accounts. Examine indication of internal verification.	Compare classification with chart of accounts or procedures manual. Review time card for employee department and job ticket for job assignment and trace through to labor distribution.
Payroll transactions are recorded on the correct dates (timing).	Procedures require recording transactions as soon as possible after the payroll is paid. Dates are internally verified.	Examine procedures manual and observe when recording takes place. Examine indication of internal verification.	Compare date of recorded check in the payroll journal with date on cancelled check and time card. Compare date on check with date the check cleared the bank.†
Payroll transactions are properly included in the payroll master file and are properly summarized (posting and summarization).	Payroll master file contents are internally verified. Payroll master file totals are compared with general ledger totals.	Examine indication of internal verification. Examine initialed summary total reports indicating that comparisons have been made.	Test clerical accuracy by footing the payroll journal and tracing postings to the general ledger and the payroll master file.

*This analytical procedure can also apply to other objectives, including completeness, accuracy, and timing.
†If check is direct deposited, other procedures are used to verify existence, accuracy, and timing of payment.

based on piece rate or other incentive systems. For many companies, time records must be adequate to accumulate payroll costs by job or assignment. Prenumbered documents for recording time are less of a concern in the payroll area because the completeness of payroll is not normally a concern.

Physical Control Over Assets and Records Access to unsigned payroll checks should be restricted. Checks should be signed by a responsible employee, and payroll should be distributed by someone independent of the payroll and timekeeping functions. Any unclaimed checks should be returned for redeposit. If checks are signed by a signature machine, access to the machine should be restricted.

Independent Checks on Performance Payroll computations should be independently verified, including comparison of batch totals to summary reports. A member of management or other responsible employee should review the payroll output for any obvious misstatements or unusual amounts. When manufacturing labor affects inventory valuation or when it is necessary to accumulate costs by job, adequate controls are necessary to verify the proper assignment of costs.

Several additional concerns for the payroll and personnel cycle are discussed in the following sections. These relate to payroll tax and other withholdings, the allocation of payroll costs to inventory, and the potential for fraudulent payroll transactions.

Payroll taxes are an important consideration in many companies, both because the amounts are often material and because the potential liability for failure to file timely tax forms can be severe.

Payroll Tax Forms and Payments

Preparation of Payroll Tax Forms As a part of understanding internal control, the auditor should review the preparation of at least one of each type of payroll tax form that the client is responsible for filing. There is a potential liability for unpaid taxes, penalty, and interest if the client fails to prepare the tax forms properly. The payroll tax forms are for such taxes as federal income and FICA withholding, state and city income withholding, and federal and state unemployment.

A detailed reconciliation of the information on the tax forms and the payroll records may be necessary when the auditor believes that there is a reasonable chance that the tax returns may be improperly prepared. Indications of potential misstatements in the returns include the payment of penalties and interest in the past for improper payments, new personnel in the payroll department who are responsible for the preparation of the returns, the lack of internal verification of the information, and the existence of serious cash flow problems for the client.

Payment of the Payroll Taxes Withheld and Other Withholdings on a Timely Basis It is desirable to test whether the client has fulfilled its legal obligation in submitting payments for all payroll withholdings as a part of the payroll tests even though the payments are usually made from general cash disbursements. The withholdings of concern in these tests are such items as taxes, 401(K) and other retirement savings, union dues, insurance, and payroll savings. The auditor must first determine the client's requirements for submitting the payments. The requirements are determined by reference to such sources as tax laws, union contracts, and agreements with employees. After the auditor knows the requirements, it is easy to determine whether the client has paid the proper amount on a timely basis by comparing the subsequent cash disbursement with the payroll records.

Auditors often extend their procedures considerably in the audit of payroll under the following circumstances: when payroll significantly affects the valuation of inventory and when the auditor is concerned about the possibility of material fraudulent payroll transactions.

Inventory and Fraudulent Payroll Considerations

Relationship Between Payroll and Inventory Valuation In audits in which payroll is a significant portion of inventory, a common occurrence for manufacturing and construction companies, the improper account classification of payroll can significantly affect asset valuation for accounts such as work in process, finished goods, or construction in process. For example, the overhead charged to inventory at the balance sheet date can be overstated if the salaries of administrative personnel are inadvertently or intentionally charged to indirect manufacturing overhead. Similarly, the valuation of inventory is affected if the direct labor cost of individual employees is improperly charged to the wrong job or process. When some jobs are billed on a cost-plus basis, revenue and the valuation of inventory are both affected by charging labor to incorrect jobs.

When labor is a material factor in inventory valuation, special emphasis should be placed on testing the internal controls over proper classification of payroll transactions. Consistency from period to period, which is essential for classification, can be tested by reviewing the chart of accounts and procedures manuals. It is also desirable to trace job tickets or other evidence of an employee's having worked on a job or process to the accounting records that affect inventory valuation. For example, if employees must account for all of their time on a weekly basis by assigning it to individual job numbers, a useful test is to trace the recorded hours of several employees for a week to the related job-cost records to make sure each has been properly recorded. It may also be desirable to trace from the job-cost records to employee summaries as a test for nonexistent payroll charges being included in inventory.

Tests for Nonexistent Payroll Because auditors have significant responsibility for the detection of fraud, they must extend audit procedures when they become concerned about the possibility of material fraud. There are several ways in which employees can significantly defraud a company in the payroll area. This discussion is limited to tests for the two most common types: nonexistent employees and fraudulent hours.

The issuance of payroll checks to individuals who do not work for the company (nonexistent employees) often results from the continuance of an employee's check after employment has been terminated. Usually, the person committing this type of defalcation is a payroll clerk, foreman, fellow employee, or perhaps the former employee. For example, under some systems a foreman could clock in daily for an employee and approve the time card at the end of the time period. If the foreman also distributes paychecks, considerable opportunity for defalcation exists.

Certain procedures can be performed on cancelled checks as a means of detecting defalcation. A procedure used on payroll audits is to compare the names on cancelled checks with time cards and other records for authorized signatures and reasonableness of the endorsements. It is also common to scan endorsements on cancelled checks for unusual or recurring second endorsements as an indication of a possible fraudulent check. The examination of checks that are recorded as voided is also desirable to make sure that they have not been fraudulently used.

A test for nonexistent employees is to trace selected transactions recorded in the payroll journal to the human resources department to determine whether the employees were actually employed during the payroll period. The endorsement on the cancelled check written out to an employee can be compared with the authorized signature on the employee's withholding authorization forms.

A procedure that tests for proper handling of terminated employees is to select several files from the personnel records for employees who were terminated in the current year to determine whether each received termination pay in accordance with company policy. Continuing payments to terminated employees is tested by examining the payroll records in the subsequent period to ascertain that the employee is no longer being paid. Naturally, this procedure is not effective if the human resources department is not informed of terminations.

In some cases, the auditor may request a surprise payroll payoff. This is a procedure in which each employee must pick up and sign for his or her check or direct deposit payroll record in the presence of a supervisor and the auditor. Any checks that have not been claimed must be subject to an extensive investigation to determine whether an unclaimed check is fraudulent. Surprise payoff is often expensive and in some cases may even cause problems with a labor union, but it may be the only likely means of detecting a defalcation.

Fraudulent hours occur when an employee reports more time than was actually worked. Because of the lack of available evidence, it is usually difficult for an auditor to discover fraudulent hours. One procedure is to reconcile the total hours paid according to the payroll records with an independent record of the hours worked, such as those often maintained by production control. Similarly, it may be possible to observe an employee clocking in more than one time card under a buddy approach. However, it is ordinarily easier for the client to prevent this type of defalcation by adequate controls than for the auditor to detect it.

Assessing control risk and performing tests of controls and substantive tests of transactions are done during the first two phases of the audit. After completing these tests and assessing the likelihood of misstatement in financial statement accounts in the payroll and personnel cycle, the auditor will follow the methodology of designing tests of details of balances.

METHODOLOGY FOR DESIGNING TESTS OF DETAILS OF BALANCES

Figure 18-3 summarizes the methodology for deciding the appropriate tests of details of balances for payroll liability accounts. This methodology is the same as that followed in Chapter 16 for accounts receivable.

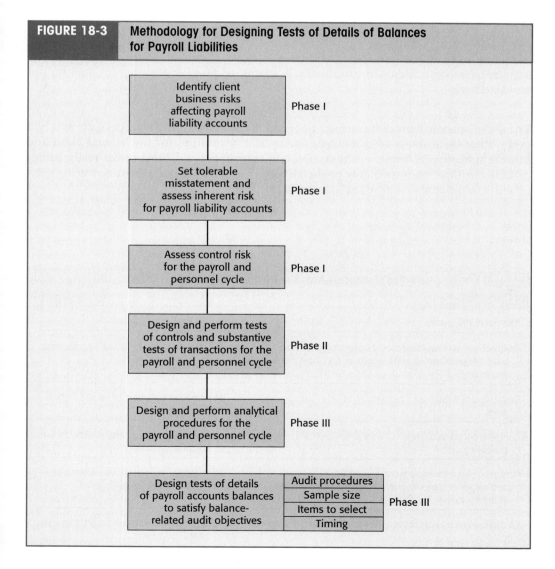

FIGURE 18-3 Methodology for Designing Tests of Details of Balances for Payroll Liabilities

Identify Client Business Risks Affecting Payroll (Phase I)

Significant client business risks affecting payroll are unlikely for most companies. However, client business risk may exist for complex compensation arrangements, including bonus and stock option plans and other deferred compensation arrangements. For example, many technology companies provide extensive stock options as part of their compensation packages for key employees that significantly impact compensation expense and shareholders' equity. Examples of other risks include events such as renegotiation of union contracts and discrimination claims. The auditor should understand the likelihood of these events and determine their potential effects on the financial statements, including footnote disclosures.

Set Tolerable Misstatement and Assess Inherent Risk (Phase I)

Most companies have a large number of transactions involving payroll, often with large total amounts. However, balance sheet accounts are normally insignificant, except for labor charged to inventory.

Except for the potential for fraud, inherent risk is typically low for all balance-related audit objectives. There is inherent risk of payroll fraud because most transactions involve cash. The existence objective is therefore often considered to be important. Also, for manufacturing companies with significant labor charged to inventory, there is potential for misclassification between payroll expense and inventory or among categories of inventory. As a part of gaining an understanding of the client, the auditor may identify complex payroll-related issues, such as stock-based compensation plans, that may increase inherent risks related to the accounting and disclosure of those arrangements.

Assess Control Risk and Perform Related Tests (Phases I and II)

Assessing control risk and the related tests of controls and substantive tests of transactions have been discussed extensively in earlier sections of the chapter and are not repeated here.

Perform Analytical Procedures (Phase III)

OBJECTIVE 18-4

Design and perform analytical procedures for the payroll and personnel cycle.

The use of analytical procedures is as important in the payroll and personnel cycle as it is in every other cycle. Table 18-3 illustrates analytical procedures for the balance sheet and income statement accounts in the payroll and personnel cycle. Most of the relationships included in Table 18-3 are highly predictable and are therefore useful for uncovering areas in which additional investigation is desirable.

TABLE 18-3	Analytical Procedures for the Payroll and Personnel Cycle
Analytical Procedure	**Possible Misstatement**
Compare payroll expense account balance with previous years (adjusted for pay rate increases and increases in volume).	Misstatement of payroll expense accounts
Compare direct labor as a percentage of sales with previous years.	Misstatement of direct labor and inventory
Compare commission expense as a percentage of sales with previous years.	Misstatement of commission expense and commission liability
Compare payroll tax expense as a percentage of salaries and wages with previous years (adjusted for changes in the tax rates).	Misstatement of payroll tax expense and payroll tax liability
Compare accrued payroll tax accounts with previous years.	Misstatement of accrued payroll taxes and payroll tax expense

The verification of the liability accounts associated with payroll, often termed **accrued payroll expenses,** is ordinarily straightforward if internal controls are operating effectively. When the auditor is satisfied that payroll transactions are being properly recorded in the payroll journal and the related payroll tax forms are being accurately prepared and promptly paid, the tests of details of balances should not be time consuming.

The two major balance-related audit objectives in testing payroll liabilities are (1) accruals in the trial balance are stated at the correct amounts (accuracy), and (2) transactions in the payroll and personnel cycle are recorded in the proper period (cutoff). The primary concern in both objectives is to make sure that there are no understated or omitted accruals. The major liability accounts in the payroll and personnel cycle are now discussed.

Design and Perform Tests of Details of Balances for Liability and Expense Accounts (Phase III)

OBJECTIVE 18-5

Design and perform tests of details of balances for accounts in the payroll and personnel cycle.

Amounts Withheld from Employees' Pay Payroll taxes withheld but not yet disbursed can be tested by comparing the balance with the payroll journal, the payroll tax form prepared in the subsequent period, and the subsequent period cash disbursements. Other withheld items such as retirement savings, union dues, savings bonds, and insurance can be verified in the same manner. If internal controls are operating effectively, cutoff and accuracy can easily be tested at the same time by these procedures.

Accrued Salaries and Wages The accrual for salaries and wages arises whenever employees are not paid for the last few days or hours of earned wages until the subsequent period. Salaried personnel usually receive all of their pay except overtime on the last day of the month, but often, several days of wages for hourly employees are unpaid at the end of the year.

The correct cutoff and accuracy of accrued salaries and wages depend on company policy, which should be followed consistently from year to year. Some companies calculate the exact hours of pay that were earned in the current period and paid in the subsequent period, whereas others compute an approximate proportion. For example, if the subsequent payroll results from 3 days of employment during the current year and 2 days of employment during the subsequent year, the use of 60 percent of the subsequent period's gross pay as the accrual is an example of an approximation.

Once the auditor has determined the company's policy for accruing wages and knows that it is consistent with that of previous years, the appropriate audit procedure to test for cutoff and accuracy is to recalculate the client's accrual. The most likely misstatement of any significance in the balance is the failure to include the proper number of days of earned but unpaid wages.

Accrued Commissions The same concepts used in verifying accrued salaries and wages are applicable to accrued commissions, but the accrual is often more difficult to verify because companies often have several different types of agreements with salespeople and other commission employees. For example, some salespeople might be paid a commission every month and earn no salary, whereas others will get a monthly salary plus a commission paid quarterly. In some cases, the commission varies for different products and may not be paid until several months after the end of the year. In verifying accrued commissions, it is necessary first to determine the nature of the commission agreement and then test the calculations based on the agreement. It is important to compare the method of accruing commissions with that of previous years for purposes of consistency. If the amounts are material, the auditor may confirm the amount that is due directly with the employees.

Accrued Bonuses In many companies, the year-end unpaid bonuses to officers and employees are such a major item that the failure to record them would result in a material misstatement. The verification of the recorded accrual can usually be accomplished by comparing it with the amount authorized in the minutes of the board of directors.

Accrued Vacation Pay, Sick Pay, or Other Benefits The consistent accrual of these liabilities relative to those of the preceding year is the most important consideration in evaluating the fairness of the amounts. The company policy for recording the liability must first be determined, and then the recorded amounts must be recalculated. The company policy should be in accordance with SFAS 43, which deals with compensated absences.

Accrued Payroll Taxes Payroll taxes, such as FICA and state and federal unemployment taxes, can be verified by examining tax forms prepared in the subsequent period to determine the amount that should have been recorded as a liability at the balance sheet date.

Tests of Details of Balances for Expense Accounts Several accounts on the income statement are affected by payroll transactions. The most important are officers' salaries and bonuses, office salaries, sales salaries and commissions, and direct manufacturing labor. There is often a further breakdown of costs by division, product, or branch. Fringe benefits such as medical insurance may also be included in the expenses.

There should be relatively little additional testing of the income statement accounts in most audits beyond the analytical procedures, tests of controls, substantive tests of transactions, and related tests of liability accounts, which have already been discussed. Extensive additional testing should be necessary only when there are significant deficiencies or material weaknesses in internal control, significant misstatements are discovered in the liability tests, or major unexplained variances are found in the analytical procedures. Nevertheless, some income statement accounts are often tested in the payroll and personnel cycle. These include officers' compensation, commissions, payroll tax expense, total payroll, and contract labor.

Officers' Compensation It is common to verify whether the total compensation of officers is the amount authorized by the board of directors, because their salaries and bonuses must be included in the SEC's 10-K report and federal income tax return. Verification of officers' compensation is also warranted because some individuals may be in a position to pay themselves more than the authorized amount. The usual audit test is to obtain the authorized salary of each officer from the minutes of the board of directors meetings and compare it with the related earnings record.

Commissions Commission expense can be verified with relative ease if the commission rate is the same for each type of sale and the necessary sales information is available in the accounting records. The total commission expense can be verified by multiplying the commission rate for each type of sale by the amount of sales in that category. If the desired information is not available, it may be necessary to test the annual or monthly commission payments for selected salespeople and trace those to the total commission payments. When the auditor believes it is necessary to perform these tests, they are normally done in conjunction with tests of accrued liabilities.

Payroll Tax Expense Payroll tax expense for the year can be tested by first reconciling the total payroll on each payroll tax form with the total payroll for the entire year. Total payroll taxes can then be recomputed by multiplying the appropriate rate by the taxable payroll. The calculation is often time-consuming because the tax is usually applicable on only a portion of the payroll and the rate may change partway through the year if the taxpayer's financial statements are not on a calendar-year basis. On most audits, the calculation is costly and is not necessary unless analytical procedures indicate a problem that cannot be resolved through other procedures. When the auditor believes that the test is necessary, it is ordinarily done in conjunction with tests of payroll tax accruals.

Total Payroll A closely related test to the one for payroll taxes is the reconciliation of total payroll expense in the general ledger with the payroll tax returns and the W-2 forms. The objectives of the test are to determine whether payroll transactions were charged to a non-payroll account or not recorded in the payroll journal at all. Because the payroll tax records and the payroll are both usually prepared directly from the payroll master file, the misstatements, if any, are likely to be in both records. Tests of controls and substantive tests of transactions are a better means of uncovering these two types of misstatements in most audits.

Contract Labor To reduce payroll costs, many organizations contract with outside organizations to provide staffing. The individuals providing the services are employed by the outside organization. For example, companies frequently contract with information technology services firms to handle the company's IT management and staffing functions. The fees paid to the outside organization are tested by comparing the amounts with the signed contract arrangement between the company and the outside services firm.

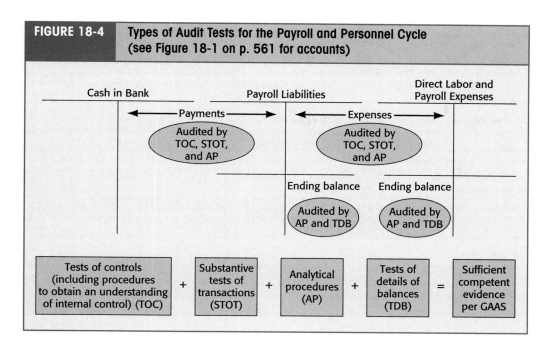

FIGURE 18-4 | **Types of Audit Tests for the Payroll and Personnel Cycle (see Figure 18-1 on p. 561 for accounts)**

SUMMARY

This chapter described the audit of the payroll and personnel cycle. Figure 18-4 illustrates the major accounts in the payroll and personnel cycle and the types of audit tests used to audit these accounts. Emphasis is on tests of controls and substantive tests of transactions because of the significance of transactions and the high quality of internal controls in most companies. Tests of details of balances are normally limited to analytical procedures and verification of accrued liabilities related to payroll.

ESSENTIAL TERMS

Accrued payroll expenses—the liability accounts associated with payroll; these include accounts for accrued salaries and wages, accrued commissions, accrued bonuses, accrued benefits, and accrued payroll taxes

Imprest payroll account—a bank account to which the exact amount of payroll for the pay period is transferred by check or wire transfer from the employer's general cash account

Payroll and personnel cycle—the transaction cycle that begins with the hiring of personnel, includes obtaining and accounting for services from the employees, and ends with payment to the employees for the services performed and

to the government and other institutions for withheld and accrued payroll taxes and benefits

Payroll master file—a computer file for recording each payroll transaction for each employee and maintaining total employee wages paid and related data for the year to date

Personnel records—records that include such data as the date of employment, personnel investigations, rates of pay, authorized deductions, performance evaluations, and termination of employment

Time card—a document indicating the time that the employee started and stopped working each day and the number of hours worked

REVIEW QUESTIONS

18-1 (Objective 18-1) Identify five general ledger accounts that are likely to be affected by the payroll and personnel cycle in most audits.

18-2 (Objectives 18-1, 18-3) Explain the relationship between the payroll and personnel cycle and inventory valuation.

18-3 (Objective 18-3) List five tests of controls that can be performed for the payroll and personnel cycle and state the purpose of each control being tested.

18-4 (Objective 18-3) Explain why the percentage of total audit time in the cycle devoted to performing tests of controls and substantive tests of transactions is usually far greater for the payroll and personnel cycle than for the sales and collection cycle.

18-5 (Objectives 18-2, 18-3) Evaluate the following comment by an auditor: "My job is to determine whether the payroll records are fairly stated in accordance with generally accepted accounting principles, not to find out whether they are following proper hiring and termination procedures. When I conduct an audit of payroll, I keep out of the human resources department and stick to the time cards, journals, and payroll checks. I don't care whom they hire and whom they fire, as long as they properly pay the ones they have."

18-6 (Objective 18-3) Distinguish between the following payroll audit procedures and state the purpose of each: (1) trace a random sample of prenumbered time cards to the related payroll checks in the payroll register and compare the hours worked with the hours paid, and (2) trace a random sample of payroll checks from the payroll register to the related time cards and compare the hours worked with the hours paid. Which of these two procedures is typically more important in the audit of payroll? Why?

18-7 (Objective 18-5) In auditing payroll withholding and payroll tax expense, explain why emphasis should normally be on evaluating the adequacy of the payroll tax return preparation procedures rather than the payroll tax liability. If the preparation procedures are inadequate, explain the effect this will have on the remainder of the audit.

18-8 (Objective 18-4) List several analytical procedures for the payroll and personnel cycle and explain the type of misstatement that might be indicated when there is a significant difference in the comparison of the current year with previous years' results for each of the tests.

18-9 (Objective 18-3) Explain the circumstances under which an auditor should perform audit tests primarily designed to uncover fraud in the payroll and personnel cycle. List three audit procedures that are primarily for the detection of fraud and state the type of fraud the procedure is meant to uncover.

18-10 (Objective 18-2) Distinguish among a payroll master file, a W-2 form, and a payroll tax return. Explain the purpose of each.

18-11 (Objectives 18-2, 18-3) List the supporting documents and records the auditor will examine in a typical payroll audit in which the primary objective is to detect fraud.

18-12 (Objective 18-3) List five types of authorizations in the payroll and personnel cycle and state the type of misstatement that is likely to occur when each authorization is lacking.

18-13 (Objective 18-5) Explain why it is common to verify total officers' compensation even when the tests of controls and substantive tests of transactions results in payroll are excellent. What audit procedures can be used to verify officers' compensation?

18-14 (Objective 18-2) Explain what is meant by an imprest payroll account. What is its purpose as a control over payroll?

18-15 (Objective 18-3) List several audit procedures that the auditor can use to determine whether payroll transactions are recorded at the proper amounts.

18-16 (Objective 18-3) Explain how audit sampling can be used to test the payroll and personnel cycle.

MULTIPLE CHOICE QUESTIONS FROM CPA EXAMINATIONS

18-17 (Objective 18-3) The following questions concern internal controls in the payroll and personnel cycle. Choose the best response.

a. A factory foreman at Steblecki Corporation discharged an hourly worker but did *not* notify the payroll department. The foreman then forged the worker's signature on time cards and work tickets and, when giving out the checks, diverted the payroll checks drawn from the discharged worker to his own use. The most effective procedure for preventing this activity is to
   (1) require written authorization for all employees added to or removed from the payroll.
   (2) have a paymaster who has *no* other payroll responsibility distribute the payroll checks.
   (3) have someone other than persons who prepare or distribute the payroll obtain custody of unclaimed payroll checks.
   (4) from time to time, rotate persons distributing the payroll.

b. The CPA reviews Pyzi's payroll procedures. An example of an internal control deficiency is to assign to a department supervisor the responsibility for
   (1) distributing payroll checks to subordinate employees.
   (2) reviewing and approving time reports for subordinates.
   (3) interviewing applicants for subordinate positions before hiring is done by the personnel department.
   (4) initiating requests for salary adjustments for subordinate employees.

c. From the standpoint of good internal control, distributing payroll checks to employees is best handled by the
(1) accounting department.
(2) personnel department.
(3) treasurer's department.
(4) employee's departmental supervisor.

18-18 (Objective 18-3) The following questions concern audit testing of the payroll and personnel cycle. Choose the best response.

a. A computer operator perpetrated a theft by preparing erroneous W-2 forms. The operator's FICA withheld was overstated by $500, and the FICA withheld from all other employees was understated. Which of the following audit procedures would detect such a fraud?
(1) Multiplying the applicable rate by the individual's gross taxable earnings.
(2) Using form W-4 and withholding charts to determine whether deductions authorized per pay period agree with amounts deducted per pay period.
(3) Footing and cross-footing of the payroll register followed by tracing postings to the general ledger.
(4) Vouching cancelled checks to federal tax form 941.

b. In the audit of which of the following types of profit-oriented enterprises would the auditor be most likely to place special emphasis on tests of controls for proper classifications of payroll transactions?
(1) A manufacturing organization.
(2) A retailing organization.
(3) A wholesaling organization.
(4) A service organization.

c. A common audit procedure in the audit of payroll transactions involves tracing selected items from the payroll journal to employee time cards that have been approved by supervisory personnel. This procedure is designed to provide evidence in support of the audit proposition that
(1) only proper employees worked and their pay was properly computed.
(2) jobs on which employees worked were charged with the appropriate labor cost.
(3) internal controls over payroll disbursements are operating effectively.
(4) all employees worked the number of hours for which their pay was computed.

DISCUSSION QUESTIONS AND PROBLEMS

18-19 (Objectives 18-2, 18-3) Items 1 through 9 are selected questions typically found in internal control questionnaires used by auditors to obtain an understanding of internal control in the payroll and personnel cycle. In using the questionnaire for a client, a "yes" response to a question indicates a possible internal control, whereas a "no" indicates a potential weakness.

1. Does an appropriate official authorize initial rates of pay and any subsequent changes in rates?
2. Are written notices required documenting reasons for termination?
3. Are formal records such as time cards used for keeping time?
4. Is approval by a department head or foreman required for all time cards before they are submitted for payment?
5. Does anyone verify pay rates, overtime hours, and computations of gross payroll before payroll checks are prepared?
6. Does an adequate means exist for identifying jobs or products, such as work orders, job numbers, or some similar identification provided to employees to ensure proper coding of time records?
7. Are employees paid by checks prepared by persons independent of timekeeping?
8. Are employees required to show identification to receive paychecks?
9. Is a continuing record maintained of all unclaimed wages?

Required

a. For each of the questions, state the transaction-related audit objective(s) being fulfilled if the control is in effect.

b. For each control, list a test of control to test its effectiveness.

c. For each of the questions, identify the nature of the potential financial misstatement(s) if the control is not in effect.

d. For each of the potential misstatements in part c, list a substantive audit procedure for determining whether a material misstatement exists.

18-20 (Objectives 18-2, 18-3) Following are some of the tests of controls and substantive tests of transactions procedures often performed in the payroll and personnel cycle. (Each procedure is to be done on a sample basis.)

1. Reconcile the monthly payroll total for direct manufacturing labor with the labor cost distribution.
2. Examine the time card for the approval of a foreman.
3. Recompute hours on the time card and compare the total with the total hours for which the employee has been paid.
4. Compare the employee name, date, check number, and amounts on cancelled checks with the payroll journal.
5. Trace the hours from the employee time cards to job tickets to make sure that the total reconciles and trace each job ticket to the job-cost record.
6. Account for a sequence of payroll checks in the payroll journal.
7. Select employees from the personnel file who have been terminated, and determine whether their termination pay was in accordance with the union contract. As part of this procedure, examine two subsequent periods to determine whether the terminated employee is still being paid.

Required

a. Identify whether each of the procedures is primarily a test of control or a substantive test of transactions.

b. Identify the transaction-related audit objective(s) of each of the procedures.

18-21 (Objectives 18-2, 18-3) The following misstatements are included in the accounting records of Lathen Manufacturing Company:

1. Direct labor was unintentionally charged to job 620 instead of job 602 by the payroll clerk when he key-entered the labor distribution sheets. Job 602 was completed and the costs were expensed in the current year, whereas job 620 was included in work-in-process.
2. Joe Block and Frank Demery take turns "punching in" for each other every few days. The absent employee comes in at noon and tells his foreman that he had car trouble or some other problem. The foreman does not know that the employee is getting paid for the time.
3. The foreman submits a fraudulent time card for a former employee each week and delivers the related payroll check to the employee's house on the way home from work. They split the amount of the paycheck.
4. Employees often overlook recording their hours worked on job-cost tickets as required by the system. Many of the client's contracts are on a cost-plus basis.
5. The payroll clerk prepares a check to the same nonexistent person every week when he key-enters payroll transactions in the computer system, which also records the amount in the payroll journal. He submits it along with all other payroll checks for signature. When the checks are returned to him for distribution, he takes the check and deposits it in a special bank account bearing that person's name.
6. In withholding payroll taxes from employees, the computer operator deducts $.50 extra federal income taxes from several employees each week and credits the amount to his own employee earnings record.
7. The payroll clerk manually prepares payroll checks but often forgets to record one or two checks in the computer-prepared payroll journal.

Required

a. For each misstatement, state a control that should have prevented it from occurring on a continuing basis.

b. For each misstatement, state a substantive audit procedure that could uncover it.

18-22 (Objectives 18-3, 18-4, 18-5) The following audit procedures are typical of those found in auditing the payroll and personnel cycle:

1. Examine evidence of double-checking payroll wage rates and calculations by an independent person.
2. Obtain a schedule of all payroll liabilities and trace to the general ledger.
3. Select a sample of 20 cancelled payroll checks and account for the numerical sequence.
4. Foot and cross-foot the payroll journal for two periods and trace totals to the general ledger.
5. For payroll liabilities, examine subsequent cash disbursements and supporting documents such as payroll tax returns, depository receipts, and tax receipts.
6. Select a sample of 20 cancelled payroll checks and trace to payroll journal entries for name, date, and amounts.
7. Compute direct labor, indirect labor, and commissions as a percentage of net sales and compare with prior years.

8. Examine owner approval of rates of pay and withholdings.
9. Compute payroll tax expense as a percentage of total wages, salaries, and commissions.
10. Discuss with management any payroll liabilities recorded in the prior year that are not provided for currently.
11. Scan journals for all periods for unusual transactions to determine whether they are recorded properly.
12. Select a sample of 40 entries in the payroll journal and trace each to an approved time card.

a. Select the type of test for each audit procedure from the following: **Required**

   (1) Test of control
   (2) Substantive test of transactions
   (3) Analytical procedure
   (4) Test of details of balances

b. For each test of control or substantive test of transactions, identify the applicable transaction-related audit objective(s).

c. For each test of details of balances, identify the applicable balance-related audit objective(s).

18-23 (Objectives 18-3, 18-5) The following are steps in the methodology for designing tests of controls, substantive tests of transactions, and tests of details of balances for the payroll and personnel cycle:

1. Design tests of details of balances for the payroll and personnel cycle.
2. Evaluate risk and materiality for payroll expense and liability accounts.
3. Evaluate the cost-benefit of assessing control risk as low for payroll.
4. Design and perform payroll- and personnel-related analytical procedures.
5. Identify controls and deficiencies in internal control for the payroll and personnel cycle.
6. Obtain an understanding of the payroll and personnel cycle internal controls.
7. Evaluate tests of controls and substantive tests of transactions results.
8. Design payroll and personnel cycle tests of controls and substantive tests of transactions.
9. Assess inherent risk for payroll-related accounts.

a. Identify (1) those steps that are tests of controls or substantive tests of transactions and   **Required**
   (2) those that are tests of details of balances.

b. Put steps that are tests of controls and substantive tests of transactions in the order of their performance in most audits.

c. Put the tests of details of balances in their proper order.

18-24 (Objective 18-4) In comparing total payroll tax expense with that of the preceding year, Merlin Brendin, CPA, observed a significant increase, even though the total number of employees increased only from 175 to 195. To investigate the difference, he selected a large sample of payroll disbursement transactions and carefully tested the withholdings for each employee in the sample by referring to federal and state tax withholding schedules. In his test, he found no exceptions; therefore, he concluded that payroll tax expense was fairly stated.

a. Evaluate Brendin's approach to testing payroll tax expense.   **Required**

b. Discuss a more suitable approach for determining whether payroll tax expense was properly stated in the current year.

18-25 (Objective 18-5) As part of the audit of McGree Plumbing and Heating, you have responsibility for testing the payroll and personnel cycle. Payroll is the largest single expense in the client's trial balance, and hourly wages make up most of the payroll total. A unique aspect of its business is the extensive overtime incurred by employees on some days. It is common for employees to work only 3 or 4 days during the week but to work long hours while they are on the job. McGree's management found that this actually saves money, despite the large amount of overtime, because the union contract requires payment for all travel time. Because many of the employees' jobs require long travel times and extensive start-up costs, this policy is supported by both McGree and the employees.

You carefully evaluated and tested the payroll and personnel cycle's internal control and concluded that it contains no significant deficiencies. Your tests included tests of the time cards, withholdings, pay rates, the filing of all required tax returns, payroll checks, and all other aspects of payroll.

As part of the year-end tests of payroll, you are responsible for verifying all accrued payroll as well as accrued and withheld payroll taxes. The accrued payroll includes the last 6 working days of the current year. The client calculated accrued wages by taking 60 percent of the subsequent period's gross payroll and recorded it as an adjusting entry to be reversed in the subsequent period.

List all audit procedures you would follow in verifying accrued payroll, withheld payroll taxes, and   **Required**
accrued payroll taxes.

18-26 (Objective 18-3) In the audit of Larnet Manufacturing Company, the auditor concluded that internal controls were inadequate because of the lack of segregation of duties. As a result, the decision was made to have a surprise payroll payoff 1 month before the client's balance sheet date. Because the auditor had never been involved in a payroll payoff, she did not know how to proceed.

Required
a. What is the purpose of a surprise payroll payoff?

b. What other audit procedures can the auditor perform that may fulfill the same objectives?

c. Discuss the procedures that the auditor should require the client to observe when the surprise payroll payoff is taking place.

d. At the completion of the payroll payoff, there are often several unclaimed checks. What procedures should be followed for these?

18-27 (Objective 18-4) Archer Uniforms, Inc., is a distributor of professional uniforms to retail stores that sell work clothing to professionals, such as doctors, nurses, security guards, etc. Traditionally, most of the sales are to retail stores throughout the United States and Canada. Most shipments are processed in bulk for delivery directly to retail stores or to the corporate office warehouse distribution facilities for retail store chains. In early 2005, Archer Uniforms began offering the sale of uniforms directly to professionals through its company Web site. Professionals can access online information about uniform styles, sizes, and prices. Purchases are applied to the customer's personal credit card, and the credit card agencies wire funds to Archer's bank account periodically throughout the month. Management made this decision based on its conclusion that the online sales would tap a new market of professionals who do not have easy access to retail stores. Thus, the volume of shipments to retail stores is expected to remain consistent.

Given that Archer's IT staff lacked the necessary experience to create and support the online sales system, management engaged an information technology consulting firm to design and maintain the online sales system.

Required
Before performing analytical procedures related to the payroll and personnel cycle accounts, develop expectations of how these recent events at Archer Uniforms, Inc., will affect payroll expense for the following departments during 2005 compared to prior years. Indicate the degree (extensive, moderate, little) to which you expect the payroll expense account balance to increase or decrease during 2005.

1. Warehouse and Shipping Department
2. IT Department
3. Accounts Receivable Department
4. Accounts Payable Department
5. Receiving Department
6. Executive Management
7. Marketing

18-28 (Objectives 18-4, 18-5) During the first-year audit of Jones Wholesale Stationery, you observe that commissions amount to almost 25 percent of total sales, which is somewhat higher than in previous years. Further investigation reveals that the industry typically has larger sales commissions than Jones and that there is significant variation in rates depending on the product sold.

At the time a sale is made, the salesperson records the commission rate and the total amount of the commissions on the office copy of the sales invoice. When sales are entered into the computer system for the recording of sales, the debit to sales commission expense and credit to accrued sales commission are also recorded. As part of recording the sales and sales commission expense, the accounts receivable clerk verifies the prices, quantities, commission rates, and all calculations on the sales invoices. Both the accounts receivable and the salespersons' commission master files are updated when the sale and sales commission are recorded. On the fifteenth day after the end of the month, the salesperson is paid for the preceding month's sales commissions.

Required
a. Develop an audit program to verify sales commission expense, assuming that no audit tests have been conducted in any audit area to this point.

b. Develop an audit program to verify accrued sales commissions at the end of the year, assuming that the tests you designed in part a resulted in no significant misstatements.

CASE

18-29 (Objective 18-3) Roost and Briley, CPAs, are doing the audit of Leggert Lumber Co., an international wholesale lumber broker. Because of the nature of their business, payroll and telephone expense are the two largest expenses.

You are the in-charge auditor on the engagement responsible for writing the audit program for the payroll and personnel cycle. Leggert Lumber uses a computer service company to prepare weekly payroll checks, update earnings records, and prepare the weekly payroll journal for its 30 employees. The president maintains all personnel files, knows every employee extremely well, and is a full-time participant in the business.

All employees, except the president, check into the company building daily using a time clock. The president's secretary, Mary Clark, hands out the time cards daily, observes employees clocking in, collects the cards, and immediately returns them to the file. She goes through the same process when employees clock out on their way home.

At the end of each week, employees calculate their own hours. Clark rechecks those hours, and the president approves all time cards. Each Tuesday, Clark prepares a payroll input form for delivery to the computer service center. She files a copy of the form. The form has the following information for each employee:

Information	Source
Employee name	Time card
Social Security number	Employee list
Hourly labor rate*	Wage rate list (approved by president)
Regular hours	Time card
Overtime hours	Time card
Special deductions*	Special form (prepared by employee)
W-4 information*	W-4 form
Termination of employment*	President

*Included on input form only for new employees, terminations, and changes.

The service center enters the information from the payroll input form into its computer, updates master files, and prints out payroll checks and a payroll register. The payroll register has the following headings:

Employee name	FICA taxes withheld
Social Security number	Medicare withheld
Regular hours	Federal taxes withheld
Overtime hours	State taxes withheld
Regular payroll dollars	Other deductions
Overtime payroll dollars	Net pay
Gross payroll	Check number

A line is prepared for each employee and the journal is totaled.

Payroll checks and the journal are delivered to Clark, who compares the information on the journal with her payroll input form and initials the journal. She gives the checks to the president, who signs them and personally delivers them to employees.

Clark re-adds the journal and posts the totals to the ledger. Cancelled checks are mailed to the president, and he prepares a monthly bank reconciliation.

a. Is there any loss of documentation because of the computer service center? Explain.

Required

b. For each transaction-related audit objective for the payroll and personnel cycle, write appropriate tests of controls and substantive tests of transactions audit procedures. Consider both controls and deficiencies in writing your program. Label each procedure as either a test of control or a substantive test of transactions.

c. Rearrange your design format audit program in requirement b into a performance format audit program.

d. Prepare a sampling data sheet using either nonstatistical or attributes sampling, such as the ones shown in Chapter 15, for the audit program in part b. Set ARACR and other factors required for sampling as you consider appropriate. Do not assume that you actually performed any tests.

INTERNET PROBLEM 18-1: OUTSOURCING THE PAYROLL FUNCTION

Reference the CW site. Many organizations outsource their payroll function by contracting with external payroll services firms. In this problem, students use Internet resources to find answers to questions related to the decision on whether to outsource payroll-related activities.

AUDIT OF THE ACQUISITION AND PAYMENT CYCLE: TESTS OF CONTROLS, SUBSTANTIVE TESTS OF TRANSACTIONS, AND ACCOUNTS PAYABLE

FALSE PURCHASES CAMOUFLAGE OVERSTATED PROFITS

Comptronix Corporation announced that senior members of its management team had overstated profits, and there would be material adjustments to the prior years' audited financial statements. Central to the fraud was the use of fictitious accounts payable purchases for large equipment items to overstate fixed assets and hide fictitious sales.

The senior executives circumvented Comptronix's existing internal controls by bypassing the purchasing and receiving departments so that no one at Comptronix could discover the scheme. Comptronix employees usually created a fairly extensive paper trail for equipment purchases. Company internal controls over acquisition and cash disbursement transactions typically required a purchase order, receiving report, and vendor invoice before payment could be authorized by the Chief Operating Officer or the controller/treasurer, who were both participants in the fraud. As a result, the executives were able to bypass controls related to cash disbursements and authorize payment for nonexistent purchases without creating any documents for the fictitious transactions.

The company also created fictitious sales and related receivables. The company issued checks to pay for the false purchase transactions. The checks were then redeposited into the company's account and recorded as collections on the fictitious receivables. As a result, it appeared that the fictitious sales were collected, and that payment was made to support the false fixed asset purchases.

The fraud scheme grossly exaggerated the company's performance by reporting profits when the company was actually incurring losses. On the day that the public announcement of the fraud was made, Comptronix's common stock price declined abruptly by 72 percent! The SEC ultimately charged the executives with violating the antifraud provisions of the Securities Act of 1933 and the Securities Exchange Act of 1934. The SEC permanently barred the executives from serving as officers or directors of any public company, ordered them to repay bonuses and trading losses avoided, and imposed civil monetary penalties against them.

Source: *Accounting and Auditing Enforcement Release No. 543*, Commerce Clearing House, Inc., Chicago.

LEARNING OBJECTIVES

After studying this chapter, you should be able to

19-1 Identify the accounts and the classes of transactions in the acquisition and payment cycle.

19-2 Describe the business functions and the related documents and records in the acquisition and payment cycle.

19-3 Describe how e-commerce affects the acquisition of goods and services.

19-4 Understand internal control, and design and perform tests of controls and substantive tests of transactions for the acquisition and payment cycle.

19-5 Describe the methodology for designing tests of details of balances for accounts payable using the audit risk model.

19-6 Design and perform analytical procedures for accounts payable.

19-7 Design and perform tests of details of balances for accounts payable, including out-of-period liability tests.

19-8 Distinguish the reliability of vendors' invoices, vendors' statements, and confirmations of accounts payable as audit evidence.

The third major transaction cycle discussed is the **acquisition and payment cycle.** The acquisition of goods and services includes such items as the acquisition of raw materials, equipment, supplies, utilities, repairs and maintenance, and research and development. This chapter first discusses assessing control risk and designing tests of controls and substantive tests of transactions for the classes of transactions in the acquisition and payment cycle. It also covers performing tests of details of balances for several accounts in the cycle.

Before studying assessing control risk and designing tests of controls and substantive tests of transactions for each class of transactions, two related topics are covered. First, it is important to know the acquisition and payment cycle classes of transactions and account balances in a typical company. Second, because a considerable portion of the audit of transactions in the acquisition and payment cycle involves documents and records, it is essential to understand the typical documents and records used in the cycle. Then, if faced with auditing recorded transactions where documents such as purchase orders, receiving reports, and vendor invoices are missing—like the situation described in the Comptronix vignette—the auditor will be more likely to detect misstatements.

ACCOUNTS AND CLASSES OF TRANSACTIONS IN THE ACQUISITION AND PAYMENT CYCLE

OBJECTIVE 19-1

Identify the accounts and the classes of transactions in the acquisition and payment cycle.

The overall objective in the audit of the acquisition and payment cycle is to evaluate whether the accounts affected by the acquisitions of goods and services and the cash disbursements for those acquisitions are fairly presented in accordance with generally accepted accounting principles. Figure 19-1 shows the way accounting information flows through the various accounts in the acquisition and payment cycle. This figure shows that there are three classes of transactions included in the cycle:

1. Acquisitions of goods and services
2. Cash disbursements
3. Purchase returns and allowances and purchase discounts

Typical accounts included in the acquisition and payment cycle are shown by T accounts in Figure 19-1. Note the large number of accounts affected by this cycle. To keep the illustration manageable, only the control accounts are shown for the three major categories of expenses used by most companies. For each control account, examples of the subsidiary expense accounts are also given. Because of the large number of accounts in the cycle, it is not surprising that it often takes more time to audit the acquisition and payment cycle than any other.

Figure 19-1 shows that every transaction is either debited or credited to accounts payable. Because many companies make acquisitions directly by check or through petty cash, the figure is an oversimplification. We assume that cash disbursement acquisitions are processed in the same manner as all other acquisitions.

BUSINESS FUNCTIONS IN THE CYCLE AND RELATED DOCUMENTS AND RECORDS

OBJECTIVE 19-2

Describe the business functions and the related documents and records in the acquisition and payment cycle.

The acquisition and payment cycle involves the decisions and processes necessary for obtaining the goods and services for operating a business. The cycle typically begins with the initiation of a purchase requisition by an authorized employee who needs the goods or services, and it ends with payment for the benefits received. Although the discussion that follows deals with a small manufacturing company that makes tangible products for sale to third parties, the same principles apply to a service company, a government unit, or any other type of organization.

There are four business functions shown in the third column of Table 19-1 (p. 584). These functions occur in every business in the recording of the three classes of transactions in the acquisition and payment cycle. Observe that the first three business functions are for

FIGURE 19-1   Accounts in the Acquisition and Payment Cycle

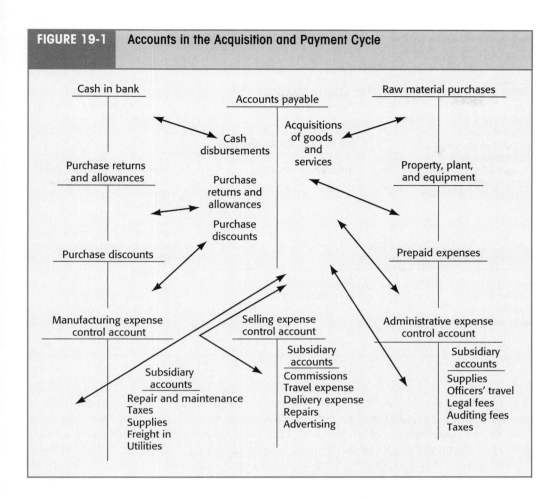

recording the acquisition of goods and services on account, and the last process is for recording the cash disbursements for payments to vendors. Processing purchase returns and allowances and purchase discounts are also business functions in the cycle, but these are not separately shown in Table 19-1 because the amounts are not significant for most companies.

This section explains the four business functions in Table 19-1 and describes typical documents and records for each function. These documents and records are shown in the fourth column of Table 19-1. It is essential to understand the business functions and documents and records in a company before assessing control risk and designing tests of controls and substantive tests of transactions.

The request for goods or services by the client's personnel is the starting point for the cycle. The exact form of the request and the required approval depend on the nature of the goods and services and company policy.

Processing Purchase Orders

Purchase Requisition A **purchase requisition** is a request for goods and services by an authorized employee. It may take the form of a request for such acquisitions as materials by a foreman or the storeroom supervisor, outside repairs by office or factory personnel, or insurance by the vice president in charge of property and equipment. Companies also rely on prespecified reorder points used by the computer to initiate purchase requisitions automatically.

Purchase Order A **purchase order** is a document identifying the description, quantity, and related information for goods and services the company intends to purchase. This document is often used to indicate authorization to acquire goods and services. Companies often submit purchase orders electronically to vendors who have made arrangements for electronic data interchange (EDI).

TABLE 19-1 | Classes of Transactions, Accounts, Business Functions, and Related Documents and Records for the Acquisition and Payment Cycle

Classes of Transactions	Accounts	Business Functions	Documents and Records
Acquisitions	Inventory Property, plant, and equipment Prepaid expenses Leasehold improvements Accounts payable Manufacturing expenses Selling expenses Administrative expenses	Processing purchase orders	Purchase requisition Purchase order
		Receiving goods and services	Receiving report
		Recognizing the liability	Acquisitions transaction file Acquisitions journal or listing Vendor's invoice Debit memo Voucher Accounts payable master file Accounts payable trial balance Vendor's statement
Cash disbursements	Cash in bank (from cash disbursements) Accounts payable Purchase discounts	Processing and recording cash disbursements	Check Cash disbursements transaction file Cash disbursements journal or listing

Receiving Goods and Services

The receipt by the company of goods or services from the vendor is a critical point in the cycle because it is the point at which most companies first recognize the acquisition and related liability on their records. When goods are received, adequate control requires examination for description, quantity, timely arrival, and condition. A **receiving report** is a paper or electronic document prepared at the time tangible goods are received. The receiving report includes a description of the goods, the quantity received, the date received, and other relevant data. The receipt of goods and services in the normal course of business represents the date companies normally recognize the liability for an acquisition.

Recognizing the Liability

The proper recognition of the liability for the receipt of goods and services requires *prompt and accurate* recording. The initial recording has a significant effect on the recorded financial statements and the actual cash disbursement; therefore, great care must be taken to include only existing company acquisitions at the correct amounts.

Acquisitions Transaction File A computer-generated file that includes all acquisition transactions processed by the accounting system for a period, such as a day, week, or month. It contains all information entered into the system and includes information for each transaction, such as vendor name, date, amount, account classification or classifications, and description and quantity of inventory purchased. The file can also include purchase returns and allowances or there can be a separate file for those transactions.

The information in the acquisitions transaction file is used for a variety of records, listings, or reports, depending on the company's needs. Examples include an acquisitions journal, accounts payable master file, and transactions for a certain account balance or division.

Acquisitions Journal or Listing A report generated from the acquisitions transaction file that typically includes the vendor name, date, amount, and account classification or classifications for each transaction, such as repair and maintenance, inventory, or utilities. It also identifies whether the acquisition was for cash or accounts payable. The journal or listing can be for any time period but is often for a month. Typically, the journal or listing includes totals of every account number included for the time period. The same transactions included in the journal or listing are also posted simultaneously to the general ledger and, if they are on account, to the accounts payable master file.

Vendor's Invoice A **vendor's invoice** is a document that indicates such things as the description and quantity of goods and services received, price (including freight), cash discount terms, and date of the billing. It is an essential document because it specifies the amount of money owed to the vendor for an acquisition. For companies using EDI, the vendor invoice is transmitted electronically rather than in paper form.

Debit Memo A **debit memo** is a document indicating a reduction in the amount owed to a vendor because of returned goods or an allowance granted. It often takes the same general form as a vendor's invoice, but it supports reductions in accounts payable rather than increases.

Voucher This document is commonly used by organizations to establish a formal means of recording and controlling acquisitions. Vouchers include a cover sheet or folder for containing documents and a package of relevant documents such as the purchase order, copy of the packing slip, receiving report, and vendor's invoice. After payment, a copy of the check is added to the voucher package.

Accounts Payable Master File An **accounts payable master file** is used for recording individual acquisitions, cash disbursements, and acquisition returns and allowances for each vendor. The master file is updated from the acquisition, returns and allowances, and cash disbursement computer transaction files. The total of the individual account balances in the master file equals the total balance of accounts payable in the general ledger. A printout of the accounts payable master file shows, by vendor, the beginning balance in accounts payable, each acquisition, acquisition returns and allowances, cash disbursements, and the ending balance. Many companies do not maintain an accounts payable master file by vendor. These companies pay on the basis of individual vendor's invoices. Therefore, the total of unpaid vendors' invoices in the master file equals total accounts payable.

Accounts Payable Trial Balance An **accounts payable trial balance** lists the amount owed to each vendor or for each invoice or voucher at a point in time. It is prepared directly from the accounts payable master file.

Vendor's Statement A **vendor's statement** is prepared monthly by the vendor and indicates the beginning balance, acquisitions, returns and allowances, payments to the vendor, and ending balance. These balances and activities are the vendor's representations of the transactions for the period and not the client's. Except for disputed amounts and timing differences, the client's accounts payable master file should be the same as the vendor's statement.

Processing and Recording Cash Disbursements

For most companies, payment is made by computer-prepared checks from information included in the acquisition transactions file at the time goods and services are received. Checks are typically prepared in a multicopy format, with the original going to the payee, one copy filed with the vendor's invoice and other supporting documents, and another filed numerically. In most cases, individual checks are recorded in a cash disbursements transactions file.

Check The document used to pay for the acquisition when payment is due. After the check is signed by an authorized person, it is an asset. Therefore, signed checks should be mailed by the signer or a person under the signer's control. When cashed by the vendor and cleared by the client's bank, it is called a cancelled check. In some EDI arrangements, the company submits payments to the vendor electronically through an electronic funds transfer (EFT) between the company's bank and the vendor's bank.

Cash Disbursements Transaction File A computer-generated file that includes all cash disbursements transactions processed by the accounting system for a period, such as a day, week, or month. It includes the same type of information discussed for the acquisitions transaction file.

Cash Disbursements Journal or Listing A report generated from the cash disbursements transaction file that includes all transactions for any time period. The same transactions, including all relevant information, are included in the accounts payable master file and general ledger.

HOW E-COMMERCE AFFECTS THE ACQUISITION AND PAYMENT CYCLE

OBJECTIVE 19-3

Describe how e-commerce affects the acquisition of goods and services.

E-procurement

Companies use the Internet and other e-commerce options to streamline processes for the acquisition of goods and services and other processes surrounding supply-chain management. While EDI has been used for years by larger suppliers and customers, Internet-based technologies now allow for electronic linkages between smaller suppliers and customers.

Information about product descriptions, pricing, delivery schedules, and other terms are readily available over the Internet through supplier Web sites and other easily accessible databases. Purchasing agents access information about products needed from a host of providers before making acquisition decisions. Often, the actual purchase decision can be initiated through company Web site portals hosted by the supplier or independent providers, bypassing the traditional paper-based procurement process.

Some companies use extranets, which are private networks built on Internet technology, allowing business suppliers and customers to communicate and conduct business directly in a secure setting. Companies access the extranet to link to preapproved suppliers to order products or services and to obtain information useful in making future purchasing decisions. The use of an extranet often increases the ability to conduct business with remote business partners who once were not feasible business partners. Even companies who compete with one another for the sale of goods and services are actually partnering to build online marketplaces that integrate common suppliers.

Other companies use business-to-business auctions hosted on the Internet to negotiate the purchase of needed supplies and services in open auctions. These Internet-based auctions often bring in a larger pool of suppliers and customers, who negotiate through the auction portal for the purchase and sale of products and services. There are a variety of auction styles, with some of the auctions being hosted by independent third-party specialists, while others are hosted privately by company suppliers.

Many argue that the use of the Internet to acquire goods and services leads to market efficiencies and cheaper prices because the online markets enable a greater number of suppliers and customers to negotiate for the purchase and sale of products and services. In addition, the use of the Internet for the acquisition of goods and services often enables a faster delivery of products and services because of the time-savings associated with placing the order online. The online availability of product and other supply-chain information, such as order status, helps reduce payroll-related costs once associated with staffing customer service and other sales functions.

METHODOLOGY FOR DESIGNING TESTS OF CONTROLS AND SUBSTANTIVE TESTS OF TRANSACTIONS

OBJECTIVE 19-4

Understand internal control, and design and perform tests of controls and substantive tests of transactions for the acquisition and payment cycle.

In a typical audit, the most time-consuming accounts to verify by substantive tests of details of balances are accounts receivable, inventory, fixed assets, accounts payable, and expense accounts. Of these five, four are directly related to the acquisition and payment cycle. The net time saved can be dramatic if the auditor can reduce the tests of details of the account balances by using tests of controls and substantive tests of transactions to verify the effectiveness of internal controls for acquisitions and cash disbursements. Therefore, it should not be surprising that tests of controls and substantive tests of transactions for the acquisition and payment cycle receive a considerable amount of attention in well-conducted audits, especially when the client has effective internal controls.

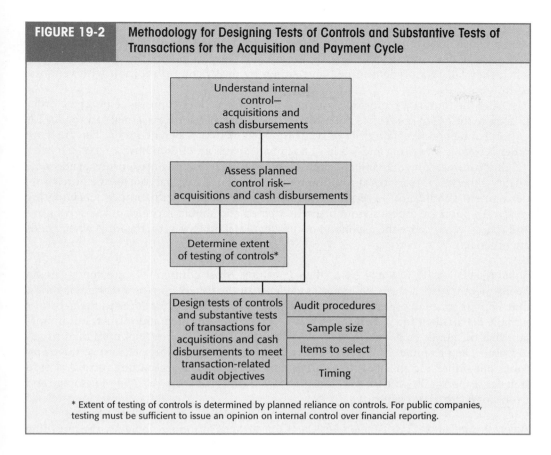

FIGURE 19-2 | Methodology for Designing Tests of Controls and Substantive Tests of Transactions for the Acquisition and Payment Cycle

Understand internal control—acquisitions and cash disbursements

Assess planned control risk—acquisitions and cash disbursements

Determine extent of testing of controls*

Design tests of controls and substantive tests of transactions for acquisitions and cash disbursements to meet transaction-related audit objectives

Audit procedures

Sample size

Items to select

Timing

* Extent of testing of controls is determined by planned reliance on controls. For public companies, testing must be sufficient to issue an opinion on internal control over financial reporting.

Tests of controls and substantive tests of transactions for the acquisition and payment cycle are divided into two broad areas: tests of acquisitions and tests of payments. Acquisition tests concern three of the four business functions discussed earlier in this chapter: processing purchase orders, receiving goods and services, and recognizing the liability. Tests of payments concern the fourth function, processing and recording cash disbursements.

Figure 19-2 shows the methodology for designing tests of controls and substantive tests of transactions for the acquisition and payment cycle. It is the same methodology used in earlier chapters. The following sections deal with each part of Figure 19-2, starting with understanding internal control.

The auditor gains an understanding of internal control for the acquisition and payment cycle by studying the client's flowcharts, preparing internal control questionnaires, and performing walkthrough tests for acquisitions and cash disbursements. The procedures for understanding internal control in the acquisition and payment cycle are similar to the procedures performed in other transaction cycles.

Understand Internal Control

There are key internal controls for each of the business functions described earlier in this chapter. Key internal controls are for the authorization of purchases, the separation of the custody of the received goods from other functions, the timely recording and independent review of transactions, and the authorization of payments to vendors. We now examine each of these key controls.

Assess Planned Control Risk

Authorization of Purchases Proper authorization for acquisitions is essential because it ensures that the goods and services acquired are for authorized company purposes and it avoids the acquisition of excessive or unnecessary items. Most companies permit general authorization for the acquisition of regular operating needs, such as inventory, at one level and acquisitions of capital assets or similar items at another. For example, acquisitions of fixed assets in excess of a specified dollar limit may require approval from the board of directors; items acquired relatively infrequently, such as insurance policies and long-term service contracts, are approved by certain officers; supplies and services costing less than a designated amount are approved by supervisors and department heads; and some types of raw materials and supplies are reordered automatically when they fall to a predetermined level, often by direct communication with vendors' computers.

After the purchase requisition for an acquisition has been approved, a purchase order to acquire the goods or services must be initiated. A purchase order is issued to a vendor for a specified item at a certain price to be delivered at or by a designated time. The purchase order is usually in writing and is a legal document that is an offer to buy.

It is common for companies to establish purchasing departments to ensure an adequate quality of goods and services at a minimum price. For good internal control, the purchasing department should not be responsible for authorizing the acquisition or receiving the goods. All purchase orders should be prenumbered and should include sufficient columns and spaces to minimize the likelihood of unintentional omissions on the form when goods are ordered.

Separation of Asset Custody from Other Functions Most companies have the receiving department initiate a receiving report as evidence of the receipt and examination of goods. One copy is normally sent to the raw materials storeroom and another to the accounts payable department for their information needs. To prevent theft and misuse, it is important that the goods be *physically controlled* from the time of their receipt until their use or disposal. The personnel in the receiving department should be independent of the storeroom personnel and the accounting department. Finally, the accounting records should transfer responsibility for the goods as they are transferred from receiving to storage and from storage to manufacturing.

Timely Recording and Independent Review of Transactions In some companies, the recording of the liability for acquisitions is made on the basis of the receipt of goods and services, and in other companies, it is deferred until the vendor's invoice is received. In either case, the accounts payable department typically has responsibility for verifying the propriety of acquisitions. This is done by comparing the details on the purchase order, the receiving report, and the vendor's invoice to determine that the descriptions, prices, quantities, terms, and freight on the vendor's invoice are correct. Typically, extensions, footings, and account distributions are also verified. In some cases, the matching of documents and verification of invoice accuracy are done automatically by computer.

An important control in the accounts payable and information technology departments is to require that those personnel who record acquisitions do not have access to cash, marketable securities, and other assets. Adequate documents and records, proper procedures for record keeping, and independent checks on performance are also necessary controls in the accounts payable function.

Authorization of Payments The most important controls over cash disbursements include the signing of checks by an individual with proper authority, separation of responsibilities for signing the checks and performing the accounts payable function, and careful examination of the supporting documents by the check signer at the time the check is signed.

The checks should be prenumbered and printed on special paper that makes it difficult to alter the payee or amount. Care should be taken to provide physical control over blank, voided, and signed checks. It is also important to have a method of cancelling the supporting documents to prevent their reuse as support for another check at a later time. A common method is to write the check number on the supporting documents.

Determine Extent of Testing of Controls

After the auditor identifies the key internal controls and weaknesses and assesses control risk, it is appropriate to decide whether substantive tests will be reduced sufficiently to justify the cost of performing tests of controls. It makes little sense to incur the cost of identifying controls and assessing control risk below the maximum if there will be no reduction of substantive tests. Of course, if the client is a public company, the auditor must document and test controls sufficiently so as to issue an opinion on internal control.

Key internal controls, common tests of controls, and common substantive tests of transactions for each transaction-related audit objective are summarized in Table 19-2. An assumption underlying the internal controls and audit procedures is the existence of a separate acquisitions journal or listing for recording all acquisitions.

Design Tests of Controls and Substantive Tests of Transactions for Acquisitions

TABLE 19-2	Summary of Transaction-Related Audit Objectives, Key Controls, Tests of Controls, and Substantive Tests of Transactions for Acquisitions		
Transaction-Related Audit Objective	**Key Internal Control**	**Common Test of Control**	**Common Substantive Tests of Transactions**
Recorded acquisitions are for goods and services received, consistent with the best interests of the client (existence).	Purchase requisition, purchase order, receiving report, and vendor's invoice are attached to the voucher.* Acquisitions are approved at the proper level. Computer accepts entry of purchases only from authorized vendors in the vendor master file. Documents are cancelled to prevent their reuse. Vendors' invoices, receiving reports, purchase orders, and purchase requisitions are internally verified.*	Examine documents in voucher package for existence. Examine indication of approval. Attempt to input transactions with valid and invalid vendors. Examine indication of cancellation. Examine indication of internal verification.	Review the acquisitions journal, general ledger, and accounts payable master file for large or unusual amounts.† Examine underlying documents for reasonableness and authenticity (vendors' invoices, receiving reports, purchase orders, and purchase requisitions).* Examine vendor master file for unusual vendors. Trace inventory acquisitions to inventory master file. Examine fixed assets acquired.
Existing acquisition transactions are recorded (completeness).	Purchase orders are prenumbered and accounted for. Receiving reports are prenumbered and accounted for.* Vouchers are prenumbered and accounted for.	Account for a sequence of purchase orders. Account for a sequence of receiving reports. Account for a sequence of vouchers.	Trace from a file of receiving reports to the acquisitions journal.* Trace from a file of vendors' invoices to the acquisitions journal.
Recorded acquisition transactions are accurate (accuracy).	Calculations and amounts are internally verified. Batch totals are compared with computer summary reports. Acquisitions are approved for prices and discounts.	Examine indication of internal verification. Examine file of batch totals for initials of data control clerk; compare totals to summary reports. Examine indication of approval.	Compare recorded transactions in the acquisitions journal with the vendor's invoice, receiving report, and other supporting documentation.* Recompute the clerical accuracy on the vendor's invoice, including discounts and freight.
Acquisition transactions are properly classified (classification).	An adequate chart of accounts is used. Account classifications are internally verified.	Examine procedures manual and chart of accounts. Examine indication of internal verification.	Compare classification with chart of accounts by referring to vendors' invoices.
Acquisition transactions are recorded on the correct dates (timing).	Procedures require recording transactions as soon as possible after the goods and services have been received. Dates are internally verified.	Examine procedures manual and observe whether unrecorded vendors' invoices exist. Examine indication of internal verification.	Compare dates of receiving reports and vendors' invoices with dates in the acquisitions journal.*
Acquisition transactions are properly included in the accounts payable and inventory master files and are properly summarized (posting and summarization).	Accounts payable master file contents are internally verified. Accounts payable master file or trial balance totals are compared with general ledger balances.	Examine indication of internal verification. Examine initials on general ledger accounts indicating comparison.	Test clerical accuracy by footing the journals and tracing postings to general ledger and accounts payable and inventory master files.

*Receiving reports are used only for tangible goods and are therefore not used for services, such as utilities and repairs and maintenance. Often, vendors' invoices are the only documentation available.

†This analytical procedure can also apply to other objectives, including completeness, accuracy, and timing.

In studying Table 19-2, it is important to relate internal controls to transaction-related audit objectives, tests of controls to internal controls, and substantive tests of transactions to monetary misstatements that would be absent or present due to controls and weaknesses in the system. The audit evidence for an audit engagement will vary with the internal controls and other circumstances. Significant audit efficiencies may be realized when controls are operating effectively.

Four of the six transaction-related audit objectives for acquisitions deserve special attention. A discussion of each of these objectives follows.

Recorded Acquisitions Are for Goods and Services Received, Consistent with the Best Interests of the Client (Existence) If the auditor is satisfied that the controls are adequate for this objective, tests for improper and nonexistent transactions can be greatly reduced. Adequate controls are likely to prevent the client from including as a business expense or asset those transactions that primarily benefit management or other employees rather than the entity being audited. In some instances, improper transactions are obvious, such as the acquisition of unauthorized personal items by employees or the actual embezzlement of cash by recording a fraudulent acquisition in the acquisitions journal. In other instances, the propriety of a transaction is more difficult to evaluate, such as the payment of officers' memberships to country clubs, expense-paid vacations to foreign countries for members of management and their families, and management-approved illegal payments to officials of foreign countries. If the controls over improper or nonexistent transactions are inadequate, more extensive examination of supporting documentation is necessary.

Existing Acquisitions Are Recorded (Completeness) Failure to record the acquisition of goods and services received directly affects the balance in accounts payable and may result in an overstatement of net income and owners' equity. Therefore, auditors are usually very concerned with the completeness objective. In some instances, it may be difficult to perform tests of details to determine whether there are unrecorded transactions, and the auditor must rely on controls for this purpose. In addition, because the audit of accounts payable generally takes a considerable amount of audit time, effective internal controls, properly tested, can significantly reduce audit costs.

Acquisitions Are Accurately Recorded (Accuracy) Because the accuracy of many asset, liability, and expense accounts depends on the correct recording of transactions in the acquisitions journal, the extent of tests of details of many balance sheet and expense accounts depends on the auditor's evaluation of the effectiveness of the internal controls over the accuracy of recorded acquisitions transactions. For example, if the auditor believes that the fixed assets are correctly recorded in the acquisitions journal, it is acceptable to vouch fewer current period acquisitions than if the controls are inadequate.

When a client uses perpetual inventory records, the tests of details of inventory can also be significantly reduced if the auditor believes the perpetual records are accurate. The controls over the acquisitions included in the perpetual records are normally tested as a part of the tests of controls and substantive tests of transactions for acquisitions. The inclusion of both quantity and unit costs in the inventory perpetual records permits a reduction in the tests of the physical count and the unit costs of inventory if the controls are operating effectively.

Acquisitions Are Correctly Classified (Classification) The tests of details of certain individual accounts can be reduced if the auditor believes that internal controls are adequate to provide reasonable assurance of correct classification in the acquisitions journal. Although all accounts are affected to some degree by effective controls over classification, the two areas most affected are current period acquisitions of fixed assets and all expense accounts, such as repairs and maintenance, utilities, and advertising. Because performing documentation tests of current period fixed asset acquisitions and expense accounts for accuracy and classification are relatively time-consuming audit procedures, the time-savings can be significant when controls are effective.

The same format used in Table 19-2 (p. 589) for acquisitions is also used in Table 19-3 for cash disbursements. The assumption underlying these controls and audit procedures is separate cash disbursements and acquisitions journals. The comments about the methodology and process for developing audit procedures for acquisitions apply equally to cash disbursements.

Once the auditor has decided on procedures, the acquisitions and cash disbursements tests are typically performed concurrently. For example, for a transaction selected for

Design Tests of Controls and Substantive Tests of Transactions for Cash Disbursements

TABLE 19-3	Summary of Transaction-Related Audit Objectives, Key Controls, Tests of Controls, and Substantive Tests of Transactions for Cash Disbursements		
Transaction-Related Audit Objective	**Key Internal Control**	**Common Test of Control**	**Common Substantive Tests of Transactions**
Recorded cash disbursements are for goods and services actually received (existence).	There is adequate segregation of duties between accounts payable and custody of signed checks.	Discuss with personnel and observe activities.	Review the cash disbursements journal, general ledger, and accounts payable master file for large or unusual amounts.*
	Supporting documentation is examined before signing of checks by an authorized person.	Discuss with personnel and observe activities.	Trace the cancelled check to the related acquisitions journal entry and examine for payee name and amount.
	Approval of payment on supporting documents is given at the time checks are signed.	Examine indication of approval.	Examine cancelled check for authorized signature, proper endorsement, and cancellation by the bank.
			Examine supporting documents as part of the tests of acquisitions.
Existing cash disbursement transactions are recorded (completeness).	Checks are prenumbered and accounted for.	Account for a sequence of checks.	Reconcile recorded cash disbursements with the cash disbursements on the bank statement (proof of cash disbursements).
	The bank reconciliation is prepared monthly by an employee independent of recording cash disbursements or custody of assets.	Examine bank reconciliations and observe their preparation.	
Recorded cash disbursement transactions are accurate (accuracy).	Calculations and amounts are internally verified.	Examine indication of internal verification.	Compare cancelled checks with the related acquisitions journal and cash disbursements journal entries.
	The bank reconciliation is prepared monthly by an independent person.	Examine bank reconciliations and observe their preparation.	Recompute cash discounts.
			Prepare a proof of cash disbursements.
Cash disbursement transactions are properly classified (classification).	An adequate chart of accounts is used.	Examine procedures manual and chart of accounts.	Compare classification with chart of accounts by referring to vendors' invoices and acquisitions journal.
	Account classifications are internally verified.	Examine indication of internal verification.	
Cash disbursement transactions are recorded on the correct dates (timing).	Procedures require recording of transactions as soon as possible after the check has been signed.	Examine procedures manual and observe whether unrecorded checks exist.	Compare dates on cancelled checks with the cash disbursements journal.
	Dates are internally verified.	Examine indication of internal verification.	Compare dates on cancelled checks with the bank cancellation date.
Cash disbursement transactions are properly included in the accounts payable master file and are properly summarized (posting and summarization).	Accounts payable master file contents are internally verified.	Examine indication of internal verification.	Test clerical accuracy by footing journals and tracing postings to general ledger and accounts payable master file.
	Accounts payable master file or trial balance totals are compared with general ledger balances.	Examine initials on general ledger accounts indicating comparison.	

*This analytical procedure can also apply to other objectives, including completeness, accuracy, and timing.

examination from the acquisitions journal, the vendor's invoice and the receiving report are examined at the same time as the related cancelled check. Thus, the verification is done efficiently without reducing the effectiveness of the tests.

Attributes Sampling for Tests of Controls and Substantive Tests of Transactions

Because of the importance of tests of controls and substantive tests of transactions for acquisitions and cash disbursements, the use of attributes sampling is common in this audit area. The approach is similar to that used for the tests of controls and substantive tests of transactions for sales discussed in Chapter 15. With reference to the most essential transaction-related audit objectives presented earlier, however, it should be noted that most of the important attributes in the acquisition and payment cycle have a direct monetary effect on the accounts. Furthermore, many of the types of errors and fraud that may be found represent a misstatement of earnings and are of significant concern to the auditor. For example, there may be inventory cutoff misstatements or an incorrect recording of an expense amount. Because of this, the tolerable exception rate selected by the auditor in tests of many of the attributes in this cycle is relatively low. Because the dollar amounts of individual transactions in the cycle cover a wide range, it is also common to segregate large and unusual items and to test them on a 100 percent basis.

METHODOLOGY FOR DESIGNING TESTS OF DETAILS OF BALANCES FOR ACCOUNTS PAYABLE

OBJECTIVE 19-5

Describe the methodology for designing tests of details of balances for accounts payable using the audit risk model.

Managing A/P

Because all acquisition and payment cycle transactions typically flow through accounts payable, this account is critical to any audit of the acquisition and payment cycle. If tests of controls and related substantive tests of transactions show that controls are operating effectively, the auditor may be able to reduce analytical procedures and tests of details of balances for accounts payable. However, because accounts payable tend to be material for many companies, auditors almost always perform extensive analytical procedures and some tests of details of balances of that account.

Accounts payable are *unpaid obligations* for goods and services received in the ordinary course of business. It is sometimes difficult to distinguish between accounts payable and accrued liabilities, but it is useful to define a liability as an account payable if the total amount of the obligation is *known and owed at the balance sheet date*. The accounts payable account therefore includes obligations for the acquisition of raw materials, equipment, utilities, repairs, and many other types of goods and services that were received before the end of the year. Most accounts payable can also be identified by the existence of vendors' invoices for the obligation. Accounts payable should also be distinguished from interest-bearing obligations. If an obligation includes the payment of interest, it should be recorded as a note payable, contract payable, mortgage payable, or bond payable.

The methodology for designing tests of details for accounts payable is summarized in Figure 19-3. This methodology is the same as that used for accounts receivable in Chapter 16.

Identify Client Business Risks Affecting Accounts Payable (Phase I)

The recent focus by many companies on improving their supply-chain management activities has led to numerous changes in the design of systems used to initiate and record acquisition and payment activities. Efforts to streamline the purchasing of goods and services, including greater emphasis on just-in-time inventory purchasing, increased sharing of information with suppliers, and the use of technology and e-commerce to transact business, are changing all aspects of the acquisition and payment cycle for many companies. These arrangements and systems can be complex.

Significant client business risks are likely to arise from these changes. For example, suppliers may have greater access to accounts payable records, allowing them to continually monitor the status of payable balances and to perform detailed reconciliations of transactions. Also, increased focus on improving the logistics of physically moving inventory throughout a company's distribution chain may increase the difficulty of establishing effective cutoff of accounts payable balances at period end. The auditor should understand the nature of changes to these systems to identify whether client business risks and related management controls affect the likelihood of material misstatements in accounts payable.

FIGURE 19-3

Methodology for Designing Tests of Details of Balances for Accounts Payable

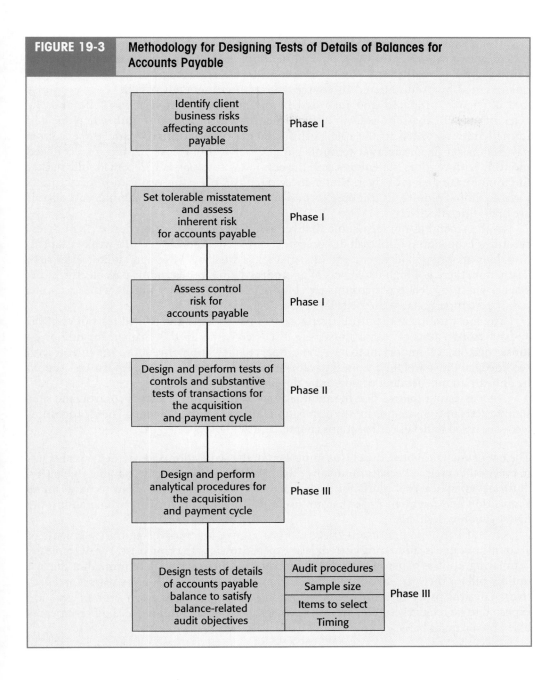

Like accounts receivable, there are typically a large number of transactions affecting accounts payable, the balance is often made up of a large number of accounts, the balance is large, and it is relatively expensive to audit the account. For these reasons, auditors typically set tolerable misstatement for accounts payable relatively high. For the same reasons, the auditor often assesses inherent risk as medium or high. Auditors are especially concerned about the completeness and the cutoff balance-related audit objectives for accounts payable because of the potential for understatements in the account balance.

Set Tolerable Misstatement and Assess Inherent Risk (Phase I)

As shown in Figure 19-3, once the auditor sets tolerable misstatement and inherent risk for accounts payable, the auditor uses his or her understanding of internal control to assess control risk. The auditor's ultimate substantive tests depend on the relative effectiveness of internal controls related to accounts payable. Therefore, it is important to have an understanding of how these controls relate to accounts payable.

Assess Control Risk and Design and Perform Tests of Controls and Substantive Tests of Transactions (Phases I and II)

The effects of the client's internal controls on accounts payable tests can be illustrated by two examples. In the first, assume that the client has highly effective internal controls over recording and paying for acquisitions. The receipt of goods is promptly documented by prenumbered receiving reports; prenumbered vouchers are promptly and efficiently prepared and recorded in the acquisition transactions file and the accounts payable master file. Cash disbursements are also made promptly when due and immediately recorded in the cash disbursements transactions file and the accounts payable master file. Individual accounts payable balances in the master file are reconciled monthly with vendors' statements, and the computer automatically reconciles the master file total to the general ledger. Under these circumstances, the verification of accounts payable should require little audit effort once the auditor concludes that internal controls are operating effectively.

In the second example, assume that receiving reports are not used, the client defers recording acquisitions until cash disbursements are made, and because of a weak cash position, bills are often paid several months after their due date. When an auditor faces such a situation, there is a high likelihood of an understatement of accounts payable; therefore, extensive tests of details of accounts payable are necessary to determine whether accounts payable is properly stated on the balance sheet date.

The most important controls over accounts payable and the related tests of controls and substantive tests of transactions were discussed earlier in this chapter. In addition to those controls, it is important to have a monthly reconciliation of vendors' statements with recorded liabilities and the accounts payable master file with the general ledger. This should be done by an independent person or by the computer.

After assessing control risk, the auditor designs and performs tests of controls and substantive tests of transactions for the acquisitions and cash disbursements. These procedures were discussed in detail earlier in this chapter and are not repeated here.

Design and Perform Analytical Procedures (Phase III)

OBJECTIVE 19-6

Design and perform analytical procedures for accounts payable.

The use of analytical procedures is as important in the acquisition and payment cycle as it is in every other cycle, especially for uncovering misstatements in accounts payable. Table 19-4 illustrates analytical procedures for the balance sheet and income statement accounts in the acquisition and payment cycle that are useful for uncovering areas in which additional investigation is desirable.

One of the most important analytical procedures for uncovering misstatements of accounts payable is comparing current year expense totals with prior years. For example, by comparing utilities expense with the prior year, the auditor may determine that the last utilities bill for the year was not recorded. Comparing expenses with prior years is an effective analytical procedure for accounts payable when expenses from year to year are expected to be relatively stable. Typical examples include rent, utilities, and other expenses billed on a regular basis.

TABLE 19-4	Analytical Procedures for the Acquisition and Payment Cycle
Analytical Procedure	**Possible Misstatement**
Compare acquisition-related expense account balances with prior years.	Misstatement of accounts payable and expenses.
Review list of accounts payable for unusual, nonvendor, and interest-bearing payables.	Classification misstatement for nontrade liabilities.
Compare individual accounts payable with previous years.	Unrecorded or nonexistent accounts, or misstatements.
Calculate ratios, such as purchases divided by accounts payable, and accounts payable divided by current liabilities.	Unrecorded or nonexistent accounts, or misstatements.

The overall objective in the audit of accounts payable is to determine whether the accounts payable balance is fairly stated and properly disclosed. Eight of the nine balance-related audit objectives discussed in Chapter 6 are applicable to accounts payable. Realizable value is not applicable to liabilities.

The auditor should recognize the difference in emphasis between the audit of liabilities and the audit of assets. When assets are being verified, attention is focused on making certain that the balance in the account is not overstated. The existence of recorded assets is constantly questioned and verified by confirmation, physical examination, and examination of supporting documents. The auditor should not ignore the possibility of assets being understated but should be more concerned about the possibility of overstatement than understatement. The opposite approach is taken in verifying liability balances; that is, the main focus is on understated or omitted liabilities.

The difference in emphasis in auditing assets and liabilities results directly from the *legal liability of CPAs.* If equity investors, creditors, and other users determine subsequent to the issuance of the audited financial statements that owners' equity was materially overstated, a lawsuit against the CPA firm is fairly likely. Because an overstatement of owners' equity can arise either from an overstatement of assets or from an understatement of liabilities, it is natural for CPAs to emphasize those two types of misstatements. The probability of a successful lawsuit against a CPA for failing to discover an understatement of owners' equity is far less likely.

Nevertheless, the auditing profession must avoid too much emphasis on protecting users from overstatements of owners' equity at the expense of ignoring understatements. If assets are consistently understated and liabilities are consistently overstated for large numbers of audited companies, the decision-making value of financial statement information is likely to decline. Therefore, even though it is natural for auditors to emphasize the possibility of overstating assets and understating liabilities, uncovering the opposite types of misstatements is also a significant responsibility.

The same balance-related audit objectives that were used as a frame of reference for verifying accounts receivable in Chapter 16 are also applicable to liabilities, with three minor modifications. The most obvious difference in verifying liabilities is the nonapplicability of the realizable value objective. The second difference is in the rights and obligations objective. For assets, the auditor is concerned with the client's rights to the use and disposal of the assets. For liabilities, the auditor is concerned with the client's obligations for the payment of the liability. If the client has no obligation to pay a liability, it should not be included as a liability. The third difference was discussed earlier: In auditing liabilities, the emphasis is on the search for understatements rather than for overstatements.

Table 19-5 (p. 596) includes the balance-related audit objectives and common tests of details of balances procedures for accounts payable. The actual audit procedures will vary considerably depending on the nature of the entity, the materiality of accounts payable, the nature and effectiveness of internal controls, and inherent risk.

Out-of-Period Liability Tests Because of the emphasis on understatements in liability accounts, *out-of-period liability tests* are important for accounts payable. The extent of tests to uncover unrecorded accounts payable, often called the *search for unrecorded accounts payable,* depends heavily on assessed control risk and the materiality of the potential balance in the account. The same audit procedures used to uncover unrecorded payables are applicable to the accuracy objective. The audit procedures that follow are typical tests.

Examine Underlying Documentation for Subsequent Cash Disbursements The purpose of this audit procedure is to uncover cash disbursements made in the subsequent accounting period that represent liabilities at the balance sheet date. Supporting documentation is examined to determine whether a cash disbursement was for a current period obligation. The receiving report indicates the date inventory was received and is therefore an especially useful document. Similarly, the vendor's invoice often indicates the date services were provided. Often, documentation for cash disbursements made in the subsequent period is

OBJECTIVE 19-7

Design and perform tests of details of balances for accounts payable, including out-of-period liability tests.

TABLE 19-5	**Balance-Related Audit Objectives and Tests of Details of Balances for Accounts Payable**	

Balance-Related Audit Objective	Common Tests of Details of Balances Procedures	Comments
Accounts payable in the accounts payable list agree with related master file, and the total is correctly added and agrees with the general ledger (detail tie-in).	Re-add or use the computer to total the accounts payable list. Trace the total to the general ledger. Trace individual vendors' invoices to master file for names and amounts.	All pages need not ordinarily be footed if footing manually. Unless controls are weak, tracing to master file should be limited.
Accounts payable in the accounts payable list exist (existence).	Trace from accounts payable list to vendors' invoices and statements. Confirm accounts payable, emphasizing large and unusual amounts.	Ordinarily receives little attention because the primary concern is with understatements.
Existing accounts payable are included in the accounts payable list (completeness).	Perform out-of-period liability tests (see discussion).	These are essential audit tests for accounts payable.
Accounts payable in the accounts payable list are accurate (accuracy).	Perform same procedures as those used for existence objective and out-of-period liability tests.	Ordinarily, the emphasis in these procedures for accuracy is understatement rather than omission.
Accounts payable in the accounts payable list are properly classified (classification).	Review the list and master file for related parties, notes or other interest-bearing liabilities, long-term payables, and debit balances.	Knowledge of the client's business is essential for these tests.
Transactions in the acquisition and payment cycle are recorded in the proper period (cutoff).	Perform out-of-period liability tests (see discussion). Perform detailed tests as part of physical observation of inventory (see discussion). Test for inventory in transit (see discussion).	These are essential audit tests for accounts payable. These are called *cutoff* tests.
The company has an obligation to pay the liabilities included in accounts payable (obligations).	Examine vendors' statements and confirm accounts payable.	Normally, not a concern in the audit of accounts payable because all accounts payable are obligations.
Accounts in the acquisition and payment cycle are properly presented and disclosed (presentation and disclosure).	Review statements to make sure material related parties and long-term and interest-bearing liabilities are segregated.	Ordinarily not a problem.

examined for several weeks, especially when the client does not pay bills on a timely basis. Any cash disbursement that is for a current period obligation should be traced to the accounts payable trial balance to make sure that it has been included as a liability.

Examine Underlying Documentation for Bills Not Paid Several Weeks After the Year-End This procedure is carried out in the same manner as the preceding one and serves the same purpose. The only difference is that it is done for unpaid obligations near the end of the audit field work rather than for obligations that have already been paid. For example, in an audit with a March 31 year-end, if the auditor examines the supporting documentation for checks paid until June 28, bills that are still unpaid at that date should be examined to determine whether they are obligations at March 31.

Trace Receiving Reports Issued Before Year-End to Related Vendors' Invoices All merchandise received before the year-end of the accounting period, indicated by the issuance of a receiving report, should be included as accounts payable. By tracing receiving reports issued at and before year-end to vendors' invoices and making sure that they are included in accounts payable, the auditor is testing for unrecorded obligations.

Trace Vendors' Statements That Show a Balance Due to the Accounts Payable Trial Balance If the client maintains a file of vendors' statements, any statement indicating a balance due at the balance sheet date can be traced to the listing to make sure that it is included as an account payable.

Send Confirmations to Vendors with Which the Client Does Business Although the use of confirmations for accounts payable is less common than for accounts receivable, it is sometimes used to test for vendors omitted from the accounts payable list, omitted transactions, and misstated account balances. Sending confirmations to active vendors for which a balance has not been included in the accounts payable list is a useful means of searching for omitted amounts. This type of confirmation is commonly called zero balance confirmation. Additional discussion of confirmation of accounts payable is deferred until the end of this chapter.

Cutoff Tests **Cutoff tests** for accounts payable are intended to determine whether transactions recorded a few days before and after the balance sheet date are included in the correct period. The five out-of-period liability audit tests just discussed are directly related to cutoff for acquisitions, but they emphasize understatements. For the first three procedures, it is also appropriate to examine supporting documentation as a test of overstatement of accounts payable. For example, the third procedure is to trace receiving reports issued before year-end to related vendors' invoices in order to test for unrecorded accounts payable. To test for overstatement cutoff amounts, the auditor should trace receiving reports issued *after* year-end to related invoices to make sure that they are not recorded as accounts payable (unless they are inventory in transit, which is discussed shortly).

Because most cutoff tests have already been discussed, only two aspects are expanded on here: the relationship of cutoff to physical observation of inventory and the determination of the amount of inventory in transit.

Relationship of Cutoff to Physical Observation of Inventory In determining that the accounts payable cutoff is correct, *it is essential that the cutoff tests be coordinated with the physical observation of inventory.* For example, assume that an inventory acquisition for $400,000 is received late in the afternoon of December 31, after the physical inventory is completed. If the acquisition is included in accounts payable and purchases but excluded from inventory, the result is an understatement of net earnings of $400,000. Conversely, if the acquisition is excluded from both inventory and accounts payable, there is a misstatement in the balance sheet, but the income statement is correct. The only way the auditor will know which type of misstatement has occurred is to coordinate cutoff tests with the observation of inventory.

The cutoff information for acquisitions should be obtained *during the physical observation* of the inventory. At this time, the auditor should review the procedures in the receiving department to determine that all inventory received was counted, and the auditor should record in the audit documentation the last receiving report number of inventory included in the physical count. During the year-end field work, the auditor should then test the accounting records for cutoff. The auditor should trace receiving report numbers to the accounts payable records to verify that they are correctly included or excluded.

For example, assume that the last receiving report number representing inventory included in the physical count was 3167. The auditor should record this document number and subsequently trace it and several preceding numbers to their related vendors' invoices and to the accounts payable list or the accounts payable master file to determine that they are all included. Similarly, accounts payable for acquisitions recorded on receiving reports with numbers larger than 3167 should be excluded from accounts payable.

When the client's physical inventory takes place before the last day of the year, it is still necessary to perform an accounts payable cutoff at the time of the physical count in the manner described in the preceding paragraph. In addition, the auditor must verify whether all acquisitions taking place between the physical count and the end of the year were added to the physical inventory and accounts payable. For example, if the client takes the physical count on December 27 for a December 31 year-end, the cutoff information is taken as of December 27. During the year-end field work, the auditor must first test to determine whether the cutoff was accurate as of December 27. After determining that the December 27 cutoff is accurate, the auditor must test whether all inventory received subsequent to the physical count, but on or before the balance sheet date, was added to inventory and accounts payable by the client.

Inventory in Transit A distinction in accounts payable must be made between acquisitions of inventory that are on an **FOB destination** basis and those that are made **FOB origin**. With the former, title passes to the buyer when it is received for inventory. Therefore, only inventory received on or before the balance sheet date should be included in inventory and accounts payable at year-end. When an acquisition is on an FOB origin basis, the inventory and related accounts payable must be recorded in the current period if shipment occurred on or before the balance sheet date.

Determining whether inventory has been acquired on an FOB destination or origin basis is done by examining vendors' invoices. The auditor should examine invoices for merchandise received shortly after year-end to determine whether they were on an FOB origin basis. For those that were, and when the shipment dates were on or before the balance sheet date, the inventory and related accounts payable must be recorded in the current period if the amounts are material.

Reliability of Evidence

OBJECTIVE 19-8

Distinguish the reliability of vendors' invoices, vendors' statements, and confirmations of accounts payable as audit evidence.

In deciding the appropriate evidence for verifying accounts payable, it is essential that the auditor understand the relative reliability of the three primary types of evidence ordinarily used: vendors' invoices, vendors' statements, and confirmations.

Distinction Between Vendors' Invoices and Vendors' Statements In verifying the amount due to a vendor, the auditor should make a distinction between vendors' invoices and vendors' statements. In examining vendors' invoices and related supporting documents, such as receiving reports and purchase orders, the auditor gets highly reliable *evidence about individual transactions*. A vendor's statement is not as desirable as invoices for verifying individual transactions because a statement includes only the total amount of the transaction. The units acquired, price, freight, and other data are not included. However, a statement has the advantage of including the ending balance according to the vendor's records. Which of these two documents is better for verifying the correct balance in accounts payable? *The vendor's statement is superior for verifying accounts payable* because it includes the ending balance. The auditor could compare existing vendors' invoices with the client's list and still not uncover missing ones, which is the primary concern in accounts payable. Which of these two documents is better for testing acquisitions in tests of controls and substantive tests of transactions? *The vendor's invoice is superior for verifying transactions* because the auditor is verifying individual transactions and the invoice shows the details of the acquisitions.

Difference Between Vendors' Statements and Confirmations The most important distinction between a vendor's statement and a confirmation of accounts payable is the source of the information. A vendor's statement has been prepared by an independent third party but is in the hands of the client at the time the auditor examines it. This provides the client with an opportunity to alter a vendor's statement or to not make certain statements available to the auditor. A confirmation of accounts payable, which normally is a request for an itemized statement sent directly to the CPA's office, provides the same information but can be regarded as more reliable. In addition, confirmations of accounts payable often include a request for information about notes and acceptances payable as well as consigned inventory owned by the vendor but stored on the client's premises. An illustration of a typical accounts payable confirmation request is given in Figure 19-4.

Because of the availability of vendors' statements and vendors' invoices, which are both relatively reliable evidence because they originate from a third party, the confirmation of accounts payable is less common than confirmation of accounts receivable. If the client has adequate internal controls and vendors' statements are available for examination, confirmations are normally not sent. However, when the client's internal controls are weak, when statements are not available, or when the auditor questions the client's integrity, it is desirable to send confirmation requests to vendors. Because of the emphasis on understatements of liability accounts, the accounts confirmed should include large, active, zero balance accounts and a representative sample of all others.

In most instances in which accounts payable are confirmed, it is done shortly after the balance sheet date. However, if assessed control risk is low, it may be possible to confirm

FIGURE 19-4   Accounts Payable Confirmation Request

ROGER MEAD, INC.   January 15, 2006
Jones Sales, Inc.
2116 Stewart Street
Wayneville, Kentucky 36021

To Whom It May Concern:

Our auditors, Murray and Rogers, CPAs, are conducting an audit of our financial statements. For this purpose, please furnish them with the following information as of December 31, 2005.

(1)   Itemized statements of our accounts payable to you showing all unpaid items;
(2)   A complete list of any notes and acceptances payable to you (including any which have been discounted) showing the original date, dates due, original amount, unpaid balance, collateral, and endorsers; and
(3)   An itemized list of your merchandise consigned to us.

Your prompt attention to this request will be appreciated. An envelope is enclosed for your reply.

Yours truly,

Phil Geriovini

Phil Geriovini, President

accounts payable at an interim date as a test of the effectiveness of internal controls. Then if the confirmations indicate that the internal controls are ineffective, it is possible to design other audit procedures to test accounts payable at year-end.

When vendors' statements are examined or confirmations are received, there must be a *reconciliation* of the statement or confirmation with the accounts payable list. Differences are often caused by inventory in transit, checks mailed by the client but not received by the vendor at the statement date, and delays in processing the accounting records. The reconciliation is of the same general nature as that discussed in Chapter 16 for accounts receivable. The documents typically used to reconcile the balances on the accounts payable list with the confirmations or vendors' statements include receiving reports, vendors' invoices, and cancelled checks.

Sample Size

The discussion of tests of details of the accounts payable balance has focused heavily on the typical audit procedures performed, the documents and records examined, and the timing of the tests. The auditor must also consider sample sizes in the audit of accounts payable.

Sample sizes for accounts payable tests vary considerably, depending on such factors as the materiality of accounts payable, number of accounts outstanding, assessed control risk, and results of the prior year. When a client's internal controls are weak, which is not uncommon for accounts payable, almost all population items must be verified. In other situations, minimal testing is needed.

Statistical sampling is less commonly used for the audit of accounts payable than for accounts receivable. It is more difficult to define the population and determine the population size in accounts payable. Because the emphasis is on omitted accounts payable, it is essential that the population include all potential payables.

SUMMARY

Figure 19-5 (p. 600) summarizes how the five types of audit tests are used to obtain audit assurance for transactions and accounts in the acquisition and payment cycle. Procedures to gain an understanding of internal control and tests of controls evaluate whether controls over transactions in the

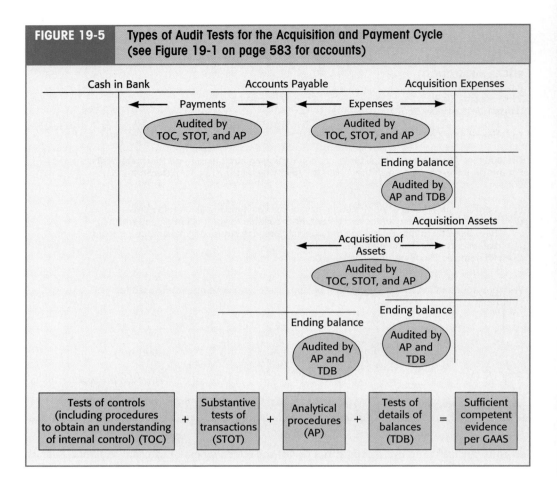

FIGURE 19-5 Types of Audit Tests for the Acquisition and Payment Cycle (see Figure 19-1 on page 583 for accounts)

cycle are operating effectively to reduce control risk and thereby reduce substantive testing of ending balances in the related accounts. By combining all types of audit tests shown in Figure 19-5, the auditor obtains a higher overall assurance for transactions and accounts in the acquisition and payment cycle than the assurance obtained from any one test. To increase overall assurance for the cycle, the auditor can increase the assurance obtained from any one of the tests.

ESSENTIAL TERMS

Accounts payable master file—a computer file for maintaining a record for each vendor of individual acquisitions, cash disbursements, acquisition returns and allowances, and vendor balances

Accounts payable trial balance—a listing of the amount owed to each vendor at a point in time; prepared directly from the accounts payable master file

Acquisition and payment cycle—the transaction cycle that includes the acquisition of and payment for goods and services from suppliers outside the organization

Cutoff tests—tests to determine whether transactions recorded a few days before and after the balance sheet date are included in the correct period

Debit memo—a document indicating a reduction in the amount owed to a vendor because of returned goods or an allowance granted

FOB destination—shipping contract in which title to the goods passes to the buyer when the goods are received

FOB origin—shipping contract in which title to the goods passes to the buyer at the time that the goods are shipped

Purchase order—a document prepared by the purchasing department indicating the description, quantity, and related information for goods and services that the company intends to purchase

Purchase requisition—request by an authorized employee to the purchasing department to place an order for inventory and other items used by an entity

Receiving report—a document prepared by the receiving department at the time tangible goods are received, indicating the description of the goods, the quantity received, the date received, and other relevant data; it is part of the documentation necessary for payment to be made

Vendor's invoice—a document that specifies the details of an acquisition transaction and amount of money owed to the vendor for an acquisition

Vendor's statement—a statement prepared monthly by the vendor, which indicates the customer's beginning balance, acquisitions, payments, and ending balance

REVIEW QUESTIONS

19-1 (Objective 19-1) List five asset accounts, three liability accounts, and five expense accounts included in the acquisition and payment cycle for a typical manufacturing company.

19-2 (Objective 19-4) List one possible internal control for each of the six transaction-related audit objectives for cash disbursements. For each control, list a test of control to test its effectiveness.

19-3 (Objective 19-4) List one possible control for each of the six transaction-related audit objectives for acquisitions. For each control, list a test of control to test its effectiveness.

19-4 (Objective 19-4) Evaluate the following statement by an auditor concerning tests of acquisitions and cash disbursements: "In selecting the acquisitions and cash disbursements sample for testing, the best approach is to select a random month and test every transaction for the period. Using this approach enables me to thoroughly understand internal control because I have examined everything that happened during the period. As a part of the monthly test, I also test the beginning and ending bank reconciliations and prepare a proof of cash for the month. At the completion of these tests I feel I can evaluate the effectiveness of internal control."

19-5 (Objective 19-4) What is the importance of cash discounts to the client and how can the auditor verify whether they are being taken in accordance with company policy?

19-6 (Objective 19-4) What are the similarities and differences in the objectives of the following two procedures? (1) Select a random sample of receiving reports and trace them to related vendors' invoices and acquisitions journal entries, comparing the vendor's name, type of material and quantity acquired, and total amount of the acquisition. (2) Select a random sample of acquisitions journal entries and trace them to related vendors' invoices and receiving reports, comparing the vendor's name, type of material and quantity acquired, and total amount of the acquisition.

19-7 (Objectives 19-2, 19-4) If an audit client does not have prenumbered checks, what type of misstatement has a greater chance of occurring? Under the circumstances, what audit procedure can the auditor use to compensate for the weakness?

19-8 (Objective 19-2) What is meant by a voucher? Explain how its use can improve an organization's internal controls.

19-9 (Objective 19-2) Explain why most auditors consider the receipt of goods and services the most important point in the acquisition and payment cycle.

19-10 (Objectives 19-4, 19-7) Explain the relationship between tests of the acquisition and payment cycle and tests of inventory. Give specific examples of how these two types of tests affect each other.

19-11 (Objectives 19-4, 19-5) Explain the relationship between tests of the acquisition and payment cycle and tests of accounts payable. Give specific examples of how these two types of tests affect each other.

19-12 (Objective 19-7) The CPA examines all unrecorded invoices on hand as of February 28, 2006, the last day of field work. Which of the following misstatements is most likely to be uncovered by this procedure? Explain.

   a. Accounts payable are overstated at December 31, 2005.

   b. Accounts payable are understated at December 31, 2005.

   c. Operating expenses are overstated for the 12 months ended December 31, 2005.

   d. Operating expenses are overstated for the two months ended February 28, 2006.*

19-13 (Objective 19-8) Explain why it is common for auditors to send confirmation requests to vendors with "zero balances" on the client's accounts payable listing but uncommon to follow the same approach in verifying accounts receivable.

*AICPA adapted.

19-14 (Objectives 19-2, 19-8) Distinguish between a vendor's invoice and a vendor's statement. Which document should ideally be used as evidence in auditing acquisition transactions and which for verifying accounts payable balances? Why?

19-15 (Objective 19-8) It is less common to confirm accounts payable at an interim date than accounts receivable. Explain why.

19-16 (Objective 19-7) In testing the cutoff of accounts payable at the balance sheet date, explain why it is important that auditors coordinate their tests with the physical observation of inventory. What can the auditor do during the physical inventory to enhance the likelihood of an accurate cutoff?

19-17 (Objective 19-7) Distinguish between FOB destination and FOB origin. What procedures should the auditor follow concerning acquisitions of inventory on an FOB origin basis near year-end?

MULTIPLE CHOICE QUESTIONS FROM CPA EXAMINATIONS

19-18 (Objective 19-4) The following questions concern internal controls in the acquisition and payment cycle. Choose the best response.

a. Effective internal control over the purchasing of raw materials should usually include all of the following procedures except
   (1) systematic reporting of product changes that will affect raw materials.
   (2) determining the need for the raw materials prior to preparing the purchase order.
   (3) obtaining third-party, written quality and quantity reports prior to payment for the raw materials.
   (4) obtaining financial approval prior to making a commitment.

b. Budd, the purchasing agent of Lake Hardware Wholesalers, has a relative who owns a retail hardware store. Budd arranged for hardware to be delivered by manufacturers to the retail store on a COD basis, thereby enabling his relative to buy at Lake's wholesale prices. Budd was probably able to accomplish this because of Lake's poor internal control over
   (1) purchase requisitions.
   (2) cash receipts.
   (3) perpetual inventory records.
   (4) purchase orders.

c. Which of the following is an internal control that would prevent paid cash disbursement documents from being presented for payment a second time?
   (1) Unsigned checks should be prepared by individuals who are responsible for signing checks.
   (2) Cash disbursement documents should be approved by at least two responsible management officials.
   (3) The date on cash disbursement documents should be within a few days of the date that the document is presented for payment.
   (4) The official signing the check should compare the check with the documents and should deface the documents.

19-19 (Objectives 19-7, 19-8) The following questions concern accumulating evidence in the acquisition and payment cycle. Choose the best response.

a. In auditing accounts payable, an auditor's procedures most likely would focus primarily on management's assertion of
   (1) existence or occurrence.
   (2) presentation and disclosure.
   (3) completeness.
   (4) valuation or allocation.

b. Which of the following audit procedures is best for identifying unrecorded trade accounts payable?
   (1) Examining unusual relationships between monthly accounts payable balances and recorded cash payments.
   (2) Reconciling vendors' statements to the file of receiving reports to identify items received just prior to the balance sheet date.
   (3) Reviewing cash disbursements recorded subsequent to the balance sheet date to determine whether the related payables apply to the prior period.
   (4) Investigating payables recorded just prior to and just subsequent to the balance sheet date to determine whether they are supported by receiving reports.

c. When using confirmations to provide evidence about the completeness assertion for accounts payable, the appropriate population most likely is
   (1) vendors with whom the entity has previously done business.
   (2) amounts recorded in the accounts payable subsidiary ledger.
   (3) payees of checks drawn in the month after year-end.
   (4) invoices filed in the entity's open invoice file.

DISCUSSION QUESTIONS AND PROBLEMS

19-20 (Objective 19-4) Questions 1 through 8 are typically found in questionnaires used by auditors to obtain an understanding of internal control in the acquisition and payment cycle. In using the questionnaire for a client, a "yes" response to a question indicates a possible internal control, whereas a "no" indicates a potential weakness.

1. Is the purchasing function performed by personnel who are independent of the receiving and shipping functions and the payables and disbursing functions?
2. Are all vendors' invoices routed directly to accounting from the mailroom?
3. Are all receiving reports prenumbered and the numerical sequence checked by a person independent of check preparation?
4. Are all extensions, footings, discounts, and freight terms on vendors' invoices checked for accuracy?
5. Does a responsible employee review and approve the invoice account distribution before the transaction is entered in the computer?
6. Are checks automatically posted in the cash disbursements journal as they are prepared?
7. Are all supporting documents properly cancelled at the time the checks are signed?
8. Is the custody of checks after signature and before mailing handled by an employee independent of all payable, disbursing, cash, and general ledger functions?

a. For each of the preceding questions, state the transaction-related audit objective(s) being fulfilled if the control is in effect.   **Required**

b. For each internal control, list a test of control to test its effectiveness.

c. For each of the preceding questions, identify the nature of the potential financial misstatement(s) if the control is not in effect.

d. For each of the potential misstatements in part c, list a substantive audit procedure that can be used to determine whether a material misstatement exists.

19-21 (Objective 19-4) Following are some of the tests of controls and substantive tests of transactions procedures commonly performed in the acquisition and payment cycle. Each is to be done on a sample basis.

1. Trace transactions recorded in the acquisitions journal to supporting documentation, comparing the vendor's name, total dollar amounts, and authorization for acquisition.
2. Account for a sequence of receiving reports and trace selected ones to related vendors' invoices and acquisitions journal entries.
3. Review supporting documents for clerical accuracy, propriety of account distribution, and reasonableness of expenditure in relation to the nature of the client's operations.
4. Examine documents in support of acquisition transactions to make sure that each transaction has an approved vendor's invoice, receiving report, and purchase order included.
5. Foot the cash disbursements journal, trace postings of the total to the general ledger, and trace postings of individual cash disbursements to the accounts payable master file.
6. Account for a numerical sequence of checks in the cash disbursements journal and examine all voided or spoiled checks for proper cancellation.
7. Prepare a proof of cash disbursements for an interim month.
8. Compare dates on cancelled checks with dates on the cash disbursements journal and the bank cancellation date.

a. State whether each procedure above is primarily a test of control or substantive test of transactions.   **Required**

b. State the purpose(s) of each procedure.

19-22 (Objective 19-3) Donnen Designs, Inc. is a small manufacturer of women's casual-wear jewelry, including bracelets, necklaces, earrings, and other moderately priced accessory items. Most of their products are made from silver, various low-cost stones, beads, and other decorative jewelry pieces. Donnen Designs is not involved in the manufacturing of high-end jewelry items, such as those made of gold and semiprecious or precious stones.

Personnel responsible for purchasing raw material jewelry items for Donnen Designs would like to place orders directly with suppliers who offer their products for sale through Internet Web sites. Most suppliers provide pictures of all jewelry components on their Web sites, along with pricing and other sales-term information. Customers who have valid business licenses are able to purchase the products at wholesale, rather than retail prices. Customers can place orders online and pay for those goods immediately by using a valid credit card. Purchases made by credit card are shipped by the suppliers once the credit approval is received from the credit card agency, which usually occurs the same day. Customers can also place orders online with payment being later made by check. However, in that event, purchases are not shipped until the check is received and cashed by the supplier. Some of the suppliers allow a 30-day full-payment refund policy, whereas other suppliers accept returns but only grant credit toward future purchases from that supplier.

Required

a. Identify advantages for Donnen Designs if management allows purchasing personnel to order goods online through supplier Web sites.

b. Identify potential risks associated with Donnen Designs' purchase of jewelry pieces through supplier Internet Web sites.

c. Describe advantages of allowing purchasing agents to purchase products online using a Donnen Designs credit card.

d. Describe advantages of allowing purchasing agents to purchase products online with payment made only by check.

e. What internal controls could be implemented to ensure that
   (1) purchasing agents do not use Donnen credit cards to purchase nonjewelry items for their own purposes, if Donnen allows purchasing agents to purchase jewelry using Donnen credit cards?
   (2) purchasing agents do not order jewelry items from the suppliers and ship those items to addresses other than Donnen addresses?
   (3) Donnen does not end up with unused credits with jewelry suppliers as a result of returning unacceptable jewelry items to suppliers who only grant credit toward future purchases?

19-23 (Objectives 19-4, 19-7) The following misstatements are included in the accounting records of Westgate Manufacturing Company.

1. Telephone expense (account 2112) was unintentionally charged to repairs and maintenance (account 2121).

2. Acquisitions of raw materials are often not recorded until several weeks after the goods are received because receiving personnel fail to forward receiving reports to accounting. When pressure from a vendor's credit department is put on Westgate's accounting department, it searches for the receiving report, records the transactions in the acquisitions journal, and pays the bill.

3. The accounts payable clerk prepares a monthly check to Story Supply Company for the amount of an invoice owed and submits the unsigned check to the treasurer for payment along with related supporting documents that have already been approved. When she receives the signed check from the treasurer, she records it as a debit to accounts payable and deposits the check in a personal bank account for a company named Story Company. A few days later, she records the invoice in the acquisitions journal again, resubmits the documents and a new check to the treasurer, and sends the check to the vendor after it has been signed.

4. The amount of a check in the cash disbursements journal is recorded as $4,612.87 instead of $6,412.87.

5. The accounts payable clerk intentionally excluded from the cash disbursements journal seven larger checks written and mailed on December 26 to prevent cash in the bank from having a negative balance on the general ledger. They were recorded on January 2 of the subsequent year.

6. Each month, a fraudulent receiving report is submitted to accounting by an employee in the receiving department. A few days later, he sends Westgate an invoice for the quantity of goods ordered from a small company he owns and operates in the evening. A check is prepared, and the amount is paid when the receiving report and the vendor's invoice are matched by the accounts payable clerk.

Required

a. For each misstatement, identify the transaction-related audit objective that was not met.

b. For each misstatement, state a control that should have prevented it from occurring on a continuing basis.

c. For each misstatement, state a substantive audit procedure that could uncover it.

19-24 (Objectives 19-6, 19-7, 19-8) The following auditing procedures were performed in the audit of accounts payable:

1. Examine supporting documents for cash disbursements several days before and after year-end.
2. Examine the acquisitions and cash disbursements journals for the last few days of the current period and first few days of the succeeding period, looking for large or unusual transactions.
3. Trace from the general ledger trial balance and supporting documentation to determine whether accounts payable, related parties, and other related assets and liabilities are properly included on the financial statements.
4. For liabilities that are payable in a foreign currency, determine the exchange rate and check calculations.
5. Discuss with the bookkeeper whether any amounts included on the accounts payable list are due to related parties, debit balances, or notes payable.
6. Obtain vendors' statements from the controller and reconcile to the listing of accounts payable.
7. Obtain vendors' statements directly from vendors and reconcile to the listing of accounts payable.
8. Obtain a list of accounts payable. Re-add and compare with the general ledger.

a. For each procedure, identify the type of audit evidence used. **Required**
b. For each procedure, use the following matrix to identify which balance-related audit objective(s) were satisfied. (Procedure 1 is completed as an illustration.)
c. Evaluate the need to have certain objectives satisfied by more than one audit procedure.

AUDIT PROCEDURE	BALANCE-RELATED AUDIT OBJECTIVE							
	Detail tie-in	Existence	Completeness	Accuracy	Classification	Cutoff	Obligations	Presentation and disclosure
1			X			X		
2								
3								
4								
5								
6								
7								
8								

19-25 (Objectives 19-4, 19-5) In testing cash disbursements for the Jay Klein Company, you obtained an understanding of internal control. The controls are reasonably good, and no unusual audit problems arose in previous years.

Although there are not many individuals in the accounting department, there is a reasonable separation of duties in the organization. There is a separate purchasing agent who is responsible for ordering goods and a separate receiving department that counts the goods when they are received and prepares receiving reports. There is a separation of duties between recording acquisitions and cash disbursements, and all information is recorded in the two journals independently. The controller reviews all supporting documents before signing the checks, and he immediately mails the checks to the vendors. Check copies are used for subsequent recording.

All aspects of internal control seem satisfactory to you, and you perform minimum tests of 25 transactions as a means of assessing control risk. In your tests, you discover the following exceptions:

1. Two items in the acquisitions journal have been misclassified.
2. Three invoices had not been initialed by the controller, but there were no dollar misstatements evident in the transactions.
3. Five receiving reports were recorded in the acquisitions journal at least 2 weeks later than their date on the receiving report.
4. One invoice has been paid twice. The second payment was supported by a duplicate copy of the invoice. Both copies of the invoice had been marked "paid."
5. One check amount in the cash disbursements journal was for $100 less than the amount stated on the vendor's invoice.
6. One voided check was missing.
7. Two receiving reports for vendors' invoices were missing from the transaction packets. One vendor's invoice had an extension error, and the invoice had been initialed that the amount had been checked.

Required
a. Identify whether each of 1 through 7 was a control test deviation, a monetary misstatement, or both.
b. For each exception, identify which transaction-related audit objective was not met.
c. What is the audit importance of each of these exceptions?
d. What follow-up procedures would you use to determine more about the nature of each exception?
e. How would each of these exceptions affect the balance of your audit? Be specific.
f. Identify internal controls that should have prevented each misstatement.

19-26 (Objective 19-4) You are the staff auditor testing the combined acquisitions and cash disbursements journal for a small audit client. The internal controls are regarded as reasonably effective, considering the number of personnel.

The in-charge auditor decided that a sample of 30 items should be sufficient for this audit because of the excellent controls. He gives you the following instructions:

1. All transactions selected must exceed $1,000.
2. At least 15 of the transactions must be for acquisitions of raw material because these transactions are typically material.
3. It is not acceptable to include the same vendor in the sample more than once.
4. All vendors' invoices that cannot be located must be replaced with a new sample item.
5. Both checks and supporting documents are to be examined for the same transactions.
6. The sample must be random, after modifications for instructions 1 through 5.

Required
a. Evaluate each of these instructions for testing acquisition and cash disbursements transactions.
b. Explain the difficulties of applying each of these instructions to attributes sampling.

19-27 (Objective 19-7) You were in the final stages of your audit of the financial statements of Ozine Corporation for the year ended December 31, 2005, when you were consulted by the corporation's president, who believes there is no point to your examining the year 2006 acquisitions journal and testing data in support of year 2006 entries. He stated that (a) bills pertaining to 2005 that were received too late to be included in the December acquisitions journal were recorded as of the year-end by the corporation by journal entry, (b) the internal auditor made tests after the year-end, and (c) he would furnish you with a letter certifying that there were no unrecorded liabilities.

Required
a. Should a CPA's test for unrecorded liabilities be affected by the fact that the client made a journal entry to record 2005 bills that were received late? Explain.
b. Should a CPA's test for unrecorded liabilities be affected by the fact that a letter is obtained in which a responsible management official certifies that to the best of his or her knowledge all liabilities have been recorded? Explain.
c. Should a CPA's test for unrecorded liabilities be eliminated or reduced because of the internal audit tests? Explain.
d. Assume that the corporation, which handled some government contracts, had no internal auditor but that an auditor for a federal agency spent 3 weeks auditing the records and was just completing his work at this time. How would the CPA's unrecorded liability test be affected by the work of the auditor for a federal agency?
e. What sources in addition to the year 2006 acquisitions journal should the CPA consider to locate possible unrecorded liabilities?*

*AICPA adapted.

19-28 (Objectives 19-2, 19-4, 19-5, 19-7) Because of the small size of the company and the limited number of accounting personnel, the Dry Goods Wholesale Company initially records all acquisitions of goods and services at the time cash disbursements are made. At the end of each quarter, when financial statements for internal purposes are prepared, accounts payable are recorded by adjusting journal entries. The entries are reversed at the beginning of the subsequent period. Except for the lack of an acquisitions journal, the controls over acquisitions are excellent for a small company. (There are adequate prenumbered documents for all acquisitions, proper approvals, and adequate internal verification wherever possible.)

Before the auditor arrives for the year-end audit, the bookkeeper prepares adjusting entries to record the accounts payable as of the balance sheet date. A list of all outstanding balances is prepared, by vendor, on an accounts payable listing and is given to the auditor. All vendors' invoices supporting the list are retained in a separate file for the auditor's use.

In the current year, the accounts payable balance has increased dramatically because of a severe cash shortage. (The cash shortage apparently arose from expansion of inventory and facilities rather than lack of sales.) Many accounts have remained unpaid for several months and the client is getting pressure from several vendors to pay the bills. Because the company had a relatively profitable year, management is anxious to complete the audit as early as possible so that the audited statements can be used to obtain a large bank loan.

Required

a. Explain how the lack of an acquisitions journal will affect the auditor's tests of controls and substantive tests of transactions for acquisitions and cash disbursements.

b. What should the auditor use as a sampling unit in performing tests of acquisitions?

c. Assuming no misstatements are discovered in the auditor's tests of controls and substantive tests of transactions for acquisitions and cash disbursements, how will that result affect the verification of accounts payable?

d. Discuss the reasonableness of the client's request for an early completion of the audit and the implications of the request from the auditor's point of view.

e. List the audit procedures that should be performed in the year-end audit of accounts payable to meet the cutoff objective.

f. State your opinion as to whether it is possible to conduct an adequate audit in these circumstances.

19-29 (Objectives 19-7, 19-8) Mincin, CPA, is the auditor of the Raleigh Corporation. Mincin is considering the audit work to be performed in the accounts payable area for the current year's engagement.

The prior year's audit schedules show that confirmation requests were mailed to 100 of Raleigh's 1,000 suppliers. The selected suppliers were based on Mincin's sample, which was designed to select accounts with large dollar balances. A substantial number of hours were spent by Raleigh and Mincin resolving relatively minor differences between the confirmation replies and Raleigh's accounting records. Alternative audit procedures were used for those suppliers who did not respond to the confirmation requests.

Required

a. Identify the accounts payable balance-related audit objectives that Mincin must consider in determining the audit procedures to be followed.

b. Identify situations in which Mincin should use accounts payable confirmations and discuss whether Mincin is required to use them.

c. Discuss why the use of large dollar balances as the basis for selecting accounts payable for confirmation might not be the most effective approach and indicate what more effective procedures could be followed when selecting accounts payable for confirmation.*

19-30 (Objective 19-8) As part of the June 30, 2005, audit of accounts payable of Milner Products Company, the auditor sent 22 confirmations of accounts payable to vendors in the form of requests for statements. Four of the statements were not returned by the vendors, and five vendors reported balances different from the amounts recorded in Milner's accounts payable master file. The auditor made duplicate copies of the five vendors' statements to maintain control of the independent information and turned the originals over to the client's accounts payable clerk to reconcile the differences. Two days later, the clerk returned the five statements to the auditor with the information on the audit schedule on page 608.

Required

a. Evaluate the acceptability of having the client perform the reconciliations, assuming that the auditor intends to perform adequate additional tests.

b. Describe the additional tests that should be performed for each of the five statements that included differences.

c. What audit procedures should be performed for the nonresponses to the confirmation requests?

*AICPA adapted.

Statement 1	Balance per vendor's statement	$ 6,618.01
	Payment by Milner on June 30, 2005	(4,601.01)
	Balance per master file	$ 2,017.00
Statement 2	Balance per vendor's statement	$ 9,618.93
	Invoices not received by Milner	(2,733.18)
	Payment by Milner on June 15, 2005	(1,000.00)
	Balance per master file	$ 5,885.75
Statement 3	Balance per vendor's statement	$26,251.80
	Balance per master file	(20,516.11)
	Difference cannot be located because the vendor failed to provide details of its account balance	$ 5,735.69
Statement 4	Balance per vendor's statement	$ 6,170.15
	Credit memo issued by vendor on July 15, 2005	(2,360.15)
	Balance per master file	$ 3,810.00
Statement 5	Balance per vendor's statement	$ 8,619.21
	Payment by Milner on July 3, 2005	(3,000.00)
	Unlocated difference not followed up because of minor amount	215.06
	Balance per master file	$ 5,834.27

19-31 (Objective 19-7) The physical inventory for Ajak Manufacturing was taken on December 30, 2004, rather than December 31, because the client had to operate the plant for a special order the last day of the year. At the time of the client's physical count, you observed that acquisitions represented by receiving report number 2631 and all preceding ones were included in the physical count, whereas inventory represented by succeeding numbers was excluded. On the evening of December 31, you stopped by the plant and noted that inventory represented by receiving report numbers 2632 through 2634 was received subsequent to the physical count but before the end of the year. You later noted that the final inventory on the financial statements contained only those items included in the physical count. In testing accounts payable at December 31, 2004, you obtain a schedule from the client to aid you in testing the adequacy of the cutoff. The following schedule includes the information that you have not yet resolved:

Receiving Report Number	Amount of Vendor's Invoice	Amount Presently Included in or Excluded from Accounts Payable*	INFORMATION ON THE VENDOR'S INVOICE		
			Invoice Date	Shipping Date	FOB Origin or Destination
2631	$2,619.26	Included	12-30-04	12-30-04	Origin
2632	3,709.16	Excluded	12-26-04	12-15-04	Destination
2633	5,182.31	Included	12-31-04	12-26-04	Origin
2634	6,403.00	Excluded	12-16-04	12-27-04	Destination
2635	8,484.91	Included	12-28-04	12-31-04	Origin
2636	5,916.20	Excluded	01-03-05	12-31-04	Destination
2637	7,515.50	Excluded	01-05-05	12-26-04	Origin
2638	2,407.87	Excluded	12-31-04	01-03-05	Origin

*All entries to record inventory acquisitions are recorded by the client as a debit to purchases and a credit to accounts payable.

Required

a. Explain the relationship between inventory and accounts payable cutoff.

b. For each of the receiving reports, state the misstatement in inventory or accounts payable, if any exists, and prepare an adjusting entry to correct the financial statements, if a misstatement exists.

c. Which of the misstatements in part b are most important? Explain.

CASE

19-32 (Objectives 19-2, 19-4, 19-5, 19-7) The following tests of controls and substantive tests of transactions audit procedures for acquisitions and cash disbursements are to be used in the audit of Ward Publishing Company. You concluded that internal control appears effective and a reduced assessed control risk is likely to be cost beneficial. Ward's active involvement in the business, good separation of duties, and a competent controller and other employees are factors affecting your opinion.

Ward Publishing Company—Part I (See below for Part II and Case 20-28 on page 632 for Part III)

Tests of Controls and Substantive Tests of Transactions Audit Procedures for Acquisitions and Cash Disbursements

1. Foot and cross-foot the acquisitions and cash disbursements journals for 2 months and trace totals to postings in the general ledger.
2. Scan the acquisitions and cash disbursements journals for all months and investigate any unusual entries.
3. Reconcile cash disbursements per books to cash disbursements per bank statement for 1 month.
4. Examine evidence that the bank reconciliation is prepared by the controller.
5. Inquire and observe whether the accounts payable master file balances are periodically reconciled to vendors' statements by the controller.
6. Examine the log book as evidence that the numerical sequence of checks is accounted for by someone independent of the preparation function.
7. Inquire and observe that checks are mailed by D. Ward or someone under his supervision after he signs checks.
8. Examine initials indicating that the controller balances the accounts payable master file to the general ledger monthly.
9. Select a sample of entries in the cash disbursements journal, and
   a. obtain related cancelled checks and compare with entry for payee, date, and amount and examine signature endorsement.
   b. obtain vendors' invoices, receiving reports, and purchase orders, and
      (1) examine vendors' invoices to determine that all supporting documents are attached.
      (2) determine that documents agree with the cash disbursements journal.
      (3) compare vendors' names, amounts, and dates with entries.
      (4) determine whether a discount was taken when appropriate.
      (5) examine vendors' invoices for initials indicating an independent review of chart of account codings.
      (6) examine reasonableness of cash disbursements and account codings.
      (7) review invoices for approval of acquisitions by Ward.
      (8) review purchase orders and/or purchase requisitions for proper approval.
      (9) verify prices and recalculate footings and extensions on invoices.
      (10) compare quantities and descriptions on purchase orders, receiving reports, and vendors' invoices to the extent applicable.
      (11) examine vendors' invoices and receiving reports to determine that the check numbers are included and the documents are marked "paid" at the time of check signing.
   c. Trace postings to the accounts payable master file for name, amount, and date.
10. Select a sample of receiving reports issued during the year and trace to vendors' invoice and entries in the acquisitions journal.
    a. Compare type of merchandise, name of vendor, date received, quantities, and amounts.
    b. If the transaction is indicated in the acquisitions journal as paid, trace the check number to the entry in the cash disbursements journal. If unpaid, investigate reasons.
    c. Trace transactions to accounts payable master file, comparing name, amount, and date.

Required

Prepare all parts of a sampling data sheet (such as the one in Figure 15-2 on page 455) through the planned sample size for the preceding audit program, assuming that a line item in the cash disbursements journal is used for the sampling unit. Use either nonstatistical or attributes sampling. For all procedures for which the line item in the cash disbursements journal is not an appropriate sampling unit, assume that audit procedures were performed on a nonsampling basis. For all tests of controls, use a tolerable exception rate of 5%, and for all substantive tests of transactions, use a rate of 6%. Use an ARACR of 10%, which is considered medium. Plan for an estimated population exception rate of 1% for tests of controls and 0% for substantive tests of transactions.

Prepare the data sheet using the computer (instructor option—also applies to Part II).

Part II

Assume a sample size of 50 for all procedures, regardless of your answers in Part I. For other procedures, assume that an adequate sample size for the circumstance was selected. The only exceptions in your audit tests for all tests of controls and substantive tests of transactions audit procedures are as follows:

1. Procedure 2—Two large transactions were identified as being unusual. Investigation determined that they were authorized acquisitions of fixed assets. They were both correctly recorded.

2. Procedure 9b(1)—A purchase order had not been attached to a vendor's invoice. The purchase order was found in a separate file and determined to be approved and appropriate.
3. Procedure 9b(5)—Six vendors' invoices were not initialed as being internally verified. Three actual misclassifications existed. The controller explained that he often did not review codings because of the competence of the accounting clerk doing the coding and was surprised at the mistakes.

Required

a. Complete the sampling data sheet from Part I using either nonstatistical or attributes sampling.

b. Explain the effect of the exceptions on tests of details of accounts payable. Which balance-related audit objectives are affected, and how do those objectives, in turn, affect the audit of accounts payable?

c. Given your tests of controls and substantive tests of transactions results, write an audit program for tests of details of balances for accounts payable. Assume:
   (1) The client provided a list of accounts payable, prepared from the master file.
   (2) Acceptable audit risk for accounts payable is high.
   (3) Inherent risk for accounts payable is low.
   (4) Analytical procedure results were excellent.

INTERNET PROBLEM 19-1: MANAGING THE ACCOUNTS PAYABLE FUNCTION

Reference the CW site. Many companies have hundreds, if not thousands, of vendors who supply products and services. This problem uses the Internet to expose students to important issues associated with evaluating how well a company manages its vendor information as part of the acquisition and payment cycle.

COMPLETING THE TESTS IN THE ACQUISITION AND PAYMENT CYCLE: VERIFICATION OF SELECTED ACCOUNTS

IMPROPER CLASSIFICATIONS HIDE A GREATER NET LOSS

TV Communications Network (TVCN), a Denver-based wireless cable television company, materially understated losses in its financial statements by improperly recording $2.5 million of expenses as a direct decrease in stockholders' equity. The misstatement took the company from an actual net loss of $4.7 million to a reported loss of only $2.2 million.

According to the investigation by the SEC, the expenses charged to equity were from disbursements for the development and distribution of brochures promoting the company's business prospects. The payments should have been expensed and reflected in the income statement as advertising expenses.

The internal controls associated with the advertising expenses were clearly inadequate. TVCN typically did not have invoices or other documentation available when payments were made by the company's president, who controlled the bank account. Because of the lack of adequate documentation, when the financial statements were prepared, TVCN employees responsible for recording the expenses did not have sufficient information to properly classify the disbursements. The SEC found that even when documentation was available, the accounts where the transactions were recorded conflicted with the supporting documentation.

Unfortunately, TVCN's auditor relied on inquiry of the company president as the primary evidence about the nature of the advertising payments. In his substantive testing of transactions exceeding $10,000, the auditor relied on the company controller to identify all transactions meeting the criteria for review. Needless to say, the controller did not present all transactions meeting the $10,000 scope. As you might expect, the SEC brought charges against the auditor for failing to comply with auditing standards.

Source: *Accounting and Auditing Enforcement Release No. 534*, Commerce Clearing House, Inc., Chicago.

The last chapter noted that transactions in the acquisition and payment cycle affect several accounts. Acquisitions of assets affect supplies, property, plant and equipment, and prepaid expenses accounts, to name a few. In addition, payments made for services incurred affect many expense accounts. This chapter continues the discussion of the acquisition and payment cycle by highlighting unique audit issues related to other accounts commonly found in the acquisition and payment cycles of most businesses.

The opening vignette about TVCN highlights the importance of understanding the nature of acquisition and payment cycle transactions. Because transactions in this cycle affect numerous accounts in both the balance sheet and the income statement, improperly classified transactions may significantly affect reported results, as they did for TVCN. Therefore, auditors must understand the nature of transactions flowing through the acquisition and payment cycle so that they can effectively evaluate the accounts in the cycle.

TYPES OF OTHER ACCOUNTS IN THE ACQUISITION AND PAYMENT CYCLE

OBJECTIVE 20-1

Recognize the many accounts in the acquisition and payment cycle.

Federal Acquisitions Regulations

Table 20-1 highlights many of the typical accounts associated with transactions in the acquisition and payment cycle. These accounts are common in many types of businesses. As the nature of the industry or the client's business becomes more specialized, however, the types of assets, expenses, and liabilities change.

The methodology associated with auditing these accounts is similar to the audits of other accounts discussed in earlier chapters. Figure 20-1 highlights that methodology, which is similar to the methodology shown for the audit of accounts payable in Chapter 19.

The last chapter presented an overview of typical tests of controls and substantive tests of transactions for acquisition and payment cycle transactions, as well as commonly used analytical procedures and tests of details of balances for accounts payable. Later chapters highlight audit issues unique to cash, inventory, and costs of goods sold, which are accounts commonly associated with acquisition and payment cycle transactions. This chapter discusses unique issues for some of the other key accounts in this cycle. In this chapter, we take a closer look at the audit of property, plant, and equipment; prepaid expenses; other liabilities; and income and expense accounts.

AUDIT OF PROPERTY, PLANT, AND EQUIPMENT

OBJECTIVE 20-2

Design and perform audit tests of property, plant, and equipment and related accounts.

We focus first on issues associated with auditing property, plant, and equipment accounts because many transactions in the acquisition and payment cycle are likely to affect these accounts. Property, plant, and equipment are assets that have expected lives of more than 1 year, are used in the business, and are not acquired for resale. The intent to use the assets as part of the operation of the client's business and their expected lives of more than 1 year are the significant characteristics that distinguish these assets from inventory, prepaid expenses, and investments. Table 20-2 (p. 614) shows examples of some of the typical classifications of property, plant, and equipment accounts.

TABLE 20-1	**Accounts Typically Associated with Acquisition and Payment Cycle Transactions**	
Assets	**Expenses**	**Liabilities**
Cash	Cost of goods sold	Accounts payable
Inventory	Rent expense	Rent payable
Supplies	Property taxes	Accrued professional fees
Property, plant, and equipment	Income tax expense	Accrued property taxes
Patents, trademarks, and copyrights	Insurance expense	Other accrued expenses
Prepaid rent	Professional fees	Income taxes payable
Prepaid taxes	Retirement benefits	
Prepaid insurance	Utilities	

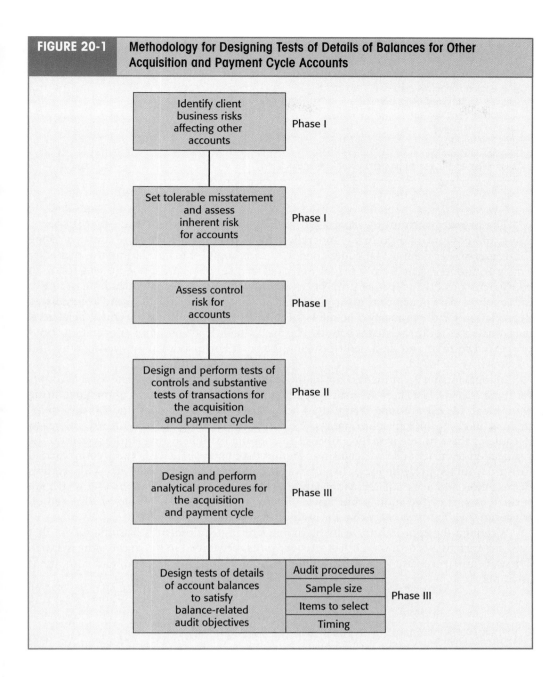

| FIGURE 20-1 | Methodology for Designing Tests of Details of Balances for Other Acquisition and Payment Cycle Accounts |

Identify client
business risks
affecting other
accounts
Phase I

Set tolerable misstatement
and assess
inherent risk
for accounts
Phase I

Assess control
risk for
accounts
Phase I

Design and perform tests of
controls and substantive
tests of transactions for
the acquisition
and payment cycle
Phase II

Design and perform
analytical procedures for
the acquisition
and payment cycle
Phase III

Design tests of details
of account balances
to satisfy
balance-related
audit objectives

Audit procedures
Sample size
Items to select
Timing
Phase III

Because the audits of these property, plant, and equipment accounts are similar, this section focuses on auditing manufacturing equipment to illustrate an approach to auditing all types of property, plant, and equipment accounts. When there are significant differences in the verification of other types of property, plant, and equipment accounts, the differences are briefly discussed.

The accounts commonly used for manufacturing equipment are illustrated in Figure 20-2 (p. 614). The relationship of manufacturing equipment to the acquisition and payment cycle is apparent by examining the debits to the asset account. Because the source of debits in the asset account is the acquisitions journal, the accounting system has already been tested for recording current period additions to manufacturing equipment as part of the tests of the acquisition and payment cycle studied in the last chapter. Because equipment additions are infrequent and may be subject to special controls, such as board of directors approval, the auditor may decide not to rely heavily on these tests.

**Overview of Equipment-
Related Accounts**

TABLE 20-2	Classifications of Property, Plant, and Equipment Accounts

Land and land improvements
Buildings and building improvements
Manufacturing equipment
Furniture and fixtures
Autos and trucks
Leasehold improvements
Construction-in-process for property, plant, and equipment

Fixed Asset Management

The primary accounting record for manufacturing equipment and other property, plant, and equipment accounts is generally a **fixed asset master file.** The contents of the fixed asset master file must be understood for a meaningful study of the audit of manufacturing equipment. The master file is composed of a set of records, one for each piece of equipment and other types of property owned. In turn, each record includes descriptive information, date of acquisition, original cost, current year depreciation, and accumulated depreciation for the property. The totals for all records in the master file equal the general ledger balances for the related accounts. The master file will also contain information about property acquired and disposed of during the year. For disposals, proceeds, gains, and losses will be included.

Manufacturing equipment is normally audited differently from current asset accounts for three reasons: (1) There are usually fewer current period acquisitions of manufacturing equipment, (2) the amount of any given acquisition is often material, and (3) the equipment is likely to be kept and maintained in the accounting records for several years. Because of these differences, the emphasis in auditing manufacturing equipment is on the verification of current period acquisitions rather than on the balance in the account carried forward from the preceding year. In addition, the expected life of assets over 1 year requires depreciation and accumulated depreciation accounts, as shown in Figure 20-2, which are verified as part of the audit of the assets. Finally, equipment may be sold or disposed of, triggering a gain or loss entry that the auditor may need to verify.

Although the approach to verifying manufacturing equipment is dissimilar from that used for current assets, several other asset accounts are verified in much the same manner. These include patents, copyrights, catalog costs, and all property, plant, and equipment accounts.

FIGURE 20-2	Manufacturing Equipment and Related Accounts

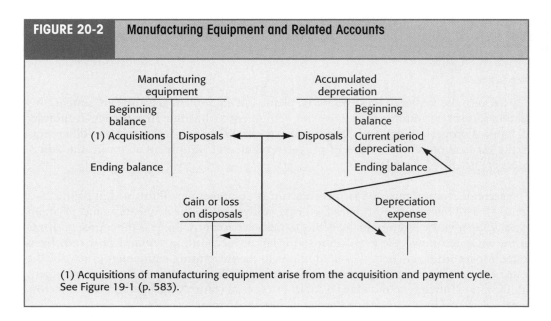

(1) Acquisitions of manufacturing equipment arise from the acquisition and payment cycle. See Figure 19-1 (p. 583).

In the audit of manufacturing equipment and related accounts, it is helpful to separate the tests into the following categories:

- Analytical procedures
- Verifying current year acquisitions
- Verifying current year disposals
- Verifying the ending balance in the asset account
- Verifying depreciation expense
- Verifying the ending balance in accumulated depreciation

The next several sections highlight the use of these categories of tests in the audit of manufacturing equipment, depreciation expense, accumulated depreciation, and gain or loss on disposal accounts.

As in all audit areas, the nature of the analytical procedures depends on the nature of the client's operations. Table 20-3 illustrates the type of ratio and trend analysis often performed for manufacturing equipment.

Analytical Procedures

As you can see, most of the typical analytical procedures performed relate to assessing the likelihood of material misstatements in the depreciation expense and accumulated depreciation accounts. In a later section, we focus on other substantive tests that are often performed for these accounts.

The proper recording of current year additions is important because of the long-term effect the assets have on the financial statements. The failure to capitalize a fixed asset, or the recording of an acquisition at the improper amount, affects the balance sheet until the company disposes of the asset. The income statement is affected until the asset is fully depreciated.

Verifying Current Year Acquisitions

Because of the importance of current period acquisitions in the audit of manufacturing equipment, seven of the nine balance-related audit objectives for tests of details of balances are used as a frame of reference. (Realizable value and presentation and disclosure are discussed in connection with verifying ending balances.)

The balance-related audit objectives and common audit tests are shown in Table 20-4 (p. 616). As in all other audit areas, the actual audit tests and sample size depend heavily on tolerable misstatement, inherent risk, and assessed control risk. Tolerable misstatement is of special importance for verifying current year additions. These transactions vary from immaterial amounts in some years to a large number of significant acquisitions in others. Completeness, accuracy, and classification are usually the major objectives for this part of the audit.

The starting point for the verification of current year acquisitions is normally a schedule obtained from the client of all acquisitions recorded in the general ledger during the year. A typical schedule lists each addition separately and includes the date of the acquisition, vendor,

TABLE 20-3	Analytical Procedures for Manufacturing Equipment	
Analytical Procedure	**Possible Misstatement**
Compare depreciation expense divided by gross manufacturing equipment cost with previous years.	Misstatement in depreciation expense and accumulated depreciation.
Compare accumulated depreciation divided by gross manufacturing equipment cost with previous years.	Misstatement in accumulated depreciation.
Compare monthly or annual repairs and maintenance, supplies expense, small tools expense, and similar accounts with previous years.	Expensing amounts that should be capitalized.
Compare gross manufacturing cost divided by some measure of production with previous years.	Idle equipment or equipment that was disposed of but not written off.

TABLE 20-4   Balance-Related Audit Objectives and Tests of Details of Balances for Manufacturing Equipment Additions

Balance-Related Audit Objective	Common Tests of Details of Balances Procedures	Comments
Current year acquisitions in the acquisitions schedule agree with related master file amounts, and the total agrees with the general ledger (detail tie-in).	Foot the acquisitions schedule. Trace the individual acquisitions to the master file for amounts and descriptions. Trace the total to the general ledger.	Footing the acquisitions schedule and tracing individual acquisitions should be limited unless controls are weak. All increases in the general ledger balance for the year should reconcile to the schedule.
Current year acquisitions as listed exist (existence).	Examine vendors' invoices and receiving reports. Physically examine assets.	It is uncommon to physically examine acquisitions unless controls are weak or amounts are material.
Existing acquisitions are recorded (completeness).	Examine vendors' invoices of closely related accounts such as repairs and maintenance to uncover items that should be manufacturing equipment. Review lease and rental agreements.	This objective is one of the most important for manufacturing equipment.
Current year acquisitions as listed are accurate (accuracy).	Examine vendors' invoices.	Extent depends on inherent risk and effectiveness of internal controls.
Current year acquisitions as listed are properly classified (classification).	Examine vendors' invoices in manufacturing equipment account to uncover items that should be classified as office equipment, part of the buildings, or repairs. Examine vendors' invoices of closely related accounts such as repairs to uncover items that should be manufacturing equipment. Examine rent and lease expense for capitalizable leases.	The objective is closely related to tests for completeness. It is done in conjunction with that objective and tests for accuracy.
Current year acquisitions are recorded in the proper period (cutoff).	Review transactions near the balance sheet date for proper period.	Usually done as part of accounts payable cutoff tests.
The client has rights to current year acquisitions (rights).	Examine vendors' invoices.	Ordinarily no problem for equipment. Property deeds, abstracts, and tax bills are frequently examined for land or major buildings.

description, notation of new or used, life of the asset for depreciation purposes, depreciation method, and cost. The client obtains this information from the property master file.

In studying Table 20-4, it is apparent that the most common audit test to verify additions is to examine vendors' invoices and receiving reports. Additional testing beyond that which is done as part of the tests of controls and substantive tests of transactions is often necessary because of the complexity of many equipment transactions and the materiality of the amounts. It is normal to verify large and unusual transactions for the entire year as well as a representative sample of typical additions. The extent of the verification depends on the auditor's assessed control risk for acquisitions and the materiality of the additions. The events described in the box on the following page highlight the importance of the auditor understanding the nature of large acquisitions.

In testing acquisitions, the auditor must know the client's capitalization policies to determine whether acquisitions are recorded in accordance with generally accepted accounting principles (GAAP) and are treated consistently with those of the preceding year. For example, many clients automatically expense items that are less than a certain amount, such as $1,000. The auditor should be alert for the possibility of material transportation and installation costs, as well as the trade-in of existing equipment.

Testing current period additions should also include reviewing recorded transactions for proper classification. In some cases, amounts recorded as manufacturing equipment should be classified as office equipment or as a part of the building. There is also the possibility that the client has improperly capitalized repairs, rents, or similar expenses. Recall from the opening vignette how poor internal controls over document preparation at TVCN resulted in significant misclassifications of disbursement transactions.

The inclusion of transactions that should properly be recorded as assets in repairs and maintenance expense, lease expense, supplies, small tools, and similar accounts is a common client error. The error results from lack of understanding GAAP and some clients' desire to avoid income taxes. If the auditor concludes that this type of material misstatement is likely, it may be necessary to vouch the larger amounts debited to the expense accounts. It is a common practice to do so as part of the audit of the property, plant, and equipment accounts.

Intangible Assets

Transactions involving the disposal of manufacturing equipment are often misstated when company internal controls lack a formal method to inform management of the sale, trade-in, abandonment, or theft of recorded machinery and equipment. If the client fails to record disposals, the original cost of the manufacturing equipment account will be overstated indefinitely, and net book value will be overstated until the asset is fully depreciated. Formal methods of tracking disposals and provisions for proper authorization of the sale or other disposal of manufacturing equipment help reduce the risk of misstatement. There should also be adequate internal verification of recorded disposals to make sure that assets are correctly removed from the accounting records.

Verifying Current Year Disposals

The auditor's main objectives in the verification of the sale, trade-in, or abandonment of manufacturing equipment are to gather sufficient evidence that (1) existing disposals are recorded and (2) disposals are accurately recorded. The starting point for verifying disposals is the client's schedule of recorded disposals. The schedule typically includes the date when the asset was disposed of, the name of the person or firm acquiring the asset, the selling price, the original cost of the asset, the acquisition date, and the accumulated depreciation of the asset. Detail tie-in tests of the schedule are necessary, including footing the schedule, tracing the totals on the schedule to the recorded disposals in the general ledger, and tracing the cost and accumulated depreciation of the disposals to the property master file.

Because the failure to record disposals of manufacturing equipment no longer used in the business can significantly affect the financial statements, *the search for unrecorded disposals is essential*. The nature and adequacy of the controls over disposals affect the extent of the search. The following procedures are often used for verifying disposals:

- Review whether newly acquired assets replace existing assets.
- Analyze gains and losses on the disposal of assets and miscellaneous income for receipts from the disposal of assets.
- Review plant modifications and changes in product line, property taxes, or insurance coverage for indications of deletions of equipment.
- Make inquiries of management and production personnel about the possibility of the disposal of assets.

When an asset is sold or disposed of without having been traded in for a replacement asset, the *accuracy* of the transaction can be verified by examining the related sales invoice and property master file. The auditor should compare the cost and accumulated depreciation in the master file with the recorded entry in the general journal and recompute the gain or loss on the disposal of the asset for comparison with the accounting records. When *trade-in of an asset for a replacement* occurs, the auditor should be sure that the new asset is properly capitalized and the replaced asset properly eliminated from the records, considering the book value of the asset traded in and the additional cost of the new asset.

Verifying Ending Balance of Asset Account

Two of the auditor's objectives when auditing manufacturing equipment include determining that (1) all equipment owned is recorded and (2) all recorded equipment physically exists on the balance sheet date. In designing audit tests to meet these objectives, the auditor first considers the nature of internal controls over manufacturing equipment. Ideally, the auditor is able to conclude that controls are sufficiently strong to allow the auditor to rely on balances carried forward from the prior year. Important controls include the use of a master file for individual fixed assets, adequate physical controls over assets that are easily movable (such as computers, tools, and vehicles), assignment of identification numbers to each plant asset, and periodic physical count of fixed assets and their reconciliation by accounting personnel. A formal method of informing the accounting department of all disposals of fixed assets is also an important control over the balance of assets carried forward into the current year.

Usually, the auditor does not obtain a list from the client of all assets included in the ending balance of manufacturing equipment. Instead, audit tests are determined on the basis of the master file.

Typically, the first audit step concerns the detail tie-in objective: Manufacturing equipment as listed in the master file agrees with the general ledger. Examining a printout of the master file that totals to the general ledger balance is ordinarily sufficient. The auditor may choose to use audit software to foot an electronic version of the master file or manually test-foot a few pages.

After assessing control risk for the existence objective, the auditor must decide whether it is necessary to verify the existence of individual items of manufacturing equipment included in the master file. If the auditor believes there is a high likelihood of significant missing fixed assets that are still recorded on the accounting records, an appropriate procedure is to select a sample from the master file and examine the actual assets. In rare cases, the auditor may believe it is necessary for the client to take a complete physical inventory of fixed assets to make sure they exist. If a physical inventory is taken, the auditor normally observes the count.

Ordinarily, it is unnecessary to test the accuracy or classification of fixed assets recorded in prior periods because presumably they were verified in previous audits at the time they were acquired. But the auditor should be aware that companies may occasionally have manufacturing equipment on hand that is no longer used in operations. If the amounts are material, the auditor should evaluate whether they should be written down to net realizable value (realizable value objective) or at least disclosed separately as "nonoperating equipment."

A major consideration in verifying the ending balance in fixed assets is the possibility of *legal encumbrances* (presentation and disclosure objective). Methods to determine whether manufacturing equipment is encumbered include reading the terms of loan and credit agreements, mailing loan confirmation requests to banks and other lending institutions, and having discussions with the client or sending letters to legal counsel.

The *proper presentation and disclosure* of manufacturing equipment in the financial statements must be evaluated carefully to make sure that GAAP is followed. Manufacturing equipment should include the gross cost and should ordinarily be separated from other fixed assets. Leased property should also be disclosed separately, and all liens on property must be included in the footnotes.

Depreciation expense is one of the few expense accounts that is not verified as part of tests of controls and substantive tests of transactions. The recorded amounts are determined by *internal allocations* rather than by exchange transactions with outside parties. When depreciation expense is material, more tests of details of depreciation expense are required than for an account that has already been verified through tests of controls and substantive tests of transactions.

Verifying Depreciation Expense

The most important objective for depreciation expense is accuracy. Two major concerns are involved in the accuracy objective: determining whether the client is following *a consistent depreciation policy* from period to period and whether the client's *calculations are correct*. In determining the former, there are four considerations: the useful life of current period acquisitions, the method of depreciation, the estimated salvage value, and the policy of depreciating assets in the year of acquisition and disposition. The client's policies can be determined by discussions with appropriate personnel and comparing the responses with the information in the auditor's permanent files.

In deciding on the reasonableness of the useful lives assigned to newly acquired assets, the auditor must consider the physical life of the asset, the expected life (taking into account obsolescence or the company's normal policy of upgrading equipment), and established company policies on trading in equipment. Occasionally, changing circumstances may necessitate a reevaluation of the useful life of an asset. When this occurs, a change in accounting estimate rather than a change in accounting principle is involved. The effect of this on depreciation must be evaluated.

A useful method of auditing depreciation is an overall reasonableness test made by multiplying the undepreciated fixed assets by the depreciation rate for the year. In making these calculations, the auditor must make adjustments for current year additions and disposals, assets with different lengths of life, and assets with different methods of depreciation. Many CPA firms include an electronic spreadsheet in their permanent file that includes a breakdown of the fixed assets by method of depreciation and length of life. If the calculations using the software are reasonably close to the client's totals and if assessed control risk for depreciation expense is low, tests of details for depreciation can be eliminated.

When an overall reasonableness test cannot be accomplished, more detailed tests are usually needed. This is done by recomputing depreciation expense for selected assets to determine whether the client is following a proper and consistent depreciation policy. To be relevant, the detailed calculations should be tied in to the total depreciation calculations by footing the depreciation expense on the property master file and reconciling the total with the general ledger. If the client maintains computerized depreciation and amortization records, it may be desirable to consider using the computer in testing the calculations.

The debits to accumulated depreciation are normally tested as a part of the audit of disposals of assets, whereas the credits are verified as a part of depreciation expense. If the auditor traces selected transactions to the accumulated depreciation records in the property master file as a part of these tests, little additional testing should be required for the ending balance in accumulated depreciation.

Verifying Ending Balance in Accumulated Depreciation

Two objectives are usually emphasized in the audit of the ending balance in accumulated depreciation:

1. Accumulated depreciation as stated in the property master file agrees with the general ledger. This objective can be satisfied by test-footing the accumulated depreciation in the property master file and tracing the total to the general ledger.
2. Accumulated depreciation in the master file is accurate.

In some cases, the life of manufacturing equipment may be significantly reduced because of such changes as reductions in customer demands for products, unexpected physical deterioration, or a modification in operations. Because of these possibilities, it is necessary to evaluate the adequacy of the allowances for accumulated depreciation each year to make sure that the net book value does not exceed the realizable value of the assets.

AUDIT OF PREPAID EXPENSES

OBJECTIVE 20-3

Design and perform audit tests of prepaid expenses.

Prepaid expenses, deferred charges, and intangibles are assets that vary in life from several months to several years. Their inclusion as assets results more from the concept of matching expenses with revenues than from their resale or liquidation value. The following are examples:

- Prepaid rent
- Organization costs
- Prepaid taxes
- Patents

- Prepaid insurance
- Trademarks
- Deferred charges
- Copyrights

One typical difference between these assets and others, such as accounts receivable and inventory, is their immateriality in many audits. Analytical procedures are often sufficient for prepaid expenses, deferred charges, and intangibles. However, in certain audits, some of these assets can be significant. We therefore discuss some of the typical internal controls and related audit tests commonly associated with prepaid expenses.

In this section, the audit of prepaid insurance is discussed as an account representative of this group because (1) it is found in most audits—virtually every company has some type of insurance, (2) it is typical of the problems commonly encountered in the audit of this class of accounts, and (3) the auditor's responsibility for the review of insurance coverage is an additional consideration not encountered in the other accounts in this category.

Overview of Prepaid Insurance

The accounts typically used for prepaid insurance are illustrated in Figure 20-3. The relationship between prepaid insurance and the acquisition and payment cycle is apparent in examining the debits to the asset account. Because the source of the debits in the asset account is the acquisitions journal, the payments of insurance premiums have already been partially tested by means of the tests of controls and substantive tests of acquisition and cash disbursement transactions.

FIGURE 20-3	Prepaid Insurance and Related Accounts

	Prepaid insurance		Insurance expense
	Beginning balance	Current period insurance expense	
(1)	Acquisitions (insurance premiums)		←——→
	Ending balance		

(1) Acquisitions of insurance premiums arise from the acquisition and payment cycle. This can be observed by examining Figure 19-1 (p. 583).

The internal controls for prepaid insurance and insurance expense can be conveniently divided into three categories: controls over the acquisition and recording of insurance, controls over the insurance register, and controls over the charge-off of insurance expense.

Controls over the acquisition and recording of insurance are part of the acquisition and payment cycle. These include proper authorization for new insurance policies and payment of insurance premiums consistent with the procedures discussed in that cycle.

An **insurance register** is a record of insurance policies in force and the expiration date of each policy. Use of an insurance register is an essential control to ensure that the company has adequate insurance. The control should include a provision for periodic review of the adequacy of the insurance coverage by an independent qualified person.

After the detailed records of the information in the prepaid insurance register have been completed, they should be verified by someone independent of the person preparing them. A closely related control is the use of monthly standard journal entries for insurance expense. If a significant entry is required to adjust the balance in prepaid insurance at the end of the year, it indicates a potential misstatement in the recording of the acquisition of insurance throughout the year or in the calculation of the year-end balance in prepaid insurance.

Throughout the audit of prepaid insurance and insurance expense, the auditor should keep in mind that the amount in insurance expense is a residual based on the beginning balance in prepaid insurance, the payment of premiums during the year, and the ending balance. The only verification of the balance in the expense account that is ordinarily necessary are analytical procedures and a brief test to be sure that the charges to insurance expense arose from credits to prepaid insurance. Because the payments of premiums are tested as part of the tests of controls and substantive tests of transactions and analytical procedures, the emphasis in the tests of details of balances is on prepaid insurance.

In the audit of prepaid insurance, a schedule is obtained from the client or prepared by the auditor that includes each insurance policy in force, policy number, insurance coverage for each policy, premium amount, premium period, insurance expense for the year, and prepaid insurance at the end of the year.

A major consideration in the audit of prepaid insurance is the frequent *immateriality* of the beginning and ending balances. Furthermore, few transactions are debited and credited to the balance during the year, most of which are small and simple to understand. Therefore, the auditor can generally spend little time verifying the balance. When the auditor plans not to verify the balance in detail, analytical procedures become increasingly important as a means of identifying potentially significant misstatements. The following are commonly performed analytical procedures of prepaid insurance and insurance expense:

- Compare total prepaid insurance and insurance expense with previous years as a test of reasonableness.
- Compute the ratio of prepaid insurance to insurance expense and compare it with previous years.
- Compare the individual insurance policy coverage on the schedule of insurance obtained from the client with the preceding year's schedule as a test of the elimination of certain policies or a change in insurance coverage.
- Compare the computed prepaid insurance balance for the current year on a policy-by-policy basis with that of the preceding year as a test of an error in calculation.
- Review the *insurance coverage* listed on the prepaid insurance schedule with an appropriate client official or insurance broker for adequacy of coverage. The auditor cannot be an expert on insurance matters, but the auditor's understanding of accounting and the valuation of assets is important in making certain that a company is not underinsured.

For many audits, no additional tests need be performed beyond the review for overall reasonableness unless the tests indicate a high likelihood of a significant misstatement or assessed control risk is high. The remaining audit procedures should be performed only when there is a special reason for doing so. The discussion of these tests is organized around the balance-related audit objectives for performing tests of details of asset balances. Realizable value is not applicable.

Insurance Policies in the Prepaid Insurance Schedule Exist and Existing Policies Are Listed (Existence and Completeness) The verification of existence and tests for omissions of the insurance policies in force can be performed in one of two ways: by referring to supporting documentation or by obtaining a confirmation of insurance information from the company's insurance agent. The first approach entails examining insurance invoices and policies in force. If these tests are performed, they should be done on a limited test basis. Sending a confirmation to the client's insurance agent is preferable because it is usually less time-consuming than vouching tests and it provides 100 percent verification.

The Client Has Rights to All Insurance Policies in the Prepaid Insurance Schedule (Rights) The party who will receive the benefit if an insurance claim is filed has the rights. Ordinarily, the recipient named in the policy is the client, but when there are mortgages or other liens, the insurance claim may be payable to a creditor. The review of insurance policies for claimants other than the client is an excellent test of unrecorded liabilities and pledged assets.

Prepaid Amounts on the Schedule Are Accurate and the Total Is Correctly Added and Agrees with the General Ledger (Accuracy and Detail Tie-in) The accuracy of prepaid insurance involves verifying the total amount of the insurance premium, the length of the policy period, and the allocation of the premium to unexpired insurance. The amount of the premium for a given policy and its time period can be verified simultaneously by examining the premium invoice or the confirmation from an insurance agent. Once these two have been verified, the client's calculations of unexpired insurance can be tested by recalculation. The schedule of prepaid insurance can then be footed and the totals traced to the general ledger to complete the detail tie-in tests.

The Insurance Expense Related to Prepaid Insurance Is Properly Classified (Classification) The proper classification of debits to different insurance expense accounts should be reviewed as a test of the income statement. In some cases, the appropriate expense account is obvious because of the type of insurance (such as insurance on a piece of equipment), but in other cases, allocations are necessary. For example, fire insurance on the building may require allocation to several accounts, including manufacturing overhead. Consistency with previous years is the major consideration in evaluating classification.

Insurance Transactions Are Recorded in the Proper Period (Cutoff) Cutoff for insurance expense is normally not a significant problem because of the small number of policies and the immateriality of the amount. If the cutoff is checked at all, it is reviewed as part of accounts payable cutoff tests.

Prepaid Insurance Is Properly Presented and Disclosed (Presentation and Disclosure) In most audits, prepaid insurance is combined with other prepaid expenses and included as a current asset. The amount is usually small and not a significant consideration to statement users.

AUDIT OF ACCRUED LIABILITIES

OBJECTIVE 20-4

Design and perform audit tests of accrued liabilities.

A third major category of accounts in the acquisition and payment cycle is accrued liabilities. **Accrued liabilities** are estimated unpaid obligations for services or benefits that have been received before the balance sheet date. Many accrued liabilities represent future obligations for unpaid services resulting from the passage of time but are not payable at the balance sheet date. For example, the benefits of property rental accrue throughout the year; therefore, at the balance sheet date, a certain portion of the total rent cost that has not been paid should be accrued. If the balance sheet date and the date of the termination of the rent agreement are the same, any unpaid rent is more appropriately called rent payable than an accrued liability.

A second type of accrual is one in which the amount of the obligation must be estimated due to the uncertainty of the amount due. An illustration is the obligation for federal income taxes when there is a reasonable likelihood that the amount reported on the tax return will be changed after an audit has been conducted by the Internal Revenue Service. Other examples include accrued payroll, accrued payroll taxes, accrued officers' bonuses, and accrued commissions, which were discussed in Chapter 18. The following are other common accrued liabilities:

- Accrued income taxes
- Accrued interest
- Accrued pension costs
- Accrued professional fees
- Accrued rent
- Accrued warranty costs

The verification of accrued expenses varies depending on the nature of the accrual and the circumstances of the client. For most audits, accruals take little audit time, but in some instances, accounts such as accrued income taxes, warranty costs, and pension costs are material and require considerable audit effort. To illustrate, the audit of accrued property taxes is discussed in this section.

The accounts typically used by companies for accrued property taxes are illustrated in Figure 20-4. The relationship between accrued property taxes and the acquisition and payment cycle is the same as for prepaid insurance and is apparent from examining the debits to the liability account. Because the source of the debits is the cash disbursements journal, the payments of property taxes have already been partially tested by means of the tests of the acquisition and payment cycle transactions.

Auditing Accrued Property Taxes

As for insurance expense, the balance in property tax expense is a residual amount that results from the beginning and ending balances in accrued property taxes and the payments of property taxes. Therefore, the emphasis in the tests should be on the ending property tax liability and payments. In verifying accrued property taxes, all nine balance-related audit objectives except realizable value are relevant. Two are of special significance:

1. Existing properties for which accrual of taxes is appropriate are on the accrual schedule. The failure to include properties for which taxes should be accrued would understate the liability (completeness). A material misstatement could occur, for example, if taxes on property were not paid before the balance sheet date and not included as accrued property taxes.
2. Accrued property taxes are accurately recorded. The greatest concern in accuracy is the consistent treatment of the accrual from year to year (accuracy).

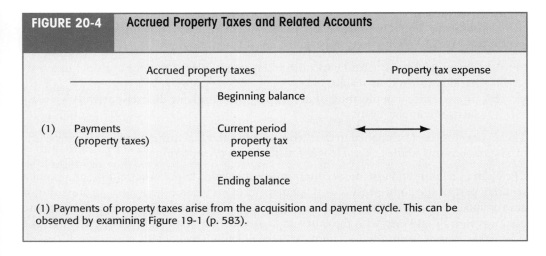

FIGURE 20-4   Accrued Property Taxes and Related Accounts

	Accrued property taxes		Property tax expense
		Beginning balance	
(1)	Payments (property taxes)	Current period property tax expense	←——→
		Ending balance	

(1) Payments of property taxes arise from the acquisition and payment cycle. This can be observed by examining Figure 19-1 (p. 583).

The primary methods of testing for the inclusion of all accruals are (1) to perform the accrual tests in conjunction with the audit of current year property tax payments and (2) to compare the accruals with those of previous years. In most audits, there are few property tax payments, but each payment is often material, and therefore it is common to verify each one.

First, the auditor should obtain a schedule of property tax payments from the client and compare each payment with the preceding year's schedule to determine whether all payments have been included in the client-prepared schedule. The fixed asset audit schedules also must be examined for major additions and disposals of assets that may affect the property taxes accrual. If the client is expanding its operations, all property affected by local property tax regulations should be included in the schedule, even if the first tax payment has not yet been made.

After the auditor is satisfied that all taxable property has been included in the client-prepared schedule, it is necessary to evaluate the reasonableness of the total amount of property taxes on each property being used as a basis to estimate the accrual. In some instances, the total amount has already been set by the taxing authority, and it is possible to verify the total by comparing the amount on the schedule with the tax bill in the client's possession. In other instances, the preceding year's total payments must be adjusted for the expected increase in property tax rates.

The auditor can verify the accrued property tax by recomputing the portion of the total tax applicable to the current year for each piece of property. The most important consideration in making this calculation is to use the same portion of each tax payment as the accrual that was used in the preceding year unless justifiable conditions exist for a change. After the accrual and property tax expense for each piece of property have been recomputed, the totals should be added and compared with the general ledger. In many cases, property taxes are charged to more than one expense account. When this happens, the auditor should test for proper classification by evaluating whether the proper amount was charged to each account.

AUDIT OF INCOME AND EXPENSE ACCOUNTS

OBJECTIVE 20-5

Design and perform audit tests of income and expense accounts.

The final look at key accounts in the acquisition and payment cycle includes an overview of procedures auditors typically use to determine whether the income and expense accounts in the financial statements are fairly presented in accordance with GAAP. The auditor must be satisfied that each of the income and expense totals included in the income statement as well as net earnings are not materially misstated.

In conducting audit tests of the financial statements, the auditor must be aware of the importance of the income statement to users of the statements. Many users rely more heavily on the income statement than on the balance sheet for making decisions. Equity investors, long-term creditors, union representatives, and often even short-term creditors are more interested in the ability of a firm to generate profit than in the historical cost or book value of the individual assets.

Considering the purposes of the income statement, the following are two essential concepts in the audit of income and expense accounts:

1. The matching of periodic income and expense is necessary for a proper determination of operating results.
2. The consistent application of accounting principles for different periods is necessary for comparability.

These concepts must be applied to the recording of individual transactions and to the combining of accounts in the general ledger for statement presentation.

Approach to Auditing Income and Expense Accounts

The audit of income and expense accounts is directly related to the balance sheet and is not a separate part of the audit process. A misstatement of an income statement account almost always equally affects a balance sheet account, and vice versa. The audit of income and expense accounts is so intertwined with the other parts of the audit that it is necessary to interrelate different aspects of testing these accounts with the different types of tests previously discussed.

A brief description of these tests serves as a review of material covered in other chapters; more important, it shows the interrelationship of different parts of the audit with income and expense account testing. The parts of the audit directly affecting these accounts are as follows:

- Analytical procedures
- Tests of controls and substantive tests of transactions
- Tests of details of account balances

The emphasis in this section is on income and expense accounts directly related to the acquisition and payment cycle, but the same concepts apply to the income statement accounts in all other cycles.

Analytical procedures were discussed in Chapter 8 as a general concept and have been referred to in subsequent chapters as part of specific audit areas. Analytical procedures should be thought of as part of the test of the fairness of the presentation of both balance sheet and income statement accounts. A few analytical procedures and the possible misstatements they may uncover in the audit of income and expense accounts are shown in Table 20-5.

Analytical Procedures

Tests of controls and substantive tests of transactions both have the effect of simultaneously verifying balance sheet and income statement accounts. For example, when an auditor concludes that internal controls are adequate to provide reasonable assurance that transactions in the acquisitions journal exist, are accurately recorded, correctly classified, and recorded in a timely manner, evidence exists as to the correctness of individual balance sheet accounts such as accounts payable and fixed assets and income statement accounts such as advertising and repairs. Conversely, inadequate controls and misstatements discovered through tests of controls and substantive tests of transactions are an indication of the likelihood of misstatements in both the income statement and the balance sheet.

Understanding internal control and the related tests of controls and substantive tests of transactions to determine the appropriate assessed control risk are the most important means of verifying many of the income statement accounts in each of the transaction

Tests of Controls and Substantive Tests of Transactions

TABLE 20-5	Analytical Procedures for Income and Expense Accounts
Analytical Procedure	**Possible Misstatement**
Compare individual expenses with previous years.	Overstatement or understatement of a balance in an expense account.
Compare individual asset and liability balances with previous years.	Overstatement or understatement of a balance sheet account that would also affect an income statement account (for example, a misstatement of inventory affects cost of goods sold).
Compare individual expenses with budgets.	Misstatement of expenses and related balance sheet accounts.
Compare gross margin percentage with previous years.	Misstatement of cost of goods sold and inventory.
Compare inventory turnover ratio with previous years.	Misstatement of cost of goods sold and inventory.
Compare prepaid insurance expense with previous years.	Misstatement of insurance expense and prepaid insurance.
Compare commission expense divided by sales with previous years.	Misstatement of commission expense and accrued commissions.
Compare individual manufacturing expenses divided by total manufacturing expenses with previous years.	Misstatement of individual manufacturing expenses and related balance sheet accounts.

cycles. For example, if the auditor concludes after adequate tests that assessed control risk can be reduced to low, the only additional verification of income statement accounts such as utilities, advertising, and purchases should be analytical procedures and cutoff tests. However, certain income and expense accounts are not verified at all by tests of controls and substantive tests of transactions, and others must be tested more extensively by other means. These are discussed next.

Tests of Details of Account Balances—Expense Analysis

The amounts included in certain income statement accounts must be analyzed even though the previously mentioned tests have been performed. The meaning and methodology of analysis of accounts are described first, followed by a discussion of when expense account analysis is appropriate.

Expense account analysis is the examination of underlying documentation of the individual transactions and amounts making up the detail of the total of an expense account. The underlying documents are of the same nature as those used for examining transactions as part of tests of acquisition transactions and include invoices, receiving reports, purchase orders, and contracts. Figure 20-5 illustrates a typical audit schedule showing expense analysis for legal expenses.

Expense account analysis concentrates on transactions that make up the details of an individual expense account. Although the focus of expense account analysis is on transactions, these tests differ from tests of controls and substantive tests of transactions. Because the tests of controls and substantive tests of transactions are meant to assess the appropriate control risk, they are tests of classes of transactions, such as acquisitions, that include many different accounts. In the analysis of expense and other income statement accounts, the auditor verifies the transactions in specific accounts to determine the propriety, classification, accuracy, and other specific information of each account analyzed.

Assuming satisfactory classification results are found in tests of controls and substantive tests of transactions, auditors normally restrict expense analysis to those accounts with a relatively high likelihood of material misstatement. For example, auditors often analyze repairs and maintenance expense accounts to determine whether they erroneously include property, plant, and equipment transactions; rent and lease expenses are analyzed to determine the need to capitalize leases; and legal expense is analyzed to determine whether there are potential contingent liabilities, disputes, illegal acts, or other legal issues that may affect the financial statements. Accounts such as utilities, travel expense, and advertising are rarely analyzed unless analytical procedures indicate high potential for material misstatement.

Expense account analysis is often done as part of the verification of the related asset. For example, it is common to analyze repairs and maintenance as part of verifying fixed assets, rent expense as part of verifying prepaid or accrued rent, and insurance expense as part of testing prepaid insurance.

Tests of Details of Account Balances—Allocation

Several expense accounts result from the **allocation** of accounting data rather than discrete transactions. These include expenses such as depreciation, depletion, and the amortization of copyrights and catalog costs. The allocation of manufacturing overhead between inventory and cost of goods sold is an example of a different type of allocation that affects expenses.

Allocations are important because they determine whether an expenditure is an asset or a current period expense. If the client fails to follow GAAP or fails to calculate the allocation properly, the financial statements can be materially misstated. The allocation of many expenses such as the depreciation of fixed assets and the amortization of copyrights is required because the life of the asset is greater than 1 year. The original cost of the asset is verified at the time of acquisition, but the charge-off takes place over several years. Other types of allocations directly affecting the financial statements arise because the life of a short-lived asset does not expire on the balance sheet date. Examples include prepaid rent and insurance. Finally, the allocation of costs between current period manufacturing expenses and inventory is required by GAAP as a means of reflecting all costs of making a product.

In auditing the allocation of expenditures such as prepaid insurance and manufacturing overhead, the two most important considerations are adherence to GAAP and consistency with the preceding period. The two most important audit procedures for allocations

FIGURE 20-5 | Expense Analysis for Legal Expense

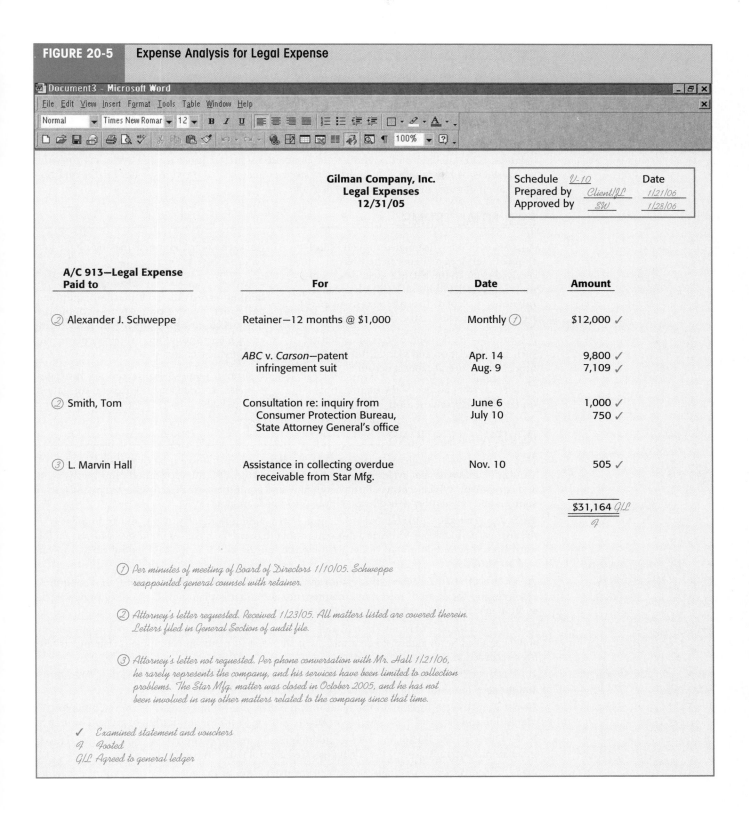

are tests for overall reasonableness using analytical procedures and recalculation of the client's results. It is common to perform these tests as part of the audit of the related asset or liability accounts. For example, depreciation expense is usually verified as part of the audit of property, plant, and equipment; amortization of patents is tested as part of verifying new patents or the disposal of existing ones; and allocations between inventory and cost of goods sold are verified as part of the audit of inventory.

SUMMARY

This chapter concludes the discussion of accounts and transactions in the acquisition and payment cycle. Auditors need an understanding of key accounts, classes of transactions, business functions, documents, and records related to acquisition and payment cycle transactions to adequately audit the numerous accounts associated with this cycle. Many of these accounts, such as accounts payable, property, plant, and equipment, depreciation expense, and prepaid expenses, have unique characteristics that affect how the auditor gathers sufficient competent evidence about related account balances. The analysis of the audit tests associated with accounts in this cycle has provided an overview of how audit tests in different cycles interrelate to provide a basis for the auditor's verification of many financial statement accounts.

ESSENTIAL TERMS

Accrued liabilities—estimated unpaid obligations for services or benefits that have been received prior to the balance sheet date; common accrued liabilities include accrued commissions, accrued income taxes, accrued payroll, and accrued rent

Allocation—the division of certain expenses, such as depreciation and manufacturing overhead, among several expense accounts

Expense account analysis—the examination of underlying documentation of individual transactions and amounts making up the total of an expense account

Fixed asset master file—a computer file containing records for each piece of equipment and other types of property owned; the primary accounting record for manufacturing equipment and other property, plant, and equipment accounts

Insurance register—a record of insurance policies in force and the expiration date of each policy

REVIEW QUESTIONS

20-1 (Objective 20-2) Explain the relationship between substantive tests of transactions for the acquisition and payment cycle and tests of details of balances for the verification of property, plant, and equipment. Which aspects of property, plant, and equipment are directly affected by the tests of controls and substantive tests of transactions and which are not?

20-2 (Objective 20-2) Explain why the emphasis in auditing property, plant, and equipment is on the current period acquisitions and disposals rather than on the balances in the account carried forward from the preceding year. Under what circumstances will the emphasis be on the balances carried forward?

20-3 (Objective 20-2) What is the relationship between the audit of property, plant, and equipment accounts and the audit of repair and maintenance accounts? Explain how the auditor organizes the audit to take this relationship into consideration.

20-4 (Objective 20-2) List and briefly state the purpose of all audit procedures that might reasonably be applied by an auditor to determine that all property, plant, and equipment retirements have been recorded in the accounting system.

20-5 (Objective 20-2) In auditing depreciation expense, what major considerations should the auditor keep in mind? Explain how each can be verified.

20-6 (Objective 20-3) Explain the relationship between substantive tests of transactions for the acquisition and payment cycle and tests of details of balances for the verification of prepaid insurance.

20-7 (Objective 20-3) Explain why the audit of prepaid insurance should ordinarily take a relatively small amount of audit time if the client's assessed control risk for acquisitions is low.

20-8 (Objective 20-3) Distinguish between the evaluation of the adequacy of insurance coverage and the verification of prepaid insurance. Explain which is more important in a typical audit.

20-9 (Objective 20-3) What are the major differences between the audit of prepaid expenses and other asset accounts such as accounts receivable or property, plant, and equipment?

20-10 (Objective 20-4) Explain the relationship between accrued rent and substantive tests of transactions for the acquisition and payment cycle. Which aspects of accrued rent are not verified as part of the substantive tests of transactions?

20-11 (Objective 20-4) In verifying accounts payable, it is common to restrict the audit sample to a small portion of the population items, whereas in auditing accrued property taxes, it is common to verify all transactions for the year. Explain the reason for the difference.

20-12 (Objective 20-4) Which documents will be used to verify accrued property taxes and the related expense accounts?

20-13 (Objective 20-5) List three expense accounts that are tested as part of the acquisition and payment cycle or the payroll and personnel cycle. List three expense accounts that are not directly verified as part of either of these cycles.

20-14 (Objective 20-5) What is meant by the analysis of expense accounts? Explain how expense account analysis relates to the tests of controls and substantive tests of transactions that the auditor has already completed for the acquisition and payment cycle.

20-15 (Objectives 20-2, 20-5) How would the approach for verifying repair expense differ from that used to audit depreciation expense? Why would the approach be different?

20-16 (Objective 20-5) List the factors that should affect the auditor's decision whether to analyze an account balance. Considering these factors, list four expense accounts that are commonly analyzed in audit engagements.

MULTIPLE CHOICE QUESTIONS FROM CPA EXAMINATIONS

20-17 (Objective 20-2) The following questions concern internal controls in the acquisition and payment cycle. Choose the best response.

a. Which of the following controls most likely would justify a reduced assessed level of control risk concerning plant and equipment acquisitions?
   (1) Periodic physical inspection of plant and equipment by the internal audit staff.
   (2) Comparison of current-year plant and equipment account balances with prior-year balances.
   (3) Review of prenumbered purchase orders to detect unrecorded trade-ins.
   (4) Approval of periodic depreciation entries by a supervisor independent of the accounting department.

b. Which of the following is not an internal control deficiency related to factory equipment?
   (1) Checks issued in payment of acquisitions of equipment are *not* signed by the controller.
   (2) All acquisitions of factory equipment are required to be made by the department in need of the equipment.
   (3) Factory equipment replacements are generally made when estimated useful lives, as indicated in depreciation schedules, have expired.
   (4) Proceeds from sales of fully depreciated equipment are credited to other income.

c. With respect to an internal control measure that will ensure accountability for fixed asset retirements, management should implement controls that include
   (1) continuous analysis of miscellaneous revenue to locate any cash proceeds from sale of plant assets.
   (2) periodic inquiry of plant executives by internal auditors as to whether any plant assets have been retired.
   (3) continuous use of serially numbered retirement work orders.
   (4) periodic observation of plant assets by the internal auditors.

20-18 (Objectives 20-2, 20-5) The following questions concern analytical procedures in the acquisition and payment cycle. Choose the best response.

a. Which of the following comparisons would be most useful to an auditor in auditing an entity's income and expense accounts?
   (1) Prior year accounts payable to current year accounts payable.
   (2) Prior year payroll expense to budgeted current year payroll expense.
   (3) Current year revenue to budgeted current year revenue.
   (4) Current year warranty expense to current year contingent liabilities.

b. The controller of Excello Manufacturing, Inc., wants to use analytical procedures to identify the possible existence of idle equipment or the possibility that equipment has been disposed of without having been written off. Which of the following ratios would best accomplish this objective?
   (1) Depreciation expense/book value of manufacturing equipment.
   (2) Accumulated depreciation/book value of manufacturing equipment.
   (3) Repairs and maintenance cost/direct labor costs.
   (4) Gross manufacturing equipment cost/units produced.

c. Which of the following analytical procedures should be applied to the income statement?
   (1) Select sales and expense items and trace amounts to related supporting documents.

(2) Ascertain that the net income amount in the statement of cash flows agrees with the net income amount in the income statement.

(3) Obtain from the proper client representatives the beginning and ending inventory amounts that were used to determine costs of sales.

(4) Compare the actual revenues and expenses with the corresponding figures of the previous year and investigate significant differences.

20-19 (Objective 20-2) The following questions concern the audit of asset accounts in the acquisition and payment cycle. Choose the best response.

a. In testing for unrecorded retirements of equipment, an auditor most likely would
   (1) select items of equipment from the accounting records and then locate them during the plant tour.
   (2) compare depreciation journal entries with similar prior-year entries in search of fully depreciated equipment.
   (3) inspect items of equipment observed during the plant tour and then trace them to the equipment master file.
   (4) scan the general journal for unusual equipment additions and excessive debits to repairs and maintenance expense.

b. Which of the following is the *best* evidence of real estate ownership at the balance sheet date?
   (1) Title insurance policy.   (3) Paid real estate tax bills.
   (2) Original deed held in the client's safe.   (4) Closing statement.

20-20 (Objectives 20-2, 20-4, 20-5) The following questions concern the audit of liabilities or income and expense accounts. Choose the best response.

a. Which of the following audit procedures is *least* likely to detect an unrecorded liability?
   (1) Analysis and recomputation of interest expense.
   (2) Analysis and recomputation of depreciation expense.
   (3) Mailing of standard bank confirmation forms.
   (4) Reading of the minutes of meetings of the board of directors.

b. Which of the following *best* describes the independent auditor's approach to obtaining satisfaction concerning depreciation expense in the income statement?
   (1) Verify the mathematical accuracy of the amounts charged to income as a result of depreciation expense.
   (2) Determine the method for computing depreciation expense and ascertain that it is in accordance with GAAP.
   (3) Reconcile the amount of depreciation expense to those amounts credited to accumulated depreciation accounts.
   (4) Establish the basis for depreciable assets and verify the depreciation expense.

c. Before expressing an opinion concerning the audit of income and expenses, the auditor would *best* proceed with the audit of the income statement by
   (1) applying a rigid measurement standard designed to test for understatement of net income.
   (2) analyzing the beginning and ending balance sheet inventory amounts.
   (3) making net income comparisons to published industry trends and ratios.
   (4) auditing income statement accounts concurrently with the related balance sheet accounts.

DISCUSSION QUESTIONS AND PROBLEMS

20-21 (Objective 20-2) For each of the following misstatements in property, plant, and equipment accounts, state an internal control that the client could install to prevent the misstatement from occurring and a substantive audit procedure that the auditor could use to discover the misstatement:

1. The asset lives used to depreciate equipment are less than reasonable, expected useful lives.
2. Capitalizable assets are routinely expensed as repairs and maintenance, perishable tools, or supplies expense.
3. Computer equipment that is abandoned or traded for replacement equipment is not removed from the accounting records.
4. Depreciation expense for manufacturing operations is charged to administrative expenses.
5. Tools necessary for the maintenance of equipment are stolen by company employees for their personal use.
6. Acquisitions of property are recorded at improper amounts.

7. A loan against existing equipment is not recorded in the accounting records. The cash receipts from the loan never reached the company because they were used for the down payment on a piece of equipment now being used as an operating asset. The equipment is also not recorded in the records.

20-22 (Objective 20-2) The following types of internal controls are commonly used by organizations for property, plant, and equipment:

1. A fixed asset master file is maintained with a separate record for each fixed asset.
2. Written policies exist and are known by accounting personnel to differentiate between capitalizable additions, freight, installation costs, replacements, and maintenance expenditures.
3. Acquisitions of fixed assets in excess of $20,000 are approved by the board of directors.
4. When practical, equipment is labeled with metal tags and is inventoried on a systematic basis.
5. Depreciation charges for individual assets are calculated for each asset; recorded in a fixed asset master file that includes cost, depreciation, and accumulated depreciation for each asset; and verified periodically by an independent clerk.

Required

a. State the purpose of each of the internal controls just listed. Your answer should be in the form of the type of misstatement that is likely to be reduced because of the control.

b. For each internal control, list one test of control the auditor can use to test for its existence.

c. List one substantive procedure for testing whether the control is actually preventing misstatements in property, plant, and equipment.

20-23 (Objectives 20-1, 20-2, 20-3, 20-5) The following audit procedures were planned by Linda King, CPA, in the audit of the acquisition and payment cycle for Cooley Products, Inc.:

1. Review the acquisitions journal for large and unusual transactions.
2. Send letters to several vendors, including a few for which the recorded accounts payable balance is zero, requesting them to inform us of their balance due from Cooley. Ask the controller to sign the letter.
3. Examine a sample of receiving report numbers and determine whether each one has an initial indicating that it was recorded as an account payable.
4. Select a sample of equipment listed on fixed asset master files and inspect the asset to determine that it exists and to determine its condition.
5. Refoot the acquisitions journal for 1 month and trace all totals to the general ledger.
6. Calculate the ratio of equipment repairs and maintenance to total equipment and compare with previous years.
7. Obtain from the client a written statement that all mortgages payable have been included in the current period financial statements and have been accurately recorded and that the collateral for each is included in the footnotes.
8. Select a sample of cancelled checks and trace each one to the cash disbursements journal, comparing the name, date, and amount.
9. For 20 nontangible acquisitions, select a sample of line items from the acquisitions journal and trace each to related vendors' invoices. Examine whether each transaction appears to be a legitimate expenditure for the client and that each was approved and recorded at the correct amount and date in the journal and charged to the correct account per the chart of accounts.
10. Examine invoices and related shipping documents included in the client's unpaid invoice file at the audit report date to determine whether they were recorded in the appropriate accounting period and at the correct amounts.
11. Recalculate the portion of insurance premiums on the client's prepaid insurance schedule that is applicable to future periods.
12. When the check signer's assistant writes "paid" on supporting documents, watch whether she does it after the documents are reviewed and the checks are signed.

Required

a. For each procedure, identify the type of evidence being used.

b. For each procedure, identify whether it is an analytical procedure, a test of control, a substantive test of transactions, or a test of details of balances.

c. For each test of control or substantive test of transactions, identify the transaction-related audit objective(s) being met.

d. For each test of details of balances, identify the balance-related audit objective(s) being met.

20-24 (Objective 20-2) Hardware Manufacturing Company, a closely held corporation, has operated since 2001 but has not had its financial statements audited. The company now plans to issue additional capital stock to be sold to outsiders and wishes to engage you to audit its year

2005 transactions and render an opinion on the financial statements for the year ended December 31, 2005.

The company has expanded from one plant to three and has frequently acquired, modified, and disposed of all types of equipment. Fixed assets have a net book value of 70% of total assets and consist of land and buildings, diversified machinery and equipment, and furniture and fixtures. Some property was acquired by donation from stockholders. Depreciation was recorded by several methods using various estimated lives.

Required

a. May you confine your audit solely to year 2005 transactions as requested by this prospective client whose financial statements have not previously been audited? Why?

b. Prepare an audit program for the January 1, 2005, opening balances of the land, building, and equipment and accumulated depreciation accounts of Hardware Manufacturing Company. You need not include tests of year 2005 transactions in your program.*

20-25 (Objective 20-4) The following program has been prepared for the audit of accrued real estate taxes of a client that pays taxes on 25 different pieces of property, some of which have been acquired in the current year:

1. Obtain a schedule of accrued taxes from the client and tie the total to the general ledger.
2. Compare the charges for annual tax payments with property tax assessment bills.
3. Recompute accrued/prepaid amounts for all bills on the basis of the portion of the year expired.

Required

a. State the purpose of each procedure.

b. Evaluate the adequacy of the audit program.

20-26 (Objective 20-4) As part of the audit of different audit areas, it is important to be alert for the possibility of unrecorded liabilities. For each of the following audit areas or accounts, describe a liability that could be uncovered and the audit procedures that could uncover it:

a. Minutes of the board of directors meetings

b. Land and buildings

c. Rent expense

d. Interest expense

e. Cash surrender value of life insurance

f. Cash in the bank

g. Officers' travel and entertainment expenses

20-27 (Objective 20-5) While you are having lunch with a banker friend, you become involved in explaining to him how your firm conducts an audit in a typical engagement. Much to your surprise, your friend is interested and is able to converse intelligently in discussing your philosophy of emphasizing the study of internal control, analytical procedures, tests of controls, substantive tests of transactions, and tests of details of balance sheet accounts. At the completion of your discussion, he says, "That all sounds great except for a couple of things. The point of view we take these days at our bank is the importance of a continuous earnings stream. You seem to be emphasizing fraud detection and a fairly stated balance sheet. We would rather see you put more emphasis than you apparently do on the income statement."

Required

How would you respond to your friend's comments?

CASES

Ward Publishing Company—Part III (See Case 19-32 for Parts I and II)

20-28 (Objectives 20-1, 20-2, 20-5) Examine the tests of controls and substantive tests of transactions results, including the sampling application in Case 19-32 (pp. 608–610), for Ward Publishing Company. Assume that you have already reached several conclusions.

1. Your tests of details of balances for accounts payable are completed, and you found no exceptions.
2. Acceptable audit risk for property, plant, and equipment and all expenses is high.
3. Inherent risk for property, plant, and equipment is high because in the current year, the client has acquired a material amount of new and used printing equipment and has traded in older equipment. Some of the new equipment was ineffective and returned; an allowance was received on others. Inherent risk for expense accounts is low.
4. New computer equipment and some printing equipment are being leased. The client has never leased equipment before.
5. Analytical procedures for property, plant, and equipment are inconclusive because of the large increases in acquisition and disposal activity.

*AICPA adapted.

6. Analytical procedures show that repairs, maintenance, and small tools expenses have increased materially, both in absolute terms and as a percentage of sales. Two other expenses have also materially increased, and one has materially decreased.

7. In examining the sample for tests of controls and substantive tests of transactions, you observe that no sample items included any property, plant, and equipment or lease transactions.

Required

a. Explain the relationship between the tests of controls and substantive tests of transactions results in Case 19-32 and the audit of property, plant, and equipment and leases.

b. How would the tests of controls and substantive tests of transactions results and your conclusions (1 through 7) affect your planned tests of details for property, plant, and equipment and leases? State your conclusions for each balance-related audit objective. Do not write an audit program.

c. Explain the relationship between the tests of controls and substantive tests of transactions results in Case 19-32 and the audit of expenses.

d. How would the tests of controls and substantive tests of transactions results and your conclusions (1 through 7) affect your planned tests of details of balances for expenses? Do not write an audit program.

20-29 (Objective 20-2) You are doing the audit of the UTE Corporation, for the year ended December 31, 2005. The following schedule for the property, plant, and equipment and related allowance for depreciation accounts has been prepared by the client. You have compared the opening balances with your prior year's audit working papers.

UTE Corporation Analysis of Property, Plant, and Equipment and Related Allowance for Depreciation Accounts
Year Ended December 31, 2005

Description	Final 12/31/04	Additions	Retirements	Per Books 12/31/05
Assets				
Land	$ 225,000	$ 50,000		$ 275,000
Buildings	1,200,000	175,000		1,375,000
Machinery and equipment	3,850,000	404,000	260,000	3,994,000
	$5,275,000	$629,000	$260,000	$5,644,000
Allowance for Depreciation				
Building	$ 600,000	$ 51,500		$ 651,500
Machinery and equipment	1,732,500	392,200		2,124,700
	$2,332,500	$443,700		$2,776,200

The following information is found during your audit:

1. All equipment is depreciated on the straight-line basis (no salvage value taken into consideration) based on the following estimated lives: buildings, 25 years; all other items, 10 years. The corporation's policy is to take one-half year's depreciation on all asset acquisitions and disposals during the year.

2. On April 1, the corporation entered into a 10-year lease contract for a die-casting machine with annual rentals of $50,000, payable in advance every April 1. The lease is cancelable by either party (60 days' written notice is required), and there is no option to renew the lease or buy the equipment at the end of the lease. The estimated useful life of the machine is 10 years with no salvage value. The corporation recorded the die-casting machine in the machinery and equipment account at $404,000, the present value at the date of the lease, and $20,200, applicable to the machine, has been included in depreciation expense for the year.

3. The corporation completed the construction of a wing on the plant building on June 30. The useful life of the building was not extended by this addition. The lowest construction bid received was $175,000, the amount recorded in the buildings account. Company personnel were used to construct the addition at a cost of $160,000 (materials, $75,000; labor, $55,000; and overhead, $30,000).

4. On August 18, $50,000 was paid for paving and fencing a portion of land owned by the corporation and used as a parking lot for employees. The expenditure was charged to the land account.

5. The amount shown in the machinery and equipment asset retirement column represents cash received on September 5, upon disposal of a machine acquired in July 2001 for $480,000. The bookkeeper recorded depreciation expense of $35,000 on this machine in 2005.

6. Crux City donated land and building appraised at $100,000 and $400,000, respectively, to the UTE Corporation for a plant. On September 1, the corporation began operating the plant. Because no costs were involved, the bookkeeper made no entry for the foregoing transaction.

Required

a. In addition to inquiry of the client, explain how you would have found each of these six items during the audit.

b. Prepare the adjusting journal entries with supporting computations that you would suggest at December 31, 2005, to adjust the accounts for the preceding transactions. Disregard income tax implications.*

20-30 (Objective 20-5) You are the manager in the audit of Vernal Manufacturing Company and are turning your attention to the income statement accounts. The in-charge auditor assessed control risk for all cycles as low, supported by tests of controls. There are no major inherent risks affecting income and expense accounts. Accordingly, you decide that the major emphasis in auditing the income statement accounts will be to use analytical procedures. The client prepared a schedule of the key income statement accounts that compares the prior-year totals with the current year totals. The in-charge auditor completed the last column of the audit schedule, which includes explanations of variances obtained from discussions with client personnel. The audit schedule is included on page 635.

Required

a. Examine the schedule prepared by the client and your staff and write a memorandum to the in-charge that includes criticisms and concerns about the audit procedures performed and questions for the in-charge auditor to resolve.

b. Evaluate the explanations for variances provided by client personnel. List any alternative explanation to those given.

c. Indicate which variances are of special significance to the audit and how you believe they should be responded to in terms of additional audit procedures.

INTERNET PROBLEM 20-1: MANAGING FIXED ASSETS

Reference the CW site. There are a number of software programs available for managing and accounting for fixed assets. This problem uses the Internet to explore an online directory that summarizes features of different fixed asset software packages. Students use the directory to compare and contrast various packages.

*AICPA adapted.

Vernal Manufacturing Co.
Income Statement Accounts
12/31/05

Account	Per G/L 12/31/04	Per G/L 12/31/05	Change Amount	Change Percent	Explanations by Client
Sales	$8,467,312	$9,845,231	$1,377,919	16.3	Sales increase due to two new customers who
Sales returns and allowances	(64,895)	(243,561)	(178,666)	275.3	account for 20% of volume. Larger returns due
Gain on sale of assets	43,222	(143,200)	(186,422)	−431.3	to need to cement relations with these
Interest income	243	223	(20)	−8.2	customers.
Miscellaneous income	6,365	25,478	19,113	300.3	Trade-in of several sales cars that needed
	8,452,247	9,484,171	1,031,924	12.2	replacement.
Cost of goods sold:					
Beginning inventory	1,487,666	1,389,034	(98,632)	−6.6	
Purchases	2,564,451	3,430,865	866,414	33.8	Increase in these accounts due to increased
Freight in	45,332	65,782	20,450	45.1	volume with new customers as indicated above.
Purchase returns	(76,310)	(57,643)	18,667	−24.5	
Factory wages	986,755	1,145,467	158,712	16.1	
Factory benefits	197,652	201,343	3,691	1.9	
Factory overhead	478,659	490,765	12,106	2.5	
Factory depreciation	344,112	314,553	(29,559)	−8.6	
Ending inventory	(1,389,034)	(2,156,003)	(766,969)	55.2	Inventory being held for new customers.
	4,639,283	4,824,163	184,880	4.0	
Selling, general and administrative:					
Executive salaries	167,459	174,562	7,103	4.2	Normal salary increases.
Executive benefits	32,321	34,488	2,167	6.7	
Office salaries	95,675	98,540	2,865	3.0	
Office benefits	19,888	21,778	1,890	9.5	
Travel and entertainment	56,845	75,583	18,738	33.0	Sales and promotional expenses increased in an
Advertising	130,878	156,680	25,802	19.7	attempt to obtain new major customers. Two
Other sales expense	34,880	42,334	7,454	21.4	obtained and program will continue.
Stationery and supplies	38,221	21,554	(16,667)	−43.6	Probably a misclassification; will investigate.
Postage	14,657	18,756	4,099	28.0	Normal increase.
Telephone	36,551	67,822	31,271	85.6	Normal increase.
Dues and memberships	3,644	4,522	878	24.1	Normal increase.
Rent	15,607	15,607	0	0.0	
Legal fees	14,154	35,460	21,306	150.5	Timing of billing for fees.
Accounting fees	16,700	18,650	1,950	11.7	Normal increase.
Depreciation, SG&A	73,450	69,500	(3,950)	−5.4	Normal change.
Bad debt expense	166,454	143,871	(22,583)	−13.6	Haven't reviewed yet for the current year.
Insurance	44,321	45,702	1,381	3.1	Normal change.
Interest expense	120,432	137,922	17,490	14.5	Normal change.
Other expense	5,455	28,762	23,307	427.3	Amount not material.
	1,087,592	1,212,093	124,501	11.4	
	5,726,875	6,036,256	309,381	5.4	
Income before taxes	2,725,372	3,447,915	722,543	26.5	
Income taxes	926,626	1,020,600	93,974	10.1	Increase due to increased income before tax.
Net income	$1,798,746	$2,427,315	$ 628,569	34.9	

AUDIT OF THE INVENTORY AND WAREHOUSING CYCLE

PHANTOM INVENTORY

Mickey Monus was the local hero in Youngstown, Ohio. He acquired a local drugstore, and within 10 years, added 299 more stores to form the national deep-discount retail chain, Phar-Mor, Inc. The company was viewed as the rising star by some retail experts and was considered to be the next Wal-Mart. Even Sam Walton announced that the only company he feared in the expansion of Wal-Mart was Phar-Mor.

Phar-Mor sold a variety of household products and prescription drugs at substantially lower prices than other discount stores. Monus described the company's strategy as "power buying," whereby Phar-Mor loaded up on products when suppliers were selling at rock-bottom prices and passed those savings to cost-conscious customers through deeply discounted prices.

Actually, Phar-Mor's prices were so low that the company was selling goods for less than their cost, causing the company to lose money. However, Monus continued to argue internally that through Phar-Mor's power buying, it would get so large that it could sell its way out of trouble. Unwilling to allow these shortfalls to damage Phar-Mor's appearance of success, Monus and his team began to engage in creative accounting so that Phar-Mor never reported these losses in its financial statements.

Management dumped the losses into "bucket accounts," only to reallocate those amounts to the company's hundreds of stores in the form of phantom increases in inventory costs. Monus' team issued fake invoices for merchandise purchases, made fraudulent journal entries to increase inventory and decrease cost of goods sold, and overcounted and double-counted inventory items.

Unfortunately, the auditors never uncovered the fraud. They allegedly observed inventory in only four stores out of 300, and they informed Phar-Mor management months in advance about the stores they would visit. Phar-Mor executives fully stocked the four selected stores but allocated the false inventory increases to the other 296 stores.

The fraud was ultimately uncovered when a travel agent received a Phar-Mor check signed by Monus paying for expenses that were unrelated to Phar-Mor. The agent showed the check to her landlord, who happened to be a Phar-Mor investor, and he contacted David Shapiro, Phar-Mor's CEO. Subsequent investigation of the invalid expenditure eventually led to the discovery of the inventory fraud.

Monus was eventually convicted and went to jail for 5 years. The CFO, who did not profit personally, was sentenced to 33 months in prison. The audit failure cost the audit firm over $300 million in civil judgments.

Sources: Adapted from Beasley, Buckless, Glover, and Prawitt, *Auditing Cases: An Interactive Learning Approach*, 2nd edition, Prentice-Hall, 2003, pp. 25–41 and Joseph T. Wells, "Ghost Goods: How to Spot Phantom Inventory," *Journal of Accountancy* (June 2001), pp. 33–36.

The **inventory and warehousing cycle** is unique because of its close relationships to other transaction cycles. Raw material and direct labor enter the inventory and warehousing cycle from the acquisition and payment cycle and the payroll and personnel cycle, respectively. The inventory and warehousing cycle ends with the sale of goods in the sales and collection cycle.

The audit of inventory, especially tests of the year-end inventory balance, is often the most complex and time-consuming part of the audit. As the example involving the audit of Phar-Mor in the opening vignette demonstrates, detecting misstatements in inventory accounts can be challenging. Factors affecting the complexity of the audit of inventory include the following:

- Inventory is generally a major item on the balance sheet, and it is often the largest item making up the accounts included in working capital.
- The inventory is in different locations, which makes physical control and counting difficult. Companies must have their inventory accessible for the efficient manufacture and sale of the product, but this dispersal creates significant auditing problems.
- The diversity of the items in inventories creates difficulties for the auditor. Such items as jewels, chemicals, and electronic parts present problems of observation and valuation.
- The valuation of inventory is also difficult because of such factors as obsolescence and the need to allocate manufacturing costs to inventory.
- There are several acceptable inventory valuation methods, but any given client must apply a method consistently from year to year. Moreover, an organization may prefer to use different valuation methods for different parts of the inventory, which is acceptable under GAAP.

This chapter begins the discussion of the audit of the inventory and warehousing cycle by reviewing the business functions in the cycle and the related documents and records.

Inventory Fraud

BUSINESS FUNCTIONS IN THE CYCLE AND RELATED DOCUMENTS AND RECORDS

OBJECTIVE 21-1

Describe the business functions and the related documents and records in the inventory and warehousing cycle.

Inventory takes many different forms, depending on the nature of the business. For retail or wholesale businesses, the most important inventory is merchandise on hand, available for sale. For hospitals, it includes food, drugs, and medical supplies. A manufacturing company has raw materials, purchased parts and supplies for use in production, goods in the process of being manufactured, and finished goods available for sale. We have selected manufacturing company inventories for presentation in this text. However, most of the principles discussed apply to other types of businesses as well.

The physical flow of goods and the flow of costs in the inventory and warehousing cycle for a manufacturing company are shown in Figure 21-1. The direct tie-in of the inventory and warehousing cycle to the acquisition and payment cycle and the payroll and personnel cycle can be seen by examining the debits to the raw materials, direct labor, and manufacturing overhead T accounts. The direct tie-in to the sales and collection cycle occurs at the point where finished goods are relieved (credited) and a charge is made to cost of goods sold.

The inventory and warehousing cycle can be thought of as comprising two separate but closely related systems, one involving the actual *physical flow of goods* and the other the *related costs*. As inventories move through the company, there must be adequate controls over both their physical movement and their related costs. The six functions that make up the inventory and warehousing cycle are discussed in the following sections.

Process Purchase Orders

The inventory and warehousing cycle begins with the acquisition of raw materials for production. Whether inventory purchases relate to raw materials for a manufacturer or finished goods for a retailer, it is essential that adequate controls over purchasing are maintained. Purchase requisitions are used to request that the purchasing department place orders for inventory items. Requisitions may be initiated by stockroom personnel or

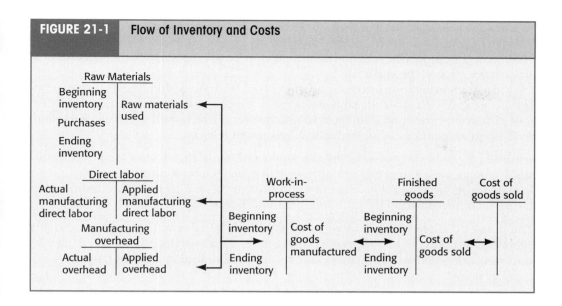

FIGURE 21-1   Flow of Inventory and Costs

by computer when inventory reaches a predetermined level, orders may be placed for the materials required to produce a customer order, or orders may be initiated on the basis of a periodic inventory count by a responsible person. Regardless of the method followed, the controls over purchase requisitions and the related purchase orders are evaluated and tested as part of the acquisition and payment cycle.

Receipt of the ordered materials is also part of the acquisition and payment cycle. Material received should be inspected for quantity and quality. The receiving department produces a receiving report that becomes a part of the necessary documentation before payment is made. After inspection, the material is sent to the storeroom and the receiving documents or electronic notifications of the receipt of goods are typically sent to purchasing, the storeroom, and accounts payable. Control and accountability are necessary for all transfers.

Receive Raw Materials

When materials are received, they are stored in the stockroom until needed for production. Materials are issued out of stock to production upon presentation of a properly approved materials requisition, work order, or similar document or electronic notice that indicates the type and quantity of materials needed. This requisition document is used to update the perpetual inventory master files and to make book transfers from the raw materials to work-in-process accounts. These updates occur automatically by computer for organizations that have integrated their inventory management and accounting systems.

Store Raw Materials

The processing portion of the inventory and warehousing cycle varies greatly from company to company. The determination of the items and quantities to be produced is generally based on specific orders from customers, sales forecasts, predetermined finished goods inventory levels, and economic production runs. A separate production control department often is responsible for the determination of the type and quantities of production. Within the various production departments, provision must be made to account for the quantities produced, control of scrap, quality controls, and physical protection of the material in process. The production department is often responsible for the review of computer-generated production and scrap reports, which provide useful information for accounting to reflect the movement of materials in the books and determine accurate costs of production.

Process the Goods

In any company involved in manufacturing, an adequate cost accounting system is an important part of the processing of goods function. The system is necessary to indicate the relative profitability of the various products for management planning and control and to value inventories for financial statement purposes. Two types of cost systems exist, although many variations and combinations of these systems are used: **job cost systems** and **process cost systems.** The main difference is whether costs are accumulated by individual jobs when material is issued and labor costs incurred (job cost) or whether they are accumulated by processes, with unit costs for each process assigned to the products passing through the process (process cost).

Cost accounting records consist of master files, worksheets, and reports that accumulate material, labor, and overhead costs by job or process as the costs are incurred. When jobs or products are completed, the related costs are transferred from work-in-process to finished goods on the basis of production department reports.

<table>
<tr><td>Store Finished Goods</td><td>As finished goods are completed by the production department, they are placed in the stockroom to await shipment. In companies with good internal controls, finished goods are kept under physical control in a separate, limited-access area. The control of finished goods is often considered part of the sales and collection cycle.</td></tr>
<tr><td>Ship Finished Goods</td><td>Shipping of completed goods is an integral part of the sales and collection cycle. Any shipment or transfer of finished goods must be authorized by a properly approved shipping document. The controls for shipment have already been studied in previous chapters.</td></tr>
</table>

The physical movement and related documentation in a typical inventory and warehousing cycle are shown in Figure 21-2. The figure reemphasizes the important point that the recording of costs and movement of inventory as shown in the books must correspond to the physical movements and processes.

Perpetual Inventory Master Files

One of the records used for inventory that has not been previously discussed is a **perpetual inventory master file.** Separate perpetual records are normally kept for raw materials and finished goods. Most companies do not use perpetuals for work-in-process.

Perpetual inventory master files can include only information about the units of inventory acquired, sold, and on hand, or they can also include information about unit costs. The latter is more typical of well-designed computerized systems.

For acquisitions of raw materials, the perpetual inventory master file is updated automatically when acquisitions of inventory are processed as part of recording acquisitions.

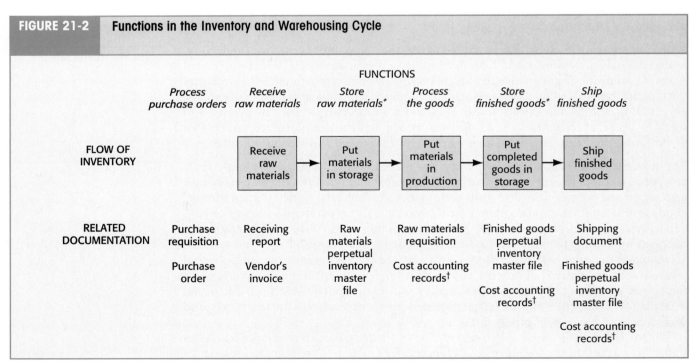

FIGURE 21-2   Functions in the Inventory and Warehousing Cycle

*Inventory counts are taken and compared with perpetual and book amounts at any stage of the cycle. The auditor must determine that cutoff for recording documents corresponds to the physical location of the items. A count must ordinarily be taken once a year. If the perpetual inventory system is operating well, this can be done on a cycle basis throughout the year.

†Includes cost information for materials, direct labor, and overhead.

For example, when the computer system enters the number of units and unit cost for each raw material acquisition, this information is used to update perpetual inventory master files along with the acquisitions journal and accounts payable master file.

Transfers of raw material from the storeroom must be separately entered into the computer to update the perpetual records. Typically, only the units transferred need to be entered because the computer can determine the unit costs from the master file. Raw material perpetual inventory master files that have unit costs include, for each raw material, beginning and ending units on hand and unit costs, units and unit cost of each acquisition, and units and unit cost of each transfer into production.

Finished goods perpetual inventory master files include the same type of information as raw materials perpetuals but are considerably more complex if costs are included along with units. Finished goods costs include raw materials, direct labor, and manufacturing overhead, which often requires allocations and detailed record keeping. When finished goods perpetuals include unit costs, the cost accounting records must be integrated into the computer system.

HOW E-COMMERCE AFFECTS INVENTORY MANAGEMENT

OBJECTIVE 21-2

Describe how e-commerce affects inventory management.

Chapter 19 highlighted how the Internet and other e-commerce applications are used to purchase and acquire goods and services, including inventory materials. This section briefly discusses how clients use the Internet and other e-commerce applications to manage inventories.

One of the key advantages the Internet provides for inventory management is to enable clients to provide expanded descriptions of their inventory products on a real-time basis to key business partners, including inventory suppliers and customers. Information about quantities on hand, the location of products, and other key inventory data helps inventory suppliers work with management to monitor the flow of inventory items. Customers often demand online access to key inventory data, such as information about product availability, back order and shipping status, product quality and reliability ratings, and compatibility specifications for integration with other products. The Internet, as well as internal local area networks, also assist client management by providing intracompany access to key inventory status reports. Managers use these systems to track the movement of goods throughout the organization by accessing online information about the location of specific inventory items.

Expanded access to information may increase business risks, such as the risk that sensitive proprietary information may unintentionally be made available to unauthorized users. The use of the Internet and other e-commerce applications may lead to financial reporting risks if access to inventory databases and systems is not adequately controlled. The use of security access restrictions such as passwords, firewalls, and other IT management controls described in Chapter 12 are critical to reducing the risk of external parties manipulating a company's inventory records that are used to prepare financial statement information.

PARTS OF THE AUDIT OF INVENTORY

OBJECTIVE 21-3

Explain the five parts of the audit of the inventory and warehousing cycle.

Now that you are familiar with the business functions and the related documents and records in the inventory and warehousing cycle, we are ready to turn our attention to the audit of the cycle. The overall objective in the audit of the inventory and warehousing cycle is to determine that raw materials, work-in-process, finished goods inventory, and cost of goods sold are fairly stated on the financial statements. The audit of the inventory and warehousing cycle can be divided into five distinct parts.

Acquire and Record Raw Materials, Labor, and Overhead

This part of the audit of the inventory and warehousing cycle includes the first three functions in Figure 21-2: process purchase orders, receive raw materials, and store raw materials. The internal controls over these three functions are first understood and then tested as a part of performing tests of controls and substantive tests of transactions in the acquisition and payment cycle and the payroll and personnel cycle. At the completion of the acquisition and payment cycle, the auditor is likely to be satisfied that acquisitions of raw materials and manufacturing costs are correctly stated, and samples should be designed to ensure that these systems are adequately tested. Similarly, when labor is a significant part of inventory, the payroll and personnel cycle tests should verify the proper accounting for these costs.

Transfer Assets and Costs

Internal transfers include the fourth and fifth functions in Figure 21-2 (p. 640): process the goods and store finished goods. These activities are accounted for in the cost accounting records. These records are independent of other cycles and are tested as part of the audit of the inventory and warehousing cycle.

Ship Goods and Record Revenue and Costs

Recording of shipments and related costs, the last function in Figure 21-2, is part of the sales and collection cycle. Therefore, internal controls over the function are understood and tested as a part of auditing the sales and collection cycle. Tests of controls and substantive tests of transactions should include procedures to verify the accuracy of the perpetual inventory master files.

Physically Observe Inventory

Observing the client taking a physical inventory count is necessary to determine whether recorded inventory actually exists at the balance sheet date and is properly counted by the client. Inventory is the first audit area for which physical examination is an essential type of evidence used to verify the balance in an account. The example at the beginning of the chapter involving the audit of Phar-Mor demonstrates the importance of physically observing on a surprise basis inventories that are material to the financial statements.

Price and Compile Inventory

Costs used to value the physical inventory must be tested to determine whether the client has correctly followed an inventory method that is in accordance with GAAP and is consistent with previous years. Audit procedures used to verify these costs are called price tests. In addition, the auditor must verify whether the physical counts were correctly summarized, the inventory quantities and prices were correctly extended, and the extended inventory was correctly footed. These tests are called compilation tests.

Figure 21-3 summarizes the five parts of the audit of the inventory and warehousing cycle. Because of the interrelationships of the inventory and warehousing cycle with other cycles, some parts of the audit of inventory are most efficiently tested with the audit tests of other cycles. As noted in Figure 21-3, the acquisition and recording of raw materials, labor, and overhead are tested as part of the audit of the acquisition and payment and payroll and personnel cycles. The shipment of goods and recording of revenue and related costs are

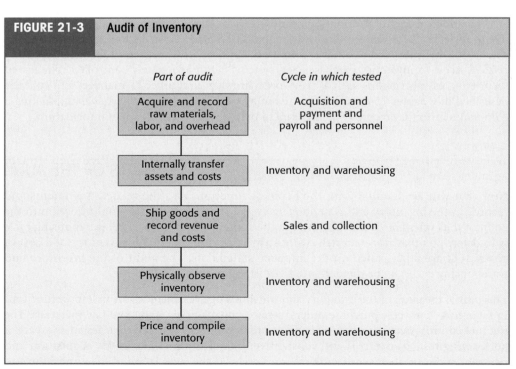

FIGURE 21-3   Audit of Inventory

Part of audit	Cycle in which tested
Acquire and record raw materials, labor, and overhead	Acquisition and payment and payroll and personnel
Internally transfer assets and costs	Inventory and warehousing
Ship goods and record revenue and costs	Sales and collection
Physically observe inventory	Inventory and warehousing
Price and compile inventory	Inventory and warehousing

addressed in the audit of the sales and collection cycle. Because these activities involving the audit of other cycles have previously been discussed, they are not addressed in this chapter. However, the results of these tests of other cycles are important to the overall evaluation of the audit of inventory.

The following section discusses the audit of cost accounting. We begin by discussing the internal transfer of assets and costs, which are accounted for in the cost accounting records. The internal transfer of assets and costs is one of the three parts of the audit of the inventory and warehousing cycle that is not tested in other cycles.

AUDIT OF COST ACCOUNTING

OBJECTIVE 21-4

Design and perform audit tests of cost accounting.

Cost accounting systems and controls of different companies vary more than most other areas because of the wide variety of items of inventory and the level of sophistication desired by management. For example, a company that manufactures an entire line of farm machines will have a completely different kind of cost records and internal controls than a steel fabricating shop that makes and installs custom-made metal cabinets. It should also not be surprising that small companies with owners who are actively involved in the manufacturing process will need less sophisticated records than will large, multiproduct companies.

Cost Accounting Controls

Cost accounting controls are those related to the physical inventory and the related costs from the point at which raw materials are requisitioned to the point at which the manufactured product is completed and transferred to storage. It is convenient to divide these controls into two broad categories: (1) physical controls over raw materials, work-in-process, and finished goods inventory, and (2) controls over the related costs.

Almost all companies need physical controls over their assets to prevent loss from misuse and theft. The use of physically segregated, limited-access storage areas for raw material, work-in-process, and finished goods is one major control to protect assets. In some instances, the assignment of custody of inventory to specific responsible individuals may be necessary to protect the assets. Approved prenumbered documents for authorizing movement of inventory also protect the assets from improper use. Copies of these documents should be sent directly to accounting by the persons issuing them, bypassing people with custodial responsibilities. An example of an effective document of this type is an approved materials requisition for obtaining raw materials from the storeroom.

Perpetual inventory master files maintained by persons who do not have custody of or access to assets are another useful cost accounting control. Perpetual inventory master files are important for a number of reasons: They provide a record of items on hand, which is used to initiate production or acquisition of additional materials or goods; they provide a record of the use of raw materials and the sale of finished goods, which can be reviewed for obsolete or slow-moving items; and they provide a record that can be used to pinpoint responsibility for custody as a part of the investigation of differences between physical counts and the amount shown on the records.

Another important consideration in cost accounting is the existence of adequate internal controls that integrate production and accounting records for the purpose of obtaining accurate costs for all products. The existence of adequate cost records is important to management as an aid in pricing, controlling costs, and costing inventory.

Acquire and record raw materials, labor, and overhead

Internally transfer assets and costs

Ship goods and record revenue and costs

Physically observe inventory

Price and compile inventory

Tests of Cost Accounting

The concepts in auditing cost accounting are no different from those discussed for any other transaction cycle. Figure 21-4 (p. 644) shows the methodology the auditor should follow in deciding which tests to perform. In auditing cost accounting, the auditor is concerned with four aspects: physical controls over inventory, documents and records for transferring inventory, perpetual inventory master files, and unit cost records.

Physical Controls An auditor's tests of the adequacy of the physical controls over raw materials, work-in-process, and finished goods must be restricted to observation and inquiry. For example, the auditor can examine the raw materials storage area to determine whether the inventory is protected from theft and misuse by the existence of a locked storeroom. An adequate storeroom with a competent custodian in charge also ordinarily results in the orderly storage of inventory. If the auditor concludes that the physical controls are so

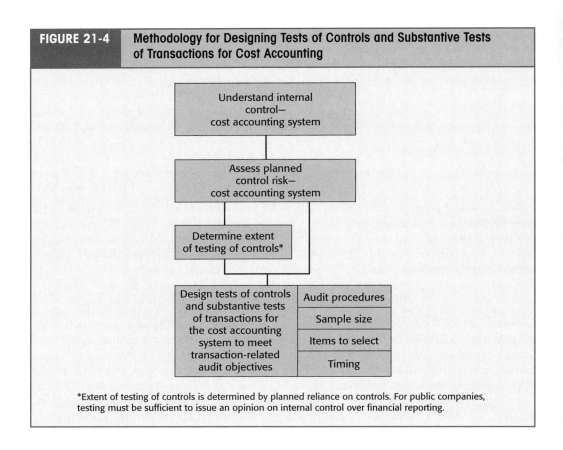

FIGURE 21-4 Methodology for Designing Tests of Controls and Substantive Tests of Transactions for Cost Accounting

Understand internal control—cost accounting system

Assess planned control risk—cost accounting system

Determine extent of testing of controls*

Design tests of controls and substantive tests of transactions for the cost accounting system to meet transaction-related audit objectives
- Audit procedures
- Sample size
- Items to select
- Timing

*Extent of testing of controls is determined by planned reliance on controls. For public companies, testing must be sufficient to issue an opinion on internal control over financial reporting.

inadequate that the inventory will be difficult to count, the auditor should expand observation of physical inventory tests to make sure that an adequate count is carried out.

Documents and Records for Transferring Inventory The auditor's primary concerns in verifying the transfer of inventory from one location to another are that the recorded transfers exist, the transfers that have actually taken place are recorded, and the quantity, description, and date of all recorded transfers are accurate. First, it is necessary to understand the client's internal controls for recording transfers before relevant tests can be performed. Once the internal controls are understood, the tests can easily be performed by examining documents and records. For example, a procedure to test the existence and accuracy of the transfer of goods from the raw material storeroom to the manufacturing assembly line is to account for a sequence of raw material requisitions, examine the requisitions for proper approval, and compare the quantity, description, and date with the information on the raw material perpetual inventory master files. Similarly, completed production records can be compared with perpetual inventory master files to be sure that all manufactured goods were physically delivered to the finished goods storeroom.

Technology has improved the ability to track the movement of goods throughout production. For example, products are labeled with standardized bar codes that can be scanned by laser to track the movement of inventory items.

Inventory Technology Tools

Perpetual Inventory Master Files Adequate perpetual inventory master files have a major effect on the *timing* and *extent* of the auditor's physical examination of inventory. When there are accurate perpetual inventory master files, it is often possible to test the physical inventory before the balance sheet date. An interim physical inventory can result in significant cost savings for both the client and the auditor, and it enables the client to get the audited statements earlier. Perpetual inventory master files also enable the auditor to reduce the extent of the tests of physical inventory when the assessed control risk related to physical observation of inventory is low.

Tests of the perpetual inventory master files for the purpose of reducing tests of physical inventory or changing their timing are done through the use of documentation.

Documents to verify the acquisition of raw materials can be examined when the auditor is verifying acquisitions as part of the tests of the acquisition and payment cycle. Documents supporting the reduction of raw material inventory for use in production and the increase in the quantity of finished goods inventory when goods have been manufactured are examined as part of the tests of the cost accounting records in the manner discussed in the preceding section. Support for the reduction in the finished goods inventory through the sale of goods to customers is ordinarily tested as part of the sales and collection cycle. Usually, it is relatively easy to test the accuracy of the perpetuals after the auditor determines how the internal controls are designed and decides to what degree assessed control risk should be reduced.

For many companies, traditional documents exist only in electronic form. Also, the perpetual inventory system is often integrated with other accounting cycles and is automatically updated with activity in those cycles. As a result, there may be opportunities to test computer-performed controls to support a reduction in control risk, which reduces the extent of substantive testing. This, in turn, may lead to audit efficiencies in the testing of the inventory and warehousing cycle.

Unit Cost Records Obtaining accurate cost data for raw materials, direct labor, and manufacturing overhead is an essential part of cost accounting. Adequate cost accounting records must be integrated with production and other accounting records to produce accurate costs of all products. Cost accounting records are pertinent to the auditor in that the valuation of ending inventory depends on the proper design and use of these records.

In testing the inventory cost records, the auditor must first develop an understanding of internal control. This is often somewhat time-consuming because the flow of costs is usually integrated with other accounting records, and it may not be obvious how the internal controls provide for the internal transfers of raw materials and for direct labor and manufacturing overhead as production is carried out.

Once the auditor understands internal control, the approach to internal verification involves the same concepts that were discussed in the verification of sales and acquisition transactions. When possible, it is desirable to test cost accounting records as a part of the acquisition, payroll, and sales tests to avoid testing the records more than once. For example, when the auditor is testing acquisition transactions as a part of the acquisition and payment cycle, it is desirable to trace the units and unit costs of raw materials to the perpetual inventory master files and the total cost to cost accounting records. Similarly, when payroll costs data are maintained for different jobs, it is desirable to trace from the payroll summary directly to job cost records as a part of testing the payroll and personnel cycle.

A major difficulty in the verification of inventory cost records is determining the reasonableness of cost allocations. For example, the assignment of manufacturing overhead costs to individual products entails certain assumptions that can significantly affect the unit costs of inventory and therefore the fairness of the inventory valuation. In evaluating these allocations, the auditor must consider the reasonableness of both the numerator and the denominator that result in the unit costs. For example, in testing overhead applied to inventory on the basis of direct labor dollars, the overhead rate should approximate total actual manufacturing overhead divided by total actual direct labor dollars. Because total manufacturing overhead is tested as part of the tests of the acquisition and payment cycle, and direct labor is tested as part of the payroll and personnel cycle, determining the reasonableness of the rate is not difficult. However, if manufacturing overhead is applied on the basis of machine hours, the auditor must verify the reasonableness of the machine hours by separate tests of the client's machine records. The major considerations in evaluating the reasonableness of all cost allocations, including manufacturing overhead, are compliance with GAAP and consistency with previous years.

Because the internal controls over cost accounting records vary significantly among organizations, specific tests of controls are not presented here. The auditor should design appropriate tests based on the understanding of the nature of the cost accounting records and the extent to which they will be relied on to reduce substantive tests. The quality of the cost accounting records also affects the use of analytical procedures, which is discussed in the next section.

ANALYTICAL PROCEDURES

OBJECTIVE 21-5

Apply analytical procedures to the accounts in the inventory and warehousing cycle.

Analytical procedures are as important in auditing inventory and warehousing as in any other cycle. Table 21-1 includes several common analytical procedures and possible misstatements that may be indicated when fluctuations exist. Several of those analytical procedures have also been included in other cycles. An example is the gross margin percentage.

In addition to performing analytical procedures that examine the relationship of inventory account balances with other financial statement accounts (as shown in Figure 21-1 on page 639), auditors often use nonfinancial information to assess the reasonableness of inventory-related balances. For example, knowledge about the size and weight of inventory products, their methods of storage (stacks, tanks, etc.), and the capacity of storage facilities (such as available square footage) can be used to determine whether recorded inventory is consistent with available inventory storage.

After performing the appropriate tests of the cost accounting records and analytical procedures, the auditor is prepared to design and perform tests of details of the ending inventory balance.

TABLE 21-1	Analytical Procedures for the Inventory and Warehousing Cycle
Analytical Procedure	**Possible Misstatement**
Compare gross margin percentage with that of previous years.	Overstatement or understatement of inventory and cost of goods sold.
Compare inventory turnover (cost of goods sold divided by average inventory) with that of previous years.	Obsolete inventory, which affects inventory and cost of goods sold. Overstatement or understatement of inventory.
Compare unit costs of inventory with those of previous years.	Overstatement or understatement of unit costs, which affect inventory and cost of goods sold.
Compare extended inventory value with that of previous years.	Misstatements in compilation, unit costs, or extensions, which affect inventory and cost of goods sold.
Compare current year manufacturing costs with those of previous years (variable costs should be adjusted for changes in volume).	Misstatements of unit costs of inventory, especially direct labor and manufacturing overhead, which affect inventory and cost of goods sold.

METHODOLOGY FOR DESIGNING TESTS OF DETAILS OF BALANCES

The methodology for deciding which tests of details of balances to perform for inventory and warehousing is essentially the same as that discussed for accounts receivable, accounts payable, and all other balance sheet accounts. It is shown in Figure 21-5.

Obtaining an understanding of the client's business is even more important for inventory than for most aspects of the audit because inventory varies so significantly for different companies. A proper understanding of the client's business and its industry enables the auditor to ask about and discuss such problems as inventory valuation, potential obsolescence, and the existence of consignment inventory intermingled with owned inventory. A useful starting point for becoming familiar with the client's inventory is for the auditor to tour the client's facilities, including receiving, storage, production, planning, and record-keeping areas. The tour should be led by a supervisor who can answer questions about production, especially about any changes in the past year.

As part of gaining an understanding of the effect of the client's business and industry on inventory in the planning phase of the audit, the auditor assesses client business risk. There may be significant sources of business risk related to inventory because of such factors as short product cycles and the risk of obsolescence, use of just-in-time inventory

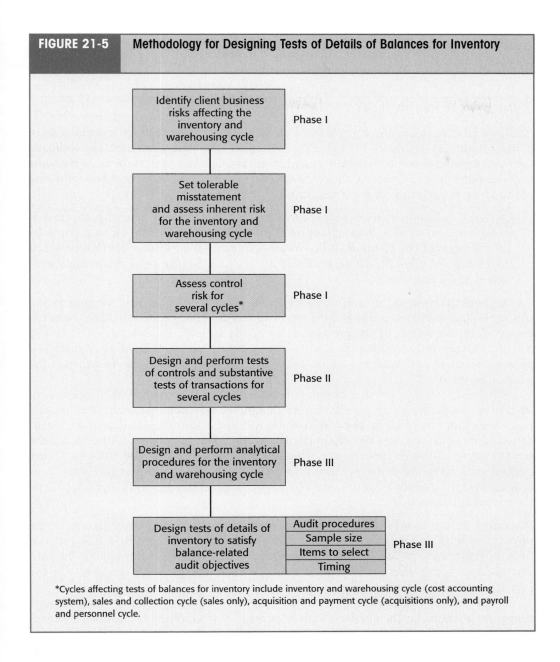

Identify client business risks affecting the inventory and warehousing cycle   Phase I

Set tolerable misstatement and assess inherent risk for the inventory and warehousing cycle   Phase I

Assess control risk for several cycles*   Phase I

Design and perform tests of controls and substantive tests of transactions for several cycles   Phase II

Design and perform analytical procedures for the inventory and warehousing cycle   Phase III

Design tests of details of inventory to satisfy balance-related audit objectives — Audit procedures / Sample size / Items to select / Timing   Phase III

*Cycles affecting tests of balances for inventory include inventory and warehousing cycle (cost accounting system), sales and collection cycle (sales only), acquisition and payment cycle (acquisitions only), and payroll and personnel cycle.

and other supply-chain management techniques, reliance on a few key suppliers, and use of sophisticated inventory management technology.

After assessing client business risk, the auditor then sets tolerable misstatement and assesses inherent risk for inventory. Inventory is typically one of the most material items in the financial statements for manufacturing, wholesale, and retail companies. Inherent risk is often assessed at a relatively high level for companies with significant inventory. Inventory may be stored in multiple locations, increasing concerns about the existence of inventory, including the potential for theft. The pricing of inventory is often complex, increasing the risk of misstatement for the accuracy objective. There may also be concerns about inventory obsolescence, which relates to the net realizable value objective.

In assessing control risk, the auditor is primarily concerned about internal controls over perpetual records, physical controls, inventory counts, and inventory pricing. The nature and extent of controls vary widely from company to company. Note that the test results from several cycles other than inventory and warehousing also affect tests of details of balances for inventory.

Because of the complexity of auditing inventory, two aspects of tests of details of balances are discussed separately: (1) physical observation and (2) pricing and compilation. These topics are studied in the next two sections.

PHYSICAL OBSERVATION OF INVENTORY

OBJECTIVE 21-6

Design and perform physical observation audit tests for inventory.

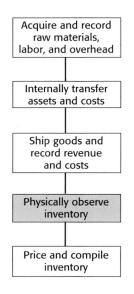

Auditors have been required to perform physical observation tests of inventory since a major fraud was uncovered in 1938 at the McKesson & Robbins Company. The company recorded significant amounts of nonexistent inventory. This was possible because the auditors did not physically observe the inventory. SAS 1 (AU 331) states that the following requirement exists for inventory observation:

> . . . it is ordinarily necessary for the independent auditor to be present at the time of count and, by suitable observation, tests, and inquiries, satisfy himself respecting the effectiveness of the methods of inventory-taking and the measure of reliance which may be placed upon the client's representations about the quantities and physical condition of the inventories.

An essential point in the SAS 1 requirement is the distinction between the observation of the physical inventory count and the responsibility for taking the count. The client has responsibility for setting up the procedures for taking an accurate physical inventory and actually making and recording the counts. The auditor's responsibility is to evaluate and observe the client's physical procedures and draw conclusions about the adequacy of the physical inventory.

The requirement of physical examination of inventory is not applicable in the case of inventory in a public warehouse. Inventory in a public warehouse or with other outside custodians is normally verified by confirmation with the custodian. However, if the inventory amounts involved are a significant portion of current assets or total assets, the auditor should apply additional procedures. These may include investigating the custodian's performance, receiving an independent accountant's report on the custodian's control procedures over the custody of goods, and observing the physical count of the goods held by the custodian, if practical.

Controls

Regardless of the client's inventory record-keeping method, there must be a periodic physical count of the inventory items on hand. The client can take the physical count at or near the balance sheet date, at a preliminary date, or on a cycle basis throughout the year. The last two approaches are appropriate only if there are adequate controls over the preparation and maintenance of perpetual inventory master files.

In connection with the client's physical count of inventory, adequate controls include proper instructions for the physical count, supervision by responsible personnel, independent internal verification of the counts, independent reconciliations of the physical counts with perpetual inventory master files, and adequate control over count sheets or tags.

An important aspect of the auditor's understanding of the client's physical inventory controls is complete familiarity with them before the inventory begins. This is obviously necessary to evaluate the effectiveness of the client's procedures, but it also enables the auditor to make constructive suggestions beforehand. If the inventory instructions do not provide adequate controls, the auditor must spend more time making sure that the physical count is accurate.

Audit Decisions

The auditor's decisions in the physical observation of inventory are similar to those made for other audit areas and include selecting audit procedures, deciding the timing of the procedures, determining sample size, and selecting items for testing. The last three decisions are discussed next, followed by a discussion of selecting the appropriate audit procedures.

Timing The auditor decides whether the physical count can be taken before year-end primarily on the basis of the accuracy of the perpetual inventory master files. When an interim physical count is permitted, the auditor observes it at that time and also tests the perpetuals for transactions from the date of the count to year-end. When the perpetuals are accurate, it may be unnecessary for the client to count the inventory every year. Instead, the auditor can compare the perpetuals with the actual inventory on a sample basis at a convenient time. When there are no perpetuals and the inventory is material, a complete physical inventory must be taken by the client near the end of the accounting period and tested by the auditor at the same time.

Sample Size Sample size in physical observation is usually impossible to specify in terms of the number of items because the emphasis during the tests is on observing the client's procedures rather than on selecting items for testing. A convenient way to think of sample size in physical observation is in terms of the total number of hours spent rather than the number of inventory items counted. The most important determinants of the amount of time needed to test inventory are the adequacy of the internal controls over the physical counts, accuracy of the perpetual inventory master files, total dollar amount and type of inventory, number of different significant inventory locations, nature and extent of misstatements discovered in previous years, and other inherent risks. In some situations, inventory is such a significant item that dozens of auditors are necessary to observe the physical count, whereas in other situations, one person can complete the observation in a short time. Special care is warranted in the observation of inventory because of the difficulty of expanding sample sizes or reperforming tests after the physical inventory has been taken.

Selection of Items The selection of items for testing is an important part of the audit decision in inventory observation. Care should be taken to observe the counting of the most significant items and a representative sample of typical inventory items, to inquire about items that are likely to be obsolete or damaged, and to discuss with management the reasons for excluding any material items.

Physical Observation Tests

The same balance-related audit objectives that have been used in previous sections for tests of details of balances provide the frame of reference for discussing the physical observation tests. However, before the objectives are discussed, some comments that apply to all the objectives are appropriate.

The most important part of the observation of inventory is determining whether the physical count is being taken in accordance with the client's instructions. To do this effectively, *it is essential that the auditor be present* while the physical count is taking place. When the client's employees are not following the inventory instructions, the auditor must either contact the supervisor to correct the problem or modify the physical observation procedures. For example, if the procedures require one team to count the inventory and a second team to recount it as a test of accuracy, the auditor should inform management if both teams are observed counting together.

THE CRAZY EDDIE, INC., FRAUD

By 1970, Crazy Eddie, Inc., a consumer electronics retail company, had 43 consumer sales outlets, sales of $350 million, reported net income before taxes of $21 million, and a market value of more than $500 million. Consumer electronics is a highly cyclical and competitive industry, with significant client business risk. Crazy Eddie seemed to be bucking industry trends by growing as other electronics retailers were struggling, but it was an illusion. By the end of 1989, the company had filed for bankruptcy, closed all stores, and liquidated all assets at a huge loss to investors.

Investigation by regulatory authorities found extensive financial fraud, the most important being a $65 million overstatement of inventory. There were extensive lawsuits against many parties, including the CEO, who was found guilty of fraud and sent to prison.

Naturally, the question arose as to why the auditors failed to uncover the fraud in their annual audit.

The defense used by the auditor was the difficulty of uncovering the well-conceived fraud. The parties involved in or who knew of the fraud included the acting controller, the director of internal auditing, and the director of accounts payable. One example of fraud was the shipment of inventory from store to store immediately before the auditor arrived to count the inventory. Another was the destruction of documentation to conceal inventory shortages at various locations. The auditor argued that it is almost impossible to uncover fraud when there is extensive collusion. The suit against the CPA firm and other defendants was settled out of court in 1993.

Sources: Adapted from 1. Michael C. Knapp, *Contemporary Auditing: Issues and Cases*, 4th edition. West Publishing, 2001, pp. 71–81. 2. Joseph T. Wells, "Crazy Eddie and the $120 Million Ripoff," *Journal of Accountancy* (October 2000), pp. 93-95.

Balance-Related Audit Objective	Common Inventory Observation Procedures	Comments
Inventory as recorded on tags exists (existence).	Select a random sample of tag numbers and identify the tag with that number attached to the actual inventory. Observe whether movement of inventory takes place during the count.	The purpose is to uncover the inclusion of nonexistent items as inventory.
Existing inventory is counted and tagged, and tags are accounted for to make sure none are missing (completeness).	Examine inventory to make sure it is tagged. Observe whether movement of inventory takes place during the count. Inquire as to inventory in other locations. Account for all used and unused tags to make sure none are lost or intentionally omitted. Record the tag numbers for those used and unused for subsequent follow-up.	Special concern should be directed to omission of large sections of inventory. This test should be done at the completion of the physical count. This test should be done at the completion of the physical count.
Inventory is counted accurately (accuracy).	Recount client's counts to make sure the recorded counts are accurate on the tags (also check descriptions and unit of count, such as dozen or gross). Compare physical counts with perpetual inventory master file. Record client's counts for subsequent testing.	Recording client counts in the audit files on *inventory count sheets* is done for two reasons: to obtain documentation that an adequate physical examination was made, and to test for the possibility that the client might change the recorded counts after the auditor leaves the premises.
Inventory is classified correctly on the tags (classification).	Examine inventory descriptions on the tags and compare with the actual inventory for raw material, work-in-process, and finished goods. Evaluate whether the percent of completion recorded on the tags for work-in-process is reasonable.	These tests would be done as a part of the first procedure in the accuracy objective.
Information is obtained to make sure sales and inventory purchases are recorded in the proper period (cutoff).	Record in the audit files for subsequent follow-up the last shipping document number used at year-end. Make sure the inventory for the above item was excluded from the physical count. Review shipping area for inventory set aside for shipment but not counted. Record in the audit files for subsequent follow-up the last receiving report number used at year-end. Make sure the inventory for the above item was included in the physical count. Review receiving area for inventory that should be included in the physical count.	Obtaining proper cutoff information for sales and acquisitions is an essential part of inventory observation. The appropriate tests during the field work were discussed for sales in Chapter 16 and for acquisitions in Chapter 19.
Obsolete and unusable inventory items are excluded or noted (realizable value).	Test for obsolete inventory by inquiry of factory employees and management and alertness for items that are damaged, rust- or dust-covered, or located in inappropriate places.	
The client has rights to inventory recorded on tags (rights).	Inquire about consignment or customer inventory included on client's premises. Be alert for inventory that is set aside or specially marked as indications of nonownership.	

Common tests of details of balances audit procedures for physical inventory observation are shown in Table 21-2. Detail tie-in and presentation and disclosure are the only balance-related audit objectives not included in the table. These objectives are discussed under compilation of inventory. The assumption throughout is that the client records inventory on prenumbered tags on the balance sheet date.

In addition to the detailed procedures included in Table 21-2, the auditor should walk through all areas where inventory is warehoused to make sure that all inventory has been counted and properly tagged. When inventory is in boxes or other containers, these should be opened during test counts. It is desirable to compare high-dollar-value inventory to counts in the previous year and inventory master files as a test of reasonableness. These two procedures should not be done until the client has completed the physical counts.

AUDIT OF PRICING AND COMPILATION

OBJECTIVE 21-7

Design and perform audit tests of pricing and compilation for inventory.

An important part of the audit of inventory is to perform all the procedures necessary to make certain that the physical counts or perpetual record quantities were properly priced and compiled. **Inventory price tests** include all the tests of the client's unit prices to determine whether they are correct. **Inventory compilation tests** include all the tests of the summarization of the physical quantities, the extension of price times quantity, footing the inventory summary, and tracing the totals to the general ledger.

Pricing and Compilation Controls

The existence of adequate internal controls for unit costs that are integrated with production and other accounting records is important to ensure that reasonable costs are used for valuing ending inventory. One important internal control is the use of **standard cost records** that indicate variances in material, labor, and overhead costs and can be used to evaluate production. When standard costs are used, procedures must be designed to keep the standards updated for changes in production processes and costs. The review of unit costs for reasonableness by someone independent of the department responsible for developing the costs is also a useful control over valuation.

An internal control designed to prevent the overstatement of inventory through the inclusion of obsolete inventory is a formal review and reporting of obsolete, slow-moving, damaged, and overstated inventory items. The review should be done by a competent employee by reviewing perpetual inventory master files for inventory turnover and holding discussions with engineering or production personnel.

Compilation internal controls are needed to provide a means of ensuring that the physical counts are properly summarized, priced at the same amount as the unit records, correctly extended and totaled, and included in the general ledger at the proper amount. Important compilation internal controls are adequate documents and records for taking the physical count and proper internal verification. If the physical inventory is taken on prenumbered tags and carefully reviewed before the personnel are released from the physical examination of inventory, there should be little risk of misstatement in summarizing the tags. The most important internal control over accurate determination of prices, extensions, and footings is internal verification by a competent, independent person.

| Acquire and record raw materials, labor, and overhead |
| Internally transfer assets and costs |
| Ship goods and record revenue and costs |
| Physically observe inventory |
| Price and compile inventory |

Pricing and Compilation Procedures

Balance-related audit objectives for tests of details of balances are also useful in discussing pricing and compilation procedures. The objectives and related tests are shown in Table 21-3 (p. 652), except for the cutoff objective. Physical observation, which was previously discussed, is a major source of cutoff information for sales and purchases. Tests of the accounting records for cutoff are done as a part of sales (sales and collection cycle) and acquisitions (acquisition and payment cycle).

The frame of reference for applying the objectives is a listing of inventory obtained from the client that includes each inventory item's description, quantity, unit price, and extended value. The inventory listing is in inventory item description order, with raw material, work-in-process, and finished goods separated. The totals equal the general ledger balance.

Valuation of Inventory

The proper valuation (pricing) of inventory is often one of the most important and time-consuming parts of the audit. In performing pricing tests, three things about the client's method of pricing are extremely important: The method must be in accordance with GAAP, the application of the method must be consistent from year to year, and cost versus market value (replacement cost or net realizable value) must be considered. Because the

TABLE 21-3   Balance-Related Audit Objectives and Tests of Details of Balances for Inventory Pricing and Compilation

Balance-Related Audit Objective	Common Inventory Pricing and Compilation Procedures	Comments
Inventory in the inventory listing schedule agrees with the physical inventory counts, the extensions are correct, and the total is correctly added and agrees with the general ledger (detail tie-in).	Perform compilation tests (see existence, completeness, and accuracy objectives). Foot the inventory listing schedules for raw materials, work-in-process, and finished goods. Trace the totals to the general ledger. Extend the quantity times the price on selected items.	Unless controls are weak, extending and footing tests should be limited.
Inventory items in the inventory listing schedule exist (existence).	Trace inventory listed in the schedule to inventory tags and auditor's recorded counts for existence and description.	The next six objectives are affected by the results of the physical inventory observation. The tag numbers and counts verified as a part of physical inventory observation are traced to the inventory listing schedule as a part of these tests.
Existing inventory items are included in the inventory listing schedule (completeness).	Account for unused tag numbers shown in the auditor's documentation to make sure no tags have been added. Trace from inventory tags to the inventory listing schedules and make sure inventory on tags is included. Account for tag numbers to make sure none have been deleted.	
Inventory items in the inventory listing schedule are accurate (accuracy).	Trace inventory listed in the schedule to inventory tags and auditor's recorded counts for quantity and description. Perform price tests of inventory. For a discussion of price tests, see text material on pages 651–654.	
Inventory items in the inventory listing schedule are properly classified (classification).	Verify the classification into raw materials, work-in-process, and finished goods by comparing the descriptions on inventory tags and auditor's recorded test counts with the inventory listing schedule.	
Inventory items in the inventory listing are stated at realizable value (realizable value).	Perform tests of lower of cost or market, selling price, and obsolescence.	
The client has rights to inventory items in the inventory listing schedule (rights).	Trace inventory tags identified as nonowned during the physical observation to the inventory listing schedule to make sure these have not been included. Review contracts with suppliers and customers and inquire of management for the possibility of the inclusion of consigned or other nonowned inventory, or the exclusion of owned inventory.	
Inventory and related accounts in the inventory and warehousing cycle are properly presented and disclosed (presentation and disclosure).	Examine financial statements for proper presentation and disclosure, including: Separate disclosure of raw materials, work-in-process, and finished goods. Proper description of the inventory costing method. Description of pledged inventory. Inclusion of significant sales and purchase commitments.	Pledging of inventory and sales and purchase commitments are usually uncovered as a part of other audit tests.

method of verifying the pricing of inventory depends on whether items are acquired or manufactured, these two categories are discussed separately.

Pricing Purchased Inventory The primary types of inventory included in this category are raw materials, purchased parts, and supplies. As a first step in verifying the valuation of purchased inventory, it is necessary to establish clearly whether LIFO, FIFO, weighted average, or some other valuation method is being used. It is also necessary to determine which costs should be included in the valuation of an item of inventory. For example, the auditor must find out whether freight, storage, discounts, and other costs are included and compare the findings with the preceding year's audit documentation to make sure that the methods are consistent.

In selecting specific inventory items for pricing, emphasis should be put on the larger dollar amounts and on products that are known to have wide fluctuations in price, but a representative sample of all types of inventory and departments should be included as well. Stratified variables or monetary unit sampling is commonly used in these tests.

The auditor should list the inventory items intended to be verified for pricing and request the client to locate the appropriate vendors' invoices. It is important that sufficient invoices be examined to account for the entire quantity of inventory for the item being tested, especially for the FIFO valuation method. Examining sufficient invoices is useful to uncover situations in which clients value their inventory on the basis of the most recent invoice only and, in some cases, to discover obsolete inventory. As an illustration, assume that the client's valuation of an inventory item is $12.00 per unit for 1,000 units, using FIFO. The auditor should examine the most recent invoices for acquisitions of that inventory item made in the year under audit until the valuation of all of the 1,000 units is accounted for. If the most recent acquisition of the inventory item was for 700 units at $12.00 per unit, and the immediately preceding acquisition was for 600 units at $11.30 per unit, the inventory item in question is overstated by $210.00 (300 × $0.70).

When the client has perpetual inventory master files that include unit costs of acquisitions, it is usually desirable to test the pricing by tracing the unit costs to the perpetuals rather than to vendors' invoices. In most cases, the effect is to reduce the cost of verifying inventory valuation significantly. Naturally, when the perpetuals are used to verify unit costs, it is essential to test the unit costs on the perpetuals to vendors' invoices as a part of the tests of the acquisition and payment cycle.

Pricing Manufactured Inventory The auditor must consider the cost of raw materials, direct labor, and manufacturing overhead in pricing work-in-process and finished goods. The need to verify each of these has the effect of making the audit of work-in-process and finished goods inventory more complex than the audit of purchased inventory. Nevertheless, such considerations as selecting the items to be tested, testing for whether cost or market value is lower, and evaluating the possibility of obsolescence also apply.

In pricing raw materials in manufactured products, it is necessary to consider both the unit cost of the raw materials and the number of units required to manufacture a unit of output. The unit cost can be verified in the same manner as that used for other purchased inventory—by examining vendors' invoices or perpetual inventory master files. Then it is necessary to examine engineering specifications, inspect the finished product, or find a similar method to determine the number of units it takes to manufacture a product.

Similarly, the hourly costs of direct labor and the number of hours it takes to manufacture a unit of output must be verified while testing direct labor. Hourly labor costs can be verified by comparison with labor payroll or union contracts. The number of hours needed to manufacture the product can be determined from engineering specifications or similar sources.

The proper manufacturing overhead in work-in-process and finished goods is dependent on the approach being used by the client. It is necessary to evaluate the method being used for consistency and reasonableness and to recompute the costs to determine whether the overhead is correct. For example, if the rate is based on direct labor dollars, the auditor can divide the total manufacturing overhead by the total direct labor dollars to determine the actual overhead rate. This rate can then be compared with the overhead rate used by the client to determine unit costs. Testing of pricing for work-in-process and finished goods is often done in conjunction with tests of standard costs. When standard costs have been tested with satisfactory results, testing of unit costs for ending inventory can be limited to tracing the price used to value ending inventory to the standard cost records.

When the client has standard costs records, an efficient and useful method of determining valuation is by the review and analysis of variances. If the variances in material, labor, and manufacturing overhead are small, it is evidence of reliable cost records.

Cost or Market In pricing inventory, it is necessary to consider whether replacement cost or net realizable value is lower than historical cost. For purchased finished goods and raw materials, the most recent cost of an inventory item as indicated on a vendor's invoice of the subsequent period is a useful way to test for replacement cost. All manufacturing costs must be considered for work-in-process and finished goods for manufactured inventory. It is also necessary to consider the sales value of inventory items and the possible effect of rapid fluctuation of prices to determine net realizable value. Finally, it is necessary to consider the possibility of obsolescence in the valuation process.

INTEGRATION OF THE TESTS

OBJECTIVE 21-8

Integrate the various parts of the audit of the inventory and warehousing cycle.

The most difficult part of understanding the audit of the inventory and warehousing cycle is grasping the interrelationships of the many different tests the auditor makes to evaluate whether inventory and cost of goods sold are fairly stated. Figure 21-6 and the discussions that follow are designed to aid the reader in perceiving the audit of the inventory and warehousing cycle as a series of integrated tests.

Tests of the Acquisition and Payment Cycle When the auditor verifies acquisitions as part of the tests of the acquisition and payment cycle, evidence is being obtained about the accuracy of raw materials acquired and all manufacturing overhead costs except labor. These acquisition costs either flow directly into cost of goods sold or become the most significant part of the ending inventory of raw material, work-in-process, and finished goods. In audits involving perpetual inventory master files, it is common to test these as a part of tests of controls and substantive tests of transactions procedures in the acquisition and payment cycle. Similarly, if manufacturing costs are assigned to individual jobs or processes, they are usually tested as a part of the same cycle.

Tests of the Payroll and Personnel Cycle When the auditor verifies labor costs, the same comments apply as for acquisitions. In most cases, the cost accounting records for direct and indirect labor costs can be tested as part of the audit of the payroll and personnel cycle, if there is adequate advance planning.

Tests of the Sales and Collection Cycle Although the relationship is less close between the sales and collection cycle and the inventory and warehousing cycle than between the two previously discussed, it is still important. Most of the audit testing in the storage of finished goods as well as the shipment and recording of sales takes place when the sales and collection cycle is tested. In addition, if standard cost records are used, it may be possible to test the standard cost of goods sold at the same time that sales tests are performed.

Tests of Cost Accounting Tests of cost accounting are meant to verify the controls affecting inventory that were not verified as part of the three previously discussed cycles. Tests are made of the physical controls, transfers of raw material costs to work-in-process, transfers of costs of completed goods to finished goods, perpetual inventory master files, and unit cost records.

Physical Inventory, Pricing, and Compilation In most audits, the underlying assumption in testing the inventory and warehousing cycle is that cost of goods sold is a residual of beginning inventory plus acquisitions of raw materials, direct labor, and other manufacturing costs minus ending inventory. When the audit of inventory and cost of goods sold is approached with this idea in mind, the importance of ending inventory becomes obvious. Physical inventory, pricing, and compilation are each equally important in the audit because a misstatement in any one results in misstated inventory and cost of goods sold.

In testing the physical inventory, it is possible to rely heavily on the perpetual inventory master files if they have been tested as a part of one or more of the previously discussed tests. In fact, if the perpetual inventory master files are considered reliable, the auditor can observe and test the physical count at some time during the year and rely on the perpetuals to keep adequate records of the quantities.

FIGURE 21-6   Interrelationship of Various Audit Tests

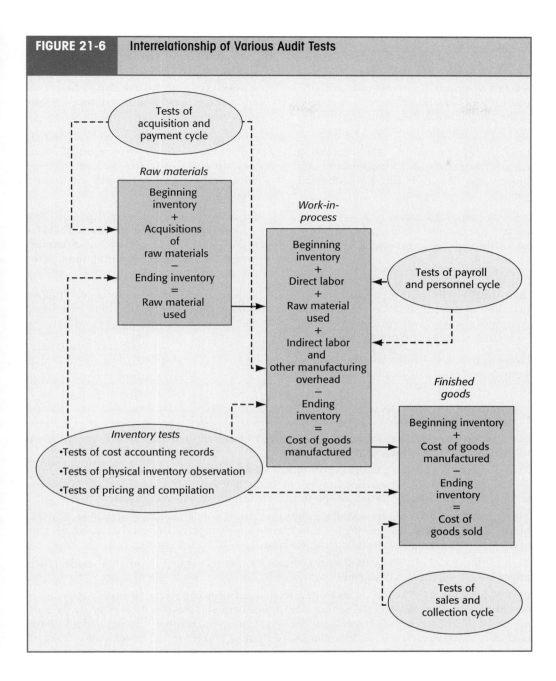

When testing the unit costs, it is also possible to rely, to some degree, on the tests of the cost records made during the substantive tests of transactions. The existence of standard cost records is also useful for the purpose of comparison with the actual unit costs. If the standard costs are used to represent historical cost, they must be tested for reliability.

SUMMARY

This chapter discussed the audit of the inventory and warehousing cycle. Because of the difficulties associated with establishing the existence and valuation of inventories, the cycle is often the most time-consuming and complex part of the audit. The cycle is also unique because many of the tests of the inputs to the cycle are tested as part of the audit of other cycles. Tests performed as part of the inventory and warehousing cycle focus on the cost accounting records, physical observation, and tests of the pricing and compilation of the ending inventory balance.

ESSENTIAL TERMS

Cost accounting controls—controls over physical inventory and the related costs from the point at which raw materials are requisitioned to the point at which the manufactured product is completed and transferred to storage

Cost accounting records—the accounting records concerned with the manufacture and processing of the goods and storing finished goods

Inventory and warehousing cycle—the transaction cycle that involves the physical flow of goods through the organization, as well as related costs

Inventory compilation tests—audit procedures used to verify whether physical counts of inventory are correctly summarized, inventory quantities and prices are correctly extended, and extended inventory is correctly footed

Inventory price tests—audit procedures used to verify the costs used to value physical inventory

Job cost systems—systems of cost accounting in which costs are accumulated by individual jobs when material is used and labor costs are incurred

Perpetual inventory master file—a continuously updated computerized record of inventory items purchased, used, sold, and on hand for merchandise, raw materials, and finished goods

Process cost systems—systems of cost accounting in which costs are accumulated for a process, with unit costs for each process assigned to the products passing through the process

Standard cost records—records that indicate variances between projected material, labor, and overhead costs and the actual costs

REVIEW QUESTIONS

21-1 (Objective 21-1) Give the reasons why inventory is often the most difficult and time-consuming part of many audit engagements.

21-2 (Objectives 21-1, 21-2, 21-8) Explain the relationship between the acquisition and payment cycle and the inventory and warehousing cycle in the audit of a manufacturing company. List several audit procedures in the acquisition and payment cycle that support your explanation.

21-3 (Objective 21-2) Give reasons why companies provide online access to descriptions of inventory products and on-hand quantity levels to key inventory suppliers. Discuss risks associated with making that information available on an online basis.

21-4 (Objectives 21-1, 21-4) State what is meant by cost accounting records and explain their importance in the conduct of an audit.

21-5 (Objectives 21-3, 21-4) Many auditors assert that certain audit tests can be significantly reduced for clients with adequate perpetual records that include both unit and cost data. What are the most important tests of the perpetual records that the auditor must make before reducing assessed control risk? Assuming the perpetuals are determined to be accurate, which tests can be reduced?

21-6 (Objective 21-6) Before the physical examination, the auditor obtains a copy of the client's inventory instructions and reviews them with the controller. In obtaining an understanding of inventory procedures for a small manufacturing company, these deficiencies are identified: Shipping operations will not be completely halted during the physical examination, and there will be no independent verification of the original inventory count by a second counting team. Evaluate the importance of each of these deficiencies and state its effect on the auditor's observation of inventory.

21-7 (Objective 21-6) At the completion of an inventory observation, the controller requested the auditor to give him a copy of all recorded test counts to facilitate the correction of all discrepancies between the client's and the auditor's counts. Should the auditor comply with the request? Why?

21-8 (Objective 21-6) What major audit procedures are involved in testing for the ownership of inventory during the observation of the physical counts and as a part of subsequent valuation tests?

21-9 (Objectives 21-5, 21-6, 21-7) In the verification of the amount of the inventory, one of the auditor's concerns is that slow-moving and obsolete items be identified. List the auditing procedures that could be used to determine whether slow-moving or obsolete items have been included in inventory.

21-10 (Objective 21-6) During the taking of physical inventory, the controller intentionally withheld several inventory tags from the employees responsible for the physical count. After the auditor left the client's premises at the completion of the inventory observation, the controller recorded nonexistent inventory on the tags and thereby significantly overstated earnings. How could the auditor have uncovered the misstatement, assuming that there are no perpetual records?

21-11 (Objective 21-6) Explain why a proper cutoff of purchases and sales is heavily dependent on the physical inventory observation. What information should be obtained during the physical count to make sure that cutoff is accurate?

21-12 (Objective 21-7) Define what is meant by compilation tests. List several examples of audit procedures to verify compilation.

21-13 (Objective 21-5) List the major analytical procedures for testing the overall reasonableness of inventory. For each test, explain the type of misstatement that could be identified.

21-14 (Objective 21-7) Included in the December 31, 2005, inventory of the Wholeridge Supply Company are 2,600 deluxe ring binders in the amount of $5,902. An examination of the most recent acquisitions of binders showed the following costs: January 26, 2006, 2,300 at $2.42 each; December 6, 2005, 1,900 at $2.28 each; November 26, 2005, 2,400 at $2.07 each. What is the misstatement in valuation of the December 31, 2005, inventory for deluxe ring binders, assuming FIFO inventory valuation? What would your answer be if the January 26, 2006, acquisition was for 2,300 binders at $2.12 each?

21-15 (Objectives 21-7, 21-8) The Ruswell Manufacturing Company applied manufacturing overhead to inventory at December 31, 2005, on the basis of $3.47 per direct labor hour. Explain how you would evaluate the reasonableness of total direct labor hours and manufacturing overhead in the ending inventory of finished goods.

21-16 (Objective 21-8) Each employee for the Gedding Manufacturing Co., a firm using a job-cost inventory costing method, must reconcile his or her total hours worked with the hours worked on individual jobs using a job time sheet at the time weekly payroll time cards are prepared. The job time sheet is then stapled to the time card. Explain how you could test the direct labor dollars included in inventory as a part of the payroll and personnel tests.

21-17 (Objective 21-6) Assuming that the auditor properly documents receiving report numbers as a part of the physical inventory observation procedures, explain how the proper cutoff of purchases, including tests for the possibility of raw materials in transit, should be verified later in the audit.

MULTIPLE CHOICE QUESTIONS FROM CPA EXAMINATIONS

21-18 (Objective 21-1) The following questions concern internal controls in the inventory and warehousing cycle. Choose the best response.

a. In a company with materials and supplies that include a great number of items, a fundamental deficiency in control requirements would be indicated if
   (1) a perpetual inventory master file is not maintained for items of small value.
   (2) the storekeeping function were to be combined with production and record keeping.
   (3) the cycle basis for physical inventory taking was to be used.
   (4) minor supply items were to be expensed when acquired.

b. For control purposes, the quantities of materials ordered may be omitted from the copy of the purchase order that is
   (1) forwarded to the accounting department.
   (2) retained in the purchasing department's files.
   (3) returned to the requisitioner.
   (4) forwarded to the receiving department.

c. Which of the following procedures would *best* detect the theft of valuable items from an inventory that consists of hundreds of different items selling for $1 to $10 and a few items selling for hundreds of dollars?
   (1) Maintain a perpetual inventory master file of only the more valuable items with frequent periodic verification of the validity of the perpetuals.
   (2) Have an independent CPA firm prepare an internal control report on the effectiveness of the administrative and accounting controls over inventory.
   (3) Have separate warehouse space for the more valuable items with sequentially numbered tags.
   (4) Require an authorized officer's signature on all requisitions for the more valuable items.

21-19 (Objectives 21-1, 21-4) The following questions concern testing the client's internal controls for inventory and warehousing. Choose the best response.

a. When an auditor tests a client's cost accounting records, the auditor's tests are *primarily* designed to determine that

(1) quantities on hand have been computed based on acceptable cost accounting techniques that reasonably approximate actual quantities on hand.

(2) physical inventories are in substantial agreement with book inventories.

(3) the internal controls are in accordance with generally accepted accounting principles and are functioning as planned.

(4) costs have been properly assigned to finished goods, work-in-process, and cost of goods sold.

b. The accuracy of perpetual inventory master files may be established, in part, by comparing perpetual inventory records with

(1) purchase requisitions.

(2) receiving reports.

(3) purchase orders.

(4) vendor payments.

c. When evaluating inventory controls with respect to segregation of duties, a CPA would be *least* likely to

(1) inspect documents.

(2) make inquiries.

(3) observe procedures.

(4) consider policy and procedure manuals.

21-20 (**Objectives 21-1, 21-5, 21-6, 21-7**) The following questions deal with tests of details of balances and analytical procedures for inventory. Choose the best response.

a. An auditor would be *most* likely to learn of slow-moving inventory through

(1) inquiry of sales personnel.

(2) inquiry of store personnel.

(3) physical observation of inventory.

(4) review of perpetual inventory master files.

b. An inventory turnover analysis is useful to the auditor because it may detect

(1) inadequacies in inventory pricing.

(2) methods of avoiding cyclical holding costs.

(3) the optimum automatic reorder points.

(4) the existence of obsolete merchandise.

c. A CPA auditing inventory may appropriately apply attributes sampling to estimate the

(1) average price of inventory items.

(2) percentage of slow-moving inventory items.

(3) dollar value of inventory.

(4) physical quantity of inventory items.

DISCUSSION QUESTIONS AND PROBLEMS

21-21 (**Objectives 21-1, 21-4, 21-6, 21-7, 21-8**) Items 1 through 8 are selected questions typically found in questionnaires used by auditors to obtain an understanding of internal control in the inventory and warehousing cycle. In using the questionnaire for a client, a "yes" response to a question indicates a possible internal control, whereas a "no" indicates a potential weakness.

1. Does the receiving department prepare prenumbered receiving reports and account for the numbers periodically for all inventory received, showing the description and quantity of materials?

2. Is all inventory stored under the control of a custodian in areas where access is limited?

3. Are all shipments to customers authorized by prenumbered shipping documents?

4. Is a detailed perpetual inventory master file maintained for raw materials inventory?

5. Are physical inventory counts made by someone other than storekeepers and those responsible for maintaining the perpetual inventory master file?

6. Are standard cost records used for raw materials, direct labor, and manufacturing overhead?

7. Is there a stated policy with specific criteria for writing off obsolete or slow-moving goods?

8. Is the clerical accuracy of the final inventory compilation checked by a person independent of those responsible for preparing it?

Required

a. For each of the preceding questions, state the purpose of the internal control.

b. For each internal control, list a test of control to test its effectiveness.

c. For each of the preceding questions, identify the nature of the potential financial misstatement(s) if the control is not in effect.

d. For each of the potential misstatements in part c, list a substantive audit procedure to determine whether a material misstatement exists.

21-22 (Objective 21-4) The cost accounting records are often an essential area to audit in a manufacturing or construction company.

Required

a. Why is it important to review the cost accounting records and test their accuracy?

b. For the audit of standard cost accounting records in which 35 parts are manufactured, explain how you would determine whether each of the following were reasonable for part no. 21:
   (1) Standard direct labor hours
   (2) Standard direct overhead rate
   (3) Standard overhead rate
   (4) Standard units of raw materials
   (5) Standard cost of a unit of raw materials
   (6) Total standard cost

21-23 (Objectives 21-1, 21-4, 21-6, 21-7) Following are audit procedures commonly performed in the inventory and warehousing cycle for a manufacturing company:

1. Compare the client's count of physical inventory at an interim date with the perpetual inventory master file.
2. Trace the auditor's test counts recorded in the audit files to the final inventory compilation and compare the tag number, description, and quantity.
3. Compare the unit price on the final inventory summary with vendors' invoices.
4. Read the client's physical inventory instructions and observe whether they are being followed by those responsible for counting the inventory.
5. Account for a sequence of raw material requisitions and examine each requisition for an authorized approval.
6. Trace the recorded additions on the finished goods perpetual inventory master file to the records for completed production.
7. Account for a sequence of inventory tags and trace each tag to the physical inventory to make sure it actually exists.

Required

a. Identify whether each of the procedures is primarily a test of control or a substantive test.

b. State the purpose(s) of each of the procedures.

21-24 (Objectives 21-1, 21-6, 21-7) The following misstatements are included in the inventory and related records of Westbox Manufacturing Company:

1. An inventory item was priced at $12 each instead of at the correct cost of $12 per dozen.
2. In taking the physical inventory, the last shipments for the day were excluded from inventory and were not included as a sale until the subsequent year.
3. The clerk in charge of the perpetual inventory master file altered the quantity on an inventory tag to cover up the shortage of inventory caused by its theft during the year.
4. After the auditor left the premises, several inventory tags were lost and were not included in the final inventory summary.
5. When raw material acquisitions were recorded, the improper unit price was included in the perpetual inventory master file. Therefore, the inventory valuation was misstated because the physical inventory was priced by referring to the perpetual records.
6. During the physical count, several obsolete inventory items were included.
7. Because of a significant increase in volume during the current year and excellent control over manufacturing overhead costs, the manufacturing overhead rate applied to inventory was far greater than actual cost.

Required

a. For each misstatement, state an internal control that should have prevented it from occurring.

b. For each misstatement, state a substantive audit procedure that could be used to uncover it.

21-25 (Objective 21-2) Technology Parts, Inc., is a retailer of computer hardware components. The company purchases inventory items in bulk directly from parts manufacturers and sells the parts to computer and other technology equipment manufacturers that use them as components in their products. Technology Parts, Inc., grants suppliers access to its inventory management system through its Internet Web site. Suppliers have real-time access to information about the parts inventory, including information about quantities held, storage locations, and forecasted product demand. In addition, customers have online access through the Web site to information containing product descriptions, price, delivery estimates, availability status, and quality and reliability ratings. Customers can also access information to assess the compatibility of selected parts with other components used in their production processes.

Required

a. Identify business objectives that Technology Parts' management may be able to achieve by providing this information online to key suppliers and customers.

b. How might the availability of the information to suppliers and customers increase Technology Parts' business risk?

c. What processes should Technology Parts' management implement to minimize business risks?

d. How might the availability of the information increase the risk of material misstatements in the financial statements?

21-26 (Objectives 21-6, 21-7) Often, an important aspect of a CPA's audit of financial statements is observation of the taking of physical inventory.

Required
a. What are the general objectives or purposes of the CPA's observation of the taking of the physical inventory? (Do not discuss the procedures or techniques involved in making the observation.)

b. For what purposes does the CPA make and record test counts of inventory quantities during observation of the taking of the physical inventory? Discuss.

c. A number of companies employ outside service companies that specialize in counting, pricing, extending, and footing inventories. These service companies usually furnish a certificate attesting to the value of the inventory.

Assuming that the service company took the inventory on the balance sheet date:
(1) How much reliance, if any, can the CPA place on the inventory certificate of outside specialists? Discuss.
(2) What effect, if any, would the inventory certificate of outside specialists have upon the type of report the CPA would render? Discuss.
(3) What reference, if any, would the CPA make to the certificate of outside specialists in the audit report?*

21-27 (Objective 21-6) You encountered the following situations during the December 31, 2005, physical inventory of Latner Shoe Distributor Company:

Required
a. Latner maintains a large portion of the shoe merchandise in 10 warehouses throughout the eastern United States. This ensures swift delivery service for its chain of stores. You are assigned alone to the Boston warehouse to observe the physical inventory process. During the inventory count, several express trucks pulled in for loading. Although infrequent, express shipments must be attended to immediately. As a result, the employees who were counting the inventory stopped to assist in loading the express trucks. What should you do?

b. (1) In one storeroom of 10,000 items, you have test-counted about 200 items of high value and a few items of low value. You found no misstatements. You also note that the employees are diligently following the inventory instructions. Do you think you have tested enough items? Explain.
(2) What would you do if you test-counted 150 items and found a substantial number of counting errors?

c. In observing an inventory of liquid shoe polish, you note that one lot is 5 years old. From inspection of some bottles in an open box, you find that the liquid has solidified in most of the bottles. What action should you take?

d. During your observation of the inventory count in the main warehouse, you found that most of the prenumbered tags that had been incorrectly filled out are being destroyed and thrown away. What is the significance of this procedure and what action should you take?

21-28 (Objective 21-6) In connection with his audit of the financial statements of Knutson Products Co., an assembler of home appliances, for the year ended May 31, 2005, Ray Abel, CPA, is reviewing with Knutson's controller the plans for a physical inventory at the company warehouse on May 31, 2005.

Finished appliances, unassembled parts, and supplies are stored in the warehouse, which is attached to Knutson's assembly plant. The plant will operate during the count. On May 30, the warehouse will deliver to the plant the estimated quantities of unassembled parts and supplies required for May 31 production, but there may be emergency requisitions on May 31. During the count, the warehouse will continue to receive parts and supplies and to ship finished appliances. However, appliances completed on May 31 will be held in the plant until after the physical inventory.

Required
What procedures should the company establish to ensure that the inventory count includes all items that should be included and that nothing is counted twice?*

*AICPA adapted.

21-29 (Objective 21-5) The following are sales, cost of sales, and inventory data for Aladdin Products Supply Company, a wholesale distributor of cleaning supplies. Dollar amounts are in millions.

	2005	2004	2003	2002
Sales	$23.2	$21.7	$19.6	$17.4
Cost of sales	17.1	16.8	15.2	13.5
Beginning inventory	2.3	2.1	1.9	1.5
Ending inventory	2.9	2.3	2.1	1.9

Required

a. Calculate the following ratios, using an electronic spreadsheet program (instructor's option):
   (1) Gross margin as a percentage of sales
   (2) Inventory turnover

b. List several logical causes of the changes in the two ratios.

c. Assume that $500,000 is considered material for audit planning purposes for 2005. Could any of the fluctuations in the computed ratios indicate a possible material misstatement? Demonstrate this by using the spreadsheet program to perform a sensitivity analysis.

d. What should the auditor do to determine the actual cause of the changes?

21-30 (Objective 21-6) In an annual audit at December 31, 2005, you find the following transactions near the closing date:

1. Merchandise costing $1,822 was received on January 3, 2006, and the related acquisition invoice recorded January 5. The invoice showed the shipment was made on December 29, 2005, FOB destination.

2. Merchandise costing $625 was received on December 28, 2005, and the invoice was not recorded. You located it in the hands of the purchasing agent; it was marked "on consignment."

3. A packing case containing products costing $816 was standing in the shipping room when the physical inventory was taken. It was not included in the inventory because it was marked "Hold for shipping instructions." Your investigation revealed that the customer's order was dated December 18, 2005, but that the case was shipped and the customer billed on January 10, 2006. The product was a stock item of your client.

4. Merchandise received on January 6, 2006, costing $720 was entered in the acquisitions journal on January 7, 2006. The invoice showed shipment was made FOB supplier's warehouse on December 31, 2005. Because it was not on hand December 31, it was not included in inventory.

5. A special machine, fabricated to order for a customer, was finished and in the shipping room on December 31, 2005. The customer was billed on that date and the machine excluded from inventory, although it was shipped on January 4, 2006.

Assume that each of the amounts is material.

Required

a. State whether the merchandise should be included in the client's inventory.

b. Give your reason for your decision on each item.*

21-31 (Objective 21-7) As a part of your clerical tests of inventory for Martin Manufacturing, you have tested about 20% of the dollar items and have found the following exceptions:

1. Extension errors:

Description	Quantity	Price	Extension as Recorded
Wood	465 board feet	$ 0.12/board foot	$ 5.58
Metal-cutting tools	29 units	30.00 each	670.00
Cutting fluid	16 barrels	40.00/barrel	529.00
Sandpaper	300 sheets	0.95/hundred	258.00

2. Differences located in comparing last year's costs with the current year's costs on the client's inventory lists:

*AICPA adapted.

Description	Quantity	This Year's Cost	Preceding Year's Cost
TA-114 precision-cutting torches	12 units	$500.00 each	Unable to locate
Aluminum scrap	4,500 pounds	5.00/ton	$65.00/ton
Lubricating oil	400 gallons	6.00/gallon	4.50/barrel

3. Test counts that you were unable to find when tracing from the test counts to the final inventory compilation:

Tag No.	Quantity	Current Year Cost	Description
2958	15 tons	$75.00/ton	Cold-rolled bars
0026	2,000 feet	2.25/foot	4-inch aluminum stripping

4. Page total, footing errors:

Page No.	Client Total	Correct Total
14	$1,375.12	$1,375.08
82	8,721.18	8,521.18

Required

a. State the amount of the actual misstatement in each of the four tests. For any item for which the amount of the misstatement cannot be determined from the information given, state the considerations that would affect your estimate of the misstatement.

b. As a result of your findings, what would you do about clerical accuracy tests of the inventory in the current year?

c. What changes, if any, would you suggest in internal controls and procedures for Martin Manufacturing during the compilation of next year's inventory to prevent each type of misstatement?

21-32 (Objective 21-6) You have been engaged for the audit of the Y Company for the year ended December 31, 2005. The Y Company is in the wholesale chemical business and makes all sales at 25% over cost.

Following are portions of the client's sales and purchases accounts for the calendar year 2005.

SALES

Date	Reference	Amount		Date	Reference	Amount
					Balance Forward	
12-31	Closing entry	$699,860				$658,320
				12-27	*SI#965	5,195
				12-28	SI#966	19,270
				12-28	SI#967	1,302
				12-31	SI#969	5,841
				12-31	SI#970	7,922
				12-31	SI#971	2,010
		$699,860				$699,860

PURCHASES

Date	Reference	Amount		Date	Reference	Amount
	Balance Forward					
		$360,300		12-31	Closing entry	$385,346
12-28	†RR#1059	3,100				
12-30	RR#1061	8,965				
12-31	RR#1062	4,861				
12-31	RR#1063	8,120				
		$385,346				$385,346

*SI = Sales invoice.
†RR = Receiving report.

You observed the physical inventory of goods in the warehouse on December 31, 2005, and were satisfied that it was properly taken.

When performing a sales and purchases cutoff test, you found that at December 31, 2005, the last receiving report that had been used was no. 1063 and that no shipments have been made on any sales invoices with numbers larger than no. 968. You also obtained the following additional information:

1. Included in the warehouse physical inventory at December 31, 2005, were chemicals that had been acquired and received on receiving report no. 1060 but for which an invoice was not received until the year 2006. Cost was $2,183.
2. In the warehouse at December 31, 2005, were goods that had been sold and paid for by the customer but which were not shipped out until the year 2006. They were all sold on sales invoice no. 965 and were not inventoried.
3. On the evening of December 31, 2005, there were two cars on the Y company siding:
   (a) Car AR38162 was unloaded on January 2, 2006, and received on receiving report no. 1063. The freight was paid by the vendor.
   (b) Car BAE74123 was loaded and sealed on December 31, 2005, and was switched off the company's siding on January 2, 2006. The sales price was $12,700 and the freight was paid by the customer. This order was sold on sales invoice no. 968.
4. Temporarily stranded at December 31, 2005 on a railroad siding were two cars of chemicals en route to the Z Pulp and Paper Co. They were sold on sales invoice no. 966, and the terms were FOB destination.
5. En route to the Y Company on December 31, 2005, was a truckload of material that was received on receiving report no. 1064. The material was shipped FOB destination, and freight of $75 was paid by the Y Company. However, the freight was deducted from the purchase price of $975.
6. Included in the physical inventory were chemicals exposed to rain in transit and deemed unsalable. Their invoice cost was $1,250, and freight charges of $350 had been paid on the chemicals.

a. Compute the adjustments that should be made to the client's physical inventory at December 31, 2005.   **Required**

b. Prepare a worksheet of adjusting entries that are required as of December 31, 2005.*

CASE

21-33 (Objective 21-7) You are assigned to the December 31, 2004, audit of Sea Gull Airframes, Inc. The company designs and manufactures aircraft superstructures and airframe components. You observed the physical inventory at December 31 and are satisfied that it was properly taken. The inventory at December 31, 2004, has been priced, extended, and totaled by the client and is made up of about 5,000 inventory items with a total valuation of $8,275,000. In performing inventory price tests, you have decided to stratify your tests and conclude that you should have two strata: items with a value over $5,000 and those with a value of less than $5,000. The book values are as follows:

	No. of Items	Total Value
More than $5,000	500	$4,150,000
Less than $5,000	4,500	4,125,000
	5,000	$8,275,000

In performing your pricing and extension tests, you have decided to test about 50 inventory items in detail. You selected 40 of the over $5,000 items and 10 of those under $5,000 at random from the population. You find all items to be correct except for items A through G at the top of page 664, which you believe may be misstated. You have tested the following items, to this point, exclusive of A through G:

	No. of Items	Total Value
More than $5,000	36	$360,000
Less than $5,000	7	2,600

Sea Gull Airframes uses a periodic inventory system and values its inventory at the lower of FIFO cost or market. You were able to locate all invoices needed for your examination. The seven inventory items in the sample you believe may be misstated, along with the relevant data for determining the proper valuation, are shown next.

*AICPA adapted.

INVENTORY ITEMS POSSIBLY MISSTATED

Description	Quantity		Price	Total*
A. L37 spars	3,000	meters	$ 8.00/meter	$24,000
B. B68 metal formers	10,000	inches	1.20/foot	12,000
C. R01 metal ribs	1,500	yards	10.00/yard	15,000
D. St26 struts	1,000	feet	8.00/foot	8,000
E. Industrial hand drills	45	units	20.00 each	900
F. L803 steel leaf springs	40	pairs	69.00 each spring	276
G. V16 fasteners	5.50	dozen	10.00/dozen	55

*Amounts are as stated on client's inventory.

INFORMATION FOR PRICING FROM INVOICES (SEA GULL AIRFRAMES)

Voucher Number	Voucher Date	Date Paid	Terms	Receiving Report Date	Invoice Description
7-68	8-01-99	8-21-99	Net FOB destination	8-01-99	77 V16 fasteners at $10 per dozen
11-81	10-16-04	11-15-04	Net FOB destination	10-18-04	1,100 yards R01 metal ribs at $9.50 per yard; 2,000 feet St26 struts at $8.20 per foot
12-06	12-08-04	12-30-04	2/10, n/30 FOB S.P.	12-10-04	180 L803 steel leaf springs at $69 each
12-09	12-10-04	12-18-04	Net FOB destination	12-11-04	45 industrial hand drills at $20 each; guaranteed for 4 years
12-18	12-27-04	12-27-04	2/10, n/30 FOB S.P.	12-21-04	4,200 meters L37 spars at $8 per meter
12-23	12-24-04	1-03-05	2/10, n/30 FOB dest.	12-26-04	12,800 inches B68 metal formers at $1.20 per foot
12-61	12-29-04	1-08-05	Net FOB destination	12-29-04	1,000 yards R01 metal ribs at $10 per yard; 800 feet St26 struts at $8 per foot
12-81	12-31-04	1-20-05	Net FOB destination	1-06-05	2,000 meters L37 spars at $7.50 per meter; 2,000 yards R01 metal ribs at $10 per yard

In addition, you noted a freight bill for voucher 12-23 in the amount of $200. This bill was entered in the freight-in account. Virtually all freight was for the metal formers.

This is the first time Sea Gull Airframes has been audited by your firm.

Required

a. Review all information and determine the inventory misstatements of the seven items in question. State any assumptions you consider necessary to determine the amount of the misstatements.

b. Prepare an audit schedule to summarize your findings. Use the computer to prepare the schedule (instructor's option).

INTERNET PROBLEM 21-1: USING INVENTORY COUNT SPECIALISTS

Reference the CW site. Many organizations hire outside inventory count specialists to conduct physical counts of their inventory balances. This problem uses the Internet to expose students to inventory count specialists' organizations. Based on this exposure, students address issues related to a company's use of these specialists to count inventory.

AUDIT OF THE CAPITAL ACQUISITION AND REPAYMENT CYCLE

A DISHONEST CLIENT WILL GET THE BEST OF THE AUDITOR ALMOST EVERY TIME

Able Construction Company entered into long-term construction contracts, recognizing income using the percentage of completion method of accounting. To finance its operations, Able borrowed funds from the bank and agreed to comply with restrictive loan covenants dependent on reported income from the long-term contracts. The percentage of completion method of accounting requires, among other things, an agreement with well-defined, enforceable terms, a reliable method of estimating costs to complete the contracts, and recognition of losses at the time they become known. As part of the audit of Able, its auditors read the contracts for all projects in progress, test costs incurred to date, and assess the ultimate profitability of the contracts, including discussing them with management. A significant part of verifying income under percentage of completion is auditing costs incurred.

In the current year, management's records and schedules of projects indicate that all projects will result in a profit. For each project, there is a separate schedule showing estimated total revenue from the project, costs incurred in the current period, costs incurred to date, estimated total costs, percentage of completion, and profit recognized in the current period. The auditor discussed each project with management, performed audit tests to support the schedule, and concluded that the revenue, expenses, and profit were reasonably stated. Reported income allowed Able to meet several of the restrictive covenants in its loan agreement with the bank.

In fact, Able had incurred a significant loss on one of its major projects. Able engaged a subcontractor to do reconstructive work not anticipated in the original contract bid. In awarding the subcontract, Able entered into an agreement with the subcontractor that the work would not be paid for until after its audit was completed in an effort to defer recording losses associated with the additional work. Management hid the subcontractor's invoices from the auditors as they were received. During the next year, management recognized this loss but doctored the invoices so that it appeared the "unexpected" additional cost was incurred during that year, and that the previous year's statements were correct and that all loan covenants with the bank were satisfied.

The fraudulent misstatement was discovered several years later when Able went bankrupt and the CPA firm was sued by the bank for performing inadequate audits. The firm was ultimately found not responsible, but only after spending extensive time and large amounts of money defending its audit.

The final transaction cycle discussed in this text relates to the acquisition of capital resources in the form of interest-bearing debt and owners' equity and the repayment of the capital. The **capital acquisition and repayment cycle** also includes the payment of interest and dividends. The cycle is important because it is the primary source of financing for most businesses.

Four characteristics of the capital acquisition and repayment cycle significantly influence the audit of these accounts:

1. Relatively few transactions affect the account balances, but each transaction is often highly material in amount. For example, bonds are infrequently issued by most companies, but the amount of a bond issue is normally large. Because of their size, it is common to verify each transaction taking place in the cycle for the entire year as a part of verifying the balance sheet accounts. It is not unusual to see audit schedules that include the beginning balance of every account in the capital acquisition and repayment cycle and documentation of every transaction that occurred during the year.

2. The exclusion of a single transaction could be material in itself. For example, the omission or incorrect recording of a single debt transaction could have a material effect on the financial statements. Accordingly, a primary emphasis in auditing debt is on the completeness and accuracy of debt.

3. There is a legal relationship between the client entity and the holder of the stock, bond, or similar ownership document. As the example involving Able Construction Company in the opening vignette demonstrates, the auditor must be concerned with whether the client has met the requirements of debt or equity agreements. In the audit of the transactions and amounts in the cycle, the auditor must take great care in making sure that the significant legal requirements affecting the financial statements have been properly fulfilled and adequately presented and disclosed in the statements.

4. There is a direct relationship between the interest and dividends accounts and debt and equity. In the audit of interest-bearing debt, it is desirable to simultaneously verify the related interest expense and interest payable. This holds true for owners' equity, dividends declared, and dividends payable.

Auditors often learn about capital acquisition transactions while gaining an understanding of the client's business and industry. Because of the significance and complexity of these transactions, auditors often assist clients in planning and addressing financial reporting issues for capital transactions. Thus, auditors frequently identify business risk issues for capital acquisition activities early in the planning process that should be considered in the design of audit procedures for transactions and account balances in the capital acquisition and repayment cycle.

We begin by describing the accounts in the cycle, and how the unique characteristics of the cycle impact the audit of these accounts.

ACCOUNTS IN THE CYCLE

OBJECTIVE 22-1

Identify the accounts and the unique characteristics of the capital acquisition and repayment cycle.

The accounts in a company's capital acquisition and repayment cycle depend on the type of business the company operates and how it is financed. For example, all corporations have capital stock and retained earnings, but some may also have preferred stock, additional paid-in capital, and treasury stock. As with other cycles, cash is an important account in the cycle because both the acquisition and repayment of capital affect the cash account. The following are accounts often found in the cycle:

- Notes payable
- Contracts payable
- Mortgages payable
- Bonds payable
- Interest expense
- Accrued interest

- Cash in the bank
- Capital stock—common
- Capital stock—preferred
- Paid-in capital in excess of par
- Donated capital
- Retained earnings

- Appropriations of retained earnings
- Treasury stock
- Dividends declared
- Dividends payable
- Proprietorship—capital account
- Partnership—capital account

The methodology for designing tests of details of balances for accounts in the capital acquisition and repayment cycle is the same as that followed for other accounts. Figure 22-1 is an example of the methodology applied to notes payable, but it is equally applicable to other accounts in the cycle.

In determining the tests of details of balances for notes payable, the auditor considers business risk, tolerable misstatement, inherent risk, control risk, the results of tests of controls and substantive tests of transactions, and the results of analytical procedures. Tolerable misstatement is often set at a low level because it is often possible to completely audit the account balance or the transactions affecting the account balance. Inherent risk is also typically set at a low level because it is usually easy to determine the correct account value. Auditors are normally most concerned about the adequacy of disclosures, such as collateral and covenant restrictions for notes payable.

Because there are usually few transactions in the cycle, control risk and the results of substantive tests of transactions are normally less important for designing tests of details of

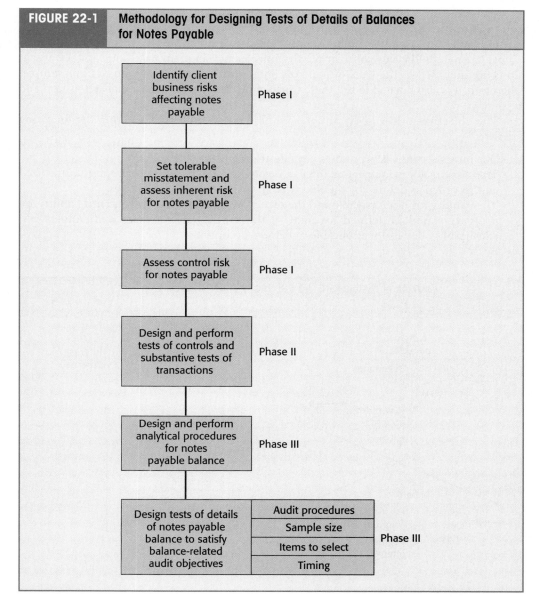

FIGURE 22-1 | **Methodology for Designing Tests of Details of Balances for Notes Payable**

balances for accounts such as notes payable. For most transactions in the cycle, an important consideration is that they are properly authorized.

The audit procedures for many of the accounts in the capital acquisition and repayment cycle are best understood by studying representative accounts that are significant parts of the cycle for a typical business. The following sections discuss (1) the audit of notes payable and related interest expense to illustrate interest-bearing capital and (2) the audit of common stock, paid-in capital in excess of par, dividends, and retained earnings.

NOTES PAYABLE

OBJECTIVE 22-2

Design and perform audit tests of notes payable and related accounts and transactions.

A **note payable** is a legal obligation to a creditor, which may be unsecured or secured by assets. Typically, a note is issued for a period somewhere between 1 month and 1 year, but there are also long-term notes of over a year. Notes are issued for many different purposes, and the pledged property includes a wide variety of assets, such as securities, accounts receivable, inventory, and fixed assets. The principal and interest payments on the notes must be made in accordance with the terms of the loan agreement. For short-term loans, a principal and interest payment is usually required only when the loan becomes due; but for loans over 90 days, the note usually calls for monthly or quarterly interest payments.

The accounts used for notes payable and related interest are shown in Figure 22-2. It is common to include tests of principal and interest payments as a part of the audit of the acquisition and payment cycle because the payments are recorded in the cash disbursements journal. But because of their relative infrequency, in many cases, no capital transactions are included in the tests of controls and substantive tests of transactions sample. Therefore, it is also normal to test these transactions as a part of the capital acquisition and repayment cycle.

The objectives of the audit of notes payable are to determine whether the following are true:

- The internal controls over notes payable are adequate.
- Transactions for principal and interest involving notes payable are properly authorized and recorded as defined by the six transaction-related audit objectives.
- The liability for notes payable and the related interest expense and accrued liability are properly stated as defined by eight of the nine balance-related audit objectives. (Realizable value is not applicable to liability accounts.)

FIGURE 22-2	Notes Payable and the Related Interest Accounts

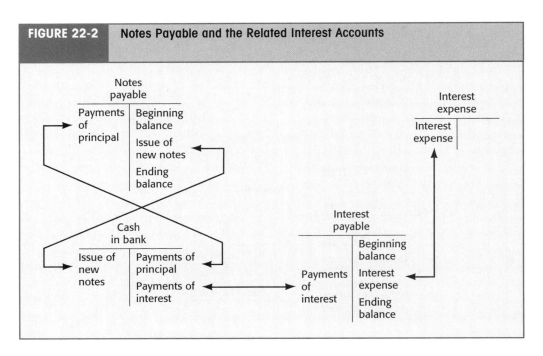

There are four important controls over notes payable:

1. Proper authorization for the issue of new notes. Responsibility for the issuance of new notes should be vested in the board of directors or high-level management personnel. Generally, two signatures of properly authorized officials are required for all loan agreements. The amount of the loan, the interest rate, the repayment terms, and the assets pledged are all part of the approved agreement. When notes are renewed, it is important that they be subject to the same authorization procedures as those for the issuance of new notes.

2. Adequate controls over the repayment of principal and interest. The periodic payments of interest and principal should be controlled as a part of the acquisition and payment cycle. At the time the note was issued, the accounting department should have received a copy in the same manner in which it receives vendors' invoices and receiving reports. The accounts payable department should automatically issue checks or electronic fund transfers for the notes when they become due, again in the same manner in which it prepares payments for acquisitions of goods and services. The copy of the note is the supporting documentation for payment.

3. Proper documents and records. These include the maintenance of subsidiary records and control over blank and paid notes by a responsible person. Paid notes should be cancelled and retained under the custody of an authorized official.

4. Periodic independent verification. Periodically, the detailed note records should be reconciled with the general ledger and compared with the note holders' records by an employee who is not responsible for maintaining the detailed records. At the same time, an independent person should recompute the interest expense on notes to test the accuracy and propriety of the record keeping.

Tests of notes payable transactions involve the issue of notes and the repayment of principal and interest. These audit tests are a part of tests of controls and substantive tests of transactions for cash receipts (see Chapter 14) and cash disbursements (see Chapter 19). Additional tests of controls and substantive tests of transactions are often done as a part of tests of details of balances because of the materiality of individual transactions.

Tests of controls for notes payable and related interest should emphasize testing the four important internal controls discussed in the previous section. In addition, the accurate recording of receipts from note proceeds and payments of principal and interest is emphasized.

Analytical procedures are essential for notes payable because tests of details for interest expense and accrued interest can often be eliminated when results are favorable. Table 22-1 illustrates typical analytical procedures for notes payable and related interest accounts.

The auditor's independent estimate of interest expense, using average notes payable outstanding and average interest rates, tests the reasonableness of interest expense and also tests for omitted notes payable. An illustration of an auditor's schedule where such an

TABLE 22-1	Analytical Procedures for Notes Payable
Analytical Procedure	**Possible Misstatement**
Recalculate approximate interest expense on the basis of average interest rates and overall monthly notes payable.	Misstatement of interest expense and accrued interest, or omission of an outstanding note payable
Compare individual notes outstanding with those of the prior year.	Omission or misstatement of a note payable
Compare total balance in notes payable, interest expense, and accrued interest with prior-year balances.	Misstatement of interest expense and accrued interest or notes payable

FIGURE 22-3 Schedule of Notes Payable and Accrued Interest

Microsoft Excel - Book2

File Edit View Insert Format Tools Data Window Help Acrobat

Arial   10   **B** *I* U ≡ ≡ ≡ $ % , ⁺⁰ ·⁰⁰ 田 · ⬥ · **A** ·

A1   =

XYZ Company, Inc.
Notes Payable
12/31/05

Schedule   *AA-4*   Date
Prepared by   *Client/DB*   *1/12/06*
Approved by   *JL*   *1/16/06*

Payee	Date Made	Due	Face Amount of Note	SECURITY Description	Valuation	Balance at Beginning of Period
First National Bank	9/30/04	9/30/05	10000	Investments	15000	10000
Second National Bank	9/30/05	9/30/06	10000	Investments	16000	
Third National Bank	10/31/05	10/31/06	10000	Fixed Assets	22000	
			30000		53000	10000 ①

① — *Traced to prior year audit schedule.*   ⑤ — *Traced to general ledger.*
② — *Obtained copy of note included in permanent file.*   ⑥ — *Recomputed expense and accrued interest; no differences noted.*
③ — *Examined cancelled note and/or check.*   ⋀ — *Footed*
④ — *Agreed to confirmation received from bank.*   *X* — *Cross-footed*

analytical procedure has been performed is illustrated in Figure 8-8, page 214. If actual interest expense had been materially larger than the auditor's estimate, one possible cause would be interest payments on unrecorded notes payable.

Tests of Details of Balances

The normal starting point for the audit of notes payable is a schedule of notes payable and accrued interest obtained from the client. A typical schedule is shown in Figure 22-3 above and on page 671. The usual schedule includes detailed information of all transactions that took place during the entire year for principal and interest, the beginning and ending balances for notes and interest payable, and descriptive information about the notes, such as the due date, the interest rate, and the assets pledged as collateral.

When there are numerous transactions involving notes during the year, it may not be practical to obtain a schedule of the type shown in Figure 22-3. In that situation, the auditor is likely to request that the client prepare a schedule of only those notes with unpaid balances at the end of the year. This would show a description of each note, its ending balance, and the interest payable at the end of the year, including the collateral and interest rate.

The balance-related audit objectives and common audit procedures are summarized in Table 22-2 (p. 672). Realizable value is not included in the table because it is not applicable to notes payable. The schedule of notes payable is the frame of reference for the procedures. Again, the amount of testing depends heavily on the materiality of notes payable and the effectiveness of internal controls.

The three most important balance-related audit objectives in notes payable are as follows:

1. Existing notes payable are included (completeness).
2. Notes payable in the schedule are accurately recorded (accuracy).
3. Notes payable are properly presented and disclosed (presentation and disclosure).

FIGURE 22-3   Schedule of Notes Payable and Accrued Interest *(Continued)*

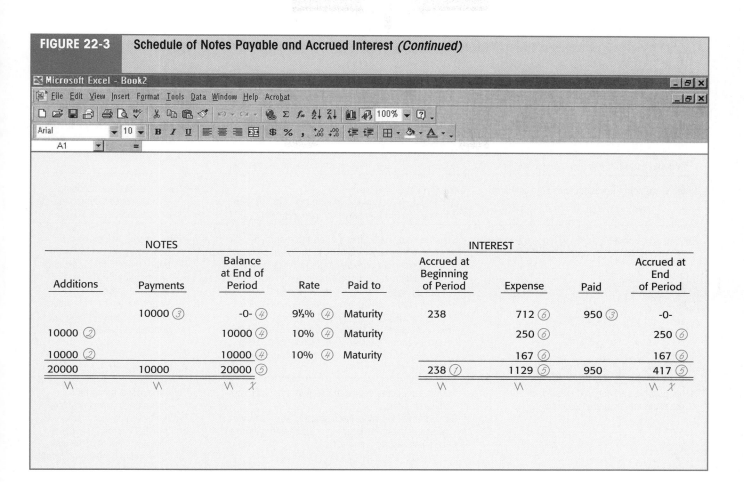

NOTES					INTEREST			
Additions	Payments	Balance at End of Period	Rate	Paid to	Accrued at Beginning of Period	Expense	Paid	Accrued at End of Period
	10000 ③	-0- ④	9½% ④	Maturity	238	712 ⑥	950 ③	-0-
10000 ②		10000 ④	10% ④	Maturity		250 ⑥		250 ⑥
10000 ②		10000 ④	10% ④	Maturity		167 ⑥		167 ⑥
20000	10000	20000 ⑤			238 ⑦	1129 ⑤	950	417 ⑤
⋈	⋈	⋈ ✗			⋈	⋈		⋈ ✗

The first two objectives are important because a misstatement can be material if even one note is omitted or incorrect. Table 22-2 indicates common procedures to test for the completeness of notes payable. When internal controls over notes payable are weak, it may be necessary to perform extended procedures to test for omitted notes payable. For example, the auditor might send confirmations to creditors that have held notes from the client in the past but are not currently included in the notes payable schedule. The auditor might also analyze interest expense for payments to creditors that are not included in the notes payable schedule, and review the minutes of the board of directors meetings for authorized but unrecorded notes.

DON'T FORGET THE LIABILITIES!

Through a series of closely timed purchase transactions, NECO Enterprises, Inc., a public utility holding company based in Providence, Rhode Island, rapidly expanded its holdings of other utilities in the New England area. Under the new leadership of David LaRoche as chairman and chief executive officer, the company purchased the outstanding stock of several corporations wholly owned by LaRoche, who also happened to be NECO's majority shareholder.

Within two years of the related party purchases, the SEC filed a complaint against the company and LaRoche accusing them of violating the antifraud provisions of federal securities laws in conjunction with quarterly financial statements filed when the acquisitions were made. According to the SEC, the quarterly reports failed to disclose over $16 million in liabilities acquired as a result of the purchases, which also led to overstatements of NECO's retained earnings and total capital balances.

Following the SEC's investigation, the company restated the filings to comply with GAAP, relocated to Vermont, and disposed of its utility subsidiary, Newport Electric Company. LaRoche consented to the issuance of a permanent injunction against future violations of all the provisions of the securities laws associated with the SEC's complaint.

Source: *Accounting and Auditing Enforcement Release No. 335*, Commerce Clearing House, Inc., Chicago.

Balance-Related Audit Objective	Common Tests of Details of Balances Procedures	Comments
Notes payable in the notes payable schedule agree with the client's notes payable register or master file, and the total is correctly added and agrees with the general ledger (detail tie-in).	Foot the notes payable list for notes payable and accrued interest. Trace the totals to the general ledger. Trace the individual notes payable to the master file.	These are often done on a 100 percent basis because of the small population size.
Notes payable in the schedule exist (existence).	Confirm notes payable. Examine duplicate copies of notes for authorization. Examine corporate minutes for loan approval.	The existence objective is not as important as completeness or accuracy.
Existing notes payable are included in the notes payable schedule (completeness).	Examine notes paid after year-end to determine whether they were liabilities at the balance sheet date. Obtain a *standard bank confirmation* that includes specific reference to the existence of notes payable from all banks with which the client does business. (Bank confirmations are discussed more fully in Chapter 23.) Review the *bank reconciliation* for new notes credited directly to the bank account by the bank. (Bank reconciliations are also discussed more fully in Chapter 23.)	This objective is important for uncovering both errors and fraud. These three procedures are done on most audits. Additional procedures to search for omitted liabilities may be necessary if internal controls are weak.
Notes payable and accrued interest on the schedule are accurate (accuracy).	Examine duplicate copies of notes for principal and interest rates. Confirm notes payable, interest rates, and last date for which interest has been paid with holders of notes. Recalculate accrued interest.	In some cases, it may be necessary to calculate, using present-value techniques, the imputed interest rates or the principal amount of the note. An example is when equipment is acquired for a note.
Notes payable in the schedule are properly classified (classification).	Examine due dates on duplicate copies of notes to determine whether all or part of the notes are a noncurrent liability. Review notes to determine whether any are related party notes or accounts payable.	
Notes payable are included in the proper period (cutoff).	Examine duplicate copies of notes to determine whether notes were dated on or before the balance sheet date.	Notes should be included as current period liabilities when dated on or before the balance sheet date.
The company has an obligation to pay the notes payable (obligations).	Examine notes to determine whether the company has obligations for payment.	
Notes payable, interest expense, and accrued interest are properly presented and disclosed (presentation and disclosure).	Examine duplicate copies of notes. Confirm notes payable. Examine notes, minutes, and bank confirmations for restrictions. Examine balance sheet for proper presentation and disclosure of noncurrent portions, related parties, assets pledged as security for notes, and restrictions resulting from notes payable.	Proper financial statement presentation, including footnote disclosure, is an important consideration for notes payable.

Presentation and disclosure is important because GAAP requires that the footnotes adequately describe the terms of notes payable outstanding and the assets pledged as collateral for the loans. If there are significant restrictions on the activities of the company required by the loans, such as compensating balance provisions or restrictions on the payment of dividends, these must also be disclosed in the footnotes.

Figure 22-4 illustrates the major accounts related to notes payable in the capital acquisition and repayment cycle and the types of audit tests used to audit these accounts.

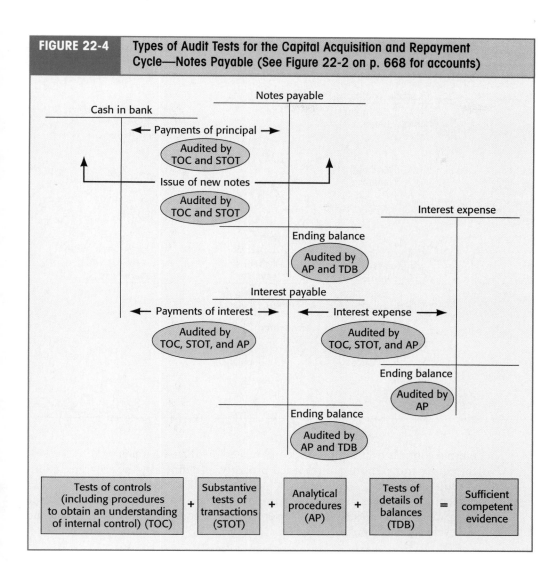

FIGURE 22-4 | Types of Audit Tests for the Capital Acquisition and Repayment Cycle—Notes Payable (See Figure 22-2 on p. 668 for accounts)

| Tests of controls (including procedures to obtain an understanding of internal control) (TOC) | + | Substantive tests of transactions (STOT) | + | Analytical procedures (AP) | + | Tests of details of balances (TDB) | = | Sufficient competent evidence |

OWNERS' EQUITY

OBJECTIVE 22-3

Identify the primary concerns in the audit of owners' equity transactions.

The previous section discussed the audit of notes payable and related accounts for debt financing. We now turn our attention to the audit of owners' equity. A major distinction must be made in the audit of owners' equity between a **publicly held corporation** and a **closely held corporation.** In most closely held corporations, there are few if any transactions during the year for capital stock accounts and there are typically only a few shareholders. The only transactions entered in the owners' equity section are likely to be the change in owners' equity for the annual earnings or loss and the declaration of dividends, if any. Closely held corporations rarely pay dividends. The amount of time spent verifying owners' equity is often minimal for closely held corporations, even though the auditor must test the existing corporate records.

For publicly held corporations, the verification of owners' equity is more complex because of the larger numbers of shareholders and frequent changes in the individuals holding the stock. In this section, the appropriate tests for verifying the major accounts—capital and common stock, paid-in capital in excess of par, retained earnings, and the related dividends—in a publicly held corporation are discussed. The other accounts in owners' equity are verified in much the same way as these.

An overview of the specific owners' equity accounts discussed in this section is given in Figure 22-5 (p. 674). The objectives of the audit of owners' equity are to determine whether the following are true:

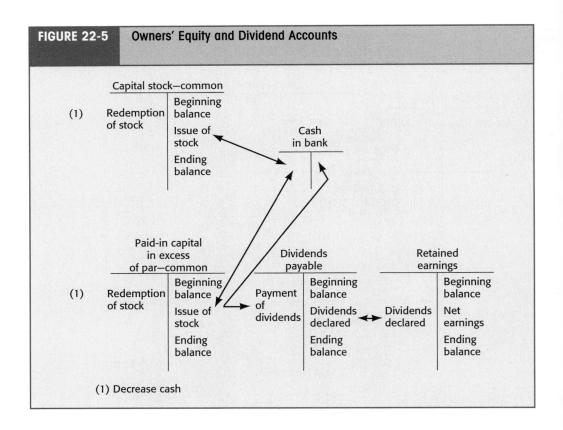

FIGURE 22-5   Owners' Equity and Dividend Accounts

Capital stock—common
(1) Redemption of stock	Beginning balance
	Issue of stock
	Ending balance

Cash in bank

Paid-in capital in excess of par—common
(1) Redemption of stock	Beginning balance
	Issue of stock
	Ending balance

Dividends payable
Payment of dividends	Beginning balance
	Dividends declared
	Ending balance

Retained earnings
	Beginning balance
Dividends declared	Net earnings
	Ending balance

(1) Decrease cash

- The internal controls over capital stock and related dividends are adequate.
- Owners' equity transactions are recorded properly, as defined by the six transaction-related audit objectives.
- Owners' equity balances are properly presented and disclosed, as defined by the balance-related audit objectives for owners' equity accounts (rights/obligations and realizable value are not applicable).

Internal Controls

Several important internal controls are of concern to the independent auditor in owners' equity: proper authorization of transactions, proper record keeping, adequate segregation of duties between maintaining owners' equity records and handling cash and stock certificates, and the use of an independent registrar and stock transfer agent.

Proper Authorization of Transactions Because each owners' equity transaction is typically material, many of these transactions must be approved by the board of directors. The following types of owners' equity transactions usually require specific authorization:

Issuance of Capital Stock The authorization includes the type of the equity to issue (such as preferred or common stock), number of shares to issue, par value of the stock, privileged condition for any stock other than common, and date of the issue.

Repurchase of Capital Stock The repurchase of common or preferred shares, the timing of the repurchase, and the amount to pay for the shares should all be approved by the board of directors.

Declaration of Dividends The board of directors should authorize the form of the dividends (such as cash or stock), the amount of the dividend per share, and the record and payment dates of the dividends.

Proper Record Keeping and Segregation of Duties When a company maintains its own records of stock transactions and outstanding stock, the internal controls must be adequate to ensure that the actual owners of the stock are recognized in the corporate records, the correct amount of dividends is paid to the stockholders owning the stock as of the dividend record date, and the potential for misappropriation of assets is minimized. The proper assignment of personnel and adequate record-keeping procedures are useful controls for these purposes.

The most important procedures for preventing misstatements in owners' equity are (1) well-defined policies for preparing stock certificates and recording capital stock transactions and (2) independent internal verification of information in the records. The client must be certain when issuing and recording capital stock that both the state laws governing corporations and the requirements in the corporate charter are being complied with. For example, the par value of the stock, the number of shares the company is authorized to issue, and the existence of state taxes on the issue of capital stock all affect issuance and recording.

A control over capital stock used by most companies is the maintenance of stock certificate books and a shareholders' capital stock master file. A **capital stock certificate record** captures the issuance and repurchase of capital stock for the life of the corporation. The record for a capital stock transaction includes such information as the certificate number, the number of shares issued, the name of the person to whom it was issued, and the issue date. When shares are repurchased, the capital stock certificate book should include the cancelled certificates and the date of their cancellation. A **shareholders' capital stock master file** is the record of the outstanding shares at any given time. The master file acts as a check on the accuracy of the capital stock certificate record and the common stock balance in the general ledger. It is also used as the basis for the payment of dividends.

The disbursement of cash for the payment of dividends should be controlled in much the same manner as has been described in Chapter 18 for the preparation and payment of payroll. Dividend checks should be prepared from the capital stock certificate record by someone who is not responsible for maintaining the capital stock records. After the checks are prepared, it is desirable to have an independent verification of the stockholders' names and the amount of the checks and a reconciliation of the total amount of the dividend checks with the total dividends authorized in the minutes. The use of a separate *imprest dividend account* is desirable to prevent the payment of a larger amount of dividends than was authorized.

Independent Registrar and Stock Transfer Agent Any company with stock that is listed on a securities exchange is required to engage an **independent registrar** as a control to prevent the improper issue of stock certificates. The responsibility of an independent registrar is to make sure that stock is issued by a corporation in accordance with the capital stock provisions in the corporate charter and the authorization of the board of directors. The registrar is responsible for signing all newly issued stock certificates and making sure that old certificates are received and cancelled before a replacement certificate is issued when there is a change in the ownership of the stock.

Most large corporations also employ the services of a **stock transfer agent** for the purpose of maintaining the stockholder records, including those documenting transfers of stock ownership. The employment of a transfer agent not only serves as a control over the stock records by putting them in the hands of an independent organization but reduces the cost of record keeping by the use of a specialist. Many companies also have the transfer agent disburse cash dividends to shareholders, thereby further improving internal control.

Stock Transfer Agents

There are four main concerns in auditing capital stock and paid-in capital in excess of par:

1. Existing capital stock transactions are recorded (completeness).
2. Recorded capital stock transactions exist and are accurately recorded (existence and accuracy).
3. Capital stock is accurately recorded (accuracy).
4. Capital stock is properly presented and disclosed (presentation and disclosure).

The first two concerns involve tests of controls and substantive tests of transactions, and the last two, tests of details of balances.

Audit of Capital Stock and Paid-in Capital

OBJECTIVE 22-4

Design and perform tests of controls, substantive tests of transactions, and tests of details of balances for capital stock and retained earnings.

Existing Capital Stock Transactions Are Recorded This objective is easily satisfied when a registrar or transfer agent is used. The auditor can confirm with them whether any capital stock transactions occurred and the accuracy of existing transactions. Review of the minutes of the board of directors meetings, especially near the balance sheet date, and examination of client-held stock record books are also useful to uncover issuances and repurchases of capital stock.

Certificate Printers

Recorded Capital Stock Transactions Exist and Are Accurately Recorded The issuance of new capital stock for cash, the merger with another company through an exchange of stock, donated shares, and the purchase of treasury shares each require extensive auditing. Regardless of the controls in existence, it is normal practice to verify all capital stock transactions because of their materiality and permanence in the records. Existence can ordinarily be tested by examining the minutes of the board of directors meetings for proper authorization.

Accurate recording of capital stock transactions for cash can be readily verified by confirming the amount with the transfer agent and tracing the amount of the recorded capital stock transactions to cash receipts. (In the case of treasury stock, the amounts are traced to the cash disbursements journal.) In addition, the auditor must verify whether the correct amounts were credited to capital stock and paid-in capital in excess of par by referring to the corporate charter to determine the par or stated value of the capital stock.

When capital stock transactions involve stock dividends, acquisition of property for stock, mergers, or similar noncash transfers, the verification of amounts may be considerably more difficult. For these types of transactions, the auditor must be certain that the client has correctly computed the amount of the capital stock issue in accordance with GAAP. For example, in the audit of a major merger transaction, the auditor has to evaluate whether the transaction has been properly accounted for. Considerable research is often necessary to determine the appropriate accounting treatment for the existing circumstances. After the auditor reaches a conclusion as to the appropriate method, it is necessary to verify that the amounts were correctly computed.

Capital Stock Is Accurately Recorded The ending balance in the capital stock account is verified by first determining the number of shares outstanding at the balance sheet date. A confirmation from the transfer agent is the simplest way to obtain this information. When no transfer agent exists, the auditor must rely on examining the stock records and accounting for all shares outstanding in the stock certificate records, examining all cancelled certificates, and accounting for blank certificates. After the auditor is satisfied that the number of shares outstanding is correct, the recorded par value in the capital account can be verified by multiplying the number of shares by the par value of the stock. The ending balance in the capital in excess of par account is a residual amount. It is audited by verifying the amount of recorded transactions during the year and adding them to or subtracting them from the beginning balance in the account.

A major consideration in the accuracy of capital stock is verifying whether the number of shares used in the calculation of earnings per share is accurate. It is easy to determine the correct number of shares to use in the calculation when there is only one class of stock and a small number of capital stock transactions. The problem becomes much more complex when there are convertible securities, stock options, or stock warrants outstanding. A thorough understanding of SFAS 128 is important before verifying the number of shares for determining basic and diluted earnings per share.

Capital Stock Is Properly Presented and Disclosed The most important sources of information for determining proper presentation and disclosure are the corporate charter, the minutes of board of directors meetings, and the auditor's analysis of capital stock transactions. The auditor should determine that there is a proper description of each class of stock, including such information as the number of shares issued and outstanding and any special rights of an individual class. The proper presentation and disclosure of stock options, stock warrants, and convertible securities should also be verified by examining legal documents or other evidence of the provisions of these agreements.

Audit of Dividends

The emphasis in the audit of dividends is on the transactions rather than on the ending balance. The exception is when there are dividends payable.

The six transaction-related audit objectives for transactions are relevant for dividends. But typically, dividends are audited on a 100 percent basis and cause few problems. The following are the most important objectives, including those concerning dividends payable:

1. Recorded dividends exist (existence).
2. Existing dividends are recorded (completeness).
3. Dividends are accurately recorded (accuracy).
4. Dividends as paid to stockholders exist (existence).
5. Dividends payable are recorded (completeness).
6. Dividends payable are accurately recorded (accuracy).

Existence of recorded dividends can be checked by examining the minutes of board of directors meetings for authorization of the amount of the dividend per share and the dividend date. When the auditor examines the board of directors minutes for dividends declared, the auditor should be alert to the possibility of unrecorded dividends declared, particularly shortly before the balance sheet date. A closely related audit procedure is to review the permanent audit documentation file to determine whether there are restrictions on the payment of dividends in bond indenture agreements or preferred stock provisions.

The accuracy of a dividend declaration can be audited by recomputing the amount on the basis of the dividend per share and the number of shares outstanding. If the client uses a transfer agent to disburse dividends, the total can be traced to a cash disbursement entry to the agent and also confirmed.

When a client keeps its own dividend records and pays the dividends itself, the auditor can verify the total amount of the dividend by recalculation and reference to cash disbursed. In addition, it is necessary to verify whether the payment was made to the stockholders who owned the stock as of the dividend record date. The auditor can test this by selecting a sample of recorded dividend payments and tracing the payee's name on the cancelled check to the dividend records to make sure that the payee was entitled to the dividend. At the same time, the amount and the authenticity of the dividend check can be verified.

Tests of dividends payable should be done in conjunction with declared dividends. Any unpaid dividend should be included as a liability.

Audit of Retained Earnings

For most companies, the only transactions involving retained earnings are net earnings for the year and dividends declared. But there may also be corrections of prior-period earnings, prior-period adjustments charged or credited directly to retained earnings, and the setting up or elimination of appropriations of retained earnings.

The starting point for the audit of retained earnings is an analysis of retained earnings for the entire year. The audit schedule showing the analysis, which is usually a part of the permanent file, includes a description of every transaction affecting the account.

The audit of the credit to retained earnings for net income for the year (or the debit for a loss) is accomplished by simply tracing the entry in retained earnings to the net earnings figure on the income statement. The performance of this procedure must, of course, take place fairly late in the audit after all adjusting entries affecting net earnings have been completed.

An important consideration in auditing debits and credits to retained earnings other than net earnings and dividends is determining whether the transactions should have been included. For example, prior-period adjustments can be included in retained earnings only if they satisfy the requirements of APB opinions and FASB statements.

After the auditor is satisfied that the recorded transactions are appropriately classified as retained earnings transactions, the next step is to decide whether they are accurately recorded. The audit evidence necessary to determine accuracy depends on the nature of the transactions. If there is a requirement for an appropriation of retained earnings for a bond sinking fund, the correct amount of the appropriation can be determined by examining the bond indenture agreement. If there is a major loss charged to retained earnings because of a material nonrecurring abandonment of a plant, the evidence needed to determine the amount of the loss could include significant numbers of documents and records of the plant.

Another important consideration in the audit of retained earnings is evaluating whether any transactions should have been included but were not. If a stock dividend was declared, for instance, the market value of the securities issued should be capitalized by

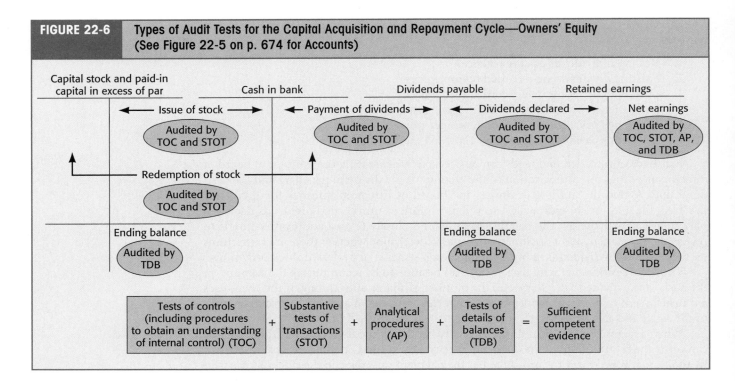

FIGURE 22-6 Types of Audit Tests for the Capital Acquisition and Repayment Cycle—Owners' Equity (See Figure 22-5 on p. 674 for Accounts)

a debit to retained earnings and a credit to capital stock. Similarly, if the financial statements include appropriations of retained earnings, the auditor should evaluate whether it is still necessary to have the appropriation as of the balance sheet date. As an example, an appropriation of retained earnings for a bond sinking fund should be eliminated by crediting retained earnings after the bond has been paid off.

The primary concern in determining whether retained earnings is correctly presented and disclosed in the financial statements is the existence of any restrictions on the payment of dividends. Often, agreements with bankers, stockholders, and other creditors prohibit or limit the amount of dividends the client can pay. These restrictions must be disclosed in the footnotes to the financial statements.

Figure 22-6 illustrates the major accounts related to owners' equity in the capital acquisition and repayment cycle and the types of audit tests used to audit these accounts.

E-COMMERCE AND CAPITAL ACQUISITION

OBJECTIVE 22-5

Identify capital acquisition issues for technology-based companies.

Throughout the late 1990s, new market opportunities created by the Internet led to the creation of many new technology-based start-up companies. These companies sought to link their businesses directly to consumers by being one of the first to offer their industry's products and services online.

In addition to acquiring capital through traditional lending institutions and private equity sources, many of these start-up companies subsequently obtained large amounts of capital by becoming publicly held companies. Favorable stock market reactions to Internet-based businesses allowed many of these businesses to sell shares to the public at high stock prices, generating significant cash proceeds. Many start-ups used the proceeds to quickly liquidate debt, reward existing private equity holders, and build significant cash reserves for future investment in the business. Often, founders of these businesses were significantly rewarded for their efforts. This occurred despite no history of profitability for many of these start-up companies.

During 2000, the favorable stock market view of Internet-based companies began to deteriorate as the economy slowed and as the initial excitement about new Internet market opportunities weakened. The resulting downturn in the technology sector of the stock market made it difficult for new start-ups to obtain capital. The decline in stock prices for Internet companies increased the pressure for start-up company management to generate profits.

As auditors of technology-based clients gain an understanding of the business and industry, they may identify specific business risks associated with the method used by start-up companies to acquire capital and the use of proceeds generated through capital acquisition. As a part of the risk assessment process, auditors should consider how the process of acquiring capital, particularly through public markets, may create significant pressure for management to generate profits, which increases the risk of material misstatements in the financial statements. In some cases, the complexity of the capital transactions may create unique financial reporting and disclosure issues that need to be addressed by the auditor.

SUMMARY

This chapter discussed the audit of the capital acquisition and repayment cycle. The cycle is important because it includes the primary sources of financing for most businesses. The cycle often involves few transactions, but the individual transactions are often material, which influences the design and performance of tests in the cycle. The approach to auditing the cycle was illustrated for notes payable, related interest expense and accrued interest, and for owners' equity and related accounts.

ESSENTIAL TERMS

Capital acquisition and repayment cycle—the transaction cycle that involves the acquisition of capital resources in the form of interest-bearing debt and owners' equity, and the repayment of the capital

Capital stock certificate record—a record of the issuance and repurchase of capital stock for the life of the corporation

Closely held corporation—corporation with stock that is not publicly traded; typically, there are only a few shareholders and few, if any, capital stock account transactions during the year

Independent registrar—outside person engaged by a corporation to make sure that its stock is issued in accordance with capital stock provisions in the corporate charter and autho-

rizations by the board of directors; required by the SEC for publicly held corporations

Note payable—a legal obligation to a creditor, which may be unsecured or secured by assets

Publicly held corporation—corporation with stock that is publicly traded; typically, there are many shareholders and frequent changes in the ownership of the stock

Shareholders' capital stock master file—a record of the issuance and repurchase of capital stock for the life of a corporation

Stock transfer agent—outside person engaged by a corporation to maintain the stockholder records and often to disburse cash dividends

REVIEW QUESTIONS

22-1 (Objective 22-1) List four examples of interest-bearing liability accounts commonly found in balance sheets. What characteristics do these liabilities have in common? How do they differ?

22-2 (Objectives 22-1, 22-2) Why are liability accounts included in the capital acquisition and repayment cycle audited differently from accounts payable?

22-3 (Objective 22-2) It is common practice to audit the balance in notes payable in conjunction with the audit of interest expense and interest payable. Explain the advantages of this approach.

22-4 (Objective 22-2) Which internal controls should the auditor be most concerned about in the audit of notes payable? Explain the importance of each.

22-5 (Objective 22-2) Which analytical procedures are most important in verifying notes payable? Which types of misstatements can the auditor uncover by the use of these tests?

22-6 (Objective 22-2) Why is it more important to search for unrecorded notes payable than for unrecorded notes receivable? Suggest audit procedures that the auditor can use to uncover unrecorded notes payable.

22-7 (Objective 22-2) What is the primary purpose of analyzing interest expense? Given this purpose, what primary considerations should the auditor keep in mind when doing the analysis?

22-8 (Objective 22-2) Distinguish between (a) tests of controls and substantive tests of transactions and (b) tests of details of balances for liability accounts in the capital acquisition and repayment cycle.

22-9 (Objective 22-2) List two types of restrictions long-term creditors often put on companies when granting them a loan. How can the auditor find out about these restrictions?

22-10 (Objective 22-3) What are the primary objectives in the audit of owners' equity accounts?

22-11 (Objectives 22-3, 22-4) Evaluate the following statement: "The corporate charter and the bylaws of a company are legal documents; therefore, they should not be examined by the auditors. If the auditor wants information about these documents, an attorney should be consulted."

22-12 (Objective 22-3) What are the major internal controls over owners' equity?

22-13 (Objective 22-3) How does the audit of owners' equity for a closely held corporation differ from that for a publicly held corporation? In what respects are there no significant differences?

22-14 (Objective 22-3) Describe the duties of a stock registrar and a transfer agent. How does the use of their services affect the client's internal controls?

22-15 (Objective 22-4) What kinds of information can be confirmed with a transfer agent?

22-16 (Objective 22-4) Evaluate the following statement: "The most important audit procedure to verify dividends for the year is a comparison of a random sample of cancelled dividend checks with a dividend list that has been prepared by management as of the dividend record date."

22-17 (Objective 22-4) If a transfer agent disburses dividends for a client, explain how the audit of dividends declared and paid is affected. What audit procedures are necessary to verify dividends paid when a transfer agent is used?

22-18 (Objective 22-4) What should be the major emphasis in auditing the retained earnings account? Explain your answer.

22-19 (Objectives 22-3, 22-4) Explain the relationship between the audit of owners' equity and the calculations of earnings per share. What are the main auditing considerations in verifying the earnings per share figure?

MULTIPLE CHOICE QUESTIONS FROM CPA EXAMINATIONS

22-20 (Objective 22-2) The following multiple choice questions concern interest-bearing liabilities. Choose the best response.

    a. The audit program for long-term debt should include steps that require the
        (1) verification of the existence of the bondholders.
        (2) examination of any bond trust indenture.
        (3) inspection of the accounts payable master file.
        (4) investigation of credits to the bond interest income account.

    b. During the year under audit, a company has completed a private placement of a substantial amount of bonds. Which of the following is the *most* important step in the auditor's program for the audit of bonds payable?
        (1) Confirming the amount issued with the bond trustee.
        (2) Tracing the cash received from the issue to the accounting records.
        (3) Examining the bond records maintained by the transfer agent.
        (4) Recomputing the annual interest cost and the effective yield.

    c. Several years ago, Conway, Inc., secured a conventional real estate mortgage loan. Which of the following audit procedures would be *least* likely to be performed by an auditor auditing the mortgage balance?
        (1) Examine the current year's cancelled checks.
        (2) Review the mortgage amortization schedule.
        (3) Inspect public records of lien balances.
        (4) Recompute mortgage interest expense.

22-21 (Objectives 22-2, 22-3, 22-4) The following questions concern the audit of accounts in the capital acquisition and repayment cycle. Choose the best response.

    a. During an audit of a publicly held company, the auditor should obtain written confirmation regarding debenture transactions from the
        (1) debenture holders.
        (2) client's attorney.
        (3) internal auditors.
        (4) trustee.

b. An audit program for the audit of the retained earnings account should include a step that requires verification of
   (1) market value used to charge retained earnings to account for a 2-for-1 stock split.
   (2) approval of the adjustment to the beginning balance as a result of a write-down of an account receivable.
   (3) authorization for both cash and stock dividends.
   (4) gain or loss resulting from disposition of treasury shares.

c. When *no* independent stock transfer agents are employed and the corporation issues its own stocks and maintains stock records, cancelled stock certificates should
   (1) be defaced to prevent reissuance and attached to their corresponding stubs.
   (2) *not* be defaced, but be segregated from other stock certificates and retained in a cancelled certificates file.
   (3) be destroyed to prevent fraudulent reissuance.
   (4) be defaced and sent to the secretary of state.

DISCUSSION QUESTIONS AND PROBLEMS

22-22 (Objective 22-2) Items 1 through 6 are questions typically found in a standard internal control questionnaire used by auditors to obtain an understanding of internal control for notes payable. In using the questionnaire for a client, a "yes" response indicates a possible internal control, whereas a "no" indicates a potential weakness.

1. Are liabilities for notes payable incurred only after written authorization by a proper company official?
2. Is a notes payable master file maintained?
3. Is the individual who maintains the notes payable master file someone other than the person who approves the issue of new notes or handles cash?
4. Are paid notes cancelled and retained in the company files?
5. Is a periodic reconciliation made of the notes payable master file with the actual notes outstanding by an individual who does not maintain the master file?
6. Are interest expense and accrued interest recomputed periodically by an individual who does not record interest transactions?

a. For each of the preceding questions, state the purpose of the control.   **Required**

b. For each of the preceding questions, identify the type of financial statement misstatement that could occur if the control were not in effect.

c. For each of the potential misstatements in part b, list an audit procedure that can be used to determine whether a material misstatement exists.

22-23 (Objective 22-2) The following are frequently performed audit procedures for the verification of bonds payable issued in previous years:

1. Obtain a copy of the bond indenture agreement and review its important provisions.
2. Determine that each of the bond indenture provisions has been met.
3. Analyze the general ledger account for bonds payable, interest expense, and unamortized bond discount or premium.
4. Test the client's calculations of interest expense, unamortized bond discount or premium, accrued interest, and bonds payable.
5. Obtain a confirmation from the bondholder.

a. State the purpose of each of the five audit procedures listed.   **Required**

b. List the provisions for which the auditor should be alert in examining the bond indenture agreement.

c. For each provision listed in part b, explain how the auditor can determine whether its terms have been met.

d. Explain how the auditor should verify the unamortized bond discount or premium.

e. List the information that should be requested in the confirmation of bonds payable with the bondholder.

22-24 (Objective 22-2) The Fox Company is a medium-sized industrial client that has been audited by your CPA firm for several years. The only interest-bearing debt owed by Fox Company is $200,000 in long-term notes payable held by the bank. The notes were issued 3 years previously and will mature in 6 more years. Fox Company is highly profitable, has no pressing needs for additional financing, and has excellent internal controls over the recording of loan transactions and related interest costs.

Required

a. Describe the auditing procedures that you think would be necessary for notes payable and related interest accounts in these circumstances.

b. How would your answer differ if Fox Company were unprofitable, had a need for additional financing, and had weak internal controls?

22-25 (Objective 22-2) The ending general ledger balance of $186,000 in notes payable for the Sterling Manufacturing Company is made up of 20 notes to eight different payees. The notes vary in duration anywhere from 30 days to 2 years, and in amounts from $1,000 to $10,000. In some cases, the notes were issued for cash loans; in other cases, the notes were issued directly to vendors for the acquisition of inventory or equipment. The use of relatively short-term financing is necessary because all existing properties are pledged for mortgages. Nevertheless, there is still a serious cash shortage.

Record-keeping procedures for notes payable are not good, considering the large number of loan transactions. There is no notes payable master file or independent verification of ending balances; however, the notes payable records are maintained by a secretary who does not have access to cash.

The audit has been done by the same CPA firm for several years. In the current year, the following procedures were performed to verify notes payable:

1. Obtain a list of notes payable from the client, foot the notes payable balances on the list, and trace the total to the general ledger.
2. Examine duplicate copies of notes for all outstanding notes included on the listing. Compare the name of the lender, amount, and due date on the duplicate copy with the list.
3. Obtain a confirmation from lenders for all listed notes payable. The confirmation should include the due date of the loan, the amount, and interest payable at the balance sheet date.
4. Recompute accrued interest on the list for all notes. The information for determining the correct accrued interest is to be obtained from the duplicate copy of the note. Foot the accrued interest amounts and trace the balance to the general ledger.

Required

a. What should be the emphasis in the verification of notes payable in this situation? Explain.

b. State the purpose of each of the four audit procedures listed.

c. Evaluate whether each of the four audit procedures was necessary. Evaluate the sample size for each procedure.

d. List other audit procedures that should be performed in the audit of notes payable in these circumstances.

22-26 (Objective 22-2) The following covenants are extracted from the indenture of a bond issue. The indenture provides that failure to comply with its terms in any respect automatically makes the loan immediately due (the regular date is 20 years hence). List any audit steps or reporting requirements you think should be taken or recognized in connection with each one of the following:

a. The debtor company shall endeavor to maintain a working capital ratio of 2 to 1 at all times, and in any fiscal year following a failure to maintain said ratio, the company shall restrict compensation of officers to $100,000 per individual. Officers for this purpose shall include chairman of the board of directors, president, all vice presidents, secretary, and treasurer.

b. The debtor company shall keep all property that is security for this debt insured against loss by fire to the extent of 100% of its actual value. Policies of insurance comprising this protection shall be filed with the trustee.

c. The debtor company shall pay all taxes legally assessed against property that is security for this debt within the time provided by law for payment without penalty and shall deposit receipted tax bills or equally acceptable evidence of payment of same with the trustee.

d. A sinking fund shall be deposited with the trustee by semiannual payments of $300,000, from which the trustee shall, in his discretion, purchase bonds of this issue.*

22-27 (Objective 22-2) The Redford Corporation took out a 20-year mortgage on June 15, 2005, for $2,600,000 and pledged its only manufacturing building and the land on which the building stands as collateral. Each month subsequent to the issue of the mortgage, a payment of $20,000 was paid to the mortgagor. You are in charge of the current year audit for Redford, which has a balance sheet date of December 31, 2005. The client has been audited previously by your CPA firm, but this is the first time Redford Corporation has had a mortgage.

Required

a. Explain why it is desirable to prepare an audit schedule for the permanent file for the mortgage. What type of information should be included in the schedule?

*AICPA adapted.

b. Explain why the audit of mortgage payable, interest expense, and interest payable should all be done together.

c. List the audit procedures that should ordinarily be performed to verify the issue of the mortgage, the balance in the mortgage and interest payable accounts at December 31, 2005, and the balance in interest expense for the year 2005.

22-28 (Objectives 22-3, 22-4) Items 1 through 6 are common questions found in internal control questionnaires used by auditors to obtain an understanding of internal control for owners' equity. In using the questionnaire for a client, a "yes" response indicates a possible internal control, whereas a "no" indicates a potential deficiency.

1. Does the company use the services of an independent registrar or transfer agent?
2. Are issues and retirements of stock authorized by the board of directors?
3. If an independent registrar and transfer agent are not used:
   (a) Are unissued certificates properly controlled?
   (b) Are cancelled certificates mutilated to prevent their reuse?
4. Are common stock master files and stock certificate books periodically reconciled with the general ledger by an independent person?
5. Is an independent transfer agent used for disbursing dividends? If not, is an imprest dividend account maintained?
6. Are all entries in the owners' equity accounts authorized at the proper level in the organization?

a. For each of the preceding questions, state the purpose of the control. **Required**

b. For each of the preceding questions, identify the type of potential financial statement misstatements if the control is not in effect.

c. For each of the potential misstatements in part b, list an audit procedure that the auditor can use to determine whether a material misstatement exists.

22-29 (Objectives 22-3, 22-4) The following audit procedures are commonly performed by auditors in the verification of owners' equity:

1. Review the articles of incorporation and bylaws for provisions about owners' equity.
2. Review the minutes of the board of directors' meetings for the year for approvals related to owners' equity.
3. Analyze all owners' equity accounts for the year and document the nature of any recorded change in each account.
4. Account for all certificate numbers in the capital stock book for all shares outstanding.
5. Examine the stock certificate book for any stock that was cancelled.
6. Recompute earnings per share.
7. Review debt provisions and senior securities with respect to liquidation preferences, dividends in arrears, and restrictions on the payment of dividends or the issue of stock.

a. State the purpose of each of these seven audit procedures. **Required**

b. List the type of misstatements the auditors could uncover by the use of each audit procedure.

22-30 (Objectives 22-3, 22-4) You are engaged in the audit of a corporation whose records have not previously been audited by you. The corporation has both an independent transfer agent and a registrar for its capital stock. The transfer agent maintains the record of stockholders and the registrar checks that there is no overissue of stock. Signatures of both are required to validate certificates.

It has been proposed that confirmations be obtained from both the transfer agent and the registrar as to the stock outstanding at the balance sheet date. If such confirmations agree with the books, no additional work is to be performed as to capital stock.

If you agree that obtaining the confirmations as suggested would be sufficient in this case, give the **Required** justification for your position. If you do not agree, state specifically all additional steps you would take and explain your reasons for taking them.*

22-31 (Objective 22-4) You are a CPA engaged in an audit of the financial statements of Pate Corporation for the year ended December 31, 2005. The financial statements and records of Pate Corporation have not been audited by a CPA in prior years.

The stockholders' equity section of Pate Corporation's balance sheet at December 31, 2005, follows:

---

*AICPA adapted.

Stockholders' Equity		
Capital stock—10,000 shares of $10 par value		$ 50,000
authorized; 5,000 shares issued and outstanding		
Capital contributed in excess of par value of capital stock		32,580
Retained earnings		47,320
Total stockholders' equity		$129,900

Pate Corporation was founded in 1998. The corporation has 10 stockholders and serves as its own registrar and transfer agent. There are no capital stock subscription contracts in effect.

Required
a. Prepare the detailed audit program for the audit of the three accounts comprising the stockholders' equity section of Pate Corporation's balance sheet. (Do not include in the audit program the verification of the results of the current year's operations.)

b. After every other figure on the balance sheet has been audited, it might appear that the retained earnings figure is a balancing figure and requires no further verification. Why does the CPA verify retained earnings as is done with the other figures on the balance sheet? Discuss.*

22-32 (Objective 22-5) E-Antiques Inc., is an Internet-based market maker for buyers and sellers of antique furniture and jewelry. The company allows sellers of antique items to list descriptions of those items on the E-Antiques Web site. Interested buyers review the Web site for antique items and then enter into negotiations directly with the seller for purchase. E-Antiques receives a commission on each transaction.

The company, founded in 2001, initially obtained capital through equity funding provided by the founders and through loan proceeds from financial institutions. In early 2004, E-Antiques became a publicly held company when it began selling shares on a national stock exchange. Although the company had never generated profits, the stock offering generated large proceeds based on favorable expectations for the company, and the stock quickly increased to above $100 per share.

Management used the proceeds to pay off loans to financial institutions and to reacquire shares issued to the company founders. Proceeds were also used to fund purchases of hardware and software used to support the online market. The balance of unused proceeds is currently held in the company's bank accounts.

Required
a. Before performing analytical procedures related to the capital acquisition and repayment cycle accounts, consider how the process of becoming publicly held would affect accounts at E-Antiques Inc. Describe whether each of the following balances would increase, decrease, or experience no change between 2003 and 2004 because of the public offering:
  (1) Cash
  (2) Accounts receivable
  (3) Property, plant, and equipment
  (4) Accounts payable
  (5) Long-term debt
  (6) Common stock
  (7) Additional paid-in capital
  (8) Retained earnings
  (9) Treasury stock
  (10) Dividends
  (11) Revenues

b. During 2005, the stock price for E-Antiques plummeted to around $19 per share. No new shares were issued during 2005. Describe the impact of this drop in stock price on the following accounts for the year ended December 31, 2005:
  (1) Common stock
  (2) Additional paid-in capital
  (3) Retained earnings

c. How does the decline in stock price affect your assessment of client business risk and acceptable audit risk?

INTERNET PROBLEM 22-1: STOCK EXCHANGE REQUIREMENTS

Reference the CW site. Many organizations seek to go public in order to sell shares on one of the national stock exchanges. In this problem, students use Internet resources to identify the general listing requirements for companies seeking to sell shares on the New York Stock Exchange or the American Stock Exchange.

*AICPA adapted.

CHAPTER 23

AUDIT OF CASH BALANCES

SOCIETY EXPECTS A LOT FROM AUDITORS

Bert Sampson was the controller of Pardoe Manufacturing Company. From 2000 through 2004, Bert paid himself an extra $2 million in "bonuses." He did this by transferring funds from the general account, writing checks to himself from the payroll account, destroying the checks when received from the bank, and making entries directly into the company's computer files to disguise the cash theft. Bert was able to do this because he had almost complete control of the company's accounting process.

Jack Baker of Tramenier and Baker, CPAs, was the partner on the Pardoe audit. Although Baker found a strong control environment at Pardoe and a good budgeting and reporting system, he assessed control risk at maximum because there was limited segregation of duties. Accordingly, Baker used a "substantive" approach to the audit. Baker applied tests of details of balances and analytical procedures to the year-end financial statements. He did no tests of controls or substantive tests of transactions.

Because Sampson had lost all of the $2 million and Pardoe had no fidelity bond insurance, the company sued Tramenier and Baker, CPAs, for the stolen funds, claiming breach of contract. Baker's defense was that he had done the audit in accordance with auditing standards.

The trial revolved around the testimony of two expert witnesses. The witness for the company argued that even though the auditors took a substantive approach to the audit, they should have seen that Sampson had the opportunity to commit the embezzlement, extended their audit, and found it.

The expert for the defense argued that a substantive audit approach is allowed by auditing standards. Sampson manipulated the records so carefully that the substantive procedures of the various payroll accounts did not indicate that the theft had occurred. Because no "red flags" were evident that would have caused the auditors to extend their tests, the audit was clearly satisfactory.

The jury found against the auditors, and Tramenier and Baker, CPAs, was required to pay approximately $2.3 million in damages. When jury members were interviewed about their decision, they indicated that they didn't really understand the technical nature of the arguments made by the expert witnesses, but it was apparent to them that the people who did the audit were extremely bright and competent. Accordingly, the jury members believed that *the auditors certainly had the ability to find the cash theft* and the fact that they didn't meant that they failed to perform up to their potential.

LEARNING OBJECTIVES

After studying this chapter, you should be able to

23-1 Show the relationship of cash in the bank to the various transaction cycles.

23-2 Identify the major types of cash accounts maintained by business entities.

23-3 Design and perform audit tests of the general cash account.

23-4 Recognize when to extend audit tests of the general cash account to test further for material fraud.

23-5 Design and perform audit tests of the imprest payroll bank account.

23-6 Design and perform audit tests of imprest petty cash.

Cash is the only account that is included in several cycles. It is a part of every cycle except inventory and warehousing. The audit of cash balances is the last audit area studied because the evidence accumulated for cash balances depends heavily on the results of the tests in other cycles. For example, if the understanding of internal control and tests of controls and substantive tests of transactions in the acquisition and payment cycle lead the auditor to believe that it is appropriate to reduce assessed control risk to low, the auditor can reduce detailed tests of the ending balance in cash. If, however, the auditor concludes that assessed control risk should be higher, extensive year-end testing may be necessary.

Cash is important primarily because of the potential for fraud but also because there may be errors. The opening vignette provides one example of what can happen if an auditor is not careful in assessing risks in auditing the cash account.

CASH IN THE BANK AND TRANSACTION CYCLES

OBJECTIVE 23-1

Show the relationship of cash in the bank to the various transaction cycles.

A brief discussion of the relationship between cash in the bank and the other transaction cycles serves a dual function: It clearly shows the importance of the tests of various transaction cycles to the audit of cash, and it aids in further understanding the integration of the different transaction cycles. Figure 23-1 illustrates the relationships of the various transaction cycles, the focal point being the general cash account.

An examination of Figure 23-1 indicates why the general cash account is considered significant in almost all audits, even when the ending balance is immaterial. The amount of cash *flowing* into and out of the cash account is often larger than that for any other account in the financial statements. Furthermore, the susceptibility of cash to defalcation is greater than for other types of assets because most other assets must be converted to cash to make them usable.

In the audit of cash, an important distinction should be made between verifying the client's reconciliation of the balance on the bank statement to the balance in the general ledger and verifying whether recorded cash in the general ledger correctly reflects all cash transactions that took place during the year. It is relatively easy to verify the client's reconciliation of the balance in the bank account to the general ledger, but a significant part of the total audit of a company involves verifying whether cash transactions are properly recorded. For example, each of the following misstatements ultimately results in the improper payment of or the failure to receive cash, but none will normally be discovered as a part of the audit of the bank reconciliation:

- Failure to bill a customer
- Billing a customer at a lower price than called for by company policy
- A defalcation of cash by interception of cash receipts from customers before they are recorded, with the account charged off as a bad debt
- Duplicate payment of a vendor's invoice
- Improper payments of officers' personal expenditures
- Payment for raw materials that were not received
- Payment to an employee for more hours than he or she worked
- Payment of interest to a related party for an amount in excess of the going rate

If these misstatements are to be uncovered in the audit, their discovery must come about through the tests of controls and substantive tests of transactions that were discussed in the preceding chapters. The first three misstatements could be discovered as part of the audit of the sales and collection cycle, the next three in the audit of the acquisition and payment cycle, and the last two in the tests of the payroll and personnel cycle and the capital acquisition and repayment cycle, respectively.

Entirely different types of misstatements are normally discovered as a part of the tests of a bank reconciliation. For example,

- Failure to include a check that has not cleared the bank on the outstanding check list, even though it has been recorded in the cash disbursements journal
- Cash received by the client subsequent to the balance sheet date but recorded as cash receipts in the current year

FIGURE 23-1 Relationships of Cash in the Bank and Transaction Cycles

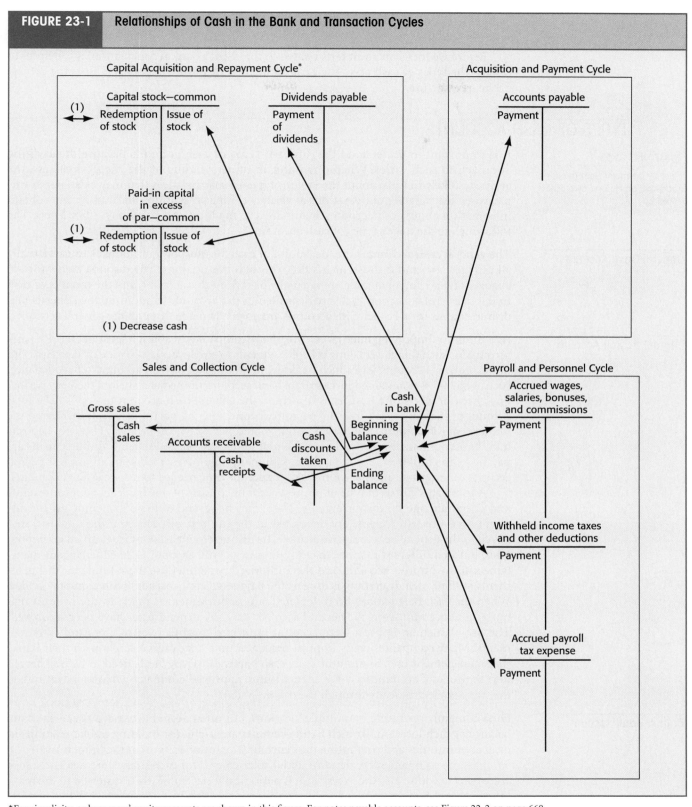

*For simplicity, only owners' equity accounts are shown in this figure. For notes payable accounts, see Figure 22-2 on page 668.

- Deposits recorded as cash receipts near the end of the year, deposited in the bank in the same month, and included in the bank reconciliation as a deposit in transit
- Payments on notes payable debited directly to the bank balance by the bank but not entered in the client's records

• Deposits received by the bank on behalf of the company from credit card agencies and other vendors making payments electronically, but not recorded in the client's records

Before we focus on audit tests related to the client's bank reconciliation, it is helpful to discuss the types of cash accounts commonly used by most companies. This is the subject of the next section.

TYPES OF CASH ACCOUNTS

OBJECTIVE 23-2

Identify the major types of cash accounts maintained by business entities.

It is important to understand the different types of cash accounts because the auditing approach to each varies. When obtaining an understanding of the client's business, the auditor is likely to learn about the various types of cash balances that may exist. For example, when learning about operations at various company locations, the auditor may obtain information about cash accounts maintained at the local and corporate office levels. The following are the major types of cash accounts.

General Cash Account

The **general cash account** is the focal point of cash for most organizations because virtually all cash receipts and disbursements flow through this account. The disbursements for the acquisition and payment cycle are normally paid from this account, and the receipts of cash in the sales and collection cycle are deposited in the account. In addition, the deposits and disbursements for all other cash accounts are normally made through the general account.

Imprest Payroll Account

As a means of improving internal control, many companies establish a separate imprest bank account for such things as making payroll payments to employees or separate cash receipts and disbursements accounts for branch banking. In an **imprest payroll account**, a fixed balance, such as $5,000, is maintained in a separate bank account. Immediately before each pay period, one check or electronic transfer is drawn on the general cash account to deposit the total amount of the net payroll into the payroll account. After all payroll checks have cleared the imprest payroll account, the bank account should have a $5,000 balance. The only deposits into the account are for the weekly and semimonthly payroll, and the only disbursements are paychecks to employees. For companies with many employees, the use of an imprest payroll account can improve internal control and reduce the time needed to reconcile bank accounts.

Electronic Funds Transfer

A somewhat different type of imprest account consists of one bank account for receipts and a separate one for disbursements. There may be several of these in a company for different divisions. All receipts are deposited in the imprest account, and the total is transferred to the general account periodically. The disbursement account is set up on an *imprest basis*, but in a different manner than an imprest payroll account. A fixed balance is maintained in the imprest account, and the authorized personnel use these funds for disbursements at their own discretion as long as the payments are consistent with company policy. When the cash balance has been depleted, a reimbursement is made to the imprest disbursement account from the general account *after* the expenditures have been approved. The use of such an imprest bank account improves controls over receipts and disbursements. Many companies using imprest bank accounts have online access with their banks that management uses to monitor daily cash balances. When funds need to be transferred into the general account to cover expenditures, approved company personnel can initiate the transfer electronically through the online system.

Branch Bank Account

For a company operating in multiple locations, it is often desirable to have a separate bank balance at each location. **Branch bank accounts** are useful for building public relations in local communities and permitting the centralization of operations at the branch level.

In some companies, the deposits and disbursements for each branch are made to a separate bank account, and the excess cash is periodically electronically transferred to the main office general bank account. The branch account in this instance is much like a general account, but at the branch level.

Imprest Petty Cash Fund

An **imprest petty cash fund** is actually not a bank account, but it is sufficiently similar to cash on deposit to merit inclusion. A petty cash account is often something as simple as a preset amount of cash set aside in a strong box for incidental expenses. It is used for small cash acquisitions that can be paid more conveniently and quickly by cash than by check, or for the

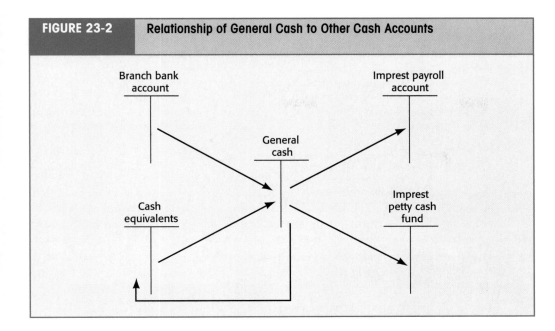

convenience of employees in cashing personal or payroll checks. An imprest cash account is set up on the same basis as an imprest branch bank account, but the expenditures are normally for a much smaller amount. Typical expenses include minor office supplies, stamps, and small contributions to local charities. A petty cash account usually does not exceed a few hundred dollars and may not be reimbursed more than once or twice each month.

Excess cash accumulated during certain parts of the operating cycle that will be needed in the reasonably near future is often invested in short-term, highly liquid **cash equivalents**. Examples include time deposits, certificates of deposit, and money market funds. Cash equivalents, which can be highly material, are included in the financial statements as a part of the cash account only if they are short-term investments that are readily convertible to known amounts of cash within a short time and there is insignificant risk of a change of value from interest rate changes. Marketable securities and longer-term interest-bearing investments are not cash equivalents.

    Figure 23-2 shows the relationship of general cash to the other cash accounts. All cash either originates from or is deposited in general cash. The remainder of this chapter focuses on auditing three types of accounts: the general cash account, imprest payroll bank account, and imprest petty cash. The others are similar to these and need not be discussed.

Cash Equivalents

AUDIT OF THE GENERAL CASH ACCOUNT

On the trial balance of Hillsburg Hardware Co. on page 141, there is only one cash account. Notice, however, that all cycles, except inventory and warehousing, affect cash in the bank.

    In testing the year-end balance in the general cash account, the auditor must accumulate sufficient evidence to evaluate whether cash, as stated on the balance sheet, is fairly stated and properly disclosed in accordance with six of the nine balance-related audit objectives used for all tests of details of balances. Rights to general cash, its classification on the balance sheet, and the realizable value of cash are not a problem.

    The methodology for auditing year-end cash is essentially the same as that for all other balance sheet accounts. The methodology is shown in Figure 23-3 (p. 690) and then discussed in detail.

Most companies are unlikely to have significant client business risks affecting cash balances. However, client business risk may arise from inappropriate cash management policies or handling of funds held in trust for others. For example, one financial services firm was recently found to have engaged in fraud by intentionally overdrawing cash balances by significant amounts.

OBJECTIVE 23-3

Design and perform audit tests of the general cash account.

Identify Client Business Risks Affecting Cash (Phase I)

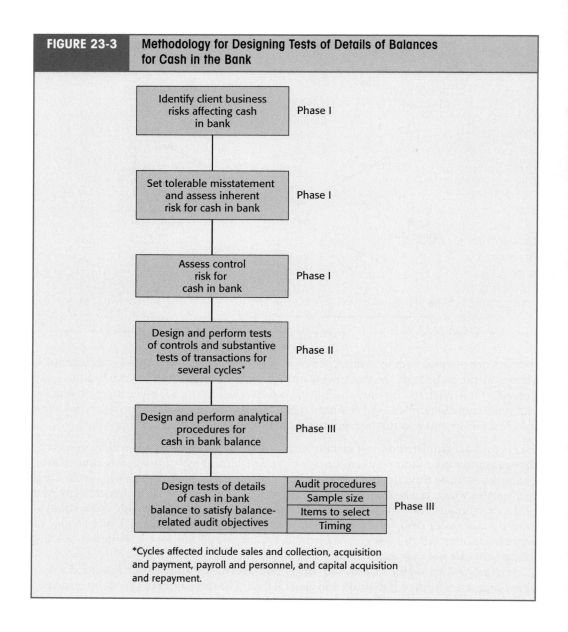

FIGURE 23-3 | **Methodology for Designing Tests of Details of Balances for Cash in the Bank**

Identify client business risks affecting cash in bank — Phase I

Set tolerable misstatement and assess inherent risk for cash in bank — Phase I

Assess control risk for cash in bank — Phase I

Design and perform tests of controls and substantive tests of transactions for several cycles* — Phase II

Design and perform analytical procedures for cash in bank balance — Phase III

Design tests of details of cash in bank balance to satisfy balance-related audit objectives | Audit procedures / Sample size / Items to select / Timing — Phase III

*Cycles affected include sales and collection, acquisition and payment, payroll and personnel, and capital acquisition and repayment.

Client business risk is more likely to arise from cash equivalents and other types of investments. Many governmental units and other entities suffered losses from repurchases of government securities in the ESM Government Securities case described in Chapter 5. Several financial services firms have suffered large trading losses from the activities of individual traders that were hidden by misstating investment and cash balances. The auditor should understand the risks from the client's investment policies and strategies, as well as management controls that mitigate these risks.

Set Tolerable Misstatement and Assess Inherent Risk (Phase I)

The cash balance is immaterial in most audits, but cash transactions affecting the balance are almost always extremely material. Therefore, there is often potential for material misstatement of cash.

Because cash is more susceptible to theft than other assets, there is high inherent risk for the existence, completeness, and accuracy objectives. These objectives are usually the focus in auditing cash balances. Typically, inherent risk is low for all other objectives.

Assess Control Risk (Phase I)

Internal controls over year-end cash balances in the general account can be divided into two categories: *controls over the transaction cycles* affecting the recording of cash receipts and disbursements and *independent bank reconciliations*.

Controls affecting the recording of cash transactions have been discussed in preceding chapters, but they are essential in deciding control risk for cash. For example, in the acquisition and payment cycle, major controls include adequate segregation of duties between the check signing and accounts payable functions, signing of checks only by a properly authorized person, use of prenumbered checks printed on special paper, adequate control of blank and voided checks, careful review of supporting documentation by the check signer before checks are signed, adequate control over the initiation and approval of wire transfer funds, and adequate internal verification. If controls affecting cash-related transactions are adequate, it is possible to reduce control risk and therefore the audit tests for the year-end bank reconciliation.

A monthly **bank reconciliation** of the general bank account on a timely basis by someone independent of the handling or recording of cash receipts and disbursements is an essential control over the cash balance. If a business defers preparing bank reconciliations for long periods, the value of the control is reduced and may affect the auditor's assessment of control risk for cash. The reconciliation is important to ensure that the books reflect the same cash balance as the actual amount of cash in the bank after considering reconciling items, but even more important, the *independent* reconciliation provides a unique opportunity for an internal verification of cash receipts and disbursements transactions. If the bank statements are received unopened by the reconciler, and physical control is maintained over the statements until the reconciliations are complete, the cancelled checks, duplicate deposit slips, and other documents included in the statement can be examined without concern for the possibility of alterations, deletions, or additions. A careful bank reconciliation by competent client personnel includes the following:

Cash Handling Procedures

- Compare cancelled checks with the cash disbursements records for date, payee, and amount.
- Examine cancelled checks for signature, endorsement, and cancellation.
- Compare deposits in the bank with recorded cash receipts for date, customer, and amount.
- Account for the numerical sequence of checks, and investigate missing ones.
- Reconcile all items causing a difference between the book and bank balance and verify their propriety.
- Reconcile total debits on the bank statement with the totals in the cash disbursements records.
- Reconcile total credits on the bank statement with the totals in the cash receipts records.
- Review month-end interbank transfers for propriety and proper recording.
- Follow up on outstanding checks and stop-payment notices.

Most accounting software packages incorporate a bank reconciliation as a part of end-of-month procedures. Even though the software reduces the clerical efforts in performing the bank reconciliations, it does not eliminate the need for the preparer to do most of the procedures just identified.

Because of the importance of monthly reconciliation of bank accounts, another common control for many companies is to have a responsible employee review the monthly reconciliation as soon as possible after its completion.

Because the cash balance is affected by all other cycles except inventory and warehousing, an extremely large number of transactions affect cash. The appropriate tests of controls and substantive tests of transactions have been discussed in detail in several earlier chapters as the audit of each cycle was studied.

Design and Perform Tests of Controls and Substantive Tests of Transactions (Phase II)

In many audits, the year-end bank reconciliation is extensively audited. Using analytical procedures to test the reasonableness of the cash balance is therefore less important than it is for most other audit areas.

Design and Perform Analytical Procedures (Phase III)

It is common for auditors to compare the ending balance on the bank reconciliation, deposits in transit, outstanding checks, and other reconciling items with the prior-year reconciliation. Similarly, auditors normally compare the ending balance in cash with previous months' balances. These analytical procedures may uncover misstatements in cash.

The starting point for the verification of the balance in the general bank account is to obtain a bank reconciliation from the client for inclusion in the auditor's documentation. Figure 23-4 shows a bank reconciliation after adjustments. Notice that the bottom figure in the audit schedule is the adjusted balance in the general ledger, which is the balance that should appear on the financial statements. The auditor must determine that the client has made adjustments such as those at the bottom of Figure 23-4 if they are material.

The frame of reference for the audit tests is the bank reconciliation. The balance-related audit objectives and common tests of details of balances are shown in Table 23-1 on page 694. As in all other audit areas, the actual audit procedures depend on the materiality and the risks the auditor has identified in other parts of the audit that are related to cash. Also, because of their close relationship in the audit of year-end cash, the existence of recorded cash in the bank, accuracy, and inclusion of existing cash (completeness) are combined. These three objectives are the most important ones for cash and therefore receive the greatest attention.

The following three procedures merit additional discussion because of their importance and complexity.

Receipt of a Bank Confirmation The direct receipt of a confirmation from every bank or other financial institution with which the client does business is typically done but not required by auditing standards for every audit except when there is an unusually large number of inactive accounts. If the bank does not respond to a confirmation request, the auditor should send a second request or ask the client to telephone the bank. As a convenience to auditors as well as to bankers who are requested to fill out bank confirmations, the AICPA has approved the use of a **standard bank confirmation form**. Figure 23-5 on page 695 is an illustration of a completed standard confirmation. As shown in Figure 23-5, it is called a standard form to confirm account balance information with financial institutions. This standard form has been agreed upon by the AICPA and the American Bankers Association.

The importance of bank confirmations in the audit extends beyond the verification of the actual cash balance. It is typical for the bank to confirm loan information and bank balances on the same form. The confirmation in Figure 23-5 includes three outstanding loans. Information on liabilities to the bank for notes, mortgages, or other debt typically includes the amount of the loan, the date of the loan, its due date, interest rate, and the existence of collateral.

Banks are *not responsible* for searching their records for bank balances or loans beyond those included on the form by the CPA firm's client. A sentence near the bottom of the form obligates banks to inform the CPA firm of any loans not included on the confirmation *about which the bank has knowledge*. The effect of this limited responsibility is to require auditors to satisfy themselves about the completeness objective for unrecorded bank balances and loans from the bank in another manner. Similarly, banks are not expected to inform auditors of such things as open lines of credit, compensating balance requirements, or contingent liabilities for guaranteeing the loans of others. If the auditor wants confirmation of this type of information, a separate confirmation addressing the matters of concern should be obtained from the financial institution.

After the bank confirmation has been received, the balance in the bank account confirmed by the bank should be traced to the amount stated on the bank reconciliation. Similarly, all other information on the reconciliation should be traced to the relevant audit schedules. In any case, if the information is not in agreement, an investigation must be made of the difference.

Receipt of a Cutoff Bank Statement A **cutoff bank statement** is a partial-period bank statement and the related cancelled checks, duplicate deposit slips, and other documents included in bank statements, mailed by the bank directly to the CPA firm's office. The purpose of the cutoff bank statement is to verify the reconciling items on the client's year-end bank reconciliation with evidence that is inaccessible to the client. To fulfill this purpose, the auditor requests the client to have the bank send directly to the auditor the statement for 7 to 10 days subsequent to the balance sheet date.

Many auditors verify the subsequent period bank statement if a cutoff statement is not received directly from the bank. The purpose of this verification is to test whether the client's employees have omitted, added, or altered any of the documents accompanying

FIGURE 23-4 Audit Schedule for a Bank Reconciliation

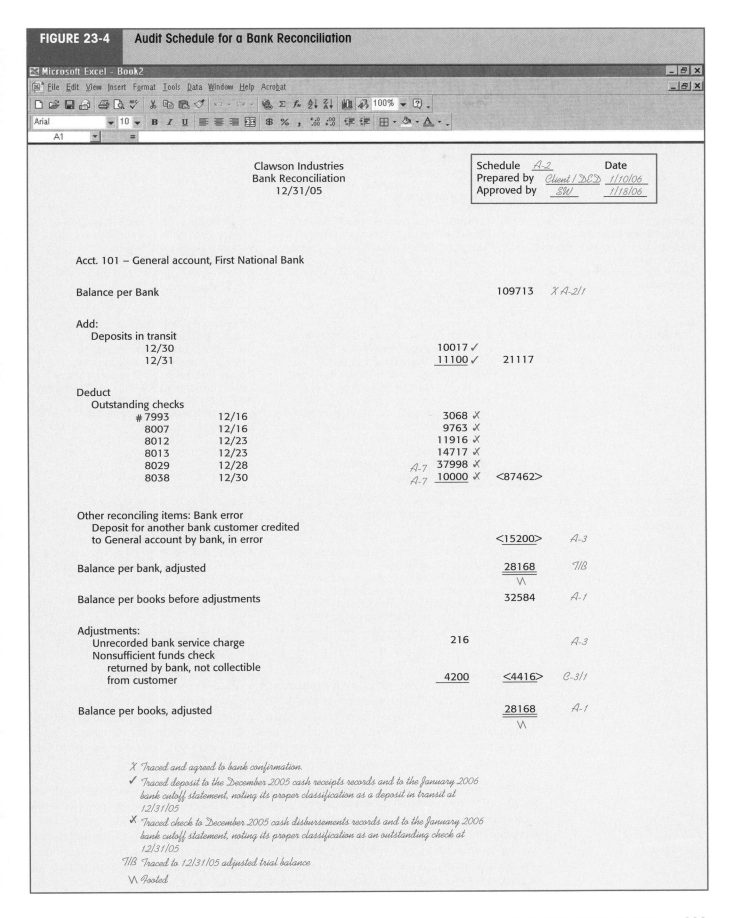

Clawson Industries
Bank Reconciliation
12/31/05

Schedule _A-2_   Date
Prepared by _Client / DED_ 1/10/06
Approved by _SW_   1/18/06

Acct. 101 – General account, First National Bank

Balance per Bank   109713   X A-2/1

Add:
  Deposits in transit
      12/30   10017 ✓
      12/31   11100 ✓   21117

Deduct
  Outstanding checks
      # 7993   12/16   3068 X
        8007   12/16   9763 X
        8012   12/23   11916 X
        8013   12/23   14717 X
        8029   12/28   A-7   37998 X
        8038   12/30   A-7   10000 X   <87462>

Other reconciling items: Bank error
  Deposit for another bank customer credited
  to General account by bank, in error   <15200>   A-3

Balance per bank, adjusted   28168   T/B
                                                            ᴧ

Balance per books before adjustments   32584   A-1

Adjustments:
  Unrecorded bank service charge   216   A-3
  Nonsufficient funds check
    returned by bank, not collectible
    from customer   4200   <4416>   C-3/1

Balance per books, adjusted   28168   A-1
                                                            ᴧ

X Traced and agreed to bank confirmation.
✓ Traced deposit to the December 2005 cash receipts records and to the January 2006
   bank cutoff statement, noting its proper classification as a deposit in transit at
   12/31/05
X Traced check to December 2005 cash disbursements records and to the January 2006
   bank cutoff statement, noting its proper classification as an outstanding check at
   12/31/05
T/B Traced to 12/31/05 adjusted trial balance
ᴧ Footed

Balance-Related Audit Objective	Common Tests of Details of Balances Procedures	Comments
Cash in the bank as stated on the reconciliation foots correctly and agrees with the general ledger (detail tie-in).	Foot the outstanding check list and deposits in transit. Prove the bank reconciliation as to additions and subtractions, including all reconciling items. Trace the book balance on the reconciliation to the general ledger.	These tests are done entirely on the bank reconciliation, with no reference to documents or other records except the general ledger.
Cash in the bank as stated on the reconciliation exists (existence). Existing cash in the bank is recorded (completeness). Cash in the bank as stated on the reconciliation is accurate (accuracy).	*(See extended discussion for each of these.)* Receipt and tests of a bank confirmation. Receipt and tests of a cutoff bank statement. Tests of the bank reconciliation. Extended tests of the bank reconciliation. Proof of cash. Tests for kiting.	These are the three most important objectives for cash in the bank. The procedures are combined because of their close interdependence. The last three procedures should be done only when there are internal control weaknesses.
Cash receipts and cash disbursements transactions are recorded in the proper period (cutoff).	*Cash receipts:* Count the cash on hand on the last day of the year and subsequently trace to deposits in transit and the cash receipts journal. Trace deposits in transit to subsequent period bank statement (cutoff bank statement). *Cash disbursements:* Record the last check number used on the last day of the year and subsequently trace to the outstanding checks and the cash disbursements journal. Trace outstanding checks to subsequent period bank statement.	When cash receipts received after year-end are included in the journal, a better cash position than actually exists is shown. It is called "holding open" the cash receipts journal. Holding open the cash disbursements journal reduces accounts payable and usually overstates the current ratio. The first procedure listed for receipts and disbursements cutoff tests requires the auditor's presence on the client's premises at the end of the last day of the year.
Cash in the bank is properly presented and disclosed (presentation and disclosure).	Examine minutes, loan agreements, and obtain confirmation for restrictions on the use of cash and compensating balances. Review financial statements to make sure (a) material savings accounts and certificates of deposit are disclosed separately from cash in the bank, (b) cash restricted to certain uses and compensating balances are adequately disclosed, and (c) bank overdrafts are included as current liabilities.	An example of a restriction on the use of cash is cash deposited with a trustee for the payment of mortgage interest and taxes on the proceeds of a construction mortgage. A compensating balance is the client's agreement with a bank to maintain a specified minimum in its checking account.

the statement. It is obviously a test for intentional misstatements. The auditor performs the verification in the month subsequent to the balance sheet date by (1) footing all the cancelled checks, debit memos, deposits, and credit memos; (2) checking to see that the bank statement balances when the footed totals are used; and (3) reviewing the items included in the footings to make sure that they were cancelled by the bank in the proper period and do not include any erasures or alterations.

Tests of the Bank Reconciliation As stated earlier, a well-prepared independent bank reconciliation is an essential internal control over cash. The reasons for testing the bank reconciliation are to determine whether client personnel have carefully prepared the bank reconciliation and to verify whether the client's recorded bank balance is the same amount as the actual cash in the bank except for deposits in transit, outstanding checks, and other reconciling items. In testing the reconciliation, the auditor can obtain the information for conducting the tests from the cutoff bank statement. Several major procedures are involved:

- Verify that the client's bank reconciliation is mathematically accurate.
- Trace the balance on the bank confirmation and/or the beginning balance on the cutoff statement to the balance per bank on the bank reconciliation; a reconciliation cannot take place until these balances are the same.
- Trace checks written before year-end and included with the cutoff bank statement to the list of outstanding checks on the bank reconciliation and to the cash disbursements journal in the period or periods prior to the balance sheet date. All checks that cleared

FIGURE 23-5   Standard Confirmation of Financial Institution Account Balance Information

Clawson Industries
Bank Confirmation
12/31/05

Schedule	A-2/1	Date
Prepared by	DCS	1/10/06
Approved by	SW	1/18/06

STANDARD FORM TO CONFIRM ACCOUNT BALANCE INFORMATION WITH FINANCIAL INSTITUTIONS

Clawson Industries
CUSTOMER NAME

[   ]

Financial Institution's Name and Address

First National Bank
200 Oak Street
Midvale, Illinois 40093

[   ]

We have provided to our accountants the following information as of the close of business on **December 31, 2005,** regarding our deposit and loan balances. Please confirm the accuracy of the information, noting any exceptions to the information provided. If the balances have been left blank, please complete this form by furnishing the balance in the appropriate space below.* Although we do not request nor expect you to conduct a comprehensive, detailed search of your records, if during the process of completing this confirmation additional information about other deposit and loan accounts we may have with you comes to your attention, please include such information below. Please use the enclosed envelope to return the form directly to our accountants.

1. At the close of business on the date listed above, our records indicated the following deposit balance(s):

ACCOUNT NAME	ACCOUNT NUMBER	INTEREST RATE	BALANCE*
General account	*19751-974*	*None*	*109,713.11* A-2

2. We were directly liable to the financial institution for loans at the close of business on the date listed above as follows:

ACCOUNT NO./ DESCRIPTION	BALANCE*	DATE DUE	INTEREST RATE	DATE THROUGH WHICH INTEREST IS PAID	DESCRIPTION OF COLLATERAL
N/A	*50,000.00*	*1/9/06*	*10%*	*N/A*	*General*
N/A	*90,000.00*	*1/9/06*	*10%*	*N/A*	*Security*
N/A	*60,000.00*	*1/23/06*	*11%*	*N/A*	*Agreement*

A L Moore   *January 3, 2006*
(Customer's Authorized Signature)   **(Date)**

The information presented above by the customer is in agreement with our records. Although we have not conducted a comprehensive, detailed search of our records, no other deposit or loan accounts have come to our attention except as noted below.

Margaret Davis   *January 10, 2006*
(Financial Institution Authorized Signature)   **(Date)**

Vice President
(Title)

EXCEPTIONS AND/OR COMMENTS
None

Please return this form directly to our accountants:

Jones and Smith CPAs
2111 First Street
Detroit, Michigan 48711

Approved 1990 by American Bankers Association, American Institute of Certified Public Accountants, and Bank Administration Institute. Additional forms available from: AICPA-Order Department, P.O. Box 1003, NY, NY 10108-1003

*Ordinarily, balances are intentionally left blank if they are not available at the time the form is prepared.

the bank after the balance sheet date and were included in the cash disbursements journal should also be included on the outstanding check list. If a check was included in the cash disbursements journal, it should be included as an outstanding check if it did not clear before the balance sheet date. Similarly, if a check cleared the bank before the balance sheet date, it should not be on the bank reconciliation.

- Investigate all significant checks included on the outstanding check list that have not cleared the bank on the cutoff statement. The first step in the investigation should be to trace the amount of any items not clearing to the cash disbursements journal. The reason for the check not being cashed should be discussed with the client, and if the auditor is concerned about the possibility of fraud, the vendor's accounts payable balance should be confirmed to determine whether the vendor has recognized the receipt of the cash in its records. In addition, the cancelled check should be examined before the last day of the audit if it becomes available.
- Trace deposits in transit to the cutoff bank statement. All cash receipts not deposited in the bank at the end of the year should be traced to the cutoff bank statement to make sure that they were deposited shortly after the beginning of the new year.
- Account for other reconciling items on the bank statement and bank reconciliation. These include such items as bank service charges, bank errors and corrections, and unrecorded transactions debited or credited directly to the bank account by the bank. These reconciling items should be investigated carefully to be sure that they have been treated properly by the client.

Figure 23-6 illustrates how the types of audit tests are used to audit the general cash account. Observe in the figure that tests of controls, substantive tests of transactions, and analytical procedures are done for each transaction cycle involving the cash account.

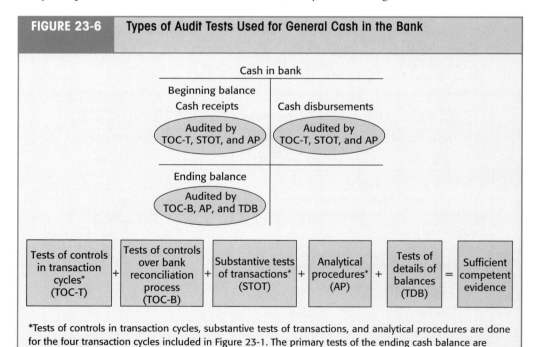

| FIGURE 23-6 | Types of Audit Tests Used for General Cash in the Bank |

Cash in bank

Beginning balance

Cash receipts — Audited by TOC-T, STOT, and AP

Cash disbursements — Audited by TOC-T, STOT, and AP

Ending balance — Audited by TOC-B, AP, and TDB

Tests of controls in transaction cycles* (TOC-T) + Tests of controls over bank reconciliation process (TOC-B) + Substantive tests of transactions* (STOT) + Analytical procedures* (AP) + Tests of details of balances (TDB) = Sufficient competent evidence

*Tests of controls in transaction cycles, substantive tests of transactions, and analytical procedures are done for the four transaction cycles included in Figure 23-1. The primary tests of the ending cash balance are tests of details of balances.

FRAUD-ORIENTED PROCEDURES

OBJECTIVE 23-4

Recognize when to extend audit tests of the general cash account to test further for material fraud.

A major consideration in the audit of the general cash balance is the possibility of fraud. The auditor must extend the procedures in the audit of year-end cash to determine the possibility of a material fraud when there are inadequate internal controls, especially the improper segregation of duties between the handling of cash and the recording of cash transactions in the accounting records.

In designing audit procedures for uncovering fraud, careful consideration should be given to the nature of the weaknesses in internal control, the type of fraud that is likely to result from the weaknesses, the potential materiality of the fraud, and the audit procedures that are most effective in uncovering the fraud. When auditors are specifically testing for fraud, they should keep in mind that audit procedures other than tests of details of cash balances can also be useful. Examples of procedures that may uncover fraud in the cash receipts area include the confirmation of accounts receivable, tests for lapping, reviewing the general ledger entries in the cash account for unusual items, tracing from customer orders to sales and subsequent cash receipts, and examining approvals and supporting documentation for bad debts and sales returns and allowances. Similar tests can be used for testing for the possibility of fraudulent cash disbursements.

Even with reasonably elaborate fraud-oriented procedures, it is extremely difficult to detect fraud, especially omitted transactions and account balances. If, for example, a company has illegal offshore cash accounts and makes deposits to those accounts from unrecorded sales, it is unlikely that an auditor will uncover the fraud. Nevertheless, auditors are responsible for making a reasonable effort to detect fraud when they have reason to believe it may exist. The following procedures for uncovering fraud that are directly related to year-end cash balances are discussed in this section: extended tests of the bank reconciliation, proofs of cash, and tests of interbank transfers.

When the auditor believes that the year-end bank reconciliation may be intentionally misstated, it is appropriate to perform extended tests of the year-end bank reconciliation. The purpose of the extended procedures is to verify whether all transactions included in the journals for the last month of the year were correctly included in or excluded from the bank reconciliation and to verify whether all items in the bank reconciliation were correctly included. Let us assume that there are material internal control weaknesses and the client's year-end is December 31. A common approach is to start with the bank reconciliation for November and compare all reconciling items with cancelled checks and other documents in the December bank statement. In addition, all remaining cancelled checks and deposit slips in the December bank statement should be compared with the December cash disbursements and receipts journals. All uncleared items in the November bank reconciliation and the December cash disbursements and receipts journals should be included in the client's December 31 bank reconciliation. Similarly, all reconciling items in the December 31 bank reconciliation should be items from the November bank reconciliation and December's journals that have not yet cleared the bank.

In addition to the tests just described, the auditor must carry out procedures subsequent to the end of the year with the use of the bank cutoff statement. These tests would be performed in the same manner as previously discussed.

Extended Tests of the Bank Reconciliation

CASH FRAUD SCHEMES

The Association of Certified Fraud Examiners (ACFE) 2002 study of 663 occupational frauds found that while the largest losses tended to result from fraudulent financial reporting, asset misappropriations were by far the most common type of fraud scheme, accounting for over 80% of the cases studied. As expected, the asset most likely to be targeted by dishonest employees is cash. Cash fraud schemes can generally be divided into three categories:

1. **Fraudulent disbursements**—Examples include the submission of false invoices, false timecards, or false reimbursement requests and the recording of false entries in the cash disbursements journal to conceal the theft of cash.

2. **Skimming**—Cash is stolen from an organization before it is recorded in the accounting records.

3. **Cash larceny**—Cash is stolen from an organization after it has been recorded in the accounting records.

Among these three categories, fraudulent disbursements were reported most frequently in the ACFE study and had the highest median loss, with an average cost of $100,000 per occurence.

Source: 2002 Report to the Nation: Occupational Fraud and Abuse, Association of Certified Fraud Examiners, 2002, Austin, Texas.

Proof of Cash

Auditors sometimes prepare a proof of cash when the client has material internal control weaknesses in cash. The auditor uses a proof of cash to determine whether the following were done:

- All recorded cash receipts were deposited.
- All deposits in the bank were recorded in the accounting records.
- All recorded cash disbursements were paid by the bank.
- All amounts that were paid by the bank were recorded.

A **proof of cash** includes the following:

- A reconciliation of the balance on the bank statement with the general ledger balance at the beginning of the proof-of-cash period
- A reconciliation of cash receipts deposited per the bank with the cash receipts journal for a given period
- A reconciliation of cancelled checks clearing the bank with the cash disbursements journal for a given period
- A reconciliation of the balance on the bank statement with the general ledger balance at the end of the proof-of-cash period

A proof of cash of this nature is commonly called a four-column proof of cash—one column is used for each of the types of information just listed. A proof of cash can be performed for one or more interim months, the entire year, or the last month of the year. Figure 23-7 shows a four-column proof of cash for an interim month.

The concern in an interim-month proof of cash is not with adjusting account balances, but rather with reconciling the amounts per books and bank.

When a proof of cash is done, the auditor is combining substantive tests of transactions and tests of details of balances. For example, a proof of cash receipts is a test of recorded transactions, whereas a bank reconciliation is a test of the balance in cash at a point in time. A proof of cash is an excellent method of comparing recorded cash receipts and disbursements with the bank account and with the bank reconciliation. However, the auditor must recognize that a proof of cash disbursements is not effective for discovering checks written for an improper amount, fraudulent checks, or other misstatements in which the dollar amount appearing on the cash disbursements records is incorrect. Similarly, proof-of-cash receipts is not useful for uncovering the theft of cash receipts or the recording and deposit of an improper amount of cash.

Tests of Interbank Transfers

Embezzlers occasionally cover a defalcation of cash by a practice known as **kiting**: transferring money from one bank to another and improperly recording the transaction. Near the balance sheet date, a check is drawn on one bank account and immediately deposited in a second account for credit before the end of the accounting period. In making this transfer, the embezzler is careful to make sure that the check is deposited at a late enough date so that it does not clear the first bank until after the end of the period. If the interbank transfer is not recorded until after the balance sheet date, the amount of the transfer is recorded as an asset in both banks. Although there are other ways of perpetrating this fraud, each involves the device of increasing the bank balance to cover a shortage by the use of interbank transfers.

A useful approach to test for kiting, as well as for unintentional errors in recording interbank transfers, is to list all interbank transfers made a few days before and after the balance sheet date and to trace each to the accounting records for proper recording. An example of an interbank transfer schedule is included in Figure 23-8 (p. 700). The schedule shows that four interbank transfers were made shortly before and after the balance sheet date.

There are several things that should be audited on the interbank transfer schedule.

- *The accuracy of the information on the interbank transfer schedule should be verified.* The auditor should compare the disbursement and receipt information on the schedule to the cash disbursements and cash receipts records to make sure that it is accurate. Similarly, the dates on the schedule for transfers that were received and disbursed should be compared with the bank statement. Finally, cash disbursements and receipts records should be examined to make sure that all transfers a few days before and after the balance sheet date have been included on the schedule. The tick mark explanations on the schedule in Figure 23-8 indicate that these steps have been taken.

FIGURE 23-7	Interim Proof of Cash

Clawson Industries
Interim Proof of Cash
6/30/05

Schedule	A-5	Date	
Prepared by	JG	7/15/05
Approved by	RP	7/17/05

Acct. 101 – General account, First National Bank

		5/31/05	Receipts	Disbursements	6/30/05
Balance per Bank	①	121782.12	627895.20	631111.96	118565.36
Deposits in transit					
5/31	②	21720.00	<21720.00>		
6/30	②		16592.36		16592.36
Outstanding checks					
5/31	③	<36396.50>		<36396.50>	
6/30	③			14800.10	<14800.10>
NSF checks	④		<4560.00>	<4560.00>	
To allow for effect of a cash disbursement recorded as a credit item in cash receipts journal			<8500.00>	<8500.00>	
Balance per bank, adjusted		107105.62	609707.56	596455.56	120357.62
Balance per books, unadjusted		107105.62	609707.56	597957.04	118856.14
Bank debit memos	⑤			120.00	<120.00>
Payroll checks erroneously entered in General Disbursements Journal	⑥			<1621.48>	1621.48
Balance per books, adjusted		107105.62	609707.56	596455.56	120357.62

① Per 6/30/05 bank statement.
② Detailed listing filed below; traced to subsequent bank statements.
③ Outstanding-check list filed below; examined cancelled checks.
④ Detailed listing filed below; all NSF items were redeposited in June and had all cleared as of 6/30/05.
⑤ Safety deposit rentals; traced to recording via journal entry.
     Requested list of contents of safety deposit boxes.
⑥ Traced to journal entry correcting error.

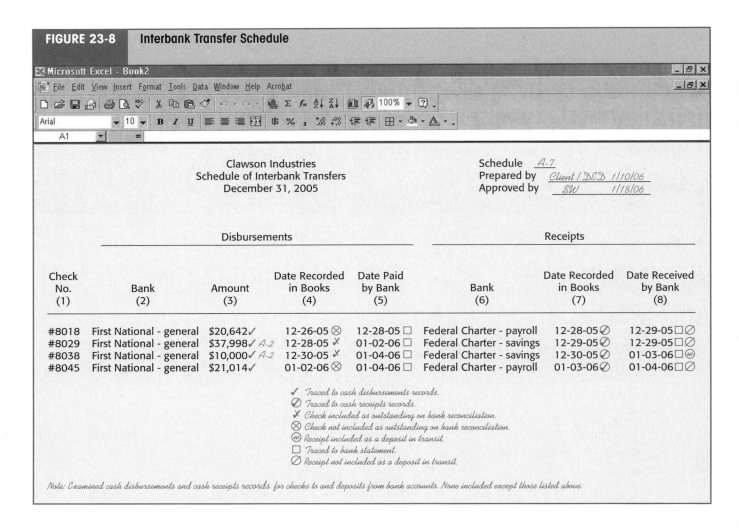

FIGURE 23-8 | **Interbank Transfer Schedule**

Clawson Industries
Schedule of Interbank Transfers
December 31, 2005

Schedule _A-7_
Prepared by _Client / DCD 1/10/06_
Approved by _SW   1/18/06_

	Disbursements					Receipts		
Check No. (1)	Bank (2)	Amount (3)	Date Recorded in Books (4)	Date Paid by Bank (5)	Bank (6)	Date Recorded in Books (7)	Date Received by Bank (8)
#8018	First National - general	$20,642✓	12-26-05 ⊗	12-28-05 ☐	Federal Charter - payroll	12-28-05 ⊘	12-29-05 ☐⊘
#8029	First National - general	$37,998✓ A-2	12-28-05 ✗	01-02-06 ☐	Federal Charter - savings	12-29-05 ⊘	12-29-05 ☐⊘
#8038	First National - general	$10,000✓ A-2	12-30-05 ✗	01-04-06 ☐	Federal Charter - savings	12-30-05 ⊘	01-03-06 ☐ⓦ
#8045	First National - general	$21,014✓	01-02-06 ⊗	01-04-06 ☐	Federal Charter - payroll	01-03-06 ⊘	01-04-06 ☐⊘

✓ Traced to cash disbursements records.
⊘ Traced to cash receipts records.
✗ Check included as outstanding on bank reconciliation.
⊗ Check not included as outstanding on bank reconciliation.
ⓦ Receipt included as a deposit in transit.
☐ Traced to bank statement.
⊘ Receipt not included as a deposit in transit.

Note: Examined cash disbursements and cash receipts records for checks to and deposits from bank accounts. None included except those listed above.

- *The interbank transfers must be recorded in both the receiving and disbursing banks.* If, for example, there was a $10,000 transfer from Bank A to Bank B but only the disbursement was recorded, this is evidence of an attempt to conceal a cash theft.
- *The date of the recording of the disbursements and receipts for each transfer must be in the same fiscal year.* In Figure 23-8, the dates in the two "date recorded in books" columns [columns (4) and (7)] are in the same period for each transfer; therefore, they are correct. If a cash receipt was recorded in the current fiscal year and the disbursement in the subsequent fiscal year, it may be an attempt to cover a cash shortage.
- *Disbursements on the interbank transfer schedule should be correctly included in or excluded from year-end bank reconciliations as outstanding checks.* In Figure 23-8, the 12-31-05 bank reconciliation for the general cash account should include outstanding checks for the second and third transfers but not the other two. [Compare the dates in columns (4) and (5).] Understating outstanding checks on the bank reconciliation indicates the possibility of kiting.
- *Receipts on the interbank transfer schedule should be correctly included in or excluded from year-end bank reconciliations as deposits in transit.* In Figure 23-8, the 12-31-05 bank reconciliations for the savings and payroll accounts should indicate a deposit in transit for the third transfer but not for the other three. (Compare the dates for each transfer in the last two columns.) Overstating deposits in transit on the bank reconciliation indicates the possibility of kiting.

Even though audit tests of interbank transfers are usually fraud oriented, they are often performed on audits in which there are numerous bank transfers, regardless of internal controls. When there are numerous interbank transfers, it is difficult to be sure that each is

ELECTRONIC TRANSFER OF CASH	Many organizations use electronic transfer when they are transferring cash among banks, collecting from customers, and paying vendors. Companies engaging in e-commerce sales activities may receive electronic funds from credit card agencies submitting payments on behalf of customers. Under these systems, cash is transferred instantly. For example, when Company A collects from Credit Card Agency X, the cash is instantly transferred from Credit Card	Agency X's bank account to Company A's. There is no check. Electronic transfers have the potential to improve internal controls in that no cash is handled by employees. However, there is also potential risk of cash thefts through inappropriate cash transfers. It is essential that excellent internal controls be in place for electronic transfers.

correctly handled unless a schedule of transfers near the end of the year is prepared and each transfer is traced to the accounting records and bank statements. In addition to the possibility of kiting, inaccurate handling of transfers could result in a misclassification between cash and accounts payable. The materiality of transfers and the relative ease of performing the tests make many auditors believe they should always be performed.

AUDIT OF THE IMPREST PAYROLL BANK ACCOUNT

OBJECTIVE 23-5

Design and perform audit tests of the imprest payroll bank account.

Tests of the payroll bank reconciliation should take only a few minutes if there is an imprest payroll account and an independent reconciliation of the bank account such as that described for the general account. Typically, the only reconciling items are outstanding checks, and for most audits, the great majority clear shortly after the checks are issued. In testing the payroll bank account balances, it is necessary to obtain a bank reconciliation, a bank confirmation, and a cutoff bank statement. The reconciliation procedures are performed in the same manner as those described for general cash except that tests of the outstanding checks are normally limited to a reasonableness test. Naturally, extended procedures are necessary if the controls are inadequate or if the bank account does not reconcile with the general ledger imprest cash balance.

Keep in mind that these procedures pertain only to the imprest bank account, not to the overall payroll cycle. Auditing the payroll cycle was discussed in detail in an earlier chapter.

AUDIT OF IMPREST PETTY CASH

OBJECTIVE 23-6

Design and perform audit tests of imprest petty cash.

Petty cash is a unique account because it is often immaterial in amount, yet it is verified on many audits. The account is verified primarily because of the potential for defalcation and the client's expectation of auditor consideration even when the amount is immaterial.

Internal Controls Over Petty Cash

The most important internal control for petty cash is the use of an imprest fund that is the responsibility of *one individual*. In addition, petty cash funds should not be mingled with other receipts, and the fund should be kept separate from all other activities. There should also be limits on the amount of any expenditure from petty cash, as well as on the total amount of the fund. The type of expenditure that can be made from petty cash transactions should be well defined by company policy.

When a disbursement is made from petty cash, adequate internal controls require a responsible official's approval on a prenumbered petty cash form. The total of the actual cash and checks in the fund plus the total unreimbursed petty cash forms that represent actual expenditures should equal the total amount of the petty cash fund stated in the general ledger. Periodically, surprise counts and a reconciliation of the petty cash fund should be made by the internal auditor or other responsible official.

When the petty cash balance runs low, a check payable to the petty cash custodian should be written on the general cash account for the reimbursement of petty cash. The check should be for the exact amount of the prenumbered vouchers that are submitted as evidence of actual expenditures. These vouchers should be verified by the accounts payable clerk and cancelled to prevent their reuse.

Audit Tests for Petty Cash

The emphasis in verifying petty cash should be on testing controls over petty cash transactions rather than the ending balance in the account. Even if the amount of the petty cash fund is small, there is potential for numerous improper transactions if the fund is frequently reimbursed.

An important part of testing petty cash is first to determine the client's procedures for handling the fund by discussing internal controls with the custodian and examining the documentation of a few transactions. As a part of obtaining an understanding of internal control, it is necessary to identify internal controls and weaknesses. Even though most petty cash systems are not complex, it is often desirable to use a flowchart and an internal control questionnaire, primarily for documentation in subsequent audits.

Tests of controls and substantive tests of transactions depend on the number and size of the petty cash reimbursements and the auditor's assessed control risk. When control risk is assessed as low and there are few reimbursement payments during the year, it is common for auditors not to test any further, for reasons of immateriality. When the auditor decides to test petty cash, the two most common procedures are to count the petty cash balance and to carry out detailed tests of one or two reimbursement transactions. In such a case, the primary procedures should include footing the petty cash vouchers supporting the amount of the reimbursement, accounting for a sequence of petty cash vouchers, examining the petty cash vouchers for authorization and cancellation, and examining the attached documentation for reasonableness. Typical supporting documentation includes cash register tapes, invoices, and receipts.

Petty cash tests can ordinarily be performed at any time during the year, but as a matter of convenience, they are typically done on an interim date. If the balance in the petty cash fund is considered material, which is rarely the case, it should be counted at the end of the year. Unreimbursed expenditures should be examined as a part of the count to determine whether the amount of unrecorded expenses is material.

SUMMARY

We have seen in this chapter that transactions in most cycles affect the cash account. Because of the relationship between transactions in several cycles and the ending cash account balance, the auditor typically waits to audit the ending cash balance until the results of tests of controls and substantive tests of transactions for all cycles are completed and analyzed. As shown in this chapter, tests of the cash balance normally include tests of the bank reconciliations of key cash accounts, such as the general cash account, imprest payroll account, and imprest petty cash fund. If the auditor assesses a high likelihood of fraud in cash, additional tests may also be performed, such as extended bank reconciliation procedures, a proof of cash, or tests of interbank transfers.

ESSENTIAL TERMS

Bank reconciliation—the monthly reconciliation, usually prepared by client personnel, of the differences between the cash balance recorded in the general ledger and the amount in the bank account

Branch bank accounts—separate bank accounts maintained at local banks by branches of a company

Cash equivalents—excess cash invested in short-term, highly liquid investments such as time deposits, certificates of deposit, and money market funds

Cutoff bank statement—a partial-period bank statement and the related cancelled checks, duplicate deposit slips, and other documents included in bank statements, mailed by the bank directly to the auditor; the auditor uses it to verify reconciling items on the client's year-end bank reconciliation

General cash account—the primary bank account for most organizations; virtually all cash receipts and disbursements flow through this account at some time

Imprest payroll account—a bank account to which the exact amount of payroll for the pay period is transferred by check or electronic transfer from the employer's general cash account

Imprest petty cash fund—a fund of cash maintained within the company for small cash acquisitions or to cash employees' checks; the fund's fixed balance is comparatively small and is periodically reimbursed

Kiting—the transfer of money from one bank to another and improperly recording the transfer so that the amount is recorded as an asset in both accounts; this practice is used by embezzlers to cover a defalcation of cash

Proof of cash—a four-column audit schedule prepared by the auditor to reconcile the bank's record of the client's beginning balance, cash deposits, cleared checks, and ending balance for the period with the client's records

Standard bank confirmation form—a form approved by the AICPA and American Bankers Association through which the bank responds to the auditor about bank balance and loan information provided on the confirmation

REVIEW QUESTIONS

23-1 (Objectives 23-1, 23-2) Explain the relationships among the initial assessed control risk, tests of controls and substantive tests of transactions for cash receipts, and the tests of details of cash balances.

23-2 (Objectives 23-1, 23-2) Explain the relationships among the initial assessed control risk, tests of controls and substantive tests of transactions for cash disbursements, and the tests of details of cash balances. Give one example in which the conclusions reached about internal controls in cash disbursements would affect the tests of cash balances.

23-3 (Objective 23-3) Why is the monthly reconciliation of bank accounts by an independent person an important internal control over cash balances? Which individuals would generally not be considered independent for this responsibility?

23-4 (Objective 23-3) Evaluate the effectiveness and state the shortcomings of the preparation of a bank reconciliation by the controller in the manner described in the following statement: "When I reconcile the bank account, the first thing I do is to sort the checks in numerical order and find which numbers are missing. Next I determine the amount of the uncleared checks by referring to the cash disbursements journal. If the bank account reconciles at that point, I am all finished with the reconciliation. If it does not, I search for deposits in transit, checks from the beginning outstanding check list that still have not cleared, other reconciling items, and bank errors until it reconciles. In most instances, I can do the reconciliation in 20 minutes."

23-5 (Objective 23-3) How do bank confirmations differ from positive confirmations of accounts receivable? Distinguish between them in terms of the nature of the information confirmed, the sample size, and the appropriate action when the confirmation is not returned after the second request. Explain the rationale for the differences between these two types of confirmations.

23-6 (Objective 23-3) Evaluate the necessity of following the practice described by an auditor: "In confirming bank accounts I insist upon a response from every bank the client has done business with in the past 2 years, even though the account may be closed at the balance sheet date."

23-7 (Objective 23-3) Describe what is meant by a cutoff bank statement and state its purpose.

23-8 (Objective 23-3) Why are auditors usually less concerned about the client's cash receipts cutoff than the cutoff for sales? Explain the procedure involved in testing for the cutoff for cash receipts.

23-9 (Objective 23-2) What is meant by an imprest bank account for a branch operation? Explain the purpose of using this type of bank account.

23-10 (Objective 23-4) Explain the purpose of a four-column proof of cash. List two types of misstatements it is meant to uncover.

23-11 (Objective 23-3) When the auditor fails to obtain a cutoff bank statement, it is common to verify the entire statement for the month subsequent to the balance sheet date. How is this done and what is its purpose?

23-12 (Objective 23-4) Distinguish between lapping and kiting. Describe audit procedures that can be used to uncover each.

23-13 (Objective 23-5) Assume that a client with excellent internal controls uses an imprest payroll bank account. Explain why the verification of the payroll bank reconciliation ordinarily takes less time than the tests of the general bank account, even if the number of checks exceeds those written on the general account.

23-14 (Objective 23-6) Distinguish between the verification of petty cash reimbursements and the verification of the balance in the fund. Explain how each is done. Which is more important?

23-15 (Objectives 23-3, 23-4) Why is there a greater emphasis on the detection of fraud in tests of details of cash balances than for other balance sheet accounts? Give two specific examples that demonstrate how this emphasis affects the auditor's evidence accumulation in auditing year-end cash.

23-16 (Objective 23-3) Explain why, in verifying bank reconciliations, most auditors emphasize the possibility of a nonexistent deposit in transit being included in the reconciliation and an outstanding check being omitted rather than the omission of a deposit in transit and the inclusion of a nonexistent outstanding check.

23-17 (Objective 23-3) How would a company's bank reconciliation reflect an electronic deposit of cash received by the bank from credit card agencies making payments on behalf of customers purchasing products from the company's online Web site, but not recorded in the company's records?

MULTIPLE CHOICE QUESTIONS FROM CPA EXAMINATIONS

23-18 (Objectives 23-3, 23-4) The following questions deal with auditing year-end cash. Choose the best response.

a. A CPA obtains a January 10 cutoff bank statement for his client directly from the bank. Few of the outstanding checks listed on his client's December 31 bank reconciliation cleared during the cutoff period. A probable cause for this is that the client
   (1) is engaged in kiting.
   (2) is engaged in lapping.
   (3) transmitted the checks to the payees after year-end.
   (4) has overstated its year-end bank balance.

b. The auditor should ordinarily mail confirmation requests to all banks with which the client has conducted any business during the year, regardless of the year-end balance, because
   (1) the confirmation form also seeks information about indebtedness to the bank.
   (2) this procedure will detect kiting activities that would otherwise not be detected.
   (3) the mailing of confirmation forms to all such banks is required by auditing standards.
   (4) this procedure relieves the auditor of any responsibility with respect to nondetection of forged checks.

c. The usefulness of the standard bank confirmation request may be limited because the bank employee who completes the form may
   (1) not believe the bank is obligated to verify confidential information to a third party.
   (2) sign and return the form without inspecting the accuracy of the client's bank reconciliation.
   (3) not have access to the client's bank statement.
   (4) be unaware of all the financial relationships that the bank has with the client.

23-19 (Objective 23-4) The following questions deal with discovering fraud in auditing year-end cash. Choose the best response.

a. Which of the following is one of the better auditing techniques to detect kiting?
   (1) Review composition of authenticated deposit slips.
   (2) Review subsequent bank statements and cancelled checks received directly from the banks.
   (3) Prepare a schedule of bank transfers from the client's books.
   (4) Prepare year-end bank reconciliations.

b. The cashier of Baker Company covered a shortage in his cash working fund with cash obtained on December 31 from a local bank by cashing an unrecorded check drawn on the company's New York bank. The auditor would discover this manipulation by
   (1) preparing independent bank reconciliations as of December 31.
   (2) counting the cash working fund at the close of business on December 31.
   (3) investigating items returned with the bank cutoff statements.
   (4) confirming the December 31 bank balances.

c. A cash shortage may be concealed by transporting funds from one location to another or by converting negotiable assets to cash. Because of this, which of the following is vital?
   (1) Simultaneous bank confirmations.
   (2) Simultaneous bank reconciliations.
   (3) Simultaneous four-column proofs of cash.
   (4) Simultaneous surprise cash counts.

DISCUSSION QUESTIONS AND PROBLEMS

23-20 (Objectives 23-3, 23-4) The following are misstatements that might be found in the client's year-end cash balance (assume that the balance sheet date is June 30):

1. A check was omitted from the outstanding check list on the June 30 bank reconciliation. It cleared the bank July 7.

2. A check was omitted from the outstanding check list on the bank reconciliation. It cleared the bank September 6.
3. Cash receipts collected on accounts receivable from July 1 to July 5 were included as June 29 and 30 cash receipts.
4. A loan from the bank on June 26 was credited directly to the client's bank account. The loan was not entered as of June 30.
5. A check that was dated June 26 and disbursed in June was not recorded in the cash disbursements journal, but it was included as an outstanding check on June 30.
6. A bank transfer recorded in the accounting records on July 1 was included as a deposit in transit on June 30.
7. The outstanding checks on the June 30 bank reconciliation were underfooted by $2,000.

a. Assuming that each of these misstatements was intentional (fraud), state the most likely motivation of the person responsible.

b. What control could be instituted for each fraud to reduce the likelihood of occurrence?

c. List an audit procedure that could be used to discover each fraud.

23-21 (Objectives 23-3, 23-4) The following audit procedures are concerned with tests of details of general cash balances:

1. Compare the bank cancellation date with the date on the cancelled check for checks dated on or shortly before the balance sheet date.
2. Trace deposits in transit on the bank reconciliation to the cutoff bank statement and the current year cash receipts journal.
3. Obtain a standard bank confirmation from each bank with which the client does business.
4. Compare the balance on the bank reconciliation obtained from the client with the bank confirmation.
5. Compare the checks returned along with the cutoff bank statement with the list of outstanding checks on the bank reconciliation.
6. List the check number, payee, and amount of all material checks not returned with the cutoff bank statement.
7. Review minutes of the board of directors meetings, loan agreements, and bank confirmation for interest-bearing deposits, restrictions on the withdrawal of cash, and compensating balance agreements.
8. Prepare a four-column proof of cash.

Explain the objective of each.

Required

23-22 (Objective 23-3) You are auditing general cash for the Pittsburg Supply Company for the fiscal year ended July 31, 2005. The client has not prepared the July 31 bank reconciliation. After a brief discussion with the owner, you agree to prepare the reconciliation, with assistance from one of Pittsburg Supply's clerks. You obtain the following information:

	General Ledger	Bank Statement
Beginning balance 7/1/05	$ 4,611	$ 5,753
Deposits		25,056
Cash receipts journal	25,456	
Checks cleared		(23,615)
Cash disbursements journal	(21,811)	
July bank service charge		(87)
Note paid directly		(6,100)
NSF check		(311)
Ending balance 7/31/05	$ 8,256	$ 696

June 30 Bank Reconciliation

**Information in General
Ledger and Bank Statement**

Balance per bank	$5,753
Deposits in transit	600
Outstanding checks	1,742
Balance per books	4,611

CHAPTER 23 / AUDIT OF CASH BALANCES   705

Additional information obtained is as follows:

1. Checks clearing that were outstanding on June 30 totaled $1,692.
2. Checks clearing that were recorded in the July disbursements journal totaled $20,467.
3. A check for $1,060 cleared the bank but had not been recorded in the cash disbursements journal. It was for an acquisition of inventory. Pittsburg Supply uses the periodic-inventory method.
4. A check for $396 was charged to Pittsburg Supply but had been written on a different company's bank account.
5. Deposits included $600 from June and $24,456 for July.
6. The bank charged Pittsburg Supply's account for a nonsufficient check totaling $311. The credit manager concluded that the customer intentionally closed its account and the owner left the city. The check was turned over to a collection agency.
7. A note for $5,800, plus interest, was paid directly to the bank under an agreement signed 4 months ago. The note payable was recorded at $5,800 on Pittsburg Supply's books.

Required

a. Prepare a bank reconciliation that shows both the unadjusted and adjusted balance per books.

b. Prepare all adjusting entries.

c. What audit procedures would you use to verify each item in the bank reconciliation?

d. What is the cash balance that should appear on the July 31, 2005, financial statements?

23-23 (Objectives 23-3, 23-4) In the audit of the Regional Transport Company, a large branch that maintains its own bank account, cash is periodically transferred to the central account in Cedar Rapids. On the branch account's records, bank transfers are recorded as a debit to the home office clearing account and a credit to the branch bank account. Similarly, the home office account is recorded as a debit to the central bank account and a credit to the branch office clearing account. Gordon Light is the head bookkeeper for both the home office and the branch bank accounts. Because he also reconciles the bank account, the senior auditor, Cindy Marintette, is concerned about the internal control weakness.

As a part of the year-end audit of bank transfers, Marintette asks you to schedule the transfers for the last few days in 2004 and the first few days of 2005. You prepare the following list:

Amount of Transfer	Date Recorded in the Home Office Cash Receipts Journal	Date Recorded in the Branch Office Cash Disbursements Journal	Date Deposited in the Home Office Bank Account	Date Cleared the Branch Bank Account
$12,000	12-27-04	12-29-04	12-26-04	12-27-04
26,000	12-28-04	01-02-05	12-28-04	12-29-04
14,000	01-02-05	12-30-04	12-28-04	12-29-04
11,000	12-26-04	12-26-04	12-28-04	01-03-05
15,000	01-02-05	01-02-05	12-28-04	12-31-04
28,000	01-07-05	01-05-05	12-28-04	01-03-05
37,000	01-04-05	01-06-05	01-03-05	01-05-05

Required

a. In verifying each bank transfer, state the appropriate audit procedures you should perform.

b. Prepare any adjusting entries required in the home office records.

c. Prepare any adjusting entries required in the branch bank records.

d. State how each bank transfer should be included in the December 31, 2004, bank reconciliation for the home office account after your adjustments in part b.

e. State how each bank transfer should be included in the December 31, 2004, bank reconciliation of the branch bank account after your adjustments in part c.

23-24 (Objective 23-3) In connection with an audit you are given the following worksheet:

Bank Reconciliation, December 31, 2005

Balance per ledger December 31, 2005		$17,174.86
Add:		
Cash receipts received on the last day of December and charged to "cash in bank" on books but not deposited		2,662.25
Debit memo for customer's check returned unpaid (check is on hand but no entry has been made on the books)		200.00
Debit memo for bank service charge for December		5.50
		$20,142.61
Deduct:		
Checks drawn but not paid by bank (see detailed list below)	$2,267.75	
Credit memo for proceeds of a note receivable that had been left at the bank for collection but which has not been recorded as collected	400.00	
Checks for an account payable entered on books as $240.90 but drawn and paid by bank as $419.00	178.10	(2,945.85)
Computed balance		17,196.76
Unlocated difference		(200.00)
Balance per bank (checked to confirmation)		$16,996.76

Checks Drawn but Not Paid by Bank

No.	Amount
573	$ 67.27
724	9.90
903	456.67
907	305.50
911	482.75
913	550.00
914	366.76
916	10.00
917	218.90
	$2,267.75

Required

   a. Prepare a corrected reconciliation.

   b. Prepare journal entries for items that should be adjusted prior to closing the books.*

23-25 (Objective 23-4) You are doing the first-year audit of Sherman School District and have been assigned responsibility for doing a four-column proof of cash for the month of October 2005. You obtain the following information:

1. Balance per books	September 30	$8,106
	October 31	3,850
2. Balance per bank	September 30	5,411
	October 31	6,730
3. Outstanding checks	September 30	916
	October 31	1,278
4. Cash receipts for October	per bank	26,536
	per books	19,711
5. Deposits in transit	September 30	3,611
	October 31	693

   6. Interest on a bank loan for the month of October, charged by the bank but not recorded, was $596.

*AICPA adapted.

7. Proceeds on a note of the Jones Company were collected by the bank on October 28 but were not entered on the books:

Principal	$3,300
Interest	307
	$3,607

8. On October 26, a $407 check of the Billings Company was charged to Sherman School District's account by the bank in error.

9. Dishonored checks are not recorded on the books unless they permanently fail to clear the bank. The bank treats them as disbursements when they are dishonored and deposits when they are redeposited. Checks totaling $609 were dishonored in October; $300 was redeposited in October and $309 in November.

Required

a. Prepare a four-column proof of cash for the month ended October 31. It should show both adjusted and unadjusted cash.

b. Prepare all adjusting entries.

CASE

23-26 (Objective 23-4) The following information was obtained in an audit of the cash account of Tuck Company as of December 31, 2005. Assume that the CPA has satisfied himself as to the propriety of the cash book, the bank statements, and the returned checks, except as noted.

1. The bookkeeper's bank reconciliation at November 30, 2005.

Balance per bank statement		$19,400
Add: Deposit in transit		1,100
Total		$20,500
Less: Outstanding checks		
#2540	$140	
#1501	750	
#1503	580	
#1504	800	
#1505	30	(2,300)
Balance per books		$18,200

2. A summary of the bank statement for December 2005.

Balance brought forward	$ 19,400
Deposits	148,700
	168,100
Charges	(132,500)
Balance, December 31, 2005	$ 35,600

3. A summary of the cash book for December 2005 before adjustments.

Balance brought forward	$ 18,200
Receipts	149,690
	167,890
Disbursements	(124,885)
Balance, December 31, 2005	$ 43,005

4. Included with cancelled checks returned with the December bank statement were the checks listed on page 709.

5. The Tuck Company discounted its own 60-day note for $9,000 with the bank on December 1, 2005. The discount rate was 6%. The accountant recorded the proceeds as a cash receipt at the face value of the note.

6. The accountant records customers' dishonored checks as a reduction of cash receipts. When the dishonored checks are redeposited, they are recorded as a regular cash receipt. Two N.S.F. checks for $180 and $220 were returned by the bank during December. Both checks were redeposited and were recorded by the accountant.

7. Cancellations of Tuck Company checks are recorded by a reduction of cash disbursements.

8. December bank charges were $20. In addition, a $10 service charge was made in December for the collection of a foreign draft in November. These charges were not recorded on the books.

9. Check 2540 listed in the November outstanding checks was drawn in 2003. Because the payee cannot be located, the president of Tuck Company agreed to the CPA's suggestion that the check be written back into the accounts by a journal entry.
10. Outstanding checks at December 31, 2005, totaled $4,000, excluding checks 2540 and 1504.
11. The cutoff bank statement disclosed that the bank had recorded a deposit of $2,400 on January 2, 2006. The accountant had recorded this deposit on the books on December 31, 2005, and then mailed the deposit to the bank.

Number	Date of Check	Amount of Check	Comment
1501	November 28, 2005	$ 75	This check was in payment of an invoice for $750 and was recorded in the cash book as $750.
1503	November 28, 2005	$ 580	This check was in payment of an invoice for $580 and was recorded in the cash book as $580.
1523	December 5, 2005	$ 150	Examination of this check revealed that it was unsigned. A discussion with the client disclosed that it had been mailed inadvertently before it was signed. The check was endorsed and deposited by the payee and processed by the bank even though it was a legal nullity. The check was recorded in the cash disbursements journal.
1528	December 12, 2005	$ 800	This check replaced 1504, which was returned by the payee because it was mutilated. Check 1504 was not cancelled on the books.
—	December 19, 2005	$ 200	This was a counter check drawn at the bank by the president of the company as a cash advance for travel expense. The president overlooked informing the bookkeeper about the check.
—	December 20, 2005	$ 300	The drawer of this check was the Tucker Company.
1535	December 20, 2005	$ 350	This check had been labeled N.S.F. and returned to the payee because the bank had erroneously believed that the check was drawn by the Luck Company. Subsequently, the payee was advised to redeposit the check.
1575	January 5, 2006	$10,000	This check was given to the payee on December 30, 2005, as a postdated check with the understanding that it would not be deposited until January 5. The check was not recorded on the books in December.

Required

Prepare a four-column proof of cash of the cash receipts and cash disbursements recorded on the bank statement and on the company's books for the month of December 2005. The reconciliation should agree with the cash figure that will appear in the company's financial statements.*

INTERNET PROBLEM 23-1: ELECTRONIC MONEY

Reference the CW site. The U.S. Treasury Department's Financial Management Service has developed Pay.gov to provide electronic collection methods that facilitate the ability of Federal agencies to conduct transactions online. This problem requires students to access the Pay.gov Web site to answer questions about Pay.gov services.

*AICPA adapted.

COMPLETING THE AUDIT

The last of the four phases of an audit is completing the audit, which is covered in Chapter 24, the only chapter in Part 5. Even when the other phases of the audit are done well, if the completion phase is done poorly, the quality of the audit will be low. If the planning phase (phase I) and the two testing phases (phases II and III) are done well, the completion phase is typically relatively easy.

COMPLETING THE AUDIT

GOOD REVIEW REQUIRES MORE THAN LOOKING AT AUDIT FILES

Larry Lenape, an audit senior of Santro, Best & Harmon, assigned staff assistant Clawson Little the audit of accounts payable for Westside Industries, a large equipment manufacturer. Accounts payable is a major liability account for a manufacturing company, and testing accounts payable cutoff is an important audit area. Testing primarily involves reviewing the liability recorded by the client by examining subsequent payments to suppliers and other creditors to ensure that they were properly recorded.

Lenape observed that Little was spending a lot of time on the phone, apparently on personal matters. Shortly before the audit was completed, Little announced that he was leaving the firm. Despite Little's distractions due to his personal affairs, he completed the audit work he was assigned within the budgeted time.

Because of Lenape's concern about Little's work habits, he decided to review the audit files with extreme care. Every schedule he reviewed was properly prepared, with tick marks entered and explained by Little, indicating that he had made an extensive examination of underlying data and documents and had found the client's balance to be adequate as stated. Specifically, there were no payments subsequent to year-end for inventory purchases received during the audit period that had not been accrued by the company.

When Lenape finished the audit, he notified Kelsey Mayburn, an audit manager on the engagement, that the files were ready for her review. She had considerable knowledge about equipment manufacturers and also about Westside Industries. Mayburn reviewed all of the audit files, including analytical procedures performed during the audit. After calculating additional analytical procedures during her review, she contacted Lenape and told him accounts payable did not seem reasonable to her. She asked him to do some additional checking. Lenape went back and looked at all the documents that Little had indicated in the audit files that he had inspected. It was quickly apparent that Little had either not looked at the documents or did not know what he was doing when he inspected them. There were almost $1 million of documents applicable to the December 31, 2005, audit period that had not been included as liabilities. Mayburn's review probably saved Santro, Best & Harmon significant embarrassment or worse.

LEARNING OBJECTIVES

After studying this chapter, you should be able to

24-1 Conduct a review for contingent liabilities and commitments.

24-2 Obtain and evaluate letters from the client's attorneys.

24-3 Conduct a post-balance-sheet review for subsequent events.

24-4 Design and perform the final steps in the evidence-accumulation segment of the audit.

24-5 Integrate the audit evidence gathered, and evaluate the overall audit results.

24-6 Communicate effectively with the audit committee and management.

24-7 Identify the auditor's responsibilities when facts affecting the audit report are discovered after its issuance.

The entire textbook starting with Chapter 6 has dealt with the first three phases of the audit process shown in the margin below. The last of the four phases of an audit, which is shaded in the figure, is completing the audit. Although completing the audit is covered in only one chapter, the topic is extremely important to auditors. The opening vignette illustrates the importance of careful and thoughtful review of the audit by an experienced and knowledgeable person. There are several other aspects of completing the audit besides reviewing the results that are critical to the success of an audit. The figure in the margin on page 713 shows the six parts of the completing the audit phase that are discussed in this chapter.

REVIEW FOR CONTINGENT LIABILITIES AND COMMITMENTS

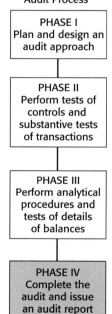

OBJECTIVE 24-1

Conduct a review for contingent liabilities and commitments.

Summary of the Audit Process

PHASE I
Plan and design an audit approach

PHASE II
Perform tests of controls and substantive tests of transactions

PHASE III
Perform analytical procedures and tests of details of balances

PHASE IV
Complete the audit and issue an audit report

A **contingent liability** is a potential future obligation to an outside party for an unknown amount resulting from activities that have already taken place. Three conditions are required for a contingent liability to exist: (1) There is a potential future payment to an outside party or the impairment of some other asset that would result from an existing condition, (2) there is uncertainty about the amount of the future payment or impairment, and (3) the outcome will be resolved by some future event or events. For example, a lawsuit that has been filed but not yet resolved meets all three of these conditions.

This uncertainty of the future payment can vary from extremely likely to highly unlikely. SFAS 5 describes three levels of likelihood of occurrence and the appropriate financial statement treatment for each likelihood. These requirements are summarized in Table 24-1. The decision as to the appropriate treatment requires considerable professional judgment.

When the proper disclosure in the financial statements of a material contingency is through a footnote, the footnote should describe the nature of the contingency to the extent it is known and the opinion of legal counsel or management as to the expected outcome. Figure 24-1 is an illustration of a footnote for pending litigation and company guarantees of debt.

Certain contingent liabilities are of considerable concern to the auditor:

- Pending litigation for patent infringement, product liability, or other actions
- Income tax disputes
- Product warranties
- Notes receivable discounted
- Guarantees of obligations of others
- Unused balances of outstanding letters of credit

Auditing standards make it clear that management, not the auditor, is responsible for identifying and deciding the appropriate accounting treatment for contingent liabilities. In many audits, it is impractical for auditors to uncover contingencies without management's cooperation.

TABLE 24-1	Likelihood of Occurrence and Financial Statement Treatment
Likelihood of Occurrence of Event	**Financial Statement Treatment**
Remote (slight chance)	No disclosure is necessary.
Reasonably possible (more than remote, but less than probable)	Footnote disclosure is necessary.
Probable (likely to occur)	• If the amount can be reasonably estimated, financial statement accounts are adjusted. • If the amount cannot be reasonably estimated, note disclosure is necessary.

FIGURE 24-1	Contingent Liability Footnote

There are various suits and claims pending against the company and its consolidated subsidiaries. It is the opinion of the company's management, based on current available information, that the ultimate liability, if any, resulting from such suits and claims will not materially affect the consolidated financial position or results of operations of the company and its consolidated subsidiaries.

The company has agreed to guarantee the repayment of approximately $14,000,000 loaned by a bank to several affiliated corporations in which the company owns a minority interest.

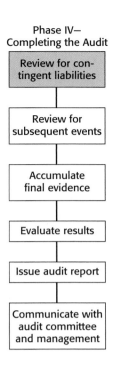

Phase IV— Completing the Audit

- Review for contingent liabilities
- Review for subsequent events
- Accumulate final evidence
- Evaluate results
- Issue audit report
- Communicate with audit committee and management

The auditor's objectives in verifying contingent liabilities are to evaluate the accounting treatment of known contingent liabilities and to identify, to the extent practical, any contingencies not already identified by management.

Closely related to contingent liabilities are **commitments** to purchase raw materials or to lease facilities at a certain price, agreements to sell merchandise at a fixed price, bonus plans, profit-sharing and pension plans, royalty agreements, and similar items. In a commitment, the most important characteristic is the *agreement to commit the firm to a set of fixed conditions* in the future, regardless of what happens to profits or the economy as a whole. In a free economy, presumably the entity agrees to commitments as a means of bettering its own interests, but they may turn out to be less or more advantageous than originally anticipated. All commitments are ordinarily either described together in a separate footnote or combined in a footnote related to contingencies.

Audit Procedures for Finding Contingencies

Many of these potential obligations are ordinarily verified as an integral part of various segments of the engagement rather than as a separate activity near the end of the audit. For example, unused balances in outstanding letters of credit may be tested as a part of confirming bank balances and loans from banks. Similarly, income tax disputes can be checked as a part of analyzing income tax expense, reviewing the general correspondence file, and examining revenue agent reports. Even if contingencies are verified separately, it is common to perform the tests well before the last few days of completing the engagement to ensure their proper verification. Tests of contingent liabilities near the end of the engagement are more a review than an initial search.

The appropriate audit procedures for testing contingencies are less well defined than those already discussed in other audit areas because the primary objective at the initial stage of the tests is to determine the *existence* of contingencies. As you know from the study of other audit areas, it is more difficult to discover unrecorded transactions or events than to verify recorded information. Once the auditor is aware that contingencies exist, evaluation of their materiality and disclosure requirements can ordinarily be satisfactorily resolved.

The following are some audit procedures commonly used to search for contingent liabilities. The list is not all-inclusive, and each procedure is not necessarily performed on every audit.

- Inquire of management (orally and in writing) about the possibility of unrecorded contingencies. In these inquiries, the auditor must be specific in describing the different kinds of contingencies that may require disclosure. Naturally, inquiries of management are not useful in uncovering the intentional failure to disclose existing contingencies, but if management has overlooked a certain type of contingency or does not fully comprehend accounting disclosure requirements, the inquiry can be fruitful. At the completion of the audit, management is typically asked to make a written statement as a part of the letter of representation, which is discussed later in this chapter, that it is aware of no undisclosed contingent liabilities.
- Review current and previous years' internal revenue agent reports for income tax settlements. The reports may indicate areas or years in which there are unsettled disagreements. If a review has been in progress for a long time, there is an increased likelihood of a tax dispute.
- Review the minutes of directors' and stockholders' meetings for indications of lawsuits or other contingencies.

- Analyze legal expense for the period under audit and review invoices and statements from legal counsel for indications of contingent liabilities, especially lawsuits and pending tax assessments.
- Obtain a letter from each major attorney performing legal services for the client as to the status of pending litigation or other contingent liabilities. This procedure is discussed in more depth shortly.
- Review audit documentation for any information that may indicate a potential contingency. For example, bank confirmations may indicate notes receivable discounted or guarantees of loans.
- Examine letters of credit in force as of the balance sheet date and obtain a confirmation of the used and unused balances.

Evaluation of Known Contingent Liabilities

Litigation and Claims Disclosure

If the auditor concludes that there are contingent liabilities, the significance of the potential liability and the nature of the disclosure needed in the financial statements must be evaluated. The potential liability is sufficiently well known in some instances to be included in the statements as an actual liability. In other instances, disclosure may be unnecessary if the contingency is highly remote or immaterial. The CPA firm may obtain a separate evaluation of the potential liability from its own legal counsel rather than relying on management or management's attorneys. The client's attorney is an advocate for the client and often loses perspective in evaluating the likelihood of losing the case and the amount of the potential judgment.

Audit Procedures for Finding Commitments

The search for unknown commitments is usually performed as a part of the audit of each audit area. For example, in verifying sales transactions, the auditor should be alert for sales commitments. Similarly, commitments for the purchase of raw materials or equipment can be identified as a part of the audit of each of these accounts. The auditor should also be aware of the possibility of commitments when reading contracts and correspondence files.

Inquiry of Client's Attorneys

OBJECTIVE 24-2

Obtain and evaluate letters from the client's attorneys.

A major procedure that auditors rely on for evaluating known litigation or other claims against the client and identifying additional ones is the **inquiry of the client's attorneys**. The auditor relies on the attorney's expertise and knowledge of the client's legal affairs to provide a professional opinion about the expected outcome of existing lawsuits and the likely amount of the liability, including court costs. The attorney is also likely to know of pending litigation and claims that management may have overlooked.

As a matter of general practice, many CPA firms analyze legal expense for the entire year and have the client send a standard inquiry letter to every attorney the client has been involved with in the current or preceding year, plus any attorney the firm occasionally engages. In some cases, this involves a large number of attorneys, including some who deal in aspects of law that are far removed from potential lawsuits.

The standard inquiry to the client's attorney, which should be prepared on the client's letterhead and signed by one of the company's officials, should include the following:

- *A list including (1) pending threatened litigation and (2) asserted or unasserted claims or assessments with which the attorney has had significant involvement.* This list is typically prepared by management, but management may request that the attorney prepare the list.
- *A request that the attorney furnish information or comment about the progress of each item listed.* The desired information includes the legal action the client intends to take, the likelihood of an unfavorable outcome, and an estimate of the amount or range of the potential loss.
- *A request for the identification of any unlisted pending or threatened legal actions or a statement that the client's list is complete.*
- *A statement informing the attorney of the attorney's responsibility to inform management of legal matters requiring disclosure in the financial statements and to respond directly to the auditor.* If the attorney chooses to limit a response, reasons for doing so are to be included in the letter.

An example of a typical standard letter sent to the attorney for return directly to the CPA's office is shown in Figure 24-2. Notice in the first paragraph that the attorney is requested to communicate about contingencies up to approximately *the date of the auditor's report.*

FIGURE 24-2	Typical Inquiry of Attorney

Microsoft Word

File Edit View Insert Format Tools Table Window Help Acrobat

HILLSBURG HARDWARE CO.
2146 Willow St.
Gary, Indiana 46405

March 1, 2005

Bailwick & Bettle, Attorneys
11216 Michigan Avenue
Chicago, IL 60606

Gentlemen:

Our auditors, Berger and Anthony, CPAs (P.O. Box 8175, Gary, Indiana 46405), are conducting an audit of our financial statements for the fiscal year ended December 31, 2004. In connection with their audit, we have prepared and furnished to them a description and evaluation of certain contingencies, including those attached, involving matters with respect to which you have been engaged and to which you have devoted substantive attention on behalf of the company in the form of legal consultation or representation. For the purpose of your response to this letter, we believe that as to each contingency an amount in excess of $100,000 would be material, and in total, $700,000. However, determination of materiality with respect to the overall financial statements cannot be made until our auditors complete their audit. Your response should include matters that existed at December 31, 2004, and during the period from that date to the date of the completion of their audit, which is anticipated to be on or about March 15, 2005.

Please provide to our auditors the following information:

(1) Such explanation, if any, that you consider necessary to supplement the listed judgments rendered or settlements made involving the company from the beginning of this fiscal year through the date of your reply.

(2) Such explanation, if any, that you consider necessary to supplement the listing of pending or threatened litigation, including an explanation of those matters as to which your views may differ from those stated and an identification of the omission of any pending or threatened litigation, claim, and assessment or a statement that the list of such matters is complete.

(3) Such explanation, if any, that you consider necessary to supplement the attached information concerning unasserted claims and assessments, including an explanation of those matters as to which your views may differ from those stated.

We understand that whenever, in the course of performing legal services for us with respect to a matter recognized to involve an unasserted possible claim or assessment that may call for financial statement disclosure, you have formed a professional conclusion that we should disclose or consider disclosure concerning such possible claim or assessment, as a matter of professional responsibility to us, you will so advise us and will consult with us concerning the question of such disclosure and the applicable requirements of Statement of Financial Accounting Standards No. 5. Please specifically confirm to our auditors that our understanding is correct.

Please specifically identify the nature of and reasons for any limitations in your response.

Yours very truly,
Hillsburg Hardware Co.

Rick Chulick, Pres.

Attorneys in recent years have become reluctant to provide certain information to auditors because of their own exposure to legal liability for providing incorrect or confidential information. The nature of the refusal of attorneys to provide auditors with complete information about contingent liabilities falls into two categories: the refusal to respond due to a lack of knowledge about matters involving contingent liabilities and the refusal to disclose information that the attorney considers confidential. As an example of the latter, the attorney might be aware of a violation of a patent agreement that could result in a significant loss to the client if it were known (**unasserted claim**). The inclusion of the information in a footnote could actually cause the lawsuit and therefore be damaging to the client. Review the attorney concerns described in the box "The Legal View."

If an attorney refuses to provide the auditor with information about material existing lawsuits (asserted claims) or unasserted claims, *the auditor must modify the audit report to reflect the lack of available evidence.* This requirement in SAS 12 (AU 337) has the effect of requiring management to give its attorneys permission to provide contingent liability information to auditors and to encourage attorneys to cooperate with auditors in obtaining information about contingencies.

Congress included provisions in the Sarbanes–Oxley Act of 2002 directing the SEC to issue rules requiring attorneys serving public companies to report material violations by the company of federal securities laws. Under the Act, an attorney must report violations to the public company's chief legal counsel or chief executive officer. If the legal officer or CEO fails to appropriately respond, the attorney must report violations to the company's audit committee. In response to these new requirements, the American Bar Association subsequently amended its attorney–client confidentiality rules to permit attorneys to breach confidentiality if a client is committing a crime or fraud. Under the previous rules, an attorney who became aware of a potential crime on the part of a client could turn clients in only when there was a threat of physical harm or death or release of hazardous materials or defective products.

THE LEGAL VIEW

The lawyer is the expert on litigation, yet differences in lawyers' and CPAs' responsibilities with respect to common clients have resulted in contentious difficulties. Although CPAs are responsible for determining there is "adequate disclosure" under Statement no. 5 [SFAS 5] ... lawyers are responsible for "winning the case." Because information provided by lawyers may affect a case adversely, these responsibilities may conflict.

Many lawyers believe that, despite a client's request they provide the auditor with information, they should be less than candid in letters to CPAs because of concern their replies may

- Impair the client-lawyer confidentiality privilege.
- Disclose a client confidence or secret.
- Prejudice the client's defense of a claim.
- Constitute an admission by the client.

The authoritative guidance for lawyers ... warns lawyers they must be careful in communications with auditors. Indeed, the first sentence of the ABA statement says, "The public interest in protecting the confidentiality of lawyer–client communications is fundamental."

The ABA statement also says lawyers normally should refrain from expressing judgments on outcome—either likelihood or amount of loss. The net effect is CPAs generally can obtain relatively complete responses on the existence of litigation and the dates when the underlying cause occurred ... but less complete responses on the likelihood of an unfavorable outcome and the amount of potential loss.

In addition to an implicit hesitancy to provide evidential matter on likelihood and amount of loss, the ABA statement gives lawyers definitions of *probable* and *remote* that are different from those in Statement no. 5:

- **Remote.** The ABA says an unfavorable outcome is remote if the prospects for the client not succeeding in its defense are judged to be extremely doubtful and the prospects of success by the claimant are judged to be slight.

- **Probable.** The ABA says an unfavorable outcome for the client is probable if the claimant's prospects of not succeeding are judged to be extremely doubtful and the client's prospects for success in its defense are judged to be slight.

Source: Excerpted from an article by Bruce K. Behn and Kurt Pany, "Limitations of Lawyers' Letters," *Journal of Accountancy* (February 1995), pp. 62-63.

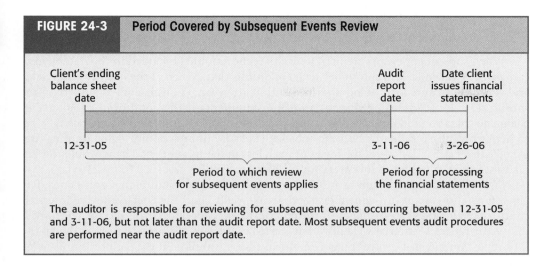

FIGURE 24-3	Period Covered by Subsequent Events Review

The auditor is responsible for reviewing for subsequent events occurring between 12-31-05 and 3-11-06, but not later than the audit report date. Most subsequent events audit procedures are performed near the audit report date.

REVIEW FOR SUBSEQUENT EVENTS

The second part of completing the audit is the review for subsequent events. The auditor must review transactions and events occurring after the balance sheet date to determine whether anything occurred that might affect the fair presentation or disclosure of the current period statements. PCAOB Standard 2 requires auditors of public companies to also inquire about changes in internal control over financial reporting occurring subsequent to the end of the fiscal period that might significantly affect internal control over financial reporting. The auditing procedures required by SAS 1 (AU 560) to verify these transactions and events are commonly called the **review for subsequent events** or **post-balance-sheet review**.

Business & Industry Insights

The auditor's responsibility for reviewing for subsequent events is normally limited to the period beginning with the balance sheet date and ending with the date of the auditor's report. Because the date of the auditor's report corresponds to the completion of the important auditing procedures in the client's office, the subsequent events review should be completed near the end of the engagement.[1] Figure 24-3 shows the period covered by a subsequent events review and the timing of that review.

Two types of **subsequent events** require consideration by management and evaluation by the auditor: those that have a direct effect on the financial statements and require adjustment and those that have no direct effect on the financial statements but for which disclosure is advisable.

Types of Subsequent Events

Those That Have a Direct Effect on the Financial Statements and Require Adjustment These events or transactions provide additional information to management in determining the fair presentation of account balances as of the balance sheet date and to auditors in verifying the balances. For example, if the auditor is having difficulty determining the correct valuation of inventory because of obsolescence, the sale of raw material inventory as scrap in the subsequent period would indicate the correct value of the inventory as of the balance sheet date.

Such subsequent period events as the following require an adjustment of account balances in the current year's financial statements if the amounts are material:

• Declaration of bankruptcy by a customer with an outstanding accounts receivable balance because of deteriorating financial condition
• Settlement of a litigation at an amount different from the amount recorded on the books

---

[1]When the auditor's name is associated with a registration statement under the Securities Act of 1933, the auditor's responsibility for reviewing subsequent events extends beyond the date of the auditor's report to the date the registration becomes effective.

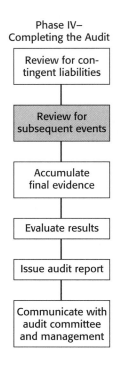

Phase IV–
Completing the Audit

- Disposal of equipment not being used in operations at a price below the current book value
- Sale of investments at a price below recorded cost

When subsequent events are used to evaluate the amounts included in the statements, care must be taken to distinguish between conditions that existed at the balance sheet date and those that came into being after the end of the year. The subsequent information should not be incorporated directly into the statements if the conditions causing the change in valuation did not take place until after year-end. For example, assume one type of a client's inventory suddenly becomes obsolete because of a technology change after the balance sheet date. The sale of the inventory at a loss in the subsequent period would not be relevant in the valuation of inventory for obsolescence in this case.

PCAOB Standard 2 requires public company auditors to inquire about and consider any information about subsequent events that materially affect the effectiveness of internal control over financial reporting as of the end of the fiscal period. If the auditor concludes the events reflect a material weakness that existed at the end of the fiscal period, the auditor's report on internal control must contain an adverse opinion. If the auditor is unable to determine the effect of the subsequent event on the effectiveness of internal control, the auditor must disclaim the opinions on internal control.

Those That Have No Direct Effect on the Financial Statements but for Which Disclosure Is Advisable Subsequent events of this type provide evidence of conditions that did not exist at the date of the balance sheet being reported on but are so significant that they require disclosure even though they do not require adjustment. Ordinarily, these events can be adequately disclosed by the use of footnotes, but occasionally, one may be so significant as to require *supplementing the historical statements* with statements that include the effect of the event as if it had occurred on the balance sheet date.

Following are examples of events or transactions occurring in the subsequent period that may require disclosure rather than an adjustment in the financial statements:

- Decline in the market value of securities held for temporary investment or resale
- Issuance of bonds or equity securities
- Decline in the market value of inventory as a consequence of government action barring further sale of a product
- Uninsured loss of inventories as a result of fire
- A merger or an acquisition

Public company auditors may also identify events related to internal control over financial reporting that arose subsequent to year-end. If the auditor determines that the subsequent event has a material effect on the company's internal control over financial reporting, the auditor's report on internal control over financial reporting must include an explanatory paragraph either describing the event and its effect or directing the reader to a disclosure in management's report on internal control of the event and its effect.

Audit Tests

Audit procedures for the subsequent events review can be conveniently divided into two categories: procedures normally integrated as a part of the verification of year-end account balances and those performed specifically for the purpose of discovering events or transactions that must be recognized as subsequent events.

The first category includes cutoff and valuation tests done as a part of the tests of details of balances. For example, subsequent period sales and acquisition transactions are examined to determine whether the cutoff is accurate. Similarly, many valuation tests involving subsequent events are also performed as a part of the verification of account balances. As an example, it is common to test the collectibility of accounts receivable by reviewing subsequent period cash receipts. It is also a normal audit procedure to compare the subsequent period purchase price of inventory with the recorded cost as a test of lower of cost or market valuation. The procedures for cutoff and valuation have been discussed sufficiently in preceding chapters and are not repeated here.

The second category of tests is performed specifically to obtain information to incorporate into the current year's account balances or footnotes. These tests include the following.

Inquire of Management Inquiries vary from client to client but normally are about potential contingent liabilities or commitments, significant changes in the assets or capital structure of the company, the current status of items that were not completely resolved at the balance sheet date, and unusual adjustments made subsequent to the balance sheet date. Public company auditors must also include specific inquiries of management about any changes in internal control over financial reporting made subsequent to the end of the fiscal period.

Inquiries of management about subsequent events must be held with the proper client personnel to obtain meaningful answers. For example, discussing tax or union matters with the accounts receivable supervisor would not be appropriate. Most inquiries should be held with the controller, the vice presidents, and the president, depending on the information desired.

Correspond with Attorneys Correspondence with attorneys, which was previously discussed, takes place as a part of the search for contingent liabilities. In obtaining letters from attorneys, the auditor must remember the responsibility for testing for subsequent events up to the date of the audit report. A common approach is to request the attorney to date and mail the letter as of the expected completion date for field work.

Review Internal Statements Prepared Subsequent to the Balance Sheet Date The emphasis in the review should be on (1) changes in the business relative to results for the same period in the year under audit and (2) changes after year-end. The auditor should pay careful attention to major changes in the business or environment in which the client is operating. The statements should be discussed with management to determine whether they are prepared on the same basis as the current period statements, and there should be inquiries about significant changes in the operating results.

Review Records Prepared Subsequent to the Balance Sheet Date Journals and ledgers should be reviewed to determine the existence and nature of significant transactions related to the current year. If the journals are not kept up-to-date, documents relating to the journals should be reviewed.

PCAOB Standard 2 also requires public company auditors to inquire about and examine such things as relevant internal audit reports and regulatory agency reports on the company's internal control over financial reporting that have been issued during the subsequent events review period.

Examine Minutes Issued Subsequent to the Balance Sheet Date The minutes of stockholders and directors meetings subsequent to the balance sheet date must be examined for important subsequent events affecting the current period financial statements.

Obtain a Letter of Representation The letter of representation written by the client's management to the auditor formalizes statements that management has made about different matters throughout the audit, including discussions about subsequent events. This letter is mandatory and includes other relevant matters too. This letter is discussed in detail during the discussion of evidence accumulation, which is the next part discussed in completing the audit.

Dual Dating

Occasionally, the auditor determines that an important subsequent event occurred after the field work was completed but *before the audit report was issued.* The source of such information is typically management or the media. An example using the dates in Figure 24-3 on page 717 is the acquisition of another company by an audit client on March 23, when the last day of field work was March 11. In such a situation, SAS 1 (AU 530) requires the auditor to extend audit tests for the newly discovered subsequent event to make sure that it is correctly disclosed. The auditor has two equally acceptable options for expanding subsequent events tests: expand all subsequent events tests to the new date, or restrict the subsequent events review to matters related to the new subsequent event. For the first option, the audit report date is changed to the new date. For the second option, the auditor issues a **dual-dated audit report**, which means that the audit report includes two dates. The first date is the date for the completion of field work except for a specific exception. The second date, which is always later, deals with the exception. In the example of the acquisition, assume that the auditor returned to the client's premises and completed audit tests on March 31 pertaining only to the acquisition. The audit report is dual-dated as follows: March 11, 2006, except for note 17, as to which the date is March 31, 2006.

FINAL EVIDENCE ACCUMULATION

OBJECTIVE 24-4

Design and perform the final steps in the evidence-accumulation segment of the audit.

In addition to the review for subsequent events, the auditor has several final accumulation responsibilities that apply to all cycles. Five types of final evidence accumulation that are discussed in this section are (1) perform final analytical procedures, (2) evaluate the going-concern assumption, (3) obtain a management representation letter, (4) consider information accompanying the basic financial statements, and (5) read other information in the annual report. Each of these is done late in the engagement.

Perform Final Analytical Procedures

Analytical procedures done during the completion of the audit are useful as a final review for material misstatements or financial problems not noted during other testing and to help the auditor take a final objective look at the financial statements. It is common for a partner to do the analytical procedures during the final review of audit documentation and financial statements. Typically, a partner has a good understanding of the client and its business because of ongoing relationships. Knowledge of the client's business combined with effective analytical procedures help identify possible oversights in an audit.

When performing analytical procedures during the final review stage, the partner would generally read the financial statements, including footnotes, and consider (1) the adequacy of evidence gathered about unusual or unexpected account balances or relationships identified during planning or while conducting the audit and (2) unusual or unexpected account balances or relationships that were not previously identified. Results from final analytical procedures may indicate that additional audit evidence is necessary.

Evaluate Going-Concern Assumption

SAS 59 (AU 341) requires the auditor to evaluate whether there is a substantial doubt about a client's ability to continue as a going concern for at least 1 year beyond the balance sheet date. That assessment is initially made as a part of planning but is revised when significant new information is obtained. For example, if the auditor discovered during the audit that the company had defaulted on a loan, lost its primary customer, or decided to dispose of substantial assets to pay off loans, the initial assessment of going concern may need revision. A final assessment is desirable after all evidence has been accumulated and proposed audit adjustments have been incorporated into the financial statements.

Analytical procedures are one of the most important types of evidence to assess going concern. Discussions with management and a review of future plans are important considerations in evaluating analytical procedures. Knowledge of the client's business gained throughout the audit is important information used to assess the likelihood of financial failure within the next year.

When the auditor has reservations about the going-concern assumption, it is necessary to evaluate management's plans to avoid bankruptcy and the feasibility of achieving these plans. Making the final decision whether to issue a report with a going-concern explanatory paragraph is typically time-consuming and difficult. Going-concern explanatory paragraphs were discussed in Chapter 3.

Obtain Management Representation Letter

SAS 85 (AU 333) requires the auditor to obtain a **letter of representation** documenting management's most important oral representations during the audit. The client representation letter is prepared on the client's letterhead, addressed to the CPA firm, and signed by high-level corporate officials, usually the president and chief financial officer.

There are two purposes of the client letter of representation:

1. To impress upon management its responsibility for the assertions in the financial statements. For example, if the letter of representation includes a reference to pledged assets and contingent liabilities, honest management may be reminded of its unintentional failure to disclose the information adequately. To fulfill this objective, the letter of representation should be sufficiently detailed to act as a reminder to management.

2. To document the responses from management to inquiries about various aspects of the audit. This provides written documentation of client representations in the event of disagreement or a lawsuit between the auditor and client. Because it is more formal than oral communication, a letter of representation also helps reduce misunderstandings between management and the auditor.

The letter should be dated no earlier than the date of the auditor's report to make sure that there are representations related to the subsequent events review. The letter implies that it has originated with the client, but it is common practice for the auditor to prepare the letter and request the client to type it on the company's letterhead and sign it. Refusal by a client to prepare and sign the letter would require a qualified opinion or disclaimer of opinion.

SAS 85 suggests four categories of specific matters that should be included. The four categories are as follows, with examples in each category.

1. *Financial statements*
   - Management's acknowledgment of its responsibility for the fair presentation in the financial statements of financial position, results of operations, and cash flows in conformity with generally accepted accounting principles
   - Management's belief that the financial statements are fairly presented in conformity with generally accepted accounting principles
2. *Completeness of information*
   - Availability of all financial records and related data
   - Completeness and availability of all minutes of meetings of stockholders, directors, and committees of directors
   - Absence of unrecorded transactions
3. *Recognition, measurement, and disclosure*
   - Management's belief that the effects of any uncorrected financial statement misstatements are immaterial to the financial statements
   - Information concerning fraud involving (1) management, (2) employees who have significant roles in internal control, or (3) others where the fraud could have a material effect on the financial statements
   - Information concerning related party transactions and amounts receivable from or payable to related parties
   - Unasserted claims or assessments that the entity's lawyer has advised are probable of assertion and must be disclosed in accordance with Financial Accounting Standards Board (FASB) Statement No. 5, *Accounting for Contingencies*
   - Satisfactory title to assets, liens or encumbrances on assets, and assets pledged as collateral
   - Compliance with aspects of contractual agreements that may affect the financial statements
4. *Subsequent events*
   - Bankruptcy of a major customer with an outstanding account receivable at the balance sheet date
   - A merger or acquisition after the balance sheet date

For audits of public companies, PCAOB Standard 2 requires the auditor to obtain specific written representations from management about internal control over financial reporting. Some of those representations are noted next:

5. *Internal control*
   - Management's acknowledgment of its responsibilities for establishing and maintaining effective internal control over financial reporting
   - Management's conclusion about the effectiveness of internal control over financial reporting as of the end of the fiscal period
   - Disclosure to the auditor of all deficiencies in the design or operation of internal control over financial reporting identified as part of management's assessment, including separate disclosure of significant deficiencies or material weaknesses

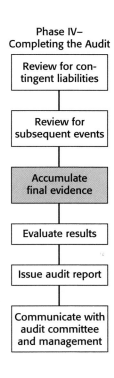

Phase IV–
Completing the Audit

Review for contingent liabilities

Review for subsequent events

Accumulate final evidence

Evaluate results

Issue audit report

Communicate with audit committee and management

- Management's knowledge of any material fraud or other fraud involving senior management or other employees who have a significant role in the company's internal control over financial reporting

Auditors of public companies may obtain a combined representation letter for both the audit of the financial statements and the audit of internal control.

A client representation letter is a written statement from a nonindependent source and therefore *cannot be regarded as reliable evidence.* The letter does provide documentation that management has been asked certain questions to make sure that management understands its responsibilities and to protect the auditor if there are claims against the auditor by management.

In some audits, the auditor may find other evidence that contradicts statements in the letter of representation. In such cases, the auditor should investigate the circumstances and consider whether representations in the letter are reliable.

Consider Information Accompanying the Basic Financial Statements

Clients often request auditors to include additional information beyond the basic financial statements in the set of materials prepared for management or outside users. SAS 29 (AU 551) refers to this additional information as *information accompanying the basic financial statements in auditor-submitted documents.* In the past, the same information was called a *long-form report.* Figure 24-4 illustrates the basic financial statements and additional information.

The profession has intentionally refrained from defining or restricting the appropriate supplementary information included to enable auditors to individualize the information to meet the needs of statement users. However, several types of information are commonly included in the additional information section:

- Detailed comparative statements supporting the control totals on the primary financial statements for accounts such as cost of goods sold, operating expenses, and miscellaneous assets
- Supplementary information required by the Financial Accounting Standards Board or the SEC
- Statistical data for past years in the form of ratios and trends
- A schedule of insurance coverage
- Specific comments on the changes that have taken place in the statements

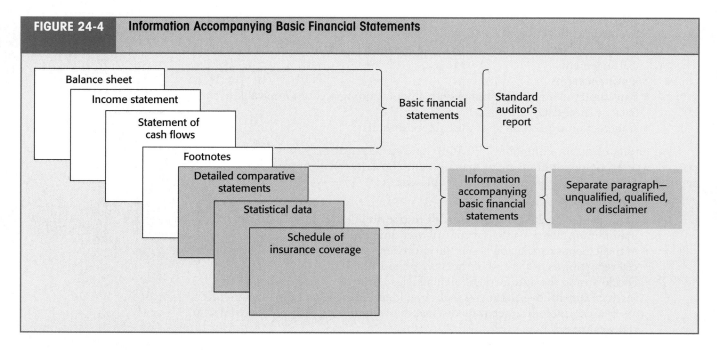

FIGURE 24-4   Information Accompanying Basic Financial Statements

It is important that the auditor clearly distinguish between responsibility for the primary financial statements and for additional information. Usually, the auditor has not performed a sufficiently detailed audit to justify an opinion on the additional information, but in some instances, the auditor may be confident that the information is fairly presented. The profession's reporting standards require the auditor to make a clear statement about the degree of responsibility taken for the additional information. Two types of opinions are allowed: a positive opinion indicating a high level of assurance or a disclaimer indicating no assurance. When the auditor issues an opinion on additional information accompanying the financial statements, materiality is the same as that used in forming an opinion on the basic financial statements. As a result, the additional procedures required are less extensive than if the auditor were issuing an opinion on the information taken by itself, such as in a report on specified elements or accounts. The following is an example of the additional wording to be added to the auditor's standard report when expressing an opinion on the additional information:

- Our audit was conducted for the purpose of forming an opinion on the basic financial statements taken as a whole. The accompanying information on pages x through y is presented for purposes of additional analysis and is not a required part of the basic financial statements. Such information has been subjected to the auditing procedures applied in the audit of the basic financial statements and, in our opinion, is fairly stated in all material respects in relation to the basic financial statements taken as a whole.

If the auditor decided that sufficient evidence had *not* been accumulated for the additional data to justify an unqualified opinion, SAS 29 requires that a disclaimer paragraph such as the following be added to the standard audit report:

- Our audit was made for the purpose of forming an opinion on the basic financial statements taken as a whole. The accompanying information on pages x through y is presented for purposes of additional analysis and is not a required part of the basic financial statements. Such information has not been subjected to the auditing procedures applied in the audit of the basic financial statements, and, accordingly, we express no opinion on it.

SAS 8 (AU 550) requires the auditor to read **other information included in annual reports** pertaining directly to the financial statements. For example, assume that the president's letter in the annual report refers to an increase in earnings per share from $2.60 to $2.93. The auditor is required to compare that information with the financial statements to make sure it corresponds.

Read Other Information in the Annual Report

SAS 8 pertains only to information that is not a part of the financial statements but is published with them. Examples are the president's letter and explanations of company activities included in annual reports of nearly all publicly held companies. It usually takes the auditor only a few minutes to make sure that the nonfinancial statement information is consistent with the statements. If the auditor concludes that there is a material inconsistency, the client should be requested to change the information. If the client refuses, which would be unusual, the auditor should include an explanatory paragraph in the audit report or withdraw from the engagement.

EVALUATE RESULTS

After performing all audit procedures in each audit area, including the review for contingencies and subsequent events and accumulating final evidence, the auditor must integrate the results into *one overall conclusion* about the financial statements. Ultimately, the auditor must decide whether sufficient audit evidence has been accumulated to warrant the conclusion that the financial statements are stated in accordance with generally accepted accounting principles, applied on a basis consistent with those of the preceding year. Similarly, auditors of public companies must also arrive at an overall conclusion about the effectiveness of internal control over financial reporting. The five main aspects of evaluating the results are discussed next.

OBJECTIVE 24-5

Integrate the audit evidence gathered, and evaluate the overall audit results.

The final evaluation of the adequacy of the evidence is a review by the auditor of the entire audit to determine whether all important aspects have been adequately tested, considering all circumstances of the engagement. A major step in this process is to review the entire

Sufficiency of Evidence

audit program to make sure that all parts have been accurately completed and documented and that all audit objectives have been met. This review includes deciding whether the audit program is adequate, considering problem areas identified as the audit progressed. For example, if misstatements were discovered during tests of sales, the initial plans for tests of details of accounts receivable may have been insufficient. The final review should evaluate whether the revised audit program is adequate.

As an aid in drawing final conclusions about the adequacy of the audit evidence, auditors often use a **completing the engagement checklist**. Such a checklist is a reminder of aspects of the audit that must not be overlooked. An illustration of part of a completing the engagement checklist is given in Figure 24-5.

If the auditor concludes that sufficient evidence has *not* been obtained to draw a conclusion about the fairness of the client's representations, there are two choices: Additional evidence must be obtained or either a qualified opinion or a disclaimer of opinion must be issued.

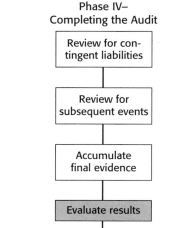

Evidence Supports Auditor's Opinion

Phase IV–
Completing the Audit

Review for contingent liabilities

Review for subsequent events

Accumulate final evidence

Evaluate results

Issue audit report

Communicate with audit committee and management

An important part of evaluating whether the financial statements are fairly stated is summarizing the misstatements uncovered in the audit. When the auditor uncovers misstatements that are in themselves material, entries should be proposed to the client to correct the statements. It may be difficult to determine the appropriate amount of adjustment because the true value of a misstatement may be unknown; nevertheless, it is the auditor's responsibility to decide on the required adjustment. In addition to the material misstatements, there are often a large number of immaterial misstatements discovered that are not adjusted at the time they are found. It is necessary to combine individually immaterial misstatements to evaluate whether the combined amount is material. The auditor can keep track of these misstatements and combine them in several different ways, but many auditors use a convenient method called an **unadjusted misstatement audit schedule** or **summary of possible misstatements**. It is relatively easy to evaluate the overall significance of several immaterial misstatements with this type of audit schedule. An example of an unadjusted misstatement worksheet is given in Figure 24-6.

The schedule in Figure 24-6 includes both known misstatements that the client has decided not to adjust and projected misstatements, including sampling error. Observe that in the bottom left portion of the audit schedule there is a comparison of possible adjustments to materiality. A summary of this audit schedule is often included with management's representation that the uncorrected misstatements are immaterial.

	YES	NO
FIGURE 24-5 Completing the Engagement Checklist		

1. Examination of prior year's audit documentation
   a. Were last year's audit files examined for areas of emphasis in the current year audit? ___ ___
   b. Was the permanent file reviewed for items that affect the current year? ___ ___
2. Internal control
   a. Has internal control been adequately understood? ___ ___
   b. Is the scope of the audit adequate in light of the assessed control risk? ___ ___
   c. Have all major weaknesses been included as reportable conditions in a letter to the audit committee or to senior management? ___ ___
3. General documents
   a. Were all current year minutes and resolutions reviewed, abstracted, and followed up? ___ ___
   b. Has the permanent file been updated? ___ ___
   c. Have all major contracts and agreements been reviewed and abstracted, copied, or downloaded to ascertain that the client complies with all existing legal requirements? ___ ___

FIGURE 24-6   Unadjusted Misstatement Audit Schedule

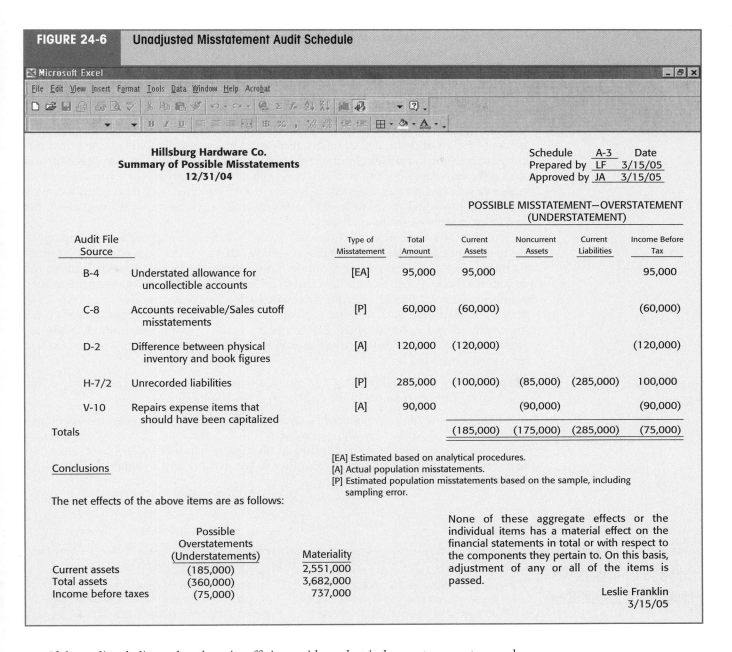

Hillsburg Hardware Co.
Summary of Possible Misstatements
12/31/04

Schedule __A-3__ Date
Prepared by __LF__ __3/15/05__
Approved by __JA__ __3/15/05__

Audit File Source		Type of Misstatement	Total Amount	POSSIBLE MISSTATEMENT—OVERSTATEMENT (UNDERSTATEMENT)			
				Current Assets	Noncurrent Assets	Current Liabilities	Income Before Tax
B-4	Understated allowance for uncollectible accounts	[EA]	95,000	95,000			95,000
C-8	Accounts receivable/Sales cutoff misstatements	[P]	60,000	(60,000)			(60,000)
D-2	Difference between physical inventory and book figures	[A]	120,000	(120,000)			(120,000)
H-7/2	Unrecorded liabilities	[P]	285,000	(100,000)	(85,000)	(285,000)	100,000
V-10	Repairs expense items that should have been capitalized	[A]	90,000		(90,000)		(90,000)
Totals				(185,000)	(175,000)	(285,000)	(75,000)

Conclusions

[EA] Estimated based on analytical procedures.
[A] Actual population misstatements.
[P] Estimated population misstatements based on the sample, including sampling error.

The net effects of the above items are as follows:

	Possible Overstatements (Understatements)	Materiality
Current assets	(185,000)	2,551,000
Total assets	(360,000)	3,682,000
Income before taxes	(75,000)	737,000

None of these aggregate effects or the individual items has a material effect on the financial statements in total or with respect to the components they pertain to. On this basis, adjustment of any or all of the items is passed.

Leslie Franklin
3/15/05

If the auditor believes that there *is* sufficient evidence but it does not warrant a conclusion of fairly presented financial statements, the auditor again has two choices: The statements must be revised to the auditor's satisfaction or either a qualified or an adverse opinion must be issued. Notice that the options here are different from those in the case of insufficient evidence obtained.

A major consideration in completing the audit is to determine whether the disclosures in the financial statements are adequate. Throughout the audit, the emphasis is most often on verifying the accuracy of the balances in the general ledger by testing the most important accounts on the auditor's trial balance. Another important task is to make sure that the account balances on the trial balance are correctly aggregated and disclosed on the financial statements. Naturally, adequate disclosure includes consideration of all of the statements, including related footnotes.

Financial Statement Disclosures

The auditor actually prepares the financial statements from the trial balance in many small audits and submits them to the client for approval. Performing this function may seem to imply that the client has been relieved of responsibility for the fair representation in the statements, but that is not the case. The auditor acts in the role of advisor when preparing financial statements, but *management retains the final responsibility for approving the issuance of the statements.*

Review for adequate disclosure in the financial statements at the completion of the audit is not the only time the auditor is interested in proper disclosure. Unless the auditor is constantly alert for disclosure problems, it is impossible to perform the final disclosure review adequately. For example, as part of the audit of accounts receivable, the auditor must be aware of the need to separate notes receivable and amounts due from affiliates and trade accounts due from customers. Similarly, there must be a segregation of current from non-current receivables and a disclosure of the factoring or discounting of notes receivable if such is the case. An important part of verifying all account balances is determining whether generally accepted accounting principles were properly applied on a basis consistent with that of the preceding year. The auditor must carefully document this information in the audit files to facilitate the final review.

As part of the final review for financial statement disclosure, many CPA firms require the completion of a **financial statement disclosure checklist** for every engagement. These questionnaires are designed to remind the auditor of common disclosure problems encountered in audits and also to facilitate the final review of the entire audit by an independent partner. An illustration of a partial financial statement disclosure checklist is given in Figure 24-7. Naturally, it is not sufficient to rely on a checklist to replace the auditor's own knowledge of generally accepted accounting principles. In any given audit, some aspects of the engagement require much greater expertise in accounting than can be obtained from such a checklist.

Audit Documentation Review

There are three main reasons why it is essential that audit documentation be thoroughly reviewed by another member of the audit firm at the completion of the audit:

1. *To evaluate the performance of inexperienced personnel.* A considerable portion of most audits is performed by audit personnel with less than 4 or 5 years of experience. These people may have sufficient technical training to conduct an adequate audit, but their lack of experience affects their ability to make sound professional judgments in complex situations.

UNRECORDED ADJUSTMENTS PROVE COSTLY TO AUDIT FIRM

In March 2002, the SEC announced it had completed its investigation of the accounting practices at Waste Management, Inc. and had filed suits against the company and several of its top executives charging them with perpetrating a massive financial statement fraud lasting more than 5 years. The SEC alleged that management manipulated the company's financial results using a multitude of improper accounting practices to meet predetermined earnings targets.

As part of the investigation, the SEC noted that Waste Management's auditors, Arthur Andersen, had identified the company's improper accounting practices and quantified much of the impact of those practices on the company's financial statements. According to SEC filings, Andersen annually presented company management with "Proposed Adjusting Journal Entries (PAJEs)" to correct errors that understated expenses and overstated earnings in the company's financial statements. Management consistently refused to make the adjustments called for by the PAJEs, and, instead, entered into an agreement with Andersen to write off the accumulated errors over periods of up to 10 years. However, as

time progressed, management never complied with the terms of their secret agreement.

The SEC eventually settled charges with Andersen and four of its partners related to the 1992 through 1996 audited financial statements. Andersen agreed to pay a penalty of $7 million, the largest ever assessed against an accounting firm at the time. Commenting on the SEC's actions, Richard Walker, SEC Director of Enforcement, noted:

> Arthur Andersen and its partners failed to stand up to company management and thereby betrayed their ultimate allegiance to Waste Management's shareholders and the investing public. Given the positions held by these partners and the duration and gravity of the misconduct, the firm itself must be held responsible for the false and misleading audit reports.

Source: Beasley, Buckless, Glover, and Prawitt, *Auditing Cases: An Interactive Learning Approach*, pp. 145–153, published by Prentice Hall.

FIGURE 24-7 — Financial Statement Disclosure Checklist: Property, Plant, and Equipment

1. Are the following disclosures included in the financial statements or notes (APB 12, para. 5):
   a. Balances of major classes of depreciable assets (land, building, equipment, and so forth) at the balance sheet date?
   b. Allowances for depreciation, by class or in total, at the balance sheet date?
   c. General description of depreciation methods for major classes of PP&E (APB 22, para. 13)?
   d. Total amount of depreciation charged to expense for each income statement presented?
   e. Basis of evaluation (SAS 32, AU 431.02)?
2. Are carrying amounts of property mortgaged and encumbered by indebtedness disclosed (FASB 5, para. 18)?
3. Are details of sale and leaseback transactions during the period disclosed (FASB 13, para. 32–34)?
4. Is the carrying amount of property not a part of operating plant—for example, idle or held for investment or sale—segregated?
5. Has consideration been given to disclosure of fully depreciated capital assets still in use and capital assets not presently in use?

Note: Information in parentheses refers to authoritative professional literature.

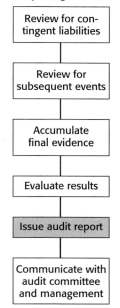

2. To make sure that the audit meets the CPA firm's standard of performance. Within any organization, the performance quality of individuals varies considerably, but careful review by top-level personnel in the firm assists in maintaining a uniform quality of auditing.

3. To counteract the bias that often enters into the auditor's judgment. Auditors must attempt to remain objective throughout the audit, but it is easy to lose proper perspective on a long audit when there are complex problems to solve.

Except for a final independent review, which is discussed shortly, the **review of audit documentation** should be conducted by someone who is knowledgeable about the client and the unique circumstances in the audit. Therefore, the initial review of the audit files prepared by any given auditor is normally done by the auditor's immediate supervisor. For example, the least experienced auditor's work is ordinarily reviewed by the audit senior. The senior's immediate superior, who is normally a supervisor or manager, reviews the senior's work and also reviews less thoroughly the schedules of the inexperienced auditor. Finally, the partner assigned to the audit must ultimately review all audit documentation, but the partner reviews those prepared by the supervisor or manager more thoroughly than the others. While performing the review, the reviewer will frequently interview the auditor responsible for preparing the audit documentation to learn how significant audit issues were resolved. Except for the final independent review, most of the audit documentation review is done as each segment of the audit is completed.

Independent Review

At the completion of larger audits, it is common to have the financial statements and the entire set of audit files reviewed by a completely independent reviewer who has not participated in the engagement. An **independent review** is required for SEC engagements, including the review of interim financial information and the audit of internal controls. This reviewer often takes an adversary position to make sure that the conduct of the audit was adequate. The audit team must be able to justify the evidence it has accumulated and the conclusions it reached on the basis of the unique circumstances of the engagement.

Summary of Evidence Evaluation

Figure 24-8 (p. 728) summarizes the evaluation of the sufficiency of the evidence and the decision as to whether the evidence supports the opinion on the financial statements. It shows that the auditor evaluates the sufficiency of actual evidence by first evaluating achieved audit risk, by account and by cycle, and then making the same evaluation for the overall financial statements. The auditor also evaluates whether the evidence supports the audit opinion by first estimating misstatements in each account and then for the overall financial statements. In practice, the evaluation of achieved audit risk and estimated misstatement are made at the same time. On the basis of these evaluations, the audit report is issued for the financial statements.

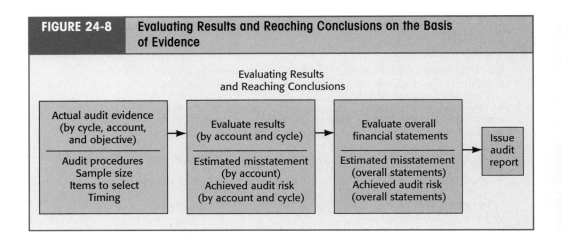

FIGURE 24-8 | Evaluating Results and Reaching Conclusions on the Basis of Evidence

Evaluating Results
and Reaching Conclusions

Actual audit evidence
(by cycle, account,
and objective)

Audit procedures
Sample size
Items to select
Timing

Evaluate results
(by account and cycle)

Estimated misstatement
(by account)
Achieved audit risk
(by account and cycle)

Evaluate overall
financial statements

Estimated misstatement
(overall statements)
Achieved audit risk
(overall statements)

Issue
audit
report

ISSUE THE AUDIT REPORT

The auditor should not decide the appropriate audit report to issue until all evidence has been accumulated and evaluated, including all parts of completing the audit discussed so far. Because the audit report is the only thing that most users see in the audit process, and the consequences of issuing an inappropriate report can be severe, it is critical that the report be correct.

In most audits, the auditor issues an unqualified report with standard wording. Firms usually have an electronic template of this report and need to change only the name of the client, title of the financial statements, and date.

When a CPA firm decides that a standard unqualified report is inappropriate, there will almost certainly be extensive discussions among technical partners in the CPA firm and often with client personnel. Most CPA firms have comprehensive audit reporting manuals to assist them in selecting the appropriate wording of the report they decide to issue.

COMMUNICATE WITH THE AUDIT COMMITTEE AND MANAGEMENT

OBJECTIVE 24-6

Communicate effectively with the audit committee and management.

After the audit is completed, there are several potential communications from the auditor to client personnel. The first three of these communications discussed in this section are required by auditing standards to make certain that the audit committee and senior management are informed of audit findings and auditor recommendations. The fourth item discussed in this section, management letters, is often communicated to operating management.

Communicate Fraud and Illegal Acts

SAS 99 (AU 316) and SAS 54 (AU 317) require the auditor to communicate all fraud and illegal acts to the audit committee or similarly designated group, regardless of materiality. The purpose is to assist the audit committee in performing its supervisory role for reliable financial statements. This requirement indicates the increased concern of the profession over the auditor's responsibility for the detection and prevention of fraud.

Communicate Internal Control Deficiencies

As discussed in Chapter 10, the auditor must also communicate significant deficiencies and material weaknesses in the design or operation of internal control. In larger companies, this communication is made to the audit committee and in smaller companies, to the owners or senior management. The nature and form of that communication were discussed in Chapter 10.

Other Communication with Audit Committee

SAS 61 (AU 380) and amendments require the auditor to communicate certain additional information obtained during the audit for all SEC engagements and other audits where there is an audit committee or similarly designated body. This communication is not required for most small, nonpublic companies. As with all communications to the audit committee, the purpose is to keep the committee informed of auditing issues and findings that will assist it in performing its supervisory role for financial statements.

The following are major items that must be communicated to the audit committee or similarly designated body under SAS 61:

- Auditor's responsibilities under auditing standards, including responsibility for evaluating internal control and the concept of reasonable rather than absolute assurance
- Significant accounting policies selected and applied to the financial statements, including management's judgments and estimates of accounting-related issues
- Significant financial statement adjustments found during the audit and the implications of both those that management has chosen to record and those proposed but not recorded, as well as uncorrected misstatements determined by management to be immaterial both individually and in the aggregate
- Auditor's judgment about the quality, not just the acceptability, of the client's accounting principles
- Disagreements with management about the scope of the audit, applicability of accounting principles, or wording of the audit report
- Difficulties encountered in performing the audit, such as lack of availability of client personnel and failure to provide necessary information
- Significant issues discussed with management prior to the retention of the auditor, especially those related to the application of accounting principles and auditing standards
- Auditor's responsibilities for other information included in documents containing audited financial statements, if applicable

The Sarbanes–Oxley Act of 2002 expands these communication requirements by also requiring the auditor of a public company to timely report the following items to the audit committee:

- All critical accounting policies and practices to be used
- All alternative treatments of financial information within generally accepted accounting principles that have been discussed with management, ramifications of the use of such alternative disclosures and treatments, and the treatment preferred by the auditor
- Other material written communications between the auditor and management, such as any management letter or schedule of unadjusted differences

As the audit of the public company is completed, the auditor should determine that the audit committee is informed about the initial selection of and changes in significant accounting policies or their application during the current audit period. When changes have occurred, the auditor should inform the committee of the reasons for the change. The auditor should also communicate information about methods used to account for significant unusual transactions and the effect of significant accounting policies in controversial or emerging areas.

Communication with the audit committee normally takes place more than once during each audit and can be oral, written, or both. For example, issues dealing with the auditor's responsibilities and significant accounting policies are usually discussed early in the audit, preferably during the planning phase. Disagreements with management and difficulties encountered in performing the audit are communicated after the audit is completed, or earlier if the problems hinder the auditor's ability to complete the audit. The most important matters are communicated in writing to minimize misunderstanding and to provide documentation in the event of subsequent disagreement.

Audit Committee Membership

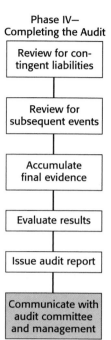

Management Letters

A **management letter** is intended to inform client personnel of the CPA's recommendations for improving any aspect of the client's business. The recommendations focus on suggestions for more efficient operations. The combination of the auditor's experience in various businesses and a thorough understanding gained in conducting the audit places the auditor in a unique position to provide management with assistance.

Many CPA firms write a management letter for every audit to demonstrate to management that the firm adds value to the business beyond the audit service provided. The intent is to encourage a better relationship between the CPA firm and management and to suggest additional tax and management services that the CPA firm can provide. Some CPA firms generate considerable additional revenue from the additional services.

A management letter is different from a letter reporting significant deficiencies in internal control, which was discussed in Chapter 10. The latter is required when there are significant deficiencies or material weaknesses in internal control, and must follow a prescribed format and be sent in accordance with the requirements of auditing standards. A management letter is optional and is intended to help the client operate its business more effectively.

There is no standard format or approach for writing management letters. Each letter should be developed to meet the style of the auditor and the needs of the client, consistent with the CPA firm's concept of management letters. It should be noted that many auditors combine the management letter with the letter about significant deficiencies and material weaknesses. On smaller audits, it is common for the auditor to communicate operational suggestions orally rather than by a management letter.

SUBSEQUENT DISCOVERY OF FACTS

OBJECTIVE 24-7

Identify the auditor's responsibilities when facts affecting the audit report are discovered after its issuance.

After the auditor issues the audit report and completes all communications with management and the audit committee, the audit is finished. The next major contact the auditor has with the client is when the planning process for next year's audit begins. Although it rarely happens, if the auditor becomes aware *after the audited financial statements have been issued* that some information included in the statements is materially misleading, the auditor has an obligation to make certain that users who are relying on the financial statements are informed about the misstatements. If the auditor had known about the misstatements before the audit report was issued, the auditor would have insisted that management correct the misstatements or, alternatively, a different audit report would have been issued. When this occurs, it is referred to as subsequent discovery of facts. Although subsequent discovery of facts is not a part of completing the audit, it is included in this chapter because it is easier to understand when compared and contrasted with subsequent events.

The most likely case in which the auditor is faced with this problem occurs when the financial statements are determined to include a material misstatement subsequent to the issuance of an unqualified report. Some possible causes of misstatements are the inclusion of material nonexistent sales, the failure to write off obsolete inventory, or the omission of an essential footnote. Regardless of whether the failure to discover the misstatement was the fault of the auditor or the client, the auditor's responsibility remains the same.

The most desirable approach to follow if the auditor discovers that the statements are misleading after they have been issued is to request that the client issue an immediate revision of the financial statements containing an explanation of the reasons for the revision. If a subsequent period's financial statements are completed before the revised statements would be issued, it is acceptable to disclose the misstatements in the subsequent period's statements. When pertinent, the client should inform the SEC and other regulatory agencies of the misleading financial statements. The auditor has the responsibility for making certain that the client has taken the appropriate steps in informing users of the misleading statements.

If the client refuses to cooperate in disclosing the misstated information, the auditor must inform the board of directors of this fact. The auditor must also notify regulatory agencies having jurisdiction over the client and, when practical, each person who relies on the financial statements, that the statements are no longer trustworthy. If the stock is publicly held, it is acceptable to request the SEC and the stock exchange to notify the stockholders.

It is important to understand that the subsequent discovery of facts requiring the recall or reissuance of financial statements *does not arise from business events occurring after the date of the auditor's report*. For example, if an account receivable is believed to be collectible after an adequate review of the facts at the date of the audit report, but the customer subsequently files bankruptcy, a revision of the financial statements is not required. The statements must be recalled or reissued only when information that would indicate that the statements were not fairly presented *already existed at the audit report date*. If, in the

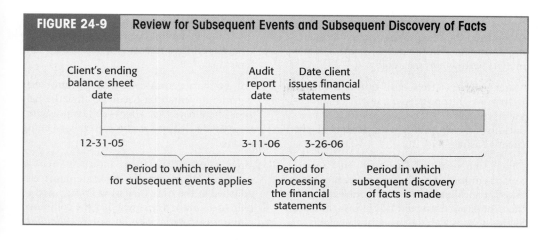

FIGURE 24-9   Review for Subsequent Events and Subsequent Discovery of Facts

Client's ending
balance sheet
date

Audit
report
date

Date client
issues financial
statements

12-31-05   3-11-06   3-26-06

Period to which review
for subsequent events applies

Period for
processing
the financial
statements

Period in which
subsequent discovery
of facts is made

previous example, the customer had filed for bankruptcy before the audit report date, there is a subsequent discovery of facts.

In an earlier section, it was shown that the auditor's responsibility for subsequent events review begins as of the balance sheet date and ends on the date of the completion of the field work. Any pertinent information discovered as a part of the review can be incorporated in the financial statements before they are issued. Note that the auditor has no responsibility to search for subsequent facts of the nature discussed in this section, but if the auditor discovers that issued financial statements are improperly stated, the auditor must take action to correct them. The auditor's responsibility for reporting on improperly issued financial statements does not start until the date of the audit report. Typically, an existing material misstatement is found as a part of the subsequent year's audit, or it may be reported to the auditor by the client.

Figure 24-9, which includes the same dates as Figure 24-3 on page 717, shows the difference in the period covered by the review for subsequent events and that for the discovery of facts after the audit report date. If the auditor discovers subsequent facts after the audit report date but before the financial statements are issued, the auditor will require that the financial statements be revised before they are issued.

The auditor's responsibility for the period from 3-11-06 to 3-26-06 is the same as that for the period after 3-26-06. If a subsequent event is discovered in this period, one of the two options discussed under the "Dual Dating" heading on page 719 should be followed.

ESSENTIAL TERMS

Commitments—agreements that the entity will hold to a fixed set of conditions, such as the purchase or sale of merchandise at a stated price, at a future date, regardless of what happens to profits or to the economy as a whole

Completing the engagement checklist—a reminder to the auditor of aspects of the audit that may have been overlooked

Contingent liability—a potential future obligation to an outside party for an unknown amount resulting from activities that have already taken place

Dual-dated audit report—the use of one audit report date for normal subsequent events and a later date for one or more subsequent events that come to the auditor's attention after the field work has been completed

Financial statement disclosure checklist—a questionnaire that reminds the auditor of disclosure problems commonly encountered in audits and that facilitates final review of the entire audit by an independent partner

Independent review—a review of the financial statements and the entire set of audit files by a completely independent reviewer to whom the audit team must justify the evidence accumulated and the conclusions reached

Inquiry of the client's attorneys—a letter from the client's legal counsel informing the auditor of pending litigation or any other information involving legal counsel that is relevant to financial statement disclosure

Letter of representation—a written communication from the client to the auditor formalizing statements that the client has made about matters pertinent to the audit

Management letter—an optional letter written by the auditor to a client's management containing the auditor's recommendations for improving any aspect of the client's business

Other information included in annual reports—information that is not a part of published financial statements but is published with them; auditors must read this information for inconsistencies with the financial statements

Review for subsequent events—the auditing procedures performed by auditors to identify and evaluate subsequent events; also known as a *post-balance-sheet review*

Review of audit documentation—a review of the completed audit files by another member of the audit firm to ensure quality and counteract bias

Subsequent events—transactions and other pertinent events that occurred after the balance sheet date that affect the fair presentation or disclosure of the statements being audited

Unadjusted misstatement audit schedule—a summary of immaterial misstatements not adjusted at the time they were found, used to help the auditor assess whether the combined amount is material; also known as a *summary of possible misstatements*

Unasserted claim—a potential legal claim against a client where the condition for a claim exists but no claim has been filed

REVIEW QUESTIONS

24-1 (Objective 24-1) Distinguish between a contingent liability and an actual liability and give three examples of each.

24-2 (Objective 24-1) In the audit of the James Mobley Company, you are concerned about the possibility of contingent liabilities resulting in income tax disputes. Discuss the procedures you could use for an extensive investigation in this area.

24-3 (Objective 24-1) Explain why an auditor would be interested in a client's future commitments to purchase raw materials at a fixed price.

24-4 (Objective 24-2) Explain why the analysis of legal expense is an essential part of every audit engagement.

24-5 (Objectives 24-1, 24-2) During the audit of the Merrill Manufacturing Company, Ralph Pyson, CPA, has become aware of four lawsuits against the client through discussions with the client, reading corporate minutes, and reviewing correspondence files. How should Pyson determine the materiality of the lawsuits and the proper disclosure in the financial statements?

24-6 (Objective 24-2) Distinguish between an asserted and an unasserted claim. Explain why a client's attorney may not reveal an unasserted claim.

24-7 (Objective 24-2) Describe the action that an auditor should take if an attorney refuses to provide information that is within the attorney's jurisdiction and may directly affect the fair presentation of the financial statements.

24-8 (Objective 24-3) Distinguish between the two general types of subsequent events and explain how they differ. Give two examples of each type.

24-9 (Objectives 24-2, 24-3) In obtaining letters from attorneys, Bill Malano's aim is to receive the letters as early as possible after the balance sheet date. This provides him with a signed letter from every attorney in time to properly investigate any exceptions. It also eliminates the problem of a lot of unresolved loose ends near the end of the audit. Evaluate Malano's approach.

24-10 (Objective 24-3) What major considerations should the auditor take into account in determining how extensive the review of subsequent events should be?

24-11 (Objective 24-3) Identify five audit procedures normally done as a part of the review for subsequent events.

24-12 (Objectives 24-3, 24-7) Distinguish between subsequent events occurring between the balance sheet date and the date of the auditor's report, and subsequent discovery of facts existing at the date of the auditor's report. Give two examples of each and explain the appropriate action by the auditor in each instance.

24-13 (Objective 24-4) Miles Lawson, CPA, believes that the final summarization is the easiest part of the audit if careful planning is followed throughout the engagement. He makes sure that each segment of the audit is completed before he goes on to the next. When the last segment of the engagement is completed, he is finished with the audit. He believes this may cause each part of the audit to take a little longer, but he makes up for it by not having to do the final summarization. Evaluate Lawson's approach.

24-14 (Objectives 24-4, 24-5) Compare and contrast the accumulation of audit evidence and the evaluation of the adequacy of the disclosures in the financial statements. Give two examples in which adequate disclosure could depend heavily on the accumulation of evidence and two others in which audit evidence does not normally significantly affect the adequacy of the disclosure.

24-15 (Objectives 24-4, 24-6) Distinguish between a client letter of representation and a management letter and state the primary purpose of each. List some items that might be included in each letter.

24-16 (Objective 24-4) Explain what is meant by information accompanying basic financial statements. Provide two examples of such information. What levels of assurance may the CPA offer for this information?

24-17 (Objective 24-4) What is meant by reading other financial information in annual reports? Give an example of the type of information the auditor is examining.

24-18 (Objective 24-5) Distinguish between regular audit documentation review and independent review and state the purpose of each. Give two examples of important potential findings in each of these two types of review.

24-19 (Objective 24-6) Describe matters that the auditor must communicate to audit committees of public companies.

MULTIPLE CHOICE QUESTIONS FROM CPA EXAMINATIONS

24-20 (Objective 24-1) The following questions deal with contingent liabilities. Choose the best response.

a. The audit step most likely to reveal the existence of contingent liabilities is
   (1) a review of vouchers paid during the month following the year-end.
   (2) accounts payable confirmations.
   (3) an inquiry directed to legal counsel.
   (4) mortgage-note confirmation.

b. When obtaining evidence regarding litigation against a client, the CPA would be *least* interested in determining
   (1) an estimate of when the matter will be resolved.
   (2) the period in which the underlying cause of the litigation occurred.
   (3) the probability of an unfavorable outcome.
   (4) an estimate of the potential loss.

c. When a contingency is resolved subsequent to the issuance of audited financial statements, which correctly contained disclosure of the contingency in the footnotes based on information available at the date of issuance, the auditor should
   (1) insist that the client issue revised financial statements.
   (2) inform the audit committee that the report cannot be relied on.
   (3) take no action regarding the event.
   (4) inform the appropriate authorities that the report cannot be relied on.

24-21 (Objective 24-4) The following questions concern letters of representation. Choose the best response.

a. A principal purpose of a letter of representation from management is to

(1) serve as an introduction to company personnel and an authorization to examine the records.

(2) discharge the auditor from legal liability for the audit.

(3) confirm in writing management's approval of limitations on the scope of the audit.

(4) remind management of its primary responsibility for financial statements.

b. The date of the management representation letter should coincide with the

(1) date of the auditor's report.

(2) balance sheet date.

(3) date of the latest subsequent event referred to in the notes to the financial statements.

(4) date of the engagement agreement.

c. Management's refusal to furnish a written representation on a matter that the auditor considers essential constitutes

(1) prima facie evidence that the financial statements are not presented fairly.

(2) a violation of the Foreign Corrupt Practices Act.

(3) an uncertainty sufficient to preclude an unqualified opinion.

(4) a scope limitation sufficient to preclude an unqualified opinion.

24-22 (Objective 24-3) The following questions deal with review of subsequent events. Choose the best response.

a. Subsequent events for reporting purposes are defined as events that occur subsequent to the

(1) balance sheet date.

(2) date of the auditor's report.

(3) balance sheet date but before the date of the auditor's report.

(4) date of the auditor's report and concern contingencies that are not reflected in the financial statements.

b. An example of an event occurring in the period of the auditor's field work subsequent to the end of the year being audited that normally would not require disclosure in the financial statements or auditor's report would be

(1) decreased sales volume resulting from a general business recession.

(2) serious damage to the company's plant from a widespread flood.

(3) issuance of a widely advertised capital stock issue with restrictive covenants.

(4) settlement of a large liability for considerably less than the amount recorded.

c. Karr has audited the financial statements of Lurch Corporation for the year ended December 31, 2005. Karr's field work was completed on February 27, 2006; Karr's auditor's report was dated February 28, 2006, and was received by the management of Lurch on March 5, 2006. On April 4, 2006, the management of Lurch asked that Karr approve inclusion of this report in their annual report to stockholders, which will include unaudited financial statements for the first quarter ended March 31, 2006. Karr approved the inclusion of the auditor's report in the annual report to stockholders. Under the circumstances, Karr is responsible for inquiring as to subsequent events occurring through

(1) February 27, 2006.   (3) March 31, 2006.

(2) February 28, 2006.   (4) April 4, 2006.

24-23 (Objective 24-4) The following questions concern information accompanying basic financial statements. Choose the best response.

a. Which of the following best describes the auditor's reporting responsibility concerning information accompanying the basic financial statements in an auditor-submitted document?

(1) The auditor has no reporting responsibility concerning information accompanying the basic financial statements.

(2) The auditor should report on the information accompanying the basic financial statements only if the auditor participated in its preparation.

(3) The auditor should report on the information accompanying the basic financial statements only if the auditor did not participate in its preparation.

(4) The auditor should report on all the information included in the document.

b. Ansman, CPA, has been requested by a client, Rainco Corp., to prepare information in addition to the basic financial statements for this year's audit engagement. Which of the following is the best reason for Rainco's requesting the additional information?

(1) To provide an opinion about the supplemental information when certain items are not in accordance with GAAP.

(2) To provide Rainco's creditors a greater degree of assurance as to the financial soundness of the company.

(3) To provide Rainco's management with information to supplement and analyze the basic financial statements.

(4) To provide the documentation required by the SEC in anticipation of a public offering of Rainco's stock.

c. Ansman, CPA, has been requested by a client, Rainco Corp., to prepare additional information accompanying the basic financial statements for this year's audit engagement. In issuing the additional information, Ansman must be certain to

(1) issue a standard short-form report on the same engagement.

(2) include a description of the scope of the audit in more detail than the description in the usual short-form report.

(3) state the source of any statistical data and that such data have not been subjected to the same auditing procedures as the basic financial statements.

(4) maintain a clear-cut distinction between management's representations and the auditor's representations.

DISCUSSION QUESTIONS AND PROBLEMS

24-24 (Objective 24-1) Elizabeth Johnson, CPA, has completed the audit of notes payable and other liabilities for Valley River Electrical Services and now plans to audit contingent liabilities and commitments.

a. Distinguish between contingent liabilities and commitments and explain why both are important in an audit. **Required**

b. Identify three useful audit procedures for uncovering contingent liabilities that Johnson would likely perform in the normal conduct of the audit, even if she had no responsibility for uncovering contingencies.

c. Identify three other procedures Johnson is likely to perform specifically for the purpose of identifying undisclosed contingencies.

24-25 (Objective 24-1) In an audit of the Marco Corporation as of December 31, 2005, the following situations exist. No entries have been made in the accounting records in relation to these items.

1. The Marco Corporation has guaranteed the payment of interest on the 10-year, first mortgage bonds of the Newart Company, an affiliate. Outstanding bonds of the Newart Company amount to $150,000 with interest payable at 5% per annum, due June 1 and December 1 of each year. The bonds were issued by the Newart Company on December 1, 2003, and all interest payments have been met by that company with the exception of the payment due December 1, 2005. The Marco Corporation states that it will pay the defaulted interest to the bondholders on January 15, 2006.

2. During the year 2005, the Marco Corporation was named as a defendant in a suit for damages by the Dalton Company for breach of contract. An adverse decision to the Marco Corporation was rendered and the Dalton Company was awarded $40,000 damages. At the time of the audit, the case was under appeal to a higher court.

3. On December 23, 2005, the Marco Corporation declared a common stock dividend of 1,000 shares with a par value of $100,000 of its common stock, payable February 2, 2006, to the common stockholders of record December 30, 2005.

a. Define contingent liability. **Required**

b. Describe the audit procedures you would use to learn about each of the situations listed.

c. Describe the nature of the adjusting entries or disclosure, if any, you would make for each of these situations.*

24-26 (Objectives 24-3, 24-7) The field work for the June 30, 2005, audit of Tracy Brewing Company was finished August 19, 2005, and the completed financial statements, accompanied by the signed audit reports, were mailed September 6, 2005. In each of the highly material independent events (a through i), state the appropriate action (1 through 4) for the situation and justify your response. The alternative actions are as follows:

*AICPA adapted.

1. Adjust the June 30, 2005, financial statements.
2. Disclose the information in a footnote in the June 30, 2005, financial statements.
3. Request the client to recall the June 30, 2005, statements for revision.
4. No action is required.

The events are as follows:

a. On December 14, 2005, the auditor discovered that a debtor of Tracy Brewing went bankrupt on October 2, 2005. The sale had taken place April 15, 2005, but the amount appeared collectible at June 30, 2005, and August 19, 2005.

b. On August 15, 2005, the auditor discovered that a debtor of Tracy Brewing went bankrupt on August 1, 2005. The most recent sale had taken place April 2, 2004, and no cash receipts had been received since that date.

c. On December 14, 2005, the auditor discovered that a debtor of Tracy Brewing went bankrupt on July 15, 2005, due to declining financial health. The sale had taken place January 15, 2005.

d. On August 6, 2005, the auditor discovered that a debtor of Tracy Brewing went bankrupt on July 30, 2005. The cause of the bankruptcy was an unexpected loss of a major lawsuit on July 15, 2005, resulting from a product deficiency suit by a different customer.

e. On August 6, 2005, the auditor discovered that a debtor of Tracy Brewing went bankrupt on July 30, 2005, for a sale that took place July 3, 2005. The cause of the bankruptcy was a major uninsured fire on July 20, 2005.

f. On May 31, 2005, the auditor discovered an uninsured lawsuit against Tracy Brewing that had originated on February 28, 2005.

g. On July 20, 2005, Tracy Brewing settled a lawsuit out of court that had originated in 2002 and is currently listed as a contingent liability.

h. On September 14, 2005, Tracy Brewing lost a court case that had originated in 2004 for an amount equal to the lawsuit. The June 30, 2005, footnotes state that in the opinion of legal counsel there will be a favorable settlement.

i. On July 20, 2005, a lawsuit was filed against Tracy Brewing for a patent infringement action that allegedly took place in early 2005. In the opinion of legal counsel, there is a danger of a significant loss to the client.

24-27 (Objective 24-5) Mel Adams, CPA, is a partner in a medium-sized CPA firm and takes an active part in the conduct of every audit he supervises. He follows the practice of reviewing all audit files of subordinates as soon as it is convenient, rather than waiting until the end of the audit. When the audit is nearly finished, Adams reviews the audit files again to make sure that he has not missed anything significant. Because he makes most of the major decisions on the audit, there is rarely anything that requires further investigation. When he completes the review, he prepares a draft of the financial statements, gets them approved by management, and has them assembled in his firm's office. No other partner reviews the audit documentation because Adams is responsible for signing the audit reports.

Required

a. Evaluate the practice of reviewing the audit files of subordinates on a continuing basis rather than when the audit is completed.

b. Is it acceptable for Adams to prepare the financial statements rather than make the client assume the responsibility?

c. Evaluate the practice of not having a review of the audit documentation by another partner in the firm.

24-28 (Objective 24-4) Leslie Morgan, CPA, has prepared a letter of representation for the president and controller to sign. It contains references to the following items:

1. Inventory is fairly stated at the lower of cost or market and includes no obsolete items.
2. All actual and contingent liabilities are properly included in the financial statements.
3. All subsequent events of relevance to the financial statements have been disclosed.

Required

a. Why is it desirable to have a letter of representation from the client concerning these matters when the audit evidence accumulated during the course of the engagement is meant to verify the same information?

b. To what extent is the letter of representation useful as audit evidence? Explain.

c. List several other types of information commonly included in a letter of representation.

24-29 (Objective 24-6) In a letter to the audit committee of the Cline Wholesale Company, Jerry Schwartz, CPA, informed them of material weaknesses in the control of inventory. In a separate letter to senior management, he elaborated on how the material weaknesses could result in a significant misstatement of inventory by the failure to recognize the existence of obsolete items. In addition, Schwartz made specific recommendations in the management letter on how to improve internal control and save clerical time by installing a computer system for the company's perpetual records. Management accepted the recommendations and installed the system under Schwartz's direction. For several months, the system worked beautifully, but unforeseen problems developed when a master file was erased. The cost of reproducing and processing the inventory records to correct the error was significant, and management decided to scrap the entire project. The company sued Schwartz for failure to use adequate professional judgment in making the recommendations.

a. What is Schwartz's legal and professional responsibility in the issuance of management letters? **Required**

b. Discuss the major considerations that will determine whether he is liable in this situation.

24-30 (Objective 24-3) The following unrelated events occurred after the balance sheet date but before the audit report was prepared:

1. The granting of a retroactive pay increase
2. Determination by the federal government of additional income tax due for a prior year
3. Filing of an antitrust suit by the federal government
4. Declaration of a stock dividend
5. Sale of a fixed asset at a substantial profit

a. Explain how each of the items might have come to the auditor's attention. **Required**

b. Discuss the auditor's responsibility to recognize each of these in connection with the report.*

24-31 (Objective 24-3) The philosophy of Irene Hatton, CPA, is to intensively audit transactions taking place during the current audit period but to ignore subsequent transactions. She believes that each year should stand on its own and be audited in the year in which the transactions take place. According to Hatton, "If a transaction recorded in the subsequent period is audited in the current period, it is verified twice—once this year and again in next year's audit. That is a duplication of effort and a waste of time."

a. Explain the fallacy in Hatton's argument. **Required**

b. Give six specific examples of information obtained by examining subsequent events that are essential to the current period audit.

24-32 (Objective 24-2) In analyzing legal expense for the Boastman Bottle Company, Mary Little, CPA, observes that the company has paid legal fees to three different law firms during the current year. In accordance with her CPA firm's normal operating practice, Little requests standard attorney letters as of the balance sheet date from each of the three law firms.

On the last day of field work, Little notes that one of the attorney letters has not yet been received. The second letter contains a statement to the effect that the law firm deals exclusively in registering patents and refuses to comment on any lawsuits or other legal affairs of the client. The third attorney's letter states that there is an outstanding unpaid bill due from the client and recognizes the existence of a potentially material lawsuit against the client but refuses to comment further to protect the legal rights of the client.

a. Evaluate Little's approach to sending the attorney letters and her follow-up on the responses. **Required**

b. What should Little do about each of the letters?

24-33 (Objective 24-4) As a part of the audit of Ren Gold Manufacturing Company, a nonpublic company, management requests basic financial statements and separately, the same basic financial statements accompanied by additional information. Management informs you that the intent is to use the basic financial statements for bankers, other creditors, and the two owners who are not involved in management. The basic financial statements accompanied by the additional

*AICPA adapted.

information are to be used only by management. Management requests the inclusion of specific information but asks that no audit work be done beyond what is needed for the basic financial statements. The following is requested:

1. A schedule of insurance in force.
2. The auditor's feelings about the adequacy of the insurance coverage.
3. A 5-year summary of the most important company ratios, with the appropriate ratios to be determined at the auditor's discretion.
4. A schedule of notes payable accompanied by interest rates, collateral, and a payment schedule.
5. An aged trial balance of accounts receivable and evaluation of the adequacy of the allowance for uncollectible accounts.
6. A summary of fixed asset additions.
7. Material weaknesses in internal control and recommendations to improve internal control.

Required

a. What is the difference between basic financial statements and additional information?

b. What are the purposes of additional information accompanying basic financial statements?

c. For the previously listed items (1 through 7), state which ones could appropriately be included as additional information. Give reasons for your answer.

d. Identify three other items that may appropriately be included as additional information.

e. Assume that an unqualified opinion is proper for the basic financial statements report, that no testing was done beyond that required for the basic financial statements report, and that only appropriate information is included in the additional information. Write the proper auditor's report.

CASE

24-34 (Objective 24-5) In your audit of Aviary Industries for calendar year 2005, you found a number of matters that you believe represent possible adjustments to the company's books. These matters are described below. Management's attitude is that "once the books are closed, they're closed," and management does not want to make any adjustments. Planning materiality for the engagement was $100,000, determined by computing 5% of expected income before taxes. Actual income before taxes on the financial statements prior to any adjustments is $1,652,867.

Possible adjustments:

1. Several credit memos that were processed and recorded after year-end relate to sales and accounts receivable for 2005. These total $23,529.
2. Inventory cutoff tests indicate that $22,357 of inventory received on December 30, 2005, was recorded as purchases and accounts payable in 2006. These items were included in the inventory count at year-end and therefore were included in ending inventory.
3. Inventory cutoff tests also indicate several sales invoices recorded in 2005 for goods that were shipped in early 2006. The goods were not included in inventory but were set aside in a separate shipping area. The total amount of these shipments was $36,022. (Ignore cost of sales for this item.)
4. The company wrote several checks at the end of 2005 for accounts payable that were held and not mailed until January 15, 2006. These totaled $48,336. Recorded cash and accounts payable at December 31, 2005, are $2,356,553 and $2,666,290, respectively.
5. The company has not established a reserve for obsolescence of inventories. Your tests indicate that such a reserve is appropriate in an amount somewhere between $20,000 and $40,000.
6. Your review of the allowance for uncollectible accounts indicates that it may be understated by between $25,000 and $50,000.

Required

a. Determine the adjustments that you believe must be made for Aviary's financial statements to be fairly presented. Include the amounts and accounts affected by each adjustment.

b. Why may Aviary Industries' management resist making these adjustments?

c. Explain what you consider the most positive way of approaching management personnel to convince them to make your proposed changes.

d. Describe your responsibilities related to unadjusted misstatements that management has determined are immaterial individually and in the aggregate.

e. Assuming Aviary Industries is a public company, describe how the noted adjustments might impact your audit report on internal control over financial reporting.

INTERNET PROBLEM 24-1: SUBSEQUENT EVENTS

Reference the CW site. This problem requires students to use the Internet to research and classify actual subsequent event disclosures reported in SEC filings.

PART 6

OTHER ASSURANCE AND NONASSURANCE SERVICES

Chapter 1 introduced assurance and nonassurance services offered by CPA firms and other types of auditors. The chapters in Part 6 expand that discussion. Assurance services other than audits and nonassurance services are increasingly important to both CPA firms and other auditors.

Chapter 25 deals with assurance and nonassurance services, both traditional and emerging, that CPA firms offer. Chapter 26 covers services performed most often by governmental and internal auditors, including internal financial auditing, governmental financial auditing, and operational auditing.

OTHER ASSURANCE SERVICES

SKEPTICISM APPLIES TO ALL TYPES OF ENGAGEMENTS

Barnhart Construction Company was a contractor specializing in apartment complexes in the Southwest. The owner of the construction company, David Barnhart, reached an agreement with a promoter named Alton Leonard to serve as a contractor on three construction projects Leonard was currently marketing. One problem with the agreement was that Barnhart would not receive final payment for the construction work until all the partnership units were sold.

The first partnership offering was completely sold and Barnhart was paid. Unfortunately, the next two partnerships were not completely sold. To solve this problem, Barnhart loaned money to relatives and key employees who bought the necessary interests for the partnerships to close so that Barnhart would receive the final payment.

Renee Lathrup, CPA, a sole practitioner, was engaged to conduct a review of Barnhart Construction's financial statements. She noticed that the accounting records showed loans receivable from a number of employees and individuals named Barnhart. She also observed that the loans were made just before the second and third partnerships closed and that they were in multiples of $15,000, the cost of a partnership unit. Renee asked Barnhart to explain what happened. Barnhart told Renee, "When I received the money from the first partnership escrow, I wanted to do something nice for relatives and employees who had been loyal to me over the years." He told Renee, "This is just my way of sharing my good fortune with the ones I love. The equality of the amounts is just a coincidence."

When Renee considered the reasonableness of this scenario, she found it hard to believe. First, the timing was odd. Second, the amounts seemed to be an unusual coincidence. Third, if he really had wanted to do something special for these folks, why didn't he give them something, rather than loan them money? Renee asked that the promoter, Leonard, send her detailed information on the subscriptions for each partnership. Leonard refused, stating that he was under legal obligation to keep all information confidential. When Renee pressed Barnhart, he also refused further cooperation, although he did say he would "represent" to Renee that the loans had nothing to do with closing the partnerships so that he could get his money. At this point, Renee withdrew from the engagement.

LEARNING OBJECTIVES

After studying this chapter, you should be able to

25-1 Distinguish AICPA attestation standards from auditing standards and know the type of engagements to which they apply.

25-2 Understand the nature of *WebTrust* assurance services.

25-3 Understand the nature of *SysTrust* assurance services.

25-4 Describe special engagements to attest to prospective financial statements.

25-5 Describe agreed-upon procedures engagements.

25-6 Understand the level of assurance and evidence requirements for review and compilation services.

25-7 Describe special engagements to review interim financial information for public companies.

25-8 Describe other audit and limited assurance engagements related to historical financial statements.

The text material to this point has been primarily about the performing of audits of historical financial statements that are presented in conformance with generally accepted accounting principles (GAAP). We now discuss other types of assurance services offered by CPAs. The example that opened the chapter involved a review of historical financial statements, a limited assurance engagement involving historical financial statements that was first introduced in Chapter 1. CPAs provide many other types of assurance services related to historical financial statements to meet the specific needs of financial statement users. With increases in technology and information, CPAs are increasingly asked to attest to controls and other types of forward-looking information. The level of assurance, extent of evidence, and type of report depend upon the nature of the service offered.

This chapter examines other assurance services related to several types of attestation engagements, such as *WebTrust* and *SysTrust* engagements, and reports on forecasted financial statements. The chapter also discusses reviews and compilations of historical financial statements and other types of assurance services engagements.

ATTESTATION ENGAGEMENTS

OBJECTIVE 25-1

Distinguish AICPA attestation standards from auditing standards and know the type of engagements to which they apply.

Chapter 1 described assurance services as independent professional services that improve the quality of information for decision makers. Individuals who are responsible for making business decisions seek assurance services to help improve the reliability and relevance of the information used as the basis for their decisions. One category of assurance services provided by CPAs is attestation services.

CPAs have increasingly been asked to perform a variety of audit-like, or attest, services for different purposes. In an **attestation engagement**, the CPA reports on the reliability of information or an assertion made by another party. An example is a bank that requests a CPA to report in writing whether an audit client has adhered to all requirements of a loan agreement.

Attestation Standards

There are 11 attestation standards that parallel the 10 generally accepted auditing standards. They are included in Table 25-1 along with generally accepted auditing standards for comparison. The attestation standards are stated in sufficiently general terms to enable practitioners to apply them to any attestation engagement, including new types of engagements that may arise.

The most notable differences in the attestation and generally accepted auditing standards are in general attestation standards 2 and 3. Standard 2 requires that the practitioner have adequate knowledge of the subject matter over which there is attestation. For example, if a practitioner is to attest to a company's compliance with environmental protection laws, the practitioner needs a thorough knowledge of the laws and methods that companies use to assure compliance. Standard 3 requires that the subject matter be able to be evaluated against criteria that are suitable and available to users. Again, using the example of environmental protection laws, it may be difficult for the practitioner to conclude whether there is compliance because of measurement difficulties and the lack of specific criteria.

Additional guidance for the performance of specific attestation engagements is provided through the issuance of **Statements on Standards for Attestation Engagements (SSAE)**. The Auditing Standards Board attempts to distinguish between issues that should be addressed by auditing standards and others that should be addressed by attestation standards, even though both are attestations. In general, attestations that deal with providing assurance on historical financial statements, including one or more parts of those statements, are addressed in auditing standards. Examples include audits of financial statements prepared in accordance with GAAP or some other comprehensive basis of accounting, audits of only a balance sheet, and audits of individual accounts. All other forms of attestation are addressed in the attestation standards [an exception is reviews of historical financial statements of a nonpublic entity, which are addressed in SSARS (see p. 752)]. Attestation standards are established by the Auditing Standards Board following the same process used for auditing standards. Attestation standards are labeled as AT rather than AU. As of the date of publication of this text, standards through SSAE 10 have been issued.

TABLE 25-1	Comparison of Attestation Standards and Generally Accepted Auditing Standards

Attestation Standards	**Generally Accepted Auditing Standards**
General Standards	
1. The engagement shall be performed by a practitioner having adequate technical training and proficiency in the attest function. 2. The engagement shall be performed by a practitioner having adequate knowledge in the subject matter. 3. The practitioner shall perform an engagement only if he or she has reason to believe that the subject matter is capable of evaluation against criteria that are suitable and available to users. 4. In all matters relating to the engagement, an independence in mental attitude shall be maintained by the practitioner. 5. Due professional care shall be exercised in the planning and performance of the engagement.	1. The audit is to be performed by a person or persons having adequate technical training and proficiency as an auditor. 2. In all matters relating to the assignment, an independence in mental attitude is to be maintained by the auditor or auditors. 3. Due professional care is to be exercised in the performance of the audit and the preparation of the report.
Standards of Field Work	
1. The work shall be adequately planned and assistants, if any, shall be properly supervised. 2. Sufficient evidence shall be obtained to provide a reasonable basis for the conclusion that is expressed in the report.	1. The work is to be adequately planned and assistants, if any, are to be properly supervised. 2. A sufficient understanding of internal control is to be obtained to plan the audit and to determine the nature, timing, and extent of tests to be performed. 3. Sufficient competent evidential matter is to be obtained through inspection, observation, inquiries, and confirmations to afford a reasonable basis for an opinion regarding the financial statements under audit.
Standards of Reporting	
1. The report shall identify the subject matter or assertion being reported on and state the character of the engagement. 2. The report shall state the practitioner's conclusion about the subject matter or the assertion in relation to the criteria against which the subject matter was evaluated. 3. The report shall state all of the practitioner's significant reservations about the engagement, the subject matter, and, if applicable, the assertion related thereto. 4. The report shall state that the use of the report is restricted to specified parties, in certain circumstances.	1. The report shall state whether the financial statements are presented in accordance with generally accepted accounting principles. 2. The report shall identify those circumstances in which such principles have not been consistently observed in the current period in relation to the preceding period. 3. Informative disclosures in the financial statements are to be regarded as reasonably adequate unless otherwise stated in the report. 4. The report shall either contain an expression of opinion regarding the financial statements, taken as a whole, or an assertion to the effect that an opinion cannot be expressed. When an overall opinion cannot be expressed, the reasons therefor should be stated. In all cases where an auditor's name is associated with financial statements, the report should contain a clear-cut indication of the character of the auditor's work, if any, and the degree of responsibility the auditor is taking.

The Auditing Standards Board has consciously made the decision to not attempt to define the potential boundaries of attestation engagements except in conceptual terms because new services are likely to arise. For example, PricewaterhouseCoopers has been attesting to the balloting for the Miss America contest for decades, but attesting to compliance with environmental protection laws started only in recent years.

Types of Attestation Engagements

The AICPA and the Canadian Institute of Chartered Accountants (CICA) have jointly developed assurance services related to e-commerce and information technology. These groups of services, known as *WebTrust* and *SysTrust*, are performed under the attestation standards. In addition, specific attestation standards have been developed in the following areas: prospective financial statements, pro forma financial information, reports on internal control over financial reporting for private companies, compliance with laws and regulations, agreed-upon procedures engagements, and management's discussion and analysis.

Standards have been developed for these types of engagements because practitioners are performing these services in sufficiently large numbers to need more specific guidance than is provided by the general attestation standards. The absence of specific standards for a type of service is not intended to imply that it is inappropriate to perform such a service.

Levels of Service

The attestation standards define three levels of engagements and related forms of conclusions: examinations, reviews, and agreed-upon procedures. In addition, compilation engagements are defined for prospective financial statements.

An **examination** results in a conclusion that is in a *positive* form. In this type of report, the practitioner makes a direct statement as to whether the presentation of the assertions, taken as a whole, conforms with the applicable criteria. An example of an examination report written under the general guidance of the attestation standards is shown in Figure 25-1. This is for an engagement to determine that the rate of return on a hypothetical portfolio, based on a brokerage firm's buy–sell recommendations, is correct as represented in the firm's promotional materials. A report on an examination is unrestricted as to distribution by the client after it is issued. This means that a client can provide the information being examined and the related report to anyone.

In a **review**, the practitioner provides a conclusion in the form of a *negative assurance*. In this form, the practitioner's report states whether any information came to the practitioner's attention to indicate that the assertions are not presented in all material respects in conformity with the applicable criteria. A review report is also unrestricted in its distribution. It is interesting that review engagements are prohibited in most of the engagements where specified attestation standards have been issued. The reason for the prohibition is the difficulty of setting standards for the limited assurance provided by reviews.

In an **agreed-upon procedures engagement**, the procedures to be performed are agreed upon by the practitioner, the responsible party making the assertions, and the specific persons who are the intended users of the practitioner's report. The degree of assurance being conveyed in such a report varies with the specific procedures agreed to and performed. Accordingly, such reports are limited in their distribution to only the involved parties, who would have the requisite knowledge about those procedures and the level of assurance resulting from them. The report should include a statement of what procedures management and the practitioner agreed to and what the practitioner found in performing the procedures.

FIGURE 25-1	Example of an Examination Report under the Attestation Standards

To Management
Akron Securities, Inc.

We have examined the accompanying statement for investment performance statistics of the Akron Securities Model Portfolio for the year ended December 31, 2005. Akron Securities' management is responsible for the statement of investment performance statistics. Our responsibility is to express an opinion based on our examination.

Our examination was conducted in accordance with attestation standards established by the American Institute of Certified Public Accountants and, accordingly, included examining, on a test basis, evidence supporting Akron Securities Model Portfolio's statement for investment performance statistics and performing such other procedures as we considered necessary in the circumstances. We believe that our examination provides a reasonable basis for our opinion.

In our opinion, the schedule referred to above presents, in all material respects, the investment performance statistics of Akron Securities Model Portfolio for the year ended December 31, 2005, based on the actual results that would have been obtained if the buy-and-sell recommendations for the portfolio were followed as described in the buy–sell recommendations set forth in Note 1.

Farnsworth & Jackson, P.C.
Certified Public Accountants
Akron, Ohio
February 12, 2006

FIGURE 25-2	Types of Engagements and Related Reports				
Type of Engagement	Amount of Evidence	Level of Assurance	Form of Conclusion	Distribution
Examination	Extensive	High	Positive	General
Review	Significant	Moderate	Negative	General
Agreed-upon procedures	Varying	Varying	Findings	Limited

Figure 25-2 summarizes the reporting levels for attestation engagements.

Four common types of engagements for which detailed attestation standards have been issued are *WebTrust* services, *SysTrust* services, prospective financial statements, and agreed-upon procedures. These engagements are discussed in the next four sections of this chapter.

WebTrust SERVICES

In a **WebTrust** assurance services engagement, a client engages a CPA to provide reasonable assurance that a company's Web site complies with certain *Trust Services* principles and criteria for one or more aspects of e-commerce activities. A site that meets the *Trust Services* principles is eligible to display the *WebTrust* electronic seal on its transaction or order page. At least once every 12 months, the CPA firm updates its testing of the e-commerce aspects to ensure that the site continues to comply with the *Trust Services* principles and criteria. The CPA firm also updates its report. If the site does not comply, the seal can be revoked. The presumption is that Web site users believe the *WebTrust* seal adds credibility to the information in the Web site.

Trust Services

The *WebTrust* service is a specific service developed under the broader *Trust Services* principles and criteria jointly issued by the AICPA and CICA. When performing *WebTrust* assurance services, the CPA firm assesses whether the company's Web site complies with the five *Trust Services* principles, which are shown in Table 25-2. These *Trust Services* principles represent broad statements of objectives. To provide more specific guidance, there are related *Trust Services* criteria for each of the five principles. A company must conform with these criteria related to its Web site to obtain and maintain its *WebTrust* seal.

The *WebTrust* assurance services and related *Trust Services* principles and criteria were jointly created by the AICPA and the CICA as an attestation engagement service to be

TABLE 25-2	Five *Trust Services* Principles
Principle	**The entity discloses and maintains compliance with its**
Security	security practices, ensuring that the system is protected against unauthorized access (both physical and logical).
Availability	availability practices, ensuring that the system is available for operation and use as committed or agreed.
Processing Integrity	processing integrity, ensuring that system processing is complete, accurate, timely, and authorized.
Online Privacy	online privacy practices, ensuring that personal information obtained as a result of e-commerce is collected, used, disclosed, and retained as committed or agreed.
Confidentiality	confidentiality practices, ensuring that information designated as confidential is protected as committed or agreed.

performed under AICPA attestation standards. The *WebTrust* services include best practices for business-to-consumer and business-to-business electronic commerce.

CPAs can issue a *WebTrust* opinion on an individual principle or on combinations of principles. In addition to issuing seals for individual principles, some special *WebTrust* programs can result in a special *WebTrust* seal. An entity that meets both the *WebTrust* online privacy principle and the processing integrity principle can display the *WebTrust Consumer Protection* seal. There are also separate *WebTrust* principles and criteria for certification authorities. Entities that meet all of those separate principles and criteria can display the *WebTrust Certification Authorities* seal.

Figure 25-3 provides an example of a *WebTrust* report covering both the *Trust Services* security and online privacy principles.

FIGURE 25-3	Example of a Report on *WebTrust* Security and Online Privacy Principles

Independent Accountant's Report

To the Management of Cullen Company, Inc.:

We have examined management's assertion *[hotlink to management's assertion]* that Cullen Company, Inc. (Cullen Company), during the period October 1, 2005, through December 31, 2005,

- disclosed its key security and online privacy practices for electronic commerce transactions,

- complied with such security and online privacy practices, and

- maintained effective controls to provide reasonable assurance that

    — access to the electronic commerce system and data was restricted only to authorized individuals in conformity with its disclosed security practices, and

    — personally identifiable information obtained as a result of electronic commerce was protected in conformity with its disclosed online privacy practices

based on the AICPA/CICA *Trust Services* Security Criteria *[hot link to security principle and criteria]* and the *Trust Services* Online Privacy Criteria *[hot link to online privacy principle and criteria]*. These practices, disclosures, compliance, and controls are the responsibility of Cullen Company's management. Our responsibility is to express an opinion based on our examination.

Our examination was conducted in accordance with attestation standards established by the American Institute of Certified Public Accountants and, accordingly, included (1) obtaining an understanding of Cullen Company's disclosed security and online privacy practices for electronic commerce transactions and the related controls over security and online privacy, (2) testing compliance with its disclosed security and online privacy practices, (3) testing and evaluating the operating effectiveness of the controls, and (4) performing such other procedures as we considered necessary in the circumstances. We believe that our examination provides a reasonable basis for our opinion.

In our opinion, Cullen Company management's assertion referred to above is fairly stated, in all material respects, based on the AICPA/CICA *Trust Services* Security and Online Privacy Criteria.

Because of inherent limitations in controls, error or fraud may occur and not be detected. Furthermore, the projection of any conclusions, based on our findings, to future periods is subject to the risk that the validity of such conclusions may be altered because of (1) changes made to the system or controls, (2) changes in processing requirements, (3) changes required because of the passage of time, or (4) a deterioration in the degree of compliance with the policies or procedures.

The *WebTrust* seal of assurance on Cullen Company's Web site constitutes a symbolic representation of the contents of this report and it is not intended, nor should it be construed, to update this report or provide any additional assurance.

Dunn and Dunn, LLP
Charlotte, North Carolina
February 1, 2006

SysTrust SERVICES

OBJECTIVE 25-3

Understand the nature of *SysTrust* assurance services.

As more organizations become dependent on information technology, the security, availability, and accuracy of computer systems are critical. An unreliable system can trigger a chain of business events that negatively affect the company, its customers, suppliers, and other business partners. The AICPA and CICA jointly developed the *SysTrust* service to provide assurance that a system is reliable.

In a **SysTrust** engagement, the *SysTrust* licensed accountant evaluates a company's computer system using *Trust Services* principles and criteria and determines whether controls over the system exist. The accountant then performs tests to determine whether those controls were operating effectively during a specified period. If the system meets the requirements of the *Trust Services* principles and criteria, an examination-level unqualified attestation report is issued under AICPA attestation standards. A licensed *SysTrust* accountant may report on only one *Trust Services* principle or any combination of *Trust Services* principles.

An organization may request a *SysTrust* engagement for a system that is in the preimplementation phase. For this type of engagement, the accountant reports on the suitability of the design of controls, and the report is at a point in time rather than for a period of time.

PROSPECTIVE FINANCIAL STATEMENTS

OBJECTIVE 25-4

Describe special engagements to attest to prospective financial statements.

As implied by the term, **prospective financial statements** refer to predicted or expected financial statements in some future period (income statement) or at some future date (balance sheet). An example is management's predictions of the income statement and balance sheet one year in the future.

Most practitioners believe that there are significant opportunities and potential risks for auditors to provide credibility to prospective financial information. It is well accepted that users want reliable prospective information to aid them in their decision making. If auditors can improve the reliability of the information, information risk is reduced in the same way as in audits of historical financial statements. The risks arise because the actual results obtained may significantly differ from the predicted results in the prospective financial statements. Regulators, users, and others may criticize and sue auditors, even if the prospective statements were fairly stated given the available information at the time they were prepared.

Forecasts and Projections

There are two general types of prospective financial statements defined in AICPA attestation standards: forecasts and projections. **Forecasts** are prospective financial statements that present an entity's expected financial position, results of operations, and cash flows, to the *best* of the responsible party's knowledge and belief. These are commonly required by banks as a part of loan applications. **Projections** are prospective financial statements that present an entity's financial position, results of operations, and cash flows, to the best of the responsible party's knowledge and belief, given one or more *hypothetical assumptions*. An example is the preparation of projected financial statements assuming that the company is able to increase the price of its primary product by 10 percent with no reduction in units sold.

Both types of prospective financial statements are commonly prepared by management, but CPA firms have begun to associate their names with these statements only in recent years. A considerable body of literature has been developed to assist responsible parties in the preparation of both forecasts and projections. This guidance, along with guidance for independent accountants, is presented in the AICPA *Guide for Prospective Financial Statements.* The guidance to preparers constitutes a set of established criteria against which an attestation engagement can be framed.

Use of Prospective Financial Statements

Prospective financial statements are for either *general* or *limited* use. General use refers to use by any third party. An example of general use is the inclusion of a financial forecast in a prospectus for the sale of hospital bonds. Limited use refers to use by third parties with whom the responsible party is negotiating directly. An example of limited use is the inclusion of a financial projection in a bank loan application document.

Forecasts can be provided for both general and limited use, but projections are restricted to the latter. This is because limited users are in a position to obtain a better understanding of the prospective statements and related circumstances than other parties. For example, a limited user such as a potential venture capital investor can ask the responsible party about the hypothetical assumptions in a projection, whereas a removed user such as a reader of a prospectus cannot. Because users may have difficulty dealing with the meaning of hypothetical assumptions without obtaining additional information, the standards prohibit their general use. An exception to this rule is that a projection may be issued as a supplement to a forecast for general use.

Types of Engagements

The following types of engagements are permissible for prospective financial statements: an examination, a compilation, or an agreed-upon procedures engagement. Only an examination, which is studied in the next section, is dealt with in this chapter.

An engagement to review a forecast or projection is prohibited. The reason is that a forecast or projection is essentially the result of mechanically applying a set of significant assumptions. It is relatively easy to define an examination as obtaining satisfaction as to the completeness and reasonableness of all the assumptions and to define a compilation as primarily involving the computational accuracy of the statements, and not the reasonableness of the assumptions. It is difficult to define a meaningful middle ground. For example, none of the assumptions could be excluded because they are all significant. Therefore, being "moderately satisfied" about the assumptions, which is implied by a review service, is likely to confuse users. Rather than confuse users with this dilemma, the AICPA decided in the attestation standards to allow only the clearer alternatives.

Examination of Prospective Financial Statements

AICPA attestation standards make it clear that the practitioner is not attesting to the accuracy of the prospective financial statements. Instead, the focus is on examining the underlying assumptions and the preparation and presentation of the forecast or projection. Accordingly, the following are the four elements of an examination of forecasts and projections:

1. Evaluating the preparation of the prospective financial statements
2. Evaluating the support underlying the assumptions
3. Evaluating the presentation of the prospective financial statements for conformity with AICPA presentation guidelines
4. Issuing an examination report

These elements are based primarily on accumulating evidence about the completeness and reasonableness of the underlying assumptions as disclosed in the prospective financial statements. This requires the accountant to become familiar with the client's business and industry, to identify the significant matters on which the client's future results are expected to depend ("key factors"), and to determine that appropriate assumptions have been included with respect to these.

The accountant's report on an examination of prospective financial statements should include the following:

- A title that includes the word *independent*
- An identification of the prospective financial statements presented
- An identification of the responsible party and a statement that the prospective financial statements are the responsibility of the responsible party
- A statement that the practitioner's responsibility is to express an opinion on the prospective financial statements based on the practitioner's examination
- A statement that the examination of the prospective financial statements was conducted in accordance with attestation standards established by the American Institute of Certified Public Accountants and, accordingly, included such procedures as the accountant considered necessary in the circumstances
- A statement that the accountant believes that the examination provides a reasonable basis for an opinion
- The accountant's opinion that the prospective financial statements are presented in conformity with AICPA presentation guidelines, and that the underlying assumptions provide a reasonable basis for the forecast or a reasonable basis for the projection, given the hypothetical assumptions
- A caveat that the prospective results may not be achieved
- A statement that the accountant assumes no responsibility to update the report for events and circumstances occurring after the date of the report
- The manual or printed signature of the accountant's firm
- The date of the examination report

Figure 25-4 is an example of a report on an examination of a forecast with an unqualified opinion. Note that the date of the forecasted balance sheet is more than a year later than the report date.

FIGURE 25-4	Example of a Report on a Forecast

Independent Accountant's Report

We have examined the accompanying forecasted balance sheet, statements of income, retained earnings, and cash flows of Allstar, Inc., as of December 31, 2006, and for the year then ending. Allstar's management is responsible for the forecast. Our responsibility is to express an opinion on the forecast based on our examination.

Our examination was conducted in accordance with attestation standards established by the American Institute of Certified Public Accountants and, accordingly, included such procedures as we considered necessary to evaluate both the assumptions used by management and the preparation and presentation of the forecast. We believe that our examination provides a reasonable basis for our opinion.

In our opinion, the accompanying forecast is presented in conformity with guidelines for presentation of a forecast established by the American Institute of Certified Public Accountants, and the underlying assumptions provide a reasonable basis for management's forecast. However, there will usually be differences between the forecasted and actual results, because events and circumstances frequently do not occur as expected, and those differences may be material. We have no responsibility to update this report for events and circumstances occurring after the date of this report.

Manford & Brown
Certified Public Accountants
October 15, 2005

AGREED-UPON PROCEDURES ENGAGEMENTS

OBJECTIVE 25-5

Describe agreed-upon procedures engagements.

Agreed-Upon Procedures
Engagement Report

When the auditor and management or a third-party user agree that the audit will be limited to certain specific audit procedures, it is referred to as an agreed-upon procedures engagement. Many practitioners refer to these as procedures and findings engagements because the report emphasizes the audit procedures performed and the findings when the procedures were completed.

The primary appeal to practitioners of agreed-upon procedures engagements is making management or a third-party user specify the procedures they want performed. Imagine the difficulty a CPA firm would face if it agreed to issue an opinion to a federal agency that a company complied with federal affirmative action laws for a 2-year period under compliance attestation standards. Now assume that the federal agency was willing to specify 10 audit procedures the CPA firm was to perform, which would satisfy the agency. For example, one procedure is to determine that the standard company's employment application form had no reference to age, gender, or race. Assuming the CPA firm and federal agency could agree on the procedures, many CPA firms would be willing to perform the procedures and issue a report of the related findings.

SAS 75 and SSAE 10 are the primary professional standards addressing agreed-upon procedures engagements. SAS 75 and SSAE 10 are referred to as mirror standards because of their similarity. The primary difference in such mirror standards is that SASs deal with financial statement items, whereas the SSAEs deal with nonfinancial statement subject matter.

An example of an agreed-upon procedures engagement under the attestation standards is calculating the internal rate of return, beta risk for measuring volatility, and other relevant information pertinent to investors for a mutual fund. An example of an SAS 75 engagement is performing agreed-upon procedures on the gross sales account for a lease agreement. These engagements are commonly performed for retail stores when the store leases from the building owner on the basis of a percent of gross sales. Figure 25-5 illustrates a report for such an engagement, including the three procedures agreed upon and the two findings resulting from the procedures performed.

REVIEW AND COMPILATION SERVICES

OBJECTIVE 25-6

Understand the level of assurance and evidence requirements for review and compilation services.

Many nonpublic companies have their financial statements reviewed or compiled by a CPA, instead of having them audited. A company's management may believe that an audit is unnecessary because of the active involvement of owners, and the company may not have significant amounts of debt or other regulatory requirements. The company may engage the CPA to assist in the preparation of financial statements, either for internal use or to provide to creditors or lenders under loan agreements. Depending on the size of the loan, a lender may require compiled or reviewed financial statements, rather than an audit. A review provides limited assurance on the financial statements, whereas a compilation provides no expressed assurance.

The standards for compilations and reviews of financial statements are called **Statements on Standards for Accounting and Review Services (SSARS)**. These statements are issued by the Accounting and Review Services Committee of the AICPA, which has

Report of Independent Certified Public Accountants

Board of Directors and Management of Morgil Company

We have performed the procedures enumerated below, which were agreed to by the Board of Directors and management of Morgil Company, solely to assist you in determining the amount of gross sales as defined in the lease agreement dated September 1, 2001, between Rocklin, Inc., lessor, and Morgil Company, lessee, for the year ended December 31, 2005. This agreed-upon procedures engagement was performed in accordance with standards established by the American Institute of Certified Public Accountants. The sufficiency of these procedures is solely the responsibility of the Board of Directors and management of Morgil Company. Consequently, we make no representation regarding the sufficiency of the procedures described below either for the purpose for which this report has been requested or for any other purpose.

The procedures we performed are summarized as follows:

1. We obtained a schedule prepared by management, which reflected gross sales, as defined above, for the year ended December 31, 2005, of $35,675,000.
2. We obtained the weekly cash reports submitted by the store manager for the year. These reports show information on gross sales, cash register readings, sales taxes, returns, and allowances for discounts and other information.
3. We compared monthly summarizations of these reports with the schedule of gross sales and compared approximately 5 percent of the daily cash net receipts shown in the weekly cash reports with the bank statements.

Based solely on the foregoing procedures, we found:

1. The daily cash net receipts shown in the weekly cash reports that we compared with the bank statements to be in agreement.
2. The monthly summarizations to be in agreement with the schedule of gross sales we obtained from management.

We were not engaged to, and did not, perform an examination, the objective of which would be the expression of an opinion on the schedule of gross sales of Morgil Company. Accordingly, we do not express such an opinion. Had we performed additional procedures, other matters might have come to our attention that would have been reported to you.

This report is intended solely for the information and use of the specified users listed and is not intended to be and should not be used by anyone other than those specified parties.

Renfor Malik and Co. CPAs, LLP
Chicago, Illinois
March 1, 2006

authority equivalent to the Auditing Standards Board for services involving unaudited financial statements of nonpublic companies.

The assurance provided by compilations and reviews is considerably below that of audits. As a result, less evidence is required for these services and they can be provided at a lower fee than an audit. It is interesting to note that the SSARS refer to practitioners performing review and compilation services as accountants, not auditors. Figure 25-6 (p. 752) illustrates the difference in evidence accumulation and level of assurance for audits, reviews, and compilations. The actual amount of evidence and assurance for each engagement is not well defined by the profession and depends on the practitioner's judgment.

Because review and compilation services provide less assurance than audits, it is important that the accountant establish an understanding with the client, preferably in a written engagement letter, about the services to be performed. The understanding should include a description of the nature and limitations of the services and a description of the compilation or review report expected to be rendered at the completion of the

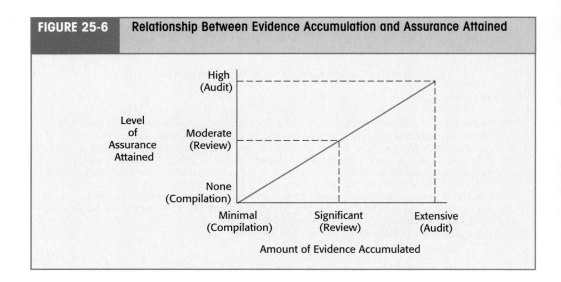

FIGURE 25-6 Relationship Between Evidence Accumulation and Assurance Attained

engagement. The next two sections discuss the requirements for review and compilation services in greater detail.

Review Services

A **review service (SSARS review)** engagement is designed to allow the accountant to express limited assurance that the financial statements are in accordance with GAAP, including appropriate informative disclosures, or an other comprehensive basis of accounting (OCBOA), such as the cash basis of accounting. Accountants performing review services must be independent of the client.

Procedures Suggested for Reviews The evidence for a review engagement consists primarily of inquiries of management and analytical procedures. It should be apparent that the required procedures for a review are substantially less than those required for an audit. A review engagement does not include obtaining an understanding of internal control, tests of controls, substantive tests of transactions, or specific tests of balances such as confirmation of receivables or physical examination of inventory. The following are recommended procedures for a review engagement:

- *Obtain knowledge of the accounting principles and practices of the client's industry.* The accountant can study AICPA industry guides or other sources to obtain industry knowledge. The level of knowledge for reviews can be somewhat less than for an audit.
- *Obtain knowledge of the client.* The information should be about the nature of the client's business transactions, its accounting records and employees, and the basis, form, and content of the financial statements. The level of knowledge can be less than for an audit.
- *Make inquiries of management.* The objective of these inquiries is to determine whether the financial statements are fairly presented, assuming that management does not intend to deceive the accountant. Inquiry is the most important of the review procedures. The following are illustrative inquiries:
    1. Inquire as to the company's procedures for recording, classifying, and summarizing transactions and disclosing information in the statements.
    2. Inquire into actions taken at meetings of stockholders and the board of directors.
    3. Inquire of persons having responsibility for financial and accounting matters whether the financial statements have been prepared in conformity with GAAP consistently applied.
- *Perform analytical procedures.* These are meant to identify relationships and individual items that appear to be unusual. The appropriate analytical procedures are no different from the ones already studied in Chapters 7 and 8 and in those chapters dealing with tests of details of balances.

- *Obtain letter of representation.* The accountant is required to obtain a letter of representation from members of management who are knowledgeable about financial matters.

Based on these procedures, the accountant may become aware that information is incorrect, incomplete, or otherwise unsatisfactory. Under these circumstances, additional procedures should be performed before the accountant expresses a standard review services report.

Form of Report Figure 25-7 provides an example of the review report issued when the accountant has completed a review engagement and determined that no material modifications are necessary to the financial statements. Three aspects of the report are worth noting:

1. The first paragraph is similar to an audit report except for its reference to a review service rather than an audit.
2. The second paragraph notes that a review consists primarily of inquiries and analytical procedures. This paragraph also notes that a review is substantially less in scope than an audit and that no opinion is expressed.
3. The third paragraph expresses limited assurance *in the form of a negative assurance* that "we are not aware of any material modifications that should be made to the financial statements."

The date of the review report should be the date of completion of the accountant's inquiry and analytical procedures. Each page of the financial statements reviewed should include the reference "See accountant's review report."

Failure to Follow GAAP If a client has failed to follow GAAP in a review engagement, a modification of the report is needed. The effects of the departure should be disclosed in the report if they have been determined by management or are known as a result of the accountant's review procedures. If the effects have not been determined, that should be stated in the report. The disclosure must be made in a *separate paragraph* in the report. The following is an example of suggested wording:

- As disclosed in note X to the financial statements, generally accepted accounting principles require that land be stated at cost. Management has informed us that the company has stated its land at appraised value and that, if generally accepted accounting principles had been followed, the land account and stockholders' equity would have been decreased by $500,000.

Compilation Services

A **compilation service** engagement is defined in SSARS as one in which the accountant presents to a client or third party financial statements that the accountant has prepared. In a compilation engagement, the CPA firm does not express any assurance on the statements.

FIGURE 25-7	Example of Review Report

We have reviewed the accompanying balance sheet of Archer Technologies, Inc., as of December 31, 2005, and the related statements of income, retained earnings, and cash flows for the year then ended, in accordance with Statements on Standards for Accounting and Review Services issued by the American Institute of Certified Public Accountants. All information included in these financial statements is the representation of the management of Archer Technologies, Inc.

A review consists principally of inquiries of company personnel and analytical procedures applied to financial data. It is substantially less in scope than an audit in accordance with generally accepted auditing standards, the objective of which is the expression of an opinion regarding the financial statements taken as a whole. Accordingly, we do not express such an opinion.

Based on our review, we are not aware of any material modifications that should be made to the accompanying financial statements in order for them to be in conformity with generally accepted accounting principles.

Many CPA firms prepare monthly, quarterly, or annual financial statements for their clients. These statements are usually for internal use by management, although they may also be provided to external users. When an accountant submits financial statements that the CPA expects will be used by a third party, the CPA is required to at least compile the statements. When the accountant does not expect the financial statements to be used by a third party, the CPA does not have to issue a compilation report in accordance with the provisions of SSARS as long as the CPA documents in the engagement letter with the client an understanding regarding the services to be performed and the limitations on the use of those financial statements. The CPA is not required to be independent to perform a compilation and the financial statements can be issued without additional disclosures.

Requirements for Compilation Compilation does not mean that the accountant has no responsibilities. The accountant is always responsible for exercising due care in performing all duties. In a compilation engagement, the accountant must do the following:

- Establish an understanding with the client about the nature and limitations of the services to be performed and a description of the report, if a report is to be issued.
- Possess knowledge about the accounting principles and practices of the client's industry.
- Know the client; the nature of the client's business transactions, accounting records, and employees; and the basis, form, and content of the financial statements. The knowledge can be less than that for a review.
- Make inquiries to determine whether the client's information is satisfactory.
- Read the compiled financial statements and be alert for any obvious omissions or errors in arithmetic and GAAP.

The accountant does not have to make other inquiries or perform other procedures to verify information supplied by the entity. But if the accountant becomes aware that the statements are not fairly presented, additional information should be obtained. If the client refuses to provide the information, the accountant should withdraw from the compilation engagement.

Form of Report The form of the compilation report depends on whether management elects to include all the required disclosures with the financial statements. It is also permissible to issue a compilation report when the auditor is not independent, but this must be clearly stated in the report.

- *Compilation with full disclosure.* A compilation of this type requires disclosures in accordance with GAAP, the same as for audited financial statements or reviews. Figure 25-8 shows the appropriate wording in such circumstances.
- *Compilation that omits substantially all disclosures.* This type of compilation is acceptable *if the report indicates the lack of disclosures* and the absence of disclosures *is not*, to the CPA's knowledge, *undertaken with the intent to mislead users.* This type of statement is usually expected to be used primarily for management purposes only.

FIGURE 25-8	Compilation Report with Full Disclosure

We have compiled the accompanying balance sheet of Williams Company as of December 31, 2005, and the related statements of income, retained earnings, and cash flows for the year then ended, in accordance with Statements on Standards for Accounting and Review Services issued by the American Institute of Certified Public Accountants.

A compilation is limited to presenting in the form of financial statements information that is the representation of management. We have not audited or reviewed the accompanying financial statements and, accordingly, do not express an opinion or any other form of assurance on them.

We have compiled the accompanying balance sheet of Williams Company as of December 31, 2005, and the related statements of income and retained earnings for the year then ended, in accordance with Statements on Standards for Accounting and Review Services issued by the American Institute of Certified Public Accountants.

A compilation is limited to presenting in the form of financial statements information that is the representation of management. We have not audited or reviewed the accompanying financial statements and, accordingly, do not express an opinion or any other form of assurance on them.

Management has elected to omit substantially all of the disclosures and the statement of cash flows required by generally accepted accounting principles. If the omitted disclosures were included in the financial statements, they might influence the user's conclusions about the company's financial position, results of operations, and cash flows. Accordingly, these financial statements are not designed for those who are not informed about such matters.

Figure 25-9 shows the appropriate wording when the accountant compiles statements without disclosures. In this example, management has also elected not to present the statement of cash flows.

• *Compilation without independence.* A CPA firm can issue a compilation report even if it is not independent with respect to the client, as defined by the *Code of Professional Conduct.* When the accountant lacks independence, the following should be included as a separate last paragraph in either of the two previously discussed reports: "We are not independent with respect to Williams Company."

For any of the three types of compilation reports, the following are also required: The date of the accountant's report is the date of completion of the compilation, and each page of the financial statements compiled by the accountant should state "See accountant's compilation report." If the client fails to follow GAAP, the same report modifications exist that were discussed for reviews.

This section discussed the requirements for compilation and review services under SSARS for nonpublic companies. The next section describes reviews of interim financial information for public companies.

REVIEW OF INTERIM FINANCIAL INFORMATION FOR PUBLIC COMPANIES

OBJECTIVE 25-7

Describe special engagements to review interim financial information for public companies.

Quarterly Financial Information

The SEC requires quarterly financial statements to be reviewed by the company's external auditor prior to the company's filing of the Form 10-Q with the SEC. The SEC also requires a footnote in the annual audited financial statements disclosing quarterly sales, gross profit, income, and earnings per share for the past two years. Typically, the footnote in the annual statements is labeled unaudited, but at a minimum, the CPA firm must perform review procedures of the footnote information.

The requirements for a **public company interim review** include the five requirements for review service engagements previously discussed for SSARS reviews. Like reviews under SSARS, a review for a public company does not provide a basis for expressing a positive-form opinion. There are ordinarily no tests of the accounting records, independent confirmations, or physical examinations. There are some differences, however, between the two types of reviews:

• Because an annual audit is also performed for the public company client, the auditor must obtain sufficient information about the client's internal control for both annual and interim financial information.

• Similarly, because the client is audited annually, the auditor's knowledge of the results of these audit procedures is used in considering the scope and results of the inquiries and analytical procedures.

• Under SSARS, the auditor makes inquiries about actions of directors and stockholders' meetings; for a public company, the auditor reads the minutes of those meetings.

FIGURE 25-10 | **Example of a Report for Interim Financial Statements for a Public Company**

Report of Independent Registered Public Accounting Firm

We have reviewed the consolidated balance sheet of Rainer Company and consolidated subsidiaries as of September 30, 2005, and the related statements of earnings, retained earnings, and cash flows for the three-month and nine-month periods then ended. These financial statements are the responsibility of the company's management.

We conducted our review in accordance with the standards of the Public Company Accounting Oversight Board (United States). A review of interim financial information consists principally of applying analytical procedures and making inquiries of persons responsible for financial and accounting matters. It is substantially less in scope than an audit conducted in accordance with the standards of the Public Company Accounting Oversight Board, the objective of which is the expression of an opinion regarding the financial statements taken as a whole. Accordingly, we do not express such an opinion.

Based on our review, we are not aware of any material modifications that should be made to the accompanying interim financial statements for them to be in conformity with accounting principles generally accepted in the United States of America.

- The auditor must also obtain evidence that the interim financial information agrees or reconciles with the accounting records. For example, the auditor might compare the interim financial information to the general ledger or a consolidating schedule derived from the accounting records.

The standard report for a review of interim financial statements included in Form 10-Q is illustrated in Figure 25-10. The review is conducted according to the standards of the PCAOB, and there is no reference to the SSARS in a review report of interim financial information for a public company. Each page of the interim financial information should be clearly marked as "unaudited."

When the auditor determines that there has been a departure from GAAP, the report should be modified. This modification is similar to that used in a review under SSARS, except that the effect of the departure should, if feasible, be stated.

The quarterly data reviewed by the auditor and included as a footnote in the annual audited statements should be labeled "unaudited." A separate review report for this information is not required.

OTHER AUDITS OR LIMITED ASSURANCE ENGAGEMENTS

OBJECTIVE 25-8

Describe other audit and limited assurance engagements related to historical financial statements.

Earlier in this chapter, we discussed compilation and review services for nonpublic companies, as well as reviews of interim financial information for public companies. We now examine other types of audit and attestation services that fall within the auditing standards but are not audits of historical financial statements in accordance with GAAP. Some of the more important of these services include audits of financial statements prepared on an other comprehensive basis of accounting (OCBOA); audits of specified elements, accounts, or items; and debt compliance letters. We now discuss each of these services in greater detail.

Other Comprehensive Basis of Accounting

Auditors often audit statements prepared on a basis other than GAAP. SAS 62 (AU 623) provides that generally accepted auditing standards apply to these audit engagements, but the reporting requirements differ somewhat from those described in Chapter 3. The following are bases other than GAAP for which reports may be issued according to the requirements of SAS 62:

- *Cash or modified cash basis.* With cash basis accounting, only cash receipts and disbursements are recorded. Under the modified cash basis of accounting, the cash basis is followed except for certain items, such as fixed assets and depreciation. Physicians and attorneys often follow this accounting method.

- *Basis used to comply with the requirements of a regulatory agency.* Common examples include the uniform system of accounts required of railroads, utilities, and some insurance companies.
- *Income tax basis.* The same measurement rules used for filing tax returns are often used for financial statement preparation, even though this is not in accordance with GAAP. Many small businesses use this method.
- *A definite set of criteria having substantial support.* An example would be the price-level basis of accounting. The method of accounting must be applied to all material items in the financial statements.

For the most part, these audits are done in the same way as those in which GAAP is followed. Naturally, the auditor must fully understand the accounting basis that the client is required to follow. For example, in auditing a railroad, there are complex accounting requirements that require the auditor to have specialized accounting knowledge to conduct the audit.

A concern in reporting on a comprehensive basis is to make sure that the statements clearly indicate that they are prepared on a basis other than GAAP. If the statements imply that GAAP is followed, the reporting requirements of Chapter 3 apply. Consequently, terms such as *balance sheet* and *statement of operations* must be avoided by the client. Instead, a title such as "statement of assets and liabilities arising from cash transactions" would be appropriate for a cash basis statement.

The reporting requirements for audits of these comprehensive bases of accounting include the following.

Introductory Paragraph This paragraph is equivalent to the introductory paragraph of a report on statements that follow GAAP. The statements are identified, and the paragraph states that they were audited. The paragraph also states that the statements are the responsibility of management and that the auditor's responsibility is to express an opinion on them based on the audit.

Scope Paragraph This paragraph is equivalent to the scope paragraph in the ordinary report. It states that the audit was conducted in accordance with generally accepted auditing standards and describes the nature of the audit process.

Middle Paragraph Stating the Accounting Basis This paragraph is unique to this type of report. It states the basis of presentation and refers to a note to the financial statements that describes the basis of accounting followed. It states that such basis is a comprehensive basis of accounting other than GAAP. The note referred to will describe not only the basis followed but also how that basis differs from GAAP. It need not state the effects of the differences in quantitative terms. It is important for the auditor to consider whether the financial statements include all informative disclosures that are appropriate for the basis of accounting used.

Opinion Paragraph The opinion paragraph is comparable to that used in the standard report. It expresses the auditor's opinion with regard to conformity with the basis of accounting described.

If the financial statements are prepared in conformity with requirements of a governmental regulatory agency, a paragraph must be added that restricts the distribution of the report to those within the entity and for filing with the regulatory agency.

Figure 25-11 is a common example of a report prepared on an entity's income tax basis.

Specified Elements, Accounts, or Items

Auditors are often asked to issue reports on their audit of specific aspects of financial statements. A common example is a special report on the audit of sales of a retail store in a shopping center to be used as a basis for rental payments. Other common examples are reports on royalties, profit participation, and provision for income taxes. The authority for auditing specified elements, accounts, or items is SAS 62 (AU 623) Special Reports.

The type of engagement to be undertaken for specified elements, accounts, or items is usually an audit. Thus, it is typically like an ordinary audit but is applied to less than the full

FIGURE 25-11   Example of a Report on Income Tax Basis

Independent Auditor's Report

We have audited the accompanying statements of assets, liabilities, and capital—income tax basis of Triangle Partnership as of December 31, 2005 and 2004, and the related statements of revenue and expenses—income tax basis and of changes in partners' capital accounts—income tax basis for the years then ended. These financial statements are the responsibility of the Partnership's management. Our responsibility is to express an opinion on these financial statements based on our audits.

We conducted our audits in accordance with generally accepted auditing standards. Those standards require that we plan and perform the audit to obtain reasonable assurance about whether the financial statements are free of material misstatement. An audit includes examining, on a test basis, evidence supporting the amounts and disclosures in the financial statements. An audit also includes assessing the accounting principles used and significant estimates made by management, as well as evaluating the overall financial statement presentation. We believe that our audits provide a reasonable basis for our opinion.

As described in Note X, these financial statements were prepared on the basis of accounting the Partnership uses for income tax purposes, which is a comprehensive basis of accounting other than generally accepted accounting principles.

In our opinion, the financial statements referred to above present fairly, in all material respects, the assets, liabilities, and capital of Triangle Partnership as of December 31, 2005 and 2004, and its revenue and expenses and changes in partners' capital accounts for the years then ended, on the basis of accounting described in Note X.

financial statements. There are two primary differences between audits of specified elements, accounts, or items and audits of complete financial statements:

1. Materiality is defined in terms of the elements, accounts, or items involved rather than in relation to the overall statements. The effect is to ordinarily require more evidence than would be needed if the item being verified were just one of many parts of the statements. For example, if the sales account is being reported on separately, a smaller misstatement would be considered material than when sales is just one account of many being reported on as a part of a regular audit.

2. The first standard of reporting under GAAS does not apply because the presentation of elements, accounts, or items is not a financial statement prepared in accordance with GAAP.

In addition, the auditor must be careful to extend audit efforts to include other elements, accounts, or items that are interrelated with those that are the subject of the engagement. This will cause an increase in audit effort as well. For example, in expressing an opinion on sales, the auditor must also consider the effect of accounts receivable on sales.

Figure 25-12 illustrates a report for royalties, which is a specified account. The format and contents of the report are similar to the standard audit report on the audit of financial statements in accordance with GAAP. However, it must also reflect the following requirements for reporting on specified elements, accounts, or items:

- The specified elements, accounts, or items must be identified.
- The basis on which the specified elements, accounts, or items are presented and the agreements specifying the basis must be described.
- The source of significant interpretations made by the client about the provisions of a relevant agreement must be indicated and described.
- If the specified element, account, or item is presented on a basis that is not in conformity with GAAP or another comprehensive basis of accounting, a paragraph that restricts the distribution of the report to those within the entity and the parties to the contract or agreement must be added.

FIGURE 25-12 Example of a Report for Royalties

Independent Auditor's Report

We have audited the accompanying schedule of royalties applicable to engine production of the Q Division of Doman Company for the year ended December 31, 2005, under the terms of a license agreement dated May 14, 2003, between Garrett Company and Doman Company. This schedule is the responsibility of Doman Company's management. Our responsibility is to express an opinion on this schedule based on our audit.

We conducted our audit in accordance with generally accepted auditing standards. Those standards require that we plan and perform the audit to obtain reasonable assurance about whether the schedule of royalties is free of material misstatement. An audit includes examining, on a test basis, evidence supporting the amounts and disclosures in the schedule. An audit also includes assessing the accounting principles used and significant estimates made by management, as well as evaluating the overall schedule presentation. We believe that our audit provides a reasonable basis for our opinion.

We have been informed that, under Doman Company's interpretation of the agreement referred to in the first paragraph, royalties were based on the number of engines produced after giving effect to a reduction for production retirements that were scrapped, but without a reduction for field returns that were scrapped, even though the field returns were replaced with new engines without charge to customers.

In our opinion, the schedule of royalties referred to above presents fairly, in all material respects, the number of engines produced by the Q Division of Doman Company during the year ended December 31, 2005, and the amount of royalties applicable thereto, under the license agreement referred to above.

This report is intended solely for the information and use of the boards of directors and managements of Doman Company and Garrett Company and should not be used for any other purpose.

It is important to realize that the circumstances and requirements that exist for modifying a report on an audit of GAAP financial statements also apply to special reports on both specific elements, accounts, or items and financial statements prepared on another comprehensive basis of accounting. These modifications would include not only departures from an unqualified opinion but also an explanatory paragraph where appropriate. The form of the modifications would essentially be the same as discussed in Chapter 3.

Debt Compliance Letters and Similar Reports

Clients occasionally enter into loan agreements that require them to provide the lender with a report from a CPA as to the existence or nonexistence of some condition. For example, borrowing arrangements may require maintenance of a certain dollar amount of working capital at specified times and an independent accountant's report as to the compliance with the requirement.

Reports on debt compliance and similar engagements may be issued as separate reports or as part of a report that expresses the auditor's opinion on the financial statements by adding a paragraph after the opinion paragraph. In either case, the following matters are important for the auditor to observe in such engagements:

- The engagement and report should be limited to compliance matters the auditor is qualified to evaluate. Some of the provisions of debt compliance agreements the auditor is normally in a position to verify are whether principal and interest payments were made when due; whether the proper limitations were maintained on dividends, working capital, and debt ratios; and whether the accounting records were adequate for conducting an ordinary audit. However, determining, for example, whether the client has properly restricted its business activities to the requirements of an agreement or if it has title to pledged property are legal questions that the CPA is not qualified to answer. Furthermore, the *Code of Professional Conduct* prohibits the auditor from practicing as an attorney in such circumstances.
- The auditor should provide a debt compliance letter only for a client for whom the auditor has done an audit of the overall financial statements. A debt compliance letter on a matter such as the existence of a current ratio of 2.5 or better would be difficult to do without having conducted a complete audit.

- The auditor's opinion is in the form of a *negative assurance*, stating that nothing came to the auditor's attention that would lead the auditor to believe there was noncompliance.

Figure 25-13 is an example of a separate report on debt compliance. Note that the final paragraph restricts distribution of the report to the directly affected parties.

Although debt compliance letters are common, they are only part of a broader set of special reports arising from contractual or regulatory requirements. These types of reports also include (1) presentations of financial statements that are in a form required by contract or regulation that are not in conformity with GAAP or another comprehensive basis of accounting and (2) presentations that are in conformity with one of those bases but are incomplete. In such cases, the auditor's report should include a separate paragraph clearly stating what the presentation is intended to present. The separate paragraph should also indicate that the statements are not intended to be a complete presentation or are not a presentation in accordance with GAAP. An additional paragraph should also restrict the distribution of the report to the client and appropriate contractual parties or regulatory agencies, except for certain filings with regulatory agencies that are to be included in a document that is distributed to the general public.

TABLE 25-3 | **Primary Categories of Other Assurance Services Engagements**

Type of Engagement	Example	Source of Authoritative Support
Audits of historical financial statements prepared in accordance with GAAP	Audit of General Mills' financial statements	Auditing standards
Attestation engagements under the attestation standards	Attestation of General Mills' e-commerce system availability	Attestation standards and *Trust Services* availability principles and criteria
Reviews or compilations of historical financial statements prepared in accordance with GAAP	Review of Ron's Shoe Store's quarterly financial statements	Accounting and review services standards for nonpublic companies; auditing standards for public companies
Audits or limited assurance engagements other than audits, reviews, or compilations of historical financial statements prepared in accordance with GAAP	Audit of Ron's Shoe Store's ending balance in inventory	Auditing standards

SUMMARY

This chapter described many of the other assurance services offered by CPAs. The types of services offered continue to grow and expand as society demands assurance on new and different types of information. Depending on the nature of the service, the guidance for performance of the service may come from auditing standards, attestation standards, or the accounting and review services standards. Table 25-3 (p. 760) provides a summary and examples of the primary categories of services discussed in this chapter.

ESSENTIAL TERMS

Agreed-upon procedures engagement—an engagement in which the procedures to be performed are agreed upon by the practitioner, the responsible party making the assertions, and the intended users of the practitioner's report; the practitioner's report is presented in the form of a negative assurance

Attestation engagement—a type of assurance service in which the CPA firm issues a report about the reliability of subject matter or of an assertion that is the responsibility of another party

Compilation service—a nonaudit engagement in which the accountant undertakes to present, in the form of financial statements, information that is the representation of management, without undertaking to express any assurance on the statements

Examination—an attest engagement that results in a positive assurance as to whether or not the assertions under examination conform with the applicable criteria

Forecasts—prospective financial statements that present an entity's expected financial position, results of operations, and cash flows for future periods, to the best of the responsible party's knowledge and belief

Projections—prospective financial statements that present an entity's financial position and results of operations and cash flows for future periods, to the best of the responsible party's knowledge and belief, given one or more hypothetical assumptions

Prospective financial statements—financial statements that deal with expected future data rather than with historical data

Public company interim review—reviews of interim, unaudited financial information performed to help public companies meet their reporting responsibilities to regulatory agencies

Review—an attestation engagement that results in a negative assurance as to the practitioner's awareness of any information indicating that the assertions are not presented in conformity with the applicable criteria

Review service (SSARS review)—a review of unaudited financial statements designed to provide limited assurance that no material modifications need be made to the statements in order for them to be in conformity with generally accepted accounting principles or, if applicable, with another comprehensive basis of accounting

Statements on Standards for Accounting and Review Services (SSARS)—standards issued by the AICPA Accounting and Review Services Committee that govern the CPA's association with unaudited financial statements of non-public companies

Statements on Standards for Attestation Engagements (SSAE)—statements issued by the AICPA to provide a conceptual framework for various types of attestation services

SysTrust—an attestation service designed to provide reasonable assurance that a company's computer system complies with *Trust Services* principles and criteria

WebTrust—an attestation service designed to provide reasonable assurance that a company's Web site complies with *Trust Services* principles and criteria for business-to-consumer electronic commerce

REVIEW QUESTIONS

25-1 (Objective 25-1) Define what is meant by attestation standards. Distinguish between attestation standards and generally accepted auditing standards.

25-2 (Objective 25-2) List the five *Trust Services* principles and explain whether a *WebTrust* licensed CPA can report on an entity's compliance with those principles individually or in combination.

25-3 (Objective 25-3) Describe the purpose of a *SysTrust* assurance services engagement.

25-4 (Objective 25-4) Explain what is meant by prospective financial statements and distinguish between forecasts and projections. What four things are involved in an examination of prospective financial statements?

25-5 (Objective 25-6) What is meant by the term level of assurance? How does the level of assurance differ for an audit of historical financial statements, a review, and a compilation?

25-6 (Objective 25-6) What is a negative assurance? Why is it used in a review engagement report?

25-7 (Objective 25-6) Distinguish between compilation and review of financial statements. What is the level of assurance for each?

25-8 (Objective 25-6) Distinguish the three forms of compilation reports that a CPA can provide to clients.

25-9 (Objective 25-6) List five things that are required of an auditor by SSARS for a compilation.

25-10 (Objective 25-6) What steps should auditors take if during a compilation engagement they become aware that the financial statements are misleading?

25-11 (Objective 25-6) What procedures should the auditor use to obtain the information necessary to give the level of assurance required of reviews of financial statements?

25-12 (Objective 25-6) What should auditors do if during a review of financial statements they discover that generally accepted accounting principles are not being followed?

25-13 (Objectives 25-6, 25-7) What are the differences between the review reports for a private company under SSARS and for the interim financial statements of a public company?

25-14 (Objective 25-7) Explain why a review of interim financial statements for a public company may provide a greater level of assurance than do SSARS reviews.

25-15 (Objective 25-8) What is the purpose of an engagement of specified elements, accounts, or items? List the four special requirements for reports on specified elements, accounts, or items.

25-16 (Objective 25-8) State the reporting requirements for statements prepared on a basis other than GAAP.

25-17 (Objective 25-8) The Absco Corporation has requested that Herb Germany, CPA, provide a report to the Northern State Bank as to the existence or nonexistence of certain loan conditions. The conditions to be reported on are the working capital ratio, dividends paid on preferred stock, aging of accounts receivable, and competency of management. This is Herb's first experience with Absco. Should Herb accept this engagement? Substantiate your answer.

MULTIPLE CHOICE QUESTIONS FROM CPA EXAMINATIONS

25-18 (Objectives 25-1, 25-4) The following questions concern attestation engagements. Choose the best response.

a. Which of the following professional services would be considered an attestation engagement?
 (1) A management consulting engagement to provide IT advice to a client.
 (2) An engagement to report on compliance with statutory requirements.
 (3) An income tax engagement to prepare federal and state tax returns.
 (4) A compilation of financial statements from a client's accounting records.

b. Which of the following statements concerning prospective financial statements is correct?
 (1) Only a financial forecast would normally be appropriate for limited use.
 (2) Only a financial projection would normally be appropriate for general use.
 (3) Any type of prospective financial statements would normally be appropriate for limited use.
 (4) Any type of prospective financial statement would normally be appropriate for general use.

25-19 (Objective 25-6) The following are miscellaneous questions about compilation and review services. Choose the best response.

a. A CPA has been engaged to perform review services for a client. Identify which of the following is a correct statement:
 (1) The CPA must perform the basic audit procedures necessary to determine that the statements are in conformity with GAAP.
 (2) The financial statements are primarily representations of the CPA.
 (3) The CPA may prepare the statements from the books but may not assist in adjusting and closing the books.

(4) The CPA is performing an accounting service rather than an audit of the financial statements.

b. It is acceptable for a CPA to be associated with financial statements when not independent with respect to the client and still issue a substantially unmodified report for which of the following:
(1) Audits of companies following GAAP.
(2) Audits of companies on a comprehensive basis of accounting other than GAAP.
(3) Compilation of financial statements following GAAP.
(4) Review of financial statements following GAAP.

c. A CPA is performing review services for a small, closely held manufacturing company. As a part of the follow-up of a significant decrease in the gross margin for the current year, the CPA discovers that there are no supporting documents for $40,000 of disbursements. The chief financial officer assures her that the disbursements are proper. What should the CPA do?
(1) Include the unsupported disbursements without further work in the statements on the grounds that she is not doing an audit.
(2) Modify the review opinion or withdraw from the engagement unless the unsupported disbursements are satisfactorily explained.
(3) Exclude the unsupported disbursements from the statements.
(4) Obtain a written representation from the chief financial officer that the disbursements are proper and should be included in the current financial statements.

d. Which of the following best describes the responsibility of the CPA in performing compilation services for a company?
(1) The CPA must understand the client's business and accounting methods and read the financial statements for reasonableness.
(2) The CPA has to satisfy only himself or herself that the financial statements were prepared in conformity with GAAP.
(3) The CPA should obtain an understanding of internal control and perform tests of controls.
(4) The CPA is relieved of any responsibility to third parties.

e. Frank, CPA, performed compilation services omitting substantially all disclosures for a client and issued the appropriate report. Three months after the statements were issued, the client informed Frank that the statements had been given to a bank for a secured loan. Which of the following is appropriate under these circumstances?
(1) Frank must revise the statements to include appropriate footnotes and attach a revised disclaimer of opinion.
(2) The client may give the statements to the banker as long as Frank's disclaimer of opinion accompanies the statements.
(3) The client should retype the statements on plain paper and send them to the banker without Frank's report.
(4) The client may let the banker review the statements and take notes but should not give the banker a copy of the statements.

f. In performing a compilation of financial statements of a nonpublic entity, the accountant decides that modification of the standard report is not adequate to indicate deficiencies in the financial statements taken as a whole, and the client is not willing to correct the deficiencies. The accountant should therefore
(1) perform a review of the financial statements.
(2) issue a special report.
(3) withdraw from the engagement.
(4) express an adverse audit opinion.

25-20 (Objective 25-8) The following questions concern reports issued by auditors, other than those on historical financial statements. Choose the best response.

a. Which of the generally accepted auditing standards of reporting would *not* normally apply to special reports such as cash basis statements?
(1) First standard.
(2) Second standard.
(3) Third standard.
(4) Fourth standard.

b. An auditor is reporting on cash basis financial statements. These statements are best referred to in the opinion of the auditor by which of the following descriptions?
(1) Cash receipts and disbursements and the assets and liabilities arising from cash transactions.

(2) Financial position and results of operations arising from cash transactions.

(3) Balance sheet and income statements resulting from cash transactions.

(4) Cash balance sheet and the source and application of funds.

c. Which of the following statements with respect to an auditor's report expressing an opinion on a specific item on a financial statement is correct?

(1) Materiality must be related to the specific item rather than to the financial statements taken as a whole.

(2) Such a report can be expressed only if the auditor is also engaged to audit the entire set of financial statements.

(3) The attention devoted to the specified item is usually less than it would be if the financial statements taken as a whole were being audited.

(4) The auditor who has issued an adverse opinion on the financial statements taken as a whole can never express an opinion on a specified item in these financial statements.

d. When asked to perform an audit to express an opinion on one or more specified elements, accounts, or items of a financial statement, the auditor

(1) may *not* describe auditing procedures applied.

(2) should advise the client that the opinion can be issued only if the financial statements have been audited and found to be fairly presented.

(3) may assume that the first standard of reporting with respect to GAAP does *not* apply.

(4) should comply with the request only if they constitute a major portion of the financial statements on which an auditor has disclaimed an opinion based on an audit.

DISCUSSION QUESTIONS AND PROBLEMS

25-21 (Objectives 25-2, 25-3) Each of the following represents different client requests for engagements related to *WebTrust* and *SysTrust* assurance services.

a. MoonBay.com's management requested that their auditor perform a *WebTrust* assurance service on their assertion about MoonBay.com e-commerce policies' compliance with the five *Trust Services* principles and criteria. Although the auditor is not a registered *WebTrust* provider, the CPA firm is a member of the AICPA.

b. The board of directors of Ferguson Hardware Company has requested that their auditor perform a *SysTrust* assurance services engagement on its information technology system. The board has requested that the auditor, who is a licensed *SysTrust* provider, report solely on the company's IT availability policies and controls using the *Trust Services* availability principle and criteria.

c. Management of Greenshield Technology, Inc. requested that its auditors perform a *WebTrust* assurance services engagement on its e-commerce security policies. The CPA firm performed the *WebTrust* services as of April 30, 2005, and has not updated its work. Management wants its *WebTrust* seal to stay posted on its Web site through May 31, 2006.

d. Ware Hospital Systems, Inc. is in the process of developing a new patient records system. Management has approached a licensed *SysTrust* accountant to perform a *SysTrust* engagement on its new system. Specifically, management wants the CPA to examine the system's processing integrity using the *Trust Services* processing integrity principle and criteria. The examination will be scheduled prior to the new system's implementation.

Required   Consider each request separately. Describe whether the requested assurance service can be performed.

25-22 (Objective 25-4) Carl Monson, the owner of Major Products Manufacturing Company, a small, successful, longtime audit client of your firm, has requested you to work with his company in preparing 3-year forecasted information for the year ending December 31, 2005, and two subsequent years. Monson informs you that he intends to use the forecasts, together with the audited financial statements, to seek additional financing to expand the business. Monson has had little experience in formal forecast preparation and counts on you to assist him in any way possible. He wants the most supportive opinion possible from your firm to add to the credibility of the forecast. He informs you that he is willing to do anything necessary to help you prepare the forecast.

First, he wants projections of sales and revenues and earnings from the existing business, which he believes could continue to be financed from existing capital.

Second, he intends to buy a company in a closely related business that is currently operating unsuccessfully. Monson states that he wants to sell some of the operating assets of the business and replace them with others. He believes that the company can then be made highly successful. He has made an offer on the new business, subject to obtaining proper financing. He also informs you that he has received an offer on the assets he intends to sell.

a. Explain circumstances under which it would and would not be acceptable to undertake the engagement.

Required

b. Why is it important that Monson understand the nature of your reporting requirements before the engagement proceeds?

c. What information will Monson have to provide to you before you can complete the forecasted statements? Be as specific as possible.

d. Discuss, in as specific terms as possible, the nature of the report you will issue with the forecasts, assuming that you are able to properly complete them.

25-23 (Objective 25-8) You have been requested by the management of J. L. Lockwood Co. to issue a debt compliance letter as a part of the audit of Taylor Fruit Farms, Inc. J. L. Lockwood Co. is a supplier of irrigation equipment. Much of the equipment, including that supplied to Taylor, is sold on a secured contract basis. Taylor Fruit Farms is an audit client of yours, but Lockwood is not. In addition to the present equipment, Lockwood informs you they are evaluating whether they should sell another $500,000 of equipment to Taylor Fruit Farms.

You have been requested to send Lockwood a debt compliance letter concerning the following matters:

1. The current ratio has exceeded 2.0 in each quarter of the unaudited statements prepared by management and in the annual audited statements.
2. Total owners' equity is more than $800,000.
3. The company has not violated any of the legal requirements of California fruit-growing regulations.
4. Management is competent and has made reasonable business decisions in the past 3 years.
5. Management owns an option to buy additional fruit land adjacent to the company's present property.

a. Define the purpose of a debt compliance letter.

Required

b. Why is it necessary to conduct an audit of a company before it is acceptable to issue a debt compliance letter?

c. For which of the five requested items is it acceptable for a CPA firm to issue a debt compliance letter? Give reasons for your answer.

25-24 (Objective 25-6) Evaluate the following comments about compiled financial statements: "When CPAs associate their name with compiled financial statements, their only responsibility is to the client and that is limited to the proper summarization and presentation on the financial statements of information provided by the client. The opinion clearly states that the auditor has not conducted an audit and does not express an opinion on this fair presentation. If users rely on compiled financial statements, they do so at their own risk and should never be able to hold the CPA responsible for inadequate performance. Users should interpret the financial statements as if they had been prepared by management."

25-25 (Objective 25-6) The following items represent a series of unrelated procedures that an accountant may consider performing in an engagement to review or compile the financial statements of a nonpublic entity. Procedures may apply to only one, both, or neither type of engagement.

1. The accountant should establish an understanding with the entity regarding the nature and limitations of the services to be performed.
2. The accountant should make inquiries concerning actions taken at the board of directors meetings.
3. The accountant should obtain a level of knowledge of the accounting principles and practices of the entity's industry.
4. The accountant should obtain an understanding of the entity's internal control.
5. The accountant should perform analytical procedures designed to identify relationships that appear to be unusual.
6. The accountant should send a letter of inquiry to the entity's attorney to corroborate the information furnished by management concerning litigation.
7. The accountant should obtain a management representation letter from the entity.
8. The accountant should make inquiries about events subsequent to the date of the financial statements that would have a material effect on the financial statements.
9. The accountant should perform a physical examination of inventory.

a. Indicate which procedures are required to be performed on a review engagement.

b. Indicate which procedures are required to be performed on a compilation engagement.*

25-26 (Objective 25-6) You are doing review services and the related tax work for Regency Tools, Inc., a tool and die company with $2 million in sales. Inventory is recorded at $125,000. Prior-year unaudited statements, presented by the company without assistance from a CPA firm, disclose that the inventory is based on "historical cost estimated by management." You determine four facts:

1. The company has been growing steadily for the past 5 years.
2. The unit cost of the typical material used by Regency Tools has increased dramatically for several years.
3. The inventory cost has been approximately $125,000 for 5 years.
4. Management intends to use a value of $125,000 again for the current year.

When you discuss with management the need to get a physical count and an accurate inventory, the response is negative. Management is concerned about the effect on property and income taxes of a more realistic inventory. The company has never been audited and has followed this practice for years. You are convinced, based on inquiry and ratio analysis, that a conservative evaluation would be $500,000 at historical cost.

Required

a. What are the generally accepted accounting principle requirements for valuation and disclosure of inventory for unaudited financial statements?

b. Identify the potential legal and professional problems that you face in this situation.

c. What procedures would you normally follow for review services when the inventory is a material amount? Be as specific as possible.

d. How should you resolve the problem in this situation? Identify alternatives and evaluate the costs and benefits of each.

25-27 (Objective 25-6) SSARS provide illustrative review procedures for accountants to use as a guideline for conducting reviews. The introduction to the illustrative inquiries states:

> The inquiries to be made in a review of financial statements are a matter of the accountant's judgment. In determining his or her inquiries, an accountant may consider (a) the nature and materiality of the items, (b) the likelihood of misstatement, (c) knowledge obtained during current and previous engagements, (d) the stated qualifications of the entity's accounting personnel, (e) the extent to which a particular item is affected by management's judgment, and (f) inadequacies in the entity's underlying financial data. The following list of inquiries is for illustrative purposes only. The inquiries do not necessarily apply to every engagement, nor are they meant to be all-inclusive.

The inquiry procedures included in SSARS for the sales and collection cycle are as follows:

Revenue

1. Are revenues from the sale of major products and services recognized in the appropriate period?

Receivables

1. Has an adequate allowance been made for doubtful accounts?
2. Have receivables considered uncollectible been written off?
3. If appropriate, has interest been reflected?
4. Has a proper cutoff of sales transactions been made?
5. Are there any receivables from employees and related parties?
6. Are any receivables pledged, discounted, or factored?
7. Have receivables been properly classified between current and noncurrent?

Required

a. What other information about accounts receivable and revenue, besides the items listed, would the accountant have to obtain?

b. Compare the illustrative procedures for review services and those commonly performed for audits. What are the major differences?

c. Of whom should the accountant make inquiries in a small, closely held company?

d. Under what circumstances would procedures beyond those illustrated likely be performed? Be specific.

*AICPA adapted.

e. Compare the levels of achieved assurance for review services and audits. Is the achieved level much higher for audits, somewhat higher, or approximately the same? Give reasons for your answer.

25-28 (Objective 25-7) Lucia Johnson, of Johnson and Lecy, CPAs, has completed the first-year audit of Tidwell Publishing Co., a publicly held company, for the year ended December 31, 2005. She is now working on a review of interim financial statements for the quarter ended March 31, 2006.

Johnson has never done an interim review of a public company, but her firm does extensive compilation and review work. She therefore has one of her most experienced assistants, Fred Blair, do the work. She instructs him to follow the firm's standard review services procedures for SSARS reviews and to do high-quality work because Tidwell is a high-risk client.

Blair completes the review of Tidwell's statements and Johnson carefully reviews Blair's work. No exceptions are found. Each page of the client's financial statements is marked "reviewed." The following report is issued.

SECURITIES AND EXCHANGE COMMISSION

We have reviewed the accompanying balance sheet of Tidwell Publishing Co. as of March 31, 2006, and the related statements of income, retained earnings, and changes in financial position for the year then ended, in accordance with the standards of the Public Company Accounting Oversight Board (United States). All information included in these financial statements is the representation of the management of Tidwell Publishing Co.

A review consists principally of inquiries of company personnel and analytical procedures applied to financial data. It is substantially less in scope than an audit in accordance with the standards of the Public Company Accounting Oversight Board, the objective of which is the expression of an opinion regarding the financial statements taken as a whole. Accordingly, we do not express such an opinion.

Based on our review, we are not aware of any material modifications that should be made to the accompanying financial statements in order for them to be in conformity with generally accepted accounting principles.

Johnson & Levy, CPAs
March 31, 2006

Required

a. Is it appropriate to do a review service for a publicly held company? Explain.

b. Evaluate the approach taken by Johnson and Blair on the engagement.

c. Evaluate the report.

25-29 (Objective 25-8) Bengston, CPA, is conducting the audit of Pollution Control Devices, Inc. In addition, a supplemental negative assurance report is required to a major mortgage holder. The supplemental report concerns indenture agreements to keep the client from defaulting on the mortgage. Total assets are $14 million and the mortgage is for $4 million. The major provisions of the indentures are as follows:

1. The current ratio must be maintained above 2.3 to 1.
2. The debt/equity ratio must be maintained below 3.0.
3. Net earnings after taxes must exceed dividends paid by at least $1 million.

Required

a. Write the appropriate supplemental report if all three indenture agreement provisions have been satisfied.

b. How would the supplemental report change if net earnings after taxes were $1,010,000 and dividends paid were $60,000?

c. Assume the same situation as in part b and also assume that the client refuses to modify the financial statements or disclose the violation of the indenture agreement provisions on the grounds that the amount is immaterial. What is the nature of the appropriate auditor's report?

d. What is the nature of the appropriate supplemental report if all the indenture agreement provisions have been satisfied but there is a lawsuit against the company that has resulted in disclosure of the lawsuit in a footnote to the financial statements?

25-30 (Objective 25-8) Quality CPA Review is the franchisor of a national CPA review course for candidates taking the CPA examination. Quality CPA Review is responsible for providing all materials, including cassettes and video material, doing all national and local advertising, and giving assistance in effectively organizing and operating local franchises. The fee to the participant is $1,500 for the full course if all parts of the examination are taken. There are lower rates for candidates taking selected parts of the examination. Quality CPA Review gets 50% of the total fee.

The materials for the review course are purchased by Quality CPA Review from Ronnie Johnson, CPA, a highly qualified writer of CPA review materials. Quality CPA Review receives one copy of those materials from Johnson and reproduces them for candidates. Quality CPA Review must pay Johnson a $60 royalty for each full set of materials used and 12% of the participant fee for partial candidates. The contract between Johnson and Quality CPA Review requires an audited report to be provided by Quality CPA Review on royalties due to Johnson. Recorded gross fees for the 2005 review course are $1,500,000.

Even before the audit is started, there is a dispute between Quality CPA Review and Johnson. Quality CPA Review does not intend to pay royalties on certain materials. Johnson disagrees with that conclusion but the contract does not specify anything about it. The following are the disputed sales on which Quality CPA Review refused to pay royalties:

1. Materials sent to instructors for promotion	$31,000
2. Uncollected fees due to bad debts	6,000
3. Candidates who paid no fee because they performed administrative duties during the course	16,000
4. Refunds to customers who were dissatisfied with the course	22,000
Total	$75,000

Required

a. Assume that you are engaged to do the ordinary audit of Quality CPA Review and the special audit of royalties for Johnson. What additional audit testing beyond the normal tests of royalties is required because of the special audit?

b. Assume that the financial statements of Quality CPA Review are found to be fairly stated except for the unresolved dispute between Johnson and Quality CPA Review. Write the appropriate audit report.

c. Write the report for total royalties to Johnson, assuming that the information as stated in the case is all correct and the dispute is not resolved.

25-31 (Objective 25-8) Jones, CPA, has completed the audit of Sarack Lumber Supply Co. and has issued a standard unqualified report. In addition to a report on the overall financial statements, the company needs a special audited report on three specific accounts: sales, net fixed assets, and inventory valued at FIFO. The report is to be issued to Sarack's lessor, who bases annual rentals on these three accounts. Jones was not aware of the need for the report on the three specific accounts until after the overall audit was completed.

Required

a. Explain why Jones is unlikely to be able to issue the audit report on the three specific accounts without additional audit tests.

b. What additional tests are likely to be needed before the report on the three specific accounts can be issued?

c. Assuming that Jones is able to satisfy all the requirements needed to issue the report on the three specific accounts, write the report. Make any necessary assumptions.

INTERNET PROBLEM 25-1: REPORTING ON QUARTERLY FINANCIAL INFORMATION

Reference the CW site. SEC rules require public companies to have their external auditor perform a timely review of the company's quarterly financial statements. This problem uses the Internet to expose students to important issues associated with the SEC's rules.

INTERNAL AND GOVERNMENTAL FINANCIAL AUDITING AND OPERATIONAL AUDITING

GOOD AUDITING OFTEN RESULTS IN IMPROVED CASH FLOWS

Sandy Previtz is an experienced internal audit staff person with Erhardt Freight Company (EFC), a long-haul trucking company. EFC has been growing rapidly, adding customers and shipping agents daily, and volume exceeds several thousand shipments per day. To address the growing volume of freight bills and related receivables, EFC implemented a new state-of-the-art computerized information system.

Previtz was assigned to test the accuracy of the aging of the accounts receivable system and the adequacy of the allowance for doubtful accounts. She took an initial sample of 300 freight bills selected at random from a population of 20,000 outstanding freight bills. She used the sample to project an aging and develop an estimate of the required allowance for doubtful accounts. Her tests indicated the allowance could be understated by as much as $1 million.

Previtz informed Martha Harris, the head of internal audit, of the situation. Harris informed the chief financial officer that as long as the tests indicated there could be a material misstatement, EFC must expand the sample until it was clear whether the allowance was materially misstated.

Previtz's second sample increased the total sample to 600 items, with essentially the same results. However, at Harris's request, she analyzed the items from *both* a management standpoint and an accounting standpoint. When Harris and Previtz met with the CFO to discuss the updated information, Harris pointed out that the real problem was not the allowance but that receivables were out of control, and EFC faced a significant loss in cash flows if management didn't do something about it. The CFO quickly agreed and responded by hiring a team of temporary workers to analyze the aging of all 20,000 freight bills and to institute a large-scale collection effort. Not only did the analysis and collection efforts improve cash flows, it also showed that Previtz's estimate was right on target.

The last chapter discussed other assurance services provided by external auditors. This chapter examines the activities of other types of auditors. As Sandy Previtz of Erhardt Freight Company demonstrates in the introductory vignette, internal auditors can have a significant impact on a company's operational efficiency and effectiveness, as well as on earnings and cash flow.

Internal and government auditors perform a significant amount of financial auditing similar to that done by CPA firms. CPA firms also do considerable financial auditing of governmental units. The concepts and methodologies discussed throughout this book apply to audits by internal and government auditors. We begin this chapter by examining the role of internal auditors in financial auditing.

INTERNAL FINANCIAL AUDITING

OBJECTIVE 26-1

Explain the role of internal auditors in financial auditing.

As discussed in Chapter 1, internal auditors are employed by companies to do both financial and operational auditing. Their role in auditing has increased dramatically in the past two decades, primarily because of the increased size and complexity of many corporations. Because internal auditors spend all of their time with one company, their knowledge about the company's operations and internal controls is much greater than the external auditors' knowledge. That kind of knowledge can be critical to effective corporate governance. In fact, the New York Stock Exchange now requires its registrants to have an internal audit function.

The Institute of Internal Auditors professional practices framework provides the following definition of internal auditing:

> Internal auditing is an independent, objective assurance and consulting activity designed to add value and improve an organization's operations. It helps an organization accomplish its objectives by bringing a systematic, disciplined approach to evaluate and improve the effectiveness of risk management, control, and governance processes.

This definition reflects the changing role of internal auditors. Internal auditors are expected to provide value to the organization through improved operational effectiveness, in addition to traditional responsibilities such as reviewing the reliability and integrity of information, ensuring compliance with policies and regulations, and safeguarding assets.

The objectives of internal auditors are considerably broader than the objectives of external auditors. This provides flexibility for internal auditors to meet company needs. Different companies vary in the extent of internal auditing and the areas on which the internal auditors focus. For example, at one company, internal auditors may focus exclusively on documenting and testing controls as required by Section 404 of the Sarbanes–Oxley Act. At another company, internal auditors may serve primarily as consultants and focus on recommendations that improve organizational performance. Also, internal audit reports are not standardized because (1) the reporting needs vary for each company and (2) the reports are not relied on by external users.

Institute of Internal Auditors

Professional guidance for internal auditors is provided by the **Institute of Internal Auditors (IIA).** The IIA is an organization similar to the AICPA that establishes ethical and practice standards, provides education, and encourages professionalism for its approximately 100,000 worldwide members. The IIA has played a major role in the increasing influence of internal auditing. For example, the IIA has established a highly regarded certification program resulting in the designation of Certified Internal Auditor (CIA) for those who meet the testing and experience requirements.

The IIA professional practice framework includes a code of ethics and **IIA International Standards for the Professional Practice of Internal Auditing** (the "Red Book"). All IIA members and Certified Internal Auditors agree to follow the Institute's Code of Ethics, which requires compliance with the Standards. The IIA Code of Ethics is included in Figure 26-1, and is based on the ethical principles of integrity, objectivity, confidentiality, and competency.

IIA

FIGURE 26-1   Institute of Internal Auditors Ethical Principles and Code of Ethics

ETHICAL PRINCIPLES

Integrity   The integrity of internal auditors establishes trust and thus provides the basis for reliance on their judgment.

Objectivity   Internal auditors exhibit the highest level of professional objectivity in gathering, evaluating, and communicating information about the activity or process being examined. Internal auditors make a balanced assessment of all the relevant circumstances and are not unduly influenced by their own interests or by others in forming judgments.

Confidentiality   Internal auditors respect the value and ownership of information they receive and do not disclose information without appropriate authority unless there is a legal or professional obligation to do so.

Competency   Internal auditors apply the knowledge, skills, and experience needed in the performance of internal auditing services.

RULES OF CONDUCT

1. Integrity   Internal auditors:
   - 1.1. Shall perform their work with honesty, diligence, and responsibility.
   - 1.2. Shall observe the law and make disclosures expected by the law and the profession.
   - 1.3. Shall not knowingly be a party to any illegal activity, or engage in acts that are discreditable to the profession of internal auditing or to the organization.
   - 1.4. Shall respect and contribute to the legitimate and ethical objectives of the organization.

2. Objectivity   Internal auditors:
   - 2.1. Shall not participate in any activity or relationship that may impair or be presumed to impair their unbiased assessment. This participation includes those activities or relationships that may be in conflict with the interests of the organization.
   - 2.2. Shall not accept anything that may impair or be presumed to impair their professional judgment.
   - 2.3. Shall disclose all material facts known to them that, if not disclosed, may distort the reporting of activities under review.

3. Confidentiality   Internal auditors:
   - 3.1. Shall be prudent in the use and protection of information acquired in the course of their duties.
   - 3.2. Shall not use information for any personal gain or in any manner that would be contrary to the law or detrimental to the legitimate and ethical objectives of the organization.

4. Competency   Internal auditors:
   - 4.1. Shall engage only in those services for which they have the necessary knowledge, skills, and experience.
   - 4.2. Shall perform internal auditing services in accordance with the International Standards for the Professional Practice of Internal Auditing.
   - 4.3. Shall continually improve their proficiency and the effectiveness and quality of their services.

The International Standards for the Professional Practice of Internal Auditing are divided into attribute standards for the internal auditor and internal audit department and performance standards for the performance and reporting of internal audit activities. The general categories of the attribute and performance standards are included in Figure 26-2 (p. 772).

The standards also include several specific standards in each category. For example, Attribute Standard 1100 on Independence and Objectivity includes three standards that address organizational independence (1110), individual objectivity (1120), and impairments to independence and objectivity (1130). In addition, specific implementation standards have been developed for assurance and consulting engagements. For example, Implementation Standard 1110.A1 provides guidance for applying Attribute Standard 1110 on organizational independence for assurance engagements, and it states that the internal audit activity should be free from interference in determining the scope of internal auditing, performing work, and communicating results.

A comparison of these standards to the AICPA generally accepted auditing standards on page 34 shows both similarities and differences. **Statements on Internal Auditing Standards (SIASs)** are issued by the Internal Auditing Standards Board to provide authoritative interpretations of the standards.

ATTRIBUTE STANDARDS

1000 Purpose, Authority, and Responsibility. The purpose, authority, and responsibility of the internal audit activity should be formally defined in a charter, consistent with the *Standards*, and approved by the board.

1100 Independence and Objectivity. The internal audit activity should be independent, and internal auditors should be objective in performing their work.

1200 Proficiency and Due Professional Care. Engagements should be performed with proficiency and due professional care.

1300 Quality Assurance and Improvement Program. The chief audit executive should develop and maintain a quality assurance and improvement program that covers all aspects of the internal audit activity and continuously monitors its effectiveness. This program includes periodic internal and external quality assessments and ongoing internal monitoring. The program should be designed to help the internal auditing activity add value and improve the organization's operations and to provide assurance that the internal audit activity is in conformity with the *Standards* and the *Code of Ethics*.

PERFORMANCE STANDARDS

2000 Managing the Internal Audit Activity. The chief audit executive should effectively manage the internal audit activity to ensure it adds value to the organization.

2100 Nature of Work. The internal audit activity should evaluate and contribute to the improvement of risk management, control, and governance processes using a systematic and disciplined approach.

2200 Engagement Planning. Internal auditors should develop and record a plan for each engagement including the scope, objectives, timing and resource allocations.

2300 Performing the Engagement. Internal auditors should identify, analyze, evaluate, and record sufficient information to achieve the engagement's objectives.

2400 Communicating Results. Internal auditors should communicate the engagement results.

2500 Monitoring Progress. The chief audit executive should establish and maintain a system to monitor the disposition of results communicated to management.

2600 Management's Acceptance of Risks. When the chief audit executive believes that senior management has accepted a level of residual risk that may be unacceptable to the organization, the chief audit executive should discuss the matter with senior management. If the decision regarding residual risk is not resolved, the chief audit executive and senior management should report the matter to the board for resolution.

Source: From *The International Standards for the Professional Practice of Auditing*, Copyright © 2004 by The Institute of Internal Auditors, Inc. 247 Maitland Avenue, Altamonte Springs, FL 32701-4201. Reprinted with permission.

Relationship of Internal and External Auditors

There are both differences and similarities between the responsibilities and conduct of audits by internal and external auditors. The primary difference is whom each party is responsible to. The external auditor is responsible to financial statement users who rely on the auditor to add credibility to the statements. The internal auditor is responsible to management. Even with this important difference, there are many similarities between the two groups. Both must be competent as auditors and remain objective in performing their work and reporting their results. They both, for example, follow a similar methodology in performing their audits, including planning and performing tests of controls and substantive tests. Similarly, they both use the audit risk model and materiality in deciding the extent of their tests and evaluating results. Their decisions about materiality and risks may differ, however, because external users may have different needs than management has.

External auditors rely on internal auditors through the use of the audit risk model. Auditors significantly reduce control risk and thereby reduce substantive testing if internal auditors are effective. The fee reduction of the external auditor is typically substantial when there is a highly regarded internal audit function. External auditors typically consider internal auditors effective if they are independent of the operating units being evaluated, competent and well trained, and have performed relevant audit tests of the internal controls and financial statements.

SAS 65 (AU 322) also permits the external auditor to use the internal auditor for direct assistance on the audit. Relying on the internal audit staff for performance of some of the audit testing may allow the audit to be completed in less time and for a lower fee. When direct assistance is provided, the external auditor should assess the internal auditors' competence and objectivity. The work of the internal auditors should be supervised and evaluated as appropriate under the circumstances.

OBJECTIVE 26-2

Describe the auditing and reporting requirements under Government Auditing Standards and the Single Audit Act.

The previous section discussed the role of internal auditors. This section examines the activities of government auditors. The federal and state governments employ their own auditing staffs to perform audits in much the same way as internal auditors. Chapter 1 briefly discussed the United States Government Accountability Office (GAO). All states have their own audit agencies, similar to but smaller than the GAO. In addition, CPA firms do considerable financial auditing of governmental units. For example, some states require the audit of all city and school district financial statements by CPA firms.

GAO

The primary source of authoritative literature for the performance of **government audits** is *Government Auditing Standards*, which is issued by the GAO. Because of the color of the cover, it is usually referred to as the **"Yellow Book"** rather than by its more formal name. The Yellow Book was initially issued in 1972, with subsequent revisions in 1981, 1994, and 2003. The initial Yellow Book standards were similar to the GAAS standards but have been expanded in subsequent revisions to provide guidance standards for performance audits. The Yellow Book standards are often called generally accepted government auditing standards (**GAGAS**).

Financial auditing under the Yellow Book includes audits of financial statements of governmental units, government contracts and grants, internal control, fraud, and other noncompliance with laws and regulations. These categories of information are broader than audits under auditing standards and encompass the types of attestation work discussed in Chapter 25 under the attestation standards. It is not surprising, however, that governmental units are as concerned with compliance with laws and regulations as with the reliability of financial statements.

Financial Audit and Reporting Requirements— Yellow Book

The financial auditing standards of the Yellow Book are consistent with the 10 generally accepted auditing standards of the AICPA, and also contain extensive additional guidance. The following are some of the important additions and modifications:

- *Materiality and significance.* The Yellow Book recognizes that in government audits the thresholds of acceptable audit risk and materiality may be lower than in an audit of a commercial enterprise. This is because of the sensitivity of government activities and their public accountability.
- *Quality control.* CPA firms and other organizations that audit government entities in compliance with the Yellow Book must have an appropriate system of internal quality control and participate in an external quality control review program. The latter requirement exists for some CPAs, but only as a requirement for membership in the AICPA, and for the audit of public companies.

  Auditors involved in planning, conducting, or reporting on audits under GAGAS must complete 80 hours of continuing professional education in each 2-year period. At least 24 of these 80 hours of training must be in subjects related to the government environment and government auditing.
- *Compliance auditing.* The audit should be designed to provide reasonable assurance of detecting material misstatements resulting from noncompliance with provisions of contracts or grant agreements that have a material and direct effect on the financial statements. The auditor must also apply additional procedures if information comes to the auditor's attention concerning possible noncompliance that would have a material indirect effect on the financial statements.
- *Reporting.* The audit report must state that the audit was made in accordance with generally accepted government auditing standards. In addition, the report on financial statements must describe the scope of the auditors' testing of compliance with laws and regulations and internal controls and present the results of those tests or refer to a separate report containing that information.
- *Audit files.* Audits done in accordance with government auditing standards are subject to review by other auditors and oversight officials. The Yellow Book indicates that audit files should contain sufficient information to enable an auditor reviewer with no

previous connection to the audit to ascertain from the audit files evidence that supports the auditors' significant conclusions and judgments.

The additional requirements reflect the emphasis on compliance in governmental audits and the need for quality control due to the complexities of the governmental accounting and auditing environment.

Audit and Reporting Requirements—Single Audit Act and OMB Circular A-133

Before 1980, each federal financing agency had its own audit requirements. As a result, recipients of federal funds received multiple audits. This was remedied in 1984 with the passage of the **Single Audit Act**, which provided for a single coordinated audit to meet the audit requirements of all federal agencies. The Single Audit Act of 1984 applied only to audits of state and local governments. The requirements of the act were extended in 1990 to higher-education institutions and other not-for-profit organizations by the Office of Management and Budget (OMB) through the issuance of OMB Circular A-133.

Congress passed the Single Audit Act Amendments of 1996 to relieve the audit burden on small entities receiving federal financial assistance. Some of the significant provisions of the 1996 Amendments include the following:

- The threshold for requiring a single audit was raised from $100,000 to $300,000 to exempt many smaller entities from single audit requirements. The OMB increased the single audit threshold to $500,000 beginning in 2004.
- Statutory coverage of the single audit was extended to not-for-profit organizations as well as to state and local governments.
- A risk-based approach is to be used in selecting programs for testing.

The Office of Management and Budget issued a revised Circular A-133, *Audits of States, Local Governments, and Non-Profit Organizations,* to provide administrative guidance for implementing the single audit requirements.

Audit Requirements The 1996 Single Audit Act Amendments and OMB Circular A-133 (hereafter referred to collectively as the Act) contain requirements for the scope of the audit, including the following:

- The audit should be in accordance with generally accepted government auditing standards (GAGAS).
- The auditor must obtain an understanding of internal control over federal programs sufficient to support a low assessed level of control risk for major programs.
- The auditor should determine whether the client has complied with laws, regulations, and the provisions of contracts or grant agreements that may have a direct and material effect on each of its major programs.

The compliance requirements to be met are described in the A-133 *Compliance Supplement,* along with suggested audit procedures. Fourteen types of compliance requirements are identified that should be considered in every audit. In addition, specific requirements for individual federal programs are identified. The following are examples of some specific compliance objectives:

- Whether the amounts reported as expenditures were for allowable services.
- Whether the records show that those who received services or benefits were eligible to receive them.
- Whether matching requirements (where the government unit matches federal funds), levels of effort, and earmarking limitations were met.

www

Association
of Government Accountants

CHANGES IN SINGLE AUDIT THRESHOLD RELIEVE BURDEN ON SMALL ENTITIES

The Office of Management and Budget (OMB) is required to review the dollar threshold for requiring a single audit under OMB Circular A-133 every two years. The 1996 Single Audit Act Amendments permit the OMB to raise the threshold if it determines it is in the best interest of the federal gpvernment, federal assistance recipients, and the public. Increasing the threshold from $300,000 to $500,000 relieved nearly 6,000 entities from the single audit requirement, but affected less than one-half of 1 percent of the dollar amount of federal awards subject to single audit requirements.

774 PART SIX / OTHER ASSURANCE AND NONASSURANCE SERVICES

FIGURE 26-3   Example of a Government Audit Report

We have audited the accompanying financial statements of the governmental activities, the business-type activities, the aggregate discretely presented component units, each major fund, and aggregate remaining fund information of Redwood City as of and for the year ended June 30, 2005, which collectively comprise the City's basic financial statements as listed in the table of contents. These financial statements are the responsibility of Redwood City's management. Our responsibility is to express opinions on these financial statements based on our audit.

We conducted our audit in accordance with auditing standards generally accepted in the United States of America and the standards applicable to financial audits contained in *Government Auditing Standards,* issued by the Comptroller General of the United States. Those standards require that we plan and perform the audit to obtain reasonable assurance about whether the financial statements are free of material misstatement. An audit includes examining, on a test basis, evidence supporting the amounts and disclosures in the financial statements. An audit also includes assessing the accounting principles used and the significant estimates made by management, as well as evaluating the overall financial statement presentation. We believe that our audit provides a reasonable basis for our opinions.

In our opinion, the financial statements referred to above present fairly, in all material respects, the respective financial position of the governmental activities, the business-type activities, the aggregate discretely presented component units, each major fund, and aggregate remaining fund information of Redwood City as of June 30, 2005 and the respective changes in financial position and cash flows, where applicable, thereof for the year then ended, in conformity with accounting principles generally accepted in the United States of America.

The management's discussion and analysis and budgetary comparison schedules as identified in the table of contents are not a required part of the basic financial statements but are supplemental information required by the Governmental Accounting Standards Board. We have applied certain limited procedures, which consisted primarily of inquiries of management, regarding the methods of measurement and presentation of the required supplemental information. However, we did not audit the information and express no opinion on it.

Our audit was conducted for the purpose of forming opinions on the financial statements that collectively comprise Redwood City's basic financial statements. The accompanying introductory section, other supplemental information, and statistical section, as identified in the table of contents, are presented for the purpose of additional analysis and are not a required part of the basic financial statements. The combining financial statements have been subjected to the auditing procedures applied in the audit of the basic financial statements and, in our opinion, are fairly stated in all material respects in relation to the basic financial statements taken as a whole. The introductory section, budgetary comparison schedules, and statistical section have not been subjected to the auditing procedures applied by us in the audit of the basic financial statements and, accordingly, we express no opinion on them.

In accordance with *Government Auditing Standards,* we have also issued our report dated *[date of report]* on our consideration of Redwood City's internal control over financial reporting and on our tests of its compliance with certain provisions of laws, regulations, contracts, and grants. That report is an integral part of an audit performed in accordance with *Government Auditing Standards* and should be read in conjunction with this report in assessing the results of our audit.

- Whether federal financial reports and claims for advances and reimbursements contain information that is supported by the books and records from which the basic financial statements have been prepared.
- Whether amounts claimed or used for matching were determined in accordance with the cost principles and administrative requirements in relevant OMB circulars.

Reporting Requirements The following reports are required under OMB Circular A-133:

- An opinion on whether the financial statements are in accordance with GAAP. Figure 26-3 is an example of a governmental audit report.
- An opinion as to whether the schedule of federal awards is presented fairly in all material respects in relation to the financial statements as a whole.
- A report on internal control related to the financial statements and major programs.
- A report on compliance with laws, regulations, and the provisions of contracts or grant agreements, where noncompliance could have a material effect on the financial statements. This report can be combined with the report on internal control.
- A schedule of findings and questioned costs.

Note that the auditor's report in Figure 26-3 refers to government auditing standards and also refers to the report on internal control and compliance. The report also addresses supplemental information, including requirements of the Governmental Accounting Standards Board. The opinion on this supplemental information is consistent with the auditor's reporting on additional information accompanying the basic financial statements discussed in Chapter 24.

AICPA Guidance for Auditors

From the preceding discussion, one can see that entering the arena of government auditing is a complex undertaking. The auditor must be familiar with both generally accepted auditing standards and a series of government audit documents, laws, and regulations. Thus, the first step in preparing for such an engagement is extensive professional development. Sources of AICPA guidance include the audit guide *Government Auditing Standards and Circular A-133 Audits* and SAS 74 (AU 801), *Compliance Auditing Considerations in Audits of Governmental Entities and Recipients of Governmental Financial Assistance.*

OPERATIONAL AUDITING

Operational Audits

Previous sections of this chapter discussed the financial auditing activities of internal auditors and government auditors. Internal and government auditors, as well as CPA firms, are also involved in operational auditing.

Although **operational auditing** is generally understood to deal with efficiency and effectiveness, there is less agreement on the use of that term than one might expect. Many people prefer to use the terms **management auditing** or **performance auditing** instead of *operational auditing* to describe the review of organizations for efficiency and effectiveness. Those people typically describe operational auditing broadly and include evaluating internal controls and even testing those controls for effectiveness (tests of controls) as a part of operational auditing. Others do not distinguish among the terms *performance auditing, management auditing,* and *operational auditing.*

We prefer to use *operational auditing* broadly, as long as the purpose of the test is to determine the effectiveness or efficiency of any part of an organization. Testing the effectiveness of internal controls by an internal auditor is therefore a part of operational auditing if the purpose is to help an organization operate its business more effectively or efficiently. Similarly, the determination of whether a company has adequately trained assembly line personnel is also operational auditing if the purpose is to determine whether the company is effectively and efficiently producing products.

Differences Between Operational and Financial Auditing

OBJECTIVE 26-3

Distinguish operational auditing from financial auditing.

Three major differences exist between operational and financial auditing: the purpose of the audit, distribution of the reports, and inclusion of nonfinancial areas in operational auditing.

Purpose of the Audit The major distinction between financial and operational auditing is in the purposes of the tests. Financial auditing emphasizes whether historical information was correctly recorded. Operational auditing emphasizes effectiveness and efficiency. The financial audit is oriented to the past, whereas an operational audit concerns operating performance for the future. An operational auditor, for example, may evaluate whether a type of new material is being purchased at the lowest cost to save money on future raw material purchases.

Distribution of the Reports For financial auditing, the report typically goes to many users of financial statements, such as stockholders and bankers, whereas operational audit reports are intended primarily for management. As indicated in Chapter 3, well-defined wording is needed for financial auditing reports as a result of the widespread distribution of the reports. Because of the limited distribution of operational reports and the diverse nature of audits for efficiency and effectiveness, operational auditing reports vary considerably from audit to audit.

Inclusion of Nonfinancial Areas Operational audits cover any aspect of efficiency and effectiveness in an organization and can therefore involve a wide variety of activities. For example, the effectiveness of an advertising program or efficiency of factory employees would be part of an operational audit. Financial audits are limited to matters that directly affect the fairness of financial statement presentations.

Effectiveness refers to the accomplishment of objectives, whereas efficiency refers to the resources used to achieve those objectives. An example of effectiveness is the production of parts without defects. Efficiency concerns whether those parts are produced at minimum cost.

Effectiveness Versus Efficiency

Effectiveness Before an operational audit for effectiveness can be performed, there must be specific criteria for what is meant by **effectiveness**. An example of an operational audit for effectiveness would be to assess whether a governmental agency has met its assigned objective of achieving elevator safety in a city. Before the operational auditor can reach a conclusion about the agency's effectiveness, criteria for elevator safety must be set. For example, is the objective to see that all elevators in the city are inspected at least once a year? Is the objective to ensure that no fatalities occurred as a result of elevator breakdowns or that no breakdowns occurred?

OBJECTIVE 26-4

Provide an overview of operational audits.

Efficiency Like effectiveness, there must be defined criteria for what is meant by doing things more efficiently before operational auditing can be meaningful. It is often easier to set efficiency than effectiveness criteria if **efficiency** is defined as reducing cost without reducing effectiveness. For example, if two different production processes manufacture a product of identical quality, the process with the lower cost is considered more efficient. The following are several types of inefficiencies that commonly occur and often are uncovered through operational auditing.

Types of Inefficiency	*Example*
• Acquisition of goods and services is excessively costly.	• Bids for purchases of materials are not required.
• Raw materials are not available for production when needed.	• An entire assembly line must be shut down because necessary materials were not ordered.
• There is duplication of effort by employees.	• Identical production records are kept by both the accounting and production departments because they are unaware of each other's activities.
• Work is done that serves no purpose.	• Copies of vendors' invoices and receiving reports are sent to the production department where they are filed without ever being used.
• There are too many employees.	• The office work could be done effectively with one less administrative assistant.

In Chapter 10, it was stated that management establishes internal controls to help it meet its own goals. The following three concerns in setting up good internal controls were identified and discussed in Chapter 10:

Relationship Between Operational Auditing and Internal Controls

  • Reliability of financial reporting
  • Efficiency and effectiveness of operations
  • Compliance with applicable laws and regulations

The second of these three client concerns is obviously directly related to operational auditing, but the other two also affect efficiency and effectiveness. For example, reliable cost accounting information is important to management in deciding such things as which products to continue and the billing price of products. Similarly, failure to comply with a law such as the Sarbanes–Oxley Act could result in a large fine to the company.

There are two significant differences in internal control evaluation and testing for financial and operational auditing: the purpose of the evaluation and testing of internal controls and the normal scope of internal control evaluation.

The primary purposes of internal control evaluation for financial auditing are to determine the extent of substantive audit testing required and report on the effectiveness of internal control over financial reporting for public companies. The purpose of operational auditing is to evaluate efficiency and effectiveness of internal control and make recommendations to management. The control procedures might be evaluated in the same way for both financial and operational auditing, but the purpose is different. To illustrate, an operational auditor might determine whether internal verification procedures for duplicate sales invoices are effective to ensure that the company does not offend customers but also receives all money owed. A financial auditor often does the same internal control evaluation, but the primary purpose is to reduce confirmation of accounts receivable or other substantive tests. However, a secondary purpose of many financial audits is also to make operational recommendations to management.

The scope of internal control evaluation for financial audits is restricted to the effectiveness of internal control over financial reporting and its effect on the fair presentation of financial statements, whereas operational auditing concerns any control affecting efficiency or effectiveness. Therefore, for example, an operational audit could be concerned with policies and procedures established in the marketing department to determine the effectiveness of catalogs used to market products.

Types of Operational Audits

There are three broad categories of operational audits: functional, organizational, and special assignments. In each case, part of the audit is likely to concern evaluating internal controls for efficiency and effectiveness.

Functional Audits Functions are a means of categorizing the activities of a business, such as the billing function or production function. There are many different ways to categorize and subdivide functions. For example, there is an accounting function, but there are also cash disbursement, cash receipt, and payroll disbursement functions. There is a payroll function,

---

MAJOR CHANGES SEEN IN ROLE OF INTERNAL AUDITORS

The control environment of major financial institutions has changed dramatically in the face of shifting regulations, complex financial instruments, technological breakthroughs, and accelerating customer and stockholder demands. Crippling losses resulting from control failures are prompting far-reaching changes in the internal audit function. Some major changes:

Tension Between Roles Traditionally, internal auditors have been the organization's "control conscience," but they are now being asked to provide strategic and operational input. These conflicting roles of both creating and enforcing rules have resulted in tension that must be effectively managed. They also demand new types of skill sets, requiring that auditors have not only technical expertise, but also "live" skills such as communication, decision making, and business analysis.

Risk Management There are two major interrelated trends in the area of risk management: (1) the need for more audit attention to control operational risk, and (2) the movement toward integrated financial risk management, a central

component of which is "value at risk"—the potential loss from adverse changes in market factors for a specified time period and confidence level.

Electronic Commerce Conducting financial activity in a "paperless" electronic environment poses a major concern. As reliance on computer networks increases, institutions must design and implement control systems that can adequately manage risk, particularly in areas such as data security and integrity, and vulnerability to viruses. Early involvement of internal auditors is important in designing and developing new data systems and products, allowing institutions to build internal controls *into* new procedures and systems, as opposed to controlling them after the fact.

Sources: 1. Adapted from Luc Aerts, "A Framework for Managing Operational Risk," *Internal Auditor* (August 2001), pp. 53–59. 2. "Major Changes Seen in Role of Internal Auditors," *Deloitte & Touche Review* (February 5, 1996), p. 2.

but there are also hiring, timekeeping, and payroll disbursement functions. As the name implies, a **functional audit** deals with one or more functions in an organization. It could concern, for example, the payroll function for a division or for the company as a whole.

A functional audit has the advantage of permitting specialization by auditors. Certain auditors within an internal audit staff can develop considerable expertise in an area, such as production engineering. They can more efficiently spend all their time auditing in that area. A disadvantage of functional auditing is the failure to evaluate interrelated functions. The production engineering function interacts with manufacturing and other functions in an organization.

Organizational Audits An operational audit of an organization deals with an entire organizational unit, such as a department, branch, or subsidiary. An **organizational audit** emphasizes how efficiently and effectively functions interact. The plan of organization and the methods to coordinate activities are especially important in this type of audit.

Special Assignments In operational auditing, **special assignments** arise at the request of management. There are a wide variety of such audits. Examples include determining the cause of an ineffective IT system, investigating the possibility of fraud in a division, and making recommendations for reducing the cost of a manufactured product.

Operational audits are usually performed by one of three groups: internal auditors, government auditors, or CPA firms.

Who Performs
Operational Audits

Internal Auditors Internal auditors are in such a unique position to perform operational audits that some people use the terms *internal auditing* and *operational auditing* interchangeably. It is, however, inappropriate to conclude that all operational auditing is done by internal auditors or that internal auditors do only operational auditing. Many internal audit departments do both operational and financial audits. Often, they are done simultaneously. An advantage that internal auditors have in doing operational audits is that they spend all their time working for the company they are auditing. They thereby develop considerable knowledge about the company and its business, which is essential to effective operational auditing.

To maximize their effectiveness for both financial and operational auditing, the internal audit department should report to the board of directors or president. Internal auditors should also have access to and ongoing communications with the audit committee of the board of directors. This organizational structure helps internal auditors remain independent. For example, if internal auditors report to the controller, it is difficult for the internal auditor to evaluate independently and make recommendations to senior management about inefficiencies in the controller's operations.

Government Auditors Different federal and state government auditors perform operational auditing, often as a part of doing financial audits. As already discussed, the most widely recognized government auditor group is the GAO, but there are also many state government auditors. Most of these auditors are concerned with both financial and operational audits.

The Yellow Book, which was discussed earlier, defines and sets standards for performance audits, which are essentially the same as operational audits. Performance audits include the following:

- *Economy and efficiency audits.* An **economy and efficiency audit** has as its purpose determining (1) whether an entity is acquiring, protecting, and using its resources economically and efficiently; (2) the causes of inefficiencies or uneconomical practices; and (3) whether the entity has complied with laws and regulations concerning matters of economy and efficiency.
- *Program audits.* A **program audit** has as its purpose determining (1) the extent to which the desired results or benefits established by the legislature or other authorizing body are being achieved; (2) the effectiveness of organizations, programs, activities, or functions; and (3) whether the entity has complied with laws and regulations applicable to the program.

The first two objectives of each of these types of performance audits are clearly operational in nature. The final objective in each is compliance in nature, and was discussed earlier.

To illustrate specific operational activities of a state governmental audit, the following three examples are taken from an article in the publication *Internal Auditor*, discussing auditing for economy and efficiency:

- A separate hospital with its own administrative staff occupied three buildings on the grounds of another state hospital. Our audit showed that the limited workload of the administrative activities of this separate hospital and its proximity to the offices of the main hospital would permit consolidation of the administrative functions of the two hospitals at a savings of $145,000 a year.
- A local school district exercised control over 29 individual facilities. Our audit showed that the unused classroom facilities amounted to about 28 percent or the equivalent of eight schools and that enrollment was continuing to decline. We recommended consolidating and closing of individual facilities to the extent possible. Such action would not only reduce costs but also provide greater flexibility in class sizes and course offerings.
- The outstanding accounts receivable at a teaching hospital increased from $7 million to $11 million during a two-year period. An audit showed that this serious situation was caused, in part, by a lack of aggressive follow-up action, insufficient supervision, and insufficient staff to keep up with an increasing workload.[1]

CPA Firms When CPA firms do an audit of historical financial statements, part of the audit usually consists of identifying operational problems and making recommendations that may benefit the audit client. The recommendations can be made orally, but they are typically made by use of a management letter. Management letters were discussed in Chapter 24.

The background knowledge about a client's business that an external auditor must obtain in doing an audit often provides useful information for giving operational recommendations. For example, suppose that the auditor determined that inventory turnover for a client slowed considerably during the current year. The auditor is likely to determine the cause of the reduction to evaluate the possibility of obsolete inventory that would misstate the financial statements. In determining the cause of the reduced inventory turnover, the auditor may identify operational causes, such as ineffective inventory acquisition policies, that can be brought to the attention of management. An auditor who has a broad business background and experience with similar businesses is more likely to be effective at providing clients with relevant operational recommendations than a person who lacks those qualities.

It is also common for a client to engage a CPA firm to do operational auditing for one or more specific parts of its business. Usually, such an engagement would occur only if the company does not have an internal audit staff or if the internal audit staff lacks expertise in a certain area. In most cases, a management consulting staff of the CPA firm, rather than the auditing staff, performs these services. For example, a company can ask the CPA firm to evaluate the efficiency and effectiveness of its computer systems.

Independence and Competence of Operational Auditors

The two most important qualities for an operational auditor are *independence* and *competence.* Whom the auditor reports to is important to ensure that investigation and recommendations are made without bias. Independence is seldom a problem for CPA firm auditors because they are not employed by the company being audited. As stated earlier, independence of internal auditors is enhanced by having the internal audit department report to the board of directors or president. Similarly, government auditors should report to a level above the operating departments. The GAO, for example, reports directly to Congress as a means of enhancing independence.

The responsibilities of operational auditors can also affect their independence. The auditor should not be responsible for performing operating functions in a company or for correcting deficiencies when ineffective or inefficient operations are found. For example, it would negatively affect auditors' independence if they were responsible for designing an IT system for acquisitions or for correcting it if deficiencies were found during an audit of the acquisitions system.

[1] From *Round Table*, © 1982 by The Institute of Internal Auditors, Inc., 249 Maitland Avenue, Altamonte Springs, Fla. 32701. Reprinted with permission.

It is acceptable for auditors to recommend changes in operations, but operating personnel must have the authority to accept or reject the recommendations. If auditors had the authority to require implementation of their recommendations, auditors would actually have the responsibility for auditing their own work the next time an audit was conducted. Independence would therefore be reduced.

Competence is, of course, necessary to determine the cause of operational problems and to make appropriate recommendations. Competence is a major problem when operational auditing deals with wide-ranging operating problems. For example, imagine the difficulties of finding qualified internal auditors who can evaluate both the effectiveness of an advertising program and the efficiency of a production assembly process. The internal audit staff doing that type of operational auditing would presumably have to include some personnel with backgrounds in marketing and others in production.

A major difficulty found in operational auditing is in deciding on specific criteria for evaluating whether efficiency and effectiveness have occurred. In auditing historical financial statements, GAAP are the broad criteria for evaluating fair presentation. Audit objectives are used to set more specific criteria in deciding whether GAAP have been followed. In operational auditing, no such well-defined criteria exist.

One approach to setting criteria for operational auditing is to state that the objectives are to determine whether some aspect of the entity could be made more effective or efficient and to recommend improvements. This approach may be adequate for experienced and well-trained auditors, but it would be difficult for most auditors to follow such a poorly defined approach.

Specific Criteria More specific criteria are usually desirable before operational auditing is started. For example, suppose that you are doing an operational audit of the equipment layout in plants for a company. The following are some specific criteria, stated in the form of questions, that might be used to evaluate plant layouts:

- Were all plant layouts approved by home office engineering at the time of original design?
- Has home office engineering done a reevaluation study of plant layout in the past 5 years?
- Is each piece of equipment operating at 60 percent of capacity or more for at least 3 months each year?
- Does layout facilitate the movement of new materials to the production floor?
- Does layout facilitate the production of finished goods?
- Does layout facilitate the movement of finished goods to distribution centers?
- Does the plant layout effectively use existing equipment?
- Is the safety of employees endangered by the plant layout?

Sources of Criteria The operational auditor can use several sources in developing specific evaluation criteria. These sources include the following:

- *Historical performance.* A simple set of criteria can be based on actual results from prior periods (or audits). The idea behind using these criteria is to determine whether things have become "better" or "worse" in comparison. The advantage of these criteria is that they are easy to derive; however, they may not provide much insight into how well or poorly the audited entity is really doing.
- *Benchmarking.* Most entities subject to an operational audit are not unique; there are many similar entities within the overall organization or outside it. In those cases, the performance data of comparable entities are an excellent source for developing criteria for benchmarking. For internal comparable entities, the data are usually readily available. When the comparable entities are outside the organizations, they will often be willing to make such information available. It is also often available through industry groups and governmental regulatory agencies.
- *Engineered standards.* In many types of operational auditing engagements, it may be possible and appropriate to develop criteria based on engineered standards—for example, time and motion studies to determine production output rates. These criteria

---

Criteria for Evaluating Efficiency and Effectiveness

OBJECTIVE **26-5**

Plan and perform an operational audit.

are often time-consuming and costly to develop because they require considerable expertise; however, they may be effective in solving a major operational problem and well worth the cost. It is also possible that some standards can be developed by industry groups for use by all their members, thereby spreading the cost and reducing it for each participant. These may be groups in the industry of the subject organization or functional groups such as an IT users' organization.

- *Discussion and agreement.* Sometimes objective criteria are difficult or costly to obtain, and criteria are developed through simple discussion and agreement. The parties involved in this process should include management of the entity to be audited, the operational auditor, and the entity or persons to whom the findings will be reported.

Phases in Operational Auditing

There are three phases in an operational audit: planning, evidence accumulation and evaluation, and reporting and follow-up.

Planning The planning in an operational audit is similar to that discussed in earlier chapters for an audit of historical financial statements. Like auditors of financial statements, the operational auditor must determine the scope of the engagement and communicate it to the organizational unit. It is also necessary to staff the engagement properly, obtain background information about the organizational unit, understand internal control, and decide on the appropriate evidence to accumulate.

The major difference between planning an operational audit and a financial audit is the extreme diversity in operational audits. Because of the diversity, it is often difficult to decide on specific objectives for an operational audit. The objectives will be based on the criteria developed for the engagement. As discussed in the preceding sections, these will depend on the specific circumstances at hand. For example, the objectives for an operational audit of the effectiveness of internal controls over petty cash would be dramatically different from those of an operational audit of the efficiency of a research and development department.

Another difference is that staffing is often more complicated in an operational audit than in a financial audit. This again is because of the breadth of the engagements. Not only are the areas diverse—for example, production control, advertising, and strategy planning—but the objectives within those areas often require special technical skills. For example, the auditor may need an engineering background to evaluate performance on a major construction project.

Finally, it is important to spend more time with the interested parties agreeing on the terms of the engagement and the criteria for evaluation in an operational audit than in a financial audit. This was alluded to in the preceding section for criteria developed through discussion. Regardless of the source of the criteria for evaluation, it is essential that the auditee, the auditor, and the sponsor of the engagement be in clear and complete agreement on the objectives and criteria involved. That agreement will facilitate effective and successful completion of the operational audit.

Evidence Accumulation and Evaluation The seven types of evidence studied in Chapter 7 and used throughout this book are equally applicable to operational auditing. Because internal controls and operating procedures are a critical part of operational auditing, it is common to extensively use documentation, client inquiry, and observation. Confirmation and reperformance are used less extensively for most operational audits than for financial audits because accuracy is not the purpose of most operational audits.

To illustrate evidence accumulation in operational auditing, we return to the example discussed earlier about evaluating the safety of elevators in a city. Assume there is agreement that the objective is to determine whether the inspection is made annually of each elevator in the city by a competent inspector. To satisfy the completeness objective, the auditor would, for example, examine blueprints of city buildings and elevator locations and trace them to the agency's list to ensure that all elevators are included in the population. Additional tests on newly constructed buildings would be appropriate to assess the timeliness with which the central listing is updated.

Assuming that the agency's list is determined to be complete, the auditor can select a sample of elevator locations and evidence can be collected as to the timing and frequency of inspections. The auditor may want to consider inherent risk by doing greater sampling of older elevators or elevators with previous safety defects. The auditor may also want to examine evidence to determine whether the elevator inspectors were competent to evaluate elevator safety. The auditor may, for example, evaluate inspectors' qualifications by reviewing resumes, training programs, competency examinations, and performance reports. It is also likely that the auditor would want to reperform the inspection procedures for a sample of elevators to obtain evidence of inconsistencies in reported and actual conditions.

In the same manner as for financial audits, operational auditors must accumulate sufficient competent evidence to afford a reasonable basis for a conclusion about the objectives being tested. In the elevator example, the auditor must accumulate sufficient evidence about elevator safety inspections. After the evidence is accumulated, the auditor must decide whether it is reasonable to conclude that an inspection is made annually of each elevator in the city by a competent inspector.

Reporting and Follow-Up Two major differences in operational and financial auditing reports affect operational auditing reports. First, in operational audits, the report is usually sent only to management, with a copy to the unit being audited. The lack of third-party users reduces the need for standardized wording in operational auditing reports. Second, the diversity of operational audits requires a tailoring of each report to address the scope of the audit, findings, and recommendations. The combination of these two factors results in major differences in operational auditing reports. Report writing often takes a significant amount of time to clearly communicate audit findings and recommendations.

When reports are being rendered on performance audits in accordance with the Yellow Book, specific contents are required. The Yellow Book permits considerable freedom on the form of the report.

Follow-up is common in operational auditing when recommendations are made to management. The purpose is to determine whether the recommended changes were made, and if not, why.

Each issue of the *Internal Auditor,* a bimonthly publication of the Institute of Internal Auditors, includes several internal operational audit findings submitted by practicing internal auditors. Most of the findings relate to efficiency rather than effectiveness. Readers of the journal likely find efficiency findings more interesting reading than those related to effectiveness. If someone can state, for example, that an operational audit resulted in a savings of $68,000, it is likely to be more interesting than reporting on improved accuracy of financial reporting. The following examples from the *Internal Auditor* include examples related to effectiveness and to efficiency:

Examples of Operational Audit Findings

Outside Janitorial Firm Saves $160,000

- An internal auditor reviewed the efficiency and effectiveness of the janitorial services furnished by state employees for the buildings in the state capitol complex. The audit disclosed the costs of the janitorial services were excessive when compared with similar services performed by outside janitorial firms. In addition, the auditors found many janitorial tasks were not completed as required, resulting in unacceptable quality. A study of alternative janitorial services indicated equal or better service could be provided by an outside janitorial firm and at a savings of $137,000 a year. The auditor recommended the state seek competitive bids and contract with the janitorial firm submitting the lowest bid that meets the specifications. The resultant contract actually saved more than $160,000, and the quality of the cleaning improved noticeably.

More Timely Credit Memo Processing

- A frequent complaint heard by the internal auditor concerned the inordinate amount of time required to process customers' credit memos. The auditor found the complaint was justified because an average of 14 working days elapsed between the receipt of the request and the actual issuance of the memo. In some cases, as many as 21 working days elapsed before the memo was issued.

  Using a time-phased flowchart, the auditor determined the requests were not moving in an efficient linear flow. As a matter of fact, the time-phased flowchart looked like a zigzag with a bad case of hiccups. The requests moved from the originator for removal of the supporting documents. The request then went back again to one of the approving departments for sorting, coding, and batching. Finally, the request was transmitted to the computer to issue the memo. Each step required from 1 to 5 working days, depending on the workload and complexity of the request.

The auditor recommended each approving department perform all the required functions the first time it handled the request and substitute well-controlled procedures for after-the-fact approvals in place of the preapprovals. The recommendation was adopted, and credit memos are now being issued within 5 working days after the request is received. The auditor noted a higher degree of customers' satisfaction, and complaints have ceased.

Use the Right Tool

- The company leased 25 heavy-duty trucks for use by service employees who installed and repaired about 20,000 vending machines in a large metropolitan area. All of the trucks were equipped with hydraulic lift-gates for loading and unloading vending machines.
- The internal auditor found that only a few of the trucks were actually delivering and picking up vending machines. Most of the trucks were used for service calls, which consisted of on-the-scene repair of coin boxes or other simple adjustments not requiring the hydraulic lift-gates.
- The auditor recommended most of the heavy-duty trucks be phased out and replaced by conventional light vans. Management agreed and the savings in lease rates and operating expenses were estimated at $25,000 a year.

Computer Programs Save Manual Labor

- ERISA requires an annual audit of profit-sharing plans. These internal auditors not only tested the finances but also performed an operational review, which provided a number of valuable recommendations to management.

The IT auditors devised a number of computer-assisted audit programs to test control over enrollment in and termination from the company's profit-sharing plan. The computer assistance saved much manual labor and detected a number of findings such as employees on the plan with less than the required 1 year of service and terminated employees still on the plan. The computer portion of the audit program also detected conflicting data between the payroll and profit-sharing plan master files.

When shown the results of the audit, management corrected all of the problems and instituted additional controls to prevent the problems in the future. And the additional controls were . . . well, guess. Yep, they wanted the IT auditors to leave their computer programs in the machine. The profit-sharing plan manager uses the programs periodically as a control to detect enrollment errors.[2]

SUMMARY

This chapter discussed the financial auditing activities of internal auditors and the effect of internal auditors on external audits. We also discussed government auditors and the auditing and reporting requirements under government auditing standards. Increasingly, internal auditors and government auditors, as well as CPA firms, are also asked to perform operational audits of the efficiency or effectiveness of a company or government unit. In these engagements, it is important to determine the appropriate criteria for evaluating efficiency or effectiveness.

ESSENTIAL TERMS

Economy and efficiency audit—a government audit to determine whether an entity is acquiring, protecting, and using its resources economically and efficiently; the causes of any inefficiencies or uneconomical practices; and whether the entity has complied with laws and regulations concerning matters of economy and efficiency

[2]Ibid.

Effectiveness—the degree to which the organization's objectives are accomplished

Efficiency—the degree to which costs are reduced without reducing effectiveness

Functional audit—an operational audit that deals with one or more specific functions within an organization, such as the payroll function or the production engineering function

Government Auditing Standards (GAGAS)—see Yellow Book

Government audits—financial or operational audits of government agencies or government-funded institutions

IIA International Standards for the Professional Practice of Internal Auditing—guidelines issued by the Institute of Internal Auditors covering the attributes and performance of internal auditors

Institute of Internal Auditors (IIA)—organization for internal auditors that establishes ethical and practice standards, provides education, and encourages professionalism for its members

Operational auditing—the review of an organization for efficiency and effectiveness. The terms *management auditing, performance auditing,* and *operational auditing* are often synonymous terms

Organizational audit—an operational audit that deals with an entire organizational unit, such as a department, branch, or subsidiary, to determine how efficiently and effectively functions interact

Program audit—a government audit to determine the extent to which the desired results or benefits established by the legislature or other authorizing body are being achieved; the effectiveness of organizations, programs, activities, or functions; and whether the entity has complied with laws and regulations applicable to the program

Single Audit Act—federal legislation that provides for a single coordinated audit to satisfy the audit requirements of all federal funding agencies

Special assignments—management requests for an operational audit for a specific purpose, such as investigating the possibility of fraud in a division or making recommendations for reducing the cost of a manufactured product

Statements on Internal Auditing Standards (SIASs)—statements issued by the Internal Auditing Standards Board of the IIA to provide authoritative interpretations of the IIA Practice Standards

Yellow Book—a publication of the GAO that is widely used as a reference by government auditors and CPAs who do governmental audit work; the official title is *Government Auditing Standards*

REVIEW QUESTIONS

26-1 (Objective 26-1) Explain the role of internal auditors for financial auditing. How is it similar to and different from the role of external auditors?

26-2 (Objective 26-1) What is the nature of the two categories of standards in the IIA International Standards for the Professional Practice of Auditing?

26-3 (Objective 26-1) Explain the difference in the independence of internal auditors and external auditors in the audit of historical financial statements. How can internal auditors best achieve independence?

26-4 (Objective 26-2) Explain how governmental financial auditing is similar to and different from audits of commercial companies. Who does governmental auditing?

26-5 (Objective 26-2) Explain what is meant by the Single Audit Act. What is its purpose?

26-6 (Objective 26-2) In what ways is the Yellow Book consistent with generally accepted auditing standards, and what are some additions and modifications?

26-7 (Objective 26-2) Identify the primary specific objectives that must be incorporated into the design of audit tests under the Single Audit Act.

26-8 (Objective 26-2) Identify the key required reports of the Single Audit Act and OMB Circular A-133.

26-9 (Objective 26-3) Describe what is meant by an operational audit.

26-10 (Objective 26-3) Identify the three major differences between financial and operational auditing.

26-11 (Objective 26-4) Distinguish between efficiency and effectiveness in operational audits. State one example of an operational audit explaining efficiency and another explaining effectiveness.

26-12 (Objective 26-4) Distinguish among the following types of operational audits: functional, organizational, and special assignment. State an example of each for a not-for-profit hospital.

26-13 (Objective 26-4) Explain why many people think of internal auditors as the primary group responsible for conducting operational audits.

26-14 (Objective 26-4) Explain the role of government auditors in operational auditing. How is this similar to and different from the role of internal auditors?

26-15 (Objective 26-4) Under what circumstances are external auditors likely to be involved in operational auditing? Give one example of operational auditing by a CPA firm.

26-16 (Objective 26-5) Explain what is meant by the criteria for evaluating efficiency and effectiveness. Provide five possible specific criteria for evaluating effectiveness of an IT system for payroll.

26-17 (Objective 26-5) Identify the three phases of an operational audit.

26-18 (Objective 26-5) Explain how planning for operational auditing is similar to and different from financial auditing.

26-19 (Objective 26-5) What are the major differences between reporting for operational and financial auditing?

MULTIPLE CHOICE QUESTIONS FROM CPA, IIA, AND CMA EXAMINATIONS

26-20 (Objectives 26-1, 26-4) The following questions deal with independence of auditors. Choose the best response.

a. The operational auditor's independence is most likely to be compromised when the internal audit department is responsible directly to the
    (1) Vice president of finance.
    (2) President.
    (3) Controller.
    (4) Executive vice president.
    (5) Audit committee of the board of directors.

b. The independence of the internal audit department will most likely be assured if it reports to the
    (1) President.
    (2) Controller.
    (3) Treasurer.
    (4) Audit committee of the board of directors.
    (5) Vice president of finance.

c. Which of the following may compromise the independence of an internal auditor?
    (1) Reviewing IT systems before implementation.
    (2) Performing an audit where the auditor recently had operating responsibilities.
    (3) Failing to review the audit report with the auditee prior to distribution.
    (4) Following up on corrective action in response to audit findings.

d. Internal auditors should be objective in performing audits. Which of the following situations violates standards concerning objectivity?
    (1) The auditor who reviews accounts receivable worked in that department for three months as a trainee 2 years ago.
    (2) The auditor reviews a department that continues to use procedures recommended by that auditor when the department was established.
    (3) The auditor reviews the same department for 2 years in succession.
    (4) The auditor reviews a department in which the auditor has the responsibility for cosigning checks.

26-21 (Objective 26-2) The following questions deal with governmental auditing. Choose the best response.

a. Which of the following bodies promulgates standards for audits of recipients of federal awards?
    (1) Governmental Accounting Standards Board.
    (2) Financial Accounting Standards Board.
    (3) Government Accountability Office.
    (4) Governmental Auditing Standards Board.

b. When performing the audit of a city that is subject to the requirements of the federal Single Audit Act, an auditor should adhere to
   (1) Governmental Accounting Standards Board General Standards.
   (2) Governmental Finance Officers Governmental Accounting, Auditing, and Financial Reporting Principles.
   (3) Government Auditing Standards.
   (4) Securities and Exchange Commission Regulation S-X.

c. When engaged to audit a governmental entity in accordance with Government Auditing Standards, an auditor prepares a written report on internal control
   (1) on all audits, regardless of circumstances.
   (2) only when the auditor has noted material weaknesses.
   (3) only when requested by the governmental entity being audited.
   (4) only when requested by the federal government funding agency.

d. Ward is auditing an entity's compliance with requirements governing a major federal financial assistance program in accordance with the Single Audit Act. Ward detected noncompliance with requirements that have a material effect on the program. Ward's report on compliance should express
   (1) no assurance on the compliance tests.
   (2) reasonable assurance on the compliance tests.
   (3) a qualified or adverse opinion.
   (4) an adverse opinion or a disclaimer of opinion.

26-22 (Objectives 26-3, 26-4, 26-5) The following questions deal with operational auditing. Choose the best response.

a. Which of the following best describes the operational audit?
   (1) It requires constant review by internal auditors of the administrative controls as they relate to the operations of the company.
   (2) It concentrates on implementing financial and accounting controls in a newly organized company.
   (3) It attempts and is designed to verify the fair presentation of a company's results of operations.
   (4) It concentrates on seeking aspects of operations in which waste would be reduced by the introduction of controls.

b. The evaluation of audit field work of an operating unit should answer the following questions:
   1. What are the reasons for the results?
   2. How can performance be improved?
   3. What results are being achieved?
   What is the chronological order in which these questions should be answered?
   (1) 3—1—2   (4) 1—2—3
   (2) 1—3—2   (5) 2—3—1
   (3) 3—2—1

c. Complaints from the public were received about processing automobile license applications in the state department of motor vehicles. You were assigned by the legislative auditor to review this operation. Which of the following should be your first audit step?
   (1) Send out questionnaires to recent licensees.
   (2) Test the system by licensing a vehicle.
   (3) Discuss the nature of the complaints with the chief of the licensing office.
   (4) Discuss the nature of the complaints with several licensing clerks.
   (5) Discuss the nature of the complaints with the director of the state department of motor vehicles.

d. The first step an operational auditor should take in performing a management study to help the director of marketing determine the optimum allocation of the advertising budget to company products is to
   (1) Analyze prior-years' advertising costs.
   (2) Hold discussions with media personnel.
   (3) Establish and discuss with the director the key objectives of the study.
   (4) Determine the amount of projected sales for the purpose of establishing the proposed sales budget.
   (5) Do both (1) and (2).

26-23 (Objectives 26-1, 26-4, 26-5) The following questions deal with internal auditing departments and their responsibilities. Choose the best response.

a. Which of the following is generally considered to be a major reason for establishing an internal auditing function?
   (1) To relieve overburdened management of the responsibility for establishing effective systems of internal control.
   (2) To ensure that operating activities comply with the policies, plans, and procedures established by management.
   (3) To safeguard resources entrusted to the organization.
   (4) To ensure the accuracy, reliability, and timeliness of financial and operating data used in management's decision making.
   (5) To assist members of the organization in the measurement and evaluation of the effectiveness of established systems of internal control.

b. Which of the following is generally considered to be the primary purpose of an internal auditor's evaluation of the adequacy of internal control?
   (1) To determine whether the established internal controls are functioning as intended by management.
   (2) To determine the extent of reliance the internal auditor can place on the established internal controls in the process of evaluating the financial statements prepared by the organization.
   (3) To determine whether all risks and exposures of the enterprise have been reduced or eliminated by the established internal controls.
   (4) To determine whether the established internal controls provide reasonable assurance that the objectives and goals of the organization will be met in an efficient and economical manner.

c. With regard to corrective action on audit results, which of the following is not the internal auditor's responsibility?
   (1) Soliciting auditees' suggestions for corrective actions.
   (2) Recommending possible alternative corrective actions.
   (3) Directing the corrective actions.
   (4) Determining that the corrective actions are responsive to the audit results.
   (5) Evaluating new policy statements to determine whether they address the unsatisfactory conditions disclosed in the audit results.

CASES

26-24 (Objectives 26-1, 26-4) Lajod Company has an internal audit department consisting of a manager and three staff auditors. The manager of internal audits, in turn, reports to the corporate controller. Copies of audit reports are routinely sent to the audit committee of the board of directors as well as to the corporate controller and the individual responsible for the area or activity being audited.

The manager of internal audits is aware that the external auditors have relied on the internal audit function to a substantial degree in the past. However, in recent months, the external auditors have suggested there may be a problem related to the objectivity of the internal audit function. This objectivity problem may result in more extensive testing and analysis by the external auditors.

The external auditors are concerned about the amount of nonaudit work performed by the internal audit department. The percentage of nonaudit work performed by the internal auditors in recent years has increased to about 25% of their total hours worked. A sample of five recent nonaudit activities are as follows:

1. One of the internal auditors assisted in the preparation of policy statements on internal control. These statements included such things as policies regarding sensitive payments and standards of control for internal controls.
2. The bank statements of the corporation are reconciled each month as a regular assignment for one of the internal auditors. The corporate controller believes this strengthens internal controls because the internal auditor is not involved in the receipt and disbursement of cash.
3. The internal auditors are asked to review the budget data in every area each year for relevance and reasonableness before the budget is approved. In addition, an internal auditor examines the variances each month, along with the associated explanations. These variance analyses are prepared by the corporate controller's staff after consultation with the individuals involved.
4. One of the internal auditors has recently been involved in the design, installation, and initial operation of a new computer system. The auditor was primarily concerned with the design and implementation of internal accounting controls and the computer application controls for the new system. The auditor also conducted the testing of the controls during the test runs.
5. The internal auditors are often asked to make accounting entries for complex transactions before the transactions are recorded. The employees in the accounting department are not

adequately trained to handle such transactions. In addition, this serves as a means of maintaining internal control over complex transactions. The manager of internal audits has always made an effort to remain independent of the corporate controller's office and believes that the internal auditors are objective and independent in their audit and nonaudit activities.

Required

a. Define *objectivity* as it relates to the internal audit function.

b. For each of the five situations outlined, explain whether the objectivity of Lajod Company's internal audit department has been materially impaired. Consider each situation independently.

c. The manager of audits reports to the corporate controller.
   (1) Does this reporting relationship result in a problem of objectivity? Explain your answer.
   (2) Would your answer to any of the five situations in requirement b have changed if the manager of internal audits reported to the audit committee of the board of directors? Explain your answer.*

26-25 (Objectives 26-1, 26-4, 26-5) Lado Corporation has an internal audit department operating out of the corporate headquarters. Various types of audit assignments are performed by the department for the eight divisions of the company. The following findings resulted from recent audits of Lado Corporation's White Division:

1. One of the departments in the division appeared to have an excessive turnover rate. Upon investigation, the personnel department seemed to be unable to find enough workers with the specified skills for this department. Some workers are trained on the job. The departmental supervisor is held accountable for labor efficiency variances but does not have qualified staff or sufficient time to train the workers properly. The supervisor holds individual workers responsible for meeting predetermined standards from the day they report to work. This has resulted in a rapid turnover of workers who are trainable but not yet able to meet standards.

2. The internal audit department recently participated in a computer feasibility study for this division. It advised and concurred on the purchase and installation of a specific computer system. Although the system is up and operating, the results are less than desirable. The software and hardware meet the specifications of the feasibility study, but there are several functions unique to this division that the system has been unable to accomplish. Linking of files has been a problem. For example, several vendors have been paid for materials not meeting company specifications. A revision of the existing software is probably not possible, and a permanent solution probably requires replacing the existing computer system with a new one.

3. One of the products manufactured by this division was recently redesigned to eliminate a potential safety defect. This defect was discovered after several users were injured. At present, there are no pending lawsuits because none of the injured parties has identified a defect in the product as a cause of the injury. There is insufficient information to determine whether the defect was a contributing factor.

The director of internal auditing and assistant controller is in charge of the internal audit department and reports to the controller in corporate headquarters. Copies of internal audit reports are sent routinely to Lado's board of directors.

Required

a. Explain the additional steps in terms of field work, preparation of recommendations, and operating management review that ordinarily should be taken by Lado Corporation's internal auditors as a consequence of the audit findings in the first situation (excessive turnover).

b. Discuss whether there are any objectivity problems with Lado Corporation's internal audit department as revealed by the audit findings. Include in your discussion any recommendations to eliminate or reduce an objectivity problem, if one exists.

c. The internal audit department is part of the corporate controllership function, and copies of the internal audit reports are sent to the board of directors.
   (1) Evaluate the appropriateness of the location of the internal audit department within Lado's organizational structure.
   (2) Discuss who within Lado should receive the reports of the internal audit department.*

26-26 (Objectives 26-4, 26-5) Haskin Company was founded 40 years ago and now has several manufacturing plants in the Northeast and Midwest. The evaluation of proposed capital expenditures became increasingly difficult for management as the company became geographically dispersed and diversified its product line. Thus, the Capital Budgeting Group was organized in 2004 to review all capital expenditure proposals in excess of $50,000.

The Capital Budgeting Group conducts its annual planning and budget meeting each September for the upcoming calendar year. The group establishes a minimum return for investments (hurdle

*CMA adapted.

rate) and estimates a target level of capital expenditures for the next year based on the expected available funds. The group then reviews the capital expenditure proposals that have been submitted by the various operating segments. Proposals that meet either the return on investment criterion or a critical need criterion are approved to the extent of available funds.

The Capital Budgeting Group also meets monthly, as necessary, to consider any projects of a critical nature that were not expected or requested in the annual budget review. These monthly meetings allow the Capital Budgeting Group to make adjustments during the year as new developments occur.

Haskin's profits have been decreasing slightly for the past 2 years despite a small but steady sales growth, a sales growth that is expected to continue through 2006. As a result of the profit stagnation, top management is emphasizing cost control and all aspects of Haskin's operations are being reviewed for cost reduction opportunities.

Haskin's internal audit department has become involved in the companywide cost reduction effort. The department has already identified several areas where cost reductions could be realized and has made recommendations to implement the necessary procedures to effect the cost savings. Tom Watson, internal audit director, is now focusing on the activities of the Capital Budgeting Group in an attempt to determine the efficiency and effectiveness of the capital budgeting process.

In an attempt to gain a better understanding of the capital budgeting process, Watson decided to examine the history of one capital project in detail. A capital expenditure proposal of Haskin's Burlington Plant that was approved by the Capital Budgeting Group in 2005 was selected randomly from a population of all proposals approved by the group at its 2004 and 2005 annual planning and budget meetings.

The Burlington proposal consisted of a request for five new machines to replace equipment that was 20 years old and for which preventive maintenance had become expensive. Four of the machines were for replacement purposes, and the fifth was for planned growth in demand. Each of the four replacement machines was expected to result in annual maintenance cost savings of $10,000. The fifth machine was exactly like the other four and was expected to generate an annual contribution of $15,000 through increased output. Each machine had a cost of $50,000 and an estimated useful life of 8 years.

Required

a. Identify and discuss the issues that Haskin Company's internal audit department must address in its examination and evaluation of Burlington Plant's 2005 capital expenditure project.

b. Recommend procedures to be used by Haskin's internal audit department in the audit review of Burlington Plant's 2005 capital expenditure project.*

26-27 (Objectives 26-4, 26-5) Lecimore Company has a centralized purchasing department that is managed by Joan Jones. Jones has established policies and procedures to guide the clerical staff and purchasing agents in the day-to-day operation of the department. She is satisfied that these policies and procedures are in conformity with company objectives and believes there are no major problems in the regular operations of the purchasing department.

Lecimore's internal audit department was assigned to perform an operational audit of the purchasing function. Their first task was to review the specific policies and procedures established by Jones. The policies and procedures are as follows:

- All significant purchases are made on a competitive bid basis. The probability of timely delivery, reliability of vendor, and so forth, are taken into consideration on a subjective basis.
- Detailed specifications of the minimum acceptable quality for all goods purchased are provided to vendors.
- Vendors' adherence to the quality specifications is the responsibility of the materials manager of the inventory control department and not the purchasing department. The materials manager inspects the goods as they arrive to be sure that the quality meets the minimum standards and then sees that the goods are transferred from the receiving dock to the storeroom.
- All purchase requests are prepared by the materials manager based on the production schedule for a 4-month period.

The internal audit staff then observed the operations of the purchasing function and gathered the following findings:

- One vendor provides 90% of a critical raw material. This vendor has a good delivery record and is reliable. Furthermore, this vendor has been the low bidder over the past few years.
- As production plans change, rush and expedite orders are made by production directly to the purchasing department. Materials ordered for cancelled production runs are stored for future use. The costs of these special requests are borne by the purchasing department. Jones considers

*CMA adapted.

the additional costs associated with these special requests as "costs of being a good member of the corporate team."

- Materials to accomplish engineering changes are ordered by the purchasing department as soon as the changes are made by the engineering department. Jones is proud of the quick response by the purchasing staff to product changes. Materials on hand are not reviewed before any orders are placed.
- Partial shipments and advance shipments (that is, those received before the requested date of delivery) are accepted by the materials manager, who notifies the purchasing department of the receipt. The purchasing department is responsible for follow-up on partial shipments. No action is taken to discourage advance shipments.

Based on the purchasing department's policies and procedures and the findings of Lecimore's internal audit staff,

Required

a. Identify weaknesses and/or inefficiencies in Lecimore Company's purchasing function.

b. Make recommendations for those weaknesses/inefficiencies that you identify.*

Use the following format in preparing your response:

Weaknesses/Inefficiencies	Recommendations
1.	1.

26-28 (Objectives 26-4, 26-5) Superior Co. manufactures automobile parts for sale to the major U.S. automakers. Superior's internal audit staff is to review the internal controls over machinery and equipment and make recommendations for improvements when appropriate. The internal auditors obtained the following information during the assignment:

- Requests for purchase of machinery and equipment are normally initiated by the supervisor in need of the asset. The supervisor discusses the proposed acquisition with the plant manager. A purchase requisition is submitted to the purchasing department when the plant manager is satisfied that the request is reasonable and that there is a remaining balance in the plant's share of the total corporate budget for capital acquisitions.
- Upon receiving a purchase requisition for machinery or equipment, the purchasing department manager looks through the records for an appropriate supplier. A formal purchase order is then completed and mailed. When the machine or equipment is received, it is immediately sent to the user department for installation. This allows the economic benefits from the acquisition to be realized at the earliest possible date.
- The property, plant, and equipment ledger control accounts are supported by lapse schedules organized by year of acquisition. These lapse schedules are used to compute depreciation as a unit for all assets of a given type that are acquired in the same year. Standard rates, depreciation methods, and salvage values are used for each major type of fixed assets. These rates, methods, and salvage values were set 10 years ago during the company's initial year of operation.
- When machinery or equipment is retired, the plant manager notifies the accounting department so that the appropriate entries can be made in the accounting records.
- There has been no reconciliation since the company began operations between the accounting records and the machinery and equipment on hand.

Identify the internal control weaknesses and recommend improvements that the internal audit staff of Superior Co. should include in its report regarding the internal controls over fixed assets. Use the following format in preparing your answer:*

Required

Weaknesses	Recommendations
1.	1.

INTERNET PROBLEM 26-1: INSTITUTE OF INTERNAL AUDITORS

Reference the CW site. Professional guidance for internal auditors is provided by the Institute of Internal Auditors (IIA). The IIA Web site [**http://www.theiia.org**] contains links to sites for continuing education, certification requirements, professional standards and other guidance, as well as other information. This problem requires students to visit the IIA Web site to answer questions related to IIA position papers.

*CMA adapted.

Note: Essential terms appear in boldface.

general controls, 354
IT controls, 355
matrix, 288–290, 427 (figure)
planned
acquisitions, 587–588
sales, 416–419
for sales and collection cycle, 389, 486–487
Corporate charter, 202
Corporate governance oversight, to reduce fraud
risks, 322–327
Corporations
general, of CPA firms, 29
professional, 29
publicly held and closely held, 673
COSO
components of internal control, 274–283
Internal Control-Integrated Framework, 271
Enterprise Risk Management-Integrated Framework,
205
Cost
of audit test types, 380–381
of evidence types, 173
persuasiveness and, 166–167
Section 404, 274
Cost accounting, audit of, 643–645
Cost systems, in inventory and warehousing cycle,
639–640
Covered members, Rule 101 and, 86–87
CPA firms, 15
activities of, 27–28
AICPA division of, 37
and client, litigation between, 88
ethical conduct by, 79
operational audits performed by, 780
professional conduct in, 40 (figure)
quality control, 37–39
size categories, 26–27
structure of, 28–30
CPAs
assurance services provided by, 8–13
legal liability, 111
protection from, 124
professional conduct by, 79–80
requirements to becoming, 17–18
CPA Vision Project, 33
Credit Alliance *v.* Arthur Andersen & Co., 115
Credit approval, 412
Credit memo, 415
timely processing, 783–784
Criminal liability, 121–122
Criteria
established, information and, 4
for evaluating efficiency and effectiveness, 781–782
Current files
adjusting and reclassification entries, 179–180
supporting schedules, 180–182
working trial balance, 178–179
Current year
acquisitions and disposals, verifying, 615–618
balance, comparison with preceding year's, 210
Customer
billing, and recording of sales, 412–414
business risk for, 6
order processing, 412
Cutoff
for accounts receivable, 492–494
back statement, 692, 694
testing for, 149, 597–598
Cycle approach to audit segmentation, 140, 142–143

D

Database management systems, 361–362
Data comparisons, client, 209–215

Debit memo, 585
Debt compliance letters, 759–760
Decisions
audit evidence, 163–164, 173
auditors'
in observation of inventory, 648–649
regarding audit reports, 62–64
materiality, 57–58
Deficiencies in control
identification of, 288–291
letter regarding, 298 (figure)
Depreciation expense, verifying, 619
Detail tie-in, 149
Difference estimation, 542, 544–550
Directed sample selection, 446
Direct-effect illegal acts, 138
Disclaimer of opinion report, 55–56, 296
Discovery of facts, subsequent, 730–731
Discreditable acts (Rule 501), 94–95
Dividends, audit of, 676–677
Documentary discrepancies, 331
Documentation. *See also* Evidence; Information
adequate, 463–465
audit, review of, 726–727
as audit evidence, 170, 174–183
of fraud assessment, 322
of understanding of internal control, 283–287
Documents and records
acquisition and payment cycle, 582–586
adequate, 280, 418
examination of, 287, 293
inventory and warehousing cycle, 638–641
payroll and personnel cycle, 560–564
sales and collection cycle, 411–415
Dual dating, 719–720
Due professional care, as GAAS, 34

E

Earnings, retained, 677–678
E-Commerce
and capital acquisition, 678–679
and CPA firm operations, 30
effect on
acquisition and payment cycle, 586
audit evidence, 182–183
audit reporting, 64
inventory management, 641
sales and collection cycle, 415
IT systems issues, 362
Effectiveness
audit committee, 275
criteria for evaluating, 781–782
vs. efficiency, 777
operating, of controls, 272
of operations, 270
Electronic transfer of cash, 701
Embedded audit module approach, 359
Emphasis of a matter, 53
Employees, appropriate, hiring and promoting, 324
Employment relationships, conflicts arising from, 84
Enforcement of rules of conduct, 97, 99
Engagement checklist, 724 (figure)
Engagement letter, 197
Engagement risk, 243
Engagements
attestation, 742–745
initial *vs.* repeat, 246
staff selection for, 197, 199
Enron, 85, 193
Enterprise risk management, 205
Equipment-related accounts, 613–615
Error *vs.* fraud, 137
Estimated population exception rate, 456–457

Ethical conduct
elements of, 323 (table)
need for, 78–80
Ethical dilemmas, 75–78
Ethical rulings, 82
Ethical values, as subcomponent of control environment, 275
Ethics
code of, 202–203, 771 (figure)
principles of, 74 (figure), 81
and reducing fraud risks, 322–325
and unethical behavior, 74–75
Evaluating audit results, 252–254, 723–727
Evidence. *See also* Documentation; Information
accumulation
and evaluation of, 5, 782–783
final, 720–723
decisions regarding, 163–164
differing, among cycles, 240 (table)
vs. legal and scientific evidence, 162–163
modification in relation to risk, 254
persuasiveness of, 164–167
from prior year's audit, 294
relationship to risk, 248–252
reliability of, 598–599
sufficiency of, 723–724
sufficient competent (as GAAS), 35
terms related to, 394–395
types of, 167–174
audit tests involving, 380
Evidence mix, 384–385
Evidence-planning worksheet, 464 (figure)
Exception rates
population, 538
estimated, 456–457
sampling for, 449–450
tolerable, 454–456
Exchange transactions, complex, 7
Existence
as balance-related audit objective, 148
management assertions about, 145
recorded acquisitions and, 590
of recorded sales, 421–423
as transaction-related audit objective, 146
Expected results, and client data comparisons,
213–215
Expense accounts, tests of details of balances for, 572,
626
Explanatory paragraph, of unqualified audit report,
51–54
External document, 170

F

Family members, Rule 101 and, 87–88
Fees
audit, payment by management, 86
contingent (Rule 302), 93–94
referral (Rule 503), 95–96
unpaid, 90
Fictitious revenues, 330
Final evidence accumulation, 720–723
Financial interests, Rule 101 and, 86–88
Financial ratios, common, 215–216
Financial reporting
fraudulent, 314
internal control over, 9
reliability of, 270, 273
risk assessment for, 277–278
Financial statements
auditable, 287
audited, 8
audit reports on, 49–50
audits of, 15, 134–135

ethical, 75
of field work, 34–35
general (Rule 201), 91
international, on auditing (ISAs), 36–37
of reporting, 35
set by AICPA, 32–33
Standard unqualified audit report, 46–49
Statements on Auditing Standards (SASs),
36
Statistical audit sampling, 466
Statistical inferences, 541–542
Stock transfer agent, 675
Strategic systems audit, 15
Stratified sampling, 522
Subpoenas, 92
Subsequent discovery of facts, 730–731
Subsequent events
audit tests, 718–719
dual dating, 719–720
types of, 717–718
Substantive tests of transactions
in audit plan development, 377–378
designing for
acquisition and payment cycle, 586–592
cash receipts, 426–429
payroll and personnel cycle, 564–569
sales, 416–425
in design of audit program, 385–386
effect of results of, 431
IT controls effect on, 355
for notes payable, 669
in phase II of audit process, 152, 395
relationship to
analytical procedures, 382
tests of controls, 381–382
trade-off with tests of controls, 382–383
Sufficiency of audit evidence, 165–166, 723–724
Supporting schedules, 180–182
Systematic sample selection, 449
Systems development, 351
SysTrust **services,** 11–12, 747

T

Tax return
audit of, 5 (figure)
payroll, 563–564
Tax services, by CPA firms, 28
Technical training, adequate (as GAAS), 33–34
Test data approach, in IT environments, 356–357
Tests of controls
in audit plan development, 377
designing for
acquisition and payment cycle, 586–592
cash receipts, 426–429
payroll and personnel cycle, 564–569
sales, 416–425

in design of audit program, 385–386
effect of results of, 431
extent of, 299
illustration of, 379 (table)
in phase II of audit process, 152, 395
procedures for, 293–294
purpose of, 292–293
relationship to
procedures to obtain understanding, 294
substantive tests, 381–382
trade-off with substantive tests, 382–383
Tests of details of balances
for accounts payable, 592–599
in audit plan development, 380
audit program, 502–504
of cash, 692–696
designing for
accounts receivable, 484–496
inventory and warehousing cycle, 646–648
in design of audit program, 388–390
evidence-planning worksheet, 251–252
expense account analysis, 626
for notes payable, 667 (figure), 670–672
payroll and personnel cycle, 564–569
in phase III of audit process, 152, 397
Tests of reasonableness, 181
Third parties
legal liability to, 114–116
suits by, auditor defenses against, 116
Time cards, 562
Timeliness of audit evidence, 165
Timing
of audit tests, 397 (table)
of confirmations, 499
difference, 494
evidence decisions and, 163–164
as transaction-related audit objective,
147
Tolerable exception rate, 454–456
Tolerable misstatements, 236–238, 250, 389, 486, 570,
593, 690
Training, fraud awareness, 324
Transaction classes
controls over, 273–274
in sales and collection cycle, 410–411
Transaction cycles, 143–144
cash in the bank and, 686–688
Transaction file
acquisitions, 584
cash receipts, 414
payroll, 562
sales, 413
Transaction-related audit objectives, 144, 146–147,
288, 291–292, 393–394, 420–421 (table),
428–429 (table), 566 (table), 589 (table)
Trial balance
accounts payable, 585
accounts receivable, 414

aged, 491
or list, 180
working, 178–179

U

Ultramares **doctrine,** 115
Uncollectible accounts
audit tests for, 430–431
authorization form, 415
Unethical behavior, 74–76
Unit cost records, 645
United States *v.* Andersen, 121–122
Unqualified opinion, 295
Unusual fluctuations, 171
Unusual transactions, significant, 328

V

Vacation pay, accrued, 571
Valuation
inventory, payroll and, 567–568
of inventory, 651–654
management assertions about, 145–146
Variables sampling
comparison with nonstatistical sampling, 539
difference estimation, 542
mean-per-unit estimation, 542–543
ratio estimation, 542
sampling distributions, 539–541
sampling risks, 543–544
statistical inference, 541–542
stratified statistical methods, 543
Vendor's statement, 585, 596–598
Verbal cues, during inquiry, 336 (table)
Verification
in acquisition and payment cycle, 615–620
of information, by user, 7
internal procedures for, 419
Viruses, computer, 361
Vouchers, 585
Vouching, 170

W

Walkthrough, 287
WebTrust assurance services, 11–12, 745–746
Wide area networks (WANs), 360
Working trial balance, 178–179
Workplace environment, positive, 324

Y

Yellow Book, 773–774